i

LUGHAT-UL-QURAN

QURANIC DICTIONARY

ENGLISH EDITION

Volume I

ا ـ ش

ISBN: **978-1505394979**

Author: Ghulam Ahmad Parwez

Translator and editor: Sheraz Akhtar

Cover design: Sheraz Akhtar

Published by: Quranic Education Society, Oslo - Norway

In association with Tolu-e-Islam Trust, Lahore - Pakistan

www.qes.no

Translators note

The journey of translating *Lughat-ul-Quran* into English has been a long one.

It all started several years ago when *Liaqat Ali* and *Saim Khawaja* in USA felt the need to have the dictionary of the Quranic terms translated from Urdu to English. For this great task, they contacted and hired *Javed Rafiq*, a retired journalist in Karachi, who took on the job to translate this book from Urdu to English. Our friends in the USA compensated his time against an agreed fee. *Javed Rafiq* had never done any translation work of such kind before, and was not familiar with the teachings and philosophy of *Allama Ghulam Ahmad Parwez* in relation to the Quran. This was clearly reflected in the early pages of his translation, but gradually he improved the translation as he moved along. This work was done gradually and handed over in parts to our contacts in the USA. When all the work was done, *Liaqat Ali* distributed it to others around the world. Some held on to it for their study, while some of this translation ended up on the internet. However, this work never got published in a book form because of several reasons. Many people felt that the work was not satisfying, and the English did not meet the desired quality and fluency. There were many linguistic, as well as cosmetic changes required. There were many missing sentences, paragraphs/pages, without any clear overview. Many readers had this opinion that the standard of the translation required review and needed thorough editing in order to make it readable and comprehensible for the western and the wider readership.

Dr. Sohail Alam (son of *Dr. Mansoor Alam)* was of the opinion that to re-write the whole book could be better and quicker time wise than editing grammatically the English translation of *Javed Rafiq*. The limitation was that although *Dr. Sohail's* English was excellent (as seen in the introduction chapter to this book) he had very little time for the complete translation.

All this contributed to the delay in the publication of this translation and the whole project came to a standstill.

I got more determined to have this book translated in English without knowing the above mentioned background. My quest for the Quranic knowledge had convinced me that in order to understand the Quran, some basic knowledge of the Arabic grammar is helpful and also knowing the root meanings of the Arabic words/terms. When I found out about the *Lughat-ul-Quran* I was pleasantly surprised to find out that such a marvelous piece did exist, I accepted this challenge to complete the translation work into English. For any serious student of the Quran this is an extremely useful book and it needed to be published in English to enhance the Quranic understanding as its author always intended. To make this happen, it was essential to present it to people on a global basis. I myself had tried to understand several chapters of the Quran by studying the *Lughat-ul-Quran*, but in order to present arguments in support of my understanding; I had to present the *Lughat-ul-Quran* in a language that other researchers of Truth may find useful.

Since I became a member of the Quranic Education Society – Norway, I wanted to present the Quran to people in a language they could understand. When I suggested that the *Lughat-ul-Quran* should be translated into English, our chairman *Khadim Malik* agreed. We both agreed on the importance of this dictionary to be presented to wider public in English. Later we found out that a preliminary translation had already been done earlier, and learnt that the project was on hold for some reason. We were fortunate that the late brother *Farhat Maqbool* (London Bazm) provided us with all the material on the work which had been done so far. This saved us a lot of time. The translated material I got was not in a presentable form by any means. The layout was poor, the grammar was not always correct, and some spelling errors were also present. The biggest limitation was of the Arabic text. I started to refine this translation. I knew that some pages were missing and hence translated those later. Another major concern with this initial translation was that it was done by someone who was not fully familiar with the philosophy of the Quran as explained by *Allama Parwez*. The translator was merely translating without understanding, and therefore the literal translation did not do justice to the original Urdu version and I had to take this into consideration.

After completion, I got the help of *Khalid Sayed* and *Ejaz Rasool* (London Bazm) who went through all four volumes very thoroughly and made further corrections while reviewing the draft and ensuring to keep the explanations closer to the Urdu version especially where human thought process was referred.

Now this work has been finalised, and we can appreciate and take advantage of the final product. I have included my name as the main editor of this translation for convenience and for any correspondence; I would like to acknowledge the contributions of all those who helped to put this together.

To conclude I would like to summarise the names of all the brothers who took part in this great challenge and helped to complete it successfully:

- *Liaqat Ali and Saim Khawaja* in USA, who initiated the translation work.
- *Javed Rafiq* in Karachi, who did the preliminary translation.
- *Farhat Maqbool* from London Bazm who provided me the raw material and encouragement.
- *Khadim Malik* of Quranic Education Society Norway who helped and provided encouragement.
- *Khalid Syed* of London Bazm, who helped to review some part of the dictionary and also kept encouraging and motivating me.
- *Ejaz Rasool* of London Bazm who reviewed the remaining part of the dictionary where Khalid Syed had handed over.

Finally, I am sure this book will help many English readers to understand the Quran, like the Urdu version enhanced my understanding of the Quranic Truth.

My only regret is that this project did not come to fruition in the lifetime of late *Farhat Maqbool*, who would have appreciated it as he showed great desire to see this project through. My father, late *Mahmood Ahmad Akhtar,* who was a long time devotee of the Tolueislam movement and the real reason behind my inspiratoin and interest in the Quranic study in the first place, would also have been very pleased with this work. They will get their rewards from Allah as promised in the Quran.

On a last note, I fully appreciate the work done for the Urdu edition by *Allama Ghulam Ahmad Parwez*, who did all the work mostly by himself, where he researched several books to help create such an encyclopaedia of the Quranic words and terms. It took him many years to research to write the Urdu version. I am grateful to Allah for giving strength and knowledge to *Allama Ghulam Ahmad Parwez* to publish the Urdu work which helped many like myself and others to spread the Quranic message for the good of mankind for all times to come. He will be getting his reward from Allah as promised in the Quran.

It should also be mentioned that the names of the messengers has been written as they appear in the Quran, and not the biblical way which is commonly known for English readers. This has been done to keep the Quranic terms under focus. All messengers are sacred to us and we do not distinguish between them with regards to respect and status (2:136). The term "peace be upon him" has not been used after any messengers name, but it is implied.

Finally, let us all keep making effort to understand the Quran and benefit from its guidance.

Sincerely

Sheraz Akhtar
Quranic Education Society
Oslo - Norway

Note: This is Volume I only and Volume II is published separately with

ISBN: 978-1506147468

Index

XV

xvi

Introduction

"The correct and the only meaning of the Quran lies, and is preserved, within itself, and a perfect and detailed exegesis of its words is within its own pages. One part of the Quran explains the other. It needs neither philosophy, nor wit, nor lexicography, nor even hadith."…. Inayat Allah Khan Mashriqi

The Quran, the final book of revelation from Allah, comprises the sole complete system of life for all mankind. This system, based on the deep eternal laws that govern and hold the fabric of our universe together, is not affected by the changing winds of time. It is so comprehensive that it encompasses, in every era, all facets of human existence, leading the charge in the quest for knowledge and wisdom. Consequently, a book with such far-ranging capabilities must be of a language that is equally comprehensive, deep, and capable of conveying the most complex and abstract thought, while at the same time maintaining clarity and precision.

Upon reflection, it becomes evident that since Allah had chosen the Arab nation to inherit and implement the revolutionary message of the Quran, then even centuries before the actual revelation of the Quran, the Arabs had a tremendous responsibility to; step by step evolve a language that would be capable of expressing and containing its wisdom. When Abraham's children were split into two branches, one branch (**Bani Israel**) received continuous revelation through the Messengers and gained authority throughout the land, whereas the other branch (**Bani Ishmael**) was settled in the barren deserts of Arabia, where following Ishmael, they received no more messengers or revelation, nor any power or authority. This apparently forgotten branch, however, bit by bit, maturing and growing in the arms of nature, grew into a nation that would hold the honour of being the first people to address the final message delivered by the final Messenger, in their own language.

These people held their tongue in such high regard that they called themselves *Arabs* (meaning clear in speech) and others *Aajam* (meaning mute). The word Arab means clean, clear and precise. An important point, however, is that during the centuries that **Bani-Israel** was occupied with the development of their civilization to the heights of their ancient world (including the glorious reigns of David and Solomon), their brothers, **Bani Ishmael**, for this entire period, either consciously or subconsciously, were engaged and occupied with the arrangement and development of a language that had no peer in the entire world. In the literature of linguistic scientists, one can find a claim that to estimate the intellectual capacity of a nation at a given time; one should examine their language to determine how many of their words are conceptual. Regarding the Indo-European languages, their research was that "every thought that has passed through the mind of India may be reduced to 121 root-concepts" (**Max Mueller**). When Sanskrit was a living language, at a time when the sun and fire were considered deities, there were a total of 37 words for sun and 35 words for fire.

Now let us compare that with the language of the Arabs. These desert dwellers had 80 words for honey, 200 for snake, 500 for lion, 1000 for sword, and for a camel they had a total of 5, 744 words (Cosmic Consciousness). These facts illustrate the depth of conceptual thought and the wide range of expression of which the Arabic language was capable. This was the language in which the Quran was revealed.

26:192	And verily this Quran is a revelation from the Sustainer of all the worlds	وَإِنَّهُ لَتَنزِيلُ رَبِّ الْعَالَمِينَ
26:193	The Spirit, faithful to the trust, has descended with it	نَزَلَ بِهِ الرُّوحُ الْأَمِينُ
26:194	On thy heart, that thou may be a Warner	عَلَى قَلْبِكَ لِتَكُونَ مِنَ الْمُنذِرِينَ
26:195	In plain and clear Arabic tongue	بِلِسَانٍ عَرَبِيٍّ مُّبِينٍ

This illustrates the position of Arabic vis-à-vis the Quran. As far as the Quran itself, it is written:

(12:2) (43:2)	We have made it a Book to be oft read in clear, eloquent language that you may understand	إِنَّا أَنزَلْنَاهُ قُرْآنًا عَرَبِيًّا لَّعَلَّكُمْ تَعْقِلُونَ
(20:113)	Thus have We revealed it as an Arabic Quran (Quraanan Arabiyyan). In it, we turned around and turned on the warnings, so people may show understanding, or that it may create reflection in them.	وَكَذَلِكَ أَنزَلْنَاهُ قُرْآنًا عَرَبِيًّا وَصَرَّفْنَا فِيهِ مِنَ الْوَعِيدِ لَعَلَّهُمْ يَتَّقُونَ أَوْ يُحْدِثُ لَهُمْ ذِكْرًا
(39:28)	An Arabic Quran, without any ambiguity, so they had to meet understanding.	قُرْآنًا عَرَبِيًّا غَيْرَ ذِي عِوَجٍ لَّعَلَّهُمْ يَتَّقُونَ
(18:01)	Praise be to Allah, Who revealed the font for its contractor, and it contains no ambiguity or uncertainty, but is straight and erect,	الْحَمْدُ لِلَّهِ الَّذِي أَنزَلَ عَلَى عَبْدِهِ الْكِتَابَ وَلَمْ يَجْعَل لَّهُ عِوَجَا
(41:3)	this is a book whose verses are well-defined and able to be analysed separately, allowing the Quran precisely to clarify itself for those who undertake its study with knowledge and insight	كِتَابٌ فُصِّلَتْ آيَاتُهُ قُرْآنًا عَرَبِيًّا لِّقَوْمٍ يَعْلَمُونَ

The key words in the above verses are "**Quraanan Arabiyyan**" (see also 42:7, 46:12).

The term "**Quraanan Arabiyyan**" can be interpreted in two ways.

- The general understanding is "an Arabic Quran ", i.e. on the Arabic language, but
- It can also be understood as "a Quran which explains itself very clearly and precisely." This is with regard to the meaning of the word **Arabi**.

This has often been repeated throughout the Quran also says phrases like "**Hukman Arabiyyan**" Thus, a clear and precise judgment. (13:37).

- The 39:28 is the clarity of the Quran underlined in the statement that it does not contain any ambiguity.

- This is repeated at 6:01 p.m., "*wa lam yaj'al lahu i'waja*," and it contains no ambiguity and uncertainty.
- This point is further elaborated in 41:3, which says that this is a book where the verses are well defined and able to be analysed separately, to prepare the Quran itself for making their assessment of knowledge and insight.

39:28	An Arabic Quran , that does not contain any ambiguity	قُرْآنًا عَرَبِيًّا غَيْرَ ذِي عِوَجٍ لَعَلَّهُمْ يَتَّقُونَ
18:01	Praise be to Allah, Who revealed the font for its contractor, and it contains no ambiguity or uncertainty, but straight and tall,	اَلْحَمْدُ لِلَّهِ الَّذِي أَنْزَلَ عَلَى عَبْدِهِ الْكِتَابَ وَلَمْ يَجْعَل لَّهُ عِوَجَا
41:3	a Book, whose word is prepared as an Arabic Koran, for people with insight.	كِتَابٌ فُصِّلَتْ آيَاتُهُ قُرْآنًا عَرَبِيًّا لِّقَوْمٍ يَعْلَمُونَ

The values espoused in the Quran, lofty and sublime though may be, have still been elaborated and described in a simple manner.

44:58	Verily, We have made this (Quran) easy, in thy tongue, in order that they may give heed.	فَإِنَّمَا يَسَّرْنَاهُ بِلِسَانِكَ لَعَلَّهُمْ يَتَذَكَّرُونَ
54:17	And We have indeed made the Quran easy to understand and remember: then is there any that will receive admonition?	وَلَقَدْ يَسَّرْنَا الْقُرْآنَ لِلذِّكْرِ فَهَلْ مِن مُّدَّكِرٍ

Based on the above observations, it is evident that the Quran asserts that it is sent in a clear and easily understood Arabic tongue. One might then conclude that a native speaker of Arabic, therefore, would easily be able to comprehend even its deepest principles. Practical experience though, reveals that this is definitely not the case. Undoubtedly, a grasp of the Arabic language is a prerequisite for interpreting the Quran (no book in the world can be understood without knowing the language it was written in), but if that was all that was required, then native speakers of Arabic would automatically become experts of Quranic knowledge. We will not discuss here the extent to which Arabs understand Quranic principles (this includes not only the general Arab populous but also the educated and the scholars). When this is the situation with native Arabic speakers, one can only imagine the multiplication of difficulties for non-Arabs.

This observation raises a vital question: why is it that the Quran describes itself as a clear, easily understood book in a clear Arabic tongue, yet very few of those who are native Arabic speakers or have learned Arabic seem truly to comprehend Quranic teachings? The answer is crucially important, a firm grasp of which is of the utmost importance in arriving at the true Quranic message.

The pre-Islamic Arabs possessed a culture with much greater affinity for poetry than prose, and that was the medium in which their entire linguistic treasure was passed on from generation to generation. In contrast, what today is called "Arabic literature" was primarily composed during the Abbasid period, the same period during which were compiled the various books of hadith, Quranic *tafseer*, history and biography. Many volumes of Arabic literature, grammar and linguistic science were produced and extensive Arabic lexicons were compiled. It is quite interesting and ironic that all these works (with few exceptions) that comprise the earliest written or prose literature of the Arabic language were actually produced by non-Arabs.

The student of history would be well aware that during the Abbasid period of Islamic history, numerous foreign concepts began to permeate all facets of life. These foreign concepts influenced and shaped society in ways that ripened the climate for the seizure of political power by the Abbasids. Their politics were infused with these new foreign concepts and ideals, further helping to perpetuate them. It is only natural that once this happened, tremendous political pressure would then be applied to inculcate these ideals into every other facet of society. It is precisely because of this fact that the literary products of that time, despite their outward appearance of Arabic form, were actually foreign/non-Arabic in their inner true nature. This is how the Arabic language, in the earliest stages of its systematization and study, was turned into a vehicle of non-Arabic ideals. A more formal description and study of this phenomenon has been excellently provided in the work of the late *Ahmed Amin Misri*, "*Fajr al-Islam*." In it, he claims "*Undoubtedly, you will agree with me that Persian literature had cast Arabic literature in a new light.*"

It follows that once the meanings of Arabic words were affected in this manner, as expected, the understanding and interpretation of the Arabic words of the Quran were impacted as well. Since the books of Quranic interpretation (*tafseer*) were compiled during this period, they too became prey to these external influences. This is how the Arabic words of the Quran came to take on altogether different meanings than the ones existing at the time of its revelation. In addition to this general external (*Aajami*) influence upon Arabic, there was also another very important reason leading to this mutation of meanings.

When the first books of Quranic exegesis were compiled in the 3rd and 4th century A. H., one major technique used to interpret any important verse of the Quran was to examine its so-called "*sabab nuzool*," the reason for the revelation of the verse as recorded in narratives. These narratives would claim that some matter would come to pass, and in answer, a verse of the Quran would then be revealed. In this way, the stories ascribed to a Quranic verse became a more important focus of commentary than the actual words of the Quran. As a result, the meanings of the Arabic words in those Quranic verses were shaped and moulded to fit the narrations ascribed to it. As time went on, newer books of *tafseer* would not dare depart too far from the original and oldest books, and in this way, this style of Quranic commentary was perpetuated through history, gaining a semblance of credence and authority. By claiming the narrations, and hence, the exegesis sprang from none other than the mouths of the beloved Messenger(s) and his companions, these *tafseer* were made all the more irrefutable. All of this is in spite of the fact that the majority of the involved narrations are weak or unreliable (according to the hadith sciences), leading the occasional frustrated scholar, such as **Ahmad Ibn Hanbal**, to lament that "narrations of war and slaughter and *tafseer* are totally unreliable." Despite these facts, these narrations continue to dominate books on Quranic commentary and its resulting philosophy; therefore, it is not difficult to conceive that if these untrustworthy narrations are the basis for determining the meaning of a Quranic verse and of the Arabic words used in that verse, this would lead to a distortion of the true meanings of the words, thus obscuring the true meaning of the verse from the eyes of the reader. This point is best explained through a specific example in the Quran.

(04:34)	Men are in charge of women, because Allah hath made the one of them to excel the other... (*Pickthall*)	الرِّجَالُ قَوَّامُونَ عَلَى النِّسَاء بِمَا فَضَّلَ اللّهُ بَعْضَهُمْ عَلَى بَعْضٍ وَبِمَا أَنفَقُواْ مِنْ أَمْوَالِهِمْ

Here, the word "*qawwaamoon*" is taken to mean "in charge of," even though according to the language, the meaning is "those who provide the daily bread." This latter meaning implies that there is a division of labor between men and women, and men are duty-bound to earn a means of living for the family. So how did the meaning shift from provider to dominator or ruler?

A glance at one of the most highly authoritative books of *tafseer*, written by **Ibn-Kathir**, will shed light on exactly how this transformation of meaning took place. In his *tafseer* of the above verse, **Ibn Kathir** relates various accounts connected to the revelation of this verse.

Ibn Abbas claimed that "*qawwamoon*" refers to the fact that women should obey men... **Hasal al-Basri** relates a story in which a woman came complaining to the Messenger that her husband had struck her. Just as the Messenger was about to pronounce that her husband should be punished, the above Quranic verse was revealed, and then the Messenger said that there would be no punishment for her husband... In another narration, a man and his wife came before the Messenger. The woman complained to the Messenger that her husband had struck her and there was still a mark on her face. Just as the Messenger began to say that the husband should not have done so, the above verse was revealed. Upon this, the Messenger claimed "I willed something but Allah willed something else."

...There is a hadith in which the Messenger is reported to have said "Don't beat Allah's slave women (referring to women in general)." Thereafter **Umar** came to him and said "Oh Messenger! Having heard your command, the women have become bold towards their husbands." Upon hearing this, the Messenger allowed the beating of women. When the men began beating their wives, many complaints arose from the women to the Messenger. The Messenger then said "Many women have appealed to me complaining of their husbands' abuse. Those men are not the best of you." ... **Ishat ibn Qays** relates "I was once a guest of **Umar**. It happened that an argument broke out between him and his wife, and he hit her. He then said to me 'Ishat, remember three things I will tell you that I learned from the Messenger. Do not ask a man why he beats his wife, do not go to sleep until you have prayed the *Witr* prayer, and I have forgotten the third (i.e. the narrator could not recall the third) … In one narration, the Messenger is reported to have said "If I could have ordered that any person bow to another person, I would have ordered the women to bow to their husbands because of the tremendous weight of right the husband has upon her."

So as one can see, traditional Quranic commentary made on the basis of narration and tradition changed the meaning of the word "*qawwamoon*" to mean ruler or dominator, perhaps even something beyond that. This interpretation is not unique to **Ibn Kathir** but is repeated in other works as well, such as **Zamakhshari's al-Kashshaaf**, in which he equates "*qawwamoon*" with "*musaytireen*" (dominators or overlords). In **tafsir Jalaalayn**, the synonym "*mutasalliteen*" is used, in other words those who control, command and rule women. With such a predominance of this interpretation, not surprisingly, this meaning of "*qawwamoon*" eventually worked its way into books of language, eventually pervading the literature of the Islamic world and the education of Islamic scholars and the masses. In this way, Arabic speakers and Arabs alike lost touch with the true message of the Quran.

These facts lead us towards a very important question, that:

If the Arabic language was tainted in the Abbasid period by non-Arabs and, If all the Arabic works (tafseer, history, lexicons, or literature) that we possess today were produced in that era (usually by non-Arabs), plus the fact that the books of tafseer used unreliable narrations to fortify the incorrect usage and meaning of Arabic words, Then how can there be any possibility of recovering the true meaning of Arabic words, as understood at the time of the revelation of the Quran?

This question is answered with the following points.

1. If this happened in any other language (or to any other book), there is no doubt that the above difficulties would be insurmountable; however, certain elements of the Arabic language (and the Quran) allow a solution to this challenging problem. Firstly, as was mentioned above, the entirety of the Arabic language was contained within the works of poetry prevalent in pre-Islamic Arabia. Poets had a special status in that society, as their poetry was often used to extol the virtues of a tribe as well as to degrade and humiliate enemy tribes. As such, these poems were a heritage of a tribe and were taught even to its children. Prose, when transmitted orally, is difficult to protect from gradual alterations as the narrators pass the message onwards adding their own understanding and/or wording. This is because the form is not considered important in prose, only the meaning. Poetry, however, is quite different since the form and meaning are both integrated in the work. Thus, whenever poetry is learned and memorized, it is always transmitted forward with its form intact.

   This is how and why pre-Islamic Arabic poetry was preserved until the time of the Abbasids, when it was finally compiled into writing. Undoubtedly though, numerous apocryphal works of poetry were also created during the Abbasid period and were mixed in with genuine pre-

Islamic poetry; however, this should not impede our purpose since that poetry must have used exactly the same language (both form and vocabulary) as true pre-Islamic poetry, otherwise the counterfeits would be immediately discovered. Thus, pre-Islamic Arabic poetry was eventually preserved in the various books of Arabic literature, the analysis of which allows deduction of the pre-Islamic usage of Arabic words. The way in which Arabic words were used in that poetry is largely how the Quran uses it (and would have been how the Arabs at the time of the Quran's revelation would have understood it).

Pre-Islamic poetry, in addition to being preserved in books of Arabic literature, are also documented in the various Arabic lexicons. These works make use of pre-Islamic poetry in an attempt to systematically derive the original meanings of the words. These lexical works are of great value in understanding the Quran the way it would have been understood at the time of its revelation.

2. Above is a description of how to arrive at the true pre-Islamic meaning of Arabic words using external literary sources; however, the Arabic language also has a tremendously useful internal characteristic that both protects the meanings of words from external forces of change as well as aids one in determining the true meaning of a particular word. Arabic words are all constituted from a single root. The essence of the meaning is contained within the root and regardless of how its appearance may change according to the rules of grammar; its derivatives will always be inextricably bound to the essence of that root (It is this very characteristic that allows Arabic to continue to create new words through time as the need arises. For this, one need only find the appropriate root meaning and consider its various grammatical derivations; there would be no concept for which an appropriate word could not be generated.) To take this concept a step further, not only are words based on a fundamental root meaning, but even within root meanings, it is known that if certain letters appear in that root (such as HA and BA) then that group of roots will have related meanings, or if the root contains another two letters (such as SAAD and RA) then another group of related roots will result. Such a high degree of hierarchical and derivational vocabulary results in an unparalleled level of protection from the adulteration of the language. If, through the winding passage of time, a word changes in meaning or usage, it will be immediately discovered against the backdrop of its relatives within which are preserved the changed word's original meaning. This is how one can analyse the various words of the Quran to arrive at the meanings that would have been prevalent among the pre-Islamic Arab society at the time of its revelation.

3. The third element that helps us to rediscover Arabic is actually a result of the very simple and plain lives of the pre-Islamic Arabs. They lived with an expansive sky above their heads decorated by the sun, moon, and the twinkling of the stars, a vast desert before them with never-ending dunes, the landscape occasionally punctuated by mountains, streams of water with lush growth of greenery serving as oases of life in the barren desert, providing its dwellers with date palms and occasionally grapevines and pomegranate trees. Near these oases, one might find the tents of these desert dwellers, serving to house their meagre few

precious possessions, of which the most prized are their weapons, swords, arrows, bows, spears, shields, and daggers. With their few camels, horses, cattle and goats grazing in the sparse meadows nearby, this simple life comprised the entire sphere of existence for those simple desert dwelling Arabs of that forgotten time. This atmosphere is what served as the basis for the development of their entire language; in other words, their vocabulary evolved from the simple concrete and perceptible things around which their whole lives were based, and this is why the words used to describe them are comprehended and even visualized easily. Confusion and ambiguity in meaning usually arise in relation to the abstract, immaterial or philosophical, which are of little use in the harsh conditions of the desert. Indeed, it is the pure and simple language of the desert Bedouins that is considered the purest Arabic tongue.

The way in which the fundamental meaning of a root can be brought to light by the practical use of the word by desert Arabs is best illustrated by an example.

(2:153)	O you, who believe, seek help in patience (Sabre) and *Salaat*. God is with those with patience (*Sabireen*).	يَا أَيُّهَا الَّذِينَ آمَنُواْ اسْتَعِينُواْ بِالصَّبْرِ وَالصَّلاَةِ إِنَّ اللّهَ مَعَ الصَّابِرِينَ

SABR, commonly translated as patience, is usually applied to a situation from which an individual cannot escape, leading to desperation and helplessness. When there is no hope of actively affecting the situation, the advice given is "has patience," to the extent that even someone suffering great injustice at the hands of another, when he can do nothing to improve the situation, calms his inner struggle through the mantra of "patience." In other words, this interpretation of "*sabr*" carries a connotation of passivity.

The root meaning of **SABR**, however, is constantly and continuously to struggle towards a goal or purpose, to stand steadfastly. This root meaning is derived based on its usage by the desert Arabs in their daily lives. In other words, it means a connotation of activity.

A part of a cloud, if it stays in exactly the same spot for 24 hours without apparently shifting, is called **AS-SABEER**. **AL-ASBIRAH** is the word used to describe camels or goats that leave during the day to graze, and later return retracing their footsteps exactly, without a single one of them going astray or being left behind {T}. These concrete examples allow one to visualize how the Arabs understood **SABR** to mean steadfastness, persistence and perseverance, to firmly adhere to a principle or way, commitment to an action. It is this unshakable resolution towards a way or principle that was considered **SABR** by the Arabs.

Moving on, if passengers or goods created an uneven balance on a boat such that it begins to be unstable, the boatman would place a heavy rock in order to balance the load. This rock would be called **AS-SABOORAH** {T}. Therefore, the second characteristic of **SABR** is that if one's footsteps begin to waver from the path, it is SABR that provides the support upon which balance is regained, keeping the footsteps firmly on the chosen path. Because this kind of steadfastness leads to success and accomplishment, *AS-SABRAH* is used to describe a pile of grain that is unmeasured (*Muheet*).

In the face of the forces of change through time, the aforementioned features of Arabic greatly facilitate arriving at the true, original meanings of words; however, while the above form a fundamental basis for the meanings that is inescapable, there is yet another level of depth to attaining the full and true meaning of a book like the Quran. The reason for this is that this book is an outline for the eternal values of life, unchanging and all-encompassing upon whose truths our entire belief is based. It is, therefore, necessary that its understanding be complete and without doubt, something that can be difficult to attain if relying purely on the language as mentioned above.

Language (or linguistic science) is the product of human efforts, and thus, is inherently open to mistakes and external influences. In addition, there are certain words that the Quran uses as a form of terminology. These terms represent very important core Quranic principles and concepts cannot be adequately elucidated by pure language alone.

For example, *SALAT, ZAKAT, TAQWA, IMAN, ISLAM, KUFR, FISQ,* etc. all these terms are a comprehensive condensation of fundamental Quranic concepts that contain depth beyond (but linked to) their linguistic understanding. By carefully studying the whole Quran, linguistic ambiguities can be eliminated and the full extent of the terminological meanings can be brought to light.

As far as how this is achieved in practice, one must bear in mind that the Quran is written in such a way that if a topic is mentioned in one place, it often will be further alluded to in another place in such a way that the former is clarified. The Quran refers to this as "*tasreef-ul-ayaat.*" This means that a topic is brought back in several verses in such a way that the complete meaning of the concept emerges.

Hence, whether for an Arabic word or for specific Quranic terminology, the true meaning may be found by bringing all the pertinent Quranic verses together within which the word is found.

Based on what has been discussed above, it is evident that to determine the meaning of a word:

1. One must first identify and study the root meaning and characteristics, keeping in mind that despite however much the appearance of the word changes, it generally carries within it the essence of the root.
2. The word must be viewed in terms of how the simple desert Arabs employed it in their daily lives. By taking those concrete examples, one can often deduce how those folk conceptualized the word. It should be kept in mind that until the concept behind a word is discovered, one cannot truly understand the meaning of the word. The modern science of semantics has shed tremendous light on this area. This particular branch of linguistics is of great value in attaining the deepest possible understanding of a word.

3. All the passages of the Quran containing the word should be investigated to determine the various shades of meaning attached to it. By doing this, one can develop an understanding of the Quranic concept for that word.

4. Most importantly, one must keep in mind the overall teaching of the Quran. It should always be borne in mind that the Quran's vocabulary and terminology should not be contrary to its basic teachings because the Quran also declares that it contains no contradictions (e.g. that if multiple meanings are possible linguistically, ones that lead to contradictions should be avoided. This does not imply that meanings of words should be changed in order to avoid contradictions, thus making it a self-fulfilling claim.). This is only truly possible when one frees his or her mind of all external biases and concentrates on deriving the meaning of the Quran in its own light. Allah has declared that the Quran is a guiding light (*Noor*), and light has no need for external sources to make itself manifest.

Using the mentioned techniques, the true meaning of the Quranic words and passages can be understood.

In this connection, *Allama Jamaluddin Afghani*'s student, and the teacher of *Syed Rashid Raza*, *Imam Sheikh Mohammad Abdohu* has written a book *Tafseerul Manar*. We present certain elements from this book's foreword, with respect to high standards of understanding Quran.

The first step is to understand the meaning of individual words. One needs to understand how words were used by the ancient Arabs and not depend on anyone's explanation or understanding as to what they mean today. But it is also essential to not depend solemnly upon this, because many words were used to express certain meanings during the revelation of the Quran, but later with passage of time, they began to mean something else. One example is the word "*taweel*" which has come to mean explanation, but the Quran uses it for a different meaning, which is of being the final result, or the result of Quranic promises. It is essential for a researcher to investigate the original meaning of a word, as compared to its current use which appeared later, and differentiate between these. Most of those who has written explanations of Quran, define the terminology of the noble Quran as per the meanings which prevailed during the first three centuries after the revelation of Quran. It is essential for researchers to take those meanings into account which prevailed at the time of Quranic revelation.

In this connection it is better to take the help of the Quran and study the words which appear repeatedly, in order to determine their meanings. If one does that, one will find that the same word has been used to express several meanings, for example, the word "*hidayah*". With deliberation, it is possible to determine its meaning at a particular place. That is why it is said that one place of the Quran explains another. Thus in order to determine the particular meaning of a word, it is imperative to see whether it jives with the foregoing text, agrees with the entire text and subject, and is in line with the overall purpose of the Quranic message.

I am a student of the Quran. My entire lifetime, from childhood to the current time, has been an association with this great Book. In the beginning I too studied the Quran in in the traditional way, but it made no impact. Later when I gave it a critical review, I realized that the real meaning of the Quran was different one then generally accepted. I was lucky to get some insight of the thoughts of the great poet *Allama Iqbal*, just as when I was struggling with this. From his insights I came to know, among other things, that Quran should be understood in the Arabic language and with the help of explanation of the verses, while external influences should be shunned. To understand the Quranic verses, one had to use "*tabveeb al-Quran*" i.e. compiling all verses regarding one subject at one place. But in respect of "*tabveeb al-Quran*", what was conceptualised by *Allama Iqbal*, and which he related to me in detail, was not found in any book. This needed the compilation of an entirely new book.

I tried my best to induce some groups or individuals to undertake the task so they could to a better job at this task then I ever could, but did not succeed in finding any. Ultimately I had to take the burden of this task on my own shoulders. For this, I compiled verses under several subjects. This took me several years. After classification of the verses on the lines of an encyclopaedia, I compiled every subject into an integrated document.

Thus came into a series of books, such as

- "*Mutaraf-ul-Quran*" (Exposition of Quran).
- "*I and God*"
- "*Iblees and Adam*"
- "*Jooye Noor*"
- "*Burq Toor*"
- "*Shola Mastoor*"
- "*Mairaj Insaniyaat*"

I am working on some other titles as well and they as well be published in due course.

The publication of my book "*Mutar-ul-Quran*" and other writings, and papers, resulted in rekindling the greatness and value of the noble Quran in the hearts of the country's educated, young folk (especially those who had turned away from religion). The main purpose of my toil of years' waste very same i.e. to bring the young folk (who had run away from the self-made religions of man and thus were also running away from Allah's sayings) to come close to the Quran and deliberate directly in it. (With God's help) The result of my humble efforts was beyond my expectations. A large number of young people came closer to the Quran, thank God.

These young people came close to the Quran alright, but when they were told to understand it directly, they complained that no present translation, nor explanation that would help them in understanding the Quran , existed. And they were right in saying so, because they meant that they must be shown the way by which they could comprehend the Quran directly. This included those who knew the Arabic language and those too who didn't. After deliberating for some time,

I arrived at the decision that there should be a dictionary of the noble Quran in which the meanings of the Quranic words and phrases were explained. I tried my best, but could not find any such dictionary. Dictionaries aside, but except some sayings of **Imam Raghib**, I could not even find any book which could even be called a proper Quranic dictionary.

Recently some books have appeared under the title "**Lughat-ul-Quran**", but they fail to fulfil the mentioned purpose.

Allama Hameeduddin Farahi had tried to organize a dictionary of this sort, and even determined the meaning of some words in this manner. If he had compiled such a dictionary for the entire Quran, then no doubt that it would be a very useful book. According to my consciousness, I have taken the help of his Quranic work. Due to the circumstances, there was no other way but to compile a fresh Quranic dictionary. The difficulty of compiling such a dictionary for the Quranic words and terms on the pattern above can be well understood by scholars. I tried very hard to get together some group, as I had tried before, to do this very difficult and challenging great work. But I failed once again. On one hand this was the situation, and on the other was the demand of those people (whom I had brought closer to the Quran). They were getting more intense as to how to understand the Quran more directly. When I considered myself for the job, I didn't seem to find either the courage or the ability to undertake such important task. This went on for quite some time.

At last, it was decided that no matter what quality, the work should be undertaken. Once the foundation was laid, men with better ability could work on this foundation and produce something better. These were the circumstances under which I decided to compile such a dictionary, and after the toil of many years, this dictionary is before your eyes. During this difficult journey, I also consulted scholars, those who were willing.

I cannot but mention **Mr. Habib Mukarram** (former ambassador of Egypt) and **Dr. Abdul Wahab Uzam** who had great knowledge of the Arabic language and love for the Quran. I was lucky to have known these two gentlemen. I had close relations with them in connection with the translation and meanings of **Allama Iqbal's** poetry. I can't express enough the extent to which I benefited from their knowledge of the Arabic language

After compiling the dictionary, I had it gone over by scholars whose knowledge of the Arabic language and love for the Quran was known to me. I am grateful from the core of my heart to all such friends. But nevertheless, I declare that whatever is contained in this book is solemnly my responsibility. I am sorry that **Allama Aslam Jerajpuri** died before this dictionary was completed. I wish he had lived to go through it. I am indebted grateful to him for the Quranic insight he gave me for my book "**Mafhoum-ul-Quran** ".

Sincerely

G. A. Parwez (1960)

References

Taj-ul-Uroos *{T}*

In the compiling and editing of this book, the question was as to which book of Arabic dictionary should be made its fundament. Three dictionaries are very famous, "*Lissan-ul-Arab*", "*Taj-ul-Uroos*" and "*Qamoos*". Some other books are famous as well, and in certain matters enjoy even more importance than the three mentioned here. After studying the benefits and good points of these three, it was decided to choose "*Taj-ul-Uroos*". *Taj-ul-Uroos* explains *Qamoos* and since it was compiled after *Lissan-ul-Arab*, it contains the linguistic details. Thus it can be said that *Taj-ul-Uroos* is the latest, detailed and authentic dictionary which contains the all formerly published authentic dictionaries.

Lissan-ul-Arab is compiled by *Ibn Mukarram*, who died in 711 Hijri.
Qamoos is compiled by *Allama Ferozabadi* who died in 816 Hijri.

Taj-ul-Uroos is compiled by *Mohibuddin Ibnul Faiz Alsyed Muhammad Murtaza Alhuseni Alwasti Alzubedi Alhanafi* who died in 1205 Hijri or 1701A.D. He edited his renowned dictionary in Egypt. It was published in 10 big volumes. The book we are referring to is published by *Matba'ul Khairia* and the date of publishing written on it is 1306 A.D. (First Edition).

According to *Edward William Lane*, except *Lissan-ul-Arab*, one hundred dictionaries have been consulted in compiling *Taj-ul-Uroos*. In the English language, the Arab dictionary (Lane's Lexicon) is also based on *Taj-ul-Uroos*. As such, this dictionary is very scientific.

Raghib *{R}*

We referred also to *Imam Raghib Isfahani's* famous book, "*Almafrudaat fi gharibul Quran*" or "The sayings of the Quran".

This is a dictionary of Quranic words and so famous that it needs no introduction. But this book is very brief. The edition we are referring to was printed in Egypt in 1324 A.D.

Ibn Faris *{F}*

The third important book we refer to is *Ibn Faris*' "*Muqabeesul Lugha*" which details the root of every word and its meaning. Since the central idea of our dictionary is the basic meaning of the root of words, substantial reference has been made from this book of *Ibn Faris*'. The book we are talking about was initially printed in Egypt in the year 1902 A.D in six volumes.

Muheet {M}

After this the book which was consulted most was ***Pitra Bostani's*** "***Muheet-ul-Muheet***".

It is a brief book (has only two volumes) but it is very beneficial. The book we are referring to was printed in Beirut in 1870 A.D.

These are the books of reference, commonly referred to in this dictionary. Besides these, the following books have been consulted as well

a) "***Fikah ul lugha***"   ***Abu Mansoor's*** brief i book which despite its brevity is thought to be very authentic. Our reference book was printed in 1938 in Egypt.

b) "***Aqrabul Muaarid***"   A famous dictionary which was compiled by ***Saeed Alkhouri Alshartuni Allebani***. The book in reference was printed in Beirut in 1889.

c) "***Muntahil Arab***"   A famous Arabic-Persian dictionary. Our reference is to version printed by Islamic Publications, Lahore in 1920.

d) "***Kitabul Ashtaqaq***"   ***Nawab Siddiq Hasan Khan's*** brief magazine, but it details the characteristics of the letters of the roots of words very well.

e) "***Al-fazul Mutaradifa***" ***Ali Ibn Isa Alrumani's*** brief magazine, who died in 384 Hijri and describes the superficial and deep difference between alternate words.

f) "***Latayeful lugha***"   This is a book by ***Ahmed Bin Mustafa Allaba Bedi*** (of Damascus) which discusses the linguistic niceties in detail.

g) "***Kitabul Qartain***"   This is a book based on a book by ***Imam Din Kutaiba Aldeenwari*** who died in 277 Hijri, printed in Egypt in 1355. ***Ibn kutaiba*** enjoys a good reputation among scholars.

h) "***Al-bustan***"   This dictionary is by ***Abdullah Albustani Allebnani*** who died in 1930, printed in 1927. Its foreword is quite good.

Besides the above mentioned dictionaries, reference has also been made to ***Zamkhashwi's tafser*** (***Kashaf***), ***tafseer Jalaleen*** and ***Allama Muhammad Abdohu's*** famous ***Tafseer-al-manar***.

Some other books have also been referred to.

A _____ أ

This letter is used to symbolize a question, as well as to call out (to someone). The following examples will make this clear:

1. To ask someone a question:

Is Zaid standing?	أَزَيْدٌ قَائِمٌ
Is that Zaid standing or *Umaro*?	أَزَيْدٌ قَائِمٌ أَمْ عَمْرٌ

The answer is likely to be:

Yes / No	لَا / نَعَمْ

Describing the story of *Ibrahim* (Abraham), the Quran says

21:63	Is it you who have done this to our gods?	أَأَنْتَ فَعَلْتَ هَذَا بِآلِهَتِنَا
79:27	Are you more difficult to create or is the sky?	أَأَنْتُمْ أَشَدُّ خَلْقًا أَمِ السَّمَاء

2. A question which is followed by a denial to invigorate positivity.

95:8	Isn't Allah the greatest of all rulers?	أَلَيْسَ اللَّهُ بِأَحْكَمِ الْحَاكِمِينَ

Thereby the meaning here is not to say that Allah is not the greatest of all rulers, but to assert the opposite, that He is in fact exactly that. Here *Hamza* is followed by *lays* for a denial, but the denial does not denote a denial of what is being said - later, but it is indeed its assertion, which is said with force.

3. A question in which a sense of scolding exists.

3:82	Do they prefer some other *Deen* (way of life) than the *deen* of Allah?	أَفَغَيْرَ دِينِ اللَّهِ يَبْغُونَ

The aim of the above is to be sarcastic and ask if they really want such a thing. The indication is that they should not desire it.

4. A question which is tinged with ridicule.

From the story of *Shoaib's* (Jethro of the Bible) nation, they tell the following to him.

11:87	Does your *salah* ask us to abandon the gods of our forefathers?	أَصَلَاتُكَ تَأْمُرُكَ أَن نَّتْرُكَ مَا يَعْبُدُ

This sentence contains satire, ridicule and even amazement.

5. For expressing amazement

25:45	Haven't you wondered how your Sustainer elongates the shadows?	أَلَمْ تَرَ إِلَى رَبِّكَ كَيْفَ مَدَّ الظِّلَّ

Here "أَلَمْ تَرَ" (*alam tara*) has been said to portray wonder, but this phrase usually means an invitation to reflect or deliberate. Similar are "أَفَلَا" (*afala*), "أَوَلَا" (*awala*), "أَفَلَمْ" (*afalam*) and "أَوَلَمْ" (*awalam*).

6. To warn if something has been delayed.

57:16	Has the time not come for the Believers to…?	أَلَمْ تَرَ إِلَى رَبِّكَ كَيْفَ مَدَّ الظِّلَّ

Thereby, the meaning of the above verse is that the time has indeed come.

7. A question which actually is an order.

Like when we say: "will you do this or not?"
The real purpose of such a question is to order someone to actually do this.

Ibrahim's (Abraham) father said to him:

19:46	Do you (dare to) avoid my gods?	أَرَاغِبٌ أَنتَ عَنْ آلِهَتِي
19:46	I'll punish you humiliatingly.	لَأَرْجُمَنَّكَ

The meaning here is that "I order you not to do this, otherwise I will punish you."

8. To equalize two things, but only when it appears after the word "sawaye"

2:6	Whether you warn them or not, (against the devastating results of their path), is the same (useless).	سَوَاءٌ عَلَيْهِمْ أَأَنذَرْتَهُمْ أَمْ لَمْ تُنذِرْهُمْ

9. For calling out:

"اَزَيْدَ أَقْبِلْ" (*azaida aqbil*) would mean: O Zaid, forge ahead! The Quran has not used this format.

10. *Alif as a Hamza* - أ

Hamza always appears in the beginning of a sentence, "أَفَلَمْ يَسِيرُوْا" (*aolam yanzoro*), "أَوَلَمْ يَنْظُرُوْا" (*afalam yasiro*)

Sometimes it is even omitted, for instance: before 'whether' "أَمْ" (*am*)

This is the case in the tale of Ibrahim on the night when the moon appeared and he asked his nation:

| 6:77 | He said, is this my Sustainer? | قَالَ هَذَا رَبِّي |

The meaning is off course sarcastic, and means to say; "do you want me to worship it?" Here, the letter *alif* which is the questioner has been omitted. Some people think that this "هَذَا رَبِّي" (*haza rabbi*) is not said by **Ibrahim** but his father (*Azar*) and the portion following thereafter in the same verse is the answer given by **Ibrahim.**

| 6:77 | Then he said, "this is my Sustainer", but when it descended, he said "If the Sustainer does not guide me, then I shall become one of the unfair" | فَلَمَّا أَفَلَ قَالَ لَئِن لَّمْ يَهْدِنِي رَبِّي لَأَكُونَنَّ مِنَ الْقَوْمِ الضَّالِّينَ |

In other words, it is a dialogue. If so, then there is no need to consider the *alif* as omitted. Note that when one *hamza* is followed by a word which begins with another *hamza*, then the two *hamzas* together become an *alif* with a *mudda'a*. آ As in آلْآنَ (what now?). This actually sounds like the beginning with two *alifs* with 'zabar'.

A-B-B   أ ب ب

"الْأَبُّ" (*al-abbu*): grass, whether dry or fresh. This word is used for all kinds of grass on which animals graze.

The Quran says:

| 80:31 | And fruits and green grass | وَفَاكِهَةً وَأَبًّا |

Mujahid says that "فَاكِهَةً" (*fakiha*) is fruit eaten by men; and "أَبًّا" (*abba*) are things that animals eat. This includes green grass, fodder, dry grass etc.

Ibn Faris says the basic meaning of the term is of grazing land, and intent. This is probably because animals go to the grazing land with a definite intent of eating.

Some others maintain that "أَبًّا" (*abba*) for animals is the same as "فَاكِهَةً" (*fakiha*) for Man. In short, it is used for something which is eaten happily. Therefore أَبًّا are those things which animals love to eat.

A-B-D   أ ب د

"اَلْأَبَدُ" (*al-abad*): 'unlimited period of time', or 'always'. *Ibn Faris* says it means 'elongated time'.

Raghib says it means 'a long time which cannot be measured'. Hence' it means 'time that cannot be divided into segments, or be measured'.

Against this we have "زَمَانٌ" (*zaman*) which means measurable time. As such, there should be no feminine gender or plural for this word but even then, it has a plural, which is "آبَادٌ" (*aabad*). Some say that the word "آبَادٌ" (*aabad*) is never used by Arab poets.

"اَلْأَوَابِدُ" (*al-awabid*): 'wild beasts', because the Arabs thought that they don't die their own deaths but die only because of some trouble. "آوَابِدٌ" (*aawabid*) also means 'trouble'.

Nawab Siddiq Hasan Khan writes that when "*ba*" is accompanied by *hamza*, it implies hatred, wildness, enmity and separation. "آبَدَالْوَحَشٌ" (*aabdalwahash*) would mean 'wild animals fled after rearing up'.

The Quran uses "اَلْأَبَدُ" (*alabad*) in the meaning we usually take i.e. "always".

| 2:95 | They can never wish for that (*jannah*) | وَلَن يَتَمَنَّوْهُ أَبَدًا |
| 4:169 | And they will live there forever | خَالِدِينَ فِيهَا أَبَدًا |

"ابدی" (*abdi*) and "ازلی" (*azli*) are not Quranic terms. "ازلی" (*azli*) has not even been mentioned in the Quran. As such, "ابد" (*abd*) would mean 'a long time'. So, while it is a mention of the dwellers of *jahannam*, in 4:169, it is also said that they shall abide there for a very long time. See heading H-Q-B)

This has also been elaborated by:

| 11:106 | till there is the sky and the earth | مَا دَامَتِ السَّمَاوَاتُ وَالْأَرْضُ |

From this it becomes clear that "ابد" (*abad*) does not mean a never-ending period. The debate about "*zaman*" as 'Time' is very scholastic, deep and technical. That is why we will not enter such a debate here. Here, I only want to say that when we say *abdi* or *azli*, we only attribute these traits to Allah and no one else. Do not take the last part to mean that *jahannam* ends after some period: that *jahannam* will expire after a time and those who dwell in it will go to some other place after being extricated from it.

At several places in the Quran it has been made clear that there is no question of getting out of *jahannam*.

Ibrahim اِبْرَاهِيْمُ

Ibrahim's time comes chronologically after *Nooh*, *Hoodh* and *Saleh*. (For tales about them see relevant headings.)

But, as the founder of the nation of *Ibrahim* and the builder of the *Kaba* (House of Allah), the Quran mentions him in detail. The Holy *Tarah* states that in the eighth generation of *Noah*, *Nahur* was born, whose son was *Azar*, and *Azar*'s son was *Ibrahim*. *Azar's* family was settled in a Chaldean city named *Ur*.

At that time, the Chaldean civilization was at its peak. According to a historical estimate, his time can be fixed at 2200 B.C. His nation was engaged in idol and star worship. *Ibrahim's* father was a great idol-worshipper. He started his call to worship One Allah from his own (father's) home (6:75). The father vehemently opposed it (16:46).

Then *Ibrahim* addressed his people and told them that they were indulging themselves in sin (21:52). This tension rose to such a peak that one day he went to their temple and smashed their idols (21:58). During this, there was also a dialogue between him and the king and he left the king speechless with his arguments and reasoning (2:258).

One after another, their defeats kindled the fires of vengeance in the nation and they were after his blood.

But Allah foiled all their schemes and he (*Ibrahim*) along with his nephew Loot (Lot) who was also a Messenger, left for Egypt (21:67-68). He settled in Palestine.

He settled his son *Is-haq* (Isaac) in *Falasteen*, and took his other son *Ismail* along with him. With Allah's blessings they went to a *ghair zi zarah* (uncultivable) valley and built the *Ka'ba* (2:125). He made *Ismail* its administrator.

All messengers of Israelites belonged to the progeny of *Is-haq*, and *Muhammad* was the flower of the dynasty of *Ismail*.

This was *Ibrahim* about whom Allah says:

16:120	Undoubtedly, *Ibrahim* (in his personae) was not an individual but an entire nation, bowing before Allah, and he was not among the "*mushrekeen*" (those who believe in more than one God).	إِنَّ إِبْرَاهِيمَ كَانَ أُمَّةً قَانِتًا لِلَّهِ حَنِيفًا وَلَمْ يَكُ مِنَ الْمُشْرِكِينَ

A-B-Q   أ ب ق

"أَبَقَ اَلْعَبْدَ اَبْقًا وَ اِبَاقًا" (*abaqa-la'bda abqa wa ibaqa'a*) is the fleeing of a slave (leaving behind his work). Neither he is given very hard work, nor is there any fear, still the slave opts to run away.

Nawab Siddiq Hasan Khan says that when *bah* and *hamza* come together they give the sense of wildness, enmity, hatred, separation etc. Here, too, "أَبَقَ" (*abaq*) imparts the same sense.

Ibn Faris says that the basic meaning of it is running away of a slave, or to perpetrate violence in some matter.

"اَلْآبَقَ" (*al-abaq*): one who leaves one's duty behind and flees, or one who hides.
"تَأَبَّقَ الشَّيَّ" (*tabbaqashi*) is someone who stays away from something considering it to be unpleasant.
"عَبَدَ آبِقٌ" (*abadan aabiqun*): a slave who has run away.

The Quran has used this expression for *Yunus*:

37:140	When he ran towards the boat that was full	إِذْ أَبَقَ إِلَى الْفُلْكِ الْمَشْحُونِ

A *rasool* (messenger) was sent towards a nation with a particular mission.

He had to suffer hundreds of ignominies and he never left his place under any circumstances. But when Deity feels that it is no longer conducive for the mission for him to stay at a place any longer, it orders him to leave the place and go somewhere else. This is called "*hijra*" (migration).

It seems that when *Yunus* felt that his nation was not ready to give up its insolence towards Allah, he decided, on his own, that the environment was not good for the Message of Allah. Thus he left the place.

His decision came before the time planned according to the Deity's program, (and he had left his place without Allah's orders to do so). That is why this act of his was called "أَبَقَ" (*abaq*). In other words, he left his duty. It may be noted that he had not flouted any of Allah's orders. He had simply made a decision on his own. But since this decision was made before the right time, Allah didn't approve.

This gives an idea as to how much the life of a *rasool* is subservient to Allah's will, and matters in which the decision is laid in the hands of Allah, the *rasool* could not even take one step on his own. However, he had permission in other matters to decide his line of action according to the rules of *wahi* (Revelation).

A-B-L   أ ب ل

"الْإِبِلْ" (*al-ibil*) and "الْإِبْلُ" (*al-iblu*) are used for a large number of camels. These words do not have a singular. Clouds also find reference to camels.

The Quran says:

88:17	Do they not see the clouds, as to how they have been created?	أَفَلَا يَنظُرُونَ إِلَى الْإِبِلِ كَيْفَ خُلِقَتْ

Here, "الْإِبْلُ" (*al-iblu*) could also mean "clouds". "اِبِلٌ أَبَابِيلٌ" (*abilun ababili*): herd after herd of camels.

105:3	Did He not send flocks and flocks of birds?	وَأَرْسَلَ عَلَيْهِمْ طَيْرًا أَبَابِيلَ

"الْإِيَالْ" (*al-ibal*), "الْأَبُوْلْ" (*al-abol*), "الْإِبِيْلْ" (*al-ibil*), "الْإِبَالَةْ" (*al-ibalah*): bunch of birds, horses and camels which come one after another in waves.
"أَبَالَ" (*abal*): 'he was bewildered.'

According to **Ibn Faris**, it has three basic meanings: camel, to be sufficient, load or overwhelming.

A-B-W   أ ب و

"آبَاءٌ" (*aaba*) is the plural of "آبٌ" (*aab*) which in fact was "أَبَوٌّ" (*abu*) which means "father" or the person who is instrumental in siring another of his species, or a person who is the manifest, or invention of such a person. This word is also used for someone older, such as an uncle. Besides that, due to seniority and age, every elderly person is called "آبٌ" (*aabun*).

"أَبَوْتَهُ أَبْوًا" (*abaota abwa*): "his upbringing was done by me".
"تَأَبَّاهُ" (*tabbah*): "I made him my father".

In the Quran the word "آبَاءٌ" (*aabau*) is used for forefathers.

2:170	what we found our forefathers to be doing	مَا أَلْفَيْنَا عَلَيْهِ آبَاءَنَا

This word is also used for uncles and grandfather, as in surah **Al-Baqrah**, when **Yaqoob** [Jacob] asked his sons, "Who will you worship when I am gone?"

| 2:133 | who will you worship when I am gone" and they replied "We will worship your God, and the God of your forefathers Ibrahim, Ismail and *Ishaq*" | لِبَنِيهِ مَا تَعْبُدُونَ مِن بَعْدِي قَالُواْ نَعْبُدُ إِلَهَكَ وَإِلَهَ آبَائِكَ إِبْرَاهِيمَ وَإِسْمَاعِيلَ وَإِسْحَقَ |

Ishaq was *Yaqoob's* father, *Ismail* was his uncle and Ibrahim was his grandfather. For all of them, the word "آبَاءٌ" (*aabau*) has been used.

In surah *Yusuf* we find the word "أَبَوَيْهِ" (*abawaeh*) which means parents (mother and father) 12:99.

When calling out to the father, "يَا أَبَتِ" (*ya abat*) has also been used instead of "يَا أَبِيْ" (*ya abiy*) as in 12:4
"الْأَبَا" (*al-aba*) is a form of "الْأَبُ" (*al-abu*) and means 'father'.

A-B-Y   أ ب ي

According to *Ibn Faris*, the basic meaning of this root is to dislike something, to abstain from something, abstain, to refuse with vehemence. "أَبَى الشَّيْءَ يَأْبَاهُ" (*abasheia yabah*)

"أَخَذْهُ أَبَاءٌ مِنَ الطَّعَامِ" (*akhazho abao minata'am*): he hated the food.
"رَجُلٌ أَبَيَانٌ" (*rajulun abyan*): one who abstains from food.
"الْإِبَاءُ" (*al-ibao*): hatred, displeasure, pride etc.

In other words, it means to refuse something because of not being up to expected standards. It also means to do something that one likes, and not allow it to anyone else.

Nawab Siddiq Hasan Khan says that when "*ba*" and "*hamza*" appear together, they convey a sense of wildness, hatred, enmity and separation.

"الْأَبَيَ" (*al-aabiya*) is used for a lion, because he too does what he wants without heeding anybody else.
"أَبِيْ" (*abiya*) conveys this sense. "أَبَيْ وَاسْتَكْبَرَ" (*abai wastakbar*) appears against "سَجْدَةٌ" (*sajdah*) "genuflection" in 2:34. This means that *Iblees* ignored Allah's orders and was unfaithful.

| 2:282 | when witnesses are called (to give evidence), they should not refuse, shouldn't stop (from giving evidence) | وَلَا يَأْبَ الشُّهَدَاء إِذَا مَا |

There is another manner in which it has been used in the Quran. Surah *Bani Israel* says that God has stated the Quranic truths in different ways.

| 17:89 | And We have certainly diversified for the people in this Quran from every kind of example, but most of the people refused anything except disbelief. | وَلَقَدْ صَرَّفْنَا لِلنَّاسِ فِي هَذَا الْقُرْآنِ مِن كُلِّ مَثَلٍ فَأَبَى أَكْثَرُ النَّاسِ إِلَّا كُفُورًا |
| 25:50 | And We have certainly distributed it among them that they might be reminded, but most of the people refuse and accept disbelief. | وَلَقَدْ صَرَّفْنَاهُ بَيْنَهُمْ لِيَذَّكَّرُوا فَأَبَى أَكْثَرُ النَّاسِ إِلَّا كُفُورًا |

In other words, they abstain from deliberating and hence are unable to find Allah's path.

Similarly, in surah *At-Tauba*, it is said:

| 9:32 | Allah doesn't accept anything except to complete his light | وَيَأْبَى اللَّهُ إِلَّا أَن يُتِمَّ نُورَهُ |

These examples make it clear that with the word "اِلَّا" (*illa*), the words mean that "nothing else, besides this is acceptable".

In surah *Al-Kahaf*, *Moosa* and his companion's tale have the following:

| 18:77 | the residents (thinking them to be lowly) refused to be their hosts | فَأَبَوْا أَن يُضَيِّفُوهُمَا |

A-T-Y   أ ت ي

"آتَي" (*aatai*) or "يَأْتِي" (*yatai*): "to come".

Raghib says, "اِتْيَانٌ" (*ityanun*): to come comfortably.

Muheet has given the example of "آتَى الْمَاءَ" (*atayolama'a*) which means, "made the water's path easy".

"مَأْتِيًّا" (*matiyan*): "one who comes definitely", (as if he has arrived). 19:61
"مَأْتِيًّا" (*matiyan*) is in fact past tense, and it means the object which one approached, or the thing which has already arrived. In this way, it would mean that everything meets the fate ordained by God.

"آتَى إِلَيْهِ الشَّيَّ" (*atya ileihishai*): something was sent towards him.
"آتَى فُلَا نَاشْيًا" (*atyafulana shyan*): he gave him that thing.

Abu al-Qasim Mahmud ibn Umar al-Zamakhshari writes in his book *Al-Kashaaf* that "آتَى" (*atya*) is often used for "اِعْطَاءٌ" (*i'taun*), but "اِيتَاءٌ" (*iytaun*) actually means to present someone something. .
That is why the word "اِيتَاءٌ" (*iytaun*) has been used to describe *sadaqat* (benevolence), in the Quran, according to *Raghib*. Reason for this can be that *sadaqat* may have been given with ease and the need to investigate, as to what had been given by whom, was simply not there.

The compiler of **Taj-ul-Uroos** give the examples of different sayings and maintains that "اِعْطَاءٌ" (**i'taun**) and "اِيتَاءٌ" (**iytaun**) differ in meanings that because in "اِعْطَاءٌ" (**i'taun**) the giver holds a slightly upper position but in "اِيتَاءٌ" (**iytaun**) the recipient's position may be better than the giver, or at least the same.

But we cannot take it as a rule because both words have been used as alternates, as in surah **At-Tauba**. It is said:

9:58	Some of them criticize you regarding the **sadqaat**. If they are given some of it, then they are pleased, if they do not get of it, they get angry	وَمِنْهُم مَّن يَلْمِزُكَ فِي الصَّدَقَاتِ فَإِنْ أُعْطُوا مِنْهَا رَضُوا وَإِن لَّمْ يُعْطَوْا مِنْهَا إِذَا هُمْ يَسْخَطُونَ
9:59	And (how nice it would be) if they were happy with what God and his Messenger had given them.	وَلَوْ أَنَّهُمْ رَضُوا مَا آتَاهُمُ اللَّهُ وَرَسُولُهُ

Regarding booty distribution, it is said in the Quran:

59:7	Whatever is given to you by the Messenger, take it and resist from taking what he forbids.	وَمَا آتَاكُمُ الرَّسُولُ فَخُذُوهُ وَمَا نَهَاكُمْ عَنْهُ فَانتَهُوا

This has been further explained in 9:59. This means the principle regarding war booty is not that one gets to keep whatever he collects.

All booty belongs to Allah's system, and it is disbursed by a central figure. In surah **Aal-e-Imran** this word appears apropos "نزع" (**naz'a**) which means "to take".

3:25	you give power to whom you wish and take away power from whom you wish	الْمُلْكَ مَن تَشَاء وَتَنزِعُ الْمُلْكَ مِمَّن تَشَاء

"اَتَي الرَّجُلُ" (**atayorrajolo**): that he did something, or performed some act.

The Quran says:

20:69	thereby, no matter what a sorcerer does, he can never succeed	وَلَا يُفْلِحُ السَّاحِرُ حَيْثُ أَتَى

Or, as it appears at another location

26:165	Contrary to universal practice, you perform this act with males.	أَتَأْتُونَ الذُّكْرَانَ مِنَ الْعَالَمِينَ

The writer of **Taj-ul-uroos** says that "اِعْطَاءٌ" (**i'taun**) and "اِيتَاءٌ" (**iytaun**) also differ in that "اِيتَاءٌ" (**iytaun**) refers to what is given to somebody does reach him and he also accepts it, whereas "اِعْطَاءٌ" (**i'taun**): that what is given to somebody doesn't necessarily reach him.

The Quran says:

17:20	what has been given by God is common, but God does not take it to every individual	وَهَؤُلَاءِ مِنْ عَطَاءِ رَبِّكَ وَمَا كَانَ عَطَاءُ رَبِّكَ مَحْظُورًا

This means that one has to struggle to get it. Nobody has the right to prevent His benevolence from reaching anyone, or act as a barrier to that benevolence.

Taj-ul-uroos also mentions that "اِيتَانٌ" (*iytanun*) means 'to kill'.

59:2	Allah annihilated them in a way of which that they hadn't even thought of	فَأَتَاهُمُ اللَّهُ مِنْ حَيْثُ لَمْ يَحْتَسِبُوا

A-Th-Th   أ ث ث

"اَلْأَثَاثُ" (*al-athath*): a large part of something, unbounded wealth, household goods, every kind of goods i.e. camels, goats, slaves, etc. "أَثَاثَةٌ" (*athathah*) is the singular. Some say it is used for all kinds of household goods but not goods for trading.

Ibn Dureed says, "أَثَاثُ الْبَيْتِ" (*athathul-baiti*): "الْمَتَاعُ الْجَيِّدُ" (*al-mata'ol-jayadu*) i.e. precious goods.

Ibn Faris says that it basically means 'gathering and softness', as in "اَثَّ النَّبْتُ أَثًّا" (*athanabtun aatha*) which means that 'the plants have become lush.

In the Quran "أَثَاثًا وَ مَتَاعًا" (*athathawa mta'a*) appears in meaning of 'goods'.

A-Th-R   أ ث ر

"اَلْأَثَرُ" (*a-athar*): remaining part of ruins etc. It also means remaining scar after that wound has healed.
"اَلْأَثِيرَةُ" (*al-athirah*): an animal that leaves tracks behind on the ground it has walked upon.
"اَلْأَثْرُ نُورُ وَالْمَيْثَرُ" (*al-totharru nooro walmaytharru*): an iron implement which is used to mark the underside of a camel's foot so that the camel can be branded, and can be identified later on, with the help of that mark if it gets lost.

The writer of **Muheet** says that "أَثَر" (*athar*) has four meanings:
1) Result of something
2) A sign
3) News
4) An order.

| 30:50 | So notice the signs of Allah's *rahmat* | فَانظُرْ إِلَى آثَارِ رَحْمَتِ اللَّهِ |

Here "أَثَر" means symbol, mark or sign.

| 48:29 | Mark on their faces | أَثَرِ السُّجُودِ |

The heartfelt peace and tranquillity is the result of obeying Allah, and gets evident from facial expressions.

Surah **Al-Momin** says:

| 40:21 | They were greater than them to plant tracks in the land | أَشَدَّ مِنْهُمْ قُوَّةً وَآثَارًا فِي الْأَرْضِ |

In surah **Yasin**, the word "قَدَّمُوا" appears with "آثَارَهُمْ"

| 36:12 | Whatever they have sent forth and the tracks they have left behind | مَا قَدَّمُوا وَآثَارَهُمْ |

In surah **Al-Kahaf**, this word appears in the sense of "footsteps".

| 18:6 | Back on the marks of their footsteps | عَلَى آثَارِهِمْ |

The same surah states further on:

| 18:64 | retraced their footsteps | فَارْتَدَّا عَلَى آثَارِهِمَا قَصَصًا |

Surah **Al-Hadeed** says:

| 57:27 | Then We sent other messengers behind them on their footsteps. (following them) | ثُمَّ قَفَّيْنَا عَلَى آثَارِهِم بِرُسُلِنَا |

Ibn Faris says that "الْأَثَرُ" (*al-atharu*) basically means to follow someone's tracks. This applies to both forms i.e. "أَثْرُ" (*athru*) and "إِثْرُ" (*ithru*).

The Quran says:

20:96	I gained a little from this messenger (**Moosa**) belief.	فَقَبَضْتُ قَبْضَةً مِّنْ أَثَرِ الرَّسُولِ
20:84	they follow my tracks (beliefs)	هُمْ أُولَاء عَلَى أَثَرِي
46:4	O symbol of knowledge	أَثَارَةٍ مِّنْ عِلْمٍ

This means scholastic reasoning (that which remains of knowledge).

"أَثَرُ" (*atharu*): to mark something as someone's own or somebody else's.

From this comes "اِيثَارُ" (*iytharu*) which means to give someone priority over one's own self. ***Ibn Faris*** has also endorsed this meaning.

Apropos the earlier meaning, it appears in the Quran

| 87:16 | Instead, you prefer these immediate benefits. (only the benefits of the physical life) | بَلْ تُؤْثِرُونَ الْحَيَاةَ الدُّنْيَا |
| 79:38 | And prefer the physical life | وَآثَرَ الْحَيَاةَ الدُّنْيَا |

The second meaning appears in surah ***Al-Hashr***:

| 59:9 | And they prefer others over themselves | وَيُؤْثِرُونَ عَلَى أَنْفُسِهِمْ |

The Quran says:

| 12:91 | Indeed, God has preferred you over us | لَقَدْ آثَرَكَ اللَّهُ عَلَيْنَا |
| 20:72 | what has come to us, we will not prefer over you | نُؤْثِرَكَ عَلَى مَا جَاءَنَا |

"حَدِيثٌ مَأْثُورٌ" (*hadethun mathorun*): a story that people have been passing on by telling it to one another.

Ibn Faris writes: "أَلْمَأْثُورَةٌ" (*al-mathorah*): a well which is now buried, but the bucket and rope are still there as a sign of its existence.

A-Th-L أ ث ل

"أَلْأَثْلُ" means a tree that cast shadow, or a tree that has strong roots.

According to ***Ibn Faris***, it means the reality of something or to gather things together. In other words, it means to have a strong base. Quran has used the word of "أَثْلٍ" in the sense of shadow casting tree (34:16).

A-Th-M أ ث م

"أَلْأَثِمَةٌ" (*al-athimah*) is used for a female camel that gets tired and hence walks very slowly.
"أَلْمُوَاثِمُ" (*al-mowathim*) is used to define a camel that can't go any further because of exhaustion.

Hence the term "اِثْمٌ" (*ithmun*) basically means:
- Exhaustion,
- Sadness,
- Loss of energy,
- Slow tread,
- Weakness.

Ibn Faris says it means "delay" or "to stay behind".

The Quran uses "اِثْمٌ" (*ithmun*) and "عُدْوَانٌ" (*a'dwanun*) for 'crime'. It refers to all acts which cause weakness in man and weaken his will to act and thus render him unable to traverse through life. To see the relevant elaboration of the word, please see the heading Ain-D-W where the difference between these two words has been illustrated. For this, the Quran has given the example of "خَمْرٌ" (*khamrun*) and "مَيْسِرٌ" (*mayasirun*) which means drinking and gambling, respectively. Here it says that though these do have their benefits, their use weakens human body and mind, and the damage caused is far more than their benefits.

2:219	They ask you regarding drinking and gambling; tell them "In them is great sin, and some profit for men; but the sin is greater than the profit."	يَسْأَلُونَكَ عَنِ الْخَمْرِ وَالْمَيْسِرِ قُلْ فِيهِمَا إِثْمٌ كَبِيرٌ وَمَنَافِعُ لِلنَّاسِ وَإِثْمُهُمَا أَكْبَرُ مِن نَّفْعِهِمَا

"خَمْرٌ" (*khamrun*) (intoxicating items) are well known for their debilitating effect on the human body; that is why it is said that heavenly wine will not have any "تَأْثِيمٌ" (*tathimun*) - intoxication.

56:25 56:26	No frivolity will they do not hear therein, nor any taint of ill— Only the saying "Peace! Peace."	لَا يَسْمَعُونَ فِيهَا لَغْوًا وَلَا تَأْثِيمًا إِلَّا قِيلًا سَلَامًا سَلَامًا

The word "مَيْسِرٌ" (*mayasirun*) comes from the word "يُسْرٌ" (*yosrun*) meaning "with ease". Thus "يُسْرٌ" (*yosrun*) is all earning acquired without due effort. How one becomes lethargic and unable to do hard work due to such income is widely known. Those who earn by claiming interest are also called "أَثِيمٌ" (*athimun*) 2:276.

Under the heading Ain-D-W, it has been said that "عُدْوَانٌ" (*a'dwanun*) also means such crimes that have a contagious effect. In other words, other people in society are also affected by it. As such, "أَثِيمٌ" (*athimun*) would mean such crimes whose effect is confined to the doer. For example, a man takes opium and lies down quietly. It is obvious that his act affects only him and no one else. But the Quran says even that is a crime, because the purpose of life is to grow and develop. As such, anything which causes weakness is a crime, even if it is self-induced. According to the Quran, it is also a crime to hurt oneself deliberately. Suicide is also murder (of self) and hence falls in the category of "أَثِيمٌ" (*athimun*).

Fornication needs no proof to be seen as a crime.

That is why it has been said for illegal/forbidden murder and fornication:

25:68	And the one, who does that, gets rewarded as a sinner.	وَمَن يَفْعَلْ ذَلِكَ يَلْقَ أَثَامًا

Similarly, if someone acquires wealth without working hard (no matter how he gets it) and he doesn't even hurt anybody in doing so, even then it is "أَثِيْمٌ" (*athimun*) (a crime) because by not working, his faculties will be weakened and according to the Quran, that, too, is a crime.

These, then, are the basic meanings of "أَثِيْمٌ" (*athimun*).

With the passage of time, people also started to use this word to describe ordinary crime. Some say that it means such act which takes time in producing a result. This, too, is included in its basic meanings, like slowness, delaying in producing result, producing result slowly, like the use of drugs.

Raghib says that "أَثِيْمٌ" (*athimun*) and "ذَنَبْ" (*zanab*) differ because "ذَنَبْ" (*zanab*) can occur unwittingly as well as deliberately but "أَثِيْمٌ" (*athimun*) is only with intent. But the definition of "بُطُوَّ" (*buto'an*) i.e. to take time is always included in its connotation.

In respect of "أَثِيْمٌ" (*athimun*), also see the heading (**B-R-R**), because it has also appeared against it as in

5:2	Co-operate with each other in works of *birr* and *taqwa* and do not co-operate (in acts of) *ism* and *udwan*.	وَتَعَاوَنُوا عَلَى الْبِرِّ وَالتَّقْوَى وَلَاتَعَاوَنُوا عَلَى الإِثْمِ وَالْعُدْوَانِ

<h2 style="text-align:center">A-J-J   أ ج ج</h2>

"اَلْأَجَّةُ" (*al-ajjah*) and "اَلْأَجِيْجْ" (*al-ajiju*): 'flare up, to be angered'. It also means the sound of burning fire.

"أَجَّ" (*ajja*), "يَوَجَ" (*yawaja*), "أَجَّا" (*ajja*): 'he walked fast'. "سَمِعْتُ أَجَّتَهُمْ" (*sami'tu ajjatahum*) would mean "I heard them walking" or "a mixed sound".

Ibn Faris says that its basic meanings are 'hear sounds' and 'intensity'.

"اَلْأَجَّةُ" (*a-ajjah*): unease, intense heat.
"مَاءٌ أَجَاجٌ" (*ma un ajajun*): very bitter water.
"وَ هَذَا مِلْعَ أَجَاجٌ" (*wa haaza mil'a ajaajun*): this water is very brackish (25:53, 35:12).
"أَجَاجَ فُلَانٌ" (*ajaaja flanun*): he attacked the enemy.
"سَمِعْتُ أَجَّةَ الْقَوْمِ" (*sami'ta-ajjattal qaum*): I heard mixed sound of movements and people's voices.

The words "يَاجُوْج" (*yajuj*) and "مَاجُوْج" (*majuj*) appear (Gog and Magog) twice in the Quran: (18:94) and in (21:96).

The former is in respect of King **Zulqarnain** whom the people of a nation pleaded to build a wall so that **Yajuj** and **Majuj** could not come and devastate their abodes. So **Zulqarnain** built them such a wall which surah **Al-Kahaf** mentions.in 18:96.

The latter is in reference to surah **Anbia** in which it is said:

21:95	There is a ban on a city which we have destroyed. They shall not return….	وَحَرَامٌ عَلَى قَرْيَةٍ أَهْلَكْنَاهَا أَنَّهُمْ لَا يَرْجِعُونَ
21:96	… until it is open for **Yajuj** and **Majooj**, and they stream down from all heights.	حَتَّى إِذَا فُتِحَتْ يَأْجُوجُ وَمَأْجُوجُ وَهُم مِّن كُلِّ حَدَبٍ يَنسِلُونَ

Yajuj and **Majuj** are also mentioned in the Torah and they are also mentioned in the prediction about the Messenger **Hazqeel** (Ezekiel).

(It may be remembered that Nebuchadnezzar had taken messenger **Hazqeel** to Babylon after destroying **Bait-ul-Muqaddas** (The Temple of Solomon) where he was alive till the time of the Persian king Cyrus who is called **Dhulqarnain** in the Quran.)

To the Europeans, **Yajuj** and **Majuj** are known as Gog and Magog. These are said to be Greek names and entered other European languages from there. As to which nations these are, researchers differ. But a majority of them seem to think that these were the desert-dwelling wild tribes of Mongolia who used to loot others. They used to appear like a wild storm and destroy everything before them. Genghis Khan and Helga Khan's warrior tribes are well known.

Mongolia's ancient name is "**Mog**" which turned to **Megog** in Greek and **Majuj** in the Israeli language.

Another tribe of this area was "**Yuachi**" which turned to **Yajuj** in the Israeli language. To avoid their attacks, nations used to build walls around them. These were the plateaus from which these tribes used to come and plunder the nations around them.

Although in surah **Al-Anbia** the names of **Yajuj** and **Majuj** are mentioned, they are meant to signify the plunderers and devastating traits of these tribes, no matter which nation they belong to.

The Quran has said that a nation which falls into ignominy shall not rise again. The only exception is in cases were conquering nation reach an under-developed nation, whose nationalism will be aroused and they will come alive again. But this does not mean that God wishes nations to subjugate nations so that the weaker nations undergo renaissance. Instead the Quran teaches that strong nations must help remove the weaknesses of the weaker nations so that they too can come up. The Quran says that if stronger nations do not do this, then the weaker nations will one day rise and throw away the yoke of slavery or subjugation.

Our era is witness to the fact as to how European nations reached weaker nations (especially Muslim countries) to exploit them, but gradually the weak nations rose against them and thus became lively once again. As such, the devastation of the tribes of *Yajuj* and *Majuj* became the harbinger of a new life for the weak nations and the fact described in (21:95-96) became evident.

Even if we take *Yajuj* and *Majuj* to be particular to their area, then it can also mean to point the fact that the current Russian designs to rule the world could be the reason for the rise of Muslim countries. But this can only happen if the Muslim nations adopt Quranic economic system.

Note: In the above mentioned verse of surah *Al-Anbia* 21:95 and 96, *hatta* has been translated to "up to here", but at other places it has also been used to start a speech and has no meaning. See the word ***hatta***.

A-J-R   أ ج ر

Ibn Faris says that this word means 'to pay' or repairing fractured bones. A labourer's pay is also called "أَجْرٌ" (*ajar*) because it helps him heal the wounds of labouring. The bones that are stretched in labour are healed by the justified pay.

"اَلْأَجْرُ" (*al-ajar*) is the justified compensation of someone's work.
"اَلْأَجْرَةُ" (*al-ajrah*) is the justified salary that one receives as compensation for his work.
"اِسْتِئْجَارٌ" (*istijarun*) is to employ someone for a salary.

It is said in surah ***Qasas***

28:26	O father, employ him for a salary.	يَا أَبَتِ اسْتَأْجِرْهُ

"أَجْرٌ" (*ajar*) or "كِنايَةٌ" (*knayah*) is used for such a gift which a husband gives to his wife on the wedding night. This is generally called "***Mehar***".

The Quran says:

33:50	Those whom you have given wedding presents to	آتَيْتَ أُجُورَهُنَّ

The Quran has given a firm principal: whatever a man gets (in this life and the hereafter) is the compensation of his own work or actions. Those who don't work don't get paid. This world is a place of work, which has no place for teetotallers. Societies in which people get something without working (except not being able to work) are not formulated according to Quranic laws.

A-J-L   أ ج ل

"اَلْأَجَلُ" (*al-ajal*): the fixed time period for something

"اَلتَّأْجِلُ" (*at-tajitil*): To fix a time period for something.

"مُوَجَّلٌ" (*muwajjal*): The one for whom a time period has been fixed

"تَأَجَّلَ" (*ta-ajjal*): he delayed.

"أَجِلَ" (*ajila*), "آجَلَ" (*aajla*): He was delayed.

"اَلْآجَلُ" (*al-aajil*): the opposite of "عاجل". See heading (*Ain-J-L*)

"أَجَلْ" (*ajl*): reason of, because of, due to.

"أَجَلٌ" (*ajl*) means a fixed period and also the limit where that period ends.

The Quran says

| 5:32 | Due to that reason | مِنْ أَجْلِ ذَلِكَ |
| 7:34 | Every nation has a fixed period (for rise and progress). | وَلِكُلِّ أُمَّةٍ أَجَلٌ |

But this "أَجَلٌ" (*ajal*) or fixed time is determined according to a law.

| 13:38 | For every fixed period, there is a law | لِكُلِّ أَجَلٍ كِتَابٌ |

And that law is

| 13:17 | Any nation will live as long as it is beneficial to mankind. | مَا يَنْفَعُ النَّاسَ فَيَمْكُثُ فِي الْأَرْضِ |

The Quran has given a detailed program for the rise and fall of nations. This means that the rise and fall of nations is not co-incidental. It happens according to an established principle. The Quran says that the result of any act starts formulating with the beginning but it appears as a tangible result only after a fixed period. The time between an act and its result is also called "أَجَلٌ" (*ajal*). This can also be called "Period of grace". This grace period too is fixed according to God's laws like the time between a seed becoming a tree.

About death, the Quran says in surah *Aal-e-Imran* that its time period is also fixed according to a law and it is the very same law that fixes its period.

| 3:145 | No living creature dies but in accordance to God's law (i.e. death comes as the law of nature) | وَمَا كَانَ لِنَفْسٍ أَنْ تَمُوتَ إِلَّا بِإِذْنِ اللهِ كِتَابًا مُؤَجَّلاً |

This very law determines the period of a man's life; by abusing one's health, one's age is decreased and by healthy living and avoiding hazardous living, life can be prolonged.

| 35:11 | No man is given a long(er) life nor is anybody's age decreased, but all this happens according to a law. | وَمَا يُعَمَّرُ مِنْ مُعَمَّرٍ وَلَا يُنْقَصُ مِنْ عُمُرِهِ إِلَّا فِي كِتَابٍ |

In other words, the extension or decreasing of age is all according to the laws created by God.

A woman's period of *idda* (the waiting period) i.e. isolation after her husband's death, is also called "أَجَلّ" (*ajal*)

2:221	When you divorce the women and they reach their (*idda*) period.	وَإِذَا طَلَّقْتُمُ النِّسَاءَ فَبَلَغْنَ أَجَلَهُنَّ

A-H-D أ ح د

"أَلْأَحَدُ" (*al-ahadu*): one, the first number.
"أَحَدٌ" (*ahad*): any one. The feminine is "إِحْدَى" (*ihdi*).
"أَلْأَحَدُ" (*al-ahadu*): one of God's attributes, and has not been used for anyone else in this connotation.

For the difference between "أَحَدٌ" (*ahad*) and "وَاحَدٌ" (*wahad*) see heading W-H-D.
"أَحَدٌ" (*ahad*) has the uniqueness of being the only one.

Therefore it is said "أَحَدُ الأَحَدَيْنِ" (*ahadul ahadain*) which means "He has no parallel or similar". This can be the most gracious praise for somebody.

"اِتَّحُدَ" (*ittahud*): to gather
"اِتَّحَادَ" (*ithad*): come together and agree upon something.
"اِسْتَاحَدَ" (*istahad*): individual and alone.

The Quran says:

2:102	but they did not teach anyone	وَمَا يُعَلِّمَانِ مِنْ أَحَدٍ

A-Kh-Dh أ خ ذ

"أَلْأَخْذُ" (*al-ikhaz*) is the opposite of 'to bestow' or 'to give'; it means 'to take'; to surround something.
Some say that "أَخْذٌ" (*akahz*) also encompasses the sense of anger and overwhelming. This word is used to mean annihilate or uproot, and also punishment as in "مُوَاخَذَةٌ" (*moakhazah*).

Ibn Faris says that it means "to surround", "to receive" and "to gather".

With reference to *Ibn Faris, Abu Ubaida* says, that:
"أَلْإِخَاذُ" (*al-akhaz*): a pool-like place where water gets collected.
"أَلْأَخِيذُ" (*al-akhiz*): a prisoner.
"أَلْأَخِيذَةُ" (*al-akhizah*): something which is usurped.

In the Quran, this word has been used in different meanings. In surah **Aal-e-Imran** it is said:

| 3:80 | Do you accept and take as binding on you this My Covenant? | وَأَخَذْتُمْ عَلَى ذَلِكُمْ إِصْرِي |

In surah **Yusuf**, it has been used to mean to arrest or to prevent

| 12:78 | Then arrest one of us in his place | فَخُذْ أَحَدَنَا مَكَانَهُ |

In surah **Hood**, it is used in the sense of the result or return which one gets for his act as per the laws of Nature

| 11:102 | And in this way does God hold (makes them pay) those dwellers which are *zalim* (unjust). Verily, his hold is woe begetting and very severe. | وَكَذَلِكَ أَخْذُ رَبِّكَ إِذَا أَخَذَ الْقُرَى وَهِيَ ظَالِمَةٌ إِنَّ أَخْذَهُ أَلِيمٌ شَدِيدٌ |
| 40:5 | And thereafter each nation plotted against their messenger to seize him | وَهَمَّتْ كُلُّ أُمَّةٍ بِرَسُولِهِمْ لِيَأْخُذُوهُ |

Here "أَخْذَ" (*akhza*): every type of opposition, in order to stop the Messenger's mission from progressing.

The Quran says:

| 8:68 | What you did or took | فِيمَا أَخَذْتُمْ |
| 18:86 | Be kind to them in behaviour | تَتَّخِذَ فِيهِمْ حُسْنًا |

A-Kh-R   أ خ ر

"آخِرٌ" (*aakhir*) is the opposite of "أَوَّلٌ" (*awwal*). The meaning of this word is of being last.

| 57:3 | The one who is the first and the last | هُوَ الْأَوَّلُ وَالْآخِرُ |

The author of **Muheet** says that it means 'something which follows something else, but does not get followed by anything'. This shows that "آخِرٌ" (*akhirun*) is the end of a chain, where there is no other link after it.

That is why the Quran has equated this life with a second life as "خَلْقٌ جَدِيدٌ" (*khalaqun jadeedun*) (17:49,98 and 42:10). This means that the Afterlife will come as a continuation of and as such, the last link of, this life. But it will come at the natural end of this life and a new life will begin. In this way, it will be the first link to a new life.

Likewise, when after the Quranic revolution, a new civilization begins, which is although linked to the former life, is the last link to that life. This makes a new kind of human civilization.

Therefore "آخِرَةٌ" (*aakhirah*) is the last segment of any sequence, after which a new sequence begins.

"آخِرَةُ الرَّحْلِ" (*aakhiraturrahli*) is used for the back part of a howdah, and is the opposite of "قَادِمَةُ الرَّحْلِ" (*qadimaturrahli*)

"آخِرَةُ الْعَيْنِ" (*aakhiratula'een*) is that corner of the eye which is adjacent to the cheek, and "قَادِمَةُ الْعَيْنِ" (*qadimatula'een*) is that part of the eye which is adjacent to the nose.

"أُخْرٌ" (*okhr*) is the opposite of "قُدُمٌ" (*qadamun*), which means to be in front. Therefore, "أُخْرٌ" (*akhir*) means to be behind.

"تَأَخُّرُ" (*takhar*) is the opposite of "تَقَدَّمَ" (*taqaddam*). The meanings of "مُتَقَدِّمٌ" (*motaqadim*) and "مُتَأَخِّرٌ" (*mutakhir*) can be gauged from this.

In the Quran, "يَسْتَأْخِرُونَ" (*yastakhirona*) appears opposite to "مَا تَسْبِقُ" (*ma tasbiqu*) in 18:5, and "مُسْتَأْخِرِينَ" (*mustakhirina*) appears against "مُسْتَقْدِمِينَ" (*mustaqdinu*) in 17:24.

"أَخَرٌ" (*akhar*): outsider or different from others. In this fashion "رَجُلٌ أَخَرٌ" (*rajalun akharun*) would mean, another man. If six men are standing in a queue, then the man opposite to the first man will be "آخَرُ" (*aakhar*). And after the second, the third will be "آخَرُ" (*aakhar*). This process will continue till the last.

After this, it became normal to use the word "آخَرُ" (*aakharu*) to mean "being different from the last link".

In surah **Al-Mominoon**, this has been explicitly defined. Regarding human birth, it has been said that it began with essence of the earth, and then the sperm was formulated. Then the sperm turned into a lump of flesh, then the bones were formed, then the bones were covered with flesh; these are the different stages which take place according to the laws of birth, not one link in this chain comes into being without the former link (in other words, no link can be omitted). (Up to this stage, animal and human foetuses are still with no differences between them).

Later, it is said:

| 23:14 | And We then raised Man as a new creation | ثُمَّ أَنْشَأْنَاهُ خَلْقًا آخَرَ |

This means that this link in the creative chain is totally different.

This point is towards the human personae, which is not subservient to the physical laws of Nature. This is known as "emergent evolution", i.e. the existence of a new species with is totally different from all former links that it follows during the process of evolution.

Therefore, the concept that comes fore is of human life which (at this stage) is transformed into a creation totally different from its former links. This will continue till his biological death. The death symbolizes the last link of the sequence of life. Life will then start a new sequence in a totally different and new style.

Those who think about our "physical laws" being applicable to that life can't believe in that life. But those who have eyes and ears, i.e. those who are observant and think, and those who have their eyes on the sudden creative revolutions of nature, can't do anything else but believe in a life hereafter.

"آخِرَةٌ" (*aakhirah*) is that future, which comes as a product of revolution and not according to ordinary circumstances, and that revolution takes place (in its life) through the Quran, and life after death also comes into being due to a revolution.

As against "الْحَيَاةِ الدُّنْيَا" (*alhayatid-dunya*) - the life of this world, the Quran uses words like "الْقِيَامَةِ" (*al-qyamah*) and "آخَرَ" (*aakhira*).

For instance:

2:85	Embarrassment in this life, and harsher punishment in period of the last one.	خِزْيٌ فِي الْحَيَاةِ الدُّنْيَا وَيَوْمَ الْقِيَامَةِ يُرَدُّونَ
2:86	These are the ones who have traded this life, in exchange for that last one.	أُولَئِكَ الَّذِينَ اشْتَرَوُاْ الْحَيَاةَ الدُّنْيَا بِالآخِرَة

"الدُّنْيَا" (*ad-dunya*): that which is nearby, and is therefore against "آخَرَ" (*aakhir*) which is that comes quickly. The Quran uses "آخَرَ" (*aakhir*) - that which comes later in 17:18-19 and 75:20-21.
Similarly, "تَعَجَّلُ" (*ta'ajjalu*) and "تَأَخَّرَ" (*ta-akhara*) have been used as opposites, as in 2:203. "آخِرَةٌ" (*aakhirah*) has also been used against "أُوْلِي" (*aolay*) in other words, e.g. the afterword against this world, as in 79:25.

As stated above, in surah *Al-Hijr* "مُسْتَأْخِرِينَ" (*mustakhirina*) has been used as against "مُسْتَقْدِينَ" (*mustaqdina*) 15:24, meaning those who came later and those who departed earlier, respectively

This has been further expounded as

15:5	No one among peoples can escape the time limit or postpone it.	مَّا تَسْبِقُ مِنْ أُمَّةٍ أَجَلَهَا وَمَا يَسْتَأْخِرُونَ

In surah *Al-Shora*, "فِي الآخِرِينَ" (*fil aakhirina*) means "those generations that come later" (26:84). As such, the word "آخِرَةٌ" (*aakhira*) includes the concepts of all the happiness in the hereafter, future generations (of man) as against the present humanity, a new life beginning after a revolution, and a new life after this life.

"أَخَّرَ" (*akhara*) or "يُوَخِّرُ" (*yowakhiru*): 'to do something later, to delay, postpone, and give it time'. "تَأَخَّرَ" (*ta-akhara*): to stay behind or come after another.

2:204	And who hurries in a couple of days (and goes away)....and he who stays behind	فَمَن تَعَجَّلَ فِي يَوْمَيْنِ فَلَا إِثْمَ عَلَيْهِ وَمَن تَأَخَّرَ

The Quran says that the **Momineen** (Believers) believe in "آخِرَةٌ" (**aakhirah**) which is 'the future'. They never care for the present (quick) benefits but stay focused on the future.

The grower who grinds wheat seeds meant to be used in the future for sowing, in order to make bread for instant use, gets to eat it instantly, but faces a future of hunger. Contrary to that, the farmer who sows seeds and waits a few months with great patience for the crop to be ready brightens up his future. When this becomes a repeated cycle, then his present becomes bright too. This is because of believing in "آخِرَةٌ" (**aakhira**-future) and for not jumping at the immediate benefits.

Reflect for a while and you will come to the conclusion that only those nations which have the betterment of the future in mind, prosper in this world. A believer is one who believes in the future. But today, under the sky, the believers (the Muslims) are probably the most negligent of the future and thus lag behind most nations although their future was supposed to be so bright that, even in the hereafter, they were supposed to be ahead of everybody. In the life of an individual, every next breath is the future. For a nation, its future is its coming generation. For human kind, the generation to follow is the future, and for all of them, the life after this biological life is the future. Give it a thought as to what the Quran means when it advises to keep the afterlife in mind as compared to the immediate benefits of the present life (biological life).

Therefore, every individual, or a nation, should:
1) Not think only of the present, but also keep the future in mind.
2) Not only focus on the welfare of the present generations but also keep an eye on the well-being of the next generations.
3) Not consider this biological life as the only life, but have faith in life after death as well.

Also see heading (**D-N-W**).

A-Kh-W   أ خ و

The word of "اَلْأَخُ" (*al-akhu*) has been derived from "أَخِيَّةٌ" (*akhiyah*) which means burying both ends of a rope or steel wire in the ground; thus the loop formed by the rope or wire remaining above the ground was used to tie animals to. As such, "أَخُّ" (*akhu*): to be tied to a loop or stake.

This term is used for 'brother', or for people who have a common bond of tribalism, religion, trait, love, or some other common issue. Some think that this word has come from "وَخَى" (*wakhi*) which means "intent" and hence this way "أَخُّ" (*akhu*) would mean "common intent". The feminine of the word is "أُخْتٌ" (*ukhtu*).

The Quran has used "اِخْوَانٌ" (*ikhwanun*) against "أَعْدَاءٌ" (*a'daun*). Such as:

| 3:103 | Once you were each other's enemies, then with His benevolence, He turned you into each other's brothers | إِذْ كُنتُمْ أَعْدَاء فَأَلَّفَ بَيْنَ قُلُوبِكُمْ فَأَصْبَحْتُم بِنِعْمَتِهِ إِخْوَانًا |

"أَعْدَاءٌ" (*a'ada*): those who have a wedge in-between. Therefore "اِخْوَانٌ" (*ikhwan*) are those who have nothing (no barrier) in between.

As such, "*momineen*" are those people whose hearts are joined like one cloud is joined to another. Quran says that all Momineen are each other's "اِخْوَةٌ" (*ikhwah*).

| 49:10 | Verily all **Momineen** are each other's peers. | إِنَّمَا الْمُؤْمِنُونَ إِخْوَةٌ |

And they all are tied together with the rope of the Quran.

| 3:102 | All of you must hold God's rope strongly | وَاعْتَصِمُواْ بِحَبْلِ اللّهِ جَمِيعًا |

That is the correct relation between the **Momineen**.

The Quran also uses this word for persons of the same tribe.

| 27:45 | Towards **Thamod**, we sent their brother, **Saleh** | وَلَقَدْ أَرْسَلْنَا إِلَى ثَمُودَ أَخَاهُمْ صَالِحًا |

And also for those of the same faith:

| 17:27 | Wasters are the brothers of **Shaitan**. | إِنَّ الْمُبَذِّرِينَ كَانُواْ إِخْوَانَ الشَّيَاطِينِ |

Similarly, "أُخْتٌ" (*ukhtu*) has been used for women of the same tribe. **Maryam** has been called **Haroon's** sister.

| 19:28 | **O Haroon's** sister, your father was no bad man. | يَا أُخْتَ هَارُونَ مَا كَانَ أَبُوكِ امْرَأَ سَوْءٍ |

And, also nations of the same faith have been called each other's "أُخْتٌ" (*akhtu*).

A-D-D   أ د د

"اَلْإِدُّ" (*al-idda*): wonder, disturbing issue, surprise. "اَلْإِدِيْدُّ" (*al-ideedun*): shouting, and the sound of falling water. Meaning thereby, such talk which people dislike so much that an opposition is created and which makes people talk {R}.

"اَدَّ اَلْبَعِيْرُ" (*adda-al-ba'yru*): murmuring of a camel.
"اَدَّتِ النَّاقَةُ" (*addatin-naqah*): sighing by a female camel, and to cry out loud;
"اَدَّتْهُ الدَّاهِيَةُ" (*addathud-dahiyah*): he got worried due to a problem.
"تَاَدَّ دَا اَلْاَمْرُ" (*tadda daa al-amru*) the matter got complicated.

The Quran tells the Christians that by believing that Christ was God's son, they have complicated the matter.

| 19:89 | Indeed, you come up with a very sad and painful statement. | لَقَدْ جِئْتُمْ شَيْئًا إِدًّا |

In other words, they have invented a very dangerous and fictitious belief.

According to **Ibn Faris**, the basic meaning of this root is of becoming very big, grand, in repeated manner; something to get grand and get out of control.

Idrees   إِدْرِيْسُ

The Quran has mentioned **Idrees** as one of the Messengers.

| 19:56 | And mention **Idrees** in the Book, verily he was a true Messenger | وَاذْكُرْ فِي الْكِتَابِ إِدْرِيسَ إِنَّهُ كَانَ صِدِّيقًا نَّبِيًّا |
| 21:85 | And **Ismael**, **Idris** and **Dhul Kifl**, they were all steadfast, | وَإِسْمَاعِيلَ وَإِدْرِيسَ وَذَا الْكِفْلِ كُلٌّ مِّنَ الصَّابِرِينَ |

But his detailed account does not appear anywhere. It is guessed that his time was even earlier than **Nooh's**. In the **Torah** he has been named as **Hanuk** or **Akhnuh**. If he is indeed **Hanuk**, then he falls into the 4th generation of **Nooh's** forefathers. The **Torah** mentions his genealogical tree as following: **Nooh**, Son of **Lamuk**, Son of **Methuselah**, and Son of **Hanuk** {the book of Genesis 5:21-29}.

A-D-M أ د م

Ibn Faris says that it means, love, harmony, compatibility.

"أَدْمَةٌ" (*admato*): closeness, in agreement, to live together, or inter mingling.

"أَدَمَةٌ" or "أَدْمَةٌ" (*adamto or admato*): to mix together, to be in agreement, to love each other.

"أَدَمَ اَللّهُ بَيْنَهُمْ يَأْدِمُ" means that Allah created mutual harmony among them.

"الْإِدَامُ" (*al-idamo*) is anything that agrees (with), or which can co-exist.

In reality it means something which is eaten, or goes together, with bread i.e. curry, vegetables etc.

"اَلْأَدَمَةُ" (*aladma*): wheat. It also means the inside of the skin.

"إِدَامٌ" (*idam*) is such a person by whom one can recognize his tribe.

"آدَامِىٌّ" (*aadami*) the one associated with "أَدَمَ" (*adama*) which is "human".

We generally think that Adam (who was expelled from Heaven) was a Messenger (2:3). The Quran does not support this assumption. From the various places in which the Quran mentions his tale, it appears that he was not a particular person but a symbol of the human race. In other words, the tale of Adam is not about a particular pair, but the tale of humans themselves, which the Quran has presented in an allegory.

The tale begins during the time when Man began to live a social life after shunning individualistic life. The word "أَدْمَةٌ" (*admatu*) itself points to that social life. Thus "humanism" indicates that condition of human life when humans began to live (together) in society. Living together led to a conflict of interests.

The solution to this conflict was beyond the grasp of human intellect. The solution was given through revelation. Details can be seen in my book *Iblees aur Aadam.*

Even so, there is one place in the Quran where Adam is mentioned as if it was an individual.

3:33	Verily Allah had given priority to *Adam* and *Nooh* and the progenies of Ibrahim and Imran (over other nations during their time).	إِنَّ اللّهَ اصْطَفَى آدَمَ وَنُوحًا وَآلَ إِبْرَاهِيمَ وَآلَ عِمْرَانَ عَلَى الْعَالَمِينَ

Here *Adam* is mentioned with *Nooh* that makes one think that this is an individual and he (like *Nooh*) was also a messenger although *istefa* has also been used for non-messengers in the Quran. Maybe Adam is the name of some personality towards which this name has been linked in this tale of the Quran, or somebody had been called by this name during this era. I have not called him a Messenger because the Quran has not mentioned him in respect of Messengers.

See 3:41 regarding **Maryam**. Also see 35:32 regarding the followers of the Messenger **Mohammad**. However, Adam mentioned in verse number 3:33 is different from the Adam "who was expelled from Heaven". Maybe he was a messenger (and his name could be Adam), but the Quran has not elaborated further. The tales of messengers generally begin with reference to **Nooh**.

Surah **An-Nisa** says:

| 4:163 | Verily we have sent **wahi** (Revelation) towards you as we did towards **Nooh** and the messenger after him. | إِنَّا أَوْحَيْنَا إِلَيْكَ كَمَا أَوْحَيْنَا إِلَى نُوحٍ وَالنَّبِيِّينَ مِن بَعْدِهِ |

However, the Quran also indicates that there had been other Messengers in his nation before him. See 25:37.

The reason for mentioning the tale about Adam in the Quran is to tell man what he would face if he followed any path except shown in the revelation and to tell him that the only way to get back towards a heavenly life is to adhere to Allah's ways. But at the same time it has refuted through this tale the false belief that the Christians had propagated that every child is born a sinner and he comes burdened with the sins of the first parents, and these sins cannot be washed away without having faith on the atonement of Jesus, or that a woman is the fountainhead of all evil because she induced Adam to sin, or to refute the belief as the Hindus propagate that the forces of nature are gods, and man should worship them etc. Through this tale all false beliefs have been refuted.

A-D-W/Y   أ د و/ى

"أَدَوْتَ تَفْعَلُ كَذَا" (*adauta taf'al kaza*) - 'you kept on planning this'. Its root is "أَدَاةٌ" (*ada*) which means a way or scheme by which one can be reached.

Ibn Faris says that its basic meaning is 'to take something to someone', or 'for a thing to reach something else on its own'.

"أَدَّاهُ" (*addahu*) or "تَأْدِيَةٌ" (*ta-adih*): 'to take to him'.
"أَدَّى دَيْنَهُ" (*addi dinahu*) he paid.

The Quran says:

| 2:178 | and pay (back) debt with nicety | وَأَدَاءٌ إِلَيْهِ بِإِحْسَانٍ |

It also means 'to hand something over to someone'. **Moosa** told Pharaoh: "*aduwa ila-un ibadallah*" ('hand over the slaves of God to me').

It is also used for handing back "**amana**" (that which is kept in trust for safe keeping).

| 2:283 | He who has been trusted (with something) must give back the *amana* (that which has been given in trust for safe keeping). | فَلْيُؤَدِّ الَّذِي اؤْتُمِنَ أَمَانَتَهُ |

Idh   إِذ

"إِذْ" (*iz*) is used for when, at the time, at the place. It is usually used in the past tense.

| 2:30 | When your Sustainer told the *Malaika*… | وَإِذْ قَالَ رَبُّكَ لِلْمَلَائِكَة |
| 2:127 | when Ibrahim was raising the foundations | وَإِذْ يَرْفَعُ إِبْرَاهِيمُ الْقَوَاعِدَ |

Sometimes the word means, "Therefore" or "because". For instance,

| 43:39 | Today it will not be of any use because you used to transgress. | يَنفَعَكُمُ الْيَوْمَ إِذ ظَّلَمْتُمْ |

With reference to *Suhahi* (another linguist), *William Lane* says that sometimes "إِذْ" (*iz*) is redundant, like:

| 2:51 | It is a fact that We ordered Musa for forty nights | وَإِذْ وَاعَدْنَا مُوسَى أَرْبَعِينَ لَيْلَةً |

At these places, "إِذْ" (*iz*) creates a new topic.

| 99:4 | that day it will relate all its news | يَوْمَئِذٍ تُحَدِّثُ أَخْبَارَهَا |
| 56:84 | and at that time you were watching | وَأَنتُمْ حِينَئِذٍ تَنظُرُونَ |

A-Dh-A   أ ذ أ

"إِذَا" (*iza*): different things, for instance:

1)   Sometimes it is used to mean "suddenly". In other words it is used when something happens suddenly.

"خَرَجْتُ فَإِذَا الْأَسَدُبِالْبَابِ" (*kharajtu fa iza alasadbilbaab*): when I came out I saw a lion in front of the door.

| 20:21 | Suddenly he saw that it was a snake and it was moving. | فَإِذَا هِيَ حَيَّةٌ تَسْعَى |

2)   Sometimes "إِذَا" also means "so" or "thus". In other words, the result of something,

| 30:36 | And they are visited by woe that is of their own doing, and then they lose hope. | وَإِن تُصِبْهُمْ سَيِّئَةٌ بِمَا قَدَّمَتْ أَيْدِيهِمْ إِذَا هُمْ يَقْنَطُونَ |

3)   Sometimes it means "when" in a conditional mode and is used both in the past and future tense.

| 110:1 | When God's help arrived | إِذَا جَاءَ نَصْرُ اللَّهِ وَالْفَتْحُ |
| 3:159 | When you decide firmly then have full faith in God's law. | فَإِذَا عَزَمْتَ فَتَوَكَّلْ عَلَى اللَّهِ |

"إِذَا" (iza) is also used when we say: 'if this happens, then this will be like this or this.'

Surah *Al-Mominoon* says:

| 23:34 | If you follow one like you (then be warned) in that case you will be a great loser | وَلَئِنْ أَطَعْتُم بَشَرًا مِّثْلَكُمْ إِنَّكُمْ إِذًا لَّخَاسِرُونَ |

"إِذَا" (iza) also means 'when', 'at which time'. Surah *Shoora* says:

| 42:37 | When they are angered then they protect others from the damaging influence of their anger. | وَإِذَا مَا غَضِبُوا هُمْ يَغْفِرُونَ |

A-Dh-N   أ ذ ن

"أُذْنٌ" (aznun) and "أُذُنٌ" (uznun): ears, the plural of which is "آذَانٌ" (aazaan). "آذَن" (aazan): a person who has large ears, and "أُذُنٌ" (azan): somebody who listens to (obeys), and accepts whatever is said. Quran says:

| 9:61 | (Opponents say about) the Messenger that he believes everything he hears | النَّبِيَّ وَيَقُولُونَ هُوَ أُذُنٌ |

"آذَانٌ" (aazan): an announcement.

| 9:3 | This is an announcement from Allah and His Messenger to the people | وَأَذَانٌ مِّنَ اللَّهِ وَرَسُولِهِ إِلَى النَّاسِ |

"آذِنَ اِلَيْهِ وَلَهُ" (aazina ileihi walahu): to listen attentively, willingly, but some feel that the liking or disliking is not implied. Some dictionary scholars say that this has a connotation of obeying along with listening. As such, to them: "وَأَذِنَتْ لِرَبِّهَا وَحُقَّتْ" (84:2, 84:5): not only 'to listen' but also 'to obey'.
"تَأَذَّنَ" (ta-azana): announce or give some news to somebody. But some others think it means to swear {T}.

Actually it does have the connotation of swearing and belief. The teller says, verily I'll do it. As such where Surah *Al-Ahzaf* says:

| 7:167 | And your Sustainer announced that He will do it. | وَإِذْ تَأَذَّنَ رَبُّكَ |

(By God's announcement or saying something definitely would mean that he has made a law (for something).

"اَذِنَ بِالشَّيْئِ" means 'to find out about something'; 'to be aware of it' *{T}*.

| 2:279 | for God has announced war against you | فَأْذَنُوْا بِحَرْبٍ مِّنَ اللّهِ |

"اَذِنَ لَهُ فِى الشَّيْئِ" (*azina lahu fishai-i*): 'to give permission', and "اِسْتَيْذَانٌ" (*istaezan*): 'to seek permission'.

"اِذْنٌ" (*izn*): permission, announcement and awareness. "فَعَلَهُ بِاِذْنِي" (*fa'alahu bi izni*): 'he did it with my knowledge'. *{T}*

Ibn Faris says that it means 'ear' as well as and 'knowledge'.

Raghib says "اِذْنٌ" (*izn*) and "عِلْمٌ" (*ilm*) (knowledge) differ as "اِذْنٌ" (*izn*) is used when the intent and willingness of the one with knowledge is included, but it is not necessarily the case with "عِلْمٌ" (*ilm*), therefore, ***iznillah*** would mean both the knowledge and permission of Allah. Ordinarily this is known as God's law or rule. (Its details will be found under the heading "Sh-Y"). Thus, in the Quran, wherever "اِذْنُ الله" (*iznu-llahi*) appears, both His knowledge and Will are intended.

Surah ***Al-Airaaf*** says,

| 7:58 | And good result comes forth from it, according to Steiner's "اِذْنٌ" (rule). | وَالْبَلَدُ الطَّيِّبُ يَخْرُجُ نَبَاتُهُ بِاِذْنِ رَبِّهِ |

It is obvious that God has a law regarding agriculture, and crops appear according to this law.

The Quran says:

| 22:65 | He holds back the clouds (rain) so that it doesn't fall onto the earth without his "اِذْنٌ" | وَيُمْسِكُ السَّمَاءَ أَن تَقَعَ عَلَى الْأَرْضِ إِلَّا بِاِذْنِهِ |
| 3:145 | No ***nafs*** comes to rest, unless according to Allah's laws | وَمَا كَانَ لِنَفْسٍ أَنْ تَمُوتَ إِلَّا بِاِذْنِ الله |

This means that all living things die according to a law (of God / Nature).

Surah ***Al-Baqrah*** says:

| 2:102 | But they hurt no one, except according to Allah's law | وَمَا هُم بِضَآرِّينَ بِهِ مِنْ أَحَدٍ إِلَّا بِاِذْنِ اللّهِ |

This means that Allah has enabled man to be hurt by the harm inflicted by another.

Stones do not have this characteristic. This is what "اِذْنْ" (*izn*) is. This is the announced law of God. Different things having different characteristics that determine their existence, is called God's law which manifests itself in the form of Law of Nature. And as far the life of human society is concerned, this "اِذْنْ" (*izn*) is written in the Book of God (the Quran).

Surah **Al-Baqrah** says:

| 2:213 | And guides those who are **Momineen** towards the truth about things that they (people) differ in, according to the law (in the book) | فَهَدَى اللَّهُ الَّذِينَ آمَنُوا لِمَا اخْتَلَفُوا فِيهِ مِنَ الْحَقِّ بِإِذْنِهِ |

Here "اِذْنْ" (*izn*): the Book of God (the Quran) which holds the announced law.

If it is taken to mean ordinary law, then it would mean that God guides people (believers) according to the law of guidance and guidance is begotten by those who seek guidance. Those who don't seek guidance, remain astray. However, "اِذْنْ" (*izn*) of Allah means God's law or the rule of guidance as contained in the Quran.

A-Dh-Y   أ ذ ي

"اَلأَذِيَّةٌ" (*al-aziyah*): something that is unpleasant, unwanted, slight botheration. When this increases, it becomes "ضَرَرٌ" (*zarar*) which means much pain, or trouble. "أَذِيَ" (*aziy*) or "يُوْذِيْ" (*yoziy*): to hurt somebody. In other words, to say something that is unpleasant for others to hear {T}.

Taj-ul-Uroos says that its derivation could be "اِيْذَاءْ" (*iyza*), but this word has not been noticed anywhere in the Arabic language. "نَاقَةٌ أَذِيَّةٌ" (*naqata aziyah*) is used for a female camel which is restless by disposition.

Regarding a woman's menstruation, the Quran says:

| 2:222 | Tell them that it is a setback. | قُلْ هُوَ أَذًى |

Here the word gives the sense of displeasure, dirtiness, and slight unease. That is why men have been advised to stay away from women during these times.

The same surah states ahead:

| 2:264 | After meeting other's need, don't create an unpleasant situation….. | لَا تُبْطِلُوا صَدَقَاتِكُم بِالْمَنِّ وَالأَذَى |

If you do so, then your help will have a destructive effect instead of constructive results, or your act will come to naught.

In a sense of punishing, this word appears in following verse

| 4:16 | And the two among you who commit this act, punish them. | وَاللَّذَانَ يَأْتِيَانِهَا مِنكُمْ فَآذُوهُمَا |

Regarding the pain (in sickness) surah **Al-Baqrah** says:

2:196	Then whoso among you who are sick or have a headache.	فَمَن كَانَ مِنكُم مَّرِيضاً أَوْ بِهِ أَذًى مِّن رَّأْسِهِ

A-R-B   أ ر ب

Ibn Faris says it has four basic meanings: need, intellect, a part, to tie a knot or to make something harder.

"ٱلْأَرَب" (*al-arab*), "ٱلْإِرْبَة" (*al-irbah*) or "ٱلْأُرْبَة" (*al-urbah*): cunningness, insight, wittiness, complete organ from which nothing is missing, intellect, and expanse.

"أَرِبَ بِالشَّيْء" (*araba bishaiy*): to be expert of something.

"أَرِبَ اِلَيْهِ" (*ariba ileihi*): "he felt urgent need of", or "lacked it".

"ٱلْأَرْبُ" (*al-arbu*): that distance (expanse) between the forefinger and the human middle finger.

"أَرَّبُ الشَّيْءَ" (*arrabusheiyu*): "to strengthen something, to make it complete" {M}.

"ٱلْأَرَبُ" (*al-arabu*): intensity, need, or requirement.

"ٱلْإِرْبَة" (*al-irbah*) or "ٱلْمَأْرَبَة" (*al-marabah*): need or requirement.

"أَرَاب" (*aarabun*) is the most essential organ. {R}

Surah **Tahaa** says:

20:18	"This will fulfill my many other needs" or "I will solve many other problems with this" or "I will get such insight from it as will help widen my understanding" or "I will get help from it in many different matters."	وَلِيَ فِيهَا مَآرِبُ أُخْرَى

Surah **An-Noor** says:

24:31	Such servants (among men) who don't (have) the need (to marry).	غَيْرِ أُولِي الْإِرْبَةِ مِنَ الرِّجَالِ

This may include servants who do lowly chores, or do not possess much intellect and who are not bothered with anything other than their meals, or who cannot in any way be attractive. This term of the Quran is very composite.

A-R-Zd أ ر ض

Anything that is low is called "أَرْضٌ" (*arz*), opposite to "سَمَاءٌ" (*sama*). As such, "أَرْضُ النَّعْلِ" (*arzun-na'li*): the sole of the shoe. Besides that, the part of the leg below the knee is also called "أَرْضٌ" (*arz*). The earth is also called "أَرْضٌ" (*arz*) because it is under one's feet. *{T}*

Since the basis of all human economics is the earth, the word "الْأَرْضَةُ" (*al-arzah*): wellbeing *{T}*. "أَرْضَتِ الْأَرْضُ" (*arzatil-arz*): that the land has become productive. Since it has become very productive it has also become pleasing to the eye. "جَدْيٌ أَرِيْضٌ" (*jadyun arizun*): a fat kid (young goat). "الْأَرْضُ" (*arzu*) also means a termite *{T}*.

Since "أَرْضٌ" (*arzun*): something below, that is why "أَرَضَةٌ" (*arazah*): humble and obedient. "أَرِيْضٌ" (*ariza*) also means a kind man, or nation, or fine land. *{F}*

In the Quran, the word "أَرْضٌ" appears along with the word "جِبَالٌ"

18:47	During when we move the "جِبَالٌ", then you shall see "أَرْضٌ" come forth	وَيَوْمَ نُسَيِّرُ الْجِبَالَ وَتَرَى الْأَرْضَ بَارِزَةً

Here *jibaal* would mean the prominent people and *arz* the common people.

"أَرْضٌ وَ سَمَوَاتٌ" (*arzun wa samawatun*) would mean the highs and lows of the universe.

Where ever these words have anything to do with any segment of human life, then "سَمَاءٌ" (*sama*) would mean God's law for the universe and "أَرْضٌ" (*arz*) would mean man's economic life. Quran says:

7:10	We have kept the means of economy in it (the earth)	وَجَعَلْنَا لَكُمْ فِيهَا مَعَايِشَ

Deliberation on this will bring one to the conclusion that the real basis of human economy is the earth. That is why this word has also been used for channels of food. If economic life is separated from God's universal law or the way of life which the Quran has ordained, then human life is degraded to a very low level of animal life in which benefits of the biological life may be attained, but the high ideals of human life are not. This economic life has been described by the Quran as benefits of this near (short) life, and it has been described as depth against height.

7:169	Benefits of this low (life)	عَرَضَ هَذَا الْأَدْنَى
7:176	If We would have desired, We could have raised him, but he was attached to the earth.	وَلَوْ شِئْنَا لَرَفَعْنَاهُ بِهَا وَلَكِنَّهُ أَخْلَدَ إِلَى الْأَرْضِ

So, what the verses are saying is that "We wanted to give loftiness to him (Man) through our law of economics but he clung to lowliness."

In other words, considering the interests of this biological life as the only reason of life has been described as selfishness or self-interest and vested interest.

In the language of the Quran:

| 7:176 | And he gave in to his own will | وَاتَّبَعَ هَوَاهُ |

Tauheed (to follow God) is that the external universal laws are to be implemented in the human economic life. This law is attained through *wahi* (Revelation) and is to be found in the Quran. *Tauheed* demands the same order of things to operate in the universe as well as on earth.

| 43:84 | He is the Lord in the skies and the earth | وَهُوَ الَّذِي فِي السَّمَاءِ إِلَهٌ وَفِي الْأَرْضِ إِلَهٌ |

If Man, instead of Allah's law, adopts his self-made laws, then inequities make life unbearable.

| 21:21 | Have they raised gods from earth they raise? | أَمِ اتَّخَذُوا آلِهَةً مِّنَ الْأَرْضِ هُمْ يُنشِرُونَ |
| 21:22 | If there were gods in them, besides Allah, they would surely have been ruined | لَوْ كَانَ فِيهِمَا آلِهَةٌ إِلَّا اللَّهُ لَفَسَدَتَا |

If there be in the skies and the earth any other power (other than Allah) then this whole system would be destroyed.

As mentioned earlier, "أَرْضٌ" (the earth) is the source of food for all humanity. This means that it cannot be owned by any individual.

| 55:10 | the earth has been created for the creatures | وَالْأَرْضَ وَضَعَهَا لِلْأَنَامِ |

At another place, it is said:

| 80:32 | for you and your animals | مَّتَاعًا لَّكُمْ وَلِأَنْعَامِكُمْ |

Not only the earth but other elements which combine to produce crop from the land, are "وَمَتَاعًا لِّلْمُقْوِينَ" 56:73 (life's sustenance for the hungry). Thus, any system in which, instead of for the benefit of the entire humanity, the earth becomes the tool for a particular group or individuals' benefit is against God's will. As such, the Quran says that this fountainhead of all "*rizq*" (sustenance) must remain accessible to all the needy.

| 41:10 | He placed the solid rock high up on it, and blessed it, and arranged a way for the four seasons, to all who seek (on an equal footing). | وَجَعَلَ فِيهَا رَوَاسِيَ مِن فَوْقِهَا وَبَارَكَ فِيهَا وَقَدَّرَ فِيهَا أَقْوَاتَهَا فِي أَرْبَعَةِ أَيَّامٍ سَوَاءً لِّلسَّائِلِينَ |

The factors of production and life's sustenance i.e. light, wind, water, earth etc. should be under a Quranic society which adopts a system that provides for all. This revolutionary program was given by the Quran when the world thought of "feudalism" as being "very natural".

The world at that time was unable to grasp the importance of this message (and later it was put on the back burner by even the Muslims) but once again, due to the exigencies of time, the world is striving towards that very goal (abolishing feudalism).

This is the fact pointed out by the Quran saying:

13:41	do they not see how we snatch the land from the big feudal and diminish it	أَوَلَمْ يَرَوْا أَنَّا نَأْتِي الْأَرْضَ نَنْقُصُهَا مِنْ أَطْرَافِهَا

Gradually, the time will come when land will not belong to any particular person and will provide sustenance for everybody. This will be the time about which it has been said:

39:66	The earth will glow with the light of its sustained.	وَأَشْرَقَتِ الْأَرْضُ بِنُورِ رَبِّهَا

A-R-K   أ ر ك

Ibn Faris says that the basic meaning of this root is "to rest".

Raghib says that four legged bed is called "آرِيْكَةٌ" (*aarikah*) because it generally is made from a wood called "أَرَاكَ" (*aarak*).

"ٱلْأَرِيْكَةُ" (*al-arikah*), with plural "أَرَائِكْ" (*araika*): a throne or resting place surrounded by curtains, or any other thing used for leaning.
"ٱلْأَرَاكُ" (*al-arak*): a kind of bitter fodder. This fodder is not sour but salty and bitter. Camels eat it after taking their meal so that it can help them digest their food.

The Quran says:

18:31	they will rest against boards with cushions (or on beds)	مُتَّكِئِينَ فِيهَا عَلَى الْأَرَائِكِ

Its meaning is that they will be comfortable. Moreover, beside the type of wood or tree, "أَرَاكْ" (*arak*) or "رِكْ" (*rik*) is that wound which heals and the skin gets levelled again, because it has come back to its original shape.

A-R-M   أ ر م

Ibn Faris says that it means 'to stack things on one another'. This has both connotations i.e. arrangement (order) and loftiness (height).

"ٱلْأَرَامُ" (*al-aramu*) with singular "أَرَمٌّ" (*aram*): footprints, or to mark something so as to recognize it. Stones too, are called "أَرَّمٌّ" (*arram*). {M}

Quran says about the nation of *Aad*:

| 89:7 | With the pillar raised *Iram* | إِرَمَ ذَاتِ الْعِمَادِ |

"إِرَمَ" (*iram*) is perhaps the name of the place they dwelled.

Raghib says that 89:7 means those lofty pillars which were engraved. Some researchers think that *Iram* was their chief who was the son of *Saam*. This would mean that *Iram* and *Aad* is the name of the same nation. The compiler of *Muheet* says that "اَلْأَرُومَةُ" (*al-aromah*): 'the roots of a tree' or 'human descent'.

A-Z-R أ ز ر

"اَلْإِزْرُ" (*alizru*): backup force, strength to rely upon.

Quran says:

| 20:31 | Strengthen my back by it | اشْدُدْ بِهِ أَزْرِي |

"اَلْإِزْرُ" (*al-izru*): the basic backup strength.
"اَلْإِزَارُ" (*al-izaru*): anything that can work as cover for your body (especially for the genitals).
"اَلْمُوَازَرَةُ" (*al-mowazarah*): to confront, or to help each other; bundling of crops with each other in such a manner that the bigger plants support the smaller ones.
"أَزَرَ" (*azara*): to strengthen the roots or basis of something.

Surah *Al-Fateh* says (about the tree of Islam):

| 48:29 | (Like the crops that first takes out its needle) and then strengthens its roots and so keeps getting thick. | فَآزَرَهُ فَاسْتَغْلَظَ |

"أَزَرُ" (*azaru*) was the name of the idol protected by Ibrahim's father *Tarukh* (the Biblical *Terah*). With reference to the idol, his title was "*Azar*". Some say that "*Azar*" was Ibrahim's uncle or some other elder relative.

But the Quran says:

| 6:74 | Once said Ibrahim to his father *Azar*... | وَإِذْ قَالَ إِبْرَاهِيمُ لِأَبِيهِ آزَرَ |

Since no other meaning can be taken, "*Azar*" was indeed his father. Some even say that it was "*Tarukh*" which was transformed into the name "*Azar*". But this is a weak argument. Some have said that "*Azar*" means "*zal'al*" (astray) but this word has not been used in the Quran for this meaning.

A-Z-Z   أ ز ز

Ibn Faris says that this root basically means 'to move', movement, or 'to dislodge'. In short, it means to instigate someone in such a way r that they can't realize that they are being instigated.

"اَلْأَزِيزُ" (***al-azeer***): sharpness, heat or thunder.
"اَلْأَزِيزُ" (***al-azeer***): sharpness, heat or thunder.
"أَزَّ النَّا زَبِزُوْزُهَا" (***azzanna zabzuha***): he lit the fire and stoked it
"أَزَّتِ الْقِدْرَ" (***azzati-lqamar***): the pot boiled up
"أَزَّتِ السَّحَابَةُ" (***azzati-ssahabah***): the clouds thundered loudly
"اَلْأَزُّ" (***al-azzu***): the twitching of a vein, or to rouse (in anger)
Surah ***Maryam*** says:

19:83	they instigate and arouse	تَؤُزُّهُمْ أَزَّا

A-Z-F   أ ز ف

Ibn Faris says the basic concept of the word is of nearness and being close by.

"أَزِفَ الرُّحَلُ" (***azfarrahal***): time to depart has come near.
"أَزِفَ الرَّجُلُ" (***azfarrajul***): the man hurried up.
"اَ لتَّأْزُفُ" (***at-tazuf***) is 'to take short, measured step's.
"اَلْأَزِفُ" (***al-azif***): 'that will happen shortly'.

The Quran says:

83:57	The moment to be approached, has approached	أَزِفَتِ الْآزِفَةُ

Or, in other words, the time for results (of one's acts) has come.

At another place, it is said:

20:18	the moment which was due (the time for revolution)	يَوْمَ الْآزِفَةِ

Nawab Siddiq Hasan Khan writes that words in which "ز" (***za***) comes together with "أ" (***hamza***), have a connotation of harshness, and narrowness.

Istabrak   استبرق

"اِسْتَبْرَقٌ" (*istabraq*): 'thick silk cloth'. Some say that it is a thick silk cloth on which there is gold embroidery.

The Quran says

18:31	Clothes of silk and embroidery	سُنْدُسٍ وَإِسْتَبْرَقٍ

The author of **Taj-ul-Uroos** reports that, according to an author Jowhari, the word's root is "بَرَقٌ" (*baraq*) meaning lightning. If so, then it may carry the connotation of bright as lightning.

Is-haaq   إِسْحَقَ

Two sons of **Ibrahim** have been mentioned in the Quran. The elder one, **Ismail**, was from his wife **Haajar** and the younger son, **Ishaaq** "اِسْحٰقَ" (*is-haaq*), was from his wife **Sarah**.

Ismail settled in the valley of **Hijaz** and **Is-haaq** led the Palestinians. God has mentioned **Is-haaq** in the category of messengers.

2:140	and that which was bestowed (revealed) unto **Ibrahim**, **Ismail** and **Is-haaq**	أَمْ تَقُولُونَ إِنَّ إِبْرَاهِيمَ وَ إِسْمَاعِيلَ وَ إِسْحَقَ

The Israelite messengers were from among their progeny.

A-S-R   ا س ر

Ibn Faris says that the basic meaning of this root is to stop, or to imprison someone.

"اَلْأَسَارُ" (*al-asaru*): the string or shoelace by which something is bound.
"اَلْأَسْرُ" (*al-asru*): to bind something with a rope etc. It also means 'to be bound', 'form' and 'creation'.
"اَلْأَسِيْرٌ" (*al-aseer*): a prisoner, a tied up man.

The plural is "أَسَارىَ" (*asariy*) or "اَسْرَىَ" (*asariy*).

The connotation of tying can also indicate meanings like 'strong' and 'stable'.
The Quran has used the word "أُسَارىَ" (*usara*) for 'prisoners'.

The Quran says:

2:85	And when they come before you as prisoners	وَإِن يَأْتُوكُمْ أُسَارَى
76:29	We created them (human beings) and bound their *"asr"* strongly	نَحْنُ خَلَقْنَاهُمْ وَشَدَدْنَا أَسْرَهُمْ

In this sense *asr* means the human body, or its form.

In the light of modern day science, it is seen that this points towards a very important fact. We cannot feel something if it doesn't have a form. Science tells us that matter in reality is not something solid. This is a conglomeration of atoms which cling to each other or are bound together according to some laws of nature or of God, and if this binding force was to be absent, then nothing would have a shape or form. Thus it is this *asr* or mutual binding force which gives form to things.

Sir James Jeans says that everything is connected, by "bottled up waves".

Nawab Siddiq Hasan Khan writes that in words where a *sin* "س" appears along with a *hamza* "أ", a connotation of strength and intensity is present.

Israel   اسرايل

This was the title of **Yaqoob** as in 3:94. For details, see the heading "**Yaqoob**". For Bani Israel, see the heading "**Bani Israel**".

A-S-S   ا س س

Ibn Faris says that its basic meaning is for something to remain in its place, or to be well-established.

"أَلْأَسُّ" (*al-assu*) or "أَلْأَسَاسُ" (*al-asaasu*) is the foundation of a building. Plural is "أَسَاسٌ" (*asaasu*).
"أَلْأَسِيسُ" (*al-asysu*): the core of something;
"أَلتَّأْسِيسُ" (*at-tasisu*) is to lay the foundation of a building.

Nawab Siddiq Hasan Khan writes that in words where a *sin* "س" appears along with a *hamza* "أ", a connotation of strength and intensity is present.

Surah **At-Tauba** says:

9:108	A mosque which is founded (based) on *taqwa*	أَبَدًا لَّمَسْجِدٌ أُسِّسَ عَلَى التَّقْوَى

"اَلْأَسُّ" (*al-assu*) is also used to describe the human heart, and also the dust or ashes that are left behind by a departing caravan. This actually signifies some influence or mark of something.

"خُذَّاسُّ الطَّرِيْقِ" (*khuzassu tareeq*) is said to someone when he is told to reach the destination with the help of the right indications or markings along the road.

<h1 style="text-align:center">A-S-F   ا س ف</h1>

Ibn Faris says it means to lose something and then feel sorrow and longing for it.

"اَلْأَسَفْ" (*al-asaf*): the great grief and sorrow one feels on losing something or someone.

Nawab Siddiq Hasan Khan writes that in words where a *sin* "س" appears along with a *hamza* "أ", a connotation of strength and intensity is present.

Surah *Al-Ahzaf* says that the following about *Moosa* (Moses) when he came back towards his nation:

7:150	And when *Moosa* came back he was furious and in sorrow	وَلَمَّا رَجَعَ مُوسَى إِلَى قَوْمِهِ غَضْبَانَ أَسِفًا

According to *Raghib*, it means the boiling of one's blood due to vengeful emotions.

If one feels this way for someone beneath his position, it is called "غَضَبٌ" (*ghazab*). And if is felt for a superior/higher person, it is called "حُزْنٌ" (*huzn*).

The Quran says the following about Allah:

43:55	When they unpleased Us, We punished them for their crimes.	فَلَمَّا آسَفُونَا انتَقَمْنَا مِنْهُمْ

For the details around the subject of unpleasing Allah, see the topic of *(Gh-Zd-B)*.

In surah Yusuf, *Yaqoob* says:

12:84	O how I grief for *Yosef*.	يَا أَسَفَى عَلَى يُوسُفَ

In ordinary circumstances, therefore, it means woe and sorrow.

"اَرْضٌ أَسِيْفَةٌ" (*arzun asifah*): that land which is barren.
"اَلْجَمَلُ الْأَسِيْفُ" (*aljamalu al-asifu*): the camel which doesn't fatten (*Ibn Faris*).
"أَسِيْفُ" (*asifu*) also means slave, because the slave is always sorrowful about the loss of his freedom.

Besides this, this word is also used for one who becomes sad easily.

Ismail اسمَعیل

The Quran mentions the two sons of Ibrahim. Ismail was the elder son who was from the first wife Hajar. He is the one whom Ibrahim meant to sacrifice, in accordance with a dream from Allah (37:102). But God kept him alive for a lifetime of sacrifice instead of the immediate sacrifice. (37:107)

That great sacrifice was the (re) birth of the **Kaba** (the House of God) and its safe keeping. As such, both father and son (**Ibrahim** and **Ismail**) together built the **Kaba** (21:127). Afterwards, **Ismail** settled there for its safe keeping, and God endowed him with Messenger hood (2:136), and called him "صَادِقُ الْوَعْدِ" (*sadiq-ul-wa'di*) 19:54.

Ismail is a combination of the Hebrew word "*shamah*" (to listen or obey) and the word "*ahl*" the people of God. Since his birth was in answer to Ibrahim's prayer, his name was Ismail (or one who listens or obeys God).

The last Messenger **Muhammad** was born among his descendants.

A-S-N ا س ن

"أَسَنَ الْمَاءُ يَأْسُنُ" (*asanal ma-o yasuun*): when the taste, color or smell of something goes bad. "آلْأَسِنْ" (*al-asin*): the water which has been petrified as result of being motionless. *{T, M, R}*

The Quran says the following about the canals in heaven:

| 47:15 | In which there are canals of water which do not deteriorate | فِيهَا أَنْهَارٌ مِّن مَّاء غَيْرِ آسِنٍ |

The meaning is that in a heavenly society, nothing is stagnant. Each and every thing that is useful circulates.

On the contrary, the society of **Jahannum** is described as where:

| 107:7 | (And they) Refuse to reach out. | وَيَمْنَعُونَ الْمَاعُونَ |

The above verse means that, in a society opposite to the Quranic society, people with power take control over the sources of production, money and things that are beneficial. They stop their circulation or flow within the people. This is done by those who enjoy power and hegemony, but this results in pollution in these resources due to lack of motion. (It is not possible for us to comprehend the conditions of next stage of life in this world but) the Quran also tells us about the Heaven and Hell on this earth. We can see such societies with our own eyes. The Heaven and Hell in the Hereafter are the basis of our Belief. Quran only describes them allegorically as in 47:15 and 13:35.

A-S-W/Y   ا س و/ ی

Ibn Faris says that "أَسُوّ" (*asu*) basically means to treat an ill condition and it also means to woe and feel sorrow.

"أَسِيتُ عَلَيْهِ" (*aseetu a'laihi*): I felt sorry for that.
"رَجُلٌ آسٍ وَ أَسْيَانٌ" (*rajlun asi wa asyan*): a grieving man.
"الآسُ" (*al-as*): a physician or doctor.
"امْرَأَةٌ أَسِيَّةٌ" (*imratun aseeh*): a grieving woman.
"أَسَّاهُ بِمُصِيبَةٍ تَأْسِيَةً" (*as-sahu bimuseebatin ta'aseyah*): sympathized with him in his woe
"فَتَأَسَّىَ" (*fata'as-saya*): so he got solace

The Quran says:

5:26	Therefore, don't be grieved at the destruction of the nation of *faseqeen*	فَلَا تَأْسَ عَلَى الْقَوْمِ الْفَاسِقِينَ

Raghib says that "أَسَّي" (*asann*): sorrow and "تَأْسِيَةٌ" (*tasiya*): to remove that sorrow. As such, "الآسُوّ" (*al-aswu*) also means a healing medicine.

"الآسِيَةٌ" (*al-asiyatun*): medicines, which is the plural of "الآسُوّ" (*al-asu*). "الآسِيّ" (*al-asiyo*) is the subject that gets treated.
"أَسَوْتَهُ بِهِ" (*asautohu behi*): "I considered it to be an example to be followed".

Raghib says that "إِسْوَةٌ" (*asa*) or "أُسْوَةٌ" (*uswatun*) is the condition of a person while obeying a command whether good or bad, pleasant or unpleasant. Besides this, it also means something that gives solace to a grieving man, something that mitigates his sorrow, something that can be the answer to one's troubles. {T}{R}

Those who were weak and unstable during the *Ahzaab* battle were told:

33:21	you should have done what Allah's Messenger did	لَقَدْ كَانَ لَكُمْ فِي رَسُولِ اللَّهِ أُسْوَةٌ حَسَنَةٌ

In other word, the way in which he faced all troubles according to the laws of God and with solidarity and strong will, you should do likewise. His example was the best example for you. You should have found solace in it. Likewise, it has been mentioned about Ibrahim at another place that he told the opponents of God's order publicly that "there is no relationship between you and me."

In this context it was said:

60:4	In Ibrahim and those who were with his, is a balanced example for you	قَدْ كَانَتْ لَكُمْ أُسْوَةٌ حَسَنَةٌ فِي إِبْرَاهِيمَ وَالَّذِينَ مَعَهُ

This act of Ibrahim and his companions is an example for you to follow. This will redress your sorrow. As such, the believers have been told at many places in the Quran, to not keep any relation with the opponents of God's order. They are told to not make them their confidantes.

3:118	Don't make anyone as confidantes except your own (believers).	لاَتَتَّخِذُواْ بِطَانَةً مِّن دُونِكُمْ

"أَلْمُوَاسَاةُ" (*almu-asato*): to consider the other in your place (and strive for as much benefit for him as you would for yourself, and strive to remove as much ill effect from him as from yourself). It is considered as sacrifice when you prefer someone else above self.

The Quran teaches sacrifice:

59:9	they prefer others over themself	وَيُؤْثِرُونَ عَلَى أَنفُسِهِمْ

The Quranic social order of **Rabubiya** (welfare) is based upon this principle.

A-Sh-R   ا ش ر

The basic meanings of this root are 'heat' and 'intensity'. *{F}*

"أَشِرَ" (*ashira*), "يَأْشَرُ" (*yasharu*), "أَشْرًا" (*ushran*): to be overly proud and vain; to be pleased with oneself.

The term "أَشَرُ الْمِنْجَلِ" (*usharul minjal*) is used to signify the teeth of a saw, while "أَلْمِنْشَارُ" (*al-minshar*): "saw".

As such "أَشْرٌ" (*ashrun*) is such a self-liking, that cuts into others; liking oneself in such a way that it bothers other people, and is disliked; in other words, such pride that goes beyond the norms of human act.

The Quran says:

54:25	On the contrary, he is denier of pride. (He is a great denier and a narcissist).	بَلْ هُوَ كَذَّابٌ أَشِرٌ

This "أَشِرَ" (*ashira*) is derived from "يَأْشَرُ" (*ya-shiro*) which means great pride and narcissism.

Al-Ukhdod   الاخدود

It refers to the army of *Zunawas*, the ruler of the *Tubba* nation, who threw the Christians in big, burning trenches (85:49). For details, see heading *(T-B-Ain)* and *(Kh-D-D)*.

Al-Aikah   الايكه

The nation towards which *Shoaib* (Jethro) was sent has been called *Ashab-ul-Aikah*. 15:78 For details see heading "*Shoaib*".

Al-Hijr   الحجر

Ismail's elder son was named *Nabayeth*. His family is called *Nabath* (plural Anbat). The ruins of his kingdom can be found all over Syria and Arabia. The Torah mentions *Nabath* in the chapter about the Messenger *Hizqeel*. At first, his capitol was *Raqeem*, but when it was occupied by the Romans, he migrated to the city of *Hijr* in the valley of Qura'a. They (the people) have been called *Ashab-ul-Hijr* in this context. They denied God's orders and were involved in *Azaaab* (God's punishment).
Since the nation of *Samuud* was also in the city of Hijr, some historians think that Ashabul-Hijr means the nation of *Samuud*. But the guess prevails that Ashab-ul-Hijr means the nation of *Nabath* whose tales of rise and fall can still be traced in the ruins of Hijr.

Al-Rass   الرس

Ismail settled in *Hijaz*. He had twelve sons who were the head of their dynasties. One of them was *Qaidmah*. *Ashab-ur-Rass* are said to be from among his descendants. Some think that it was one of the tribes of the nation *Samuud*. In connection with the denial of God's orders, they have been mentioned at two places in the Quran (25:48) and (50:12).

Ar-Raqeem   الرقيم

Those young men who were preparing for a celestial revolution while they sought refuge in a cave, have been mentioned in Surah *Al-Kahaf* (18:9-26). Details will be found in my book *Shola'eh Mastoor*.

The city of *Raqeem* was the capital of the *Nabti* [Nubia] government during ancient times. When the Romans conquered Syria and Palestine, this city came to the limelighbut not as *Raqeem* city but as *Petra* city which was called *Batra* by the Arabs. Modern archaeology has found the ruins. This city was situated on the highway from Hijaz to Syria. As such, at the time of the revelation (of the Quran), the Arabs were aware of the tales of the *Ashab-ul-Kahaf*

(Companions of the Cave) or the *Ashab-ur-Raqeem* (Companions of Batra) but only so much as was known to the common man.

The Quran (without going into the details) revealed what in fact their purpose was and what people later took them to be. For more details see heading R-Q-M.

A-Sd-D   أ ص د

Ibn Faris says that the basic meaning of this root is 'merging of one thing into another'.

"آصُدُ" (*asud*): – 'he closed (the door etc)'.
"اَلأَصِيدُ" (*al-aseed*): a cage where animals are kept locked up.

The Quran has used "مُوْصَدَةٌ" (*musadatun*) which means 'closed', or 'constituting of'.

Compilers of dictionaries maintain that it is a part of the root "وَصَدُّ" (*wasad*), so we have also mentioned it there (i.e under the heading *W-Sd-D*) even though we think that it is a permanent root.

A-Sd-R   ا ص ر

The basic meaning of this root is to make someone stop or bow, that is, to subjugate somebody *{F}*.

"اَلأَصْرُ" (*al-asr*): to tie something up; forcibly stop.*{T}*
"اَلأَصِرَةُ" (*al-aseerato*) is a small rope with which the lower part of a tent is bound firmly *{M}*.
"اَلأَصِرُ" (*al-isro*): a firm command to which a human being is firmly bound (adherent). It also means 'burden'.

Surah *Al-Araaf* says about the Messenger:

7:157	He will ease the burden which mankind has been burdened with	وَيَضَعُ عَنْهُمْ إِصْرَهُمْ

That means that he will lift the severe prohibitions that are unbearable for humans and, in this way, will give Mankind the real freedom of thought and action.

It is this very "إِصْرٌ" (*isrun*) with which we have been taught to think freely.

The Quran says:

2:286	And do not burden us with such load	وَلَاتَحْمِلْ عَلَيْنَا إِصْرًا

This is the real freedom granted by the Quran. In other words, only God's orders, nobody else's, not even of religious figures or worldly leaders (if their orders are against God's orders), will be obeyed in this world (3:78).

Raghib says that "الإصْرّ" (**al-isr**): those elements which prevent or stop someone from following the path of virtuousness.

A-Sd-L   أ ص ل

"الأَصْلْ" (**al-asl**) is the lowest part of something. "أَصّلْ" (**asl**) is the basis or foundation of something.

This word has appeared in the Quran as against "فَرْعٌ" (**far-un**) which means the highest point of something.

14:24	Strong foundation and peaks in the heights	أَصْلُهَا ثَابِتٌ وَفَرْعُهَا فِي السَّمَاء

"اِسْتَأصَلَهُ" (**asta-slah**) – 'it was rooted out', 'pulled from its roots' or 'cut'. "الأَصِيّلُ" (**al-aseel**) is used for the time from **asr** to **maghrib** (from afternoon till twilight).

The Quran says:

7:205	… Morning and evening…	بِالْغُدُوِّ وَالآصَالِ

Ibn Faris says that it means the time after the evening. This is probably said in the context of the basic part of the night.

According to **Ragib**, "أَصّلْ" (**as-lun**) means the basic part of a thing which, if removed, destroys that thing. Thus the time between **asr** and **maghrib** is called "الأَصِيّلْ" (**al-aseel**) because when that ends, the day ends as well.

A-F-F   ا ف ف

Ibn Faris says it basically means something being unpleasant.

"اَلأُفُّ" (*al-uff*) is used for every dirty, acrimonious, and degraded thing, such as dirt, nail pairing, the dirt between the nails, ear wax etc. The word "أُفْتَبِ" (*uftabin*) is used when you rub off, or blow away dirt or ash from your clothes.

It seems that in connection with blowing away, "اَلأُفْتَهُ" (*al-uftah*): a coward, or somebody who has nothing of significance, one who has little wealth, a dirty man.

"اَلأَفَفُ" (*al-afaf*): to be tired of.
"اَلأَفُّ" (*al-uf*): bad smell.
"أَفَّ" (*u-ofo*): unease, tire of, or due to some pain say "*uf*." It is used to express tiredness (of somebody), or to degrade somebody "أُفْتِ لَهُ" (*uffin lahu*) will be used.

About parents, the Quran says:

17:23	Do not degrade them or do not scold them (talk to them harshly).	فَلَاتَقُل لَّهُمَآ أُفٍّ وَلَاتَنْهَرْهُمَا وَقُل لَّهُمَا قَوْلاً كَرِيمًا

Present time is also described by this word, but the Quran has not used it in this meaning.

A-F-Q   ا ف ق

Ibn Faris says it basically means the expanse or polarization between two ends of a thing.

"اَلأُفُقْ" (*al-ufaq*): corner (horizon). The plural is "آفَقٌ" (*aafaqun*), meaning everything in between heaven and earth that is in your visual range.

The Quran says:

41:53	we will show them our signs around the world and also within themselves	سَنُرِيهِمْ آيَاتِنَا فِي الْآفَاقِ وَفِي أَنفُسِهِمْ

Meaning is of national and international calamities. It could also mean the external universe and the human world.

"أُفُقُ الْبَيْتِ" (*ufaqul bait*) is a tent's front porch.
"فَرَسٌ أُفُقٌ" (*farasun ufaq*): a delightful horse with amazing speed.
"أَفِقَ الرَّجُلُ" (*ufaqir rajul*): that he reached excellence in knowledge, nobility and other traits.

Regarding great loftiness and expanse, it is said about the Messenger:

81:23	and He found him in great loftiness (God found the Messenger at a high place in character)	وَلَقَدْ رَآهُ بِالْأُفُقِ الْمُبِينِ
53:7	(The messenger) is at a high pedestal (of knowledge and humanism).	وَهُوَ بِالْأُفُقِ الْأَعْلَى

A-F-K   ا ف ك

Ibn Faris says it basically means to overturn something or divert something from its path.

"أَفَكَ" (*afak*) or "يَأْفِكُ" (*yafiko*): to tell a lie, to fabricate, to divert someone from his rightful path {T}.

"اِئْتَفَكَ" (*i'tafak*): can hold the connotation of deviating from the right path and fabricating lies.

"الْمُؤْتَفِكَاتُ" (*al-mutafikaat*) also mean the winds which have deviated from their right path, therefore it may mean those dwellings (those who live in them) who have not stayed on the right path or who perform wrong deeds, fabricated lies. The Quran's style reflects that they were certain dwellings where people lived and got destroyed.

46:11	They will say this is the same lie which has been fabricated since old times	فَسَيَقُولُونَ هَذَا إِفْكٌ قَدِيمٌ
54:2	The lie that has been perpetrated since old times	سِحْرٌ مُسْتَمِرٌّ

In Surah **An-Noor** the Quran warns the muslims not to fabricate false accusations and not to propagate such things in society (24:18, 24:4). It has also related an instance in this regard when a group falsely accused another group:

24:11	The people who have fabricated these lies is a group among you	إِنَّ الَّذِينَ جَاؤُوا بِالْإِفْكِ عُصْبَةٌ مِنْكُمْ

In this entire narration the Quran does not mention as to who it was who was falsely accused. It has only said that when the news (which was fabrication of false accusation) reached the **momineen**, they should have reacted by saying "هَذَا إِفْكٌ مُبِينٌ" (*haaza ifkun mubeen*) in 24:14, or "هَذَا بُهْتَانٌ عَظِيمٌ" (*haaza buhtanun azeem*) in 24:16 this is the same thing which has been clarified at another place by saying that when some *faasiq* tells you something, then investigate it (47:6).

Only this much has been said by the Quran but this event has been referred to Aisha (one of the wives of the messenger) and a whole story seems to have been built around it. It has said that even the Messenger himself was very troubled about this event, so much so that he had sent Aisha to her parents' house and only when God had absolved her through a verse, had he brought her back.

It can be clearly seen that it was a fabricated tale, which was fabricated with ulterior motive. But we **Muslims** treat it as an historical event. When the opponents of Islam argue about it we tend to get angry, although in answer to such allegations we must say what the Quran has said:

| 24:12 | This so-called event is an open lie and a big accusation | هَٰذَا إِفْكٌ مُبِينٌ |

The Quran says about the staff of **Moosa**:

| 7:117 | it destroyed (devoured) all that they had created | تَلْقَفُ مَا يَأْفِكُونَ |

In surah **As-Saff'at** it is said about the lying deniers:

| 37:86 | Do you want to (go on) a diversion……. | أَئِفْكًا |

Surah **Ash-Shura** says:

| 26:222 | Sinful liars | أَفَّاكٍ أَثِيمٍ |

The Quran has explained this in surah **Al-Jasiya** by saying:

| 45:8 | he listens to the laws of God, which are presented before him, then through pride, insists on what he believes, as if he didn't even hear the laws of God | يَسْمَعُ آيَاتِ اللَّهِ تُتْلَىٰ عَلَيْهِ ثُمَّ يُصِرُّ مُسْتَكْبِرًا كَأَن لَّمْ يَسْمَعْهَا |

"اِفْكٌ" (**ifkun**): to overturn something, to change something from how it should have been like. **Raghib** too, thinks it has this meaning.

In this context, it appears in surah **Az-Zariyat**:

| 51:9 | One only turns away when he himself wants to turn away | يُؤْفَكُ عَنْهُ مَنْ أُفِكَ |

This means that if one is willing, only then he can be turned away (from some teaching, belief etc.).

This points to a great fact that God doesn't lead anyone astray; it is man himself who lets him be led astray. God's law ordains that one who wants to go astray is not forced to select the right path. The initiative is in Man's hands. Whatever he does, right or wrong, God's law accordingly is applied on him. If he becomes hard like stone, then every glass that strikes him will be blown to smithereens, and if he becomes delicate like glass, then even a small stone will be enough to shatter it. God does not change one's direction forcibly.

| 61:5 | When they went astray then A's law (the laws of nature) turned their hearts…." | فَلَمَّا زَاغُوا أَزَاغَ اللَّهُ قُلُوبَهُمْ |
| 5:75 | the dwellings that were overturned | أَنَّىٰ يُؤْفَكُونَ |

"اَلْآفِكَةُ" (*al-ifkatoh*): the draught years. {T}{R}

"اَلْمَأْفُوْكَ" (*al-mafuk*) is a place which is barren, due to lack of rain {T, R}.

A-F-L   ا ف ل

"اَفَلَ ٱلْقَمَرُ افُوْلاً" (*afalal qamaro ufula*): the appearance and disappearance of the moon (or other heavenly bodies).

"اَلْمُوَفِّلُ" (*al-muaffil*): defective or weak.

"رَجَلٌ مَاءٍ فُوْلُ الرَّاْي" (*rajaloon ma fulur ra'ee*): a dim witted man.

Raghib says that "اَلْأُفُوْلُ" (*al-ufool*): the sinking of bright stars.

Ibn Faris says it means sinking as well as to become small or dim.

The Quran says **Ibrahim** deliberated deeply over the system of the universe. He studied them (the heavenly bodies) and their strengths deeply.

6:75	and in this way we showed Ibrahim the highs and lows of the universe	وَكَذَلِكَ نُرِي إِبْرَاهِيمَ مَلَكُوتَ السَّمَاوَاتِ وَالأَرْضِ

In this way strengthened his belief in God. As such, he saw the stars, deliberated on the moon, the sun and found out that at one time they burn very bright but at other times they are lost in darkness. As such, these things, which are subject to change, could not be his god. Only that which is not subject to change could be his God.

Therefore, he said:

6:75	I am not ready to worship things which are subject to change	لا أُحِبُّ الآفِلِينَ
6:79	For me, God is one who is the Creator of all of them	فَطَرَ السَّمَاوَاتِ وَالأَرْضَ

This declaration that something which is subject to change cannot be worshipped points to a great reality. The basic characteristic of personality is that it is not subject to external factors, in the words of Bergson [the famous French philosopher (1859-1941)], this is "changelessness in change". Therefore, God, which is the most complete and perfect personality will be totally devoid of change. Therefore, that which is subject to change or "اَفَلَ" (*afal*) cannot be God.

Change is against the basic traits of personality. A person, whose personality is groomed, also bears this characteristic. He becomes firm in his principles and is not affected by external influences (like a weather cock). This is what is called firmness of belief and solidarity of actions. Such are the men who can be trusted. Those men whose God is not "اَفَلَ" (*afal*) are not

"أَقَلْ" (*afal*) either. Like God, like individual or nation. The concept of God has a deep impression on a man's personality or that of a nation. The concept of God, as presented by the Quran, is that the believers can be matched by no other, neither in strength and solidarity, nor in honor.

A-K-L   أ ك ل

Ibn Faris says that this root basically means to diminish gradually, like when you eat a thing, it gets diminished gradually.

Hence "أَكُلْ" (*akul*): to chew something and then eat it. Something which one drinks or swallows without chewing is not called "مَأْكُوْلْ" (*ma-kool*), "أَلْمَأْكُوْلْ" (*al-makool*): an animal which is eaten by a wild beast.

Surah *Al-Kahaf* says:

105:5	eaten, and cut (into small pieces of) fodder	كَعَصْفٍ مَّأْكُولٍ

Hence it means fodder or leaves eaten by insects (moth-eaten).

"أَلْأَكِيْلْ" (*al-akeel*): a king and "أَلْمَأْكُوْلْ" (*al-makool*) are the subjects. "أَلْأُكُوْلْ" (*al-ukul*) is generally used for fruits but any part of plants that is eaten is "أَلْأُكُوْلْ" (*al-ukul*).

About the *Jannah* the Quran says:

13:35	its fruits will always remain (it will always have, or bear, fruit)	أُكُلُهَا دَآئِمٌ

Provisions (*rizq*), intellect, opinion, and profound intellect are also called "أَلْأُكْلْ" (*al-ukul*).

"آكُلْ" (*aakul*) actually means "to eat", but it also means "to take":

3:129	do not "take" (charge) interest	لَا تَأْكُلُوْا الرِّبَا

Raghib writes that "أَكْلُ الْمَالْ" (*akal maal*) means charity because most of one's money is spent on edibles and for meeting economic needs.

In surah *Al-Ma'ida* it is said in reference to *haram* (forbidden) items:

5:3	Carrion, unless you do a proper *zibah* [slaughter]	أَكَلَ السَّبُعُ إِلَّا مَا ذَكَّيْتُمْ

Carrion is an animal which has been devoured partly by beasts, and there is still life in it. This is followed by that if you slaughter in the Islamic way while saying Allah's name (but not cutting off the throat completely)) then it is allowed. If beasts have eaten it (some animal) completely, then there is no question of it being **haram** or **halal** (i.e. permissible or not). And if the animal has died then it becomes **haram** (forbidden).

A-L أَلْ

This is used to specify a particular thing, exactly as "the" or "this" is used in English. "رَجُلٌ" (*rajul*) is some man. "الرَّجُلُ" (*al-rajul*) is "the" or "this" man. The closest English expression is the Definite Article 'the.' Following examples will clarify its usage:

- First mention or talk about someone/something is used ordinarily. Then, when mentioned again, "*al*" is added as prefix.

Example:

| 73:15 | we sent a Messenger to **Firoun** | كَمَا أَرْسَلْنَا إِلَى فِرْعَوْنَ رَسُولًا |
| 73:16 | Then **Firoun** disobeyed this Messenger | فَعَصَى فِرْعَوْنُ الرَّسُولَ |

Here, "الرَّسُولَ" (*ar-rasul*): the afore-mentioned **rasul**.

To mention something/someone which or who the listener is already familiar with
For instance:

| 9:40 | When the two were inside that cave | إِذْ هُمَا فِي الْغَارِ |

Here at first no cave was mentioned. It has been called "**al-ghaar**" even the very first time. This means that the listeners knew which "**ghaar**" or cave was being mentioned.

- When time or period is being fixed. As in

| 5:3 | During this period, we have completed your **deen** (way of life or religion) | الْيَوْمَ أَكْمَلْتُ لَكُمْ دِينَكُمْ |

- When the entire humanity is being discussed, or meaning full or entire as.

| 4:28 | Man is created in such a way so as to become overwhelmed with emotions | وَخُلِقَ الْإِنْسَانُ ضَعِيفًا |

Here the characteristic of the entire human race is being described.

- When all things of its kind have been included in something, also then "al" is used. For example:

| 2:2 | This book | ذَلِكَ الْكِتَابُ |

Here "**al-kitab**" or this book means the book which includes the special characteristics of all celestial books.

However the "al" in "هُوَالْحَقُّ" (*huwal haqq*): that all specialties of its kind have been included in it.

- When something is meant to be referred in context to a particular person, "al" is used. For example "اَلْمَدِيْنَة" (*al-medina*): the city of Medina, The city of the Messenger. With this reference, that city became well known and famous.

Sometimes, it gives the meaning of "اَلَّذِيْ" (*al-lazi*), for instance "اَلضَّرِبُ" (*az-zaribu*), which is a person who beats or hits.

A-L-A   اَ لَا

This is a combination of *hamza* for questioning or enquiry, and *la* of denial.

Quran says:

| 24:22 | Don't you desire that God should arrange your protection? | اَلَا تُحِبُّونَ أَن يَغْفِرَ اللَّهُ لَكُمْ |

Or:

| 9:13 | Won't you wage war on those who have not kept their words (promises)? | اَلَا تُقَاتِلُونَ قَوْمًا نَّكَثُوا أَيْمَانَهُمْ |

This is also a word of warning. It is also used to warn or assure somebody. For example:

| 2:12 | Be warned that these (people) are *mufsideen* | اَلَا إِنَّهُمْ هُمُ الْمُفْسِدُونَ |

Or it is a fact that these people are *mufsideen*. Both have the same meaning.

A-L-F   أ ل ف

Ibn Faris says that the basic meaning is for two things to mix and intermingle with each other.

"أَلْفٌ" (*alf*): 'one thousand'. Plural is "أَلَافٌ" (*alafun*) or "أُلُوفٌ" (*ulufun*).

Since a thousand has four digits, "الْإِلْفُ" (*al-ilfu*): co-ordination and being intertwined, or a companion who intermingles. (Or the word "أَلْفٌ" (*alfun*) is from the word "إِلْفٌ" (*ilfun*).

"أَلَّفَ بَيْنَهُمْ" (*al-lafa bainahoom*): "created co-ordination between them" Co-ordination similar to the intermingling that clouds make with each other.

| 24:43 | Haven't you seen how Allah drives the clouds, adds them together and stacks them in piles? | أَلَمْ تَرَ أَنَّ اللَّهَ يُزْجِي سَحَابًا ثُمَّ يُؤَلِّفُ بَيْنَهُ |

"أَلْمُؤَلَّفُ" (*al-mu'allifu*): something that is compiled.

"أَلْأُلْفَةُ" (*al-ulfah):* to intermingle with each other.

"أَلْمُؤَلَّفَةُ قُلُوبُهُمْ" (*al-mu-allafat-o qulubuhum*): in whose hearts love and brotherhood needs to be kindled.

"أَلْإِيلَافُ" (*al-eelaaf*): to familiarize with and make friendly with.

| 106:1 | Collaboration with **Quresh** | لِإِيلَافِ قُرَيْشٍ |

As such, it means mutual promises, the agreement which binds two parties together. These were the agreements between the **Quresh** and others so that the **Quresh** (a tribe of Mecca) caravans will not be looted as they were the keepers of Mecca.

About the **Momineen**, the Quran says:

| 3:103 | you were each other's enemy, God created harmony between you and thus through His Benevolence you became brothers | إِذْ كُنتُمْ أَعْدَاء فَأَلَّفَ بَيْنَ قُلُوبِكُمْ فَأَصْبَحْتُم بِنِعْمَتِهِ |

Hence the true meaning gets clarified from this. "اِنْتِلَافٌ" (*intilaaf*) is a step ahead of co-operation. With this, individuals intermingle with each other and a spirit of homogeneity prevails. If a society doesn't have such relationship between individuals, then that society does not comprise of **Momineen** or Believers. Co-operation and homogeneity is the natural outcome or essential result of **Imaan** (belief). When different persons have the same purpose in life, their destination is the same, the path is the same, and then why would not their hearts be intertwined as well?

A-L-K   أ ل ك

Ibn Faris says that the basic meaning of this root is to chew something in the mouth. A message is hence called "أَلْأَلُوْكَةُ" (*al-aluk*) because it is chewed out from the mouth.

Many people believe that this is the correct root for the word "مَلَٰٓئِكَةٌ" (*malaika*) which according to them means "angel" or "messenger", with respect to the meaning of "أَلَكَ" (*alak*) as delivering a message.

"أَلَكْنِيْ اِلَى فُلَانٍ" (*alikni ala falanin*): give him this message from me.

But other researchers think that its root is **(M-L-K)** which means strength and authority. **Raghib** thinks that "مَلَٰٓئِكَةٌ" (*malaika*) is actually plural of "مَلَكٌ" (*malak*). Those angels, who are entrusted with administrative duties, are called "مَلَك" *malak* and humans who do the planning are called "مَلِكٌ" (*malikun*).

Mufti Muhammad Abdohu writes in his explanation of the Quran, (*Al-Manar*) that it is a fact that everything has a strength (nucleus) on which the thing depends. Those who do not believe on **Wahi** (Revelation) they call it the "physical force" and in the Quranic language it is called "*malaikah*". But call it whatever you desire, the truth remains the same, and an intelligent person is one whom names do not prevent from getting to the truth.

Quran calls the "*malaika*" "messengers".

22:75	Allah picks messengers from among the *malikah* and from among *ins*.	اللَّهُ يَصْطَفِي مِنَ الْمَلَائِكَةِ رُسُلًا وَمِنَ النَّاسِ

But this (relaying messages) is only one of the duties of the *malaika*. Comprehensively, they have been called "مُدَبِّرَاتِ أَمْرً" (*mudabbbiraateh amran*) 79:5 and "مُقَسِّمَتِ أَسْرً" (*muqassimateh isran*) 51:4. In other words, they are forces or groups which plan and execute different chores. There are different forces at work in the universe as ordained by God. The forces which bring into practicality those schemes according to the laws of God have been called "*malaika*".

This way the more probable root for "*malaika*" is M-L-K, instead of A-L-K.

These forces are not free to do what they want at their own will (God has granted this ability only to Man.) This is why these forces carry out God's will without fail and without any questioning.

16:50	whatever is said to them, they carry out	وَيَفْعَلُونَ مَا يُؤْمَرُونَ

The laws according to which these forces carry out their tasks have been made known to Man. In other words, Man has been enabled to find out about the laws of nature if he wants to. Therefore, these forces can be controlled by Man. This is what is meant by the "*malaika*" bowing before **Adam**. This is what is known as conquering Nature.

But "*malaika*" are not only the forces which act in the external affairs of this world; they also influence Man's internal (psychological) life.

41:30	It is a fact that those who believe in the *raboobiya* (sustaining power) of God, and are steadfast in this belief, have *malaika* coming down to them saying 'do not have fears or woe of any kind.'	إِنَّ الَّذِينَ قَالُوا رَبُّنَا اللَّهُ ثُمَّ اسْتَقَامُوا تَتَنَزَّلُ عَلَيْهِمُ الْمَلَائِكَةُ أَلَّا تَخَافُوا وَلَا تَحْزَنُوا

Here, by coming down or "*nuzool*" means the psychological change that is produced within Man due to unshaken belief in God's sustaining power. Contrary to this, forces which produce fear and hopelessness in Man, whether they are external or psychological, have been called the "*Shaitans*".

These were the "*malaika*" which gave heart to the *mujahideen* in the fields of *Badr* and *Hunain* (8:12 and 9:16).

These are the forces which cause changes in Man's body till death plays its part (4:97; 16:28). Besides, *malaika* are the also the "registrars" of human acts. In other words, they are responsible for the natural cause and effect of these acts 1(0:21; 43:80). These registers of acts have been referred as *malaika,* but at another place it has been mentioned that God himself also takes care of it (19:79); it has also been said that 'Man hangs this "register of actions" around his neck' (17:13; 14). Deliberating on these verses, one can easily understand that *malaika* are those celestial forces which create the result of everything according to God's law of cause and effect and that result affects human personality.

Since *malaika* are meta-physical, they are invisible to the human eye (9:40; 9:26). As regarding the system by which *malaika* used to bring *wahi* (Revelation) to the Messengers, we cannot understand how it was done because that is beyond our comprehension. We are duty- bound to have faith on in it and act according to it though the greatness and veracity of what has been revealed can be understood with knowledge. Not only *wahi*, but also how these forces work is also beyond our comprehension. We can only know what we feel or see. In other words, we can only understand so far as our senses allow us.

The Quran says one of the elements of belief (faith) is belief in *malaika* (2:285), meaning thereby that, in order to be a Muslim, one must believe in God, the [divinely-revealed] Books, the Messengers and the Day of Judgment along with belief in *malaika.* Now, what does belief in *malaika* mean? It means that one must have the same concept about them and to hold them in the same esteem (position) as the Quran has held for them.

About the *malaika* the Quran says that they bowed (performed *sajdah*) before Adam (4:43). As said before, Adam allegorically means the human race. Therefore, their bowing before Man means man can subjugate them (the forces). Keep the forces of Nature which we have not, as yet discovered or able to master to one side. Let us talk about the forces which have come to light so far. The correct belief would be that they are subservient to man.

Therefore, according to the Quran, the nation to whom these forces do not subjugate themselves are not fit to be in the human race itself leave alone *Momineen* (Believers) because believers are the best of the human race. This is a moment of reflection. A nation whose belief (part of its faith) is that these forces must bow before Man, are today themselves bowing before those forces, nay, even before those who have subjugated these forces. It is a dismal measure of their degradation.

Remember: Man's place is such that all forces of the universe must bow before him. And a *Momin's* place is to master these forces for the betterment of Mankind. A little thought is enough to make one realize that we Muslims in today's world don't even enjoy Man's honor, leave alone a *Momin's* honor.

A-L-L   ل ل أ

Ibn Faris says it basically means 'to sparkle with movement', and also produce a sound at the same time.

"أَلْأَلّ" (*al-illa*): anything that should be honored and its rights fulfilled; for instance, relationships, pity, neighborliness, pact etc. anything so specified and concluded that it cannot be denied. The real meaning of this word is 'to sparkle'.

Besides that, it also means 'a reason which is protected'. "أَلْأَلُّ" (*al-illu*): such things in society which are clear, distinct, and open and need no religion or criterion to be proven true; something that is true and respectable for all. For instance, good behavior with neighbors or relatives is an established norm in society and needs no proof.

The Quran says about the *Quresh* (the tribe to which the Messenger belonged):

6:8	They have gone so far in their opposition (that in your case) they do not even respect or observe the norms normally observed in society; nor do they respect any right being sanctimonious.	لاَ يَرْقُبُواْ فِيكُمْ إِلاًّ وَلاَ ذِمَّةً

There was also an indication towards those about whom the Messenger had said:

42:23	I don't demand any compensation for relaying (God's) message to you, but you should not go so far in your opposition so as to ignore even the rights that ordinarily are due a relative	لَّا أَسْأَلُكُمْ عَلَيْهِ أَجْرًا إِلَّا الْمَوَدَّةَ فِي الْقُرْبَى

It should be noted that he doesn't even demand this (right) as a payment for the message (of God). All Messengers never asked for compensation. They only drew attention to common social rights which should be respected.

This may also mean that if they were kind among themselves, it can be the return for the Messenger's being sent as a messenger because at another place it is said:

34:47	The return that I ask of you is for your own good.	مَا سَأَلْتُكُم مِّنْ أَجْرٍ فَهُوَ لَكُمْ

Al-la   أَلَّا أَنْ+لَا

| 27:31 | (the thing is that) you should not mutiny against me. | أَلَّا تَعْلُوا عَلَيَّ |

Sometimes it is preceded by a "ل" (*laam*) and becomes "لِئَلَّا" (*li-alla*) which means "so that"

| 2:150 | So that nobody has any argument or reasoning against you. | لِئَلَّا يَكُونَ لِلنَّاسِ عَلَيْكُم حُجَّةٌ |

Il-la   أَلَّا

"أَلَّا" (*Il-la*) ordinarily means 'exept', 'but for', 'other than', etc. The following examples will explain:

Example 1:

| The whole nation stood up, except Zaid. | قَامَ الْقَوْمُ إِلَّا زَيْدَا |

This means that Zaid is a part of the nation, but he did not stand up.

The Quran says:

| 2:249 | Few among them drank form it. | فَشَرِبُوا مِنْهُ إِلَّا قَلِيلاً مِّنْهُمْ |

Example 2:

| Everyone stood up but the donkey didn't. | قَامَ الْقَوْمُ إِلَّا حِمَارًا |

This means that the donkey is not included among the people of the nation. In other words, nation is one thing and the donkey another. This is contrary to the first example.

The Quran says:

| 2:34 | Once we told the **malaika** to bow before **Adam,** then they all did so, but Iblees did not. | وَإِذْ قُلْنَا لِلْمَلَائِكَةِ اسْجُدُوا لآدَمَ فَسَجَدُوا إِلاَّ إِبْلِيسَ |

In other words, **Iblees** was something else besides the **malaika.** Hence he was not one of them. Ergo it means that all **malaika** except **Iblees** prostrated. The command towards **Iblees** gets clarified from other verses like 7:12.

Likewise, the Quran says

| 42:23 | Tell them I demand no compensation for this invitation (to accept Islam): I only want you to respect my rights as your relative (or each other's rights.) | قُل لَّا أَسْأَلُكُمْ عَلَيْهِ أَجْرًا إِلَّا الْمَوَدَّةَ فِي الْقُرْبَى |

Surah **Yunus** says:

| 10:98 | Then why wasn't there such a habitat that accepted peace, so its peace could be beneficial for it, except nation of **Yunus**?" | فَلَوْلَا كَانَتْ قَرْيَةٌ آمَنَتْ فَنَفَعَهَا إِيمَانُهَا إِلَّا قَوْمَ يُونُسَ |

Example 3: Sometimes it is used to mean "وَ" (*waw*). For instance, as the Quran says:

| 27:10 27:11 | In front of Us, Our Messengers do not need to have any fear, and neither do those (people) who sometimes transgress and later exchange that evil with virtue. | لَا تَخَفْ إِنِّي لَا يَخَافُ لَدَيَّ الْمُرْسَلُونَ إِلَّا مَن ظَلَمَ ثُمَّ بَدَّلَ حُسْنًا بَعْدَ سُوءٍ |

Example 4: The Quran says:

| 38:14 | None (of the groups among them) was such that it did not deny the messengers | إِن كُلٌّ إِلَّا كَذَّبَ الرُّسُلَ |

All of them denied the Messengers. All of them did so. In other words, "*in kullun illa*" means all of them.

Example 5: Sometimes, it is used to mean "if not". For instance:

| 9:40 | Even if you didn't help him, so what? It is a fact that God helped him. | إِلَّا تَنصُرُوهُ فَقَدْ نَصَرَهُ اللَّهُ |

Example 6: *Mufti Abdohu* (and his dear disciple the late *Syed Rashid Raza*) have written in *Tafseer al Manar* (vol. 1, pp. 404-419) that whenever "*illa*" appears with God's will, then it means a total NO.

As in:

| 87:6 | When we teach you the Quran, you will forget nothing | سَنُقْرِؤُكَ فَلَا تَنسَى |
| 87:7 | Absolutely. God so ordain. | إِلَّا مَا شَاءَ اللَّهُ |

This has been supported by 18:76.

| 17:86 | "if we wanted, we would have taken away what we have sent to you as Wahi | وَلَئِن شِئْنَا لَنَذْهَبَنَّ بِالَّذِي أَوْحَيْنَا إِلَيْكَ |
| 17:87 | Absolutely. This is your God's *rahma* | إِلَّا رَحْمَةً مِّن رَّبِّكَ |

This makes it clear that it was never God's will that anything in the Quran would be unsafe.

Al-Manar also gives some other examples, such as:

| 11:108 | (The Hell-dwellers) will live there as long as the skies and earth remain (and the Heaven-dwellers in Heaven). Nobody can get out of one to go to the other. | خَالِدِينَ فِيهَا مَا دَامَتِ السَّمَاوَاتُ وَالْأَرْضُ إِلَّا مَا شَاءَ رَبُّكَ عَطَاءً غَيْرَ مَجْذُوذٍ |

Al-lazi   أَلَّذِيْ

"ٱلَّذِيْ" (**al-lazi**): that one (maculine)
"ٱلَّذَانِ" (**al-lazaan**): those two (masculine)
"ٱلَّذِيْنَ" (**al-lazeena**): those more than two (masculine)
"ٱلَّتَانِي" (**al-taani**): those two (feminine)
"ٱلَّتَانِ" (**al-latee**): that one (feminine)
"ٱلَّاتِيْ" (**al-lati**) or (**al-layee**): those two (feminine).

| 59:22 | Allah is that one, except which there is no God | هُوَ اللَّهُ الَّذِي لَا إِلَهَ إِلَّا هُوَ |

A-L-M   ا ل م

"ٱلَّمّ" (**alam**) and "أَيْلَمَةٌ" (**ailama**): means "pain". "ٱلَيْمٌ" (**aleem**): someone or something that inflicts pain, or is "painful". "ٱلَيْمُ الْعَذَابِ" (**aleemul azaab**) is ia pain that has reached its height.

The writer of Muheet says that the unpleasantness in life is called "ٱلَّمّ" (**alam**). The opposite is "لَذَّةٌ" (**lazza**) i.e. enjoyment or pleasure.{M}

"ٱلْوَمَةٌ" (**alumatun**) also means meanness. {T}

The Quran mentions "ٱلَيْمُ الْعَذَابِ" (**aleemul azaab**) at several places. It means the result of wrong human deeds, or the insulting destruction in this life.

Nooh (Noah) told his nation that if they rebel against the laws of God then:

| 11:26 | I fear of a painful *azaab* (punishment) on you | إِنِّي أَخَافُ عَلَيْكُمْ عَذَابَ يَوْمٍ أَلِيمٍ |

They faced this punishment in the shape of a great flood which destroyed them.

Surah **Al-Baqrah** says about the hypocrites (munafiqeen)

| 2:10 | There will be a painful punishment for them. | وَلَهُم عَذَابٌ أَلِيمٌ |

ه ل أ

A-L-He

A-L-He   ه ل أ

Ibn Faris writes that it basically means 'to accept someone's subjugation'.

"أَلِهَ" (*aleha*), "أَلَيْهِ" (*ilaiheh*), "يَأْلَه" (*yalah*), mean "to seek some one's refuge in distress".
"أَلِيْةَ" (*aaleha*) also means "to be surprised".
"أَلَهَ" (*aalaha*) or "يَأْلَه" (*yaloh*): "to give refuge to someone in distress", or "to take someone under one's protection". As such "أَلَهَ بِالْمَكَانِ" means "to live in some house peacefully". {T}

Under these circumstances, "إِلهُ" (*ilahun*) would mean "someone whose refuge may be sought in danger", or "someone who can be requested to save one from difficulties and the concept of whose loftiness surprises one". Some think that this word has been extracted from "لَاه يَلِيْه" (*laha yaleeheh*), which means "to be lofty in stature and be hidden from the naked eye" {T}.

Some others say that "أَلِهَ" (*alah*): "that person became a slave" and "أَلَّهَهُ" (*al-lahahu*): "he enslaved him". From this come "تَأْلِيْهٌ" (*taleehun*) or "تَعْبِيْدٌ" (*ta'beed*) which mean "to enslave". Also from this we have "إِلهُ" (*ilah*) which as a verb, turns into "مَألُوْهٌ" (*maaluhun*), as "*kitab*" and "*maktoob*")

This way, "إِلهُ" (*ilah*) would mean 'a being whose rules must be accepted and whose laws must be followed and obeyed'.

As such, when the *Pharoah* told *Moosa*:

26:29	If you accept someone else as your "*ilah*" then I will have you imprisoned	قَالَ لَئِنِ اتَّخَذْتَ إِلهًا غَيْرِي لَأَجْعَلَنَّكَ مِنَ الْمَسْجُونِينَ

Here "*ilah*" means someone who is in power.

In the same manner, it is said:

25:43	Have you wondered about the man who became subservient to his own desires(emotions)?	أَرَأَيْتَ مَنِ اتَّخَذَ إِلهَهُ هَوَاهُ

Similarly, about God it is said:

43:84	He is the One who is in the heights of the skies as well as the depths of the universe	وَهُوَ الَّذِي فِي السَّمَاء إِلَةٌ وَفِي الْأَرْضِ إِلَةٌ

Or, the one who is the ruler of the skies as well as of this world.

So the word also means 'the one with power' or 'one who rules'.

Since in pagan times, people worshipped the sun and the moon etc. as being powerful, therefore "الْاهَةٌ" (*ilaaha*): the moon, while "أَلِهَةٌ" (*aalaha*): the sun. This way, anything which is worshipped is called "إِلهُ" (*ilah*). Even the idols which are worshipped are called "إِلهُ" (*ilah*).

Lughat-ul-Quran - Volume I   Page 91 of 800

There is a school of thought that says that Allah is a static word, which has not been derived from any other word, but others say that this word was actually "الْإِلٰه" (*al-ilah*) that gradually became "الله" (*Allah*) *{T}*

In the noble Quran, the word "*Allah*" has been used to describe the identity of Almighty. Therefore, Allah (the *Ilah* in the Quran) is that lofty being which is hidden from human eyes, but compared to whose Greatness human intellect and comprehension are quite disabled. He is the One who rules the entire universe and whose obedience is a must. And we can obey Him only as per His dictates which He has endowed us with through *wahi* (Revelation) and which is now capsuled safely in the Quran.

As such, "أَطِيْعُو اَلله" (*ati-ullaha*) would mean "follow Allah's law". In the same way, whatever takes place in the universe, takes place according to Allah's law. The world of meta-physics and this world too (*alam amar, alameh khalq*) are ruled by this law. These laws have been made as He wished them to be, and they work under his control and authority. This is the "سُنَّةُ الله" (*sunnatul Allah*), way of Allah which undergoes no changes. (The details can be seen under the heading (*Sh-Y-A*).

 The Quran is the sum of Allah's attributes, Allah's laws, Allah's orders, Allah's Tact, Allah's guidance, etc. All His teachings have a central point which is His Oneness or "*wahdaniya*". That is to announce that nothing except God's rule is Supreme in the universe.

So far as His composition or form is concerned, that is beyond our grasp because we are all finite and no finite can comprehend the infinite. However, while remaining within our mental limits, we can have some idea about Him from His 99 attributes. According to the Quran, the correct Belief is that which is according to the requirements in the Quran. Those who believe in God according to their own interpretation are not Believers, as per the Quran. This is a very important point and must be clearly understood. "God worship" and "virtuous actions" is only right, if done according to the Quran and not according to what different people, nation or religion thinking.

A-L-W/Y   أل و/ي

"آلَا" (*ala*), "يَألُوْ" (*yaluh*), "أَلُوَّا الِيّا" (*uluwan wa ilayya*): to be short of, to delay, to be lackadaisical, to abstain:

3:117	these people will not delay in your detriment	لاَ يَأْلُونَكُمْ خَبَالاً

"آلأَلِيَّةُ" means 'to swear'
"الإِيْلَاءِ" is 'swear to abstain' e.g. swear not to go near a woman {T}.

2:226	those people who for swear to go near their wives (forswear having sex with their wives)	نِّسَآئِهِمْ مِن يُؤْلُونَ لِّلَّذِينَ

Surah **An-Noor** says:

24:22	And they should not forswear helping others.	وَلَا يَأْتَلِ أُوْلُوا

From these examples it is clear that this forswearing is of a kind which is harmful to others.

Raghib says that is the characteristic (of such swearing or forswearing). "مَا أَلَوْتُهُ" means "I don't have the capacity for it."
Ibn-ul-Erabi says that it means "to be slack" as well as "to have the capacity and strength" or "to stop" as well "to endow". That is why "أَلْوَّ" (which is the plural): "strength" as well as "endowment" or "gift".

The Quran says:

55:13	which might and strength of your Provider will you belie (which gift and benevolence will you belie)	فَبِأَيِّ آلَاءِ رَبِّكُمَا تُكَذِّبَانِ

At every place, the meaning according to the context will prevail.

Note: "الأَلْءُ" (*alo-o*) as singular as "أَلْوَّ" (*uloo*) was not found anywhere else other than in **Tajul Uroos**. In other dictionaries, it has appeared as "الِيْ" (*ilya*), or "الِيّْ" (*ilyun*), although the meaning is still endowment and strength (capacity).

Allama Hameedud Deen Farahi, while writing in his compilation **Ta'leefal Quran** page 11, says: Although "آلَاءُ" (*ala-u*) is said to mean (with consensus) benevolence, its usage in the Quran and in Arabic poetry shows that this is not its meaning. Apparently it means "strange workings" for which the Persian word "miracle" can be used…'

With reference to **Johri** he says that "آلَاءِ" (*ala'a*) means the good qualities. He has presented many Arabic verses as proof of this.

Ilay   الىٰ

It means "up to", "towards", "according to time", and also "house".

| 2:187 | then you must fast until night and | ثُمَّ أَتِمُّواْ الصِّيَامَ إِلَى الَّيْلِ |
| 17:1 | From **masjid haram** to **masjid aqsa** | الْمَسْجِدِ الْحَرَامِ إِلَى الْمَسْجِدِ الْأَقْصَى |

One thing is notable in the above verse. Here the word "الَّيْلِ" means "till the beginning of night", which means when the day ends and night begins. The night is not included.

But in regards to the guidance of **wudu** (ritual ablution), the Quran says:

| 5:6 | up to your elbows | إِلَى الْمَرَافِقِ |

Here, the meaning is including the elbows. Hence this distinction should be noted.

It also means "with". For instance,

| 4:2 | and don't devour (usurp) their wealth by mixing it with your own | وَلاَ تَأْكُلُواْ أَمْوَالَهُمْ إِلَى أَمْوَالِكُمْ |

It also appears in the meaning of 'for me, before me'. Like:

| 12:33 | He said: O my Sustainer, jail is much better than what they draw me to. | قَالَ رَبِّ السِّجْنُ أَحَبُّ إِلَيَّ مِمَّا يَدْعُونَنِي إِلَيْهِ |

It is also used to mean: "it is for him"

| 27:33 | and it is for you to take the final decision | إِلَيْكِ |

Sometimes, it is also used to have the meaning of (ala) which means to talk against someone.

| 17:4 | And we had decided this against the **Bani Israel** | وَقَضَيْنَا إِلَى بَنِي إِسْرَائِيلَ |

But it could also mean "We had informed the **Bani Israel** about it. In the latter case, (ila) would not be used in the meaning of (ala) but it would mean "towards it". The word is commonly used in this sense.

Sometimes it is also used to mean "in," for example:

| 4:87
6:12 | He will collect you (all) on the day of **qayama** | لَيَجْمَعَنَّكُمْ إِلَى يَوْمِ الْقِيَامَةِ |

Sometimes, it is also used in the sense of **minn**, meaning "from". But such an example is not to be found in the Quran.

Ilyas   إِلْيَاسَ

He has been discussed by the Quran as a messenger:

6:85	And *Zikriyya*, *Yahya* and *Isa* and *Ilyas*. All these were the righteous people	وَزَكَرِيَّا وَيَحْيَى وَعِيسَى وَإِلْيَاسَ كُلٌّ مِّنَ الصَّالِحِينَ
37:123	And indeed, *Ilyas* was one of the messengers.	وَإِنَّ إِلْيَاسَ لَمِنَ الْمُرْسَلِينَ

In the same surah he has been called "*il yaseen*"

37:130	Peace be upon *il yaseen*	سَلَامٌ عَلَى إِلْيَاسِينَ

It has been said that the nation towards which it was sent used to worship "*Ba-al*".

37:125	Do you worship *Ba-al*?	أَتَدْعُونَ بَعْلًا

He is probably the same Messenger as *Elijah* in the Torah. Some others think that *Ilyas* is another name for messenger *Idrees*.

But (as it is mentioned under the heading *Idrees*) if *Idrees* was among the forefathers of *Nooh*, then *Ilyas* couldn't be *Idrees*.

Because in verse 6:85, *Ilyas* has been told to be from *Nooh's* (or *Ibrahim's*) progeny, hence he was probably one of the *Bani Israel's* Messengers.

Il Yaseen   يَاسِين

This is another name for *Ilyas*. For details, see heading "*Ilyas*". The Quran uses this name for him in 37:130.

Alayasa-o   اَلْيَسَعُ

This is the same Messenger as "*Elisha*" in the Torah. The Quran, while mentioning him as a messenger in 6:87, has said in 6:90 that they were all given the Book. Besides, he has been mentioned by name in 38:49. Detailed introduction is not given.

Am   أَمْ

It means "or". At times, it is used for a rhetorical question and, at others, as superfluous.

The following examples will make it clear:

79:27	Is it more difficult to create you or the celestial bodies?	أَأَنتُمْ أَشَدُّ خَلْقًا أَمِ السَّمَاءُ بَنَاهَا
2:6	It is the same for them, whether you warn them or not.	سَوَاءٌ عَلَيْهِمْ أَأَنذَرْتَهُمْ
13:16	Ask them whether a blind man and one who can see are equal (or rather) can darkness and light be equal?	قُلْ هَلْ يَسْتَوِي الْأَعْمَى وَالْبَصِيرُ أَمْ هَلْ تَسْتَوِي الظُّلُمَاتُ وَالنُّورُ
43:52	I am better than this (Am I not better than this?)	أَمْ أَنَا خَيْرٌ مِّنْ هَذَا الَّذِي
18:9	Do you know that the men of the cave and those with the tablets were from among our strange signs	أَمْ حَسِبْتَ أَنَّ أَصْحَابَ الْكَهْفِ وَالرَّقِيمِ كَانُوا مِنْ آيَاتِنَا عَجَبًا

A-M-Th   أ م ت

Ibn Faris says it means something which is slim at one end and thick at the other.

"أَمَتَ" (*amat*), "يَأْمِتُ" (ya-mit), "أَمْتًا" (*umta*) mean "to estimate, to assess".
"أَمَتَهُ، أَمْتًا" (*amatahu amta*): "he intended (to do) this".
"الْأَمْتُ" (*al-amt*): "small dunes, vicissitude, height and depth" *{T, M, R}*.

The Quran says:

| 20:107 | Without waves or being uneven | لَا تَرَى فِيهَا عِوَجًا وَلَا أَمْتًا |

"أَمْتًا" (*amtha*) is the opposite of clean and even. It is also used to mean "to oppose" and also "doubt".

As such, it is said "الْخَمْرُ حَرُمَتْ لَأَمْتَ فِيْهَ" (*al-hamru hurman la amta fiha*): Intoxication has been declared as *haram* (forbidden). There is no doubt about it.

A-M-D   أ م د

Ibn Faris says its basic meaning is "being extreme".

"أَمَدٌ" (*amad*): 'a period (of time)'.

Raghib says that "أَمَدٌ" (*amad*) and *abad* are close in meaning as *abad* is used for an unlimited period of time and "أَمَدٌ" (*amad*) has to have an ending.
"زَمَانٌ" (*zaman*) "time" is used for the beginning or ending or both, of time, but "أَمَدٌ" (*amad*) is used only for the last (or extreme) limit of time. *{T, M, R}*
"اَلْأَمَدُ" (*al-amad*): 'the extreme end of life'.

The Quran says:

3:29	he would want a long period of time between him and the Day of the Judgment	تَوَدُّ لَوْ أَنَّ بَيْنَهَا وَبَيْنَهُ أَمَدًا بَعِيدًا

The compiler of *Muheet* says that in this verse "أَمَدٌ" (*amad*): distance.

In 72:25 the word has been used against closeness, where it has been said:

72:25	Tell them I do not know whether what I promise you (the Day) is near or whether my Sustainer will extend the period.	قُلْ إِنْ أَدْرِي أَقَرِيبٌ مَّا تُوعَدُونَ أَمْ يَجْعَلُ لَهُ رَبِّي أَمَدًا

As such, it would mean "a long time".

A-M-R   ا م ر

"أَمَرٌ" (*amr*): 'order, situation, matter, work,' etc. *{F}*

Ibn Faris also includes "mark" among its basic meanings.

"اَلْأَمَرَةُ وَالتَّأْمُورُ" (*al-amrat-o wat'tamoor*): A sign made of small stones in the desert to mark boundaries or a path. As such, it basically means a mark, a sign, indication pointing towards a way. From this, it has come to mean 'consult'.
"اَلْائْتِمَارُ" (*al-atimaar*) means "to discuss", "to seek advice".

Surah *Airaaf* says that the Pharoah discussed the matter of Musa (Moses) with his officials and said:

7:110	So, what do you suggest?	فَمَاذَا تَأْمُرُونَ
26:35	So, what do you suggest?	فَمَاذَا تَأْمُرُونَ
65:6	Consult each other	وَأْتَمِرُوا بَيْنَكُم

Similarly, surah **Al-Qasas** says that a man came running from the opposite direction and said to **Moosa**:

28:20	The chiefs are discussing among themselves about murdering you.	إِنَّ الْمَلَأَ يَأْتَمِرُونَ بِكَ لِيَقْتُلُوكَ

But **Tajul Uroos** says that here it means 'to firmly decide'. These days this word means "conference".

"أَمِيْرٌ" (*ameer*) is the person whose advice is sought. One who leads the blind is also called the same.
"أَمَرَ" (*amar*): for something to become more than needed.
"أَمِرَ الرَّجَلُ" (*amir rajul*): "that man's animals became too many (proliferated)"
"الْأَمِرُ" (*al-amir*): a man with proliferation.

Ibn Faris says that with this meaning, where in surah **Bani Israel** it says *amirna mutrafeeha* in 17:16, it means "We proliferate wealth for the **mutrafeen**". But I think that it means that God's law in regard to destruction of nations is that such nations become prone to a life of luxury, demand abundance, lazy and of capitalist mentality. There is increase of well-to-do people who create imbalances in society and thus destroy the nation or cause its deterioration.

Where it means an order, the plural is "أَوَمِرٌ" (*awamir*), (*awamir*) and (*nawahi*), where *awamir* is the opposite of **nahi**) and where it means matter, situation, or accident, or event, then the plural is "أَمُوْرٌ" (*umoor*), but word "أَوَمِرٌ" (*awamir*) appears nowhere in the Quran.

According to these meanings, "الْأَمِيْرُ" (*al-ameer*) would mean a ruler.

2:67	Allah orders you	إِنَّ اللَّهَ يَأْمُرُكُمْ
24:62	On a collective matter.	عَلَى أَمْرٍ جَامِعٍ

"الْإِمْرَةُ" (*al-imratu*): government. {T}
"إِمَارَةُ" (*imaratu*) also means the same, that is, government.
"أَمْرٌ عَظِيْمٌ" (*amrun azeem*): great incident. {T}

16:33	a decisive stage	أَوْ يَأْتِيَ أَمْرُ رَبِّكَ
18:71	a very obnoxious thing	جِئْتَ شَيْئًا إِمْرًا

"الْأَمَّرَةُ" (*al-ammarah*) is one who orders a lot, one who disturbs a lot.

12:33	Opinion, willingness, whish	مَا آمُرُهُ
18:82	I didn't do it willingly	وَمَا فَعَلْتُهُ عَنْ أَمْرِي

The Quran uses "أَمْرٌ" (*amr*) as against "خَلْقْ" (*khalq*) or creation in 7:54.

And it has a special meaning to comprehend while its root has to be kept in mind i.e. sign, symbol, leading the way.

Ibn Faris says its basic meaning is also 'to nurture'.

As it has been mentioned under the heading *(Kh-L-Q)*, "خَلْقْ" (*khalq*) also means "to create new things in new ways".
"خَلْقْ" (*khalq*) is that stage of birth (or creation) when we can feel or sense those things, but obviously there is a stage before this stage as well.

That is when these things are in the process of becoming. This planning stage is about the world of "أَمَرٌ" (*amar*).

One other thing must be noted here. The universe has many things, such as the sun, the moon, the stars, the trees etc. Then there is an order in the universe according to which these things operate. This law or order is also called "*amar*". A detailed explanation will be found under the heading *(Sh-Y-A)*.

About the planning situation the Quran says:

2:117	when he decides about some planning "*amar*" then He tells the "*amar*" to be and it happens	وَإِذَا قَضَى أَمْرًا فَإِنَّمَا يَقُولُ لَهُ كُنْ فَيَكُونُ

What this "أَمْرٌ" (*amr*) is and how it is formulated, we are not able to say.

Our knowledge is confined to a sensory world only, and these things are beyond their purview. The famous philosopher and thinker Pringle Patterson acknowledges that it is a shortcoming of the English language that it has only one word for "*takhleeq*" and that is "creation." Although the physical world's creation and the meta-physical world's creation demanded that there should have been two separate words, but no. Quran has done this and used two different words, the words of "*khalq*" and "*amar*", respectively.

The other part of "أَمْرٌ" (*amr*) i.e. the law or God's order, which is operative in the universe, is before us and can be known about (in fact, we do know about many scientific facts). But only so far as to know how the law works in certain cases. Why any law is the way as it is, we are unable to say. For instance, we know that water flows towards the slope, that is the scientific fact or the law, and we know this, but we don't know why this law has been made for water!

The Quran is full of such "*amar*" i.e. the laws of God:

| 7:54 | the sun, the moon, the stars, are all bound in God's law or follow God's law | وَالشَّمْسَ وَالْقَمَرَ وَالنُّجُومَ مُسَخَّرَاتٍ بِأَمْرِهِ |
| 22:65 | ships sail on the seas according to His law | وَالْفُلْكَ تَجْرِي فِي الْبَحْرِ بِأَمْرِهِ |

In verse 34:12 "*izn*" and "*amar*" have been used in homogenous meanings. See heading "*Izn*".

The Quran says that just as in the physical world, everything works according to a particular law, and every result is subject to a particular order. In the same way, in the social world of humans too, the destruction and rise and fall of a nation also take place according to a law. This is the 'law of consequences' or 'result of actions', and this too has been called "*amar*"

| 8:42 | So Allah decided the matter in the way it got settled, so the fallen one fell, and the survivor survived. | لِّيَقْضِيَ اللَّه أَمْرًا كَانَ مَفْعُولًا لِّيَهْلِكَ مَنْ هَلَكَ عَن بَيِّنَةٍ وَيَحْيَى مَنْ حَيَّ عَن بَيِّنَةٍ |

Meaning thereby that whosoever has to be destroyed will be destroyed according to a law and whoso-ever has to live will do so according to the law. This is the law of consequence in whose result Man can do nothing.

Not even a **rasul** or Messenger can make any changes in this law:

| 3:127 | O rasul, you have no intervention in this law | لَيْسَ لَكَ مِنَ الْأَمْرِ شَيْءٌ |

This "*amar*" or law is about human actions and is given to Messengers through the knowledge revealed to them and through them to the other human beings:

| 45:17 | We have told them the clear things about *amar*. | وَآتَيْنَاهُم بَيِّنَاتٍ مِّنَ الْأَمْرِ |
| 65:5 | this is Allah's *amar* or law which He has revealed to you | ذَلِكَ أَمْرُ اللَّهِ أَنزَلَهُ إِلَيْكُمْ |

Thus Allah's "أَمْرٌ" (*amr*) has three stages, one where every law is fixed and everything is planned. We cannot find out about this stage. The second niche of God's *amar* or law is manifest in the universe and the knowledge about it can be gained through experiment, intellect, observation and insight. The third niche is that which deals with humans. This is granted to Messengers through **Wahi** (Revelation) and through them to other humans. It is preserved in the Quran and according to which the life or death of nations is decided. Every human can climb the evolutionary stages of life in accordance with its understanding.

In the first niche, Allah makes and operates the laws as He wishes. In the second niche, He operates the universe according to the laws framed by Him and the things in the universe are bound to follow His laws. In the third niche, His laws are given to Mankind through **Wahi** but they are given the choice to accept them or not, as they wish. But whatever path a man chooses will result accordingly. Allah's decisions, be they about the universe or about human life, are not subject to any change. This too is God's decision.

A-M-S   ا م س

"اَمْسِ" (*ams*) or "اَلْأَمْسِ" (*al-ams*): 'yesterday'. In surah *Qasas*, it has been used in this very meaning

| 28:18 | the man who asked him for help, yesterday | فَإِذَا الَّذِي اسْتَنصَرَهُ بِالْأَمْسِ |

But as is meant by "those who asked him for help till yesterday…" doesn't really mean the past day, but it means till some days back.

"اَلْأَمْس" (*al-ams*) is also used in this sense. In the same surah, a little ahead, it is said:

| 28:82 | The people who till yesterday wished to attain that position (*Qaroon's*)…. | وَأَصْبَحَ الَّذِينَ تَمَنَّوْا مَكَانَهُ بِالْأَمْسِ |

A-M-L   ا م ل

Ibn Faris says that its basic meaning is 'to wait for something or somebody, and 'have a doubtful expectation or hope'. To hopefully wait for a result that is expected but is late.

"اَلْأَمَلُ" (*al-aml*): expectation or hope, hence used for expectation of something not very probable. As such, a person who wishes to travel to a distant place will use "اَمَلْتُ" (*amalto*), but if the place is nearby and it is easy to go there, then he will use "طَمِعْتُ" (*ta-meto*) .This shows the difference between these two words. {M}. The word "رَجَاءٌ" (*rajao*) is used with regards to both. {T}

"اَلْأَمِيْلُ" (*al-ameel*) is a sand dune which is a day's travel away.

"تَأَمَّلَ الرَّجُلُ" (*ta ammala rajul*): to wait and think about a matter.

Surah *Al-Hijr* says:

| 15:3 | Their extended wishes (hopes) keeps them away from the real purpose of life. | وَيَتَمَتَّعُواْ وَيُلْهِهِمُ الْأَمَلُ |

A-M-M ا م م

Ibn Faris says that this root has four basic meanings:
- Fundament
- Junction
- Group
- Deen (system of life).

"اُمّ" (*um*) is that syllable which a child utters before learning to speak, according to *Muheet*'s compiler which leads to its meaning as 'mother'. Some also call "اُمّ" (*um*) as "اَمَّة" (*ummah*) and some even call "اَمَّیْة" (*ummya*) whose plural is "اُمَّهَاتٌ" (*ummahaat*). As regards to a mother's lap, a man's abode is also called "اُمّ" (*um*).

A nation is also called "اَمَّة" (*ummah*), specially the one of similar sect or group.

Surah *Al-Baqra* after mentioning various things about the Messengers says:

| 2:134 | It was an *umma* (nation) which has passed (is no more). | تِلْكَ أُمَّةٌ قَدْ خَلَتْ |
| 21:92 | Surely your nation is unique. | إِنَّ هَذِهِ أُمَّتُكُمْ أُمَّةً وَاحِدَةً |

Besides this, its meaning is of being the base or fundament of something.

"أُمُّ الْقَوْمِ" (*ummul qaum*): the chief of his nation.
"أُمُّ النُّجُومِ" (*ummul nujum*): galaxy.
"أُمُّ الرَّأْسِ" (*ummur raas*): the mind.
"اُمّ" (*um*) is also used to describe the point or junction where all things meet. In this regard Mecca is called "أُمُّ الْقُرَىَ" (*ummul Qura*).
"أُمُّ الْكِتَابِ" (*ummul kitab*): the basis of law. {*T*}
"الْأُمَّة" (*al-ummah*): condition, gift, grandeur, time, period, *sharia* (the laws of life according to Islam) and deen.

This word has appeared as meaning period of time in following verse:

| 12:45 | The one, who had been released, said after thinking a period | وَقَالَ الَّذِي نَجَا مِنْهُمَا وَادَّكَرَ بَعْدَ أُمَّةٍ |

It also means "اِمَام" (*imam*) meaning leader and "هَادِي" (*hadi*), meaning one who shows the right path.

As *Abu Obaidah* has said in his translation:

| 16:120 | Indeed, Abraham was a humble leader | إِنَّ إِبْرَاهِيمَ كَانَ أُمَّةً قَانِتًا |

Here the word *imam* would mean leader, as well as follower. Although it might also mean that Ibrahim was an individual, he was so complete as if to encompass an entire nation.

"أُمَّةٌ" (*ummat*), "نُعْلَةٌ" (*fu'lat*) or "فُعْلَةٌ" (*fu'alaht*), "فُعْلَةٌ" (*fu'la*) means something which is much intended. It may therefore mean the leader.

"فُعْلَةٌ" (*fu'ala*): he who thinks a lot about someone. As such with this meaning, "" (*ummah*) in 16:120 would mean one who turns to God time and again.

Ibn Qateebah has written that "أُمَّةً" (*ummah*), means "way of life, leader or group".

Lataiful Lughaat (a dictionary) also says that it means "a man who has all the best traits", and it also means "***Imam***". For more details see ***Tatammah*** vol.VI pub 1812.

"اَلْإِمَامَةٌ" (*al imama*): to be in front, to lead.

"إِمَامٌ" (*imam*) is the person who is in front, that is, in leadership. It also means a man who is the embodiment and fountainhead of all types of goodness. At another place the Quran verifies the meaning:

2:124	Indeed, I am the one to have appointed you to be a leader to the mankind.	إِنِّي جَاعِلُكَ لِلنَّاسِ إِمَامٌ

This is also the name of the thread or string which masons use to determine whether all bricks are laid in a straight line or not. In Arabic, the instrument for doing this is called ***faadin*** and in Urdu, *sahil*. Besides, a wide street is also called "إِمَامٌ" (*imam*). 15:79

"أَمَامٌ" (*amam*): of being in front, future. For example:

75:5	Mankind will continue to live in evil	بَلْ يُرِيدُ الْإِنسَانُ لِيَفْجُرَ أَمَامَهُ

"أَمَّهُ" (*amahu*), "يَؤُمَّهُ" (*yau-umo-hu*), "أَمَّا" (*amma*): 'to decide to, to be of the intent'.

"أَمِّينَ" (*ammeen*): those who intend to, those who decide to. Quran uses "*amma*" and all its derivatives, which appear above in all the meanings given above. As such, there is no need for examples.

"اَلْأُمِّيّ" (*al-ummi*) is one word whose meanings must be understood correctly. It basically means one who is in the state of his birth (to stay as innocent as at the time of birth) and who doesn't learn to read or write. {L}

Our messenger ***Muhammad*** is also called "أُمِّيّ" (*ummi*) because he didn't know how to read or write. But this is before his Messenger-hood. He had learnt to read and write after being endowed with Messenger-hood. There is distinct evidence to that effect in the Quran.

Surah **Al-Ankabut** says:

29:48	(Before the revelation of the Quran) you did not read nor write this with your hand.	وَمَا كُنتَ تَتْلُو مِن قَبْلِهِ مِن كِتَابٍ وَلَا تَخُطُّهُ بِيَمِينِكَ

From this, it is evident that before revelation of the Quran he did not read or write but this condition changed after revelation. That is why the Quran explained "**min qiblehi**" (before this). But in the Quran, even the common Arabs have been called "أُمِّيّ" (**ummi**). This means the people who were not given any Code before the Quran because, this word has appeared against "**ahley kitab**" that is, those with the Code.

See 3:19 and 3:74. The **Christians** and the Jews were called "those with the Code" in the Arab world, and those who didn't claim to have any celestial Book or Code, were called "**ghair ahley kitab**" that is, those without a Book or "**ummi**". This doesn't mean that they were completely illiterate.

This was only a figure of speech for the "**ahley kitab**" to distinguish them from others. Thus at several places in the Quran "أُمِّيّ" (**ummi**): illiterate and at other places "those people without any celestial Code."

Besides this, "أُمِّيّ" (**ummi**) also means an inhabitant of Mecca "أُمّ الْقُرَىئَ" (**ummul Qura**). Like an inhabitant of **Hazarmaut** is called a **Hazarmi**.

Note: **Amma** is a letter which has been kept separate.

It may be kept in mind that the Quran has called Muslims who have been given this Book of Quran):

74:31	but only those who have the right knowledge of this Book	الَّذِينَ أُوتُوا الْكِتَاب

llah is used only for God. All his other names are based on some trait or the other.

Amma أَمَّا

This word is used in sense of:
- as far as this is concerned
- so far as this thing is concerned

Example 1.

2:26	So far as the Believers are concerned, they know that...	فَأَمَّا الَّذِينَ آمَنُواْ فَيَعْلَمُونَ
80:5	as far as he who considers himself an exception	أَمَّا مَنِ اسْتَغْنَى
18:79	So far as the boat is concerned....	أَمَّا السَّفِينَةُ

| 18:80 | And as far as the boy is concerned | وَأَمَّا الْغُلَامُ |

Example 2.

Sometimes, **amma** means "or the thing that" or which. This is that very um which appears after a questioning **hamza**, for instance, as in surah **Anaam**:

| 6:144 | Tell them that both males are made haram (forbidden) or both females, or that which is in their wombs. | قُلْ آلذَّكَرَيْنِ حَرَّمَ أَم الْأُنثَيَيْنِ أَمَّا اشْتَمَلَتْ عَلَيْهِ أَرْحَامُ الْأُنثَيَيْنِ |

A-M-N   ا م ن

Ibn Faris says its basic meaning are:

-   The opposite of being dishonest for breaking someone's trust
-   Peace and safety
-   To verify

"أَمَنْ" (*aman*): fearlessness, solace, to be protected from any fear.

Surah *Al-Baqrah* and Surah *Al-An'am* says:

| 2:240 | When you are safe | فَإِذَا أَمِنتُم |
| 6:81 | so which group among these two deserves security the most | فَأَيُّ الْفَرِيقَيْنِ أَحَقُّ بِالْأَمْنِ |

"أَمَنْ" (*aman*): to free somebody of worries and unease, to give peace to somebody, to take the responsibility of protecting someone.

"الْإِنْتَمَانْ" (*itemaan*): to trust someone, or to make someone trustworthy.

"نَاقَةٌ آمُونٌ" (*naqatun amoon*) is a female camel which is pretty strong, as such its limbs and habits are trust worthy. Something one can be sure about, that with continuous use, it will not weaken and not stumble and fall on the way.

"مُؤْمِنٌ" (*momin*) is someone who guarantees peace, one on whom a person can depend with equanimity, the guarantor of world peace.

"آمَانَةٌ" (*amanat*) is something which is kept in trust *{M}*

"حَمَلَ أَمَانَةً" (*hamal amanat*) means to break the trust of *amanat* (see heading H-M-L).

"أَمِيْنٌ" (*ameen*) is someone without fear, as regards one's safety or trust. One who is dependable.

"بَلَدٌ أَمِيْنٌ" (*baladun amen*) is the city which has peace and security (95:3)

"مَقَامٌ أَمِيْنٌ" (*maqamun amen*) the place where there is complete contentment (in the above meaning) and security (44:52) *{L}*

The Quran says:

26:162	I am the Messenger of peace for you	إِنِّي لَكُمْ رَسُولٌ أَمِينٌ
16:112	Allah narrates the tale of a dwelling which was content and in peace. It had the accoutrements of life coming in from other places in plenty. Then it did not appreciate Allah's benevolence. So Allah made them taste the punishment of hunger and fear.	وَضَرَبَ اللّهُ مَثَلاً قَرْيَةً كَانَتْ آمِنَةً مُّطْمَئِنَّةً يَأْتِيهَا رِزْقُهَا رَغَدًا مِّن كُلِّ مَكَانٍ فَكَفَرَتْ بِأَنْعُمِ اللّهِ فَأَذَاقَهَا اللّهُ لِبَاسَ الْجُوعِ وَالْخَوْفِ بِمَا كَانُواْ يَصْنَعُونَ
15:82	For security, they used to carve out mountains to make houses	وَكَانُواْ يَنْحِتُونَ مِنَ الْجِبَالِ بُيُوتًا آمِنِينَ
3:154	then he endowed you with peace after sorrow.	ثُمَّ أَنزَلَ عَلَيْكُم مِّن بَعْدِ الْغَمِّ أَمَنَةً

Here "أَمَنْ" (*aman*) has come as the opposite of sorrow.

The Quran has used this word's root to mean trust at various places.

2:283	if one of you trust the other	فَإِنْ أَمِنَ بَعْضُكُم بَعْضًا
12:11	then he doesn't trust us	لاَ تَأْمَنَّا
12:17	And you will not believe us	وَمَا أَنتَ بِمُؤْمِنٍ لَّنَا
12:64	He said that I do not trust you like I trusted you	قَالَ هَلْ آمَنُكُمْ عَلَيْهِ إِلاَّ كَمَا أَمِنتُكُمْ

At all these places the word *Amn* has been used to mean trust, and belief.

"أَمَنْ" (*aman*) also means to accept (agree).

Regarding the Bani Israel, surah *Al-Baqrah* says:

2:55	we will not agree upon what you say	لَن نُّؤْمِنَ لَكَ

This has the connotation of trustworthiness, belief and obedience, all together. When ـب (*beh*) comes after it, then it means to trust upon it.

2:285	All trusted upon Allah	كُلٌّ آمَنَ بِاللّهِ

"أَمَنْ" (*aman*) therefore means:
- To trust
- To accept, or not deny
- To certify, to agree of something being the truth, not to deny it.
- To trust and e secure about something
- To accept, to obey, to bow one's head in acceptance.

There are five basic facts on which one must trust, that is, have *Iman*, which makes one Momin.

Surah *Al-Baqrah* says:

| 2:177 | Open is the path for him who has trust in God, on the time of judgement, on the *malaikah*, on the Book (the Quran) and the Messengers | وَلَكِنَّ الْبِرَّ مَنْ آمَنَ بِاللَّهِ وَالْيَوْمِ الآخِرِ وَالْمَلآئِكَةِ وَالْكِتَابِ وَالنَّبِيِّينَ |

Denying any one of the above mentioned is *kufr.*

| 4:136 | One who denies Allah, and his *malaikah*, This Book, Messengers and the time of the Judgement, goes far in denial. | وَمَن يَكْفُرْ بِاللَّهِ وَمَلآئِكَتِهِ وَكُتُبِهِ وَرُسُلِهِ وَالْيَوْمِ الآخِرِ فَقَدْ ضَلَّ ضَلاَلاً بَعِيدًا |

Belief or *Eemaan* on Allah means to have total faith in Him, to believe whatever he says, belief in all His laws, and to agree to obey them. To believe in the time of Judgement means to have complete faith in the laws of cause and effect (in human affairs as well), and belief in Life after Death. Belief on the *malaikah* means to have faith that these celestial forces are engaged in carrying out God's program in the universe and God has subjugated them before Man.

He has conquered them for Man. Therefore, there is no force among them for Man to bow to. Faith on the Messenger means that Man's intellect alone is not enough to go through life successfully. The guidance for this comes through *Wahi*, and *Wahi* does not come direct, but through selected individuals who are called Messengers. This *Wahi* system ended with Messenger Muhammed. Faith on the Books means that this way of life has been received through *Wahi* and by following it Man can reach his ultimate destination. There is no other way through which one can reach the destination. To act according to this Book is an active display of faith on the Messenger (*peace be upon him*). But after the revelation of the Quran, no other book can be Man's beacon of light for a successful life.

As such, a Momin is one who believes unshakably the laws of God which are at play in the universe and the laws that have been given to us through *Muhammad* , and is now preserved in the Quran. Belief on the results of all human acts (in this world as well as in the Hereafter).

A group consisting of such persons as having these beliefs have been called by the Quran as " يَا أَيُّهَا الَّذِينَ آمَنُوا" (*ya ayyohal lazeena amenu*), but warns at the same time lest only the name remains and the spirit is not there. To ensure that they remain so, they were told that like the others, the rest of humanity (the Christians and the Jews) they too, must have faith in the laws of God and on repayment (of human deeds).

They can have a fearless and content life only in this way, and not simply by being born into a Muslim family:

2:62	Verily those who call themselves the **Momins**, and those who are the Christians, the Jews and the **sabiens** whosoever will entrust on Allah and do good deeds, will have their repayment with their Sustainer, and they will have no woe nor fear	إِنَّ الَّذِينَ آمَنُواْ وَالَّذِينَ هَادُواْ وَالنَّصَارَى وَالصَّابِئِينَ مَنْ آمَنَ بِاللَّهِ وَالْيَوْمِ الآخِرِ وَعَمِلَ صَالِحاً فَلَهُمْ أَجْرُهُمْ عِندَ رَبِّهِمْ وَلاَ خَوْفٌ عَلَيْهِمْ وَلاَهُمْ يَحْزَنُونَ

Also see 4:136.

Along with this, God also said that the Christians and the Jews must not think that since they already believe in God and Life after Death, they do not need to have renewed trust in order to become **Momin**.

They were told clearly that until they believe in all matters as the Quran has laid out, nobody's belief will be called true belief:

2:137	if they trust the way you do, then they will be considered to be on the right path	فَإِنْ آمَنُواْ بِمِثْلِ مَا آمَنتُم بِهِ فَقَدِ اهْتَدَواْ

Eeman is that belief which is according to the Quran and good deeds are also only those which are as the Quran has ordained.

Quran also says that there are people who do believe that God is the creator of the universe and the universe runs according to His laws, but they do not think it necessary to follow God's dictates in their matters (matters of human life) as laid out in the **Wahi** (God's message through the Messenger). Such people, according to the Quran are not true **Momin**. To be a true **moumin**, it is necessary for one to believe in God, and at the same time to believe in the **Wahi** and to lead one's life according to it.

For details see 23:82 to 90.

Also remember, that either due to some exigency, or since the **Momins** are in power, it is not **Eeman** to have faith. **Eeman** means to have faith in the lordship and truths of God from the core of the heart.

Surah **Al-Hijr** says:

49:14	Arabs say they have accepted **eeman**. Tell them they haven't. Say that you have accepted our subjugation, because **eeman** has not yet entered your hearts.	قَالَتِ الْأَعْرَابُ آمَنَّا قُل لَّمْ تُؤْمِنُوا وَلَكِن قُولُوا أَسْلَمْنَا وَلَمَّا يَدْخُلِ الْإِيمَانُ فِي قُلُوبِكُمْ

It must be clearly understood that **eeman** does not only mean acknowledging these facts, it also means to act accordingly.

Surah **Rome** says:

| 30:53 | You can only recite (make them understand the Quran) only to those people who believe our orders and are subservient to them | إِن تُسْمِعُ إِلَّا مَن يُؤْمِنُ بِآيَاتِنَا فَهُم مُّسْلِمُونَ |

This is why **eeman** has been treated as the opposite of **kufr** as in verse 2:3-6. It has also been made out as the opposite of (making inroads into) avoiding **Imaan**:

3:110	they are also the opposites of wrongdoers	مِّنْهُمُ الْمُؤْمِنُونَ وَأَكْثَرُهُمُ الْفَاسِقُونَ
3:166	So that he can find out who are Momin	وَلِيَعْلَمَ الْمُؤْمِنِينَ
3:167	and who are hypocrites	وَلِيَعْلَمَ الَّذِينَ نَافَقُوا

Quran calls God as **Al-momin** in 59:23, because He is the Protector of the entire universe. And whosoever believes on his laws is protected by Him from destructive forces. This way an individual is a **momin** when the entire human race can trust him and who is responsible for keeping peace.

From the above deposition, it can be well understood as to what a **momin** is, hat his place in society is and what his duties and responsibilities are.

Imma   أَمِّا

"أَمَّا" (*imma*): either, or whether, and can be explained with the following examples:

| 9:106 | Whether he punish them, or whether He listens to them. | إِمَّا يُعَذِّبُهُمْ وَإِمَّا يَتُوبُ عَلَيْهِمْ |
| 20:65 | They said, O **Moosa**, would you rather go first, or shall we do? | قَالُوا يَا مُوسَى إِمَّا أَن تُلْقِيَ وَإِمَّا أَن نَّكُونَ أَوَّلَ مَنْ أَلْقَى |

Sometimes it gives the meaning of condition. In that case the sentence also contains "ma":

| 19:26 | Then, if you see any person….. | فَإِمَّا تَرَيِنَّ مِنَ الْبَشَرِ أَحَدًا |

A-M-W   ا م و

"أَمَةٌ" (*amah*): a slave girl. It is the opposite of "حُرَّةٌ" (hurrah) which is used for a free woman. Actually this word was "أَمَوَةٌ" (*amawuh*) or "أَمْوَةٌ" (*amwah*) {T}. Quran uses the word "عَبْدٌ" (*abd*) for the masculine and "أَمَةٌ" (*amah*) for the feminine. (2:228). The plural of "أَمَةٌ" (*amah*) is "إِمَاءٌ" (*imaa*) (24:32).

An   أَنْ

"أَنْ" (*an*) usually means that or which:

9:32	What they wish, is to extinguish Allah's light	يُرِيدُونَ أَن يُطْفِؤُواْ نُورَ اللَّهِ
2:184	and that if you observe the fast, it will be better for you	وَأَن تَصُومُواْ خَيْرٌ لَّكُمْ
26:33	When they came towards **Lout** whom we had sent. (here "**un**" is redundant)	وَلَمَّا أَن جَاءتْ رُسُلُنَا لُوطًا
11:77	(Same verse as 26:33 except أَن)	وَلَمَّا جَاءتْ رُسُلُنَا لُوطًا

Sometimes "un" is used to state the reason.

38:4	And they are surprised that somebody from among them had come to make them aware	وَعَجِبُوا أَن جَاءهُم مُّنذِرٌ مِّنْهُمْ

In other words they are surprised that a Messenger has come from amongst them. But some say that here "**an**" is actually "**le an**" which means "so that" or because of, but it has not been written. It also means "so that".

16:15	And he has made mountains on the earth to provide you with sustenance.	وَأَلْقَى فِي الأَرْضِ رَوَاسِيَ أَن تَمِيدَ بِكُمْ

Or you stay comfortably on it as it turns round or revolves.

Some think "**laam**" or "**le**" is not written here as well.

Sometime it means "saying that" as in:

16:36	And we sent a messenger to every nation, saying that people should only accept Allah's subjugation.	وَلَقَدْ بَعَثْنَا فِي كُلِّ أُمَّةٍ رَّسُولاً أَنِ اعْبُدُواْ اللَّهَ

It also means "so that it may not" as in:

4:176	Allah tells you these things openly so that you may not be at fault.	يُبَيِّنُ اللّهُ لَكُمْ أَن تَضِلُّواْ

Also means: so that if this happens, then... For instance:

2:282	If it so happens that one of them makes a mistake, then....	أَن تَضِلَّ إْحْدَاهُمَا

In   إِنْ

Means "if":

8:38	Say to the opposers that if they stop, then what has been shall be corrected	قُل لِّلَّذِينَ كَفَرُواْ إِن يَنتَهُواْ إِن يُغْفَرْ لَهُم

Sometimes it means "no" as in:

37:15	And they said, no, this is clear deception.	وَقَالُوا إِنْ هَذَا إِلَّا سِحْرٌ مُبِينٌ
35:41	if they move (away) then nobody can stop them.	وَلَئِن زَالَتَا إِنْ أَمْسَكَهُمَا

Also see the heading (**S-H-R**)

Sometimes it is the abbreviation of "*inna*" and means surely, indeed. As in:

87:9	Then keep reminding them, surely this reminder is beneficial	فَذَكِّرْ إِن نَّفَعَتِ الذِّكْرَى

Some think that "*in*" here is conditional and the verse means that one should only speak of Allah when it is beneficial or else one should wait for the right time.

When "*in*" is the abbreviation of "*inna*", then it definitely asserts something as in:

62:2	and verily they were, before this, in clear digress	وَإِن كَانُوا مِن قَبْلُ لَفِي ضَلَالٍ مُّبِينٍ

Sometimes it is redundant or additional. That is, it bears no meaning at all. Therefore some people think that in the following verse, "un" is redundant.

46:26	and verily we had endowed them with such grandeur as we had granted you	وَلَقَدْ مَكَّنَّاهُمْ فِيمَا إِن مَّكَّنَّاكُمْ فِيهِ

But if here "in" is taken to mean "no" then the meaning would be: we gave them such grandeur as have not even given you.

Sometime it means "*iz*" which means "because":

5:112	Guard (be the sentinel to) God's law because you are a Momin	اتَّقُواْ اللَّهَ إِن كُنتُم مُّؤْمِنِينَ
2:172	And be thankful for God's bounties to you, because you are obedient to Him.	وَاشْكُرُواْ لِلَّهِ إِن كُنتُمْ إِيَّاهُ تَعْبُدُونَ

"إِلَّا" (*illa*) is the same as (لَا + إِنْ) (*in+la*). See heading "إِلَّا" (*illa*)

Ana اَنَا

It is used for both masculine and feminine.
"اَنَا رَجُلٌ" (*ana rajul*): I am a man.
"اَنَا اِمْرَأَةٌ" (*ana imra'a*): I am a woman.

Quran says:

2:258	I give life and death	اَنَا اُحْيِي وَأُمِيتُ

The feminine plural for "اَنَا" (*ana*), is "نَحْنُ" (*nahno*).

Anta اَنْتَ

"اَنْتَ رَجُلٌ" (*anta rajal*): that you are a man.

Surah *Al-Baqrah* says:

2:35	Let you and your partners live in the garden	اسْكُنْ أَنْتَ وَزَوْجُكَ الْجَنَّةَ

Its feminine is "اَنْتُمَا" (*antuma*) and plural is "اَنْتُنَّ" (*antun*).

Anti اَنْتِ

"اَنْتِ اِمْرَأَةٌ" (*anteh imrah*): that you are a woman. The feminine is "اَنْتُمَا" (*antuma*) and plural is "اَنْتُنَّ" (*antoon*).

Antam اَنْتُم

"اَنْتُم رِجَالٌ" (*antum rijal*) meant that you are all men. The singular is "اَنْتَ" (*ant*).

The Quran says:

2:132	you are all Muslims	وَأَنْتُم مُّسْلِمُونَ

Antama اَنْتُمَا

It is used for masculine as well as feminine. "اَنْتُمَا رُجْلَانِ" (*antuma rojalan*): you are both men. "اَنْتُمَا اِمْرَأَتَانِ" (*antuma imrataan*): you are both women.
Surah *Al-Qasas* says:

28:35	you two, and whosoever follows you will prevail	أَنْتُمَا وَمَنِ اتَّبَعَكُمَا الْغَالِبُونَ

Antan اَنْتُنَّ

"اَنْتُنَّ" (*antun*) is the deviation for plural feminine. "اَنْتُنَّ نِسْوَةٌ" (*antunn-niswah*): you are all women. The singular is "اَنْتِ" (*anti*).

A-N-Th أ ن ث

"اَنْثُنَّ" (*anthun*) basically means "soft".
"حَدِيْدٌ اَنِثٌ" (*hadeedun anees*): soft iron.
"اَرْضٌ اَنِيثَة" (*ardun aneesa*) is soft earth.
"سَيْفٌ اَنِيثٌ" (*saifun anees*) is soft sword which doesn't cut.
"اَنَثَ لَهُ" (*anasa lahu*): that he became soft for him, which means that he developed a soft corner for him {T}.

Raghib says since the female as against the male of all species is softer, as such the female is called "اُنْثَى" (*unsa*). Therefore all things, in which there is some weakness, are called "اَنِيْثٌ" (*anees*). This is also why all soft stones are called "اَلْاِنَاثٌ" (*al inaas*). And all such things which are worshipped as against God are called (with reference to their weakness in contrast to God) "اِنَاثٌ" (*inaas*).

As surah **An-Nisa** says:

| 4:117 | They call upon the weak ones, instead of it | إِن يَدْعُونَ مِن دُونِهِ إِلَّا إِنَاثًا |

Here "اِنَاثٌ" (*inaas*): weak even if they are stone idols.

Quran uses "ذَكَرٌ" (*zakar*) as against feminine of "اُنْثَى" (*unsa*) in 4:11. As against "بَنِيْنَ" (*baneen*) meaning sons, is also used "اِنَاثٌ" (*inaas*) meaning daughters, in 17:40.

Injeel إِنْجِيْلٌ

Injeel has many meanings. Besides them it also means "flowing water" and "نَجَلَتِ الْأَرْضُ" (*najalatal ard*): that land became fertile.

"نَجَلَ الشَّيَّءَ" (*najalas shaiyi*): he disclosed it. Some say "اَلْاِنْجِيْلٌ" (*al-injeel*) has been derived from this {T}.

But **Muheet** says that this word has been derived from "اَوَنْجِلِيُوْنَ" (*awaljiloon*) which means good news or happy tidings.

Ibn Faris says "اَلْإِنْجِيلٌ" (*al-injeel*) has come from "نَجَلَتِ الشَّيْءَ" (*najalas shaiyi*) which means, I extracted him, meaning "made clear" or "described openly." Its basic meaning is wideness or vastness in something.

The Quran has used this word for the Book (Bible) which was presented to *Isa* (Jesus). (57:27)

The history of this Book, *al-anjeel* or Bible can be viewed in the first chapter of my book "*Meraj Insaniyat*". This will make it clear that the book is totally not in its original form. *Isa's* Holy Book which he left with his friends is not to be found anymore. Later when the church became the battle ground of Jews and non-Jewish elements, people of different schools of thought began compiling their own version of the bible. The Encyclopaedia Britannica says that as many as thirty four Bibles can be traced from that period. These were actually the biographies of the Christ as culled from tradition. Jesus and his band's language was Irami but it is surprising that all the 34 bibles (excepting one which is now found nowhere) were not in the Irami language. They were all in the Greek language. *Niqa's* famous council (held in 325 B.C.) selected four out of these 34 bibles and the rest were declared false.

These four selected *Injeels* and the letters which are linked to St. Paul and the band (the 12 friends of Christ) are called the New Testaments. But none of them is found on this earth in its original shape. At present, there are only three ancient volumes of the bible. One is with the Vatican, the second in the British Museum and the third was sold by Russia to England. The first two volumes are of the Fifth Century whereas the third one is of the Fourth Century. In the fourth century, Gerome translated it from Greek to Latin. This translation is the basis of the translation which was published during King James' rule (1611) and which translation is considered authentic.

In 1870 there was a conference in Canterbury of 27 big Christian scholars who decided that since this translation was not correct, a new translation was needed. This was called the Revised Edition. But this does not mean that the translations now available are according to those two translations. Not at all. Every new volume which is published by the Bible Societies is different from the previous one. The difference is so pronounced that when Dr. Mel collected some revised edition volumes, he found thirty thousand differences! And when he probed deeper, then he found as many as one million differences. For details see the chapter named Gospel of the Encyclopaedia Britannica and the chapter titled Bible of the book Encyclopaedia of Religions and Ethics.

This, briefly, is the Bible which the Christians think is a celestial book. Remember that these differences do not appear in the bibles as errors. They have been made deliberately as a virtuous deed which is thought to invoke the Blessings. As such even St. Paul is on record as stating:

"*If God's truth was manifest due to his omnipotence, then why am I ordered like a sinner?*" (Letters to the Romans 2:7)

How this was possible, only one example will suffice (to make the contradiction clear): Dr. Jude, in his book God and Evil, writes that: *"The thing that is most condemnable is the character of Christ that the bibles present (page 319)."* This will make one realize that Quran did the Christian world a great favour when it described *Maryam* and *Isa's* tales in the right perspective.

A-N-S   ا ن س

"أُنْسٌ" (*uns*): to be familiar with.
"اَلْحُمْرُ الْإِنْسِيَّةُ" (*alhumurul insiyato*): pet donkeys.
"حِمَارٌ وَحْشِيٌّ" (*himarun wahshiun*): wild donkeys.
"إِسْتَنَاسُ الْوَحْشِيِّ" (*istanasal wahshi*): that the wild animal is familiarized.
"اِنْسُ فُلَانٍ" (*insun fulaan*): man's special friend.

"اِنْسٌ" (*ins*) is used for "man" and the singular is "اِنْسِيٌّ" (*insiun*). "النَّاسُ" (*an-nas*) is that tribe which is settled somewhere *{T}{L}*.

Those gypsy tribes which move from place to place and stay away from one's vision are called "جِنٌّ" (*jinn*). See heading *(J-N-N)*.

Ibn Faris says that the basic meaning of "اِنْسٌ" (*ins*) is to be evident as against "جِنٌّ" (*jinn*) which means to be non-evident. The plural is "أُنَاسٌ" (*unas*) and "أَنَاسِيٌّ" (*anasi*). Some think that "النَّاسُ" (*an-nas*) is also its plural.

Surah *Al-Baqrah* says:

2:60	all the tribes found their drinking spot.	قَدْ عَلِمَ كُلُّ أُنَاسٍ مَّشْرَبَهُمْ

Here *onas* means tribes. In the sense of the human race, *unasi* and *an-naas* appear in surah *Al-Furqan* 25:50, and 25:49.

About the word "اِنْسَانٌ" (*insaan*), there are many versions, but some think that it has come from the word "اِنْسٌ" (*ins*). Quran uses "اِنْسَانٌ" (*insaan*), and "بَشَرٌ" (*bashar*) as alternatives.15:26 and 15:28. Besides this, the word "اِنْسِيًّا" (*inseyan*) has also appeared along with *bashar* in 19:26.

For the difference between *insaan* and *bashar*, see heading *(B-Sh-R)*.

As said before, "النَّاسُ" (*an-anas*) is the plural of "اِنْسٌ" (*ins*). Some also think that it is a collective noun like "قَوْمٌ" (*qaum*). Some believe that "النَّاسُ" (*an-anas*) was "أُنَاسٌ" (*onaas*) to start with, which is the plural of *ins*. Some also think that it was "الْأَنَاسُ" (*al-unasi*) at first, and gradually only *an-naas* remained. *{T}*

"أَنَاسٌ" (*anas*): to see and feel.

In **Moosa's** tale it is said:

20:10 27:7	I have seen a **naar**	إِنِّي آنَسْتُ نَارًا

Here "أَنَاسَ" (**anas**): to see.

Muheet says that "اِيْنَاسٌ" (**in-naas**): to comprehend and believe something.
"مُسْتَأْنِيْسٌ" (**mustanis**): something that is familiar and well known, and without protocol.

Surah **Al-Ahzaab** says:

33:53	talk without protocol or freely	مُسْتَأْنِسِينَ لِحَدِيثٍ

"اِسْتَأْنَسٌ" (**istaanus**) is to seek permission.

Surah **An-Noor** says:

24:27	Until you seek permission	حَتَّى تَسْتَأْنِسُوا

"اِسْتَأْنَسٌ" (**istanasu**): to seek information. A man who knocks at a door tries to find out if someone is at home, and if so, if he can enter. This word, in this manner, began to be used as **istayizan** i.e. seeking permission; this sort of seeking permission is meant to familiarize the one who has come at the door with the inmates of the house.

God in the Quran is **Rabb-in-naas**, **Malak-in-naas**, **Ilah-in-naas**:

114:1	Proclaim that I am under close protection of the provider of the **naas**	قُلْ أَعُوذُ بِرَبِّ النَّاسِ
114:2	The security holder over the **naas**	مَلِكِ النَّاسِ
114:3	The protector of the **naas**	إِلَهِ النَّاسِ

The Quran says about itself:

45:20	This is the provider of insight for the **naas**	هَذَا بَصَائِرُ لِلنَّاسِ

So the invitation (to accept Islam), has no bounds of time or place and God's superiority is for the whole universe. The Quran also mentions the **jinn** and **naas**, i.e. the gypsies and civilized people together (in the same verse), and also about the creation of **jinns** before **naas** (15:27). This means that the rural villages were created before the civilizations of cities.

For details, see heading (**J-N-N**).

A-N-F   ا ن ف

"اَلْأَنْفُ" (*al-anf*): the nose, or tip, the strongest and hardest part of something, which is in the front. {T}{R}

5:45	And the nose for nose	وَالْأَنفَ بِالْأَنفِ

"اَلْإِسْتِنَافُ" (*al-istenafu*): to begin something new. {T}{R}

The Arabs apply both wealth and disgrace to it. As "حَمِيَ أَنْفُهُ" (*hamiya anfahu*): that he became respected, and "رَغِمَ أَنْفُهُ" (*raghema anfahu*) he became disgraced: {M}.

"آنَفًا" (*anefan*): "just now". The Quran uses this meaning in 47:16.

A-N-M   ا ن م

"اَلْأَنَام" (*al-anaam*): creations (creatures), or only *ins* and *jinn*. Some say all things on earth are called *anaam*. This is probably derived from "أَنَام" (*annam*) and can mean all things which are subjects to sleep {T, R}. Some say all living things are called "اَلْأَنَامُ" (*al-anaam*) {M}.

The Quran says:

55:10	The earth has been created for the benefit of the creations	وَالْأَرْضَ وَضَعَهَا لِلْأَنَام

It is evident from this that any system in which the earth (the fountainhead of all sustenance is reserved for a few only (or lies waste) would be against God's wishes.

To explain this, the Quran at another place says:

41:10	it should be open (available) for all needy	سَوَاء لِّلسَّائِلِينَ

For more details, see heading *(A-R-Dh)*.

Inna   إِنَّ

"إِنَّ" (*inna*) is used for assertion and assurance:

2:6	it is a fact that those who deny this (system of life)	إِنَّ الَّذِينَ كَفَرُواْ

"إِنَّمَا" (*innama*) is used to mean "only":

9:10	*Sadaqat* are only for those who are *fuqra*	إِنَّمَا الصَّدَقَاتُ لِلْفُقَرَاء

It also means reiteration. See under heading "*ma*". *Inni* is also called *innani* and *inna* is also spoken as *innana*.

Anna اَنَّ

"اَنَّ" (*anna*) is actually like "اِنَّ" (*inna*). It is used for reiteration. When it has a *kaaf* in front, it reads "كَاَنَّ" (*ka-anna*). See heading (*ka-anna*).

"اَنَّمَا" (*annama*) also means the same as "اَنَّ" (*anna*), and means reiteration.

21:108	Verily, your *ilah* is a unique *ilah*.	اَنَّمَا إِلَهُكُمْ إِلَهٌ وَاحِدٌ

"اَنَّ" (*anna*) and "اِنَّ" (*inna*) differ only in that *anna* is used in between a sentence while inna is used in the beginning of the sentence.

Anna اَنَّى

"اَنَّى كَيْفَ" (*anna kaifa*): how.

89:23	(and that day) how can he be reminded of the law?	وَاَنَّى لَهُ الذِّكْرَى

"مَتَى" (*mata*): when:

19:8	(Zakariah) said: O my Sustainer, when will a son be born to me?	قَالَ رَبِّ اَنَّى يَكُونُ لِي غُلَامٌ

"مِنْ اَيْنَ" (*min aina*):, from where?

3:36	From where did you get this?	اَنَّى لَكِ هَذَا
6:96	where are you going backwards	فَاَنَّى تُؤْفَكُونَ

Surah *Al-Baqrah* says:

2:223	Your *nisa* are your fields. Come to your fields when you want to	نِسَاؤُكُمْ حَرْثٌ لَكُمْ فَأْتُوا حَرْثَكُمْ اَنَّى شِئْتُمْ

Here "اَنَّى" (*anaa*): whenever.

Ibn Abbas says it means, whenever in the day or night you want. *Taj-ul-Uroos* also says it means "when" (ever). In *Gharibul Quran*, *Mirza Abul Fazl* writes that it means "if you want".

A-N-Y   ا ن ي

"أَنَى الشَّيْءُ" (*anish shaiyi*): the time for something has come, time for something to be strengthened, for something to be completed or reach its end.

This (thing) has reached its completion (has matured)	بَلَغَ هَذَا آنَاهُ وَ إِنَاهُ

Surah *Al-Ahzaab* says:

33:53	those who wait for meal time	نَاظِرِينَ إِنَاهُ

That is, if called for a meal, come at the scheduled time (and not too much earlier), or continue idle gossip till it is meal time and you are included for the meal (out of courtesy).

Surah *Al-Hadeed* says:

57:16	Hasn't the time for its completion come for the Momineen?	أَلَمْ يَأْنِ لِلَّذِينَ آمَنُوا

Surah *Al-Ghashiya* says:

88:5	the stream water which has reached its extreme	عَيْنٍ آنِيَةٍ

"الْأَنَاءُ" (*al-inaa*): utensils {T}. Its plural is "أَنِيَّةٌ" (*aneyah*) as used in 76: 15.
"الْأَنَاءُ" (*al-inaa*) is the plural of "أَنِيٌّ" (*aniyun*) which means a part of time:
"آنَاءُ اللَّيْلِ" (*anaul lail*): some time (moments) in the night. (20:130) and (3:112).

Ibn Faris says "أَنِيٌّ" (*ini*): sometime in the night.
"أَنَيْتُ الشَّيْءَ" (*anaiyto shaiyi*): that I postponed something from its scheduled time.

A-H-L   ا ه ل

Muheet says that this root means "tent" in the Hebrew language. As such it means "the people who live under the same tent". Thereafter, as *Raghib* says, it began to be used for people of the same race, religion or profession, house and city.

"أَهْلُ الرَّجُلِ" (*ahlur rajul*) is commonly used for a man's close relatives and family, and is also used for ones wife and children. "أَهْلُ الْبَيْتِ" (*ahlul bait*): those who live in the same house.

Muheet says that it means a lot of things. Then with reference to *Abu Hanifa*, he says that it basically means wife.

"أَهْلِيٌّ" (*ahli*) is that four-legged pet animal which becomes familiar with the house.

The Quran does give respect to relationship but the basic criteria for distinguishing people is *eeman* and *kufr* i.e. trust and denial. Those who are bound within the same system of life, are of the same group or party, and are the individuals of the same nation, but those who are outside this bondage are members of the other group and as such "others" or strangers.

If relatives belong to the same group, then their relationship becomes stronger, but if they are not of the same group then they do not stay as one's own. This was the truth which was revealed to *Nooh* when he was told that his son was:

11:46	O *Nooh*, he is not one of your group, his acts are not virtuous	يَا نُوحُ إِنَّهُ لَيْسَ مِنْ أَهْلِكَ إِنَّهُ عَمَلٌ غَيْرُ

Before this, *Nooh* was told that his son was not included in the Momin group. As such whether it be *Ibrahim's* father or *Nooh's* son, *Lot's* wife or the closest relative of *Muhammad,* for example his uncle, if they are not bound within the same way of life, then they cannot be considered *ahl* or family. Such people will not be hated but will be treated humanely and justly. The *ahl* will be members of the group which will be the torch bearer of God's system, His Lordship and which will nurture the human race.

"هُوَ أَهْلٌ لِكَذَا" (*huwa hazun lekaza*): that he deserves it, this is where he belongs.

Surah *An-Nisa* says:

4:58	Allah orders you to return the security to those who have given you security	إِنَّ اللَّهَ يَأْمُرُكُمْ أَن تُؤدُّواْ الأَمَانَاتِ إِلَى أَهْلِهَا

If this means items that have been given for secure keeping, then it would mean: "don't misappropriate them and return them to the owners." If *amanaat* means other things which the elite have been given as trust, such as power, then it would mean to give it to those who deserve it and not those who don't.

Some say that *ahl* here means those who deserve, befitting whom.

The Noble Quran mentions the *Ahlil Kitab* very often. At that time there were two groups of Arabs. One of them had a claim to some celestial book or the other. These were the *Ahlil Kitab* or "those with the Book", and the other group which did not believe in any celestial book. They have commonly been called *mushrikeen*, i.e. who include others to Gods authority.

But *shirk* was not limited to *mushrikeen*. There were even those among *Ahlil Kitaab* who committed *shirk*. They believed on other gods too. For details see heading (Sh-R-K). Those without the Book were also called *ummiyeen*. See heading (A-M-M). From among all these, those who had belief in *Muhammed* were called *momineen*. And those who did not, were called *kafireen*. The *ahl* of the Messenger were those who obeyed him or followed him (7:83). It also means (as mentioned earlier) those who have the right, the owners, and those who have the capability (of doing something) 4:58.

Aw   أو

"أو" (*aw*) is used to mean "or".

1) To mean doubt, as in:

18:19	we have stayed for a day or some part of the day	لَبِثْنَا يَوْمًا أَوْ بَعْضَ يَوْمٍ

This means that the speaker doesn't know which one is correct.

2) When a choice between two things is given as:

	Either marry *Hindan* or her sister	تَزَوَّجْ هِنْدًا أَوْ اَخْتَهَا

3) When "أو" (*aw*) is preceded by a negative, then it means neither of the two things:

76:24	You will neither obey or follow any *Aasim* or *Kafur*	وَلَا تُطِعْ مِنْهُمْ آثِمًا أَوْ كَفُورًا

4) To mean "perhaps":

37:147	And we sent him to hundreds of thousands; perhaps they were even more than that.	وَأَرْسَلْنَاهُ إِلَى مِئَةِ أَلْفٍ أَوْ يَزِيدُونَ

5) To mean "until now":

48:16	fight them until they become obedient	تُقَاتِلُونَهُمْ أَوْ يُسْلِمُونَ

6) Sometimes it happened thus; and sometimes it happened otherwise: in this meaning:

7:4	so our devastation sometimes appeared at night and sometimes when they were resting in the afternoon	فَجَاءَهَا بَأْسُنَا بَيَاتًا أَوْ هُمْ قَائِلُونَ

A-W-B   ا و ب

"اَلْأَوْبُ" (*al-aob*): to bring the legs back while running very fast.

"اَلْأَوْبَاتُ" (*al-aobaat*): legs.

"اَلتَّأْوِيبُ" (*at-taweeb*): to travel the whole day and to stay foot at night.

"رِيْحٌ مُوَّوِبَةٌ" (*reehun mu-awwebah*): the wind that blows the entire day. {T}

"أَوْبُ" (*aob*) also means to return.

"أَوْبُ" (*aob*) and "رُجُوعٌ" (*rujooh*) differ only in that the last mentioned is said to return with or without intent, while *aub* is only with intent.

"اَلْمَآبُ" (*almaab*): to return, also junction, and when something becomes oblivious, or the place from where something turns back.

"بَيْنَهُمَا ثَلَاثُ مَآوِبَ" (*bainahuma salaso ma aub*): there are three places to stop between the two places.

| 88:25 | they will return but to us | إِنَّ إِلَيْنَا إِيَابَهُمْ |

This means that they are traversing the path that will take them to life's happiness. They are wrong in doing so. Every step they take is moving towards the destination which we have ordained as a result of their deeds. No step of theirs can go beyond our law of consequence, which is the result of cause and effect. They are moving towards that goal, because:

| 88:26 | every deed of theirs is subject tour laws | عَلَيْنَا حِسَابَهُمْ |

According to this system, the results of good deeds have been called "حُسْنُ الْمَآبِ" (*husnul maab*) in 3:13.

In other words, good result for good deeds, but that is not the last destination. It is to stay only momentarily, because according to the Quran, *jannah* is one of the evolutionary destinations for Man. For details see heading *(J-N-N)*.

About *Ayub* (a messenger) the Quran says:

| 38:44 | turn towards the law of God | إِنَّهُ أَوَّابٌ |

In similar meaning, the leaders of *Dawood's* nation were told:

| 34:11 | O you leaders, turn over | يَا جِبَالُ أَوِّبِي |

Usually, *jibaal* is translated to *mountains*, but its other meanings are the leaders of the nation. See heading *(J-B-L)*. If *jibaal* is taken to mean mountains, then it would mean that *Daud* used to employ the mountains for which nature has created them, i.e. for protection, to let the forests grow on then to make wood available and to provide minerals and stones. These are some of the purposes for which God has created the mountains and by doing this, the mountains obey Him.

A-W-D   ا و د

The basic meaning of the word is for something to bend or become crooked (*Ibn Faris*). In other words, it means to get bent due to a heavy load or burden.

"اَلْأَوَدُ" (*al-awad*): to bend.
"اَلْأَوْدُ" (*al-awad*): to bend or make crooked, to offend, to be a burden.
"اَلْأَوْدَةُ" (*al-audah*): load, or to become a burden (for something).
"اَدَهُ الْأَمْرُ" (*aadahul amr*): that some burden has bent his back.
"تَأَوَّدَهُ الْأَمْرُ" (*ta-awwadal amr*): that this matter has burdened him.

The Quran says:

| 2:255 | the control of the universe is no burden to God | وَلَا يَؤُودُهُ حِفْظُهُمَا |

A-W-L   ا و ل

Ibn Faris says it means both the beginning and end of some work.

"آلَ اِلَيْهِ اَوْلاً" (*ala ilaihey awla*): he went back to him, returned to him.

"آلَ عَنْهُ" (*ala-unhu*) turned from him. Basically the word means to return and focus.

"اَوَّلَ اللهُ عَلَيْكَ ضَالَّكَ" (*awwal-allahu a'laika zalaka*): Let Allah return your lost thing to you.

"مَآلٌ" (*maal*) is the point to which a thing at last returns, or the last result of anything.

"تَاوِيْلٌ" (*ta'weelun*): to return something to its right path.

"اَوَّلَ الْكَلاَمَ تَاوِيْلاً" (*awwala alklama taweela*): he explained the results and assessment.

"آلَ عَلِيَّ الْقَوْمُ" (*aala a'liyya-al-qoum*):he became the friend of the nation.

"آلَ الْمَالَ وَ اِنْتَالَهُ" (*aala al-mala wa antalahu*): he looked after the wealth, arranged for it, corrected it.

"اَلْاِيَالَةُ" (*al-iyalah*): politics, limits of the state.

"آلَ" (*aala*): to be reduced, to get rid of.

"اَوَّلُ" (*awwal*) is the opposite for "آخِرٌ" (last). 57:3. this means that *awwal* means the very first.

Raghib says that "اَنَا اَوَّلُ الْمُسْلِمِيْنَ" (*ana awwalul muslemeen*): that I am the first to bow before the laws of Allah and thus am an example for others.

Quran says Allah is *al-awwal* (the first) in 57:3. This indicates his infinity which human concept cannot grasp.

"اَوِلَ الرَّجُلُ يَأْوُلُ آوَلاً" (*awilar-rajulu yawalu aawalaa*): he became precede, he attained number one (position). "اُوْلَى" (*Oola*) is the feminine gender *{T}*.

Quran says:

| 79:25 | The last and the first | الْآخِرَةَ وَالْأُولَى |

"آلٌ" (*al*) mean the members of one's family, his friends, or those who are obedient to him. "آلٌ" (*al*) is used among gentlemen only, not among the dregs of society. *{T}*

When Quran says "آلِ يَعْقُوبَ" (*ale Yaqub*) in 19:6, it means the children, friends or obedient of *Yaqob*.

"آلِ فِرْعَوْنَ" (*ala firoun*): likewise the obedient one of the Pharaoh.

"اَلْآلَةُ" (*ala lateh*): situation, instruments or gadgets. The plural is "اَلْآلَاتُ" (*aalaat*).

Quran uses the word "تَاوِيْلٌ" (*taweel*) to mean the last result, outcome, last verdict:

| 4:59 | This is the right way (of living) and it will have a good result | ذَلِكَ خَيْرٌ وَأَحْسَنُ تَأْوِيلاً |
| 7:53 | now they are waiting for the veracity of this book? | هَلْ يَنظُرُونَ إِلاَّ تَأْوِيلَهُ |

I.e. they are waiting for what this book says will take place to take place. In the narrative about **Moosa** (Moses) and his traveling companion (elder), the companion says in the end:

| 18:78 | I will now tell you about the things about which you were so eager and restless. | سَأُنَبِّئُكَ بِتَأْوِيلِ مَا لَمْ تَسْتَطِع عَّلَيْهِ صَبْرًا |

Yaqoob had said about **Yusuf**:

| 12:6 | God will give you such insight that you will get to the bottom of things instantly | وَيُعَلِّمُكَ مِن تَأْوِيلِ الأَحَادِيثِ |

This means that he will reach the final result by knowing the beginning. That is why interpretation of dreams is also called *taweel*.

| 12:36 | Inform us about the interpretations | نَبِّئْنَا بِتَأْوِيلِهِ |

About *ayaateh mutashabehaat,* those verses or sentences which are inexplicable by us because they are beyond human comprehension, it has been said in the Quran:

| 3:7 | Whatever the interpretation of this knowledge is, lies with none other than Allah and those who keep acquiring substance in this knowledge | وَمَا يَعْلَمُ تَأْوِيلَهُ إِلاَّاللَّهُ وَالرَّاسِخُونَ فِي الْعِلْمِ |

For details, see heading *(Sh-B-He)* and *(H-K-M)*.

Oulai   أُوْلَاء

"أُوْلَاء" (*oulai*) is a noun and means "all this". Its singular is "ذَا" (*za*). See also heading "ذَا" (*za*).
"أُولَئِكَ" (*oulaikah*): *they all*. Its singular is "ذَاكَ" (*zaak*) and "ذَالِكَ" (*zalik*).
"أُولَئِكُمْ" (*oulaikum*): *all of them* as in 4:91. It is used for both masculine and feminine genders.

It also appears as a warning such as:

| 11:78 | These are my daughters? | هَؤُلاء بَنَاتِي |

Oulu   أُولُوا

"أُولُوا" (*oulu*) is also a noun and means "with" such as:

| 38:43 | those with intellect and insight | لِأُوْلِي الأَلْبَابِ |

The singular is "ذُوْ" (*zu*). "اَوْلَاتُ" (*oulaat*) is plural and feminine in gender. The singular is "ذَاتُ" (*zaat*)

| 65:6 | those with burden (responsibility or pregnancy) | أُوْلَاتِ حَمْلٍ |

A-W-N   ا و ن

"اَلْآنُ" (*al-aan*) is the present time, now, at this time. *{T}*.

| 2:71 | Now you are telling the truth. | الآنَ جِئْتَ بِالْحَقِّ |

A-W-He   ا و ه

"آهِ" (*ah*), "أَوْهُ" (*auho*), "آوِهِ" (*awihi*). All these are expressions of pain and complaint. "اَلْأَوَّاهُ" (*al-awwah*) is a person who uses the expression of "تَأَوُّهُ" (*taawoho*) very much, which means to express anger and sorrow. As such it signifies a person who is easily brought to tears and very commiserate and sorrowful at people's plight *{T}*. It is also used for a very understanding person and for one who prays a lot. *{T}*

Ibrahim is called "أَوَّاهٌ حَلِيْمٌ" (*awwahun haleem*) 9:114 which means commiserate, one who grieved over other's plight.

A-W-Y   ا و ی

Ibn Faris says the word basically means "to gather", and "to pity and fear".

"أَوَيْتُ مَنْزِلِيْ" (*awaito manzili*): I got down (landed) at my house, or returned to it, or lived in it.
"آوَيَ اِلَيْهِ" (*awa ilaih*): to lean towards someone and become enamoured.
"آوَيْتَ لَهُ" (*awaito lahu*): I felt pity for him.
"رَجَعْتُ اِلَيْهِ بِقَلْبِيْ" (*rajata ilaihi biqalbi*): I became enamoured of him from the heart. *{R}*
"اَلْمَاوَىٰ" (*al-mawa*): place to returns during day or night, a place where a camels return at night to rest. *{T}*
"اَلْأَوِيُّ" (*al-awyo*): birds that remain in flocks
"اَلْمَاوِيَ" (*al mawia*): the garden where one can spend the night.
"أَوَيْتُهُ" (*awaitohu*): I got him down at my house *{T}*. Also see heading (*Th-W-Y*)

The Quran says:

| 11:43 | I will go towards the mountain to escape | سَآوِي إِلَى جَبَلٍ |
| 23:50 | We gave shelter to (Jesus and Mary) | آوَيْنَاهُمَا |

| 33:51 | to give shelter near oneself | تُرْجِي مَن تَشَاءُ مِنْهُنَّ وَتُؤْوِي |
| 8:26 | God sheltered you | فَآوَاكُمْ |

Quran calls *jannah* as *Al-mawa* in 53:15 which means the place where one can live in peace and without any fear. Where one does not need to fear that somebody will snatch it away:

But the same word has also been used for *Jahannum*:

| 3:151 | You will live permanently in fire | وَمَأْوَاهُمُ النَّارُ |

Because as per the root, *mawa* is any place that is a destination, center, or living place.

I-Y   ا ي

"إِيْ" (*Iy*): yes, as in:

| 10:53 | tell them, yes, it is undoubtedly so | قُلْ إِي وَرَبِّي إِنَّهُ لَحَقٌّ |

"إِيْ" (*Iy*) must be followed by words of swearing.

A-Y-D   ا ي د

Ibn Faris says its basic meanings are protection and strength.

"أَدُّ" (*ad*), "يَئِيدُ" (*yaid*), "آيْدًا" (*aida*), they all mean to be strengthened, to become hard.
"اَلْأَدُّ" (*al-aado*): hardness or strength.
"اَلْأَيْدُ" (*al-ayd*): the same.
"ذَا الْأَيْدُ" (*za al-ayd*): strong man.
"اَيَّدْتُه قَابِيْدًا" (*ayyatohu tayeeda*): to strengthen something very much.
"اَلْأِيَادُ" (*al iyad*): that which is used to give strength.

It also means mud which is placed around the edges of a tent so that rain water does not enter. It also means high dune, or strong mountain.

| 2:87 | And We strengthened *Isa* (Jesus) through *Rooh-ul-Qudus* (Holy Spirit) | وَأَيَّدْنَاهُ بِرُوحِ الْقُدُسِ |
| 51:47 | We have built the universe with great strength | وَالسَّمَاءَ بَنَيْنَاهَا بِأَيْدٍ |

"أَيْدٍ" (*aiyd*) is the plural of "يَدٌ" (*yad*) (hand). See heading (**Y-D-Y**).

A-Y-K   ا ى ك

"أَلْأَيْكُ" (*al aiyk*): a lot of trees, a bunch of trees, a wood which has berry trees etc. proliferation of any kind of trees. "أَيْكَةٌ" (*aikah*) is its singular.

Quran says:

15:78	People of the woods	أَصْحَابُ الْأَيْكَةِ

It is said for the people of **Madyan** who lived in dense forests.

A-Y-M   ا ى م

"أَلْأَيَامُّ" (*al iyaam*): "smoke".

"أَم يَئِيْمُ وَ يَوُوْمُ إِيَامًا" (*aama yaimu wa yauwmu iyaama*): in order to get to the beehive he smoked it so that the bees fly away and the hive is left alone.

"أَلْأَيِّمُ" (*al-ayim*): a woman with no husband. Its plural is "أَلْأَيَامَى" (*al-ayama*).

There was an Arab proverb that said "أَلْحَرْبُ مَا يَمَةٌ لِلْنِسَاءِ" (*alharbu ma yamatun lillanisa*) which mean that war turns women into widows.

The Quran says:

24:32	Those among you who are single, let them be married. (Either bachelors, or spinsters, married or unmarried, widowers or widows, all are included) *{T, M}*	وَأَنكِحُوا الْأَيَامَى

It is evident from this that it is also among the duties of an Islamic society to create an environment in which individuals are able to live a life of connubial bliss.

Ain   أَيْنَ

"أَيْنَ" (*ain*): where, whither, which place.

"أَيْنَمَا" (*ainama):*, where, wherever.

75:10	There is no escape	أَيْنَ الْمَفَرُّ
2:148	Wherever you be, God will collect you (all).	أَيْنَ مَا تَكُونُوْا يَأْتِ بِكُمُ اللَّهُ جَمِيعًا

Ayyi   أَيَّ

"أَيٌّ" (*ayyon*): who, which, which one:

| 7:185 | Then besides this hadith, on what will these people believe? | فَبِأَيِّ حَدِيثٍ بَعْدَهُ يُؤْمِنُونَ |
| 17:110 | Call him by what name you will, all well balanced named belongs to him. | أَيًّا مَّا تَدْعُواْ فَلَهُ الأَسْمَاء الْحُسْنَى |

It is also used to call someone, to call out, like "يَا أَيُّهَا النَّاسُ" (*ya ayyo han-naas*) which means O people.

Iyya   أَيَّا

There is a sense of abbreviation in it, it doesn't come by itself but has a pronoun with it.

1:4	4 we accept only your subjugation	إِيَّاكَ نَعْبُدُ
16:51	so keep following me	فَإِيَّايَ فَارْهَبُونِ
6:152	we give you *rizq* as well as them i.e. we feed you as well as them	نَّحْنُ نَرْزُقُكُمْ وَإِيَّاهُمْ

Ayyaan   أَيَّانَ

It means "when":

| 7:187 | they ask of you when will the moment of revolution come? | يَسْأَلُونَكَ عَنِ السَّاعَةِ أَيَّانَ مُرْسَاهَا |

Ayyub   أَيُّوْبَ

Ishaq had two sons, *Yaqub* and *Eesu*. *Eesu* went to his uncle *Ismail* and married his daughter. He had several children among whom *Amaliq* and *Eewaz* became well known. *Eesu's* nickname was *Adoom* (pinkish) and hence his dynasty was called *Adoomi*. The area in the centre between the Dead Sea and the *Uqaba* Gulf was where he lived. In the Torah it is called the *Koh* or Mount *Siir*. The capital was *Raqeem*. *Ayub* belonged to the *Eewaz* tribe. In the Torah, *Ayyub's* travel is mentioned. *Yubab*, *Oub* and *Aayub* are the same name (*Ayyub*). The period was between 700 and 1000 B.C. Although some researchers think that his period was prior to Moses. His tale is written therein and as is usual with the Torah, the tale has been garnished a lot. The Quran has mentioned only one phase of his life when he was in severe difficulties but he tolerated them with great courage and perseverance. For details see 21: 83 and 84 and 38: 44 and 49.

A-Y-Y   أ ي ي

"آيَةٌ" (*ayah*): visible evidence, symbol or sign. As such, landmarks are called *ayah*. Actually, *ayah* is necessarily the visible part of anything that is hidden, and when one can understand or comprehend the visible part, and then he can even guess as to what the invisible part means. {R, T, M}. God's personality cannot come within the purview of human comprehension, therefore, it can only be guessed from the visible signs which abound in the universe. As such, this universe and everything within it are called *ayah* of Allah. These verses are the marks of which we can have some idea of (man's) "destiny". The biggest *ayah* in the human world is "*wahi*" or revelation. It is therefore also an *ayah* of Allah. Every part or verse of the Noble Quran is called an "*ayah*". The message brought by a Messenger is also called the *ayah* {L}

Saleh said to his nation "whether you honour Allah's law or not, I have decided to let this camel go free. This camel is here called *ayah*:

| 7:73 | this (female) camel is a sign for you | هَذِهِ نَاقَةُ اللّهِ لَكُمْ آيَةً |

Similarly the Quran calls **Nooh's** Ark *ayah* as well

| 29:15 | A sign for all the world | آيَةً لِّلْعَالَمِينَ |

It was called a sign because it was a sign that the nation which will obey the law of God will be safe from harm. In short, everything which draws Man's attention towards God is an ayat.

Besides that, even reasoning could be an *ayah*:

| 17:12 | points to these very reasoning | وَجَعَلْنَا اللَّيْلَ وَالنَّهَارَ آيَتَيْنِ |

In other words, by deliberating Man can reach the understanding that the universe is not static, but dynamic. In surah **Ash-Shoa'ra**, the word *ayah* has also been used for a memorial. 26:128

Iyan nabaat means that *ayaah* is the beauty of flowers of plants. {L}
"أَيَا الشَّمْسِ" (*aiya-ash-shamsi*): rays or indications of the sun {T, M}.
"تَأَيَّأَ" (*ta ayah*): to stop at someplace.
"تَأَيَّأَبِالْمَكَانِ" (*ta ayah bil makan*): he stopped at that place and got late.

Ibn Faris says its basic meanings are to stop and deliberate, or to intend and decide.

"To wait and deliberate" throws a very illuminating light on the particularities of *ayahs*. The phrase would mean that all of the various things in the world are *ayahs,* every one of them. But they can be *ayahs* (signs) only for those who stop and deliberate on them. By deliberating on them, one's mind will naturally go towards their Creator. Similarly, by deliberating on the Quranic *ayah* s, a human being can reach his rightful destiny. If one does not stop and think about it, then the *ayah* cannot lead to the real meaning of life. In this way, it would not be an *ayah* in the real sense.

B   ب

The following examples will make the use of this letter clear:

"أَمْسَكْتُ بِزَيْدٍ" (*amsaktu bi zaid*): I caught Zaid

"مَرَرْتُ بِزَيْدٍ" (*marartu bi zaid*): I went past Zaid

"ذَهَبَ زَيْدٌ" (*zahaba zaid*): Zaid went

"ذَهَبْتُ بِزَيْدٍ" (*zahabtu bi zaid*): I went with Zaid, or I took Zaid with me.

The Quran says:

4:43	do the "*masah*" on your faces (wipe one's hands over the face without water, while performing ablution).	فَامْسَحُوا بِوُجُوهِكُمْ
25:72	When they walk past by fault.	إِذَا مَرُّوا بِاللَّغْوِ
2:17	Allah deprived them of their light	ذَهَبَ اللَّهُ بِنُورِهِمْ
2:54	You have been unkind to yourself due to worshipping a calf.	ظَلَمْتُمْ أَنْفُسَكُمْ بِاتِّخَاذِكُمْ
11:48	*Nooh*, dismount with safety	نُوحُ اهْبِطْ بِسَلَامٍ مِّنَّا
96:4	he taught with (through) the pen	عَلَّمَ بِالْقَلَمِ

To indicate time or place, meaning "in":

| 54:34 | We saved them in the morning | نَجَّيْنَاهُم بِسَحَرٍ |
| 3:123 | truly Allah has helped you in the field of *Badr* | وَلَقَدْ نَصَرَكُمُ اللَّهُ بِبَدْرٍ |

In exchange for something, as in:

| 12:20 | And they sold him (*Yusuf*) in exchange for a small price. | وَشَرَوْهُ بِثَمَنٍ بَخْسٍ |

To mean "عَلَى" (*a'la*) or "over", the Quran says:

| 4:42 | If the earth could be levelled over them. | لَوْ تُسَوَّى بِهِمُ الْأَرْضُ |

To mean "from", as in:

| 25:59 | About him, inquire from someone who knows | فَاسْأَلْ بِهِ خَبِيرًا |
| 76:6 | the stream from which servants of Allah drink | عَيْنًا يَشْرَبُ بِهَاعِبَادُ الله |

Some think that the way "مِنْ" (*min*) is used here, means "some". Not full, but a part. As such, some people maintain that the following verse should be translated as shown below:

| 5:6 | Do the "*masaah*" over a part of the head | وَامْسَحُوْا بِرُءُ وْسِكُمْ |

At some places this letter is additional and doesn't mean anything, as in:

| 13:43 | Allah is witness enough | كَفَى بِاللهِ شَهِيْداً |

Even if "*beh*" had not been used in the above verse, it would generate the same meaning.

Mirza Abul Fazal writes in his book ***Gharib-ul-Quran*** that the "*beh*" in "بِسْمِ اللهِ" (*bismillah*) is to invoke help.

"بِاللهِ" (*billah*): to swear on Allah. This means that "*beh*" is also used to swear.

B-A-R   ب أ ر

"أَلْبِئَرُ" (*al-bi'aro*): "water well".

Its actual meaning is of a hole which has its opening camouflaged so if someone goes over it, he may fall into it. In other words, a dug trap. Although, it is not unthinkable that the use of this word can apply to other meanings as well.

The Quran says:

| 22:45 | blind (useless) wells | وَبِئْرٍ مُّعَطَّلَةٍ |

B-A-S   ب أ س

"بِئْسَ" (*beys*): "bad". It is usually used in past tense, but has no definitive derivate. Its forms are formed by combining the root letters directly, as "نَعِمَ" (*naima*) from "نِعْم" (*ni'm*). It is sometimes accompanied with "مَا" (*ma*), for instance "بِءْسَمَا" (*bi'usama*) in 2:90.

"أَلْبَأْسُ" (*al-basu*): severe plight, raging battle, hardness, strength etc.

"لَاَبَأْسَ عَلَيْکَ" (*la basa alaika*) or, "لَاَخَوْفَ بُوْسَ الرَّجُلُ" (*la khaufa bo- sa rajal*): the man became brave.

"بَئِسَ الرَّجُلُ يُوْسَا" (*ba'esar rajulu yu-sa*): the man became very needy.

"أَلْبَأْسَاءُ" (*al-ba'sa'o*): intensity.

"عَذَابٌ بَئِيْسٌ" (*azabun ba'is*): severe punishment, a punishment in which economy is affected.

"أَلْبَأْسَاءُ" (*al-ba'sao*) also means hunger {*M*}.

"أَلْبَأْسَاءُ" (*al-basa'o*): the loss of wealth {*M*}.

"أَلضَّرَّاءُ" (*az-zarrao*): physical harm, like disease etc. {*M*}.

"أَلْمُبْتَئِسُ" (*al-mubtaus*): a sad person {*M*}.

The Quran says:

| 18:2 | unpleasant results of wrong deeds | بَأْساً شَدِيداً بِمقابله اَجْراً حَسَناً |
| 7:4 | When Our punishment came to that dwelling | فَجَاءَهَابَأْسُنَا |

This implies that due to their wrong deeds, the law of nature was activated, and severe plight was encountered. In surah **Bani Israel**, there is mention of a warring tribe which used to bring ''اُولِیْ بَأْسٍ'' (**ooli baas**), that is, severe plight.

Surah **Al-Hadeedh** says:

| 57:25 | there is great hardness in it | فِيْهِ بَأْسٌ شَدِيْدٌ |

''اِبْتِئَاسٌ'' (**ibteasun**): to take offend, to be sad.

In surah **Hoodh**, **Noah** has been addressed:

| 11:37 | Don't worry about a thing of what these opponents do | فَلَا تَبْتَئِسْ بِمَا كَانُوْا يَفْعَلُوْنَ |

Babel   بَابِلُ

The city of **Babel** (Babylon) was the centre of ancient Caledonian civilization. The Quran has mentioned this city and denied the mythical stories that are related with it in reference to **Solamon** in Jewish literature:

| 2:102 | And in **Babel**, no such revelation was made to **Haroot** and **Marut** (two angels, supposedly). | وَمَاأُنْزِلَ عَلَى الْمَلَكَيْنِ بِبَابِلَ هَارُوْتَ وَ مَارُوْتَ |

These were all tales fabricated by those resistors themselves.

B-T-R   ب ت ر

''اَلْبَتْرُ'' (**al-butar**): to cut something, before it is complete or matures {**Ibn Faris**}.
It also means to cut off a tail at its root.
''سَيْفٌ بَاتِرٌ'' (**saifun batir**): the sword which cuts.
''اَلْاَبْتَرُ'' (**al-abtaro**) unrequited, a pauper who has nothing, childless, one whose dynasty has its root cut off, after whose death, no trace of his name or good deeds shall remain {**T, M, R**}.

The Quran says:

| 108:3 | no trace of your opponent | إِنَّ شَانِئَكَ هُوَ الْأَبْتَرُ |

The meaning of "no trace" in this context is that their strength and grandeur, due to which they so oppose you, will end and they will have no part from the better things of life.

B-T-K   ب ت ک

Ibn Faris says it basically means to cut. The basic meaning of "بَتَکَ" (***batak***) is to cut, or to get hold of feathers and wrench them out. As such "اَلْبِتْکَةُ" (***al-bitkah***): the rooted out feathers. This would mean that "بَتَکَ" (***batak***): to root out, but it figuratively means to cut the ears of animals, or split them and let them go free in the name of idols *{T, M, R}*. This was the practice in heathen Arabia.

Surah ***An-Nisaa*** says:

4:219	So they will split the ears of animals.	فَلَيُبَتِّكُنَّ اَذَانَ الْاَنْعَام

"اَلسَّيْفُ الْبَاتِکُ" (***as-aaiful batik***): a sword that cuts *{T}*.

B-T-L   ب ت ل

Ibn Faris says it basically means to differentiate something from other things.

"بَتَلَهُ" (***batalau***) or "يَبْتُلُهُ" (***yabtolohu***): he separated her.
"فَانْبَتَلَ" (***fa'anbatal***): hence he was separated.
"تَبَتَّلَ" (***tabattal***) also means the same as above.
"اَلْبَتُوْلُ" (***al-batool***) is a woman who stays away from men, or who stays away from marriage.
"اَلْمُبَتَّلَةُ" (***al-mubattala***) is a beautiful woman, who has fine (beautiful) limbs.
"تَبَتَّلَتِ الْمَرْأَةُ" (***tabattalatil mar'aa***): the woman finished her make-up.
"اَلْمُبْتِلُ" (al-mubtil): being different from others.
"اَلْبَتْلُ" (***al-batl***) is the truth, or one's right. *{T}*
"اِنْبَتَلَ فِیْ سَیْرِہ" (***inbatala fee sairih***): he tried to walk fast.

Quran says:

73:8	To cut off from everybody (everything) and to follow Allah only, and engage oneself in efforts to establish His system	وَتَبَتَّلْ اِلَيْهِ تَبْتِيلاً

When the Messenger was given the principles of Allah's system, he was ordered to form a group of those who were loyal to him, and to carry out its implementation, and in doing so, not to heed the opponents in any way:

6:92	Proclaim to Allah, and leave the opponents aside	قُلِ اللہُ ثُمَّ ذَرْهُمْ

When a man decides upon the end (goal), then he should shelve ifs and buts, and with the goal in mind, take every step towards that goal. All this should be done in a nice way, because "تَبَتَّل" (*tabattul*) has a connotation of décor as well.

B-Th-Th   ب ث ث

"بَثٌّ" (*bus*) is to spread out and disturb something, thus it also means to spread, as well as increase (proliferate). *{T}*

Muheet's compiler says that it means to invent and create. While asserting these meanings, *Raghib* has added that "بَثٌّ" (*bus*) also means to disclose something which was previously hidden. Therefore, it also means to make such things obvious, which were unclear earlier. {T, L}

Ibn Faris also says that its basic meaning is to disclose or distribute (without any pattern).

"بَثُّ الْغُبَارَ" (*bus alghubar*): to raise dust.
"بَثَثْتُکَ السِّرّ" (*basastokash shir*): I disclosed the secret to you.
"اَبْثَثْتُکَ" (*absustoka*): I disclosed (the reason of) my sorrow to you. *{T}*
"اَلْبَثُّ" (*al-basso*) is that sorrow which cannot remain hidden. *{T}*

The Quran says:

2:164	God spread out every kind of living thing on earth, and proliferated them (created them abundantly).	وَبَثَّ فِيهَا مِنْ كُلِّ دَابَّةٍ
101:4	like flies spread around	كَالْفَرَاشِ الْمَبْثُوثِ
56:7	the spread particles in the air	هَبَاءً مُنْبَثًّا
12:86	I complain due to my suffering and my grief	أَشْكُو بَثِّي وَحُزْنِي

This makes it clear that "بَثٌّ" (*bus*) is sadness other than sorrow, and means such sadness which cannot be kept hidden.

B-J-S   ب ج س

"بَجَسَ الْمَاءُ" (**bajasal ma'a**): for the water to split something, and to flow out.
"مَاءٌ بَجِسٌ" (**ma'un bajus**): water that flows out in this manner {**T**}.

The Quran mentions:

7:160	streams of water flowed out of it	فَانْبَجَسَتْ مِنْهُ
2:60	Then gushed forth	فَانْفَجَرَتْ

Raghib says when water flows from a narrow opening it is called "انْبِجَاسٌ" (**inbijaas**), and "انْفِجَارٌ" (**infijaar**) is a common condition. But the Quran has used both words to mean the same thing.

B-H-Th   ب ح ث

According to **Ibn Faris** the basic meaning of "اَلْبَحْثُ" (**al –bahs**) is to look for something in the dirt, or to scratch the earth.

"اَلْبُحَاثَةُ" (**al-bohasa**) is dust or mud which has been scratched out of the ground.
"اَلْبَحُوثُ" (**al-bohos**) is a camel which kicks up dust with his feet behind him, which it digs out while running.
"اَلْبَحْثُ" (**al-bahso**) is the mine in which gold or silver is prospected. {**M**}

Surah **Al-Maidah** mentions:

5:31	a crow was scratching the earth	غُرَابًا يَبْحَثُ فِى الْأَرْضِ

"اَلْبَحِيثُ" (**al-bahees**): a secret.

Nawab Siddiq Hasan Khan writes that words in which "بَاء" (**ba**) and "حَاء" (**ha**) appear together, carry the connotation of investigation, or to take out (make out) one thing of the other.

B-H-R   ب ح ر

"اَلْبَحْرُ" (**al-bahr**): to split, or tear on a large scale. Seas or rivers are called "بَحْرٌ" (**bahr**) because they have apparently been dug into the earth. The female camel which had given birth to ten camels was let to roam freely in the name of the idols after splitting its ears, and was called "بَحِيرَةٌ" (**baheera**).

Nawab Siddiq Hasan Khan writes that words in which "بَاء" (**ba**) and "حَاء" (**ha**) appear together carry the connotation of investigation, or to take one thing out of the other.

Ibn Faris, with reference to **Khalil,** says that the sea is called "بَحْرٌ" (**bahr**) because of its vastness. A river which flows continuously is also called "**bahr**". The sea is called "بَحْرٌ كَبِيرٌ" (**bahr kabeer**) or bigger **bahr** in comparison.

Kitabul Ashqaq says that a great body of water (whether brackish or drinkable) is called "بَحْرٌ" (**bahr**).

"بَحْرٌ" (**bahr**) actually means the place where a lot of water has accumulated. Cultivable land is also called "بَحْرٌ" (**bahr**), as well as cities, especially the cities which are situated near sea or rivers.

Quran says:

30:41	Those societies which exist on land and those which exist on **bahr**, all have become inequitable	ظَهَرَ الْفَسَادُ فِى الْبَرِّ وَالْبَحْرِ

It also means that all societies of the world on land and water have been infested with vile. In the meaning of land and water (the sea and dry land) these words have appeared in 17: 67. Also see heading **(Y-M-M).**

In the tale about **Moosa** crossing the river, and the Pharaoh's drowning, the words "بَحْرٌ" (**bahr**) and "يَمَّ" (**yum**) have been used in 2:50, 2:77 and 2:78.

The Quran has termed fishing as permitted:

5:96	That (fish) which you catch yourself and that which the water throws out or that is left behind on the land when the water recedes	صَيْدُ الْبَحْرِ وَطَعَامُه '

Also see heading **(Th-Ain-M).**

B-Kh-S   ب خ س

Ibn Faris says the basic meaning of this root is of shortcoming or reduction.

"اَلْبَخْسُ" (**al-bakhs**): to reduce, to oppress, reduction in rights. That is why **Ibnul Sakeet** says that "بَخْسٌ" (**bakhs**): to grant less than what is rightful, that is, reduction in rights **{T}.**

"اَلْبَاخِسُ" (**al-bakhis**): something that is slightly bad **{R}.**

"اَلْبَخْسُ" (**al-bakhs**) is the tax received by the ruler **{T}.**

Surah **Al-Baqarah** says:

2:282	and makes no reduction whatsoever in it	وَلَا يَبْخَسْ مِنْهُ شَيْئًا
72:13	he will not fear reduction of his rights, nor will he fear any oppression	فَلَا يَخَافُ بَخْسًا وَّلَا رَهَقًا
12:20	(they) sold him for a low price	شَرَوْهُ بِثَمَنٍ بَخْسٍ

But **Zajaj** says that verse 12:20 means that the act of selling him was equal of exceeding human rights, because selling humans is forbidden.

Nawab Siddiq Hasan Khan says that words where "باء" (**ba**) and "خاء" (**kha**) appear together give the meaning of knocking out someone's eye, which gives a sense of committing excess.

B-Kh-Ain   ب خ ع

"اَلْبِخَاعُ" (**al-bikha**) is a vein inside the back of the neck.
"بَخَعَ بِالشَّاةِ" (**bakha'a bish shaat**): he cut the goat's throat with such vigour that even its "بِخَاعُ" (**bikha**) was cut through. This is the real meaning. Later it was used to mean other things too.
"بَخَعَ نَفْسَهُ يَبْخَعُ" (**bakha'a nafsahu**) is to kill oneself in anger and sorrow, (in frustration).
"بَخَعَ الْأَرْضَ بِالزِّرَاعَةِ" (**bakha'al arda biz zira'a**): he kept on tilling the soil till it lost its fertility completely.

About the Messenger, the Quran has said:

18:6	you will kill yourself (in the grief as to why these people do not believe).	لَعَلَّكَ بَاخِعٌ نَفْسَكَ عَلَى آثَارِهِمْ

Note how a preacher of God grieves for his nation, like a kind physician.

B-Kh-L   ب خ ل

"اَلْبُخْلُ" (**al-bukhl**): to stop the justified use of things that you have acquired.

Raghib thinks that there are two types of "بخل" (**bukhl**). One is to be miserly with what one has acquired, i.e. abstain when spending is needed. The second kind is the one who is pained to see someone else spending what he has acquired when needed. This is more condemnable. Then he presents 4:37 in support of his contention.

Muheet says that "بخل" (**bukhl**): to stop things from being spent, and "شُحَّاس" (**shohas**) is the desire which forces one to do just that. In other words, "شُحَّاس" (**shohas**) indicates both greed and "بخل" (**bukhl**).

Quran says:

4:37	the people who stop *rizq* (sustenance or wealth) from being spent and order others to desist from spending (life's accoutrements, or necessities), and hide whatever Allah has endowed them with..	الَّذِينَ يَبْخَلُونَ وَيَأْمُرُونَ النَّاسَ بِالْبُخْلِ وَيَكْتُمُونَ مَا آتَاهُمُ اللهُ مِنْ فَضْلِهِ

The central idea of the noble Quran is that man should strive up to his utmost, but keep only what he needs. The rest should be kept open and available for sustenance of all mankind. See heading (N-F-Q).

"بُخْل" (*bukhl*) or "miserliness" is the exact opposite of the teaching in which Man keeps everything for himself and doesn't give anything to others. This way he denies the happiness and equities in society. (92:6 – 92:9). Quran stresses "اِنْفَاق" (*infaaq*) (spending for others' benefit) and discourages "بُخْل" (*bukhl*) (miserliness) in several ways.

Islam's basic teaching includes keeping one's fruits of labor (after fulfilling one's bare needs) available to others, and for spending according to Allah's dictum. This is called *taqwa*. It solves life's problems and makes the life of the Hereafter better. The Quran clearly states that a nation which adopts "بُخْل" (*bukhl*) or miserliness as a trait is removed from the chessboard of life and replaced by another nation, which is not like the one removed (47:38).

That is because the unchangeable law of Allah is that:

13:17	Only those things are long lasting in this world, that are beneficial for mankind	مَا يَنْفَعُ النَّاسَ فَيَمْكُثُ فِى الْأَرْضِ

The system which is for the good of only one individual, one group, or one nation, and not for the entire humanity, will not have a long-lasting effect. When something is stopped from being beneficial to Mankind, it is "بُخْل" (*bukhl*) and that will create havoc for individuals as well as for nations.

B-D-A   ب د أ

"بَدَأَبِمْ" (*badabih*), "بَدَأَوَابْتَدَأَ" (*bad-unwa'atda'a*) :to begin with something.
"بَدَاَالشَّيِّئَ" (*bada aash shaiyi*): He initiated this, he started it.
"فَلَانٌ مَا يُبْدِىُٔ وَمَا يُعِيْدُ" (*fulan ma yubdiyo wama yu eed*): that man neither initiates talk nor answers anything.
"الْبَدِئُ" (*al-badi*): the head man, the leader or chief.
"بَدَأَ مِنْ أَرْضِهِ اِلَى أُخْرَىٰ" (*bada min ardehi ila ukhra*) He left his own land for another. He left his country.
"الْبَدْءُ" (*al-bad-u*), "اَلْإِبْدَاءُ" (*al-ibda'a*); to give priority to something over basic things {*T*}.
"بَادِئُ الرَّأْىِ" (*baadi ar rayee*) is the initial opinion.
"بَادِىَ الرَّأْىِ" (*baadiar rayee*) is an opinion that is obvious {*R*}. See heading (B-D-W).

The Quran says:

9:13	They are the ones who began (to fight) with you. (they are the initiators)	وَهُمْ بَدَءُ وَكُمْ أَوَّلَ مَرَّةٍ

In the context of the creation of the universe, Quran mention:

10:4	He is the One who initiates (the creations) and keeps them revolving	اِنَّهُ يَبْدَؤُا الْخَلْقَ ثُمَّ يُعِيْدُهُ

It is obvious that everything gets created from the point of its initiation, and then passes through different stages to its completion. Its initiation is according to Allah's laws and its completion after different stages is also according to His laws. Also see headings (F-Th-R), (B-D-Ain), (Ain-W-D).

Surah **Saba** says:

34:49	Tell them that the constructive Allah's law is here and no destructive program can stand against it, because a destructive program doesn't have the acumen to begin any scheme and then take it to completion	قُلْ جَاءَ الْحَقُّ وَمَا يُبْدِئُ الْبَاطِلُ وَمَا يُعِيْدُ

Baatil (Untruth) does not do anything which is result-oriented.

Surah **Hoodh** says:

11:27	Immature opinion	بَادِئَ الرَّأْیِ

For this, see heading **(B-D-W)**.

B-D-R   ب د ر

"بَادَرَه" (*baadara*), "مُبَادَرَةً" (*mubaadarah*), "بِدَارًا" (*bidara*): all these words mean to hurry about some work which is to one's liking.

Surah **An-Nisa** says:

4:6	being a spendthrift in a hurry	إِسْرَافًا وَّ بِدَارًا

Zajaj says it means to fill up or be completely filled.
"مُبَادَرَةً" (*muBadratun*) is a man who uses all his strength in a hurry *{T}*.

Ibn Faris says it has two basic meanings
1) for something to be complete and filled to the brim
2) to rush towards something.

"اَلْبَدْرُ" (*al-badr*): a full moon, fully grown. Besides this "بَدْرُ" (*badr*) is the name of a place between **Mecca** and **Madina**, as described in 3:123 *{T}*. This was the place of a battle with the opponents.

Raghib thinks that the root of this word actually is "أَلْبَدْرُ" (*al-badr*) i.e. full moon.

Nawab Siddiq Hasan Khan writes that in words where "باء" (*ba*) and "دال" (*daal*) appear together, they give the sense of beginning, or advent.

"بَدَرَالَيْهِ بِكَذَا" (*Badra ilaihi bikaziba*): that he disclosed a thing to him {*K*}.
This makes the meaning of "أَلْبَدْرُ" (*al-badr*) clear i.e. complete advent or appearance.

B-D-Ain   ب د ع

Ibn Faris says that "أَلْبِدْغُ" (*al-bido*) is something which has occurred for the first time and has no precedence.
"أَلْبَدِيْعُ" (*al'badii*): a new rope which has been woven for the first time with new threads.
"رَكِىٌّ بَدِيْعَةٌ" (*raki yun badiatun*) is a newly dug well {*T*}.

Nawab Siddiq Hasan Khan writes that in words where "باء" (*ba*) and "دال" (*daal*) appear together, they give the sense of beginning, or advent.

Raghib writes that "أَلْإِبْدَاغُ" (*al-ibda-o*): to create or give birth to something without following anybody i.e. without any example or model. And when this word is used for God, it means to create something without any tool, without any matter and without reference to time and place.

The Quran says:

2:117	He is the Originator of the Heavens and earth.	بَدِيْعُ السَّمٰوٰتِ وَالْأَرْضِ

Only God can bring something from oblivion into existence, but this quality is also reflect-able in Man, which allows him to discover and invent new things in the universe. This is the reason for human dominance over other creatures, the condition being that these inventions and discoveries will be used for the benefit of Mankind and not for human destruction. But all these inventions will be in the biological or physical world. God's laws are for the benefit of mankind, and are contained in the Quran.

These laws will never change, because these laws were not made by Man's intellect, instead given to him by revelation. This revelation is found in the Quran, and has reached completion. The lifestyle of Islam does not require any addition. It is complete and no addition or change is permitted. That is why the Quran has condemned *Rahbaniyat* (monasticism), as in 57:37, although while remaining within those unchangeable principals, laws that follow up can be formulated, according to the needs of the times.

About the Messenger, it is said:

| 46:9 | Say "I am not a new *rasool*" | قُلْ مَا كُنْتُ بِدْعًا مِنَ الرُّسُلِ |

Meaning of the above verse is at what I am presenting is not something new, and has already been presented previously by others.

B-D-L ب د ل

"بَدَلٌ" (*badal*), "بِدْلٌ" (*bidl*), "بَدِيلٌ" (*badeel*): all these words mean anything that replaces something else.

"اَبْدَلْتُ الْخَاتَمَ بِالْحَلْقَةِ" (*bdaltal khatama bil khalqata*): I took off the ring and in its place put on a band.

"بَدَّلْتُ الْخَاتَمَ بِالْحَلْقَةِ" (*baddaltul khatama bil khalqata*): I had the ring melted and in its place had a band.

"تَبْدِيلٌ" (*tabdeel*): for something to change form while its substance remains the same.

"اِبْدَالٌ" (*ibdaal*): to replace one substance with another.

"مُبَادَلَةٌ" (*mubadala*): to replace the kind of thing that was taken.

"تَبَدَّلَ" (*tabaddal*): something underwent change.

"تَبَدَّلَه، و تَبَدَّلَ بِهِ" (*tabaddalahu wa tabaddala bi*): that something took its place, or changed it.

"تَبْدِيلٌ" (*tabdeel*) also means to change.

In the Quran, "بَدَلًا" (*badala*) has been used to mean in exchange for (remuneration, return and price) in 18:50. "بَدَّلَ" (*baddal*) has been used to denote to change one thing with another in 27:11.

Quran says:

30:30	Allah's way of creation never changes	لَا تَبْدِيلَ لِخَلْقِ اللهِ
6:34	there is none who can change Allah's laws (neither can they be changed nor replaced)	لَا مُبَدِّلَ لِكَلِمَاتِ اللهِ
66:5	If he divorces you then Allah may give him better wives than you in exchange	إِنْ طَلَّقَكُنَّ اَنْ يُبْدِلَهُ، اَزْوَاجاً خَيْراً مِنْكُنَّ
33:52	neither that you take other wives in their place	وَلَاۤ اَنْ تَبَدَّلَ بِهِنَّ
4:20	to wish to change (replace) one wife with another	اِسْتِبْدَالَ زَوْجٍ مَكَانَ زَوْجٍ

For the change in situation of a nation, see 47:38.

B-D-N   ب د ن

"أَلْبَدَنْ" (*al-badan*): the body i.e. exept the head, hands and legs. Although, *Azhari* says it means the entire body *{T}*.

Raghib says the word "بَدَنّ" (*badan*) is used for the body as per the hulk, and according to its color.
Ibn Faris says it means a thing by itself, not its surroundings.

Quran says while talking of the Pharaoh:

10:92	Today we will preserve your body	فَالْيَوْمَ نُنَجِّيکَ بِبَدَنِکَ

The pharaohs of ancient Egypt used to mummify their dead and they can still be seen. The pharaoh who followed *Moosa* was drowned in the river. So it was probably how his body was lost. But Quran had stated some fourteen hundred years ago that the body was retrieved from the sea and had been preserved. Therefore those mummies which have been recovered also include his mummy. Refer to Encyclopedia Britannica and also my book *Birk-e-Tour*. Although "بَدَنّ" (*badanun*) also refers to armor because it is worn on the body *{R}*.

"أَلْبَادِنْ" (*al-baadinu*), "أَلْمُبَدَّنْ" (*al-mubaddanu*): large and fuller bodied person.
"بَدُنَ وبَدَنَ" (*baduna wa badana*): that he became fuller and bigger.
"أَلْبَدَنَةُ" (*al-badanatuh*), that cow or camel that was taken to slaughter, that is because those animals which were taken to *Mecca* for slaughter, were fattened. Its plural is "بُدْنّ" (*budnun*).

Quran says in surah *Al-Hajj*:

22:36	And the camels and cattle	وَالْبُدْنَ

B-D-W   ب د و

"بَدْوّ" (*badwun*) and "بُدُوّ" (*budooun*): to appear
"أَبْدَيْتُهُ" (*abdaitahu*): I exposed it.
"بَدَاوَةُ الشَّیْءِ" (*badaawatuh sahai*): the part of something that appear first.

The Quran has used "تُبْدُوْنَ" (*tubdona*) "you show", in contrast to "تَكْتُمُوْنَ" (*tuktumona*) "you hide" in 2:33. Likewise in verse 2:71, the word "تُبْدُوْا" (*tubdona*) "you show" has come against "تُخْفُوْ" (*tukhfoo*) "you keep secret".

In surah *An-Noor* the Quran says:

24:31	they should not display their adornments	وَلَا يُبْدِيْنَ زِيْنَتَهُنَّ

"اَلْبَدْو" (*al-abadoo*), "اَلْبَادِيَةْ" (*al baadiyatuh*), "اَلْبَدَاوَةْ" (*al badaawatuh*): desert or village.
"اَلْبَدَاوَةْ" (*al-badaawatuh*) is the urban life as opposed to village or desert life. Desert is said to be "بَادِيَةٌ" (*baadiyatun*) because it is exposed and open, as in 12:100. {T}

In Quran "اَلْبَادِ" (*al-baadi*) appears in contrast to "اَلْعَاكِفُ" (*al a'kifu*) in verse 22:25, which means one who comes from outside.

Quran mention in surah **Hood** that opponents of **Noah** said the following to him:

11:27	We cannot see that other than those of the lower class (of our society) follow you.	مَانَرَاكَ اتَّبَعَكَ إِلَاالَّذِيْنَ هُمْ أَرَاذِ لُنَا بَادِىَ الرَّأْى

This saying has a hidden meaning, that those who follow you have a clear appearance of being outcasts of normal standards. Their looks reveal their condition. (We have it as a phrase meaning of "first sight"). This verse can also mean the opponents are trying to say that those people, who followed Noah, were not doing so because of their intellect but rather because of emotions.

B-Dh-R   ب ذ ر

"بَذَرْتُهُ بَذْرًا" (*bazartahu bazran*): I scattered it, separated it, spoilt it.
"اَلْبَذْرُ" (*al-bazru*), is the portion of seeds that is kept for sowing. From this it stands for agricultural cultivation. It is also used for the seedlings sown in a field, or the vegetables which just sprout out of the ground.

Nawab Sidique Hassan Khan has written that where "باء" (*ba*) and "ذال" (*dhal*) appear together, the words give meaning of extracting.

Ibn Faris has said that its fundamental meaning is to scatter and separate.

The fundamental meaning of "تَبْذِيْرٌ" (*tabzeerun*) would be to consume the grain which was saved for sowing. It also means to habitually waste wealth, because "تَبْذِيْرٌ" (*tabzeerun*) also means to separate {T}.

It is given in the Quran:

17:26-27	You should not squander wealth. Those who do so are opposition's brethren	لَاتُبَذِّرْ تَبْذِيْرًا إِنَّ الْمُبَذِّرِيْنَ كَانُوا إِخْوَانَ الشَّيْطِيْنِ

B-R-A   ب ر أ

"بَرَأَ" (**barun**): The fundamental meaning is of separating one thing away from other dissimilar things.

"بَارَأَهُ" (**baara ahu**): that he separated and distanced himself.

"تَبَرَّأَنَا" (**tabarraanaa**): we are all separate.

"بَرِئَ الْمَرِيضُ مِنْ مَرَضِهِ" (**bareeu al-mardu min maradihi**): the patient is cured, because his illness has been separated from him.

"أَنَا بَرَاءٌ مِنْهُ" (**anaa baraaun minhu**): I am free, separate from it. I have no relation with it.

Quran says:

2:166	when the leaders will become frustrated and separate themselves from their followers ...	إِذْ تَبَرَّأَ الَّذِينَ اتُّبِعُوا مِنَ الَّذِينَ اتَّبَعُوا
9:1	This is a proclamation from Allah and His Rusool (the centre of Quranic system) that we are absolutely separate (from the polytheists of Mecca, with whom there was a treaty)	بَرَاءَةٌ مِنَ اللهِ وَرَسُولِهِ

With reference to Allah, he Quran says:

| 59:24 | He is Allah, the creator, the separator, the formatter | هُوَ اللَّهُ الْخَالِقُ الْبَارِئُ الْمُصَوِّرُ |

All the elements in the Universe exist in harmony. When God has a scheme to create something, He rearranges various elements in a new form; this is called "خَلْقٌ" (**khalqun**). See heading (**Kh-L-Q**). Then He separates it from the other elements, this is "بَرَاءَةٌ" (**baraa-atun**). The vesting is then given a new visual form. This is the attribute of "مُصَوِّرِيَّت" (**musawwireeat**). See heading (**Sd-Q-R**). Hence He is called **Baari, Khaaliq** and **Musawwir** in 59:24. Some maintain that this is why the creation is called "الْبَرِيَّة" (**al-bar ya**).

The Quran says:

| 98:7 | Those are the best creations | أُولَئِكَ هُمْ شَرُّ الْبَرِيَّةِ |

The root of this word is "بَرِيَّةٌ" (**baryun**), and is derived from "الْبَرَى" (**al-bareey**), meaning the soil.

Nawab Sidque Hasan Khan has written that, whenever "باء" (**ba**) and "راء" (**raa**) appears together, its meaning is of revealing.

"بَرْءٌ" (**barun**) is to be used when an incidence occurs, or gets revealed, as in 57:22.

"مُبَرَّأ" (**mubarra**) is the same as "بَرِيْءُ الذِّمَّةِ" (**baree-uz-zimmatih**) which means "pure" (24:26).

"أَبْرَأَ" (**abraa-a**): to cure one from disease (3:48).

B-R-J بـ ر ج

"بُرُوْج" (*buooj*), singular of which is "بُرْجّ" (*burj*), means the watch posts around a palace. The same goes for watch posts that are built around a city, or a fortress. In this sense, this word can also mean a fortress, as in verse 4:78. In fact, any combination of (J-B-R) would indicate to a sense of intensity and power. *{T}*

Ibn Faris has said that the basic meanings include the sense of being apparent as well as protected.

The Quran says:

33:33	Stays seriously in your homes, and do not display your ornaments as you did in ignorant past days.	وَقَرْنَ فِي بُيُوتِكُنَّ وَلَا تَبَرَّجْنَ تَبَرُّجَ الْجَاهِلِيَّةِ الْأُولَى
24:60	Those who do not display their ornaments	غَيْرَ مُتَبَرِّجَاتٍ بِزِينَةٍ

According to *Taj-ul-uroos*, "تَبَرَّجَ" (*tabarraja*) means a woman who displays her pride and beauty in front of men in such a manner as if she intends to tease them.

Nawab Sidque Hassan Khan has written that whenever "باء" (*ba*) and "راء" (*raa*) appears together, its meaning is of "revealing".

Abu-ishaaq has claimed that "تَبَرَّجَ" (*tabarraja*) is used when a women display herself in such a manner that it would arouse men.

The compiler of *Muheet* says that "اَلْبَرُّجُ" (*al-barrojo*): to walk with a hip movement, while "اَلْبَرَجُ" (*al-baraju*): someone with a pretty face and "الْاَبْرَجُ" (*al-abraju*): someone with lovely eyes.

Raghib says that "تَبَرُّجُ" (*tabarruju*) can be used for a woman who comes out of her mansion and reveals herself. This confirms the understanding of above-mentioned verse (33:33).

But according to me, the meaning presented by *abu Ishaaq* makes more sense, which it, means to "present oneself in such a manner that it would be the cause of male arousal".

The human feelings of arousal do not get triggered automatically. They get activated by human thoughts and actions. The Quran teaches how to prevent such emotions. All the rules and regulations between man and woman that have been presented are to achieve this goal.

"بُرْجّ" (*burj*) also means the star constellations. In early astronomy, the night sky was divided into 12 different star constellations. *Ibn Darid* writes in his book that the Arabs were not familiar with these constellations. In the early texts of the Arabs, one does find mention of the different stages of the moon, but nothing regarding star constellations. Hence, when the Quran addressed them with these wordings, the meaning was not star constellations, but rather stars and planets.

Quran says in surah *Al-Hijr*:

16:15	And certainly We have created *burooj* in the heaven, and made them attractive for the spectaculars.	وَلَقَدْ جَعَلْنَا فِى السَّمَاءِ بُرُوْجاً وَّزَيَّنَّهَا لِلنَّظِرِيْنَ

Here the word *burooj* means huge stars which are more prominent than others.

In Surah *As-Safaat*, the Quran says:

37:6	Indeed We adorned the near sky with dornment of stars	إِنَّا زَيَّنَّا السَّمَاءَ الدُّنْيَا بِزِيْنَةِ نِ الْكَوَاكِبِ

From this we can conclude that Quran uses the word "بُرُوْجّ" (*burooj*) for stars.

B-R-H   ب ر ح

"أَلْبَرَاحُ" (*al-barahu*) is the open landscape where there are no trees, vegetation or buildings in sight. Hence this word is used for such a matter in which there is no uncertainty, but which is clear and open.
"لَأَبَرَاحَ" (*labaraha*): something in which there is no doubt or uncertainty.
"بَرِحَ الْخَفَاءُ" (*bariha-lkhafa*): that the secret got out and was revealed {T}.

Nawab Sidque Hassan Khan has written that, whenever "باء" (*ba*) and "راء" (*raa*) appears together, its meaning is of revealing. This supports the translation of "بَرِحَ الْخَفَاءُ" (*bariha-lkhafa*) as presented above.

Ibn Faris says that the basic meanings of this root are:
-   To appear, come forth, get open.
-   Be heavy and big.

Raghib says that "لَأَبَرَاحَ" (*labaraha*) is used to indicate something that remains steadfast, or something that keep on working continuously.

Muheet has said that "بَرَحَى" (*baroha*) is a word used when the aim is missed. Hence "أَلْبَارِحُ مِنَ الظِّبَاءِ وَالطَّيْرِ" (*albariho minatiba i dattayr*): that deer or bird which appears in front of a hunter in such a manner that aiming it becomes difficult {T}.

Quran has used this word for instruction and determination:

12:80	I shall never leave this land.	فَلَنْ أَبْرَحَ الْأَرْضَ

18:60	I shall not stop walking, until I reach the place where the two rivers meet.	لَا أَبْرَحُ حَتَّى أَبْلُغَ مَجْمَعَ الْبَحْرَيْنِ

B-R-D   ب ر د

"اَلْبَرْدُ" (*al-bardu*): to be chilled. It is the opposite of hot, which is "حَرٌّ" (*harra*).

"مَاءٌ بَرْدٌ وَبَارِدٌ" (*maobarodwbarid*): cold water.

"اَلْبَرْدُ" (*al-bardu*): sleep.

"اَلْبَرَدُ" (*al-barad*): hail.

"عَيْشٌ بَارِدٌ" (*a'eshun barid*): good and balanced life.

"بَرَدَ السَّيْفُ" (*baradassef*): the sword got corroded *{T}*.

Raghib says that as motion is associated with "حَرٌّ" (*harran*), likewise "بَرْدٌ" (*burd*) is associated with something getting motionless. For instance "بَرَدَ عَلَيْهِ دَيْنٌ" (*barada aliahi deen*) means "that load stayed with him", that is, "did not get paid off" *{T}*.

Ibn Faris says that the basic meaning of this root also includes the concepts of being at rest and without motion.

The Quran mention the following verse with regards to narration of **Ibrahim**.

21:69	O fire, become cold and secure **Ibrahim**.	يَا نَارُ كُونِي بَرْدًا وَسَلَامًا عَلَى إِبْرَاهِيمَ

This means that the opposition plotted their best efforts towards **Ibrahim**, and went neck on neck in their resistance. But the All-mighty protected **Ibrahim** against their fury, and extracted him safely from there, so he could migrate to another land.

29:24	But Allah saved him from the fire	فَأَنْجَاهُ اللهُ مِنَ النَّارِ

Above verse means that the opposition even plotted to burn him alive, but Allah failed their conspiracies and extracted **Ibrahim** to safety. Also se 37:97-99.

21:70	They planned a plot against him, but We made them to lose.	وَأَرَادُوا بِهِ كَيْدًا فَجَعَلْنَاهُمُ الْأَخْسَرِينَ

In other words, their plot did not bear any fruit. **Ibrahim** migrated safely from there to someplace else. Also see 29:26, 21:71 and 39:99.

From all these points, it is obvious that the word fire reflects the furious rivalry of the opposition, which Allah cooled down, so they could not fulfil their hateful plans.
With regards to the meaning of "hail rain", this word has been used in verse 24:43.

Surah **Al-Waqiah** says following when explaining the restrictions or punishment of **Jahannum**:

56:44	Not cooling, not pleasant nor beneficial.	لَابَارِدٍ وَّلَاكَرِيْمٍ

Surah **An-naba** says the following with regards to those in **Jahannum**:

78:24	They shall not find cool and anything to drink	لَايَذُوْقُوْنَ فِيْهَا بَرْدًا وَّلَاشَرَابًا

Taj-ul-Uroos says that the meaning of "بَرْدٌ" (**barud**) in the above verse is "sleep". The compiler of **kitab-ul-ashfaaq** has also supported this opinion. This word could also be used for "relaxation" and "ease", which are most suitable here. As the saying goes "no relaxation in punishment".

Ibn Faris has said that the basic meaning includes a sense of anxiety and motion.

B-R-R   ب ر ر

"برر" (**barar**): vastness, broadness etc. because "بَرٌّ" (**berr**) has been used against "بَحْرٌ" (**bahar**). Since we use "بَحْرٌ" (**bahar**) to define sea or river, "بَرٌّ" (**berr**) against that denotes dry land, as in 17:67.

"اَلْبَرُّ" (**al-berr**): desolate land and "بَحْرٌ" (**bahar**): such places and cities which have water. "بَرٌّ" (**berr**) also means to drive goat or sheep. Since it means vastness, it has come to mean extensive. As such "اَبَرَّالرَّجُلُ" (**abarar rajul**): that man became a man with many children.
"اَبَرَّالْقَوْمُ" (**abarral qaum**): a nation that has expanded greatly. Because of this, this word also got to be used for dominance.
"اَبَرَّعَلَيْهِمْ" (**abarra alaihim**): that he excelled them, and overwhelmed them.
"اَلْمُبِرُّ" (**ilmubirr**): someone who gains dominance.

Nawab Sidque Hassan Khan has written that whenever "باء" (**ba**) and "راء" (**ra**) appears together in a word, its meaning is of "revealing". This supports the translation of "بَرِحَ الْخَفَاءُ" (**barihalkhafa**) as presented above.

With regards to this, "بَرَّ" (**berra**) also means "he appeared". Being liberal in vision, greatness of heart, lend "بَرٌّ" (**berr**) to the meaning of good behaviour, kindness and sympathy on a grand scale. It also means truth and obedience.
"بَرٌّ" (**berru**) and "بِرٌّ" (**birru**): someone who is true to his promise.
"اَلْبَرُّ" (**al-berru**) is also one of God's attributes as defined in 52:28.

Quran has used "بِرٌّ" (**birru**) against "اِثْمٌ" (**ism**) in 5:2

"اِثْمٌ" (**ism**): weakness, tiredness. As such, "بَرٌّ" (**berr**) being the opposite would mean strength, vastness, proliferation, expanse, broadness. Since "اِثْمٌ" (**ism**) is a crime, "بِرٌّ" (**birru**) is virtue.

As such, according to the Quran, virtuous deeds will be those who open the way for expansion, produce broader vision, expansion in the heart and greatness in the human character, and overall which produces expansion in life's accoutrements. And to be expansive in different matters "بِرّ" (*birru*) and "تَقْوَى" (*taqwa*) have thus been used together in 5:2 and 2:224, because with "تَقْوَى" (*taqwa*) (observance of Allah's laws) man is distanced from narrow-mindedness and moves towards expansion. That can be achieved by Man keeping his dearest possessions (wealth, or even one's life) available according to Allah's laws, for the benefit of mankind.

It is therefore said:

3:91	until you keep your dearest possessions open for humans, you will not achieve extensiveness and broadness	لَنْ تَنَالُوا الْبِرَّ حَتَّى تُنْفِقُوا مِمَّا تُحِبُّونَ

Those who think that to observe religious dictums only superficially constitutes "بَرّ" (*berr*), or virtue, are grossly mistaken.

Quran clearly says:

2:177	Greatness cannot be achieved by turning your faces in directions of east or west.	لَيْسَ الْبِرَّ أَن تُوَلُّوا وُجُوهَكُمْ قِبَلَ الْمَشْرِقِ وَالْمَغْرِبِ

The process to reach greatness is that you, after endorsing *belief*, make your wealth available for needy people of your society, despite its attractions. Those who follow this process are called "أَبْرَارٌ" (*abrar*) against "فُجَّارٌ" (*fujjar*) which means wrongdoers in 82:11-12, and also "بَرَرَةٌ" (*bararah*) in 80:16.

About *Yahya* it is said:

19:14	he used to deal with his parents with broad heartedness (kindly)	بَرًّا بِوَلِدَيْهِ

God has been called "الْبَرُّ الرَّحِيْمُ" (*al-berrur Rahim*) in 52:28, which means the expander, provider of growth. He has provided (various things) for humanity on such a large scale that nobody can ever doubt about Him being the Provider. As such, a society that reflects upon their God's attributes, may as well, within the limits of humanity, also be "الْبَرُّ الرَّحِيْمُ" (*al-berrur Rahim*). In other words, the society must be generous and great for the provision of the human race. This is the definition of "بِرّ" (*birr*) which is commonly translated as virtue. Generally speaking, it is obvious that this word "virtue" cannot have the connotation of greatness and vastness. A virtuous person is one who avoids bad deeds. But to avoid bad deeds, is but a negative aspect. The Quran also demands positivity with it. Therefore, according to the Quran, a nation which is not open hearted and generous, and does not provide for the human race with their generosity, cannot possess "بِرّ" (*birr*).

B-R-Z   ب ر ز

"اَلْبَرَازُ" (*al-baraz*) or "اَلْبِرَازُ" (*al-biraz*): a vast expanse with no vegetation etc. Since people in early days used to go to open places for defecating, "اَلْبِرَازُ" (*al-biraz*) and "اَلْبَرَازُ" (*al-baraz*) came to mean the loo.

"بَرَزَ" (*baraz*): to become evident, to appear.
"اَلْبَارِزُ" (*al-bariz*) is the thing which has appeared completely.

Nawab Sidque Hassan Khan has written that, whenever "باء" (*ba*) and "راء" (*ra*) appears together in a word, its meaning is of appearing or revealing.

Ibn Faris writes that its fundamental meaning is to be apparent and to distinguish oneself from other similar things.

"بَارَزَ مُبَارَزَةً" (*baraza mubarazah*) is the battlefield, where men come forth face to face, by leaving the rows of soldiers.
"بَرَزَ" (*baraz*) is to exceed others in bravery, and come forth. *{T}*

The Quran says:

2:250	When they came forth to face **Jaloot** (in combat).	وَلَمَّا بَرَزُوْا لِجَالُوْتَ
18:47	you will note that the land is open (or those who have been subdued will rise and appear)	وَتَرَى الْأَرْضَ بَارِزَةً
14:21	All, big and small, will appear before Allah (Before His law of consequences)	وَبَرَزُوْ اللهِ جَمِيْعًا
40:16	nothing they do is hidden from Allah (His laws)	لَا يَخْفَى عَلَى اللهِ مِنْهُمْ شَيْءٌ

The above verse means that results of their deeds will become prominent and become apparent.

At another place it is said:

| 79:36 | And **jaheem** will rise and become evident, for those who have insight | وَبُرِّزَتِ الْجَحِيْمُ |

This means that at that time the results (of their deeds) shall appear before them, but only for those who understand.

| 79:36 | For those who have insight. | لِمَنْ يَّرَى |

As such, the criminals (the wrongdoers) are not oblivious of their current negative state. 82:16

| 29:45 | And for sure, **Jahannum** surround the **kafireen** | وَإِنَّ جَهَنَّمَ لَمُحِيْطَةٌ بِالْكَافِرِيْنَ |

But this is only obvious for those who have insight of things. This state only appears before the one who has understanding of it. For details see heading (*Jahannum*).

Barzakh   بر ز خ

"بَرْزَخٌ" (*barzakh*): the partition or limit between two things.

Raghib says it has come from "بَرْزَةٌ" (*barzah*) which means "a veil".

Ibn Faris says this is actually an Arabic word from root *(B-R-Z)* and the "خاء" (*kha*) is additional and added for exaggeration. It means such vastness that has become a limit for things. In other words, things outside are too far away to be seen. Here too it would mean a partition, which obstructs vision.

Surah *Rahman* says:

| 55:20 | there is a partition between the two rivers, beyond which they cannot proceed | بَيْنَهُمَا بَرْزَخٌ لَا يَبْغِيَانِ |

Also see 25:35. Surah *Momineen* says that when one of them dies then he says "O God, if you would return me back to the world, I will do good deeds". But the Quran says that such requests are meaningless, because no one can return to this world once he has died:

| 33:99 33:100 | they have a partition behind them, till the time of the Rising | وَمِنْ وَرَائِهِمْ بَرْزَخٌ إِلَى يَوْمِ يُبْعَثُونَ |

See headings *(W-R-Y)* and *(B-Ain-Th)*.

B-R-Sd   ب ر ص

"اَلْبَرَصُ" (*al-baras*): the white spot which appears on one's body due to some disease, such as leprosy.
"اَلْبِرَاصُ" (*al-biraas*) is desert lands which do not have any cultivation; barren land {F}.
"تَبَرَّصَ الْبَعِيْرُ الْأَرْضَ" (*tabarrasal ba'eerul ard*): the camel grazed all the grass, and didn't leave anything on ground {T}.

Surah *Aal-e-Imraan* relates what *Isa* (Jesus) told his people:

| 3:48 | I will give sight to those who are born blind and relieve a leper of his disease | وَأُبْرِئُ الْأَكْمَهَ وَالْأَبْرَصَ |

The condition of *Bani Israel* (the descendants of Israel) has been compared to that of lepers. It means either that their land was absolutely barren or that they roamed hither and thither, while nobody was ready to own them.

| 3:111 | wherever they go, they will be met with insult and demeaning behaviour | وَضُرِبَتْ عَلَيْهِمُ الَّذِلَّةُ اَيْنَ مَاثُقِفُوا |

Both meanings have the same concept. The main duty of a Messenger is in fact to liberate a nation from their state of deamination and to make its barren land fertile.

The Quran has equated moral deficiencies with diseases and referring to such people thus:

| 2:17 | deaf, mute, blind | صُمٌّ- بُكْمٌ- عُمْیٌ |

It has also been said that such people carry diseases in their hearts:

| 2:10 | There are diseases in their hearts | فِیْ قُلُوْبِهِمْ مَرَضٌ |

They have even been called "dead" in 27:80. In this context celestial teachings are called "بُدیً" "وَّشِفَاءٌ" (hudawn wa shifa) as in 41:44, which says that this guidance is a cure.

| 10:57 | cure for whatever they have in their hearts | شِفَاءٌ لِمَا فِیْ الصُّدُوْرِ |

The purpose for the advent and mission of the messengers is not to cure bodily diseases but to remove the "diseases of humanity". To grant vision to the blind and to cure the lepers is also an allegory as used in the case of **Isa**. See details in my book "**Shola-e-Mastoor**".

B-R-Q   ب ر ق

"بَرْقٌ" (**barq**) is the lightning in the sky. It basically means "flash".
"بَرِقَ بَصَرُه" (**bariqa basarooh**): that his eyes got blind sighted because of light, and due to the surprise and fear, he couldn't see (75:7).

Ibn Faris says it basically means to be surprised.

Surah **Al-Baqarah** says:

| 2:20 | The lightning nearly snatched away their vision. | يَكَادُ الْبَرْقُ يَخْطَفُ اَبْصَارَهُمْ |

"اسْتَبْرَقٌ" (**istabraq**): thick silken cloth (18:31, 55:54) {**T, M**}.
"اِبْرِیْقٌ" (**ibreeq**): a pouring pot, jug or such vessel. 56:18. This is supposed to be the Arabic form of the Persian word "آب ریز" (**aab'rez**) {**L**}

But **Ibn Faris** says that this word is derived from the word "برق" (**barq**) and it means something beautiful and shiny.

B-R-K   ب ر ک

"بَرَکَة" (*barakah*): stability with growth. In other words, it is something which is established in its origin and keeps growing at the same time. Hence the meaning includes concepts of stability and abundance, as well as development.

Nawab Siddiq Hassan Khan says that words in which "باء" (*ba*) and "راء" (*ra*) appear together give the connotation of "appearance".

The concept of development indicates towards the exposition of one's hidden abilities. Hence "بَرَکَة" (*barka*) includes the ideas of stability, growth, development, appearance and conspicuousness.

Ibn Faris also wrote that this word means stability and growth.

"مُبَارَکٌ" (*Mubarak*) or "فِیْہِ بَرَکَة" (*feehey barakah*) is said when something is felt to be growing, as well as being stable. It is derived from "بَرَکَ الْبَعِیْرُ" (*barakal bayeer*) which means "the camel sat there with a plumb and didn't leave its place". "اَلْبِرْکَة" (*al-birkah*) is "the camel's chest" which it uses to support when sitting, and it also means a goat which produces a lot of milk, and also a pool or pond in which water has stagnated {*R, M, T*}.

The plural for "بَرَکَة" (*barakah*) is "بَرَکَاتٌ" (*barakaat*). As mentioned earlier "بَرَکَة" (*barakah*): stability, growth and all kinds of good things. Since these things are obtained through the necessary means, therefore the means of this goodness will also be called "بَرَکَاتٌ" (*barakaath*).

Surah *Al-Airaaf* says that the necessary result of "ایمان" (*eeman*) and "تقوی" (*taqwa*) is that the nation which practices them is bestowed with "بَرَکَاتٌ" (*barakaat*):

7:96	**Barakaat** from the heavens and earth	بَرَکَاتٍ مِّنَ السَّمَاءِ وَالْأَرْضِ

This means that it will be endowed with the goodness of the heavens as well as the earth. This means that such a nation gets economic benefits, as well as celestial guidance.

About the earth it is said:

41:10	(God has) proliferated it with things which are the means of stability and sustenance for the humankind.	وَبَارَکَ فِیْهَا

Surah *Al-Qaf* says:

50:9	we made rain from the skies which is the means for growth and stability for humankind	نَزَّلْنَا مِنَ السَّمَاءِ مَاءً مُّبَارَکاً

The Quran has also said the following about itself:

| 38:39 | Such system of living which is a permanent source of goodness through a set of God's laws, which are directly related to the growth and nurturing of mankind. | كِتَابٌ أَنْزَلْنَاهُ إِلَيْكَ مُبَارَكٌ |

The night in which the Quran was revealed is also termed as "مُبَارَكٌ" (*mubarak*) in 44:2

Mecca city (the center of Islam) has also been called "مُبَارَكٌ" (*mubarak*). Due to His sustenance (*raboobiyat*) of the universes God Himself is called "مُبَارَكٌ" (*mubarak*).

| 7:54 | *Tabarik* is Allah, Sustainer of worlds | تَبَارَكَ اللهُ رَبُّ الْعَالَمِيْنَ |

"تَبَارَكَ" (*tabaraka*): to be the fountainhead for all kinds of goodness and benevolence.
"تَبَارَكَ الَّذِيْ" (*tabarakal lazi*): the personality in whom goodness and benevolence has reached its ultimate.

Thus the meaning of verse 7:54 would be that the personality which is the fountainhead of all kinds of goodness and benevolence is the personality of Allah, and the entire universe is provided sustenance from this fountainhead. A nation which wants to reflect this trait of Allah must also be responsible for providing sustenance to the world.

B-R-M   ب ر م

"أَبْرَمَ الْحَبْلَ" (*abramal habal*): he wove the rope tightly (in two colors or two weaves).
"الْمَبَارِمُ" (*al-mabarim*) spinning wheel etc. on which ropes are tightened.
"الْبَرِيْمُ" (*al-barim*) is a double-weaved thread which women put round their waists or arms, anything that has two colors, or rope or string with two colors.
"أَبْرَمَ الْأَمْرَ" (*ab-ramal amar*): he strengthened the matter {T}.
"قَضَاءٌ مُبْرَمٌ" (*qazaun mubrum*): solid or unchangeable decision.

The Quran says:

| 43:79 | Have they strengthened their cause (for opposing the truth)? If so, then We too will strengthen our cause. | أَمْ أَبْرَمُوا أَمْراً فَإِنَّا مُبْرِمُوْنَ |

Since a rope to be woven strongly has to be woven repeatedly, therefore "اِبْرَامٌ" (*ibraam*) is also used for being dogmatic and stubborn {M}.

Ibn Faris includes following in its basic meanings

For something to be strengthened, two different colors, to be frustrated. The word has not been used in the Quran to mean the last thing.

B-R-He ب ر ه

"اَلْبَرَهُ" (*al-barah*): plumpness along with fairness in color.

"اَلْبَرَهْرَهَةَ" (*al-bararah*): fair, young beauty, glowing fair and fresh skin {*R*}.

"اَلْبَرْهاتو" (*al-barhato*), "اَلْبُرْهَةَ" (*al-burhaa*): longer time {*T*}.

"اَلْبُرْهانُ" (*al-burhan*) according to *Khalil*, has come from the word "بَرْبَرَةَ" (*barahrah*) meaning of which is given above as laminated with clear reasoning. Or that it comes from "بُرْهَة" (*burhah*) which means to delink or cut, or in other words, the reasoning for dissociation or separation.

Raghib says that it has come from "بَرِةَ" (*bareh*) and "يَبْرَةُ" (*yabrahu*) which means "white". {*R*}

Nawab Siddiq Hassan Khan says that words in which "باء" (*ba*) and "راء" (*ra*) appear together give the connotation of "appearance".

All agree upon that it means such reasoning which is true for all times and in every situation. Clear and distinct reasoning, very evident reasoning.

The Quran has said about itself:

4:175	Distinct reasoning from your Sustainer.	بُرْهَانٌ مِّنْ رَبِّكُمْ

This is because every bit of reasoning of the Quran is based on claim and solid logic.

That is why it demands reasoning from its opponents and openly says:

2:111	if your claims are true then give reasoning in their support	هَاتُوْا بُرْهَانَكُمْ إِنْ كُنْتُمْ صَادِقِيْنَ

It is so sure about its own reasoning that along with this demand, it says that they cannot have any final reasoning:

23:117	None can give any reasoning (in support of "shirk").	لَا بُرْهَانَ لَهُ بِهِ

It is one of the particularities of the Quran to present *Deen* (which was always thought to be beyond any reasoning) with the help of knowledge, intellect and reason. It backs all its claims by solid reasoning and knowledge.

The Quran has given us *Deen* not religion. The word for *mazhab* as religion does not appear in the Quran. We have used it for general purposes. Otherwise Islam should be called a *Deen*, which means "Way of Life", or "system of society ordained by Allah".

B-Z-Gh ب ز غ

"بَزَغَ نَابُ الْبَعِيرِ" (**bazagha naabol ba'eer**): the camel's molar (teeth) pierced the flesh to make itself appear. When the sun and the moon rise, they are called "بُزُوغ" (**buzugh**) {T}.

Ibn Faris says it basically means for something to appear or make it evident.

"الرَّبِيعُ ابْتَزَغَ" (**ibtazaghar rabbi**): spring began, and the buds started blooming {T}.

Quran says:

6:78 6:79	The rising or shinning of the sun and moon	اَلْقَمَرَ بَازِغًا ، اَلشَّمْسَ بَازِغَةً

Nawab Siddiq Hassan Khan says that words in which "باء" (**ba**) and "زاء" (**za**) appear together give the connotation of "coming out and being evident", and that is what "بَزْغ" (**bazgh**) {T}.

B-S-R ب س ر

"اَلْبَسْرُ" (**basr**) basically means for something to act prematurely and incompletely.
"بَسَرَ الدُّمَّلَ" (**basaral dumal**): he popped the blister before it became ripe.
"اَلْبُسْرُ" (**al-busr**): everything that is fresh, for instance a date which is not ripe {T}.

With these meanings, the Quran says:

74:23	he made a face	ثُمَّ عَبَسَ وَبَسَرَ

"بَسَرَ" (**basar**) also means to look at someone despicably, thus it would mean raising the eyebrows and make a face. One believes that eating unripe fruit leaves distaste in the mouth. Hence "بَسَرَ" (**basar**) became to mean "distasteful".

At another place it is said:

75:24	that day there will be some distorted faces	وَوُجُوهٌ يَوْمَئِذٍ بَاسِرَةٌ

Ibn Faris thinks it means:
1) The state of something prior to ripening (completion)
2) The reduction in movement of something, or for it to stop before its time.

"بَسَرَ الرَّجُلُ الْحَاجَةَ" (**basarur rajul ool haaja**): he sought to fulfill his needs in a place where they couldn't be (fulfilled).

B-S-S   ب س س

The powder of dry bread, which can be mixed with water, and drunk. To mix with water, to crush into a powder is called "بَسَّ يَبُسُّ بَسًّا" (*bassa yaboosso bassa*). Thus it also means to reduce something into small bits or granules.

"بَسَّ الإِبِلَ بَسًّا" (*bassan ibila bassa*): he drove the camels with kindness.
"الْبَسُّ" (*al-basso*): to send the camels into different cities and scatter them. Thus this word would mean to drive something from its place *{T, R}*.
"اِنْبَسَّتِ الْحَيَّاتُ" (*inbassatil hayat*): that the snakes slithered quickly *{T, R}*.

The Quran says:

| 56:5 | The *jibaal* (leaders of the oppressors) will be blown to smithereens.
Or, they will be driven from their place and thus removed.
Or, they will themselves slither away | وَبُسَّتِ الْجِبَالُ بَسًّا |

In the same meaning, it appears at different places:

78:20	And these leaders shall lose their grip and scatter.	وَسُيِّرَتِ الْجِبَالُ فَكَانَتْ سَرَابًا
81:3	When these leaders lose their grip	وَإِذَا الْجِبَالُ سُيِّرَتْ
77:10	When these leaders get crushed	وَإِذَ الْجِبَالُ نُسِفَتْ
20:105	The Sustainer shall crush them all	يَنْسِفُهَا رَبِّى نَسْفًا

At all these places the meaning is similar i.e. the breakup of their strength, all their places (status) to be lost, to be destroyed in revolution. See also heading *(N-S-F)* and *(J-B-L)*. Note that *jabaal* literally means mountains. Therefore if these verses are taken literally then they would mean that "the mountains flew away or disintegrated". But in reference to the context, the former meanings seems to be more appropriate.

B-S-Te   ب س ط

"بَسَطَهُ" (*basatahu*), "بَسْطَهُ" (*bas'atahu*) mean to spread, broadcast, to extend, to expand, as against "قَبْض" (*kabz*) in 2: 245, and as against "قَدَر" (*qadar*) in 42:27, which means to give in measured quantities. Also against "مَغْلُولَة" (*maghloola*) or tied up in 5:64 and 17:29.

Besides this, it also means to attack, reach out, to be high handed, as in 5:11, where it is said:

| 5:11 | That they stretch their hands towards you. | أَنْ يَبْسُطُوا إِلَيْكُمْ أَيْدِيَهُمْ فَكَفَّ أَيْدِيَهُمْ عَنْكُمْ |

It may also mean domination, as in:

| 6:94 | And the angels will be spreading their hands (overwhelm them) | وَالْمَلَائِكَةُ بَاسِطُوا أَيْدِيهِمْ |

"مَبْسُوطٌ" (**mabsoot**): wide, as in 5:64

"بِسَاطٌ" (**bisatun**) spread out and lay out, as in 71:19.

About **Taloot**, the Quran says:

| 2:247 | He was given knowledge and bodily strength in abundance | زَادَهُ بَسْطَةً فِى الْعِلْمِ وَالْجِسْمِ |

Raghib says that "بَسْطَةً فِى الْعِلْمِ" (**bastatan fil ilmi**): that Man should not only benefit himself through knowledge but also be beneficial to others. And God told the Bani Israel "you employ your strengths for yourself only, but **Taloot** benefits others with his body (bodily strength) and knowledge. That is why We have selected him to be your commander". To become a commander, one needs both bodily and mental strengths, and also the capability to benefit others with his capabilities.

B-S-Q   ب س ق

"أَلْبُسَاقْ" (**al-busaaq**): mouth's saliva.

"بَسَقَ" (**basaqa**): he spat.

"بَسَقَ النَّخْلُ بُسُوقًا" (**basaqal nakhlo basuqa**): the date palms (grew) taller and higher. **Ibn Faris** says this is its basic meaning.

"بَسَقَ عَلَيْهِمْ" (**basaqa alaihim**): he exceeded them in exaltation.

"أَلْبَسُوقُ" (**al-basoqo**): a (female) goat with long teats.

"يَسَقَ الشَّئُ بُسُوقًا" (**basaqal shai-o basuqa**): the length of a thing got completed {T, R}.

The Quran says:

| 50:10 | tall date palms | وَالنَّخْلَ بَاسِقَاتٍ |

Muheet says it also means laden date palms.

B-S-L   ب س ل

The real meaning of "بَسْلٌ" (**basl**) is to stop. **Raghib** has written in this context that it means to prevent. Explaining the difference between "بَسْلٌ" (**basl**) and "حرَام" (**haram**), he writes that "حرَام" (**haram**) is general and "بَسْلٌ" (**basl**) means to prevent with force or anger.

"يَوْمٌ بَاسِلٌ" (**yaumun basil**): a hard day.

"أَلْبَاسِلُ" (**al-basil**): a lion.

"بَسَالَةٌ" (**basala**): brave, one who bravely defends himself {M}.

"أَلْبَسْلُ" (**al-basl**): deprived, as well as that which is mortgaged with somebody {R}.

"بَسْلالَهُ" (**baslalah**): let him meet destruction {T}.

"أَلْبَسْلُ" (**al-basl**): to screen in a sieve, or to take something a little at a time, or to imprison someone.

"أَبْسَلَهُ" (**absalahu**): gave him up to destruction and annihilation.

"أَبْسَلُهُ لِعَمَلِهِ" (**absalahu li `amalehi**): he was given up to his deeds (so that he gets paid for his deeds) {T}.

The Quran says:

6:70	Lest someone (due to his wrongdoings) is deprived (of Quranic blessings)	اَنْ تُبْسَلَ نَفْسٌ بِمَا كَسَبَتْ
6:70	These are the ones who have been deprived due to their deeds	أُولَئِكَ الَّذِينَ أُبْسِلُوا بِمَا كَسَبُوا

This means tasting the results of one's deeds according to the scheme of things, or to be deprived of the blessings of life and in this way stultifying of life's progress.

B-S-M   ب س م

"بَسَمَ" (**basam**), "يَبْسِمُ" (**yabsam**), "بَسْماً" (**basmah**): to smile or laugh lightly to display pleasure.

"إِبْتِسَمَ" (**ibtisim**), "تَبَسَّمَ" (**tabassam**): he laughed briefly but beautifully, or smiled.

"مَابَسَمْتُ فِى الشَّىْءِ" (**ma basamto fee shaiyi**): I have not even tasted it.

27:19	he smiled due to pleasure	فَتَبَسَّمَ ضَاحِكاً

B-Sh-R   ب ش ر

"بَشَرَةٌ" (**bashara**): the upper surface of a man's skin. As such "أَلْبَشْرُ" (**al-bashar**) means to strip the skin, i.e. to clear it of hair {T}. Later "أَلْبَشَرُ" (**al-basher**) came to mean man himself with the difference that "بَشَرٌ" (**bashar**) means only the physical part of a human being. This way, every human child or human being is a "بَشَرٌ" (**bashar**), but the ingredients (elements) of humanness would be different in each human being.

Thus the Quran says about the Messenger:

18:110	(Tell them) I too am a (**bashar**) human like you all	اَنَا بَشَرٌ مِنْلُكُمْ
23:33	(They said that) this messenger is a (**bashar**) human just like you. Whatever you eat, he eats too. Whatever you drink, he drinks too	مَاهَذَا إِلاَّ بَشَرٌ مِثْلُكُمْ يَا كُلُ مِمَّا تَا كُلُونَ مِنْهُ وَيَشْرَبُ مِمَّا تَشْرَبُونَ

If celestial guidance which he receives from God is separated from him, then the physical being of a messenger is like ordinary human beings, but messenger-hood could not be acquired by human endeavor.

The human part of a messenger may end with his death but the revelation part remains. Generally, "اِنْسَانٌ" (*insaan*) and "بَشَرٌ" (*basher*) have been used as alternates (15:26, 15:28).

"بَاشَرَبِاْ" (*baashraha*): copulation in such a way that the skin of man and woman is in contact (2:187).
Sometimes it means only necking and kissing {T}, but the Quran uses "بَاشِرُوْبُنَّ" (*basheru hunna*) in 2:187 for sexual relations.

"بِشَارَةٌ" (*bishara*) basically means tidings which change the color of a man's face, regardless of the news being unpleasant or pleasant.
"بَشَّرَ" (*basharra*): to impart such news.

The Quran uses this word for news of a great punishment (3:20). Similarly in surah *An-Nahal* it is said that when they are told about a girl child being born to them, their faces turn black (due to sadness). For such news too, the word "بُشَّرَ" (*bashar*) has been used (16:58), but ordinarily "بِشَارَةٌ" (*bisharah*) means good news.

Ibn Faris says the basic meaning of this word is to appear with beauty.

"اَبْشَرَ" (*abshara*) and "اِسْتَبْشَرَ" (*istabshara*) also mean to be happy.

Surah *Az-Zomr* uses "اِسْتِبْشَارٌ" (*istibshaar*) as against "اِشْمِيزَازٌ" (*ishmezaz*) (39:45).

"اَلْبَشَارَةٌ" (*al-basharah*) also means beauty.
"اَلْبَشِيْرُ" (*al-basheero*): one who brings good news.
"اَلْبِشْرُ" (*al-bishr*): large heartedness.
"التَّبَاشِيْرُ" (*at-tabashir*): good news, as well as the front part or the initial part of anything. It also means the first rays of the sun in the morning.
"اَلْمُبَشِّرَاتُ" (*al-mubash-sheraat*): those winds which bring tidings of rain.

The Quran has used "بَشِيْرٌ" (*basher*) and "نَذِيْرٌ" (*nazeer*) for the messengers in 5:19.
"بَشِيْرٌ" (*basheer*) means he who gives good news about happy results of good deeds.
"نَذِيْرٌ" (*nazeer*) is he who warns of the destructive results of traversing the wrong path.

In verse 17:105 "بَشِيْرٌ" (*bashar*) has also been used along with "نَذِيْرٌ" (*nazeer*). This too means one who gives good news.

B-Sd-R   ب ص ر

"بَصَرٌ" (*basar*): to touch the heart, that is why it also means "knowledge".

"بَصِيْرٌ" (*baseer*): one who sees, and also a scholar:

"بَصِيْرَةٌ" (*baseerah*): power of comprehension, or intellect. It also means reasoning, faith and intent.

"بَصِيْرَةٌ" (*baseerah*) also means witness and testifier {T}.

"بَصِيْرَةٌ" (*baseerah*): a spot of blood or blood mark to identify the prey.

"بَصَرَةٌ" (*basarah*): hard ground and also soft and white stone {T}. **Raghib** has added "shinning" to its meaning as well.

The Quran has used this root to mean easy to comprehend. Surah *Airaaf* says:

7:195	Do they not have eyes with which they may see?	اَمْ لَهُمْ اَعْيُنٌ يُبْصِرُوْنَ بِهَا

Quran has used "اَعْمٰى" (*a'amaa*) (blind) as against "بَصِيْرٌ" (*baser*) (one who can see) in 20:125. The difference between sight or vision and insight has also been made very clear.

Surah *Al-Airaaf* says:

7:198	You can see that they have their eyes towards you, but they are not actually seeing (grasping the meaning or truth).	وَتَرَاهُمْ يَنْظُرُوْنَ اِلَيْكَ وَهُمْ لاَ يُبْصِرُوْنَ

Such people have been called "" (*umyun*) or blind in surah *Yunus* (Jonah). Those who don't use their insight or "بصيرت" (*baseerat*) 10:43. In 47:16, these people have been mentioned by saying that they are (apparently) listening to you, but in fact are lost in some other thought {R, T}. Also see heading (S-M-Ain)

Having "بَصِيْرَةٌ" (*baseerah*) or insight means to utilize the directions given in to revelation with one's intelligence. This has been made clear in 6:50 {T}. **Momins** are those who possess "بَصِيْرَةٌ" (*baseerat*) i.e. who employ their intellect in the light of the revelation.

The Quran uses "بَصِيْرَةٌ" (*baseerah*) to mean witness in 75:14 and "مُبْصِرَةٌ" (*mubassirah*): the one who is illuminating and presenting clear reasoning.

The word "بَصِيْرَأ" (*baseerah*) has also been used in surah *Yusuf* 12:66. The Quran has called itself "بَصَاءِرٌ" (*basa-ir*) in 6:105 where the meaning is of being distinct reasoning, open truth, illumination of knowledge.

"اِسْتَبْصَرَ الشَّىْءَ" (*istabsharash shaiyi*): saw something very closely {T, M}.

Raghib has said that "اِسْتَبْصَرَ" (*istabsar*) means to ask for insight.

"اَبْصَرَ" (*absar*) also means this, i.e. "to see".

The Quran says:

29:38	they had insight and were wise and perceiving	وَكَانُوا مُسْتَبْصِرِيْنَ

The Quran has said that the nations of **Aad** and **Samood** despite possessing intellect and insight were destroyed. At another place this has been explained by saying:

46:26	We had granted them the power to hear, see, and think (deliberate).	وَجَعَلْنَا لَهُمْ سَمْعًا وَّ أَبْصَارًا وَّ أَفْئِدَةً
46:26	but since they were rebellious of God's laws, their hearing, or sight or insight could do them no good and they were destroyed	فَمَا أَغْنَى عَنْهُمْ سَمْعُهُمْ وَلَا أَبْصَارُهُمْ وَلَا أَفْئِدَتُهُمْ مِّنْ شَيْءٍ إِذْ كَانُوْ يَجْحَدُوْنَ بِآيَاتِ اللّهِ

The Quran has said that if intellect is not made subservient to celestial guidance then it cannot protect man from annihilation. Let's see how man's intellect works. Man is born with animal instincts in him. These create different kinds of desires in him. If his life is dominated by the intellect and empotions (without the guidance of the revelation). Then his intellect will try to justify these desires and try to satisfy the desires some way. Thus that desire will turn into a wish, and when man decides to satisfy that wish then it will turn into a will. Man's intellect will thus be a means to satisfying his desire.

If the intellect is mature, then it might try to expostulate to man how harmful the satisfaction of that desire may be, i.e. intellect can at the most protect only self interests. It can go no further. Intellect cannot distinguish between what is wrong and right. This is possible only for the celestial guidance, which is the last word on the universal good or bad for the entire mankind and also for the strength and weakness of a man himself. Therefore man can avoid destruction only if he employs the intellect under the guidance of the celestial guidance.

Today, the big nations of the world are on the brink of disaster, because they do not put their intellect under the guidance of the revelation. And we, the muslims, are in ignominy because we are neither invoking the celestial guidance nor using our intellect.

B-Sd-L ب ص ل

"بَصَلٌ" (**basal**): "onion" {T}. In the noble Quran, this word has appeared in verse 2:61

B-Zd-Ain   ب ض ع

"اَلْبَضْعُ" (*al-baz'o*): to cut.

"بَضَعْتُ اللَّحْمَ" (*bazaatul laham*): I cut the meat into pieces.

"اَلْبِضْعُ" (*al-biz'o*): a part, some part {R, T}.

The Quran says:

12:42	some years	بِضْعَ سِنِينَ

But it is used for more than three years, and less than ten {R, T}.

"اَلْبِضَاعَةُ" (*al-biza'ah*) is that part of the wealth which is used for business {R, T}. The goods for trading.

Surah *Yusuf* uses these words in this meaning:

12:19	they hid him as goods to be traded	وَ أَسَرُّوهُ بِضَاعَةً

"بِضَاعَتَهُمْ" (*biza'atahoom*): capital, as in 12:62, and 12:65.

B-Te-A   ب ط أ

"بَطُؤَ" (*bat'u*), "يَبْطُؤُ" (*yabtu'u*), "بِطَاءً" (*beta'aa*) is to delay.

"اَبْطَؤُوا" (*abatu*): their animals became slow.

Raghib says "اَلْبُطْؤُ" (*al-batoo*): to slack (delay) in coming along, or in getting up (to go). He translates this verse from surah *An-Nisa*:

4:72	Those people who shall be late, and delay others as well.	وَإِنَّ مِنْكُم لَمَن لَّيُبَطِّئَنَّ

B-Te-R   ب ط ر

"اَلْبَطَرُ" (*al-batar*) is that pride and obnoxiousness that is born in a novae riche.

"يَبْطُرُ" (*yabtur*) basically means to tear up, to split.

"اَلْبَيْطَارُ" (*al-baitar*) is a veterinary doctor who performs surgery on animals or tears them apart.

Since excess of wealth makes a shallow person arrogant, therefore this psychological state is also called "بَطَرٌ" (*batar*).

"اَبْطَرَهُ الْمَالُ" (*abtarah almaal*): wealth created obnoxiousness in him {T}.

The Quran says:

| 8:47 | Those who came out of their houses strutting and flaunting | اَلَّذِيْنَ خَرَجُوْا مِنْ دِيَارِهِمْ بَطَرًا |
| 28:58 | Which exulted in its means of livelihood | بَطِرَتْ مَعِيْشَتَهَا |

B-Te-Sh   ب ط ش

"بَطَشَ" (**batash**) or "يَبْطِشُ" (**yabtish**): to take something forcibly.

"اَلْبَطْشُ" (**al-batsho**): strong grip, or war.

"بَطَشَ عَلَيْهِ" (**batasha alaih**): he attacked him quickly.

The Quran says:

| 7:195 | Can they grip anyone with their hands? | اَمْ لَهُمْ اَيْدٍ يَبْطِشُوْنَ بِهَا |

Surah **Yousuf** says:

| 85:12 | Sustainer's grip (the grip of consequential law or the scheme of things) is very strong. | اِنَّ بَطْشَ رَبِّكَ لَشَدِيْدٌ |
| 44:16 | the day when We will catch (you) in the strongest of grips | يَوْمَ نَبْطِشُ الْبَطْشَةَ الْكُبْرٰى |

This means when the time for an outcome is here. This is the grip of the law of justice. On the other hand, it is the grip of oppression which is said to be the hallmark of the annihilated nations.

| 26:130 | when you catch somebody you do it in an oppressive way | وَاِذَا بَطَشْتُمْ بَطَشْتُمْ جَبَّارِيْنَ |

The system of your Sustainer comes to liberate weak nations from this grip which in turn grabs the oppressors.

B-Te-L   ب ط ل

"بَاطِلٌ" (**baatil**) is described as an effort which fails to produce any result. This does not mean that there are efforts in this world which are result-less. As per the consequential law created by God, every deed has a result. "بَاطِلٌ" (**baatil**) produces results which are not intended to be to start with.

The Quran has used "بَاطِلٌ" (**baatil**) against "حَقٌّ" (**haqq**), or truth, as in 2:42. As such, to comprehend the right meaning of "بَاطِلٌ" (**baatil**), see the chapter under the heading **(H-Q-Q)** where it has been dealt in detail. In other words, anything or any concept which is not "حَقٌّ" (**haqq**), is "بَاطِلٌ" (**baatil**). For instance "حَقٌّ" (**haqq**): solid, constructive results, as such the meaning of "بَاطِلٌ" (**baatil**) would be destructive efforts or efforts which have a negative or no result, i.e. "بَاطِلّ" (*baatil*) is not only destructive efforts but any effort which has no result at all. Therefore, "بَطَل الشَّي" (*batalash shaiyi*): for something to go waste *{T}*.

Ibn Faris says that "بَاطِلّ" (*baatil*): to keep reducing or to stay for a short while.

Tajul Uroos says that when something is tested according to some criterion and it doesn't come up to the mark, it is "بَاطِلّ" (*baatil*). In other words, "حَقّ" (*haqq*) is something which meets a criterion while "بَاطِلّ" (*baatil*) is something which doesn't.

"اِبْطَال" (*ibtaal*): to spoil or waste something even if it is "حَقّ" (*haqq*).
"بَطَل الأَجِيْرُ" (*batalal ajeer*): the worker became jobless *{T}*.

Muheet says that "بَاطِلّ" (*baatil*) are things in which benefits or characteristics for which they were initially made for, do not fully remain and only their form (or appearance) remains. (This is why he says that it will not be surprising if it means empty or vacant).

With this meaning in mind, all those acts of religion can be branded "بَاطِلّ" (*baatil*) which are performed formally and the benefits, for which they were suggested, are not being reaped. See the heading (H-K-M), wherein God Himself has pointed out those benefits that we may acquire by following the laws detailed in the Quran. That is why the Quran also use "بَاطِلّ" (*baatil*) against "نِعْمَة" (*ne'mata*) that stands for pleasant benefits, as in 16:72, and 29:67.

Because by acting on the principles of "حَقّ" (*haqq*), one will surely reap the "نِعْمَة" (*ne'mata*) or the good things or benefits. If you are lacking these benefits, then surely your actions are not reflecting "حَقّ" (*haqq*), but rather "بَاطِلّ" (*baatil*). It does not make any difference if you had mistaken "بَاطِلّ" (*baatil*) as "حَقّ" (*haqq*). The outcome of your actions testifies if you were on the right track or wrong.

"حَقّ" (*haqq*): something which is resolute in its place. That is why "بَاطِلّ" (*baatil*) is something which doesn't have permanence *{T}*. That may appear so, but when investigated, it is not found to have permanence *{T}*.

The Quran says:

17:81	"*haqq*" has come and "*baatil*" is perished. Indeed the "*baatil*" is destined to be perished.	جَاء الْحَقُّ وَزَهَقَ الْبَاطِلُ إِنَّ الْبَاطِلَ كَانَ زَهُوقاً

The very word "بَاطِلّ" (*baatil*) means something which is not going to last. "بَاطِلّ" (*baatil*) is there till "حَقّ" (*haqq*) arrives. When the light comes, darkness perishes. As such, to destroy "بَاطِلّ" (*baatil*) one needs to replace it simply with a solid and result producing program. Constructive efforts must be made and hence peoples positive results shall, by themselves, destroy un-constructive and futile efforts.

11:114	egalitarianism and pleasantness destroy non-egalitarianism and unpleasantness	إِنَّ الْحَسَنَاتِ يُذْهِبْنَ السَّيِّئَاتِ

When smoothness is applied over an uneven surface, the unevenness gets removed by itself. Thus, it needs to be understood what all the different meanings of "حَقٌّ" (*haqq*) against the meaning of "بَاطِلٌ" (*baatil*).

"بَاطِلٌ" (*baatil*) also means futile effort, and that which produces weakness in man. This is the result of "بَاطِلٌ" (*baatil*) which can be rectified only by adhering to truth.
"بَطَّالٌ" (*battalun*), "بَطَلَ" (*batal*) is a very brave man who doesn't value any one's blood (life), and is ready to destroy it needlessly *{T}*.

B-Te-N   ب ط ن

"بَطْنٌ" (*batan*): stomach, or the inside of something. Its plural is "بُطُونٌ" (*botoon*).
"اَلْبَطْنُ" (*al-baton*) is the opposite of "ظَهْرٌ" (*zahrun*) *{T}*.

Muheet says that the actual meaning of this root is to be empty (vacant) and to be absolved.
Raghib says the slide of everything is "بَطْنٌ" (*batan*) and rise is "ظَهْرٌ" (*zahrun*).

"اَلْبَطْنُ" (*al-batnu*) is the stomach, the internal part of anything.
"بَطْنُ الْأَمْرِ" (*batan-ul-amr*) is the internal situation of any matter *{T, R}*.
"اَلْبِطَانَةُ مِنَ الثَّوَابِ" (*al-bitanatu minas saub*) is the inside lining of clothes as in 55:52. From this, it came to mean confidante, i.e. someone who can go inside and acquire knowledge about internal matters *{T, R}*.

The Quran says:

3:117	except (from) your own group, don't allow anyone the position where he may investigate your internal secrets	لَا تَتَّخِذُواْ بِطَانَةً مِّن دُونِكُمْ

Zajaaj says "اَلْبِطَانَةٌ" (*al-bitana*) are people with authority with whom one can have talks openly and they can be included in on the secrets. Hence it also means secret.

The Quran define God as:

57:3	He is the first and the last, the obvious and the hidden	هُوَ الْأَوَّلُ وَالْآخِرُ وَالظَّاهِرُ وَالْبَاطِنُ

For the full meaning, see heading *(Ze-He-R)*.

When one deliberates upon God's creations in the universe, he can have an idea about the Creator of the universe. In other words, the creations lead him to the opinion that all this must have a Creator, and at the back of this mind-boggling machinery, there is some great and tactful power at work. In this manner God is obvious or "الظَّاهِرُ" (*az-zahiro*). But He is not visible to the eye for that matter.

| 3:104 | He cannot be comprehended through sight. (He can't be seen) | لاَّ تُدْرِكُهُ الْأَبْصَارُ |

This way, He is also "الْبَاطِنُ" (*al-baatino*) or hidden. Hence some people interoperate it to mean that, all which is visible in the universe, is God, and all which is not visible, is the hidden part of God. In other words, all that is hidden behind these manifestations is God Himself. This is a misconception and totally against the teachings of the Quran, and it is akin to the Hindu concept of *Vedant.*

The Quran says:

| 6:120 | And keep away from the obvious and hidden sin | وَذَرُواْ ظَاهِرَ الْإِثْمِ وَبَاطِنَهُ |

This means the physical sins as well as the nonphysical sins. They include the sins committed by the eyes to observe, as well as those sinful thoughts which cross our minds.

B-Ain-Th   ب ع ث

"بَعْثٌ" (*ba'as*): to remove any obstacle in the free movement of something or somebody and thus make the movement possible.
"بَعَثَ النَّاقَةَ" (*ba'asan naqah*): he let the camel loose to go free.

Surah *At-Tatfeef* says:

| 83:4
83:5 | Do they think that they shall be able to go freely on this grand duration? | أَلَا يَظُنُّ أُولَئِكَ أَنَّهُم مَّبْعُوثُونَ لِيَوْمٍ عَظِيمٍ |

In this surah the Quran has brought forth a very basic and important principle of economics. It says that in capitalism, "businessman mentality" is such that a capitalist while receiving from others takes the full due, but when he gives (to the labourer) then gives him less than he (the labourer) produces. The truth is that the whole capitalist system is dependent on this type of mentality, but Allah's law does not allow this. It doesn't allow giving anyone less than what he produces. This brings a change in the entire society.

At present, the situation is such that the capitalists think that the system which they have created cannot be changed by anyone. The Quran says that they are wrong. This system will vanish, and these people (the capitalists) have been let lose "أَنَّهُم مَبْعُوثُونَ" (*annahum maboosoon*) till such time of the great revolution "لِيَوْمٍ عَظِيمٍ" (*lee yaumey azeem*), when mankind, pestered by this wrong system, will rise for establishing God's universal sustenance.

83:6	The duration during which mankind shall face the sustenance of the world.	يَوْمَ يَقُومُ النَّاسُ لِرَبِّ الْعَالَمِينَ

The capitalist system which, like a leash less camel, is growing as it wants will ultimately result in mankind rising to establish God's system of universal sustenance, in which taking or giving will be on equal basis.

"اَلْبَعْثُ" (*al-ba'aso*): to send/post/appoint somebody'.

10:75	then We sent *Moosa* after him	ثُمَّ بَعَثْنَا مِن بَعْدِهِم مُّوسَى

It also means to make someone get up from where he is sitting, or to wake someone up from sleep {*T, M*} as in 6:60.

"اَلْبَعِثُ" (*al-bayeso*): someone who keep waking up at night.
"اِنْبَعَثَ فَلَانٌ لِشَانِهِ" (*inn ba'asa falanoon li-shanehi*) is said or spoken when someone rises up in anger and goes to do his work.
"اَلْبَعْثُ" (*ba'ass*): cause or motive, because it removes the hurdle in acting and gets man to get up and go.

Surah *Al-Baqrah* says:

2:56	then we raised you from your stupor	ثُمَّ بَعَثْنَاكُم مِّن بَعْدِ مَوْتِكُمْ

The above verse means that all hurdles that were preventing you from being sensible were removed by us and you were awakened once again. The same surah goes on to say:

2:259	then Allah kept him dead for a hundred years and then raised him again	فَأَمَاتَهُ اللّهُ مِئَةَ عَامٍ ثُمَّ بَعَثَهُ

This is a detailed allegory to the life and death of a nation. Here "بَعَثَ" (*ba'as*): to remove those hurdles preventing a resurrection of the nation. After the destruction of the *Baitul-Muqaddas*, i.e. the temple of Solomon, the *Bani-Israel* were in a bad state. Details can be found in my book *Barq-e-Toor*.

This root has been used in the meaning of sending messengers in 2:129, and to appoint someone for a given task in 4:35,

| 4:35 | appoint someone from his/her family as the arbitrator | فَابْعَثُواْ حَكَماً مِّنْ أَهْلِهِ |
| 7:5 | gave them domination over you | بَعَثْنَا عَلَيْكُمْ |

"يَوْمُ الْبَعْثِ" (*yaumul ba'sey*) or "يَوْمَ يُبْعَثُونَ" (*yaumey yubasoon*) are important phrases like " يَوْم الدِّين" (*yaum-id-din*) in the Quran. The meaning of which can only be determined with reference to context, basically they mean life anew or the time for the appearance of the results. Life anew can happen after the collective death of a nation, or a second life after death (in the form of Life Hereafter).

B-Ain-Th-R   ب ع ث ر

"بَعْثَرَهُ" (*ba'sara*): sought him and looked for him.
"بَعْثَرَ الشَّيْئِىَ" (*ba'sarah shaiyi*): he took the thing out and opened it.
"بَعْثَرَ الْحَوْضَ" (*ba'saral hauz*): he demolished the (small) pool and brought the lower portion upwards.
"يَعْثَرَ مَتَاعَهُ" (*ba'sara mata-oo*): he ransacked his belongings.
"الْبَعْثَرَةَ" (*al-ba'sara*): nausea {T, M}. This too has the connotation of something being upside down.

The Quran says:

| 82:4 | when the quboor will be turned upside down | وَإِذَا الْقُبُورُ بُعْثِرَتْ |

This means that after search and investigation the things that are buried will be taken out. For "قُبُورٌ" (*quboor*) see heading (*Q-B-R*).

| 100:9 | Whatever there is in the *quboor* will all be taken out. | إِذَا بُعْثِرَ مَا فِي الْقُبُور |

B-Ain-D   ب ع د

"بُعْدٌ" (*boa'd*): distance, to be distanced. It is the opposite of "قُرْبٌ" (*qurbun*) that means close, as used in 21:109.
"بَعِدَ" (*ba'id*), "يَبْعَدُ" (*yab'id*), "بَعَدًا" (*ba-ada*), "بُعْدٌ" (*boa'dan*) to be killed, to be destroyed {T, M}. It means to be removed from the pleasantries of life.

Quran says:

| 11:44 | There is destruction for the oppressing nation (They will be removed from life's happiness) | بُعْداً لِّلْقَوْمِ الظَّالِمِينَ |

"بَعِيدٌ وباعِدٌ و بُعَادٌ" (*ba'yeedun wa ba'eedun wa bu'aad*): which is to be distance (removed), which will be destroyed *{T, M}*.

"بَعْدُ" (*ba'd*) is the opposite of past, or the times to come after a period that has passed *{T, M}*.

"اْلأَبْعَدُ" (*al-abad'o*) is the opposite of "أَقْرَبُ" (*al-aqrab*) or that which is near. It also means a renegade, and hence "اْلبُعَدَاءُ" (*al-bu'ada*) is used for foreigners. It also means "غَيْرُ" (*ghair*), which means something strange, not familiar.

45:23	Who else (except Allah) can show him the way (the right guidance can only be given by Allah)	فَمَن يَهْدِيهِ مِن بَعْدِ اللَّهِ

It also means "despite":

2:178	The one who rebels despite this, for him there is painful punishment.	فَمَنِ اعْتَدَى بَعْدَ ذَلِكَ فَلَهُ عَذَابٌ أَلِيمٌ

B-Ain-R   ب ع ر

"اْلبَعِيرٌ" (*al-baeer*): camel, a young camel.

"اْلبَعِيرٌ" (*al-baeer*) also means donkey. It is said for an animal which is used for loading.

"اْلبَعْرُ" (*al-ba'ro*) is the droppings of a goat *{T}*.

Surah *Yusuf* says:

12:72	a camels (or donkeys) load	حَمْلُ بَعِيرٍ

B-Ain-Zd   ب ع ض

"بَعْضٌ" (*ba'z*) is a part of something, whether big or small, as in 2:85. For example, eight is the "بَعْضٌ" (*ba'az*) of ten and so is two.

"بَعَضَ الشَّىءَ" (*ba'dus shai-aa*): the thing was divided up.

"تَبْعِيضٌ" (*taba eezun*): to separate, or divide *{T}*.

Surah *Al-Baqrah* says:

2:72	when some of them meet their own in private, (or go to them)	إِذَا خَلاَ بَعْضُهُمْ إِلَى بَعْضٍ

"بَعْضُنَا" (*ba'zo-na*) is someone among us. Some dictionary scholars think that "بَعْضٌ" (*ba'zo*) also means total or whole and quote this following verse as proof:

40:28	all that you are warned of will visit upon you	يُصِبْكُم بَعْضُ الَّذِى يَعِدُكُم

But, in this verse, the meaning of "all" may also be taken as "some". Also see 43:63.

"بَعُوْضَةٌ" (*ba'uza*), the plural of which is "بَعُوْضٌ" (*ba'ooz*): mosquito as in 2:26, since it is very small in comparison to other creatures *{M}*.

B-Ain-L   ب ع ل

"بَعْلٌ" (*ba'al*) is high land which cannot be reached (inundated) by flood water. It also means every tree, plant or crop that sucks water for irrigation with its own roots. From the connotation of loftiness and not being dependent on anyone, this word has come to mean owner or lord.

Ibn Faris writes that it basically means *sahib* which also includes the meanings of friend and companion in addition to "lord". It also means "surprise" and "bewilderment", as well as "loftiness".

Raghib says the Arabs used to call their idols "بَعْلٌ" (*ba'al*) because they thought that they were high and mighty. Their society had the concept that man is dominant over women, which is why husbands too were called "بَعْلٌ" (*ba'al*). Its plural is "بُعُوْلَة" (*ba'ula*). Everything which overwhelmed or dominated others was also called "بَعْلٌ" (*ba'al*). But they also knew that all dominant figures become a burden after sometime, and so a load or burden was also called "بَعْلٌ" (*ba'al*). As such "أَصْبَحَ فُلانٌ بَعْلاً عَلیٰ أَهْلِہِ" (*asbaha falanun ba'ala ala ahlehi*): a person who has become a burden for his folks *{T}*.

Since the Arabs called the husband "بَعْلٌ" (*ba'al*), the Quran also uses this word in this meaning in 2:228, 24:31. So here the word does not mean dominance but husband.

William Lane has written (with several references) that "بَعْلٌ" (*ba'al*) is used for both husband and wife in the same manner as "زَوْجٌ" (*zauj*). Just as "زَوْجٌ" (*zauj*) can have "زَوْجَہ" (*zauja*), which is the specific female form, "بَعْلٌ" (*ba'al*) can have "بَعْلَہ" (*ba'lah*). Therefore, there is no connotation of dominance in this word, but only of husband and wife.

As the Quran has declared "نکاح" (*nikah*) which is marriage according to the Islamic way, as a sacred pact, there is no question of dominance of one over the other.

The writer of *Muheet* says that the difference between "بَعْلٌ" (*ba'al*) and "زَوْجٌ" (*zauj*) is that latter means every husband, but he becomes "بَعْلٌ" (*ba'al*) after he has consummated the marriage.

Ilyas' (Elijah's) nation used to call its idol "بَعْلٌ" (*ba'al*) as it appears in 37:125. It was the most favorite of all among the Semitic tribes. It used to be worshipped in Syria. The *Torah* also mentions it (33:2 - 33:3).

B-Gh-T   ب غ ت

"اَلْبَغْتُ" (*al-baghto*) and "اَلْبَغْتَـةُ" (*al-baghta*): suddenly.

"اَلْمُبَاغَتَةُ" (*al-mubaghata*): to reach one another suddenly *{T}*.

Raghib says it means for something to appear from an unexpected place.

The Quran says:

6:31	when the moment (اَلسَّاعَةُ) sneaks up upon them suddenly	إِذَا جَاءَ تْهُمُ السَّاعَةُ بَغْتَةً

(To understand the concept of "اَلسَّاعَةُ" (*assa'ah*) see heading (S-Ain-W).

The same surah says further ahead:

6:47	God's punishment can come suddenly, or there may come signs first and then the punishment itself	إِنْ أَتَاكُمْ عَذَابُ اللَّهِ بَغْتَةً أَوْ جَهْرَةً

It is hence clear that "بَغْتَةً" (*bagh-tatan*) means a situation in which some event happens revolutionarily or as an emergent evolution, not evolutionary. It must be understood that the result of an action starts to register right at the beginning of the action but it takes time to fully manifest itself.

Surah *Al-Anbia* says:

21:12	when they felt our punishment	فَلَمَّا أَحَسُّوا بَأْسَنَا

In other words, the punishment was being prepared and could be felt only afterwards. In some cases signs of the impending punishment start appearing before its actual advent, this is called "جَهْرَةً" (*jahra*). Sometimes the punishment is sudden, and is called "بَغْتَةً" (*bagh-ta*).

39:25	They were visited by the punishment from a place they had no knowledge about. (Which could not be comprehended by them earlier.)	فَأَتَاهُمُ الْعَذَابُ مِنْ حَيْثُ لَا يَشْعُرُونَ

The nations which view only the superficial indicators try to assess the causes of a disaster from the physical causes that were present at the time of the punishment or disaster; in fact, however, the causes go back.

B-Gh-Zd   ب غ ض

"اَلْبُغْضُ" (*al-bughz*): this word is opposite of "الحُبُّ" (*al-hoobb*) – 'love'; to be unloved or disgusted with something. "اَلْبَغْضَاءُ" (*al-baghzao*) is 'the height of disgust' as used in 3:117 *{T, R, M}*.

B-Gh-L   ب غ ل

"اَلْبَغْلُ" (*al-baghlo*): an ass *{T}*. The plural is "بِغَالٌ" (*bi-ghaal*) as in 16:8.

Ibn Faris says its basic meaning is of physical strength.

The ass is called "اَلْبَغْلُ" (*al-baghl*) because of its physical strength.
"اَلتَّبْغِيلُ" (*at-tabgheel*) is used for a body that is big and strong *{T}*. Since an ass is born of a mare and a donkey, therefore "بَغْلٌ" (*baghl*) is used for any crossbred animal.

Since a mule comes into being through the mating of a mare and a donkey, therefore this animal is also called "بَغْلٌ" (*baghl*) because is born out of the coupling of two different genres.

B-Gh-Y   ب غ ى

"اَلْبَغْى" (*al-baghyi*) is the wish to overstep the middle path (regardless of whether one can actually do or not).
"اَلْبَغْىُ" (*al-baghyo*): too much rain that exceeds all measures.
"بَغَتِ السَّمَاءُ" (*baghatis samai*) is the cloud that exceeds its limit, meaning that it rained a lot. These are the basic meanings of this word.

Ibn Faris says it basically means to ask for something and to be spoilt.

"فِءَةٌ بَاغِيَةٌ" (*fe'ateh baghia*) is a party or group that opposes the order and rebel.
"اَلْبَغَايَا" (*al-baghya*) are those soldiers who move ahead for making prior arrangements.
"بَغَى يَبْغِى" (*bagha yabgha*): he became too proud and exceeded his limits.
"تَبَاغَوْا" (*tabaghau*): to commit excesses on one another.
"بَغَتِ الْمَرْأَةُ بِغَاءً" (*baghatil mar'ato begha'a*): the woman exceeded the limits of decency.
"بَغْيٌ" (*baghyun*) and "بَغُوٌّ" (*baghu'a*) is a fornicating woman.
"بَغَى عَلَيْهِ" (*bagha alaih*) is to commit excess against or on someone, to oppress someone, to be high handed against somebody, and be jealous of someone. If the envy is for a good thing then the envy also becomes good otherwise not *{T}*.
"اِبْتِغَاءٌ" (*ibtigha*): to struggle in pursuit of something. If the search is for something good, then the search becomes limited, otherwise a wild chase *{T}*.

"اَلْبِغْیَة" (al-bighyah) and "اَلْبُغْیَة" (al-bughiya) is the thing which is being looked for, which one intends to possess. It also means something which is lost and for which a great search is mounted.

"اَلْبَاغِیْ" (al-ba'ghi) also means one who searches {T}.

"اِنْبَغَی الشَّیْیٌ" (in bagh-ash shaiyi) is for something to become easy, to be acquired, or to be befitting.

"مَا یَنْبَغِیْ" (ma yanbaghi): this is not correct or proper, or this is not possible, or this is not permitted {T}.

Muheet says it signifies leaning towards one of two things and the justification for the other.

Surah *Yaseen* says:

| 36:69 | We did not teach the Messenger poetry | وَمَا عَلَّمْنَاهُ الشِّعْرَ وَمَا یَنْبَغِی لَهُ |

Nor can the psychological makeup of a revolutionary preacher be such that emotions rule over the truths (and this is what a poet's psychology is based upon).

| 36:69 | what he has been given are the facts of history and clear cut laws for life | إِنْ هُوَ إِلَّا ذِكْرٌ وَقُرْآنٌ مُبِینٌ |

How can then there be room for emotional leanings? For details see heading (Sh-Ain-R).

The Quran says:

22:60	the oppressed	بُغِیَ عَلَیْهِ
4:104	Don't be slack in pursuing the enemy (try your best to pursue him)	وَلَاتَهِنُوْا فِیْ ابْتِغَاء
3:6	The intention to create fitna (mayhem)	ابْتِغَاءَ الْفَتْنَةَ

About *Qaroon* it is said:

| 28:70 | he used to commit excesses on them. (wanted to stay ahead of them) (*Gharibul Quran by Mirza Abul Fazal*) | فَبَغَی عَلَیْهِمْ |

It also means to demand power and kingdom.

Surah *An-Noor* uses the word "الْبِغَاءُ" (al-ibghao) for fornication in 24:33, but in surah *Maryam* it is used for transgressing. In Surah Mariam this word has been used for committing crime in 19:20, and not specifically for fornication. That is, Maryam said "I am living like a nun, and the law is that a nun should live a life of celibacy, I have hence not broken that law." It is to be remembered there were allegations against Maryam that she had adopted an ordinary life (and not a celibate life as was required of her) and this was against the law. That is why they said to her that her mother was not one to break laws (19:28). Then, could she break the law?

Isa (Jesus) in reply had said "your laws are self-made. I have been made a messenger by God, and given the book (The Bible). This book contains no such law (i.e. of celibacy). That is why my mother has not done anything against Gods law.

But if "بَغِيًّا" (*baghiyyan*) is taken to mean "evil-doer" then this verse would mean that Maryam said that "I am living a life of celibacy (under the Temple) therefore there is no question of my mating with anyone". Another meaning can be of "wrong-doing" . Then this verse would mean "but I am not corrupt either, så how can I give birth to a child?" This is during the time when Maryam was living a celibate life as a nun under the Temple rules. Later when she came to know of the teachings of Allah, she left the life of a nun and started living a normal life with the child. Since it was un-thinkable, i.e. leaving sisterhood and living a family life, therefore , they considered Maryam's life as a life of corruption. *Isa* had refuted their self made laws and defended his mother even as a child.

Surah *Al-Baqrah* says that the Jews oppose the Quran because they are jealous as to why the Quran, instead of being revealed to the dynasty of *Bani Israel*, was revealed to one from *Bani Ismail* (i.e. *Muhammed*). For this (jealousy) "بَغْيًا" (*baghyan*) has been used in 2:90.

The Quran, after discussing "*haram* and *halal*" (permissible and non-permissible) in edibles says:

2:173	due to hunger if someone faces death then he has done no crime	فَمَنِ اضْطُرَّ غَيْرَ بَاغٍ وَلاَعَادٍ فَلا إِثْمَ عَلَيْهِ

This means that he is absolved and is permitted to eat the forbidden things, provided that he takes only as much as necessary to save his life and doesn't exceed the limit, and also if his intention is not to break the law. In other words, neither should he take just because he wants to nor should he take more than necessary (just enough to save his life).

Note that although "بَغِيٌّ" (*baghiy*) is masculine in gender, it is also used in feminine terms.

B-Q-R   ب ق ر

"بَقْرٌ" (*baqar*): to tear up/ apart something like cutting up some animal's stomach.
"بَقَرَ الْعِلْمَ" (*baqaral-ilm*): deep research and inquiry.
"بَاقِرٌ" (*baqir*): a lion and also a scholar {T, M}.

Baqar can either mean a cow or a bull {T}. It is the plural while the singular is "بَقَرَةٌ" (*baqarah*). This word appears in the tale of *Bani Israel* in 2:67. Whatever that is written in the verses that follow shows that this word was meant for the bulls which were not meant for work but were let to roam free, in the name of the their gods. They used to worship the bull in Egypt and this emotion had embedded itself, consciously or subconsciously in the minds of *Bani Israel*. In order to eradicate this emotion, the order for slaughtering cows was given.

B-Q-Ain   ب ق ع

"اَلْبَاقِعُ" (*al-baqey*) is a spotted crow or a dog.

Ibn Faris says it basically means the difference in colors.

"اَلْبَاقِعَةُ" (*al-bage'a*) is a bird which is very alert and looking around finds out whether it is being hunted. In order to drink, unlike other birds, it goes to some unfamiliar spot *{T, M}*.

According to the earlier stated meaning, "أَرْضٌ بَقِعَةٌ" (*arzun baq-eta*) is a land with greenery at some places while other spots are barren (spotted land).

"اَلْبُقْعَةُ" (*al-buga't*) is the land which is not similar to the surrounding land *{T, M}*.

The Quran says:

28:30	in the ***mubarak*** (established and developing) land with the trees (which is different than its surroundings)	فِى الْبُقْعَةِ الْمُبَارَكَةِ مِنَ الشَّجَرَةِ

"اَلْبَقْعَةُ" (*al-baq'ato*) is also a place where water has accumulated.

B-Q-L   ب ق ل

"بَقَلَ الشَّىْءُ" (*baqalash-shaiyi*): the thing appeared.
"بَقَلَتِ الْأَرْضُ" (*baqalatil ard*): vegetables appeared on the land.

Raghib says that "بَقْلٌ" (*baqlun*) are vegetables which lose their branches and roots in winter. ***Ibn Faris*** says that this word basically means "fertility".

Abu Ziad says whatever first appears (grows) on land is "بَقْلٌ" (*baql*).

According to ***Aqrabul Muwarid***, "بَقْلٌ" (*baql*): such vegetables which do not grow under the soil (like potato, carrot, turnip etc.) but above the soil like cauliflower, tomato, etc.

The Quran uses this word to mean "vegetables" in 2:61.

B-Q-Y   ب ق ى

"بَقِيَ" (*baqiyu*), "يَبْقَى" (*yabqa*), "بَقَاءٌ" (*baqa'a*) is used for something to remain in its state and not undergo change. It is the opposite of "فَنَاءٌ" (*fanah*) which means to undergo change. "اِبْقَاءٌ" (*ibaqa*), "اِسْتِبْقَاءٌ" (*istibqa*) is to remain unchanged {*T, M*}. It also means to protect and guard.

Everything in the universe is undergoing change, but God's personae are above changes, and so are His laws. These are permanent values. The acts which are according to his laws also beget unchangeable results. By following these laws, the human personality also becomes stable and above change. The basic characteristic of personality is that it remains unchanged in a changing world. For details see my book "*Nizam Raboobiyat*" and also "*Mun O Yazdan*" and the 5th Volume of "*Ma'aruf-ul- Quran*" with the title "*What Man Thought*".

See this word in the light of these meanings and how the noble Quran has used words from this root, and its use shall become absolutely clear.

18:46	wealth, progeny, are things for the worldly life (physical life) of Man	الْمَالُ وَالْبَنُونَ زِينَةُ الْحَيَاةِ الدُّنْيَا
18:46	According to God's Law the best acts are those whose enabling results never change. To hope for these is life's best goal.	وَالْبَاقِيَاتُ الصَّالِحَاتُ خَيْرٌ عِندَ رَبِّكَ ثَوَاباً وَخَيْرٌ أَمَلاً
16:96	whatever you have, according to your concepts, is gradually lost, but that which accrues to you according to the law of God, (whether they are the pleasantries of life or the growth of human personality) is foreign to change	مَا عِندَكُمْ يَنفَدُ وَمَا عِندَ اللّهِ

Surah *Al-Kahaf* says: These things are not bad and should not be avoided.

Surah *Hood* says:

| 11:86 | wealth and goods which are acquired according to Allah's law | بَقِيَّةُ اللّهِ |
| 11:116 | Those possessing a remnant | أُوْلُواْ بَقِيَّةٍ |

This has been said for those who obey the laws of Allah

| 43:28 | A lasting word | كَلِمَةً بَاقِيَةً |

The lasting word is the book about the uniqueness of Allah (the basis for all Quranic teachings) which the messengers leave behind for their followers, and which never changes. The advisers of Pharaoh's court had termed it as "خَيْرٌ وَأَبْقَى" (*khairun wa abqa*) in 20:73, which means "the most unchanging".

Surah **Ar-Rahman** says:

| 55:26 | Everything in this universe changes. (The universe is changing all the time.) | كُلُّ مَنْ عَلَيْهَا فَانٍ |
| 55:27 | But Sustainer's personae is above all changes, and His laws, and their results too do not change | وَ يَبْقَى وَجْهُ رَبِّكَ ذُوالْجَلَالِ وَالْإِكْرَامِ |

The meaning of the word "فَنَا" (*fana*) as understood today to be "perishing", is not correct. For details, see heading **(F-N-Y)**. For other meanings of "وَجْمِ رَب" (*wajhey rabbey*) see heading **(W-J-He)**.

"بَقِيَّةُ الشَّيْئِ" (*baqiyyatush shaiyi*) is the remaining part of anything, but of the same kind. That is why a brother cannot be called "بَقِيَّةُ الْأَبِ" (*baqiyyatul ab*) (the remaining part of father) **{M}**.

About **Bani Israel's** Arc of the Covenant, it is said:

| 2:248 | The remaining part of the progenies of **Moosa** and **Haroon,** which they had left behind. | وَ بَقِيَّةٌ مِّمَّا تَرَكَ آلُ مُوسَى وَآلُ هَارُونَ |

B-K-R ب ک ر

"اَلْبِكْرُ" (*al-bikro*) with plural "اَبْکَارٌ" (*abkaar*) is used for an unmarried woman, a spinster; also a man who has not had sex with any woman (a male virgin); the mother of the first baby or camel; the first child; any first thing. It also means a cow which has not yet become pregnant, a young cow.

Ibn Faris says these are its basic meanings.

| 2:68 | nor old nor in her prime (young) | لَافَارِضٌ وَلَابِكْرٌ |

"اَلْبُكْرَةُ صبح" (*al-bukrah sub-ha*) is the first part of the day, in other words, i.e. morning. The compiler of **Muheet** says that it is the time from dawn to the *chaasht* (a prayer which is performed before noon). See 3:40 and 3:19. Besides this the root of the word means "to pierce" or "cut" **{T}**. Things which have no precedence are also "اَلْإِبْکَارُ" (*abkaar*) **{Qamoos}** as in 56:35, 56:36.

The Quran uses the word in this meaning, i.e. with the right teachings and with the acts of virtue the women became totally different from the women of pre-Islam age of ignorance, which had no precedence.

B-K-K   ب ک ک

"بَكَّةٌ" (*bakkah*), "يَبُكُّ" (*yabakkah*), "بَكَّاً" (*bakka*) is to tear something up, to separate, to resist. "بَكَّ عُنُقَهُ" (*bakka anooqahu*): he broke his neck {T}.

Mecca is also called "بَكَّةٌ" (*bakkah*):

3:59	The first house for Humanity is that which is in **Bakkah**, (a house with blessings).	إِنَّ أَوَّلَ بَيْتٍ وُضِعَ لِلنَّاسِ لَلَّذِى بِبَكَّةَ مُبَارَكاً

There are different opinions about this name of the city. Some think that people come to it in droves and there is a big crowd in the surroundings, which is why it is called "بَكَّةٌ" (*bakkah*). Some think that the oppressors and the rebels had their necks broken here (lost their power), hence the city is named "بَكَّةٌ" (*bakkah*), but *Raghib* thinks that "بَكَّةٌ" (*bakkah*) is a different form of "مَكَّةٌ" (Mecca). There are many examples in Arabic of M being substituted for B {M}.

For example, *Sabad* and *Samad*, *Laazib* and *Laazim*. These words have the same meaning regardless if there is B or M in them.

B-K-M   ب ک م

"بَكَمٌ" (*bakam*): to be unable to speak, dumb. *Azhari* says that "أَبْكَمُ" (*abkum*) and "أَخْرَسُ" (*akhrus*) differ in that the last mentioned means someone who cannot speak from birth, while the first word means one who can speak but is not outspoken, and due to this inability to speak properly, cannot make himself understood. But "أَبْكَمُ" (*abkum*) also means a person who is deaf, dumb and blind {T}.

Ibn Faris says that "أَبْكَمُ" (*abkum*), plural of which is "بُكْمٌ" (*bekum*), is one who abstains from speaking either on his own will or due to his uncouthness, and also one who cannot describe something clearly.

The Quran says:

2:18	Deaf, dumb, blind	صُمٌّ بُكْمٌ عُمْىٌ فَهُمْ

Here "بُكْمٌ" (*bukum*) only means dumb, because for deaf and blind the words "صُمٌّ" (*summon*) and "عُمْىٌ" (*umyun*) have been used additionally.

In surah *Al-Anfaal*, it is said:

8:22	According to Allah, the worst creatures are those who are deaf and dumb and hence do not comprehend.	إِنَّ شَرَّ الدَّوَابِّ عِندَ اللّهِ الصُّمُّ الْبُكْمُ الَّذِينَ لَايَعْقِلُونَ

Here with the words "صُمّ" (*summon*) and "عُمْیٌ" (*umyun*) has been made it clear that the words do not mean those who are physically deaf and dumb, but those who dot employ their intellect.

Surah *An-Nahal* says:

| 16:76 | One of them is dumb and does not understand anything. | أَحَدُهُمَا أَبْكَمُ لَایَقْدِرُ عَلَی شَیْءٍ |

This means one who doesn't have the ability to do anything, and is a burden on his boss. If he goes on an errand, he doesn't do it right. Compared to him is one who is powerful or with authority, and who orders justice. He treads the right path. These explanations make it clear that the use of "صُمُّ بُکْمٌ" (*summun bukmun*): those who instead of employing their intellect go blindly along their wrong path.

B-K-Y   ب ک ی

"بُکَاءٌ" (*bukaa*): to cry tearfully in sorrow. Sometimes only sorrow or to cry is "بُکَاء" (*bukaa*) *{T, R}*.

Ibn Faris says its basic meanings are to cry, and for something to lessen.

The Quran uses "ضَحِکَ" (*zahika*) against "بَکَی" (*ba'kaa*) in 9:82. Therefore it means "to lessen sadness".

Surah *Ad-Dukhan* says:

| 44:29 | neither the sky nor the earth cried at their destruction | فَمَا بَکَتْ عَلَیْهِمُ السَّمَاء وَالْأَرْضُ |

This means that nobody felt sorrow on their behalf because their destruction took place according to the scheme of things, so they just faced consequences of their own actions.

Ergo, their destruction was just.

| 19:58 | When they were told about the words of their Sustainer, they bowed down with their full leaning | إِذَا تُتْلَی عَلَیْهِمْ آیَاتُ الرَّحْمَن خَرُّوا سُجَّدًا وَبُکِیًّا |
| 25:73 | Those who when reminded of their Sustainer's signs, accept them, but not as dumb and blind. | وَالَّذِینَ إِذَا ذُکِّرُوا بِآیَاتِ رَبِّهِمْ لَمْ یَخِرُّوا عَلَیْهَا صُمًّا وَعُمْیَانًا |

This verse is about those who obey God's law with full knowledge and understanding, and accept them from the bottom of their heart because their acceptance is based upon their intellect.

Bal   بَل

"بَل" (*bal*): instead, on the contrary. The following examples will make the meanings clear.

When it comes in the middle of a sentence, it denies the first part and asserts the second.

21:26	And they say that God has taken sons (for Himself). On the contrary, they are His respected missionaries.	وَقَالُوا اتَّخَذَ الرَّحْمَنُ وَلَداً سُبْحَانَهُ بَلْ عِبَادٌ مُّكْرَمُونَ

The assertion of one thing without the denial of another:

23:62 23:63	We have a book which speaks the truth, and there is no excess on them, on the contrary their hearts are in sixes and seven and uncouthness.	وَلَدَيْنَا كِتَابٌ يَنطِقُ بِالْحَقِّ وَهُمْ لَا يُظْلَمُونَ بَلْ قُلُوبُهُمْ فِي غَمْرَةٍ مِّنْ هَذَا

This means that the second part of the verse is separate from the first. Also study 87:14-16, and 85:20-21. Here this word is used to mean "and". Similarly in 21:62-63 too, this word might begin a new sentence. Details can be found under the relevant headings.

B-L-D   ب ل د

"أَلْبَلَدُ" (*al-balad*): any part of land, or earth which has a boundary, whether inhabited or unhabited. The plural is "بِلَادٌ" (*bilad*) and "بُلْدَانٌ" (*buldaan*). It has been used to mean "a village" or "a dwelling".

Surah *Al-Baqrah* says: "هَذَا بَلَدًا" (*haaza balada*) in 2:126. Here it can mean either dwelling or a plot of land.

In surah *Al-Balad*, "بِهَذَ الْبَلَدِ" (*bihaazal balad*) refers to the city of Mecca (90:102). The city at another place, 95:3, has been called "الْبَلَدِ الْأَمِيْنِ" (*al-baladil amen*) which means "the City of Peace".

Ibrahim had prayed for it to be a place of peace for the oppressed of the world (2:126). That it would become the Centre of Allah's system of universal sustenance and of the *Momineens*, who are the guarantors of peace in the world he wished that it would indeed become a City of Peace. For more details see headings related to *Hajj* and *Ka'aba*.

"بَلَدَ الْفَرَسَ" (*balladal faras*): the horse lagged behind in the race, or couldn't surge ahead *{M}*.
"بَلِيْدٌ" (*baleed*): an idiot or moron (who stays behind) *{M}*.

Ibn Faris says its basic meaning is "chest"

"بَلَّدَ الرَّجُلُ بِالْأَرْضِ" (*baladar rojolo bil ard*): the man put his chest against the earth, i.e. he hugged the ground.

B-L-S   ب ل س

Ibn Faris has said that the basic meaning of "أَبْلَسَ" (*ablas*) is of becoming disappointed and hopeless.

21:77	they will lose hope without cause	إِذَا هُمْ فِيهِ مُبْلِسُونَ

It also means to be surprised or shocked. In ancient Semitic lexicon it meant "to kill by trampling, or trample" *{Ghareeb-ul-Quran}*.

Some believe that "أَبْلِيس" (*Iblees*) has been derived from "أَبْلَسَ" (*ablas*) which means "permanently without hope about God's benevolence", but some other dictionary scholars say that it is not an Arabic word and has been Arabised *{T}*.

The Quran has presented ***Iblees*** as the embodiment of rebelliousness and mutiny:

2:34	He refused to obey orders, was rebellious and mutinous, became among the disobeyers.	أَبَى وَاسْتَكْبَرَ وَكَانَ مِنَ الْكَافِرِينَ

This word has come against *malaika* who are obedient by nature:

38:73	All the *malaika* bowed to him	فَسَجَدَ الْمَلَائِكَةُ كُلُّهُمْ أَجْمَعُونَ

Man is the only creature in the entire universe who has been given the freedom of choice, when it comes to obeying the laws of God or disobey them if he so chooses. No other creation has been given the right to disobey (go against God's laws). Man disobeys God when his emotions get the better of him. These emotions rouse him towards personal benefit as against the universal good, and thus he lays God's laws aside and follows such emotions. Hence his intellect tells him how to achieve those ends.

The Quran has called such emotions and such intellect, which leads him on to this end "أَبْلِيس" (*Iblees*), and due to its rebelliousness said that it has been created out of fire (*naar*) 7:12.

And since these emotions are hidden from the naked eye, and work in the subconscious, they are called "كَانَ مِنَ الْجِنّ" (*kaana minal djinn*) in 18:50 (*djinn* means hidden). Since these emotions (due to which Man can disobey God's laws) are born with him and stay with him as long as he lives, the Quran says that "أَبْلِيس" (*Iblees*) and Man co-exist (see heading ***Adam***). "أَبْلِيس" (*Iblees*) has been given time along with Man till the very last moment.

15:36	He said "My Sustainer, give me time till they are reawaken"	رَبِّ فَأَنْظِرْنِي إِلَى يَوْمِ يُبْعَثُونَ

But if you look at the depth of the meaning of the word "بَعْثَ" (*ba'as*), then the meaning of "يوم يُبْعَثُونَ" (*youm ba'asoon*) becomes something else. "بَعْثَ" (*ba'as*) means "to remove obstacles from the way of someone's freedom", hence "to grant freedom". So what *Iblees* was told is that his activity was to break loose the moral codes of the people. Hence as long as people do not break their moral codes and get towards a common freedom, its presence shall be required. When they shall be able to do so by themselves, then the services of *Iblees* shall no longer be required. *Iblees* needs this due, and hence it is granted. It is a fact that it takes some effort to break loose from moral principles at first. But when it finally happens, its comes very natural for man to simply go with the flow.

The person who mutinies against God's laws is deprived of all the happiness which would have accrued to him by following His laws. Therefore "اَبْلِيْس" (*Iblees*) has been termed deprived and hopeless.

Those who live according to the laws of Allah:

2:38	they will have no fear nor sorrow	فَلاَحَوْفٌ عَلَيْهِمْ وَلاَهُمْ يَحْزَنُونَ

About them it is also said that they will not be overwhelmed by *Iblees* in any way (15:42). The Quran has described "اَبْلِيْس" (*Iblees*) and "شیطان" (*Shaitan*) as two sides of the same coin when, for example, it refers to the tale of Adam. In this tale *Iblees* refuses to bow before Adam, commits mutiny, shows pride and challenges God to mislead the mankind. These are all actions of *Iblees*. But where *Adam's* fault is mentioned, it has been linked to *Shaitaan* (the opposer).

2:36	Then the *Shaitan* made them (both) slip	فَاَزَلَّهُمَا الشَّيْطَانُ

Also see 7:11-20 and 20:116-120.

This makes it obvious that *Shaitan* is actually a particular sort of mentality (not a person or being) and the way it works or operates is called *shaitan*. For details on *Shaitan* see heading **(Sh-Te-N)**. For details of all these terms, see my book "*Iblees O Adam*" which is one in my series to an introduction to the Quran i.e. *Muarif-ul-Quran*.

Iblees and *Shaitan* are those obstacles which hamper human intellect in its natural growth. If the human intellect overcomes these hurdles and thus proves itself to be solid and steadfast, the evolutionary system moves ahead, but if these hurdles prove insurmountable, then that intellect is confined to the lower (or animal) level of life. Life, in fact, is the name of this very struggle between Man and *Iblees*, and that is why the existence of *Iblees* along with Man is inevitable. The human personality cannot find stability without opposition and clashes, or in other words, its solidarity cannot be tested without these. For the continuous flow of water, a waterfall is most essential. What remains to be seen is whether the water becomes a stagnant pol due to this (fall) obstacle or keeps its flow despite the hurdle. To select such a path, in which the hurdles of sect, celibacy, etc. are not present, is to stultify your own flow. So, life is a continuous struggle between Man and *Iblees*.

And it is said that *Iblees* (hopelessness) and *Shaitan* (rebelliousness) are two sides of the same coin. Modern psychology supports the theory that hopelessness leads to rebelliousness or aggressiveness. When Man finds something not being according to his wishes, he gets frustrated. If he takes out the frustration on himself, the result is worry or gloominess which might end in self-destruction. When the frustration is against the cause of frustration, it appears as vengeance, but if that is not plausible, then he takes out his anger or frustration against things which are not even related to the cause. This is the beginning of madness, thus this shows how closely hopelessness and rebelliousness, and in other words *Iblees* and *Shaitaan*, are related.

These are the psychological frames of the human mind. The Quranic laws create a society which has no room for hopelessness for its members.

| 39:53 | don't lose hope in Allah's benevolence | لَا تَقْنَطُوا مِن رَّحْمَةِ اللَّهِ |
| 7:156 | and this benevolence encompasses everything necessary for the growth of life | وَرَحْمَتِى وَسِعَتْ كُلَّ شَىْءٍ |

Thus in such a society hopelessness cannot overwhelm anyone. This is why the Quran says:

| 15:42 | Surely you cannot overwhelm My mission takers. | إِنَّ عِبَادِئ لَيْسَ لَكَ عَلَيْهِمْ سُلْطَانٌ |

Also see headings *(Q-N-Te)*, and *(Y-A-S)*.

B-L-Ain   ب ل ع

"بَلَعَ" (*bale'a*), "يَبْلَعُ" (*yablah*): to swallow something.
"اَلْمُبْلَعُ" (*al-mabla'o*) is the place from where food gets down to the stomach.
"اَلْبَلُوعُ" (*al-baloo'o*): something which is meant to be drunk.
"اَلْبُلْعَةُ" (*al-bul'a*): a sip *{T}*.

Besides this, it also means the opening of a grain mill down which the grain is put *{M}*.

About the storm during *Nooh's* time, God commands the ground to:

| 11:44 | Swallow your water (absorb it) | ابْلَعِى مَاءَكِ |

B-L-Gh   ب ل غ

"بَلَغَ الْمَكَانَ بُلُوغاً" (*balagh-al-makana bulugha*): that he reached the spot. It is said that "بُلُوْغٌ" (*bulugh*) and "بَلاغٌ" (*balagh*) mean to reach the ultimate end, whether that is with regards to right place or time. It also means something estimated, but sometimes this word is used for just getting close.

As the Quran has said:

2:231	when they are getting close to completion of *idda* (When they reach the last limit of the appointed time)	فَإِذَا بَلَغْنَ اَجَلَهُنَّ

The Waiting Period (*'idda*) in 2:231 is not for a widow, but for a divorcee, and it is 3 months/menstruation (given in 2:228). A widow's *'idda* (4 months and 10 days) is given in 2:234.

"اَلْبَلاغُ" (*al-balgh*) is for something to be enough or sufficient in order to make a man realise his goal through it, so he may not require any further means for this *{T}*.
"اَلْبُلْغَةُ" (*al-bulgha*) is any such thing with which one can reach some goal *{T}*.

The Arab tent-dwellers used to roam the desert, since their lives depended on water. There were some wells in the desert, and a rope and a bucket used to be kept on the well wall. However, the water level of the wells was not constant in warm areas. Sometimes the level was so low that the bucket (with its rope) could not reach the water. As a counter measure these Arabs used to keep a rope with them and in such cases tied it to the existing rope "الرِّشَاءُ" (*ar-risha*) of the bucket so that the bucket could reach the water. This piece of extra rope was called "التَّبْلِغَةُ" (*at-tabligha*). This makes the meaning of the word "تبليغ" (*tableegh*) or preaching clear, which means that a man lacks the capacity to reach a meaning himself, then this shortcoming is overcome somehow by some preacher so that he can grasp the meaning. But if he doesn't want to use his piece of rope "الرِّشَاءُ" (*ar-risha*) then only "التَّبْلِغَةُ" (*tabligha*) cannot alone take him to the water. "تبليغ" (*tableegh*) can only benefit those who use their own intellect and insight. "مَبْلَغٌ" (*mablagh*) is the last destination which somebody may reach (53:30)

God has termed the Quran as "بَلاغٌ لّلنَّاسِ" (*balaghun naas*) in 14:52. In other words, it is the medium through which man can reach his goal and does not require the presence of any other medium to do so. So the Quran is the medium through which Man can reach his destiny, but it can only take those to their ultimate destination who obey it, those who live according to its dictates.

This is because the Quran says:

21:106	This *balgh* is only for those who truly accept the mission of God	إِنَّ فِىْ هَذَا لَبَلاغاً لَّقَوْمٍ عَابِدِيْنَ

It has been left to Man's discretion to take the right path according to the Quran or take some other (the wrong path). Nobody can be forced to choose a particular way of life. If they had meant to be forced, then God would have created Man in a way in which he couldn't disobey Him. All the other creations in the universe are compelled to traverse a certain path only. Therefore the messengers came to deliver Allah's message to the people, not to force them to follow those laws.

16:35	Messengers have no more responsibility than to explain and deliver God's laws to the people.	فَهَلْ عَلَى الرُّسُلِ إِلاَّ الْبَلاغُ الْمُبِينُ

"بَالِغَةٌ" (*baligha*) in 68:39, means something that reaches its goal.

B-L-W   ب ل و

"بَلاءٌ" (*balaun*), "أَبْتَلاءٌ" (*ibtela-un*).

Raghib says this word has two meanings:
- To obtain information about one's welfare or to acquire information about him.
- For the real condition of something to become known, whether good or bad.

When the word is used for God, it would have only the second meaning, because God knows it all, and one cannot even imagine that He is unaware of any condition *{T, R}*. Therefore, the word's basic meaning is to portray the reality.

"بَلِيَ" (*bali*), "يَبْلَى" (*yabla*) is used for a cloth to become old and worn. Because when a cloth has been worn out, its real condition comes to light. Therefore "ابَلاءٌ" (*bala*) is used for a man's real personality to come out during times of difficulties and misery. But it does not necessarily mean that identity of everything has to be bad. It can also be good. That is why it could also mean the real personality of someone during happy times. There are two times when a man's reality becomes manifest, times of misery and times of happiness. At both these times, his real self appears.

"أَلْمُبَالاَةٌ" (*al-mubalah*): to boast, or to pride oneself as to the better position in life against another *{M}*. "أَبْتَلاَ" (*ibtelaa*): to select, to choose *{T}*.

In surah **Al-Baqrah**, the **Bani Israel** has been told Pharaoh's nation perpetrated different excesses on you, but We delivered you from their oppression.

2:49	the deliverance from their oppression provided the opportunity to watch how you behave upon getting freedom	وَفِى ذَلِكُم بَلاءٌ مِّن رَّبِّكُمْ عَظِيمٌ

Surah *Al-Anfaal* says that God granted victory to the Momineen in the battle field of *Badr*:

8:17	so it is through successes in this world that they are given the opportunity to show the world how to behave during good times	لِيُبْلِيَ الْمُؤْمِنِيْنَ مِنْهُ بَلَاء حَسَناً

Some dictionaries have combined the roots *(B-L-W)* and *(B-L-Y)*. But we have presented them as separate headings, though they have only a very fine difference between them, so fine that at times they are difficult to differentiate.

Surah *Ad-Dukhan* says that the *Bani Israel* are told that they have been given all this " مَا فِيْهِ بَلَاء مُبِيْنٌ " (*ma feehey balawun mubeen*) in 44:33, which had everything needed for their growth. It also means "to make evident".

The Quran says:

86:9	The day when every hidden thing will be made evident	يَوْمَ تُبْلَى السَّرَائِر
3:153	So that Allah may make those things evident which were in your heart	لِيَبْتَلِيَ اللّٰهُ مَا فِيْ صُدُورِكُم
10:30	There every one's act shall be made evident for him, that he had committed	هُنَالِكَ تَبْلُو كُلُّ نَفْسٍ مَّا أَسْلَفَتْ

In surah *Al-mominoon*, after describing things about the nation of *Nooh*, it is said:

23:30	This is how We make (the tales about former nations) evident	وَإِن كُنَّا لَمُبْتَلِيْنَ

The struggle between Right and Wrong goes on. In this struggle we get familiar with different facts of life. Sometimes one is faced with trying aspects and at other times with peaceful aspect of life's happiness. This has been described by the Quran as "اَبْتَلَى" (*ibtela*), meaning the different faces of life which keep appearing. In surah *Al-Fajr*, this meaning is made clear (see 89:15-16). This way man can determine as to see how far his capabilities go, because he can only face the difficult aspects of life to the extent to which his latent qualities have developed. These hurdles that he faces are actually a man's opportunities for development of his own personality. This is what "اَبْتَلَى" (*ibtela*).

Surah *Al-Baqrah* says:

2:144	And when his Sustainer provided *Ibrahim*, opportunities to develop his personality, through various laws...	وَإِذِ ابْتَلَى إِبْرَاهِيْمَ رَبُّهُ بِكَلِمَاتٍ

When, as per the laws of God, life's many events (difficulties) came into his (*Ibrahim's*) life, so that He viewed how far *Ibrahim's* capabilities had developed. The way *Ibrahim* faced these difficulties (the way he reacted) made clear that his capabilities had developed to the utmost. That his capabilities had developed fully.

"فَأَتَمَّهُنَّ" (*fatamahunna*) as in 2:124, makes it clear that the concept of "اَبْتَلٰى" (*ibtela*) being a "test" from God, as we usually believe, is not what Quran thinks it to be. God doesn't test anyone, He only provides man with opportunities so he can judge how capable he is, and may strive to do better.

In surah *Ad-Dahar*, the Quran has used the word "اَبْتَلٰى" (*ibtela*), from which the meaning of latent capabilities becoming evident. It says that the human birth takes place due to the interaction of the male and female. The sperm is composed of such minute germs that they cannot even be seen without a microscope, but the whole human child is hidden in those tiny germs.

To explain this truth the Quran says:

76:2	we give birth (initiate the birth) of Man with a mixed sperm and arrange it, so in the womb its latent capabilities gets developed and he grows into a seeing and hearing human child	إِنَّا خَلَقْنَا الْإِنسَانَ مِن نُّطْفَةٍ أَمْشَاجٍ نَّبْتَلِيهِ فَجَعَلْنَاهُ سَمِيعاً بَصِيراً

This is what "اَبْتِلَاءٌ" (*ibtelaa*) is and its correct definition is for latent elements to become evident and grow.

Bala   بَلٰى

"بَلٰى" (*bala*) is used if the question is negative, so it can refute it.

7:172	Am I not your Sustainer?	اَلَسْتُ بِرَبِّكُمْ
7:172	They said, yes off course, we testify to that.	قَالُوا بَلَى شَهِدْنَا

This means that they are actually saying "You are our Sustainer".

43:80	Do they think that We are unaware of their secrets and private discussions?	أَمْ يَحْسَبُونَ أَنَّا لَا نَسْمَعُ سِرَّهُمْ وَنَجْوَاهُم
43:80	But yes, our messengers are with them, writing it all down	بَلَى وَرُسُلُنَا لَدَيْهِمْ يَكْتُبُونَ

And the answer is "بَلٰى" (*bala*) why not? We definitely are (aware).

There may not be any question, and refutation of something negative is meant. For instance:

| 16:38 | They swear, and swear profusely by Allah that one who dies is not resurrected by Allah (but they are totally wrong) | وَأَقْسَمُوا بِاللَّهِ جَهْدَ أَيْمَانِهِمْ لَايَبْعَثُ اللَّهُ مَن يَمُوتُ |
| 16:38 | But yes, He has made a binding promise (law), but people are not aware. | بَلَى وَعْدًا عَلَيْهِ حَقًّا وَلَكِنَّ أَكْثَرَ النَّاسِ لَايَعْلَمُونَ |

This is His promise (His law) that there will be life after death, and this promise will be fulfilled by all counts. Here, "بَلَى" (*bala*) refutes the first part of the sentence.

Similarly, surah *Al-Baqrah* says that the Jews and the Christians say that none other than their people will go to Heaven.

After this, it is said:

| 2:112 | No, this is wrong. The fact is that anyone who bows to the laws of Allah (The Quran) can go to Heaven | بَلَى مَنْ أَسْلَمَ وَجْهَهُ لِلَّهِ وَهُوَ مُحْسِنٌ فَلَهُ أَجْرُهُ عِندَ رَبِّهِ وَلَاخَوْفٌ عَلَيْهِمْ وَلَاهُمْ يَحْزَنُونَ |

B-L-Y ب ل ى

"بَلِيَ يَبْلَى بِلَى الثَّوْبُ" (*yabliya yabla balius saub*): that the cloth became old and fragile. Any cloth which has become old and fragile will be called "بَالٍ" (*baalin*) {T}.

The Quran says:

| 20:120 | Such government that does not diminish or deteriorate. (a state which always stays fresh and which does not deteriorate) | مُلْكٍ لَّا يَبْلَى |

Every human being nurses the wish to live forever and become immortal. In its own particular way, the Quran states that this hope was exploited by *Iblees* who was told that:

| 20:120 | Shall I tell you, Adam, about immortality and point out a state which never gets old? | قَالَ يَا آدَمُ هَلْ أَدُلُّكَ عَلَى شَجَرَةِ الْخُلْدِ وَمُلْكٍ لَّا يَبْلَى |

Then through discreet pointers, the Quran tells about the idea planted by *Iblees* that immortality could only be possible through one's children (progeny), ergo a man should try to keep his name alive. But this is an *Ibleesian* misconception. Eternal life is only possible through development of man's personality for which the Quran has given a specific program (it includes to have *Imaan* and do righteous deeds). It is true that one's dynasty is essential for extending one's race, but this doesn't produce growth in the individual's personality. Those who exist on the level of animals think that this (the progeny) is the key to immortality.

B-N-N   ب ن ن

"بَنُّ بِالْمَكَانِ" (*banu bilmakan*), "يَبِنَّ" (*babni*), "بَنَّاَ" (*ban'aa*): to stay foot somewhere, to stop.
"اَبَنَّتِ السَّحَابَةَ" (*abannatis sahaba*): the cloud remained at a spot for several days.
"تَبَنَّنَ" (*tabannana*): he stayed put.
"اَلْبَنَانِیُ" (*al-banani*): the fingers, or their environs {*T*}, because it is the fingers with which one hold something strongly. It is a fact that the thumb is a strong element for holding something tightly, which is why this word is used for human strength, the power to grasp, and strong grip.

Surah *Al-anfaal* says:

8:12	hit every *banan* of theirs	وَاضْرِبُوٓا مِنْهُمْ كُلَّ بَنَانٍ

Here the word *banan* means "fingers". The meaning is to hit everything which signifies the enemy's power and strength.

Surah *Al-Qiyamah* says:

75:4	We can also complete all of Man's limbs and strengths	بَلَى قَادِرِينَ عَلَىٰ اَن نُّسَوِّىَ بَنَانَهُ

This means to complete every such thing with which he grabs other things, or all those strengths which are responsible for human acts. *Ibn Faris* says that *banan* means hands and legs.

B-N-W/Y   ب ن و/ى

"بَنَاءٌ" (*bnaa*): a building, or anything that is constructed, even the tents in which the Arab gypsies live. It also means a roof. *Abu Hanifa* thinks "بِنَاءٌ" (*binaa*): anything which is inorganic, like stone, earth etc.

"بَنَاءٌ" (*banna*) is a constructor, as well as an architect.
"بَانٍ" (*banin*) also means constructor of a building. Its plural is "بُنَاةٌ" (*bunah*).
"بَانِيَةٌ" (*baaniah*) is the bent bone of the chest.
"بُنْيَانٌ" (*buniyan*): walls. Some think that this word is plural.
"بِنْيَةٌ" (*baniyah*) is the form of construction:
"اَرْضٌ مَبْنِيَّةٌ" (*ardun maniyah*): land on which a building is constructed {*T, L*}.

Ibn Faris says this root means to build by linking a part of one thing to another.

"اِبْنٌ" (*Ibn*): man's son, because a son is in a way a father's construction as well, or because a son has some part of the father in him. The plural is "اَبْنَاءٌ" (*abna'a*), or "بَنُونَ" (*banoon*), or "بَنِين" (*baneen*).

"بِنْتٌ" (*bint*) is the daughter of which "بَنَاتٌ" (*banat*) is plural.

"تَبَنَّاهُ" (*tabannah*): to adopt someone as one's son. It also means having interest or relations with someone, for example "اِبْنُ حَرْبٍ" (*ibn herb*) is a fighter. "اِبْنُ السَّبِيْلِ" (*ibnas sabeel*) is a passenger {R}.

The Quran says:

| 2:22 | Who spread the earth below you and the sky above | الَّذِیْ جَعَلَ لَكُمُ الأَرْضَ فِرَاشاً وَالسَّمَاءِ بِنَاء |

Here "بَنَاءٌ" (*bina'aa*): something which is laid down, so "بَنَاءٌ" (*bina'aa*) would mean something which is hovering above or spread out above, like a tent.

Surah *An-Nahal* says:

| 16:26 | Allah made their constructions fall on them from their foundations, and their roofs caved in over them | فَأَتَى اللّٰهُ بُنْيَانَهُم مِّنَ الْقَوَاعِدِ فَخَرَّ عَلَيْهِمُ السَّقْفُ |

Here "بُنْيَانٌ" (*bunyaan*): buildings which have foundations beneath and roofs above.

In the tale about the *Bani Israel*, the word of "أَبْنَاءٌ" (*ibna*) has been used against "نِسَاءٌ" (*nisa*).

| 14:6 | They used to *qatal* (degrade) your *Ibna* and "kept alive" your *nisa* | وَيُذَبِّحُونَ أَبْنَاءَكُمْ وَيَسْتَحْيُونَ نِسَاءَكُمْ |

If "أَبْنَاءٌ" (*abna*) is to be translated as sons, then "نِسَاءٌ" (*nisa*) should mean daughters, and if "أَبْنَاءٌ" (*abna*) is taken to mean men, then "نِسَاءٌ" (*nisa*) would mean women. These meanings are also supported by verse 17:40 where "نِسَاءٌ" (*nisa*) has been used against "بَنِيْنَ" (*baneen*). Figuratively "أَبْنَاءٌ" (*abna*) would mean the strong or well-constructed individuals of a society. Also see under heading (N-S-W) and (Dh-B-Ain).

Surah *Al-Luqman* says "يَٰبُنَیَّ" (*ya bunaiya*) in 39:16 which means, "O my little son". Here "بُنَیٌّ" (*bunaiyun*) is the abbreviated form of "اَبْنٌ" (*ibn*).

Bani Israel   بنی اسرائیل

Bani Israel are the descendants of *Israel* or *Yaqoob*.

This was the title for *Yaqoob* who was *Ibrahim*'s grandson. *Israel* means "Man of God". His progeny or dynasty is called *Bani Israel*.

His fourth son was named *Yahuda* (Judas). The tribe of *Yahuda* and *Bin Yamin* ruled *Judea* in *Palestine*. That is why the tribe was called *Yahudi* (which is even today the word a Jew) and the other tribes were called *Bani Israel.* Later, the difference mitigated and they both came to be identified as *Bani Israel*.

Yaqoob's motherland was *Kana'aan* (Palestine), but when his son *Yusuf* attained a lofty position in Egypt, the entire family was called to Egypt, due to it being *Yusuf's* tribe, who was most respected in Egypt. For four hundred years, the tribe remained in Egypt, and the tribe which was comprised of a few individuals became a big nation. But at the same time the pharaohs of Egypt enslaved them and treated them like slaves are treated, which is shabbily. When their ignominy reached its peak, *Moosa* was sent to them (as a messenger) and he, after liberating them from the enslavement of the pharaohs, took them back to Palestine. This event happened close to 1600 B.C. Here they reached new heights. They were also blessed with exalted messengers like *Daud* and *Suleman*. But then this nation became mutinous of Allah's laws, and this resulted in chaos which made them weaker and weaker as a nation.

In 599 B.C. *Babul's* (Babylon's) king, *Banu Kid Naser* (Nebuchadnezzar) attacked Jerusalem and ransacked this national center of *Yahudis* (Jews). They were imprisoned and taken to *Babul* where they lived in ignominy. The Quran has pointed to this first devastation of the Jews in verse 17:5. For nearly eighty years, they lived in this sorry state when three kings, *Zulqarnain* (Cyrus), *Dara* (Darius) and *Artakhshasha* (Artaxerxes) became ready to help them one after another. They deliberated them from the imprisonment in Babylon and allowed them to resettle once again in Palestine around 515 BC. Palestine was then rebuilt and the expelled Jews settled in their center again. The Quran has pointed to this in verse 17:6 and placed this (nearly) 100 years' period in allegorical form. Some years later, the Jews reverted to their degenerated state. In year 332 BC first Alexander attacked them and dispersed them. Later, in year 320 BC *Batlemoos* (Ptolemy) captured Jerusalem and broke whatever power they had left.

During Antigonus' rule, the whole area came under the Greeks. Then in 66 BC Pompeii (a Roman) destroyed Jerusalem in 01 BC. Another attack on Jerusalem completely destroyed their morale (the Quran has pointed to this second destruction of the Jews in verse 17:7).

At this stage, Nature gave them another chance to recuperate, and *Isa* (Jesus) was sent to them, but the Jewish scholars and leaders hatched a conspiracy against him and in this way self-destructed.

In 70 A.D, the Roman governor Tyson attacked them for the last time due to which there was no trace left of them. In the words of *Encyclopedia Brittanica*:

"On the tenth of the month in 70 A.D, in a state of fear which is without parallel in the world, the fall of Jerusalem took place, and the Jewish state was no more."

As to why the Jewish scholars and leaders had conspired against *Isa*, the following statement from the gospel of Barnabas can throw light. On page 142 of Barnabas' Bible it is said:

"Then they discussed with the leaders of the astrologers and said,"Iif this Man (Christ) becomes king, what are we then going to do? It will be a big difficulty for us. Because he wants to reform the way God is worshipped. At this moment he doesn't hold the power to annul our practices and traditions, but (if he comes into power) what will happen to us under his control? Surely we and our children will all be destroyed, because the moment we lose our positiion, we will have to beg for our bread. Although at this time the king and our ruler are both without any care about what we do, as we also do not have anything to do with their practices. That is why we can do whatever we please. At this time, if we make any mistake, we can please our God with fasting and sacrifice, but if this man (Christ) becomes king, God will not be pleased until he finds worship to be what Moses has written".

Such a nation, which has degenerated to this level, has no other fate than destruction and ignominy. During the time of our Messenger Muhammed, they (the Jews) were given another opportunity to redeem themselves by obeying the laws of Allah, but due to their dogmatism, they opposed this too and as a result had to leave the Arab peninsula. The Quran has mentioned this in verse 59:2, thereafter this nation was known as the *"Wandering Jews"* till such time (now) that the political reformers of some strong states have made a home for them in Palestine. (We will not go into this political discussion because it is outside our scope)

It must be noted that religion among the Jews was only hereditary or national. One could only be a Jew by dint birth into a Jew family. None other than one of *Bani Israel* could be a Jew. This alone is enough to show that this was not the religion which had been given to them by the messengers. Allah's *Deen* (system) is for the entire human race. That is why when the advisors of Pharaoh's court accepted *Imaan* (became believers), they were not rejected by *Moosa* because they were not from among the *Bani Israel* (i.e. the dynasty of *Jacob*). But later, the Jews made it a national religion. More details about the *Bani Israel* can be found in my book *"Barq-e-Toor"*.

B-He-T   ب ه ت

"بَهِتَ" (**bahit**) is to be shocked or surprised. It means to be quieted due to surprise.
"اَلْبَهْتُ" (**al-bahto**) is to catch someone suddenly.

The Quran says:

2:258	He who had denied, was grabbed by this ultimate reasoning, (due to surprise he became quiet, he shut up as he was shocked)	فَبُهِتَ الَّذِى كَفَرَ
21:40	the revolution will come so suddenly that it will stun them	فَتَبْهَتُهُمْ

"بُهْتَانٌ" (**bohtan**) is to accuse someone, at which he becomes shocked, as in 24:16

24:12	Clearly false talk	إِفْكٌ مُبِينٌ

Surah **Al-Mumtehana** uses this word "بُهْتَانٌ" (**bohtan**) as every unpleasant act:

60:12	and will not commit any unpleasant act	وَلَا يَأْتِينَ بِبُهْتَانٍ يَفْتَرِينَهُ

B-He-J   ب ه ج

"اَلْبَهْجَةُ" (**al-bahjah**) means "beauty". This word is used for freshness and bloom in vegetation and pleasantness in humans.
"اَلْإِبْتِهَاجُ" (**al-ibtehaaj**): happiness and pleasure.
"تَبَاهَجَ الرَّوْضُ" (**tabahajar-rauz**): a lot of flowers bloomed in the garden.

The Quran says:

22:5	and the earth gives birth to (grows) every kind of fresh and delightful plant	وَأَنبَتَتْ مِن كُلِّ زَوْجٍ بَهِيجٍ
27:60	Beautiful gardens	حَدَائِقَ ذَاتَ بَهْجَةٍ

B-He-L   ب ه ل

"اَبْهَلَهُ" (**abhala**): to make someone free in his opinion and intent.
"أَبْهَلَ النَّاقَةَ" (**abhan naqa**): that the camel was set free so that anyone could milk it, or she was allowed to roam free.
"اِسْتَبْهَلَ الْوَالِى الرَّعِيَّةَ" (**istabhal al way-alir raeeyah**): that the ruler let the subjects go free so they could do whatever that suited them {T}.

Raghib says that the actual meaning of the word is to leave something in an unattended state, to leave it to its own device. *Raghib* also says that

"اَلْاِبْتِهَالُ فِیْ الدُّعَاءِ" (*al-ibtehal-o fid dua yi*): to openly keep on praying for something {R}.
"اَلْبَهْلُ مِنَ الْمَالِ" (*albahl-o minal maal*): a little wealth
"اَلْبَهْلُ" (*al-bahal*) is a little something, an insignificant amount {T}.

Ibn Faris says its basic meaning includes water shortage.

This word has appeared in 3:60 where the Messenger is told that if these people do not accept (what you preach) despite all the reasoning and evidence, then tell them that we and our family gets to one side and you and your families move to another. "ثُمَّ نَبْتَهِلْ" (*summa nabtahil*).

And thus Quran says:

3:60	From now you don't interfere in our society, and we have nothing to do with you	فَنَجْعَلْ لَّعْنَةَ اللّٰهِ عَلَى الْكَاذِبِیْنَ

In other words, leave each another in order to choose and operate separate opinions and beliefs, and follow their respective programs. Time and result will make it clear which group gets deprived of Allah's blessing and becomes "ملعون" (*mal'oon*).

This is what "لعنة" (*lana*) means, that the deprived group will be proven false in its claims.

This is said at different places as:

73:10	leave them in a very nice manner	وَاهْجُرْهُمْ هَجْراً جَمِیْلاً
15:85	So be in a very nice manner	فَاصْفَحِ الصَّفْحَ الْجَمِیْلَ
3:136	You pursue your way and I will pursue mine, results shall declare successes and failure	اَعْمَلُوْا عَلَى مَكَانَتِكُمْ اِنِّیْ عَامِلٌ فَسَوْفَ تَعْلَمُوْنَ مَنْ تَكُوْنُ لَهُ عَاقِبَةُ الدَّارِ اِنَّهُ لَا یُفْلِحُ الظَّالِمُوْنَ

This will also prove the law of Allah which dictates that "the fields of disbelievers never produce a crop". This is what Allah's *lana* on the liars is.

The first revolutionary step in a Messenger's program is of preaching. The second step is to distance from those who refuse to accept the program and oppose it due to their intransigence and adamancy. At this stage they are told simply not to interfere in the messenger's program and the Messenger will not interfere in their affairs. This has been termed as "نَبْتَهِلْ" (*nabtahil*) in surah *Aal-e-Imran*. The third stage is of the clash when results are before everyone to see. In other words, good and evil are made evident irrefutably.

B-He-M ب ه م

"اَلْبُهْمَة" (**al-bohma**): a solid rock.

"اَلْأَبْهَمُ" (**al-abhamo**): solid and composite thing, dumb, ambiguous, without flow.

"بُهْمَة" (**bohma**): a matter which is difficult to understand.

"اِبْهَاماً الْأَمْرُ أَبْهَمَ" (**abhamal amro ibhama**): that the matter became ambiguous and was beyond comprehension as how to solve it.

"حَائِظٌ مُبْهَمٌ" (**ha-i-zun mubhamun**): a wall which has no opening or door *{T, M, R}*.

Ibn Faris says that its basic meaning is for something to become such that no way towards it is perceived or to become indistinct and ambiguous.

With reference to dumbness, "بَهَائِمُ" (**baha-um**), singular of which is "اَلْبَهِيْمُ" (**al-baheema**), means all animals who cannot speak, or their voices are ambiguous and they cannot be understood. All animals including aquatic animals are included in this category. However, *Muheet* and *Raghib* both maintain that wild carnivores and birds are not included in this category.

The Quran says:

5:1	**bahimatul anam** (dumb animals) have been made **halal** (permitted) for you…	أُحِلَّتْ لَكُم بِهِيْمَةُ الْأَنْعَام إِلاَمَا يُتْلَى عَلَيْكُمْ

… other than those which the Quran itself has termed as *haram* (forbidden) in 5:3. For the meanings see heading *(N-Ain-M)*.

B-W-A ب و أ

"بَاءَ" (**baa'a**), "يَبُوءُ" (**yabu-o**), "بَوْأَ" (**bawaa**) basically means to return to something, to move back, to be in agreement with, to accept, to bear the load, to be equal *{T, M, R}*.

The Quran says:

2:61	they became prone to Allah's wrath and with that burden returned	وَ بَآؤُواْ بِغَضَبٍ مِّنَ اللَّهِ

Their actions and the resulting ignominy became befitting.

In surah *Al-Maida*, in the tale about the descendants of Adam, it is said that the oppressed said to the oppressor:

5:29	I want that you bear the burden of my murder and other crimes. (Become deserving of their punishment.)	إِنِّى أُرِيْدُ أَن تَبُوءَ بِإِثْمِى وَإِثْمِكَ

"اَلْمَبَاءَ ةٌ" (*al-maba'ah*): bee hive. It also means residence, home *{T}*.

"بَوَّا الْمَكَانَ" (*bowwal makana*): he stopped somewhere, got down.

"بَوَّاهُ الْمَنْزِلَ" (*bowwahul manzil*): got him down somewhere, got him to stay somewhere.

"بَوَّأ هُ مَنْزِلاً" (*bowwahul manzila*): he made some place agreeable, corrected some place, and made it smooth *{T}*.

Raghib too says it means "to make the elements of some place smooth and agreeable".

"بَوَّأتُ لَهُ مَكَانَاً" (*bawwatu lahu makanah*): I made some place smooth for him.

Surah **Al-Hajj** says:

22:26	We appointed the **Kaba** to be the smooth place for him	وَاِذْ بَوَّأنَالاِبْرَا هِيْمَ مَكَانَ الْبَيْتِ

It can also mean that "We made it a place to be returned to, for him".

"تَبَوَّا الْمَكَانَ" (*tabawwal makan*) got down at some place and stayed there *{T, M, R}*

Surah **Al-Hashar** says:

59:9	Those who made **Medina** their abode (staying place) before them, and placed strong trust in their hearts.	وَالَّذِيْنَ تَبَوَّؤُوا الدَّارَ وَالْإِيْمَانَ مِن قَبْلِهِمْ

B-W-B   ب و ب

"بَابٌ" (*baab*) is the place of entry *{T}*, hence it means "a door". Plural is "أَبْوَابٌ" (*abwaab*). In agriculture the places from where water is opened (allowed to flow) are also called "أَبْوَابٌ" (*abwaab*) *{M}*.

"هَذَا بَابَتُهُ" (*haaza babatohu*): this is befitting, this suits him, or is his condition *{T}*.

"أَبْوَابُ السَّمَاءِ" (*abwaabus sama'a*) as used in 7:39 means "the paths of blessings".

"أَبْوَابَ جَهَنَّمَ" (*abwaaba jahannum*) as used in 16:29, means "the stages of destruction". Also see 15:44.

"أَبْوَابُ كُلِّ شَيْىءٍ" (*abwaabo kulli shaiyi*) in 6:44 means "every type of comfort".

Surah **Al-Baqrah** has used "ظُهُوْرِهَا" (*zahooraha*) against it in 2:128 to mean "backyard" against "the doors of a house".

B-W-R   ب و ر

"اَلْبَوْرُ" (*al-baur*) is the land which has not been cultivated, ergo uncultivable land.
"بَارَ عَمَلُهُ" (*baar amaloh*): his actions went waste *{T, M, R}*.

Ibn Faris says its basic meanings are annihilation and suspension.

The Quran says:

35:10	their planning will go waste (will bear no fruit)	وَمَكْرُ أُوْلَئِكَ هُوَ يَبُورُ

"بَارَتِ السُّوقُ" (*baaratis sooq*): the market cooled down (went into a depression) *{T, M, R}*.

The Quran says:

35:29	a trade which sees no loss	تِجَارَةً لَّن تَبُورَ

"اَلْبُوْرُ" (*al-boor*): useless, without benefit, idle, losers, those who are to be destroyed *{T}*.

25:18	That nation was to be annihilated.	وَكَانُوا قَوْماً بُوراً

"اَلْبَوَارُ" (*al-bawar*): destruction, loss
"بَوَارُ الْأَيِّمِ" (*bawarul aleem*) is an unmarried girl or widow not being married (and staying home) because there are no proposals for her.

The Quran says:

14:28	they brought their nation to a place where there would be no buyer for that commodity	وَأَحَلُّوا قَوْمَهُمْ دَارَ الْبَوَارِ

This means where nobody even inquires about them, where nobody gives them any message, where they are in great loss, where there is destruction and annihilation for them. Due to vested interests and wrong policies of leaders, nations reach such a state. This has been termed as *jahannum* by the Quran in 14:29.

The full verses' translation is as following: "have you pondered about those who defied Allah and led the nation to a state where there was no buyer for them (the commodity) i.e. *jahannum,* or a place of destruction, and they entered it, and it is a lousy (bad) place to stay at". The leaders that do not value the blessings of Allah lead their nations to *jahannum* of destruction and annihilation, where both the leaders and the nation meet destruction.

The Quran has stated the dialogue between these leaders and their nations in detail and they are very eye opening in 14:21, 33:67, 37:29, 40:47, and 38:60.

B-W-L   ب و ل

"أَلْبَالُ" (*al-baal*) is the condition or state about which one should ponder, i.e. a valuable matter which captures one's fantasy, wishes, emotions, thoughts that cross one's mind {T}.

Surah *Yusuf* says:

12:50	What is the condition of those women? (What is the matter with them?)	مَا بَالُ النِّسْوَةِ

"بَالٌ" (*baal*): that the matter had particular importance. *Yusuf* was worried about some matter in the above mentioned verse.

Surah *Muhammed* says:

47:2	God will smoothen out their difficulties, sort out their problems.	وَأَصْلَحَ بَالَهُمْ

B-Y-T   ب ى ت

Raghib says that "بَيْتٌ" (*bait*): a place where a man takes shelter for the night, but later this word came to mean "a house".

"بَيْتُ الرَّجُلِ" (*baitur rajul*): a man's wife and kids.
"أَلْبَيْتُ" (*al-bait*): to wed {T}.
"بَاتَ" (*baat*), "يَبِيْتُ" (*yabeet*): to work all night long.

Zajaj says that anyone who spends the night some place is "بَاتَ" (*baat*), whether he sleeps or does some work there.

"بَيَّتَ الْأَمْرَ" (*baitul amr*): to plan work at night, or to work at night.
"بَيَّتَ الْقَوْمَ" (*bayyatal qaum*) is to attack a nation at night {T}.
"أَلْبَيْتُ" (*al-beet*): food.
"أَلْبَائِتُ" (*al-ba-it*) is stale, (not fresh).

Surah *Al-Baqrah* uses "أَلْبَيْتُ" (*al-baito*) for the *Ka'ba* in 2:125.

Surah *Al-Furqan* uses "يَبِيتُونَ" (*yabeetoon*) in 25:64, which means to consult at night, or to spend the night, while its use in 27:49 indicates to mean attack at night.

"بَيَاتًا" (*bayata*): during the night.

B-Y-D   ب ى د

"بَادَ يَبِيْدُ" (**bada yabeed**): for something to diminish, to end, to be annihilated.
"بَادَتِ الشَّمْسُ بُيُوْداً" (**baadatis shamsu buyuda**): the sun set.
"أَلْبَيْدَاءُ" (**al-baida**): to travel in a barren desert or jungle, meaning annihilation.
"بَادَ الشَّىءُ" (**baadash shaiyi**): that thing was scattered. From this it has come to mean to diminish or to be destroyed.
"أَبَادَهُ اللهُ" (**abadah-ullah**): Allah annihilated him {*T, R*}.

Surah *Al-Kahaf* says:

18:35	I never thought that it would be destroyed	مَا أَظُنُّ أَن تَبِيدَ هَذِهِ أَبَداً

"أَلْبَاءِدُ" (**al-bayed**): one who is annihilated {*M*}.

B-Y-Zd   ب ى ض

"أَلْأَبْيَضُ" (**al-abyaz**): white. Plural is "بِيْضٌ" (**beez**) and feminine is "بَيْضَاءُ" (**baizaa**).
"أَلْبَيَاضُ" (**al-bayaz**): whiteness. It is the opposite of "أَسْوَادٌ" (**aswad**) and means black {*T*}.

As for the Arabs, "بَيَاضٌ" (**bayaz**) was the best regarded color. Therefore it is allegorical to good habits and blessings. As such, a man who is not soiled with any defects is called "أَبْيَضُ الوَجْهِ" (**abyazul wajhi**). It also means life's brightness and life's happiness.

The Quran says:

3:105	on that day some faces will be white and some black	يَوْمَ تَبْيَضُّ وُجُوهٌ وَتَسْوَدُّ وُجُوهٌ

Here "تَبْيَضُّ" (**tabyazzo**): to be blessed with life's happiness.
"تَسْوَدُّ" (**taswaddo**): pain and sorrow {*M*}.
"أَلْبَيْضَةَ" (**al-baizato**): egg, also the status or real place of anything, gathering, collective force, basis, the place of government or domination, group or tribe {*T*}.
"أَلْيَدُ الْبَيْضَاءُ" (**al-yadul baiza'o**): the argument which forms the basis of some reasoning, or clear and evident reasoning, also a person who do not dwell upon or stress the philanthropy after giving something. The one who gives without even asking {*T*}.

Muheet says it means blessing, power, pride and fame {*M*}.

The Quran mentions "يد بيضاء" (**yad eybaize**) several times, as in the tale of Moses (7:107, 20:22, 26:34, and 28:32). It figuratively means clear and distinct reasoning.

Lataif-ul-lugha has also supported these meanings.

About the women in *jannah*, the Quran says:

| 37:49 | consider them to be like preserved "eggs" | كَأَنَّهُنَّ بَيْضٌ مَّكْنُونٌ |

This means white, without blemish, without any defect and shiny pearls.

| 55:58 | As if they are *yaqoot* and *marjan* (rubies and pearls) (virgins whom nobody has touched earlier) | كَأَنَّهُنَّ الْيَاقُوتُ وَالْمَرْجَانُ |

"ابْيَضَّتْ" (*ibyazatto*) or "بَيَّضَتْ" (*bayyizat*): to be filled.
"ابْيَضَّتْ عَيْنَاهُ" (*ibyazzat ainah*): his eyes filled with tears {*Razi*}.

About *Yaqoob*, surah *Yusuf* says:

| 12:84 | his eyes were always full of tears due to sorrow | وَابْيَضَّتْ عَيْنَاهُ مِنَ الْحُزْنِ |

B-Y-Ain ب ى ع

"بَاعَ" (*baa*), "يَبِيْعُ" (*yabeeh*), "بَيْعًا" (*bai'a*): either to sell or buy something.

Surah *Al-Baqrah* says:

| 2:254 | The day there shall not be any buying or selling | يَوْمٌ لَا بَيْعٌ فِيهِ |

The surah goes on to say:

| 2:257 | Allah has declared *bai'a* as *halal* (permitted) and *riba* as haram (prohibited) | وَأَحَلَّ اللَّهُ الْبَيْعَ وَحَرَّمَ الرِّبَا |

Further ahead where laws about trade are given, it is said:

| 2:282 | in case of cash dealing, there is no need to write it down | أَن تَكُونَ تِجَارَةً حَاضِرَةً |
| 2:282 | when it is a matter of mutual dealing of buying and selling, then have some witnesses (and write it down as well) | وَأَشْهِدُوا إِذَا تَبَايَعْتُمْ |

From the context it is evident that it is a case where the dealing is not in cash. This shows that trade and *bai'a* are different. This is supported by the verse in surah *An-Noor*:

| 24:37 | People who trade and do *bai'a* don't ignore Allah's mention | رِجَالٌ لَّا تُلْهِيهِمْ تِجَارَةٌ وَلَا بَيْعٌ عَن ذِكْرِ اللَّهِ |

In today's language, it would mean that the difference between these two words is that "بيع" (*bai'a*) is like ordinary trading, trade or commerce {*T*}. Trade is professional trading while "بيع" (*bai'a*) is like barter.

Recall the verse in which it has been mentioned that Allah has declared "بيع" (*bai'a*) as *halal* and "ربو" (*riba*) as *haram*. *Riba* as interests will be dealt in detail in the relevant chapter. Here it is necessary to know what, according to the Quran, "بيع" (*bai'a*) is that we believe in it, and act accordingly which also includes the guidelines for trading. We cannot take as much profit as possible, this is not permitted.

Surah *At-Tatfeef* says:

83:1-3	Woe to them who (deliberately) give less or reduce. When they take measure form others, they take full, but when they give measure to others, they give less.	وَيْهِلٌ لِّلْمُطَفِّفِينَ الَّذِينَ إِذَا اكْتَالُوا عَلَى النَّاسِ يَسْتَوْفُونَ وَإِذَا كَالُوهُمْ أَو وَّزَنُوهُمْ يُخْسِرُونَ

These verses don't only mean that the measure or weight must be complete. These verses describe a very important principle of the Quranic system. Say one worker makes a pair of shoes and brings it to the shopkeeper. The shopkeeper tries his utmost to buy the pair of shoes at the lowest price possible,

That is, they take full measure, but do not give accordingly. When a customer approaches such a person, he tries to get the highest possible price from him. It is such trader's mentality which the Quran has described as the reason for social destruction. This "earning" has been called "تطفيف" (*tatfeef*). Why does the shopkeeper give the lowest possible price to the workman? Or in other words, why is the worker (the cobbler in this example) compelled to sell at the lowest price? Simply because he does not have any "capital". As such, the "profit" acquired this way on the strength of capital is not permitted.

The question now remains as to what profit the shopkeeper should get. For one thing, he employs investment; secondly he works the whole day at the shop. The rule according to the Quran is that:

53:39	for a man it is (only) what he works for	لَّيْسَ لِلْإِنسَانِ إِلَّا مَا سَعَى

Thus this shopkeeper deserves the return for his labor, not a profit on the capital. For this, it needs to be determined as to what the shopkeeper should get for a day's work. He cannot take more than this share out of this business.

The economics rule of the Quran's is:

2:279	you should not give anybody a loss nor should anyone give you a loss	لاَتَظْلِمُونَ وَلاَتُظْلَمُونَ

This means that you should not commit any excess on anybody and nobody should commit any excess on you. Since there is no labor in interest, and only an interest on the capital is received, that is why only the principal amount is allowed to be taken back. In "بيع" (*bai'a*), since there is basic plus labor, therefore it is permissible to take the basic along with the compensation for the labor, not more. This will work till the whole economic system adopts the Quranic way, thereafter the entire responsibility for the necessities of life will be on society (the state) and there would be no profit taking at all.

Therefore, where capital alone fetches an earning (without any labour) will not be permitted in an Islamic society. "رِبٰوا" (*riba*) is only with capital and "بيع" (*bai'a*) is capital plus labor. In "بيع" (*bai'a*), the compensation for labor can be earned.

"بيع" (*bai'a*) also means mutual agreement *{T}*.

According to the Quran, there is sort of trade or "بيع" (*bai'a*) between a **Momin** and God:

9:111	Verily, Allah has traded their lives and possessions for *janna* (heaven).	إِنَّ اللَّهَ اشْتَرَى مِنَ الْمُؤْمِنِينَ أَنفُسَهُمْ وَأَمْوَالَهُم بِأَنَّ لَهُمُ الْجَنَّةَ

It is obvious from this that man is actually the owner of neither his wealth, nor his life. Both things are only lent to him for safe-keeping. In return, he is granted heavenly bliss in this world as well as in the Hereafter. The details are to be found in my book *Nizaam-e-Raboobiyat*.

In reality, this pact is between Man and the central authority of the system which manifests itself to implement the laws of Allah in this world (initially with the Messenger and later on with other leaders succeeding him). This is the pact which is committed at the time of accepting Islam, as it is mentioned in surah **Al-Mumtaneha**:

60:12	O **Nabi**, when **Momin** women come to you for this pact	يَا أَيُّهَا النَّبِيُّ إِذَا جَاءَكَ الْمُؤْمِنَاتُ يُبَايِعْنَكَ

It is renewed when this system is in great difficulties and when the **Momineen** have to come out fearlessly for battle.

This was the same pact which the **Momineen** committed themselves to at **Hudaibiya** and which has been mentioned in surah **Al-Fateh** in these words:

48:10	Those who make a pact with you actually are making a pact with Allah, and apparently your hand is over theirs, but actually it is the hand of Allah.	إِنَّ الَّذِينَ يُبَايِعُونَكَ إِنَّمَا يُبَايِعُونَ اللَّهَ يَدُ اللَّهِ فَوْقَ أَيْدِيهِمْ

You see how a pact actually is made with Allah? The pact is in fact made with the system's center, which is based on the laws of Allah. This was the pact which was made in exchange for one's life and possessions, but when **Deen** (system of life) turned into religious **Sufism**, then "بيع" (*bai'a*) became a theory instead of a practical principle.

"أَلْبِيْعَة" (*al-be'a*) is the **Knesset** of the Jews or church of the Christians *{T}* as used in 22:40.

Latif-ul-lugha says that **Knesset** is the Jews' place for prayer and "أَلْبِيْعَة" (*al-be'a*) is the prayer place of the Christians.

According to **Allama Iqbal**:

Either continuous chanting towards emptiness of the sky	یا وسعتِ افلاک میں تکبیر مسلسل
Or continuous chanting while embracing the dust	یا خاک کے آغوش میں تسبیح و مناجات
That is the religion of strong men while they are lost in divine search.	وہ مذہب مردانِ خود آگاہ و خدا مست
This is merely the religion of priests suited for those who have no ability of progression.	یہ مذہب ملا و نباتات و جمادات

B-Y-N   ب ی ن

"اَلْبَیْنْ" (*al-bain*): separation, parting, to be separate or to separate. Some linguists think that it holds the contradictory meanings of both separating and meeting, but it is a weak argument. The right usage is "فَصّلٌ" (*faslun*): to separate. **Ibn Faris** says this is what the word actually means.
"اَلْبَیْنُ" (*al-baino*) is the distance between two pieces of land.
"بَانُوْا بَیْنًا" (*baanu baina*): that they parted or got separated.
"بَانَ الشَّیْیُ" (*baanush shaiyi*): the thing was cut off, parted away.
"ضَرَبَہُ فَاَبَانَ رَأْسَہُ" (*zarabahu fa"abaana rasahu*): "he hit him and separated his head from his shoulders".
"طَلَاقٌ بَائِنٌ" (*talaq bainun*) is the final divorce after which man and wife are separated {*T*}.

This is only a linguistic term, because according to the Quran "طلاق" (*talaq*) as divorce, is the ending off a contract of "نکاح" (*nikah*), meaning marriage. See heading **(Te-L-Q)**.

"بَیْنَ" (*baina*): the center between two things {*T*}.
"اَلْبَیَانْ" (*al-bayan*): for something to makes its advent, to become clear, to appear.
"بَیَّنُ الشَّجَرُ" (*bayyanush shajar*): leaves of a tree when they appear, like when buds etc. become evident.
"بَیَّنَ الْقَرْنُ" (*bainul qaran*): the horn appeared.

Muheet's compiler says "بَیَانْ" (*bayaan*) is something with logic or reasoning which clarifies a matter. The Quran uses "تَبْیِنْ" (*tabyeen*) against "کَتْمْ" (*katam*) in 3:186 and 2:159. "کَتْمْ" (*katam*): to hide something. As such, "تَبْیِیْنْ" (*tabyeen*) would mean to highlight something, make it evident. At another place this word has been used against "اِخْفَاءْ" (*ikhfaa*) which means to hide, as in 5:15. At the same place, the Quran has been called "کَتَاب مُبَیِّنْ" (*kitabun mubeen*) which means the life format which makes the hidden truths evident. It is also understood as the life's manual which contains clear truths, which are not related to this physical world and are beyond Man's comprehension. They are revealed to the Messenger by God through Revelation. To reveal the truth this way, is called "تَبْیَانْ" (*tibyaan*).

That is why the Quranic truths are called "بَيِّنَاتٌ" (*bayyenaat*) which means the truths He has manifested Himself. If He had not disclosed them, then they would have remained hidden. So far we have talked about the hidden truths which God has revealed to the Messenger through Revelation. Now, let us look at the next stage.

There is only one way in which God reveals the truths and it is known as revelation. Revelation is reserved for the Messenger only, but the human mind also gave birth to the concept of revelation from Allah to others than Messenger and called it "الہام" (*ilhaam*) or "کشف" (*kashaf*). For details see heading *(L-He-M)*. The man can only benefit from the truths of "کشف" (*kashaf*) or "الہام" (*ilham*) on whom it appears, and they cannot be transmitted. The Quran says that this concept is wrong. "کشف" (*kashaf*) from God means that the truths must be made known to others. This "کشف" (*kashaf*) is made from God through one individual (Messenger) to the whole of the human race. Whoever gets these revelations, have a duty to ponder over them and relay them to others.

This is the great truth that is mentioned in surah *An-Nahal*:

16:44	And We have revealed unto you this law of life so that what has been revealed, you may reveal to the people so that they may deliberate over it	وَأَنزَلْنَا إِلَيْكَ الذِّكْرَ لِتُبَيِّنَ لِلنَّاسِ مَا نُزِّلَ إِلَيْهِمْ وَلَعَلَّهُمْ يَتَفَكَّرُونَ

In other words, the Quran has said that "Allah revealed this Book to His messenger "أَنزَلْنَا إِلَيْكَ" (*anzalna ilaik*). But, in reality, this book has been revealed for all mankind "مَاۤ أُنزِلَ إِلَيْهِمْ" (*ma unzela ilaihium*)

Therefore, it is the Messengers duty (not to keep it to him as was wrongly believed in the case of *kashaf* and *ilham*), but to make it known to all mankind "لِتُبَيِّنَ لِلنَّاسِ" (*letubayyena lin naas*), and to take it to them "بَلِّغْ مَاۤ أُنزِلَ إِلَيْكَ مِن رَّبِّكَ" (*baligh ma unzela ilaika mir rabbik*) (5:67). Fie upon those who hide it.

Surah *Al-Baqrah* says:

2:159	Those who hide what we have openly or with guidance revealed, after that We have made it known to all in the Quran, they deserve God's *laana* and *laana* of all those who do *laana*.	إِنَّ الَّذِينَ يَكْتُمُونَ مَا أَنزَلْنَا مِنَ الْبَيِّنَاتِ وَالْهُدَى مِن بَعْدِ مَا بَيَّنَّاهُ لِلنَّاسِ فِي الْكِتَابِ أُولَٰئِكَ يَلْعَنُهُمُ اللَّهُ وَيَلْعَنُهُمُ اللَّاعِنُونَ

For the meaning of *laana*, see heading *(L-Ain-N)*. It follows that:

2:160	But those people who gave this act up, and reformed, and made evident or disclosed (whatever we had revealed), these are the people who I return to	إِلَّا الَّذِينَ تَابُوا وَأَصْلَحُوا وَبَيَّنُوا فَأُولَٰئِكَ أَتُوبُ عَلَيْهِمْ وَأَنَا التَّوَّابُ الرَّحِيمُ

The Book that was revealed to the Messenger (The Quran) was said to have the following characteristics.

| 16:89 | We have revealed this Book to you to clarify all matters | وَنَزَّلْنَا عَلَيْكَ الْكِتَابَ تِبْيَانًا لِّكُلِّ شَىْءٍ |

In other words, all was revealed through Revelation, and nothing in this context was to remain hidden.

At another place, it is said:

| 2:187 | This way God reveals His orders for the people so that they may observe them. | كَذَلِكَ يُبَيِّنُ اللّهُ آيَاتِهِ لِلنَّاسِ لَعَلَّهُمْ يَتَّقُونَ |

As such, this is the portrayal of the truth for all mankind:

| 3:138 | This is a clarification for all humanity | هَذَا بَيَانٌ لِّلنَّاسِ |

The Right and Wrong paths have both been made clear and distinct in it:

| 5:15 | This is the completely clear and distinct book | كِتَابٌ مُّبِينٌ |
| 15:79 | This is the completely clear and distinct path | إِمَامٍ مُّبِينٍ |

It is (a beacon of) light:

| 5:15 | surely you received *noor* (light) from Allah and a clear Book | قَدْ جَاءَكُم مِّنَ اللّهِ نُورٌ وَكِتَابٌ مُّبِينٌ |

Light is not dependent on anything else to manifest itself. It is intrinsically, and anyone who uses his intellect can illuminate other things with this light. It makes every other thing very clear, that is why it is also called "تَفْصِيْلَ كُلّ شَىْءٍ" (*tafseela kulli shjayi*) in 12:111.

"تَفْصِيْلَ" (*tafseel*): in detail, to display clearly by separating everything. See heading (*F-Sd-L*).

This is the truth about the Quran which has been given to mankind by God, through His Messenger. At the same time, He made it known as to what the Quranic method of "تَبْيِيْن" (*tabyeen*) or explaining is.

Surah *Al-Anaam* says:

| 6:105 | In this manner, We repeat things so that they say that you have clearly expostulated everything, and so that We disclose them to those who use their knowledge | وَكَذَلِكَ نُصَرِّفُ الآيَاتِ وَلِيَقُولُواْ دَرَسْتَ وَلِنُبَيِّنَهُ لِقَوْمٍ يَعْلَمُونَ |

In other words, the Quran can be understood with the help of deliberation and knowledge.

"أَلْبَيِّنَة" (*al-bayyinah*): reasoning which can be felt logically {T}. The plural form is "بَيِّنَاتٌ" (*bayyinaat*).

The Quran mentions one characteristic of man as "عَلَّمَهُ الْبَيَانَ" (*allamahul bayaan*) in 55:3. This means that God has endowed him with the ability to express his thoughts. In other words, Man has the ability to communicate with others through his tongue or pen. This ability discriminates man from other animals, and is a great tool when forming human civilization and evolving.

"بَيْنَ" (*bain*): to be in between.

2:113	God decides between them	فَاللَّهُ يَحْكُمُ بَيْنَهُم

For "بَيْنَ يَدَيْهِ" (*baina yadeehi*), see heading **(Y-D-Y)**.
"اِسْتَبَانَ الْأَمْرُ" (*istabanal amr*): that the matter broke open, became detailed and clear.

The Quran says:

6:55	This is how we clarify the indications to the path of criminals or wrongdoers	وَكَذَلِكَ نَفَصِّلُ الْآيَاتِ وَلِتَسْتَبِينَ سَبِيلُ الْمُجْرِمِينَ

"تَبَيَّنَ الشَّيْءُ" (*tabayyenush shaiyi*): that the thing became evident and distinct.
"تَبَيَّنْتُهُ" (*tabayyantehu*): that I opened it, made it evident and comprehended it, as used in 49:6.

T ت

21:57	Swear by Allah.	تَاللَّهِ

Al-Sualibi writes in *Fiqh-ul-Lugha* that "تَاء" (*ta*) is not used except with Allah's names.

"يَأَبَتِ" (*ya abat*) appears several places in the Quran, and means "*O my father*", as in 14:2. Here this letter has been used as "ى" (*yah*). This is exclusive with "*ab*".

Taboot تَابُوْتٌ

"تَابُوْتٌ" (*taboot*) means "box", as in 20:39 *{T}*.

Raghib says it also means "the heart" and "chest".

Lissan-ul-Arab supports this opinion, as it has been used in 2:248. Accordingly, it would mean such a heart which is full of peace and contentment and has the support of the universal forces (*malaikah*), so that it stays stable.

Taloot was endowed with such a heart, and if figurative meanings are not attributed to this word, then it would mean the coffin which the Bible mentions.

Some think that it has come from "تَابَ" (*tab*). See heading (T-W-B).

T-B-B   ت ب ب

"اَلتَّبُّ" (*at-tub*): loss.

"اَلتَّبَابُ" (*at-tabaabo*), "اَلتَّبِيبُ" (*at-tabeebo*), "اَلتَّتْبِيبُ" (*at-tatbeebo*): loss, annihilation and destruction *{T}*.

Surah *Hoodh* says:

| 11:101 | it only increased their loss (increased their destruction) | وَمَا زَادُوهُمْ غَيْرَ تَتْبِيبٍ |

Surah *Al-Momin* says:

| 40:37 | And whatever *Firoun* planned, was nothing else then destruction | وَمَا كَيْدُ فِرْعَوْنَ إِلَّا فِيْ تَبَابٍ |

"تَبَّ فُلَاناً" (*tubba fulana*): he killed that man.

"اَسْتَتَبَّ الرَّجُلُ" (*istatabbar rajal*): the man became weak and old, became unable *{T}*.

"اَلتَّابُّ" (*at-taab*): old and weak man, camel or donkey whose back has become bent, which makes him/it unable to work *{T}*.

The Quran says:

| 111:1 | *Abu Lahab's* both hands were destroyed and he too was annihilated | تَبَّتْ يَدَا أَبِيْ لَهَبٍ وَتَبَّ |

He was himself destroyed and the system due to which he opposed Allah's system was destroyed as well. He became unable to oppose, was destroyed, and encountered great loss. In *Raghib*'s words, "was in continuous loss".

T-B-R   ت ب ر

"اَلتِّبْرُ" (*at-tibr*): gold. Some say this word is also used for silver as well as gold, especially if they are in ore form and not purified.

"اَلتَّبْرُ" (*at-tabr*): to break, to annihilate *{T}*. Ibn Faris has recorded these two meanings for this word as well.

| 25:39 | We turned them into pieces, annihilated them, and destroyed them. | وَكُلًّا تَبَّرْنَا تَتْبِيْراً |

"تَبَارَأَ" (*tabara*): annihilation as used in 71:28.

"مَتَبَّرٌ" (*mutabbar*): annihilated, destroyed, and turned to pieces (all as adjectives) in 7:139.

T-B-Ain   ع ب ت

"تَبِعَ" (*ta'beh*): to walk behind, follow.

"بَقَرَةٌ مُتْبِعٌ" (*baqaratun mutbeh*): a cow which has its calf walking behind it (following it), and the following calf is called "تَبِيعٌ" (*tabeeh*).

"اَلتَّبَعُ" (*at-tabah*): those who follow. It is the plural of "تَابِعٌ" (*taabeh*).

"اَتْبَعْتُهُمْ" (*atba'tum*): I followed him, he had gone ahead but I caught up with him {T}.

The Quran has used "تَبِعَ" (*tabeh*) against "عَصَى" (*asi*) or mutiny in 14:36. As such, "اِتِّبَاع" (*ittebah*): loyalty towards Allah's laws. It means to follow His laws. Against this is the person who reverts.

3:134	And whoever turns on his heels	وَمَن يَنقَلِبْ عَلَىٰ عَقِبَيْهِ

Deen is a collective system, therefore the laws of Allah will not be obeyed individually or selectively, but obeisance will be subject to the whole system. This system was first formulated by, our Messenger, and therefore the obedience to Allah's laws was through obedience to him, as stated in 7:157. After him, the system moved ahead, and the obedience of the Caliphs (the four Caliphs who came after him) took the same place. That is why the Quran has instructed not to revert to old ways after the death of Messenger, but continue obeying. See 3:143.

Note that "اتباع" (*itbah*) and "اطاعت" (*ita'a*) have a minor difference, like to follow and to obey. Definitely "اطاعت" (*ita'a*) means following as well as obedience, which is done for the sake of the mentor, but it does have a connotation of an order or moral requirement. "اتباع" (*itbah*), on the other hand, is following at one's own will due to love, or attraction, but not due to some order or requirement.

"اَلتَّابِعُ" (*at-tabeh*) or "اَلتَّبِيْعُ" (*at-tabeeh*): a servant {T}. The plural of "تَابِعٌ" (*tabeh*) is "اَلتَّابِعِيْنَ" (*at-tab'een*) as used in 24:31. However, the meaning of "تَبِيْعاً" (*tabeeaa*) in 17:69 is of prosecutor in a case, or one who questions, somebody who demands your answers (for payment of your debt).

Surah **Ash-shura** uses the word "اَتَّبَاعٌ" (*ittebah*), which means to bring out a procession. In other words, to put the victorious sorcerers in front, and take them in a procession, as in 26:40.

"تَبَعَ" (*Taba'*): to talk about a second thing in relation to the first. For incidents to occur continuously, one after another {T}. "اَلتُّبَّع" (*at-tooba*) was the title of the kings of Yemen, because they ascended the throne in a continuous line {T}.

The Quran mentions the nation of **Tubbah** in 50:14. This has been detailed in a separate heading. See heading **Tubbah**.

The **Kitab-il-Ashqaq** mentions the meaning of "النُّبَّعُ" (*at-tubba*) as shade, perhaps because a shade moves along with the relative source of light.

Tubb'a نُبَّعٌ

Surah **Qaf** says:

50:14	The fellowship of **al-ayka** and the nation of **Tubb'a**, all denied our Messengers.	وَأَصْحَابُ الْأَيْكَةِ وَقَوْمُ نُبَّعٍ كُلٌّ كَذَّبَ الرُّسُلَ

At another place it is said with reference to the **Quresh** tribe:

44:37	Are they any better than the nation of **Tubb'a**?	أَهُمْ خَيْرٌ أَمْ قَوْمُ نُبَّعٍ

In **Suleman**'s tale, it is said that in eastern **Yemen**, the nation of **Saba** ruled. One branch of this nation, the **Himyar** was settled in western Yemen. When the Romans destroyed the economy of **Saba**, the economy of **Himyar** started to boom, and they became a wealthy and powerful nation. At first the people there were star worshippers, like the people of **Saba**, but later they became Jews. One of the kings of this dynasty adopted the title of **Tubb'a,** which means Sultan.

When during the time of king **Zunawas**, Christians started preaching Christianity, he became very angry. He attacked the centre of Christianity, which was **Najraan**. The citizens of this city resisted at first but succumbed later. **Zunawas's** bias reached its peak and turned to barbarism. Anyone who refused to accept Judaism was thrown into big pits of fire. This army of **Zunawas** has been mentioned in the Quran (85:4-9) as "أَصْحَابُ الْأُخْدُودِ" (*ashabul ukhood*), or the people of **Ukhdood**, and condemned this oppression by them. This is because the purpose of the Quran is to stop oppression, regardless who perpetrates it against whom.

T-J-R ت ج ر

"تِجَارَةٌ" (*tijarah*): professional trade which includes buying and selling.
Raghib says "تَجَارَةٌ" (*tijarah*): to employ the principal (amount) for making a profit.
Muheet says the word also means the goods which are traded.
"تَاجِرٌ" (*tajir*) is a professional buyer and seller. The Arabs also used to call one who sold wine as "تَاجِرٌ" (*tajir*). Figuratively, "تَجَارَةٌ" (*tijarah*) is also cleverness or expertise (in something), and an expert is a "تَاجِرٌ" (*tajir*) {M}.

The Quran says:

2:16	their buying and selling made them no profit	فَمَا رَبِحَت تِجَارَتُهُمْ

This means that their adoption of the wrong path as against the right one brought them no gain.

The Quran has equated **Imaan** (Islam) with "تِجَارَةٌ" (*tijarah*), or a sort of trading in which a sort of buying and selling takes place.

Surah **At-Tauba** says:

9:111	verily Allah has bought the lives and possessions of the **momineens** and endowed them with **janna** in return:	إِنَّ اللَّهَ اشْتَرَى مِنَ الْمُؤْمِنِينَ أَنفُسَهُمْ وَأَمْوَالَهُم بِأَنَّ لَهُمُ الْجَنَّةَ

In this trading, the **momineen** hand over their lives and possessions for a society that observes Allah's laws, and in turn that society provides them with a life fit for paradise in this world (and they get **janna** in the life of Hereafter as well)

This is the sort of trading about which it is mentioned in another verse:

61:10-11	O group of **momineen**! Would you like me to tell you about a trade which will deliver you from a painful punishment? That trade is for you to have faith in Allah and his Rusool. And struggle in the way of Allah with your lives and possessions. If you employ knowledge and insight, you will know how beneficial this trade is for you. The benefits of this trade are more beneficial than ordinary trade	يَا أَيُّهَا الَّذِينَ آمَنُوا هَلْ أَدُلُّكُمْ عَلَى تِجَارَةٍ تُنجِيكُم مِّنْ عَذَابٍ أَلِيمٍ تُؤْمِنُونَ بِاللَّهِ وَرَسُولِهِ وَتُجَاهِدُونَ فِي سَبِيلِ اللَّهِ بِأَمْوَالِكُمْ وَأَنفُسِكُمْ ذَلِكُمْ خَيْرٌ لَّكُمْ إِن كُنتُمْ تَعْلَمُونَ

Also see 26:11

As to how much profit can be taken from buying and selling, is mentioned under the heading (B-Y-Ain). The principle being that only remuneration for labor can be taken. No profit can be received on capital. This will apply to barter as well as trade. With this principle in mind, the following verse's meaning can be understood:

4:29	Don't gobble up on each other's wealth in a wrong way, excepting in trade with mutual agreement	لَا تَأْكُلُوا أَمْوَالَكُم بَيْنَكُم بِالْبَاطِلِ إِلَّا أَن تَكُونَ تِجَارَةً عَن تَرَاضٍ مِّنكُمْ

These days mutual agreement is taken to mean to demand as much profit as you would like from the customer and ask him to buy a thing if he can afford it. Then, if he still buys, it means that he is ready to pay as much profit as demanded. This is self-deception. The customer is forced by his need to pay the shopkeeper's demanded price. For the difference between barter (**bai**) and trade (**tijarah**) see heading (B-Y-Ain). The above mentioned situation cannot be called " تِجَارَةً عَن تَرَاضٍ مِّنكُم" (*tijaratan un tarazin minkum*). If the profit is return of one's labor only, and is fixed by the society, then every customer will gladly pay it. That will be a mutual willingness.

The Quran says:

4:29	don't degrade each other	وَلاَتَقْتُلُوٓاْ أَنفُسَكُمْ

This means to not degrade one's own people. To benefit from another's need is like killing or degrading your own people.

To demand just the compensation for labor is a practice described as:

2:279	neither are you oppressed nor are you the oppressor	لاَتَظْلِمُونَ وَلاَتُظْلَمُونَ

Trading in a society should be to fulfill each other's needs, not to annihilate others. If trade stands in the way of Quranic unchangeable values, then destruction will follow as the result of it. 9:24.

T-H-T   ت ح ت

"تَحْتُ" (*tahat*) is the opposite of "فَوْقُ" (*fauq*) which means over/above. So the meaning of this word is "below"

2:25	below which streams are flowing	تَجْرِىٰ مِن تَحْتِهَا الأَنْهَارُ

"اَلتُّحُوتُ" (*at-tahut*) is the plural of "تَحْتُ" (*tahat*) and means people of the lower strata.

Raghib says that "تَحْتُ" (*tahat*) doesn't mean the underside of a thing, but something which is below that thing. In this context "أَسْفَلُ" (*asfal*) shall be the underside of that thing. This means that when something is below another thing it is "تَحْتُ" (*tahat*), but the underside of that thing is "أَسْفَلُ" (*asfal*).

T-R-B   ت ر ب

"اَلتَّرْبُ" (*at-tarb*) or "اَلتُّرْبُ" (*at-turab*): the soil, ground, earth, dirt. As the words "عَلَيْهِ تُرَابٌ" (*alaihi turab*) has been used in 2:264. The plural form is "أَتْرِبَةٌ" (*aribah*) as well as "تِرْبَانٌ" (*tirbaan*)

"مَتْرَبَةٌ" (*matrabah*): poverty, or starvation.
"ذَامَتْرَبَةٍ" (*za matrabah*): to be covered with dust, needy, in misery as used in 90:16 {T}.
"جَمَل تَرَبُوتٌ" (*jamalan taraboot*): obedient as a pet or trained camel {T}
"اَلتَّرَائِبُ" (*at-traaib*) has been translated to ribs in 86:6.

"اَلتِّرْبُ" (*at-tirb*): being of the same age. Plural is "أَتْرَابٌ" (*at-traab*).

Ibn Turab says it means of being the same age and contemporary, and those are its basic meanings. It also means friend, beloved and companion.

Describing the ***Jannah***, the Quran mention words like "عُرُباً أَتْرَاباً" (***ooroban at raban***) in 56:37 and "كَوَاعِبَ أَتْرَاباً" (***kwaiba atraba***) in 78:33. These words are generally translated as wives of the same age, but it means companions which are homogenous in habits and hobbies which are cut from the same fabric.

"أَتْرَاباً" (***at-raaba***) is the adjective of "كَوَاعِبَ" (***kwaib***) and "عُرُباً" (***oroban***), thus it would mean such women who are of the same bent of mind. In other words, there will be no emotions of envy, or strangeness between them but agreement of thought etc. It can also mean mutual agreement between husband and wife. Hence the meaning is of such women who would have similar opinions and thoughts as their husbands. What sort of relationship it would be between them in the hereafter is beyond our comprehension, but in this world we all know how a household can be turned into a blissful heaven if husband and wife are in agreement. See 2:231. But since "أَتْرَابٌّ" (***atraab***) also means similar people and contemporaries, that is why there is an element of egalitarianism and equality in it as well. See heading ***(Z-W-J)***.

T-R-F   ت ر ف

"اَلتُّرْفَة" (***at-turfah***): the bliss of being plentiful, in abundance, delightful meal, a good thing {T}.
"تَرَفَ" (***taarif***): he became bountiful and happy. He got the luxuries of life.
"اَتْرَفَ" (***at-ruff***): made him happy.
"اَلْمُتْرَفُ" (***al-mutraf***): he who is living a life of luxury and is pursuing the road to pleasure and temptations, someone who is drunk with happiness and plentiful. Some think that it means a rich man, who with his wealth becomes a leader, and whatever he does is not challenged. It can also be used for a man who does what he pleases, and there is nobody to admonish him {T}, or he who due to excess of wealth, becomes mutinous.

The plural is "مُتْرَفُوْنَ" (***mutrafoon***) and "مُتْرَفِيْنَ" (***mutrafeen***).
"اَتْرَفَ فَلَانٌ" (***atraf falan***): he became mutinous and kept on disobeying.

"مُتْرَفِيْنَ" (***mutrafeen***) is an important term in the Quran . The Quran has said it is usual that whenever someone from Allah called people to the right path, then the "مُتْرَفِيْنَ" (***mutrafeen***) of the nation strongly opposed him. These are the people who thrive on others' labor and rule them as well. It is obvious that such people have no place in Allah's system. That is why they always oppose this system.

The Quran says:

| 34:33 | We have never sent anyone to warn a society, where the ***mutrafeen*** did not say that "we oppose this message that you have brought" | وَمَا أَرْسَلْنَا فِيْ قَرْيَةٍ مِّن نَّذِيْرٍ إِلَّا قَالَ مُتْرَفُوْهَا إِنَّا بِمَا أُرْسِلْتُم بِهِ كَافِرُوْنَ |

The following verse explains who these **mutrafeen** are:

34:34	They used to say "we have abundance of wealth and progeny, so who can touch us?"	وَقَالُوا نَحْنُ أَكْثَرُ أَمْوَالاً وَأَوْلَاداً

This is the same group which these days are called the capitalist group, and which acquires power on the basis of its wealth. This includes the religious leaders who do not do any work themselves but thrive on the earnings of others and rule the very same people. The Quran says that this group too is in the forefront of opposition to Allah's system and instigates people by saying that "see this revolutionary (**Rusool**), he opposes the religion that your forefathers maintained" 34:43, 43:23. These are all **mutrafeen** and Quran has called them mankind's worst enemies.

T-R-K ت ر ک

"تَرْکٌ" (**tarkun**) is to let go, to throw, also to insert, to empty.

"تَرِکَةُ الرَّجُلِ" (**terakut ul rijuli**) is the assets a person leaves behind after death.

"تَرِیْکَة" (**tareekatunh**) is a woman whom nobody marries. It also means an egg-shell, from which the chick has hatched out {T}.

"اَلتَّرِیْکُ" (**al-tareeku**) is a bunch which has been stripped of all its fruit or eaten up {T}.

Some maintain it to mean abandoning a job, regardless if it is done intentionally or unwillingly. It includes both scenarios. Hence it means to abandon a job one was conducting, or to become careful from doing it. To avoid it, is "تَرَکَ" (**tarka**) as well. Hence Ibn Faris says that a garden where its keeper does not pay attention to it, and avoid its maintenance, is called "اَلتَّرِیْکُ" (**at-tareek**). But the work that is abandoned because of one's weakness of not being able to do it cannot be called "تَرْکٌ" (**tarkun**) according to **Muheet**.

"تَرَکَ" (**taraka**) is also used instead of "جَعَلَ" (**ja'la**). This means "to give it a shape".

"تَارَکَهُ" (**taarakahu**) is to keep the matter in the state that it was in before {T, L}.

It also means to give a matter a state of permanence, for example as given in the following verse:

37:78	We have kept the discussion open for the next generation	وَتَرَکْنَا عَلَیْهِ فِی الْآخِرِینَ

This means that it has been given continuity.

T-S-Ain   ت س ع

"تِسْعَةُ رِجَالٍ" (*tisatun rijaalin*): nine men.

"تِسْعُ نِسْوَةٍ" (*tisu' niswatin*): nine women.

"تِسْعُ آيَاتٍ" (*tisu' aayaatin*): nine signs (27:12).

"تِسْعَةَ عَشَرَ" (*tisa'tah a'shara*): nineteen (overseers) (74-30).

"تِسْعٌ وَتِسْعُونَ نَعْجَةً" (*tis'u wa ts'ona ja'jah*): "ninety nine sheep" (38:23).

T-Ain-S   ت ع س

Ibn Faris has stated its fundamental meaning to be "to turn".

"ٱلتَّعْسَ" (*at-ta'su*): to fall flat on one's face and be incapable of getting up. It also means to stagger, death, to be degraded and deterioration.

"تَعَسَهُ الله" (*ta a'saullah*): Allah destroyed them.

"فَهُوَ مَتْعُوسٌ" (*fahuwa matu'sun*): hence he was destroyed.

"تَعْسالَهُ" (*ta'saan lahu*): to curse someone {T}.

The Quran says:

47:8	the people who opted to reject and to rebel, for them there is death and destruction, disgrace and adversity	وَالَّذِينَ كَفَرُوا فَتَعْساً لَّهُمْ

T-F-Th   ت ف ث

"ٱلتَّفَثُ" (*al-tafthu*) Taj-Ul-Uroos, has stated with reference to other dictionaries, that this word does not appear in the poetry of the pre-Islamic era. Hence its literal meaning cannot be given. In commentaries though, "تَفَثٌ" (*tafathun*) is given as, 'shaving of one's head', 'rami (casting stones)' and 'animal sacrifice' rituals of the *Hajj* {T, R}.

Muheet said that "ٱلتَّفَثُ" (*al-tafthu*) does not only mean dishevelling, but also confusion and anxiety.

Ibn Abbas said that "تَفَثٌ" (*tafathun*) stands for all the rituals of *Hajj*. He includes the cutting or shaving off the hair, trimming the moustache or the hair of the armpit in the meaning of this word.

Thus Quran says:

22:29	then it is required that they should complete their *tafath*	ثُمَّ لْيَقْضُوا تَفَثَهُمْ

"تَفِثَ لِرَّجُلُ يَتْفَثُ" (*tafitha al rijaalu yutfathu*) is when a person stops grooming his hair, thus the hair become dishevelled and disturbed {M}. As given above, the Quran states in verse 22:29 "then it is required that they should complete their *tafath*". If this is limited to the activities of

Hajj, then it would mean the grooming of hair only. But if the metaphoric meanings are taken, then it would mean to consider the ways to remove the traumas and troubles of the whole community.

The *Hajj* is the universal gathering to consider the solution of removing traumas and troubles of the community. See heading (H-L-Q) for the details of shaving head during Hajj.

T-Q-N   ت ق ن

"التَّقَنُ" (*al-tiqnu*) is a skilled person *{T, M}*. It means all the expertise necessary to establish an economic system; the thing that helps to solve an issue; an example is of the expertise in mineralogy; anything that may help in correcting something *{T}*.

Ibn Faris gives these fundamental meanings:
-   To strengthen some thing
-   Sticky black soil.

"أَتْقَنَ الْأَمْرَ اِتْقَاناً" (*at-taqan al amra itqaa nan*): To firmly establish an issue *{T, M}*.

The Quran states in relation to Allah:

27:88	He has created everything absolutely proper and firmly	أَتْقَنَ كُلَّ شَىْءٍ

In Quran, wherein by describing the attributes of God, the true concept of His is revealed. At the same time it establishes the fact that individuals, nations, society or a system that follows Allah's laws, will develop the same attributes within the limits of its humanness.

For example:

27:88	It is Allah's attribute that He has created everything perfect	صُنْعَ اللَّهِ الَّذِىٓ أَتْقَنَ كُلَّ شَىْءٍ

It is to show that everything the community of believers produces will be as near perfect. It will have neither slack nor wrinkles in it, and it will not be weak or incomplete.

In the scheme of nature it is vehemently asserted, as is in verse 67:3

67:3	you will not find lack of proper proportion in the creation of Rahman, the most merciful	كه مَّا تَرَى فِىْ خَلْقِ الرَّحْمَنِ مِن تَفَاوُتٍ

Similarly one will have the assurance of perfection and balance in things established by the believers.

Hence, it can be deduced from this as to how much the above group would be the cause of peaceful and satisfactory coexistence for humanity. This is just one of the aspects of Allah's attributes. Imagine the condition of a nation that possesses such attributes of Allah!

Tilka   تِلْكَ

"تِلْكَا" (*tilka*) is used for something distant, 'that'. It is a feminine form.
For details see heading "ذَا" (*zaa*).

T-L-L   ت ل ل

The fundamental meaning of "تَلّ" (*tallu*) is the land that is considerably higher than the surroundings.

"اَلتَّلُّ مِنَ التُّرَاب" (*al-latllu min turaab*) is a mound of dirt.

"اَلتَّلُّ" (*at-tallo*): a pillow or mattress. It also means to spread or to put down on the mound. It may be from "تَلِيْلٌ" (*talilun*) which means the neck and cheeks. Hence it would mean, to drop someone on the neck and the face.

"تَلَّهُ" (*tallahu*), "يَتِلُّهُ" (*yatilluhu*) and "تَلًّا" (*tallan*): that he has thrown someone down.

"قَوْمٌ تَلَّى" (*qoum-un talla*) is a nation that has been thrown down.

"تَلَّ" (*tallu*), "يَتِلُّ" (*yatllu*) is to be thrown down, to fall down, to fall.

"اَلتَّلَّةُ" (*at-tallatuh*) is to fall, to put down (once).

"اَلْمِتَلُّ" (*al-mitalu*) is the place for the above; or the spear with which someone is put down.

"اَلتَّلَّى" (*allutla*) is the slaughtered goat {*T, M, R*}

In Quran is given:

37:108	he put him down on his side (on his temple)	وَتَلَّهُ لِلْجَبِيْنِ

T-L-W   ت ل و

"تَلَوْتُهُ" (*talutuhu*), "تَلَيْتُهُ" (*talaituhu*): that I followed him.

"اَتْلَيْتُهُ إِيَّاهُ" (*atlaituhu iyyaahu*): that I made him follow in his footsteps.

"تَلُوٌّ" (*taloowan*) is the person who always follows.

"اَلتُّلُوُ" (*attiloo*) is a thing that follows another, for example, the young animal that follows its mother.

"اَتْلَتِ النَّاقَةُ" (*atlati an naaqatih*) is the baby camel that follows its mother.

"اَلتَّوَالِيْ و التَّالِيَاتُ" (*at-tawaalee wat taaliyaatu*): the back parts.

"اَلتَّلِيَّةُ" (*at-taleeyatuh*) and "الثَّلاَوَةُ" (*at-tulaawatuh*) is the remaining unpaid portion of a debt.

Raghib states that "تلاوة" (*tilaawatunh*): to follow in the footsteps or to obey. This could be in a physical sense or in the sense of obedience to somebody.

"تَلَا" (tala) means to follow somebody in a way that nobody else comes in between. This sometimes occurs physically and sometimes means to follow in spirit. In this meaning the root of the word is "تُلُوٌّ" (tuluwwun) or "وَتْلُو" (watilwu). When it means to read or deliberate then its root is "تِلَاوَةٌ" (tilawah).

The example of following physically is of the Moon:

| 61:2 | the moon follows the Sun and benefits from its light | وَالْقَمَرِ إِذَاتَلَاهَا |

"تَتَلَّاهُ تَتَلِّيًا" (talaalahu tatallian): he followed behind him.
"تَتَلَّيْتُ حَقِّيْ" (tatalliyatu haqqyi): I followed him and extracted my full dues from him {T, M}

For the obedience of divine laws, it is mandated to 'study' the Quran. According to *Raghib*, "تِلَاوَةٌ" (tilaawa) is especially meant for the obedience of Divine Scriptures. In order to obey these laws, it is essential firstly to understand the given instructions in them. Hence this too is termed as "تِلَاوَةٌ" (tilaawa), but it is a particularized form of "قِرَأَةٌ" (qiraa a) (to read). However "قِرَأَةٌ" (qiraa) is inclusive of "تلاوة" (tilaawa) (to obey, but not the other way round). Therefore, "تلاوة" (tilawa) as reading of the Quran, means to study it in order to follow its instructions (not merely to recite it).

"تَلَاهُ" (talaahu) also means "he has been set free", in a way that he then follows behind (**Ibn Faris**).

In The Quran is given:

| 2:121 | Those who have been given this book, they read (*tilaawath*) it in a honest way, and these are the people who have trust in the book | الَّذِينَ آتَيْنَاهُمُ الْكِتَابَ يَتْلُونَهُ حَقَّ تِلَاوَتِهِ أُولَئِكَ يُؤْمِنُونَ بِهِ |

Therefore, obviously it can only mean to obey the book, because it has been said that 'these people have trust in the book'. If it had meant as merely to recite, then even non-believers read Quran. Hence Quran's *tilaawa* is to obey it's given instructions. It is read, so that it can be understood and it can then be obeyed. Otherwise it would be a futile exercise just to recite it. The Quran said that a **Momin** is one who follows it implicitly.

In Quran, it is given with reference to the Messenger:

| 3:163 | he presents Allah's laws to the community | يَتْلُو عَلَيْهِمْ آيَاتِهِ |

It says that he simultaneously provided the resources, for the development of their potentials. See heading **(Z-K-W)**.

It is apparent then, when it is asked to read the Quran, that Allah's system of laws should be demonstrably implemented so that it's tangible and constructive outcomes are obvious.

Therefore it is self-deception to think that just by reciting the Quran, its purpose is fulfilled. Hence it is imperative to read and understand and then to act on its teaching. Otherwise just reciting it is futile.

The Quran says in surah **As-Saffah**:

37:3	the community that obeys the Quran	فَالتَّالِيَاتِ ذِكْرًا

In surah **Al-Baqarah**, of the charge against the Jews is that:

2:102	These people follow the **Shaitan** (the enemy of Allah's way) who has spread falsehood against the kingdom of Solomon	وَاتَّبَعُوا مَا تَتْلُوا الشَّيَاطِينُ عَلَى مُلْكِ سُلَيْمَانَ

If one wishes to know, what false tales have been spread by the enemies of **bani Israil's** divine Messengers, and how the Jews have propagated these tales as divine revelations, then one should read the Old Testament of the Bible. Therein are such falsehoods against these Messengers that any self-respecting person would not like to know.

T-M-M ت م م

"تَمَامُ الشَّيْءِ" (*tamamush-shaiyi*): something that adds to the completion of a thing.

Ibn Faris gives its fundamental meaning as 'complete'.

Some maintain that "تَمَامٌ" (*tamaamun*) and "كَمَالٌ" (*kamaalun*) are synonymous, but others maintain that "تَمَامٌ" (*tamaamun*) is to contribute towards the completion of a thing and "كَمَالٌ" (*kamaalun*) is the finite limit to which a thing has developed, or to accomplish the purpose for which a thing was made. For example "رَجُلٌ تَامُ الْخَلْقِ" (*rajulun taamul khalqi*) means "such a man who has no constitutional defects".

"كَامِلُ الْخَلْقِ" (*kaamilun khalqi*): something that has attained the maximum perfection and beauty. So, it goes a step further than "تَمَامٌ" (*tamaamun*) {T}.
"تَمَّ الشَّيْءُ" (*tamma al shaiyi*): the thing is complete.
"تَمَّ عَلَيْهِ" (*tamma alaihi*): the person remained steadfast.
"أَتَمَّ الشَّيْءَ" (*at tammash-shaiyi*): he completed the thing {T}.

It is given in Quran:

2:124	When the Creator gave the resources for Ibrahim to develop himself, he with his steadfastness and persistence, achieved it to its fullest extent and proved that he had no shortcomings left in him what so ever	وَإِذِ ابْتَلَى إِبْرَاهِيمَ رَبُّهُ بِكَلِمَاتٍ فَأَتَمَّهُنَّ

In Surah **Al-Maidah** is given:

| 5:3 | Now We have established your authority and control to its fullest extent, that is to say that there was no rebellious power left to oppose you and your life system was fully developed, and whatever shortcomings were there, We removed them | اَلْيَوْمَ اَكْمَلْتُ لَكُمْ دِيْنَكُمْ وَاَتْمَمْتُ عَلَيْكُمْ نِعْمَتِيْ |

This means that the opponents who were at loggerheads with the Messenger for years have been made to surrender. Though **Deen** (the system of Allah) had made progress even after the Messenger's death. If **Deen** is taken to mean the way of Islam, then the meaning could be the completion of the **deen** which reached its zenith in the Quran.

In Surah **Al-Ana'm** it is given:

| 6:116 | Whatever was left to be implemented of Allah's laws, was done with truth and balance and so there is none to make any changes in it | وَتَمَّتْ كَلِمَتُ رَبِّكَ صِدْقاً وَّعَدْلاً لاَمُبَدِّلَ لِكَلِمٰتِهِ |

Thus the Code (**ad-Deen**) was completed so there is no need to add to the divine laws or make any change, then there is no reason for a new messenger to come.

"مُتِمٌّ" (**mutimmun**): "the one who completes a thing (61:8).

Tannaur تَنُّوْرٌ

"اَلتَّنُّوْرُ" (**at-tannawarun**), some say that its root is "نَارٌ" (**naarun**). See (**N-W-R**). But some maintain that this word is Persian. The Arabs have Arabised it. One of its meanings is the same as in Urdu, which is of the oven (**tandoor**) for baking bread. But "اَلتَّنُّوْرُ" (**tannuwaru**) is also the pond where water collects in a valley, and hence, all such places from where water springs. It also means a raised and high ground {**T, M, Lataif-ul-Lugha**}.

The Quran mentions this word with reference to Noah's flood. It has been used in 11:40 to define the place in the valley where the water collected. That is to say, it rained so heavily that the rainwater formed a flood.

T-W-B   ت و ب

"تَابَ" (*taaba*), "تَوْبًا" (*tawban*), "تَوْبَةً" (*towbatan*), "مَتَابًا" (*mataaban*): all these words include the sense of returning {T}. An example is as if you are walking on the path (of life) and come to a crossroad, so you take a turn. After some distance you realize that you have taken a wrong turn, so to get back on the right path you have to return to the crossroad where you went wrong. This action of turning back is called "تَوْبَةٌ" (*towbah*).

It is obvious that you have to walk back to the spot from where you made the error. If you stand there all your life lamenting as to why you took the wrong turn, it would not be "تَوْبَةٌ" (*towbah*). Hence "تَوْبَةٌ" (*towbah*) is the action one takes to 'undo' the wrong that one did in the first place. This then corrects the ill effects of the error.

"تَابَ عَنْہُ" (*taaba a'nhu*) and "مَنْہُ" (*minhu*): that, one has realized ones error and stopped following on the wrong path and then started on the right path. "تَوْبَةٌ" (*towbah*) comprises of the three elements, firstly the realization of one's error, secondly to stop continuing with the error and turn back and finally to follow the right way. Such a person is called "تَائِبٌ" (*taaibun*) {T}.

Therefore Quran says:

11:114	righteous actions have the reaction to eliminate the ill effects	إِنَّ الْحَسَنَاتِ يُذْهِبْنَ السَّيِّئَاتِ

This is "تَوْبَةٌ" (*towbah*). It is important to understand a particular point here. If one robs other's right, but after sometime realizes the error and repents, then the right thing to do is to restore the person's right and make a vow that one will not rob other's right again.

The second example is, if you have some liquor, and after some time you realize that in Islam it is forbidden, the "توبہ" (*tauba*) in this case would be for you to repent and never ever touch liquor again.

In the first related example, when you took the wrong turn, the right path had left you when you realized your mistake and reverted to the right path. The right path too, which had turned away from you, (as it were) was available again. Moreover, when you took one step toward it, it took two steps toward you. Two because one was the wrong step which you retracted and the second was the step you took towards it. This is known as "تَابَ عَلَيْہِ" (*taaba alaih*), and one who does this is called "تَوَّابٌ" (*tawwab*).

The Quran says the following with regards to Allah:

110:3	He is returning	اِنَّہُ کَانَ تَوَّاباً

While the following words are regarding the people:

2:222	Indeed Allah prefer those who do *tauba*	إِنَّ اللَّهَ يُحِبُّ التَّوَّابِينَ

This means when man turns away from non-divine systems and adopts the laws of Allah, then this system with all its happy results turn toward man.

That is why in 3:127 this word is used against "عَذَابٌ" (*azaab*). Also in 9:106 its meaning is that if a man sins or commits a crime then he is not distanced from life's happiness forever. Whenever he reverts to Allah's laws, they will jump towards him. That is, everyone has a chance to retract. That is why every nation has a chance for renaissance.

In a nation's life, this moment comes when life anew becomes impossible. See heading *(H-L-K)*. This is however possible only if there is a chance that man will do good deeds. When the time to act ends, so does the time to retract. Retraction is not possible in state of *Jahannum*.

To understand the difference between "توبہ" (*tauba*) and "استغفار" (*isteghfaar*), see heading *(Gh-F-R)*.

Lataiful Lugha says "توبہ" (*tauba*) is repentance at previous faults, while "استغفار" (*istegfaar*) is shunning future sins.

"اَلتَّابُوْتُ" (*at-taboot*): box, or trunk, because the things taken out of it are also put back {T}. In this sense also see heading (*Taboot*).

T-W-R   ت و ر

"اَلتَّوْرُ" (*taur*): to flow, to be issued, envoy, be ambassador.
"اَلتَّوْرَةُ" (*at-taurah*) is a slave girl who keeps on coming and going (flitting in and out) among her lovers.
"اَلتَّارَةُ" (*at-tarah*): time, status.
"جَاءَتْهُ تَارَةً أُخْرَىٰ" (*je'tohu taratun ukhra*): I went to him twice.
"آتَارَہ" (*atarah*): he defeated him repeatedly.
"اَلتَّائِرُ" (*at-taa-iro*): tired but still engaged in work {T}.

Surah *Taaha* says:

20:55	we will raise you for a second time	نُخْرِجُكُمْ تَارَةً أُخْرَى

Raghib says this is with reference to "تَارَ الْجُرْحُ" (*Taral jurah*) which means for a wound to heal. It means to flow, continue, and to be engaged in work despite being tired. Considering these meanings, imagine how meaningful this word "تَارَةً" (*taratan*) is for us. Life is continuous, only conditions keep changing. This is what "تَارَةً أُخْرَىٰ" (*taratan ukhra*) is.

Taurah   اَلتَّوْرَاةُ

Some say that this word has been derived from "وَرَى" (*wari*) which means to light up *{T}*. See heading *(W-R-Y)*.

But the correct view word is the same as *Muheet* has explained. *Muheet* says that this is the Arabised form of the Hebrew word, meaning way of life (*shariat*) and orders. The plural is "تَوْرَاتٌ" (*taurat*) i.e. orders and ways.

It is generally thought that *Taurah* is the name of the book which was revealed to *Mosa*, but the Quran does not say specifically that *Moosa's* book was named *Taurah.* About *Taurah* it has said that it was revealed after Ibrahim (3:64) and after *Yaqoob* (3:92), but before *Isa* (Jesus) (5:46).

It was celestial guidance for the Jews and contained Allah's laws (5:43). The scholars of the Jews used to adjudicate on its basis (5:44). This makes it clear that *Taurah* is the collection of books that were revealed to the Messengers of *Bani Israel* and were revealed before *Isa*. This collection is what they call the Old Testament which consists of thirty nine documents, and each document is named with reference to its Messenger. *Isfaarey Musa* (Books of Moses) are included in them

The Quran calls them '*Suhafey Musa*' or *Moses' books* (87:19), and also '*Kitaabey Musa* (46:14). According to the practice at that time, these books were written on tablets (7:145).

The New Testament contains thirty nine books but some other books have been referred to which are not in this collection. At least eleven such books can be counted. This shows that the collection is not complete.

"*Asfaarey Musa*" is linked to *Musa* (Moses) but it contains matters about his death and after. This means that at least some part of the book was added later.

Research has not yet determined as to when the New Testament was completed and who were the compilers. But this is known that at one time they had become extinct i.e. when in 6 B.C Babylon's king *Bakht Naser* (Nebuchadnezzar) destroyed Jerusalem (see heading Bani Israel). He had burnt the Torah to ashes. When the Jews returned again to *Baitul Muqaddus* (Temple of Solomon) they looked for their lost Book. As such *Azra Nabi* (Messenger Ezra) compiled the first five books as a historian but it is not known when *Azra Nabi* himself had come to Jerusalem. It is commonly believed that he compiled the books in 444 A.D.

As to how the compilation and editing etc. was done, *Azra's* own words are quoted:

"The second or next day a voice called me and said: Azra, open your mouth and drink what I give you to drink. So I opened my mouth. Then he sent me a goblet. It was filled with water but its color was fiery. I took it and drank. When I drank it, my chest became insightful and understanding and my soul made my memory strong. When I then spoke, I did not stop for forty days and the writers continued to write. They used to write the whole day and used to eat only at night. And I used to dictate to them the whole day. In 40 days they wrote down 204 books" (Book of *Azra* 2:14, 44:34:38)

This statement needs no explanation, but the only thing that can be added to it, is that Jerusalem was destroyed in 578 A.D. and *Azra* dictated these books in 444 A.D, which is about one hundred and fifty years later. Obviously *Azra* had not seen these books and had memorized them from somewhere. That is why he didn't have the memorized books rewritten, but dictated new books. Then also, according to *Azra* himself, he had dictated 204 books but now it is believed that he dictated only five books (which are called *Isfarey Musa*).

After *Azra*, *Nahmyiah Nabi* (Messenger Nehemiah) had some other books compiled, but in 168 B.C the Greek king of *Antakia*, *Antonious* again destroyed Jerusalem and destroyed their Holy Books. Then due to the courage and diligence of *Yahuda Maqabi*, they were compiled once again. But in 70 B.C. the Roman general Titus destroyed *Baitul Muqaddas* in such a way that the Jews could not settle there again. He took the Holy Books with him. Then the Jew scholars recompiled them from memory.

It was not only the celestial and earthly events destroyed those books. They were also deliberately tampered with. As such, the famous Christian historian, *Renan* writes in his book "Life of Jesus":

"During the time near to Christ, many important changes were made in the Torah. Completely new books were compiled, and these were supposed to contain the real sharia (ways) of Moses, although they were different in spirit to the old books" (page 40).

Besides this, the Jews came up with another thought. They said that *wahi* (Revelation) was of two types. One was *Torah Shabaktub* (in book form) and the other *Torah Shibulfaa* (not in book form). The Jewish scholars also collected the traditions and gave it the respect of Torah. This collection is called *Mishna*.

Then the explanatory (exegetical) books (*tafseerat*) of this book were collected, which were called *Jamrah*. Both are called *Talmud*. There are two *Talmuds*: one is Syrian, the other is Babylonian. Both are considered to be celestial and both were compiled in the fifth century.

Besides this, the Jews also believe in "insightful knowledge". The books on this are called "*safrim janosiyam*" (the books of hidden treasures).

Let us now turn to the Torah's language:

The ancient language of the Jews was **Hebrew**. Upon returning from Babylon their language turned to **Aramaic**, but none of their books was either in **Hebrew** or **Aramaic**. All their books the world knows about are in the Greek language. **Isfaarey Moosa** were translated from Greek to Hebrew. This Greek volume was in the library of Alexandria which the Romans burnt down in 394 A.D.

St. Jerome published the famous Roman translation of these works known as the Vulgate. It is not known which volume was translated by St. Jerome.

The copies of the Torah, which are currently circulated in the world, differ in that the first volume was printed in 1488, its second edition which was arranged in 1750 differed in about 12,000 points. This second edition is now considered as the Torah. (Old Testament).

To know about the differences of Jewish scholars and Christian researchers about the current Torah, see the first chapter i.e. **Zohrul Fisaad** of my book **Meraj Insaniysat**.

This is the brief description of the Torah which the Jews present as their celestial book and about which fourteen hundred years ago the Quran had said, had been badly mutilated by them.

When the Quran says one must believe in the former celestial books, it only means that one accepts that Messengers of yesteryears also used to receive Revelation. It is not demanded that you believe in the books which the Jews and the Christians (People of the Book) call celestial books today. As to how the Quran certifies these books, see **(S-D-Q)**.

T-Y-N   ت ی ن

"اَلتِّیْن" (**at-teen**): fig, or the fig tree. It is also the name of a mountain, just like "زَیْتُوْنٌ" (**Zaitoon**), which is also the name of a hill **{T, R}**.
"اَلتِّیْن" (**at-teen**) is the place where Noah began his preaching (invitation). Similarly "زَیْتُوْنٌ" (**Zaitoon**) is the place where Jesus began his preaching.

The Quran has used the names of these places (**teen, zaitoon, toor seena, and Mekkah**) as witnesses (95:1) to indicate that the struggle between good and bad is not something new, but has been continuing since time immemorial. Wherever the celestial message was delivered, the "مترفین" **mutrafeen** opposed it. Whether the invitation was from **Noah** at (**at-teen**) or **Jesus** at (**zaitoon**), or **Moses** at (**at-toor**), or **Muhammed** at (**al-baladul amen**, meaning **Mecca**), all were opposed in the same way.

T-Y-He   ت ى ه

"أَرْضٌ تَيَّةٌ" (**arzun teah**): the land where there are no dunes, nor mountains, no landmarks. Hence a traveller gets lost and worried

"تَاهَ يَتِيْهُ فِى الْأَرْضِ" (**ta'ah yateeho fil ard**): lose the way and roam around worried and harried:

"رَجُلٌ تَائِهٌ" (**rojulun taayiah**): a wandering traveller *{T}*. This has led to "تَأَهَ" (**ta'a'aha**), or "يَتِيْهُ" (**yateehu**) which means to be surprised. These are its basic meanings, according to **Ibn Faris**.

"تَأَهَ يَتِيْهُ" (**ta'aha yateeho**): to pride oneself *{T}*.
"التِّيْهُ" (**at-tiyahu**), "اَلتَّوْهُ" (**at-tauhu**): point of surprise *{R}*.

About the Bani Israel, it is said:

5:26	they will wander around (for forty years)	يَتِيْهُونَ فِى الْأَرْضِ

This condition is met by the nations that find ways to avoid Allah's laws and which proffers different arguments about it. That nation wanders around in the journey of life and it doesn't find a way out (like the Muslims of today).

Th-B-Th   ث ب ت

"ثَبَتَ" (**thabath**): to be stable, to remain in one state.
"اَلثَّبْتُ مِنَ الْخَيْلِ" (**thabot minal khail**) is a horse which keeps running at the same speed.
"اَلثِّبَاتُ" (**al-sibat**) is the strap to which a camel is tied. The camel which is tied to this strap, is called "اَلْمُثْبَتُ" (**al-musbath**) *{T}*

Ibn Faris says it means the perpetuation of a thing.

In surah **Ar-Ra'ad**, "اِثْبَاتٌ" (**isbaath**) has appeared against "مَحْوٌ" (**mahwu**) which means to wipe out (13:39). Surah **Ibrahim** uses "يُثَبِّتُ" (**yusabbith**) against "يُضِلُّ" (**yazil**). Ergo, it means something that does not go waste and produces some result. Something which is not wiped out, but does not leave its place and stays stable.
"اَلْقَوْلُ الثَّابِتُ" (**al-qaulus sabith**) is used in 14:27 for a stable concept of life
"أَصْلُهَا ثَابِتٌ" (**asloha sabith**) is used in 14:24 for a tree with roots embedded strongly. Against it, there is a tree "أُجْتُثَّتْ مَنْ فَوْقِ الْأَرْضِ مَالَهَا مَنْ مِنْ قَرَارٍ" 14:26, which is uprooted easily and has no stability.

Surah **An-Nahal** uses "ثُبُوْتٌ" (**subuth**) against "تَزِلَّ" (**tazil**), meaning not to waver and staying put.
Surah **Bani Israel** uses it against "تَرْكَنُ" (**tarkana**) which is not to bend even a little, and not to lean at all. It is in 8:11 as "وَيُثَبِّتَ بِهِ الْأَقْدَامَ" (**wa subeta behil aqdaam**).

Surah **An-Nisa** says:

4:66	more strong in giving stability	وَاَشَدَّ تَثْبِيتاً

"دَاءٌ ثُبَاتٌ" (*da-un sabat*) is a disease which leaves a man immobile *{T, M, R}*.
In this context, "اَثْبَتَ" (*asbat*): to imprison someone in a way as to make him immobile
Surah **Al-Infaal** says "لِيُثْبِتُوکَ" (*liyus betooka*) in 8:30, which also has the same meaning.

The characteristic of the group of Momineen is that t is adamant on the God given concept of life and acts according to it, so that it gains so much strength that it can be shaken by no other force from its place.

Th-B-R   ث ب ر

"اَلثَّبْرُ" (*as-sabar*): to stop (someone from something), or to prevent.
"مَاثَبَرَکَ عَنْ هٰذا" (*ma sabarak un haaza*): somewhere, something stopped him *{T, M, R}*

Ibn Faris says "اَلثَّبْرَةُ" (*sabarah*) is soil which is like lime.

"اَلثَّبْرُ" (*as-sabr*) is unrequited and unsuccessful, to be deprived of happiness.
As such "اَلْمُثَبَّرُ" (*al-musabbar*) is a person who has been found guilty and has been sentenced, and thus is deprived of freedom *{T}*.
"أَلْمُثَبَّرُ" (*al-musabbir*) is the place where camels are slaughtered. In this context "اَلثُّبُوْرُ" (*as-saboor*): annihilation and continuous destruction *{T, M. R}*.

25:13	they will call out to annihilation	دَعَوْا هُنَالِکَ ثُبُوْرًا

Here "اَلثُّبُوْرُ" (*masboor*): unsuccessful and unrequited, annihilated, idiotic, deprived *{T, M, R}*.

25:102	O Pharaoh, I notice that you lack intelligence	اِنِّى لَاَظُنُّکَ يا فِرْعَوْنُ مَثْبُوْرًا

"ثَبَرَ فُلَانٌ" (*sabar falanun*): a man was killed, or his development was curtailed. According to the Quran, both mean the same. See heading *(J-H-M)*.

Th-B-Te   ث ب ط

"تَبَطَّرَ عَنِ الْأَمْرِ" (*tabatah unil amrhe*): prevented (from doing something) and engaged in another work.

The Quran says:

9:46	so they were stopped	فَتَبَّطَهُمْ

"تَثْبِيطٌ" (*tasbeet*): to stop someone from what he was doing. Some say it means to intervene between man and his intent

"اَلثَّبْطُ" (*as-sabito*): someone who is lazy, incompetent and weak in his work. He who acts (moves) rather late {*T, M*}.

Th-B-Y   ث ب ى

"اَلتَّثْبِيَةُ" (*at-tasbiah*) is used for the following:
- to collect a heap
- to be adamant at something and be consistent
- to praise one's tribe again and again
- to narrate the various high points
- to reform something and add to it
- to complete
- to respect.
- for a man to follow his father's traits
- to collect the good and the bad.
- to criticize and condemn a lot

"ثَبَّيْتُ الْمَالَ" (*sabbaitul maal*): I deposited the wealth
"مَالٌ مُثَبَّى" (*maalun musabba*): the collected wealth
"اَلثَّبِيُّ" (*as-sabi-o*): he who praises people very much
"اَلثُّبَةُ" (*as-soobah*): the central part of a small pool, a group of people, a group of horse riders
"جَاءَتِ الْخَيْلُ ثُبَاتٍ" (*ja'atil khailo subat*): the horses came in batches.

Researchers say that it was actually "ثُبَةٌ" (*sabwah*), but the "و" (*wa*) has been dropped.

Ibn Bari says that the researchers have used this saying, that the basic of this word is "ثُبْوَةٌ" (*sabwah*).

Abu Ishaq says that it has been derived from "ثَابَ الْمَاءُ يَثُوْبُ" (*sa'abal ma-oo yasub*).

Johri says that "ثُبَةٌ" (*subat*) is the central part of the pool where water collects.

Raghib, however, says it's root is "ثَبَّى" (*sabyun*).

“تَبَّى الشَّيْءَ يَثْبِيْهِ ثَبْياً” (*sabiush shaiya yasbeehi sabya*): to collect something, to make it bigger, correct it, to increase it, to complete it.

The Quran says:

54:71	you all come out as separate groups or all together	فَانفِرُوا ثُبَاتٍ اَوِانفِرُوا جَمِيْعاً

Here “ثُبَاتٍ” (*subatin*) is the plural of “ثُبَّةٍ” (*subah*) which means a separate group or party. As against it “جَمِيْعاً” (*jameea*) has been used.
The plural is “ثُبَاتٍ” (*subatin*) and “ثُبُوْنَ ثُبِيْنَ” (*suboona subeen*), where the “ياء” (*ya*) has been omitted at the end *{R}*. See heading (Th-W-B).

Th-J-J   ث ج ج

“ثَجَّ الْمَاءُ” (*sajjal ma-o*), “يَثُجُّ” (*yasujjo*), “ثُجُوْجاً” (*sajoojan*): the flow of water, to fall forcefully.
“انْثَجَّ” (*insajja*): the water fell.
“الثَّجَّاجُ مِنَ الْمَطَرِ” (*as-sajjajo minal matar*): rain which is falling hard {T, M, F}.

The Quran says:

78:14	We brought down hard rain from the clouds	وَاَنْزَلْنَا مِنَ الْمُعْصِراتِ مَاءً ثَجَّاجاً

Th-Kh-N   ث خ ن

“ثَخُنَ” (*sakhun*), “يَثْخُنَ” (*yaskhun*): for something to become thicker or fatter, so that it cannot flow.
“اَثْخَنَ فِى الْعَدُوِّ” (*askhana fil uduway*): he killed and injured a lot of enemies.
“اسْتَثْخَنَ مِنْهُ النَّوْمُ” (*istaskhana minhum naum*): sleep overwhelmed him.
“اَثْخَنَ” (*askhana*): he overpowered, he dominated *{T}*.

Surah **Al-Infaal** says:

8:67	till he overpowers all the enemies (and prevents them from their opposition tactics)	حَتَّى يُثْخِنَ فِى الْاَرْضِ

Surah **Al-Mohammed** says:

47:4	Until you overpower them.	حَتَّى اِذَا اَثْخَنْتُمُوْهُم

According to **Ibn Faris**, the basic meaning of “ثَخَنَ” (*sakhan*) is to become so heavy, that it would restrict movement. Since the overpowered or killed cannot move from his place, this word is used in this manner. It would mean to overwhelm the enemy in such a way that it immobilizes him and surrenders due to being unable to oppose. As such "تَخِيْنٌ" (*sakhyeen*): a man who is without arms *{F}*.

Muheet says "تَخِيْنٌ" (*saheen*): to be unarmed. It is possible that the due to the basic meaning, both these meanings were created. This is perhaps because a man carrying a weapon has its burden to carry, and hence cannot move freely. In the same way, an unarmed person will also be scared from moving freely.

Th-R-B   ث ر ب

"ثَرْبٌ" (*sarb*): a thin layer of fat which is with the intestines.
"تَثْرِيْبٌ" (*tasreeb*): to get rid of this fat, to remove it.
"تَرَّبَ الثَّوْبَ" (*sarrabas sauba*): he rolled up the cloth.
"ثَرَّبَهُ و عَلَيْهِ يُثَرِّبُ تَثْرِيْباً" (*sarrabahu a alaihi yusarribo tasreeba*): to condemn him for his mistake, to admonish him *{T, M, R}*.

Surah ***Yusuf*** says:

12:9	There is no shame on you today. (I don't chide you, you are pardoned for past sins, and in future you will not be shamed.)	لَا تَثْرِيْبَ عَلَيْكُمُ الْيَوْمَ

"يَثْرِبُ" (*yasrib*) is the ancient name for Medina *{T, M, R}*.

The Quran says:

33:13	O dwellers of ***Yasrib***	يَا أَهْلَ يَثْرِبَ

Th-R-W/Y   ث ر ی (و)

"اَلثَّرَىٰ" (*asra*): moist, wet soil, soil which is moist but which has not turned into mud, the soil on top is dry but beneath it the earth is wet. This moist soil is called "ثرىٰ" (*sara*).

20:6	whatever is beneath the ***sara***	مَا تَحْتَ الثَّرَىٰ

"ثَرِيَتِ الْأَرْضُ" (*sariyatil arz*): that the earth became wet. Since this wetness of earth is necessary for agriculture, therefore "فُلَانٌ قَرِيْبُ الثَّرَىٰ" (*falanun qareebus sara*): a man who easily blesses others. Real wealth is attached to the wetness of the earth which is the fountainhead of wealth "اَنَا ثَرِىٌّ بِهِ" (*ana sariun behi*): I am pleased with him.

Th-Ain-B   ث ع ب

"ثَعَبَ الْمَاءَ" (*sa'abal ma'aa*): to make water flow.

"فَانْثَعَبَ" (*fa'ansa'ab*): the water flowed.

"مَاءٌ أُثْعُبَانٌ" (*ma'un usbaan*): water that flows.

"مَثَاعِبُ الْمَدِينَةِ" (*masa'ibun madinah*): the spots of the city from where the water flows.

"الثُّعْبَانُ" (*as-so'baan*): snake (long, thick, and male snake), since while moving a snake gives the appearance of a thin line of flowing water.

"الْأُثْعُبَانُ" (*al-usbaan*): a heavy, white and beautiful face {T}.

Ibn Faris says its basic meanings are extension and to spread out.

In the tale about *Moosa* in the Quran, it is said:

7:107	then he put down his staff and it was clearly a snake	‫فَأَلْقَى عَصَاهُ فَإِذَا هِيَ ثُعْبَانٌ مُبِينٌ--‬

For its figurative meaning, see heading *(Ain-Sd-W)*.

Th-Q-B   ث ق ب

"الثَّقْبُ" (*as-saqbo*): a hole, an incision that goes through and through.

"ثَقَبَهُ" (*saqabah*), "يَثْقُبُهُ" (*yasqubuh*): that he drilled a hole into it.

"فَانْثَقَبَ" (*fansaqab*), a hole appeared in it.

"الْمِثْقَبُ" (*almisqab*): the implement to drill a hole with.

"ثَقَبَتِ النَّارُ" (*saqabatin naar*): the fire (was) started.

"ثَقَبَ الْكَوْكَبُ" (*saqabul kaukab*): the shining star.

"شِهَابٌ ثَاقِبٌ" (*shihabun saqib*): a shooting star, as if it had drilled a hole in the blanket of darkness and come out, or its rays pierced the darkness of the atmosphere.

"الثَّقِيبُ" (*as-saqeeb*): a female camel who gives lots of milk, one whose lines of milk pierce {T}

The Quran has said "شِهَابٌ ثَاقِبٌ" (*shihabun saqib*) in 37:10 and "النَّجْمُ الثَّاقِبُ" (*an najmus saqib*) in 86: 3.

Th-Q-F   ث ق ف

"الثَّقْفُ" (*as-saqf*): expertise in sensing or getting at something or expertise in some work.

"ثَقِفْتُ كَذَا" (*saqifto kaza*): I got to the bottom of something with my expertise. Later this word started being used to mean getting something whether expertness of insight was included or not {R}. *Muheet's* compiler says it also means to acquire domination.

The Quran says:

60:2	if they dominate you, then they will become your enemy	اِنْ يَّثْقَفُوْكُمْ يَكُوْنُوْالَكُمْ اَعْدَاءً
2:191	where you can sense (their ill intentions) dominate them	وَاقْتُلُوْهُمْ حَيْثُ ثَقِفْتُمُوْ هُمْ

"اَلثِّقَافُ" (as-siqaaf): infighting and to use swords. It also means the implement with which spears are straightened.

"ثَقَّفْتُ الْقَنَاةَ" (saqqafatul qanat): I straightened the bend in the spear. As such, "اَلثَّقَافَةُ" (as-saqafah): insight, intellect, and expertise. At the same time it also means to wield the sword and to straighten the spear {T, M, R}.

The first cultural craft of nations is the sword (defence capability), but in the end only poetry and story writing remains. A living nation's cultural crafts are insight and the swiftness of the blade.

Th-Q-L   ث ق ل

"اَلثِّقَلْ" (as-siqal) is the opposite of "خِفَّةْ" (khiffah), which means to be heavy and burdensome.

Raghib says that these words are opposites. When two things are compared with each other, the heavier is called "ثَقِيْلْ" (saqeel) and the lighter is "خَفِيْفْ" (khafeef). The plural of "ثَقِيْلْ" (saqeel) is "ثِقَالْ" (siqaal).

"قَوْلاً ثَقِيْلاً" (qaulan saaqeela): some talk of great importance (73:5).
"ثَقَلَيْنِ" (saqalain): two great things, or groups.
"اَيُّهَ الثَّقَلْنِ" (ayyohas saqalaan): Oh you, two classes (55:31)

Muheet's compiler says it means the **Arabs** and the **Ajams** (non-Arabic) as both are "ثَقَلْ" (saqal) (great) on the earth.

"اَثْقَالْ" (asqaal) is the plural of "ثِقَلْ" (siqal) which means weight, load, the results of actions as used in (29:13).

Surah **Al-Zalzalah** says:

99:2	the earth will bring forth **asqaal** (whatever it has within) to the top	وَاَخْرَجَتِ الْاَرْضُ اَثْقَالَهَا

The meaning in the above verse is of minerals etc. (the treasure buried in it) and the bigwigs too (who are buried)

"مِثْقَال" (*misqaal*): anything against which anything is weighed, therefore any weight (or measure) can be called "مِثْقَال" (*misqaal*) as in 4:40 {*T*}.

"ثَقُل" (*saqul*): to be heavy {*T*}

| 7:187 | He is weighty in the skies and the earth | ثَقُلَتْ فِى السَّمٰوٰاتِ وَالْأَرْضِ |
| 7:189 | the woman's pregnancy became known | أَثْقَلَتِ الْمَرْأَةُ وَنَقَلَتْ |

"اِثَّاقَل" (*issaqal*): to bend due to weight, to be lazy, to be late, as in 9:38. {*R*}

"مُثْقَل" (*musqal*): burdened with weight as used in 52:40 or "مُثْقَلَة" (*musqalah*) as in 35:18.

Surah *At-Taubah* says:

| 9:41 | when you are called for jihad, then whether you are in abundance (i.e. well-to-do position) or whether you are pinched (in a sorry state), go for jihad | اِنْفِرُوْ اِخْفَافًا وَّ ثَقَالًا |

Taj-ul-Uros says it also means the young and the old. It can also mean the swift and the lazy, and those who are partially or fully armed. "ثَقُلَتْ مَوَازِيْنُه" (*saqolat mawazeenohu*), See heading (*Kh-F-F*).

<h1 style="text-align:center">Th-L-Th   ث ل ث</h1>

"ثَلَث" (*salas*), "الثُّلُثُ" (*as-solosu*): one third (1/3) of something.

Surah *An-Nisa* says:

| 4:11 | Then one third for his mother | فَلِأُمِّهِ الثُّلُثُ |

"الثُّلُثَانِ" (*as-solosani*) is the two third (2/3) of something.

"ثَلَّثَ" (*salasas*): the horse that finishes third in a race right after "مُصَلِّى" (*musalli*). ("مُصَلِّى" (*musalli*) is the runner up right behind the winner).

"الثَّلَاثَة" (*as-salasa*): as male, the count of three.

"ثَلَاثَ" (*salas*): feminine form of three.

The Quran says:

| 2:196 | The fasting of three days | فَصِيَامُ ثَلٰثَةِ اَيَّامٍ |

"ثُلَاثَ" (*solas*): up to three.

The Quran says:

4:3	Up to two and three and four	مَثْنَى وَثُلَاثَ وَرُبَعَ

"اَلثَّلَاثِيْنَ وَثَلَاثُوْنَ" (*as-salaseen was-salason*): thirty.

Th-L-L   ث ل ل

"اَلثَّلَّةُ" (*as-sallah*): a lot of sheep and goats. Actually it means a lot of wool, since sheep also have wool on their backs; their flock is called "ثَلَّةٌ" (*salsalah*).

"حَبْلُ ثَلَّةٍ" (*hablu salah*): a rope of wool.

"اَلثُّلَّةُ" (*as-sullah*): a group of men.

Quran says:

56:13	a big group in the antecedents	ثُلَّةٌ مِنَ الْأَوَّلِيْنَ

"ثَلَّ لَدَارَ" (*salad-daar*): to take out the earth from the foundation and then to push it (the structure) down.

"بَيْتٌ مَثْلُوْلٌ" (*baitun maslool*): a demolished house.

"اَلثِّلَّةُ" (*as-sillah*): annihilation {T, M, R}, to be turned into a heap.

Th-M-D   ث م د

"اَلثَّمْدُ" (*as-samd*), "اَلثَّمَدُ" (*as-samado*), "اَلثِّمَادُ" (*as-simaad*): a little water that accumulates somewhere, but not a stream, as rainwater.

"أَثْمَدَ الماءَ" (*asmadal ma'aa*): preserved rainwater etc. in ditches {T}.

"اَلثَّامِدُ" (*as-saamid*): four legged animal or human child which has started eating a little. This is its initial age.

Researchers have divided the human race into three big divisions:
1) Aryai (Aryans)
2) Mongol
3) Semitic.

The **Saami** nations are the **Arabs** the **Aramis** (Aramaic) are the **Hebrews**, the **Syriacs** and the Caledonians etc. The Quran has discussed the Messengers which belong to the **Saamis**. According to the **Torah**, **Saamis** was the name of one of **Noah's** sons. His descendants are called **Saamis**. According to modern research, the **Saami's** first homeland was Arabia from where they spread out to Babylon, Syria and Egypt etc. The most famous tribe among them who established their rule in inland Arabia was **Samood**. **Samood** literally means in front, before.

Some think they were called **Samood** because there was shortage of water and they existed on rainwater {T}: They ruled north western Arabia which was named **Quraa**. Hijr was their capital and was situated on the ancient road from **Hijaz** to Syria. The surrounding areas of **Quraa** are very fertile but are composes of lava flow. This nation was known for big palaces and for carving out solid mountains as forts which were sculptural masterpieces. (15:83, 7:74).

As God created Man, He also spread out means of his sustenance one earth so that each could partake as he needs, but usurpers take control of these fountainheads of sustenance, and this result in the weaker dying of hunger. The purpose of the Messengers was also to get these fountainheads of sustenance out of the control of these usurpers and to make them accessible for all.

In ancient times (and today as well with the gypsies and the mount dwellers) grazing lands and water holes are the basic fountainheads of sustenance. In the nation of **Samood** too, this was the situation. The tribal heads controlled the streams of water, and the weaker human beings had to look up to them as they were dependent on them for water. To remove this inequity from society, **Saleh** was sent to them (7:73) who told them not to create such inequities in society (7:74). The weaker section of the population supported **Saleh,** but the wealthy opposed him strongly and told him in return that they will not allow any changes in what their elders followed. It seems that **Saleh** also had some say because he got the powerful people to agree to take turns and he worked out a pact with them whereby all (the rich and the poor) could get their animals to drink in turn from the streams.

Saleh said that if they honored the pact, he would let his camel loose and if it is allowed in its turn to drink from the stream, then that would prove that they would honor the pact (7:73). However, they killed the camel and thus breached the pact (went back on their word) (7:77). This camel was a material symbol of Allah and that is why it was called "نَاقَةُ اللّهِ" (*naqatullah*), the camel of God, and hence a sign (7:73). They were living a very luxurious life when suddenly there was a blast in the volcanoes, a scream, a thunder roared in the air and the **Samood** nation's dwellings turned to dust. It became heaps of rubble (7:78). The details can be found in my book **Joo-e-Noor** in the tale about **Noah**.

Th-M-R   ث م ر

"ثَمَرٌ" (*samar*) is the fruits of a tree, goods (wealth) of all kinds, gold or silver.
"أَثْمَرَةٌ" (*as-samrah*): the tree itself, and is also used for one's offspring.
"مَالٌ ثَمَرٌ" (*maalun samar*): wealth in abundance (that which increases very quickly).
"ثَمَرَ النَّبَاتُ" (*samaran nabaat*): the plant shed the flower and in its place the fruit appeared.

Ibn Faris says the root means anything which is born of another in consolidated form. Later it was also used allegorically.

The Quran also uses this word to mean wealth and riches in 18:34 as "كَانَ لَهُ ثَمَر" (**kana lahu samara**).

It is also used for the bee that sucks juices from all the fruits or "ثَمَرَاتٌ" (**samaraat**) in 16:69.

Raghib writes that "ثَمَّر" (**samara**) is on top of all parts of the tree which can be tasted or eaten, thus "ثَمَرا" (**samara**) includes flowers etc. which can also be eaten.

Samma   ثَمَّ

"ثَمَّ" (**samma**) is used to point at something, like 'that' in English {*T, L*}.

Surah **Al-Baqrah** says:

2:165	whichever way you face, you will find before you the path that will take you to the destination destined by Allah	فَأَيْنَمَا تُوَلُّوا فَثَمَّ وَجْهُ اللهِ

Allah's law can be found in every aspect of life. Here the personality of God could also be ment, but His personality comes before us in the shape of His signs. The basis of these verses or signs is the law of Allah. See heading (*W-J-He*).

Surah **Ash-Shura**, Surah **Ad-Dahar**, and Surah **At-Takweer** says:

26:64	We brought the others near there too	وَأَزْلَفْنَا ثَمَّ الْآخَرِينَ
76:20	when you see there (or that way) you will find blessings	إِذَا رَأَيْتَ ثَمَّ رَأَيْتَ نَعِيماً
81:21	He is belonging andtrustee as well	مُطَاعٍ ثَمَّ أَمِينٍ

"ثَمَّ" (**samma**) can also be a verb with different meanings, such as to correct, to trample, to collect etc.

Summa   ثُمَّ (حرف)

"ثُمَّ" (**summa**) is usually used where some sort of arrangement is narrated, for instance, he ate the food, then drank some water.

Surah **Al-Momineen** says:

23:32	then We dimensioned another generation after that	ثُمَّ أَنْشَأْنَا مِنْ بَعْدِهِمْ قَرْناً آخَرِينَ

But it is not necessary for "ثُمَّ" (**summa**) to be used for relaying arrangement or order only. It can be used to mean 'and'. For instance in surah **Yunus** it is said:

10:46	and God is witness to what they do	ثُمَّ اللهُ شَهِيدٌ عَلَى مَا يَفْعَلُونَ

Another clear example is in surah **Al-Baqrah**:

2:26	Allah is the One who created all that is on earth, and then (summa) He turned towards the skies and corrected them in varied forms of different spheres.	هُوَ الَّذِئ خَلَقَ لَكُمْ فِى الْاَرْضِ جَمِيْعاً ثُمَّ اسْتَوَىٰ إِلَى السَّمَاءِ فَسَوَّاهُنَّ سَبْعَ سَمٰوٰتٍ

If "ثُمَّ" (**summa**) here is to be taken to mean 'then', it would mean that the order is such that He first created the earth and then the sky, but surah **An-Nazeyaat** mentions the celestial spheres first:

79:29	he raised the sky and corrected it	رَفَعَ سَمْكَهَا فَسَوَّاهَا
79:29	and threw the earth after it	وَالْاَرْضَ بَعْدَ ذٰلِكَ دَحٰهَا

This shows that first the celestials or the spheres of the skies were created, then the earth was thrown afar. That the spheres were thrown like drops is also confirmed by 21:30. It is evident therefore that"ثُمَّ" (**summa**) is not used for any sort of order, as such it will not mean order at all places. Sometimes it will also mean 'and'.

Sometimes it is redundant, as in surah **At-Taubah**:

9:118	till they came to believe that the earth despite being very vast had no place for them and they were fed up of themselves; and they came to believe that except Allah, nobody will save them from Allah's punishment, then God turned towards them.	حَتّٰى إِذَا ضَاقَتْ عَلَيْهِمُ الْاَرْضُ --- ثُمَّ تَابَ عَلَيْهِمْ

Here "ثُمَّ" (**summa**) has no meaning, it is hence redundant. See the book's foreword for the meaning of "زَائِد" (**za-id**) or redundant. "ثُمَّ" (**summa**) also means "on top of that", "despite", "even so", "although":

16:83	They recognize the favor of Allah, and then they deny it.	يَعْرِفُوْنَ نِعْمَةَ اللّٰهِ ثُمَّ يُنْكِرُوْنَهَا

Th-M-N ث م ن

"تَمَنُ الشَّیءِ" (*samanush shaiyi*): that after payment of which one can become the owner. Usually "ثَمَنٌ" (*saman*) is the price at which both buyer and seller agree upon, while "قیمۃ" (*qeema*) is the remuneration which is actually commensurate with that thing. "مَتَاعٌ ثَمِیْنٌ" (*mata-un sameen*): precious goods {T, M}.

The Quran says:

2:41	don't sell My signs for a small price	وَلَاتَشْتَرُوْا بِا یَاتِیْ ثَمَناً قَلِیْلاً

This doesn't mean that they should be sold at a high price. The meaning is that their real price or "قیمۃ" (*qeema*) is the result which is received by following them (the signs), any price beside this will be too little. It is the worst form of crime to make *Deen* a means of personal gain. Religious monasticism is based on this. As such the Quran has it that the rebellious one said:

2:118	I will definitely take an ordained share from your followers	لَاَتَّخِذَنَّ مِنْ عِبَادِکَ نَصِیْباً مَفْرُوْضاً

This is the same thing as "مَتَاعٌ فِی الدُّنْیَا" (*mataun fidduniya*) in 10:69. The benefits for a man in this physical world without considering the future, are anyway very little (4:77), regardless the level of quantity. This, because benefits and possessions which do not contribute to a man's development, do not hold any weight in the human scale. The mutual conspiracy of the religious leaders is for this very benefit (29:25). This is why monasticism and Islam are considered to be opposites.

"ثَمَانِیَۃٌ" (*samaniah*): eight (masculine).
"ثَمَانِیَۃَ اَیَّام" (*samaniah ayyam*): eight days (69:7).
"ثَمَانٍ یا ثَمَانیْ" (*samanin baa samani*): eight (feminine).
"ثَمَانیَ حِجَج" (*samaniya hijaj*): eight years (28:237).
"ثَمَانُوْنَ" (*samanoon*), "ثَمَانِیْنَ" (*samaneen*): eighty.
"ثَمَانِیْنَ جِلْدَۃ" (*samaneena jaldah*): eighty lashes (24:4).
"اَلثُّمُنْ" (*as-sumun*), "اَلثَّمْنُ" (*as-samn*), "اَلثَّمِیْنْ" (*as-sameen*): eighth part of anything.
"فَلَهُنَّ الثُّمُنْ" (*fala hunnas sumun*): for them is the eighth share or part (4:12).

Mirza Abul Fazal with reference to *Sir Syed Ahmed Khan* has written in his book *Gharibul Quran*, that this word is sometimes used merely for garnishing, where its meaning is indefinite like 'many'.

Th-N-Y   ث ن ى

"ثَنَاهُ" (*sanah*), "ثَنْياً" (*sania*): to double something or fold it, like cloth, or to double something by bending it, (like a branch of a tree).

"ثَنَى الشَّيْءِ" (*sanash shaiyi*): bend or fold something.

"تَثَنَّى" (*tasana*): the thing is bent.

"ثَنْيُ الْحَيَّةِ" (*siniul hayya*): for the snake to bend or wriggle.

"اَلثَّنْيُ مِنَ الْوَادِىْ" (*as sinyoo minal wadi*): the bend in the valley, the plural is "اَلْمَثَانِىْ مِنَ الْوَادِىْ" (*al-misani minal wadi*)

"اَلْمَثَانِىْ مِنَ الدَّابَّةِ" (*al masani minad da'abba*): the knees and forelegs of a four legged animal which are folded and doubled {T}.

"ثِنَاءٌ" (*sinaun*): the rope with which the thigh of a camel is secured after bending its knee {L}.

"ثِنْىٌّ" (*sinyun*): a thing which is repeated again and again.

"الْإِثْنَانِ" (*al-isnaan*): two, double than one {T}. "اِثْنَتَانِ" (*isnataan*), "اِثْنَتَيْنِ" (*isnatain*) are feminine forms.

"فَوْقَ اثْنَتَيْنِ" (*fauqas natain*): more than two (women) (4:11).

"أَثْنَاءُ الْكَلَامِ" (*asnaul kalam*): in the middle of some speech.

"فِىْ اَثْنَاءِ ذَالِكَ" (*fi asna-ee zalik*): in the meanwhile.

"اِسْتِثْنَاءٌ" (*istisna'a*): to exempt someone to separate {T}.

Ibn Faris says the root basically means:
1) To repeat something
2) To make two separate things out of one.

The Quran says about the hypocrites:

11:5	they have doubled their chests (they fold it so that something is on top (fold) and something else in the bottom (fold))	اَلَا اِنَّهُمْ يَثْنُوْنَ صُدُوْرَهُمْ

In other words, they have dual personality. In surah **Al-Hajj**, it is said about those who want to avoid the Quran:

22:9	he turns away his face (tries to avoid)	ثَانِىَ عِطْفِهِ

Surah **Al-Qalam** says that the capitalists who face destruction:

68:18	do not take out what is the right of others (they will keep nothing for others only themselves)	لَا يَسْتَثْنُوْنَ

In surah **Al-Hijr**, the Messenger is told to:

15:87	We endowed you with **sab'un minal misani** and the great Quran	وَلَقَدْ اٰتَيْنٰكَ سَبْعاً مِنَ الْمَثَانِىْ وَالْقُرْاٰنَ الْعَظِيْمَ

The great Quran is that set of Allah's laws according to which acts formulate their own results. See heading *(Ain-Dh-M)*, and "أَلْمَثَانِىْ" *(al-misani)* are those historic truths which keep repeating themselves. On the one hand Allah has stated those basic principles which lead to the rise or fall of nations (through the Quran), and on the other has supported them with historical events which kept taking place during every era. To test the historic truths related by the Quran, one can study the history of mankind to see that what happened to the nations when they followed the path of righteousness as described by the Quran, and what resulted when they followed the unjust, mentioned by the Quran.

For more details see the argument about "مُحْكَمَاتٌ" *(mohkamaat)* and "مُتَشَا بِهَا تِّ" *(mutashabihat)* under heading *(H-K-M)*.

Surah *Al-Zumr* says about the Quran:

39:23	A book with an inner harmony as its fundament	كِتَاباً مُتَشَا بِهاً مَثَانِىَ

As mentioned earlier, "مَثَانِىَ" *(misani)*: things which face each other (like the elbows and knees of four-legged animals which when bent, come face to face), and "مُتَشَابِهاً" *(mutashabehan)*: similar to each other.

The entire teaching of the Quran, from one end to another, is uniform. There is no contradiction in it, but in order to make its meaning clear it brings opposites face to face so that things may become clear. For instance, "ظُلُمَت" *(zulumaat)* against "نُوْر" *(noor)*, or darkness against light. Death against life. *Imaan* against *kufr*, or belief against denial. That is, it brings opposites face to face to make things explicit.
As such the Quran is "مُتَشَابِهاً" *(mutashabiha)* as well as "مَثَانِىَ" *(masani)*, which means similar and dis-similar as well. It is a book in which one thing is linked to another, but the meaning is sometimes explained by bringing opposites face to face. For more details, see headings *(Sh-B-He)*, and *(H-K-M)*.

"مَثْنَى" *(masna)*: in groups of two (35:1), (4:3).
"اثْنَا عَشَرَ" *(asna ashar)* is the masculine form.
"اثْنَتَا عَشْرَةَ" *(isnata ashrah)* is the feminine form as in (2:60) for twelve.
"كِتَاباً مُتَشَابِهاً مَثَانِىَ" *(kitaban mutashabehan masani)* can also mean "similar to the former" (books of God) and in a way their reiteration.

Th-W-B   ث و ب

"ثَابَ" *(sab-aa)*, "يَثُوْبُ" *(yasoob)*, "ثَوْباً" *(sauban)*: to return, to turn back after leaving.
"ثَابَ جِسْمُهُ ثَوَبَاناً وَأَثَابَ" *(sa'ba jismohu saubanan wa asaba)*: his body came back to its natural form after illness and thus his strength and health got recovered *{T, M}*.
"ثَابَ الْمَاءُ" *(sabal ma'o)*: took the water out but it got refilled, was restored *{T}*
"اَلثَّائِبُ مِنَ الْبَحْرِ" *(as saibo minal bahar)*: after ebbing, the water which remains of the sea.

"بِءْرٌ ثَيِّبٌ" (**berun saib**): the well in which water comes back (after drying up).

Kitabul Ashqaq says that "ثَابَ يَثُوْبُ" (**saaba yasoob**): "رَجَعَ" (**ra-jah**) or to return.
"كُلُّ رَاجِعٍ ثَائِبٌ" (**kullo raje-in sayebun**): everyone who returns. ***Ibn Faris*** too says this is its meaning.

"مَثَابَةُ الْبِئْرِ" (**masabatul beyr**): as far as the water of the well reaches.
"أَلْمَثَابَةُ" (**al-masabah**): the spot where the gathering takes place again and again, centre, house, or destination.
"ثَابَ النَّاسُ" (**saaban naas**): the people gathered *{T, M}*.
"أَلثَّوْبُ" (**as-saub**): cloth, probably because the shuttle comes and goes repeatedly in the making of a cloth. Its plural is "ثِيَابٌ" (**siyaab**).
"ثَوَّابٌ" (**sawwab**): one who sells cloth *{T, M}*.

The Arabs usually take "ثِيَابٌ" (**siyaab**) to mean a man's personality, that is, the one who wears the clothes himself. So they say "فُلَانٌ دَنِسٌ سُسُ الثِّيَابِ" (**fulan danis sus siyaab**): that man has a mean personality, his personality is very bad *{T, M}*.

"تَثْوِيْبٌ" (**tasweeb**): to call out to people, to make them assemble. As such, in the call to morning prayer, they say "أَلصَّلٰوةُ خَيْرٌ مِنَ النَّوْمِ" (**salato khairum minan naum**): praying is better than sleeping. This is also called "تَثْوِيْبٌ" (**tasweeb**) *{T}*.

"ثَابَ يَثُوْبُ" (**saaba yasoob**): to understand the right meanings, one has to recall the meanings given at first.
"ثَابَ" (**saab**): for a thing to go first and then return. Whatever you do, something is used up in it. If nothing else, then your bodily strength, time and mental faculties may be used. If the work you do is useless, then all your strengths that are used up in it also go waste. If it produces some result, then whatever strengths you invested, get compensated. This restoration is called "ثَوَابٌ" (**sawab**).

Obviously it is not just a thought. Whatever you use up, is felt very much by you; either it is time that is spent or physical or mental strength. Therefore whatever is restored must also be felt, otherwise how will you know that the restoration has taken place? That is why when the Quran says "ثَوَابَ الْآخِرَةِ" (**sawabil akhirah**), which is the compensation in Hereafter (3:144), it also mention "ثَوَابَ الدُّنْيَا" (**sawabud duniyah**) compensation in life (3:147).

In order to remove any doubts, it is also explained that this "ثَوَابٌ" (**sawab**) will be in the shape of luxuries, like power and leadership, thick and fine silken clothes, and victories etc. (18:31). Quran has said that the result of good deeds without failure, are the domination and riches in this world (24:55). Thus "ثَوَابٌ" (**sawaab**) should be manifest in this world as a first step. Later in the Hereafter as well, since all these are due to good deeds, that is why "ثَوَابٌ" (**sawaab**) is the result of our good deeds.

This word "ثَوَابٌ" (*sawaab*) is generally used for good results but sometimes it is used for the results of bad deeds as well, as in 83:36 and in 3:152. In these verses it mean for man to return to whatever he has done.

83:36	the deeds of the deniers return to them as the result	هَلْ ثُوِّبَ الْكُفَّارُ مَاكَانُوْا يَفْعَلُوْنَ

The Quran has explained this very fine point that acts are themselves their own compensation. For example, you go for morning walk, walk for two or three miles in which you use up your energy as well as time. In return you get good health and freshness etc. This health and freshness is the result of your walk, i.e. your walk itself is its own result or reward. This is "ثَوَابٌ" (*sawaab*) which makes it clear how wrong "اِيْصَالِ ثَوَابَ" (*eesaali sawaab*) (the practice of trying to transfer the "ثَوَابٌ" (*sawaab*) or result of good deeds to someone, usually dead) is. Can it be that you take the walk and transfer the results to me? It is impossible to do so! If you take the walk, the benefits will accrue only to you. If I do not take the walk, then it can do no good for me. Despite desperately wanting to transfer the benefits to another, you cannot do that. Therefore, transferring "ثَوَابٌ" (*sawaab*) to another is a dubious belief and seems to have no connection with the Quran. Everyone gets the result of their own deeds, which they can't transfer to anyone else.

"مَثُوْبَةٌ" (*masoobah*): result or the natural cycle of events (5:60).

Quran has addressed the Messenger to say:

74:4	And your *siyab* purified	وَثِيَابَكَ فَطَهِّرْ

We have seen that this word "ثِيَابٌ" (*siyab*) is used for personality. Quran itself, at another place, has used this word for personality, or human thought, as in 71:7, and 11:5. That is why it also means that you should keep your personality clean of any pollution, and if *tasweeb*'s meaning is kept in mind, then it would mean to keep your invitation (to trust in Allah and His Rusool) away from those who have the pollution of duplicity or hypocrisy in their hearts. Therefore there is a connotation of keeping your personality clean rather than keeping the clothes clean.

For another meaning of "ثَوَابٌ" (*sawaab*) see the heading "سُدىً" (*sudya*).

Th-W-R   ث و ر

"اَلثَّوَرَانْ" (*as-sauran*): agitation.

"ثَارَالشَّیْیِّ" (*saaras shaiyi*): that thing was agitated.

"ثَارَالْغُبَارْ" (*saaral ghubar*): the dust rose and spread out.

"قَدْثَأَائِرُهُ" (*qad sara sairohu*): that man got furious.

"أَثَارَهُ وَثَوَّرَهُ و اسْتَثَارَهُ" (*asarohu wa saurahu wastasarah*): he roused him, agitated him.

"أَثَارَ الْأَرْضَ" (*asaral ard*): ploughed the land and turned it upside down {T}.

The Quran says:

100:4	those horses hit the earth with their hooves and raised dust	فَأَثَرْنَ بِهِ نَقْعاً
2:71	this ox has not been harnessed in the plough	لَا ذَلُوْلٌ تُثِيْرُ الْأَرْضَ
30:38	they agitate the clouds and lift them	فَتُثِيْرُ سَحَاباً

Ibn Faris says the root means for something to be lifted.

Th-W-Y   ث و ی

"تَوَى الْمَكَانَ" (*sawal makaan*): stayed at some place for long, got down for permanent residence.
"الْمَثْوَىٰ" (*al-maswa*): residence, staying place, a place of permanent residence.
"أَبُوْ مَثْوَىٰ" (*abu-maswa*): host, guest, the resident.
"الثَّوِيُّ" (*as-savi*): guest, also guestroom.
"أَثْوَاهُ" (*aswah*): hosted him.
"الثَّوِيَّةُ" (*asuwwah*): a resting place for camels near ones house. Also see heading *(A-W-Y)*. It is also called as "الثَّوِيَّةُ" (*sawaiyah*) *{T, R, Lataiful Lugha}*.

Surah *Al-Qasas* and *Yousuf* says:

| 28:45 | You were not staying with the people of *Madyan* | وَمَاكُنْت ثَاوِياً فِيْ اَهْلِ مَدْيَنَ |
| 12:21 | Keep it with respect (give him a place of respect) | اَكْرِمِيْ مَثْوِيهُ |

The connotations of permanent residence and hosting shows that the ruler of Egypt had already hosted *Yusuf* respectfully, and that he was not kept as an ordinary slave.

Surah *Aal-e-Imraan* says:

| 3:150 | The residence of the mutinous is (hell) indeed a very bad place. | بِئْس مَثْوَىٰ الظَّالِمِيْنَ |

Th-Y-B   ث ی ب

"الثَّيِّبُ" (*as-sayib*): a woman who is no longer with her husband (either divorced or a widow) *{T}*.

The Quran uses "ثَيِّبَات" (*sayyebaat)* as against "اَبْكَار" (*abkaar*) which means an unmarried woman i.e. a spinster (66:5)
"بِئْرٌ ثَيِّبٌ" (*be'roon sayyib*): the well in which water returns after drying up.
"ثَيَّبَتِ الْمَرْأَةُ و تَثَيَّبَتْ" (*sayyabatil mar'ato wa tasayyibat*): the woman was widowed *{T}*.

J-A-R   ج أ ر

"جُؤَارٌ" (*juwaar*): to call out loudly and to make a noise, regardless if this act is carried out by a human or animal. This means that it can be used for loud chanting and also for a cow to make noises.

"اَلْجُوَارُ" (*al-juwar*) also means "خُوَارٌ" (khuwar): for an ox to make noises.
"جَأَرَ الدَّاعِىَ يَجْأَرُ" (*jaraddayi bajar*): to raise one's voice while praying.
"جَأَرُ الرَّجُلُ إِلَى اللهِ" (*jarar rajulu ilal lah*): he pleaded while praying before God {T}.
It is said at times of great stress while praying or pleading {R}.

Quran says when you are in trouble, then

16:53	You shout out, and plead before God	فَإِلَيْهِ تَجْأَرُونَ

Jaloot   جَالُوْتُ

"جَالُوْتُ" (*jaloot*) is a non-arabic word {T, R}. Jaloot was a mutinous leader in Palestine who was killed by the hands of **Dawood** (2:251).

Its hebrew diction is "جَلْيَاتُ" (*Jalyat*) {M}. Some think that this word has come from "جَالَ" (*jaala*) and "جَالَ فِىْ الْحَرْبِ" (*jaala fi hurb*): that he attacked with fierceness in battle.

In English the character of Jaloot is better known as Goliath.

J-B-B   ج ب ب

"اَلْجَبُّ" (*al-jabb*), "اَلْجِبَاتُ" (*al-jibaat*), "اَلْاِجْتِبَ" (*al-ijtebaab*): to cut, to delink.
"اَلْجُبُّ" (*al-jub*): well, very deep well, a well which is not concrete or plastered.
It is called "جُبٌّ" (*jubb*) when it has not been dug by man, but a sort of ditch or hole has been formed naturally. A well which has formed on its own and not dug by man. It was this sort of well in which **Yusuf's** brothers had put him into (12:10).

Muheet's compiler says "جُبٌّ" (*jubb*) also means a well or ditch about which it is not known how deep it is or how far down the bottom is.

Raghib says it means a deep hole or ditch whose bottom is fathomless, or a well or ditch which is dug on a hard surface.

Ibn Faris writes that the other basic meanings of this word are to collect things. This is why "اَلْجُبَّةُ" (*al- jubba*): the (gown-like dress of Arabs) dress because it sort of collects the entire body within it.

Taj-ul-Uroos says that "أَلْجُبَّةُ" (*al-jubba*): a dress which is sewn from cut pieces of cloth.

J-B-T   ج ب ت

Tajul Uroos says that "أَلْجِبْتُ" (*al-jibt*): a statue, a sorcerer, an astrologer. Hence Taj writes with reference to Shobi that it means sorcery (magic). The root is said to be "أَلْجِبْسُ" (*al-jubbs*) which means anything which has no good *{T, M}*.

Muheet says it is actually derived from Siryan and means "جَوَّف" (*maj jauf*) which means something hollow. Thereby it began to be used for any hollow or empty object. Alminar says this is as well.

Quran speaks about the people of the code (*ahli kitaab*):

4:51	They trust in sorcery and non-beneficial systems	يُؤْمِنُونَ بِالْجِبْتِ وَالطَّاغُوتِ

They trust in mutinous and the man-made laws and the forces which implement those laws and "جِبْتُ" (*jibt*) which is any unimportant thing, superstitions, spiritless traditions and which have become hollow inside.

Any nation which turns away from Allah's law thinks "جِبْتُ" (*jibt*) and "طَاغُوت" (*taghoot*), or sorcery, are powers to be worshipped.

J-B-R   ج ب ر

"أَلْجَبْرُ" (*al-jabr*) basically it means to reform something in a way which needs force.
"أَلْجَبَائِرُ" (*al-jabair*): the splints used for mending broken bones.
"بَرَ الْعَظْمَ" (*jabaral azm*): to reset broken bones.
"أَلْجَابِرُ" (*al-jabir*): one who mends broken bones *{T, M, R}*.

Nawab Siddiq Hasan Khan writes that "ج" (*jeem*), "ب" (*ba*), "ر" (ra) in their various arrangements give the meaning of intensity and strength.

Ibn Faris says that this word basically signifies greatness, loftiness and stability.

"أَلْجَبَّارُ" (*al-jabbaar*) is one of Allah's traits, which means the mender of all cosmic or human weakness. It also means to make one free of all needs. For instance:

"جَبَرَ الْفَقِيرَ مِنَ الْفَقْرِ" (*jabaral faqira minal faqir*): he made the needy free of his needs.
"تَجَبَّرَ الشَّجَرُ" (*tajabbarash shajar*): the tree became green with vegetation.
"تَجَبَّرَ الْمَرِيضُ" (*tajabbaral mareez*): the patient's condition became better.

These above examples make clear what Allah's "جَبَّارِيَّتْ" (*jabbariat*):. In other words, this too is one more aspect of His Kindness, but for this Man has to observe the path and remain within the set limit. But when human forces break the limits set by Allah, then the very streams become ferocious. That is why in this condition "جَبْر" (*jabr*): tyranny and "جَبَّار" (*jabbar*): tyrant, mutinous, and those who cross the limit.

In the Quran Hazrat Isa says:

| 19:32 | Allah has not made me mutinous, tyrant or ill-fated | وَلَمْ يَجْعَلْنِيْ جَبَّاراً شَقِيّاً |

In surah *Qaf*, about Messenger Muhammed it is said:

| 50:45 | you are not one to pressure them in any way (don't force them to agree upon anything) | وَمَا أَنتَ عَلَيْهِم بِجَبَّارٍ |

About the nation of *Aad*, it is said:

| 26:130 | when you arrest someone, then you arrest him very tyrannically | وَإِذَا بَطَشْتُم بَطَشْتُمْ جَبَّارِينَ |

This word has also been used for men with a big hulk in 5:22.

"اَلْجَبَّارُ مَن النَّخِيْل" (*al-jabbaro man-nikheel*): the long date which nobody's hand can reach

You would have noted that no force of man is good or bad in itself. It is its usage which makes it good or bad. If force is used to mend broken bones, then it is good, but if the same force is used for breaking bones, then it is bad.

"جبّار" (*jabbar*) which stops tyranny is a blessing of God, and the "جبّار" (*jabbar*) that perpetrates tyranny is the reason for punishment.

Jibreel   جِبْرِیْلُ

"جِبْرِیْلُ" (*Jibreelu*) is a Hebrew word. In Quran it is meant to be the power that inscribes Divine inspiration (*wahi*) on the Messengers heart.

Quran says:

| 2:97 | Say "if someone distances himself from Jibreel, who inscribed this Divine message on your heart"… | قُلْ مَن كَانَ عَدُوًّا لِّجِبْرِيلَ فَإِنَّهُ نَزَّلَهُ عَلَى قَلْبِكَ |

"جِبْرِيْلُ" (*jibreel*) is also called as "رُوْحُ الْقُدُسِ" (*ruhool quddus*) (16-102) and "رُوْحُ الْأَمِيْنِ" (*roohul ameen*) (26:193). The word "جِبْرِيْلُ" (*Jibreelu*) appears in **Surah Baqaraa** twice (2:97-98) and once in **Surah Tahreem** (66:4).

Since mankind cannot understand the significance of *wahi* (Divine inspiration, because *wahi* is the knowledge that has its source beyond the comprehension of mankind, therefore it cannot understand what is the essence of "جِبْرِيْلُ" (*jibreel*) is. Our connection with *wahi* exists in Quran and from there we can comprehend it. This energy "رُوْحٌّ" (*roohun*) is called "قُدُسٌ" (*quddusun*) and "أَمِيْنٌ" (*ameenun*) because the Divine inspiration (which is engraved on the heart of Messengers) is neither adulterated nor has any corruption in it. Neither is there any doubt of an emotional input of the Messenger (53:3), nor is there any corruption made by Messengers themselves (3:160). None of the worldly powers can interfere with it.

The enemies of the Messengers are the ones who introduce these elements after their death (whether they may be their own kin or others). But Quran states that no adulteration or corruption is possible, because God Himself has taken on the responsibility to safeguard it.

J-B-L   ج ب ل

"الْجَبَلُ" (*Aljabalu*) is a mountain, or nation's chief or scholar. (plural "جمع جِبَالٌ" (*jeebaalun*)).

Surah Al-Anmbiyaa says:

21:79	We made the chiefs of this nation subservient to David (for the fulfillment of the purpose of life)	وَسَخَّرْنَا مَعَ دَاوُوْدَ الْجِبَالَ

The same meaning is to me taken in (34:10). It could also mean that the Messenger David brought the mountainous area under his control and put to use. In **Surah Qaaf** the opposite of "الْجِبَالَ" (*al-jbaal*) is given as the "أَرْضٌ" (*arz*) which means lower level. (18:47). Also see heading *(A-W-B)*.

In it too "جِبَالٌ" (*jibaalu*) are meant to be the chiefs, while the "أَرْضٌ" (*arz*): the lesser group. "الْجِبِلُ" (*al-jibilu*) and "الْجِبِلَةُ" (*al-jibilatuh*) is a large group of people as in 36:62 & 26:184 {*T*}. "الْجِبِلَّة" (*al-jibillath*): a large amount, a constant mannerism, nature, crowd {*M*}.

Ibn Faris has said that its fundamental meaning is to be elevated and that all its various constituents to be collected permanently together. Hence "جِبَالٌ" (*jibaalun*) is a collection of loftiness, status, power and community.

The common meaning of "جِبَالٌ" (*jabalun*) is a mountain and its metaphorical meaning is chiefs or leaders of a nation. Thus in Quran, it is possible to ascertain which meanings are appropriate by considering the context of the verse.

J-B-N   ج ب ن

"اَلْجُبْنُ" (*al-jubnu*), is cowardice, to be weak hearted. Also its meaning is cheese. "اَلْجَبِينَان" (*al-ajabeenaani*) is temples (both sides of forehead) where the folds occur. Its singular is "الجَبِيْنُ" (*al-jabeenu*). "الجَبِيْنُ" (*al-jabhatunh*) is also the fore head (this in between the temples) [T, M,R}.

In Quran, with reference to Abraham and Ishmael it is given

37:103	Abraham put Ishmael on his side, of temple	وَتَلَّهُ لَلْجَبِينِ

Same as a slaughter lays the animal down on one side to slaughter it with ease. Thus it is obvious from Quran that Abraham laid Ishmael down in the same way.

J-B-He   ج ب ه

"اَلْجَبْهَة" (*al-jabhatuh*) is forehead. Its plural is "جَبَاة" (*jabhaau*). It also means a beautiful woman who has a broad and high forehead {T}. Muheet has said that its fundamental meaning is of lofty and tall person. Quran says "جِبَاهُهُمْ" (*jibahuhum*) in verse 9:35 to say "their foreheads".

J-B-W/Y   ج ب و (ى)

"جَبَى الْخِرَاجَ وَالْمَالَ" (*jabyi al khiraaja wal maala*): collected tribute and wealth.
"جَبَى الْمَاءَ فِى الْحَوْض" (*jabyi al maa fi al hodh*): collected water in the fountain.
"جَبَى الْمَاءَ فِى الْحَوْض" (*jabal ma'aa fil hauz*): collected water in the pool. Tts plural is "جَوَاب" (*jawabin*) or "اَلْجَوَابَة" (*al-jawabi*).

The fundamental meaning of this root is to collect {T, M, R}.

The Quran says:

34:13	asins large as reservoirs	وجِفَانٍ كَالْجَوَاب
28:57	all types of fruit would be drawn towards the Kaabaa and get collected there	يُجْبَىٰ إِلَيْهِ ثَمَرَاتُ

"جَبَا" (*jabaa*): to compile or collect.

In Surah **Al-Airaf** it is said:

7:203	when you do not take a Quranic verse to them, they say 'why don't you compose one your self	وَإِذَا لَمْ تَأْتِهِم بِآيَةٍ قَالُوا لَوْلَا اجْتَبَيْتَهَا

This is said because, the non-believers had this impression that the messenger compiled (God forbid) the Quranic verses by collecting hearsay.

Even today the Orientalist put out such ideas. This is because of their lack of knowledge regarding position of the 'Messenger-ship' or perhaps mere prejudice on their part. In both cases our educated people were badly affected by such writings.

"اَلْإِجْتِبَاءُ" (*al-ijteebaau*) is to collect wealth from the source and horde it, (meaning the collected tribute). Thus it is deduced that it means, to selectively collect {*T, M, R*}, as given in verse 3:178 "اَللهُ يَجْتَبِیْ" (Allah reclaims).

J-Th-Th   ج ث ث

"اَلْجَثُّ" (*al-jaththu*) is to uproot a tree from its roots.
"اَلْإِجْتِثَاثُ" (*al-jitithaathu*): the same, but even with more emphases {*T, M, R*}. In Quran we have "اُجْتُثَّتْ" (*ujtuthtu*) in verse 14:26, which means 'its roots and base was uprooted'.
"اَلْجُثُّ" (*al-juththu*) is a hill which is reduced to a small mound.
"جُثَّةُ الْإِنْسَانِ" (*juththul al insaani*) is when a person is sitting or lying down, and thus his body quizzes to small size (*Ibn Faris*).

Ibn Faris states that its fundamental meaning is to collect. The same applies to uprooted tree as it is collected in small bundle so that it does not sprout again.

J-Th-M   ج ث م

"جَثَمَ" (*jathama*), "يَجْثِمُ" (*yajthimu*), "جَثْماً" (*jathman*) and "ثُوْماً" (*juthoomu*) is to cling such as not to separate again. For birds etc. to sit on their chest, so as not to move from the place is said "اَلْجَاثِمُ" (*al-jaathimu*).
"اَلْجُثْمَةُ" (*al-juthmatuh*) is a mound of soil, mud or ash.
"اَلْجُثُوْمُ" (*al-juthoomu*) and "الْجَثَمَ" (*al-jathamatah*) is a hillock.
"اَلْمُجَثَّمَةُ" (*al-mujaththamatuh*) is the animal that is tethered so as to take an aim at it for the purpose of killing it {*T*}. Therefore it means to collect in a place and be made immobile {*F*}.

In Quran is given:

| 7:78 | they remained static in their houses and turned into mounds | فَاَصْبَحُوْ فِیْ دَارِهِمْ جَثِمِیْنَ |

J-Th-W ج ث و

"اَلْجَثْوَةُ" (*al-jathwatuh*) (with all three vowels on J) a mound of stones or sand, and also body.
"اَلْجَثْوَةُ" (*juthaa al harami*) is the mound of pebbles that is collected at the limits of the ""
(*haram*) to be thrown at the Devil. The idols, on which the sacrificial animals were slaughtered, during the pagan period.
"اَلْجُثَّاءُ" (*al-juthaa*) is a community (collection) of people.
"جَثَوْتُ الإِبِلَ" (*jathawtu al ibila*): 'I have collected the camels'.
"جَثَا" (*Jathaa*), "يَجْثُوْ" (*yajtho*), "جُثِيَّا" (*jutheeyan*) is to squat (for the purposes of quarrel).
"فَهُوَ جَاثٍ" (*fahuwa jaathin*): that someone squatted on knees (plural is "جُثِيٌّ" (*juthiyun*) and also "جِثِيَّ" (*jithiyan*) {T}.

In **Surah Jaathiyaa** it is given:

45:28	you will see all groups squatting on their knees (in disgrace, humility and helpless ness.)	وَتَرَىٰ كُلَّ أُمَّةٍ جَاثِىَ

In **Surah Maryam** it is given:

| 19:27 | We will place the ignorant on their knees | وَنَذَرُ الظَّالِمِيْنَ فِيْهَا جِثِيّاً |
| 19:68 | We will present them around hell on their knees (in total disgrace) | لَنُحْضِرَ نَّهُمْ حَوْلَ جَهَنَّمَ جِثِيًّا |

J-H-D ج ح د

"جَحَدَ حَقَّهُ" (*jhada haqqahu*), is to deliberately deny some one's right.
"أَرْضٌ جَحِدَةٌ" (*ardhun jahidatunh*) is dry land.
"عَامٌ جَحِدٌ" (*a'mun jahidun*) is the year with below average rain.
"أَجْحَدَ الرَّجُلُ" (*ajhadal rajulu*) is uttered when one loses everything and gets up dejected to leave {T}.

Ibn Faris has said that it means the draught (shortage) of blessings, or of good things.

Raghib and **Muheet** have said that "اَلْجَحْدُ" (*al-jahdu*): to deny that which the heart believes in, and vice versa.

In various places Quran has referred to those who deny Divine laws merely on account of the intentional stubbornness "بِآيَاتِ اللهِ يَجْحَدُوْنَ" (6:33).

This is explained elsewhere as in following verse:

| 27:14 | these people deny the truth deliberately, merely on account of their lack of knowledge and arrogance, although they know very well that it is the truth | وَجَحَدُوْ اِبَاو اَسْتَيْقَنَتْهَا اَنْفُسُهُمْ ظُلْماً وَعُلُوًّا |

Muheet has said that "جَحَدَ النِّعْمَةَ" (*hajada al ne'matih*): that he has not understood it or deliberately is ungrateful of the blessings.

J-H-M   ج ح م

"اَجْحَمَ عَنْہُ" (*ajhama anhu*): that he was stopped from whatever he was doing.

"اَلْجَحَّامُ" (*al-hjjam*) is used for a miser who stops his wealth from spreading {T}.

"اَلْبَعِيْرَ" (*al-bai'yur*): to put a muzzle on a camel's mouth to stop it from biting.

"تَجَحَّمَ الْمَكَانُ وَالْقَلْبُ" (*tajahhama al makaanu walqalbu*): the house, or the heart got constricted {M}.

Imam al Ramanyi has given "اَجْحَمَ" (*ajhama*), "اَمْسَکَ" (*amsaka*) and "اِنْتَھیٰ" (*intahaa*) as synonyms.

Ibn Faris has said that this word in its meaning is an inversion.

"تَجَحَّمَ" (*tajahamma*): to grow bitter as the consequences of one's miserliness and constriction of heart. From this is deduced as, to set aflame.

"اَلْجَحْمَةُ" (*al-jahmatuh*) is the fire in a deep place. Therefore it means a very hot place.

"اَلْجَاحِمُ مِنَ الْحَرْبِ" (*al jaahimu minal harbi*): a very fierce battle {T}.

Ibn Faris has given its meaning as very hot and intense fire.

Quran has used this word for the state of Hell (see 44:27, 37:55, 37:64, 37:68). Quran has given the result of 'wrong doing' as the fire of hell because it burns everything to ashes.

If the purpose of life is considered in the light of Quran, it will be obvious that this worldly life is a link in the chain of development and this progress has a long way yet to travel. In following the divine laws, human being reaches a certain level of progress and development eventually in the hereafter. But if its capabilities are not able to travel the distance then it is not able to reach that level. It comes to a halt. This is the fundamental rule of natural progress. This halting is referred to in Quran as "اَلْجَحِيْمُ" (*al-jaheemu*), which fundamentally means to come to a halt.

"اَلْجَحِيْمُ" (*al-jaheemu*) is hence the last stop on the path of its journey. And because this heat of realization is so intense, it burns the heart (104:7-8) to the extent that it will turn its dreams to ashes. According to Quran, an individual or a nation that come to such a halt, that place is called

"أَلْجَحِيْمُ" (*jaheem*). Life is a continuous flow that has to keep on flowing, but the flow which comes to a halt, starts getting stale.

J-D-Th   ج د ث

"أَلْجَدَثْ" (*al-jadas*): grave. Its plural form is "أَجْدُثٌ" (*ajdus*) and "أَجْدَاثٌ" (*ajudas*).

The Quran says about those in the state of *Janannum*:

36:51	They will suddenly get out of their graves and sped towards their lord.	فَإِذَاهُمْ مِنَ الْأَجْدَاثِ إِلَى رَبِّهِمْ يَنْسِلُوْنَ

This is followed up with the following verse where these same people shall say:

36:56	Who woke us up from our resting place?	كَهْمَنْ بَعَثَنَا مِنْ مَرْقَدِنَا

Hence "أَجَدَثٌ" (*ajadas*) and "مَرْقَدٌ" (*maroqad*) have same meanings. Please not that these words are not confined for some specific places, but rather conditions.
"أَلْجَدَثَةُ" (*al-dajasa*) is the sound a camels foot makes while striking the ground.

J-D-D   ج د د

"أَلْجَدُّ" (*al-jadda*). The basic meaning of this root is to complete or cut off something. For instance,
"ثَوْبٌ جَدِيْدٌ" (*saub jadeed*): the recently cut cloth. But soon its use began to mean every newly prepared or new-born thing *{T}*. "أَلْجَدِيْدُ" (*al-jadeed*) is used for a thing with you previously never had any knowledge of.

The Quran says:

14:20	If He would desire, He could replace you with a new creation. (a creation which you have no knowledge of)	إِنْ يَّشَأْ يُذْهِبْكُمْ وَيَأْتِ بِخَلْقٍ جَدِيْدٍ

"أَلْجُدَّةُ" (*al-jodda*): the way of anything, which is the way of its completion. The plural is "جُدَدٌ" (*joda*).

The Quran use this word in mention of mountains:

35:27	Roads of color red and white	جُدَدٌ بِيْضٌ وَحُمْرٌ

Here the ways are referring to the lines of rocky layers of different colors, on which the mountains are constructed. In this regard "أَلْجُدَّةُ" (*al-jodda*) is also used for the lines on a donkey back.

"أَلْجَدُّ" (*al-jaddo*) also means soil or field, and also for a very blessed man. It also means grandfather. It is to this regard that its meanings are maturity, greatness and high status as well.

The Quran hence says:

| 72:3 | The status of our **Rabb** is extremely great. | وَأَنَّهُ تَعَالَى جَدُّ رَبِّنَا |

"أَلْجِدُّ" (*al-jidda*) to make an effort in any work. It also means to hurry or do something quickly. In addition to this, this word is also used to express exaggeration, for instance "عَالِمٌ جِدَّ عَالِمٍ" (*alimun jidda alim*): he is a scholar, indeed a great scholar *{T}*.

Ibn Faris says that this root has three basic meanings:
- High status
- Well blessed
- Completion by cutting.

All three meanings have been presented with examples in the above text.

J-D-R   ر د ج

"أَلْجَدْرُ" (*al-jadro*), "أَلْجِدَارُ" (*al-jidar*): wall. "أَلْحَائِطُ" (*al-haito*) is used to cover a wall.
"أَلْجَدَرُ" (*al-jadar*): to be tall.

The real meaning of this root is in fact to be rise, to be tall. Hence "جَدَرْتُ الْجِدَارَ" (*jarad tul-ijara*): that the wall got taller.
"أَلْجَدْرُ" (*al-jadru*) is a plant that grows in sandy soil *{T}*.
Surah kahaf has uses the wird of "جَدَارٌ" (*jadar*) in the meaning of wall (18:77).
"أَلْجَدِيْرُ" (*al-jadeer*): to be in appropriate and suitable.
"قَدْجَدُرَ جَدَارَةً" (*qad jadora jadarah*): surely he got appropriate.
"إِنَّهُ مَجْدُوْرٌ أَنْ يَفْعَلَ ذٰلِكَ" (*inna majdor an yaf'al zalika*): he is indeed suitable for this.

The Quran says:

| 9:97 | They are more suited then this where they do not understand | وَأَجْدَرُ أَلَّا يَعْلَمُوْا |

"أَلْجَدِيْرَةُ" (*al-jadeerah*) is one's health condition.

J-D-L   ج د ل

"اَلْجَدْلُ" (*al-jadlo*) basically means to be twisted.

"جَدَلَ الْحَبْلَ" (*jadal-al-habla*): twisted the rope firmly.

"اَلْجَدِيْلُ" (*al-jadeel*) is the twisted leather or rope used on horses {*T*}.

"اَلْجُدَالُ" (*al-judalo*) is used for anything that is twisted firmly {*M*}.

"اَلْجَدَلَةُ" (al-jadalah): firm soil {*T*}.

"جَدَلَ الشَّىْءُ جُدُوْلاً" (*jadalashai judola*): to become firm and hard.

Ibn Faris says that the basic meaning of this root is to become long firm.

"جَدَلٌ" (*jadal*) is used for a quarrel because of its long lasting.

"اَلْجِدَالُ" (*al-jidalo*). According to **Raghib**, this word is used for such a quarrel where participants try to dominate each other, and for that reason make the discussion long without any proper reason. This is the reason why some think that the meaning of this word is the same as of "صِرَاعٌ" (*sira'o*) which means to throw your opponent on the ground {*T*}.

The Quran mention the following regarding Hajj.

2:197	Don't exercise *jidal* in hajj	لَاجِدَالَ فِىْ الْحَجِّ

With respect to the above given meaning of *jidal,* the purpose of hajj becomes clear. Hajj is an international gathering of Muslims with a practical purpose. The purpose is to get together to discuss and solve the mutual problems and issues. The Quran says that for this gathering do not adopt such a manner in which you try to throw down your encountering party, or prolong the discussion with useless inputs, in order to win an argument. Keep your discussions short and serious, and keep in mind the purpose, which is to discuss as much issues in least possible time.

Surah **Mujadilah** says "اَلَّتِىْ تُجَادِلُكَ" (*allitu tujadilko*). This is referring to that woman who used to constantly ask question regarding her husband, from **Rusool-Allah**. She was prolonging the discussion without any reason. She wanted to win the argument and hence the argument started to turn into something like a quarrel.

Surah **Al-Kahaf** says:

18:54	And We have indeed put forth in the Quran repeatedly for mankind every kind of example (alternating the styles), but man is far ahead in contention than anything else	وَلَقَدْ صَرَّفْنَا فِىْ هٰذَا الْقُرْآنِ لِلنَّاسِ مِن كُلِّ مَثَلٍ وَكَانَ الْإِنْسَانُ أَكْثَرَ شَىْءٍ جَدَلاً

The meaning is that all aspects has been clearly defined in the holy Quran, but he true way of approach is that one should not constantly try to prove the Quranic teaching wrong, no matter what. One should keep an open mind while studying Quran, and always have this objective that I am studying Quran to learn about the facts. This is the only way to actually learn something.

J-Dh-Dh   ج ذ ذ

"اَلْجَذُّ" (*al-jazz*): to break something.

"كَسَرْتُمْ أَجَذَاذاً" (*kasaratu ajazaza*): I smashed it into several pieces.

"اَلْجُذَّةُ" (*al-juzzah*) basically means the part of something that gets cut off.

"جُذَاذٌ" (*juzazu*) parts or dust of gold.

Surah **Al-Anbiya** says:

21:58	Ibrahim smashed those statues into pieces.	فَجَعَلَهُمْ جُذَاذاً

Surah **Hood** says the following regarding the status of **Jannah**:

11:108	Not breakable gift (a gift that is not going to stop or end, which shall last forever)	عَطَاءً غَيْرَ مَجْذُوذٍ

In other words

65:6	An everlasting compensation	أَجْرٌ غَيْرُ مَمْنُونٍ

J-Dh-Ain   ج ذ ع

"جِذْعٌ" (*jiz'a*) is the trunk of a palm tree. Its plural is "جُذُوعٌ" (*jozo'o*).

Some have said that this word is used for the trunk that has gone dry. Some has said that it means the trunk that has been cut off. But others think that this word does not contain concepts of drying out or get cut off.

Surah Mariam has mentioned "جِذْعِ النَّخْلَةِ" (*jiza'in nahazi*) in 19:23, to means palm tree of dates, and 19:25 has made it clear that this palm tree is flourishing, bearing fruit. But on the other hand, surah Taha has used the words of "جُذُوْعِ النَّخْلِ" (*jozo'in nahli*) for the wood of a crucifix (20:71). From this we get the indication that crucifix was made from cut off dry wood of palm trees.

"جَذَعْتُهُ" (*jaz'ah*): that I cut it off.

"جَذَعَ الدَّابَّةَ" (*jaz'addabbah*): he cut off the animal's route.

"اَلْجُذُوْعَةُ" (*al-jodo'ah*) is the young age.

Ibn Faris says that it basically means youth and freshness, trunk of a tree, to meet with something.

J-Dh-W   ج ذ و

"جَذَا عَلَى الشَّىءِ يُجْذُوْجَذواً" (*jaza a'lashai i yojazzo jazoa*): He established himself firmly on something.

"جَذَا الرَّاجُلُ عَلىٰ أَطْرَافِ أَصَابِعِهِ" (*jazzarrajolu a'la atrafi asabi'hi*): Man stood up upon his toes.

Hence it has the basic concept of standing of something on something. For that reason "جَذْوَةٌ" (*jazzwah*) is that flare of burning wood, which loses its glow. In other words, the shining and twinkling is lost and it gets settled on a condition. Quran has used "جَذْوَةٍ مِنَ النَّارِ" in 28:26 to indicate flare of a fire.

J-R-H   ج ر ح

"جَرَحَ" (*jarha*): to acquire something, to get something.

Ibn Faris says that it has two basic meanings. One is earning and second is of opening the skin (to inflict wound)

The Quran says following with respect to earning:

65:6	Those who produce unbalance	أَمْ حَسِبَ الَّذِيْنَ اجْتَرَ حُوا السَّيِّأتِ

This above verse is referring towards those who commit crime.

Surah **Al-An'am** says:

6:60	That what you do during the daytime	مَاجَرَحْتُمْ بِا لنَّهَارِ

In this context "أَلْجَوَارِحُ" (*al-javarih*) is used for the hands, feet or body members that work for a man.

Muheet says that "أَلْجَوَارِحُ" (*al-javarih*): those challenges that one makes during the daytime. Likewise, the problems that come during the night, as called "طَوَارِقْ" (*tawariq*).

In addition to this, it means the hunting animal. This because "جَرَحَ يَجْرَحُ" (*jaraha yajrah*): to wound.

"أَلْجَرَاحَةُ" (*al-jarahah*): the wound which is inflicted by a spear or sword.

Quran has used "أَلْجَوَارِح مُكَلِّبِيْنَ" (*aljawarihi mokaleen*) for those animals one train for hunting, like dogs (5:45).

J-R-D   ج ر د

"جَرَدَ" (*jarad*), "يَجْرِدُ" (*yajrid*): to peel off.

"جَرَدَ الْجِلَدَ" (*jaradaljild*): that he peeled of the hairs of the skin.

"جَرَدَ زَيْداً مَنْ ثَوْبِه" (*jaradazaid aman soba*): He stripped Zaid of his clothes.

"فَتَجَرَّدَ" (*fatajarra*): He got nude.

"اَلتَّجَرُّدُ" (*attajarro*): to get nude, undressed.

"اَلْجَرَادُ" (*al-jirad*): locust, probably because it shave of the trees and fields from crops. (7:133)

"مَكَانٌ جَرِدٌ" (*makan jarid*): such a place where there grows no grass.

"سَنَةٌ جَارُوْدٌ" (*sanaha jarod*) is a year of extreme famine.

Ibn Faris says that its basic meaning is to clean of something in such a manner that it becomes clearly visible.

J-R-Z   ج ر ز

"جَرَزَ" (*jarza*), "يَجْرُزُ" (*yajrozo*), "جَرْزأَ" (*jarza*): to eat quickly. To murder, to cut off, to uproot. The basic meaning of this root is to cut off and to be hasty about it.

"اَلْجَرُوْزُ" (*al-jarozu*): when a heavy eater sits down to eat, and leave nothing behind.

"أَرْضٌ جُرُزٌ" (*arz jorz*): field on which nothing grows, or where all vegetation has been grazed clean.

"الْجَرَزْ" (*al-jaraz*): a year when no vegetation grows.

"اَلْجَارِزْ" (*al-jariz*): an unfertile woman.

"اَلْجُرَازْ" (*al-joraz*): a sharp sword.

The Quran says:

18:8	We turn this soil into unfertile ground	وَإِنَّا لَجَاعِلُونَ مَا عَلَيْهَا صَعِيدًا جُرُزًا

This could mean that We turn this soil into unfertile ground during the season of harvest and winter. It can also mean that whatever is on earth, We keep deteriorating (the cycle of spring and autumn).

J-R-Ain   ج ر ع

"اَلْجَرْعَةُ" (*al-jar'a*): a sip of a drink (with all three vowels on J).
Lisaan-al-Arab says that "جَرْعَةٌ" (*jar'a*) is the swallowing of a drink once, while "جُرْعَةٌ" (*jor'a*) is the drink itself that gets swallowed.

"اَلتَّجَرُّعُ" (*al-jarro'o*) is the sipping of a drink in such a manner that it becomes very clear that the person who is drinking, is disliking his drink.

Hence the Quran stated regarding those in the state of *Jahannum* that whatever they get to drink there:

14:17	he will drink it loath fully and will not be able to swallow it	يَتَجَرَّعُهُ وَلَايَكَادُ يُسِيغُهُ

God Almighty! How demeaning can be the bread that one gets in ignominy and subjugation in this world. It is hard to survive without eating and the food can't even be pushed down the throat!

Muheet's compiler says, the real meaning of this root is to break or cut apart (or to collect).

"وَتَرٌّ جَرِعٌ" (*wa tarun jare-un*): the bent of a bow which is so crooked that it gets easily spotted among others. "اَلْأَجْرَعُ" (*alajra'o*): hard and rocky land.

Ibn Faris says it basically means the decreasing or lessening of anything drinkable.

J-R-F   ج ر ف

"جَرَفَ" (*jaraf*), "يَجْرُفُ" (*yajrofo*), "جَرْفاً" (*jarfan*): to take a lot, to take all or a big portion.
"جَرَفَ الطِّينَ" (*jarafat teen*): he scraped the earth.
"اَلْجَارِفُ" (*al-jaarif*): a destruction that destroys the (good) acts of a nation. It also means the plague or some other epidemic.
"سَيْلٌ جُرَافٌ" (*sailun juraaf*): the flood which washes away everything.
"اَلْجُرْفُ والْجُرُفُ" (*aljarfo wal juruf*): that land which is situated on the banks of a river and gradually is eaten away by the river or washed away in the flood {*T, R*}.

Surah *At-Tauba* says:

9:109	a bank which is gradually being washed away	شَفَاجُرُفٍ

The real meaning of this root is to cleanse, to take out, to take (water) in the palm of the hand and to cut away, or to usurp the whole thing {*F*}.

J-R-M   ج ر م

"جَرْمٌ" (*jaram*) basically means to cut something or to remove something from on top of it and lay it bare *{M}*.

Commonly it is used to cut off or pick a fruit from the tree *{R}*.

"جَرَمَ النَّخْلَ" (*jaramal nakhal*): cut off the date palm or picked its fruit.

"أَلْجِرْمَةٌ" (*al-jirmah*): the men who pick the fruits of the date palms.

"جَرَمَ الشَّاةَ جَرْماً" (*jarama lushata jarma*): he cut off the sheep's wool *{T}*.

"جَرَمَ لَّلَحَم عَنِ الْعَظْمِ" (*jaramal laham unil azm*): tore off the flesh from the bone and laid it bare *{M}*.

These examples should make the meaning of the word clear, which is to rob, exploitation, to pick somebody else's fruit for self. To rob off other people's gains and to lay them bare. The perpetrators of these acts are called "مُجْرِمُونَ" (*mujremoon*). On this basis every unpleasant effort, (displeasing earnings) are called "جَرْمٌ" (*jarm*)

"أَجْرَمَ" (*aj-ram*): he became one of the ones with "جَرْمٌ" (*jurm*) *{R}*.

Keep this meaning of the word in mind and consider that when the Quran sends a nation "مُجْرِمُونَ" (*mujremoon*) to *jahannum*, what it means. According to the Quran the worst society is one in which some people exploit others and live a luxurious life on the basis of others' hard earned incomes. Such a society is destined for the state of *jahannum*.

Surah *Al-Qalam* says:

68:35	will We equate the *muslemeen* with the *mujremeen*	اَفَنَجْعَلُ الْمُسْلِمِيْنَ كَالْمُجْرِمِيْنَ

It is therefore evident that no *Muslim* can ever be a *mujrim*. Also see heading (J-N-Y).

"لَاجَرَمَ" (*la-jaram*): essentially, of course, without doubt, what is evident or unmasked or naked *{T}*.

The Quran says:

11:22	without doubt these people will be losers in the end	لَاجَرَمَ اِنَّهُمْ فِى الْاٰخِرَةِ هُمُ الْاَخْسَرُوْنَ
5:2	Do not make a nation incite you	لَا يَجْرِمَنَّكُمْ شَنَاٰنُ قَوْمٍ

It means to not make a deal unless they makes you agree to acquire it.

Ibn Faris says "جَرَمَ" (*jaram*) means to earn.

J-R-Y ج ر ی

"جَرْیٌ وَجَرَیَانٌ" (*jariun wa jarayan*): means the flow of water, or to flow without any hindrance. *Raghib* says "اَلْجَرْیُ" (*al-jario*): to walk fast. Hence "جَرَی الْفَرَسُ" (*jaral faras*): the horse ran fast.

The Quran says:

13:2	Each sphere is moving firmly for a destined period (There is no hindrance in its path)	كُلٌّ یَجْرِیْ لِأَجَلٍ مُسَمًّی

The feminine is "اَلْجَارِیَةُ" (*al-jariah*) or "جَارٍ" (*jarin*) or "اَلْجَارِیْ" (*al-jari*) which means one which moves, flows, or one who runs fast. The plural of "جَارِیَةٌ" (*jariah*) is "جَارِیَاتٌ" (*jariyaat*), and "جَوَارٍ" (*jawarin*).

Quran says:

51:3	The easily gliding ones	اَلْجَارِیَاتُ یُسْراً

The boat which flows or sails in the river is also called "جَارِیَةٌ" (*jariah*)
"اَلْجَارِیَةُ" (*al-jaari*): the moon.
"اَلْجَوَارِیْ" (*al-jawariy*): the stars.
"جَارِیَةٌ" (*jaariah*): a girl.
"جَرَی لَهُ الشَّیْءُ" (*jaralahush shaiyi*): means that thing remained for him forever, that is, here is a connotation of perpetuity *{T}*.
For the perpetuation's meaning, see heading (J-N-N), under which the term "تَجْرِیْ مِنْ تَحْتِهَا الْأَنْهَارُ" (*tajri min tahtehal anhaat*) has been explained in the context of heaven.
"اَلْجَرِیُّ" (*al-jariyo*): counsellor and guarantor *{T, M}*.

The Quran says:

88:12	there is a flowing stream in it	فِیْهَا عَیْنٌ جَارِیَةٌ
42:32	ships in the sea	اَلْجَوَارِ فِی الْبَحْرِ

J-Z-A ج ز ا

"اَلْجُزْءُ" (*al-juzz*): a part of something.
"اَجْزَاءٌ" (*ajza*): the parts (plural) of which a thing comprises of.
"اجزاء السَّفِیْنَة" (*ajza us safeena*), "اجزاء الدَّوَاء" (*ajza ud dawa*): if some things are removed from among many things, they will also be a part of that collection and called a "جُزْءٌ" (*juzz*) of that collection *{T}*.

Surah *Az-Zakhraf* says about the Christians:

43:15	some say that some of God's followers are a part of Him (His sons)	وَجَعَلُوا لَهُ مِنْ عِبَادِهِ جُزْءًا

This is meant to deny the concept of the 'Holy Trinity", which is "One of three and three in One". This concept divides God into three! Or it is meant to show as false any notion which gives any man a share in God's domain. Jesus being the son of God also comes within the purview of this concept, or the concept that Man is God, as well.

"جَزْءٌ" (*jaz-un*): to tear into pieces or separate

"اَلْجُزْءُ" (*al-juz*) is a part of something whether it is attached to the whole or not. It is not necessary that to separate a part every individual part of the whole also be cut or broken off. A lot of individuals together may form a part of the whole.

Surah *Al-Hijr* says:

15:44	for everyone (for the humans who will enter *jahannum*) of the doors, a part has been destined	لِكُلِّ بَابٍ مِنْهُمْ جُزْءٌ مَقْسُومٌ

This does not mean that the humans have been torn to pieces and their parts have been separated but it means that every group has been separated. This makes the verse of surah *Al-Baqrah* clear in which *Ibrahim* has been told to make familiar very well with four birds

2:260	then leave them separately in the mountains ; then call out to them and they will fly towards you	ثُمَّ اجْعَلْ عَلَى كُلِّ جَبَلٍ مِنْهُنَّ جُزْءًا

The Quran uses the word "جَزَاءً" (*jazaa*) for the result of one's deeds. See its meaning in heading (J-Z-Y).

<h2 style="text-align:center">J-Z-Ain   ج ز ع</h2>

"جَزْعٌ" (*jaz-un*) actually means to cut a rope in the middle {*R*}. Then it began to be used to mean to cut anything or delink it from the whole

"جَزَعَ الْأَرْضَ وَالْوَادِيَ" (*jaza'al arda wal waadi*): he separated the land from the valley {*T*}.

"جِزْعُ الْوَادِيِّ" (*jiz-ul waadi*) actually is the place where the valley turns or ends.

"اَلْجَازِعُ" (*al-jazey*) is that main beam in the ceiling and smaller pieces join it: thus it divides these smaller pieces or the room itself into two parts {*R*}.

"اَلْجَزَعُ" (*Al-jaza'o*) is the opposite of "صَبْرٌ" (*sabar*). "صَبْرٌ" (*sabar*): perseverance, to be stable. See heading (Sd-B-R). When something is left in the middle, that is, one dissociates himself with it, then it is "اَلْجَزَعُ" (*aljaza*) that is to lose hope, to be unstable {*R*}.

Surah **Ibrahim** says:

| 14:21 | whether we lose heart or stay stable | أَجَزِعْنَا اَمْ صَبَرْنَا |

J-Z-Y   ج ز ى

"جَزَاءٌ" (*jaza'oon*), "جَازِيَةٌ" (*jaaziah*): the return for something.
"جَزَاهُ كَذَاوبِم وعَلَيْهِ" (*jaza-hu kazaubehi alaih*): he replied to something in such a way that {T}.
"مُجَازَاةٌ" (*mujazah*): to give return to each other. Ordinarily, it is used to mean a return for bad things while "مُكَافَأَةٌ" (*makafa'ah*) is used for good things.

Ibn Faris says its basic meaning is to replace i.e. for one thing to be in another's place.

This meaning points to a great truth. What is considered to be the result of deeds is actually the 'natural' result of that deed, that is, the result replaces the deed. If you put your hand into the fire, it is your act, your hand is burnt and it is very painful, this is the result of your act. The act ended soon but it was replaced by the result. This brings the Quranic concept of reward and punishment (*jaza* and *saza*) to the fore. According to this concept, neither reward comes from somewhere outside, or punishment. You abuse someone, he slaps you, and this punishment is from the outside because the abuse and slap have no connection. But if you eat poison and then die, this is a result of your act. In other words the result replaces the act.

That is why the Quran says:

| 7:147 | acts are in a way their own results (every result replaces the act) | هَلْ يُجْزَوْنَ اِلَّا مَا كَانُوا يَعْمَلُوْنَ |

"جَزَى الشَّيْئُ يَجْزِى" (*jazash shaiyu yajzi*): that thing was enough. **Ibn Faris** too, agrees with this meaning.
"مَا يُجْزِينَىْ هٰذا لثَّوْبُ" (*ma yujzaini haazas saub*): this cloth will not be enough for me.
"بٰذه ابلٌ مَجَازَىْ" (*hazehi iblun majazee*): For me, these camels will be enough for taking up the load {T}.

The Quran says:

| 2:48 | on which day the biggest of men cannot take the load for someone else's crime (no man can adopt anybody results) | يَوْماً لَا تَجْزِيْ نَفْسٌ عَنْ نَفْسٍ شَيْئاً |

Ibn Faris says it means to compensate on behalf of another.

"جِزْيَةٌ" (*jizyah*) is used in 9:29 for the tax that is taken from non-Muslims for their protection. That is, that which is thought to be enough to provide their lives, possessions, honor etc. with protection, and due to which they are to be exempted from taking part in wars. This small tax is taken in return for all the benefits that non-Muslims enjoy in an Islamic state and maintenance of which is the responsibility of the Muslims.

Imam-ur Rahmani has said that "اَلْجِزْيَةُ" (*jizyah*) is equivalent to "اَلْعَهْدُ" (*al-ahd*) (pact)
"اَلذَّمَّةُ" (*az-zimmah*): responsibility.
"اَلْأَمَانُ" (*al-aman*): peace, security
"اَلْخَرَاجُ" (*al-khiraj*): tax {*M*}

Thus it would mean the pact or agreement in which somebody is provided security in exchange for a small tax.

J-S-D   ج س د

"اَلْجَسَدُ" (*al-jasad*): means human body. Other bodies which eat and drink are not called "جَسَدٌ" (*jasad*), but the creatures which do not eat or drink but have a mind. According to the Arab's belief, *djinns* and *malaikas* etc. their bodies too may be called "جَسَدٌ" (*jasad*) {*T, R*}.

The Quran has however called **Bani Israeel's** calf as "جَسَدٌ" (*jasada*) in 7:148.

Muheet's compiler as well as **Ibn Faris** says that it means for something to be consolidated and hard. As such "جَسَدٌ" (*jasad*) is a solid and compound body. The calf made by **Sameri**, was called "جَسَدٌ" (*jasad*) perhaps because it was solid as well as made out of various jewellery and therefore compound.
Kulyaat or the Key says that "جَسَدٌ" (*jasad*) is actually a colourful body {*M*}.

Surah Anbia uses the word "جَسَدٌ" (*jasada*) in 21:8 for a human body, but at the same time, it is mentioned that those "جَسَداً" (*jasadah*) were not such so as not to eat or drink. **Suleman'** son has also been called "جَسَداً" (*jasadah*) in 38:33. That is, a piece of flesh, but only "دَابَّةٌ" (*dabbah*) 34:14.

Torah says following about this son (*Ajaam*) of *Suleman*:

"*And on the fifth year of Ajaam's government, it so happened that the Egyptian king Siiq attacked*
Jerusalem and looted the treasures of God and the King's house ...during the reign of Salomo, a man named Birbaum had conspired together with an astrologer called Haya against his government. At that time his efforts had failed, but during Ajaam's time he became very powerful and together with ten leaders of Bani Israeel, he defeated Ajaam. He had the idol house made as against the Jewish place of religion where golden and silver idols were worshipped." (**Salateen** 1, Chapter 14 - 11:12).

This son of **Suleman**, who also sat on the throne, has been called **Jasad** i.e. only a compound of flesh, in order to point to his incapability (38:34). This was known by **Suleman** during his lifetime and he had prayed to God to keep the kingdom safe.

<h2 style="text-align:center">J-S-S   ج س س</h2>

"جَسٌّ" (**jass**) basically means to touch, and to find out by touching the pulse whether one is healthy or sick. It is closer to "حَسٌّ" (**hus**) which means to find out about the things which one can feel.

"اَلْجَسُّ" (**al-jas**): to probe and investigate the internal matters and secrets.

Some say that "تَجَسَّسَ" (**tajassus**) and "تَحَسَّسَ" (**tahussus**) have the same meaning with the only difference that "تَجَسَّسَ" (**tajassus**) is to find out for another and "تَحَسَّسَ" (**tahussus**) is for self. Word "جَاسُوْسٌ" (**jasos**) meaning spy, comes from this. Some say "تَجَسَّسَ" (**tajassus**): to find out secrets and "تَحَسَّسَ" (**tahussus**): to eavesdrop *{T, R}*.

"اَلْجَاسُوْسُ" (**al-jasoos**) is a bad confidante and "اَلنَّامُوْس" (**an-namoos**) and "اَلْحَاسُوْسُ" (**al-hasoos**) is a good confidante.

Quran says:

49:12	don't investigate hidden things for nothing		لَا تَجَسَّسُوْا

This means don't try to find out for personal gain or things which he wants to keep hidden and which brook no evil. Don't waste your precious time in such useless things. These meanings also indicate an element of evil, that is, to do this for a bad purpose is not good. But for governments it is necessary to know internal things about citizens and foreigners. These do not fall into the category which Quran has forbidden.

<h2 style="text-align:center">J-S-M   ج س م</h2>

Ibn Faris says its basic meaning of "اَلْجِسْمُ" (**al-jism**) is for something to collect.

It is used for body (the overall shape), the limbs of the body *{T}*.

"تُعْجِبُكَ اَجْسَامُهُمْ" (**tu'jiboka ajsamohum**) as used in 63:4 means their stature, hulk.

Surah **Al-Baqrah** has used this word for bodily strength in 2:247 where it is said that the army can be commanded by someone who has knowledge as well as bodily strength, as well as others benefit from it.

Note how the Quran has highlighted the importance of bodily strength along with knowledge. Any individual or nation which is weak, its scholarliness cannot be of much benefit to it. In bodily strength, every type of physical force is included. No doubt the aim is to nurture the personality of Man, but at the present level of existence, it is not possible without nurturing the body. Bodily strength is as essential as for the eggshell to be intact for the egg to be formulated. Within the Quranic system, body and personality, both find ways to develop.

J-Ain-L ج ع ل

"جَعَلَ" (ja'al): means a lot of things, and according to **Raghib**, it can be used for a lot of things. Also in comparison to "فَعَلَ" (fa'al) (he did) and "صَنَعَ" (sana') (he made) etc. "جَعَلَ" (ja'al) has much broader meaning {**T, R**}:

Muheet says it means to exchange as well as to name something (2:143), and to believe (15:96). Although all these have the connotations "to do" or "to make" but these examples make the usage of the root clear.

For example the Quran says:

19:30	He made me a Nabi (Messenger)	وَجَعَلَنِي نَبِيًّا

Here it means quite different than manufacture or create. But:

6:1	He created darkness and light	جَعَلَ الظُّلُمَٰتِ وَالنُّورَ

Here "جَعَلَ" (ja'al): to invent and create.

Similarly:

21:30	and we created every living thing from water	وَجَعَلْنَا مِنَ الْمَاءِ كُلَّ شَيْءٍ حَيٍّ
16:78	God made eyes, ears and heart (mind) for you	وَجَعَلَ لَكُمُ السَّمْعَ وَالْأَبْصَارَ وَالْأَفْئِدَةَ
15:74	we exchanged its lower part with its upper part.	جَعَلْنَا عَالِيَهَا سَافِلَهَا

Here too, "جَعَلَ" (ja'al): the same. For "فى" (fi) to come after it, makes it mean for putting one thing into another:

2:19	they put their fingers into their ears	يَجْعَلُونَ أَصَابِعَهُمْ فِي آذَانِهِمْ
57:27	we created softness and sympathy in the hearts of those who obeyed that Messenger (Jesus)	وَجَعَلْنَا فِي قُلُوبِ الَّذِينَ اتَّبَعُوهُ رَأْفَةً وَرَحْمَةً

Wherever this word appears in Quran its meaning will be determined according to the context. It will not have the same meaning everywhere, because as said above, this word is like the English phrase 'to make' and has many meanings. For the other meanings of "جَعَلَ" (ja'al).

J-F-N   ج ف ن

"الْجَفْن" (*al-jafn*): eyebrow, both upper and lower, sheath for a sword.

"الْجَفْنَة" (*al-jafna*): small well, big bowl for eating. Its plural is "جِفَانٌ" (*jifaan*) as in (34:13). It is said in this verse that the people of the mountainous areas (*djinn*), whom **Suleman** had put to work for him, used to make, beside other things, big lagans.

Ibn Faris says this word means anything that encompasses some other thing, that is, takes it within its fold.

J-F-W/A   ج ف و/أ

"جَفَا" (*jafa*), "جَفَاءٌ" (*jafa'a*), "تَجَافَى" (*tajafa*): he failed to stay in his place, like the saddle which doesn't stay on the horse's back.

"اجْتَفَيْتُهُ" (*ijtafaitohu*): I removed him from his place.

"جَفَا مَالَهُ" (*jafa maalahu*): he was separated from his camels.

"الْجُفَاءُ" (*al-jufaa*): the dirt of the (cooking) which comes out and falls when the vessel boils.

"أَجْفَتِ الْقِدْرُ زَبَدَهَا" (*ajfatil qadrozabadha*): the vessel threw out its boil {T} (whatever was boiling). As such this came to mean the dirt etc. That remained in both corners of the valley, or every useless thing {T}.

Surah **Ar-Raad** says:

| 13:17 | so the foam goes totally waste | فَأَمَّا الزَّبَدُ فَيَذْهَبُ جُفَاءً |

It is from this concept that "جَفَتِ الأَرْضُ وَ أَجْفَتْ" (*jafatil ardo wa ajfat*): the land became without any good, i.e. turned useless {T}.

In the Quran, about the **Momineen** it is said:

| 32:16 | their sides leave the beds (to complete Allah's program, they lose their sleep or have very little sleep.) | تَتَجَافَى جُنُوبُهُمْ عَنِ الْمَضَاجِعِ |

J-L-B   ج ل ب

"جَلَبَهُ" (*jalabah*), "يَجْلِبُهُ" (*yajlibohu*): he drove him from one place to another {T, M. R}.

It is used to take the goods from one place to another for trading {M}.

"الْجَلَبُ" (*al-jalab*): those who drive goats or camels from one place to another for selling. The goats and camels are called "جَلَبٌ" (*jalab*) as well.

"عَبْدٌ جَلِيْبٌ" (**abdun jaleeb**): a slave who has been brought from another city, the vagaries of the weather, pangs of hunger or hard work. This has led to "اَلْجُلْبَةُ" (**al-jalb**) meaning to oppress somebody and to be harsh.

"جَلَبَ عَلَيْهِ" (**jalaba alaih**): he oppressed him.

"أَجْلَبَ الْقَوْمُ عَلَيْهِ" (**ajlabal qaumo alaih**): the nation gathered against him.

"أَجْلَبَ الْقَوْمُ" (**ajlabal qaum**): people from all sides gathered for battle.

Quran has used it in this meaning:

17:64	bring all your armies against them (storm them)	وَأَجْلِبْ عَلَيْهِمْ

Ibn Faris says the other basic meaning of this word is something which covers another.

This way "اَلْجِلْبَابُ" (**al-jilbaab**) is a cloth which is bigger than a scarf but smaller than a shawl with which women cover their heads and breasts with *{T, M, R}*.

The Quran says:

33:59	to cover themselves with their shawls	يُدْنِينَ عَلَيْهِنَّ مِنْ جَلَابِيبِهِنَّ

That too was called "جِلْبَابٌ" (**jilbaab**). By such, broad cloth was meant peace and tranquillity as a proverb.

J-L-D   ج ل د

"اَلْجِلْدُ" (**al-jild**), "جَلْدٌ" (**jald**): the skin of every living thing (16:80). The plurals are "جُلُوْدٌ" (**julud**) or "أَجْلَادٌ" (**ajlaad**).

"اَلْجِلْدُ" (**il-jild**) also allegorically means the penis.

"أَجْلَادُ الْاِنْسَانِ" (**ajlaadul insaan**): the body and the whole human skeleton.

Ibn Faris says it means strength and hardness (toughness):

"فُلَانٌ عَظِيْمُ الْأَجْلَادِ" (**falanoon azeemul ajlaad**): he has strong limbs and body.

"يَا مَاأَشْبَهَ أَجْلَادُهُ بِأَجْلَادِ أَبِيْهِ" (**yama ashbaha wa ajlaadohu bi ajlaadey aabeeh**): his body and features, face, and built is so much like his father *{T, M, R}*.

It also means stuffed skin of a baby camel which is put before a female camel prior to milking her.

"اَلْجَلَدُ" (**al-jalad**): intensity and strength, stability and toughness.

The compiler of Muheet says it means the sky, celestial spheres, and water which has fallen from above and frozen on earth.

Raghib says that just as "قُلُوبٌ" (*qulub*) it means individuals, "جُلُودٌ" (*julud*) may mean bodies *{T, R}*.

"اَلْمِجْلَدُ" (*al-mujlad*): the piece of leather which the womenfolk hit their faces with while grieving.
"جَلَدَ يَجْلِدُ" (*jalad yajlid*): to strike with a whip (24:2) *{T, M, R}*.

Raghib says it means
-   To hit with leather
-   To hit the skin

"جَلَدَةُ عَلَى الْأَمْرِ" (*jalada alil amr*): forced him to *{T, M, R}*.

Surah **An-Nisa** says:

4:56	Their *julud* (skins) wear out, we will give them other skins	كُلَّمَانَضِجَتْ جُلُودُ هُمْ بَدَّلْنَٰهُمْ جُلُوداً غَيْرَهَا لِيَذُوْ قُوْا لْعَذَابَ

This means they will feel the punishment continuously. When after facing the ordeal once they will rise again, and face defeat and ignominy again. Facing this continuously, their strength and toughness will be shattered. From the battle of Badr to the victory in Mecca, they (the opponents) faced continuous defeats and at last the toughness of the opponents ended.

In Surah Ha Miim, "سمع و بصر" (*sahahada*) has been mentioned with "جُلُودٌ" (*julud*) 41:20-22. That is, the hearing of the **mujrameen**, along with their sight and acts will testify against them. They will testify against themselves. Every act has an effect on the human personality, therefore the basic witness to every human act is the human personality itself, no matter what excuses the intellect presents

75:14 75:15	Man is proof against his own personality, no matter with how many excuses he defends himself.	بَلِ الْإِنْسَانُ عَلَى نَفْسِهِ بَصِيْرَةٌ - وَلَوْاَلْقَى مَعَاذِ يْرَهُ

This is the evidence of sight, hearing and "جلود" (*julud*). The time that the results are known is pretty difficult when man's most secret act cannot remain hidden, not even a passing thought.

J-L-S   ج ل س

"جَلَسَ" (*jalas*), "يَجْلِسُ" (*yajlis*), "جُلُوساً" (*julusa*), "مَجْلِساً" (*majlisa*): to sit

"جُلُوسٌ" (*julus*): a man who was in lying down position but sits up, while

"قُعُودٌ" (*qu'ood*): a man who is standing up but then sits down.

"اَلْجَلَسُ" (*al-jals*): hard and high ground which is its basic meaning. It is used for sitting because a man puts his backside on hard ground *{T, M, R}*.

Ibn Faris says that its basic meaning is to be higher, and since a man who sits up from lying down, does becomes higher (compared to when he is lying down). This word is thus used for him.

Quran uses the word "مَجَالِسٌ" (*majalis*) in 58:11. This means the places where people sit in a gathering.

J-L-L   ج ل ل

"جَلَّ الرَّجُلُ يَجِلُّ جَلَالَةً وَجَلَالاً" (*jallar rujulo yajullo jalalatun wa jalalah*): to be old.

"جَلِيلٌ" (*jaleel*): to be very distinguished.

"جُلَّ الشَّيْءِ" (*jallush shaiyi*): the larger part of a thing

"اَلْجُلَّى" (*al-ujalla*): great thing.

"اَلْجُلَّ" (*al-julla*): the cloth which is put on for protection on a four legged animal.

"اَلْجَلِيلُ" (*al-jaleel*): big man or camel, as against "دَقِيقٌ" (*daqeeq*) which means a goat *{T, R}*

The real meaning, according to **Muheet**, is to be round and high.

Raghib says that "جلال" (*jalaal*) has more of the meaning of an expert, than a great man.

The Quran says about God:

55:27	One who has greatness and *jalaal* (greatness)	ذُوْالْجَلَالِ وَالْاِكْرَام

For the meaning of "اِكْرَام" (*ikraam*), see heading (K-R-M).

J-L-W   ج ل و

"اَلْجَلَاءُ" (*al-jala'u*): to disperse, to separate, to exile. (56:3)

"جَلَا فُلَاناً الْأَمَرَ" (*jala fulanal amr*): he opened the matter before him, made it evident, clear.

Ibn Faris says the above mentioned are its basic meaning.

Quran says:

91:3	(the period), when it pierces the darkness and makes everything prominent and clear	وَالنَّهَارِ إِذَا جَلَّاهَا

"اَلْجَلِيُّ" (*al-jaliyo*): distinct event, opposite of secret.

"اَلْجَلَاءُ" (*al-jala'o*): distinct event.

"اَلْجِلْوَةُ" (*al-jilwah*): anything which the husband gives his wife on the wedding night {T}.

7:143	when his Sustainer disclosed himself on the mount	فَلَمَّا تَجَلَّى رَبُّهُ لِلْجَبَلِ

"جَلْوٌ" (*jalwu*) actually means to open up {R}.

J-M-H   ج م ح

"جَمَحَ الْفَرَسُ" (*jamahal faras*): the running of a horse with such a rage that its rider no longer is in control, this running a horse with his head high {T, M, R}.

The Quran says:

9:57	they are running away uncontrollably (defying the law of God)	وَهُمْ يَجْمَحُون

"اَلْجُمَاحُ" (*al-jummah*): the defeated whom it is impossible to bring back to the battle field.

"جَمَحَتِ الْمَرْأَةُ مِنْ زَوْجِهَا" (*jama-atil mar-ato min zaujeha*): a woman who is angry with her husband and leaves home for her mother's without being divorced.

"جُمَيْحٌ" (*jumeeh*): a man's phallus

"اَلْجَمُوْحُ" (*al-jumuh*): a man who follows his emotions and it is difficult to prevent him from doing so {T, M, R}

Ibn Faris says it means for a thing to move ahead with force and overwhelming ness. Later, it came to mean run away or to run.

J-M-D   ج م د

"جَمَدَ الْمَاءُ" (*jamadak ma'oo*): the water froze, became stagnant.

"اَلْجَمدُ" (*al-jamd*): ice, frozen water.

"اَلْجَمَادُ" (*al-jamaad*): a slow moving camel which has stopped giving milk.

"جَمَادة الْكَفّ" (*jamadul kaff*): a miser.

"عَيْنٌ جَمُوْدٌ" (*ainun jamood*): the eye which does not shed tears {*T*}.

"اَلْجَمَادُ" (*al-jamad*): land, anything which does not grow, which is inorganic.

"جُمَادَى الْأُوْلَى" (*jamadal awla*) and "جُمَادَى الْأَخِرَةُ" (*jamadil akhirah*): the two months after **Rabius Saani**. At that time these months were so named, because they used to fall during heavy winter. Now since one goes by the moon it is not necessary for each month, each year to fall in this season {*T*}.

Quran says about the *jibaal* (the leaders of the nation or elite):

27:88	you think they are frozen	تَحْسَبُهَا جَامِدَةً

J-M-Ain   ج م ع

"اَلْجَمْعُ" (*al-jam'o*): to gather different tribes together.

Raghib says it means to bring things closer together. It also means red coloured glue. It also means a group of people.

"اَلْجَمِيْعُ" (*al-jami'o*): army, crowd, or tribe.

"اَلْجُمَّاعُ" (*al-jumma*): anything with its elements mixed with each other, consolidated, the people of different tribes who have gathered together. It also means the place where the roots of anything converge.

"جُمْعُ الْكَفِّ" (*jum ul-kuff*): closed fist {*T*}.

"اَجْمَعُ" (*aj-maa*) (masculine),

"جَمْعَاءُ" (*jam'aa*) (feminine),

"اَجْمَعُوْنَ" (*ajma'oon*) (masculine plural),

"جُمَعٌ" (*juma'un*): (plural feminine).

These words appear only for stressing something, i.e. when we say "اَجْمَعُوْنَ" (*ajma'oon*), we would not mean everybody, the meaning would be the majority.

"اَجْمَعْتُ الْأَمْرَ" (*ajma'tul amr*): I decided firmly to do it (10:71).

Raghib says it connotes to decide on something after deliberating over it.

"اَمْرٌ جَامِعٌ" (*amrey jamey*): wonderful work for which people will gather.

"يَوْمُ لُجُمَعَةٍ" (*yaumul jumu'ati*): before the advent of Islam, the Quresh (tribe) used to gather a day every week at **Darun Nidow** (their national parliament) near the **Darun Qusi**, and called that day "يَوْمُ الْعَرُوْبَةِ" (*yaumul urubah*).

Ka'ab bin Lawi named that day "يَوْمُ الْجُمْعَةِ" (*yaumul jumuaa*). As such he began to be called "اَلْمُجَمِّعُ" (*al-jamioh*) which was the nickname of **Qussi bin Kalaab** who had built the **Darun Nidow {M}**. This makes the meaning of the word "جمعه" (*jumuaa*) (Friday) clear. It means to gather for consultation.

Quran says the group of Momineen are wont to:

42.38	they establish the system of salaat and their decide their affairs by mutual consultation	اَقَامُواْالصَّلوةَ وَاَمْرُ هُمْ شُوْرَاىٰ بَيْنَحُمْ

They bow before God in the prayer gatherings is the physical manifestation that we have gathered for obeying God's order and the purpose of our consultation too is similar.

Muheet says "اَلْجُمْعَةُ" (*al-jumah*) is derived from "اَجْتَمَاعٌ" (*ijtemah*) which means gathering just as "اَلْفُرْقَةُ" (*al-furqah*) has been derived from "اِفْتِرَاقٌ" (*ifteraaq*).

Quran uses "اَلْجُمْعَةُ" (*jami'un*) against "اَشْتَاتًا" (*astatah*) in 24:61. That is, gathering as against separately or individually.

Surah **An-Nisa** uses "جَمِيعًا" (*jami'un*) as against "ثُبَاتٍ" (*subaat*) in 4:71 which means in the shape of a whole army. For "ثُبَاتٍ" (*subaat's*) meaning see heading (Th-B-Y).

The word "اَجْمَعِيْنَ" (*ajma-een*) has been used by the Quran several times, as in 2:161. As said before it is used to stress not to mean that nobody is left out.

J-M-L   ج م ل

"اَلْجَمَلُ" (*al-jamul*), "اَلْجَمَلُ" (*al-jaml*): male camel. Plural is "جِمَالَةٌ" (*jimalah*) as used in 77:33 "جَمَالٌ" (*jamal*): beauty too as used in 16:6 *{T}*:

Ibn Faris says the basic meanings are
- to gather and to be higher in creation
- beauty.

For the Arabs, camel has most "جَمَلَّ" (*jamal*), meaning loftiness and beauty. Their own grandeur was due to (having) these camels.
"جَمِيلٌّ" (*jamel*): beautiful manner, good thing *{T}*.
"فَصَبْرٌ جَمِيْلٌ" (*fasbarun jameel*): to bear loss in a good manner and to stay stable (12:18).
"اَلْجُمَّلُ" (*al-jummal*), "اَلْجُمْلُ" (*al-juml*), "اَلْجُمَلُو" (*al-jumalo*), "اَلْجَمَلُ" (*al-jamal*): thick rope on a boat *{T, R}*

Quran says:

7:40	till the ship's rope passes through the eye of the needle (which is an impossibility)	حَتّىٰ يَلِجَ الْجَمَلُ فِيْ سَمِّ الْخِيَاطِ

"اَلْجُمْلَةُ" (*al-jumlah*): collection of things *{T, R}*.

"اَلْمُجْمَلُ" (*al-mujmal*): the collection of many things, that is, things which have not been separately detailed *{T, R}*.

Quran says:

25:32	all at once	جُمْلَةً وَاحِدَةً

For "مجمل" (*mujmal*) and "مفصل" (*mufassal*) see heading (F-Sd-L).

J-M-M ج م م

"اَلْجَمُّ" (*al-jumm*): the abundance of everything.

"مَالٌ جَمٌّ" (*maalun jumm*): much wealth

"جُمَّةُ الْمَاءِ" (*jummatul ma'a*): the place for lot of water to collect *{T}*.

Ibn Faris has said that its basic meanings are abundance and gathering.

"جَمَّتِ الْبِئْرُ" (*jammatil bey'ro*): the water returned to the well after being taken out and collected in abundance (replenished in abundance).

"اَلْجَمَمُ" (*al-jamam*): whatever is above the glass, full to the brim *{T}*.

"اَلْجَمَامَةُ" (*al-jamama*): comfort, contentment.

"جَمّاً غَفِيْراً" (*jamman ghafeera*): all of them, a big number of people which includes the big and the small, the elite and the commoners.

Quran says:

89:20	you love wealth dearly, and want it to come towards you as water collects in a ditch	وَتُحِبُّونَ الْمَالَ حُبّاً جَمّاً

This is what happens in capitalism. Wealth gets concentrated in a few hands. The Quran has come in order to erase such a system.

J-N-B   ج ن ب

Ibn Faris says the basic meanings are of avoidance, and distance.
Zajaj says that it means the path to which he invited me.

"أَلْجَنْبُ" (*al-junb*): direction, towards, side *{T, R}*. Its plural is "جُنُوبٌ" (*junub*) as in 3:190.
"اَلصَّاحِبُ بِالْجَنْبِ" (*as-sahibo bil janb*): companion, friend (4:36)
"اَلْجَارِ ذِیْ الْقُرْبٰی" (*al-jaaril junb*): *Kitabul Ashqaq* says it means "اَلْغَرِیْبُ" (*al-ghareeb*) or a stranger.

The Quran says:

| 39:56 | the shortcomings committed in following Allah's orders | مَافَرَّطْتُ فِیْ جَنْبِ اللّٰهِ |
| 5:6 | the state of fornication | وَاِنْ کُنْتُمْ جُنُبًا |

"جَنْبَةٌ" (*janbah*): to stay separate from the others.
"جُنَبَةٌ" (*junabah*): the thing which one keeps away from {Lane}
"جَنَبَ" (*janabah*), "جَانَبَہٗ" (*janabhu*): moved him away.
"جَنَّبَہٗ" (*jannabahu*), "اَجْنَبَہٗ" (*ajnabah*): removed him.
"رَجُلٌ جَنْبٌ" (*rajolin janib*): stranger etc. and a person who due to miserliness stays away from the usual life so that he won't have to be someone's host.
"سَیُجَنَّبُہَا" (*saijannoboha*) as in 92:72, "یَتَجَنَّبُہَا" (*yatajannoboha*) as in 87:11, "اِجْتَنَبَ" (*ijtanab*) as in 39:17.
All these above words have the same connotation, that is, to stay away or keep away.
"جَانَبُ الْبَرّ" (*janibul burr*) as in 17:68 means piece of dry land
"أَلْجَنَابُ" (*al-janab*): open ground in front of one's house *{T}*.

It also means some place where one alights or stays *{M}*.

Surah *Al-Qasas* says when his mother put the child into a box and pushed him out into the river, she told her daughter, *Moosa's* sister to follow the trunk down the river. She kept him in sight and the Pharaoh's people could not feel that she is following him:

| 28:11 | and she kept looking at him like a stranger so that the people couldn't understand that she is in fact looking for him | فَبَصُرَتْ بِہٖ عَنْ جُنُبٍ وَّ ہُمْ لَایَشْعُرُوْنَ |

J-N-H   ج ن ح

"اَلْجَنَاحُ" (*al-jinah*), with plural "اَجْنِحَةٌ" (*amjinha*): hand, arm, bird's wing, armpit, side.

"اَنَا فِیْ جَنَاحِهِ" (*ana fi jinahihi*): I am in his shadow and protection *{T}*

Protection of the sort like when a hen takes the chicks under her wings in danger.

"جَنَحَ اِلَیْهِ" (*janah ilaihi*): he was attracted to him, leaned towards him.

Ibn Faris says its basic meaning is to lean. This led to its meaning leaning towards sin *{T}*. Muheet contends that this word is the Arabised form of sin, and is also used to mean harm.

When the Messenger was told to move away from opponents and organize his own group, he was told:

15:88	lower your shoulder for people of your group (gather them under your wings like a hen takes her new born chicks under its wings)	كه وَاخْفِضْ جَنَاحَكَ لِلْمُؤْمِنِیْنَ

In surah **Al-Qasas**, **Moosa** has been told that in the struggle against the Pharaoh not to lose heart, but to keep himself together:

28:32	at times of fear, don't panic, keep your wits about you (protect the people of your party, or organize them)	وَاضْمُمْ اِلَیْکَ جَنَاحَکَ مِنَ الرَّهْبِ

All these things could be meant.

In surah **Bani Israeel**, regarding the upkeep and protection of parents, it is said:

17:24	lower your shoulder to them in kindness and sympathy	وَاخْفِض لَهُمَا جَنَاحَ الذُّلِّ مِنَ الرَّحْمَةِ

Look after them with great compassion because they have become (old and) dependent.

Surah **Al-Faatir** says "اُولِیْ اَجْنِحَةٍ" (*ooli ajneha*) about the **malaikah** in 35:1, where the literal meanings are with wings, because wings are used for flying. So figuratively it would mean multidimensional cosmic forces.

To mean sin or harm, the word "جُنَاحٌ" (*junnah*) has been used at several places:

2:158	there is no harm in moving between these mounts (**Safaa, Marwah**)	لَا جُنَاحَ عَلَیْهِ اَنَ یَطَّوَّفَ بِهِمَا

Ibn Faris has said its second basic meaning is 'excess'.

J-N-D   ج ن د

"اَلْجَنَدُ" (*al-janad*): hard land, stones which look like earth.
"جُنْدٌ" (*jund*): people who gather or things which are collected.

Ibn Faris says the basic meanings of this word are to gather together or help.

"اَلْجَنَدُ" (*al-jund*): army, because of its harshness. Plural is "جُنُوْدٌ" (*junud*), and every soldier a "جُنْدٌ" (*jund*).

Surah *Maryam* mention "اَضْعَفُ جُنْداً" (*az-afo junda*) in 19:75, which means those whose friends and companions, party or group is weak.

Surah *Al-Fatah* says:

48:4	The armies of the skies and the earth are for Allah	اَضْعَفُ جُنْداً

This refers to all the forces of the universe.

Muheet says this means a particular kind of creature as well.

Surah *Al-Brooj* says:

85:17	Have you heard about the armies? (tales about those with big armies)	هَلْ اَتٰكَ حَدِيثُ الْجُنُوْدِ

(The next verse then discusses the Pharaoh and the *Samood* people).

J-N-F   ج ن ف

"اَلْجَنَفُ" (*al-janaf*): to lean on one side, partiality, or predilection. This is used for straying from the path of justice.
"تَجَانَفَ عَنْ طَرِيْقِهِ" (*tajanafa un tareeqih*): moved to one side from his path {*T, M*}.

The Quran says:

2:182	Whoever fears that the maker of the will shall be partial to someone. (He will not be fair and favour one more than the other)	فَمَنْ خَافَ مِن مُّوصٍ جَنَفًا

Note that "مُجْنِفٌ" (*mujnif*) is someone who is not fair and favours someone {*T, M*}.

Surah *Al-Ma'ida* says:

5:3	who would not favour sin	غَيْرَ مُتَجَانِفٍ لِإِثْمٍ

J-N-N   ج ن ن

"جَنٌّ" (*junn*) basically means to hide. **Raghib** says "جَنٌّ" (*junn*): to hide something from one perspective.

6:77	when the darkness of the night hid it, he saw a star	فَلَمَّا جَنَّ عَلَيْهِ اللَّيْلُ رَأَى كَوْكَبًا

As it is, "قَدْ جَنَّ عَنْكَ" (*qad junnaa anka*) is said for anything which is hidden from your view. "جَنَنٌ" (*janan*): a grave, because it hides the corpse or a dead body. It means the dead body and also the shroud as well.

"جَنِينٌ" (*janeen*) is the plural as used in 53:32, and means a foetus

"جُنَّةٌ" (*junnah*) is a weapon one uses for defence, any veil or hiding place.

"جُنَّةٌ" (*junnah*) and "مِجَنَّةٌ" (*mijinnah*) also means shield *{T, M}*.

58:16	means there is no secret about it	لَا جِنَّ بِهَذَا الْأَمْرِ

"جِنَّةٌ" (*jinnah*) also means madness, as used in 23:25

Actually among the Arabs, it is thought that "مَجْنُونٌ" (*majnnon*) is one whom a "جِنٌّ" (*jinn*) has possessed. During the superstitious era, all those forces which man could not see with the naked eye nor comprehend attained the stature of gods and goddesses. These, due to their being oblivious to the eyes, were called "جِنٌّ" (*jinn*).

They used to call even the angels for "جِنٌّ" (*jinn*), although they worshipped them as well.

Raghib says "الْجِنّ" (*al-jinn*) is used in two ways. One is when you say "جِنّ" (*jinna*), which even includes angles, and secondly "جِنّ" (*jinna*) are the hidden forces (spirits), with the difference that the good ones are called *farishta* (angel), and the bad ones are known as the *shayateen* (the devils) *{T, R}*.

Those with good and bad both types are called "جِنّ" (*jinn*). As such at several places in the Quran where worship by Arabs during the dark years is mentioned, the word "جِنَّةٌ" (*jinna*): indeed angels, as in 37:158 etc. *{T, R}*.

Our earth was a big ball of fire initially and it took millions of years to cool down and be habitable. The Quran says that before Man, the creatures which lived on this earth had the capacity to bear intense heat. Thereafter they became extinct and got replaced by the humans. See heading *(Kh-L-F)*.

Since those creatures are now extinct, Quran has said:

| 15:27 | before Man We had created creatures from hot air, those creatures are not before you | وَالْجَانَّ خَلَقْنَاهُ مِنْ قَبْلُ مِنْ نَّارِ السَّمُومِ |

This can also mean that the things of the universe before coming into material form were in the state of hidden energy and are today in latent form.

Because of it being oblivious to the eyes, and due to its rebellious nature, *Iblees* is also said to be among the *jinn*. See heading *(B-L-S)*, and *(Sh-Te-N)*.

At several places in the Quran, the words "جِنّ" (*jinn*) and "أَنْس" (*ins*) have come together in the same sentence. In the heading (A-N-S) we have already said "أَنْس" (*ins*) among the Arabs meant the tribes that settled permanently at one place, and "جِنّ" (*jinn*) were the tribes which roamed from place to place and were thus not seen by many. They are also called Nomadic tribes. Even today, such tribes move about jungles and deserts away from the usual population, but due to the information explosion many things have become common between them and the general population. Therefore there is no basic enmity between them, but in the times when the information explosion had not taken place, the lives of these Nomadic tribes and the usual population differed so much in their culture and ways of living that they seemed to be from two different worlds. There were many such tribes among the Arabs. They were called *baddu* or *airaab*. Since Quranic message was for both, therefore *jinn* and *ins* both are addressed.

Upon deliberation on this, it becomes clear that by "جِنّ" (*jinn*), it was also meant the humans or "أَنْس" (*ins*), or those wild tribes who lived in the jungles or the deserts.

As in surah *An-Anaam*:

| 7:131 | You group of *jinns* and *ins*, did not our messengers come to you? | يَمَعْشَرَ الْجِنِّ وَالْإِنْسِ أَلَمْ يَأْتِكُمْ رُسُلٌ مِنْكُمْ |

The Quran has not mentioned a Messenger who was a *jinn,* and this is further explained in surah *Al-Airaaf* that Messengers were sent from the human race (7:35).

In surah *jinn* and surah *Ahqaaf*, it is said that a group of *jinns* came to the Messenger and listened to the Quran (its recital). See 46:29 and 72:1. This also proves that *jinns* too had men as Messengers. These very verses make it clear that the *jinns* which came to the Messenger for listening to the Quran were humans as well. They were from the wild tribes of Christians, Jews and the *Mushriks* (those who worshipped more than one god).

Surah *Bani Israeel* has that, if the *jinns* and the humans get together, even then they cannot bring forth something like the Quran.

Surah *Al-Anaam* says that the rebellious among the *ins* and *jinns* used to oppose the Quran (6:113).

Surah *Al-Airaaf* says that the majority of the *jinns* and *ins* do not use their intellect and therefore they are *jahan-namees* (will go to *jahannum*) (7:179).

Surah *As-Sajda* says that the dwellers of *Jahannum* will say that they were misled by many among the *jinn* and *ins* (41:29).

Surah *Al-Anaam* says the *ins* (the humans) will say that they used to benefit from the *jinns* and the *jinns* will say that they benefited from the *ins* (6:149).

Surah *An-Namal* says that *Suleman* had armies of *ins* and *jinns* (27:17).

Surah *Saba* says about these *jinns* that they used to make statues, used to make lagans i.e. watches of sorts and big cooking pots (34:13). They were kept in chains (38:37-38).

The Torah says that *Suleman* (Solomon) asked the Saur king for men from the *Saiduni* nation for cutting wood from the jungle. As such these people and the "جِبْلِيْم" (*jibleem*) i.e. mountain tribes, used to cut wood and make structures for *Suleman*. Besides this, *Suleman* had employed 70.000 men from the mountain and jungle tribes of Palestine as labourers, and 10.000 men for cutting wood and making structures.

These explanations show that by *jinn* and *ins*, the Quran means the civilized people and the wild men of the tribes who lived in the deserts and jungles. For more details see my book "*Iblees and Adam*".

"اَلْجَانُّ" (*al-jann*): a yellow coloured snake with black eyes as used in 27:10 *{T}*.
Ibn Faris says that it is used as such due to its connotation to "جَانٌّ" (*jann*)
"اَلْجِنُّ مِنَ النَّبْتِ" (*al-jinni minal nabti*): flowers and buds.
"جُنَّتِ الْأَرْضُ" (*jannatil ard*): grass grew on the land and was pleasing to the eye *{T}*.
"جَنَّ النَّبَاتُ" (*jan nun nabaat*): the plants grew tall and intertwined.
"نَخْلَةٌ مَجْنُوْنَةٌ" (*nakhlatun majnoonah*): very tall date palm *{T}*.

"جَنَّةٌ" (*jannah*) is an orchard of dates and grapes. If any orchard contains trees of some other fruits than these, it is called "حَدِيْقَةٌ" (*hadeeqah*), not "جَنَّةٌ" (jannah) *{T}*.

Raghib says "جَنَّةٌ" (*jannah*) is any garden in which one does not find bare land due to the (abundance) of trees.

The Quran has used the term "جَنَّةٌ" (*jannah*) in a very comprehensive manner. If the Quranic system is followed, it creates a society which is blissful or "جَنَّةٌ" (*jannah*), and after death, the blissful results are called "جَنَّةٌ" (*jannah*) as well. Those who act according to the Quran, the Momineen, get a heavenly society in this life.

Its details are given at different places in the Quran, but if the whole thing is to be understood in short, then one must concentrate on the verse which concerns Adam's tale and which says:

2:35	eat as you want from where you want here, but don't go near that *shajara*	وَكُلَا مِنْهَا رَغَداً حَيْثُ شِئْتُمَا وَلَا تَقْرَبَا هَذِهِ الشَّجَرَةَ

For "شجر" (*shajara*) see heading (Sh-J-R). In short "جَنَّةٌ" (*jannah*) is that society which has all the comforts of life in abundance, not only food, but dresses as well, as houses etc. That is, all the basic necessities of life. But all these comforts are to be utilized as God has directed. If this is done, then that society will be evergreen (20:118-119).

That is why this has been called:

2:25	The orchard will always have a stream flowing below it	جَرِى مِنْ تَحْتِهَا الْأَنْهَارُ

The Quran has further explained:

13:35	its fruits and other facilities will always be available	اُكُلُهَا دَائِمٌ وَظِلُّهَا

Regarding the results of good deeds after death, they have been called "جَنَّةٌ" (*jannah*) as well, but along with it, it has also been mentioned:

32:17	that result which God has saved of good deeds, that cannot come within human comprehension	فَلَا تَعْلَمُ نَفْسٌ مَا اخْفِىَ لَهُمْ مِنْ قُرَّةِ اَعْيُنٍ

We cannot have any idea about that life. That is why, despite giving so much in detail about the "جَنَّةٌ" (*jannah*), the Quran has said that all this is only allegorical (13:35).

But we can have a "جَنَّةٌ" (*jannah*) on this earth as well, provided that we build a society on the lines mentioned by the Quran. Such a society has all the happiness for blissful existence, externally and internally, but we cannot understand the Heaven after death because our consciousness cannot go beyond material things. It will suffice to understand that here we get not only physical comforts but our personality is developed as well. This makes human personality prepared to proceed to the next level and eventually to our ultimate destiny. This sort of personality reaches the stage which is called "جَنَّةٌ" (*jannah*). That is not the last stage in our lives, but the stage to move onwards, because 'His light will proceed before us' (57:12). As against this, those whose personality's development would have stopped, those who are unable to proceed ahead, they will dwell in *jahannum*. (See headings *Jahannam* and J-H-M). However, after death, Heaven or Hell, are not places as such, but the feelings of man's personality whose reality is beyond our comprehension. We should all try to change the Hell in this world (which we are all living in) into a Heaven. This can only be done through the Quranic system of living.

J-N-Y   ج ن ى

"جَنَى الثَّمَرَةَ يَجْنِيهَا" (*janas samarata yajneeha*): he picked the fruit from the tree. These are its basic meaning {*Ibn Faris*}.

"فَهُوَ جَانٍ" (*fahuwa jaanin*): he is about to pick the fruit.

"اَلْجَنَى" (*al-janah*): fresh and solid date.

"اَجْنَى الشَّجَرُ" (*ajnash shajar*): the fruits of the tree have become ripe enough to be picked.

"ثَمَرٌ جَنِيٌّ" (*samarun jani'un*): fresh fruit which has just been picked {R, T}.

Surah Maryam says "رُطَبًا جَنِيّاً" (*rutaban janiya*) in 19:25. Here it has been used to indicate fresh dates, while surah Rahman says "جَنَى" (*janaa*) in 55:54 to mean fruits. It also means to pick somebody else's fruit is as a crime. From this came "اَلْجِنَايَةُ" (*al-jinayah*) which is a punishable crime.

"جَانٍ" (*jaanin*): crime.

"جَانَى عَلَيْهِ مُجَانَاةً" (*jana alaihi mujanah*): he lodged a case of crime against him {T}. When a man can commit a crime simply by picking someone else's fruit, then those who usurp the fruits of others' labor are criminals as well. In this reference, see heading (J-R-M).

J-He-D   ج ه د

"اَلْجَهْدُ" (*al-jahdo*): *Ibn Abeer* says that it means pain and hard labor, and to take some work to its extreme.

"جُهْدٌ" (*johd*): vastness and strength, but some say that "جَهْدٌ" (*jahd*) and "جُهْدٌ" (*johd*) both mean vastness and strength.

"جَهْدٌ" (*jahd*): hard labor. In the Quran, "جُهْدٌ" (*johd*) has also come to mean hard labor (9:79).

Ibn Faris says this is the word's basic meaning.

"جِهَادٌ" (*jehad*): to spend all your energies to the full in order to achieve some goal, not to leave any stone unturned for it.

"جَهَادٌ" (*jahad*): hard land without any vegetation.

"اَجْهَدَتْ لَكَ الْأَرْضُ" (*ajhadatun lakal ard*): the earth or land appeared for you {T}.

"اَلْإِجْتِهَادُ" (*al-ijtehaad*): to spend all you energies for achieving a purpose for which troubles must be taken and hard labor practiced {M}. It has to be troublesome and difficult.

"اَلْجَاهِدُ" (*al-jahiod*): someone who is awake.

The Quran uses "مُجَاهِدِيْنَ" (*mujahideen*) as against "قَاعِدِيْنَ" (*qai-deen*) in 4:95. *Qaideen* are those who remain sitting, he lazy ones. Therefore, the "مُجَاهِدِيْنَ" (*mujahideens*) are those who struggle, those who do their utmost for the achievement of their goals. They struggle to that extend that they may even have to give their lives for the purpose. According to the Quran, the secret of life is struggle, and strife and action.

As such a "مومن" (*momin*) man remains a "مجاهد" (*mujahid*), a struggler though out his life. For the word of war, see heading (*Q-T-L*).

Surah *An-Nahal* says "جَهْدَ أَيْمَانِهِمْ" (*jahda aimanihim*) to define a strong promise in 16:38.

J-He-R   ج ه ر

"جَهْرٌ" (*jahr*): *Raghib* says it means for something to be made prominent and evident with extra force, whether that thing is to be seen or heard.

"رَأَه جَهْرَةً" (*ra ahu jahrah*): to see each other without any curtain or anything in between.

"جَهَرَ الصَّوْتَ" (*jahas saut*): he raised his voice.

"جَهَرَ الْكَلَامَ" (*jaharul kalam*): he said it clearly and openly.

"جَهْرَاءُ الْقَوْمِ" (*jahraul qaum*): the prominent persons of a nation {T}.

"جَهَرَ الْقَوْمُ الْقَوْمَ" (*jaharul qaumul qaum*): one tribe attacked another at dawn.

"مُجَاهَرَةً" (*mujahara*): to try to overwhelm one another {T}.

Quran says about Allah that He cannot be seen without a curtain in between (2:55).

Surah Al-Hadeed says that Allah is "هُوَ الظَّاهِرُ" (*az-zahiro*) in 57:3. For its meaning, see headings (*Z-He-R*) and (*B-Te-N*).

Surah *Al-Anaam* uses "جَهَرَ" (*jahr*) as against "سِرَّ" (*siirr*) in 6:3, and uses it against "كَتَمَ" (*katam*) in 21:110.

Surah *Bani Israeel* uses it against "خَفْتٌ" (*khaft*).

17:110	Don't shout during your *salah*, but don't whisper either	وَلَا تَجْهَرْ بِصَلَاتِكَ وَلَا تُخَافِتْ بِهَا

For *Salah*, see heading (Sd-L-W)

Surah *Al-Anaam* says:

6:47	If Allah's punishment would strike you suddenly, openly and clearly visible.	إِنْ أَتَاكُمْ عَذَابُ اللَّهِ بَغْتَةً أَوْ جَهْرَةً

"بَغْتَةٌ" (*baghtatan*): which has no signs etc. beforehand; therefore "جَهْرَةٌ" (*jahr*) would mean something whose signs etc. appear beforehand.

Surah *Al-Hijrat* says:

49:4	don't raise your voice to the Messenger , or do not shout while talking as you are wont to do among yourselves	لَاتَرْفَعُوا أَصْوَا تَكُمْ فَوْقَ صَوْتِ النَّبِيِّ وَ لَاتَجْهَرُوا لَهُ بِالْقَوْلِ كَجَهْرِ بَعْضِكُمْ لِبَعْضٍ

The above translation was the literal meaning of the verse. Figuratively it would mean to not try to give prominence to your opinion over his, accept his decisions with complete acquiescence. In a Quranic society, the centre's decision is the last word. During his lifetime the Messenger held this position. After him, this position will be transferred to the Caliphs or the center of the Quranic state.

J-He-Z   ج ه ز

"اَلْجَهَازُ" (*al-juhaaz*): luggage or load, anything that is needed. *{T, M}*.

Ibn Faris says it basically means anything which can be bought or acquired.

"اَلتَّجْهِيزُ" (*at-tahjeez*): to load the luggage or give it *{T}*.

Surah Yusuf says:

| 12:59 | When they were given their luggage and they got ready for travel. | وَلَمَّا جَهَّزَ هُمْ بِجَهَازِهِمْ |

"اَلْجَهْزَاءُ مِنَ الْأَرْضِ" (*al-jahza'o minal ard*): high land.

J-He-L   ج ه ل

"اَلْجَهْلُ" (*al-jahl*): to proceed in matters about which one is not familiar.

Raghib says "جَهْلٌ" (*jahl*) has three meanings
    1) Human mind to be bereft of knowledge (this is its basic meaning)
    2) To have the wrong ideas about something
    3) Not to do something the way it should be done, whether the ideas are wrong or right.

Ibn Faris says its basic meanings are
    1) The opposite of knowledge
    2) Hollowness and discomfort.

"مَجْهَلٌ" (*majhal*): a land without landmarks due to which the right way cannot be seen *{T}*.
"اَلْجَهُوْلُ" (*al-jahool*) is that simpleton who is easily hoodwinked *{M}*.

Tajul Uroos says that the word "جَاهِلٌ" (*jaahil*) is used condemningly but sometimes it means to be unaware. In this situation, the word is not used for condemnation.

The Quran says:

2:273	Unaware ones, thinks they are wealthy	يَحْسَبُهُمُ الْجَاهِلُ اَغْنِيَاءَ

The word "جَاهِلٌ" (*jahiliah*) has been used for the Arabic period before Islam.

Quran has used it in 33:33, where it does not mean that they were totally illiterate, but that they were not familiar with the **Deen** (Islam). Here "جَاهِلٌ" (*jahiliah*) does not mean their illiteracy, but not being familiar with the **Deen** (way of life) that reached them through the Messenger Muhammad. Therefore the traditions and customs of that era include not only the traditions and customs that were prevalent before the advent of Islam, but they also mean the wrong traditions and customs that are spreading due to unfamiliarity with the **Deen** among Muslims.

Besides this, to stick to these traditions even after being aware of Deen, simply because they have been practiced in the past, is "جَاهِلٌ" (*jahiliah*). It is the religion of stones, not to move from one's old stands. That is why a big rock is called "صَفَاةٌ جَيْهَلٌ" (*safatun jeehal*){M}. This is the worst form of "جَاهِلٌ" (*jihaalah*) and "جَهْلٌ" (*jahiliah*) that is why the **Tajul Uroos** calls it " جَهْلٌ مُرَكَّبٌ" (*jahlun murakkab*) or compound "جَاهِلٌ" (*jahiliah*).

Ahmed Ameen Misri has said that the word "سَلَامٌ" (*salaam*): security which is the opposite of battle or enmity.

Quranic verse is:

25:63	وَعِبَادُ الرَّحْمٰنِ الَّذِينَ يَمْشُونَ عَلَى الْاَرْضِ هَوْناً وَّاِذَا خَاطَبَهُمُ الْجٰهِلُوْنَ قَالُوْا سَلَاماً

In the above verse the word "سَلَام" (*salam*) has been used against "جَاهِلِيَّة" (*jahiliah*). Perhaps this verse will help us find the reason for which the period before the Messenger was termed "جَاهِلِيَّة" (*jahiliah*) and the period after his coming as **Islam**. This word "جَاهِلِيَّة" (*jahiliah*) has not been derived from the word "جَهْلٌ" (*jahal*) which means to be unaware, but it has been derived from the word "جَهْلٌ" (*jahal*) which means foolishness, anger and ego.

Abu Zar Ghaffari is recalled as saying that someone was shamed by naming his mother at which the Messenger said: "اِنَّكَ امْرُوءٌ فِيْكَ جَاهِلِيَّةٌ" (*innakam ruwun wafeeka jahiliah*): you still have the spirit of the "جَاهِلِيَّة" (*jahilia*) period in you.

The Arabs too have a proverb "اِسْتَجْهَلَهُ الشَّىْءُ" (*istajhalahus shaiyi*) which is, that thing made him a stranger to intellect, he has become mad.
A poet has said "دَعَاكَ الْهَوَى وَاسْتَجْهَلَتْكَ الْمَنَازِلُ" (*da'akal hawa wastajhaltaakal manazil*): love called you and the beloved's talk made you lose your senses.

Umru Bin Kulsoom has said: beware, do not commit any excess on us, or we will commit greater excesses on you:

This shows that the word "جَاهِلِيَّة" (*jahiliah*) is used for hollowness, leave of senses, bias and false pride etc. which were very important part of the Arab psyche before the advent of Islam. As such that period is called the period of "جَاهِلِيَّة" (*jahiliah*). As against these are personal satisfactions, the realization of the importance of good deeds, the transitory nature of racial pride, etc. This clarifies as to what Islam is and what "جَاهِلِيَّة" (*jahiliah*) is.

According to the Quran, it is a crime not to acquire knowledge and to keep following your wrong ways even after acquiring knowledge is a bigger crime.

For more details see headings *(Ain-L-M)* and *(Ain-Q-L)*. In surah *Al-Baqrah* this word has appeared with the word "هَزْوٌ" (*hazwun*) in 2:67. Therefore, it means people who don't take life's problems and orders and laws seriously, and take them frivolously.

Jahannum جَهَنَّمُ

Some think it is Arabic word which means 'deep'.

"رَكِيَّةٌ جَهَنَّمٌ" (*rikkaitum jahannam*): a well with a deep bottom. Some others think it is the Arabic form of the Hebrew word *Gahannaam {T}*.

Muheet says that this word is basically from Hebrew and a compound of two words, "جِى" (*ji*) which means a valley and "هَنُّوْم" (*hanoom*) which was a man's name. The valley of *Hannoom* was a famous valley in the south of Jerusalem in which the god *Molok* was paid tribute by sacrificing (burning) human beings. As such *ji-hanoom* meant a valley where humans were massacred or burnt.

In this context *jahannam* would mean a place for human sacrifice. Allah's law envisages that man's latent capabilities be developed, that humanity be respected and be fruitful. A society in which humanity develops is a heavenly society. Conversely a society in which humanity is slaughtered or burns to ashes is a *jahannami* (hellish) society. There is an Arabic word for it which is "جَحِيْم" (*jaheem*), which also means to stop from something. See heading (J-H-M). *Jaheem* is hence the point where development has stopped.

Surah *Bani Israeel* says this about the *Jahannum*:

17:8	*jahannam* is the stoppage spot (for those who live in disobedience of Allah's Law)	وَجَعَلْنَا جَهَنَّم لِلْكُفِرِيْنَ حَصِيْراً

Since life progresses continuously (although in various forms) one whose development stops here is not able to reach the next stages. As such he stays in hell or *jahannam* in this world as well as in the Hereafter. What will be the situation in that life, we cannot say anything about today, although we can feel the agony of *jahannam* in this life every day, individually as well as collectively. Collectively, a nation which traverses the wrong path finds its efforts coming to naught instead of being fruitful. This is *jahannam*. The result is ignominy and defeat. Its details will be found at different places in the Quran. In this state the capabilities of the individuals in such a society are burnt to ashes.

One should understand that *jahannam* is formulated by one's own deeds. That is why it has been said:

| 29:54 | surely *jahannam* is surrounding the deniers from all sides | كه وَاِنَّ جَهَنَّمَ لَمُحِيْطَةٌ بِالْكَافِرِيْنَ |
| 82:16 | it is not hidden from their eyes | وَمَاهُمْ عَنْهَابِغَاءِبِيْنَ |

it is watching them, even as we speak, but they do not feel it. Therefore it is oblivious to them. When their eyes open, it will jump before their eyes and become visible.

| 79:36 | for one who sees, it will be obvious | وَ بُرِّزَتِ الْجَحِيْمُ لَمْن يَرَى |

This is the situation about which it has been said that:

| 82:15 | these people will enter it during the period of the *Deen* | يَصْلَوْنَهَا يَوْمَ الدِّيْن |

"يَوْمَ الدِّيْن" (*yaumuddeen*) is the period of the results, either in this day or after death.

<h1 style="text-align:center">J-W-B   ب و ج</h1>

"اَلْجَوْبُ" (*al-jaub*): to delink, to tear up, to drill a hole. These are the basic meanings of this root.

The Quran says:

| 89:8 | and *Samood* who used to carve the mountains (and made them their homes) | وَثَمُوْدَ الَّذِيْنَ جَابُوْ الصَّخْرَ بِالْوَادِ |

"اَلْجَوْبَةُ" (*al-jaubah*): a ditch in which rainwater accumulates behind the house {*T*}.
"اَلْجَوْبُ" (*al-jaub*) also means a shield {*T*}.

"اَجَابُ" (*ajaab*), "يُجِيْبُ" (*yujib*), "اِجَابًا" (*ajaba*), "اَجَابَةٌ" (*ijabah*), they all mean 'to reply' because one answers the questioner and the answer leaves his mouth and travels to the questioner's ears, and thus cuts or shortens the distance.

A question is of two types. One is inquiring about something and secondly to ask for help or assistance. As such, replies are also of two kinds, and to satisfy and help both would constitute the answer. That is, to answer somebody's question or to fulfil someone's demand.

The question also cuts the distance but this word has become special for an answer {*R*}. This has led to "مُجِيْبٌ" (*mujeeb*), one who answers.

The Quran says:

| 11:61 | Verily my Sustainer is near and He answers as well. | اِنَّ رَبِّیْ قَرِیْبٌ مُّجِیْبٌ |

Surah *Al-Baqrah* says:

| 2:186 | I answer any caller when he calls out to me | اُجِیْبُ دَعْوَةَ الدَّاعِ اِذَا دَعَانِ |

For prayer and God's answer to it, see heading *(D-Ain-W)*. Here let it suffice to say that prayer means to observe the laws of Allah and by Allah's answering to it means the outcome of an action.

Surah *Al-Momin* says:

| 40:60 | your developer (one who sustains your growth) says call me and I will answer you | وَقَالَ رَبُّكُمُ ادْعُوْنِیْ اَسْتَجِبْ لَكُمْ |
| 40:60 | those people who are rebellious and do not obey me will be badly humiliated and enter Jahannam | اِنَّ الَّذِیْنَ یَسْتَكْبِرُوْنَ عَنْ عِبَادَتِیْ سَیَدْخُلُوْنَ جَهَنَّمَ دَاخِرِیْنَ |

This whole verse makes it evident that prayer in reality is the opposite of "یِرُوْنَ عَنْ عِبَادَتِیْ" (*yastakberoona un ibadati*). As such, prayer means God's dominance.

That is why it is said a little earlier:

| 40:50 | Those who refuse observance of Allah's laws, never have their prayers bring any results. | وَمَا دُعَاءُ الْكٰفِرِیْنَ اِلَّا فِیْ ضَلَالٍ |

This is why when it is said in surah *Al-Baqrah*:

| 2:186 | I answer every caller's call | اُجِیْبُ دَعْوَةَ الدَّاعِ اِذَا دَعَانِ |

Along with it is also said:

| 2:186 | As such they should have faith in My laws and obey me (If they do this, I will certainly make their efforts bear fruit) | فَلْیَسْتَجِیْبُوْا لِیْ وَ الْیُؤْمِنُوْا بِیْ |

This is the real meaning of prayer and the acceptance of prayer, which is, if you fulfill whatever is Allah's requirement are, then He will fulfill your demands. This is Allah's law. He does not let anyone's efforts in obeying Him go waste.

| 11:115 | and be steadfast: verily Allah does not let the *mohsineen*'s efforts go waste: and nothing can be acquired without effort | وَصْبِرْ فَاِنَّ اللهَ لَایُضِیْعُ اَجْرَ الْمُحْسِنِیْنَ |
| 53:39 | Man can get nothing but for which he has tried | وَاَنْ لَیْسَ لِلْاِنْسَانِ اِلَّا مَاسَعَی |

Questioning is of two kinds, one is to ask about something and the other to ask for some help. As such, replies too will be of two kinds, and the words used for them are to answer someone's query or to fulfill someone's demand.

J-W-D   ج و د

"اَلْجَيّدُ" (*al-jayyid*): a good thing.
"جَوْدَةٌ" (*jaudah*): to be a good thing.
"أَجَادَهُ" (*ajadah*): made it good.
"اَلْجَوَادُ" (*al-jawad*): philanthropist.
"اَلْجُوْدِيُّ" (*al-joodi*): is the name of the mount on which **Nooh's** boat came to a stop (11:44).
"جَوَّادٌ" (*jawwad*): horse of a good breed which runs fast and uses all his energy in running *{R}*. Plural is "جِيَادٌ" (*jee'aad*).

It is said that it is situated in the mountain range which divides **Armenia** and **Mesopotamia**.

Surah **Saad** says:

38:31	thorough bred speedy stallions	اَلصّٰفِنٰتُ الْجِيَادُ

J-W-R   ج و ر

"اَلْجَوْرُ" (*al-jaur*): to leave the middle path and move to one side. This made it mean injustice and oppression.
"جَارَ" (*jaar*): to leave the path of justice *{T}*.
The Quran has used "جَائِرٌ" (*jayir*) against "قَصْدُ السَّبِيْلِ" (*qasdus sabeel*) in 16:9. "قَصْدُ السَّبِيْلِ" (*qasdus sabeel*) is the middle way and "جَائِرٌ" (*jayir*) is a lopsided path.
"اَلْجَارُ" (*al-jaar*): neighbour, the person whom you have sheltered against someone's oppression. It is also used to mean companion, and helper *{T}*.

The Quran has stated "اَلْجَارِ ذِى الْقُرْبٰى" (*al-jaari zil qurba*) and "اَلْجَارِ الْجُنُبِ" (*al-jaaril junub*) in 4:36. For details see heading (J-N-B).

The Quran says:

33:60	they will not be able to live like your neighbours in this city.	لَا يُجَاوِرُوْنَكَ فِيْهَا
8:48	I am your sheltered, or supporter or helper:	اِنِّىْ جَارٌ لَكُمْ
13:4	adjacent plots of land	قِطَعٌ مُتَجٰوِرَاتٌ

"أَجَارَهُ" (*ajarah*): shelter him, provided him with shelter, took him in his protection (72:22).
"اِسْتَجَارَ" (*istajar*): to ask for shelter.

J-W-Z   ج و ز

"جَازَ الْمُوْضَعَ" (*jaazul mauzeh*): he went past that place, left it behind. If it is a river, it would mean to have crossed the river.

"جَاوَزَ" (*jawaz*): to go beyond some place or spot {*T*} (2:249, 18:62).

The real meaning of this root is to delink, cut off {*M*}.

"تَجَوَّزَ عَنْ ذَنْبِهِ" (*tajjawwaza un zambehia*): overlooked his error.

| 46:16 | We overlook their mistakes | وَنَتَجَاوَزُ عَنْ سَيِّئَاتِهِمْ |

Ibn Faris says the basic meaning is to cut off something or the middle of something.

"جَوْزُ كُلَّ شَيٍّ" (*jauzu kulla shaiyun*): the middle or center of everything.

"اَلْجَائِزُ" (*al-jayizo*): something which passes through the middle of something.

"اَلْجَائِزُ" (*al-jayizo*): one who passes through the right way {*M*}.

"اَلْمَجَازُ" (*almajaz*): road which is cut from one end to another or the road which is heavily traversed {*T*}.

"اَلْجَائِزَةُ" (*al-jayizah*): gift, reward, the goods given to a traveller for a day and night. It is possible that this led to its meaning a gift or reward.

J-W-S   ج و س

"اَلْجَوْسُ" (*al-jaus*): to search for something to the utmost, to roam around {*T, R*}.

"اَلْإِجْتِيَاسُ" (*al-ajtiyas*): to roam at night {*T*}.

Ibn Faris says its basic meaning is to penetrate something.

The Quran says:

| 17:5 | they penetrated your cities and searched everywhere for you (and in this way murdered or arrested you after seeking out each one) | فَجَاسُوْا خِلَالَ الدِّيَارِ |

Muheet has included the meanings of moving hither and thither to attack or loot.

J-W-Ain   ج و ع

"اَلْجُوْعُ" (*al-jooh*): hunger:

"جَاعَ" (*ja'a*), "يَجُوْعُ" (*yajooh*), "جُوْعاً" (*joo'a*): to be hungry.

"عَامُ مَجَاعَةٍ" (*aamu maja'ati*): year of hunger, drought.

The Quran has used it for hunger in 2:155 and one specialty of the *jannat* has been mentioned that there will never be hunger (shortage of sustenance). It also means to hide life's accoutrements or to misuse the results:

| 20:118 | you will never remain hungry there | اِنَّ لَکَ اَلَّا تَجُوْعَ فِیْہَا |
| 16:112 | the punishment of hunger and fear | لِبَاسُ الْجُوْعِ وَالْخَوْفِ |

For any nation, the shortage of sustenance or is a sort of punishment, or restriction, while its abundance is a particularity of a heavenly society. Nobody can go hungry in a society that follows the Quran. This by no count means that in a society, if no man goes hungry the society will be called a heavenly society.

God's order has many particularities and unless the society meets them all, it cannot be called a *jannati* society, but a society in which people go hungry and cannot feed their children, is by no means a *jannati* society nor is its order Allah's system. It is possible that for some time there is a shortage of food (during wars etc.), but as a permanent value, hunger is God's punishment, and a nation which does not want to get rid of such a system, wants to remain in hell forever.

J-W-F   ج و ف

"اَلْجَوْفُ" (*al-jauf*): vast low land, stomach, or the insides of something.
"جَوْفُ الْبَیْتِ" (*jaufal bait*): the inside of the house.

Ibn Faris says that it basically means the inside of something.

"جَافَہٗ" (*jafah*), "یَجُوْفُہ" (*yajoofah*), "جَوْفًا" (*jaufa*): he deepened it.
"جَوَّفَ" (*jawwaf*): something with depth, as against "مُحَدَّبٌ" (*muhaddaf*) which means a man who has no heart (coward), a man with a hollow chest {T, M}.

The Quran says:

| 33:4 | Allah has not created two hearts in anyone's chest. | مَاجَعَلَ اللّٰهُ لِرَجُلٍ مِنْ قَلْبَیْنِ فِیْ جَوْفِہٖ |

Here "جَوْفٌ" (*jauf*): chest.

J-W-W   ج و و

"اَلْجَوُّ" (*al-ajju*): the atmosphere, the space between the earth and the outer space *{T, M, R}*.

Quran uses it to refer to the celestial atmosphere:

| 16:79 | the birds have conquered (mastered) the atmosphere: | مُسَخَّرَاتٍ فِيْ جَوِّ السَّمَاءِ |

However, "اَلْجَوُّ" (*al-ajju*) also means the inside of a house *{T, M}*.

Ibn Faris says it means a thing which is encompassing another or surrounding another. The outer atmosphere is called "اَلْجَوُّ" (*al-ajju*) because it seems to be surrounding the earth.

J-Y-A   ج ی أ

"جَاءَ" (*ja'a*), "يَجِيىءُ" (*yajyi*): to come.
"أنَا أَجَأتُهُ وَجِءْتُ بِهِ" (*aja'to hu wa jey'to behi*): I brought him *{T}*.

Raghib says while differentiating between "اِتْيَانٌ" (*ityaan*) and "اَلْمَجِىءُ" (*majee*) that "اِتْيَانٌ" (*ityaan*) means to intend to do something (whether or not it can be performed) but "اَلْمَجِىءُ" (*aljiyo*) will be said when some work has been completed.

It also means to bring and to commit or do. People said to ***Maryam***:

| 19:27 | you have done a strange thing
(you have committed a strange act) | لَقَدْ جِئْتِ شَيْئًا فَرِيّاً |

Similarly in surah ***Al-Kahaf*** it is said in the tale about ***Moosa*** and the old man:

| 18:71 | You have committed a dangerous act. | لَقَدْ جِئْتَ شَيْئًا إِمْرًا |

Surah ***Maryam*** says:

| 19:23 | the labor pains brought her near the date palm | فَأَجَاءَ هَاالْمَخَاضُ إِلَى جِذْعِ النَّخْلَةِ |

This signifies a sort of compulsion.

J-Y-B   ج ى ب

"جَيْبُ الْقَمِيْصِ" (*jaibul qamees*): the neck of a loose shirt.

"الْجَيْبُ" (*al-jaib*) is also used for the chest on which the front of the shirt rests, and it also means the heart.

"بُوَنَا صُبح الْجَيْبِ" (*hauna sehool jaib*): he is a clear hearted or clean chested person, meaning that he is sincere *{T}*.

Surah **An-Noor** tells women:

23:36	they should put their long narrow cloth on their chests.	وَلَيَضرِبْنَ بِخُمُرِ هِنَّ عَلى جُيُوْبِهِنَّ

In the tale about **Moosa**, it is said:

27:12	enter your hand in your shirt	وَاَدْخِلْ يَدَکَ فِیْ جَيْبِک
28: 32	put your hand in your shirt	أُسْلُکْ يَدَکَ فِیْ جَيْبِکَ

For the meanings of these above verses, see heading *(Y-D-Y)* and *(B-Y-Zd)*.

J-Y-D   ج ى د

"جِيْدٌ" (*jeed*): the neck, the front part of the neck, or the part of the neck where necklaces hang.

According to a saying "جِيْدٌ" (*jeed*) is said when in praise, and when in condemnation, "عُنْقٌ" (*oonuq*) is used.

About **Abu Lahab's** wife, the Quran says:

111:5	her neck has a rope made out of date palm leaves	فِیْ جِيْدِ هَاحَبْلٌ مَنْ مَّسَدٍ

That is, the neck (or person) which was so respected and exalted is being humiliated in this manner. Her pride is being trampled into dust.

H-A-Sh ح أ ش

"اَلْحَاشِيَةُ" (*al-hashiyaa*): edge/border (of cloth etc.)

"حَشْوَةُ الْنَّاسِ" (*hashwatun naas*): lowly people (i.e. those who are kept on the periphery). From this it came to mean distance.

"حَاشَ لِلَّهِ" (*hasha lillah*): Allah is very far from him, or I seek Allah's protection.

"اَلْحَاشِيَةُ" (*al-hashiyaa*) also mean people who live under someone's protection {T}.

The Quran says:

| 12:31 | they said Allah is without any blemish or fault (he is flawless) | وَقُلْنَ حَاشَ لِلَّهِ |

This is used for exemption, i.e. to be exempt of any fault or blemish {R}.

H-B-B ح ب ب

Muheet says "اَلْحُبُّ" (*al-hoob*) or "اَلْمَحَبَّةُ" (*al-muhabbah*) has five meanings:

1) Whiteness and cleanliness. Hence, "حَبَبُ الْأَسْنَانِ" (*hababul asnaan*) means "the sparkle of teeth".

2) To rise or to be high, to appear "حَبَابُ الْمَائِن" (*hubaabul ma'a*) has come from it and it means a water bubble.

3) For something to be stable in its place. Hence, "حَبَّ الْبَعِيْرُ وَ أَحَبَّ" (*habbal bayeero wa ahab*) means "the camel sat down so adamantly that it did not get up after that".

4) For something to be pure or its real element, like "حَبَّةُ الْقَلْبِ" (*habbatul qalb*): pureness of heart.

5) To protect someone, to hold.

This is why "حُبُّ الْمَاءِ" (*hubbul ma'a*) is a canter or skin tank in which water can be preserved. "حَبَّ الرَّجُلُ" (*habbur rajul*) means the man stopped.

"أَحَبَّ الزَّرْعُ" (*ahabbaz zara*), the fields were sowed, that is, the results of their development began to appear {M}.

Raghib says "المَحَبَّةُ" (al-muhabbah) *means to want something which is found to be good and beneficial. This has three aspects.*

- One is for pleasure like a man loves a woman.
- Second is to like or want material things which are beneficial in some way.
- Third is to love figurative matters as scholars like each other because of the knowledge they have.

Sometimes love is also said to mean intent, but love has more of force and strength than intent {R}.

"اِسْتَحَبَّهُ" (*istahabba*): liked him//her,

"اِسْتَحَبَّهُ عَلَيْهِ" (*istahabba alaih*): preferred him over another. (12:107)

Ibn Faris says "اَلْحُبُّ" (*al-hoob*) and "اَلْمَحَبَّةُ" (*al-muhabba*) mean to think someone is essential. The basic meanings of this root are essentiality and stability. That is to think that something is essential and to stay with it with steadfastness.

The Quran has used the word "حُبُّ" (*hoob*) as against "كُرْةً" (*kurhun*). Here it means liking, as in 49:7 or 2:216. These meanings need no explanation, but where ever love for Allah is mentioned, it needs to be clarified.

Surah **Al-Baqrah** says:

2:165	and there are people who consider other forces to be Allah's contemporaries and love those forces as they love Allah although those who have **Imaan** (those who trust), love Allah in much greater degree:	وَمِنَ النَّاسِ مَنْ يَتَّخِذُ مِنْ دُوْنِ اللّٰهِ اَنْدَاداً يُحِبُّوْنَهُمْ كَحُبِّ اللّٰهِ وَالَّذِيْنَ اٰمَنُوْا اَشَدُّ حُبّاً لِّلّٰهِ

This is the general translation of this verse.

Surah **Aal-e-Imran** says:

3:30 3:31	Tell them if you love Allah then follow me; Allah will love you too, and pardon your sins: and Allah is most merciful and protector. Tell them to obey God and his messengers, but if they turn away from this, then (be warned) that Allah does not like the deniers.	قُلْ اِنْ كُنْتُمْ تُحِبُّوْنَ اللّٰهَ فَاتَّبِعُوْنِيْ يُحْبِبْكُمُ اللّٰهُ وَيَغْفِرْ لَكُمْ ذُنُوْبَكُمْ وَ اللّٰهُ غَفُوْرٌ رَّحِيْمٌ قُلْ اَطِيْعُوا اللّٰهَ وَالرَّسُوْلَ فَاِنْ تَوَلَّوْا فَاِنَّ اللّٰهَ لَا يُحِبُّ الْكَافِرِيْنَ

This is the traditional translation.

These verses are quoted as proof for the love for and by Allah's and the edifice of *tasawwuf* (Mysticism/Sufism) is built upon it. This love is so great that its height is deemed to merge with His personae. This whole concept is born due to taking love to mean as we human beings take it to mean.

A relationship of this kind with God is not Quranic. As far as God's personae are concerned, it is beyond our comprehension, and therefore, there is no question of love as one would love a beloved (even if it's one's child). To love an unseen body in this manner is psychologically impossible.

This was the difficulty which compelled Man to believe in God's incarnation in human form or to make statues of Him.

Everything will be clear if we recall the meanings of love given in the beginning.

"حُبّ" (*hoob*) means "to be steadfast". Therefore, loving Allah would mean to be stable and unwavering about Allah's orders and to follow them steadfastly, to be resolute about them and not waver over them. The verses above are testifying to these meaning.

See verse 2:165 of surah *Baqrah* which says "those who consider others to be powerful, and follow their laws and decisions as well". Therefore, here love of Allah means following His laws.

Surah *Aal-e-Imran's* verse 3:30:31 explains this: here "اِنْ كُنْتُمْ تُحِبُّونَ اللهِ" (*inn kuntum tuhibboonillaha*) has been expostulated by "أَطِيْعُوا اللهَ" (*atiullah*) which is to obey Allah.

As against it "تَوَلَّوْا" (*tuwallau*) has been used. This word further clarifies the meaning. As such, in these verses love of Allah means following His orders, which come under a centralized system, which is formed for establishing His laws.

Surah *Al-Maidah's* verse 5:54-55 supports this. In these verses, it has been said to the believers that if anyone among them turns his back from this way of life, then he should well understand that Allah's way of life is not dependent upon him. He must not think that if he leaves this way of life, then there will be nobody to take care of it.

Allah will replace them with people who are "يُحِبُّهُمْ" (*yuhibbohum*) and "يُحِبُّونَهُ" (*yuhibbunahu*), i.e. those who love Allah. Allah will also love them. This means that they will be very soft with their own and liable to dominate others. They will struggle continuously and will not be deterred by any detractor or condemner.

The next verse says:

5:55	Allah, the messenger and the believers are your friends	اِنَّمَا وَلِيُّكُمُ اللهُ وَرَسُولُهُ وَالَّذِيْنَ اٰمَنُوا

This makes it clear that by "love" here means to be close to someone, as a friend. Ahead the *Mominen* are told not to befriend the deniers in 5:57.

This too makes it clear of what 'to love Allah' means, which is to follow His laws. Now as far as Allah loving Man is concerned, one needs to recall the other meaning of the word i.e. to protect, to hold, to elicit strong capabilities, or acts to produce results. Thus, Allah's love would mean the appearance of all those results that are inevitable to obeying His laws. This is the true meaning of Man loving Allah and vice versa. This is also the meaning of being Allah's *wali* (friend) or Allah being Man's *wali*. See heading (*W-L-Y*).

"حَبّ" (*hub*) also means grain, cereal and crop, as used in 55:12
"حَبَّةٌ" (*habba*): singular of grain as used in 2:261.

H-B-R   ح ب ر

"اَلْحِبْرُ" (*al-hibr*) means ink.
"اَلْمِحْبَرَةُ" (*al-mihbarah*) means inkpot.
"اَلْحِبْرِيُّ" (*al-hibri*) means one who sells ink.
"اَلْحِبْرُ" (*al-hibr*) is the knowledge of authors, especially a Jewish scholar {*T*}.
"حْبَارٌ" (*ahbaar*) is the plural form as used in 5:44.
"اَلْحِبْرُ" (*al-hibr*) means beauty and its glow.
"اَلْحَبْرُ" (*al-habr*) means pleasure, bliss, and happiness.
"حَبْرَةٌ" (*habrah*) is complete bliss and comfort, abundance of luxury.
"اَلْحَبْرَةُ" (*al-habra*) means music in heaven or *jannat*, good song.

The Quran says:

| 30:15 | So they shall be delighted in the gardens | فَهُمْ فِىْ رَوْضَةٍ يُحْبَرُوْنَ |
| 43:70 | Enter the jannah delightfully, you and your spouses | أُدْخُلُو الْجَنَّةَ اَنْتُمْ وَ اَزْوَاجُكُمْ تُحْبَرُوْنَ |

Zajaj says the dictionary says that "اَلْحَبْرَةُ" (*al-habra*) means a good song {*T*}. Actually it encompasses all the aspects of happiness and pleasure, whether they are with the blissfulness of sight or sound, masterpieces of art or music.

Ibn Faris says it means such signs which highlight the beauty of a thing.

"حَبَّرَ الْخَطَّ وَ الشِّعَرَ" (*habbaral khatta wash-sheyr*): he polished the letter and the verse, and made it beautiful.
"تَحَبَّرَ الرَّجُلُ" (*tahabbarar rajul*): the man became handsome and beautified {*M*}.
"ثَوْبٌ حَبِيْرٌ" (*taubun habeer*): good, new cloth.
"اَلْيَحْبُوْرُ" (*al-yahboor*): a man with a delicate body {*T*}.

Raghib says that "اَلْحِبْرُ" (*al-hibr*) means a very good and beautiful sign.

"اَلْحَبْرُ" (*al-habao*) means a scholar, because his knowledge has an effect on people and his better signs and steps are followed.
The Quran enunciates the appreciation of every beautiful thing in the universe and stresses enjoying it (its beauty), with the condition that Man stays within the limits set by God and does not transgress.

A heavenly society is the one in which art and music are cause for delight in their respective places, and since all the time Allah's limits are kept in view, they are not the cause of ill effects.

The Quran has mentioned every aspect of beauty and adornment in the context of heavenly life, but life turns heavenly only when Allah's laws are implemented and followed.

H-B-S   ح ب س

"اَلْحَبْسُ" (*al-habs*): to stop, to imprison.

"اِحْتَبَسَهُ" (*ihtabasahu*): stopped him.

"فَأَحْتَبَسَ" (*fa ahtabus*): Thus, he stopped.

"اَلْمَحْبَسُ" (*al-mahbus*): the eating pot of animals {T}. It also means a ring which is put on the fingers {M}.

"حَبَسَهُ عَنْهُ" (*habasahu unhu*): to stop someone from (doing) something.

"حَبَسَهُ عَلَيْهِ" (*habasahu alaihi*) means to devote {M}.

The Quran says:

| 5:106 | (you should) stop those two witnesses | تَحْبِسُوْنَهُمَا |

H-B-Te   ح ب ط

"اَلْحَبَطُ" (*al-habat*): the scar that remains even after the wound has healed.

"اَلْحُبَاطُ" (*al-habaat*): an animal disease in which the stomach swells and the animal dies

Zamkhashri and Ibnul Atheer *say that* "حَبِطَتِ الدَّابَّةُ حَبَطاً" (*habetatin da'bbatin habata*) *means an animal overeating upon reaching a very good grazing land but not being able to digest the food it has eaten. Hence, this makes its stomach swell and it dies* {T, M}.

Ibn Faris says its basic meanings are to be proven false; pain and sorrow.

Quran has used the terms "حَبْطِ أَعْمَال" (*habatey aamaal*) (the futility of actions) rather being meaningful, as in 2:217.

If whatever an animal eats gets well digested, it becomes a part of the body and adds to the animal's health due to which it becomes strong and plump. But if its fodder is not digested, then its stomach swells, and it seems like the animal is fattening. But in fact it is a sign that the animal will die. Similarly human beings do a lot of things which appear very good to him, and he expects very good results from those acts, but they are actually the cause of his annihilation.

The Quran calls this "حَبْطِ أَعْمَال" (*habtey aamaal*) that is, not getting the good results that one expected those acts to produce. The fact is that only such acts can produce good results as which are committed under the right system of Allah's orders.

If this is not so, then all Man's efforts go waste, and the result is nothing but destruction.

| 2:217 | whose efforts go waste in this world and also in the Hereafter: | أُولَئِكَ حَبِطَتْ اَعْمَالُهُمْ فِى الدُّنْيَاوَالْآخِرَةِ |

Their efforts only leave traces, there are no results, Thus, good deeds are not those which we think are so, but the criterion for good and bad deeds is the Book of Allah. The deeds which according to Him are not good can never produce good results no matter how good they may appear to us. No matter how good our intentions are, in the universal balance, decisions are not made according to our likes or dislikes, but according to the unchanging values of Allah. That is why the Quran has not only pontificated the good deeds but also mentioned what results they will produce, so that we can judge whether we are traversing the right path or not. If our deeds are not producing the results mentioned by the Quran, then we must understand that our deeds are not according to the Quran. If we do not keep taking stock and continue in our self-deception, then all our deeds will go waste.

18:105	Thus, their deeds did not produce any result; and on the day of the judgment, we will not even ready the scales (to weigh their deeds)	فَحَبِطَتْ أَعْمَالُهُمْ فَلَا نُقِيْمُ لَهُمْ يَوْمَ الْقِيٰمَة وَزْناً

We must ponder over many of our deeds that are going to waste, and we never stop to think why this is happening, although Allah's Book (the ever true criterion of deeds) is with us.
As mentioned earlier, *Ibn Faris* has said the basic meanings of the root are not only to go to waste, but also pain and sorrow.

That means that the deeds will not only go waste, but also be cause for pain and sorrow. That is, deeds which were supposed to produce good results have been so wasted.

H-B-K   ح ب ك

"اَلْحَبَکَ" (*al-habak*): to secure tightly.

"اَلْحُبَکَةُ" (*al-habakah*): the place where a belt is tied, i.e. the waist.

"تَحَبَّکَ تَحَبُّکاً" (*tahabbaka tahheboka*): tied the *azaar* (belt) on his waist

"اَلْحُبْکَةُ" (*al-hubkah*): a rope which is tied to the waist.

"اَلْحُبُکُ مِنَ السَّمَاءِ" (*al-hoboka minas sama-ee*): the path of the stars (orbits).

"حُبُکُ الرَّمْلِ" (*hobokar raml*): waves of sand.

Fara'a says "حَبْکٌ" (*hubk*) means for something to twist and bend or break. As such, "اَلْحُبُکُ مِنَ الشَّعْرِ" (*al-hobok mina-sha'ar*) also means curly hair which grow twisted with split ends.
"اَلْحَبْکُ" (*al-habka*) means to cut and cutting of the neck {T, R, M}.

The Quran says:

51:7	the sky with pathways (or orbits):	وَالسَّمَاءِ ذاتِ الْحُبُکِ

And if it is taken to mean strength, then the verse would mean such high atmosphere where each body moves in its orbit and doesn't move away from its orbit. As such "أَلْحِبَاكْ" (*al-hibaak*) is that bunch of wooden pieces which are bound tightly together so none of the pieces moves from its place {T}, and if it is taken to mean break, then it would mean the atmosphere with celestial bodies in which they are orbiting after originally breaking away from their source (meteors).

Ibn Faris says the basic meanings include something's continuity, longevity and strength. Thus, verse 51:7 would mean such height (atmosphere) which has long or big orbits for the celestial bodies.

<h1 style="text-align:center">H-B-L   ح ب ل</h1>

"أَلْحَبْلُ" (*al-habl*): something to tie with, a rope. The plural is "حِبَالٌ" (*hibaal*).
"حَبَلَهُ" (*hablah*): tied him with a rope {T}.

Surah ***Taha*** says "حِبَالُهُمْ" (*hibalohum*) in 20:66, which means ropes.
"أَلْحَبْلُ" (*al-habl*) also means pact, responsibility, and security.

Surah ***Aal-e-Imran*** says:

3:102	all of you, hold on to the rope of Allah (be linked to Him)	وَاعْتَصِمُوْ بِحَبْلِ للّٰهِ جَمِيْعاً

Here ***Taj-ul-Uroos*** says that "حَبْلٌ" (*habal*) means 'pact'.
The author of ***Kitabil Ashqaq*** also supports this meaning.
Ibn Faris says its basic meaning is the longevity of anything.
Raghib says anything through which one reaches another thing is "حَبْلٌ" (*habal*), Thus, "حَبْلُ اللّٰهِ" (*hablullah*) means the thing which takes you to Allah i.e. the Noble Quran.
Abu Ubaid says "أَلَا إِعْتِصَامُ بِحَبْلِ اللّٰهِ" (*al-etesaamiu bihablil lah*) means following the Quran.
Ibn Masood has also taken "حَبْلُ اللّٰهِ" (*hablullah*) to mean the Quran.
Ibn Arfah says that at one place in the Quran it says:

3:111	Allah's responsibility or the responsibility given by the people.	اِلَّا بِحَبْلٍ مِنَ اللّٰهِ وَحَبْلٍ مِنَ النَّاسِ

As such in 3:102 "حَبْلُ اللّٰهِ" (*hablillah*) means responsibility towards Allah {T}.

But whatever we take the word to mean, rope or the means, responsibility or pact. It is all the same, our relationship or link is through the Quran. This is the rope that has come to us from Him and which binds us together. The next part of the verse says "وَلَا تَفَرَّقُوْ" (*wala tafarraqu*) (i.e. do not be dissected), and beyond that the ***momineen*** have been told to stay as one group or party. See 3:103 and 3:109.

Thus, "حَبْلُ اللهِ" (*habalillah*) means the collective system which is based on the Quran and whose purpose is unity of the nation and following of Allah's laws.

The Quran says about Allah:

| 50:16 | We are closer to Man than his **hablul vareed**. | وَنَحْنُ أَقْرَبُ إِلَيْهِ مِنْ حَبْلِ الْوَرِيدِ |

Fara'a says that "حَبْلٌ" (*hablil*) and "الْوَرِيْدِ" (*al-vareed*) has the same meaning and that is of lifeline {T}.

This nearness of God to Man has been explained in the first part of the verse by saying:

| 50:16 | We are even familiar with his breath | وَنَعْلَمُ مَا تُوَسْوِسُ بِهِ نَفْسُهُ |

The reference is the knowledge of Allah who is All Knowing and on which the wheel of nature depends, and no human deed, not even a passing thought, is outside His Knowledge.

| 50:17 | There is a guard (watchman) on every human deed. | مَا يَلْفِظُ مِنْ قَوْلٍ إِلَّا لَدَيْهِ رَقِيبٌ عَتِيدٌ |

This is how god is closer than one's lifeline.

H-T-M   ح ت م

"حَتَمَهُ و حَتَمَ بِكَذَا" (*hatamahu way hatama bekaza*), "يَحْتِمُ" (*behtim*), "حَتْمًا" (*hatman*): he decided about something
"حَتَمَ عَلَيْهِ الأَمْرَ" (*hatama alaihil amr*): something was made compulsory for him
"أَلْحَاتِمُ" (*al-haatim*): one who decides, one who makes a decision to be compulsory on someone {T, M}

The Quran says:

| 19:71 | This has been decided by your Sustainer. | كَانَ عَلَى رَبِّكَ حَتْمًا مَقْضِيًّا |

Ibn Faris says that this word has no root but a mutation where (*ta*) has been changed out by (*kaaf*). He claims that "حَتَمَ" (*hatam*) in fact was "حَكَمَ" (*hakam*) which means to decide.

Hatta   حَتّٰى

"حَتّٰى" (*hatta*) is used in the following meanings:

30:91	they said we will continue doing this, ***until Moosa*** doesn't return to us	قَالُوْا لَنْ نَبْرَحَ عَلَيْهِ عَاكِفِيْنَ حَتّٰى يَرْجِعَ اِلَيْنَا مُوْسٰى

Sometimes it means 'so that', as some say it means in this verse

2:217	And these people will continue fighting you ***so that*** if they may, they will force you to revert from your way of life	وَلَا يَزَالُوْنَ يُقَاتِلُوْنَكُمْ حَتّٰى يَرُدُّوْكُمْ عَنْ دِيْنِكُمْ اِنِ اسْتَطَاعُوْا

This means that their purpose is of fighting you....

Sometimes it also means the same as "اِلَّا" (*illa*) which means "rather", as quoted by both ***Taj-ul-Uroos*** and ***Muheet*** with reference to ***Ibn Maalik*** in the verse that means:

It is not largesse to give much from riches that are more than necessary, but rather to give even if you have little.

Sometimes it is also used to mean "and", as in:

47:4	So when you come against the deniers, then behead them (kill them), and when you overwhelm (conquer) them…	لَيْسَ العَطَاءُ مِنَ الْفُضُوْلِ سَمَاحَةً حَتّٰى تَجُوْدَ وَ مَا لَدَيْكَ قَلِيْلُ

No doubt that "حَتّٰى" (*hatta*) here may mean until, but 'and' also gives the requisite meaning.

Sometimes it is used only to begin talking, as:

27:18	however, when they came to the valley of the ***namal*** …	فَاِذَالَقِيْتُمُ الَّذِيْنَ كَفَرُوْ فَضَرْبَ الرِّقَابِ حَتّٰى اِذَا اَثْخَنْتُمُوْهُمْ

Here "حَتّٰى" (*hatta*) is starting a completely new topic which has no connection with the previous talk.

H-Th-Th   ح ث ث

"حَثَّ" (*hassa*), "يَحُثُّ" (*yuhusso*), "حَثًّا" (*hassan*): to hurry, to continuously ask to hurry up.
"حَثَّهُ عَلَيْهِ" (*hassahu alai*): to instigate
"الْحَثِيْثُ" (*al-haseeso*): speedy, swift in one's work {*T, M*}.

The Quran says about night and day:

7:54	the day follows the night very swiftly	يَطْلُبُهُ حَثِيْثًا

Hariri with reference to *Khalil* has written that "حَثٌّ" (*hassun*) and "حَضٌّ" (*hazzun*) are alternate words. The only difference is that "حَثٌّ" (*hassun*) means to ask to make haste and to instigate, while "حَضٌّ" (*hazzun*) means to persuade and ask to make haste *{T, M}*.

H-J-B   ح ج ب

"حَجَبَ" (*hajab*), "يَحْجِبُ" (*yahjeeb*): to cover, to hide.
"أَلْحِجَابُ" (*al-hijaab*): the thing that is used as a veil *{T}*.

7:76	there will be veil between the two	وَبَيْنَهُمَا حِجَابٌ

But *Raghib* writes that it means an obstruction that obstructs one thing from getting to another: This means that punishment meted out to those in the state of *Jahannum* will not reach those who are in the state of *Jannah*. And the dwellers of *Jahannum* will not be able to partake of the pleasures of *Jannah*. Here it means to deprive.

Surah *At-Tatfeef* says:

83:15	They will be deprived of Allah's blessings during this time. (due to their (bad) deeds)	إِنَّهُمْ عَنْ رَبِّهِمْ يَوْمَئِذٍ لَمَحْجُوبُونَ

Nawab Siddiq Hasan Khan has written that words in which "ح" (*hah*) and "ج" (*jeem*) comes together, indicate to the meaning of stopping or negating.

"أَلْحَاجِبُ مِنَ الشَّمْسِ وَالْقَمَرِ" (*al-haajib minash shamsi wal qamar*): the corner of the sun or moon which appears first *{T}*.

H-J-J   ح ج ج

"أَلْحَجُّ" (*al-hajj*): to intend, to decide.
"حَجَجْتُ فُلَانًا" (*hajajto fulanan*): I intended for it.
"أَلْحِجَّةُ" (*al-hijjah*): one year *{T, M}*.
"حِجَجٌ" (*hijaj*) is the plural form.

Some scholars say that it means to decide about some respectable thing or to decide with a majority *M}*. This is why intending to head for *Mecca* has been called "حَجٌّ" (*hajj*).

Surah *Al-Qasas* says:

28:27	eight years	ثَمَانِيَ حِجَجٍ

"اَلْحَجُّ" (*al-hajj*) also means to prevent.

"حَجَّهُ عَنِ الشَّیْءِ" (*hajjahu unish shaiyi*): stopped him from (doing) it.

"اَلْمُحَاجَّةُ" (*muhajjah*) has been lead to mean "to quarrel" {*T, M*}.

Each one of the quarrelling party tries to stop the other from his intentions.

The Quran says:

| 3:19 | if they stop you from what you intend | | فَاِنْ حَاجُّوْکَ |

Also see 6:81.

"حُجَّةٌ" (*hujjah*): reasoning.

Muheet says that reasoning is called "بَیِّنَةٌ" (*bayyenah*) because it makes the thing clear and distinct and "حُجَّةٌ" (*hujjah*) leads to victory over the opponent.
In surah **Anaam**, the Quranic reasoning and orders are called "اَلْحُجَّةُ الْبَالِغَةُ" (*al-hujjatul baalegha*) in 6:150.

For the pilgrimage at **Kaaba** the word "حَجّ" (*hajj*) is used in 2:196.
In 3:96, the same thing has been called "حِجُّ الْبَیْتِ" (*hijj-ul-bait*).
"اَلْحَاجُّ" (*al-hajjo*) is one who performs "حَجّ" (*hajj*).

"حَجّ" (*hajj*) is the universal gathering of the Islamic world, and is held in the center of this nation, so that solutions to their collective problems are sought in the light of the Quran. In this way this nation is able to see the benefits with their own eyes.

| 22:28 | so that they see what is to their benefits in material (physical) form | | لِیَشْهَدُوْا مَنَافِعَ لَهُمْ |

For the establishment of a system, centralized gatherings are very important. It is interesting to note that the Quran gave a system of consultation, as stated in 42:38, and a gathering so that when the world was in the grip of kingships and when the world thought that they were "God's gift to Mankind' and when it thought that the kings had the Divine right.

From the local congregation of prayers to the universal congregation of **Hajj**, the purpose is to establish the Quranic system and solve problems for mankind. For more details see heading **Qibla**.

H-J-R   ح ج ر

"حَجَرٌ" (*hajar*): stone.

"أَحْجَارٌ" (*ahjaar*) or "حِجَارَةٌ" (*hijaar*) is the plural form.

"اَلْحُجْرُ" (*al-hujr*), "اَلْحِجْرُ" (*al-hijr*), "اَلْحَجْرُ" (*al-hajr*): to stop from, to prevent, to protect.

"حِجْرًا مَحْجُورًا" (*hijran mahjoora*) as used in 25:54 means something that stops, a stopper, a barricade.

"حُجْرَةٌ" (*hajra*): a camels' enclosure, a room. "حُجُرَاة" (*hujraat*) is its plural.

"اَلْحِجْرُ" (*al-hijr*): the intellect that prevents man (from doing something harmful). 89:5

Nawab Siddiq Hasan Khan writes that words in which "ح" (*hah*) and "ج" (*jeem*) appear together give the meaning of preventing from, or stopping from something.

"حِجْرٌ" (*hijr*) was also the name of the dwellings of the nation ***Samood,*** because these dwellings were carved out in mountains.

"حَنْجَرَةٌ" (*hanjarah*): the throat. Its plural form is "جَنَاجِرُ" (*hanajir*) as used in 40:18, 33:10.

"حَجَرٌ" (*hajar*): gold and silver, and a very aware and clever man as well.

Quran says about "اَلنَّارَ" (*an-naar*):

2:25	Its fuel is humans and stones	وَقُودُ هَا النَّاسُ وَالْحِجَارَةُ

Raghib says it means people who are so adamant or whose hearts are as hard as stone. About the same people it is said a little further ahead:

2:74	Then your hearts (attitudes) hardened, so they became hard as stones or even harder. (or that their development capabilities had stopped)	ثُمَّ قَسَتْ قُلُوبُكُم مِّن بَعْدِ ذَلِكَ فَهِىَ كَالْحِجَارَةِ أَوْ أَشَدُّ قَسْوَةً

"اَلنَّاسُ" (*an-naas*) could also mean the commoners who follow the elite of the society, and "اَلْحِجَارَةُ" (*al-hijarah*) means those clever people who as leaders make the simple folks follow them. That is, those who traverse the wrong path, the leaders and their followers both, will go to state of ***Jahannum***. This is supported by other verses of the Quran, like 14:21, 33:67. If it is taken to mean gold and silver, then it would mean capital worship which gives birth to a hellish society. Surah ***Tauba*** says that if people keep collecting gold and silver (wealth) and do not use it for the welfare of humanity, then that gold and silver will be heated in the fire of ***Jahannum*** and be branded on their foreheads and backs. (9:34-35).

As such, the fuel of ***Jahannum*** is the capitalists and their wealth which they do not use for the benefit of mankind but for their own personal gains. On the other hand, if in 2:25 the meaning of "اَلنَّارَ" (*an-naar*) is taken to mean battle (see heading N-W-R), and then "اَلْحِجَارَةُ" (*al-hijarah*) would mean the stoning which in those days was done against the opponents (as in 105:4). That would mean that since you do not decide on the basis of knowledge and intellect, then it would mean battle, which is waged by Man and inflamed by the stones which are thrown against the opponents. This can mean battle between the *Momins* and the opponents or between the opponents themselves. (See 6:65, 6:130, 27:82-83). The supporters of Allah's laws have to go to in war in order to eradicate war from this world once for all.

Surah *Al-Anaam* says "حِجْرٌ لَا يَطْعَمُهَا" (*hijrunbla yatamoja*) in 6:139, which means forbidden, which is not permitted ordinarily to eat.

"حُجُوْرٌ" (*hujoor*) means to protect. "حِجْرٌ" (*hijr*) means 'lap'.

H-J-Z   ح ج ز

"حَجَزَهُ" (*hajazah*), "يَحْجُزُهُ" (*yah-jozuhu*), "حَجَازَةً" (*hijarah*) means to stop, to prevent.
"حَجَزَ الْبَعِيْرَ" (*haja-zal bayeer*) means to make a camel sit and tie its lower legs with a rope and tie its waist with the same rope so that it cannot move and its wound on its back can be treated.
"اَلْحِجَازُ" (*al-hijaaz*) is the rope with which the camel is Thus, bound.
"حِجَازٌ" (*hijaaz*) is called so, because this place is situated between *Najaf* and *Tuhama* and is serves as a barrier. {T, R, M}
"اَلْحَجْزُ" (*al-hajzo*) means to build an obstruction or border between two things {L}.

Ibn Faris says it basically means to be an obstruction or barrier.

The Quran says "حَاجِزاً" (*haajizan*) in 27:61. At another place it says "حَاجِزِيْنَ" (*haajizeen*) in 69:47. These words mean to prevent or stop from something.

Nawab Siddiq Hasan Khan writes that words in which "ح" (*hah*) and "ج" (*jeem*) appear together give the meaning of preventing from, or stopping from something.

H-D-B   ح د ب

"اَلْحَدَبُ" (*al-hadab*) means the stomach and chest, to cave in, and the hunch on the back to jut out.
"حَدِبَ يَحْدَبُ حَدَباً" (*hadiba yah-dabun hadaba*) means to be a hunch back.
"اَلْحَدَبُ" (*al-hadab*) means high land, plateau, and the hard and high part of land {M}.

Ibn Faris says it basically means to be high or lofty.

The Quran says about *Yajjoj Majooj*:

| 21:96 | they will jump out very fast from the plateau | وَهُمْ مَنْ كُلِّ حَدَبٍ يَنْسِلُوْنَ |

For details see the word *Yajooj* in the heading *(A-J-J)*.

H-D-Th   ح د ث

Ibn Faris says it basically means to come into existence from oblivion.

"اَلْحِدِيْثُ" (*al-hadees*): is the opposite of ancient, something new.

"حَوَادِثُ" (*hawadis*): new events that keep coming to the fore, or keep happening.

"حَدِيْثُ السِّنّ" (*hadisus-sin*): young man.

"أَحْدَثَهُ" (*ahdasa*): he did something (which was never done before).

"اِحْدَاثٌ" (*ahdaas*): to bring into existence.

"اَلْمُحَدَثُ" (*al-muhaddas*): honest and truthful man

"اَلْمُحَدِّثُ" (*al-muhaddis*): someone who relates *hadees* {T}.

"مُحْدَثٌ" (*mohdas*): unprecedented {M}.

It means something that comes into existence for the first time, unparalleled. It also means something that has not happened too long ago.

Quran has used the word "مُحْدَثٌ" (*mohdis*) in these meanings in 21:2, 26:4.

Surah *Al-Kahaf* says:

18:70	let me initiate and talk first	أُحْدِثَ لَكَ

Surah *Taha* says about the Quran:

20:113	Or so that they may think of it.	أَوْ يُحْدِثُ لَهُمْ ذِكْرًا

It can also mean that it will grant loftiness to those people. See heading (Dh-K-R). And also that it will bring the historical events of universal nations which will awaken their capacities to comprehend.

In both cases the meaning of the word "اِحْدَاثٌ" (*ihdaas*) is to bring into existence.

Surah *Az-Zuhaa* says:

93:11	you keep propagating your Sustainer's blessings	وَأَمَّا بِنِعْمَةِ رَبِّكَ فَحَدِّثْ

Here "تَحْدِيْثٌ" (*hadees*) means common propagation.

"أَحَادِيْثُ" (*ahadees*) is the plural form of "حَدِيْثٌ" (*hadees*) which can mean tales, historical records as in 12:6. It has also been used for tales in 23:44.

Ibn Faris says that "حَدَثَ" (*hadas*) means for something to come into existence, out of non-present state.

This leads to "اَلْحَدِيْثُ" (*al-hadees*) because it leads to another thing that is stories galore.

In the Islamic law, "اَلْحَدِيْثُ" (*al-hadees*) means any speech or act which has been attributed to Allah's messenger. The meaning of "حَدِيْثٌ" (*hadees*) is quite extensive, but we have briefly dealt with it here.

Faraa says that "اَحَادِيْثُ" (*ahahdeesa*) is the plural of "اُحْدُوْثَةٌ" (*uhdoosa*) which is possible, but later it became the plural of "حَدِيْثٌ" (*hadees*).

H-D-D   ح د د

"اَلْحَدُّ" (*al-hudd*): the actual meanings of this root are to prevent or stop from something {M}.
"حَدَّ الرَّجُلَ عَنِ الْأَمْرِ" (*huddar rajula unil amr*): stopped that man from (doing) it.
"حَدَدْتُ فُلَانًا عَنِ الشَّرِّ" (*ha-dadto fulanan unish shiir*): I stopped him from something bad.
"اَلْحَدَدُ" (*al-hadad*): obstruction.
"هَذَا أَمْرٌ حَدَدٌ" (*haazarun hadad*): this is a forbidden act.
"اَلْحَدُّ" (*al-hudd*): to distinguish a thing from the other, also something which becomes a barrier between two things so that one does not merge into the other, or so that one thing does not reach the other.
"اَلْحَدِيْدُ" (*al-hadeed*): "iron", because due to its hardness it becomes a barrier (especially to enemies). Also a sharp object or which goes through and though.
"حَدَّ" (*hudd*): to sharpen.
"اَلْمُحَادَّةُ" (*al-muhad'da*): infighting; to oppose each other {M}.

It actually means to prevent or stop one another from something.

Surah *Al-Ahzaab* has used "بِأَلْسِنَةٍ حَدَادٍ" (*bi al-sinatin hidaad*) 'from sharp tongues'.
"حَدَاد" (*hiddaad*) is the plural of "حَدِيْدٌ" (*hadeed*) as used in 33:19.

Surah *Qaf* says "فَبَصَرُكَ الْيَوْمَ حَدِيْدٌ" (*fa basrokal yauma hadeed*) in 50:22. It means sight that can see through the covers that are covering the truth. This is about the time of the result when eyes will be so sharp as to see the results behind the deeds.

Surah "الحديد" (*al-hadeed*) tells us to establish Allah's law, and uses the word "حَدِيْدٌ" (*hadeed*) i.e. the sword or force.

Surah *Al-Mujadlah* says:

58:5	resist those who obstruct the establishing of Allah's laws and his messenger	إِنَّ الَّذِيْنَ يُحَادُّوْنَ اللَّهَ وَرَسُوْلَهُ

For the laws of Allah, the Quran mentions a phrase at several places, like in:

2:187	these are Allah's limits, do not go near them	تِلْكَ حُدُودُ اللّهِ

Calling Allah's laws as "حُدُودُ اللّهِ" (**hudood-allah**) points to a very big reality. The Quran has generally given the orders in principle, and left it to the human beings to formulate sub laws according to the need of the times under those principles. Quranic principles will remain unchanged, but the laws under them, will change as the times change. Thus, Man has full liberty under the unchanging principles, just as the team in a game has full liberty within certain rules. Thus, Man is given a system by the Quran, in which he fulfills both, the unchanging basic principles and the changing sub-laws. This does not leave him completely unbridled or impose restrictions that curtail his freedom totally.

This is the purpose of "حُدُودُ اللّهِ" (**hudood-allah**). But we have strayed away from the truth and formulated rigid laws which have made Islam a collection of outdated and rigid laws instead of the living movement that it is.

And which cannot be compatible with modern times. Complete freedom under few limitations. This is the way of life given to us by the Quran. "حُدُودُ اللّهِ" (**hudood-allah**) are the last limits of Allah's law which should not be transgressed.

H-D-Q　　　　　　ح د ق

"أَلْحَدَقَةُ" (**al-hadaqah**): the blackness of the eye which surrounds the pupil.

Ibn Faris says it basically means for one thing to surround, encompass another.

"حَدَقُوا بِهِ يَحْدِقُونَ" (**hadaqu bihi yahaqoon**): they surrounded him.
"أَحَدَقَ بِهِ" (**ahdaq behi**) is anything which encloses another.
"حَدِيقَةُ" (**hadeeqa**) means the ditch in the valley where water gets collected.
"حَدِيقَةُ" (**hadeeqa**) is also the garden with a surrounding wall. Without the wall, it is not called "حَدِيقَةُ" (**hadeeqah**), and in addition this garden needs to grow grass. If there is no grass, then such a garden is called "رَوْضَةُ" (**rozah**) {T, R, M}.
"حَدَائِقْ" (**hada-iq**) is the plural of "حَدِيقَةُ" (**hadeeqah**) {T, R, M}.

The Quran says "حَدَائِقَ ذَاتَ بَهْجَةٍ" (**hadayiqa zaata bahjah**) which means delightful gardens. Here it means ordinary gardens without walls.

H-Dh-R   ح ذ ر

"حِذْرٌ" (*hizr*), "حَذَرٌ" (*hazar*) is to avoid something which frightens, to be careful, to be cautious.

Ibn Faris says it basically means to be aware, and avoid.

"رَجُلٌ حَذِرٌ" (*rajulun hazar*): a person who lies awake as is wary.
"ابْنُ أَحْذَار" (*ibnu aaar*): the one person who is extremely cautious {T, M}.
"حَذَار حَذَار" (*hazari hazari*): caution.
"اَلْحَاذِرُ" (*al-hazir*): a person who is armed and ready for battle {T, R, M}.
"حَاذِرُوْنَ" (*haazeroon*): the plural form of "اَلْحَاذِرُ" (*al-hazir*).

The Quran says:

| 26:56 | armed armies | وَإِنَّا لَجَمِيعٌ حَاذِرُوْنَ |
| 17:57 | Sustainer's *azaab* (the results of bad deeds) is something to be aware of | إِنَّ عَذَابَ رَبِّكَ كَانَ مَحْذُوْرًا |

Surah *Baqrah* says "فَاحْذَرُوْهُ" (*faahzuruhu*) in 2:235 which means to observe the laws of Allah.

Surah *Al-Zumr* says about a *Momin*:

| 39:9 | he keeps the life of the Hereafter in mind | يَحْذَرُ الْآخِرَةَ |

Surah *Al-Ma'ida* uses "فَخُذُوْهُ" (*fakhzohu*) against "فَاحْذَرُوْ" (*faahzuro*) (5:41) which means "to avoid".
Surah *Al-Baqrah* says "حَذَرَ الْمَوْتِ" (*hazarul maut*) in 2:243, 2:19, which means "to avoid or escape death".
Surah *An-Nisa* says "خُذُوْا حَذَرَكُمْ" (*khuzohazrakum*) which includes all precautions.

"حَذَّرَهُ تَحْذِيْرًا" (*hazzarahu taeera*): alerted him, warned him.
"حَذَّرَهُ مِنْ أَمْرٍ" (*hazzarahu min amrin*), or "حَذَّرَهُ الْأَمْرَ" (*hazzarahu-lamra*): He told him to be aware of that matter.

The Quran says:

| 3:28 | Allah tells you to be aware of the results of the natural outcome. | يُحَذِّرُكُمُ اللهُ نَفْسَهُ |
| 17:57 | verily your Sustainer's punishment is something to be cautious about | إِنَّ عَذَابَ رَبِّكَ كَانَ مَحْذُوْرًا |

H-R-B ح ر ب

Muheet says "أَلْحَرْبُ" (*al-harb*) has basic meaning of desolation, destruction and waste.

Nawab Siddiq Hasan Khan has written that words, in which "ح" (*ha*) and "ر" (*ra*) appear together, contain the meanings of hardness and hard work.

Ibn Faris writes that its basic meaning is to snatch, and this word is the opposite of peace. In other words this word means to fight.

"حَارَبَهُ" (*haraba*) means to fight and to rebel {T}.

The Quran says:

| 9:107 | For those who rebel against Allah and his messenger | لِمَنْ حَارَبَ اللَّهَ وَرَسُولَهُ |
| 5:33 | These are those who rebel against Allah and his messenger | اَلَّذِينَ يُحَارِبُونَ اللَّهَ وَرَسُولَهُ |

"حَرْبٌ" (*hurb*) means battle, war as used in 2:279.
"أَلْمِحْرَابُ" (*al-mihraab*): upper floor, high place, center, and palace.

Kitabal Ashqaq says that such high places are built for battles.

"مَحَارِيبُ بَنِى اِسْرَاءِيلَ" (*mahareebo Bani Israel*): the mosques of *Bani Israel* in which they used to meet to consult about battles etc. {T}

The Quran too while telling Muslims to establish the system of prayer mentions mutual consultation 42:38. That is, they solve their problems with mutual consultations. This clearly shows the connections between mosques and consultation.

But it seems that "مِحْرَاب" (*mihraab*) was also the place where sacrifices were made.

About *Zakariya* it is said:

| 3:38 | he was engaged in *salah* in the sacrificial place | هُوَ قَائِمٌ يُصَلِّىْ فِىْ الْمِحْرَابِ |

Surah *Saba* says in 32:13 that "مَحَارِيبُ" (*mahareeb*) used to be made for *Suleman* (Solomon). This could also mean strong fortes and palaces or mosques.

H-R-Th   ح ر ث

"ٱلْحَرْثُ" (*al-hars*) basically means to earn. Later this word became common as meaning to work on land. "حَرْثٌ" (*hars*), as such, means to do farming, since it entails hard labour along with the faculties of the mind.

"حَرَثَ الشَّىْءَ" (*harsash shaiyi*) Hence, means that he gained expertise in it.

"ٱلْحَرْثُ" (*al-hars*) also means to stoke the fire to make it burn more brightly.

"ٱلْمِحْرَاثُ" (*al-mihraas*) is the wooden poker used to stoke the fire {*T, M*}.

Quran has also called women as "حَرْثٌ" (*hars*) (cultivation, fields) in 2:223, because they are the basic means of the perpetuation of the human race. This also shows that the Quran uses this word for sexual intercourse between husband and wife which is perpetuation of the human race. For details see headings (*H-Sd-N*) and (*S-F-H*).

In surah *Waqia* "تَحْرُثُوْنَ" (*tahrosoon*) is used in 59:63 which means to sow seeds (in the earth), and then "تَزْرَعُوْنَ" (*tazra-oon*) in 56:63 which means to make the crop grow from the land. "حَرَثٌ" (*hars*) is in Man's own power, but "زَرْعٌ" (*zara*) happens according to Allah's law. Man can well sow the seed in land but to make it grow is not within his power. This happens (growth) only according to Allah's law. As such, whatever grows is not only man's doing but also the gift of God. A man can only ask for compensation for his labor, but cannot be the owner of what God has done. For details see my book, *Nizaami Raboobiyat*.

Ibn Faris says that "حَرَثَ نَاقَتَهُ" (*Harsun naaqata*) means that he weakened his she-camel, probably due to hard work.

H-R-J   ح ر ج

"ٱلْحَرَجُ" (*al-harj*) means to collect things in a manner that, a dense concentration appears. It also means where there are thick trees {*T*}.

Raghib says that from this it came to mean discomfort. It also means work which is not done whole heartedly.

"حَرَجَ الرَّجُلُ أَنْيَابَهُ" (*harajar rujolu anyaabahu*): he grinded his teeth.

"لَا حَرَجَ عَلَيْكَ" (*la haraja alaika*): there's no harm on you, or there is no objection against you {*M*}. From this, this word also came to mean 'sin'.

Nawab Siddiq Hasan Khan has written that words, in which "ح" (*ha*) and "ر" (*ra*) appear together, contain the meanings of hardness and hard work.

Surah **an-nisa** says that the characteristic of **Momineen** is that they follow Allah's laws in such manner that:

4:65	they don't feel any qualms about this obedience	لَا يَجِدُوْا فِىْ اَنْفُسِهِمْ حَرَجاً

In Surah **An-Noor** this word has appeared to mean something objectionable (24:61).

Surah **Al-Hajj** says:

22:78	he has not been narrow in affairs of this way of life towards you	وَمَاجَعَلَ عَلَيْكُمْ فِى الدِّيْنِ مِنْ حَرَجٍ

It may also means that it cannot be forced upon somebody.

2:256	It will be accepted gladly	لَا اِكْرَاَه فِى الدِّيْنِ

The laws which you observe in the way of life are not useless labor, but it is so that your personality becomes expanded and strong and stable.

2:286	Allah does not hold any person liable or responsible for anything except if it is not necessary to expand his personality	لَا يُكَلِّفُ اللّٰهُ نَفْساً اِلَّا وُسْعَهَا

Remember that there is no narrowness in this way of life. This does not mean that you claim to follow this way of life but accept only those things which you find easy, and reject the things you find difficult (to do) on the plea that there is no narrowness or coercion in way of life.

As long as you are within this system, you will have to accept all its laws with equanimity. When you feel some coercion, you are out of this system. By staying within the system, you will have to follow and observe every law and rule. This is not coercion but a limitation which one observes voluntarily. That is, to accept the limitations set by this way of life is in a way agreement that one will observe the limitations imposed by the system. This is what is meant by no (narrowness) coercion in this way of life.

H-R-D   ح ر د

"حَرَدَهُ" (*Haradah*), "يَحْرِدُهُ" (*yahridoh*), "حَرْداً" (*hardah*): he intended to, he stopped him or he prevented him from.
"اَلْحُرُوْدُ" (*al-hurudu*): to be aloof.

Ibn Faaris says it basically means to intend, to be angry, or to get to one side.

"رَجُلٌ حَارِدٌ" (*rajulun haarid*): a man who is aloof. It also means a man who is very angry.

In the Quran, it has been said about the men with the gardens (or orchard) "وَغَدَوْا عَلى حَرْدٍ قَادِرِيْنَ" (*wahadau ala hardin qaadereen*) in 68:28. This could mean that they were capable of completing their mission or purpose, and also that they had the power to prevent the poor from coming to their garden. The second meaning seems to gel with the context.

Nawab Siddiq Hasan Khan has written that words, in which "ح" (*ha*) and "ر" (*ra*) appear together, contain the meanings of hardness and hard work.

H-R-R   ح ر ر

"اَلْحَرُّ" (*al-har*), "اَلْحَرُوْرُ" (*al-haroor*), "الْحَرَارَةُ" (*al-harah*): heat.
"الْحَرُوْرُ" (*al-huroor*): the heat of the sunlight.

In the Quran this word has been used opposite to "ظِلّ" (*Zill*) as "اَلْحَرِيْرُ" (*al-hareer*) in 35:21.

"اَلْحَرِيْرُ" (*al-hareer*): silken cloth, as used in 76:12 *{T}*.
"حَرِيْرٌ" (*hareer*): every thin or fine cloth *{R}*.

The actual meaning of this root is to be absolutely pure and without any pollution *{T}*.

"اَلْحُرُّ" (*al-hur*) is the opposite of "عَبْدٌ" (*abd*) which means "someone bound by contract".
"اَلْحُرُّ" (*al-hur*): a free man removed from a contract. It also means the best part of anything, the best horse, the best land from among ordinary land and sandy soil.
"حُرُّ كُلِّ أَرْضٍ" (*hurro kulli ardin*): the best part of any land.
"مَاهَذَا مِنْكَ بِحُرٍّ" (*ma haza minka bihur*): this is not your best work *{T}*.
"حَرًّا" (*harra*), "يَحَرُّ" (*yuharro*): to be free.
"اَلتَّحْرِيْرُ" (*al-tahreero*): to free a slave man or woman.
"تَحْرِيْرُ الْكِتَابِ" (*tehrirul kitaab*): though it might mean to free one's thoughts from one's mind and bring them on to a book, the writer of *Taj* says this means "to beautify edit the words of the book", otherwise "to make the book better".
"تَحْرِيْرُ الْوَلَدِ" (*tehrirul walad*): to devote a child in the service of some place of worship.

Surah **Maryam** quotes her mother as saying:

| 3:34 | whatever is in my womb, I have promised to devote to my deity | اِنِّیْ نَذَرْتُ لَکَ مَافِیْ بَطْنِیْ مُحَرَّراً |

Here "مُحَرَّرٌ" (**harar**) means that there is the condition in this that the child can never leave the service {**T**}.

As such even today the Christian nuns have to devote their entire lives to the Church. This explains the very many allegations against **Maryam** which the Jews had leveled against her. **Maryam** had been devoted to the service of the **Kaneesa** or the holy place of the Jews. It seems that at that time **Maryam's** mother had given her to the **Kaneesa**, celibacy was not requires for the devotee. This was later formulated by the Jews, which later permeated the Christians too and is still practiced. **Maryam** defied this man-made rule and followed what God told her to do, and got married, left the holy place and began to live a normal life. This, according to the bigwigs of the Jews, was a very big crime and rebelliousness from their religion. That is why they persecuted her so. Details of this can be found in my book "**Shola e– Mastoor**".

H-R-S   ح ر س

"حَرَسَہ" (**harasa**), "یَحْرِسُہ" (**yahresahu**), "یَحْرُسُہ" (**yahrosohu**): he protected him.
"اَلْحَرَسِیُّ" (**al-harassio**): governmental guard and bodyguard.
"حَرَسَ الرَّجُلُ" (**harasur rajul**): this man committed a robbery.
"اَلْحَرِیْسَۃُ" (**al-hareesa**): stolen goods {**T**}.

The Quran says:

| 72:8 | strict guards | حَرَساً شَدِیْداً |

"حَرَسٌ" (**harasun**) and "حُرَّاسٌ" (**hurraas**) are the plural of "حَارِسٌ" (**haaris**): the protector or guard.
"حَرْزٌ" (**hurz**): the protection of goods.
"حَرْسٌ" (**hurs**) means the protection of a place {**R**}.

This will contain an element of strictness and labor because the letters "ح" (**ha**) and "ر" (**ra**) have appeared together. This is their particularity {**Al-ilmul khalaq**}.

H-R-Sd   ح ر ص

"اَلْحَرْصُ" (**al-hurs**) means to drill a hole into something, to tear something up or scrape something, like the washer beats the clothes on the stones and Thus, even tear up some clothes.

"ثَوْبٌ حَرِيصٌ" (**saubun hareesun**) means clothes torn up this way.
"اَلْحَارِصَہ" (**al-haarisa**) is the cloud which drills sort of holes into the ground with its rain, or scrapes the top surface of the earth.
"اَلْحَرْصَۃُ" (**al-harsah**) means for animals' teats to split so that the milk falls into the pots {**T, M**}.

In the light of these basic meanings, "حِرْصٌ" (**hirs**) means a wish (whether it is good or bad) which pierces the heart. It does not remain hidden in the heart and is often expressed. That is, a very earnest desire {**T**}.

The Quran says:

2:96	you will find that the wish to live forever is very intense in their hearts	وَلَتَجِدَنَّهُمْ أَحْرَصَ النَّاسِ عَلَى حَيٰوۃٍ

Another place, it is said about the Messenger (**pbuh**):

9:128	he is pained at whatever misfortune befalls you (he nurses the intense desire for your benefit)	حَرِيصٌ عَلَيْكُمْ

Azhari says that to the Arabs "حَرِيصٌ عَلَيْکَ" (**hareesun alaik**) is the same as "حَرِيصٌ عَلَى نَفْعِکَ" (**hareesun ala naf'eka**) {**T**}. That is, the wish to benefit you is very intense in his heart.

H-R-Zd   ح ر ض

"اَلْحَرَضُ" (**al-hurz**) means disorder, mutation, even if it is physical or mental. A weak and broken man who is near destruction, perhaps due to sorrow or heart break (12:85) {**R**}. A thing not worth considering, which has no good attributes {**Al-ilmul-khafaq**}.
"اَلْحَرِضُ" (**al-hariz**): the man who is weakened by disease.

Raghib says "تَحْرِيضٌ" (**tehreez**) means "اِزَالَۃُ الْحَرَضِ" (**izalatul haraz**) or to remove somebody's weakness.
"مَرَّضْتُہ" (**marraztoh**) means to remove somebody's sickness. Thus, "حَرَّضَ" (**harraz**) means to instigate someone for something which is life-giving for him and which if not done would be deadly for him.

The Quran tells the Messenger (pbuh) "وَحَرِّضِ الْمُؤْمِنِيْنَ عَلَى الْقِتَالِ" (**wa harrazil momineena alal qitaal**) in 8:65. Ordinarily it is supposed to mean "get them ready for battle", but it means that you remove all the weaknesses and faults from your companions so that they engage in struggle for life with gusto and manliness. This is what "وَيُزَكِّيْهِمْ" (*wa yuzakkihim*) means in 62:2, which is to develop, to remove the weakness, something that is the first stage of this program.

H-R-F   ح ر ف

"حَرْفٌ" (*harf*) means the end or corner of something, or limit.
"حَرْفُ الْجَبَلِ" (*harful jabal*) is the upper part of a mountain which juts out on one side.
"فُلَانٌ عَلَى حَرْفٍ مِنْ أَمْرِهِ" (*fulanun ala harfin min amrihi*): that man is standing on edge to go the way he finds beneficial {T}.

The Quran says:

22:11	in matters of observing Allah's laws they are on the border line (edge), if they find it beneficial to observe them, they do it, otherwise they leave it (the observance)	وَمِنَ النَّاسِ مَنْ يَعْبُدُ اللَّهَ عَلَى حَرْفٍ

"حَرَفَ الشَّيْئَ عَنْ وَجْهِهِ" (*harafash shaiyi un wajhehi*): to turn something away from its right path, changed.
"اَلتَّحْرِيْفُ" (*al-tahreef*) means to change or amend, whether in words or figuratively.
"اِنْحَرَافَ" (*inharaf*) means to lean to one side, to become crooked (not straight) {T}.

Quran says:

2:75	They change the word of Allah (amend it after understanding the word of Allah)	يُحَرِّفُوْنَهُ مِنْ بَعْدِ مَا عَقَلُوْهُ

"حَرَفَ لِعِيَالِهِ" (*harafa le iyaalehi*): he earned for his family {T}.
"اَلْحِرْفَةُ" (*al-hirfah*): industry or profession from which one earns.
"حَرِيْفَكَ" (*hareefoka*): your companion in your profession {R}. (We use this word in meaning of opponent or enemy due to the mutual tussle between colleagues).
"اَلْمُحَارَفُ" (*al-muhaarif*): someone who strives very hard but is unable to earn enough for his family {R}.
"اَلْمُحَرَّفُ" (*al-muharraf*): someone who has lost his goods {R}. Therefore, "تَحْرِفَةٌ" (*tehreef*) would mean to argue and explain in such a way as to miss the spirit of the thing which is actually the capital (or the main point), whether this "تَحْرِفَةٌ" (*tehreef*) is by changing the words or by changing the meaning. The changes which the nations with celestial Books have made are mentioned in the Quran.

4:46	they remove the sentences from their places	يُحَرِّفُوْنَ الْكَلِمَ عَنْ مَوَاضِعِهِ

Also see 5:41. This is the sense of "تَحريف" (*tehreef*) (change of words or meaning).

Surah *Al-Baqrah* says:

2:79	they write the Books themselves and say they have been sent by Allah:	يَكْتُبُونَ الْكِتَابَ بِأَيْدِيهِمْ ثُمَّ يَقُولُونَ هٰذَا مِنْ عِنْدِ اللّٰهِ

This means change of words. Details about how badly the Christians and the Jews both have committed "تَحْرِيْف" (*tehreef*) in their holy books can be found in the first chapter *Zahrul Fisaad* of my book *Meraaji Insaaniyat*. None of their Holy Books is in its original shape anymore.

H-R-Q   ح ر ق

"حَرَقَ الْحَدِيْدَ بِالْمِبْرَدِ" (*haraqal hadeeda bilmibrad*): filed the iron, which is the basic meaning according to **Ibn Faris.**

Since this process generates heat, it means to burn by putting in the fire.
"الْحَرَقُ" (*al-harq*): the flare of fire, or fire itself
"الْحَرِيْقُ" (*al-hariqu*): fire, or to be on fire.
"الْحَرِقُ مِنَ السَّحَابِ" (*al-hariqu mis-sahab*): cloud with a lot of lightning.

Surah *Aal-e-Imran* says:

3:180	taste the punishment of total destruction	ذُوْقُوْا عَذَابَ الْحَرِيْقِ

Surah *Al-Ambia* says about *Ibrahim*:

21:68	they said "burn him"	قَالُوْا حَرِّقُوْهُ

"الْحَرِيْقُ" (*iharaq*) means to burn as used in 2:266.

Since "ح" (*ha*) and "ر" (*ra*) have appeared together in this word, it has the connotation of hardness and hard labor which is its particularity {*Al-ilmul-khafaq*}.

H-R-K   ح ر ک

"حَرَکَ" (*harok*), "يَحْرُکُ" (*yahrok*), "حَرْکًا" (*harka*) and "حَرَکَةٌ" (*harkah*): moved, showed some movement.

It is the opposite of being still, stationary.

"حَرَّکْتُهُ فَتَحَرَّکَ" (*harraitohu fatah-harrak*): I moved it, so it became mobile. This is used for material things to be transferred from one place to another. Sometimes "تَحَرَّکَ کَذَا" (*taharraka kaza*) is said when there is a change in something, that is, there is some addition or subtraction in its elements.

The Messenger (pbuh) has been told in the Quran, with literal meanings that

| 75:16 | do not move your tongue along with it, so that you take it faster: | لَا تُحَرِّكْ بِهِ لِسَانَكَ لِتَعْجَلَ بِهِ |

It is generally thought that this is about the noble Quran, because at another place it is said:

| 30:114 | Do not act on Revelation's program until the entire program is before you. (act only when the entire program is revealed before you, not before) | وَلَا تَعْجَلْ بِالْقُرْآنِ مِنْ قَبْلِ اَنْ يُقْضَى اِلَيْكَ وَحْيُهُ |

But the Quran has not been mentioned before 75:16, but rather the context it about humans and their deeds. Thus, this verse begins on a new subject, if the context is to be kept in mind, then it will be understood that it is mankind which is being addressed, and the matter is about the catalogue of their deeds. See details in *Mafhum-ul- Quran*, because that is its right place.

H-R-M ح ر م

Ibn Faaris says that the basic meaning is to forbid or stop someone from something.

"حَرَمَهُ الشَّىْءَ" (*haramahus shaiyi*), "حَرِيْماً" (*hareeman*), "حِرْمَاناً" (*hirmanan*): to stop something from, not to let something reach it.
"اَلْحَرَامُ" (*al-haraam*): all those things which are forbidden to do.
This is the opposite of "اَلْحَلَالُ" (*al-halal*) which means to open up the ropes and remove the shackles.
"اَحْرَمَ الْحَاجُّ" (*ahramal ha'ajj*): haji (one who performs *hajj*) reached a stage where some things which he could do previously were disallowed to him. This is the situation in "اِحْرَامٌ" (*ihraam*).
"اَلْحَرِيْمُ" (*al-hareem*): anything that is haram (or forbidden), which is to be protected and supported at every place.

During the times of ignorance, it also meant all those clothes which they took off before circling the *kaaba* naked. That is, those clothes were forbidden to wear at that time.
"اَشْهُرُ الْحُرُمِ" (*ash-hurul haram*) means in the same sense those (four) months in which battle or war was forbidden *{T, M}*.
"حَرِيْمُ الدَّارِ" (*hareemud daar*) also means the inside of the house which has been roped in and included in the house *{T, M}*.
"اَلْمَحْرُوْمُ" (*al-mahroom*) is one who cannot meet his needs, who has nothing left *{T, M}*.

Actually, the connotation of labor is included in it because "ح" (*ha*) and "ر" (*ra*) have appeared together, and the word they appear together in has an element of hard labor and hardness *{Al-ilmul-khafaq}*.

Therefore, its basic meaning is to stop or prevent vehemently.

"اَلْحَرْمَةُ" (*al-hurmah*) is anything which is not permitted to be done, the prohibition which cannot be broken, and also the responsibility which needs to be protected, that which must be done {*T, M*}.

The Quran says:

6:152	Violation of those things which are a must for you is forbidden	تَعَالَوْا اَتْلُ مَا حَرَّمَ رَبُّكُمْ عَلَيْكُمْ اَلَّاتُشْرِكُوْابِهِ

Surah *Al-Ambia* says:

21:95	nation which is destroyed due to the scheme of things is forbidden from rising again	وَحَرَامٌ عَلَى قَرْيَةٍ اَهْلَكْنُهَا اَنَّهُمْ لَايَرْجِعُوْنَ

This means that salvation of such a nation is not possible. This is the destruction of nations which comes after the grace period, and due to which those nations can never raise again. But if this verse is taken with the verse that comes after it, and which begins with "حَتّٰى" (*hatta*) which means "until" then it will mean that their renaissance is possible only when the situation described in the verse prevails. Or the verse would mean that these dwellings were only destroyed because they were deserving of punishment, as they did not come towards the laws of Allah at any cost. This means that a nation deserves annihilation when it loses the capacity to progress in accordance to the laws of Allah. In this case "حَتّٰى" (*hatta*) in the next verse would be redundant.

"حُرُمٌ" (*hurum*) is the condition of prohibition, as used in 5:1.
"اَلْحُرُمَاتُ" (*al-hurmaat*): the things that have been forbidden (2:194).
"مَحْرُوْمٌ" (*mahroom*): someone who is prevented from something, as just returns for his labor (56:67). Someone who cannot meet the needs of life (51:19)
"مُحَرَّمٌ" (*muharram*): that which has been declared forbidden (2:85), that which has been made respectable or that which must be respected (14:37).

Since the question of forbidden and permitted holds a very important place in religions, so much so that sometimes it is the basic difference between two religions, they must be discussed in detail.

God has created every human as a free spirit. Every man, simply by being a human being should be respected.

17:70	we have granted respect to man	وَلَقَدْ كَرَّمْنَا بَنِيْ آدَمَ

He has clearly stated that no man has the right to subjugate another.

Ibn Qutaiba has also written that in **la yarjeoon**, the **la** is additional, or the meaning of **haram** must be taken. (**Al-qartain** volume I page 134, volume II page 26).

The second meaning is right that **la** cannot be taken as additional.

| 3:78 | no man has the right, no matter he has been given the laws of Allah or power to rule or even messenger hood, to tell other human beings to obey him rather than Allah | مَاكَانَ لِبَشَرٍ اَنْ يُّؤْتِيَهُ اللّٰهُ الْكِتَابَ وَالْحُكْمَ وَ النُّبُوَّةَ ثُمَّ يَقُوْلَ لِلنَّاسِ كُوْنُوْا عِبَاداً لِّیْ مِنْ دُوْنِ اللّٰهِ |

As such, according to the Quran, nobody has the right to curb the freedom of other human beings.

But there is need for certain limitations in life. These limitations are of different kinds.

The doctor may tell his patient not to eat meat for a certain number of days. Obviously this limitation is not obedience of someone's orders. It is a sympathetic suggestion which we can either observe or not observe. By accepting it, we will be benefited, and if we do not, then we stand to lose. We accept this limitation with grace, and it does not curb our freedom.

Our assembly is constituted of our representatives, it makes laws and the government implements them (for instance to drive on the left or right side of the road). This rule also is not obedience and is a prevention set by ourselves. This too does not curb our freedom.

But somebody says that according to Islam, the use of a certain thing is forbidden. This means that this man has imposed a restriction on millions of fellow human beings of his time, but imposes them in such a way that the violator is liable to punishment not only in this life but even in the life hereafter. Obviously for imposing such restrictions, one must do it on some competent authority. What is this authority according to the Quran?

The Quran has used the word **haram** for restriction of this nature, which is the opposite of **halal**. **Haram** means to prevent or restrict someone from something. The Quran has given distinct orders about what is **haram** and what is **halal**. The first thing it says is that all things that Allah has given humans are **halal**, except those things that are declared **haram**.

Surah **Al-Baqrah** says:

| 2:172 | O those with trust, whatever Allah has given you, eat the good things and thank Allah, if you are subservient to Him only. | يَا اَيُّهَا الَّذِيْنَ اٰمَنُوْا كُلُوْا مِنْ طَيِّبَاتِ مَا رَزَقْنٰكُمْ وَاشْكُرُوْا لِلّٰهِ اِنْ كُنْتُمْ اِيَّاهُ تَعْبُدُوْنَ |
| 2:173 | He has only forbidden you to eat dead bodies, and blood, and meat of pork and that which is attributed towards another then Allah... | اِنَّمَا حَرَّمَ عَلَيْكُمُ الْمَيْتَةَ وَالدَّمَ وَلَحْمَ الْخِنْزِيْرِ وَ مَا اُهِلَّ بِهٖ لِغَيْرِ اللّٰهِ |

Here only edibles are mentioned.

Surah *Al-Airaf* also mentions things we use, for instance:

7:32	Ask them who has forbidden life's adornments that He has created for His slaves? And the good things of life?	قُلْ مَنْ حَرَّمَ زِينَةَ اللّهِ الَّتِي أَخْرَجَ لِعِبَادِهِ وَالطَّيِّبَاتِ مِنَ الرِّزْقِ۔
7:33	tell them, my Sustainer has forbidden only shameless things, whether they are hidden or obvious	قُلْ إِنَّمَا حَرَّمَ رَبِّيَ الْفَوَاحِشَ مَا ظَهَرَ مِنْهَا وَمَا بَطَنَ

In Surah *Al-Aam* explain it further that blood is only forbidden in its liquid state:

6:146	Flowing blood	دَمًا مَّسْفُوحًا

These verses make it clear that:

- Only Allah has the right to declare something as forbidden.
- No one else besides Allah has the right to do this
- He has not declared any adornment as forbidden.
- Those edibles which have been declared forbidden have been detailed.

We have Thus, seen that only Allah has the right to declare something as forbidden, but Allah does not address each individual personally and Therefore, His decisions about forbidden or allowed were conveyed to the Messenger through Revelation).

Surah *Al-Anaam* says:

6:164	O, Messenger, tell them, that "whatever has revealed unto me, I don't find anything *haram* in it, excepting that which is dead, flowing blood, and that which has been attributed to other than Allah	قُلْ لاَ أَجِدُ فِي مَا أُوحِيَ إِلَيَّ مُحَرَّمًا عَلَى طَاعِمٍ يَطْعَمُهُ إِلاَّ أَنْ يَكُونَ مَيْتَةً أَوْ دَمًا مَّسْفُوحًا أَوْ لَحْمَ خِنزِيرٍ فَإِنَّهُ رِجْسٌ أَوْ فِسْقًا أُهِلَّ لِغَيْرِ اللّهِ

Thus, it is obvious that God himself has decided as to what is forbidden and what is not through Revelation.

Surah *Al-Hajj* says:

22:30	The four legged are allowed for you except those which have been forbidden according to the revelation which is related to you.	وَأُحِلَّتْ لَكُمُ الْأَنْعَامُ إِلَّا مَا يُتْلَى عَلَيْكُمْ۔

Surah *Al-Ankabut* says:

| 29:45 | read what has been revealed to you from the Book | أُتْلُ مَا أُوْحِيَ اِلَيْكَ مِنَ الْكِتَابِ |

This is the thing which is contained in the verses of surah *Aal-e-Imran*, the first part of which has been mentioned in the previous pages:

| 3:78 | through this book, which you teach: | بِمَا كُنْتُمْ تُعَلِّمُوْنَ الْكِتَابَ وَ بِمَا كُنْتُمْ تَدْرُسُوْنَ |

Surah *An-Namal* says clearly:

| 47:92 | I have been ordered to recite (follow) the Quran | ـ اِنَّمَا اُمِرْتُ۔ اَنْ اَتْلُوَ الْقُرْاَنَ۔ |

From these explanations, it is obvious that only God has the right to declare something as Forbidden.
Whatever was to be declared as forbidden has been mentioned in the Quran.

This makes clear as to who is the authority to declare something haram. Let us see further how the Quran has highlighted the fact that nobody except God has the authority to declare something forbidden

Surah *Al-Airaaf* says:

| 7:32 | Tell them, who can declare things of adornment and good things created by Allah for His missionaries as *haraam*? | قُلْ مَنْ حَرَّمَ زِيْنَةَ اللهِ الَّتِيْ اَخْرَجَ لِعِبَادِهِ وَالطَّيِّبٰتِ مِنَ الرِّزْقِ |

Thus, it is clear that Allah has not given anyone the right to declare stuff as forbidden.

In this connection even the Messenger (pbuh) has been told:

| 66:1 | O, messenger, why would you declare something as *haram* which Allah has declared *halal* for you (all)? | يَاَيُّهَاالنَّبِيُّ لِمَ تُحَرِّمُ مَا اَحَلَّ اللهُ لَكَ |

At this point we will not go into the matter as to what it was that the Messenger (pbuh) had forbidden for himself. We only want to say that this right has not been granted by Allah even to the Messenger (pbuh), and not only that, but even to forbid for him anything which Allah has not forbidden.

Here, a point in this connection needs to be clarified. The Quran says "طَيِّباً" (*tayyeban*) along with the things which are *halal*. As in surah *Al-Baqrah*:

| 2:168 | O mankind, the products of the land which have been made *halal* for you, eat it in a *tayyab* way | يَاَيُّهَاالنَّاسُ كُلُوْا مِمَّا فِى الْاَرْضِ حَلٰلاً طَيِّباً |

Tayyab means delightful, pure, beneficial and fine. It is not that everything that is halal must be eaten. You can select things to eat according to your taste and liking. Those which you do not like need not to be consumed. This allows for personal liking, medical use, and other particularities.

But for the Messenger (pbuh), there is caution even in terms of this allowance. That is, if *Zaid* does not like something and Therefore, does not eat it, then the effect of his decision will only affect him. But if the

Messenger (pbuh) leaves something, and leaves it like it is *haram* for him, then the effects could be far reaching. It is possible that due to simplicity or ignorance or due to excess of faithfulness, some may think that there must be some religious reason for him leaving that thing, and they may give it up altogether. In this manner, something which Allah has ordained *halal* becomes *haram* for the people. This has happened in earlier races. That is why this was specifically pointed out to our Messenger (pbuh).

The Quran says that *Yaqoob* (Jacob) had taken something to be forbidden for him alone, but the Bani Israel (the people who followed him) thought it to be God's order, and made it *haram* for them. Till such time that when they saw that the things which the Quran mentions as *haram* do not include that thing, they raised the question as to why something which was forbidden by God earlier (according to the wrong concept of theirs) had been declared halal by the Quran.

Quran answers by saying:

3:94	All this food (which has now been declared *halal* for the Muslims) was also *halal* for Bani Israel, except which, before the revelation of the Torah, *Israel* or *Yaqob* had forbidden for himself.	كُلُّ الطَّعَامِ كَانَ حِلًّا لِّبَنِيْ إِسْرَاءِيْلَ إِلَّا مَا حَرَّمَ اسْرَءِيْلُ عَلَى نَفْسِهِ مِنْ قَبْلِ اَنْ تُنَزَّلَ التَّوْرَاةُ

These things were not declared by God, but by people.

Yaqob had, for some reason, made these things forbidden for him. The Jews thought since the God's messenger had made it forbidden for him, then these must be forbidden by God. That is why it was pointed out to our Messenger that though he had left the use of something due to personal dislike or some other reason, (in the usual circumstances this is very ordinary) but it may so happen that some people, due to excessive piousness, may consider it *haram* too, like the descendants of Israel. Therefore, you must be careful in these circumstances.

This discussion will be incomplete without the real meaning of the verses of surah *al-araf,* without which the reader may be the victim of a misunderstanding.

In this surah, it is said about the real traits of the Messenger (*pbuh*):

7:157	he will declare the good and execrable things as *haram*	وَيُحِلُّ لَهُمُ الطَّيِّبَاتِ وَيُحَرِّمُ عَلَيْهِمُ الْخَبَائِثَ

This verse is believed to means that the Messenger had the right to declare things as *halal* or *haram*.

It must be first seen as to that Allah says at different places in the Quran that only Allah has the right to declare *halal* or *haram.*

But surah *Al-Ma'ida* says:

5:87	O you, who entrust, do not make such things *haram* which Allah has made *halal* for you.	يَاأَيُّهَالَّذِيْنَ آمَنُوْا لَا تُحَرِّمُوْا مَاأَحَلَّ اللّٰهُ لَكُمْ

This clearly states the things which Allah declare as *halal,* should not be declared haram by people.

The same surah (*Al-Araaf*) says:

7:33	tell them that my Sustainer has only declared *fawahish* (transgression) as *haram*	قُلْ إِنَّمَا حَرَّمَ رَبِّيَ الْفَوَاحِشَ

Here it has been said through the Messenger's mouth, to declare that only God can declare something for *haram.*

Surah *Al-Baqrah* says:

2:274	Allah has declared *bai* (profit by trading) as *halal* and declared *riba* (profit by interest) as *haram*	وَأَحَلَّ اللّٰهِ الْبَيْعَ وَ حَرَّمَ الرِّبٰوا

Therefore, where ever the Quran has attributed *halal* or *haram* towards the Messenger is as well revealed though Revelation, and is preserved in the Quran.

In his connection the following verse of Surah *At-Tauba* must be understood correctly:

9:29	Fight those who (among people of the book) do not believe in Allah and the Hereafter and do not consider forbidden that which has been declared haram by the Messenger.	قَاتِلُوا الَّذِيْنَ لَا يُؤْمِنُوْنَ بِا اللّٰهِ وَلَا بِالْيَوْمِ الْآخِرِ وَلَا يُحَرِّمُوْنَ مَا حَرَّمَ اللّٰهُ وَرَسُوْلُهُ

From this verse it is inferred that Allah and the messengers both have the right to declare *haram* or *halal*. In this verse, these words should not be taken to mean declaring something edible as *haram*. As stated earlier, the word of *haram* is also used for making something compulsory.

Thus, the verse means that Allah and his messengers declare the things that are compulsory but they do not consider them compulsory. These people avoid the Islamic laws while remaining within the Islamic system. They will have to face war untill they agree to live as subjects of an Islamic state.

This clarifies that according to the Quran:

- The right to declare something *haram* or *halal* is entirely up to God.
- Whatever that is declared as *haram* has been explained by the Quran.
- Nobody other than God has this right.

The Quran has declared it a great sin to declare something as *haram* which God has declared halal.

It has stressed that:

5:87	O you who entrust. Do not declare *haram* the good things which Allah has declared *halal* for you, and do not exceed the limit. Allah does not like those who exceed the limit.	يَا اَيُّهَاالَّذِينَ آمَنُوا لَا تُحَرِّمُوا طَيِّبٰتِ مَا اَحَلَّ اللّٰهُ لَكُمْ وَلَا تَعْتَدُوا إِنَّ اللّٰهَ لَا يُحِبُّ الْمُعْتَدِينَ

This means that to declare something halal or haram, for human beings, is to exceed the limit, because it has been said earlier that no human has the right to curb another man's freedom.

At another place it has been said with more emphasis:

16:116	And how your tongues utter falsely, that this is halal and that is haram, and accuse Allah for it. Do not do this.	وَلَاتَقُولُوا لِمَا تَصِفُ اَلْسِنَتُكُمُ الْكَذِبَ هٰذَا حَلَالٌ وَهٰذَا حَرَامٌ لِّتَفْتَرُوا عَلَى اللّٰهِ الْكَذِبَ إِنَّ الَّذِينَ يَفْتَرُونَ عَلَى اللّٰهِ الْكَذِبَ لَايُفْلِحُونَ

Here the Quran has pointed out that those religious scholars who prepare a list of what is *haram* or *halal* know fully well in their hearts that nobody except Allah has the right to declare something as *haram* or *halal* (or they know that if they declare something as *haram* or *halal* on their own (without attributing it to Allah) then people will not observe them. That is why they say that all this is according to Allah's law. Thus, they attribute such things to Allah which He has never said. This is fabrication, falsehood, great allegation.

About such people it is said:

10:59	Say: have you pondered that you declare *haram* or *halal* from the sustenance which Allah has created for you? Ask them if Allah has permitted them to do so, or dis they make these allegations to Allah?	قُلْ اَرَءَ يْتُمْ مَا اَنْزَلَ اللّٰهُ لَكُمْ مِنْ رِزْقٍ فَجَعَلْتُمْ مِنْهُ حَرَاماً وَ حَلَالاً قُلْ اَللّٰهُ اَذِنَ لَكُمْ اَمْ عَلَى اللّٰهِ تَفْتَرُونَ

The Quran says that no man has been given the right to declare something for being *halal* or *haram*. Anyone who does such a thing casts allegations upon Allah.

The Quran also tells us that many things which are *halal* (for us Muslims) were declared *haram* for the Jews as a punishment.

The Quran says:

6:147	And we had declared *haram* all animals with nails for the Jews and the fat of cows and goats too, except that stuck to their backs, or intestines or bones. This was Our punishment for them for rebelling (from His laws).	وَعَلَى الَّذِيْنَ هَادُوْا حَرَّمْنَا كُلَّ ذِىْ ظُفُرٍ --- ذَالِكَ جَزَيْنٰهُمْ بِبَغْيِهِمْ
4:160	For the transgression of the Jews, We had declared some of the good things as *haram* for them	فَبِظُلْمٍ مِّنَ الَّذِيْنَ هَادُوْا حَرَّمْنَا عَلَيْهِمْ طَيِّبٰتٍ أُحِلَّتْ لَهُمْ

The details of their transgressions follow, as punishment for which many things were declared *haram* for them. Surah **An-Nahal** says this was not oppression on them from Allah, but they had oppressed themselves by becoming deserving of this punishment (16:118). This clarifies that to declare things as *haram* which have not been so declared by Allah is to punish people for no reason.

In order to relieve the Jews from this punishment, **Isa** (Jesus) made his advent. He said that the purpose of his coming as a Messenger was this very thing:

3:49	so that I can make some things *halal* which have been declared *haram* for you	أُحِلَّ لَكُمْ بَعْضَ الَّذِىْ حُرِّمَ عَلَيْكُمْ

The Jews opposed **Isa** and Thus, became more deserving of punishment than ever. After that **Muhammed** was sent, and the purpose of sending him as a messenger is mentioned by Allah as:

7:156	He will make the good things *halal* for them and the bad things *haram*	وَيُحِلُّ لَهُمُ الطَّيِّبٰتِ وَ يُحَرِّمُ عَلَيْهِمُ الْخَبٰئِثَ

But they defied this Messenger too, and Thus, preferred to be kept captive by those inhibitions (by opposing this Messenger as well) and are still in these chains.

Those with the books had prepared lists of *haram* and *halal* according to their religious leaders, for which they had no authentication from Allah. The **mushrekeen** (those who followed others than Allah as well), had some traditions about *haram* and *halal*, and they followed them although they were based on mere superstition. The Quran opposed them too. They used to believe that this animal among the four-legged was haram, that crop was haram, that once a specific animal was permitted for riding (6:139), that thing is *halal* for the men but not for women (6:140), so and so progeny of camel is *haram*, so and so calves are haram (6:144). They were told that those lists were all "compiled by your forefathers" (6:149). You attribute them towards Allah without any reason (6:141). Then they were challenged that if they were right then they should produce witnesses to back their claims (6:151).

These discussions make it clear that there is no other authority than Allah to declare **haram** or **halal**.

Aside from edibles, the Quran has also mentioned in detail the relationships which are **halal** or **haram.** This has been mentioned in surah **An-Nisa**, verses 12 to 24. This is the Quranic version of **halal** and **haram,** and for something to be declared **halal** or **haram**, Quranic authority is essential. It may be mentioned, that the (true) Islamic state, due to some emergency or some expediency declares something as prohibited for a limited period.

For instance during the rainy season, the health officer may declare that the use of figs etc. is forbidden or during a war the government orders that something is forbidden for civil use because the army's need is greater. But it is obvious that such limitation is for a limited time period only, and declaring something as **haram** for all times is quite different because nothing can be declared **haram** by anyone except God. See heading (**H-L-L**) and (**N-Ain-M**), as well for more details.

H-R-Y   ح ر ى

"التَّحَرِّىْ" (*at-tahri*) means to intend to, to strive to get something, to intend to do something particularly.

"تَحَرَّاهُ" (*taharrah*): he intended to do it. Some say it is to strive to get the good things *{T}*.

The Quran says:

72:14	these are the people who have decided honorably to receive guidance	فَأُوْلَٰئِكَ تَحَرَّوْا رَشَداً

Ibn Faris says its basic meanings are nearness, or intent, temperature, to return or to lessen.

"حَرَاء" (*hiraa*) was a mountain in Mecca city which **Muhammed** (pbuh) is said to visit (to receive guidance) before messenger hood *{T}*. This is only mentioned historically, but the Quran says nothing about it. The Quran says only that before messenger hood, **Muhammed** (pbuh) was in search for the truth and guidance. See heading (**Zd-L-L**).

H-Z-B   ح ز ب

"اَلْحِزْبُ" (*al-hizb*): the turn to drink, people's group or party. The plural is "اَحْزَابٌ" (*aaab*).

Rabhib says that it means the condition where the feelings and acts of the people in the group or party are similar, even if they have never met each other. **Raghib** also says that there is also the condition that there is hardness and intensity among those people. This is why the Quran mentions two groups i.e. "حِزْبُ الله" (*hizbullah*) (8:22) and "حِزْبُ الشَّيْطَانِ" (*hizbush shaitan*) (58:19).

Hizbullah are those people who are strictly observant of Allah's laws, no matter in which part of the world they may be, and **Hizbush shaitaan** (the opposing party) are those who live according to contradictory laws to Allah's, no matter which nation or country they belong to. The Quran formulates nations on the basis of life or purpose of life and not on the basis of country, race and language.

In surah **Momin** the parties which opposed Allah's messengers have been called "اَلْاَحْزَابُ" (*al-ahzaab*). In surah *al-aaab*, "اَلْاَحْزَابُ" (*al-aaab*) are those parties which together fought against Allah's Messenger (40:30).

The Quran has termed sectarianism as **shirk** (that is the highest sin i.e. to worship others along with Allah). Because it then so happens that:

32:32	every group thinks that it is on the right path (and all the other sects are on the wrong path)	كُلُّ حِزْبٍ بِمَالَدَيْهِمْ فَرِحُونَ

By saying "كُلُّ حِزْبٍ" (*kullo hizbin*) (all groups), the Quran has clarified that when there are sects within this way of life, than it is wrong to assume that any one sect is right and all the others wrong. The very existence of sects is **shirk** to the Quran (30:32). As long as there is true **Deen** (Islamic system) there can be no sects within it. When that system is no longer present, then this way of life becomes an individual thing and the formation of sects is inevitable. To remove sects, there is only one way, which is the establishment of a truly Islamic system. Other than this, there is no way to get out of this shirk.

H-Z-N   ح ز ن

"حَزْنٌ" (*huzn*): this is a composite word and is used for every misfortune that may befall a human being, including economic troubles form a great part of this misfortune.

"حَزَانَةُ الرَّجُلِ" (*hazanatur rajul*): those family members whose pain is felt by a man and whom he fends for {T}.

Tajul Uroos says that in surah *Faatir's* verse 35: 34, the word "حَزَنٌ" (*hazan*) means the worry about acquiring the daily bread.

Raghib says that where in the Quran, it has been said "لَا تَحْزَنْ" (*la taan*) or "لَا تَحْزَنُوا" (*la taanu*), it does not mean to not worry, because man does not have the power 'not to worry" (i.e. man cannot help worrying). It means not let those reasons be created which create "حَزْنٌ" (*huzn*). This can happen with economic wellbeing because "حَزْنٌ" (*huzn*) means the worries which arise due to financial troubles. Also "أَلْحَزْنُ" (*al-hazn*) means hard, stony, the opposite of which is "سَهْلٌ" (*sahl*) {T}, probably because vegetation cannot grow in such harsh soil.

Ibn Faris says that this root contains an element of hardness, harshness, and intensity.

In the heading (**Kh-W-F**) you will find that "خَوْفٌ" (*khauf*) is the worry which is due to some expected danger, (i.e. it concerns some event in the future), while "حَزْنٌ" (*huzn*) is used against this meaning. It means a sadness that is due to some event in the past, something that has passed. The situation before any loss is "خَوْفٌ" (*khauf*), and after that event this fear is no more, but sadness or "حَزْنٌ" (*huzn*) begins, or remains.

The Quran says:

3:139	Do not get sad or heartbroken. If you are those with peace, you are greater.	وَلَا تَهِنُوا وَلَا تَحْزَنُوا وَأَنتُمُ الْأَعْلَوْنَ إِن كُنتُم مُّؤْمِنِينَ

Here it has appeared against greatness and loftiness, peak, overpowering.

In the tale about *Adam*, when the life of Heaven was taken away from Adam, he was told that if he spent his life according to what was revealed, the result would be:

2:38	He will not have any *khauf* and *huzn*. (any fear or worry):	لَا خَوْفٌ عَلَيْهِمْ وَلَا هُمْ يَحْزَنُونَ

When this Heavenly society of Quranic laws is established in this world, then along with other comforts of life, there remains no worry on account of the economic factor. These are the basic connotation of "حَزْنٌ" (*huzn*). Also the heaven out of which *Adam* was driven out, had the particularity that nobody had to bend his back for food, clothing or housing, nor did anyone go without these (20:118 -119)

For details of these matters see headings (*A-D-M*), (*Sh-J-R*), (*J-N-N*).

It is obvious Therefore, that any nation which is suffering from hunger, fear, and "حَزَنٌ" (*huzn*) etc. is not obeying the laws of Allah. To live in obedience of Allah's laws means inevitably that man's life in this world will be successful as well as in that of the Hereafter.

In surah *Yusuf*, "حَزَنٌ" (*huzn*) has been used to mean a sadness or worry that has been born due to some past event (12:82).
"لَا تَحْزَنْ عَلَيْهِمْ" (*la tahazzan alaihim*) in 15:88 means "do not be sad for them".
"تَحَزَّنَ عَلَيْهِ" (*tahazzan alaih*) means that he was sad for it {*T*}.

H-S-B   ح س ب

"حَسَبَ" (*hasab*), "يَحْسُبُ" (*yahsab*), "حُسْبَانًا" (*husbana*) and "حِسَابًا" (*hisaaba*) means to count, to number.
"حَسِبَ" (*hasibu*), "يَحْسَبُ" (*yahsabu*), "مَحْسَبَةً" (*mahsabah*), "حِسْبَانًا" (*hisbana*): to think, to have the opinion.
"حَسْبُ" (*hasb*): that which is enough, that which suffices, after which the need ends.
"حَاسِبٌ" (*haasib*): someone who counts.
"حُسْبَانٌ" (*husbaan*) is the plural form.
"حَسْبُكَ دِرْهُمٌ" (*hasbuka dirham*): one dirham is enough for you.
"حَسْبُنَا اللهُ" (*hasbunallah*): Allah (Allah's laws) are enough for us (9:59). With Him there, we do not need anything else, He shall suffice to meet all our needs.
"هَذَا بِحَسَبِ ذَا" (*haaza bihasabi za*): this is according to his need or this is sufficient for him {*T, M*}.
"حَسِيبٌ" (*haseeb*): one who counts, administrator.

17:14	Read your own book, today you are accountable for yourself.	اقْرَأْ كَتَابَكَ كَفَى بِنَفْسِكَ الْيَوْمَ عَلَيْكَ حَسِيبًا

According to the scheme of things created by God, at the time of the results of one's deeds, there is no need for any outside witness or accountant, as man's own self is a living testimony against him.

75:14	the effects of deeds which naturally affect the person, themselves testify as to the nature of deeds done	كَفَى بِنَفْسِكَ الْيَوْمَ عَلَيْكَ حَسِيبًا

The time of the results being made known, has been called "يَوْمُ الْحِسَابِ" (*yaumul hisaab*) (the Day of Reckoning) or in 14:41 "يَقُومُ الْحِسَابُ" (*yaqumul hisaab*), the result of every deed begins to formulate as the deed is done. But they appear after a time, like the fruit which begins to take shape when the bud appears, but the fruit actually appears after some time. This is the time for their appearance of results.

| 6:97 | We created the sun and moon for you to keep count | وَالشَّمْسَ وَالْقَمَرَ حُسْبَاناً |
| 10:5 17:12 | so that they can be used to keep track of months and years | لِتَعْلَمُوا عَدَدَ السِّنِينَ وَالْحِسَابَ |

It is obvious then that there can be a calendar based on the sun's orbiting, the lunar or solar, whichever is easier, can be used.

Surah **Kahaf** says:

| 18:40 | He can send **husbaan** on the field (cultivation) | وَيُرْسِلَ عَلَيْهَا حُسْبَاناً مِنَ السَّمَاءِ |

Here "حُسْبَان" (**husbaan**) is generally taken to be some misfortune, i.e. some celestial catastrophe which destroys the cultivation, as rain, storm strong winds, hails, or swarm of insects *{T}*. But the **Lughat Hameer** (the dictionary of **Hameer**) says it means extreme cold.

Ibn Faris says it means both, hail and swarm of locusts.

"اِحْتَسَبَ" (**ehtasab**) means to think, or have an opinion *{M}*.

The Quran says:

| 65:3 | Allah's laws provide sustenance from places not even thought of. | وَيَرْزُقْهُ مِنْ حَيْثُ لَا يَحْتَسِبُ |
| 2:212 | Someone who desires this method gets countless sustenance from Allah. | وَاللَّهُ يَرْزُقُ مَنْ يَشَاءُ بِغَيْرِ حِسَابٍ |

Raghib writes a little differently. One of them is that He gives him but does not take at all, or gives, not according to what people think, but much more than that. When society is formed according to Allah's laws, then the provision of sustenance becomes abundant and much more than common ideas.

H-S-D ح س د

"حَسَدٌ" (**hasad**) means to scrape.

"الحَسَدٌ" (**al-hasad**): the mentality which says that whatever the other one has in possession, may be taken from him and given to me. And even if I do not get it, then may it be lost to him "غِبْطَةٌ" (**ghibtah**) means that along with him, I too may get it, in other word, envy {T}.

Raghib has only added that it also includes striving for that thing.

Surah **Al-Baqrah** says that the opponents due to "حَسَدَ" (**hasad**) (jealousness) wish you to give up your trust and become a denier. So they wish that the good results of trust may be taken away from you, no matter if they gain anything from this or not (2:109).

The Quran has described jealousy as a very destructive mentality, and advised avoiding people with such mentality (113:5). This can be done through profound connection with Allah's laws.

H-S-R ح س ر

"حَسَرَ" (**hasar**), "يَحْسِرُ" (**yahsir**): basically means to open something or scrape it or to skin. "التَّحْسِيرُ" (**il-la tehseer**) means for a bird to lose its feathers {T}. This led to its meaning of being vulnerable.

"حَسَرَ الْبَعِيرْ" (**hasaral ba-eer**): the camel was made to walk so much that it became vulnerable. "الْحَسْرَةُ" (**al-hasrah**) Hence, means a situation in which a man becomes like a tired camel. The word has the connotation both of vulnerability and shamefulness, as well as sadness and repentance {T}.

Raghib says "الْحَسْرَةُ" (**al-hasrah**) means sadness and shamefulness at something's death, as if the truth has dawned upon the man and the situation in which he did something, has been removed.

That is why **Muheet** says it really means "كَشْفٌ" (**kashaf**), which means to open up. "حَسَرَ الْبَحْرُ عَنِ السَّاحِلِ" (**hasaral bahru unis sahil**) means that the river receded from the banks and the land which was below the water, openly came into view {T}. This contains the elements of "كَشْفٌ" (**kashaf**) the opening, and vulnerability.

Surah **Al-Baqrah** says:

2:167	Allah will unveil their deeds to them and this revealing will make them vulnerable	يُرِيهِمُ اللَّهُ أَعْمَالَهُمْ حَسَرَاتٍ عَلَيْهِمْ

"حَسَرْتُ الْبَيْتَ" (**hasaratul bait**) means I swept the house. "الْمِحْسَرَةُ" (**al mihsarah**) is the broom {R}. That means the previous verse can also mean that their deeds became totally unproductive and all they did was swept aside.

Surah *Anbia* says "لَا يَسْتَحْسِرُوْنَ" (*la yastahseroon*) in 21:19, which means to get tired.

Surah *Bani Israel* has used "مَلُوْماً مَحْسُوْراً" (*maluman mahsoora*) in 17:29 i.e. begging situation, a condition in which all is lost, and you repent at what you did. 67:4 says "حَسِيْرٌ" (*haseer*) which means getting tired and emaciated.

"اَلتَّحَاسِيْرُ" (*at-tahaseer*): troubles and misfortunes.
"حَسْرَةٌ" (*hasrah*): deep sadness and shame and to repent the loss of something *{T}*.
"يَاحَسْرَتَى" (*ya hasrata*): "Alas!" (39:56).

H-S-S   ح س س

"اَلْحِسُّ" (*al-hiss*) means movement, hidden voice. This leads to "اَلْحَوَاسُّ" (*al-hawass*).
"اَحَسَّ" (*ahass*): that which is to feel, to be aware of *{T}*.

Raghib says when something becomes evident, so as to be felt, we say "اَحَسَّ" (*ahass*)

| 3:51 | when he felt | فَلَمَّا اَحَسَّ |

"تَحَسَّسَ" (*tahhass*): to find out about someone (12:87). "حَسِيْسٌ" (*hasees*): a soft sound.

| 21:102 | They don't even hear a single sound from there | لَا يَسْمَعُوْنَ حَسِيْسَهَا |

"اَلْحِسُّ" (*al-hiss*): cold in which grass dries out.
"حَوَاسُّ الْاَرْضِ" (*hawaasul ard*): cold, hail, wind, swarm of insects and cattle which might destroy cultivation. As such the word means destruction
"اَلْحَاسُوْسُ" (*al-hasoos*) means drought.

Surah *Aal-e-Imran* says:

| 3:151 | when you were annihilating and destroying them | اِذْ تَحُسُّوْنَهُمْ |

Ibn Faris says that "اَلْحَسُّ" (*al-hass*) also means to kill.

H-S-M   ح س م

"حَسَمَ" (*hasamah*), "يَحْسِمُ" (*yahsimoh*): he cut it off

"حَسَمَ الْعِرْق" (*hasam-ul-irq*): he cut the vein, and branded it with iron so that the blood did not flow off {*T*}.

Ibn Faris says it means to cut off something at its root.

"أَلْحَسَامُ" (*al-husaam*): sharp cutting sword.

"أَلْحُسُوْمُ" (*al-husoom*): bad luck

Azhari says that anything which follows a thing is called "حَاسِمٌ" (*hasim*), plural of which is "حُسُوْمٌ" (*husoom*). Thus, it means things that come one after the other, things which keep coming continuously.

Raghib says "أَلْحَسْمُ" (*al-hasm*) means to remove the effects of something, that is, to destroy something in a way that no traces are left.

The Quran says that following about the punishment that came upon the nation of *Aad*:

69:7	The storm kept coming for seven nights and eight days.	سَخَّرَهَا عَلَيْهِمْ سَبْعَ لَيَالٍ وَ ثَمَنِيَةَ اَيَّامٍ حُسُوْماً

"حُسُوْماً" (*husooman*) here can also mean continuous, but with reference to the context, this meaning deems more appropriate that it was such a storm that removed even the traces of the *Aad* nation, or even removed them from their roots.

H-S-N   ح س ن

"أَلْحُسْنُ" (*al-husn*): Muheet says that "حُسْنٌ" (*husn*), or beauty means for all limbs to be in the right proportion, and generally the word "حسين" (*haseen*), or beautiful, is used for things which are pleasing to the eye due to their balanced proportions. As such "حُسْنٌ" (*husn*) means the right proportion and symmetry, and is the opposite of "سُوْءٌ" (*so'a*) which means unbalanced or bad.

This is why this word has come against "فَسَادٌ" (*fasaad*) in 28:77, which means disproportion. Thus, "أَلْإِحْسَانُ" (*al-ehsaan*) means to make some proportion right. That is, if in society, there has been a decrease or insufficiency in somebody's capability or strength, to make up for it is called "اِحْسَانٌ" (*ehsaan*). See heading (Ain-D-L) in which "عَدْلٌ" (*adl*) and "اِحْسَانٌ" (*ehsaan*) have been discussed in detail.

Raghib says that "اِحْسَانٌ" (*ehsaan*) is of two types. One is to make up for the deficiencies and correct the balance, and the second to make one's own character balanced, or to create "حُسْنٌ" (*husn*) in it.

Raghib says that "عَدْلٌ" (*adl*) is to give whatever you have and take only which is your right. On the other hand "اِحْسَانٌ" (*ehsaan*) is to give more than you are required to give and take less than what is you right. This means that in *ehsaan*, the purpose is not to focus on what is due, but on creating a balance.

Surah **Al-Qasas** says that when Moses came of age and "وَاسْتَوٰى" (*wastawa*), i.e. every type of balance was created in him, and then We bestowed him with knowledge and sagacity (i.e. decision power).

Later, it is said:

28:14	Thus, We reward the **muhsaneen** with the fruits of their (good) deeds.	كَذَالِكَ نَجْزِئ الْمُحْسِنِيْنَ

Here, it is obvious that "مُحْسِنِيْنَ" (*mohseneen*) means those who live a balanced life.

"هُوَ يُحْسِنُ الشَّىْءَ اِحْسَاناً" (*huwa yuhsinush shaiyi ehsana*): he knows it fully well {T}. Surah Yusuf relates that in prison, when two men after relating their dreams asked **Yusuf** to interpret them it is said:

12:36	We know that you are one of fully aware people	إِنَّا نَرَاكَ مِنَ الْمُحْسِنِيْنَ

Here "مُحْسِنِيْنَ" (*mohseneen*) mean people who know something very well.

The Quran has used "حَسَنَاتٌ" (*hasanaat*) as against "سَيِّئَاتٌ" (*sayye-aat*) meaning life's pleasant things, as in 7:131 and 3:119.

Surah **At-Taubah** uses "مُصِيْبَةٌ" (*musibah*) against "حَسَنَةٌ" (*hasanah*) in 9:50. As such "حَسَنَةٌ" (*hasanah*) is anything which gives comfort to human beings, goods of comfort and luxury. Since this can be achieved by being in the government, it was said that We made the Bani Israel the inheritors of the East and West of Palestine, and:

7:137	Thus, the law of balance of your Sustainer was fulfilled	تَمَّتْ كَلِمَتُ رَبِّكَ الْحُسْنٰى

"حُسْنٰى" (*husna*) is the feminine of "اَحْسَنُ" (*ahsan*).

Allah attributes are known as "اَلْاَسْمَاءُ الْحُسْنٰى" (*asma'al husna*) in 59:24, because Allah's persona is such that various attributes are present in it in complete balance. All attributes and in complete balance. This, according to the Quran, is the concept of Allah, and since the purpose of man's life is to walk in His shadow, so to speak, he is nearest to Allah whose good attributes as well develop in a very balanced manner.

This is why the Quran has said:

| 7:180 | the attributes of Allah are certainly the attributes of Allah, and they are totally balanced | لِلّٰهِ الْأَسْمَاءُ الْحُسْنٰى فَادْعُوهُ |

Therefore, call Him by those attributed, i.e. the concept of Allah is similar to the attributes that which you invoke Him with.

It is also said that:

| 7:180 | dissociate with those who go lopsided (away from the path of balance) in any one of them (attributes) | وَذَرُوا الَّذِينَ يُلْحِدُونَ فِي أَسْمَائِهِ |

Therefore, the required is not only to reflect upon attributes of Allah (i.e. the development of hidden capabilities of human personality), but also to balance them. The life which is without "حُسْنٌ" (*husn*) or balance is not a life which is in the Quranic mould. The purpose of life is to see how much balance you create in yourself and how much balance you contribute to the universe. In this world (outside the human personality) this "إِحْسَانٌ" (*ehsaan*) (creating balance) begins with dealing humanely with other individuals in society.

| 2:83 | treat people in a way so that balance is created | وَقُولُوا لِلنَّاسِ حُسْناً |

The practical way to do this is by "أَنْفِقُوْ فِىْ سَبِيْلِ اللهِ" (*anfequ fi sabi lillah*): keep the fruits of your labor open (available) for mankind and Thus, "أَحْسِنُوْا" (*ahsenu*), create balance in society (2:195). This is the definition of "إِحْسَانٌ" (*ehsaan*) 2:83.

The Quran cautions that when you are asked to create *husn* or do *ehsaan*, it must not be done to get any remuneration, because:

| 55:60 | the return for creating balance, is that balance in deed is created | هَلْ جَزَاءُ الْإِحْسَانِ إِلَّا الْإِحْسَانُ |

We generally believe that "إِحْسَانٌ" (*ehsaan*) should be returned with another *ehsaan*. For instance, a man faces hard times, he goes to somebody for help, and the other person helps him, which is assumed to be his *ehsaan*. Now the first person is on the lookout for when the other person faces bad times so that he may repay his *ehsaan*, and till that time he does so, he feels indebted. Even if he disagrees with him on a minor point, that person may recall the *ehsaan* he did on him and say "what sort of *ehsaan*-forgetting person are you?" This is the *ehsaan*, as we assume, but the above Quran ordains clearly define the difference in its use today and the real meaning.

Ehsaan means to keep on doing *ehsaan* and not even think about its compensation or return, because when *Momins* do *ehsaan* on somebody they clearly tell him:

| 7:6 | we want no compensation, nor thanks (gratitude) from you | لَا نُرِيدُ مِنْكُمْ جَزَاءً وَّ لَا شُكُوْرًا |

Thus, the teachings of the Quran are aimed at creating "حُسْنّ" (*husn*) in Man's own soul as well as in other human beings and the external universe. To make all these more beautiful, will be its own reward. That is why the Quran has said that when you feel that the balance has gone out, correct the balance. This will remove any bad effects.

| 23:96 | Take stock of yourself first. If your personality is not balanced then try to balance it | اِدْفَعْ بِالَّتِيْ هِيَ اَحْسَنُ السَّيِّئَةَ |

When the society loses its balance, try to rectify it. Thus, keep on beautifying the external universe through knowledge and inventions. Your efforts towards this end will be their own reward. The result of trying to create "حُسْنّ" (*husn*) or to restore balance is that "حُسْنّ" (*husn*) or balance will ultimately be established.

Hence, the purpose of life is to maintain balance, and God's personality is one in which "حُسْنّ" (*husn*) or balance has reached its peak.
"الاَسْمَاءُ الْحُسْنٰى" (*al asma ul husna*): the objective standard for man is Therefore, God's personae for the proper development of his own faculties.

H-Sh-R ح ش ر

"اَلْحَشْرُ" (*al-hashr*) means to gather people and drive them towards some direction.

Ibn Faris says its basic meaning is to drive, to life, to get up and go.

Experts of dictionaries say that "اَلْحَشْرُ" (*al-hashr*) means to collect and drive.
"اَلْمَحْشَرُ" (*al-mahshar*), "اَلْمَحْشِرُ" (*al-mahshir*) is a place to gather.

Muheet says people use this word for a crowd and to create narrowness (lack of space) for each other {M}. This means such crowd or gathering which creates difficulty for others.

The Quran has also used this word to mean "to gather for war", as in:

| 27:17 | as per **Sulemans's** orders, the armies were collected and taken | وَحُشِرَ لِسُلَيْمٰنَ جُنُوْدُهٗ |

And about the Jews, it is said in surah *Al-Hashr*:

| 52:6 | Allah is He who, among those who had the Book, took the rebellious out of the houses for *hashr* | هُوَ الَّذِىْ اَخْرَجَ الَّذِيْنَ كَفَرُوْا مِنْ اَهْلِ الْكِتٰبِ مِنْ دِيَارِهِمْ لِاَوَّلِ الْحَشْرِ |

This too refers to a gathering for war or exile, which was the outcome of this battle.

Surah *Aal-e-Imraan* says to tell these opponents:

3:11	you will be overpowered soon, and will be collected in the ground of destruction and then taken towards *jahannam*	سَتُغْلَبُوْنَ وَ تُحْشَرُوْنَ اِلٰى جَهَنَّمَ

Its next 3:12 verse details the battle.

Surah *Shura* says about the Pharaoh that he sent "حَاشِرِيْنَ" (*haashereen*) to different cities (26:36). This means that representatives who would collect people and bring them (to him) were sent to different cities.

"اَلْحَشْرُ" (*al-hashr*): to sharpen the blade and to take from one place to another after collect them together, as drought gets people out of the villages and into the cities *{T}*.
"اَلْحَشَرَةُ" (*al-hashara*) means that which is hunted and is edible, i.e. which can be eaten. It also means insects. That is why "حشرات" (*hasharaat*) means insects and small animals. In the Yemen dialect, it means "saw dust" *{T}*.
"اَلْحَشْرُ" (*al-hashr*) also means death. It is also the fine part of the ear.

Surah *Tahaa* says:

20:124	and We will raise him blind on *youm-ul-qiyamah*	وَنَحْشُرُهُ يَوْمَ الْقِيٰمَةِ اَعْمٰى

This means to give return for deeds. That is, the results of deeds continue to be formulated very discreetly.

"مَحْشُوْرَةٌ" (*mahshoorah*): gathered together (38:19).

50:44	it is easy for us to gather them	ذَالِكَ حَشْرٌ عَلَيْنَا يَسِيْرٌ
46:6	And when mankind are gathered	وَاِذَا حُشِرَ النَّاسُ

In these places, the connotation of taking them somewhere along with gathering together must be borne in mind.

We generally take "حَشْرٌ" (*hashr*) to mean reckoning (after death on the Day of the Judgment), like *Aakhirah*, *qiyamah*, *sa'ah*, *bo'as* etc. These are composite terms of the Quran and mean not only to rise after death but also the renaissance of nations. As such, *Shah Waliullah* says (in *Hujjatulaahi Baligha - Kitabul Fatan*) that in Islamic (*sharia*), "حَشْرٌ" (*hashr*) has two meanings. One is the gathering or collection of people in Syria, that is, before the *Qiyamat*, this will happen when people are sparse and either due to various ceremonies or due to battle, people will gather there, and the second is to rise after death.

Wherever these words appear in the Quran, it must be noted with reference to the context whether they mean life after death, or a revolution in this world.

H-Sd-B   ح ص ب

"الْحَصَبَةُ" (*al-hasabah*) means gravel, small stones.
"الْحَصَبُ" (*al-hasab*) means fuel, or whatever is put into the fire to make it burn brighter, as firewood.
"حَصَبٌ" (*hasab*) can be used if the fire is stoked.
"الْحَاصِبُ" (*al-hasib*): the strong wind which raises dust and gravel {*T*}.

The Quran says:

| 17:68 | Send towards you a wind that raises gravel or stones | يُرْسِلَ عَلَيْكُمْ حَاصِباً |
| 21:98 | you and your gods whom you worship other than Allah are the fuel for hell | إِنَّكُمْ وَمَا تَعْبُدُونَ مِن دُونِ اللَّهِ حَصَبُ جَهَنَّمَ أَنتُمْ لَهَا وَارِدُونَ |

Here "حَصَبٌ" (*hasab*) means fuel. The fiery wind which blew from a volcano towards the nation of *Loot* was also called "حَاصِباً" (*haaseba*). It has a mix of both, small stones and the heat of the fire.

H-Sd-D   ح ص د

"حَصَدَ" (*hasad*) means to cut cultivated crop or plants with a shears {*R*}.

| 12:47 | let the corn remain in the ear of the crop you cut | فَمَا حَصَدتُّمْ فَذَرُوهُ فِي سُنبُلِهِ |

"حَصَادٌ" (*hasaad*): to cut the crop, as used in (6:142), or the time to cut the crop.
"الْحَصِيْدُ" (*al-haseed*): the crop that is cut.

About the annihilated nations, the Quran says:

| 21:15 | We made them motionless and quiet like the crop which has been cut. | جَعَلْنَاهُمْ حَصِيداً خَامِدِينَ |

H-Sd-R   ح ص ر

"اَلْحَصْرُ" (*al-hasr*): to stop, to imprison, to create narrowness *{T}*.

Raghib says that "حَصْرٌ" (*hasr*) and "اِحْصَارٌ" (*ihsaar*) are said when the stoppage is due to some visible obstruction (like if the enemy has stopped you) or if there is some internal reason (like disease which has prevented you). When the obstruction is only internal then "حَصْرٌ" (*hasr*) is used *{R}*.

Surah **An-Nisa** says:

4:90	or they may come to you in the condition that their chests are constricted and hearts narrow (frustrated)	اَوْجَاءُ وَكُمْ حَصِرَتْ صُدُوْرُهُمْ

"حَصِيْرٌ" (*haseer*) as used in 17:8 means a prison, as well as a narrow-minded person. It also means that miser who does not drink, only due to his miserliness.
"اَلْحَصُوْرُ" (*al-hasoor*) as used in 3:38 means one who refrains, especially one who refrains from going to women *{T}*.
"حَصُوْرٌ" (*hasoor*) can also mean a man who has control over his libido.
"مُحَاصَرَةٌ" (*muhasarah*) means to surround the enemy and stop it.
"حَصَرَ الْقَوْمُ بِفُلَانٍ" (*hasarun qaumun bi fulani*): the nation surrounded somebody *{T}*.

Surah **Baqrah's** verse "أُحْصِرُوْا فِىْ سَبِيْلِ اللّٰهِ" (*ahsiru fi sabeelil lah*) has been explained by " لَا يَسْتَطِيْعُوْنَ ضَرْبًا فِى الْأَرْضِ" (*la yastati-oona zarban fil ard*) in 2:273. It is about those who are stopped in a way that they cannot move, that is, their movements are restricted.

Surah **Bani Israel** states "جَهَنَّمَ" (*Jahannam*) as "حَصِيْرًا" (*haseera*) in 17:8. This means a place or condition where one's development stops, or where somebody is forbidden to go forth. For the right meaning of *jahannam*, see heading *jahannam* and (*J-H-M*).

H-Sd-Sd   ح ص ص

"اَلْحَصُّ" (*al-hass*): to shave the head so that the head is cleaned.
"اَلْحَصَّاءُ مِنَ الرِّيَاحِ" (*al-mohassa'a minar riyah*): clean air without any dust or pollution etc.
"حَصَّصَ الشَّىْءُ تَحْصِيْصًا وَحَصْحَصَ" (*hus-hasa shaiyo tahseesnan wah hus-hus*): The thing became evident, became distinct. In other words, it was previously hidden but got clearly visible *{T, R}*.

"حَصْحَصَ" (*hushus*) is a four-lettered word (ح ص ح ص) but we have dealt with it as three-letter sections.

Surah **Yusuf** says:

12:51	now the reality is clear (the reality has now become evident)	اَلْآنَ حَصْحَصَ الْحَقُّ

But **Muheet**, with reference to **Baizawi** says that this is from "حَصْحَصَ الْبَعِيْرُ" (**husasil aabeer**) which means that the camel, in order to sit down, rested his knees and chest firmly on the ground.

"حَصْحَصَ الْحَقُّ" (**hus hasal haq**): the truth is proven and become well evident {M}.

"حِصَّةٌ" (**hissah**): that which is cut off from the thing itself, a part of the whole {T, R}.

Ibn Faris says its basic meanings include being a part, to become clear, and also for something to end or lessen.

H-Sd-L   ح ص ل

"اَلْحَاصِلُ مِنْ كُلِّ شَيْءٍ" (**al-haasilo min kulli shaiyi**): that which remains of something.

"اَلتَّحْصِيْلُ" (**at-tahseel**): whatever that is received, to separate it.

"تَحْصِيْلٌ" (**tahseel**) actually means to pick the kernel out of the skin, for instance wheat from chaff, or to pick out small stones from the wheat.

"تَحَصَّلَ الشَّيْءَ" (**tahassala shaiyi**): the thing was collected and was proven.

"اَلْحَوْصَلَةٌ" (**al-hauslah**): a bird's stomach {T, R}.

The Quran says:

100:1	whatever is hidden in the chest (or anywhere else) will be brought out like kernel from the skin	وَحُصِّلَ مَا فِى الصُّدُوْرِ

Ibn Faris writes that "تَحْصِيْلٌ" (**tahseel**) means to take out gold or silver from the mine.

H-Sd-N   ح ص ن

"اَلْإِحْصَانُ" (**al-ihsaan**) means to safe keep something, protect it. This is its basic meaning.

"حَصُنَ الْمَكَانُ يَحْصُنْ" (**hasanul makanu yahsun**): for a place to be safe in a way that there is no way it can be reached, a place as safe as this, would be called "اَلْحِصْنْ" (**al-hisn**).

"حَصَّنَهُ" (**hassanahu**) and "أَحْصَنَهُ" (**ahsanah**): he made it safe.

"اَلْحِصْنْ" (**al-hisn**): every safe place which cannot be reached, plural is "حُصُوْنٌ" (**husoon**) as used in 59:2.

"مُحَصَّنَةٌ" (**muhssana**): protected, as in 59:14.

"اَلْمِحْصَنْ" (**al-miihsun**): lock for protection.

Surah *Al-Anbia* says:

21:80	So that it keeps you safe.	لِتُحْصِنَكُمْ

Surah *Yusuf* says for wheat that was safe kept:

12:48	Unless that which you keep safe.	مِّمَّا تُحْصِنُوْنَ

"حَصَانٌ" (*hasaan*) is a woman who protects her chastity {*T, R, M*}. It also means a pearl (because it is safe in a clam). There are two ways a woman can be chaste. One is that she is unmarried and protects her chastity, and secondly that she gets married and belongs to only one man. Thus, she protects her chastity from other men. A chaste woman is called "مُحْصِنٌ" (*mohsin*) or "مُحْصَنٌ" (*mohsan*).

Raghib says "مُحْصَنٌ" (*mohsin*) (protector) is used when she protects her chastity in an unmarried state, while "مُحْصَنٌ" (*mohsan*) when she (who is protected) is married (and Thus, is protected by marriage). Therefore, "أَلْمُحْصَنَاتُ" (*al-mohsinaat*) mean married women.

"أَحْصَنَ" (*ahsan*) means to get married.

But *Taj-ul-Uroos*, with reference to *Johri* and *Sa'lab*, writes that chaste women are called "مُحْصِنَةٌ" (*mohsinah*) as well as "مُحْصَنَةٌ" (*mohsanah*) both. On the other hand, a married woman is only called "مُحْصِنَةٌ" (*mohsinah*).

The Quran uses "أَلْمُحْصَنَاتُ" (*al-mohsinah*) for chaste women in 24:4, which includes both married and unmarried women. As such when "مُحْصَنَةٌ" (*mohsinah*) is used, it will have to be seen with reference to the context whether it means a spinster or a chaste woman or a married woman.

This word has been used in the Quran in 5:5, 234:4, and 24:23. In surah *Nisaa* verse 4:25, this word has been used against "فَتَيَت" (*fayyaat*), where it means free women (as removed from slavery). In the same surah's verse 4:24, it has been used to mean chaste or 'with husband'. According to the first meaning of this word, the verse would mean that all chaste women except those in your marriage are unlawful for you. While according to the second meaning the verse would mean that all women with husbands are unlawful for you, except those slave women which you already possess. Except women with husbands who have already been excepted (60:10). Here, the meaning of women with husbands is more appropriate.

The Quran has used two words for the sexual relations between man and woman, "مُحْصِنِيْنَ غَيْرَ مُسَافِحِيْن" (*mohseneena ghaira musafeheen*) in 4:24.
See the detailed meaning of "سَفَحَ" (*safah*) under heading (*S-F-H*).

Here it suffices to know that it means to wash away or waste your sperm uselessly. If it is only for taking out the sperm, that is, for pleasure, or the satisfaction of sexual desire, then it is called "زنا" (*zina*) or illegal fornication. This is not permitted, and if it is intended to give the sperm a spot to stay i.e. pregnancy, and not be wasted, then it is allowed. This is called "نِکاَحٌ" (*nikaah*). As such the Arabs used the word *nikaah* against *siffah*. They also used to gamble with arrows where every arrow was for a particular spot, but one arrow was extra. It had no part in play. This arrow was called "السَّفِیْح" (*as-safeeh*) {T}. This shows what "مُحْصِنِیْنَ غَیْرَ مُسَافِحِیْنَ" (*mohseneena ghaira musafeheen*) means.

"اَلْمَسْفُوْحُ مِنَ الزَّرْع" (*al-masfooh minaz zar'a*) was a cultivation whose leaves yellowed due to extreme cold and its seeds withered down {M}. In this way, the whole cultivation got lost. This too shows what the Quran means by sexual intercourse.

That is why it has called women as cultivation in 2:223 that means, a man and woman's sexual intercourse should be "مُحْصَنِیْن" (*mohseneen*), which is to protect the responsibilities that are imposed (though willingly) on each other through marriage. This aim at the protection and perpetuation of the human race is not just sexual satisfaction, or unproductive sex. *Nikaah* for a limited period is also "سَفْحٌ" (*safah*) not "اِحْصَانٌ" (*ihsaan*). See also heading (*Kh-D-N*).

As to how much the nature of sexual relationships affect a society, see my book "*Letters to Tahira*".

H-Sd-Y ح ص ى

"اَلْحَصٰى" (*al-hasa*): small gravel, like stones. Since the Arabs used small stones to keep count, as is done on the fingers, therefore, "اِحْصَاءٌ" (*ihsaa*) means to count as used in 14:34. It also means to count, and procure and surround.

The Quran says:

72:28	he has counted each and every thing and surrounds it	وَاَحْصٰی کُلَّ شَیْءٍ عَدَداً

This includes the elements of counting as well as taking into protection.

Surah *Al-Muzammil* says:

73:28	he knows that you cannot have the perseverance to do it regularly	عَلِمَ اَنْ لَّنْ تُحْصُوْهُ

Surah *Al-Kahaf* says:

18:12	has anyone of the two groups taken the period into consideration (or kept track of): or kept it in one's control	اَیُّ الْحِزْبَیْنِ اَحْصٰی لِمَا لَبِثُوْا اَمَداً

We think it is better to take the word as a past tense. *Kishaaf* has also written so.

Ibn Faris has written that its basic meaning is to abstain (from something), also to count and to have the capacity to do something with difficulty. This too means to surround and to persevere.

H-Zd-R   ح ض ر

"حَضَرَ" (*hazar*), "يَحْضُرُ" (*yahzuru*), "حُضُوْراً" (*huzura*) means to be present. It is the opposite of being absent.
"حَاضِرٌ" (*haazir*) means present.
"اَحْضَرَ الشَّىْءَ" (*ahzarash-shaiyi*): presented the thing {*T, R*}.

"حَضَرَهُ" (*hazarahu*), "اَحْضَرَهُ" (*aaraha*), "اَحْتَضَرَهُ" (*ahazarah*): presented him, made him present, came to him and reached {*M*}.

Ibn Faris says this root means to reach, to deliver, to make present.

"اَلْاِحْتِضَارُ" (*al-ihtezaaru*) means the time of death, when death becomes present.

In verse 23:98 "يَحْضُرُوْن" (*yaaroon*) means to hurt; or to do badly.
"اَلْحَضَارَةُ" (*al-hazaarato*): stay in the city, as against "بَدَاوَةٌ" (*badawah*) which means to reside in the village.
"اَلْحَاضِرَةُ" (*al-hazirah*): means green habited areas, cities, group of dwellings.

The Quran says:

2:133	when death faced *Yaqoob* (when his time to die had come)	اِذْ حَضَرَ يَعْقُوْبَ الْمَوْتُ

"حَاضِرَةَ الْبَحْرِ" (*haaziratil bahr*): to be situated on the bank of a river (7:163).
"تِجَارَةٌ حَاضِرَةٌ" (*tijarato haazirah*): cash transaction or cash trade (2:282).
"مُحْضَرُوْن" (*mohzaroon*): those who were made to be present, to undergo punishment (30:16).
"مُحْتَضَرٌ" (*mohtazar*): the one who is made to be present (54:28). There will be a drinking place for whosoever the turn is, and nobody else would have besieged it.

H-Zd-Zd   ح ض ض

"اَلْحَضُّ" (**al-hazz**): to instigate something.

Khalil says "اَلْحَضُّ" (**al-hazz**) means to drive and also to instigate for other things (with reference to **Ibn Faris**) "حَضَّهُ" (**hazzahu**), "يَحُضُّهُ على أَمْرٍ" (**yahuzzuhu alaa amr**): to instigate someone for something.

"حَضِيضٌ" (**hazeez**): means low land, because man goes towards a slope quite fast {T, R}.

The actual meaning of "حَضٌّ" (**huzz**) is to drive or steer an animal towards the low or sloping land {R}. Later on the word came to be used to mean instigate, prompt.

The Quran says:

69:34	he does not instigate or persuade towards feeding the poor	وَلَا يَحُضُّ عَلَى طَعَامِ الْمِسْكِينِ

Surah **Fajar** says:

86:18	They do not motivate or instigate each other. Those who do so deny this way of life.	وَلَا تَحَاضُّونَ

Also see 107:1-4. Note how deeply the Quran is linked to economics.

H-Te-B   ح ط ب

"اَلْحَطَبُ" (**al-hatab**): firewood, fuel. When alighted, this fuel will be called "وَقُودٌ" (**waqood**).

"حَطَبَ يَحْطِبُ" (**hataba yahtib**): to collect firewood.

"مَكَانٌ خَطِيبٌ" (**makanun hateeb**): the place where there is a lot of wood.

"هُوَ حَاطِبُ لَيْلٍ" (**huwa haatibul lail**): he relates all sorts of things, good and bad, useful and useless, like in the darkness of the night, a collector of wood, thinking a snake to be some wood, picks it up.

"فُلَانٌ يَحْطِبُ عَلَى فُلَانٍ" (**fulaan yahtibu alaa fulaan**): so and so man instigates people against so and so.

"حَطِبَ فُلَانٌ بِصَاحِبِهِ" (**hatiba fulanu besahibehi**): so and so squealed against his companion.

The Quran has used "حَطَبًا" (**hatiba**) in 72: 15 to mean fuel, and **Abu Lahab's** wife has been called "حَمَّالَةَ الْحَطَبِ" (**hamma latal hatab**) in 111: 4 which may mean enmity or squalor. The meaning 'who speaks against someone (untruthfully)' seems to be more appropriate, or the one who increases the tools or means of opposition.

H-Te-Te   ح ط ط

"اَلْحَطُّ" (*al-hutt*): the root actually means to take down from above and place it down *{M}*.

"اَلْحَطُّ" (*alhutto*), "اَلْإِحْتِطَاطُ" (*al-ihtetaat*): to unload luggage etc. from a transport as a camel or donkey or some vehicle.

"حَطَّ فِىْ مَكَانٍ" (*hutta fi makan*): he got down somewhere.

"اَلْمَحَطُّ" (*al-mahutt*): destination, a place to stay.

"حَطَّ الرَّجُلُ يَحُطُّ" (*hutar rajulo yahut*): he got down from above.

"اَلْحُطَاءِطُ" (*al-hutaa-it*): man of small height *{T}*.

In surah *Al-Baqrah* verse 2:58 where the **Bani Israel** have been told to enter the city victoriously, it is also said "وَقُوْلُوْا حِطَّةٌ" (*waqulu hitta*) which means to go and settle in this city, and pray that days of our wandering in the wilderness may come to an end. Let our traveling goods be unloaded and let us live comfortably.

Raghib says "حِطَّةٌ" (*hitta*) is the same as "حُطَّ عَنَّاذُنُوْبَنَا" (*hutta unna zunubana*): unload our sins from us, remove our sins from us. This too means that we may be pardoned and our days of gypsy life may be over.

H-Te-M   ح ط م

"اَلْحَطْمُ" (*al-hatm*) means to break, no matter how. To break something dry, like the bones

"انْحَطَمَ" (*inhatama*): that thing broke.

"اَلْحِطْمَةُ" (*al-hitma*), "اَلْحُطَامَةُ" (*al-hutama*): whatever that breaks off a thing.

"اَلْحَطِيْمُ" (*al-hateem*): the part which has been left aside from the **Ka'ba**.

"اَلْحَطْمَةُ" (*al-hatma*): severe drought year.

"اَلْحُطَمَةُ" (*al-hutama*): camels or goats in large number who trample the crops. It also means intense fire which burns everything down to its ashes. It is also used for a shepherd who oppresses his flock.

Surah *An-Namal* says:

27:18	lest they trample you:	لَا يَحْطِمَنَّكُمْ

Surah *Az-Zumr* says:

39:12	then He breaks into very small pieces, like something trampled upon:	ثُمَّ يَجْعَلُهُ حُطَامًا

Surah *Al-hamzah* uses "اَلْحُطَمَةُ" (*al-hutamah*) for *jahannam* in 104:4, that is, the condition in which humanity is trampled down.

H-Ze-R ح ظ ر

"حَظَرَهُ الشَّىْءَ يَحْظُرُهُ" (*hazarhush shaiya yah-zarohu*): to stop him from something, to lock, to stop.

"حَظَرَهُ عَلَيْكَ" (*hazarahu alaika*) is said when something becomes an obstruction between two things.

"اَلْحَظِيْرَةُ" (*al-hazeerah*): the boundary around a field (of crops), boundary, a circle of sorts which is made from branches of date palms etc. and dates are put inside after being picked, a camel pen etc.

"اَلْحِظَارُ" (*al-hizaar*): a wall.

"اَلْحَظِيْرُ" (*al-khazeer*): also means a miser because he keeps his wealth to himself and does not open it (makes it available) for the rest of human race.

"اَلْمَحْظُوْرُ" (*al-mahzoor*): stopped, obstructed, and prevented, one who has been stopped from receiving something *{T}*.

The Quran says that as per God's physical laws, worldly wealth, according to one's efforts, can be acquired by anyone who strives, whether **Kaafir** (denier) or **Momin** (believer).

17:20	God has not limited his Benevolence (to the Momin only)	مَاكَانَ عَطَاءُ رَبِّكَ مَحْظُوْراً

It has been kept open for all mankind, and there for they should be open for all. The system which puts curbs on God-given fountains of sustenance by putting them in individual ownership violates the universality of God's principles. That is why it can never succeed. This has been called "يَمْنَعُوْنَ الْمَاعُوْنَ" (*yamna-oonal ma-oon*) in 107:7 that is, the sustenance which should flow like water, has been curbed by putting dams.

Surah **Qamar** says about the destruction of the nation of **Samood**:

53:31	they became like the leftover broken pieces in an old pen (or like the sawdust which a man makes an enclosure to keep) (**Ibn Faris**).	فَكَانُوا كَهَشِيْمِ الْمُحْتَظِرِ

H-Ze-Ze ح ظ ظ

"اَلْحَظُّ" (*al-huzz*): luck, ordained part.

"اَحَظَّ فَلاَنٌ" (*ahuzza falan*): that man became rich and lucky.

"اَلْحَظِيْظُ" (*al-hazeez*): lucky and well to do *{T}*.

The Quran calls a very lucky man as "ذُوْحَظٍّ عَظِيْمٍ" (*zuhazzan azeem*) in 41:35. He is the man who removes with goodness whatever that is bad, and treads steadfastly on the right path (41:34-35).

H-F-D   ح ف د

"حَفَدَ" (*hafad*), "يَحْفِدُ" (*yahfad*): to be quick in work, to serve.
"أَلْحَفْدُ وَألْحَفَدَةُ" (*alhafado walhafadah*) means servants. It is the plural of "حَافِدٌ" (*haafid*), and a
"حَافِدٌ" (*haafid*) is one who does some work with alacrity and obedience {*T*}.

The Quran says:

| 16:72 | he made your wives give birth to you progeny (sons) and servants as well | وَجَعَلَ لَكُم مِّنْ أَزْوَاجِكُم بَنِينَ وَحَفَدَةً |

Some say that "حِفَادُ الرَّجُلِ" (*hifaadur rajul*) means man's progeny. Some others say that it means
relatives by law. Still some others say this means grandsons {*Lataif-ul-Lugha*}. The majority
however, thinks it means servants, and the verse means that He gave birth to your progeny from
your wives and created servants to serve you. This word is taken to mean grandsons because
they are more sincere in service.

By servants, it is meant those who help in work, not slaves or low status citizens whom you do
not even give the status of human beings.

H-F-R   ح ف ر

"حَفَرَ الشَّىْءَ يَحْفِرُهُ" (*hafarash shaiya yahferuh*) means to dig. The place which is dug is called
"حُفْرَةٌ" (*hufrah*), and with which tool you dig, is called "مِحْفَارٌ" (*mihfaar*) {*T, R*}.
"أَلْحُفْرَةُ" (*al-hufra*): a dug hole {*T, R*} as used in 3:102.
"أَلْحَافِرُ" (*al-haafir*): an animal's hooves, because when the animal walks his hooves dig the
ground.
"حَافِرَةٌ" (*haafirah*) is a road or path with landmarks.
"رَجَعْتُ عَلَى حَافِرَتِىْ" (*raja'to ala haafirati*): I returned to the path I was on. That is, to return to
one's former state.

Ibn Faris says it also means the first task besides digging.

Surah *An-Nazeaat* says that when they are told that their power and wealth will be lost to them
and they will return to their former state when they were without it, they make fun of this.

| 79:10 | and they say' listen to this, they say that we will return to our former state (as if this was possible) | يَقُولُونَ ءَ إِنَّا لَمَرْدُودُونَ فِى الْحَافِرَةِ |

Taj says that "حَافِرَةٌ" (*haafirah*) means for the last part to return to the first part. In other words,
to become as you were, or to return towards life after that even your bones have become hollow,
or to relive.

H-F-Ze   ح ف ظ

"حَفِظَ" (*hafezah*), "حِفْظاً" (*hifzan*) means to guard, to protect {*T*}.
"أَلْحِفْظُ" (*al-hifzo*) means the same in (37:7).

Nawab Siddiq Hasan Khan writes that words in which "ح" (*ha*) and "ف" (*fa*) appear together have the connotation of collecting or gathering together.

One aspect of protection is not to let something be scattered, be divided, to keep together.
"حَافِظ" (*hafiz*), "حَفِيْظ" (*hafeez*): the man who is appointed to guard something, a guard {*T*}.

| 86:4 | there is a guard or overseer appointed for everyone: | إِنْ كُلُّ نَفْسٍ لَمَّا عَلَيْهَا حَافِظٌ |
| 11:57 | my Sustainer is overseer of everything | إِنَّ رَبِّيْ عَلَى كُلِّ شَيْءٍ حَفِيْظٌ |

In surah ***Qaf***, a ***Momin*** has also been called "حَفِيْظ" (*hafeez*). It would mean one who guards or oversees Allah's laws. The plural is "حَفَظَةٌ" (*hafazah*).

In the Quran, this word has also been used for those celestial powers (*malaikah*) which according to Allah's law control everything (6:61).

"اِسْتَحْفَظَ" (*istahfaz*): to wish for protection.
"مَحْفُوْظٌ" (*mahfooz*): kept in protection.

The Quran says:

| 5:44 | the Book of Allah which was given to them for safekeeping: which they were required to protect: | بِمَا اسْتُحْفِظُوا مِنْ كِتَابِ اللهِ |
| 21:31 | We made the sky a safe roof | وَجَعَلْنَا السَّمَاءَ سَقْفاً مَحْفُوْظًا |

Fathal Qadeer says that it means "مَرْفُوْعاً" (*marfoo-a*) or high. But we did not get confirmation of this in the dictionaries. Perhaps these meanings were taken with regards for protection of something, is kept so high that it is beyond people's approach or reach, but this is only a guess. For the meaning in detail see heading (S-M-W)

Nasir says that "أَلْحَافِظُ" (*al-haafiz*) also means straight and clear path.

H-F-F   ح ف ف

"أَلْحِفَافُ" (*al-hifaaf*): the ring of hair on a bald man's head: Otherwise this word means everything which surrounds something.

"حَفَّ بِالشَّيءِ" (*haffa bish shaiyi*): he surrounded him with something.

"حَفَّفَ حَوْلَهُ" (*haf-fafo haulahu*): he surrounded him {T, M}.

The words in which "ح" (*ha*) and "ف" (*fa*) appear together, contain the meaning of gathering together or collecting.

Surah *Al-Kahaf* talks about two orchards:

| 18:32 | We placed date palms around them | حَفَفْنٰهُمَا بِنَخْلٍ |

Surah *Al-Zumr* says:

| 39:75 | you will find that the *malaika* surround the sky | وَتَرَى الْمَلٰئِكَةَ حَافِّيْنَ مِنْ حَوْلِ الْعَرْشِ |

The sky (*arsh*) is the center of the universe's control, and *malaika* are the forces which put God's program into action. All these forces work according to God's celestial control.

H-F-Y/W   ح ف ى-و

"أَلْحَفَا" (*al-hafa*): man's or camel's foot and animals' hooves which due to excessive walking get injured or scraped, or to walk barefoot without shoes or socks.

"إِحْتَفَى" (*ihtafa*): he walked bare foot {M}. Since a man gets up and leaves barefoot only for some work which he deems urgently and think of as most essential, therefore, this word is also used for intensity and exaggeration.

"حَفِيَ بِهِ" (*hafia behi*): treated him very kindly, respected him, and expressed pleasure at seeing him {M}.

"حَفِيَ عَنْهُ يَحْفَى" (*hafia anhu yahfaa*): to find out about someone's welfare time and again.

"أَحْفَى السُّوَالَ" (*ahfas suwaal*): he repeated the question again and again. He asked insistently.

"أَلْحَفِيُّ" (*al-hafee*): a scholar who has acquired knowledge with great endeavor or someone who can get to the bottom of things.

"اِسْتَحْفَى الرَّجُلُ" (*istahfar rajul*): he found out with much effort {M}.

"أَلْحَافِيْ" (*al-haafi*): judge who gets to the bottom of the matter and decides the case.

"أَلْحَفِيُّ" (*al-hafee*): someone who knows thing very well {T}, or someone with vast and comprehensive knowledge.

Surah *Al-Airaaf* says:

| 7:187 | they ask you about the *sa-a* (the moment i.e. *qiyamat*) as if you are researching this subject beside everything else | يَسْئَلُوْنَكَ كَأَنَّكَ حَفِيٌّ عَنْهَا |

Surah **Maryam** says about God:

| 19:47 | He is very kind to me. He looks after my needs | اِنَّهُ كَانَ بِى حَفِيًّا |

"حَفِىَ بِهِ" (**hafio behi**) means to exaggerate in someone's respect. **Samai** says "حَفِىَ بِهِ" (**hafia behi**) means to be when needed, and to make him stay with respect **{T}**.

| 47:37 | If he asks you (for wealth) and insists on his demand: pursues you or sticks to you or keeps after you bare footed. | اِنْ يَسْئَلْكُمُوْهَا فَيُحْفِكُمْ |

Ibn Faris has said that the root basically means to prevent, to be excessive in asking, and to be bare-foot.

This root also contains the connotation of uprooting something.
"اِحْفَاءُ الشَّوَارِب" (**ihfa-ush shawarib**): to shave off the moustache from the roots.

Muheet has quoted a verse by **Abu Faras inb Hamdan Advi**:

اَغَايَةُ الدِّيْنِ اَنْتُحْفُوا شَوَارِ بَكُمْ ۔ يَا اُمَّةً ضَحِكَتْ مَنْ جَهْلِهَا الأُمَمُ

Which means: *"Has the importance of Deen (this way of life) been reduced to shaving off your mustache only? The nations of the world are laughing at your idiocy."*

H-Q-B   ح ق ب

"اَلْحَقَبُ" (**al-haqab**): the strap that passes under the camel's belly and is fastened to the 'howdah'.

Ibn Faris says that the basic meanings of the word are to prevent or imprison.

"اَلْحَقِيْبَةُ" (**al-haqeebah**) means sack, especially the sack which dangles at the back side of the camel's seat.
"اَلْمُحْقِبُ" (**al-mohqib**): a man who allows someone else to ride at his back on the camel.
"اِحْتَقَبَ فُلاَنٌ" (**ihteqab fulan**): that man tied something to the camel's seat and let it dangle.
"اِحْتَقَبَ فُلاَنٌ الْإِثْمَ" (**ihteqaba fulanul ism**): that man tied a bundle of sins behind him.
"اَلْحِقْبَةُ مِنَ الدَّاهْرِ" (**al-hiqba minad dahar**): a period of time which cannot be measured.
"اَلْحُقْبُ" (**al-huqbu**), "اَلْحُقُبُ" (**al-huqub**): time, a period of 80 years, a year and many years. The plural is "اَحْقَابٌ" (**ahqaab**). This word denotes an unlimited period of time **{R}**.

Lataif-ul-Lugha has written that it means "اَلدَّهْرُ" (**ad-dahr**), which is indefinite time.

Surah **Al-Kahaf** says:

18:60	Keep walking (moving on) for years and years.	اَوْ اَمْضِىَ حُقُباً
78:23	they will live in it (*jahannum*) for an indefinite time	لبِثِيْنَ فِيْهَا اَحْقَاباً
11:107	As long as the sky and the earth exist.	مَادَامَتِ السَّمٰوٰتُ وَ الْاَرْضُ

H-Q-F   ح ق ف

"اَلْحِقْفُ" (*al-hiqfu*): means long, high or big, round sand dune. Plural is "اَحْقَافٌ" (*ahqaaf*). Also means a winding, sandy land.

"اَحْقَافٌ" (*ahqaaf*) is used in 46:21 for the dunes and mountains between **Oman** and **Hazarmot** in Yemen where the nation of **Aad** used to live {L}.

H-Q-Q   ح ق ق

"حَقٌّ" (*haqq*) means for something to be present, happen or to be proven in way which cannot be denied {L}. It means for something to present itself in concrete form, or to be established.

Words in which "ح" (*ha*) and "ق" (*qaf*) appear together give a positive meaning.

Ibn Faris says its basic meanings include health (good health), stability and establishment.

"عِنْدَ حَقٌّ لِقَاحِهَا" (*inda haq liqaa-heha*): after a she camel's pregnancy was established.

"رَجُلٌ حَاقُّ الرَّجُلِ" (*rajulun ha-aqqar rajul*): means that man's manliness is an undeniable truth

"رَمٰى فَاَحَقَّ الرَّمِيَّةَ" (*rama fa-ahaqqar ramiyyah*): he shot the arrow and the animal died, Thus, it was proven that his arrow had hit the target. The dead animal Hence, proved that the arrow had found its mark.

"اِحْتَقَّتْ بِهِ الطَّعْنَةُ" (*ihtaqqat behit ta'nah*): spear injured him, and proved that the attack was indeed fruitful.

"طَعْنَةٌ مُحَقَّقَةٌ" (*ta'na mohaqaqa*), or "مُحْتَقَّةٌ" (*mohtaqqa*): it is said when the spear goes through and leaves no doubt that it had hit its target.

"حَقٌّ" (*haqq*) Thus, means for something to be established as a solid event or reality.

Surah **Al-Ahqaaf** says that the criminals will be made to stand before their punishment and asked:

| 46:34 | Say if the law of consequences is a reality or not? | اَلَيْسَ هٰذَا بِالْحَقِّ |

Similarly when **Yusuf** gained prominence in Egypt, he said to his father:

| 12:100 | this is the reality behind the dream which I had in my childhood, my Sustainer has presented it in the form of a solid event | هَذَا تَأْوِيلُ رُؤْيَايَ مِنْ قَبْلُ قَدْ جَعَلَهَا رَبِّي حَقًّا |

Similarly surah **Hijr** says that when **Ibrahim's** guests gave him the good news about a son in old age, Ibrahim was surprised, and they said:

| 15:55 | the good news we are giving you will come before you as a solid reality | بَشَّرْنَاكَ بِالْحَقِّ |

Thus, "حَقّ" (*haqq*) means for something to appear as a solid event or reality.

A solid reality can incorporate changes only if its development is constructive, therefore, *haqq* means the positive and constructive results of deeds.

"تَحْقِيق" (*tehqeeq*) means to weave cloth very strongly {L}.
"ثَوْبٌ مُحَقَّقٌ" (*saubun muhaqqaq*) is a cloth which has a strong weave {M}.
"أَلْحِقّ" (*al-hiqq*) are the camels which have completed three years (of age) and entered the fourth, and are now able to bear a load, and they are now also capable of making female camels pregnant and Thus, are productive {T}.
"احْتَقَّ الْفَرَسُ" (*ehtaqqal faras*) means that the horse became weak, or emaciated.
"احْتَقَّ الْمَالُ" (*ihtaqqal maal*) means that the cattle fattened.
"انْحَقَّتِ الْعُقْدَةُ" (*inhaqqatil uqdah*): the knot was very tight {T}. Hence, *haqq* means solid, constructive event, which is established and solid, which cannot be erased.

The Quran uses "يُحِقّ" (*yuhiqqo*) as against "يَمْحُ" (*yamho*):

| 42:24 | Allah's laws of the universe, destroy the results of destructive forces, and maintains the results of the constructive forces, which keep their presence in solid shape: | وَيَمْحُ اللَّهُ الْبَاطِلَ وَيُحِقُّ الْحَقَّ بِكَلِمَاتِهِ |

Anything can last only if it is according to the laws of protection and permanence, also which can meet the needs of times which is right in its own place and also meets the need of the changing times. Therefore, another meaning of *haqq* is intellect and knowledge, fair play and justice, and to be right in accordance with the times.

Raghib has explained this through an example. Nowadays there are locks on doors but in older times there used to be a projected wooden bar which used to fit the socket in such manner that it used to stay in place as well as swing with the door. **Raghib** says that *haqq* is like that. Therefore, *haqq* also means an inventor who invents keeping the needs of sagacity in mind.

"أَلْحَقُّ مِنَ الْفَرَسِ" (*alhaqqo minal faras*): means a horse which steps with its hind legs right where it foreleg fell {*T*}.

In the light of the above meanings, the right connotation of "حَقٌّ" (*haqq*) and "بَاطِلٌّ" (*baatil*) may be comprehended.

"حَقَّ الْأَمْرُ يَحُقُّ" (*haqqul amro yahaqqo*) and "يَحِقُّ" (*yahiqqo*) mean that that act became compulsory.
"حَقِيقَةٌ" (*haqiqah*) is something whose protection is compulsory for you.
"حَقَّاً عَلَى الْمُتَّقِيْنَ" (*haqqa alal muttaqeen*) as used in 2:180 means this very thing, that the **muttaqeen** are under compulsion not only to follow those laws, but also to protect them.

The flag of a country is also called "حَقِيقَةٌ" (*haqiqah*) because it establishes the presence of a country and its protection is compulsory on its citizens.

"حَقَّ الطَّرِيْقَ" (*haqqal tareeq*) means that he mounted and walked in the middle of the road, and Thus, his presence became prominent {*T*}.

Surah **Yunus** has used the word *haqq* as against "ظَنّ" (*zann*) in 10:36 where it has been said that *zann* does not work against *haqq* at all. Therefore, *haqq* should be followed and not *zann*. **Deen** is totally *haqq* and there is no place for *zann* in it, as said in 10:30. God is *haqq* Himself, and his messenger is *haqq* as well.
The Quran which He has sent is *haqq* (34:6). Its promises (laws) are also *haqq* (10:55). Its way of live is *haqq* (9:33), and this universe has been created with *haqq* (39:5).

Since *haqq* is higher than *zann* or doubts, and it is present in a solid constructive event, therefore, the appearance of results is also called "أَلْحَاقَّةُ" (*al-haqqah*), as in 69:1.

The above explanations show that *haqq* is not something mental, intellectual, or conceptual. This is the name for the concept and beliefs in life that make their appearance in solid shape, which are compatible with the times and which are not dependent on external reasoning for their truth, but are like the sun, which are proof of their own. No belief about this world can be proven *haqq* until its constructive results appear in the form of reality.

The Quran says that the sky will be torn asunder and the earth will become empty. For details see Mafoomul Quran.

After this it is said:

84:2-5	It will act upon the laws made by its Sustainer and it has been so (to act so) created.	وَأَذِنَتْ لِرَبِّهَا وَ حُقَّتْ

Similarly for making the results of deeds becoming compulsory, it has been said:

7:30	(a group) was committed to go astray	حَقَّ عَلَيْهِمُ الضَّلَالَةُ
17:16	So was proven against it their word	فَحَقَّ عَلَيْهَا الْقَوْلُ
50:14	So was proven my promise	فَحَقَّ وَعِيدِ
38:14	So was proven my penalty	فَحَقَّ عِقَابِ
10:103	to protect the *momineen* from the conspiracies of the opponents is incumbent upon us	حَقًّا عَلَيْنَا نُنْجِ الْمُؤْمِنِينَ

"حَقِيقٌ" (*haqeeq*): proper, essential, compulsory, or must (7:105).

"اِسْتَحَقَّا اِثْمًا" (*istahaqqa innama*): that they committed a crime. Here too, this word has been used for the act to be committed, for it to become an event (5:107).

These are the basic meanings of *haqq*. See heading (*B-Te-L*) for "بَاطِلٌ" (*baatil*) as against *haqq* so that the meaning of *haqq* becomes more clear.

H-K-M   ح ك م

"اَلْحَكَمَةُ" (*al-hakamah*) means the horse's rein {*T*}, rather the bit which is then tied to the leather so that it tightens both the jaws, so that they do not move. It is called "حَكَمَةٌ" (*hakamah*).

"اَحْكَمَ الْفَرَسَ" (*ahkamal faras*) means to rein a horse like this, since this rein is to keep the horse in check. Hence, it is said:

"حَكَمْتُ الْفَرَسَ" (*hakamtul faras*): I stopped the horse and (with the help of the reign) controlled him.

"اَحْكَمَهُ عَنِ الْأَمْرِ" (*ahkamahu unil amr*): he prevented him from it, stopped him.

Ibn Faris says that its basic meaning is to stop or prevent, to tell a person, which are his limits that he cannot exceed. This is, making a decision in controversial matters. That is to ascertain the limits of one's rights and responsibilities, and not allow them to exceed them. This is the meaning of "حُكْمٌ" (*hookum*), which is order, or decision {*T*}.

"حَاكِمٌ" (*haakim*) means one who decides, one who orders something as foregoing.

"حَكَمَ بَيْنَهُمْ كَذَالِكَ" (*hakama bainahum kazalik*) means he decided Thus, between them {*T*}.

"اَلْحُكُومَةُ" (*al-hukumah*) is the noun.

"اَلْحَكَمُ" (*al-hakamo*): arbitrator with authority or reach, one who can decide finally for or against, one who imposes the law (6:115, 4:35).

"اَلْحِكْمَةُ" (*al-hikmah*) means to keep fair play and justice in mind while deciding. That is, to fix everyone's limits and not allow them to transgress. This is why a "حَكِيمٌ" (*hakeem*) is a person who deals with matters in a balanced way, keeping all aspects in mind {*T*}.

"حَكَمٌ" (*hakam*): stop something at one spot, anything which stops firmly at one place.

"اَحْكَمَهُ" (*ahkamah*): made it stolid, made it immoveable from that spot {*T, M*}.

Ibn Faris says that "حِكْمَة" (***hikmah***) is called so, because it prevents from unawareness.

In ***Allama Iqbal's*** view (a very famous poet of the East); "حِكْمَة" (***hikmah***) is an opinion with authority, that is, the power to decide and the power to implement the decision. This is nowadays called 'governance'.

The Quran has been described as "حَكِيْم" (***hakeem***) in 36:2, because it fixes the right point for everything and does not let it transgress. It decides all controversial affairs. God too has been called "حَكِيْم" (***hakeem***) in 2:32 because He operates the universe on sound grounds and creates everything in the right proportion and controls everything with his laws.

2:113	He decides affairs controversial among men	يَحْكُمُ بَيْنَهُمْ فِيْمَا كَانُوْا فِيْهِ يَخْتَلِفُوْنَ

The Quran has said that its verses are of two kinds, "مُحْكَمٰتٌ" (***mohkamaat***) and "مُتَشَابِهَاتٌ" (***mutashabehaat***). This is a very important point and must be well understood.

Surah ***Aal-e-Imraan*** says the following in ordinary language:

3:7	Allah is the One who has revealed this Book to you. One kind of verses it contains is '***mohkam***', and these are the basis of the Book. The other kind is '***mutashabihaat***' (figurative). Therefore, those who have some mischief in their hearts, latch on to the '***mutashabihaats***' to make them controversial by attributing different meanings to them, although their true meaning is known only to Allah and those who are solid in knowledge. Those say that we have trust in all of them (the verses) and these are all from our Sustainer. The truth is that truth can be understood only by those who have insight and intellect.	هُوَالَّذِىْ اَنْزَلَ عَلَيْكَ الْكِتَابَ مِنْهُ آيَاتٌ مُحْكَمٰتٌ هُنَّ أُمُّ الْكِتَابِ وَ أُخَرُ مُتَشٰبِهٰتٌ - فَاَمَّا الَّذِيْنَ فِىْ قُلُوْبِهِمْ زَيْغٌ فَيَتَّبِعُوْنَ مَا تَشَابَهَ مِنْهُ ابْتِغَاءَ الْفِتْنَةِ وَ ابْتِغَاءَ تَأْوِيْلِهِ وَمَايَعْلَمُ تَأْوِيْلَهُ إِلَّا اللّٰهُ وَالرّٰسِخُوْنَ فِىْ الْعِلْمِ يَقُوْلُوْنَ اٰمَنَّا بِهِ كُلٌّ مِنْ عِنْدِ رَبِّنَا وَمَا يَذَّكَّرُ إِلَّا أُولُوا الْأَلْبَابِ

As seen above, ***mohkam*** means resolute, unmoving in its place, one who decides clearly and solidly, but here it has been used as against ***mutashabehaat***. Thus, ***mohkam*** would mean that which is not ***mutashaabeha*** or similar. ***Mutashabehaa*** would mean that which is not ***mohkam***. This means that ***mohkamaat*** and ***mutashabehaat*** are two types of verses in the Quran.

For detailed meaning of "مُتَشَابِهٌ" (***mutashaabeh***) see under heading (Sh-B-H). Briefly, it means similar or like one another.

Mohkam would Therefore, mean firstly the verses which mean exactly what they say. For instance, in the case of **nikaah** (the marriage contract) it is said:

4:23	your mothers are forbidden for you (you all are forbidden to wed your mothers)	حُرِّمَتْ عَلَيْكُمْ أُمَّهٰتُكُمْ

Here "أُمّ" (**umm**) means mother, that is, the woman who gives birth to a child, but as mentioned earlier under verse 3:7, "هُنَّ أُمُّ الْكِتَابِ" (**hunna ummul kitaab**) is not that kind of mother. The word **umm** has been used metaphorically and it means the basis and real. This is the explanation of the word.

"تَأْوِيْل" (**ta'weel**) means end result, the ultimate reality of anything. The Quran contains the guiding principles for Mankind. Obviously, the words and meaning of such principles and rules should be such whose meanings are evident from the very words, as in "حُرِّمَتْ عَلَيْكُمْ أُمَّهٰتُكُمْ" (**hurremat alaikum umma-haatekum**) (4:23). These verses are '**mohkamaats**'. But at the same time, the Quran also contains such truths which are beyond our comprehension, as Allah's personality and His traits, life after death and the results of our deeds, the concepts of **jannah** and **jahannam** or the end purpose of human life. It is obvious that such truths can only be told allegorically.

This means that they will be related symbolically. For instance, it has been said about Allah:

7:54	He sat on the **arsh** (came to stay on the throne)	ثُمَّ اسْتَوٰى عَلَى الْعَرْشِ
11:7	His **arsh** (throne) is on water	كَانَ عَرْشُهُ عَلَى الْمَاءِ

Obviously in these verses "عَرْشٌ" (**arsh**) is not a throne made of wood or some other material, and "مَاءٌ" (**ma'a**) also does not mean water. This is an allegory, that is, these facts have been related in an allegorical or symbolic way. Thus, these verses are **mutashabehaat**. Meaning that these verses are such in which truths have been related in an allegorical way.

It is also true that the truths which are beyond our senses cannot be comprehended by us. Although by deliberating on similar things which have been related, we can get some, not total, idea as to what they may be. As from the word we can understand, that it means authority or control, or in 11:7 "مَاءٌ" (**ma'a**) means the fountainhead of life, because at another place in the Quran, it is said:

21:30	we made every living thing from water:	وَجَعَلْنَا مِنَ الْمَاءِ كُلَّ شَيْءٍ حَيٍّ

But we cannot understand how He exercises His control or how He created the life form. We have been given a very small part of these truths:

17:85	And of knowledge ye have been vouchsafed but little.	وَمَا أُوْتِيْتُمْ مِنَ الْعِلْمِ إِلَّا قَلِيْلاً

However, we can exercise our intellect, knowledge and insight to reach the level of guidance meant for us by these indications:

| 3:7 | And not will they take heed, except men of understanding. | وَمَا يَذَّكَّرُ أُولُو الْأَلْبَابِ |

Two types of mentalities have been mentioned about such verses, i.e. **mutashabehaat**. One belongs to those who are out to create controversies, that is, by leading mankind away from the basic truths about life and into mere rhetoric and into spending their energy in futile pursuits. In order to understand these beyond-comprehension truths, they keep on projecting different concepts and thoughts, and consider all this to be the height of knowledge. They consider human matters as lowly and are always engaged in celestial matters. This Quran says is the wrong path, and makes one oblivious of practical life.

On the contrary, people with the other type of mentality are those whom the Quran calls ''رَاسِخُونَ فِى الْعِلْمِ'' (*raasekhoona fil ilm*) and ''أُولِى الْأَلْبَابِ'' (*oolil albaab*), which is those who exercise their intellect and thought, and go on becoming more mature in their knowledge. They, it has been said, build their thoughts on the structure of trust. This means that they say that all these truths have been related by God who has the knowledge about all things. As such, there can be no doubt about their being the truths.

Therefore, there is no doubt that they are the truth but we cannot grasp their real connotation. However, the human guidance that they can provide us, we can certainly reach through the use of our intellect and understanding, but this is the limit of our understanding of these truths. Only Allah is aware of the real connotation of these truths and people can only understand them as far as human guidance is concerned.

The Quran has said at several places that man can derive the right results from knowledge if he uses his intellect under the guidance of the celestial revelation. For example see 46:26 or 25:23. It must also be understood that there are two types of believers. One type will be of those people who believe in the celestial message as it is, and the other is of those people of knowledge and perception who use their intellect to deliberate on the truths of the celestial message.

Surah **Al-Mudassar** has called the latter group ''أَلَّذِينَ أُوتُوا الْكِتَبَ'' (*al-lazeena ootul kitab*), which are those with more understanding of the book, whereas common folk have been called ''الْمُؤْمَنُونَ'' (*al-muminoon*), or just the believers (72:31).

Surah **Al-Mudassar** talks in detail about the two groups mentioned above and their mentality.

Also it has been said about ''سَقَرٌ'' (*saqar*) or hellish state that:

| 74:31 | nineteen angels are posted there | عَلَيْهَا تِسْعَةَ عَشَرَ |

Obviously, this is only a parable and after that it has been said:

| 74:31 | And not we have made their number, unless a trial for those who deny | وَمَا جَعَلْنَا عِدَّتَهُمْ الْفِتْنَةً لِّلَّذِينَ كَفَرُوا |

Their count i.e. the count of 19 is a cause for chaos for those who deny the truths of the Quran. But conversely:

74:31	those who have been given the knowledge of the Book strengthen their belief through this Book and the common believers increase their faith through it	وَلَا يَرْتَابَ الَّذِيْنَ أُوْتُوا الْكِتَابَ وَ الْمُؤْمِنُوْنَ

However, whether it is the elite of the believers or the commoners they never find the allegorical tales of the Quran as doubtful, but:

74:31	Those whose hearts are diseased and also those who do not believe in the Quran ask as to what does Allah really mean when He presents these allegories?	لِكَنْوَلِيَقُوْلَ الَّذِيْنَ فِيْ قُلُوْبِهِمْ مَرَضٌ وَ الْكَافِرُوْنَ مَاذَا اَرَادَ اللّٰهُ بِهٰذا

After that it is said that the truths in the Quran have been related through parables. Whoever wants to derive guidance from these can do so and whoever wants to be misled can also do so.

After that it has been said:

74:31	these are the soldiers of Allah about whose reality and connotation only He can tell	وَمَا يَعْلَمُ جُنُوْدَ رَبِّكَ اِلَّاهُوَ

And then it is also said:

74:31	but their allegorical mention is there for the guidance of human beings	وَمَاهِىَ اِلَّا ذِكْرٰى لِلْبَشَرِ

As such those who are convinced that they are the truth do not try to find their exact connotation etc. but through the use of intellect and deliberation, reach the guidance that is meant for them. This is the first meaning of the verses that are called "مُحْكَمٰتٌ" (*muh-kamaah*) and "مُتَشَابِهَاتٌ" (*muta- shabihaat*).

Muta-shabihaat also include truths that have been related in words that are similar to others but the meaning of which every person can derive as per his own knowledge level and intellect or the persons of different eras can glean according to the advancement of that time. The Quran is guidance for every level of human being and person in every era. We find that even during the same era people possess intellect and knowledge that is different from others of the same era, and if the Quran had related its truths which only a particular set of people could understand, then it could not have been meant for eternity as at present nor be universal and could have been suited to only people of a certain era or people of a certain level only. Then it would have been useless for all others. It was Therefore, necessary to describe the truths in a way that could be interpreted in many different ways so that people with all mental levels during all eras could benefit from it.

Actually the choice of words is also a characteristic of the Quran. These words not only represent the truth at all times but men of all mental levels can benefit from it. For instance the Quran says about the celestial system:

| 36:40 | Everything is progressing in its own circle. | كُلٌّ فِىْ فَلَكٍ يَسْبَحُوْنَ |

And about the sun the Quran says:

| 36:38 | the sun is travelling towards its destiny | وَالشَّمْسُ تَجْرِىْ لِمُسْتَقَرٍّ لَّهَا |

Obviously till the ancient beliefs about the universe were prevalent there could be no right concept about the planets and the stars. When later the astronomer *Copernicus* came out with his theory about the universe and the celestial bodies, then it was known as to how the celestial bodies revolve in their respective circles. Similarly, until *Herschel's* theory came to light, nobody could imagine that the sun along with all bodies within its system was travelling towards its destiny. Until human knowledge had not reached this far, the Quranic verses regarding these were *mutashabihaat* or metaphors, but after the discoveries and revelations, the related verses entered the realm of *muhkimaat*.

Now these verses hold the status of *muhkimaat* for persons of a certain mental level. For people below that level they still hold the status of *mutashabihaat*. Till these verses were included among the *mutashabihaat*, and the discoveries were not made only Allah knew about the truth in them. When these discoveries were made then these verses entered the realm of *muhkumaat*, and their reality was disclosed to some people of thought and knowledge. It is due to such instances that it has been said that Allah has revealed the Quran, and Who is aware of the highs and lows in the universe (25:6).

After a few verses, it is said that if you want to know anything about these matters then:

| 25:59 | ask the One who is aware | فَسْئَلْ بِهِ خَبِيْراً |

Until human knowledge reaches a certain stage, only Allah is aware of those truths. He is the one who has related the truths in parables through the celestial revelation. When human knowledge reaches that level, then human beings too, those who are in a position to know, will become aware of those truths as well. As such, this is also one meaning of *mutashabihaat* and *muhkumaat*.

These are the various meaning of *mutashabihaat* and *muhkumaat* of the Quranic verses. But whether it is *mutashabihaat* or *muhkumaat*, all verses are strong and authoritative in their own right. Every single word of the Quran is like a rock, established in its place.

That is why Surah **Hood** says:

11:1	This is a book of which all verses are authoritative for this book, comprises of permanent values.	كِتَبٌ أُحْكِمَتْ آيَاتُهُ

The truths it contains are unchangeable and its principles too do not know change. The truths that have been related in parables are also unchangeable in their veracity. From this point of view, all verses of the Quran are **muhkumaat**.

On the contrary, Surah **Al-Zumr** says that the whole book is comprised of '**muta-shabihaat**':

39:23	Allah has presented the most balanced narrations in this **kitaab** that are **mutashibihaat** rather than **masani**	اَللَّهُ نَزَّلَ أَحْسَنَ الْحَدِيثِ كِتَباً مُّتَشَابِهاً مَثَانَي

But here the word **mutashabihan** has not been used opposite the word of **muhkimun**, but it has been used opposite the word "مَثَانَي" (**masani**). For the meaning of "مَثَانَي" (**masani**), see heading (Th-N-Y).

But briefly, it is mentioned here that '**masani**' is used for two things that are opposite one another. It is the style of the Quran that it brings two opposites to face each other to make the meaning clear. For example "نور" (**noor**) or light is explained by bringing its opposite "ظلم" (**darkness**) in front of it. These two, light and darkness are each other's '**masani**', or opposite of each other. By explaining things this way, it can make everything very clear. As such some philosophers think that things are known by their opposites. But this may lead one to think that the Quran mentions only opposites to which Allah said "No!" There is no contradiction in the Quran (4:83). All its verses are similar '**mutashabiha**' to each other. The opposites are mentioned only to make things clear. Therefore, the verses of the Quran are similar or '**mutashabiha**' besides being opposite.

In this way, the Quran is a book that is **kitaban muta-shabihan masani**. Alternatively, it can be said that similar or **muta-shabihan** is the style in which truths have been mentioned, such as '**noorun wa hadyun**' that is light and guidance, and opposites or '**masani**' is the style where a thing has been explained by bringing an opposite before it. "سَبْعاً مِنَ الْمَثَانَي" (**sab-un minas saani**) as in 15:28. See heading (Th-N-Y).

The Quran has used the word "حِكْمَة" (**hikmah**) along with the word "كَتَابٌ" (**kitaban**) which means a book of wisdom.

2:151	And teaches your about the book (law) and the **hikmah**	وَيُعَلِّمُكُمُ الْكِتَابَ وَ الْحِكْمَةَ

Law is one thing and there is another which is the reason or (why of it). The law has been called "كَتَابَ" (**kitab**). See heading (K-T-B), and its why, or reason it is called the "حِكْمَة" (**hikmah**). Because it is '**hikmah**' that tells us why that particular law has been made. If the Quran wanted to impose that law by force, then only the book of law or '**kitab**' would have been enough, but since the Quran wants believers to act on the laws with equanimity and fully voluntarily, it is necessary to impart the reasoning of the law along with the law. These are both given by Allah through the divine revelation, and are safe in the Quran.

Surah *An-Nisaa* says:

4:113	Allah has revealed the book and its reasoning towards you	وَأَنْزَلَ اللّٰهُ عَلَيْكَ الْكِتَابَ وَالْحِكْمَةَ

Also see 17:39.

At some place the Quran has been called "أَلْحِكْمَةْ" (*al-hikmah*) only as in 17:39. At others places it has been called both the *kitab* and *al-hikmah,* and only one pronoun has been used for both, as in 2:231. So that it can be made clear that these two are one and the same thing.

Surah *Azhaab* has made it clear by saying that '*al-hikmah*' is also to be followed. All these things make it evident that reasoning or '*hikmah*' is within the Quran, not outside of it.

Revealing the '*hikmah*' through divine revelation also had a special purpose. The Quran has given us laws and rules in order to achieve results. That is, its laws and rules are not there just for the sake of it, but have been given in order to produce definite results. If only laws were received from Allah and it was not revealed as to what results can be achieved through them, then maybe we would have acted upon those laws as we deemed fit, and would be content that we had done Allah's will. However, this was not the case. He gave us laws and also told us what results they would produce if followed faithfully. As such, we will always have to ensure that those laws are indeed producing the results that Allah has ordained. If yes, then the laws are being followed correctly. But if not, then we will have to review and find out where we are going wrong and why the desired results as ordained by Allah are not being produced.

For instance, the Quran says:

29:45	Establish *as-salah*, indeed, *as-salah* prevents *fahsha* and evil deeds.	أَقِمِ الصَّلٰوةَ إِنَّ الصَّلٰوةَ تَنْهٰى عَنِ الْفَحْشَاءِ وَالْمَنْكَرِ

Here "أَقِمَ الصَّلٰوةَ" (*aaqimis salat*) or the establishing of "صلٰوة" (*salat*) is an order (*kitab*), and the second part that "صلٰوة" (*salat*) will prevent forbidden things i.e. "فحشاء" (*fah-sha*) and negate all that is undesirable its reasoning. If *salat* is not producing this result, then we should find out where we are going wrong, because when Allah Himself says that *salat* will produce such and such result, then if *salat* is being established in the right way, it should produce that result.

Because the result has also been created by Allah, it can never be wrong. In *Deen,* or the Quranic way of life, or system, every command of Allah which is followed correctly, produces its result as ordained by Allah. This was the meaning of *kitab* and *hikmah*. Also see heading (*K-T-B*).

Hukman also means that strength of decision making power, or understanding that is available to a common person even without the knowledge of revelation.

Surah *Al-Qasas* says about *Moosa*:

28:14	When he reached maturity and his limbs became balanced, then We endowed him with *hokum* (understanding or decision power and knowledge).	وَلَمَّا بَلَغَ أَشُدَّهُ وَاسْتَوَىٰ آتَيْنَاهُ حُكْماً وَّ عِلْماً

The context reveals that this is before *Moosa* was given messenger hood, and Therefore, does not mean that this *hikmat* was the same as the one made available through divine revelation. This is the reasoning or *hikmat* that enables one to apply Allah's order and principle to details or to mundane things as it is suitable to the era and situation in general. Or, the application of which command or principle will be most appropriate. But all this deliberation and reasoning is quite different from that *hikmah* which is acquired through the '*wahi*' and which is found in the Quran.

About the Messenger Muhammed, the Quran says:

62:2	Reciting to them its verses, and purifying them, and teaching them the book and the wisdom.	يَتْلُو عَلَيْهِمْ آيَاتِهِ وَيُزَكِّيهِمْ وَيُعَلِّمُهُمُ الْكِتَابَ وَالْحِكْمَةَ

All four aspects as '*tilawa*' (following the verses), '*aaya*' (signs of Allah), '*tazkiyah*' (cleansing of the body and soul with education) and '*kitab*' (laws), are present here.

It means that you, (Messenger Muhammed) impart the teaching of the '*kitab*' or the book and the reasoning behind the verses that are found within the Quran, and towards the formation of that system practically, and in this way decide the correct application and implementation of Allah's system. Through this education and training he desires to teach the followers that they too should employ this strategy in their lives.

The reasoning related by the Quran is unchangeable as are its laws, but this reasoning or '*hikmah*' will continue to change, as it is applied to changing circumstances.

Governance: the Quran says in principle that no human being has the right to govern another, even if he may enjoy full authority to do so (3:78). The right to adjudicate between people and to make decisions accepted belongs only to Allah (12:40). This governance of Allah is established through His book (6:115). But the need to implement practically the decisions of the Quran a living and present authority is inevitable. This is called the Islamic system or Islamic republic which was first established by our Messenger Muhammed (pbuh). The central authority of this system was the obedience of Allah because the authority made everyone obey the laws and commands of Allah and not the decisions of anyone else (4:65, 5:48).

After *Muhammed*, this system was carried forward by the *Khalifas* (caliphs) of Islam and was called the path of the messenger (3:143). The '*deen*' or the way of Islam can only be found in an

Islamic republic. It is not an individual matter. 'Allah's governance' means this very thing, i.e. to govern as per the dictates of the Quran. Those who do not do this are called **kafirs,** or the deniers by the Quran (5:44).

Contrary to what many say today, an Islamic government can certainly be established at any time as demonstrated by our beloved Messenger Muhammed.

H-L-F ح ل ف

"اَلْحَلْفُ" (*al-halfu*), "اَلْحَلِفُ" (*al-halif*) means a promise that is made between two individuals in order to seal a deal. Later it began to mean any ordinary promise *{M}*.
"اَلْحِلْفُ" (*al-hilf*) is a promise made between people. It also means friendship and friend.
"اَلْحَلِيْفُ" (*al-haleef*): someone with whom a pact has been made.
"حَلَّافٌ" (*halaaf*) means one who makes too many promises *{T}* 68:10.
"حَلَفَ" (*halafa*), "يَحْلِفَ" (*yahlifa*) means to promise *{T}* 4:62.

Ibn Faris says its basic meaning is to stick with another. This led to its meaning to abide by.

H-L-Q ح ل ق

"حَلْقَةٌ" (*halqah*): any circle whether it is of human beings or of gold, silver or iron.
"اَلْحَلْقَةُ" (*al-halqa*): armor, weapon, and rope, round mark atop a camel *{T}*.

Ibn Faris says its basic meaning includes cleaning of hair, or to shave the head.
This led to "حَلَقَ يَحْلِقُ" (*halaqa yahliqu*) which means to shave the head *{T}*.

Raghib also says that "حَلْقٌ" (*halq*) actually means to cut off hair.
"اَلْحَلْقُ" (*al-halq*): the place where animals are slaughtered *{T}*. The inner part of it is called
"حُلْقُوْمٌ" (*hulqum*), "حَلَقَ" (*halaqa*), "يَحْلِقُ" (*yahliqu*).

The Quran says:

48:27	those who shave off their heads	مُحَلِّقِينَ رُءُوْسَكُمْ

"حُلْقُوْمٌ" (*hulqum*) also means the throat as in 56:83.

Maulana Abeedullah Sindhi writes that among the descendants of *Ibrahim,* the hair on the forehead was thought to be sacred just like the **khes** (head hair) among **Sikhs** and the **bodi** or tail among Hindus. The Arabs at that time also used to maintain hair with great sanctity and used to have them cut at the point of *Mina* during *Hajj* and this shave was thought to be equal to sacrificing the head {*Maulana Sindhi's tafseer* or explanation named *Al-maqaamul Mehmood*}.

H-L-L   ح ل ل

The real meaning of "حَلَّ" (*hall*) is to open a knot.

| 20:27 | Open the knots in my tongue. | وَاحْلُلْ عُقْدَةً مِنْ لِسَانِيْ |

"حَلَّ" (*hall*) also means to melt something which has been frozen, that is, its knot was opened and it was solved. Later "حَلَّ الْمَكَانَ" (*hal lul makan*) came to mean to arrive at some place and stay.

Raghib says that "حَلَّ الْأَحْمَالَ" (*halla-al-ahmal*) means to open the knots of ropes tyding the luggage in order to dismount them from camels.

"حَالَهُ" (*hallah*) means to dismount or stay along with someone.

"حَلِيْلٌ" (*haleel*) has been derived from this root, which means husband and "حَلِيْلَةٌ" (*haleelah*) means wife. Because these two live people in the same house with each other, or they are "حلال" (*halal*) or permissible for each other.

The Quran says "حَلَائِلُ أَبْنَائِكُمْ" (*hala-eelu abna'ikum*) in 4:23. "حَلَائِلُ" (*halail*) is the plural of "حَلِيْلَةٌ" (*haleelah*) i.e. the wives of your sons.

"اَلْحِلَّةُ" (*al-halla*): neighborhood, the destination of the nation.

"اَلْحِلَّةُ" (*al-hilla*): a nation which has come down. It also means neighborhood

"اَلْحُلَّةُ" (*al-hulla*): a pair of clothes, as shirt, blanket or cloak. It also means wife by implication.

"اَلْحِلُّ" (*al-hillu*) is the place outside or the sacred place of Muslims.

"اَلتَّحِلَّةُ" (*al-tahilla*): something used to atone for broken promises and in this way their knots are opened.

"حَلَّ أَمْرُ اللهِ عَلَيْهِ" (*halla amarullah alaih*) means that the matter of Allah was made incumbent upon him.

Ubab says that "يَحِلُّ" (*yahillu*) means to be incumbent and "يَحُلُّ" (*ya-hullu*) means to be revealed or to come down {*T*}.

"اَلْحَلَالُ" (*al-halal*) is the opposite of "حرام" (*haram*) or impermissible or that which does not have the knot of impermissibility on it. That is things which are allowed to be eaten and which have not been declared impermissible.

"اَلْحِلُّ و اَلْحَلِيْلُ" (*al-hillu wal haleel*) also means this {*T, M*}.

Surah **Al-Ma'idah** says:

| 5:2 | Do not open the knots that have been tied in respect and reverence. (Respect them). | لَاتُحِلُّوْ اشَعَائِرَ اللهِ |

Regarding becoming incumbent it is said:

20:81	My wrath shall become incumbent upon you	فَيَحِلَّ عَلَيْكُمْ غَضَبِى

About the place of animals sacrificed during *Al-Hajj* it is said:

22:23	the place of their slaughter is the Kaaba	ثُمَّ مَحِلُّهَا إِلَى الْبَيْتِ الْعَتِيقِ

Surah *Al-badar* says:

90:2	you are resident in this city	وَأَنْتَ حِلٌّ بِهَٰذَا الْبَلَدِ

Here "حِلٌّ" (*hillun*) may be taken as "حَلَالٌ" (*halal*) or permissible {*R*}, and it may also mean that they did not respect even this city of peace and persecuted you by being inimical to your life.

Maulana Mehmoodul Hasan writes that this phrase means 'and there will be no bar on you in this city'.

As far as **halaal** and **haraam** i.e. permissible and impermissible are concerned in Islam, the Quran teaches that everything that the Quran has declared as **haraam** (see heading (H-R-M), all other edibles are **halaal** or permissible. That there is no bar on their consumption, nor has anyone been given the right to declare anything as forbidden or impressible or **haram**. See 5:78, 6:146, 6:119-120, 10:59, 16:116, and 22:30.

Even the Messenger Muhammed has not been given this right to declare anything **haraam** (66:1).

Surah *Al-Airaaf* says about **Muhammed**:

7:157	he will declare the pure things as **halaal** or permissible and the impure things as **haraam** or impermissible	يُحِلُّ لَهُمُ الطَّيِّبَاتِ وَيُحَرِّمُ عَلَيْهِمُ الْخَبَائِثَ

There it means that he (the Messenger) will do it through celestial guidance or **wahi**, through the Quran 6:146, 5:1.

But the Quran has also said "طَيِّبًا" (*tayyiban*) along with **halaal** in 2:168 that is, you can choose from among the things that you like among the permissible things and need not necessarily take all things that are permissible even if you do not favor them; and do not eat things which are not pleasant for you. The things that are permissible must also be pleasant for you. The edibles should be tasty and good for health as well. They should be delightful in every way. The Quran has made allowances for the taste and likes of every individual and for collective benefit.

Here one point must be understood. According to the Quran, every pure or *tayyab* edible is *halal* or permissible and every impure thing is *haram* or impermissible. This means that everything that Allah has declared as *halal* is by itself pure or *Tayyab*. This does not mean however that all *halal* things should be eaten or consumed even if they do not cater to one's taste. If someone doesn't like something which is *Tayyab*, then he is permitted not to eat it. But it should not be considered *haram* or impermissible. In the same way the Islamic society for greater or collective benefit can declare some things as impermissible for some time, and there is nothing wrong with imposing these prohibitions if necessary but it is not allowed to declare that thing as *haram*. In the same manner nobody is allowed to declare something as *halal* or permissible if it has been declared impure or *haram* by the Quran.

As per Allah's system of sustenance, pure and impure i.e. *halal* and *haram* could also mean that ordinary edibles in nature which Allah has made sustenance for human beings should be allowed to remain available (*halal*), and they should not be withheld and kept away from benefiting people. This is also like making Allah's *halal* as *haram*. This is the basis of the Quranic system which is that free goods should never be turned into economic goods or a commodity for sale. For more details of *halal* and *haram* see heading (H-R-M) and (N-Ain-M). For *Saidul bahar* (catch of the sea) to be *halal*, see heading (*B-H-R*), and verse no 5:96.

"مُحِلٌّ" (*muhillun*) means he who thinks that a thing which has been declared as *haram*, or forbidden to be *halal* or permissible.

| 5:1 | those who think that the hunted animal or bird is not *halal* or permitted to be eaten | غَيْرَ مُحِلِّى الصَّيْدِ |

"حِلٌّ" (*hillun*) means *halal* as in 5:5.
"تَحِلَّةٌ" (*tahilla*) is a kind of atonement, that which frees one from the binding of a promise (66:2).

H-L-M ح ل م

"ٱلْحُلْمُ" (*al-hulm*), "ٱلْحُلُمُ" (*al-hulum*) means "a dream". The plural is "أَحْلَامٌ" (*ahlaam*) as used in 12:44. It also means copulation in a dream, and since this condition i.e. copulation is a testimony to one being an adult, it also means adulthood 24:59. And since adulthood also brings understanding "ٱلْحُلُمُ" (*al-hulum*) began to be used to mean peace and tranquility, intelligence and deliberation, and self-control.

| 52:32 | do their understanding and deliberation, their seriousness and sobriety order them or drive them to obey this | أَمْ تَأْمُرُهُمْ أَحْلَامُهُمْ بِهَذا |

"ٱلْحِلْمُ" (*al-hilm*) means to have self-control so as not to flare up even in anger {*R*}.

Ibn Faris says its basic meaning is not to hurry, i.e. not to flare up instantly over some trivial thing. Thus, it led to the word "تَحَلَّمَ الْمَالُ" (*tahallamal maal*) which is said when the animals become fat and corpulent, and they become more sturdy too.

"الْحَلِيْمُ" (*al-haleem*) is a trait of Allah and is used to mean that neither the disobedience of the unfaithful makes Him flare up nor He is aroused by anger to take some step hastily. Rather, He has framed a law for everything which that thing or being reaches ultimately in any case. This means that every deed has a result, good or bad. Therefore, "حَلِيْمٌ" (*haleem*) means understanding, authentic, stable, always one to act according to law and principle, one who does not flare up emotionally.

About *Ibrahim* the Quran says:

11:75	Verily Abraham was sympathetic, being one to revert to Allah	إِنَّ إِبْرَاهِيْمَ لَحَلِيْمٌ أَوَّاهٌ مُنِيْبٌ

And about *Ismael* it is said:

37:101	We gave Abraham the good tidings about a *haleem* (or an understanding son)	فَبَشَّرْنَاهُ بِغُلَامٍ حَلِيْمٍ

We use "حِلْمٌ" (*hilm*), or "حليم الطبع" (*hileemut taba-a*) to mean humility, self-effacing, soft spoken but these are the meanings of our own language (Urdu). Simple selflessness is the product of weakness but "حِلْمٌ" (*hilm*) encompasses a feeling of strength and energy within it, but which is under full control and which does not allow for loss of this control even under very stringent circumstances and does nothing that is cause for repentance. One who cannot face an opponent bows due to weakness and insult, but to have the power to rebel and still bend before law and principle is the height of humility and humanity.

H-L-Y   ح ل ى

"الْحَلْىُ" (*al-hali*) means jewelry or ornaments, which are made by melting metals or with precious stones {T}. The plural is "حُلِىٌّ" (*hulliun*)

7:128	made a calf out of their ornaments	مِنْ حُلِيِّهِمْ عِجْلاً

It means that they melted their gold to frame a calf out of it.
"الْحِلْيَةُ" (*al-hilya*) means a thing or ornament.

16:14	which you recover things of ornaments (such as pearls from the sea)	تَسْتَخْرِجُوا مِنْهُ حِلْيَةً

"حَلَّا هَا تَحْلِيَةً" (*hillahu tahliya*) means he adorned the woman with jewelry {T}.

| 18:31 | they will get to wear things of adornment there | يُحَلَّوْنَ فِيْهَا |

Ibn Faris says it basically means luxury.

H-M-A   ح م أ

"اَلْحَمْأَةُ" (*al-hamatu*), "اَلْحَمَاءُ" (*al-hama*) means black smelly mud, spoiled earth.
"حَمِئَ الْمَاءُ" (*hamial ma-oo*) means water that has become murky with the amalgamation of black smelly mud. A place which has such water will be covered with a layer of caked "حَمِىءٌ" (*hamiyun*). The feminine is "حَمِئَةٌ" (*haminah*).

About the early stages of man's creation, the Quran says:

| 15:26 | black transformed earth on which a crust has formed, Allah began man's creation from it | خَلَقَ الْإِنْسَانَ مِنْ صَلْصَالٍ مِنْ حَمَإٍ مَسْنُوْنٍ |

This very thing has been called "طِيْنٍ لَّازِبٍ" (*teenil lazib*) in 37:11. This means that the earliest living cell was created from the amalgamation of earth and water. Details can be found in my book (*Iblees O Adam*).

The Quran has called the Black Sea as "عَيْنٍ خَمِئَةٍ" (*ainin hamiatin*) in 18:81.

Note: see also last part of heading (H-M-Y).

H-M-D   ح م د

"حَمْدٌ" (*hamd*) is the feeling that is created within the human breast at seeing a very rare and very delightful sight or thing. This *hamd* is an appreciation of the Creator of that beautiful thing. This has few conditions which have been related by the author of *Muheet* as follows.

1} the thing that is being acclaimed and lauded must be a palpable and physical thing. That which cannot be felt can never gain our acclamation i.e. which is good in concept only, such as "مقام محمود" (*maqami mahmod*), "صفات محمود" (*sifaat mahmood*) etc. even though they have been mentioned in the Quran.

For example we can only appreciate an artist or painter through his works which come before our eyes in palpable form and we cannot laud his concept only. As such, the Quran has as sarcasm upon those who merely want praise for themselves instead of doing something constructive and then let their works be praised.

3:187	They want to be praised on the basis of the work that they do not produce.	يُحِبُّونَ اَنْ يُحْمَدُوْا بِمَا لَمْ يَفْعَلُوْا

2} the praise for somebody's work must be voluntary, so that the individual ego of he who is praising can also be gauged i.e. whether it is magnanimous enough to praise good work by another. Automatic work or quality which is inherent or incumbent even if it is good does not produce the right occasion for hamd. So much so that the word hamd is not used for beauty and excellence that is present inherently and has necessarily to be acquired. If the qualities are present of their own, then the word "مَدَحَ" (madah) is used instead of hamd.

"مَدَحَ الْجَمَالَ" (*madah-al jamal*): if a machine is producing fine things then that machine is not fit for *hamd* but *madah*, but producer of the will be deserving *hamd*. This is also the case with a peacock's dance. The peacock deserves *madah* for the dance and the peacock's Creator deserves *hamd*.

3} For true *hamd* it is also necessary that the thing that is being praised is also actually liked by the one who is praising or is close to his heart; to praise someone because of some pressure is not *hamd* but it is *madah*. *Hamd* does not encompass any sort of deceit, fabrication, pretense or hypocrisy or soft-soaping. In *hamd* the acclaim comes to the surface involuntarily.

4} the thing that is being praised must also be very much correct i.e. it must deserve to be praised. *Hamd* cannot take place only on the basis of some vague concept. *Hamd* can never be done for un-clear concepts, ambiguous outlines, and on the basis of doubt and hesitation. *Hamd* does not arise out of deceit, concept, superstition and blind faith. It is based on solid belief and faith, but *madah* can also be done for opinions, but not *hamd*.

5} the things of benefit, delight and balanced beauty that are being praised or for which *hamd* is being undertaken must have reached perfection and their benefit must be felt and acknowledged. At which is not beneficial to human beings or art which has not reached perfection cannot be praised. For instance the sleight of hand of a pick pocket cannot be praised because it is not beneficial for human beings although it may be perfect.

Hamd is a feeling which meets the conditions given above. If even one of the above conditions is not there then it will be *madah* and not *hamd*. It must be mentioned that the word "ثناء" (*sana*) can be used both for praise and criticism.

"تسبيح" (*tasbeeh*) means to be engaged in its duty with full attention.

The Quran says:

13:13	The thunder lauds Him with its loud sound	وَيُسَبِّحُ الرَّعَدُ بِحَمَدِهِ
30:18	In the highs and lows of the universe all **hamd** or praise is for Him.	وَلَهُ الْحَمَدُ فِى السَّمَوٰتِ وَالْأَرْضِ
17:22	that is, there is nothing that does not praise Allah along with performing His **tasbeeh**	وَإِن مِّن شَىْءٍ إِلَّا يُسَبِّحُ بِحَمَدِهِ

This means that nothing in the entire universe can abstain from following His laws along with conducting His **hamd** or praise. Therefore, it means that all forces in the universe are busy in producing beneficial results that are living examples of Allah's creativity and His praise. This so much that when destructive forces are removed out of the way then that work by itself deserves praise.

As such it is said about the destruction of oppressive nations:

6:25	The oppressive nations were routed and Allah the nurturer of the universe deserves all praise or **hamd**.	فَقُطِعَ دَابِرُ الْقَوْمِ الَّذِينَ ظَلَمُوا وَالْحَمَدُ لِلّٰهِ رَبِّ الْعَٰلَمِينَ

That is why it has been said about Allah that He is "عَزِيزٌ" (**aziz**) as well as "حَمِيدٌ" (**hadeed**). This means that He is fine or delicate, as well as hard and tough (14:1). He is the remover of destructive forces out of the way to make the beneficial aspects manifest so that they become living examples of Allah's **hamd** and praise.

At another place it is said:

64:1	every sort of authority belongs to Him	لَهُ الْمُلْكُ وَلَهُ الْحَمَدُ

He is also the fountainhead of every kind of grandeur and beauty. It is also one of the traits of the believers that they are "حَامِدُونَ" (**hamidoon**) as described in 9:112. This means that they are known to do **hamd** or sing Allah's praise, for this purpose man has been given the knowledge of the names (or qualities) of Allah, or the knowledge of natural elements, because when the **malaika** or the forces of the universe said to Allah:

2:30	we are always busy in Your **hamd** or praise (Allah's praise).	وَنَحْنُ نُسَبِّحُ بِحَمَدِكَ

Then it was said in reply from Allah:

2:31	Adam [man] has been given the knowledge about all things in nature or in the universe	وَعَلَّمَ آدَمَ الْأَسْمَاءَ كُلَّهَا

But this knowledge can become operational only if he keeps this knowledge under obedience of the celestial message or the **wahi**.

That is why he was told that:

2:38	the nation that follows the guidance of Allah will be safe from fear and grief	فَمَنْ تَبِعَ هُدَايَ فَلَا خَوْفٌ عَلَيْهِمْ وَلَا هُمْ يَحْزَنُوْنَ

This is the said "مَقَامًا مَحْمُوْدًا" (*maqaman mahmoodan*) or the happy place situation (17:79). This means a position which is completely deserving of *hamd* or praise, and that was attained by our beloved Messenger Muhammed. He himself was called "أَحْمَدُ" (*Ahmad*) in (61:6), which means one who was given greatly to conduct *hamd* or praise (of Allah). Some think that it means who himself is greatly praised, and this later became "مُحَمَّدٌ" (*Muhammed*) (48:26), that means one who is continuously the reason for *hamd* and praise, i.e. one who is praised for one quality after the other. The messenger of Allah was also named "مُحَمَّدٌ رَّسُوْلُ اللهِ" (*muhammadar-rasul Allah*) 48:26 i.e. *Muhammed*, the Messenger of Allah.

The book named **Kitabul Ashqaaq** says that *Muhammed* means the one who is praised constantly, while *Mahmood* is the one who gets praised only once. The book **Aqrabul Muwarid** says that *Muhammed* means one who possesses many different praiseworthy traits.

If we deliberate on the meanings of the first verse of the Quran that is:

1:1	Allah is the praiseworthy Sustainer of the worlds.	اَلْحَمْدُ لِلّٰهِ رَبِّ الْعَالَمِيْنَ

In the light of the above given definitions of the word *hamd* then we can see how the Quran has revealed the universal truth before man, that every creation in the universe is a season or occasion for *hamd* or praiseworthiness of Allah who is nurturing everything from its initial stages to its ultimate end. Obviously then *hamd* is not just a reason for emotional response but a living truth that is arrived at by deliberation upon things in the universe. Thus, a nation that does not deliberate upon the system of the universe cannot be able to appreciate the excellence of the Creator. How can he then hope to understand how things in the universe are praiseworthy? For example we can only appreciate an artist or painter through his works which come before our eyes in palpable form and we cannot laud his concept only. As such the Quran has as sarcasm upon those who merely want praise for themselves instead of doing something constructive and then let their works be praised.

"To sing the praises of Allah" is not just a verbal praising session but it is in fact a practical program i.e.to sing praises of Allah means to give practical shape to a system in society that Allah has ordained (and that which has been manifested by the last messenger of Allah i.e. *Muhammed*) and to make it produce miraculous results such as those which the whole world instantly recognizes and appreciates and cries out that undoubtedly the God or Allah Who has given such laws to humanity following which can produce such results indeed deserves unlimited praise.

H-M-R   ح م ر

"أَلأَحْمَرُ" (*al-ahmar*) means red. Its plural is "حُمْرٌ" (*humr*).

| 35:27 | the layers of red color or lines | خُدَدٌ بِيضٌ وَ حُمْرٌ |

"أَلْحِمَارُ" (*al-himaar*) means donkey as used in 2:259. The plural is "حُمُرٌ" (*humur*).

Surah *Al-Mudassar* says:

| 74:50 | donkeys which rear up after being frightened or disturbed | حُمُرٌ مُسْتَنْفِرَةٌ |

H-M-L   ح م ل

"حَمَلَ" (*hamal*), "يَحْمِلُ" (*yahmil*), "حَمْلاً" (*hamla*), all mean to lift a burden, or carry a burden, to be laden with.

"اِحْتَمَلَ" (*ihtamal*) means to lift.

"أَلْحَمْلَةُ" (*al-hamalah*) means to revert in battle and attack *{T}*.

"حَمَّلَ" (*hammal*) means to burden with, or to make one lift a burden, or to allocate some work to someone.

| 62:5 | the people to whom the responsibility of obeying the orders of the *Taurah* was designated | مَثَلُ الَّذِينَ حُمِّلُوا التَّوْرَاةَ |

"اِحْتَمَلَ" (*ihtamal*) means to burden oneself with as in 4:112.

"حَمُولَةٌ" (*hamulatun*) means an animal for lifting burden *{T}*.

| 6:143 | And some of these animals are to carry burden while others to eat | وَمِنَ الأَنْعَامِ حَمُولَةً وَفَرْشًا كُلُوا |
| 111:4 | one who snitches *{T}* | حَمَّالَةَ الْحَطَبِ |

Hence, it means someone who passes information unnecessarily from one to another, one who gathers information for opposing.

"حَمَلَ" (*hamala*) means to make someone leave his place of seating, i.e. to destroy him *{M}*.

| 69:14 | the earth carries the burden of the mountains | وَحُمِلَتِ الْأَرْضُ وَ الْجِبَالُ |

"حَمَلَ الأَمَانَةَ" (*hamala al-amanata*) means to misappropriate in that which is entrusted *{T, M}*.

Surah *Al-Azaab* says:

| 33:72 | We presented the **amana** or that which was to be kept safe to the sky, the earth and to the mountains but they all refused and became afraid lest there be some misappropriation in it, but man does misappropriate in it; he is very oppressive and foolish | إِنَّا عَرَضْنَا الْأَمَانَةَ عَلَى السَّمٰوٰتِ وَ الْأَرْضِ وَ الْجِبَالِ فَأَبَيْنَ اَنْ يَّحْمِلْنَهَا وَ اَشْفَقْنَ مِنْهَا وَ حَمَلَهَا الْإِنْسَانُ إِنَّهُ كَانَ ظَلُوماً جَهُوْلاً |

This means that Allah presented His laws to be kept safe to the universe but it did not do any misappropriation in it i.e. the entire universe is engaged faithfully in carrying out the orders of Allah as He has ordered them to but man does misappropriate in these laws i.e. he does not carry them out faithfully i.e. does not follow them faithfully, he is very foolish and is oppressive to himself by being foolish and committing this misappropriation.

Surah *Al-Anka'buut* says:

| 26:60 | How many animals aren't there who carry their own needs? | وَكَاَيِّنْ دَابَّةٍ لَّا تَحْمِلُ رِزْقَهَا |

The author of the book **Taj-ul-Uroos** says that here "حمل رزق" (**hamala rizq**) means to hoard {T, M}. The Quran has pointed to a very important reality here. To hoard is inherent within human nature but not within animals. The hoarding that we see ants and mice indulge in is only due to their habits, as research has shown us, and not due to a purpose.

Besides, whatever they hoard is used by all of them and not just an individual. They do not hoard so that they can sell it at a higher price or to earn more profit as humans do. When a cow has eaten its fill, then it does not hoard the left over feed for the evening. Only humans can do this. It is this greed for more that has become the cause of such conflict in human society. The strong or the clever ones hoard the wealth etc. and the poor and the weak suffer deprivation.

The Quran says:

| 29:60 | Allah provides for the animals (who do not hoard), as well for the humans (who do hoard) | اللّٰهُ يَرْزُقُهَا وَاِيَّاكُمْ |

Animals only fulfill their need but you [man] indulge in hoarding for making a profit. This is caused chaos in human society. Details can be found in my book **Nizami Rabubiyat.**

Surah *Al-Airaaf* says:

| 7:176 | As example of a dog, if you attack him, he lolls out his tongue, or if you leave him, he lolls out his tongue | كَمَثَلِ الْكَلْبِ اِنْ تَحْمِلْ عَلَيْهِ يَلْهَثْ اَوْ تَتْرُكْهُ يَلْهَثْ |

"حَمَلَهُ عَلَى" (*hamalal aala*) means to tire out someone by making him walk too much {T, M}. As such the verse would mean that if you tire out a dog by making him run, he will pant but even if you don't, he will pant nevertheless. This means it cannot be at rest in any condition, and it will pant in any case. Or it could be from "حَمَلَهُ عَلَى الأَمْرِ" (*hamalahu alal amr*) which means that he was instigated {T, M}. Like a dog is told to go after the hunted bird or animal, that is, no matter whether you sic a dog onto the hunt or let him stay still or sit idle, he will continue to pant. Most scholars have said that "حَمَلَ عَلَيْهِ" (*hamalal alaih*) means to attack, to drive away or to dismiss someone.

H-M-M   ح م م

"حَمَّ التَّنُّورَ حَمَّاً" (*hammat tannura hamma*) means that he warmed up the *tandoor* oven. That is traditional among the Arabs and is used for baking bread or *naan* and is fixed in the ground, by putting fuel into it.

"حَمَّ الشَّحْمَةَ" (*hammash shah-mah*) means that he melted the fat.

"حَمَّ الْمَاءَ حَمَّاً" (*hammal ma-a hamma*) means that he warmed up the water.

"اَلْحُمَامُ" (*al-humaam*) means the fever of all animals or camels.

"حَمٌّ" (*hammun*) means worry or grief.

"اِحْتَمَّ لَهُ" (*ihtamma lahu*) means he worried for him {T, R, M}.

"اِحْتَمَّ الرَّجُلُ" (*ihtammar rajul*) means the man could not sleep due to worry.

"اِحْتَمَّتِ الْعَيْنُ" (*ihtammatil ain*) means without any pain, there was no closing the eyes i.e. couldn't sleep.

About the residents of *jahannum* it is said:

6:70	that drink which turns life into a great distress i.e. great distress or punishment	لَهُمْ شَرَابٌ مِّنْ حَمِيمٍ وَ عَذَابٌ اَلِيْمٌ

Lataif-ul-lugha says it means both hot and cold water.

Surah *Al-Waqiya* says:

56:23	shadow of hot black smoke	وَظِلٍّ مِّنْ يَّحْمُوْمٍ

"اَلْحَمِيْمُ" (*al-hameem*) means a close relative for whom one worries, or with whom there is mutual concern and love, or the one who possesses the feeling to support his close ones and who expresses that warmth and love {T, M}.

The Quran has used this word to mean a close and sympathizing friend or associate (70:10).

"حُمَّ الْأَمْرُ" (*hummal amr*) means the matter was decided.

"حَمَّ" (*hamma*), "حَمَّهُ" (*hammahu*) means he intended to do it.

"حَمَّ اللهُ كَذَا وَأَحَمَّهُ" (*hammal lahu kaza wa ahammahu*) means Allah decided it for him.

Ibn Faris says its basic meaning includes to become warm or to intend.

H-M-Y   ح م ى

"حَمَى الشَّىْءَ" (*hamash shaiyee*) means that thing was protected.

"كَلَاءٌ حَمِىٌّ" (*kallun hamiyyi*) means protected grass.

"اَلْحَمِىُّ" (*al-hamiyyun*) means the sick man who has been prohibited from taking things that might hurt him.

"اَلْحَامِيَةُ" (*al-hamiyah*) is one who protects or prevents one from hurtful actions or things. Both these things fall within the purview of support.

"حَامٍ" (*haam*) during the pre-Islamic era of ignorance, there was a tradition among the Arabs to let a camel roam free if it had made a fixed number of she-camels pregnant, just as oxen are allowed to roam free among Hindus even now. And this camel is then no more used for loading or for a lowly purpose. That camel used to roam free and eat from where it wanted.

It used to acquire a sort of superstitious sacredness. The Quran has forbidden this practice in 5:103.

56:23	the heat of the sun or the fire became intense	حَمِيَتِ الشَّمْسُ وَالنَّارُ تَحْمَى

The Quran says "نَارٌ حَامِيَةٌ" (*naarun hamiya*) in 10:11 i.e. very hot fire.

"حَمِيَتُ عَلَى فُلَانٍ" (*hameetu ala fulan*) means he was angry at someone {R}

"اَلْحُمَيَّا" (*al-humaiyya*) means height of emotion or extreme anger {T}.

"حَمِىَ الْمَسْمَارُ" (*hamiyal masmaar*) means the rod became hot {T}.

The Quran speaks of the wealth of capitalists:

9:35	the day he will be burnt in the fire of *jahannum*	يَوْمَ يُحْمَى عَلَيْهَا فِى نَارِ جَهَنَّمَ

"اَلْحَمِيَّةُ" (*al-hamiya*) means that heat which is generated in anger. This means that a man should show emotional heat to protect something that is close to his heart. If that thing is factually good then this emotion is also treated as good, and if that thing is not good then this emotion shall also not be treated as good. Before the advent of Islam, the Arabs used to be very emotional in protecting their traditions. Since most of those customs and traditions were execrable or not good Therefore, the Quran has described the emotion to protect these traditions as the "حَمِيَّةَ الْجَاهِلِيَّةِ" (*hamiyyatil jahiliyya*) in 48:26.

"اِحْمَوْمَى الشَّىْءُ" (*ah-moma ash-shaiyee*) means the thing turned black like the night and the cloud.

H-N-Th   ح ن ث

"اَلْحِنْثُ" (*al-hinsu*) means sin, disobedience *{T, R}*. It means to be disobedient to Allah or disobey His command.

Surah *Al-Waqiya* says:

56:37	these people used to insist upon committing big crimes or infidelities	وَكَانُوا يُصِرُّونَ عَلَى الْحِنْثِ الْعَظِيْمِ

"اَلْحِنْثُ" (*al-hinsu*): to make a false promise deliberately or fail to keep a promise *{T, R}*. It also means to move towards falsehood from the truth *{Aqrabul Muwarid}*.

"حَنِثَ فَلَانٌ فِى كذا" (*hanisa fulanun fee kaza*): if he gets the strength to sin, or makes some mistake.

"بَلَغَ الْغُلَامُ الْحِنْثَ" (*balaghul ghulamul hins*) is said when a child reaches adulthood, because then he himself becomes responsible for his good deeds and bad. He then violates some command, then he himself is thought to be the criminal *{Ibn Faris}*

"تَحَنَّثَ" (*tahan-nasa*) means to prevent one from committing some sin *{T, R}*.

The Quran says in the tale about *Ayub*:

38:44	(By treating your disease through superstitious means) do not leave the truth to go towards falsehood.	وَلَا تَحْنَثْ

Also see heading (*Zd-Gh-Th*).

H-N-J-R   ح ن ج ر

"اَلْحَنْجَرَةُ" (*al-hanjaratu*) means the throat *{T}*, or the windpipe *{M}*. The plural is "حَنَاجِيرٌ" (*hanajir*) as in 34:10. "حَنْجَرَہٗ" (*hanajarahu*) means he slaughtered him *{T}*.

H-N-Dh   ح ن ذ

"اَلْحَنْذُ" (*al-hanz*) means to fry meat on warm stones and make *kabab*.
"حَنِيْذٌ" (*haneez*) means the warm meat from which water is still dripping even after being fried *{T}*.

Ibn Faris says its basic meaning is to cook something.

Surah **Hoodh** says about **Ibrahim**:

11:69	he brought fried kid goat for his guests	عِجْلٌ حَنِيْذٌ

<h2 style="text-align:center">H-N-F   ح ن ف</h2>

"اَلْحَنَفْ" (*al-hanaf*): the arch of the foot.

"رِجُلٌ حَنْفَاءُ" (*rijulun hanafa-o*): for the foot to be arched. This leads to the word "حَنِيْفٌ" (*haneef*) which means to leave the wrong path (the curve) and to adopt the straight path.

Raghib says that "حَنَفْ" (*hanaf*) means "to leave the path of being astray and come to the straight path".

This encompasses the connotation of being single-minded.

The book **Tafsir-ul-Manaar** says that in the dictionary "حَنِيْفٌ" (*haneef*) means to be inclined. In his time people used to follow the path of denial or "كفر" (*kufr*), he left all the different ways and adopted the straight path {*Al-munaar*}.

The Quran after abstaining from "رِجْسٌ" (*rijs*) and "قَوْلُ الزُّوْرِ" (*qauluz zuur*) has said "حُنَفَاءَ لِلّٰه" (*hunafa'a lillah*) in 22:30-31. This makes the meaning of "حَنِيْفٌ" (*haneef*) clear i.e. to shy away from all sorts of worship, and go towards the laws of Allah.

"غَيْرَ مُشْرِكِيْنَ بِهٖ" (*ghaira mushrikeena behi*), as in 22:31 means one who accepts no other obedience but His. This is what Islam means i.e. to turn away from every Godless force "يَكْفُرْ بِا الطَّاغُوْتِ" (*yukfur bit-taghoot*), and after that to believe in the laws of Allah "يُؤْ مِنْ بِاللّٰهِ" (*yumin billah*) 2:256.

The above is exactly what "لَاإِلٰهَ اِلَّاللّٰهُ" (*la ilaha illal laah*) means, i.e. there is no authority but that of Allah. As such, every believer or "مومن" (*momin*) is a "حَنِيْفٌ" (*haneef*). This was also the way of **Ibrahim** whom the Quran has called "حَنِيْفٌ" (*haneef*) in 2:135 i.e. one who turns away from all else and starts obeying the commands or laws of Allah.

H-N-K   ح ن ک

"اَلْحَنَکُ" (*al-hanak*): some say that this means the upper inside of the mouth, but others say that it means the lower part of the mouth. However, this leads to "تَحَنَّکَ فُلَانٌ" (*tahanaka fulan*), which means that he took the twist of his turban from under his chin upwards.

"اَلْحِنَاکُ" (*al-hinak*) means the bind with which the prisoner is held, so that if he even pulls a little on it, it may cause him pain in his chin {*T, F*}.

Animals (horses, donkeys etc.) are usually held by a leash but if a leash is not available then a rope is passed through their mouths so that it can be held and directed according to the owner's wishes.

This is called "اِحْتِنَاکٌ" (*ihtinak*). The Arabs say "لَمْ اَجِدْلِجَاماً فَا حْتَنَکْتُ دَابِّئِیْ" (*lum ajid lijama fahtanakta da abbani*) that is, since I found no leash so I put a rope in my animal's mouth to control it. This has led to "اِحْتَنَکَ الْجَرَادُ الْاَرْضَ" (*ahtanakal jaradul ard*) which means the tad-flies swarmed over the land and sucked away all the produce.

"اِسْتَحْنَکَ الْعِضَاہْ" (*is-tahnakal iza-a*) means that a bush was uprooted.

The Quran says that *Iblees* has challenged that "لَاَحْتَنِکَنَّ ذُرِّيَّتَهٗ" (*lahtakinna zurriyatehi*) in 17:62, which means that I will surely tie a rope through a man's mouth. This means put him on a leash and in this way guide him where I want.

In this there is implied the meaning not only that *Iblees* will drive Man to go wherever he pleases but it also encompasses the demeaning connotation as in "اِحْتِنَاکٌ" (*ihtinaak*). Selfish ends can possess man and everyone is aware that those selfish ends serve to demean people, just as the legs of a dog follow his nose so does man follow his selfish desires and earns a bad name as a result. But if he makes these selfish emotions to be controlled by the commands of the celestial guidance or the *wahi,* then he can be greatly enriched and rewarded.

The harm which selfish ends do to a man's character is also done by rebellious nations to weak nations. This means that they drive a rope through the weaker nation's mouth and make it do whatever they the stronger nation wants. These strong nations are also like the devilish forces. As such the aforesaid verse was revealed 17:62. After that the Quran describes the machinations of the powerful nations into enticing the weaker nations. Details of these can be found in my book *Mafhoom-ul-Quran.*

H-N-N   ح ن ن

"اَلْحَنِیْنْ" (*al-haneen*) means to be attracted towards something, or to laugh or cry intensely, or the sound of involuntary emotion whether in happiness or sadness. The author of *Misbah* says that the word "حَنِیْنْ" (*haneen*) is said only of a mother's love for its child.

"اَلْحَانَّةْ" (*al-hannah*) means a she-camel which pangs for its child which is away in another land.

"اَلْحَنَّانَةْ" (*al-hannanah*) also means a woman who has been abandoned by her husband and is now worrying on account of her young kids. {*T, R*}.

The Quran says about the messenger *Yahya*:

19:12-14	We endowed him with the heart of a sympathetic and loving mother	اَتَیْنٰهُ--- حَنَاناً مَنْ لَدُنَّا

Allah's attributes include the attribute of "اَلْحَنَّانْ" (*al-hannan*), but this word has not been used in the Quran itself. It gives the impression somewhat of a Christian God in its meaning of sympathy and feeling.

"حُنَیْنْ" (*hunain*) as used in 9:25 is a valley near Mecca where Messenger Muhammed fought a battle with his opponents.

H-W-B   ح و ب

"حُوْبَ" (*hoob*) and "حَابْ" (*haab*) are words used to scold a camel {*T*}.

"اَلْحَوْبَةْ" (*al-haubah*) means need, a need that can drive the needy to commit a crime {*R*}. After that, the word also came to be used to mean a sin. It also means annihilation and worry, and also to be sympathetic or remorseful which is a necessary result after sinning {*T*}.

Ibn Faris says its basic meaning is sin, need or residence.

The Quran says "حُوْباً کَبِیْرأً" (*huban kabeera*) in 4:2, which means to usurp the wealth of an orphan which is a cardinal sin. It also means frustration, annihilation, misery and grief or disease {*M*}.

H-W-T   ح و ت

"اَلْحُوْتُ" (*al-huut*) means fish but mostly big fish. The plural is "اَحْوَاتٌ" (*ahwaat*).
"حِیْتَانْحَاوَتَهُ" (*hitanhawatahu*) means he deceives like a fish deceives.

Ibn Faris says its basic meaning is to deceive i.e. change course suddenly which deceives the onlooker.

It is for this reason that the fish is called "حُوْتٌ" (*huut*).
"حَاتَ عَلَی الشَّیءِ" (*haata alash shaiyee*) means to revolve around something {L}.

The Quran says about the **Yunus**:

37:142	the big fish made him its mouthful, or that the big fish swallowed him (literal meaning)	فَالْتَقَمَهُ الْحُوْتُ

Surah **Al-Airaaf** says

7:163	that is, their fish	حِیْتَانُهُمْ

H-W-J   ح و ج

"اَلْحَاجَةُ" (*al-hajatu*) or "اَلْجَائِجَةُ" (*al-haija*) means need. Actually, it means not being able to reach one's objective, or not being able to reach one's desired destination. Later this word began to be used commonly to mean need.

"اَلْحَاجَةُ" (*al-hajatu*): the fishing tackle.
"اَلْحَاجَةُ" (*al-hajatu*): a need which embeds itself in a man's heart like a tackle {M}.

Ibn Faris says it means to become very moved about acquiring something.

Surah **Yusuf** says:

12:68	this was a pang in **Yaqub's** heart (which was later fulfilled)	اِلَّا حَاجَةً فِیْ نَفْسِ یَعْقُوْب

Surah **Momineen** says this word has come to mean something which is desired.

40:80	that which your heart desires	حَاجَةً فِیْ صُدُوْرِكُمْ

H-W-Dh ح و ذ

"اَلْحَوْذُ" (*al-hauz*) means to encircle something *{T}*. It also means to drive an animal harshly.

Ibn Faris says it basically means speed, to be speedy in some matter.

"اِسْتَحْوَذَ عَلَى كَذَا" (*istahwaza ala hala*) means overwhelmed something; became overpowering over it.

"حَاذُ الْمَتْنِ" (*haazal matni*) means the imaginary line that can be 'seen' or imagined on a horse's back from the neck to his tail, or the line of its spine or the place where the saddle is placed on the horse's back or that part of the horse's thigh that touches the tail. Both corners as such will be called "حَاذَانِ" (*hazaan*).

"اَلْحَوْذُ" (*al-hauz*) means for the man to walk exactly aligned between the legs behind a horse from where he can easily control the animal *{R}*. If this simile can be kept in mind then this verse can well be understood:

58:19	Selfish ends rode them hard and they were driven hard all their life by these emotions (instead of following the Allah's way).	اِسْتَحْوَذَ عَلَيْهِمُ الشَّيْطَنُ

In the same way the weaker nations are driven at the stronger nation's behest. See heading (H-N-K).

Surah *Al-Nisa* says:

4:141	Say when you came to attack it was We who had encouraged you and given you the courage	قَالُوا اَمْ نَسْتَحْوِذْ عَلَيْكُمْ وَنَمْنَعْكُم مِّنَ الْمُؤْمِنِينَ

Here "نَمْنَعْكُمْ" (*nam'na'kum*) means your enemies protected you, and "نَسْتَحْوِذْ عَلَيْكُمْ" (*nastahwiz alaikum*) means that we were dominant on you.

H-W-R ح و ر

"حَارَ" (*haar*), "يَحُوْرُ" (*yahuur*), "حَوْرًا" (*hoora*) all mean to revert, to return, to be transformed from one state to another, also to be reduced after being excessive 54:14.

Ibn Faris says its basic meanings are a kind of color, to revert or return, to revolve.

"اَلْمُحَاوَرَةُ" (*al-mahawaratu*), "التَّحَاوُرُ" (*at tahawoor*) means reply to each other or retort (to return a statement) i.e. exchange of words as in 18:33, 58:1.

"اَلْمِحْوَرُ" (*al-mihwar*) means the piece of wood or iron around which something revolves.

"أَلْحَوْرُ" (*al-haur*) also means amazement and surprise. See heading (H-Y-R).

"أَلْحَوَرُ" (*al-hawar*) is a kind of wood which because of its whiteness also is called "بَيْضَاءُ" (*baiza'a*).

Saghani says this word "حَوْرٌ" (*huur*) is based on being white. Its basic meaning is to be white.

As such "أَلْحَوَارِيَّاتُ" (*hawariyyaat*): the women who are fair and also less soiled than women who work.

"أَلْحُوَّارَىٰ" (*al-hawwari*) means flour which is the essence of ground wheat. It also means any edible thing that has been whitened or cleaned *{T, M}*.

The companions of Jesus have been called "أَلْحَوَارِيُّوْنَ" (*hawariyyuun*) in the Quran 61:14. Some think that they were laundrymen and that is why they were called Thus, or they were called this because of their cleanliness. But most think that they were called *hawariyyuun* because of their clean nature and pure intent.

Shamar says that "حُوَّارَى" (*al-hawwari*) means a well-wisher, however this word has come to mean the purity of thought, the sincerity of action or deed, and the best of companionship.

The author of ***Al-Manaar*** thinks that "حُوَّارَى" (*huwwari*) means flour as it is the essence of ground wheat. The companions of Jesus were called *hawariyyuun* because they were the selected people from among their nation and were particular persons *{Al-manarr vol.3}*.

"حُوْرٌ" (*haur*) is a plural word. Its singular is "أَحْوَرُ" (*ahwar*) which is masculine, while "حَوْرَاءُ" (*haura'a*) is feminine.

"أَلْحَوَرُ" (*al-haur*) means the white of the eye to be very white and the black to be very black and for the complexion to be very clear. It may as well mean the blackness of the eye to be so intense as to look as if it has been enhanced artificially. Men and women in whom these traits are found will all be called "حُوْرٌ" (*huur*).

The Quran says about ***muttaqeen*** (those who adhere to Allah's laws):

52:20 44:54	And we unite them as *hauri ein*	وَزَوَّجْنٰهُمْ بِحُوْرٍ عِيْنٍ

Just as "حُوْرٌ" (*hoor*) is used for both masculine and feminine, so is "عِيْنٌ" (*ein*) the plural for "أَعْيَنُ" (*a'yan*) which is masculine, and "عَيْنَاءُ" (*aina*) which is feminine.

Raghib says that "زَوَّجْنٰهُمْ بِحُوْرٍ عِيْنٍ" (*zawwaj nahoom bihoorin een*) means to make companions. See heading (Z-W-J). Therefore, this does not only mean to be husband and wife but also to be companion and friend.

Husband and wife are "زَوْجٌ" (*zauj*) for each other. Accordingly the Quran has also called pure women of a heavenly society as "حُوْرٌ" (*hoor*) in 56:22, 55:72.

Besides this, *Lane* has written with reference to various sources that "أَحْوَرُ" (*ahwar*), which is singular of "حُوْرٌ" (*hoor*), means pure or clean intellect. That is not cunning intellect but pure and clean intellect without cunningness. As such "مَايَعِيْشُ بِأَحْوَرَ" (*ma yaeesh bi ahwar*) means a person who is not clean in his dealings, and does not live according to purity of intellect. As such, in heavenly life, mutual friends or companions are "حُوْرٌ عِيْنٌ" (*hoorun ein*), whether friends or wives will not use their intellect to deceive each other but their intellect will be devoid of such impurities.

H-W-T   ح و ط

"حِيْطَةٌ" (*heetah*) means to protect, to keep safe, to safe guard, to resist, fulfilling someone's need.
"لَازِلْتَ فِى حِيَاطَةِ اللّٰہ" (*la zilta fee hiyata tillah*): May you live always in Allah's protection.
"رَجُلٌ يَتَحَوَّطُ أَخَاہُ" (*rajulun yatahaw wato akhah*): he looks after his brother.
"اَلْحَاءِطُ" (*al-hayito*) means wall, because it protects the things inside it.
"اَلْمُحَاطُ" (*al-muhaat*): a place where cattle etc. are kept and which is protected from all sides {T}.

Kitabul Ashqa says that
"حُطْتُ الشَّيْءَ" (*huttosh shai-a*) means to protect, and
"اَلْإِحَاطَةُ" (*al-ihaatah*) means to protect fiercely.

Ibn Faris says its basic meaning is to surround something.

"اَلْحَيْطَةُ" (*al-haita*): a chaste and gentle woman who is extra wary {M}.
"أُحِيْطَ بِالْقَوْمِ" (*uheeta bilqaum*): the entire nation was encircled by annihilation {M}. That is, was destroyed.

The Quran says:

2:19	These people think there is no one to ask them what all they are doing; they are wrong, and their deeds can never remain without due results.	وَاللّٰہُ مُحِيْطٌ بِالْكَافِرِيْنَ

God's scheme of things covers them and results of their deeds are surrounding them and they will surely be annihilated. Thus, "مُحِيْطٌ" (*muheet*) includes both, the covering or protection of deeds and the annihilation due to the results of their deeds.

Likewise, it is said about **jahannam**:

26:54	verily, **jahannam** surrounds them	وَإِنَّ جَهَنَّمَ لَمُحِيْطَةٌ بِالْكَافِرِيْنَ
82:16	they are not oblivious to Him	وَمَاهُمْ عَنْهَا بِغَائِبِيْنَ

Surah *Al-Kahaf* says:

| 18:42 | his possessions, the fruits of the orchard etc. all were destroyed | وَأُحِيطَ بِثَمَرِهٖ |

Surah *An-Namal* says:

| 27:22 | he said, I have found out something of which you are unaware | فَقَالَ أَحَطتُّ بِمَا لَمْ تُحِطْ بِهٖ |

Here "أَحَاطَ" (*ahaat*) means to have found out about something, to bring it within the bounds of knowledge.

Surah *Al-Brooj* says:

| 85:20 | Allah is unseeingly surrounding them | وَاللّٰهُ مِنْ وَرَاءِهِمْ مُحِيطٌ |

This means the same as said in respect of "مُحِيطٌ بِالْكَافِرِيْنَ" (*muheetun bilkafireen*).

Surah *Al-Baqrah* says:

| 2:255 | they cannot understand anything out of or from within Allah's knowledge | وَلَا يُحِيطُوْنَ بِشَيْءٍ مِنْ عِلْمِهٖ |

They cannot comprehend, cannot come within the boundary of their knowledge.

H-W-L   ح و ل

"حَوْلٌ" (*haul*) basically means to change, to go from one state to another and be distinguished from other things. As such the thing which is not in its former condition but undergoes change is called "حَالَ الشَّيْءُ" (*haalalash shaiyo*) or "اِسْتَحَالَ الشَّيْءُ" (*istahaalash shaiyo*) because there is a change in its condition.
"مُسْتَحَالَاتْ" (*mustahalaat*) and "مُسْتَحِيْلَةٌ" (*mustaheelat*) means a bent bow. It also means land which has not been cultivated for many years (i.e. it becomes uneven and does not retain its former state).

Raghib says that "غَيَّرْتُ الشَّيْءَ فَتَحَوَّلَ" "حَوَّلْتُ الشَّيْءَ فَتَحَوَّلَ" (*hawwaltush shaiyia fatahawwal*) means "غَيَّرَ" (*ghaiyyartush shaiya fataghaiyyar*), Thus, "حِوَّلٌ" (*haul*) means change. In the same manner, in Quranic verse 18:108 "لَايَبْغُوْنَ عَنْهَا حِوَلًا" (*la yadhona ainha hiwala*), the meaning of "حِوَلًا" (*hiwala*) is of change and transformation.

"حَوَالُ الدَّهْرِ" (*hawalud dahar*): the changes of time.

Raghib says "حَالٌ" (*haal*): the changes in one's possessions, body or in his psyche.

"اَلْحَالُ" (*al-haal*): the present time.

"حَوَلٌ" (*hawal*): to be cross eyed because the eye is not in its former (original) state.

"حِوَلٌ" (*hiwal*): decline or death. This also has an element of change.

Ibn Faris says it basically means the movement of the times.

"حَوْلٌ" (*haul*) also means the year, because it happens due to the revolution of the earth (2:240).

"أَحَالَ الشَّىْءُ" (*ahaalush shaiyi*) means the thing passed one year, or the thing is one years old.

"اَلْحَوْلِيُّ" (*al-hauliyyo*) is a four legged animal which is one year old.

"حَوْلٌ" (*haul*) also means the surroundings.

"حَوْلُ الشَّىْءِ" (*haulush shaiyi*) means the end of a thing or the side.

"حَوَ الْيكَ" (*hawalaika*) and "حَوْليْكَ" (*haulaika*) are the ends which surround you.

"مَاحَوْلَ الشَّىْءِ" (*mahaulash shaiyi*) means the surroundings of a thing {T}.

"حَالَ بَيْنَهُمَا" (*haala bainuhuma*) is something which intervenes between two things (34:54). That which intervenes is called "حِوَالٌ" (*hiwaal*) or "حَوَلٌ" (*hawal*) or "حُوَلٌ" (*huwal*).

"تَحْوِيْلٌ" (*tehweel*) means to change something's direction or to deteriorate something (17:56) {T}. Therefore, it also means to deteriorate and to change from one state to another {M}.

"اَلْحَوَالَةُ" (*al-hawalah*) means to turn the direction of a canal to another direction.

"مُحَالٌ" (*muhaal*) means two opposites to be combined (which is impossible) {T, M}. It also means "باطل" (*baatil*) which is something untrue and diverted from its right direction.

"حَوْلَةٌ" (*haulah*) means spending power, observing power and authority. It also means to firmly sit on the back of a horse. Any load which one lifts on his back is also called "حَالٌ" (*haal*). It also means a child's walker which helps him learn to walk {T, M}.

"حِيْلَةٌ" (*heelah*): Expertness in observing, and sharpness of sight, the control over affairs and tact, and mastery in affairs.

Raghib says that "حِيْلَةٌ" (*heelah*) is the secret manner in which one reaches a conclusion.

Urdu speakers generally use it in a negative sense, but in the Quran it is used to mean "to have the power to change things" and "to deal with matters", as in 4:98 "لاَيَسْتَطِيْعُوْنَ حِيْلَةً" (*la yastatee-oona heelah*).

"حَوِيْلٌ" (*haweel*): a witness, as well as a caretaker.

"حَاوَلْتُ لَهُ بَصَرِىْ" (*hawalto lahu basri*): I looked at him sharply {R}.

H-W-W   ح و و

"اَلْحُوَّةُ" (*al-huwwah*): greenish blackness, dark green, a color like iron that is reddish and blackish.

"اَحْوَاوَتِ الْاَرْضُ" (*ihwawatil ard*): the land became green *{T, M}*. **Raghib** has supported this meaning.

The Quran says:

87:4-5	God grows fodder from the earth, then it dries up and becomes blackish rubbish	وَ الَّذِیْ اَخْرَجَ الْمَرْعٰی۔ فَجَعَلَهُ غُثَاءً اَحْوٰی

Fara'a has said when the grass dries up it is called "غُثَاءٌ" (*ghusa'oon*) and when it becomes old and moth eaten and black, then it is called "اَحْوٰی" (*ahwa*). Feminine form is "حَوَّاءُ" (*hawa'u*).

"غُثَاءٌ" (*ghusa'oon*) means garbage. See under heading (*Gh-Th-W*).

H-W-Y   ح و ی

"اَلْحَوِیَّةُ" (*al-hawaiyyah*): the roundness of anything, wound in a circle, like the intestine. Plural is "حَوَایَاَ" (*hawaya*), i.e. intestines as used in 6:147 *{T}*.

"حَوَاہُ" (*Hawah*), "یَحْوِیْہِ" (*yahweeh*) means to collect something, to gather within, to be owner, to surround it, to keep watch over it *{T}*.

Ibn Faris says that the basic meaning is to collect.

Hais   حَیْثُ

As "حِیْنٌ" (*heen*) points to time like 'when', "حَیْثُ" (*hais*) points to place i.e. like 'where'. **Akhfush** says it also points to time, that is, it can also mean 'when'. **Taj** and **Muheet** also support this.

Surah **Al-Baqrah** says:

2:58	Whenever you want and from where ever you want, eat.	فَكُلُوْا مِنْهَا حَیْثُ شِئْتُمْ

About the '*jannah*' of Adam, it is said:

2:35	eat profusely from where-ever you want	وَكُلَا مِنْهَا رَغَدًا حَیْثُ شِئْتُمَا

The heavenly society will be such that life's accoutrements will be available to every individual in abundance.

H-Y-D   ح ى د

"حَادَ عن الطَّرِيْقِ" (*haada unit tareeq*), "يَحِيْدُ" (*yaheed*): he moved to one side from the way.
"اَلرَّجُلُ يَحِيْدُ عَنِ الشَّىْءِ" (*ar rajulu yaheedo unish shaiyi*): man abstains from a thing out either of hate or fear.
"حِمَارٌ حَيْدٰى" (*himarun haida*): the donkey which balks at his own shadow.
"حَيْدُ الْجَبَلِ" (*haidul jabal*): lifted portion of a mountain which is high and jutting out; hard, bent rib {T, M}.

Ibn Faris says its basic meaning is to move to one side from the path.

The Quran says:

50:19	this is the thing from which you used to balk and avoid	ذَالِكَ مَاكُنْتَ مَنْهُ تَحِيْدُ

H-Y-R   ح ى ر

"حَارَ بَصَرُه" (*haara basaroh*), "يَحَارُ" (*yahaar*): to be blinded (temporarily) by looking at something.
"حَارَ فِى أَمْرِه" (*haara fi amrihi*): he could not find the right solution for the matter.
"حَيْرَةٌ" (*hairah*): actually means to be blinded by the glare (and Thus, to turn the eyes away from there).
"حَارَ وَاسْتَحَارَ" (*haara wus tahara*): to find no way
"فَهُوَ حَيْرَانٌ" (*fahuwa hairaan*): he was surprised, that is, being troubled at not finding the right path.
"حَارَ الْمَاءُ فِى الْمَكَانِ" (*haaral maa-oo fil makaan*): when water finds no outlet and it keeps revolving in the same place {T}.
"اَلْمُسْتَحِيْرُ" (*al-mustaheer*): a path in the middle of a barren desert about which it is not known where it will lead to {T}. It also means to be troubled and go crazy over not finding a way.

The Quran says:

6:71	like a man possessed by his desires which the *shayateen* (opposition) control, and lead him astray in the world and the man is bewildered	كَالَّذِى اسْتَهْوَتْهُ الشَّيٰطِيْنُ فِى الْأَرْضِ حَيْرَانَ

That is one who follows his desires and loses the way and does not know which way to go.

H-Y-Z   ح ى ز

"حَازَ الشَّىْءَ يَحُوْزُه" (*haazash shaiya yahuza*): to gather or collect something and take it within itself or towards oneself.

"اِنْحَازَ عَنْهُ" (*inhaaza unhu*): he moved away from it.

"اِنْحَازَ اِلَيْهِ" (*inhaaza ilaih*): he leaned towards him.

"تَحَوَّزَ" (*tahawwaz*), "تَحَيَّزَ" (*tahayyaz*): to wind like a snake, to wind, to move to one side *{T}*.

The Quran has it:

8:16	one who turns back to reach his group or party	أَوْ مُتَحَيِّزًا اِلٰى فِئَةٍ

Raghib says it means one who moves towards an open place, to an edge, to a corner. It means everything whose elements are interlocked with each other. As such "مُتَحَيِّزًا اِلٰى فِئَةٍ" (*mutahayyizan ila fi'atin*) means to regroup with his own (or some other) party.

H-Y-Sd   ح ى ص

Ibn Faris says that it contains the element of surprise along with moving.

"حَاصَ عَنْهُ" (*haasa unhu*), "يَحِيْصُ" (*yahees*): to move away from a thing, to run away to escape somebody

"اَلْمَحِيْصُ" (*al-mahees*): the place where one moves to, the place where one runs to and moves to one side *{T}*.

4:121	They will find no place to escape it. They will find no sanctuary after escaping.	وَلَا يَجِدُوْنَ عَنْهَا مَحِيْصًا

"اَلْأَحَيْصُ" (*al-ahais*) also means a person whose eye is smaller than the other.

"حَيْصَ بَيْصَ" (*hais bais*) means something to become very puzzling *{R}*, intense confusion *{T}*.

H-Y-Zd   ح ى ض

"حَاضَ السَّيْلُ" (*haazas sayl*): the flood arose, and its water rose and flooded.

This root basically means for something to start flow and then keep flowing.

"حَاضَتِ الْمَرْاَةُ" (*haazatil mar'ato*): a woman to bleed during menstruation *{T, M}*.

"اَلْمَحِيْضُ" (*al-mahez*): to menstruate as in 2:22. It also means the menstruation blood, or the days of menstruation, or the place from where the blood flows.

This word is also used for menstruation itself in (65:4).

Ibn Faris, however, says the red water that comes out of the **babool** tree (a sort of cactus) is called "حَاضَتِ السَّمُرَةُ" (**haazatis sumrah**). **Taj** has supported the meaning.

"حَاضَتْ،تَحِيْضُ" (**haazat taheez**): to flow.

65:4	The women who for some reason have not menstruated: (that is, according to their age, they should have menstruated but due to some disease they did not menstruate)	وَاللَّائِىْ لَمْ يَحِضْنَ

H-Y-F   ح ى ف

"اَلْحَائِفُ" (**al-haaif**): something crooked or bent. It also means "one who has left righteousness".
"اَلْحَائِفُ مِنَ الْجَبَلِ" (**al-haaif minal jabal**): a portion of a mountain which juts out on one side.
"اَلْحِيْفَةُ" (**al-heefah**): corner, side.

Ibn Faris says the basic meaning is leaning.

"اَلْحَيْفُ" (**al-hayf**): to be partial while making a decision, to be unjust, to be unfair, and to be oppressive.
"حَافَ عَلَيْهِ" (**haafa alaih**): was oppressive towards him {T}.

The Quran says:

24:50	Do they fear that Allah and His Messenger will be partial and won't do justice to them? (How wrong they can be)	اَمْ يَخَافُوْنَ اَنْ يَحِيْفَ اللهُ عَلَيْهِمْ وَرَسُوْلُهُ

H-Y-Q   ح ى ق

"حَاقَ بِهِ الشَّىءُ يَحِيْقُ" (**haaqa behish shaiyo yaheeq**): something encircled him {T}.

40:45	the worst type of punishment encircled the nation of **Firoun** (Pharaoh)	وَحَاقَ بِالِ فِرْعَوْنَ سُوْءُ الْعَذَابِ
6:10	The people who used to make fun of Allah's message were encircled by what they used to make fun of. (they were surrounded by the results of their deeds)	فَحَاقَ بِالَّذِيْنَ سَخِرُوْامِنْهُمْ مَاكَانُوْا بِهِ يَسْتَهْزِءُوْنَ

Ibn Faris says it basically means for one thing to overwhelm another, to cover it and stick to it.

H-Y-N   ح ى ن

"أَلْحِيْنُ" (*al-heen*): total time, whether it is little or more.

In the Arabic language, "حِيْنٌ" (*heen*) means from a moment to infinity.

Raghib says it means the time when something is achieved.

"حَانَ الْقَوْمُ" (*haanal qaum*) means that which was desired by the nation, that time for getting it had come.
"حِيْنٌ" (*heen*) also means period, and when it is meant to say that one thing happened after another then "إِذْ" (*iz*) is added.

For instance in:

| 59:84 | when it is time for death, and life reaches the throat, at that time, after that, you are watching him | اَنْتُمْ حِيْنَئِذٍ تَنْظُرُوْنَ |

The Quran says:

| 38:3 | this is not the time to run away | لَاتَ حِيْنَ مَنَاصٍ |

"حَيَّنَهُ" (*hayyenah*): fixed a time for it {T}.

Surah ***Al-Baqrah*** says:

| 2:36 | you have to stay on earth and avail of the benefits for a time, period of which or duration of which, has not been fixed | وَلَكُمْ فِى الْاَرْضِ مُسْتَقَرٌّ وَمَتَاعٌ اِلَى حِيْنٍ |

This duration will be different for various nations and individuals. The time for any nation will be fixed by its deeds. As for human presence on earth, nobody knows about that duration.

"أَلْحَيْنُ" (*al-heen*) also means murder and death.
"أَحَانَهُ اللهُ" (*ahanahi-llah*): He got killed by Allah (Allah's laws).
"أَلْحَائِنُ" (*al-hayen*) is used for an idiot
"أَلْحَانِيَّةُ" (*al-haniya*) means alcoholic brew {T}.

H-Y-Y   ح ى ى

"حَيِيَ" (*ha-yiya*), "يَحْيَىٰ" (*yahya*), "يَحُيِّى" (*ya-hayyio*): he lived or became alive.
"حَيَاةٌ" (*hayaat*): life.
"أَحْيَاهُ" (*ahyaa*): he made him alive.
"اِحْيَاءٌ" (*ihyaa*): to give life.
"تَحَيَّامِنْهُ" (*tahayya minhu*): he shrank from it.

Biologists say one sign of life is to shrink. Touch any living thing (insect etc.) and its first reaction will be to shrink itself, and if it is not living then it will remain as it is. This shrinking is actually due to its defensive instinct. From this the Arabs derived the meaning of this root as shrinking.

"حَيَاءٌ" (*hayaa*) also means shame, shyness and is also derived from this root because that too is displayed by stepping back a little.

A snake is also called "حَيَّةٌ" (*hayya*) because it moves by shrinking and expanding. *{T}.*

Raghib says "حَيَاةٌ" (*hayaa*) means the faculty of sensation, "موت" (*mout*) is its opposite. See heading (*M-W-T*)

These different perspectives are:

1. faculty of growth, which is found in animals and plants
2. faculty of sense
3. the faculty to think and act
4. freedom from sorrow
5. life after death which can be reached through life, that is the life of intellect and knowledge
6. Life which is met only by God and which has no death "أَلْحَىُّ الْقَيُّوْمُ" (*al-hayyul qayyum*).

"اِحْيَاءٌ" (*ihyaa*): to make alive.
"اِسْتِحْيَاءٌ" (*istihyaa*): to keep alive, also to make live.

But in 2:26, "لاَيَسْتَحْي" (*la yastahyi*) means that God has no qualms about giving this example here *{R}.*

"لاَحَيَّ عَنْهُ" (*la hayyia unhu*) means it is no bar.
"أَلْحَيَاءُ" (*al-haya*) means greenery as well as rain, because these are related to the land's life.
"حَىَّ عَلى يا حَىَّ بَلْ" (*hayyia ala or hayyia hal*) means make haste in this work *{R}.*
"حَيَّاهُ تَحِيَّةً" (*hayyiahu tahayyia*): to pray for somebody's longevity and a happy life *{R}.* It also means to salute as in 4:86 *{M}.*

"تَحِيَّاتٌ" (*tahiyyat*) is actually used for everlasting life {L}, and also to be safe from all evils and misfortunes.

"اَلْمَحْيَا" (*al-mahiya*) means life as life comes opposite to death in 67:2. Like this "مَمَاتٌ" (*mamat*) appears as against "مَحْيَا" (*mahya*) in 6:163.

"اَلْحَيَاةُ" (*al-hayato*) sometimes means soft or beneficial {T}.

"اَلْحَيَاةُ الطِّيِّبَةُ" (*al-hayatut tayyebah*) means *jannah* (heaven) or *halal* (permitted) sustenance {M}.

"حَيِىَ الطَّرِيْقُ" (*hayyit tareewo*) means the path became clear or distinct.

"طَرِيْقٌ حَىٌّ" (*tareeq hayyi*) means clear path {M}.

For life after death, the Quran says "وَاِنَّ الدَّارَ الْاَخِرَةَ لَهِىَ الْحَيَوَانُ" (*wa innad daral akhi-ratah*) in 64:29. Here instead of "حَيَاةٌ" (*hayah*) the word "حَيَوَانٌ" (*hayawan*) has been used which rhymes with "فَعَلَانٌ" (*fualaan*). This difference is very significant. In the Arabic language the words rhyming with "فَعَلَانٌ" (*fualaan*) have the connotation of intensity, overpowering, for something to appear suddenly, and movement and the element of being disturbed. This means that Life after death is not a link in the chain of life in this world which is governed by physical laws. Life will suddenly adopt a new form there {M}. Instead of stagnation, there will be constant movement and effort {M}.

Also see "أَخِرَةٌ" (*akhiratun*) and "قِيَامَةٌ" (*qiyamatun*) which are mentioned under the headings (*A-Kh-R)*, and (Q-W-M). Also see the word "رَحْمَنٌ" (*Rahman*) which will be found under the heading (*R-H-M*).

"حَيْوَةٌ" (*hayaah*) has different meanings as mentioned in the Quranic verses above.

He has also written that a snake is called "حَيْوَةٌ" (*hayyah*) because of its long life. The Arabs thought that the snake met its death only due to some accident, not biologically. This means that the life after death will indeed be a continuation of this life, but it will not be according to the physical laws, it will have other set of laws there.

But this fact must be well understood that the Quran does not call only the physical life as "حَيْوَةٌ" (*hayyah*). Real life, in its eyes, is that which attains the height of humanity, in which Man develops himself by acting upon the laws of Allah.

"الحَيَاةُ الدُّنْيَا" (*al-hayatud duniya*) means quick benefit, instant benefits, only present benefits, that is a life which has no eye on the future. Hence, it means the physical life in which a man exists on the animal level. He does not have in mind the delightfulness of the life after death nor believes in the continuation of life (after death).

This is "الحَيَاةُ الدُّنْيَا" (*al-hayatyud duniya*). We should keep the Quranic meanings of "الحَيَاةُ الدُّنْيَا" *hayatud duniya* and life after death in mind. Also the fact that as generally believed, life means to breathe and death means for the breath to stop. That is not so, but has a deeper meaning, and these words have been used in a wide connotation. Therefore, at every place, we must see which meaning is more befitting according to the context. As for example, when we say that that nation is dead, we do not mean that the individuals of that nation are buried in their graves. When we say that that nation is among living nations, then it does not mean that the individuals of that nation breathe. The meaning of alive and dead nations is obvious. The Quran has used these words at some places in these connotations too.

Surah *Al-Anaam* says:

6:123	And he who is dead…then We enliven him, and walk among people….	اَوَمَنْ كَانَ مَيْتًا فَاَحْيَيْنٰهُ وَ جَعَلْنَا لَهُ نُوْرًا يَّمْشِیْ بِهٖ فِی النَّاسِ

It is obvious here that life and death here are not physical and mean guidance and being led astray. This difference in the meanings of life and death must be borne in mind at every step. The messengers used to come in order to give 'life' anew to 'dead' nations with which they could achieve all the successes of life (8:24). This life can now be achieved by following the Quran, but only those who have the capacity to 'live' (36:70) and he who wants to escape disaster (2:2).

Kh-B-A ء ب خ

"خَبَأَه" (*khabah*), "يَخْبَوُه" (*yakhbawuh*), "خَبَأَ" (*khaba*) means to hide, to keep behind a veil. *Ibn Faris* says that these are its basic meanings.

"امْرَأَةٌ خَبَأَةٌ" (*imra atun khibah*): domestic woman who hardly leaves her house.
"الْخَبِيئَةُ" (*al-khabiat*): the seeds which the farmer hides in the earth, the bounties of Nature which are hidden in the earth.
"الْخَبُّ" (*al-khub*): buried or hidden thing {*T, R*}.

The Quran says:

27:25	the treasures hidden in the highs and lows of the universe	اَلْخَبُّ فِى السَّمٰوٰتِ وَالْاَرْضِ

It means their latent potentialities, the treasures of sustenance hidden in them.

Kh-B-T ت ب خ

Ibn Faris says that it means vast land in which there is no vegetation.

"الْخَبْتُ" (*al-khabt*): low, vast land {*T*}.
"أَخْبَتَ" (*akhbat*): he reached the low land. Later this word came to mean softness, humbleness, to obey, to be content {*T*}.

The Quran says about the *momineen*:

11:23	they obey Allah's law	وَاَخْبَتُوْ اِلٰى رَبِّهِمْ
22:54	before Him, their hearts bow (become soft)	فَتُخْبِتَ لَهٗ قُلُوْبُهُمْ

In verse 22:34, it is said "مُخْبِتِيْنَ" (*mukhbateen*), which means those with softness and obedience. Before that it is said "فَلَهٗ اَسْلِمُوْا" (*faklahu aslamu*) in 32:34, which means those who bend before Allah's laws, meaning, those who accept them with good grace.

Kh-B-S   خ ب ث

"اَلْخَبِیْثُ" (*al-khabiss*): opposite of "طَیِّبْ" (*tayyab*). See heading (*T-Y-B*) to see the meaning of "طَیِّبْ" (*tayyab*).

"اَلْخَبِیْثُ" (*al-khabis*): dirty, hateful and unpleasant, even if it regarding edibles, speech, actions, beliefs or thoughts.

"اَلْخَابِثُ" (*al-khabis*): cunning man, or useless thing *{T, M}*.

"خَبَثُ الْحَدِیْدِ والْفِضَّہِ" (*khabasul hadeed wal fizza*): a mixture of iron and silver which is melted and separated in the oven. Hence, it may mean mixture, adulteration. "اَلْخُبْثُ" (*al-khubs*): fornication.

Surah *Airaaf* says "خَبُثَ" (*khabus*) in 7:58. It is used for saline land which does not grow anything or if it does, then very little.

In surah *Ibrahim*, it is said "كَلِمَۃٌ طَیِّبَۃ" (*kalimatun tayyebah*) as against "كَلِمَۃٌ خَبِیْثَۃ" (*kalimatun khabisah*), which has been likened to "شَجَرَۃٌ خَبِیْثَۃ" (*shajaratun kjhabisah*), 14:24-26. It means a tree which gives no fruit, unfruitful concepts of life. Something that appears very correct but does not produce any result, and all effort is lost, although wrong concept grows very quick and has a lot of glamour (5:100), but it can never be stable, for its roots are not deep enough (14:26).

"خَبَائِث" (*khabais*), "خَبِیْثَۃ" (*khabisatun*) is the plural.

7:157 says that the messenger declares the *tayyebat*, or good and desirable things, as *halal*, while not good things as *khubais* and Hence, *haram*. This means that things as termed *haram*, or forbidden by the Quran are *khubais* and the things which are *halal* are the *tayyebat*. For details see headings (H-R-M), and (*H-L-L*).

The Quran has used the word "خبيث" (*khabiss*) also for people who commit lewd acts as well as for the bad deeds themselves.

Surah *An-Noor* says:

| 24:26 | *khabis* things are befitting *khabis* people | اَلْخَبِیْثُتُ لِلْخَبِیْثِیْنَ |

This can however also mean that *khabis* women are for *khabis* men. The second meaning is confirmed by another verse which says:

| 24:3 | a fornicating man can only wed a fornicating woman | اَلزَّانِیْ لَایَنْكِحْ اِلَاَزَانِیَۃً |

This is explained in *Mafhoom-ul-Quran*.

Kh-B-R   خ ب ر

Ibn Faris says the basic meaning of "خَبَرٌ" (*khabar*) is knowledge. As such, "خَبَرٌ" (*khabar*) must have knowledge as well as familiarity in it.

"اَلْأَخْبَارٌ" (*akhbar*) is the plural form.

"خَبَرٌ" (*khabar*) and "نَبَاءٌ" (*naba*) differ only in that the last mentioned is news about a very big event and "خَبَرٌ" (*khabar*) is news about ordinary affairs.

Some lexicologists say that ***khabar*** is something which is copied from something, but the Quran has not used this word with this distinction.

Moosa said to his family upon seeing fire:

27:7	I will bring news about it to you	سَآتِيكُمْ مِنْهَا بِخَبَرٍ

"اَلْخَبِيرُ" (*al-khabeer*): one who knows or has the news, or one who gives the news {T}.

The Quran has used this word as one of the traits of God:

2:271	Allah is aware of what you do	وَاللهُ بِمَا تَعْمَلُونَ خَبِيرٌ

"خُبْرٌ" (*khubr*) also means to know something as used in 18:68 {T}.

Muheet says this means knowledge on the basis of experience.

Kh-B-Z   خ ب ز

"اَلْخُبْزُ" (*al-khubz*) means bread as used in 12:36 {T}. The real meaning in this root is to shun and kill.

"اَلْخَبْزُ" (*al-khubz*) means for a camel to strike the earth with his pawn.

Since bread is also made by slapping the dough in the own with the hand, it is Hence, called "خُبْزٌ" (*khubz*), or perhaps because bread shuns or kills hunger.

Sometimes the word is used for edibles or means of livelihood {M, F}.

Kh-B-Te   خ ب ط

"خَبَطَ" (*khabat*) means to strike something hard, to trample something forcefully with the foot, to strike the tree with a stick and make the leaves fall.

"خَبَطَ اللَّيْلَ" (*khabat-ul-lail*): to walk at night without knowing the direction where one is going.

"تَخَبَّطَهُ الشَّيْطَنُ" (*tahabbatush shaitaan*): the devil maddened him {T}.

"خَبْطٌ" (*khabt*) also means a king's oppression {*R*}.

"اِخْتِبَاطُ الْمَعْرُوْف" (*ikhtebaatul ma'roof*) means to demand a favor from someone perforce {*R*}.

Surah *Al-Baqrah* describes those who practise usury as:

2:275	these people stand like they have bitten by the snake	لَايَقُوْمُوْنَ اِلاَكَمَا يَقُوْمُ الذِىْ يَتَخَبَّطُهُ الشَّيْطٰنُ مِنَ الْمَسِّ

This state embodies mental agony as well as a troubled heart which gives no calm to them as their hearts are afire with the greed for more wealth. If "اَلشَّيْطٰنُ" (*ash-shaitaan*) in this verse is taken to mean the wild emotions of man, then it would mean, the man who is being mad due to his desires.

Kh-B-L خ ب ل

"أَخْبَلُ" (*al-khabl*), "اَلْخَبَلُ" (*al-khabal*): it basically means for some trouble (something amiss) to appear, such as some trouble to develop in man's limbs, or to have an attack of paralysis, or to be mad.

Zajaj says it means for something to be lost. Later, it commonly meant annihilation or loss.

"رَجُلٌ مُخَبَّلٌ" (*rajulun mukhabbal*): a man whose hands and legs have been amputated {*M*}.

The Quran says:

3:117	your enemies will leave no stone unturned to hurt you	لَايَالُوْنَكُمْ خَبَالاً

This embodies all types of loss.

Kh-B-W خ ب و

"خَبَتِ النَّارُ وَ الْحَرْبُ" (*khabatin naaro wal hurb*): the fierceness of the battle dimmed, became calm, the flame became mild {*T*}.

Surah *Bani Israel* says:

17:97	when the fire will start dying	كُلَّمَا خَبَتْ
17:97	we will stoke the fire for them to make it burn brighter	زِدْنٰهُمْ سَعِيْرًا

"خِبَاءٌ" (*khibaun*): a curtain with which something is covered, and also the ear of the corn, the husk {*R*}.

"خَبْءٌ" (*khab*) as used in 27:25, see heading (*Kh-B-A*).

Ibn Faris says that "خَبْوٌ" (*khabwoon*) and "خَبٌ" (*khabun*) both mean to hide.

Kh-T-R   خ ت ر

"اَلْخَتْرُ" (*al-khatr*): going back on one's word is the worst way possible, to break an agreement and to deceive *{T, M}*. This is that break of agreement for which one works so hard that he becomes dead tired *{T, M}*. He becomes tired and weak and Hence, his limbs become weak as well *{R}*.

"اَلْخَتَرُ" (*al-khatar*) is of the same meaning as "اَلْخَدَرُ" (*al-khadar*) which means such stupor as created by taking some poison or drug that is the cause of slackness and weakness in limbs. "رَجُلٌ مُخَتَّرٌ" (*rajulun mukhatta*): a man whose limbs become slack. "خَتَّرَهُ الشَّرَابُ" (*khattarahush sharaab*): the drink has made his limbs slack *{T, M}*.

Ibn Faris says it basically means laziness and madness.

The Quran says "خَتَّارٍ كَفُوْرٍ" (*khattarin kafoor*) in 31:32. This verse may mean a con man, or a man who has become lazy, due to lack of hard labor, or the man who is lazy in carrying out Allah's orders.

Kh-T-M   خ ت م

"خَتْمٌ" (*khatum*) means to hide or cover something, to close and Hence, make something safe. As such, when land is cultivated and seeds sown, then watered for the first time, it is called as "خَتَمَ الزَّرْعَ" (*khatamuz zar'a*) by the Arabs, because after watering the mud sticks together and Thus, hides the seed which becomes safe.

The bee collects the honey in the honeycomb cells and lays a thin wax layer at the mouth to close the honey inside and keep it safe. This too is called "خَتْمٌ" (*khatum*) by the Arabs. Later, the honey itself, and the mouths of the cells too came to be called "خَتْمٌ" (*khatum*).

"خَتَمَ الشَّيْىءَ خَتْمَأً" (*khatamash shaiya khatma*): means to reach at the end of something *{T}*. *Ibn Faris* says this is its basic meaning.

"خَتْمٌ" (*khatmun*) and "طَبْعٌ" (*tabo'n*) are used in two ways:

1. To put a seal on something.
2. The mark that is made by sealing,

Later on the meaning widened and it came to mean to close and stop something. This because by sealing the thing inside, one closes it and it is not brought out anymore *{T}*.

"خِتَامٌ" (*khitaam*) is the wax which is used to seal.

"خَاتَمٌ" (*khatamun*) is the seal itself.

"خَاتَمٌ" (*khatamun*) is also used for the end of everything.

"خَاتُمُ الْقَوْمِ" (*khatamul qaum*) would as such mean the last individual of the nation.

"خِتَامٌ" (*khitaam*) means the last part of any drink {F}.

Fara thinks that "خَاتَمٌ" (*khatamun*) and "خِتَامٌ" (*khitaam*) are very similar in meaning

"فُلَانٌ خَتَمَ عَلَيْكَ بَابَهُ" (*fulan khatama alaika babehi*): that man avoids you and closes his doors on you *{T}*.

Quran says:

| 2:7 | There is a seal of Allah on their hearts | خَتَمَ اللهُ عَلَى قُلُوبِهِمْ |

It also says "طَبَعَ اللهُ" (*taba'allahu....*) other places.

When it says that the hearts of people are sealed, it means that they lose the capacity to think or comprehend.

Surah *Al-Anaam* says:

| 6:46 | If Allah take away your ability to listen and observe and seal of your heart … | أَخَذَ اللهُ سَمْعَكُمْ وَأَبْصَارَكُمْ وَخَتَمَ عَلَى قُلُوبِكُم مِّنْ |

This verse makes it clear seal on heart means to lose the abilities of comprehension. This is the condition of those who willingly adopt the wrong path, because they prefer quick benefits to the pleasantness of future (16:106-108). Then there are those who are unwilling to hear the right thing and when they are confronted with it, they turn their heads and walk away (17:45-46). Their condition is such that they attend your sittings and it appears that they are listening to you quite attentively, but they are listening to something else (they are faking that they are listening to you), and only know how to follow their desires (47:16-17) and do not deliberate on the noble Quran (27:24). Their deeds themselves turn into rust and seal their hearts *{T}*.

These explanations clarify what "خَتَمَ اللهُ عَلَى قُلُوبِهِمْ" (*khatamul lahu ala qulubehim*) means. It means that it is not Allah who seals the hearts, but their own deeds, according to the laws of nature, become the seals.

In surah *Tatfeef* verse 83:25, the drink in *jannah* has been called "رَحِيقٍ مَخْتُومٌ" (*raheeqim makhtoom*), and it is said "خِتَامُهُ مِسْكٌ" (*khitaamohu miskun*) in 83:25, also with it is 83:26 which says that its will shall remain and shall be like musk. It is followed by "مِزَاجُهُ مِنْ تَسْنِيمٍ" (*mizajohu min tasneem*) in 83:27 which means that it will be mixed with water which is coming from great heights and shall give life the strength to reach the highest destinations.

Surah *Aaab* calls the Messenger (pbuh) as "خَاتَمَ النَّبِيِّينَ" (*khaataman nabiyyin*) in 33:40. "خَاتَمٌ" (*khatam*) has been explained earlier and as per those meanings it would mean that the Messenger is the last Messenger. To think that messenger-hood continues after him is against the Quranic teachings. Since the Quran is the last Book that has been revealed by God, the Messenger is also the last messenger. See (N-B-A) for the meaning of messenger where it has also been explained that there can be no messenger without a holy Book. Therefore, there was no celestial book after the Quran and no Messenger after Mohammed (pbuh).

The concept that with the messenger's seal others can also become messenger is to be unaware of the reality of messenger-hood. Messenger-hood was endowed on any man by God not due to any effort or expertise. Nobody could acquire it, nor could any messenger relegate it to anybody. Details will be found under heading (N-B-A). As such, any claim to messenger-hood after Mohammed (pbuh) is patently untrue.

But there is another form of the claim to messenger-hood which is very complex and as such demands careful deliberation. Messenger-hood is to acquire knowledge directly from God, that is, his own intellect or knowledge has nothing to do with it. He must get the knowledge directly from God. In *sufism*, there is a concept that *aulia Allah* (Allah's friends) or *Sufis* get direct knowledge from God, and that is called *kashf* or *ilhaam*. But the difference is of name only as manifested. *Kashf, ilhaam* and *wahi* are all the same, only the names are different, Thus, inherently this concept lays open the door to messenger-hood. According to the Quran, whatever knowledge God wished to impart, He gave to the last Messenger (pbuh). This knowledge is now safe in the Quran. Now, no human can have direct knowledge from God.

Note that *kashf* and *ilhaam* are man's own psychological tribulations, they are not from God.

Kh-D-D   خ د د

"اَلْخَدُّ" (*al-khudd*) has been used in 31:18 for the cheek. Otherwise it means a rectangular hole dug in the ground. "اَلْخَدُّ" (*al-ukhdood*) means ditch {T}.

The Quran says:

85:4	Death other people of the fire-ditches	قُتِلَ اَصْحَٰبُ الْاُخْدُودِ

Muheet relates that the king of Yemen, *Zunawaas*, asked able bodied Christian young men to give up Christianity. When they refused, he had a trench built and put them in it to burn in the fire which he had started there. *Taj-ul-Uroos* relates that *Bakht-Nasr* torched religious Jews like this. But the context of the Quran shows that it means all those opponents of Islam who were fighting against the God's Messenger, and used to keep the fires of war burning. The Quran has given the news about their destruction. Also see heading *ashaabul, ukhdood* and *tubbah*.

Kh-D-Ain خ د ع

"خَدْعٌ" (*khad'a*) means hypocrisy, to secretly connive against someone *{T}*.

Ibn Faris says its basic meaning is to hide and keep secrets.

"خَدُوْعٌ" (*khad'o*) is actually that female camel which at times gives milk profusely and at others completely dries up *{L}*. Arabs were famous hosts and used to live on desert and the milk and meat of their animals was readily available with them. Imagine the chagrin of the host who goes to milk a camel only to find out that she has dried up. Thus, a camel (she) which could not be relied on was called "خَدُوْعٌ" (*kjhad'o*).

"خَيْدَعٌ" (*khada'a*) is a mirage, and also the path which is seemingly leading to one's destination but the reality is against it *{T}*.

"خَادِعَةٌ" (*khadia*) is a small room built aside a bigger room, where the valuables of the house are kept *{T}*.

Lataaif-ul-Lugha says that "اَلْخَادِعُ" (*al-khadih*) and "اَلْخَدُوْعُ" (*al-khuduh*) means the path which sometimes becomes very clear and at other times is completely lost.

"خَدْعٌ" (*khaduh*) is that way of life in which hypocrisy is practiced or which is less than expected, or that which is not stable (not on the same condition).

"خَدَعَ الْكَرِيْمُ" (*khadal karteem*) is said when a philanthropist unexpectedly turns miserly.

"خَدَعَ الْمَطَرُ" (*khada'al matar*) means when it rains less than expected.

"سُوْقٌ خَادِعَةٌ" (*sooqun khadia*) means a market which does not stay stable.

"خَدَعَتِ الْأُمُوْرُ" (*khada'atil umoor*) means for conditions to deteriorate *{T}*.

"خَدَعَ" (*khada'ah*) also means to become less.

"اَلسِّنُوْنُ الْخَوَادِعُن" (*as-sinoonal hawadeh*) are the years when sometimes there is a good crop and sometimes drought, or which years have lots of rain but little produce.

"دِيْنَارٌ خَادِعٌ" (*deenarun khadeh*) is that *Deenar* (Arab unit of currency) which looks okay but on scrutiny is found to be counterfeit *{T}*.

"خَادِعٌ" (*khadeh*) means the person who in his emotions either flares up or withdraws within himself, or that hypocrite who appears as he is not only to gain some profit, and in this way he deceives the society. Such people cannot be trusted.

Muheet says "خَدَعَ" (*khada'a*) basically means secretive and hidden-ness which cannot be judged beforehand. This is the hallmark of opportunists or emotionalists.

The Quran has described this sort of deceptive mentality as the disease of the heart in 2:10 and said further that this is psychologically a deception with one's Self, since God's scheme of things makes them deceive themselves.

| 2:9 | But they deceive none other than themself | وَمَا يَخْدَعُوْنَ اِلَّا اَنْفُسَهُمْ وَمَا يَشْعُرُوْنَ |
| 2:10 | There is a disease in their hearts | فِىْ قُلُوْبِهِمْ مَرَضٌ |

Surah **Nisaa** describes them as:

| 4:142 | these hypocrites want to deceive Allah's laws but it so happens that they deceive only themselves | اِنَّ الْمُنٰفِقِيْنَ يُخٰدِعُوْنَ اللّٰهَ وَهُوَ خَادِ عُهُمْ |
| 9:2 | Deceiving Allah is actually self-deception | وَمَا يَخْدَعُوْنَ اِلَّا اَنْفُسَهُمْ |

But people do not understand, because they do not have awareness about it. As it is, anyone who is blinded by emotions loses his understanding power.

Kh-D-N      خ د ن

"اَلْخِدْنُ" (**al-khidn**) means companion, one to talk to, friend {**T**}.

Raghib says this is used mostly for a companion who stays with one due to sexual desire.

Words which have "خ" (**kha**) and "د" (**daal**) together contain the connotation of effectiveness {**Al-ilm-ul Khafaaq**}.

Ibn Faris says it basically means to stay with someone.

The noble Quran has said about the sexual relationship of man and woman:

| 4:25 | **Mohsanaatin** instead of **musafehatin**, and not those who take secret lovers | مُحْصَنٰتٍ غَيْرَ مُسٰفِحٰتٍ وَّلَا مُتَّخِذٰاتِ اَخْدَانٍ |

The meanings of "مُخْصَنٰتٍ" (**mohsanaatin**) and "مُسٰافِحٰاتٍ" (**musafehatin**) can be found under the heading (**H-Sd-N**) and (**S-F-H**). From there it will be clear that "سَفْحٌ" (**safhun**) means sexual relationship only for pleasure seeking, for which the Arabs used to send messages to women before Islam. That was the custom in those days.

"خِدْنٌ" (**khizn**) is secretive affairs. Both ultimately came to mean the same thing. They are mentioned separately here so that all forms of sexual relations (out of wedlock) shall be rejected, and only one form remains, which is "مُحْصِنِيْنَ" (**mohseneen**), that is, protected and in wedlock. "مُسٰافِحِيْنَ" (**musafeheen**) means only for pleasure seeking. This includes illegal fornication or to fulfill the custom of marriage without accepting any of the responsibilities of wedlock.

"مُتَّخِذَاتِ أَخْدَانٍ" (*muttakhizaati akhdaan*) would simply mean illegal fornication, although the Quran has used the words in the context of slave girls, (which the Arabs used to have in those days). See heading (M-L-K). But it is commonly applicable because as per the Quran, illegal fornication is not permitted, no matter in what form.

In other words, "سَفْحٌ" (*safhun*) would be the satisfaction of sexual desires in a way acceptable to society and "خِذْنٌ" (*khidnun*) a form which the society deems impermissible. As per the Quran, however, every form of sexual intercourse would be impermissible which is against the Quranic *Nikah* (wedlock), and its purpose, which is perpetuation of the human race, whether society feels it is permissible or impermissible.

Kh-Dh-L   خ ذ ل

"خَذَلَتِ الظَّبْيَةُ" (*khazalatiz zabeeha*): the female deer lagged behind its herd. Such a deer is called "خَاذِلٌ" (*khaazil*) or "خَذُوْلٌ" (*khuzool*). Usually such deer or cow lags behind due to its young one {T}.

"تَخَاذَلَتْ رِجْلَاهُ" (*tahazalat rijlahu*): his feet got tired and he lagged behind.

Such a man is called "رَجُلٌ خَذُوْلُ الرِّجْلِ" (*rajlun khazulur rajul*).

"الْخَذْلَانُ" (*al-khazlaan*) is used when a man who thought to be very useful, backs out.

Ibn Faris says it basically means to back out and be helpful.

Surah *Aal-e-Imraan* says:

3:159	If He leaves you without being helpful, who is left there to help you?	إِنْ يَخْذُلْكُمْ فَمَنْ ذَا الَّذِئ يَنْصُرُكُمْ مِنْ بَعْدِهِ

A nation which is left un-helped by Allah's laws (resources), as against "يَنْصُرُ" (*yansur*) in 3:159, and that nation lags behind other nations, cannot be helped by others. Such an individual or nation which lags behind others is deprived of the blessings of life (17:22). Islam means that all *Monineen* progress in union. See the word *tasalam* under heading (S-L-M). However "أَثِمَ" (*ism*) means to stay behind or lag behind due to some personal weakness. See heading (A-Th-M). But if somebody due to various temptations, children's love being the greatest attraction among them, lags behind his party, it will be called "خَذَلَ" (*khazal*), which means to lag behind the group of *momineen* due to some personal benefit or emotion or to lag behind the nations of the world because of giving up Allah's system of life. These are both called "خَذَلَ" (*khazal*).

Surah *Al-furqaan* says:

25:29	The rebellious human emotions seemingly would be with one to the last, but at the time of need, give up man's company. (such emotions are only temporary)	وَكَانَ الشَّيْطٰنُ لِلْاِنْسَانِ خَذُوْلاً

Kh-R-B   خ ر ب

"أَلْخَرَابُ" (*al-kharaab*) means desolation. It is the opposite of "عُمْرَانٌ" (*umraan*) or habitation, to be uninhabited.

"خَرِبَ" (*khariba*): to become inhabited.

"أَخْرَبَ" (*akhraba*): to make inhabited, to make desolate.

"أَلْخَرِبَةُ" (*al-kharibah*): isolated or uninhabited place.

"أَلْخَرْبَةُ" (*al-kharbah*): a sieve, impairment, impairment of ***Deen***, doubt and blame.

Ibn Faris says it means for a corner to break off and Thus, create impairment, and to be full of holes, like a knife is blunted as its corner breaks off.

Ibn Faris says "أَلْخَرِبَةُ" (*al-khariba*) means hole, and "أَلْخُرَّبَةُ" (*al-khurrabah*) means the needle's eye.

The Quran says:

59:2	they make their homes desolate with their own hands	يُخْرِبُونَ بُيُوتَهُمْ بِأَيْدِيهِم

Surah ***Al-Baqrah*** says about the mosques:

2:114	He tries for them to become desolate.	سَعَى فِى خَرَابِهَا

Hence, the desolation of mosques does not just mean that they are not visited by people to pray, but also that they avoid discussions regarding Allah's and His traits. That is why the following order is related to mosques:

42:38	Establishment of ***Salaat*** and mutual consultation go hand in hand	أَقَامُوا الصَّلوةَ وَ أَمْرُهُمْ شُورَى بَيْنَهُمْ

This means that where there is one, so is the other. At another place it is said that the ***mushrekeen*** (those who involve other laws with Allah's) cannot inhabit the mosques (9:17), because they do not obey pure or chaste divine laws.

Kh-R-J   خ ر ج

"خُرُوجٌ" (**khurooj**): to exit, or come out.

"اَلْخَرْجُ" (**al-kharj**): expenditure as against income.

"خَارِجُ كُلِّ شَيْءٍ" (**kharijo kulli shaiyin**): the part of everything that sticks out, or which is evident

"اَلْخَارِجِيُّ" (**al-kharijiyyo**): a horse which is better than its parents. It also means anything that surpasses others of its species {T}.

"خَرَجَ فُلَانٌ فِى الصِّنَاعَةِ" (**kharaja fulaan fis sana'ah**): somebody became an expert in workmanship {M}.

"نَاقَةٌ مُخْتَرِجَةٌ" (**naaqatun mukh-tarijah**): a camel which surpasses others and becomes an Alfa-camel {T}.

"يَوْمُ الْخُرُوجِ" (**yaumul khurooj**): A day of festivity when people come out all decked up.

"خَرَجَتِ الرَّعِيَّةُ عَلَى الْوَالِىْ" (**kharajatir rayiyatu alal ewaali**): when the subjects rebel against the leader and stop obeying him {M}.

The Quran, saying that God enlivens the dead land with rain, goes on to say "كَذَالِكَ الْخُرُوجُ" (**kazaalikul khurooj**) in 50:12, this way there will be '**khuruj**'. Here **khuruj** means life anew. This has been called "يَوْمُ الْخُرُوجِ" (**yaumal khurooj**) a little further on in 50:42. In the Quran, the words "قيامه" (**qiyamah**), "ساعه" (**saa'ah**), "بعث" (**bo-as**), "خروج" (**khurooj**) have special connotations, but all these have the elements of life anew. This life anew could be a nation's renaissance, or for the entire humanity to stand on its own feet, or the Life after Death of an individual. All these concepts are included in the said terms and context will determine as to what they mean at a particular place.

The words "خَرْجٌ" (**kharj**) and "خَرَاجٌ" (**kharaj**) have also been used in the Quran, as in 18:64 and 23:71. It means the sum which one takes out of his wealth and gives to others.

I have not discussed "tribute" in a jurisprudential context because the term is not mentioned as such with this word in the Quran .

Among the Arabs, "خَرَاجٌ" (**kharaj**) was the amount a slave-owner had fixed for spending towards his slave (for paying him). Later, this word came to be used for land tax. Now, every tax that the government receives from the people is called "خَرَاجٌ" (**kharaj**). In the beginning "خَرَاجٌ" (**kharaj**) used to mean the produce of the land, but later it came to mean the tax received from properties as well {T}.

"خَارِجٌ" (**kharij**): that which comes out, exits, get expelled.

"مَخْرَجٌ" (**makhraj**): the place where something gets expelled from.

"اَخْرَجَ" (**akhraj**): to take out, to give birth, to produce.

"اِخْرَاجٌ" (**ikhraaj**): to get something out, to give birth.

"مُخْرِجٌ" (**mukhrij**): the one, who gives birth, produces.

"مُخْرَجٌ" (*mukhraj*): which is born, or the place or time from which something has been extracted (17:80).

"اِسْتَخْرَجَ" (*istakhraj*): to take out.

Surah **Baqrah** uses "اِخْرَاجٌ" (*ikhraaj*) as against "كِتْمَانٌ" (*kit'aan*) in 2:72, which means to make something evident. In the same surah, it is said "فَأَخْرَجَهُمَا" (*fa akhrajhuma*) in connotation to Adam's tale: "He got the two of them out of there", and later it says "وَقُلْنَا اهْبِطُوْا" (*wa qulnah betoo*) in 2:36. It is obvious then that **khurooj** and **huboot** are different. **Khurooj** simply means to get out, while **huboot** also has a demeaning connotation. For details, see my book "*Iblees O Adam*").

Kh-R-D-L   خ ر د ل

"ٱلْخَرْدَلُ" (*al-khardil*) means mustard.

"خَرْدَلَ اللَّحَم" (*khardalal laham*): he cut the meat into many small pieces {T}.

The Quran says:

| 21:27 | equal to one mustard seed | مِثْقَالَ حَبَّةٍ مِنْ خَرْدَلٍ |

Kh-R-R   خ ر ر

"ٱلْخَرِيرُ" (*al-khareer*) is the sound of water running, or wind blowing, or the sound of an eagle's wings in flight, or the sound of snoring.

"ٱلْخَرُّ" (*al-kharr*) actually means to fall from a height and the sound of the fall. Later it started meaning every type of fall.

The Quran says:

| 7:144 | Moses fainted due to the lighting and thunder | خَرَّ مُوْسَى صَعِقاً |
| 22:31 | as if he fell from the sky | فَكَأَنَّمَا خَرَّ مِنَ السَّمَاءِ |

This is the state of a **mushrik** (one who lives according to other laws as well as Allah's).

Surah **Al-Furqaan** has enumerated various qualities of a **momin**. One of them is:

| 25:73 | when the verses of the Sustainer are recited in front of them, they don't follow them, as if they are blind or deaf | إِذَا ذُكِّرُوْا بِآيَاتِ رَبِّهِمْ لَمْ يَخِرُّوْا عَلَيْهَا صُمّاً وَ عُمْيَانًا |

Muheet says that "خَرَّ عَلَى الشَّىْءِ" (*kharra alish shaiyi*) means to stick to one thing.

From this it is obvious that the Quran cannot be result producing if it is simply adhered to emotionally without any deliberation. The quality of the *momineen* is that their acting upon the Quran is based on careful thought. Imagine how can the Quran allow non-divine things to be worshipped or accepted without deliberation, when it even does not allow its own verses to be followed blindly and without understanding?

It says that a *momin* does not follow something without properly understanding it. It orders him to:

17:36	Do not follow something which you do not understand. Verily the sight, hearing and the heart (or mind) will all be questioned about their responsibilities.	وَلاَتَقْفُ مَا لَيْسَ لَكَ بِهِ عِلْمٌ إِنَّ السَّمْعَ وَالْبَصَرَ وَالْفُؤَادَ كُلُّ أُولَئِكَ كَانَ عَنْهُ مَسْؤُولاً

For knowledge, sight and hearing (i.e. the senses) and mind are necessary, and *momin* is one who follows Allah's orders after having an understanding.

Kh-R-Sd   خ ر ص

"اَلْخَرْصُ" (*al-khars*): to estimate, to form an idea, to guess without knowing something one is uncertain of.
"خَرْصُ النَّخْلِ" (*kharsun nakhal*): to guess how much dates the tree would produce.
"كَمْ خِرْصُ أَرْضِكَ" (*kam khirsu ardika*): what is the estimated produce of your land? As such, every assumption is called "اَلْخَرْصُ" (*al-khars*), even falsehood {T}.

The Quran says:

6:117	These people follow their whims and their talk is mere assumptions	إِنْ يَتَّبِعُونَ إِلَّاالظَّنَّ وَإِنْ هُمْ إِلَّا يَخْرُصُونَ

Surah *Az-Zareyah* says:

51:10	Their assumptions shall be defeated	قُتِلَ الْخَرَّاصُونَ

Truth is based on facts and Therefore, *Deen* is based entirely on truth. No guesswork can be *Deen*. Each and every word of the Quran is safe with us. Quran's internal and external historical evidence supports this theory. Therefore, it is truly *Deen* and the criterion for truth and falsehood.

Raghib says that to say something by guessing, even if it is true, is still an act of uncertainty.

Hence, "خَرَّاصٌ" (*kharras*) means the same as "كَذَّابٌ" (*kazzab*) or liar {R}.
"خَرَصَ" (*kharasa*): he lied {M}.

The Quran claims that those who follow assumptions shall be destroyed. As such those who follow assumptions in **Deen** will never succeed. Our current condition testifies to this.

Kh-R-T-M   خ ر ت م

"اَلْخُرْطُوْم" (*al-khurtoum*): the nose, or the front part of the nose *{T}*. It also means an elephant's trunk *{M}*.

Sa'ab says that "خَطْم" (*khatm*) and "خُرْطُوْم" (*khurtoum*) is generally used for the front part of the face of wild animals.

"خَرَاطِيْمُ الْقَوْمِ" (*kharateemul qaum*) means the leaders of a nation, because they are in the forefront of the nation. This is an allegory to being eminent.

The Quran says:

68:16	We shall disfigure his nose (i.e./ We shall demean him)	سَنَسِمُهُ عَلَى الْخُرْطُوْمِ

To deface the face or nose was very demeaning *{R}*. It embodies an element of disgrace which cannot be hidden.

Kh-R-Q   خ ر ق

"اَلْخَرْقُ" (*al-khurq*) means to tear something up without following any principle. This is opposite of "اَلْخَلْقُ" (*al-khalq*) which means to do something properly and disciplined *{T}*.

"خَرَقَ الثَّوْبَ" (*kharaqas saub*): he tore up the cloth without judging.

Surah **Bani Israel** says:

17:37	You cannot just tear apart the earth	إِنَّكَ لَنْ تَخْرِقَ الْأَرْضَ

This means to tear up or drill holes. Some say that it means cutting the distance (shortening it) from one end to another *{T}*.

In surah **Qahaf** it is said "خَرَقَهَا" (*kharqeha*) with regards to making a hole in the boat (18:71).

"خَرَقَ" (*kharaq*): he lied.
"خَرَقَ الكَذِبَ" (*kharaqal kizb*): he fabricated a falsehood.
"اَلتَّخَرُّقُ" (*al-taharraq*): to create falsehood.
"اَلتَّخْرِيْقُ" (*at-takhreeq*): to lie profusely *{T}*.

Surah **Anaam** says:

| 6:100 | they believe in God's progeny which is patently untrue | وَ خَرَقُواْ لَهُ بَنِينَ |

Their concept is against all factors, belief etc. It shatters the truth.

Kh-Z-N   خ ز ن

"اَلْخَزْنُ" (*al-khazn*) basically means to hoard something {*T, R*}.
"اَلْخِزَانَةُ" (*al-khazaanatu*), "الْخَزِيْنَةُ" (*al-khazeenatu*), "الْمَخْزَنَ" (*al-mazkan*) means storehouse, or the place where something is hoarded {*T, R*}.
"اَلْخَزِيْنَةُ" (*al-khazeenah*): something which is safely hidden. The plural is "خَزَائِنُ" (*khazayin*).

The Quran says:

| 6:50 | I do not claim to have the treasures of Allah | لَا أَقُوْلُ لَكُمْ عِنْدِئْ خَزَائِنُ اللهِ |

"خَازِنٌ" (*khaazin*): someone who collects, or guard or protector.
The plural is "خَازِنُوْنَ" (*khazenoon*) or "خَزَنَةٌ" (*khazanah*).

The Quran says:

| 39:72 | The guards will tell them | وَقَالَ لَهُمْ خَزَنَتُهَا |

Ibn Faris says the word means to safe-keep something.

"خَزَائِنُ اللهِ" (*kayinullah*) are those forces and treasures of the universe that have not yet come within man's knowledge.

Kh-Z-Y   خ ز ی

"خِزْیٌ" (*khizyun*) means such ignominy which puts one to shame. That is why this word is used to mean both demeaning and shame. As such, it would mean shameful and demeaning, or to disclose such faults that are shameful to disclose {*T*}.

In the Quran, the result of living against the laws of Allah has been related as:

| 2:85 | shameful ignominy in this world | خِزْیٌ فِی الْحَیٰوةِ الدُّنْیَا |

Surah **Taha** says "نَذِلَّ" (*nazilla*) and "نَخْزَیٰ" (*nakhza*) in 20:134. These two words have appeared together here and they mean shame and chagrin. In surah **Hijr**, this word has come with "تَفْضَحُوْنِ" (*tafzahoon*), in 15:69, which means shame and disgrace.

"مُخْزِى الْكَافِرِيْنَ" (*mukhzi al-kaafireen*): one who imparts shameful disgrace to the *kafirs* (deniers), as said in 9:2. A life of honor and dignity is **momin's** way of life. Ignominy and disgrace is Allah's punishment. As such, the nation which faces these in the world cannot be a party or group of **Momineen**.

Ibn Faris says that this word basically means to distance, that is, a nation which is distanced from life's happiness, which is the worst type of disgrace.

If it is to be determined whether a nation is living according to the laws of Allah, then it should be seen whether that nation is living a life of honor, success and power, or is disgraced in comparison to other nations of the world. If this nation is not living honorably in comparison to other nations of the world, then it is not following Allah's laws. The following should be well understood in this context. A nation which follows the laws of the universe but its cultural life is subject to its own laws, then although it does attain immediate benefits (that is, in this life) but its future is dark. The Western nations fall into this category.

A nation, which follows the laws of this universe as well as the laws of Allah, lives a successful life in this world and has a bright future as well. This is the particularity of the party of **Momineen,** but a nation which neither follows the laws of this universe nor follows the laws of Allah in its cultural life, faces ignominy in this world as well as the Hereafter. We (the Pakistanis) fall into this category.

2:85	ignominy in this world and disgrace on the Day of the Judgment	خِزْیٌ فِى الْحَیٰوةِ الدُّنْیَا وَیَوْمَ الْقِیٰمَةِ یُرَدُّوْنَ اِلٰى اَشَّدِ الْعَذَابِ

Kh-S-A   خ س ء

"اِلْخَسِیْیُ" (*il-khasi*): useless and waste wool which is thrown away. Thus, this word acquires the connotation of degradation and hatred.
"خَسَاَالْکَلْبَ" (*khasa'al kalba*): he shooed the dog away.
"خَسَاَالْکَلْبُ" (*khasa'al kalbo*): the dog became homeless.
"اَلْخَاسِیُء" (*al-khaasi-o*): the one who is shunned.

Ibn Faris says it basically means to distance, to remove.

The noble Quran has said "قِرَدَةً خَاسِئِیْنَ" (*qirdatan khaseyeen*) in 2:65, meaning "disgraced monkeys".
See heading (**Q-R-D).**

"خَسَاَالْبَصَرُ" (*khasa'al basaro*): the eye was surprised and tired (due to wonderment) {*T, M*}.

The Quran says:

| 67:4 | sight will become homeless and return to the eye | يَنْقَلِبْ اِلَيْكَ الْبَصَرُ خَاسِئاً |
| 23:109 | live here with ignominy and disgrace | اخْسَئُوا فِيْها |

It also means to be away from life's happiness and be deprived.

Kh-S-R   خ س ر

"خَسَرَ فُلَانٌ" (*khasera fulaan*) means that man was lost on the way, was killed *{T}*.
"الْخَسْرُ" (*al-khasru*), "الْخُسْرَانُ" (*al-khusraan*) means to make less, lessen, to fail.
"خَسَرَ الْوَزْنَ" (*khasaral wazna*), "الْكَيْلَ وَأَخْسَرَ" (*alkaila wa akhsar*): he measured less.

Some dictionary scholars say that "الْخَاسِرُ" (*al-khasir*) is a man who when giving measures gives less and while taking takes more than the measure *{T}*.

The Quran says:

| 26:181 | measure to the full and do not be among those who give less | اَوْفُوا الْكَيْلَ وَلَا تَكُوْنُوْا مِنَ الْمُخْسِرِيْنَ |
| 83:2-3 | when taking they measure fully and while giving they lessen the measure | اِذَا اكْتَالُوْا عَلَى النَّاسِ يَسْتَوْفُوْنَ وَاِذَا كَالُوْهُمْ اَوْوَّزَنُوْهُمْ يُخْسِرُوْنَ |

This last verse relates a very big economic principle. Details will be found in heading (*B-Y-Ain*).

Surah *Ar-Rahman* says:

| 55:9 | Keep the measure full according to fairness and do not measure less: also do not spoil the balance of society. | وَاَقِيْمُوا الْوَزْنَ بِالْقِسْطِ وَلَا تُخْسِرُوا الْمِيْزَانَ |

"صَفْقَةٌ خَاسِرَةٌ" (*safqatun khaserah*): unprofitable trade which incurs loss *{T}*.
"الْخَيْسَرَى" (*al-khaisarah*): deception, reneging, meanness, lops.
"خَسَّرَهُ تَخْسِيْرًا" (*khassarahu takhseera*): killed him *{T}*.
"الْخَاسِرُ" (*al-khaasir*): someone who goes missing on the way, one who gets killed, or cannot succeed *{T}*.
It also means one who suffers loss in trade.
"خُسْرٌ" (*khusr*): loss; destruction.

Raghib says that "خُسْرٌ" (*khusr*) includes both loss of material things and loss of non-material or figurative things. That is, loss of wealth as well as loss of intellect or trust, health and honor.

Ibn ul-Aarabi has said that "ٱلْخَاسِرُ" (*al-khaasir*): a man who has lost both his intellect and wealth *{T}*.

| 103:2 | (If) humanity (is left without Revelation) would be in loss. | إِنَّ الْإِنْسَانَ لَفِى خُسْرٍ |

This above mentioned loss includes all kinds.
"خَسَارٌ" (*khasaar*): annihilation, loss, one who suffers loss.
"أَخْسَرُ" (*akhsar*): someone who loses the most.
"تَخْسِيرٌ" (*takhseer*): to give loss, to shun from the good things.

Ibn Faris has said that the root basically means loss and to decrease.

Kh-S-F   خ س ف

"خَسَفَ الْمَكَانُ" (*khasafal makaan*), "يَخْسِفُ" (*yakhsefu*), "خُسُوفًا" (*khusufa*): that ground caved in *{T, M}*.

Ibn Faris says it means to go deep and hide, to cave in.

The Quran says:

| 28:81 | We buried him (*Qaroon*) and his house (destroyed him) | فَخَسَفْنَا بِهِ وَبِدَارِهِ الْأَرْضَ |

"خَسَفٌ" (*khasaf*) also means to tie up an animal without food and water. This led to its meaning of being oppressive to someone. Later this word also came to mean disgrace, insult, and to be oppressive.
"ٱلْخَاسِفُ" (*al-khaasf*): weak
"بَاتَ الْقَوْمُ عَلَى الْخَسْفِ" (*batal qaumu alal khasf*): the people spent the night hungry.
"سَامَهُ خَسْفًا" (*saamahu khasfa*): he insulted and disgraced him.
"ٱلْخَسِيفُ" (*al-khaseef*): caved-in (adjective).
"أَخْسَفَتِ الْعَيْنَ" (*akhsafatil ain*): the eye went blind *{T, R}*.

The Quran says

| 16:25 | Allah will bury them in the ground (destroy them) | يَخْسِفُ اللَّهُ بِهِمُ الْأَرْضَ |

"خُسُوفٌ" (*khusoof*): lunar eclipse *{T, R}*.
"بِئْرٌ مَخْسُوفَةٌ" (*berun makhsufah*): well whose water disappears *{R}*.

The Quran says about the revolution brought about by Messenger *Mohammed*:

| 78:8 | the moon was eclipsed, it waned (literal meaning) | خَسَفَ الْقَمَرُ |

The above verse figuratively means that the Arabs of dark ages (who had the moon ass their insignia) would weaken. They will become weak, their opposition and rebelliousness would end.

Kh-Sh-B   خ ش ب

"خَشَبٌ" (*khjashab*): thick wood. Plural is "خُشُبٌ" (*khushub*). The Quran has compared the hypocrites (*munafeqeen*) to "خُشُبٌ مُسَنَّدَةٌ" (*khushubun musannadah*) in 63:4. That is, such wood which have been standing with support of a wall.

Muheet says that "خَشَبَةٌ خَشْباء" (*khashabatun khashbah*) is a wood which has been eaten on the inside by termites.

This means that is something which only appear to be strong but is in fact eaten up inside. *Munafiqeen* has been called so, because neither do they have intellect or the power to deliberate, nor the freshness of life. Neither is their heart in right place, nor the mind. Hence, it means something useless, despite a fake appearance.

"خَشَبَ الشِّعْرَ" (*khashabash she'r*) means when somebody recites a verse without making it presentable.
"فَحْلٌ خَشِيْبٌ" (*fahlun khasheeb*) is an untrained camel.
"جَبْهَةٌ خَشْباءُ" (*jabhatun khashba-oo*): uneven forehead.

Ibn Faris says that it means to be hard and uncouth or rough.

"اَلْأَخْشَبُ" (*al-akhshab*) means a hard, rocky mountain, also a fresh sword which is not yet smooth and shiny due to being new and unused. These meanings make it clear as why the Quran has called the hypocrites "خُشُبٌ" (*khushub*).

Kh-Sh-Ain   خ ش ع

"خَشَعَ" (*khasha*) means the lowering of the eyes or voice.

20:108	voices will be lowered	خَشَعَتِ الْأَصْوَاتُ
68:43	their eye will be lowered	خَاشِعَةً أَبْصَارُهُمْ
68:43	disgrace will overtake them	تَرْهَقُهُمْ ذِلَّةٌ

This makes the meaning of "خَشَعَ" (*khasha*) clear, that it means the lowering of eyes and voice due to shame and disgrace.

"خَشَعَتِ الْأَرْضُ" (*hasha'til ard*): the land dried up and there was no rain.

"خُشُوعُ الْكَوْكَبِ" (*khushu-ul kaukab*): for the star to lower at time of setting.

"خَشَعَتِ الشَّمْسُ" (*ksha'atish shams*): the sun was in eclipse.

"اخْتَشَعَ" (*ikhtasha'a*): to drop the head and lower the eyes *{T}*.

"الْخُشَةُ" (*al-khushah*): hard rocky plot of land which does not grow any vegetation.

"الْخَاشِعُ" (*al-khashih*): dusty place where camping is not possible.

The Quran uses the word "خَاشِعَةً" (*khaashiah*) in 41:39 for dead land.

In surah *Ghashia*, the word "خَاشِعَةٌ" (*khaashiah*) has been used opposite to "نَاعِمَةٌ" (*naaimah*). Since "نَاعِمَةٌ" (*naaimah*) means green and blooming, "خَاشِعَةٌ" (*khaashiah*) would mean withered.

The Quran has after this said "عَامِلَةٌ نَاصِبَةٌ" (*aamilatun naasebah*) in 88:3, that is, emaciated, depressed.

"خَاشِعِيْنَ" (*khaashe-een*) has also been used for those who bow before Allah's laws.

The Quran says the following to elaborate what it means by *khaashe-een*:

| 2:46 | those who believe that one day they will have to meet their Sustainer, that is, they believe that they are answerable to the laws of Allah for their deeds, and Thus, they refer to His laws for every matter | الَّذِيْنَ يَظُنُّوْنَ اَنَّهُمْ مُلٰقُوْا رَبِّهِمْ وَاَنَّهُمْ اِلَيْهِ رَاجِعُوْنَ |

This is what "خُشُوْعٌ" (*khushuh*) means. To bow before Allah's laws with a willing heart.

Ibn Faris says "خَشَعَ" (*khashah*) means to bow one's head.

<h2 style="text-align:center">Kh-Sh-Y   خ ش ی</h2>

"الْخِشِيُّ" (*al-khashi*): dry plant.

"الْخَشَاءُ" (*al-khasha'a*): rocky land which does not grow anything *{T}*. Among the Arabs, the drying up of plants due to lack of water was very dangerous. Therefore, "خَشْيَةٌ" (*khashiyah*) came to mean the fear of some loss *{T}*.

Muheet says, with reference to ***Kulliyaat***, that "الْخَشَاءُ" (*khashiyah*) is more intense than fear, because it has been derived from the Arab saying "شَجَرَةٌ خَاشِيَةٌ" (*shajaratah khaashiyah*), that is, a completely dry tree which has no sign of life left. As against it, fear only means fear of some loss, because it is derived from "نَاقَةٌ خَوْفَاءُ" (*naaqatah khaufa*) which means a sick female camel who has not died. That is, there is still hope for its survival.

"الْخَشَاءُ" (*khashiyah*) also has the connotations of hope, doubt, and expectations.

As "خَشِيْتُ اَنْ يَكُوْنَ ذَالِكَ اَسْهَلَ لَکَ" (*khashiyatu un yakun zaalika ashal lak*): I had the hope or expected that it will be easier for you. Likewise, it also contains the connotation of knowledge, as used in 20:94.

"خَوْفٌ" (*khauf*) also means "to know". See heading (**Kh-W-F**).

When it is taken to mean fear, it means fear that is born out of awe *{T, R, F}*.

"خَشِيَّةٌ" (*khashiyah*), therefore, means fear of the outcome of some deed (18:80), or to dislike it.

"خَشِيَةِ اللهِ" (*khashiyatillah*) usually means fear of Allah but the right meaning of this fear can be understood from the meaning of "خَشِيَّةٌ" (*khashiyah*).

The Quran says that if Man follows Allah's laws, his fields become green or he flourishes. "هُمُ الْمُفْلِحُوْنَ" (*humul muflehoon*) as in 2:5 means that his efforts become a strong tree which has its roots in the ground and branches in the sky and it bears fruit in every season (14:24). On the contrary, if life is against the laws of Allah, then the field of his efforts dries up. The feeling that if we do not live according to Allah's laws, then our efforts will come to nothing (the fields of our efforts will dry up), is called "خَشِيَةُاللهِ" (*khashiyatillah*) or fear of Allah. For more details, see heading (**Kh-W-F**).

Surah *At-Taubah* says:

9:13	You fear as to what will happen if they oppose you whereas you should fear what will happen if you oppose Allah's laws?	اَتَخْشَوْنَهُمْ فَا اللهُ اَحَقُّ اَنْ تَخْشَوْهُ

The fear of results is the right meaning of "اَلْخَشَاءُ" (*khashiah*).

Further ahead the surah says:

9:24	the trade whose loss you fear	وَتِجَارَةٌ تَخْشَوْنَ كَسَادَهَا

Kh-Sd-Sd   خ ص ص

"اَلْخَصَاصُ" (*al-khasaas*) means a break or gap which may appear between two things. It also means a hole, since a break makes a thing weak.

"خَصَاصَةٌ" (*khasasah*) came to mean constriction, starvation, bad condition, need (59:6). When the vine grapes are picked, some grapes remain here or there, they are called "اَلْخُصَاصَةُ" (*al-khusasah*) *{T}*.

Ibn Faris has said that this root's basic meaning contains weakness and space. Hence, "اَلْخَصَاصَةُ" (*al-khasah*) means deprivation and weakness in condition.

When there is gap between two things, they are separated, and Hence, "خُصُوْصٌ" (*khusoos*) means to separate someone from the others and to treat him especially. As such "خَاص" (*khaas*) is the opposite of "عام" (*aam*) i.e. particular against common.

"خَصَّهُ" (*khassahu*), "اَخْتَصَّهُ" (*akhtassahu*) means separated him from the others and treated him specially. That is, such treatment in which others were not included, as it has been used in 8:25 *{T}*.

"خَصَّ الشَّىْءُ" (*khassun shaiyi*): something that did not become common.

"خَصَّ الرَّجُلَ خَصَاصَةً" (*khassarrajola khasasah*): he became needy and dependent on others *{M}*.

Surah **Baqrah** says:

| 2:105 | Allah selects whom he wants for his benevolence | وَاللّٰهُ يَخْتَصُّ بِرَحْمَتِهِ مَنْ يَشَاءُ |

Here **rahmat** (benevolence) means the Revelation. This means that God selects one from the common people and grants him the Revelation, which is God-given and Therefore, no amount of effort can achieve it. This is only bestowed as per God's own program; or rather it used to be bestowed, because Revelation is not going to be bestowed on anyone now.

Kh-Sd-F   خ ص ف

"اَلْخَصْفُ" (*al-khasf*): shoe or footwear which has equal sized leather pieces, one upon the other (the old kind of shoes). Every leather piece is called "خَصْفَةٌ" (*khasfah*).

"خَصَفَ النَّعْلَ يَخْصِفُهَا" (*khasafan na'ala yakhsefuha*): sewed two leather pieces by putting them on top of one another.

"خَصْفٌ" (*khasfu*): to join, to collect, to mend, or sew.

"خَصَفَ الْعُرْيَانُ الْوَرَقَ عَلَى بَدَنِهِ" (*khasafal uryaanul waraqa ala badinehi*): the naked man put the leaves on his body and put one over the other to cover his body *{T}*. In other words, he placed them one over another to hide their bodies *{T}*.

In the tale about Adam, the Quran says:

| 7.22 | they began covering themselves by putting the leaves from the garden one over another: | وَطَفِقَا يَخْصِفَانِ عَلَيْهِمَا مِنْ وَرَقِ الْجَنَّةِ |

This is a reference to the awareness about sex (organs) that is awareness about shame or shyness. Details about this matter can be found in my book "**Adam O Iblees**"

"اَلتَّخْصِيفُ" (*at-takhseef*): to try hard for acquiring something which you haven't got.

Ibn Faris says it basically means for one thing to merge with another.

Kh-Sd-M   خ ص م

"اَلْخُصُوْمَةٌ" (*al-khusuma*): quarrel.

"اَلْخَصْمُ" (*al-khasm*): one who quarrels (it is plural as well as feminine).

"اَلْخَصِيْمُ" (*al-khaseem*): the one who quarrels.

"اَلْخُصْمُ" (*al-khusm*): the corner or edge of something.

"اَلْخُصُوْمُ" (*al-khusum*): the mouth of the valleys {*T, M, R*}.

The Quran says:

2:204	highly quarrelsome	اَلَدُّ الْخِصَامِ
22:19	these are two parties that quarrel with each other	هٰذانِ خَصْمانِ

Surah *An-Nahal* says about Man:

16:4	if he is allowed to be without the light of the revelation, then he will be found to be openly quarrelsome	هُوَ خَصِيْمٌ مُبِيْنٌ

Also see heading (*J-D-L*).

Surah *Az-Zakhraf* says:

43:58-59	these people say these things only to quarrel with you; verily they are quarrelsome	مَاضَرَ بُوْهُ لَكَ اِلَّا جَدَ لاً - بَلْ هُمْ قَوْمٌ خَصِمُوْنَ

Surah *Aal-e-Imraan* says about the Jewish worshippers:

3:43	you were not there when they were quarrelling	وَمَاكُنْتَ لَدَيْهِمْ اِذْيَخْتَصِمُوْنَ

Kh-Zd-Zd   خ ض ض

"خَضْدٌ" (*khazd*): to bend or break a damp or dry thing in such a way as to break it, but not to break it off. Sometimes it also means to cut.

"خَضَدَ الشَّجَرَ" (*khazadash shajar*): he broke the needles of the tree (and in this way eliminated the harmful element).

"اِنْخَضَدَتِ الثَّمَارُ" (*inkhazadatis simaar*): the fruits dwindled and because the juice had gone out of them, did not remain fresh.

"رَجُلٌ مَخْضُوْدٌ" (*rajulun makhzood*): the man who has no more argument or who becomes disabled {*T*}.

"اِخْتَضَدَ الْبَعِيْرَ" (*ikhtazadil bayeer*): to control the camel, he resigned it and got up on his back {*M*}.

The Quran says about the dwellers of *jannah*:

56:28	Within there shall be *makhzood* plum trees	فِيْ سِدْرٍ مَّخْضُوْدٍ

It means such plum trees, the branches of which seem to be breaking under the weight of the fruit, or if this is taken allegorically, such luxuries which have been freed from all impurities. See heading (S-D-R). Then it would mean immense surprise but with no trace of doubt or any sort of trouble in it (53:14).

Kh-Zd-R   خ ض ر

"اَلْخُضْرَةُ" (*al-khuzrah*): green color. Plural is "خُضَرٌ" (*khuzarun*) and "خُضْرٌ" (*khusur*).

The Quran says:

76:21	green silken clothes	ثِيَابُ سُنْدُسٍ خُضْرٌ

Here "خُضْرٌ" (*khuzr*) is the plural of "أَخْضَر" (*akhzar*).
"اَلْخَضِرُ" (*al-khaziru*): greenery (6:100), green field.
"اَلْخَضَرُ" (*al-khazar*): to be fine and silken.
"اَلْخَضْرَاءُ" (*al-khazra'a*): goodness, broadness, benevolence, greenery and flourishing {T}. Since green when dark becomes blackish. Therefore, the Arabs also interchanged "أَسْوَدَ" (*aswad*) or black as "أَخْضَرُ" (*akhzar*) or green {R}.

Ibn Faris goes so far as to say that with the Arabs, any color which is different than white has the traces of black in it.

"مُخْضَرَّةٌ" (*mukhzarrah*) as used in 22:63 means that which is green.
"اَلْخِضْرُ" (*al-khizru*), "اَلْخَضِرُ" (*al-khaziru*): the mythical **Khizr** with his eternal life who is famous as the messenger of water and who will stay alive till Doomsday, but this is only a myth as the Quran has no mention of such a being.

Kh-Zd-Ain   خ ض ع

"اَلْخُضُوْعُ" (*al-khuzu*) means to bow down.
"خَضَعَ النَّجْمُ" (*khaza'in najam*): the star leaned to set.
"اَلْأَخْضَعُ" (*al-akhza*): the man who has lowliness and bending in his neck, who has become helpless.
"خَضَعَهُ الْكِبَرُ" (*khaza-ahul kabeer*): old age bent him.
"اَلْخَضِيْعَةُ" (*al-khazee-ah*): the (soft) sounds of the flood.
"أَخْضَعَ الرَّجُلُ" (*akhza-arrajul*): the man made his voice soft.
"اَلْخُضَعَةُ" (*al-khuz'ah*): a man who is humble and pleading before everyone.
"خَضَعَ" (*khazah*): he became motionless and obedient {T, R}.

Kh-Te-Ain   ا ط خ

"اَلْخَطْءُ" (*al-kha*), "اَلْخَطَأُ" (*al-khata*), "اَلْخَطَاءُ" (*al-khatao*): wrong, not correct, to miss {T, L}. "اَلْخَطَأُ" (*al-khata*) is the mistake that is made unwittingly and "اَلْخَطِئَةُ" (*al-khteeah*) is a wrong committed willfully.

But *Muheet's* composer writer that "اَلْخَطِيئَةُ" (*al-khateeah*) could also be unintentionally and unwittingly, but "اِثْمٌ" (*ism*) is always willful or deliberate.

The plural for "خَطِيئَةٌ" (*khateeah*) is "خَطَابَا" (*khataba*) and "خَطِيئَاتٌ" (*khateeaah*) actually means a deed which does not produce its full result.
"عَلَى النَّخْلِ خَطِيئَةٌ مِنْ رُطَبٍ" (*al-unnakhli khateeah min rutab*) means there are a few dates on the date palm {T}.

The Quran says:

| 6:81 | whosoever commits uneven (bad) deeds, is encircled by his own errors | بَلَى مَنْ كَسَبَ سَيِّئَةً وَ اَحَاطَتْ بِهِ خَطِيئَتُهُ |

This shows that "سَيِّئَاتٌ" (*sayyiaat*) means to be surrounded by errors, that is, after this, a man starts missing his targets. He cannot understand anything rightly. His date palms do not bear full fruit.

In verse 2:286, forgetfulness and error have been mentioned separately:

| 2:286 | if we forget or make a mistake, then do not hold us to it | لَاتُوَاخِذْنَا اِنْ نَسِيْنَا اَوْاَخْطَأْنَا |

But another verse says:

| 33:5 | You will not be held responsible if you err (unwittingly), it is a sin if you do it deliberately | لَيْسَ عَلَيْكُمْ جُنَاحٌ فِيْمَا اَخْطَأْتُمْ بِهِ وَلِكِنْ مَا تَعَمَّدَتْ قُلُوْبُكُمْ |

It is evident from this that "خَطَأً" (*khata*) is an error which is not committed with intent. These were the sort of errors that Ibrahim hoped God would keep him away from:

| 26:82 | the personae which I hope will keep me safe from my errors at the time of the Day of the Results | وَالَّذِىْ اَطْمَعُ اَنْ يَغْفِرَلِىْ خَطِيئَتِىْ يَوْمَ الدِّيْنِ |

Surah *Al-Haaqqa* uses the word "خَاطِئُوْنَ" (*khatey-oon*) for *jahannam* in 69:37, and "خَاطِئَةٌ" (*khate-atah*) for oppression and excesses as well in 69:9.

Surah *Al-Alaq* says:

| 96:16 | False, erring forehead | نَاصِيَةٍ كَاذِبَةٍ خَاطِئَةٍ |

At these places "خَطَأ" (*khata*) means a crime or sin which has intent and deliberation, likewise in surah Bani Israel it is said about the murder of one's children:

| 17:31 | their murder is verily a big crime | اِنَّ قَتْلَهُمْ كَانَ خِطْأً كَبِيْراً |

The above explanations make clear that "خَطَأ" (*khata*) is also used for an unintentional mistake or error, and also for those which are deliberate. It is that error which is deliberate will be a crime or sin and answerable for. The scholars of dictionary have said that "خَطِيَ" (*khatee*) means to make a deliberate error, and "أَخْطَأ" (*akhtaa*) to make the error unintentionally.

Kh-Te-B خ ط ب

"الْخَطْبُ" (*al-khatb*): to talk, some issue, condition, matter, whether big or small.
"جَلَّ الْخَطْبُ" (*jallal khatb*): the matter blew up {T}.

The Quran says:

| 12:51 | (the king asked) what was their matter (problem): | قَالَ مَا خَطْبُكُنَّ |
| 15:57 | He said, O messengers, what is your issue? | قَالَ مَا خَطْبُكُمْ أَيُّهَا الْمُرْسَلُوْنَ |

It certainly holds the importance of the issue:

"خَطَبَ الْمَرْأَةَ خَطْبًا وَ خِطْبَةً" (*khatabal mar-atah khatba wa khitbah*): sent a wedding proposal to a woman {T}.
"خِطْبَةً" (*khitbah*): wedding proposal (2:235).
"خَطِيْبَةً" (*khateebah*): fiancée (female) {T}.
"الْخِطَابُ" (*al-khitaab*): to talk to one another, or to address to someone {M}.
"فَصْلُ الْخِطَابِ" (*fasalul khitaab*): direct talk, or to decide forthrightly. See heading (F-Sd-L).
"خَاطَبَهُ" (*khaatibah*): talked to him
"خَاطَبَهُ" (*khatabah*): to talk or deal with.

| 25:63 | when illiterate (uncouth) or unknowing people talk to them or deal with them they say 'salam' | اِذَا خَاطَبَهُمُ الْجَاهِلُوْنَ قَالُوْا سَلَمًا |

That means that they said things in which they remain safe and sound from sinning or saying something hurtful (lest they say something harsh and sinful).

Ibn Faris has said that it basically means dialogue between two persons, and for two different colors to be present.

Kh-Te-Te   خ ط ط

"اَلْخَطُّ" (*al-khatt*): a lone line in something: a narrow, unclear path in soft ground.

Ibn Faris says it basically means a long mark. It also means any path.

"اَلْخِطُّ" (*al-khitt*) the land around which it has rained but not on it: the ground where no one has landed before you.

"اَلْخِطَّةُ" (*al-khittah*): the plot of land that one marks as his own for building.

"خَطَّ" (*khatt*), "يَخُطُّ" (*yakhutt*), "خَطَّاً" (*khatta*) means to write, to scribe.

"كِتَابٌ مَخْطُوْطٌ" (*kitabun makhtoot*): written book {T, R}.

Surah *Ankaboot* says about the Messenger (pbuh):

69:48	neither could you read any book before now, nor could you write with your right hand	وَمَاكُنْتَ تَتْلُوْمِنْ قَبْلِهِ مِنْ كِتٰبٍ وَّلَا تَخُطُّهُ بِيَمِيْنِكَ

This shows clearly that before the advent of the noble Quran the Messenger (pbuh) could not read or write, but later this changed. He had later learnt to read and write. Therefore, the belief that he was an illiterate all his life is not correct according to the Quran.

Kh-Te-F   خ ط ف

"خَطْفٌ" (*khatf*): to snatch or grab something quickly.

"خَاطِفُ ظِلِّهٖ" (*khaatifu zillehi*): a bird which swoops down in water upon seeing its shadow, to snatch it. {T}

"خُطَّافٌ" (*khuttaaf*): a black colored bird which swoops down in its flight {T}.

"اَلْخَاطِفُ" (*al-khaatif*): the arrow which drags along the ground and hits the target, as if it is snatching something from the ground. Hence, the following meaning:

"اَلْخَطِيْفَةُ" (*al-khateefah*): a girl who runs away with someone {T}.

The Quran says:

2:20	The lightning nearly snatches their eyesight. (It nearly blinds them).	يَكَادُ الْبَرْقُ يَخْطَفُ اَبْصَارَهُمْ
22:31	the bird flew away with it	فَتَخْطَفُهُ الطَّيْرُ
37:10	excepting if somebody snatches some bit of conversation or information:	اِلَّا مَنْ خَطِفَ الْخَطْفَةَ
29:67	We made the place where Haram is, a place of peace although people from around it are snatched away	جَعَلْنَا حَرَمًا اٰمِنًا وَيُتَخَطَّفُ النَّاسُ مِنْ حَوْلِهِمْ

"خَطِفَ الْخَطْفَةَ" (*khatefal khatfatah*) has been used in 37:10 and "اِسْتَرَقَ السَّمْعَ" (*istaraqas sama'a*) is from 15:18. The meaning is to snatch some bits of unimportant conversation or information and to eavesdrop a little. See heading (*S-R-Q*).

This is about those astrologers who claimed to know about the unknown, and still do in places where the light of Islam has not reached. The Quran says they simply employ guesswork. If something is by chance proven right, then they highlight it. Whichever is proven wrong, they find reasons for it. Besides this, they have no access to the unknown.

37:8	They may not listen.	لَا يَسَّمَّعُونَ
26:212	Indeed they have lost their ability to listen	إِنَّهُمْ عَنِ السَّمْعِ لَمَعْزُولُونَ

After the revelation of the Quran was the dawn of the era of knowledge and vision. These concepts get fiery whiplashes from God's kingdom. More details will be found in the relevant headings.

Kh-Te-W   خ ط و

"اَلْخُطْوَةُ" (*al-khutwah*) and "اَلْخَطْوَةُ" (*al-katwah*) means distance between one foot and another in a step, in other words, a pace. Plural is "خُطاً" (*khutan*) or "خُطُوَاتٌ" (*khutuwaat*). Then it came to be used for a step, or for the road or path. "خُطُوَاتِ الشَّيْطٰنِ" (*khutuwaatish shaitaan*) as used in 2:168 is the path of rebellious forces or the path of desires *{T}*. "خَطَا الرَّجُلُ يَخْطُو" (*khatar rujulu yakhtoo*): the man took a step forward.
"تَخَطَّيْتُهُ" (*takhatiyyatuh*): I stepped over him to get ahead *{T}*.

Ibn Faris says that "خَطُوٌّ" (*khatwun*) basically means to go ahead of something, to surpass.

Kh-F-T   خ ف ت

"خَفَتَ الصَّوْتُ" (*hafatas saut*): to be weak voiced due to hunger or to be voiceless.
"خَفَتَ فُلاَنٌ" (*khafata fulan*): that man died because his voice was cut off and he became soundless and motionless.
"اَلْخَفْتُ" (*al-khaft*): to talk secretively. It is the opposite of "جَهْرٌ" (*jahr*). See 17:110.

Surah *Taha* says:

20:103	have secretive conversation mutually	يَتَخَافَتُونَ بَيْنَهُمْ

Ibn Faris says that it basically means to hide and keep hidden.

Kh-F-Zd   خ ف ض

"اَلْخَفْضُ" (*al-khafz*): is the opposite of "رَفْعٌ" (*raf-un*) which means to lift or make lofty. Hence, this word means to make lower, to demean.

"خَفَّضَ رَأْسَ الْبَعِيْرِ" (*khaffaz raasil bayir*): he lowered the neck of the camel downwards to get on its back.

"اَلْخَافِضَةُ" (*al-khaafizah*): low dune.

"اَلْخَفْضُ" (*al-khafz*): slow speed.

"خَفَضَتِ الْإِبِلُ" (*khafzatil ibl*): the camel slowed its speed. This led to the word meaning hospitality, calm.

"عَيْشٌ خَافِضٌ" (*aishun khaafiz*): a carefree and calm life.

"خَفْضُ الْعَيْشِ" (*khafz-ul-aish*): a life of abundance and care-freeness {*T, R*}.

The root basically contains connotation of getting sustenance without any difficulty or effort.

The Quran says:

| 15:88 | lower your arm for those who are *momin* (take them under your wing) | وَاخْفِضْ جَنَاحَكَ لِلْمُؤْمِنِيْنَ |

"خَفَضَ الطَّائِرُ جَنَاحَهُ" (*khafazut taa-iro janaha*): when a bird closes its wings to check its flight {*T, R*}. From the above meaning it could also mean that you curtail your speed so that those in your group, who are not as fast, may keep up with you. A leader has to keep the capability of his group in mind.

Surah *Al-Waaqiha* says:

| 56:3 | that system will demean the rebels and give new heights to those who follow Allah's laws | خَافِضَةٌ رَافِعَةٌ |

Here "خَفْضٌ" (*khafz*) is the opposite of "رَفْعٌ" (*raf-ah*). This means that those who are now exalted will be lowered, and those who are lower will be held aloft or that they will be reversed (11:82)

Kh-F-F   خ ف ف

"اَلْخِفُّ" (al-kiffu), "اَلْخَفِيْفُ" (al-khafeefu): light (as against heavy).
"اَلْخُفَافُ" (al-khufaaf): light weight.

Some differentiate between "خُفَافٌ" (khufaaf) and "خَفِيْفٌ" (khafeef) by saying that "خُفَافٌ" (khufaaf) is without weight in intellect and thought; and "خَفِيْفٌ" (khafeef) is to be light in body: the plural is "خَفِيْفٌ" (khufaaf) as in 9:41.

Raghib says "خَفِيْفٌ" (khafeef) is sometimes a trait to be praised and sometimes to be condemned. This means that which is praiseworthy is "خَفِيْفٌ" (khafeef), and which is heavy is "ثَقِيْلٌ" (saqeel). Surface oriented and light is called "خَفِيْفٌ" (khafeef), and heavy and weighty is called "ثَقِيْلٌ" (saqeel).

"اِسْتَخَفَّ فُلَانٌ بِحَقِّیْ" (istakhafun fulanun bihaqqi): he did not respect my right and though it was weightless.
"تَخْفِيْفٌ" (takhfeef): to make less, or reduce.
"اَلْخُفُّ" (al-khuff): the leg of a camel or an ostrich: also a leather sock.

"خَفَّ الْقَوْمُ عَنْ وَطَنِهِمْ" (khaffal qaumu un watanihim): the people got out of their country fast and went on travel {T, R}.

The Quran says the following with regards to the desert gypsies:

16:80	you find them light weighted	تَسْتَخِفُّوْنَهَا

Surah **Ar-Rom** says:

30:60	those who do not believe in Allah's laws, let them not take you lightly	لَا يَسْتَخِفَّنَّكَ الَّذِيْنَ لَا يُوْقِنُوْنَ

This means that there must not be any element in you at all, to make the opponents feel that you are light (without weight) in your claims and aims, so that removing you from your path and to follow theirs is not at all difficult.

Surah **Al-Qaariah** has used "ثَقُلَتْ" (saqolat) as against "خَفَّتْ" (khaffat):

101:6-9	Thus, the scale of those which is heavy will live a life according to his choice and those whose scale will be light, will find themselves deep in the hole of destruction	وَاَمَّا مَنْ ثَقُلَتْ مَوَازِيْنُهُ فَهُوَ فِیْ عِيْشَةٍ رَاضِيَةٍ وَ اَمَّا مَنْ خَفَّتْ مَوَازِيْنُهُ فَاُمُّهُ هَاوِيَةٌ

A great principle of evolution has been described here. For example, for the exam of students, a percentage is fixed as the passing mark, say sixty percent. The student who obtains 60 out of

100 marks is thought to have the capability of moving ahead. 40 percent of his mistakes are overlooked and he is promoted to the next class. This represents that the scale of his capabilities is heavier than the scale of his errors. Contrary to this, the student who obtains only 40 percent marks fails because he does not meet the criteria for going ahead. In the universe, the principle of evolution is the same. He who attains the capability to move ahead, is the one whose errors are comparatively less do not stand in his way. He who does not attain this capability, whatever little capabilities of his are found wanting, and do not do him any good. He cannot move on. Life's evolution works on the same principle. Whoever has his scale of capabilities lower (heavier due to weight) than the other, will move on to the next stage.

The scale of whoever will be found wanting will not be able to move ahead. Those who will progress are called the dwellers of *jannah*, and those who cannot move on, have been called the dwellers of *jahannam*.

This fact has been stated at another place as:

11:15	truly, good deeds remove bad deeds	اِنَّ الْحَسَنٰتِ يُذْهِبْنَ السَّيِّاٰتِ

If the scale with *muhsinaat* (good deeds) is heavier, then the bad effects of the rest of bad deeds are eliminated. For determining this, every scrap or iota of man's deeds is evaluated (99:7-8), but the decision is made purely on the basis of which scale is the heavier (good or bad). If his good deeds are more, then his bad deeds are overwhelmed by the good deeds, or they do not impede or stop his progress and development, but if it is the opposite, then the good deeds, whatever they are, do not help or become the basis of his evolution. For more details see heading (*N-J-W*).

Kh-F-Y   خ ف ى

"الْخَافِيَة" (*al-khaafiah*): is the opposite of "عَلَانِيَّة" (*alaniah*), i.e. to hide, hiddenness, hidden thing.
"الْخَفَاء" (*al-khafa*): that thing which is hidden to you.
"اِخْتَفَى" (*ikhtifa*), "اَخْفَى" (*akhfaa*), "اِسْتَخْفَى" (*istakhfaa*): was/became hidden.

The Quran has used the word "اِخْفَاء" (*ikhfaa*) against "اِبْدَاء" (*ibdaa*), which means to display, make evident.

2:271	If you give charity openly, it is good, but it is even better if you give secretly	اِنْ تُبْدُوا الصَّدَقٰتِ فَنِعِمَّا هِيَ وَ اِنْ تُخْفُوْهَا

Surah *Al-Mai'dah* has used it against "تَبْيِيْنٌ" (*tabyeenun*) in 5:15. This too means to make evident.

19:3	low (hidden) voice	نِدَاءً حَفِيًّا

Surah *Taha* has used "اَخْفَى" (*akhfaa*) and "سِرّ" (*sirran*) together in 20:7.

Surah **Al-Haqqa, and An-Nisa** says:

| 69:18 | no secret will remain hidden | لَا تَخْفَى مِنْكُمْ خَافِيَةٌ |
| 4:108 | they want to hide from the people | يَسْتَخْفُونَ مِنَ النَّاسِ |

"مُسْتَخْفٍ بِاللَّيْلِ" (*mustakhfin bil lail*) as used in 13:10 means which hides at night or wants to hide.
"الْخَفِيُّ" (*al-khafiyu*): hidden, secret, which is not evident.
"طَرْفٍ خَفِيٍّ" (*tarfin khafiyin*) as used in 52:45 means to see out of the corner of the eyes.
"الْخَفِيُّ" (*akhfiyyu*) means to disclose something, to remove its "أَخْفَاهُ" (*akhfaa*), or hiddenness
{T}.

Muheet says that "خَفِيَ لَهُ" (*khafi lahu*) means to appear, and the word is used when a thing previously hidden makes an appearance, or becomes evident in some discreet manner.

Lataif-ul-Lugha says it means both "كَتَمَ" (*katam*) and "أَظْهَرَ" (*azhar*), that is, to hide and to make evident.

Ibn Faris also supports this theory about it meaning opposites.

Surah **Taha** says "أَكَادُ أُخْفِيهَا" (*akadu ukhfeeha*) in 20:15. If "أَكَادُ" (*akadu*) is taken to mean to intend here and "أُخْفِيهَا" (*ukhfeeha*) to mean make evident, then it would mean I intend to make it known or evident. If "أَكَادُ" (*akadu*) is taken to mean a negative and "أُخْفِيهَا" (*ukhfeeha*) to mean keeping hidden, then too, the verse would mean that I do not want to keep it secret, and want to make it known. In both conditions the meaning would be the same. This point has been explained under the heading (K-W-D), which must be referred to.

Kh-L-D   خ ل د

"خُلُودٌ" (*khulud*) means perpetuity.

Muheet, with reference to **Kulliyaat**, says that when something changes after a very long time, that is, it is not adulterated for a long time, and then this quality is known as "خُلُودٌ" (*khulud*). Therefore, it also means for something to stay as it is for a long period, whether it stays that way always or not *{T}*.

"رُجُلٌ مُخَلَّدٌ" (*rujulun mukhallud*): means a man who ages after a long time, while "الْبَقَاءُ" (*al-baqqa*) means to remain unchanged.

Kitabul Ashqaq says it means longevity of life and (to remain unchanged).

"اَلْخَوَالِدّ" (*al-khawalid*) means mountains, rocks and stones because they always stay in the same state. The Arab gypsies used to collect stones and make ovens out of them and when they left, the stones were left behind. They were also called "خَوَالِدّ" (*khawalid*) {*T*}.

"خَلَدَ و اَخْلَدَ بِالْمَكَانِ و اِلَى الْمَكَانِ" (*khalada wa akhlada bil makaani wailal makaan*): he resided somewhere and stayed there for quite a while.

"اَخْلَدَ الرَّجُلُ بِصَاحِبِهِ" (*akhladar rajul bisaahibehi*): stayed with his companion and did not leave him.

"اَخْلَدَ اِلَيْهِ" (*akhlada ilaih*): he leaned towards him and stuck to him {*T, M*}.

Surah *Al-Airaaf* says:

7:176	if We wished We could have granted him loftiness, but he stuck to the earth	وَلَوْشِئْنَا لَرَ فَعْنُهُ بِهَا ولكِنَّهُ اَخْلَدَ اِلَى الْأَرْضِ

Ibn Faris says it basically means stability and to stick together continuously, that is, to remain unchanged and to stick to someone.

The Quran generally says "خَالِدِيْنَ فِيْهَا" (*khaalideena feeha*) or "هُمْ فِيْهَا خَالِدُوْنَ" (*hum feeha khalidoon*) when it mentions *Jannah,* as in 2:25 where it refers to a heavenly society on earth. See heading (J-N-N). Then its "خُلُوْدّ" (*khulud*) means that till that society is according to the laws of Allah, it will not deteriorate. But where it refers to the perpetual life, it means that Life after Death which is the outcome of good deeds. Note that the Quran has used the word "خُلُوْدّ" (*khulud*) both for *Jannah* and *Jahannum*. The "خُلُوْدّ" (*khulud*) of *Jannah* is eternal life, which is the life which completes its different evolutionary stages and moves ahead. And the *jahannam's* "خُلُوْدّ" (*khulud*) is the stage where human capabilities and evolution come to a standstill and life becomes unable to complete the evolutionary stages and becomes stagnant. Therefore, this "خُلُوْدّ" (*khulud*) is like the mountains and the rocks. Details of these points can be found at different places in the Quran.

"مُخَلَّدُوْنَ" (*mukhalladoon*): the wrist and ears that are wearing jewelry. These jewelries are called "خَلَدّ" (*khaladun*). The singular is called "خَلَدَةّ" (*khaladah*).

56:17	Bedecked with jewelry	وِلْدَانٌ مُخَلَّدُوْنَ

Kitaabul Ashqaaq and *Gharibul Quran* also support these meanings.

"اَخْلَدَ" (*akhlad*): to escape destruction and bad fortune for a long time {*Gharibul Quran*}.

The Quran says the following regarding a man who collects wealth and keeps counting it:

104:3	he thinks that his wealth will save him from destruction for a long time, or give him perpetuation	يَحْسَبُ اَنَّ مَالَهُ اَخْلَدَهُ

This is a false thought. Perpetuation is not for him who collects wealth for himself and keeps others away from its benefits, but it is for one who is beneficial to the human race.

13:17	And as for what benefits the mankind, remains in the earth	وَأَمَّا مَا يَنْفَعُ النَّاسَ فَيَمْكُثُ فِي الْأَرْضِ

The perpetuity of the Afterlife must not be taken to mean that it is perpetuity like the eternalness of God. Absolutely not! There is no eternalness like God's. The human perpetuity will be according to Allah's laws. What will be its end? The human mind cannot presently comprehend anything about it. This is the reason why the Quran has along with the **khulud** of **Jannah** and **Jahannam** dispelled any thought about the infinity of God by saying "مَادَ أَمَتِ السَّمٰوٰتُ وَالْأَرْضُ" (*madamatis samawaatu fil ard*) in (11:107-108). For the meaning of "إِلَّا مَاشَاءَ رَبُّکَ" (*illa ma sha' a rabbuka*), see heading (N-S-Y).

Kh-L-Sd خ ل ص

"خَلَصَ" (*khalas*): to be rid of all adulteration and impurities and to become pure.
"خَلَصَ مِنَ الْقَوْمِ" (*khalasa minal qaum*): he separated from the nation and became a recluse *{T}*.
"اَخْلَصَ الشَّیْءَ" (*akhlasah shaiyi*): made something pure; selected it *{M}*.
"الْمُخْلَصُ" (*akhlasu*): someone who has been separated from the others and selected for some purpose *{T}*.

12:24	he (Yusuf) was not one to follow the common path	إِنَّهُ مِنْ عِبَادِ نَا الْمُخْلَصِيْنَ

This means that he had been separated from the lot, he was to follow the right path. Likewise, it is said about his brothers:

12:80	they separated from others to have mutual consultation	خَلَصُوْا نَجِيًّا

"خَالِصَةً مِنْ دُوْنِ النَّاسِ" (*khaalisatan min doonin naas*): We removed the others, purely for ourselves (2:94).
"اسْتَخْلَصَہُ" (*istakhlasahu*): made him purely my own (and for none else) (12:54)
"خَالِصٌ" (*khaalis*): pure, free from adulteration.

Raghib says "اَلْخَالِصُ" (*al-khaalis*) and "اَلصَّافِی" (*as-safee*) have the same meaning: but "اَلصَّافِی" (*as-safee*) can sometimes be used for something which is already pure. "خَالِصٌ" (*khaalis*) is that which has been purified of impurities *{M}*.

Ibn Faris says the basic meaning is to purify and separate the unwanted parts.

"اَلْخِلَاصُ" (*al-khilaas*) means butter, or gold and silver which is heated, liquefied and then purified.

"خَلَّصَ اللهُ لَهُ فُلَاناً" (*khallasal lahu fulanan*): God brought him out of the trouble he had landed into, just as a tangled thread is straightened *{T}*.

Surah *Al-Baqrah* says:

2:139	we have parted from everywhere else (have become purely the followers of Allah's laws)	وَنَحْنُ لَهُ مُخْلِصُوْنَ

It has been explained by "لَهُ مُسْلِمُوْنَ" (*lahu muslemoon*) and "لَهُ عٰبِدُوْنَ" (*lahu aabedoon*): which have appeared in the first two verses 2:136-138 i.e. followers only of His laws.
This also explains "مُخْلِصِيْنَ لَهُ الدِّيْنَ" (*mukhleseena lahud deen*): 7:29 that is, to turn away from all other forces and reserve obedience only for God.

Surah *Saad*, after mentioning the tale of the messengers says:

38:46	We separated them from others (And made them a special group).	إِنَّا اَخْلَصْنٰهُمْ بِخَالِصَةٍ ذِكْرَى الدَّارِ

Because of the particularity that they kept the end result in mind, that is, they kept the real life in mind (29:64), so that wherever it clashed with the temporary life, the real life was given priority over this physical life.

Kh-L-Te   خ ل ط

"خَلَطَ" (*khalat*), "خَلَّطَ" (*khallat*) is to mix something with another thing, even if they can be separated later (like mixing camels in a herd of sheep) or not *{T}*.

Muheet says that "اَلْمَزْجُ" (*al-mazj*) means to mix liquids together and common word for mixing is "اَلْخَلْطُ" (*al-khalt*) *{M}*. A partner in business or trade is called "خَلِيْطٌ" (*khaleet*), but *Johri* says that for one to be a partner in trade is not necessary. Those who live together without business interests and develop love for each other are also called "خَلِيْطٌ" (*khaleet*) *{T}*. This means "خَلِيْطٌ" (*khaleet*) is a living companion or even a neighbor. The plural is "خُلَطَاءُ" (*khulata'a*) according to (*Ibn Faris*).

"اِخْتَلَاطٌ" (*ikhtelaat*) also means intercourse.
"رَجُلٌ خِلْطٌ مِلْطٌ" (*rajulun khiltun milt*): a man who is the product of two races.
"الْخِلْطُ" (*al-khilt*) means a bastard *{T}*.
"خَالَطَةٌ" (*khliatah*): lived with him, intermingled.

About orphans, surah *Al-Baqara* says:

2:220	if you intermingle with them or become a partner in their trade, then remember that they are like your brethren	وَاِنْ تُخَالِطُوْ هُمْ فَاِخْوَانُكُمْ

Surah *Saad* has used the word "خُلَطَاءُ" (*khultaa*) for business partner in 38:24.

The Quran says:

9:102	those who mixed good deeds with bad deeds	خَلَطُوا عَمَلاً صَالِحاً---
6:147	the (fat) that clings to the bones	مَااخْتَلَطَ بِعَظْمٍ
18:45	That rain makes the land fertile.	فَاخْتَلَطَ بِهِ نَبَاتُ الْأَرْض

Kh-L-Ain   خ ل ع

"خَلْعٌ" (*khala*): to get rid of something. It has similar meaning as of "نَزْعٌ" (*nazaa*) but in "نَزْعٌ" (*nazaa*) there is alacrity and "خَلَعَ" (*khulaa*) is slow and delayed. Some think both words mean the same.
"اَلْخَالِعُ" (*al-khaalio*): fallen, broken tree.

Ibn Faris says it basically means something which was together along with another part, but then got separated.

"اَلْخُلْعُ" (*al-khulaa*): the divorce which a woman can take from a husband {*R*}.

Surah *Taha* says God said to *Moosa* "فَاخْلَعْ نَعْلَيْکَ" (*fakhlaa fa alaika*) in 20:12. Literally, it means "take off your shoes", but *Taj-ul-Uroos* says that it means "wait here" or "stay where you are". Like when you tell someone you know to take off his shoes and rest for some time. Thus, this verse would mean that God told *Moosa* not to be in a hurry, and to sit calmly and listen. Now your travel (that you were roaming in search of the truth) has come to an end. Now you will find your destination easily.

Qurtubi says that here "اخْلَعْ نَعْلَيْکَ" (*ikhlaa na'laika*) means complete your family chores i.e. put them out of your mind. He has said that the Arabs also mean family by the word "نَعْلٌ" (*na'al*) which usually means shoe.

Kh-L-F   خ ل ف

"خَلْفٌ" (*khalf*) means behind, at the back. It also means after.

"خَلْفَكَ" (*khalfaka*): after you.

"اَلْخَلْفُ" (*al-khalf*): an era after an era (a generation after another). It also means the human beings who replace the former people, and are more than them in number.

"اَلْخَلَفُ" (*al-khalaf*): the progeny, if good, will be called so. If they are not good, they will be called "خَلْفٌ" (*khalf*). But some think that these are alternate words.

Ibn Burri says that the word means progeny or a replacement.

"اَلْخَلَفُ" (*al-khalaf*) is used for the generation after another or the replacement of people whether they are dead or living. In other words, it means those who remain after the annihilated ones.

Ibn Aseer says that both words mean the same, with the difference that "خَلَفٌ" (*khalaf*) is used in a good way and "خَلْفٌ" (*khalf*) in bad manner.

Ibn Faris says there are three meanings for this root
1) For something to come after another and replace it
2) The opposite of front, that is, back
3) Change and amendment.

"خِلْفَةٌ" (*khilfatun*) means the leaves that appear after the old leaves have fallen. To come after another and to take its place is called "خِلْفَةٌ" (*khilfatun*).

The Quran says:

25:62	God is the One who has so created the night and day that one comes after the other	هُوَ الَّذِىْ جَعَلَ اللَّيْلَ وَ النَّهَارَ خِلْفَةً

"اَلْخَالِفُ" (*al-khaalifu*) is a man who takes the seat or throne after the former or lags behind, or does not come together (9:83).

"خَلَفَ اَبَاهُ" (*khalafa abahu*) means that he was the heir after his father.

"اَلْخَلِيْفَةُ" (*al-khalifah*): another's heir, or the ruler who is heir after the former. Plural is "خُلَفَاءُ" (*khulafaa*) and "خَلَائِفُ" (*khalaif*) {T}.

When *Moosa* went on the mount of *Toor*, he had said to his brother *Haroon*:

7:142	you be my replacement (in my absence)	اُخْلُفْنِيْ فِىْ قَوْمِىْ

Here it must be noted that *Moosa* would be absent, nobody can be a replacement in somebody's presence.

Surah **Yunus** says:

| 10:14 | We made them their heirs after them | ثُمَّ جَعَلْنَاكُمْ خَلَائِفَ فِى الْأَرْضِ مِنْ بَعْدِهِمْ |

Surah **Hoodh** says that **Hoodh** told his nation that if they go against God's orders then:

| 11:87 | my Sustainer will replace you with other people | يَسْتَخْلِفُ رَبِّى قَوْماً غَيْرَكُمْ |

This means that you will be destroyed and in your place another nation will be made your heir.

About the nation of **Aad** is said:

| 7:69 | you were made the heirs after the nation of **Nouh** | جَعَلَكُمْ خُلَفَاءَ مِنْ بَعْدِ قَوْمِ نُوحٍ |

About the **Samood** nation it is said that after the nation of **Aad**, they were made the heirs (7:74). The Quran has discussed **Adam** at several places. In verse 2:30 it is said "إِنِّى جَاعِلٌ فِى الْأَرْضِ خَلِيفَةً" (*inni ja'elun fil ardi khalifah*). This is ordinarily understood to mean that Adam is God's deputy on earth. This meaning is inherently wrong.

Firstly, nowhere in the Quran has man been called "خَلِيفَةُ اللهِ" (*khalifatullah*), or Allah's deputy. What has been said is "خَلِيفَةً فِى الْأَرْضِ" (*khalifatan fil ard*). Secondly, because we have seen earlier, that "خَلِيفَةً" (*khalifah*) means to take one's place in his absence, that is, a successor. God is present everywhere at all times. Therefore, a successor in his absence is inherently false. He who is present himself can have no successor.

Abu Bakar was the *khalifah*, or successor of the Messenger (pbuh). This means that after the death of the Messenger, he was his successor. He was not "خَلِيفَةُ اللهِ" (*khalifatullah*) i.e. Allah's successor. A person once called him *khalifatullah* after he became *khalifah*. He was corrected immediately and **Abu Bakar** said: I am the **Khalifah** (successor) of the Messenger, not Allah. {References from the book "**Abu Baker**" by author **Muhammmed Hussain Hekel**, page 580 of the Urdu translation}.

Man has not come to earth to be Allah's successor or His deputy. He has come to establish His laws and to live according to His laws.

Adam or man has been called "خَلِيفَةً فِى الْأَرْضِ" (*khlifatan fil ard*) because he replaces (is successor to) the creatures before him. See heading (**A-D-M**) and (**J-N-N**).

Since being an heir implies having authority and power, therefore, "اِسْتِخْلَافٌ فِى الْأَرْضِ" (*istakhlaafun fil ard*) means rule of a country, or the succession of some other ruling nation. Details of these matters can be found in my book "**Iblees O Adam**" where Adam has been discussed in detail.

The concept that man is Allah's deputy is also not correct according to the Quran. Being a deputy implies to be delegated the powers. Allah does not delegate His powers to anyone. Nobody has the Divine right, neither a king nor any religious leader, not even a messenger. Allah has formulated laws by using His absolute power. Allah's true slaves first implement those laws on self and then on the rest of the world.

Man's duty is to implement the laws of Allah. He has not been delegated the power to formulate the laws. Even the messengers simply brought Allah's **Deen** (laws) to mankind and implemented them. They did not MAKE the laws. Therefore, they were not **naib**, or deputies in this way, but if **naib** is taken to mean one who implements Allah's laws, then it is okay. But the word then used should not be **naib**, because the use of the word brings delegation of powers automatically to mind.

"اِخْلَافٌ" (*ikhlaaf*) means to go against a promise.
"اَخْلَفَ وَعْدَهُ" (*akhlafa wahdahu*) means that he promised but later did not fulfill it {*T, M*}.

2:80	Allah will not break His promise (He will surely fulfill His promise)	فَلَنْ يُخْلِفَ اللّٰهُ عَهْدَهُ

"اِخْتَلَافٌ" (*ikhtilaaf*): to differ. It also means to come one after another.

2:164	the coming of night and day, one after the other	اِخْتِلَافُ اللَّيْلِ وَالنَّهَارِ

It also means to oppose or differ:

19:37	then sects among them differed	فَاخْتَلَفَ الْأَحْزَابُ مِن بَيْنِهِمْ

Some however think that "خَلَفٌ" (*khalaf*) are good children and "خَلْفٌ" (*khalf*) are bad children {*T, M*}.

The Quran says:

19:59 7:169	Then succeed after them successors	فَخَلَفَ مِنْ بَعْدِهِمْ خَلْفٌ

"تَخَلَّفَ" (*takhallaf*): to lag behind (9:120)
"مُخَلَّفُوْنَ" (*mukhalladoon*): those who lagged behind (9:81).
"خَالَفَهُ" (*khaalafah*): opposed him.
"مُخْلِفُوهُ" (*mukhlifooh*): those who renegade or break a promise (92:27).
"مُخْتَلِفٌ" (*mukhtalif*): different (16:69).
"اِسْتَخْلَفَ" (*istakhlaf*): to make one to replace the other (24:55).
"مُسْتَخْلَفٌ" (*mustakhlaf*): heir (57:7).

God has said that the result of good deeds is "استخلاف فى الارض" (*istakhlaaf fil ard*) in 24:55. Therefore, the belief which does not enjoy authority and power is not real, and the good deeds are not really as such. To think that belief and good deeds will only bear fruit in the Hereafter, and they have nothing to do with this world, or it simply means the spiritual development of being only, which is not connected to the collective wellbeing of society, is against what Quran says.

Surah *Hoodh* says that *Shoaib* tried to prevent his people from the wrong way of life and said "وَمَا أُرِيدُ أَنْ أُخَالِفَكُمْ اِلَى مَا اَنْهٰكُمْ عَنْهُ" (*wama ureedu un ukhalifokum ila ma inhaakum unhu*) 11:88

Taj says that "خَالَفَهُ اِلَى الشَّىْءِ" (*khalifa alash shaiyi*) means to intend to do something after preventing others from it. As such, the verse would mean "I have no intention at all of doing what I am preventing you from doing".

According to the Quran, in-fighting is a sort of punishment (3:104), and for differences to be removed a blessing (11:118-119). The Quran intends to remove the differences among people (16:64), and as such, it is also a blessing from God. Those who do not have differences deserve the *Jannah* (3:105-106).

In-fighting and differences in *Deen* are *shirk* (to mix with one another) (42:10), but this duty will be performed by the collective system of the nation (4:65). These matters are further explained in heading (*F-R-Q*). Also, see my book "*Letters to Saleem*" vol.2).

Kh-L-Q   خ ل ق

"خَلْق" (*khalq*) basically means to measure for making or cutting something, to estimate it. This is also the meaning of "تَقْدِيْر" (*taqdeer*). See (Q-D-R). It means to see whether it is proportionate and balanced, or to model after something, to soften and smooth out something {T, L}. It also means to make one thing out of another {R}.

"خَلَقَ الاَدِيْمَ" (*halaqul adeem*): he measured or evaluated the leather for making something.
"رَجُلٌ تَامُّ الخَلْقِ" (*rajulun tammul khalq*): a man who is balanced and proportionate. It is also called "خَلِيْقٌ" (*khaleeq*).
"خُلْقَةٌ" (*khulqatun*): smoothness, to be symmetrical.
"اَلْخَلَقُ" (*al-khalaq*): to be free of gaps etc. and be smooth {T, L}.

Ibn Faris says that its basic meanings are to evaluate or measure something, and for something to become smooth (due to constant use). That is why old things are called "خَلَقَ" (*khalaq*) because due to constant use, they become smooth surfaced.

Thus, "خَلَقَ" (*khalaq*) would mean to evaluate something, to create it so that it becomes balanced and proportionate, and it becomes clean and smooth.

"بَدَعَ" (*bada'*) and "فَطَرَ" (*fatar*) mean to bring something from nothingness into existence, to create for the first time, to invent. Thus, "خَلَقَ" (*khalaq*) would mean to give different shapes and form to elements and to create things.

| 16:14 | Creation of Man has been done of surfing liquid | خَلَقَ الْإِنْسَانَ مِنْ نُطْفَةٍ |
| 55:14 | Creation of Man has been done from clay | خَلَقَ الْأَنْسَانَ مِنْ صَلْصَالٍ |

In surah *Hajj* the different stages of sperm, and genes in the mother's womb have been described and the Quran says that it transforms into "مُضْغَةٍ" (*muzgha*) which has two forms, "مُخَلَّقَةٍ" (*mukhallaqah*) and "غَيْرِ مُخَلَّقَةٍ" (*ghair mukhallaqah*) 22:5. "مُخَلَّق" (*mukhallaq*) means complete, or which is made smooth or softened (*Muheet*).

Ibn Faris says "الْمُخَلَّقُ" (*al-mukhalliq*) is that arrow which has been straightened. Therefore, the verse can be taken to mean that "مُضْغَةٍ" (*muzgha*) is either a complete child or it remains incomplete, and is aborted.

Surah *Shooraa* says:

| 26:137 | this is the same old custom or old habit, or way of old | اَنْ هٰذَا اِلاَءَ خُلُقُ الْأَوَّلِيْنَ |

Some people have said it means customs and traditions {*T, L*}. This has led to its meaning of habits and usual practices. As such, "خُلُقٌ" (*khuluqun*) is somebody's physical habits {*T, L*}, since habits are old practices, that is why "خَلَقَ" (*khalaq*) also means ancient.

"خَلَقَ الثَّوْبُ" (*khalaqas saub*): the cloth became old.
"اِنْ هٰذَا اِلاَّ اخْتِلاَقٌ" (*inn haaza illakh telaaq*) is a concoction used in (38:7)
"خِلْقَةٌ" (*khalaqatun*) means someone's natural constitution {*T*}.
"خَلاَقٌ" (*khalaaq*) means estimated portion as used in 3:76.

Raghib says "خَلاَقٌ" (*khalaaq*) means that edge which one gets due to good morals.

The Quran has also used "أَمْرٌ" (*amr*) as against "خَلْقٌ" (*khalq*), as in 7:54. See heading (A-M-R). "خَلَقَ" (*khalaqa*) also means to make the right estimate and to intend and plan accordingly. It also means to train {*Gharib-ul-Quran*}.

"خَلاَّقٌ" (*khallaq*) and "خَالِقٌ" (*khaaliq*) are two great traits of Allah (59:25, 36:81). Therefore, the individual or nation that has Allah's gift will display great creativity as well.

Having children is not creation, but pro-creation. This is a biological function which animals share with man, Thus, birth is an animal level function. Thus, man's creativity cannot be shared by animals. The nation which is bereft of creativity is devoid of Allah's quality of Creativeness.

Note that creation is not mere duplication, but demands new inventions, Thus, it is said about Allah:

38:1	He keeps adding to His creations according to his Will	يَزِيدُ فِى الْخَلْقِ مَا يَشَاءُ

Therefore, his slaves must also keep inventing newer things. This is called invention.

About the Messenger Muhammed (pbuh), the Quran says:

68:4	and verily you contain very great morals	وَإِنَّكَ لَعَلَى خُلُقٍ عَظِيمٍ

As said earlier, "خَلْقٌ" (*khalq*) means balanced and proportionate. Morals are the distinguishing trait of humanity, and our Messenger **Muhammad** was supreme in this. Those traits which are described as "morals" with us are actually the remnants of the era of hegemony. The morals as described by the Quran, which belong to a *momin*, are the true morals, and the Messenger (pbuh) is the epitome of those morals, which is the best example for the human race. This example of the Messenger is preserved in the Quran.

Kh-L-L   خ ل ل

"اَلْخَلُّ" (*al-khal*): the path that goes into desert or the path that passes between two deserts.

"اَلْخَلَلُ" (*al-khalal*): the space between two things.

"خِلَالٌ" (*khilaal*): the space between.

"خِلَالُ الدِّيَارِ" (*khilalud dyar*): the space between two houses, the space in the environment of houses.

"تَخَلَّلَ الشَّيْءَ" (*takhalash-shaiyi*): to go inside a thing, to enter.

"خَلَّ الشَّيْءَ" (*khallash shaiyi*): drilled a hole into a thing and went through it.

"اَلْخِلَالُ" (*al-khilaal*): a drill which drills through a thing.

"اَلْخَلَّةُ" (*al-khallah*): need, troubled condition {T}.

"فَجَاسُوا خِلَلَ الدِّيَارِ" (*fajasu khilalid dyaar*): 17:5 they entered the cities: penetrated them:

"خِلَالِهَا" (*khilalaha*): inside it.

"خُلَّةٌ" (*khullah*): friendship (2:254), perhaps because friends enter each other's hearts, or need each other.

"أَخِلَّاءُ" (*ikhla'a*) is the plural of "خَلِيلٌ" (*khaleel*) which means friend. (4:164, 43:67).

"خِلَالٌ" (*khilaal*): mutual friendship.

"اَلْخَلَّ" (*al-khal*): vinegar.

Kh-L-W   خ ل و

"خَلَا الْمَكَانُ" (*khala-ul makaan*): a house vacated as the occupants go away.

"خَلَا الشَّيْءِ" (*khala-ush shaiyi*): for something to pass away or go away.

"خَلْوَةٌ" (*khalwah*): means solitude.

"خَلِيَّةٌ" (*khaliyah*): bees-hive *{T}*.

Raghib says that "خُلُوٌّ" (*khulu*) is used for both place and time. Since time also passes, the scholars of dictionaries take "خَلَا الزَّمَانُ" (*khala-uz zaman*) to mean the time passed *{T}*.

Ibn Faris says it basically means for one thing to part from another.

The Quran has used "خَلَوْ" (*khalau*) against "لَقُوا" (*laqu*) in 2:76 and 2:14. Here it means solitude and to meet in solitary.

"خَلَوْا مِنْ قَبْلِكُمْ" (*khalau min qablikum*): the people who have passed away prior to you (2:214).

"تِلْكَ أُمَّةٌ قَدْ خَلَتْ" (*tilka ummatun qad khalat*): this was a group or party who had passed away (2:141).

"فِي الْأَيَّامِ الْخَالِيَةِ" (*fi al-ayyami khaliyah*): in the days that which have passed away, or past days (69:24).

Surah *Yusuf* says:

12:9	you will have full attention of your father; no one else will share it	يَخْلُ لَكُمْ وَجْهُ اَبِيكُمْ

"خَلَا فِيهَا نَذِيرٌ" (*khala feeha nazeer*) as in 35:24, means "where no one to warn has been".

"تَخَلَّتْ" (*takhallat*) as in 84:4, means to be empty and be pure.

"فَخَلُّوا سَبِيلَهُمْ" (*fakhallu sabeelahum*) in 9:5 means leave their path, do not argue with them.

"خَلَّا سَبِيلَ الْأَسِيرِ" (*khalla sabeelal aseer*): means freed the prisoner *{R}*.

Kh-M-D   خ م د

"خَمَدَتِ النَّارُ" (*khamadatin naar*): for the flames of the fire to go out even if the ambers are still glowing. If even the ambers are extinguished, then it will be "هَمَدَتِ النَّارُ" (*hamadatin naar*) *{R}*.

Ibn Faris says it basically means for movement to die down and to fall down.

"اَخْمَدْتُهَا" (*akhmad-toha*): I silenced the flames.

"اَلْخَمُّودُ" (*al-khammud*): the place where a fire is buried.

"خَمَدَ الْمَرِيضُ" (*khamadal mareez*): the patient fainted or died.

"قَوْمٌ خَامِدُونَ" (*qaumun khaamedoon*): people whose steps are too silent *{M}*, or people with no movement.

"اَخْمَدَ اللهُ اَنْفَاسَهُ" (*akhmadullahu anfaasuhu*): Allah demeaned him or gave him death *{T}*.

Surah *Ambia* and *Yaseen* say:

| 21:15 | we made them devoid of the movement of development and made them unmoving like a cut crop | جَعَلْنٰهُمْ حَصِيْدًا خٰمِدِيْنَ |
| 36:26 | so see, they became silent like the ambers | فَاِذَاهُمْ خٰمِدُوْنَ |

Zajaj says it means silent and dead. The nations that are destroyed lose any movement and they turn to ashes. Also the green fields of their life in this world are cut and only their traces remain.

Kh-M-R   خ م ر

"خَمَرٌ" (*khamr*): to cover or hide something.

"خَمَرَ الشَّيْءِ يَخْمِرُهُ" (*khamarash shaiyia yakhmir*): hid him, covered him.

"خَمَرَ فُلَانٌ أَشْهَادَةٌ" (*khamara falanun shahadah*): he hid the evidence.

"اَلْخَمَرُ" (*al-khamar*): veil, a cloth with which women cover their heads {*T*}. Plural is "خُمُرٌ" (*khumur*) (24:31).

Lataif-ul-Lugha says that initially women used to put on "اَلْغِفَارَةُ" (*al-ghifaarah*) on their heads, and "اَلْخِمَارُ" (*al-khimar*) over it. See heading (*Gh-F-R)* the meaning of *ghifaarah*.

"اَلْخَمْرُ" (*al-khamr*): every intoxicating substance, because it covers the intellect.

Caliph *Umar* has said "اَلْخَمْرُ مَا خَامَرَ الْعَقْلَ" (*al-khamro ma khamaral aqal*). It means that *khamar* is something which interferes with the intellect and spoils it. Some say "لِأَنَّهَا تَخْمِرُ الْعَقْلَ" (*lannaha takhmirul aql*): that is, liquor has been called "خَمَرٌ" (*khamr*) because it covers the intellect {*T*}.

The Arabs usually used to make wine from grapes and called it "خَمَرٌ" (*khamr*). Hence, grapes too were called "خَمَرٌ" (*khamr*).

"تَخْمِيْرٌ" (*takhmeer*) means to raise the yeast {*T*}.

"خَامَرَ الرَّجُلُ فِى الْبَيْعِ مُخَامَرَةً" (*khamarar rajulun fee bai-i mukhaamarah*): he deceived in trade and sold a free man as a slave.

Ibn Faris says it basically means to cover and with it to intermingle.

"اَلْإِسْتِخْمَارٌ" (*istikhmaar*) means to enslave, as it is necessary to seize a man's intelligence to enslave him.

About "خَمَرٌ" (*khamr*) and "مَيْسِرٌ" (*maysar*), that is, drinking and gambling, the Quran says:

| 2:164 | it has a lot of sin, and some benefits for people too | فِيْهِمَا اِثْمٌ كَبِيْرٌ وَ مَنَافِعُ لِلنَّاسِ |
| 2:219 | their sin is much greater than the benefits in them | وَ اِثْمُهُمَا اَكْبَرُ مِنْ نَفْعِهِمَا |

"اِثْمّ" (*ism*) means frustration, tiredness, laziness, such weakness that leaves a man behind in life's race. See heading (*A-Tha-M*). Wine and gambling (easily acquired wealth) surely get the adrenalin flowing.

A man temporarily becomes excited by them, but later his limbs become so exhausted or lackadaisical that they lose the ability to struggle in life. That is why they have been termed "رِجْسٌ مِنْ عَمَلِ الشَّيْطٰنِ" (*rijsun min amalish shaitaan*): the devil's work, by the Quran and warned to abstain from them (5:90). And said that they will create acrimony among you and you will become unable to establish the system of *salaah* (5:91).

"خَمْرٌ" (*khamr*): alcoholic drink. The biological research about it is that initially it increases the blood pressure and this in certain conditions (diseases) is a good thing, but later its effect slows down the blood pressure and this is a deep effect. Therefore, as against the initial benefit its later effect is very harmful.

"خَمْرٌ" (*khamr*), as well as "مَيْسِرٌ" (*maysir*) not only slacken the human body, they slacken the human personality as well, and this is a big loss.

Kh-M-S   خ م س

"اَلْخَمْسَةُ" (*al-khamsah*): five.
"يَوْمُ الْخَمِيسِ" (*yaumul khamees*): fifth day.
"خَمْسُوْنَ" (*khamsoon*): fifty
"خُمْسٌ" (*khumsun*) and "خَمْسٌ" (*khamsun*): fifth part
"خَامِسٌ" (*khaamsun*): fifth. Feminine form is "اَلْخَامِسَةُ" (*al-khamisah*) as in 24:7.

18:23	And they say they were five	وَيَقُوْلُوْنَ خَمْسَةٌ
29:14	Except for fifty years	إِلَّا خَمْسِيْنَ عَاماً
8:41	Then for Allah, one fifth of it…	فَاَنَّ لِلهِ خُمْسَهُ

The fifth part of the war booty is for Allah and His **Rusool** (8:41), **Rusool** being the central administration of Allah's system. The **ameer**, or leader of the nation will spend it to meet the needs of the nation, and it is called "فِىْ سَبِيْلِ اللهِ" (*fee sabilil Allah*).

Kh-M-Sd   خ م ص

"اَلْخَمْصَةُ" (*al-khamsah*): hunger.
"خَمِصَ الْبَطَنْ" (*khamisal batn*): the stomach became empty and caved in.
"اَلْاَخْمَصُ" (*al-khamas*): the sole of the foot whose curve is inside (concave).
"خَمِيْصٌ" (*khamees*): a hungry man who's stomach curves inside.
"زَمَنْ خَمِيصٌ" (*zamun khamees*) means the period of drought {*T*}.
The Quran has used "مَخْمَصَةٌ" (*makhmasah*) for acute hunger (5:3).

Kh-M-Te   خ م ط

"خَمَطَ اللَّحْمَ يَخْمِطُهُ" (**khamatal lahma yakhmitohu**): he fried the meat. If it is boiled in water then it will be called "مَمْطٌ" (**mamt**).

"اَلْخَمْطُ" (**al-khamt**): sour, anything bitter, every plant which is bitter, a kind of deadly poison or lethal tree, every tree without needles {T}.

In the Quran, it has been said in connection with punishment that in place of the fine orchards, such orchards grew which were "ذَوَاتَىْ أُكُلٍ خَمْطٍ" (**zu wa aati ukulin khamt**), that is, which produced bitter fruit. It also means that the pleasantness of their lives was replaced with bitterness.

Ibn Faris says it basically means to be naked and empty, and also power and authority. With these meanings the verse would mean to deprive somebody of life for evil deeds or oppression, which is exactly what, happened to the nation of **Sabaa**.

Kh-N-Z-R   خ ن ز ر

"اَلْخَنْزَرَةُ" (**al-khanzarah**): to become fat, big. This word is used for a fat hammer, used to break stones.

"اَلْخِنْزِيْرُ" (**al-khinzeer**): pig, plural of which is "خَنَازِيْرُ" (**khanazeer**).

"خَنْزَرَ" (**khanzar**): he committed several acts like a pig. This is also used for seeing out of the corner of the eye {T}.

The Quran has listed meat of pig among the things which as unlawful and Hence, forbidden (2:173). The word has also been used for people whose characters have been mutilated and turned like the worst of animal behavior (5:60).

Raghib says it can be used both for mutilated faces ad characters. See heading (Q-R-D).
The **Gharib-ul-Quran** says that it is a compound of the words "خَنِزَ" (**khaniz**) plus "نَزْرٌ" (**nazr**), which means a rotten thing.

The word swine or being a swine is generally considered to be a negative quality in most parts of the world. Even in the west, where its meat is cosumed, its name is used as a curse word. The **Bible** too uses this word in a demeaning manner.

Kh-N-S   خ ن س

"خَنَسَ عْنُه" (*khanasa unhu*), "يَخْنِسُ" (*yakhnis*), "خَنْساً" (*khansa*): to get back from it.

"خَنَسَه" (*khanasah*): to move someone back.

"اَلْخُنُسُ" (*al-khunus*): the place where deer hide. Also see "كُنُسٌ" (*kunus*).

"خَنَسَ مِنْ بَيْنِ أَصْحَابِهِ" (*khanasa min baini asaabehi*): he hid from among his friends.

"اَلْخَنَسُ فِي الْقَدَمِ" (*al-khanasu fil qadam*): for the sole of the foot to be even and have flesh {*T, R*}

"اَلْخِنِّيسُ" (*al-khinees*): a scoundrel who lies in wait for somebody, also one who makes excuses and is a deceptive person {*T, R*}.

The Quran says "فَلَا أُقْسِمُ بِالْخُنَّسِ" (*fala uksimo bil khunnas*) in 18:15, which means "those stars which recede", and since stars do not make any sound while doing so, the word has come to mean "to back down silently". This is the same sort of evidence which has been described in "وَالنَّجْمِ إِذَا هَوَىٰ" (*wan najmi iza hawa*) in 53:1 and 56:75, and this because later the description is about revelation and messenger hood (81:20-22).

Surah *an-Naas* says:

114:4	he who whispers something in the ear and silently recedes (he who quietly spreads wrong thoughts and hides)	الْوَسْوَاسِ الْخَنَّاسِ

Maulana Abeedullah Sindhi writes that "اَلْخَنَّاسُ" (*al-khannas*) means a force which hides, or one which when attacked hides.

Ibn Faris says it basically means to hide and to be hidden.

Kh-N-Q   خ ن ق

Ibn Faris says it basically means constriction.

"خَنَقَ" (*khanaq*), "يَخْنِقُ" (*yakhneq*): to strangle.

"اَلْخَانِقُ" (*al-khaaniq*) means a narrow valley.

"اَلْخَنِقُ" (*al-khaniq*): means to strangle.

"اَلْخِنَاقُ" (*al-khinaaq*): the rope with which one strangles.

"اِنْخَنَقَ" (*inkhanaq*): his throat was strangulated {*T, R*} {*Tafseerul Muqaam al Mahmud* page 221}.

"خُنَاقٌ" (*khunaaq*) is another derivation.

"اَلْمُنْخَنِقَةُ" (*al-munkhaniqah*): the strangled animal. Animal that dies of strangulation has been made forbidden to eat by the Quran (5:3).

Kh-W-R خ و ر

"خَوِرَ" (*khawir*), "يَخْوَرُ" (*yakhwar*), "خَوَراً" (*khawara*) means to be weak, to be a coward, to break down, to become slack.

"خَارَتْ قُوَّةُ الْمَرِيضِ" (*kharat quwwatil mareez*): the patient's strength lessened, that is, he became weak.

"خَوَّرَتِ الْأَرْضُ" (*khawwaratil ard*): due to the excessive rains the soil flowed out (with water) {*T, M*}.

"اَلْخُوَارُ" (*al-khuwaar*): cow, ox, or goat. It also means the sound of a deer or arrows. Actually it meant the sound of a cow or ox, but later began to be used for all kinds of sounds {*T, M*}.

Raghib says "خُوَارٌ" (*khuwaar*) means the sound of cows or oxen, but later it metaphorically also started to mean the sound of a camel. The Quran has used "لَهُ خُوَارٌ" (*lahu khuwaar*) for "عِجْلٌ" (*ijlun*) or calf in 7:148, that is, the calf that used to make sound.

Kh-W-Zd خ و ض

"خَاضَ" (*khaz*) and "يَخُوْضُ" (*yakhuz*) basically mean to get down in water, or wade in water.

Ibn Faris says it basically means to indulge. Later this word began to be used for being busy in something for long.

The Quran has used it mostly for engaging in useless things {*T, R*}.

"خَاضَ" (*khaaza*): he talked nonsense: {*Aqrabul Muwaarid*}.

The Quran says:

9:69	And you indulge like the one who indulges (engage in useless talk)	وَ خُضْتُمْ كَالَّذِىْ خَاضُوْا
52:12	Those who are engaged in falsehood and are oblivious of the truth	الَّذِيْنَ هُمْ فِىْ خَوْضٍ يَلْعَبُوْنَ
74:45	And we used to indulge in vain talk with those who talked in vain	كُنَّا نَخُوْضُ مَعَ الْخَائِضِيْنَ

This is about the type of leaders who did nothing for the common good, but only repeated statements to this effect, passed resolutions, and spent their time in planning. That is all talk and no work. It also applies to those scholars and philosophers who keep themselves busy in picking loopholes in conceptual issues and nit picking, and ignore the matters which produce practical results. These people cause destruction of their nations (70:41-42).

Kh-W-F   خ و ف

"خَوْفٌ" (*khauf*) means to fear some catastrophe due to some evidence and signs of it. Hence, it means to apprehend, just as "طَمَعٌ" (*tama-a*) means to expect some benefit from the evidence and sign before one. The Quran has used them together in 7:56.

"حُزْنٌ" (*huzn*) is the sadness that comes after an event and the loss has already been established. "خَوْفٌ" (*khauf*) is the apprehension of the loss that may take place in the future, while "حُزْنٌ" (*huzn*) is the loss which has already taken place.

Surah *An-Nisaa* says:

4:128	If a woman fears unfair treatment from her husband	وَإِنِ امْرَأَةٌ خَافَتْ مِنْ بَعْلِهَا نُشُوزًا

Thus, the fear of Allah would mean the realization that by leaving Allah's laws (their obedience) I will suffer a great loss. Hence, it means to avoid the wrong path due to the realization of the bad results it will produce.

Surah *An-Nahal* says about the things in the universe and about the *malaika*:

16:50	They fear the authority and overwhelming of their Sustainer and do whatever they are ordered to do	يَخَافُونَ رَبَّهُمْ مِنْ فَوْقِهِمْ وَيَفْعَلُونَ مَايُؤْمَرُونَ

That is, they fully follow the laws of Allah because they know that if they don't, then only chaos will result. As such, the fear of Allah is not like the fear of some tyrant. This fear is like the apprehension of being burnt due to which we do not play with fire.

"أَلْخَافَةُ" (*al-khaafah*) is the protective leather that a honey collector puts on, so that he may be protected from the bee stings. It also means a bag which is used for keeping something safe *{T}*. "خَوَافٌ" (*khawaaf*): means high level of noise *{T}*.

Ibn Faris says the root basically means worry and trouble.

"خَوْفٌ" (*khauf*) also means annihilation and war *{T}*. As such, "خَوْفٌ" (*khauf*) in 33:19 has been taken to mean killing.
"تَخَوَّفَ الشَّيْءِ" (*takhawwafash shjaiyi*): means to decrease something.
"تَخَوَّفَهُ حَقَّهُ" (*takhawwafah haqqah*): reduced his rights.
"أَوْيَأْخُذَ هُمْ عَلَى تَخَوُّفٍ" (*aw yakhuz hoom ala takhawwuf*): destroy them gradually, instead of at once (16:47).
"تَخَوُّفٌ" (*takhawwuf*) means to fear, to be apprehensive all the time, lest they are hauled up despite their fearing Him and being wary of the consequences. But the earlier meaning seems more plausible.
"أَلْخِيفَةُ" (*al-khafeefah*): the state of fear *{M}*.

Following the guidance definitely results in a fearless nation without any worries (2:38). Thus, if a nation lives in some kind of fear, then that nation is not following Allah's orders. To follow Allah's laws and feel fear, do not go together.

Kh-W-L   خ و ل

"اَلْخَالُ" (*al-khaal*): mother's brother, maternal uncle.
Plurals are "اَخْوَالٌ" (*akhwaal*), "اَخْوِلَةٌ" (*akhwilah*), "خُوُوْلٌ" (*khu'ool*).
"اَلْخَالَةُ" (*al-khaalah*): mother's sister, maternal aunt. Plurals are "خَالَاتٌ" (*khaalaat*) as in 4:23, "اَخْوَالٌ" (*akhwaal*) as in 24:61.
"اَلْخَالُ" (*al-khaal*): the sign of goodness in a man, or an army's flag, or a black camel.
"هُوَ خَالُ مَالٍ" (*huwa khalun maal*): he is the guard of the camels {T}.

Ibn Faris says it basically means to look after or guard something.

"خَوَّلَ" (*khawwal*), "تَخْوِيلٌ" (*takhweel*): to endow someone with grandeur or such things which need to be guarded {R}.
"اِذَا خَوَّلَهُ نِعْمَةً" (*iza khawwalahu ne'mah*) as in 39:8 means "when Allah endows someone with luxuries".

Kh-W-N   خ و ن

"اَلْخَوْنُ" (*al-khaun*) basically means to decrease something.
"خَوَّنَهُ" (*khawwanah*): decreased it.
"فِیْ ظَهْرِهِ خَوْنٌ" (*fi zahrihi khaun*): his back is weak, or there is weakness in his back.
"خَوْنٌ" (*khaun*) is also used for glare {T}.
"خَانَ" (*khaan*), "یَخُوْنُ" (*yakhun*), "خَوْناً" (*khauna*) is a man who is thought to be trust worthy, but turn out to not be worthy of trust.
"خِیَانَةٌ" (*khiyaanah*) is to betray or to lose someone's trust.
"خَانَ الدَّلْوَالرِّشَاءُ" (*khaanad dalur risha'a*): the rope was not faithful to the bucket and broke in the middle, due to which the bucket fell into the well {T}. We pull the bucket out of the well by depending on the strength of the rope. If the rope breaks in the middle, then it is called its "خِیَانَةٌ" (*khiyanah*). As such, "اَمَانَةٌ" (*amanah*) means to be at peace with someone or something (to be content that the trust is not lost), but in "خِیَانَةٌ" (*khiyanah*) this trust is simply not there.

This is the reason why Quran says "لَا انْفِصَامَ لَهَا" (*la infisaama laha*) in 2:256 describing the laws of Allah's. These words mean that these laws are a strong link which can never break, and can be fully depended upon. These never leave you in the lurch.

"تَخَوَّنٌ" (*takhawwan*) does not just mean to hurt or incur loss, but it also means any change, alteration, decrease, or amendment.

"خَانَهُ الدَّبْرُ" (*khaanahud dehar*): time was not on his side. That is, it treated him badly {T}.

The Quran says:

22:38	Indeed, Allah does not befriend any of those who betray in denial.	إِنَّ اللهَ لَا يُحِبُّ كُلَّ خَوَّانٍ كَفُورٍ

"خَوَّانٌ" (*khawwan*) can be used for any man who cannot be trusted or depended upon, and also the enemy who tries to deteriorate your condition. It also means a big misappropriate. The Quran instructs to stop even from misappropriation of sight (20:19).

Surah *Al-Baqrah* says:

2:187	That you used to deceive yourself.	أَنَّكُمْ كُنْتُمْ تَخْتَانُونَ أَنْفُسَكُمْ

Raghib says that "اِخْتِيَانٌ" (*ikhtiyaan*) means to prepare or intend to misappropriate. As such, one must not only try to not misappropriate others, but also oneself. One should not even let the thought of misappropriation cross one's mind. The biggest crime is to misappropriate from self. That is, to act against what you think is the right thing to do, whether it is in someone's knowledge or not. This is not only a sign of weakness of one's self-respect, but also a sign of a dual personality. The Quran forbids it.

Surah *An-Nisaa* says:

4:107	those who intend to deceive each other	الَّذِينَ يَخْتَانُونَ أَنْفُسَهُمْ

Surah *Al-Anfaal* says: do not conspire against Allah's system "لَا تَخُونُوا" (*la takhunu*), nor be found lacking (misappropriate) in any of the matters entrusted to you.

Kh-W-Y   خ و ى

"خَوَتِ الدَّارُ" (*khawatid daar*): the house became abandoned and fell down.

Ibn Faris says it basically means to be vacant and fall.

"أَرْضٌ خَاوِيَةٌ" (*ardun khawiah*): abandoned land {T}.
"الْخَوَاءُ" (*al-khawa*): means to be empty {R}.
"خَوِيَ المَكَانُ" (*khawi al-makaan*): the place became empty {M}.

About a dwelling, surah *Al-Baqrah* says:

2:256	And it overturned on its roofs	وَهِيَ خَاوِيَةٌ عَلَى عُرُوشِهَا

This verse is talking about the destroyed and desolated houses which had fallen down, or the houses that despite the roofs standing, were laid bare.

Surah *Al-Haaqqa* says:

| 69:7 | destroyed date palms which are ready to fall (hollow inside) | اَعْجَازُ نَخْلٍ خَاوِيَةٍ |

Kh-Y-B   خ ى ب

"خَابَ" (*khaab*), "يَخِيْبُ" (*yakheeb*), "خَيْبَةَ" (*khaibah*) means to remain deprived, to suffer loss, to be disappointed, not to be able to achieve that which is desired, to remain unrequited, expectations to be cut off, to be needy and beggarly. *{T, M}*.

Ibn Faris says that "اَلْخَيَّابُ" (*al-khayyab*) is a firestone which does not have the capability to start a fire.

The Quran says:

| 3:126 | let them return unrequited | فَيَنْقَلِبُوا خَائِبِيْنَ |

The Quran has used the word "خَابَ" (*khaab*) against "اَفْلَحَ" (*aflaha*) which means the crops to grow and be fruitful. As such, "خَابَ" (*khaab*) would mean to be unfruitful.

| 91:10 | He who buries it, fails | خَابَ مَنْ دَسَّهَا |

It means that he who pressured it and did not let it develop, his plate remained, desolated. His spark of life became desolate, and became such a fire stone that has no fire. This is why "خَابَ" (*khaab*) has been explained further by saying "بَلَکَ" (*halak*) in surah *Ibrahim*, which means destruction (14:13-15).

It also includes destruction in this life (rather, it is manifested first). Therefore, the nurturing or development of self-results inevitably in the happiness of this life as well. Spiritual development by giving up this world is against the Quran. Human development takes place by conquering the universe. A life without a spark is like a heap of ashes.

Kh-Y-R ر ی خ

"الخَيْرُ" (*al-khair*): anything which is favored or liked by all, also useful thing. It is the opposite of "الشَّرُّ" (*shar*).

"أَلْخَيْرُ" (*al-khair*): all types of good. Arab horses used to be called "خَيْرٌ" (*khair*) due to their usefulness (38:32).

"خَيْرَاتٌ" (*khairaat*): beautiful and courteous women {*T*}, or one who have many good traits as beauty.

"خَيَارٌ" (*khayaar*) means authority, that is, the choice to adopt whichever deed, and leave whichever.

Ibn Faris says it basically means leaning and bending.

"أَنْتَ بِالْخَيَارِ" (*anta bil khayaar*): you have the choice to work according to your wishes.

"خَيَّرَهُ بَيْنَ الشَّيْئَيْنِ" (*khaiyyarahu bainash shaiy-een*): he gave him the right to choose whichever of the two things {*T*}.

"اِسْتِخَارَةٌ" (*istikharah*) means to ask for the better of two things. Since whichever of two things is in any case thought to be better of the two, "" (*khairun*) is also used for honor, superiority and estimation.

"هُوَ خَيْرٌ مَنْکَ" (*huwa khairun mink*): he is better than you.

"خَاَرَ الرَّجُلَ عَلَى غَيْرِهِ وَ خَيَّرَهُ تَخْيِيْرًأَ" (*khaarar rajula ala ghairehi wa khaiyyarahu takhyeera*): he preferred that individual man over others.

"اِخْتَرْتُهُ عَلَيْهِمْ" (*akhtartuhu alaihim*): I gave him superiority, chose him, and selected him over all others.

"أَلْخِيَارٌ" (*al-khiyar*) is a vegetable of a kind (celery).

The Quran has used "خَيْرٌ" (*khair*) to mean wealth at several places, as in 2:272, 2:180.

"خَيْرٌ" (*khair*) has been used against "أَدْنَى" (*adna*) (2:16).

"خَيْرٌ" (*khair*) is used for something "even better" in 2:106.

Surah ***Anaam*** (6:17) uses this word against "ضُرٌّ" (*zur*), against "فِتْنَةٌ" (*fitnah*) in surah ***Al-Hajj*** (22:11) and against "شَرٌّ" (*shar*) in surah ***Al-Baqrah*** (2:216).

Surah ***An-Nahal*** has used this word for every good thing and deed (16:76).

Surah ***Aal-e-Imran*** (3:35) says about Allah that "بِيَدِکَ الْخَيْرُ" (*biyadekal khaiir*): He has the concept for all sorts of authority and every type of good thing.

Surah ***Al-Ahzaab*** (33:36) has used "خِيَرَةٌ" (*khiyarah*) for choice and right.

Surah ***Taha*** uses "يَخْتَارُ" (*yakhtaar*) for the natural selection in the universe.

About ***Moosa*** it is said in 20:13 "وَأَنَا اخْتَرْتُکَ" (*wa ana akhtartuka*). I have chosen you (selected you) for a great purpose.

In surah ***Saad*** (38:27), the word of "أَخْيَارٌ" (*akhyaar*) has been used for the Messengers who were the preferred individuals.

Ibn Faris has said "قَوْمٌ خِيَارٌ" (*qaumun khiyaar*) and "أَخْيَارٌ" (*akhyaar*) mean a nation with many capabilities.

In 55:70 "خَيْرَاتٌ حِسَانٌ" (*khairatun hisaan*) has been used to mean women with proportionate limbs and moderate character, or for proportionate and good things. Since all life's happiness and authority and expanse is availed by following Allah's orders, therefore, His revelation has also been called "خَيْرٌ" (*khair*) in 23:105. As such, the life of the *momineen* is such that all life's happiness is available to them and their authority knows no bounds. This is what "خَيْرٌ" (*khair*) is and which is the definite result of following Allah's orders. That is why when the opponents ask the *momineen*, tell us what your Sustainer has revealed, they reply "قَالُوا خَيْرًا" (*qaalu khair*) in 16:30. In this verse these words mean world's happiness and the expanse of authority.

It is explained by the words that follow:

16:30	pleasantness in this world as well as pleasantness in the Hereafter	فِي هٰذِهِ الدُّنْيَا حَسَنَةٌ وَلَدَا رُالْأَخِرَةِ خَيْرٌ

Thus, every deed which has the betterment of this world and the Hereafter is "خَيْرٌ" (*khair*) and the opposite of "الشَّرُّ" (*shar*). In pleasantness, the development of the human personality is supreme. Rather pleasantness is the development of the human personality. That which stultifies human development is "الشَّرُّ" (*shar*). The Quran gives us a program which results in pleasantness. It equates them with good deeds, which develop human capabilities and produce smoothness in the society. See heading (*Sd-L-H).*

Surah *Al-Baqrah* says about *Hajj* (pilgrimage):

2:197	you must take what is necessary to perform Hajj (pilgrimage): this will help prevent you from begging over there	وَتَزَوَّدُوا فَإِنَّ خَيْرَ الزَّادِ التَّقْوَى

Here "خَيْرٌ" (*khair*) means benefits and "تقوىٰ" (*taqwa*) means to be safe from the ignominy of being needy.

Kh-Y-Te خ ى ط

"اَلْخَیْطُ" (*al-khait*) means thread or chain etc. *{T}*.

Ibn Faris says it means to be long and thin.

"اَلْخِیَاطُ" (*al-khiyaat*) or "اَلْمِخْیَطُ" (*al-mikhyat*) means a needle *{T}*.
"فِی سَمِّ الْخِیَاطِ" (*fi sammil khiyaat*): in the needle of the eye (7:40).
"خَاطَ الثَّوْبَ" (*khaatas-saub*): to sew one part of the cloth with another *{M}*.
"خَیَّاطٌ" (*khaiyyaat*): tailor *{T}*.

The Quran, in respect of fasting says:

| 2:187 | white thread and black thread | اَلْخَیْطُ الْأَبْیَضِ وَ الْخَیْطِ الْأَسْوَدُ |

These words are relating to the light of dawn and the darkness of the night *{T}*. This shows that in the Quran, literal meanings do not apply and the meaning is with reference to the context.

As such, ***Lataif-ul-Lugha*** says that "اَلْخَیْطُ الْأَبْیَضُ" (*al-khaitul abyaz*) is taken to mean "اَلنُّوْرُ" (*an-noor*) which means light.
"اَلْخَیْطُ" (*al-khait*) also means color *{T}*, and even a group.

Kh-Y-L خ ى ل

"خَالَ" (*khaal*), "یَخَالُ" (*yakhaal*) means to conjecture, assumption.
"خَیَّلَ" (*khyyal*) means to estimate and guess.
"خُیِّلَ اِلَیْهِ اَنَّہُ کَذَا" (*khuyyila ilaihi annahu kaza*): he thought of something, something which is not as it seems but which appears so in one's thoughts.
"اَلسَّحَابَةُ الْمُخَیِّلَةُ" (*as sahabatu almuta-khayyila*) is a cloud which seems to be raining.
"اَلْخَیَالُ" (*al-khiyaal*) also means a scarecrow *{T}*.

With respect to such meanings, when the experts of the Pharaoh's court threw their ropes:

| 20:66 | due to their charm, it appeared to ***Moosa*** (Moses) as if they were moving (like snakes): | یُخَیَّلُ اِلَیْهِ مِنْ سِحْرِ ہِمْ اَنَّہَا تَسْعیٰ |

This means that they were not actually moving, but only gave the illusion of movement. Note how big a truth about illusion or "سحر" (*seher*) the Quran has revealed. It has said that due to illusion, the things do not actually change regardless what one's vision says. The effect is merely psychological.

The confusion only occurs when we take the meanings of such words literally, but if taken figuratively then the meaning would be something else. The details will be found at their own places.

See heading *(S-H-R)*.

"خُيَلَاءُ" (*khuyela*): pride without any cause (unjustifiably). That is, a man gives himself airs, but he does not have the greatness in him. He simply thinks in his mind that he is great. Someone who does this is called "مُخْتَالٌ" (*mukhtaal*), as in 31:18, which means one who is indulging in self-deceit.

Ibn Faris says it basically means an act which also includes delusion. This is the definition of "خَيَالٌ" (*khayaal*), which is actually something one dreams about. For one thing, everything in a dream is shifting, secondly the dreamers thinks that whatever he is dreaming about, is reality. This makes the meaning of this verse clearer, and elaborates the sorcery of the sorcerers, as well as earlier mentioned verse (20:66).

Raghib says this led to the word "خَيْلٌ" (*khail*) which means horses or a cavalry brigade (3:13), because a horse seems to be walking rather proudly, and a horseman also has a sort of pride in him as well.

Kh-Y-M   خ ى م

"تَخْيِيمٌ" (*takhyeem*) means to mount tents and then rest in them.

"خَيْمَةٌ" (*khaemah*) means any kind of temporary construction that Arabs used to set up for their rest. There are many definitions regarding the structure of such a construction, but the general concept is of setting up four wooden pillars covered with vegetation for shelter and shadow. Such a construction was called "خَيْمَةٌ" (*khaemah*). Those tents that were constructed with fabrics were called "مِظَلَّةٌ" (*mizallah*).

"خَيَّمَ الشَّىْءَ" (*khayyamash shay*) means that he covered on thing with another thing *{T}*.

"خِيَامٌ" (*khayaam*) is the plural form of "خَيْمَةٌ" (*khaemah*), as used in 55:72.

D-A-B   د ء ب

"اَلدَّابُ" (*ad-daab*), "اَلدَّأُبُ" (*addaobo*): to be continuously engaged in some work, to keep trying continuously.

Raghib says that it means situation, customs, and traditions.

"دَأُبَ فُلَانٌ" (*daaba folan*): that man tried continuously, became tired but kept on trying {*T, M, Aqrab al-Muwarid*}. *Kitaab-ul-Ashfaq* too says that "دَأُبٌ" (*da-ab*) means work done continuously without any break.

Ibn Faris says its basic meaning is of being persistent.

Surah *Aal-e-Imran* says:

3:10	according to the ways of the nation of the *Pharaoh*	كَدَأُبِ آلِ فِرْعَوْنَ

Surah *Yusuf* has "دَأَبًا" (*da-abba*) in verse 12:47 which means striving very hard continuously.

Surah *Ibrahim* says:

14:33	The sun and the moon revolve continuously in their orbits at their own speed. (They are continuously busy in performing their duties.)	وَالشَّمْسَ وَ الْقَمَرَ دَائِبَيْنِ

Dawood   داوُد

The Quran says that *Dawood* (David) was among the descendants of *Ibrahim* (Abraham).

6:84	And of his descendants was *Dawood*	وَمِنْ ذُرِّيَّتِهِ دَاوُدَ

Allah had given him *Zaboor*. Note that *Zaboor* also means 'a book'. But surah *Ambia* mentions *"Zaboor"* as a special book in 21:105. Perhaps this was the name of the book revealed to him. He was granted knowledge in profusion (27:15) and a stable rule (38.20), so that he could rule with equanimity and justice (38.26). The big leaders of the mountain tribes were very faithful and obedient to him and were busy in putting his program into action (38.18), as well as the gypsies of the *Tair* tribe who formed the cavalry brigade of the army (38.16).

Previously he had defeated the army of *Jaloot* (Goliath) fighting along with the army of *Bani Israel* and killed *Jaloot* as well (2:251). It seems like he was the inventor of armor, or that he had special expertise in it (21.80). His period was approximately 1000 B.C. It is said that he had a very beautiful voice. He is said to be the first person to edit Hebrew music and develop the Egyptian and Babylonian musical instruments, and Thus, invent new musical instruments. When he used to sit on the hill and play his musical instruments, even the trees swayed with the music. The **Torah** and our **Tafseer** books support this theory *{Tarjuman-ul-Quran}*.

D-B-B   د ب ب

"دَبَّ النَّمْل يَدِبُّ دَ بًّا" (***dabbal namalu yadibbu dabba***): to walk quietly.

"دَبَّ الشَّرَابُ فِى الْجِسْمِ" (***dabbah fil jism***): for wine to go down slowly in the body.

"اَلدَّابَّةُ" (***ad-dabbah***): any living thing that walks or crawls on the ground *{T, Latif-ul-Lugha}*.

"اَلدِّبَّةُ" (***adib-bah***): slow speed.

Ibn Faris says that this is the speed slower than "مَشْیًٌ" (***mashyun***).

"اَلدَّبَّابَةُ" (***addab-babah***): a big cart made of skins and wood used by soldiers to reach the fort gates to break it down *{T, Latif-ul-Lugha}*. A tank of the olden days used to move slowly and those inside were safe from the enemy's onslaught.

"اَلدَّبْدَبَةُ" (***addab-dabah***): the sound of a walk on hard ground, it also means a noise like beating the drum, and also the sound of the drum itself.

The Quran has used this word for all sorts of creatures including crawlers, two legged and four legged (24:45). The plural is "دَوَابُّ" (***dawaab***). In surah **Al-Hajj**, this word has been used for all living creatures except man (35:28)

Surah **An-Nahal** says:

16:61	If Allah held people responsible for their crimes immediately, then there would not be a ***da-abba*** (soul) (alive) on this earth.	لَوْ يُؤَاخِذُ اللهُ النَّاسَ بِظُلْمِهِمْ مَاتَرَكَ عَلَيْهَا مِنْ دَآبَّةٍ

See 35:45 as well

Here the word "دَآبَّةٌ" (***da-abbah***) has come for the humans themselves, because due to their wrong doings it is they who must be annihilated, not all other living creatures. But in a broader meaning, it could mean humans and other living beings as well.

Surah **Al-Anfaal** calls those who do not employ their intellect "شَرَّ الدَّوَابِّ" (***ash sharrad dwab***) in 8:22, that is, the worst among living things who walk, or even more astray than the other living things.

Surah **An-Namal** says:

27:82	And when the sentence against them is fulfilled, We shall bring forth a creature from the earth for them	وَإِذَا وَقَعَ الْقَوْلُ عَلَيْهِمْ أَخْرَجْنَا لَهُمْ دَآبَّةً مِنَ الْأَرْضِ تُكَلِّمُهُمْ

Raghib says it refers to those wicked people who behave like animals in their unawareness. This way this word becomes plural. But when the Quran uses the word "دَابَّةٌ" (**da-abbatun**) for humans, the example about animals is redundant. It will mean warring nations. This has been explained by "تُكَلِّمُهُمْ" (**tukallemohim**) which means to injure. But even if "تُكَلِّمُهُمْ" (**tukallemohim**) is taken to mean talk, it does not affect the meaning of "دَابَّةٌ" (**da-abbah**). See heading (K-L-W).

Surah **Saba** has used this word for **Suleman's** unworthy son (34:14). This means that he did not have the credentials of an intellectual human being, but a moving apparition. Details will be found under heading **Suleman**.

Surah **Hoodh** says:

11:6	There is not a single **da-abbah** on this earth for whose sustenance Allah is not responsible for.	وَمَا مِنْ دَآبَّةٍ فِى الْأَرْضِ اِلَّا عَلَى اللهِ رِزْقُهَا

A natural question that comes to mind after reading 11:6 is that if this statement is true, then why people die of hunger in this world. A single drought may claim millions of lives and even as it is, thousands die of hunger and starvation. If Allah is responsible for providing for them, then why does He not fulfill that responsibility? This is a very important question that demands an answer.

At such places, Allah's responsibility is fulfilled by the system set in place by following Allah's laws. This system takes upon itself all the responsibilities attributed to Allah and in this way all those rights and duties (mentioned in the Quran) are also shifted to the system which are called Allah's rights. Allah's system is followed by obeying His laws.

"عَلَى اللهِ رِزْقُهَا" (**alal lahi rizqoha**) means that the system is responsible for the sustenance of all. To provide for all living things, becomes its responsibility. The resources of sustenance are with it for safekeeping and are a trust. The system so distributes the sustenance given by Allah that nobody is deprived of it. This way Allah's responsibility is automatically fulfilled. But in the absence of such a system, hegemonic forces seize those resources, and the weaker of the human races live at their mercy. They provide as much as they want for the ones they want to provide for. The celestial revolution is for snatching these resources and hand them over to the system which provides for all.

Surah **Ash-Shura** says:

49:29	And one of Allah's signs is that He created the earth and the skies and heavenly bodies and the living things (**da- abba**) in them. And He is able to collect them according to the law of His will.	وَمِنْ اٰيٰتِهِ خَلْقُ السَّمٰوٰتِ وَالْأَرْضِ وَمَا بَثَّ فِيهِمَا مِنْ دَآبَّةٍ وَهُوَ عَلٰى جَمْعِهِمْ اِذَا يَشَآءُ قَدِيرٌ

This verse gives a clue as to creatures on other heavenly bodies. The days are coming near when one day the inhabitants of earth will intermingle with that of other planets. The Quran has clearly stated that whatever is contained in the earth and the skies has been subjugated to man. Therefore, the human effort to reach the heavenly bodies (moon, mars, etc.) is very much in keeping with the teachings of the Quran. Note how the Quranic verses provide clues to universal truths (41:35).

D-B-R   د ب ر

"اَلدُّبُرُ" (**ad-dubur**), "اَلدَّبْرُ" (**ad-dubr**): the back (end) of anything. It is also used for ones back and the anus.

Ibn Faris has said that it means the tail end of something. Plural form of it is "اَدْبَارٌ" (**ad-baar**).

The Quran says:

54:25	they will turn their backs	يُوَلُّونَ الدُّبُرَ
12:25	from behind	مِنْ دُبُرٍ
27:10	he turned his back and ran	وَلَّى مُدْبِرًا

"اِدْبَارٌ" (**idbar**): to move back, previous event.
"اِدْبَارَ النُّجُومْ" (**idbaran nujum**): the time for the stars to set at the end of night (52:49) {*T, M*}. Hence, it means the receding of the stars.

"اَلدَّابِرُ" (**ad-daabir**): the end of everything, the reality and basis {*T, M*}.

"اَلتَّدْبِيرُ" (**at-tadbeeru**), "اَلتَّدَبُّرُ" (**at-tadibbiru**): to deliberate on some issue with its end result in mind. To keep the last destination in mind while administrating.

6:45	last man of the nation was killed as well (nation was uprooted)	فَقُطِعَ دَابِرُ الْقَوْمِ
32:5	he plans matters	يُدَبِّرُ الْأَمْرَ
4:82	Do they not deliberate on what the Quran says?	أَفَلَا يَتَدَبَّرُونَ الْقُرْآنَ
38:29	so that they deliberate on its (the Quran's) verses	لِيَدَّبَّرُوا آيَاتِهِ
79:5	One who takes matters to completion (one who plans matters)	الْمُدَبِّرَاتِ أَمْرًا

Surah **Qaf** says following to the Messenger:

| 50:39 | Do not worry or be troubled by whatever his opponents said. Just continue being engaged in preparing (the people) in worshipping and praising the Lord. Strive from before the sunrise till sunset, as well as during the night, for the completion (establishment) of His system. | فَاصْبِرْ عَلَى مَا يَقُولُونَ وَسَبِّحْ بِحَمْدِ رَبِّكَ قَبْلَ طُلُوعِ الشَّمْسِ وَقَبْلَ الْغُرُوبِ۔ وَ مِنَ الَّيْلِ فَسَبِّحْهُ وَ أَدْبَارَ السُّجُودِ |

Surah **At-Toor** repeats almost the same thing in almost the same words but there it is said " أَدْبَارَ النُّجُومِ" (*adbaarin nujoom*), which means the time when stars set or recede.

Surah **Qaaf** has used "أَدْبَار" (*adbaar*) which is the plural of "دُبُرٌ" (*dubur*). The other word is "سُجُود" (*sujud*) which means to lean or bend towards someone. The ordinary exegesis books say that the meaning is "after-prayers", but this meaning does not make much sense, especially because the word used here is "أَدْبَار" (*adbaar*) not "إِدْبار" (*idbaar*). {*Lissan-ul-Arab. Tafseer Fatahul Qadeer (Shokani) - Tafseer Roohul Muani*}.

"دُبُر" (*dubur*) also means the end part of something, which is in any case included in that thing, and 'after' is used when something ends and then some other event or thing begins. We cannot say up till today with certainty what it really means.

D-Th-R   د ث ر

"اَلدَّثْرُ" (*ad-dasr*): enormous wealth.

"مَالٌ دَثْرٌ" (*maal dasr*): unbounded riches.

"اَلدِّثَارُ" (*ad-disaar*): a cloth which a man can wrap around himself.

"تَدَثَّرَ بِالثَّوْبِ" (*tadassara bis saub*): he wrapped himself in a cloth.

"دَثَرَ الشَّجَرُ دُثُورًا" (*dasarash shajaru dasoora*): the tree brought out new leaves and branches.

"هُوَ دَثْرُ مَالٍ" (*hudasru maal*): he is a good guard of the camels.

"تَدْثِيرُ الطَّائِرِ" (*tadreesut tayir*): a bird mends its nest.

"اَلدَّثُورُ" (*ad-dasoor*): slow, heavy, one who sleeps a lot, i.e. one who is wrapped in sheets.

"دَثَرَ الأَثَرُ" (*dasaral asar*): for a mark to be obliterated {*T, M, R*}.

Ibn Faris says it basically means for things to come one after the other, to be deposited layer upon layer, or to climb over.

Raghib and **Ibn Faris** have stated various meanings for this root, which include overwhelming someone.

"مَنْزَلٌ دَاثِرٌ" (*manzilun daasir*): the destination whose signs have been obliterated, or have been hidden by layer upon layer of dust.

The Quran has addressed the Messenger **Muhammad** as "يَاأَيُّهَا الْمُدَّثِّرُ" (*ya ayyohul mudassir*) in 74:1. Considering the meaning of "اَلدِّثَارُ" (*ad-disaar*) it is generally translated as. "*O, the one who has wrapped himself in a cloth*". But according to *tadreesut tayir,* it would mean "*O, one who sets his house in order*", and as per "دِثْرُ مَالِ" (*disru maal*), it would mean good caretaker. The meaning is Hence, "*O you who has the responsibility of setting humanity in order*", or "*O you who has come to solve humanity's problems with tactfulness and good scheme*". These meanings seem more appropriate. As per "دَثَرَ الشَّجَرُ" (*dasarush shajar*) it would mean "*O you whose coming heralds the dawn of a new era*", or "*O you with whose coming the garden of the world will see a new spring*"

After this address, the Messenger (*pbuh*) was told "قُمْ فَأَنْذِرْ" (*qum fa anzir*) in 74.2. This means "*rise and warn the world of the results of wrong deeds*". After this, the various elements of this revolutionary invitation have been brought forward. This too, reveals that "اَلْمُدَّثِّرُ" (*al-mudassir*) has the element of the wellbeing of humanity and the revolutionary message. This is what the responsibility and the particularity of a celestial inviter is.

Raghib's meaning has the element of overwhelming the untrue concepts, but could also mean overpowering.

The Quran says:

9:33	so that super imposes (overwhelms) it on all other religions or ways of life	لِيُظْهِرَهُ عَلَى الدِّينِ كُلِّهِ

Ibn Faris has given some examples:

"تَدَثَّرَ الرَّجُلُ فَرَسَهُ" (*tadassara-rajulu farasahu*): the man jumped and got on his horse *{Lisan-ul-Arab}*. Here "jumped up" is very important. This thing (revolution) does not take place gradually. The revolution which took place at the hands of the Messenger (*pbuh*) was also revolutionary. Thereafter the Quranic concepts are now gradually hold in the world. This is the evolutionary system. The world considers one concept, tests it and finds that the concept presented by the Quran was the correct one, and which the Messenger (*pbuh*) successfully implemented. Therefore, now gradually the Quranic concepts are replacing false concepts. But if a group takes up this concept or a government implements these concepts, then this concept can revolutionarily replace other concepts in the world. It is yet to be seen which nation initiates this noble work. That nation will be the biggest benefactor of mankind, and by its hands the universe will blossom and at its hands the flowers of life's tree will bloom once again.

Tafseer of Rohul Kuani says that "اَلْمُدَّثِّرُ" (*al-mudassir*) means one who is endowed with miracles and messenger-hood. Figuratively, it says that it also means a man who has no program before him and Hence, is free. This would mean that by saying "قُمْ فَأَنْذِرْ" (*qum fa anzar*) the Quran endowed him with a great program.

Tafseer Fatahal Qadeer says it means one who bears the responsibility of messenger-hood and its responsibilities. Some say that "اَلْمُدَّثِّرُ" (*al-mudassir*) initially was "اَلْمُتَدَّثِّرُ" (*al-mudatassir*), meaning someone from the linguistic group of "تَفَعُّلْ" (*tafa'aul*), and got transformed to its current state over time.

D-H-R   د ح ر

"اَلدَّحْرُ" (*ad-dahr*) means to get someone out, to oust someone, to remove someone, to push out or to oust insultingly *{T, R, M}*.

The Quran says:

37:8-9	And they are condemned by all sides. (they are the rejected ones of all accounts)	وَيُقْذَفُونَ مِنْ كُلِّ جَانِبٍ دُحُورًا
7:18	Ignominious, condemned, the removed one	مَذْءُ وْماً مَدْحُورًا

D-H-Zd   د ح ض

"دَحْضٌ" (*dahz*) actually means to slip. Later it came to mean to remove, obliterate or make untrue.

"دَحَضَ بِرِجْلٍ" (*dahaza berijlehi*) is said when somebody thrashes around like a slaughtered animal.

"مَكَانٌ دَحْضٌ" (*makanun dahz*) is a slippery place *{T, R, M}*.

Ibn Faris says it basically means to move out or to slip.

18:56	So they remove truth from its place through falsehood and make it useless.	لِيُدْحِضُوا بِهِ الْحَقَّ
42:16	Their reasoning and claim is very weak and transitory in the eyes of God.	حُجَّتُهُمْ دَاحِضَةٌ
7:141	He slipped, he lost strength, and he became weak and powerless.	فَكَانَ مِنَ الْمُدْحَضِينَ

D-H-W/Y   د ح و/ی

"دَحیٰ" (*daha*) is to spread out, to make vast {T}.

"دَحَاالْمَطَرُ الْحَصَا" (*dahal matarul hasa*): the rain washed out the pebbles.

"دَحَى الْإِبِلَ" (*dahal ibl*): he shooed the camels i.e. he drove them.

"مَرَّ الْفَرَسُ يَدْحُوْ دَحْواً" (*marralfarasu yadhu dahwa*): the horse ran digging his hooves in the ground {R}.

"بُوَيَدْ حُوْ بِالْحَجَرِ" (*huwaid hubilhajar*): he throws stones {Lisan-ul-Arab}.

Taj-ul-Urus says that the phrase which contains this meaning is "يَدْحُوْ الْحَجَرَ بِيَدِهٖ" (*yad hubilhajara biyadehi*).

Keep these meanings of "دَحَا" (*daha*) in mind and consider the Quranic verse in which it is said about the creation of heavenly bodies:

| 79:30 | And threw the earth after it and made it smooth | وَالْأَرْضَ بَعْدَ ذَلِكَ دَحَاهَا |

Surah *Al-Anbia* says:

| 21:30 | The heaven and the earth were previously joined together and then they got separated. | إِنَّ السَّمٰوٰتِ وَالْأَرْضَ كَانَتَا رَتْقاً فَفَتَقْنٰهُمَا |

Thus, the earth became a separate entity. Then with further changes it was made smooth (habitable). This fact has been stated as "دَحَابَا" (*dahaha*). The earth was separated as if it was a stone thrown from a sling, or as the rain washes out the pebbles afar. Note that about a thousand and five hundred years ago, such things were related about the universe only through the Revelation.

"بَعْدَ ذَالِکَ" (*ba'daa zalika*) reveals the fact that the earth was created later than the mass. That is, it came into existence in the second stage. The first stage is the mass when the earth and the sky were joined together. Then the heavenly bodies got separated from the mass and began to revolve in their own orbits (36:40).

D-Kh-R   د خ ر

"دَخَرَ" (*dakhar*), "يَدْخَرُ" (*yadkharu*), "دَخِرَ" (*dakhir*), "يَدْخَرُ" (*yadkhar*): to be humble (small), to be obedient and bow (before someone).

"اَلدَّاخِرُ" (*ad-dakhir*): someone who bows.

"دُخُوْرٌ" (*dukhur*): ignominy and smallness.

"اَلدَّخَرُ" (*adakhar*) means surprise which is actually a manifestation of the helplessness of the intellect (that reason which is unable to explain something).

"أَدْخَرَهُ" (*adkhara*): he insulted him, made him helpless {T, R, M}.

The Quran says about the things in the universe that they are "داخِرُوْن" (*daakheroon*) in 16:48. This means that they are subservient to the laws of Allah.

This meaning has been made explicit by the next adjacent verse which says:

| 16:46 | Whatever there is in the highs and lows of the universe, is subservient to Allah. | لِلّٰهِ يَسْجُدُ مَا فِى السَّمٰوٰتِ وَمَا فِى الْاَرْضِ |

For details, see heading (**S-J-D**).

D-Kh-L   د خ ل

"دَخَلَ" (*dakhala*), "يَدْخُلُ" (*yadkhulu*): entered, it is the opposite of "خَرَجَ" (*kharaja*), as in 2:111.
"اَدْخَلَ" (*adkhal*): made him enter (17:80).
"دَاخِلَةُ الْاَرْضِ" (*daakhilatul ard*): things which are hidden (buried) inside the earth.
"اَلدَّخْلُ" (*ad-dakhl*): the income from one's property.
"اَلدَّخَلُ" (*ad-dakhal*): It means deceit, as well as intellectual or physical deterioration, and also chaos {*T*}.
It also alleges internal deterioration and enmity, according to **Raghib**.

Surah *An-Nahal* says:

| 16:92 | You make your promises the basis for your mutual chaos. | تَتَّخِذُوْنَ اَيْمَانَكُمْ دَخَلًا بَيْنَكُمْ |

Here "دَخَلٌ" (*dakhal*) means chaos and conflict.

"دَخَلَ بِالْمَرْأَةِ" (*dakhal bil mar'ah*): he had sexual intercourse with a woman.

Surah *An-Nisa* says:

| 4:23 | Out from the wombs of the women with whom you have had sexual intercourse (out of wedlock) | مِنْ نِسَاءِكُمُ الّٰتِىْ دَخَلْتُمْ بِهِنَّ |

In surah *At-Tauba*, while mentioning the mentality of the hypocrites, it is said that they have come with you to the battlefield unwillingly.

Their condition is such that:

| 9:87 | If they would find some place to hide or escape to, or entrance to some hiding place, then they will run towards it madly. | لَوْ يَجِدُوْنَ مَلْجَاً اَوْ مَغٰرٰتٍ اَوْ مُدَّخَلًا لَّوَلَّوْ اِلَيْهِ وَهُمْ يَجْمَحُوْنَ |

Here the Quran has used the word "مُدَّخَلًا" (*muddakhala*) which indicates to that if they can find even a small place to hide, then they will try to enter it, no matter how much they have to strive for it.

D-Kh-N   د خ ن

"اَلدُّخَانُ" (*ad-dukhaan*): smoke.

"دَخَنَ الْغُبَارُ دُخُونًا" (*dakhanal ghubaaru dukhuna*): the dust rose {*T, M, R*}.

"دَخَنُ الْفِتْنَةِ" (*dakhanul fitna*): to disclose some *fitnah* (something that would lead to anarchy) something that instigate (people to chaos) {*T*}.

"خُلُقٌ دَاخِنٌ" (*khulqun daakhin*): bad manners.

"اَلدُّخَانُ" (*ad-dukhaan*) means drought or hunger because a hungry man perceives a sort of cloud between the earth and the sky (the atmosphere is cloudy to him). Some say that hunger is called "دُخَانٌ" (*dukhaan*) because in a drought the dust rises and makes a sort of cloud. It also means anything bad, and deterioration.

"اَلدُّخَانُ" (*ad-dukhan*) is used for something bad or dysfunctional.

"يَوْمٌ دَخْنَانٌ" (*yaumun dukhnaan*): a day of intense heat and travails {*T*}.

The Quran says that the earth was created in two stages:

41:11	Then He turned to the other heavenly bodies which were in a smoky condition (or in gaseous condition).	ثُمَّ اسْتَوَىٰ إِلَى السَّمَاءِ وَ هِيَ دُخَانٌ

Modern science confirms this although the Quran had disclosed it about fifteen hundred years ago. The earliest form of the heavenly bodies is indeed said to be nebulous.

Surah *Ad-Dukhaan* says:

44:10	When the atmosphere is filled with smoke.	يَوْمَ تَأْتِى السَّمَاءُ بِدُخَانٍ مُبِينٍ

This verse could mean the time when problems and difficulties abound. There will be chaos and anarchy everywhere, or the sky will seem filled with smoke due to hunger or drought. It will be a great punishment (44:11).

D-R-A   د ر ء

"دَرَأَهُ" (*daraa*), "يَدْرَؤُهُ" (*badra-oo*), "دَرْأَ" (*draa*): to reject and to remove angrily {*T, M, R*}.

"دَرَأَ عَلَيْهِمْ دُرُوْأ" (*dara'a alaihim durwa*): to appear before someone suddenly.

"جَاءَ الشَّيْلُ دَرْأ" (*ja'ashaylo dar'a*): the flood appeared from nowhere {*T*}.

"دَرَأْتُهُ عَنِّي" (*daratohu anni*): I removed him from my side (3:167).

"مُدَارَأَةٌ" (*mudaarah*): means opposition and defiance {*T*}.

The Quran says:

| 24:8 | this can remove (save) the woman from punishment | وَيَدْرَؤُا عَنْهَا الْعَذَابَ |
| 28:54 | Get rid of *sayyeaat* (sins, or bad things) with good things (Behavior etc.) | وَيَدْرَؤُونَ بِالْحَسَنَةِ السَّيِّئَةَ |

This is a great reality which the Quran has mentioned at different places in different styles. It says a bad thing in return for a bad thing is not the answer. If you are weak, then germs will attack you and sicken you. The cure is to increase your defiance. This way your deterioration will be checked and your constructive process will continue. In every aspect of life, this is the right way of defense. This is called the scales of goodness to tip.

"تَدَاؤُ وا فِي الْخُصُومَةِ" (*tada aoo fil khusumah*) means to push and shove each other, or to blame each other and Thus, have differences {*T*}. In these meanings this word has been used in 2:72 "فَادَّارَءَ ثُمَّ فِيْهَا" (*fa ad-dara'otum fiha*). Scholars of dictionaries say that this was in reality "تَدَارَأْتُمْ" (*tadaaratum*).

D-R-J   د ر ج

"دَرَجَ" (*daraj*): to walk very slowly, to crawl {*T*}. It means to walk like a mountaineer i.e. like climbing a mountain {*R*}.
"مَدْرَجَةُ الطَّرِيْقِ" (*madrajatut tareeq*): the distinct and open part of the road.
"دَرَجَ الْقَوْمُ" (*daraj al-qaum*): the nation dwindled gradually, and became extinct.

The Quran says:

| 7:182 | We will catch them slowly (gradually) and they will not even know where the destruction came from | سَنَسْتَدْرِجُهُمْ مِنْ حَيْثُ لَا يَعْلَمُوْنَ |

"دَرَجَ الشَّيْءَ" (*darajash shai yi*): he folded the thing and wrapped it.
"اَلدَّرْجُ" (*ad-darj*): something on which there is some writing.
"دَرْجُ الْكِتَابِ" (*darjul kitaab*): a fold of the book {*T*}.
"اَلدَّرَجَةُ" (*ad-darajah*): one of the steps of a ladder (the steps which take one upwards)
"دَرَجَاتٌ" (*darajaat*): the steps which will bring you downwards are "درکات" (*darakaat*) {*L*}.
"اَلْمَدَارِجُ" (*al-madaarij*): the mountain roads which generally get higher with every turn {*T*}.

Raghib says "دَرَجَةٌ" (*darajah*) and "مَنْزِلٌ" (*manzilah*) are almost the same, but *manzilah,* which is a place to get down to, is called *darajah* when it is being used to climb upwards. *Darajah* is also taken to mean value and estimation and Thus, means honors, or stages over one another.

The Quran says regarding those who engage themselves in *jihad* that their status, or "دَرَجَةٌ" (*darajah*) is over "قَاعِدِيْنَ" (*qa'ideen*) or those who remain seated behind (4:95).

Surah *At-Tauba* says the following regarding those who do jihad and those who migrate for this cause:

| 9:20 | Those who are peace seekers have migrated and done jihad in the way of Allah with their wealth and lives, hold a high status with Allah | الَّذِينَ آمَنُواْ وَهَاجَرُواْ وَجَاهَدُواْ فِي سَبِيلِ اللّهِ بِأَمْوَالِهِمْ وَأَنفُسِهِمْ أَعْظَمُ دَرَجَةً عِندَ اللّهِ |

The Quran says about men and women:

| 2:228 | women, according to good practices, have rights according (apropos) their responsibilities | وَلَهُنَّ مِثْلُ الَّذِي عَلَيْهِنَّ بِالْمَعْرُوفِ |

That is, just as men have rights over women, women too have rights over men. As per the responsibilities and rights, no one has superiority over the other. Both are equal in this respect.

But after this, it is said:

| 2:228 | men have superiority over women in one thing | وَلِلرِّجَالِ عَلَيْهِنَّ دَرَجَةٌ |

What is that one thing? The next verse says that a divorced woman will have to observe "عِدَّتْ" (*iddat*) or celibacy for a period during which she cannot wed another man, but men do not have to observe this period. Also if the man has divorced the woman and repents it, then he can bring the woman back into his wedlock during this period.

| 2:228 | And their husbands would do better to take them back in that case if they desire reconciliation. | وَبُعُولَتُهُنَّ أَحَقُّ بِرَدِّ هِنَّ فِي ذَالِكَ إِنْ أَرَادُوا إِصْلَاحاً |

Now consider human history. Everywhere you will find "عَلَيْهِنَّ" (*al-aihinna*) i.e. only rights for men and responsibilities for women! No right of women will be accepted as a right and a woman cannot demand any of her rights a matter of right. This revolutionary voice that women have rights as well came only from the Quran, so many years ago. These few words (of the verse) have brought a revolutionary change in man's social or civilized life. Look how composite these words are which don't leave matters at the will of any individual or society. It has been made a provision in the laws of Allah (that women have rights too). The Quran also tells you what the matter is in which men are superior.

But this does not mean that equality in rights is equality in responsibilities. According to their functions, Nature has differentiated between them. They have been created differently (according to their biology) and a woman is supposed to fulfill the responsibilities she is required to fulfill while men according to theirs. The woman's responsibility which man cannot fulfill is to give birth and bring up the children. Since this takes up most of the woman's time, earning has been made man's responsibility (2:34).

D-R-R   د ر ر

"اَلدَّرّ" (**ad-dar**): milk (but it has the connotation of a thick stream and abundance).

"اَلدَّرَّة" (**aliddarrah**): profusion of milk.

"اِسْتَدَرَّ اللَّبَنُ" (**istadar ral laban**): the milk became abundant.

"دَرَّتِ السَّمَاءُ بِالْمَطَرِ" (**darratis sama-o bil matar**): it rained heavily from the skies.

"مِدْرَارٌ" (**midrar**): clouds which cause heavy rain (6:6).

"دَرَّ السِّرَاجُ" (**darras siraaj**): the lamp became well lighted (bright).

"كَوْكَبٌ دُرِّىٌّ" (**kaukabun durriyyun**): shiny, bright star *{T, R}* which sends forth rays of light (22.35), or like a pearl.

Muheet says that "اَلدَّرُّ" (**ad-daar**) means for one thing to be born from another, like milk from animals, brightness from the stars, etc. *Ibn Faris* agrees with this meaning as well.

It also means movement and unease. Allah has termed the light of His guidance (the noble Quran) as "كَوْكَبٌ دُرِّىٌّ" (**kaukabun durriyyun**), like a star which sends forth the light of knowledge and insight, and which is not stagnant but with continuous movement. This light is born of God's Divine knowledge and spreads to all corners of the earth.

D-R-S   د ر س

"دَرَسَ الشَّيْئُ" (**daras shaiyi**) means something became old and was obliterated *{M}*.

Ibn Faris says it basically means to hide, to be low and be obliterated.

"دَرَسَهُ الْقَوْمُ" (**darasu hool qaum**): the people removed all signs of it (obliterated it).

"طَرِيْقٌ مَدْرُوْسٌ" (**tariqun madroos**) means a path (the signs) that due to the pedestrian traffic has been obliterated.

"دَرَسَ الْحِنْطَةَ" (**darasil hintah**) means to take the cereal out of the ears of corn by having oxen walk over the laid wheat crop which separates the grain from the chaff.

"دَرَسَ" (**darasa**) means to rub something so much that it becomes obliterated.

"دَرَسَ النَّاقَةَ" (**darasan naaqah**) means to walk a camel so much that it becomes obedient.

"اَلْمُدَارَسَةُ" (**al-mudarasa**) means to strive continuously for something or look after it continuously *{T}*.

"دَرَسَ الْكِتَابَ يَدْرُسُهُ" (**darasal kitaaba yarusuhu**) means to read a book so many times that one memorizes it.

Surah *Aal-e-Imraan* says:

3:79	Because you have been studying the Book	بِمَا كُنْتُمْ تَدْرُسُوْنَ الْكِتَابَ

"تَدْرُسُوْنَ" (*tadrusoon*): to (tread) or read a book in such a way that its meanings become explicitly clear. It means to read something continuously so that the truths hidden in it comes out explicitly and clearly. It may also mean the concepts that receded in Man's mind, come up to the surface.

Surah **An-Anaam** has used the word "دِرَاسَةٌ" (*diraasah*) in 6:157 for study with a lot of attention:

| 6:157 | we were truly unaware of studying them | وَاِنْ كُنَّا عَنْ دِرَاسَتِهِمْ لَغٰفِلِيْنَ |

<h1 style="text-align:center">D-R-K   د ر ک</h1>

Ibn Faris says that the basic meanings of "تَدَرَکَ" (*taraka*) is to pursue something and then join it, reach it, catch it

Surah **Taha** says:

| 20:77 | You shall not fear that (**Firoun**) shall pursue and catch you | لَا تَخَافُ دَرَكاً |

Surah **Ash-Shurah** says that the fellowship of **Moosa** said:

| 24:64 | Now we are caught | اِنَّا لَمُدْرَكُوْنَ |

So what they are saying is that they feel that the soldiers of **Firoun** have gained upon them.

"تَدَرَکَ" (*tadaraka*) means to gain upon someone. It has a connotation of keen reaching to something.

Surah **Al-Qalam** says:

| 68:49 | If the benevolence of his Sustainer had not have reached him | لَوْلَاۤ اَنْ تَدَارَكَهُ نِعْمَةٌ |

That is said with regards to the life of **Yunus** which passed through several travails, but God's benevolence and help was continuously with him.

"اَلَّدَرَاكُ" (*ad-draak*): for one thing to continuously follow another.
"اَلتَّدْرِيْكُ مِنَ الْمَطَرِ" (*at-tadrikal minal matar*): for the raindrops to fall down continuously (one after another) {*T*}.
"اَلَّدَرَکَ و لَدَّرَکَ" (*ad-daraka wad darak*): the end of something's depth, bottom of something.
"اَلَّدَرَکُ" (*ad-derku*) means the opposite of "دَرْجٌ" (*darj*). The steps of a ladder are called "دَرَجَاتٌ" (*darajaat*) when used for climbing up, while same steps are called "دَرَكَاتٌ" (*darakaat*) when used for stepping down. {*T, M*}.

This is why the Quran has termed the stages of the **jannah** as "دَرَجَاتٌ" (*darajaat*), and the stages of **jahannam** as "دَرَكَاتٌ" (*darakat*).

| 4:145 | the bottom of *jahannam* | فِى الدَّرْكِ الْاَسْفَلِ مِن لنَّارِ |

Note that a ladder has the same steps for going up or down. A man can use the very same steps for going up or coming down. Life too is the same way. Whichever way one wants to live, it can be the means of taking it to the resultant destination, whether to the heights or the depths of life.

"اَدْرَكَهُ" (*adrakahu*): reached him, got to him.

"اَدْرَكْتُهُ بِبَصَرِى" (*adaraktuhu be basari*): I found him with my eyes (I spotted him), saw him *{T}*.

"اِدْرَاكٌ" (*idraak*) is that knowledge which is acquired through the senses.

Surah *Yunus* says:

| 10:90 | When drowning overtook him. (he drowned, when he saw his drowning, when he felt that he was drowning) | حَتّى اِذَا اَدْرَكَهُ الْغَرَقُ |

"اَدْرَكَ الشَّىْءُ" (*adrakash shaiyi*): the thing completed its time and was completed, reached its climax *{T}*.

The Quran says:

| 27:66 | that their knowledge about the Hereafter ended | بَلِ ادَّرَكَ عِلْمُهُمْ فِىْ الْاخِرَةِ |

Scholars have said that the above verse means that they could not grasp its whole truth, and remained unaware of the Hereafter *{T}*.

Raghib says that along with these meanings, it could also mean that they will come to know about it in the Hereafter. But it does not seem to portray the meaning of the verse correctly.

The Quran says that knowledge about the Hereafter has reached them continuously, but still they are in doubt over its existence like the blind in the darkness.

| 27:66 | On the contrary, their knowledge of the Hereafter has declined. They are on the contrary in doubt of it. | بَلْ هُمْ فِىْ شَكٍّ مِنْهَا بَلْ هُمْ مِنْهَا عَمُونَ |

Darham   دربم

"اَلدِّرْبَمَ" (**ad-dirham**): a silver coin. The plural is "دَرَابِمُ" (**draahem**). This is not an Arabic word. Some say it is actually a **Farsi (Persian)** word, and others say it is Greek *{T}*. But it seems that it is the Arabic form of the Roman word **Drawburg**. Very similar are the words **Deenaar (Dinarins)** and **Fils**.

Surah **Yusuf** says:

12:20	(they sold **Yusuf**) for a few **Dirhams**	دَرَاهِمُ مَعْدُودَةٍ

D-R-Y   د ر ى

"دَرَيْتُهُ" (**dareetah**): I now know about him (21:109).

"اَدْرَاهُ بَمَ" (**adra'o bi**): told him about him *{T}*.

"دِرَايَةٌ" (**diraayah**) means to find out by some effort or tact or to find about something which is doubtful.

This is the reason that this word is not used for Allah *{T}*.

Ibn Faris says its basic meanings include intending and to demand or ask for. It also means "to be sharp".

As such "مِدْرًى" (**midrun**) mean a comb, because its teeth are pointy and sharp. This means "دِرَايَةٌ" (**dirayah**) contains the meaning of sharpness as well as intention.

Raghib says that wherever Quran says "مَاأَنْرَاكَ" (ma adraaka) which means "do you know?", or "has somebody made you aware?" It always follows with an explanation. For example see 97:2. But wherever it says "مَاأَنْرِيكَ" (ma yudreeka) which means "what tells you?" does not follow with an explanation. Instead, "لَعَلْ" (la-al) or perhaps has been said and the subject at hand has been discussed (see 42:17, 33:63, 80:3). This means that after "مَاأَنْرَاكَ" (ma adraaka), knowledge (about the thing) has been positively given, but after "مَاأَنْرِيكَ" (ma yudreeka) it is said that "لَعَلْ" (la'al) perhaps it can be so.

Surah **Al-Baqrah** says:

97:2	What do you know about **lailat-ul-qadr?**	وَمَا أَدْرَاكَ مَالَيْلَةُ الْقَدْرِ

After this "لَيْلَةُ الْقَدْرِ" (**lailat-ul-qadr**) has been explained.

It is the converse in surah **Ash-Shura**:

42:17	What do you know? Perhaps the time for the revolution is near.	وَمَايُدْرِيكَ لَعَلَّ السَّاعَةَ قَرِيبٌ

These examples explain the difference of "مَا أَدْرَاكَ" (*ma adraaka*) and "مَايُدْرِيْكَ" (*ma yudreeka*).

D-S-R   د س ر

"دُسُرٌ" (*dusur*) is the plural of "دِسَارٌ" (*disaar*) which means a nail or a stave.

"دَسْرٌ" (*dasr*) basically means harshness and to push hard *{R}*.

"دَسَرَ الدِّسَارُ" (*dasarud dissar*): hammered the nails very hard.

"اَلدِّسَارُ" (*ad-disaar*) also means the rope woven from the strands of the date palms with which the boards of a boat are fastened together.

Ibn Faris says this meaning is not right.

"دَسْرَاءُ" (*dasra-oo*) also means the boat itself *{T}* because it pushes the water ahead of it as it moves ahead.

The Quran has called the ark of **Nooh** as:

54:13	An ark made of boards and staves	ذَاتِ أَلْوَاحٍ وَدُسُرٍ

If "دُسُرٌ" (*dusur*) really means staves, (not a boat of date palm fiber) then it shows that in those days metal had begun to be used and boats too were not made of hollowed out trunks of trees but instead were built from boards and nails. About the boat, it is also said in the Quran that **Nooh's** ark was made under God's guidance or instructions (11:37). Perhaps in those days, this craft too was imparted through divine revelation and then its usage became common.

One hardly knows what human history may reveal. Perhaps many things which we think are the product of human intelligence are actually introduced by divine revelations.

D-S-S/W   د س س/و

"اَلدَّسُّ" (*ad-das*): to hide something underneath something or bury it *{T}*.

Raghib has added to the meaning by saying that it means to make helpless. That is to force something into something by force *{R}*.

"دَسَسْتُ الشَّيْءَ فِى التَّرَابِ" (*dasastu shaiyi fit turaab*): I hid the thing in the ground *{T}*.

Surah **An-Nahal** says that during the period of unawareness when the Arabs got news about the birth of a girl child, their thought was:

16:59	Perhaps he should bury her in the ground	أَمْ يَدُسُّهُ فِى التُّرَابِ

Surah **Ash-Shams** says about human intention:

91:10	He who developed it (on the right lines) became successful (his fields bore fruit)	قَدْ اَفْلَحَ مَنْ زَكَّهَا
91:11	He who buried it became unsuccessful	وَقَدْ خَابَ مَنْ دَسَّهَا

For a seed to develop, it must be buried in the ground. If the proportion of water, earth, air, temperature and light is correct, then the seed develops and blossoms into a strong tree. But if the same seed is buried too deep, it loses all its capabilities. The human personae have been endowed with latent capabilities to develop, but these capabilities are developed in this physical world. If physical forces are used properly then human personality's latent talents are developed. If the personality is buried under self-interests, then its capabilities are stultified.

"دَسَّىٰ" (dassa) was actually "دَسَّسَ" (dassasa). Since three "س" (seen) together are not feasible, the word has become "دسَّىٰ" (dassa).

Fara and **Zajaj** say this means miserliness. Because a miser hides himself while a philanthropist is open and prominent, this meaning is in one way right. The Quran has itself said the development of a human being is in giving, while miserliness has been described as a reason for destruction.

92:5-10	Then as for him who gives and believes in the best. Then we will ease him towards ease, but as for who withholds and considers himself free from need and denies the best. Then We will ease him towards difficulty.	فَاَمَّا مَنْ اَعْطَىٰ وَاتَّقَىٰ وَصَدَّقَ بِالْحُسْنَىٰ فَسَنُيَسِّرُهُ لِلْيُسْرَىٰ وَاَمَّا مَنْ بَخِلَ وَاسْتَغْنَىٰ وَكَذَّبَ بِالْحُسْنَىٰ فَسَنُيَسِّرُهُ لِلْعُسْرَىٰ

This is what **rabubiyah** (providence) is. That is, to develop oneself by providing for others and this is what the Quran teaches us to do.

With regards to hiding "اَلدَّسِيْسَةُ" (ad-dasyasah) is that misconception and fraud that is hidden, or a thing that enters secretly {M}.

The linguists have said "دَسَّهَا" (dassaha) comes from the root **(D-S-S)** as well as **(D-S-Y)**. This is the reason why we have included both roots under the same heading.

D-Ain-Ain د ع ع

"اَلدَّعُّ" (*ad-da'a*): to push hard.

"دَاعٍ" (*daa-ee, daa'ee*): an admonishing voice for the goatherd.

"اَلدَّعَاعُ" (*ad-da'a*): a man's small children *{T}* (for which he is pushed around in society).

The Quran says:

| 107:6 | this is him who pushes (away) the orphans | فَذَالِكَ الَّذِى يَدُعُّ الْيَتِيْمَ |

Surah *At-Toor* says:

| 52:13 | The day when they will be pushed hard towards the fire of *jahannam* (hell) | يَوْمَ يُدَعُّوْنَ إِلَى نَارِ جَهَنَّمَ دَعًّا |

Ibn Faris says the basic meaning of the word is to push and unease.

Consider the verse of surah *Al-Ma'on* once again:

107:1	Have you ever wondered about the man who denies this way of life?	أَرَءَ يْتَ الَّذِى يُكَذِّبُ بَالدِّيْنِ
107:2	this is him who pushes (away) the orphans	فَذَالِكَ الَّذِى يَدُعُّ الْيَتِيْمَ
107:3	and does not pursued (others too) for feeding the destitute	وَلَا يَحُضُّ عَلَى طَعَامِ الْمِسْكِيْنِ

Note how closely the way of Islam (*Deen*) and economics are related. This relationship is even found in *salaah* and economics as well, because the next verse says that there is destruction for those who are unaware of the true meaning of *salaah*.

People like this offer their prayers, thinking that it is *salaah*, but build barriers against the sources of sustenance and prevent them from reaching the needy, although they (the resources) should be like flowing water, available for everybody. (Further details will be found under relevant headings).

D-Ain-W د ع و

"دَعَا" (*da'a*) means to call someone.

"اَلدَّعَاءَ ةُ" (*ad-da'ah*) means the forefinger which is used as a sign to call someone.

"اَلدَّاعِيَةُ" (*ad-dayiah*) means the cry of the horses in battle.

"هُوَ مِنِّى دَعْوَةَ لِرَجُلٍ" (*huwaminni dawatar rajul*): He is at a distance where a man's voice can reach him. He is at a calling distance *{T}*.

Ibn Faris says it means to incline towards oneself through talk or voice.

"دَعَاہُ اِلَی الْاَمِیْرِ" (*dayahu ila al-ameer*): he took him towards the leader.

"دَاعٍ" (*dayi*) is not only one who calls but also someone who takes you to someone *{T}*.

"اِدَّعَاؤٗ" (*iddia'oo*), "یَدَّعُوْنَ" (*yad-da'oon*) means to wish or desire *{T}*, or to call out to someone (67:28).

"تَدَاعَوْا عَلَیْہِ" (*tadau alaih*): means they gathered against him.

"تَدَاعٰی عَلَیْہِ الْعَدُوُّ مِنْ کُلِّ جَانِبٍ" (*tada'a alaihal aduwu min kulli jaanib*) means the enemy attacked him from all sides.

"تَدَاعَتِ الْحِیْطَانُ" (*tadaa'atil haitaan*) means the walls fell down one after another *{T}*.

"دَعَوْتُہٗ زَیْدًا" (*da'autuhu zaida*): I named him *Zaid*.

"اَلدَّعِیُّ" (*ad-dayee'o*): adopted son *{T}*, plural is "اَدْعِیَاؤُ" (*addia'o*) as in 33:4.

"اَلدَّاعِیَۃُ" (*ad-daayiah*): is the milk that is left behind in the teats of animals so that with its help the animal can be milked again *{T}*. It also means the reason, or cause.

"اَلدَّوَاعِیْ" (*ad-dawa'ee*): such things as tempt or instigate people's emotions or desires *{M}*.

These meanings should be kept in mind because they throw light on the meaning of the word "دُعَاؤٌ" (*dua*), or prayer/supplication.

2:23	call those who may help you	وَادْعُوْا شُشَدَاءَکُمْ

In surah *Kahaf*, "نَادٰی" (*nadyaa*) and "دَعَا" (*da'a*) have been used in a similar meaning as in 18:25.

In surah *Airaaf*, "صَمَتَ" (*samat*), which means to be quiet, has been used against "دَعَا" (*da'a*) in 7:193.

As such "دَعَا" (*da'a*) would mean to call.

Surah *Al-Baqrah* says:

2:61	Call out to your God on our behalf	فَادْعُ لَنَا رَبَّکَ

"اَلدَّعْوٰی" (*ad-da'wyaa*): to call out, demand, require (10:10)

We have now come to that part of "دَعَا" (*da'a*), considered to be prayers, which has been taxed as the most complicated one in the world of scholars and religion, because its explicit meaning has not been given. Consider an example. In some case, *Zaid* is the Prosecution and *Bakar* the *Defence*. *Zaid* prays to God that the case is decided in his favor. This raises the following questions:

a)   One group of people believes that all matters are decided beforehand by God. If this is taken to be correct, then it would mean that it has already been decided that the case will be decided in *Zaid's* favour or against. If it was decided by God beforehand, then *Zaid's* prayer will not change God's already made decision and Zaid will now not win the case if he was already destined to lose it.

If this is not so, then it would mean that God changes His decisions according to men's prayer or bidding. This would then imply that He is obedient to men. This concept cannot be right in any case.

b)   Now if we suppose that *Zaid's* claim in the case was false or fabricated, would then God decide the case in his favor because he prayed? If this is true, then it would mean that God decided in favor of a liar and deprived the truthful from his right. This concept too about God is wrong.

c)   Suppose that *Zaid* is justified in his claim. Now if *Zaid* does not pray to God, then would the case be decided in his favor or not? If the case cannot be decided in his favor without praying then it would mean that God does not decide in favor of the truth on His own. The truthful has to plead before God in order to obtain a decision in his favor even though he did nothing wrong. This concept too about God is wrong. If God decides in favor of truth, then it does not make a difference whether *Zaid* prays or not. God in any case had to decide in his favor (that is, in favor of the truth). As such, praying is a useless effort!

d)   It is obvious that in order to win a case, a man has to make some effort, however ethical. Now if *Zaid* only prays, and does not make the required effort, will he win the case? If praying is enough to win the case then it would mean that God's stress on effort (deed) is useless? Also if one cannot win the case without making the required effort, then what is the usage of any praying?

e)   If *Zaid* prays to God and *Bakar* does it as well, then in whose favor will the case be decided? Whose prayer will God accept?

These questions and many others arise with regards to the concept of praying to God, where religions and philosophers have been trying to solve or answer these questions for centuries, but with no luck.
Please note that the term religion is a manmade concept while following Gods instructions is called *Deen*.

The Quran has said that this concept of *dua* or praying is wrong and a product of the time when man was in his infant stage and was unaware of the law of causality.

The Quran clarified that:

1)   Everything in the universe is operating according to the order created by God. He never changes His laws. "وَلَنْ تَجِدَ لِسُنَّتِ اللهِ تَبْدِيْلاً" (*walan tajeda sunnatillahi tabdeelah*) (33:64), i.e. "You will not find any change in God's laws".

2)   It is God's law which is operative in man's world as well. He who strives as much under these laws will succeed proportionately. "لَيْسَ لِلْإِنْسَانِ الَّا مَاسَعٰى۔ وَأَنَّ سَعْيَهٗ سَوْفَ يُرٰى" (*laisa lil insaana illa ma sa'a, wa unna sa'yahu saufa yura*). 53:39-40, i.e. "There is nothing for man other than what he works for, and the result of his efforts will soon be made manifest".

At the same time, the Quran has made it clear to believe that simply by praying (and not making any effort), one's wish is granted, is an erroneous concept about God.

Surah **Ar-Raad** says "لَهٗ دَعْوَةُ الْحَقِّ" (*lahu dawatul haq*). This means that human invitation which can produce successful results, which can be said to be based on truth, is the same invitation with which you invite someone towards your sustainer (according to His law and order).

"وَالَّذِيْنَ يَدْعُوْنَ مِنْ دُوْنِهٖ لَا يَسْتَجِيْبُوْنَ لَهُمْ بِشَيْءٍ" (*wallazeena yad'ona min doonehi la yastajeebuna lahum bish shaiyi*): those who attach their wishes to others beside God, that is, believe that by leaving aside the Laws of God, they can succeed on the basis of their superstitions, are wrong. These self-created forces can never fulfill their wishes.

Such people can be likened to "كَبَاسِطِ كَفَّيْهِ اِلَى الْمَاءِ لِيَبْلُغَ فَاهُ وَمَا هُوَ بِبَالِغِهٖ" (*kabasiti kaffiyahi ilal ma-ee liyab lugha fa hu wama huwa bi-balighihi*): as if a man sits beside a river and prays that the water may come into his mouth, the water will never come into his mouth on its own. As such, "وَمَادُعَاءُ الْكَافِرِيْنَ اِلَّا فِىْ ضَلَالٍ" (*wama dua-ool kafireena illa fi zalaal*) 13:14: Those who deny God's verses or God's sayings, their praying can never produce results.

Do you not see that "وَلِلّٰهِ يَسْجُدُ مَنْ فِى السَّمٰوٰتِ وَالْأَرْضِ طَوْعًا وَّ كَرْهاً" (*walil lahi mun fis samawaati wal ardi tau-an wa karha*) 3:15: everything in the universe, willingly or not, has to operate according to the Laws of God. Then how can man be an exception to this?

As such, according to the Quran, calling out to God means calling out to the Laws of God for help. That is, by obeying them in order to find the desired results. This fact has been clarified at various points in the Quran.

For example the Quran says:

| 40:60 | Your Sustainer says "Call out to me, I will respond to your call" | وَقَالَ رَبُّكُمُ ادْعُوْنِى أَسْتَجِبْ لَكُمْ إِنَّ |

The meaning of the above verse will be explained a little further ahead. After this, it is said:

| 40:60 | Indeed, those who refuse to accept my authority enter the state of *jahannum* after distress and humiliation | اِنَّ الَّذِیْنَ یَسْتَکْبِرُوْنَ عَنْ عِبَادَتِیْ سَیَدْخُلُوْنَ جَهَنَّمَ دَاخِرِیْنَ |

This explains what is meant by calling out to God. It means to accept and to obey Him and His superiority. His answer to the call means for man's efforts to bear fruit.

This fact has been described at another place as:

| 32:15 | Those who trust Us, (have faith in Us) are those who gladly bow their heads (in subservience) when they are presented with our orders, and are engaged in establishing and making praiseworthy the program given by their Sustainer, and they do not defy these orders. | اِنَّمَا یُؤْمِنُ بِاٰیٰتِنَا الَّذِیْنَ اِذَا ذُکِّرُوْا بِهَا خَرُّوْا سُجَّدًا وَّسَبَّحُوْا بِحَمْدِ رَبِّهِمْ وَهُمْ لَا یَسْتَکْبِرُوْنَ |
| 32:16 | They are so busy in this work that they do not even consider sleep, are awake at night, and Thus, call on their Sustainer for removing their problems and for His benevolence. Because they know that their efforts will cause good results, and what destruction will follow if the orders are disobeyed. Whatever We have given them, is kept open (available) to the human race (for their welfare). | تَتَجَافٰی جُنُوبُهُمْ عَنِ الْمَضَاجِعِ۔ یَدْعُوْنَ رَبَّهُمْ خَوْفاً وَّطَمَعاً وَّ مِمَّا رَزَقْنٰهُمْ یُنْفِقُوْنَ |

Surah *Al-momin* says:

| 40:65 | When you call out to God, then call Him with full and complete obedience only for Him | فَادْعُوْهُ مُخْلِصِیْنَ لَهُ الدِّیْنَ۔۔۔ |

Surah *Ash-Shura* says:

| 42:26 | He responds to the call of those people who believe on His laws and work according to them | وَیَسْتَجِیْبُ الَّذِیْنَ اٰمَنُوْا وَعَمِلُوا الصّٰلِحٰتِ۔۔۔ |

This shows too, what calling to God and His response means.

Surah *Al-Airaaf* says:

| 7:55 | Call your Sustainer with complete equanimity of heart and soul. so that the call comes from the core of your heart | اُدْعُوْا رَبَّكُمْ تَضَرُّعًا وَّخُفْيَةً اِنَّهٗ لَا يُحِبُّ الْمُعْتَدِيْنَ |

Note that those who rebel against His laws and cross the limits are disliked by Him. This also shows that "calling" Him means "obeying Him".

The next verses explain this:

| 7:56 | Do not create ripples in society after it has become smooth or calm | وَلَا تُفْسِدُوْا فِى الْاَرْضِ بَعْدَ اِصْلَاحِهَا |
| 7:57 | And call out to God for banishing your problems and ills and for acquiring benefits. Remember that those who maintain the balance in society, Allah's benevolence is very near to them | وَادْعُوْهُ خَوْفاً وَّ طَمَعاً اِنَّ رَحْمَتَ اللّٰهِ قَرِيْبٌ مِّنَ الْمُحْسِنِيْنَ |

Here Allah's benevolence is said to be 'near'. In surah *Al-Baqrah* God Himself is said to be near:

2:186	And when my obedient ask you about Me, tell them I am not far from them, and are very near.	وَاِذَا سَاَلَكَ عِبَادِيْ عَنِّيْ فَاِنِّيْ قَرِيْبٌ
2:186	Thus, they should obey Me and believe in the veracity of my laws so that they find the path to their destinations.	فَلْيَسْتَجِيْبُوْا لِيْ وَلْيُؤْ مِنُوْا بِيْ لَعَلَّهُمْ يَرْشُدُوْنَ
50:16	(I am) closer than their jugular vein	أُجِيْبُ دَعْوَةَ الدَّاعِ اِذَا دَعَانِ

This also makes explicit that "calling out" to God means "obeying" Him, and the response to that call is the result of those efforts which one makes according to His laws.

In surah *An-Namal,* first the attention has been drawn to various elements of the universal system as to how everything happens according to God's order (system). Then, the group of *momineen* has been addressed which was passing through very difficult times in its initial stages of establishing God's orders, and was calling out at every step for help from God.

"مَتٰ نَصْرُ اللّٰهِ" (*mata nasrullah*): when shall God's help come? (2:214)

They were told (through evelation, of course):

| 27:62 | (except God) who can hear or answer your cries for help; and remove your worries and difficulties, and grant you the rule on this earth but the rule on earth can only be gotten as a result of your deeds | اَمَّنْ يُّجِيْبُ الْمُضْطَرَّ اِذَادَعَاهُ وَيَكْشِفُ السُّوْءَ وَيَجْعَلُكُمْ خُلَفَاءَ الْاَرْضِ |

Thus, do not worry, keep working according to God's laws, he will turn your helplessness into dominance, and if you continue on this path (the path of God) then Our cosmic forces will save you from the harmful machinations of your opponents (40:7). Not only was the group of *momineen* told this, but the messengers as well.

In surah *Yunus*, in the tale of *Moosa*, *Moosa* and his brother *Haroon*, who also was a messenger, pray to God to confront *Firoun* successfully. They are told that:

| 10:89 | the prayers of you both have been accepted | قَدْ أُجِيبَتْ دَّعْوَتُكُمَا فَاسْتَقِيمَا |

This means that they were told to continue with their program (as given by God) with steadfastness.

Obviously if the acceptance of prayer meant only that whatever you have asked for shall be given to you, (or you will get it), then after that there was no need for any effort. However here it has been said that your prayer has been accepted. Therefore, be steadfast in your program. This makes it obvious, that *Moosa* and his brother *Haroon* were only told that their call-outs are according to God's laws, and now they should strive to achieve those ends with steadfastness and Hence, they would surely succeed.

The above explanations make it clear that calling out to God means obeying his orders and laws. The Messenger Mohammed (*pbuh*) was also asked to 'call out God', to do *dua*:

| 72:20 | Tell them that I only call out to my Sustainer and do not include anyone else with Him (do not include anyone in His Supreme authority) (18:26) | قُلْ إِنَّمَا أَدْعُوْا رَ بِّيْ وَلَا أُشْرِكْ بِهِ أَحَداً |

After this Quranic meaning of '*dua*', there is no cause left for the doubts and tribulations mentioned earlier bout '*dua*'.

The Quran also relates the things similar to what we mean by '*dua*' in the ordinary sense:

| 3:146 | O Sustainer, protect us from our faults and transgressions. Give solidarity to our feet (us) and give us success over the nation of deniers | رَ بَّنَا اغْفِرْلَنَا ذُنُوْبَنَا وَإِسْرَافَنَا فِيْ أَمْرِ نَا وَثَبِّتْ أَقْدَامَنَا وَانْصُرْنَا عَلَى الْقَوْمِ الْكَافِرِيْنَ |

That is such prayers (*dua*) in which a man desires fulfillment of his wishes. These prayers are actually a manifest of the intensity of his wishes. This intensity creates a kind of a change in his personality that gives vent to his latent capabilities and they go to work for him. Consider the meanings of the words "اَلدَّاعِيَةُ" (*ad-dayituh*) and "اَلدَّوَاعِىْ" (*ad-dawayi*) given earlier. First a man must desire that which is according to God's laws (not the obverse). Then he should create intensity in his wishes. This will create a revolutionary condition within himself and the result is indeed surprising. Note that the Quran has also said that your wishes must be according to the laws of God or you may wish for something that in reality is harmful for you (17:11).

It can be argued that by praying revolutionary changes are created in man himself which help him to attain his goals. Then what is the difference in calling out to God or praying to Him? It is correct that man's latent capabilities are aroused in this way, but the aim is not only to raise the latent forces or capabilities as such. The first thing is to determine the aim for which they are aroused. That is, the purpose for the attainment of which the effort is being made, and what sort is that aim? Then, what are the means to achieve it, and what will the purpose be, if attained? A *momin* (one who follows the Quran) decides all matters under the orders of Allah and therefore, keeps Allah before him from first to last. His wish or desire is also a link in this chain. Therefore, he calls out to God for its attainment too. Everything takes place as per God's laws, so much so that the latent forces in man are aroused too as a result of His laws.

Another point to be noted here is that God has bestowed man with that a personality with the proper development of which (to the extent that is humanly possible) can arouse the qualities which when unbounded, are attributable to God. In this manner, God's personality becomes the standard for the development of the human personality. By praying to God (by calling out to Him) a man wants to arouse the qualities within himself that will help him attain his goal. This is the difference between 'praying to God' and arousing intense desire in oneself.

We now come to the praying of the messengers mentioned in the Quran. Messenger-hood is quite different from ordinary human matters. We cannot understand anything about it. We only understand the message that they have brought to us and their obedience is our duty. As far as God talking to them in response to their prayers is concerned, it does not happen with ordinary human beings. God does not talk to anyone except the messengers to believe that He does, even after the last Messenger (pbuh), is blasphemy.

The concept that if God does not listen to our pleadings, therefore, someone close to God should be requested to pray for us before God is not correct.

As per the Quran, no power can interfere between God and His missionaries. To believe so is a big sin. To reach God or to take one's pleading to God, no media is required. Every human being by obeying God's laws can reach God or take his voice to Him. To see the meaning of "وسیلہ" (*waseela*), or means, go to relevant heading. His laws are obeyed by remaining within the bounds of a Quranic society. That is the reason that the prayers that God has taught the *momineen* are mostly collective. Such as 1:5, 1:7, 2:201, 3:7, 3:146, and 3:192 etc.).

To explain verses 2:186 and 50:16 as mentioned above. These verses contain hints to His imminence and transcendence. He is closer to every human being than his jugular vein. This shows that God is present everywhere in the universe, but not present as something is bound to some place. Since our senses are unable to grasp how God can be present somewhere in space without occupying some space, therefore, it has been said in the Quran that:

6:104	human eyes cannot comprehend Him	لَا تُدْرِكُهُ الْأَبْصَارُ ۖ وَهُوَ يُدْرِكُ الْأَبْصَارَ

But it is encircling or comprehending human sight. But we can comprehend His laws and can observe their results as well. Therefore, the Quran has said that we are connected to God's laws. We call out to His laws and when we act according to His laws, He answers our call by bringing the desired results that we have called for.

As far as God's knowledge is concerned, the thing that we term as past, present or future, have no place according to the laws of God. Before God, all the past, present and the future are revealed at the same time. There is a sort of eternal now. That is, He is aware of future events or what will take place in the future (future for us) as if they are taking place now. But it makes no difference as to our intent or authority which we have been given by God. Nor is the fact affected that whatever happens to us is the result of our own deeds. Everything is taking place before God. He also knows what we are going to do, but he does not interfere with our intent or authority. We do what we chose to, and face whatever results our own deeds bring. If we act according to God's laws then we get good results, if we go against these laws then we suffer. Nobody has the power to do wrong and reap good results. To observe God's laws is to call out to Him or pray to Him and to get good results means our prayers have been answered.

D-F-A   د ف ء

"اَلدِّفْئُ" (*ad-dif'u*): temperature and heat, or something that heats something.

"اَدْفَأَهُ" (*adfaahu*): he attired him in such clothes as to warm him.

"اَلدِّفَاءُ" (*ad-difa'u*): anything that provides heat.

The Quran says about cattle:

16:5	They have the wherewithal to provide heat and have other benefits.	لَكُمْ فِيهَا دِفْءٌ وَ مَنَافِعُ

Ibn Faris says that "دَفُى" (*dafun*) means the camel's kids, its milk and its other beneficial things.

D-F-Ain   د ف ع

"دَفَّعَ" (*dafah*): to banish something by force, to remove, as in 2:251 {*T, R*}.

Muheet says "اَلدَّفْعُ" (*ad-dafah*) means to banish something before it takes place and "اَلرَّفْعُ" (*ar-rafah*) means to remove it after it takes place.

Basa-ir says when "دَفَعَ" (*dafah*) is followed by "اِلیٰ" (*ila*) then it means to entrust or to pay back. As in:

4:9	return their goods or wealth to them	فَادْفَعُوا اِلَیْهِمْ اَمْوَالَهُمْ

When it is followed by "عَنْ" (*un*), then it means to support or protect {*T*}.

22:38	Verily God (God's law) protects those who Believe on His reality	اِنَّ اللّٰهَ یُدَافِعُ عَنِ الَّذِیْنَ آمَنُوْا

"اَلْمَدَافَعَةُ" (*al-mudaafi'atu*): to jostle one another and to push {*T*}.
"دَافِعٌ" (*daafiun*): one who removes (70:2)?

D-F-Q   د ف ق

"دَفَقَ الْمَاءَ یَدْفِقُ" (*dafaqal ma'a yudfiqu*): he spilled the water.
"دَفَقَ الْكُوْزَ" (*dafaqal kooz*): spilled the water of the cup at once.
"دَفَقَ الْمَاءُ" (*dafaqul ma'o*): the water boiled suddenly.
"سَیْلٌ دُفَاقٌ" (*sailun dafaaq*): the flood whose waters overflowed the valley.
"اَلدِّفَقُّ" (*ad-difaqqu*): a fast camel.
"اَلدِّفَقّیٰ" (*ad-difaqqa*): a fast speed in which the animal jumps when running {*T, M, R*}.

Ibn Faris says it basically means to push forward.

The Quran speaks about the creation of man.

86:6	He has been created from the surfing liquid (sperm).	خُلِقَ مِنْ مَّاءٍ دَافِقٍ

D-K-K   د ک ک

"اَلدَّكُّ" (*ad-dok*): to break, to pound, to demolish a wall or mountain. Actually it means to pound and break a thing and level it with the ground {*T, M*}.

Ibn Faris thinks it means to become low and to spread out.

"اَلدَّكَّةُ" (*ad-dakkatu*), "اَلدَّكُّ" (*ad-duk*): smooth or even place, or to level the ups and downs of the ground. (To beat them into a level with the ground) {*T, M*}.

89:21	When the land's unevenness (ups and downs) will be removed and made level.	اِذَا دُكَّتِ الْاَرْضُ دَكًّا دَكًّا

In other words when the balance of economy shall be made even, and there will be no ups and downs *{T}*.

69:14	The evenness will be made in one go	فَدُكَّتَا دَكَّةً وَاحِدَةً
7:143	Smoothed it, removed the ups and downs or high or lows or unevenness.	جَعَلَهُ دَكًّا
18:98	Will break it and make it level (here the word 'earth' is silent for which **dakka** has been said)	جَعَلَهُ دَكًّا

"اَلدَّكَّاءُ" (*ad-dakka'o*) means a mud dune or hill *{T}*.

"جَعَلَهُ دَكَّاءَ" (*ja'alahu dakka'a*) would mean that the wall becomes like a dune when demolished.

"أَرْضٌ دَكَّاءُ" (*ardun dakka'o*): smooth land *{R}*.

"اَلدُّكَّانُ" (*ad-dukaan*): a place the top of which is smoothed over for sitting *{T, M}*.

D-L-K   د ل ک

"دَلَكَهُ بِيَدِه دَلْكًا" (*dalakahu beyadehi dalka*): to rub something with the hands.

"دَلَكَتِ الشَّمْسُ دُلُوْكًا" (*dalakatis shamsu duluka*): sunset, because one who looks at it starts rubbing his eyes with his hands *{T}* (but we think that this reasoning is feeble).

"دُلُوْكًا" (*dalakat duluka*): for the sun to become yellowish and go towards sunset, or for the sun to lean towards the west (towards setting) after mid noon in the middle of the sky *{M}*.

Azhari says this is the right meaning because in Arabic "دُلُوْکٌ" (*dulook*) means decline. **Ibn Faris** too seems to agree with this as he says the word means for a thing to move away (decline) from something else. But he also says that the word contains the connotation of something moving away softly. This word is also used for rubbing because in that state hands do not stay in one place.

Alwasi writes in **Roohul Ma'ani** that the word means to transfer from one place to another. So sunrise as well as sunset is "دُلُوْکٌ" (*dulook*) because both ways it moves away. When the sun has reached its peak and starts setting, it is called "دَالِكَةٌ" (*dalikah*), as well as it has set, because in both conditions it is in decline.

Nawaderul Airaab says it means for the sun to be high or low.

Ibn Faris says that wherever "د" (*daal*) appears along with "ل" (*laam*), the word means to move, to come or go, and to decline from one place to another. As such "دَلَكَ الثَّوْبَ" (*dalakatis saub*) would mean rubbed the cloth while washing it.

„دَلَکَتِ الْمَرْأَةُ الْعَجِیْنَ‟ (*dalakatil mar-atul ajeen*): the woman prepared the dough.

„تَدَلَّکَ الرَّجُلُ‟ (*tadallakar rajul*): he rubbed his body while bathing.

„اَلدَّلُوْکُ‟ (*ad-dalook*): to rub perfume or balm etc.

„بَعِیْرٌ مَدْلُوْکٌ‟ (*baeerum medlook*): a camel which has been used for traveling constantly.

„اَلدَّالِیْکُ‟ (*ad-deek*): to walk fast without the full feet touching the ground {T}

All these meanings show that the real meaning of this root is movement. As such when the sun rises to its peak in the noon, is also called „دُلُوْکُ‟ (*dulook*) (as has been mentioned with reference to *Nawadarul Airaab* above). And when it starts setting after reaching its peak, will also be called „دُلُوْکُ‟ (*dulook*) as mentioned above.

Raghib too, says it means leaning towards the sunset

Ibn Dureed says in Jamharatil Lagha that it means to set and disappear.

The Quran says:

17:78	Establish the *salaah* from *duluk* of the sun to *ghasaqil lail*, and Quran is of the *Fajr*. (ordinary meaning)	اَقِمِ الصَّلٰوةَ لِدُلُوْکِ الشَّمْسِ اِلٰى غَسَقِ اللَّیْلِ وَ قُرْآنَ الْفَجْرِ

If „دُلُوْکُ‟ (*dulook*) here is taken to mean ordinary movement then it covers the entire time from sunrise to sunset, and „قُرْآنَ الْفَجْرِ‟ (*Quran-ul-Fajr*) i.e. before sunrise to „غَسَقِ اللَّیْلِ‟ (*ghasaqil lail*) i.e. after sunset. The meaning is obvious that this whole period is available to you for *salaah*. And if „دُلُوْکُ‟ (*duluk*) is taken to mean from the sun's decline to sunset then (according to the above meaning) the time between sunrise and half the day will be eliminated.

At another place regarding establishment of *salaah* it is said:

11:114	both ends of the day and night (in the earlier part)	طَرَفَيِ النَّهَارِ وَزُلَفاً مِّنَ اللَّیْلِ

Both ends of the day are *fajar* which is before sunrise, and *maghrib* which is time of sunset. The earlier part of the night is *ghasaqal lail*.

Surah *An-Noor* says:

24:58	The *salaah* of *fajar*	صَلٰوةُ الْفَجْرِ
24:58	the *salaah* of *ish'a*	صَلٰوةُ الْعِشَاءِ

These have been mentioned specifically. It is obvious from the above then that in the time of *Mohammed* (pbuh), *salaah* congregations were held at these two timings which was the time from morning to evening, or from the time of the decline to evening.

"دُلُوْكْ" (*dulook*) according to the earlier meaning (i.e. the time from morning to evening) seems more appropriate linguistically.

"غَسَقْ" (*ghasaq*) means twilight. See heading (*Gh-S-Q*).

Salaah does not only mean timely congregations. It also means the Quranic system or the life as determined by the Quran. According to this, if in this verse (17:78) too, *salaah* is taken to mean the duties imposed by the Quranic system, then it would mean that from the first day consider what guidance the Quran gives you (this will be *Quran ul-fajr*), and then engage in complying with the Quranic program from morning till evening. This will be establishing of *salaah* from early morning to late night.

D-L-L   د ل ل

"دَلُّ الْمَرْأَةِ وَدَلَالُهَا عَلَى زَوْجِهَا" (*dall ul-mar'ati wa dalaluha ala zaujiha*): for wife to be coy with her husband, to act as if she is defying her husband, without really doing so.

"دَلَّهُ عَلَى الشَّيْءِ" (*dallahu alash shaiyi*): told him something, led him to something.

"أَدَلَّ عَلَيْهِ" (*adalla alaih*): became informal with him, became bold with him, due to complete trust on his love even committed excesses on him/her.

"اَلدَّالَّةُ" (*ad-d'allah*): coyness.

"اَلدُّلَّى" (*ad-dulla*): distinct path.

"اَلدَّلِيْلْ" (*ad-daleel*): landmark which leads to a destination and the thing that clarifies something.

"اَلدَّلَالَةُ" (*ad-dalalah*): to show someone the way, and to herald something with the signs.

Raghib says it means something which leads to an understanding of something else {T, M, R}

Ibn Faris says it means to disclose something by its signs which you conclude after much deliberation. That is, the expression of truth through signs. It also means for movement or unease to be present in something. The Quran says you do not ponder upon the "حكمہ" (*hikmah*) or scheme of your Sustainer. That, for instance causes the elongation of shadows.

Later it is said:

25:45	The elongation or shortening of the shadows is due to the sunlight.	ثُمَّ جَعَلْنَا الشَّمْسَ عَلَيْهِ دَلِيْلاً

If there is no sunlight, then there would be no shadow, and its reduction or elongation would not be visible.

Surah *Saba* says:

34:14	Nothing made aware of *Suleman's* death except….	مَادَ هُّمْ عَلَى مَوْتِهِ إِلَّا-

I.e. that thing, after long deliberation, led to the conclusion that **Suleman** had actually expired.

(Details will be found under the heading **Suleman**). As such, reasoning is something which upon deliberation can lead gradually to a conclusion.

D-L-W/Y   د ل و/ی

"اَلدَّلْوُ" (**ad-dalwu**): bucket (of a well). When it is filled with water, it is called "ذَنُوْبٌ" (**zanoob**) {M, T}, but it is not a rule.

"دَلَوْتُ" (**daloot**), "اَدْلَيْتُ" (**adlait**): I dropped the bucket into the water {T}, or brought it out filling it with water {L}. This led to "اَدْلَى" (**adla**) which means to provide the means to reach something. Just as to reach the water of the well, one has to drop the bucket inside the well.

"اَدْلَى اِلَيْهِ بِمَالِهِ" (**adla ilaihi bimaalehi**): gave him his wealth {T}.

"اَدْلَى حَاجَتَهُ دَلْوًا" (**dala haajatuhu dalwa**): he demanded what he wanted or needed.

"دَلَى بِرَحِمِهِ" (**adla berahmehi**): he used his relationship as a means to getting his work done {T}.

Ibn Faris says it basically means to approach something with softness and ease.

The Quran has said:

2:188	To reach the authorities through wealth (via bribe) and to receive a judgment in one's favored.	تُدْلُوْا بِهَا اِلَى الْحُكَّامِ

"تَدَلَّى" (**tadalla**) also means to hang, to be near.

Surah **An-Najam** mentions:

53:8	He got near, became of the same color, and was lost in the depths of the truth.	ثُمَّ دَنَا فَتَدَلَّى

This is a particularity of messenger-hood.

Surah **Al-Airaaf** has this:

7:22	Deceived them to fall into the depths.	فَدَلَّاهُمَا بِغُرُوْرٍ

"دَالَاهُ" (**dalaahu**), "مُدَالَاةٌ" (**mudalaah**): was soft (courteous) to him {M}.

"دَلَى" (**daliya**), "يَدْلَى" (**yadla**): to be surprised {T}.

D-M-D-M   د م د م

"دَمْدَمَ الْقَوْمَ وَدَمْدَمَ عَلَيْهِمْ" (*damdamal qauma wa damdama alihim*): the nation was destroyed and annihilated.

"دَمْدَمَ عَلَيْهِ" (*damdama alaih*): was angry at him and talked to him angrily {*T*}.

"دَمْدَمَ عَلَيْهِمْ" (*damdama alihim*): they were annihilated and troubled {*T*}, {*Latif-ul-Lugha*}.

"اَلدَّمْدَمَةُ" (*ad-damdamatu*): troublesome talk, anger {*T*}. It also means to destroy {*Latif-ul-Lugha*}.

"اَلدَّمْدَمُ" (*ad-damdam*): dry grass {*T*}.

"دَمْدَمَ الرَّعْدُ" (*damdamar raad*): there was strong thunder {*L*}.

The Quran mentions:

| 91:13 | Their Sustainer (the natural turn of events) killed them in such a way that even their traces were obliterated. | فَدَمْدَمَ عَلَيْهِمْ رَبُّهُمْ |

D-M-R   د م ر

"اَلدُّمُورُ" (*ad-dumoor*), "اَلدَّمَارُ" (*ad-damaar*): to be killed, to kill.

"اَلتَّدْمِيرُ" (*at-tadmeer*): to kill, to root out.

Raghib says it means to instill destruction into something.

"دَمَرَ عَلَيْهِمْ" (*damara alihim*): he came near him without permission (and with malicious intent). He suddenly attacked him {*T*}.

The Quran says:

| 7:137 | We destroyed | وَدَمَّرْنَا |

Ibn Faris says the basic meanings are to enter a house etc. Some add that this entry is without permission.

D-M-Ain   د م ع

"اَلدَّمْعُ" (*ad-dam'o*): tears, whether they are of joy or sorrow.

"اَلدَّمْعَةُ" (*ad-dam'atuh*): a tear.

"دَمَعَتِ الْعَيْنُ" (*dama'atil ain*): the eyes became moist {*T*}.

"دَمَعَتِ السَّحَابَةُ" (*dam'atis sahabah*): *it rained from the clouds* {*T*}.

Surah *Al-Mai'dah* says:

| 5:83 | You will find that tears begin to roll down their eyes | تَرَى أَعْيُنَهُمْ تَفِيضُ مِنَ الدَّمْعِ |

D-M-Gh   د م غ

"اَلدِّمَاغُ" (*ad-dimagh*) means he brain.

"دَمَغَ" (*damagha*), "يَدْمَغُ" (*yadmagh*): he injured him in such a way that the wound reached the brain.

"اَلدَّامُوغُ" (*ad-damogh*): the thing which breaks or destroys something else.

"دَمَغَهُ" (*damagha hu*): he overpowered him {T}.

"دَمَغَ الْحَقُّ الْبَاطِلَ" (*damaghul haqqul baatil*): the truth obliterated the untruth, or destroyed it {T}.

"حُجَّةٌ دَامَغَةٌ" (*hujjatun daamigha*): mind boggling reason{R}.

Surah **Al-Ambia** says that **haqq** (undeniable truth) destroys the **baatil** (the falsehood).

In the struggle between truth and untruth (**haqq** and **baatil**), good and evil, that is perpetual in the universe, **haqq** (the constructive element) always overpowers **baatil** (destructive element) and so on. If the destructive element was overpowering then leave alone the evolution of the universe, the universe itself would cease to exist.

| 21:18 | We strike the **baatil** with **haqq**, so that **haqq** destroys the **baatil**. | بَلْ نَقْذِفُ بِالْحَقِّ عَلَى الْبَاطِلِ فَيَدْمَغُهُ فَإِذَا هُوَ زَاهِقٌ |

So see how **baatil** is being destroyed. It is the law of nature for constructive program to overcome destructive forces. It cannot be otherwise. But the speed at which these constructive forces overcome is (according to our standards) very slow. God's single day is equal to one thousand (or rather fifty thousand of our) years (32:5, 70:4). But if man becomes a friend of God, then the results start to be formulated according to our measure.

D-M-W/Y   د م و/ى

"دَمٌّ" (*dum*) means blood.

"اَلدِّمَاءُ" (*ad-dima'a*) is the plural as in 2:30 {T}.

"دَمٌّ" (*dum*) was actually "دَمَوٌّ" (*damu*) or "دَمًى" (*damun*). The Quran has declared "دَماً مَسْفُوْحاً" (*duman masfoohan*) in 6:146 i.e. flowing blood as forbidden. For more details, see under heading (S-F-H).

D-N-R   د ن ر

"دِيْنَارٌ" (*deenar*) is the name of a gold coin. The plural is "دَنَانِيْرَ" (*dananeer*). It is a non-Arabic word that has been arabized. This was used by Arabs from the days of old, so it became Arabic {T}. The Quran has used this word in 3:74.

Some say that the word was actually "دِنَّار" (*dinar*). That is why its plural is "دَنَانِيْر" (*dananeer*) *{T}*. It means a pound, or guinea which is golden as well. It is a Roman word ***Dinarins*** which has been arabized. Roman coins were generally used by the Arabs. (See heading dirham).

D-N-W   د ن و

"دَنَا" (*dun'a*), "يَدْنُوْ" (*yadnu*), "دُنُوّْ" (*dunuwa*), "دَنَاوَةٌ" (*danawah*): to get closer.

"اَلدُّنْيَا" (*ad-dunyah*): the closest thing. The masculine form is "اَدْنَى" (*adna*).

"دَنِىَ" (*dun*), "يَدْنَى" (*yadna*) means to be old and weak.

"اَدْنَى الرَّجُلُ اِدْنَاءً" (*adnar rajulu idna*): that man lived a life of deprivation and poverty.

"اَدْنَى الشَّىْءَ" (*adnash shaiya*): to bring something closer.

"اَدْنَتْ ثَوْبَهَا عَلَيْهَا" (*adnati saubiha alaiha*) he covered himself with a cloth *{L}*.

33:59	They should cover themselves with their shawls.	يُدْنِيْنَ عَلَيْهِنَّ مَنْ جَلَا بِيْبِهِنَّ

"اَلْاَدْنَى" (*aladna*) means closer. Sometimes it means small as "اَصْغَرُ" (*asghar*) and comes opposite to "اَكْبَرُ" (*akbar*) which means big. Sometimes it means bad or demeaning "اَرْذَلُ" (*arzal*) and comes opposite to "خَيْرٌ" (*khair*) which means good. Sometimes it means first "اَوَّلُ" (*awwal*) and comes against "اَخِرَةٌ" (*aakhir*) which means last. Sometimes it means closer "اَقْرَبُ" (*aqrab*) and comes opposite to "اَقْصَى" (*aqsaa*) which means far *{T, R}*.

The Quran says:

30:3	the land nearby	فِىْ اَدْنَى الْاَرْضِ
53:8-9	he again got close, or closer	ثُمَّ دَنَا--- اَوْاَدْنَى
55:54	Close	دَانٍ
69:23	Close	قُطُوْفُهَا دَانِيَةٌ
37:6 67:5	The nearest sky	اَلسَّمَاءَ الدُّنْيَا

Also see heading (S-M-W).

"اَلدُّنْيَا" (*ad-duniya*) (closest) has come against "اَلْقُصْوَى" (*al-quswa*) (farthest) in 8:42. This word has been used against "اَكْبَرُ" (*akbar*) (big) in 32:21, against "اَكْثَرُ" (*aksar*) (most) in 58:7, against "خَيْرٌ" (*khair*) (good) in 2:61.

The Quran has used "اَلْحَيٰوةُ الدُّنْيَا" (*al-hverseid dunyiah*) as against "اَخِرَةٌ" (*akhirah*), meaning the life of this world against the Hereafter. It has appeared at many places and this is the comparison which is most noteworthy, because in this comparison, life in this world "اَلْحَيٰوةُ الدُّنْيَا" (*al-hverseid duniya*) has been declared very small or of less significance than the Hereafter "اَخِرَةٌ" (*akhirah*).

In religions in general, where the concept of soul and materialism exists, the world of *duniyah* and its possession have been termed very belittling and insignificant. According to the Hindu religion, the world is nothing but *maya* or deceit, and getting rid of this deceit is *mukti* or emancipation. According to the Buddhist religion, every wish is the precursor of some difficulty or ill. Therefore, real life, it says, is to give up any desire. This is shared by the Christians where the real kingdom is in the Heavens. As such for them, giving up the world is very acceptable. This is the very core of *tasawwuf* and some of our own Muslims have been influenced by this concept and the world or *duniya* is condemnable and little. Therefore, worldly and sinful have come to mean almost the same.

To the contrary, world or *duniya* and *deen* are said to be opposites. But this concept is against the teachings of the Quran. It teaches a *momin* to pray for "فى هٰذِهِ الدُّنْيَا حَسَنَةً" (*fi haazehid duniyah hasanah*) in 7:156 (i.e. wellbeing in his world), and says clearly:

16:30	The result of good deeds is not only the good things or pleasantness in the *aakhirah* (hereafter) but this world too	لِلَّذِيْنَ اَحْسَنُوْا فِيْ هٰذِهِ الدُّنْيَا حَسَنَةٌ

Against it, it terms:

7:156	Ignominy in this world, as God's wrath	ذِلَّةٌ فِى الْحَيٰوةِ الدُّنْيَا

Such verses have appeared at different places in the Quran. As such this concept is *baatil* or untrue that this world and its luxuries and comforts are sinful.

But the Quran also contains certain verses which have termed the life of this world as transitory or impermanent and the life here as "لهو" (*lahu*) and "لعب" (*la'ab*). To understand this point, see under heading (A-Kh-R) and (Ain-J-L) in which it has been explained as to what is meant by "مَفَادِ عَاجِلَةِ" (*mufaadi aajila*) or immediate benefits) and "مَتَاع آخِرَة" (*mata-i aakhirah*) or the wealth of the Hereafter. There you will find that the Quran strongly opposes those who have "مَفَادِ عَاجِلَةِ" (*muffadi aajila*) i.e. immediate benefits of this world in sight and ignore the pleasantness of the Hereafter. This temporary benefit has been called "مَتَاعُ الدُّنْيَا" (*mata-id duniya*) or immediate benefit, and condemns those strongly who ignore the lasting benefits of the Hereafter to choose the immediate benefits of this world. As such, according to Quran condemnable is for man to ignore the lasting benefits of the future in the Hereafter for immediate gains in this world. That is to consider real life only to be in this world, and it is also condemnable to give up this world and set about building the future. This is called monasticism which according to the Quran is not permissible. See under heading (R-H-B).

The Quran says:

2:201	The good things in this life as well the good things in the life hereafter. (Good immediate	رَبَّنَا اٰتِنَا فِى الدُّنْيَا حَسَنَةً وَفِى الْاٰخِرَةِ حَسَنَةً

| | benefits as well as benefits in the future) | |

It has also said that if the present of somebody is not good, then his future too is bleak:

| 17:72 | he whoever is blind here (unseeing the truths) will be blind there too, or rather worse | وَمَنْ كَانَ فِيْ هٰذِهِ اَعْمٰى فَهُوَ فِيْ الْاٰخِرَةِ اَعْمٰى وَاَضَلُّ سَبِيْلاً |

For the meaning of "اَعْمٰى" (*aama*) see under heading (Ain-M-Y).

As such:

1)   The concept that this world's pleasant things are hateful is wrong

2)   It is wrong too that only this life is everything, and only these world's benefits or gains should be kept in mind.

3)   The right concept is that the gains of this life are also attained and human personality due to its capabilities becomes able to reap the benefits in the Hereafter too. Also not to concentrate only on personal benefits but keep an eye open for the betterment of the entire human race and coming generations too. This will be this life's future and the rest in the lie to come. (More details under heading (*A-Kh-R*).

The entire teachings of the Quran are focused on establishing values for man. It tells him what the value of everything is in the scale of humanity. After that, it advises to sacrifice petty gains for greater gains. It tells us that no doubt the pleasant things of this life are indeed attractive and they should be attained or strived for, but when the interests of this life and the life hereafter clash, then the petty interests of this physical life must be sacrificed for the greater goal in the hereafter. These are the places where Quran has termed the interests of this world lowly as compared to those of the Hereafter. This in no way means that this life is hateful. This is the Quran's teaching about this world and the Hereafter.

D-H-R   د ه ر

"اَلدَّهْرُ" (*ad-dahr*) is the period from the beginning of this world till the end. Then it began to be mean a long period as against "زَمَانٌ" (*zaman*) which means both a short or long period {R}.

The Quran says:

| 76:1 | that is, a period, or the duration of a period | حِيْنٌ مِنَ الدَّهْرِ |

Ibn Faris says it means overpowering (or hold) or forcible.

Present time conditions are called "دَهْرٌ" (*dahr*) because it encompasses everything and has a hold over it.

"اَلدَّهَارِ بْرُ" (*ad-dhariribrur*): the vicissitudes of time.

"دَهَرَهُمْ اَمْرٌ" (*daharahum amr*): some misfortune befell them {T}.

The Quran has recalled what some people say:

| 45:44 | This is only the passage of time which causes our deaths. | وَمَا يُهْلِكُنَا إِلَّا الدَّهْرُ |

As time passes one's limbs weaken and deterioration ends in his death and life ends there. There is no other life after this. This is the very concept which in today's world is known as the materialistic concept of life.

The Quran says:

| 45:24 | This concept is not based on knowledge. | وَمَا لَهُم بِذَالِكَ مِنْ عِلْمٍ إِنْ هُمْ إِلَّا يَظُنُّونَ |

This is only guess work and goes back fourteen hundreds years or so. In our time, the new concepts and philosophic and scientific that have been formulated, state that the reality of time is quite different. This is only the beginning of research on this very difficult and sensitive topic. Now research says that life continues onwards. The passage of time weakens human body indeed, but it does nothing to his personality. It is not affected by time.

According to the Quran, Man is not only the physical being, but his personality. If it is developed according to the dictates of the Quran, then death can have no effect on it and it moves ahead to cover the other stages of life. That is why "دهر" (*dahr*) or time can not affect it.

The Quran has also termed the period when man had not even come into existence as "اَلدَّبْرُ" (*ad-dahr*).

| 76:1 | There has been a time for man when he was not even a subject to be mentioned | هَلْ أَتَى عَلَى الْإِنسَانِ حِينٌ مِّنَ الدَّهْرِ لَمْ يَكُن شَيْئًا مَّذْكُورًا |

But this does not mean that time itself is to be mistaken as God. However, the debate about time or "دهر" (*dahr*) is very complex and is out of our purview. The Quran has used this word in the above meanings at two places only. At these places its meanings are very clear and distinct and simple, and to understand them no philosophical debate is required.

D-H-Q   د ه ق

"دَهَقَ الْكَاسَ" (*dahaqal kaas*): he filled the cup.

"مَاءٌ دِهَاقٌ" (*ma un dehaaq*): abundant water.

"كَأْسٌ دِهَاقٌ" (*kaasun dihaaq*): clean cup, filled cup.

"اَلدَّهْقُ" (*ad-dahq*): to press hard.

"اَلدَّهَقُ" (*ad-dahaq*): vice.

"اَلْمُدَهَّقُ" (*al-muddahaq*): that which is pressed hard {T}.

"دِهَاقًا" (*dihaaq*): something stuffed, probably because something is filled in it by pressing hard.

The Quran says "كَأْسًا دِهَاقًا" (**kasan dihaqan**) in 78:34 that is, clean and full to the brim cup. That is, this is the particularity of a *jannati* (heavenly) society. The right life should be like this. Full and pure, which contains everything that increases life, purity and movement and everything is abundant and pure. In which aside from catering to his physical needs, his latent capabilities are fully developed and purity of heart and sight are also present. The cups of life are full of pure and strengthening pleasantness.

Ibn Faris says this also contains the element of spilling over or movement aside from being full to the brim.

D-H-M   د ه م

"اَلدُّهْمَةُ" (**ad-duhma**): blackness.

"اِدْهَامَّ الشَّيْءُ" (**idhaamash shaiyi**): the thing turned black.

"اِدْهَامَّ الزَّرْعُ" (**idhaamaz zar'ah**): due to being watered the field became blackish.

"حَدِيقَةٌ دَهْمَاءُ وَمُدْهَامَّةٌ" (**hadeeqatun dahma-oo wa mud hammatah**): a green garden which seems blackish due to the vegetation. The Arabs also call dark green color as "دُهْمَةٌ" (**duhma**) because the color resembles black, while light black color is called "خُضْرَةٌ" (**khuzrah**) because it comes close to green {T, M, R}.

Ibn Faris says it means to cover something in darkness. Later, due to much usage the condition of blackness or darkness was also removed. The Quran, due to the heavy vegetation in the gardens of *jannat* (heaven) have called it "مُدْهَامَّتَانِ" (**mud hammataan**) in 55:64. It also means a life which has reached the peak in freshness, flowering and delightfulness.

D-H-N   د ه ن

"اَلدُّهْنَةُ" (**ad-duhna**): slipperiness, greasy.

"اَلدُّهْنُ" (**ad-duhn**): oil.

"اَلْمُدْهُنُ" (**ak-mudhun**): bottle of oil.

"اِدَّهَنَ" (**idhan**): he rubbed oil (on his body) {T, M, R}.

The Quran says about the olives:

| 23:20 | It comes out with oil. (It has oil inside it). | تَنْبُتُ بِالدُّهْنِ |

Ibn Faris says it means softness, ease and shortage.

"أَدْهَنَ" (**ad-han**) means to misappropriate (from something which is kept in trust).

"اَلْمُدَاهَنَةُ" (**al-mudaahana**): deceit, make believe, false, showy (as far as clever talk) is concerned.

"اَلْإِدْهَانُ" (**al-idhaan**): to deceive, to be a hypocrite, to be soft, to concede, to be unserious and untruthful {T, M, R}.

Surah *Al-Qalam* says:

| 28:9 | They want you to shift a little then they too will shift a little. | وَ دُّوْالَوْتُدْ هِنْ فَيْدْهِنُوْنَ |

It means that they want to compromise their positions if you to do the same. But the person who is on right, by shifting embraces falsehood (*baatil*). Conversely, if *baatil* or falsehood shifts from its position, then it does not matter. It remains false.

Supposing *Zaid* says three plus three are six and *Bakar* says this is not so. Now an arbitrator tells one of them to move up a little and the other to move down a little so that three and three become five. *Bakar* stands to lose nothing because he was wrong the first time and would still be so. But Zaid will move from the truth to untruth or falsehood. This is the reason that *haqq* (truth) cannot move even a little from its position. It is fixed in its position. The established principles of this way of life do not have any capacity for any leeway.

In surah *Al-Waaqiah* at first it is said how great a book the Quran is and after that it is said in (56:81):

"اَفَبِهِذَا الْحَدِيْثِ اَنْتُمْ مَدْبِنُوْنَ" (*afabihaazal hadisi antoom mudhenoon*) can have two meanings.

One is, "do you make any changes in this book by your glib talk?"
Second is "do you use this book to move people away from the right path?"

The meaning of both is actually the same. Monasticism does indeed do this. It amends the teachings of the Quran and moves people away from the right path, and only because they want to make a living (out of monasticism).

| 56:82 | You make this untruth the means of your earning? | وَتَجْعَلُوْنَ رِزْقَكُمْ اَنَّكُمْ تُكَذِّبُوْنَ |

"اَلدِّبَانُ" (*ad-dihaan*): red skin, or the dregs of oil *{T}*.

The Quran says that the sky will:

| 55:37 | (The sky) will be torn asunder | وَرْدَةً كَالدِّهَانِ |
| 70:8 | will become like molten metal | كَالْمُهْلِ |

D-H-W/Y   د ه و/ى

"دَهْأَ" (*dahah*), "دَهْيأَ" (*dahya*): he picked holes in it, criticized it, hurt him a lot.

"اَلدَّاهِيَة" (*ad-daahiyah*): great thing, great misfortune.

"دَوَاهِىَ الدَّهْرِ" (*dawahiya addahr*): the misfortunes or ills that time brings.

"اَلدَّهْىُ" (*ad-dahyo*), "اَلدَّهَاءُ" (*ad-dhaha*): surprising cleverness, fine opinion.

"دَهِىَ" (*dahiya*): he worked very cleverly {*T, M*}.

"رَجُلٌ دَاهٍ" (*rajulun daahin*) means a very astute and clever person {*T, M*}. Most of the ills of this world are created due to the deceits created by people's intellect.

The Quran says:

| 54:46 | that moment of revolution will be extremely misfortune and will come surprisingly | وَالسَّاعَةُ اَدْهَى |

Ibn Faris says that "دَهْىٌ" (*dahyun*) means for something unpleasant to make its appearance, but it comes before man so suddenly and in such a way that man is awestruck. A revolution or is something which appears suddenly and surprises onlookers.

D-W-R   د و ر

"دَارَ" (*daar*), "يَدُوْرُ" (*yadura*), "دَوْرًا" (*daura*): to revolve.

"اَلدَّوَّارَة" (*ad-dawarah*): compass.

"اَلدَّائِرَة" (*ad-dairah*): circle. Plural is "دَوَائِرُ" (*dawa-ir*).

"اَلدَّارُ" (*ad-daar*): house. Plural is "دِيَارٌ" (*diyaar*), because people move around in it, or come back to the place they have left from. It also means neighborhood, city, area, a place to stay or residence, as well as the world, and also time which keeps moving.

"دَارَةٌ" (*daarah*): cycle of misfortune.

"اَلْمَدَارُ" (*al-madaar*): orbit {*T, M, R*}.

Ibn Faris says it means for one thing to surround another from all sides.

The Quran says:

| 9:98 | Annihilation and destruction surrounded them from all sides. (Surrounded them like a circle, encircled them). | عَلَيْهِمْ دَائِرَةُ السَّوْءِ |

Surah **At-Taubah** says:

| 9:98 | They wait for you to be caught in trouble. | يَتَرَبَّصُ بِكُمُ الدَّوَائِرَ |

In surah **An-Nooh** "دَيَّارًا" (*diyaara*) in 71:26 means resident, one who dwells. It is also used to mean any one after a negative {*T, M, R*}.

"دَارُ الْاٰخِرَة" (*daarul aakhirah*) in 2:94 has been used by the Quran several times as in 2:94. It means the house of the hereafter or the residence in the hereafter. That is, the life of the future and its comforts.

See under heading (*A-Kh-R*).

Surah *Al-Baqrah* says about trade "تُدِيْرُوْنَهَا" (*tudeerunaha*) in 2:282, which you give and take. That is which you exchange mutually, move goods around.

D-W-L   د و ل

"اَلدَّالَةُ" (*ad-dalah*): fame.

"اَلدَّوْلَةُ" (*ad-daulah*): turn.

"صَارَ الْفَئْیُ دَوْلَةً بَيْنَهُمْمَال" (*saaral fai'o daulatan bainahum*): the war booty was divided and began circulating *{T}*.

"دَاوَلَ" (*dawaal*): to turn away.

Ibn Faris says it basically means for one thing to move to another place.

The Quran says:

3:139	These are the conditions which we keep changing among men. (Sometimes it is one's turn, sometimes it is another's).	تِلْکَ الْاَيَّامُ نُدَاوِلُهَا بَيْنَ النَّاسِ

"تَدَاوَلُوْهُ" (*tadawalu*): they took it in turn *{T}*.

"دُوْلَةٌ" (*doolah*) and "دَوْلَةٌ" (*daulah*): some say they mean the same thing, that is, to revolve or move around, but others contend that "دَوْلَةٌ" (*daulah*) means for two armies to win in turn, that is, first one army is victorious then the defeated army overpowers the victorious one *{T}*.

"دُوْلَةٌ" (*doolah*) means the customs that keep changing. Some say it means something which keeps changing hands, while "دَوْلَةٌ" (*daulah*) is the change that takes place *{T}*.

About the revolving of wealth, the Quran has said:

59:7	so that it does keep changing hands only among the rich or wealthy	کَیْ لَا يَكُوْنَ دُوْلَةً بَيْنَ الْاَغْنِيَاءِ مِنْكُم

This is a great economic principle which the Quran has related so simply. There is unease in the society due to wealth moving around only in the wealthy circles. According to the Quran, no one should possess extra wealth nor should wealth remain confined to certain circles. The government's money too should not only be spent among the wealthy circles. It should be spent for the common good.

D-W-M   د و م

"دَوَامّ" (*dawaam*) means for something to stay as it is.

"دَامَ الشَّيْءُ" (*daamash shaiy'o*) means when a thing lasts for a long time {*T, R*}.

"اَلْمَاءُ الدَّائِمُ" (*al-maaud-dayim*): standing or stagnant water.

"اَلْمَدَامُ" (*al-mudaam*): continuous rain.

Ibnul Aerabi says "دَامَ اَلشَّيْءُ" (*daamush shaiyi*) means the thing revolved or turned. This word is also used for getting tired or to stop.

"اَلدُّوَّامَةُ" (*ad-duwamma*) is a top which kids use to spin.

Ibn Keesaan writes that in "مَادَامَ زَيْدٌ قَائِماً" (*ma-dama zaid qaima*), ma means that when Zaid stands up, you do same {*T, R*}.

Surah **Ar-Ra'ad** says about the *jannat* (heaven), "أُكُلُهَا دَائِمٌ" (*ukuluha daayim*) in 13.35, its fruits will last (forever). That is, the gainful things of the heaven will be lasting, will never cease to exist, there will be no shortage of Sustenance.

Surah **Hoodh** says:

11:108	As long as the sky and earth remain in their present state. (for a very long time)	خَالِدِينَ فِيهَا مَادَامَتِ السَّمٰوٰتُ وَالْأَرْضُ

For details see heading (**Kh-L-D**).

Surah **Aal-e-Imraan** says:

3:74	Except if you stand at his head. (Pester him by your presence).	إِلَّا مَادُمْتَ عَلَيْهِ قَائِماً

D-W-N   د و ن

"دُوْنَ" (**doon**) is used for several meanings. As against "فَوْقُ" (**fauq**) or up, it means down. "هُوَ دُوْنَهُ" (**huwa doonahu**): he is under him, below him. Sometimes it means near. "زَیدٌ دُوْنَکَ" (**zaidun doonak**): Zaid is near you (in stature etc.). It also means to be in front. "مَشَی دُوْنَهُ" (**masha doonahu**): he led from the front, walked ahead of him. It also means being beyond as "هُوَ اَمِیرٌ عَلٰی مَادُوْنَ جَیْحُوْنَوہ" (**huwa ameerun ala ma doona jaihoon**): he is the **ameer** (head) of the area beyond **Jihoon**.

It is also used to mean 'beside'.

"وَیَعْمَلُوْنَ عَمَلاً دُوْنَ ذَالِکَ" (**wa ya'malkoona amlun doona zaalik**): they do other things beside it.

Muheet says the word means the opposites, such as in front and in back, up and down etc.

"شَیِیٌّ دُوْنٌ" (**shaiyun doon**): it means a lowly thing but it also means something respectable and good thing {T}.

"مِنْ دُوْنٍ" (**min dooni**) means beside.

The Quran says:

72:11	Some of us who do good deeds and some are at a lower level.	وَ اَنَّامِنَّا الصَّالِحُوْنَ وَمِنَّا دُوْنَ ذَالِکَ

To mean except or to mean first, this word has appeared in 33:21 where it is said:

33:21	We will make them taste the great punishment aside from or first, the smaller **azaab** (punishment).	وَلَنُذِیْقَنَّهُمْ مِنَ الْعَذَابِ الْاَدْنٰی دُوْنَ الْعَذَابِ الْاَکْبَرِ
3:37	Let not the **momins** make friends with other than **momins**. (not to be friendly with the deniers)	لَایَتَّخِذِ الْمُؤْمِنُوْنَ الْکَافِرِیْنَ اَوْلِیَاءَ مِنْ دُوْنِ الْمُؤْمِنِیْنَ

Likewise if the believers get friendly to the deniers then they too will be counted among them.

The Quran has used "مِنْ دُوْنِ اللہ" (**min dooni-llah**) at several places. This phrase may means that they worship others beside Allah, and also that they do not reach (or observe) the laws of Allah. Before reaching there, they believe on man's self-made laws and **shariah** (way of life). There are many lords that man worships instead of Allah. These are not the gods of statues or idols but that of human emotions. These are gods of religious entities, the gods of powerful people, etc. These are the gods, which prevent man from reaching the only God and His laws.

Raghib says "دُوْنَ" (**doon**) is used when somebody is unable to reach something. Hence, "مِنْ دُوْنِ اللہ" (**min dooni-llah**) would mean to worship other things even before being able to reach God.

After the revelation of the Quran, there is no question of not being able to reach God, because following the instructions in this Book, which is before everybody, is the means to reach Him.

D-Y-N   ن ى د

"دِيْنٌ" (*deen*): this word is used for a lot of meanings as overpower, power, government, state, constitution, law and order, decision, solid result, reward and punishment, return etc. This word is also used for obedience and faithfulness *{T}*.

Lataif-ul-Lugha too says it means accountability, overpower, habit etc.
Kitaab-ul-Ashqaq says it means obedience, way "دَأْبٌ" (*daa-b*) and nation.

The Quran has used the word in all these meanings.

Surah *Al-Baqrah* says:

2:13	I have submitted myself to the Lord of the Worlds	أَسْلَمْتُ لِرَبِّ الْعَالَمِيْنَ

To bow the head before the universal Sustainer has been called "اَلدِّيْنُ" (*ad-deen*) in 2:131, 2:132. It has been called "اَلْإِسْلَامُ" (*al-islam*) in 3:18.

The Quran says:

56:86	86 those who are not under anybody	غَيْرَ مَدِيْنِيْنَ
9:29	they do not follow the law of God	وَلَا يَدِيْنُوْنَ دِيْنَ الْحَقِ
12:76	the law of the authority holder	دِيْنِ الْمَلِكِ
24:2	God's law or the law of the government	دِيْنِ اللهِ
9:36	That is the law of stability	ذَالِكَ الدِّيْنُ الْقَيِّمُ
24:25	In that period, Allah shall give them their justified way of truth	يَوْمَئِذٍ يُوَفِّيْهِمُ اللَّهُ دِيْنَهُمُ الْحَقَّ

As you see in 9:36, when surah *At-tauba* talks about the twelve months on which 4 are of prohibition, there too the word of "دِيْنٌ" (*deen*) has been used for laws and authority. But in 24:25 "دِيْنٌ" (*deen*) means the tern or results of ones deeds.

"دِيْنٌ" (*deen*) means the return or result of the deeds (that is, reward or punishment).

Ibn Qateebah says that it may also mean accountability. {*Ibn Qateebah - Al-qartai vol.* 1 page 4)}

Surah *As-Saffaat* says:

37:53	Will We be accountable for your deeds? Will We get the return for your deeds?	ءَ إِنَّا لَمَدِيْنُوْنَ

The Quran has made the meaning of "يَوْمُ الدِّيْن" (*yaumud deen*) clear by asking " مَا اَدْرَاكَ مَايُوْمُ الدِّيْن" (*adraaka yaumud deen*) Do you know what the Day of the *Deen* is? And proceeded to answer it as "يَوْمَ لَا تَمْلِكُ نَفْسٌ لِنَفْسٍ شَيْئاً وَالْاَمْرُ يَوْمَئِذٍ لِلّٰهِ" (*yauma la tamliku nafsun linafsin shaiyan wal amru yaumaizinlillah*) in 82:18-19. During which time no man will hold any power or right.

In surah *Al-Fateha*, it is said:

1:3	Time during which human life will be spent according to the law of Allah	مٰلِكِ يَوْمِ الدِّيْنِ

The basic characteristic of such a life will be that no man will be superior to any other. The only authority will be that of Allah. This is a great freedom which man will enjoy under Allah's laws.

"دِيْنٌ" (*deen*) also means habit, as well as the rain which habitually comes down in one place {T}. This meaning too holds the connotation of a sort of rule. Allah's laws are called the laws of nature in the universe, while i human world Allah's laws are received (by the messengers) through the revelation. This law is safe in the Quran in its completed and unalterable form. It is called "اَلدِّيْنُ" (*ad-deen*), and to act according to it is called "اَلْاِسْلَامُ" (*al-islam*).

The fact is that in this world many different terms are used such as social system, rule of life, laws of government, constitution of the state etc. But the Quran has used one composite term instead of them all, and that is "اَلدِّيْنُ" (*ad-deen*). This is our social system, the rule or order of our lives, the law of our government and the constitution of our state. According to this constitution, only Allah can determine the limits of man permanently. Nobody else has this right, and Hence, in this way of life, the sovereignty belongs only to Allah. This sovereignty of His is exercised through the Quran. Therefore, practically speaking, sovereignty belongs to Allah's Book (the Quran) in this world. The Islamic government is only the means through which Quranic principles are implemented in this world, and since the criteria for man's deeds to be right or wrong is also this Book. Therefore, reward and punishment is also according to it. This brings Islamic justice in focus which means not only court justice but justice in all aspects of life. The constitution of an Islamic state is in other words the unalterable rules of the Quran. All matters of this Islamic state take place within the parameters of these rules. The purpose is to maintain a system of balance and justice. This is what *DEEN* is.

As such, **deen** would mean the God given system of life which determines the limits of our freedom and according to which our deeds are judged. In the era in which men become followers of this system, they will be free of all hegemony and only be subservient to Allah's laws, because the Lord of the period of **Deen** is no one else but Allah. Every decision in that period will be according to the laws of Allah, will be a **deeni** (according to the **deen**) decision and will be based on the norms of Quranic justice.

In surah **Al-Fateha**, along with the attributes of Allah of being the Sustainer, His system of justice has also been mentioned (**maaliki yaumiddeen** – the Lord of the Day of Judgment). It means that Allah has granted the accoutrements of life to man without any effort, but the determination of his stages will be according to his deeds. It is called a life according to Allah's law and justice, and this is what distinguishes man from animals.

About **Al-Medina**, some think that this word has come from the word **thi**s way of life meaning law and order. Since **Medina** is the central place from which law and order is controlled, some also think that it has come as a follow up of the word meaning obedience or following. Because in the city of **Medina** one has to be obey the law **{T}**.

Kitaab ul-Ashfaq says that this word was derived from **Deen** and was originally **madinah**.

Ibn Faris says deen **basically has the connotation of obedience and the city is called** Medina **because the government in that city is obeyed.**

"دَيْنٌ" (**dain**): a loan because a borrower has to bend before the lender.
"تَدَايُنٌ" (**tadayun**): to deal in loan mutually, as in 2:282.
"دَيْنٌ" (**dain**) is that loan which has a time frame for repayment. The loan which has no time frame for repayment is not "دَيْنٌ" (**dain**) but called "قَرْضٌ" (**qarz**) **{T}**.

Muheet, with the agreement of **Taj** says commonly "دَيْنٌ" (**dain**) is a loan which is given for a fixed period on interest, but since the Quran has forbidden interest, as such for mutual loans among **muslims**, the word loan is for interest free loans only (2:282).
As said earlier, the Quran has used the word several times and it means the order of life.

3:19	The way of life which is close to Allah, is al-Islam	اِنَّ الدِّيْنَ عِنْدَ اللهِ الْإِسْلَامُ
5:3	And I have approved for you al-Islam as your way of life	وَرَضِيْتُ لَكُمُ الْإِسْلَامَ دِيْناً
9:33	He is the one who have sent His messengers with guidance and this way of life of truth to manifest it over all other systems of life.	هُوَ الَّذِيْ أَرْسَلَ رَسُوْلَهُ بِالْهُدَىٰ وَدِيْنِ الْحَقِّ لِيُظْهِرَهُ عَلَى الدِّيْنِ كُلِّهِ

Also see 38:28

This is the **Deen** with which the Messenger (pbuh) was endowed. God is the one who sent His Messenger with the **deen of truth** (**deen-al-haqq**) so that he may implements it (system of life) over all the prevailing systems, no matter how abhorring it may be for the **mushrikeen** (those who follow other systems).

The word **mazhab** or religion has not been used even once by the Quran, therefore, the word **mazhab** or religion must not be taken for **deen-e-Islam**. **Mazhab** is the way of life that has been designed by man, while **Deen** is the system which has come from God. This is the reason that there are many sects in religion whereas **Deen** considers sectarianism as '**shirk**' which is the greatest of sins (30:32). The **Deen** given by God is the same for everyone and there is no question of any sect in it. Sects are created by man by following different paths of life. God's **Deen** came to earlier dynasties of man (through the messengers) but they destroyed their celestial Books and instead adopted the ways of life created by men. Thus, they lost the **Deen** which was replaced by Religions.

But in the Quran, God has made the **Deen** secure in its original form. This **Deen** was the constitution of the state that was later created by the Messenger **Mohammed** (pbuh). We sidetracked the Book of God and started following the teachings given by man. Thus, we too, adopted religion in place of **Deen**. We are like the earlier nations in this respect, but we are still different in a way. They do not have the God given **Deen** in its original form and cannot replace their religions with the **Deen**. But we do have the Book of God in its real form. Therefore, we can replace our religion with the original **Deen** of Allah at any time we want (similarly other nations too, if they want, can adopt the God given **Deen** in the Quran). Until we do so, we cannot reach life's destiny.

Dh-A   ذَا

"ذَا" (*za*): this. The feminine is "ذِهْ" (*zih*). "ذِهِ" (*zihi*), "ذِهِى" (*zihee*): up to. For two it is "ذَانْ" (*zaan*) or "ذَيْنْ" (*zain*). For feminine it is "تَانْ" (*taan*), "تَيْنْ" (*tain*). And plural is "أُولَاءِ" (*oolaa-i*) which is generally preceded by "هَا" (*ha*) as "هَذَا" (*haaza*) for masculine and "هَذِهِ" (*haazehi*) for feminine. This pontification is for a near thing. For a distant pontification, it is "ذَلِكَ" (*zaalika*) with feminine "تِلْكَ" (*tilka*). If we are addressing a man we will say see that thing or "ذَالِكَ" (*zaalika*). If we are addressing two men we will say "ذَالِكُمَا" (*zaalikuma*). If there are many men, we will say, "ذَالِكُمْ" (*zaalikum*). If the addressee is a woman, we will say "ذَالِكِ" (*zaaliki)*, and many women as "ذَالِكُنَّ" (*zaalikun*).

"ذَا" (*za*) has different uses. For instance:

2:255	<u>Who</u> can dare stand with anyone in his place (who can dare to support anyone in His kingdom).	مَنْ ذَاالَّذِىْ يَشْفَعُ عِنْدَهُ-
2:219	<u>They</u> ask you what should be kept open (available).	يَسْئَلُوْنَكَ مَاذَ يُنْفِقُوْنَ-
20:63	<u>They</u> are merely sorcerers	إِنْ هَذَانِ لَسَاحِرَانِ--
2:2	<u>This</u> is the book	ذَالِكَ الْكِتَابُ-
2:141	<u>This</u> was a group or party which has passed away.	تِلْكَ أُمَّةٌ قَدْخَلَتْ
28:32	<u>These</u> two are clear reasoning (signs).	فَذَانِكَ بُرْهَانِ--

As said earlier, "ذَالِكَ" (*zaalika*) is used for pointing at a distant thing as well as a near thing.

Surah *Ar-Room* says:

30:30	With the nature of Allah's laws that He has created for mankind. There can not by any change in what Allah's law creates	فِطْرَتَ اللهِ الَّتِيْ فَطَرَ النَّاسَ عَلَيْهَا لَا تَبْدِيْلَ لِخَلْقِ اللهِ
30:30	<u>This</u> is the lasting *deen*	ذَالِكَ الدِّيْنُ الْقَيِّمُ

Or in surah *Bani Israel*:

17:35	this is in the end very good	ذَالِكَ خَيْرٌ وَّأَحْسَنُ تَأْوِيْلاً

At all these places "ذَالِكَ" (*zalika*) is for pointing to a near thing i.e. "this".

As against this in the tale about *Moosa*, it is said:

18:64	that was the place we were looking for	ذَالِكَ مَاكُنَّانَبْغِ

Here "ذَالِكَ" (*zaalik*) is for pointing at a distant thing i.e. "that".

Raghib says "ذَالِک" (*zalik*) is indeed used for a distant thing but that is not the only thing meant by it. It is also used for anything which is on a higher plane and Thus, distant. No matter if that thing is physically near. So "ذَالِکَ الْكِتَابُ لَارَيْبَ فِيْهِ" (*zalika la raiba feeh*) in 2:2 would mean "*this book, about which there is no uncertainty*".

Dhalkifli   ذَالْكِفْل

This name has been used by the Quran in respect of a messenger (21:85, 38:48), but he has not been mentioned besides these verses. He is probably the messenger **Ezekiel** who has been mentioned in the **Torah**. Also see under heading (**K-F-L**).

Dhanon   ذَالنُوْن

It is the nick name of Messenger **Yunus** who probably is the same as Jonah in **Torah** (21:87). For details see headings '**Yunus**' and '**Noon**'.

Dhaab   ذ أ ب

"اَلذَّعْبُ" (*az-zeib*): wolf, as in (12:13).
"اَلذَّأْبُ" (*az-zaab*): to frighten, to condemn, using harsh voice {*T*}, to use impolite talk.
"ذَأَبَ الرَّجُلُ" (*zaabar rajul*): the man shouted loudly {*M*}.

Ibn Faris has said that it means transition, unease.

It also means a moment of a thing which is from no particular direction.
"تَذَأَّبَتِ الرِّيْح" (*tazabbatir reehu*): the breeze came from all sides.

A wolf is called "ذِعْبٌ" (*zeib*) because it sometime approaches from one side sometimes from the other.
Dh-A-M   ذ أ م
"ذَأَمَہ" (*zamah*) "يَذْأَمُہ" (*yazaamuh*): to consider somebody lowly or condemnable. It also means to accuse, or defame, or to harshly tell someone to get out {*T, M*}.

Raghib says it means condemnable.

"اَذْأُمَّ" (*azaamah*): Frightened and awed him {*T, M*}.

The Quran says about the **Iblees**.

| 7:18 | Told insulted and belittled (or harshly) to get out. | قَالَ اَخْرُجْ مِنْهَا مَذْءُوْماً مَدْحُوْرًا |

Dh-B-B   ذ ب ب

"ذُبَابٌ" (*zabaab*): flies. Singular is "ذُبَابَةٌ" (*zubaba*).

Muheet says with reference to *Jaahiz* that in addition to all kinds of common flies "ذُبَابٌ" (*zubaab*) covers bees and mosquitoes *{M}*.

The Quran has said:

22:73	they will not be able to create even a fly	لَنْ يَخْلُقُوا ذُبَاباً

Flies are called "ذُبَابٌ" (*zubaab*) because they are driven away, or because they are never at rest in one place. This root contains both connotations.

Ibn Faris says the root basically means unease and movement.

Raghib says that "اَلذَّبْذَبَةُ" (*az-zab-zaba*) means the sound of something that is hanging. Then this word began to be used for every movement and unease (that is fluctuation and uncertainty) *{R}*.

"بَعِيرٌ ذَابٌّ" (*bayeerun zaab*): a camel which does not stay in one place *{T}*.

"ذَبْذَبَةٌ" (*zab-zabah*): This word should perhaps be under heading Dh-B-Dh-B, but many linguists have placed it under Dh-B-B. Because of its meaning of being a share of something, we have also included it under this heading.

The Quran says about the *munafiqeen* (the hypocrites):

4:143	Wavering between that	مُذَبْذَبِينَ بَيْنَ ذَالِكَ
4:143	neither wholly on this side nor wholly on that side	لَا إِلَى هَؤُلَاءِ وَلَا إِلَى هَؤُلَاءِ

It is these very people about whom it is said:

22:11	who sit on the fence and observe the laws of Allah	مَنْ يَعْبُدُ اللَّهَ عَلَى حَرْفٍ

If gains are received on this side, they lean here, and if gains are perceived on the other side, then they lean towards it. Like a fly, nobody can predict where it will go next.

41:30	Once they accept God as the *Rabb* (Sustainer) then they stick to it.	إِنَّ الَّذِينَ قَالُوا رَبُّنَا اللَّهُ ثُمَّ اسْتَقَامُوا

Belief and stability are the hallmark of a *momin* (peace maker). As against a hypocrite who is opportunist.

Dh-B-H ح ب ذ

"ذَبَحَ" (*zabah*), "يَذْبَحُ" (*yazbah*): to slaughter, to split, to tear apart *{T}*.

Ibn Faris also says that these are its basic meanings.

"ذَبَحَتْهُ الْعَبْرَةُ" (*zabahatul abrah*): tears choked him.
"اَلتَّذْبِيحُ" (*at-tazbeeh*): to slaughter deeply, to bend the head so much that it gets lower than the waist.
"الذِّبْحُ" (*az-zibh*): the thing that is slaughtered *{T}*.

The Quran says about *Bani Israel* that:

2:49	(the people of the Pharaoh) killed your sons (*ibna*) and kept your daughters (*nisa*) alive.	يُذَبِّحُوْنَ اَبْنَاءَكُمْ وَيَسْتَحْيُوْنَ نِسَاءَكُمْ

This is generally taken to mean that the *Pharaoh* had ordered to kill every son that was born and to keep the baby girls alive. The question to ponder is whether "يُذَبِّحُوْنَ" (*yuzabbihoona*) means actually to slaughter or something else.

Surah *Al-Airaaf* has used "يُقَتِّلُوْنَ" (*yuqteloona*) instead of "يُذَبِّحُوْنَ" (*yuzabboon*) in 7:149. Here it says that they used to kill your sons and kept your daughters alive. It is Therefore, clear that the Quran has used "ذَبْح" (*zabah*) and "قَتَّلَ" (*qatal*) in similar meaning.

It has to be seen what "قَتَّلَ" (*qatal*) means. This word has been debated in detail under the heading (Q-T-L). There you will see that it means not only to kill, but also to weaken or demean or make ineffective. It means to make something so ineffective that its presence or absence is made the same. It means to belittle somebody. It also means to deprive someone of knowledge and training. See these meanings under heading (Q-T-L). It is thought that here "قَتَّلَ" (*qatal*) means not to kill (the sons of *Bani Israeel*), but to weaken them, demean them or make them ineffective.

The arguments against the notion that is really means "to kill" are as following.

1) In the time of *Moosa*, the nation of *Bani Israel* was huge. If the male kids in any society are killed and only the females are allowed to live, then after a time the nation will cease to exist. *
2) *Moosa*'s elder brother *Haroon* was alive and present and *Moosa* too was not killed immediately after birth. This also shows that the boys of the *Bani Israel* nation were not killed immediately after birth
3) Surah *Yunus* says in 10:83 that the youth of *Moosa's* nation believed in him. See under heading (Z-R-R). If the boys of the *Bani Israel* were killed immediately after birth then this youth would not exist.

4) When *Moosa* came to the *Pharaoh*, he said, we have nurtured you and were your benefactors and you are repaying us Thus,. In reply *Moosa* said: "you remind me of the benevolence but you have enslaved the nation of Bani Israel (26:22)". Here *Moosa* has accused the pharaoh of enslaving the nation of *Bani Israel*. If he had also ordered killing of new born boys of that nation, *Moosa* would have certainly accused the Pharaoh of this deed first. Because killing children was a much more severe crime than enslaving. But, nowhere in the Quran has *Moosa* accused the Pharaoh of so doing.

* Some books claim that Pharaoh killed 90.000 children of Bani Israel.

These facts show that the Pharaoh and his ilk did not kill the boys of the Bani Israel. It may be argued if this was not the case then why did *Moosa's* mother leave him to drift in the river in a box? First, bear in mind that the Pharaoh is said to have ordered killing of new born males at the time when *Moosa* had come with his revolutionary message. (As long as the right meanings of these verses are not made clear, we will continue with the traditional meaning i.e. to kill the children of the Bani Israel.)

Surah *Al-Airaaf* says, that seeing the effectiveness of *Moosa's* message, the leaders in the Pharaoh's nation asked the Pharaoh why no harsh measures were taken against him? Why was he left free to do as he wanted? In reply the Pharaoh said he had a plan! And that is: "we will murder their boys and let the girls live" (7:127). From this it can be seen that this was said when *Moosa's* message spread. This order did not prevail at the time of *Moosa's* birth. Surah *Al-momin* makes this clearer where it is said that when *Moosa* went to the Pharaoh with the message of God, he said: ""those who trust in *Moosa's* God, kill their sons and let their women live" (40:25). Thus, it is clear that this order was issued at the time when *Moosa* came with the message, and not at his birth. Besides, this order was not for the entire Bani Israel nation but only for those who entrusted themselves to *Moosa*, or his God.

These facts show that at the time of *Moosa's* birth, this order was not in force. When this order was not in force then it is not right to believe that God wanted to keep him alive in this manner. Why was then *Moosa* set out to drift in the river? The Quran has answered this question. The *Bani Israel* had entered Egypt in the time of Yusuf who gained an exalted position in Egypt. This respect would have reflected positively on his nation, the Bani Israel, and would have lasted some time even after Yusuf. But *Bani Israel* were later enslaved by the rulers. Even today, subjugated nations are worth almost nothing but in those days subjugated nations were almost like slaves. According to God's plan, *Moosa* was born to oppose the Pharaohs. For this purpose, he needed to be educated and trained at a high level. For this aim, it was destined that he grows up at the Pharaoh's palace itself. He should spend the early years as the Pharaoh's adopted son. This was the reason that he was set to drift and land at the Pharaoh's palace. The Quran says this was done so that he could be brought up under our watch (20:39). This meant good training from which the children of Bani Israel were barred. This was a link to the program and *Moosa* was being readied for this campaign. A little further, it is said "in this manner, O *Moosa*, you came up to Our standards" (20:41).

It will be related further ahead that those who had belief in **Moosa's** God were spared by the Pharaoh, then why did he order killing of the new born babies? What was their fault?

Surah **Al-Qasas** says that **Moosa's** mother was told to:

28:7	keep feeding him, and when you fear for him, then put him in the river	اَرْضِعِيْهِ فَاِذَا خِفْتِ عَلَيْهِ فَاَلْقِيْهِ فِي الْيَمِّ

This is taken to mean that the Pharaoh had ordered the killing of male children. But Quranic evidence is there to refute this line of thinking because the Pharaoh's order came when **Moosa** was a grown man and had brought Allah's message. We have to attribute some other cause for this fear. Further ahead it is said that when Pharaoh's people found the box (with **Moosa** in it in his infancy), the pharaoh's wife said "do not kill him, we shall adopt him" (28:9). This too is taken to mean that in those days, Israeli kids were killed. But this is not a right guess because how was it known that the baby that had been rescued from the waves, was an Israeli kid and not a kid from among the Pharaoh's nation?

As such "لَا تَقْتُلُوْهُ" (*la tuq tulu*) in 28:9 would not mean "do not kill him", but "do not throw him out as an insignificant being". See heading Q-T-L.

So what is the right meaning of "يُذَبِّحُوْنَ اَبْنَاءَ هُمْ وَيَسْتَحْيُوْنَ نِسَاءَ هُمْ" (*yuzabb-oona abna'ahum wa yastahyoona nisa'ahum*)?

We have seen that this was during the time that **Moosa's** message was spreading and the Pharaoh perceived this as a threat to his dominance. In addition when his advisers had asked him why nothing was being done about it, he had replied that he had a plan (7:127), and this was the plan (to perform *qatal* of *ibna*). The Quran has termed this scheme as "كَيْدٌ" (*kaidun*) in 40:25 which means a deep conspiracy.

About the Pharaoh, surah **Al-Qasas** says:

28:4	he used to divide and rule	وَجَعَلَ اَهْلَهَا شِيَعاً يَّسْتَضْعِفُ طَائِفَةً مِّنْهُمْ

Later it is said:

28:4	He used to *yuzabbuh* (tear apart) their *ibna* (strength), and let the *nisa* (weak) to be *yastahi* (live).	يُذَبِّحُ اَبْنَاءَ هُمْ وَيَسْتَحْيِ نَسَاءَهُمْ

He wanted to divide the nation of Israel into different parties so that they would be busy in struggling against each other. Every ruling nation indulges in this kind of conspiracy. Later after dividing them into parties he used to subjugate the party which he perceived was a strong threat to his rule. He used to humiliate and demean them, while he used to elevate the foppish or weak people. This too is practiced by every conquering nation. A dictator nation always keeps the subordinated nation divided. The strong section is always ridiculed and demeaned, while the weak and insignificant portion which they fear no danger from, get promoted.

The Quran has defined the strong and brave portion of a nation as "اَبْنَاءٌ" (*ibna*) and the weak portion of a nation as "نِسَاءٌ" (*nisa*). Hence, by "قَتْلِ اَبْنَاء" (*qatl-ibna*) the Quran means demeaning of the strong and brave section of a nation, while "وَيَسْتَحْى نَسَاءَهُمْ" (*yastahyai nisa'akum*) means to elevate weak section of a nation. In this way, he was weakening the *Bani Israel's* entire nation. The Quranic evidence points to this that *qatal* or *zabah* of *ibna'a* means this.

But this is only an assumption and can be given more thought. One can understand what the Pharaoh's order to kill the sons of those who believed in *Moosa* means (40:25). That is, his plan was to divide the entire Bani Israel into different parties so that those who were a threat to him could be made ineffective so that nobody listened to them. See this meaning of *qatal* under heading (*Q-T-L*). Otherwise, it is not reasonable to kill the sons of those who believe in Moses (and spare the believers themselves). In addition, this is a fact too that when the sorcerers of his court said that they had started believing (in *Moosa's* God), he ordered them to be hanged, not to kill their sons.

This shows that the phrase "ذَبِّح اَبْنَاءَ" (*zabhi abna'akum*) and "اسْتِحْيَاء نِسَاء" (*istahya'i nisa'akum*) has been used as a metaphor. This does not mean actually to slaughter them.

But as said earlier, this is an educated guess. If this reasoning is considered weak then "ذَبْح اَبْنَاءَ" (*zabha abna'a*) will be taken to mean what its literal meaning is i.e. the Pharaoh used to kill the boys of *Bani Israel* but up till now the history of ancient Egypt mentions no such murder or killing. Perhaps history may yet reveal such incidents. Up till now the *Torah* relates that the Pharaoh had ordered the killing of *Bani Israel's* boys (*Kitaab Khurooj*). But we all know historically how correct the *Torah* is.

In surah *Al-Ma'idah* the animals which were sacrificed on the altar of statues (gods) were called "مَا ذُبِحَ عَلَى النُّصُبِ" (*ma zubha alan nusub*) in 5:3.

Surah *As-Saffaat* says that when *Ibrahim* got ready to sacrifice his son, and his son Ismail became ready to be sacrificed, then We called out to him to desist and "فَدَيْنٰهُ بِذِبْحٍ عَظِيْمٍ" (*wafadainahu bizibhin azeem*) (37:107): saved Ismail in exchange for a great sacrifice.

As is evident from various places in the Quran, this "بِذِبْحٍ عَظِيْمٍ" (*zibhi azeem*) (great sacrifice) was that instead of the ruler ship of the green area of Syria, he was chosen for the caretaking of Kaba in the desolate land of Arabia. This was a lifelong sacrifice, not only for his own whole life, but also for the coming generations.

| 37:108 | And We left for him among the later folk | وَتَرَكْنَا عَلَيْهِ فِى الْآخِرِينَ |

(For more details see my book *Jooye Noor* and the matters about the Bani Israel in my book *Barq-e-Toor*).

Dh-Kh-R   ذ خ ر

"ذَخَرَ" (*zakhar*), "يَذْخَرُ" (*yazkhar*): to take something, to make it one's own, to hide something so that it may be used when required.

Ibn Faris says to keep something hidden for its safety.

"اِدَّخَرَ" (*ad-zakhara*), "اِدِّخَارُ" (*id-zikhaar*): also means the same as "ذَخَرَ" (*zakhar*).
"اِدِّخَارُ" (*izkhaar*) was actually "اِدْتِخَارُ" (*id-zikhaar*).
"الْمُذَّخِرُ" (*al-muzakhir*): a horse who does not use all of his strength in running but preserves some {T}.
"اَلذَّاخِرُ" (*ad-zakhir*): plump, fat. {M}

Surah *Aal-e-Imran* says:

3:49	And what you hoard in your houses	وَمَا تَدَّخِرُونَ فِي بُيُوتِكُمْ

It seems that Jesus (since he had come with a true revolutionary message) was averse to the hoarding habit of the Jews. This is a pontification of that.

Dh-R-A   ذ ر أ

"ذَرَاَالْأَرْضَ" (*zaral ard*): sowed the seed (in the ground) {T}.
"ذَرَاَاللهُ الْخَلْقَ" (*zara allah-ul-khalq*): Allah created the creatures and increased them, made it abundant.

The Quran says:

42:11	He keeps increasing you and spread you	يَذْرَؤُكُمْ فِيْهِ

Surah *Al-mominon* says:

23:79	He is the One who increased you and spread you on this on this earth.	هُوَ الَّذِئ ذَرَاَكُمْ فِى الْأَرْضِ

Some think that "ذُرِّيَّةٌ" (*zurriyyah*) has come from "ذَرَأ" (*zara*) but others say it has come from "ذَرٌّ" (*zarr*) that we have mentioned under (*Dh-R-R*).

Dh-R-R ذ ر ر

"اَلذَّرُ" (*az-zarr*): very small ants. The specks (dust) particles we see in the sunlight. The singular is "اَلذَّرُّ" (*az-zarru*). A very small and light thing is also called "ذَرَّةٌ" (*zarrah*).
"ذَرَّ" (*zarr*): to sprinkle something, to disburse or differentiate.

Surah *Al-zalzalah* says:

99:6	And whose doeth good an atom's weight	مَنْ يَعْمَلْ مِثْقَالَ ذَرَّةٍ

Ibn Faris says it means finesse and spreading.

"ذَرَّ الْمِلْخَ عَلَى اللَّحْمِ" (*zarral milha alal lahm*): He sprinkled the meat with salt.
"ذَرَّ الْحَبَّ فِى الْأَرْضِ" (*zarral hubba fil ard*): He sprinkled the seeds in the ground {T}.
"اَلذُّرِّيَّةُ" (*az-zuriyyah*): a man's progeny whether male or female. Sometimes it is also used for one's parents and grandparents. This word sometimes means the opposites {T}. (We will read more about it further ahead).

Raghib says it actually means young children but sometimes it also means both young and older children, and is used as plural as well as singular. Some say the root of this word is "ذَرِيَّةً" (*zara*) which means to create and increase {L}.

"ذَرَّ الْبَقْلُ" (*zarral baql*): the vegetable budded.

The Quran has used the word "ذُرِّيَّةٌ" (*zurriyah*) to mean descendants or generation (2:124).

Surah *Yasin* says:

36:41	And We bear their offspring in the laden ship	إِنَّا حَمَلْنَا ذُرِّيَّتَهُمْ فِى الْفُلْكِ

Here "الذُّرِّيَّةُ" (*zurriyah*) means all, big and small. Because of this verse (36:61), some attribute the meaning of progeny and grandparents to the word "الذُّرِّيَّةُ" (*zurriyah*), and this is why it has been accepted to mean the opposites. But research shows that the Quran has never used this word for grandparents, but only for descendants (6:88).

Verse 36:41 also clarifies the meaning if we take "اَلْفُلْكَ الْمَشْحُونَ" (*al-foolkil mash hoon*) as the arc of *Nouh* which was built according to the revelation and "ذُرِّيَّةٌ" (*zurriyah*) to mean the young generation of humans of that time. This will leave no ambiguity in the meanings of the verse.

Surah *Yunus* says:

10:83	So nobody believed *Moosa* except the youth of his nation	فَمَا آمَنَ لِمُوسَى إِلَّا ذُرِّيَّةٌ مِنْ قَوْمِهِ

Some say it means very small number of people {*Ibn Abbas*}. Others say it means the youth of that nation {*Abul Kalam Azad*}. We think the second meaning is clearer. The youth accept a revolutionary program more readily. The older people are more dogmatic about their previous dogmas. Also, due to the age factor, they have little capacity for adopting new things. It is the youth that accept a revolutionary program which is against oppressiveness without any fear. Also see under heading (*Dh-B-H*).

Dh-R-Ain   ذ ر ع

"اَلذِّرَاغُ" (*az-zara'a*): the part of the arm from the elbow to the end of the middle finger. It is also used to mean the wrist, and also a measure {*T*}.

Surah *Al-Kahaf* says:

| 18:18 | Their dog had both forelegs on the ground | وَكَلْبُهُم بَاسِطٌ ذِرَاعَيْهِ |

"ذَرْعُهُ كَذَا" (*zarohu kaza*): it is of such length {*M*}.

| 69:32 | it is seventy hands long | ذَرْعُهَا سَبْعُونَ ذِرَاعاً |

Ibn Faris says it basically means to be long and move forward.

"مَالِيْ بِهِ ذَرْغٌ" (*maali bi zarun*): I do not have recourse to it {*T*}.
"ضِقْتُ بِهِ ذَرْعاً" (*zdiqtu bi zar'a*): to have no capacity for doing something.

Surah *Hood* says about Loot:

| 11:77 | In their matter, he found himself in capable | ضَاقَ بِهِم ذَرْعاً |

"الذَّرِيْعَةُ" (*az-zuriyah*): the she-camel which is used as a shield while hunting {*T*}. It means any means which is used to reach the goal.

Dh-R-W   ذ ر و

"ذَرَتِ الرِّيْحُ الشَّىْءَ وَرْوًا" (*zaratir-raehoosh-shaiya warwa*): the wind blew it away.

"ذَرَا الْحِنْطَةَ يَذْرُوْبَا ذَرْوًا" (*zaralhintata yazruha zarwa*): he threw the wheat in the air to separate it from the chaff.

"فَتَذَرَّتْ" (*fatazarrat*): the wheat became free of the chaff.

"ذَرَاوَةُ النَّبْتِ" (*zarawatun nabt*): the dry parts of a plant which fall away and are blown away by the wind.

"ذُرْوَةُ الشَّىْءِ" (*zurwatush shaiyi*): the higher part of a thing *{T}*.

Surah *Al-Kaif* says:

| 18:45 | … the winds blow it around | تَذْرُوْهُ الرِّيْحُ |

Surah *Az-Zarriyat* says:

| 51:1 | By those scattering, dispersing … | وَالذَّرِيتِ ذَرْوًا |

"ذَرْوٌ" (*zaru*) means to disperse, spread around.

"ذَار" (*zaar*), "اَلذَّارِئ" (*az-zaari*): one who spreads, one who disseminates, the forces which are the means of dissemination, the force which spreads the word around in the world, the means of communication and dissemination (media).

Dh-Ain-N ذ ع ن

"اَذْعَنَ" (*az'an*): to be quick in obedience, in following, to obey a command with alacrity.

"نَاقَةٌ مِذْعَانٌ" (*naaqatun miz'an*): an obedient camel.

"مُذْعِنِيْنَ" (*mud'ineen*): those who became followers or obedient quickly (22:49) *{T}*.

"اَذْعَنَ لَهُ" (*az'ana lahu*): bowed before him and became obedient to him *{T}*.

Muheet while quoting the literal meaning of "اَلإِذْعَانُ" (*al-iz'an*) says it means heartfelt intent and solidity after deliberation or hesitation.

"اَلإِذْعَانُ" (*a-liz'an*) has different stages and the lowest is called opinion and the best is called *Iman* (trust/conviction), and between these two is the stage of mere custom and tradition *{T, L}*.

Dh-Q-N   ذ ق ن

"اَلذَّقَنُ" (*az-zaqan*): chin *{T}*. Plural is "اَذْقَانٌ" (*azqaan*) as in 36:8. It figuratively also means the face.

| 17:107 | They fall on their faces | يَخِرُّوْنَ لِلأَذْقَانِ سُجَّدًا |

Dh-K-R   ذ ک ر

"اَلذِّكْرُ" (*az-zikru*) and "اَلتَّذْكَارُ" (*at-tazkaar*): to make something safe, to make something present in the heart (to imagine something as present). This word has been used against "نَسْیٌ" (*nasee*) in 6:68.

"نَسِیٌ" (*nasiyun*) means to forget something, and as such "ذِكْرٌ" (*zikr*) would mean to recall something.

"اِذَّكَرَہُ" (*izkarahu*), "اِسْتَذْكَرَہ" (*istazkarah*), "تَذَكَّرَہ" (*tazakkirah*): ordinarily mean to memorize something, but scholars say there is a slight difference in the meaning of the words.

"اِذَّكَرَ" (*izkar*) is actually "اِذْتَكَرَ" (*iztutakar*). The "ذ" (z) has been omitted because it is heavy on the tongue. Then "ت" (*taa*) was amalgamated in "د" (*daal*). Ergo this word was created.

"اَلتَّذْكِرَۃُ" (*at-tazkirah*): something which reminds one of the need (79:29).

"الذِّكْرَای" (*az-zikra*): reminder.

"ذَکَرَحَقَّہُ" (*zakara haqquhu*): his right was protected, not lost.

"أ ذْكُرُوْنِعْمَۃَ اللهِ عَلَیْكُمْ" (*ozkuru ne'matallahi alaikum*): do not waste the benevolence (favors of) Allah on you and protect them {T}.

"ذِكْرٌ" (*zikr*): fame as well as to speak kind words about someone, and to respect. It also means "a lesson". *Zikr* also means the book which contains the details about *Deen* and laws about the nation {T}.

"اَلذَّكْرُ" (*az-zakar*): a strong and brave man, the hardness and sharpness of a sword {T}, also means male when used against "أُنْثَی" (*unsa*), as in 3:35.

"مُذَكَّرٌ" (*muzakkar*): masculine, the opposite of feminine, severe troubles which only men can face {T}.

The Quran has been called "اَلذِّكْرُ" (*az-zikr*) as in 16:42, because it contains the laws about nations and also historic events. Those who deliberate about the things in the universe have been called "لِقَوْمٍ یَذَّكَّرُوْنَ" (*liqaumin yaz zakkaroon*) as in 16:13. The struggle against anti-God forces has also been called *zikr*. That is, the struggle to bring the laws which they (the *mushrikeen*) have ignored (20:42, 20:34). Hence, to be steadfast in the battlefield and Thus, strive to give dominance to Allah's laws have been called *zikr*, as in 8:25. It also means not to ignore the laws of Allah, even in the battlefield, and to always keep them in mind. The laws of Allah themselves are *zikr* as mentioned in 39:23 to mean respect and greatness.

This word has been used in 23:70 as well as in 43:44 where it has been said about the Quran:

43:44	The secret of your greatness and that of your nation is in following the Quran.	اِنَّہُ لَذِكْرٌ لَکَ وَلِقَوْمِکَ

Surah *Al-Qamar* has said "مُذَكِّرٌ" (*muzakkir*) to mean "one who recalls" in 54:15.

Surah *Ad-Dahar* says that there has been a time when man was unremembered "لَمْ یَكُنْ شَیْاً" "مَذْكُوْرًا" (*lam yakan shaya mazkoora*) (76:1). Here *mazkoora* means something which has come into existence by itself and which is established {T, L}.

In surah *Al-Baqrah*, (2:152) God says "فَاذْ كُرُوْنِيْ اَذْكُرْكُمْ" (*fa azkuruni azkarkum*). This means that if you uphold my laws then I will protect your rights and grant you greatness and grandeur.

That is, if you follow My laws then their delightful results will certainly be in front of you. Here, it must be noted that the initiative is from Man while God only answers it. The sort of deed that is committed by man gets the same sort of result (i.e. good result for good deeds and bad result for bad deeds). Therefore, "ذِكُرُ اللہ" (*zikrullah*) or the *zikr* of Allah means the following of Allah's orders (and not merely turning the beads of the rosary). The definite result of following these orders is respect and greatness and domination over anti-God forces. For *Ibrahim* to go and confront the Pharaoh (with God's laws) is *zikr* and "تَسْبِيْحٌ" (*tasbeeh*). For the meaning of "تَسْبِيْحٌ" (*tasbeeh*), see under heading (S-B-H). To be steadfast in the battlefield is *zikr*. To deliberate upon the things of this universe is *zikr*. To keep Allah's laws before one, at every step in every aspect of life is *zikr*. To propagate these laws is also *zikr*. This in today's world is called broadcasting and publishing.

This is the very "ذِكُرُ اللہ" (*zikrullah*) which gives "real" peace to a man (13:28). The 'real' has been added because transitory and artificial peace or satisfaction can be obtained through untrue religions as well. Real peace is obtained through deep insight. The only time we reach the conclusion that something is true is when we have deliberated on something deeply, or when the final results of deeds are before us. Only under these circumstances do we achieve real peace, which is peaceful both for the heart and mind. False peace (satisfaction) is obtained by deceiving oneself. Real peace accrued to the group of *momineen* in the battlefield of *Badr* when they defeated an army three times their size (3:125). Peace is not obtained in secluded rooms or places.

Dh-K-W   ذ ک و

"ذَكَاءٌ" (*dhaka*) basically means for a thing to be completed.

Khalil says "اَلذَّكَاءُ فِى السِّنِّ" (*al-dhaaka'o fis-sin*) means mature age in which a man's capabilities reach their peak.

"اَلذَّكَاءُ" (*adh-dhaka'o*) means the sharpness and completion of intellect and wit.
"ذَكِيٌّ" (*dhakki*) is one who understands quickly, one who has very sharp intelligence.
"ذَكَتِ النَّارُ" (*dhakatin naar*): the fire flared {T}.

Ibn Faris says it basically means sharpness and implementation.

"اَلذَّكِيَةُ" (*adh-dhakiyyah*) means to slaughter an animal.
"ذَكَاءٌ" (*dhaka*) means temperature and "ذكّى" (*dhakka*) means the temperature was taken out.

The Quran says:

5:3	Excepting that which you slaughter …	إِلَّا مَا ذَكَّيْتُمْ

Dh-L-L   ذ ل ل

"ذِلَّة" (*dhillah*), "ذَلَالَة" (*dhalalah*): when hardness and dogmatisms of something gets to its end, and it becomes obedient.

Raghib says "الذُّلُّ" (*adh-dhull*) means to bend, because when anger and power bow or bend, the harshness becomes mellow on its own. He has also written that when "الذِّلُّ" (*adh-dhill*) is not due to external pressure, it is no more a condemnable trait.

"ذَلُوْلٌ" (*dhalool*), plural is "ذُلُلٌ" (*dhulul*): one who becomes obedient {T}.

Surah **Al-Baqrah** says:

2:71	The ox which has not been harnessed in the plough.	إِنَّهَا بَقَرَةٌ لَاذَلُوْلٌ

"عَيْرُ الْمَذَلَّةِ" (*air-ul-muzillah*): an ass which is laden heavily and who is being driven with the help of a stick {M}. This brings the right concept of "ذِلَّت" (*dhillat*) before you, which is used for "disgrace".

"ذَلَّلَ الْكَرْمُ تَذْلِيْلاً" (*dhullilal karmu tazlila*): bunches of grapes were made low (bent down) {T}.

The Quran has used "تُذِلُّ" (*tudhillu*) against "تُعِزُّ" (*tu-idhu*) in 3:25.

"عِزَّت" (*idhat*) means as described therein, to get the government and state (i.e. power) and "ذِلَّت" (*dhillat*) means as also described therein, to be deprived of power.

Surah **Yasin** says about cattle:

36:70	Humans have domination over them.	فَهُمْ لَهَا مَالِكُوْنَ- وَذَلَّلْنَاهَا
36:71	They have been made subservient to man	

Surah **Taha** says "نَذِلَّ وَنَخْزَىٰ" (*nadhilla wa naanadhraa*) in 20:134. It means that in the battlefield this word has come to mean weakness. Also see (3:122).

In surah **Al-Ma'idah** the particularity of the **momineen** has been described as:

5:54	Humble towards **momineen** and stern towards **kafireen**	اَذِلَّةٍ عَلَى الْمُؤْمِنِيْنَ اَعِزَّةٍ عَلَى الْكَافِرِيْنَ

Ibnul Airabi says here "اَذِلَّةٍ عَلَى الْمُؤْمِنِيْنَ" (*azillatin alal Momineen*) means the same as "رُحَمَاءَ بَيْنَهُمْ" (*ruhama bainahum*) as in 48:29. That is, they are friendly and kind to one another, while hard on the enemy.

"جَنَاحَ الذَّلّ" (*janahadhul*): It has appeared for softness and hospitality and kindness.

The Quran has termed a life of "ذلت" (*dhillat*) and weakness as punishment of God (2:61). This ignominy is in this world and can be seen by everybody (7:152). As against it, it has been said that the life of the **momineen** is a life of power and greatness.

63:8	Power and domination is for Allah, his Rusool, His group or party.	وَلِلّهِ الْعِزَّةُ وَلِرَسُوْلِهِ وَلِلْمُؤْمِنِيْنَ

The life of the **momineen** is "اَعْلَوْنَ" (*a'loon*) as it has been said in 3:138. It's a life of domination and power (24:55). Thus, a life which does not have power and domination is not a life of the **momineen**.

The ignominy in this world is a punishment from Allah.

2:61	And humiliation and misery struck on them and they drew wrath on themselves	وَضُرِبَتْ عَلَيْهِمُ الذَّلَّةُ وَالْمَسْكَنَةُ وَبَاءُ وَ بِغَضَبٍ مِنَ اللّهِ

They were hit by ignominy. That is they became deserving of Allah's punishment.

To believe that by handing this world over to others and to live a life of helplessness and deprivation and ignominy, one can attain spiritual development, is a false concept. This is a mirage that is passed on by the stronger nations to the weak and subjugated nations.

The Quran has come to shatter this false concept. It has openly declared that power, respect, grandeur, wealth, etc. is the natural result of trusting Allah's laws and doing good deeds. A life of deprivation, poverty, ignominy and subjugation is Allah's punishment. It is also said that whoever is in a bad condition in this world, cannot be near Allah in the Hereafter. He whose present is dark will also have a bleak future.

20:124	He who ignores our laws, his earnings will be constricted and on the Day of the Judgment. We will raise him blind	وَمَنْ اَعْرَضَ عَنْ ذِكْرِئ فَاِنَّ لَهُ مَعِيْشَةً ضَنْكاً وَّنَحْشُرُهُ يَوْمَ الْقِيْمَةِ اَعْمٰى

We can all judge ourselves against this criterion.

Dh-M-M   ذ م م

"ذَمَّ" (*dhammah*), "يَذُمُّهُ" (*yadhummah*), "ذَمَّا" (*dhamma*), "مَذَمَّةٌ" (*madhamma*) are all opposite of "مَدْحٌ" (*madah*) which means to praise. It means that these words mean to bad mouth someone.

"اِسْتَذَمَّ" (*istadham*): he did a condemnable thing.

"بِمَ ذَمِيمَةٌ" (*bi dhamimah*): he cannot go out of the house due to some sickness or some misfortune {*M*}.

"مَذْمُومٌ" (*madhmoom*) has been used in 68:49 in these meanings.

"ذِمَّةٌ" (*dhimmah*): any responsibility, pact, agreement, or oral agreement that is not fulfilled and Hence, is condemnable {*M*}. It is also used for breaking a pact a man is liable to, and Hence, condemned{*R*}.

"اَلذِّمَّةُ" (*adh-dhimmah*): protection, patronage, guarantee.

"ذِمِّيٌّ" (*dhimmi*): the man who is under a pact, he who has been assured of protection, or he who has been guaranteed in every way.

The Quran says:

| 9:8 | they do not respect any agreement or pact | لَا يَرْقُبُوا فِيكُمْ اِلاًّ وَلَا ذِمَّةً |

For details, see heading (A-L-L).

Dh-N-B   ذ ن ب

"اَلذَّنَبُ" (*adh-dhanab*): tail.

"ذَنَبَهُ" (*dhanbahu*): he tailed him (followed his tail).

"مُسْتَذْنِبٌ" (*mustadhnib*): a man who follows right behind a camel.

"اَلذِّنَابُ" (*adh-dhinaab*): the back part of anything.

"ذَنَبَةُ الْوَادِىْ" (*dhanbatul wadi*): the last part of the valley.

"اَلذُّنَابَةُ" (*adh-dhunabah*): one who follows behind.

Raghib says that "الذَّنْبُ" (*adh-dhunb*) basically means the back part of anything or the tail. Hence, it means every deed which has a bad ending. The result of any deed is Therefore, called "ذَنْبٌ" (*dhanb*) because it follows the act {*M*}. This word is also used to mean sin and crime.

The Quran says:

| 91:14 | they were destroyed by their Sustainer due to their crimes | فَدَمْدَمَ عَلَيْهِمْ رَبُّهُمْ بِذَنْبِهِمْ |

So in the above verse, the meaning is of crime.

"ذَنَبٌ" (*dhanab*) also means a mean person.

Since a tail is always behind an animal, therefore, "ذَنُوْبّ" (*dhunub*) is also those allegations which are in a way stuck to somebody's back. "اَلْقِفْوَةُ" (*al-qifwah*) means a tail but it also means allegation. See heading (Q-F-W)

Surah *Al-Fateh* says about the Messenger *Mohammed* (*pbuh*):

48:2	This great victory is being granted so that you are protected from all the allegations that your opponents level against you or will level against you.	لِيَغْفِرَ لَكَ اللهُ مَا تَقَدَّمَ مِنْ ذَنْبِكَ وَمَاتَاَخَّرَ

The opponents used to say that the Messenger's claims (God forbid) are false. He is demented. Somebody had worked a spell on him. He paints rosy pictures with no basis and deceives people. God says this great victory, which has broken the back of the opposing forces, is proof of the fact that at last you were proven right. See more under heading (Q-D-M).

"ذَنُوْبّ" (*dhanoob*) means a horse with a bushy tail. It also means a big bucket (used to fetch water from a well) which is full of water, while if it is empty then it is called "دَلُوّ" (*dalu*). It also means a day of unending miseries.

Surah *Adh-dhurriyaat* says:

51:59	those who are being oppressive will share the fate of those who were like them	فَاِنَّ لِلَّذِيْنَ ظَلَمُوْا ذَنُوْباً مِثْلَ ذَنُوْبِ اَصْحَابِهِمْ

Taj, *Muheet* and *Raghib* say that "ذَنُوْب" (*dhanub*) means share or luck. It is therefore, that the above verse has been translated as such.

Some people out of humbleness call themselves sinners etc. "مُذْنِبْ" (*mudhanb*) or sin is a crime against God's laws. When we do not like being called criminals, then why call ourselves sinners (even if it is only out of humility)? If we have actually committed some crime then we should be ashamed of it rather than make it a distinguishing mark!

Dh - H - B   ذ ه ب

"ذَهَابٌ" (*dhahaab*): to go, to pass by.

"ذَهَبَ بِہ" (*dhahaba behi*): to take away.

"ذَهَبَ عَلَیَّ کَذَا" (*dhahaba alayya kaza*): I forgot that thing.

If "عَنْ" (*un*) appears with "ذَهَب" (*dhahab*), then it means to leave, while if "اِلٰی" (*ila*) comes with it then it means to be attentive *{T}*.

Kashaaf says that "اَذْہَبَہُ" (*adhaabahu*) means eliminated it, pushed it away or took it away (46:20).

"ذَهَبَ بِہ" (*dhahaba behi*): took him away along with him. That is, went with him *{M}*.

The Quran says "ذَهَبَ اللهُ بِنُوْرِہِمْ" (*dhahaballahu benoorihim*) in 2:17. Here it means to take away, not to go along with him.

"اَلْمَذْہَبُ" (*al-madh-hab*): to go, a place to go to, the way to go, the method to follow, the concept towards which one leans, religion to follow. It also means the latrine where one goes for defecating. The Quran has not used this form of the word "مَذْہَبٌ" (*madh-hab*) anywhere. For "Islam" the word "دِیْنٌ" (*deen*) has been used.

"مَذْہَبٌ" (*madh-hab*) actually means "a school of thought".

In the beginning the word for Islam was only "دِیْنٌ" (*deen*), when different sects were created due to thoughts of different scholars, religion or *madh-hab* replaced *deen*.

"ذَهَبَ فِی الدِّیْنِ مَذْہَباً" (*dhahaba fiddeen madh-haba*): he followed a certain concept about *Deen*.

"فُلَانٌ یَذْہَبُ اِلٰی قَوْلِ اَبِیْ حَنِیْفَةَ" (*falanun yazhabu ila qaului abi hanifah*): man follows the sect of *Imam Hanifa {L}*.

This way the *Deen* (the way of life which Allah had given us) was lost and various religions which were attributed to different personalities began to flourish. Until and unless these religions are not erased, *Deen* will be pushed kept hidden in the background. By "erasing" the religions, it means that they should only be given the importance that they are a way of thinking, not a way to live by as *Deen* is. Alternatively, these were the details which they had determined according to their time. They were not permanent. Permanence is only for *Deen* which is contained in the Quran. As such, whatever has come to us in the form of religion from our forefathers must be judged on the criterion of the Quran. Whatever the Quran says to be right must be taken to be right, and whatever it says is false must be rejected.

As far as philosophical details are concerned, they cannot be permanent because they will be determined according to the time we are passing through, under the overall guidance of Quranic laws.

Since in the West, Christianity only holds the status of a religion, therefore, they also call Islam a religion (whereas it is a **Deen**). The concept of **Deen** has been eradicated, and Islam too was understood to be a religion among other religions of the world, although Islam is a **Deen** (way of life) not religion.

About the basic meaning of the word religion, there is a difference among scholars but they agree on the meaning "respect for the gods". Thereafter the worship of any meta-physical being was called religion and this is the meaning which currently holds sway. (See the Century Dictionary). Obviously, Islam is not a religion in this sense, because it is a complete code of life. Therefore, Islam must not be called "religion".

Religion or **madh-hab** is the product of the times when the human mind or knowledge was in its infancy. Man could not understand that the events in this universe take place according to the laws framed by God. Since he did not understand their cause, he genuflected before them and tried to woo them with presents and sacrifices. He used to find ways with which he could reach them, and looked for someone to intervene between him and them. Man's own superstition created the gods and goddesses and Thus, he began to worship them. Those who were cleverer made themselves out to be near the gods or their friends and exploited simple folk. They began to be worshipped themselves. Thus, were the institutions of religious leadership and spiritual rulers. The ruling clique too came close to them and Thus, became the 'avatar' (incarnations of God). The simple folks were taught that they (the religious and temporal rulers) had been granted powers by the gods. All these concepts together made up religion that prevails even today among humans.

To dispel this falsehood of religion, **Deen** continued to be presented by God through the Messengers. It made man realize his true place in the universe. It also said everything in the universe is working according to the laws made by God and man had been given the knowledge to harness these forces and utilize them for the benefit of the entire human race. It (**Deen**) has supported its claims with reasoning and invited man to accept them with his knowledge and insight. God's **Deen** is completely secure in the Quran and is a living challenge to religion. Since man's knowledge and insight is increasing, the supremacy of religion is being eroded. Thus, the path for the establishment of the **Deen** is being prepared. The world is gradually becoming frustrated with the concepts of capitalism, hegemonies and religious leadership. These are signs to that God's **Deen** will one day bloom with all its delights. Now man is reaching a mature era and can neither be frightened of his own superstitions nor be content with false happiness. Now it can only be content with the solid facts of life which cannot be found anywhere else but in the Quran.

"اَلذَّهَبُ" (*adh-dhahab*), as used in 18:31, means the gold which has been purified after being mined. The gold which is still within the mine and which has not been melted and purified is called "تِبْرٌ" (*tibr*).

"مُذَهَّبٌ" (*mudhahab*): anything which has gold plating.

"ذَهِبَ الرَّجُلُ" (*dhahabir rujul*) is said when a man is awestruck by seeing a lot of gold in a mine.

"اَلذِّهْبَةُ" (*adh-dhihbah*): slight rain or largesse *{T}*.

Ibn Faris says it basically means to go, as well as beauty and freshness.

Dh-He-L   ذ ه ل

"ذَهْلَةٌ" (*dhahlah*), "ذَهِلَ عَنْهُ" (*dhahala unhu*): to leave, to give up something even though there is some contact, or to give up knowingly, or to forget due to being engaged in something else.

Some say "ذُهُوْلٌ" (*dhuhool*) means for the memories of the beloved to fade away and despite its absence, for the heart to be happy and feel no loss *{T}*.

Muheet has added that "ذُهُوْلٌ" (*dhuhool*) means to give up one's beloved one due to some fright. "ذَهِلَ" (*dhahil*) means for someone to lose his/her senses *{M}*.

Ibn Faris says the word basically means to forget about something due to worries and troubles.

The Quran says:

22:2	When you see it (*Qaiyamah*) every mother will stop feeding her child and every pregnant woman will abort her fetus.	يَوْمَ تَرَوْنَهَا تَذْهَلُ كُلُّ مُرْضِعَةٍ عَمَّا أَرْضَعَتْ وَتَضَعُ كُلُّ ذَاتِ حَمْلٍ حَمْلَهَا

This is said about the frightening aspect of that 'moment' (the Day of the Judgment). But if it is taken to mean the revolutionary era, then it draws a picture of our times in which no woman wants to feed her baby and no woman (despite being married) is willing to be pregnant. And they do not feel any compunction at giving up these feminine duties but instead they are very happy. They consider these things to be a hindrance in their other engagements.

"ذَهَلَ" (*dhahal*) connotes all these meanings. It also means the troublesome lives that we lead and in this way become oblivious of our other responsibilities.

Dh-W   ذُوْ

"ذُوْ" (*dhu*) means having. Its plurals are "ذَوُوْنَ" (*dhawoon*), "ذَوِيْنَ" (*dhaween*) and "أُولُوْ" (*oolu*). Feminine form is "ذَاتّ" (*dhaat*). Feminine plural is "ذَوَاتَانِ" (*dhawataan*). According to a rule "ذُوْ" (*dhu*) can sometimes become "ذِیْ" (*dhee*) or "ذَا" (*dhaa*).

2:280	one who is poor, has poverty	ذُوْعُسْرَة
41:51	one who prays for long	فَذُوْ دُعَاءٍ عَرِیْضٍ
2:177	Relatives	ذَوِیْ الْقُرْبٰی
18:18	on the right and left side	ذَاتَ الیَمِیْنِ وَذَاتَ الشِّمَالِ
3:153	whatever is inside the heart (whatever thoughts are in the mind)	بِذَاتِ الصُّدُوْرِ
55:28	scholars of different sciences and arts	ذَوَاتَا أَفْنَانٍ

Dhulqarnain   ذو القرنین

"ذوالقرنین" (***Dhulqarnain***) was the kind king of Persia who liberated the Jews from the captivity of the Babylonians, and allowed them to settle down in Jerusalem. The Quran has discussed him in detail in surah ***Al-Kahaf*** 18:83-101. For details see heading (Q-R-N).

Dh-W-D   ذ و د

"اَلذَّوْدُ" (***adh-dhud***): to drive, push away, to scold and oust, to remove.
"اَلْمِذْوَدُ" (***al-midhwad***): the place where the animals are fed; it also means the horns of the ox with which he defends himself or keeps others away from him {*T, M, R*}.

Ibn Faris says it basically means to separate something from another and make it one sided.

Surah ***Al-Qasas*** says that when ***Moosa*** reached ***Madyan***, he saw that people's animals (which came later) drank their fill and departed, but two girls stood there and waited with their animals (presumably for their turn). "تَذُوْدَان" (***tadhudaan***) as used in 28:23 means that those animals strained at their leash to get a drink but the girls restrained them. This has been termed as "اَلذَّوْدُ" (***adh-dhood***). ***Moosa*** was surprised as to why these girls had been restraining their animals from getting a drink. He asked the girls about this and they replied:

28:23	We cannot let our animals get a drink as long as these (powerful shepherds) do not return after that their animals have had their drink.	حَتّٰی یُصْدِرَ الرِّعَاءُ

They also told him the reason for this:

28:24	(We are girls and weaker than men) and our father is very old. Therefore, we cannot dare to let our animals drink before these others.	وَأَبُونَا شَيْخٌ كَبِيرٌ

Note how the Quran has told the entire human story in a few words. This has been happening all over the world that the animals of the strong or wealthy drink first (these people are prioritized) and if later anything remains, then the poor animals can have a lifesaving drink.

Only those who come with a celestial program are the exception to this rule. It is their duty to let the weaker animals drink in their turn, exactly as **Moosa** did.

28:23	(Without any remuneration) arranged for the girls' animals to have a drink.	فَسَقَىٰ لَهُمَ

This is what the Messengers came for, and their left system will do likewise (7:22). That is, the sources of sustenance that are currently dominated by a few will be made available to entire mankind. **Moosa** had not been declared a messenger yet, but he was naturally inclined towards such (good) deeds.

Dh-W-Q   ذ و ق

"ذَاقَ" (*dhaaq*): to find out the taste of something, to taste {T}.

Raghib says this word actually means to eat a little.

Ibn Faris says it means to eat something and find out about its internal condition.

Then it began to be used for every experiment {M}. That is, to have the experience of something.

7:22	when they had experienced the "شجره" (*shajarah*) (fraction)	فَلَمَّا ذَاقَا الشَّجَرَةَ

"أَذَاقَ" (*adhaaq*): to let someone have a taste of something (16:112).
"ذَائِقٌ" (*dhaaiq*): one who tastes, one who gains the experience (3:182). Feminine form is "ذَائِقَةٌ" (*dhaa-iqah*)

In the Quran, this word has generally been used with punishment, although at some places it has also appeared with "رَحْمَةٌ" (*rahmah*). This means that man should feel his deeds in such a way as to have tasted or experienced them, so that he knows firsthand what may be the result of that deed.

Dh-Y-Ain   ذ ى ع

"ذَاعَ" (*dha'a*), "يَذِيْعُ" (*yadhi'o*): to spread something, for something to become common.
"اَذَاعَ سِرَّهُ" (*dha'a sirrah*): he disclosed his secret and made it public knowledge.

Zajaj says it means to call out and tell the people, to announce *{T, M}*.

The Quran says:

4:83	When some information about peace or fear reaches them, they spread it around	وَاِذَا جَاءَهُمْ اَمْرٌ مِنَ الْاَمْنِ اَوِ الْخَوْفِ اَذَاعُوْا بِهِ

R-A-S   ر أ س

"اَلرَّأْسُ" (*ar-raas*), plural is "رُئُوْسٌ" (*ruoos*) basically means head, or the top part of anything.
"رَئِيْسٌ" (*raiys*) can therefore be used for head or leader of a nation.

Ibn Faris says it basically means to come together and to be elevated or high.

"رَأْسُ الْمَالِ" (*raasul maal*): capital.
"اَلرَّائِسُ" (*arra-is*): ruler.
"اَلْمَرْئُوْسُ" (*al-maroos*): the subjects (the ruled) *{T}*.

The Quran says in context of the performance of *Hajj*:

2:196	Do not shave off your heads.	وَلَا تَحْلِقُوْا رُئُوْسَكُمْ

(See under heading (H-L-Q).

For capital wealth it is said:

2:279	Capital.	رُئُوْسُ اَمْوَالِكُمْ

R-A-F   ر أ ف

"اَلرَّأْفَةُ" (*ar-rafah*), "رحمت" (*rahma*) and "رافت" (*raaft*) are words with similar meanings.

Muheet says "رَأْفَةٌ" (*rafah*) means to free you of matters that are harmful, and "رَحْمَةٌ" (*rehmah*) is to benefit you.

This has been supported by *Al-minar* which says that the result of "رَأْفَةٌ" (*rafa*) is to banish the ills, while "رَحْمَةٌ" (*rahmah*) is to grant benefits in abundance. {*Al-minar* vol-II page 122}. Therefore, "رَئُوْفٌ" (*raoof*) and "رَحِيْمٌ" (*rahim*) together cover both negative and positive aspects.

Hence, it means to remove or banish such things or matters which are harmful, and prevent the smooth development of one's being, and together with that, provide such things that are helpful for development.

As to how Allah's "رَأَفَت" (*rafat*) and "رَحْمَت" (*rehmat*) are, it is said in surah *Al-Baqrah*:

2:143	Allah never lets someone's eeman (faith) go unprotected and never leaves him with no result, He is raoofur raheem.	وَمَاكَانَ اللّهُ لِيُضِيعَ إِيْمَانَكُمْ- إِنَّ اللّهَ بِالنَّاسِ لَرَؤُوفٌ رَّحِيْمٌ

That means, He removes all the obstacles that hinder a man's faith bearing result and creates good results of the faith. Therefore, his *rafat* and *rehmat* are the result of faith. This is the right way for humanity to develop. Faith means to believe in the veracity of God's laws and to make it one's life's duty to obey Him.

Since generally the feeling to banish someone's ills is created by the softening of the heart. As such "رَأْفَةٌ" (*raafeh*) also means softness.

In surah *An-Noor*, it has been said regarding the punishment for fornication:

24:2	Do not be soft in implementing God's orders. (Do not be soft thinking that the punishment will hurt them and thus not punish them (the fornicators) at all)	وَلَا تَأْخُذْكُمْ بِهِمَا رَأْفَةٌ فِى دِيْنِ اللّهِ

Because, if the criminals are not punished, then how can the victims be redressed. Christianity was soft on the criminals out of pity which made them brazen and gradually the religion had to be confined to the churches and politics became unbridled. The Quran has said about monasticism that it was a fabricated sect (or concept) and the wrong interpretation of "رَؤُوفٌ رَّحِيْمٌ" (*raofur-reheem*). 57.27

Islam teaches justice for which the forces that commit excesses have to be broken. Therefore, it requires harshness along with kindness. See under heading (Gh-L-Zd).

R-A-Y   ر أ ى

"رُؤْيَةٌ" (*rooyah*): to comprehend some material thing.

This word is used for seeing with the eyes, or have insight, or to dream or think about it.

Johri says that when it appears with one subject, only then it means seeing with the eye, and when two subjects appear with it then it means to acquire knowledge or to know.

Raghib says that when it is followed by two subjects then it means knowledge and when it is followed by "اِلٰی" (*ila*), it means to look at a thing (or deliberate on something) so that it imparts a lesson *{T}*.

Muheet says that "رَاَیْ رُوْیَۃٌ" (*ra-ai rooyah*) means to see with the eyes. "رُوْیَا" (*rowayah*) means to dream and "رَاَیًا" (*raaya*) to deliberate or see from the heart. That is, deeply deliberate on something.

"اَلْمَرَیٰ، اَلْمَرَاَۃُ" (*al-marai*, *al-mar'ah*): scene.
"اَلْمَرَاَۃُ" (*al-mirah*): mirror.
"اَلرُّوْیَا" (*arrooyah*): dream.
"اَلرَّاَیُ" (*arrayu*): opinion, thought, to have an opinion about a matter which is not definite *{T}*.
"اَرَاَیْتَکَ" (*araaitak*) as used in 107:1 is the way the Arabs usually say: "will you inform him?", or "will you tell me?"

"اَلَمْ تَرَ اِلٰی" (*alam tara ila*) is said at a time of surprise. It means "do you not see?" That is, don't you wonder about it? *{T}*. But at the times when these words are spoken, it is also an invitation to look at the thing with a view to learning a lesson.

Surah *Aal-e-Imran* says:

3:12	They were seeing them twice of them with the sight of their eyes	یَرَوْنَهُمْ رَأْیَ الْعَیْنِ

Here it comes for reiteration and to clarify, as we say "seen with my own eyes" etc.

Surah *Maryam* says "رِئْیًا" (*ri'ya*) in 19:74 where it means a scene or apparent condition. "رِئَاَالنَّاسِ" (*ria-annaas*) as in 2:264, means "for people's sake", i.e. only to show people.

4:142	show the people	رِئَاَالنَّاسِ

"هُمْ یُرَاءُوْنَ" (*hoom yuraoon*): they show the people that they are true followers but they have lost the soul of *salaah*. That is, the fountainheads of sustenance which should be kept open are blocked (for personal gains) and denied to people (107:7)

Surah *Al-Momin* says:

40:29	I tell you only that which I comprehend	مَاأُرِیْکُمْ إِلَّا مَا أَرَیٰ

Surah *Ash-Shura* says:

26:61	When both the groups or parties saw each other	فَلَمَّا تَرَاَءَ الْجَمْعٰنِ

"بَادِیَ الرَّاْیَ" (*baadiar ra'ya*) as in 11:27, but for its meaning, see under heading (B-D-W).

R-B-B   ر ب ب

"رَبٌّ" (*rabb*) means to nurture or to develop. That is, to pass a thing through ever-new changes or stages so it gradually develops and reaches its ultimate destination *{R}*. It can be explained just as Mother Nature passes a particle through several stages and changes it into a pearl while gradually nurturing it on its way *{T}*.

This method of nurturing is called "ربوبيت" (*raboobiyat*).

"رَبَّ وَلَدَهُ رَبّاً وَرَبَّبَ" (*rabba waladahu wa rabb wa rabbanah*): he brought up the child, looked after him till he became an adult.

Hisaan bin Saabit's verse says the (one who is praised) is more beautiful than the pure and white pearl that has been nurtured in the depths of the sea.

Ibn Faris says it basically means
   -      to look after something and beautify it.

"اَلرَّبُّ" (*ar-rabbu*), "مَالِكٌ" (*maalik*), "خَالِقٌ" (*khaliq*), all mean one who looks after and improves a thing.

   -      to stay unmoved and stable.

"اَرَبَّتِ السَّحَابَةُ بِهٰذِهِ الْبَلْدَةِ" (*arabbatis sahabatu behaazehil baladah*): the cloud kept hovering over the city or kept raining.

   -      To join something with something. Therefore, to continuously nurture and fine tune a thing is called "ربوبيت" (*raboobiyat*).

Figuratively, patting a child to sleep is called "رَبَّتِ الْمْرَأَةُ صَبِيَّهَا" (*rabbatil mar'atu sabiyyaha*) *{T}*, because the time a child sleeps peacefully has a direct bearing on his growth.

For correcting something and establishing its solidarity, it is said "رَبَّ" (*rabba*), "يَرُبُّ" (*yarubbu*), "رَبَّاَ" (*rabba*) *{T}* and also to gather something and increase it continuously.

"رِبَابَةٌ" (*ribaaba*) is the pack in which a lot of arrows are kept.
"رَبَّ الدُّهْنَ" (*rabbud duhn*): he improved (refined) the oil and made it perfumed {M}.

Since the result of nurturing is positive flowering, "اَلرِّبَّةُ" (*arribbah*) also means the plants which do not wither even in winter but they are evergreen *{T}*.

"اَلْمَرَبُّ" (**al-marabbu**) is the land which is evergreen with trees and plants *{T}*.

"اَلرُّبَّة" (**ar-rubbah**) means a lot of bushy trees, a very big party (nearly of ten thousand or so) or the abundance of luxuries *{T}*.

Al Qateeba writes that a party is called "رِبِّيّ" (**rabbiyi**). Its plural is "رَبِّيُّوْنَ" (**ribiyyoon**) *{T}* (See 3:145).

"اَلرَّبَابَةُ" (**ar-rababah**): layer upon layer of the clouds *{T}*.

"اَلرِّبَبُ" (**ar-ribab**): sweet (potable) water which has gathered somewhere in abundance *{T}*.

"اَلرِّبِيْنَةُ" (**ar-rabibah**): pact or agreement. It also means the state, because in a state one nation mingles with the other {M}.

"اَلرَّبِيْبَةُ" (**ar-rabibah**) is the singular of "رَبَائِبُ" (**rabayib**). It means a girl who comes with a woman and who are the progeny of the woman's first husband. The she-goat which is nurtured at home rather than the grazing fields so that its milk can be had when required *{T}*.

The above makes the meaning of "رَبّ" (**rabb**) clear, as the one who nurtures. It means one who takes something to completion, one who arranges, and one who improves. Therefore, the nation's leader is called "رَبُّ الْقَوْم" (**rabb-ul-qaum**), and the man of the house is called "رَبُّ الْبَيْتِ" (**rabb-ul-bait**) *{T}*.

"رَبَّ الْقَوْمَ" (**rabb-al-qaum**) means that he took the affairs of the state in hand and led the nation *{T}*.

"رَبّ" (**rabb**) can also mean elder brother {*Muntahil Arab*}. When the **Bani Israel** said to **Moosa**:

5:24	you and your elder brother (Haroon) should go and fight the enemy.	فَاذْهَبْ أَنْتَ وَرَبُّكَ فَقَاتِلَا

It is possible that they were being sarcastic when they said that.

"اَلرَّبَّانِيّ" (**ar-rabbani**): that which is attributed to Rabb, or the teacher who first nurtures the mind of his pupils by first giving them small doses of knowledge before giving really big ones. Every scholar is called "رَبَّانِيّ" (**rabbani**), as well as those with the right knowledge *{T}*. "رِبِّيّ" (**rabbi**) is also used in these meanings.

The Quran begins with:

1:1	every beautiful aspect of the universe is an epitome of praise for the Sustenance by the Rab	اَلْحَمْدُ لِلّٰهِ رَبِّ الْعَالَمِيْنَ

Everything in the universe is testimony to the fact that a wonderful program or scheme is at work. In this program a seed, while traversing different stages of nurturing, reaches fruition.

This is what the system of God's sustenance is. Allah is praiseworthy because He nurtures everything.

Just as this system of God's sustenance is at work automatically in the internal and external universe, so should human beings implement and establish His *Nizaam-e-raboobiyat*, that is, the system of sustenance in their social lives. The way to do it is to make the fountainheads of sustenance as well as the capabilities of the humans available to all. Thus, all of humanity's latent capabilities will flourish and reach their completion or peak. Those who establish such a system will be called *rabbaniyyoon* (3:78) and this system can be established by following the Quranic system. This is the crux of all Quranic teachings. That is, the establishment of God's sustenance. Since this involves man's physical being as well as his personality, it is the duty of an Islamic state to establish a system which caters not only to every individual's needs but is also conducive equally for the development of his capabilities. When a man's personality is nurtured in this way, then death too makes no difference, because life goes ahead to traverse other stages, i.e. the life hereafter. God's sustenance continues there as well.

Universal sustenance is the purpose and aim of an Islamic society. That is, the sustenance of mankind regardless of caste, race, color, creed, or religion. Until such system of sustenance is reflected in a human society, it cannot be called an Islamic society. This is the beginning of Quranic teaching.

He, in whom this trait of *raboobiyat* is reflected, uses all his strength to earn. Whatever part of his earning which is beyond his needs, he gives to the central authority of this system for the sustenance of others (a welfare state). That is why in such a society, no concept of building estates or accumulating wealth takes root. In such a system no one tries to hold dominance over the fountainheads of sustenance, neither does anyone usurp the fruits of others' labor. This is the sort of society that the Quran wants to build, and only such a system can show the world how praiseworthy Allah's system can be. This is the manifestation of "أَلْحَمْدُ لِلّهِ رَبِّ الْعَالَمِيْنَ" (*al-hamdo-lilla-hi rabbil aalameen*) or all praise is for Allah.

Rubba   رُبَّ

"رُبَّ" (*rubba*), "رُبَ" (*ruba*), "رُبَّمَا" (*rubbama*), "رُبَمَا" (*rubama*). It is used to express as we say 'most of the time'. 'it happens often,, 'generally, this is the condition,' etc. This is also used for reiteration and for expressing intensity, like we say "no matter how much he wanted", or "no matter how many times they tried" etc.

15:2	The deniers will wish very much to have been Muslims too	رُبَمَا يَوَدُّ الَّذِيْنَ كَفَرُوْا لَوْكَانُوْا مُسْلِمِيْنَ

Alternatively, these people will always wish that they had been Muslims. This word is also used to mean "sometimes". The context in the Quran can determine what the word means.

R-B-H   ر ب ح

"رِبْحٌ" (**rabih**): the profit that accrues in a trade {R}

Ibn Faris too says it means success or increase in trade or business.

"رِبْحٌ" (**ribhun**) and "رَبَاحٌ" (**rabah**): increase and progress in trade {T}.
"أَرْبَحَ النَّاقَةَ" (**arbahan naaqah**): it is said when a man milks the she-camel in the morning, or at noon.
"تَرَبَّحَ الرَّجُلُ" (**tarabbahal rajul**): the man was surprised, awestruck {T, M}.

The Quran says:

2:16	Their trade gave them no profit	تَرَبَّحَ الرَّجُلُ

R-B-Sd   ر ب ص

"تَرَبَّصَ" (**tarabbas**): to wait for some good or bad thing {T}, or to wait for something to be cheaper or dearer or for something to happen or disappear {R}.

In surah **Al-Baqrah** this word has been used to wait:

2:226	Those who swear not to sleep with their women should abstain or wait for four months.	لِلَّذِينَ يُؤْلَوْنَ مِنْ نِّسَاء هِمْ تَرَبُّصُ أَرْبَعَةِ أَشْهُرٍ

Within four months, they will have to decide whether they want to keep the women in their wedlock or divorce them. They cannot leave them in the lurch indefinitely.

"مُتَرَبِّصٌ" (**mutzarabbisun**): someone who waits.

R-B-Te   ر ب ط

"رَبَطَهُ" (*rabatahu*): tied him up.

"اَلرِّبَاطُ" (*ar-ribaat*): that which is used for tying.

"اَلرَّبِطَةُ" (*ar-rabitah*): relation, ties.

Ibn Faris says this root means tying or securing something tightly as well as solidarity.

"اَلرِّبَاطُ" (*ar-ribaat*): to do something continuously, to watch out for the enemy permanently.

"رِبَاطُ الْخَيْلِ" (*ribaatul khail*): to make army posts at the border to guard the frontiers *{T}* (8:60).

Surah *Aal-e-Imraan* says:

3:200	Be steadfast and patient and constant	اِصْبِرُوْا و صَابِرُوْ وَرَبِطُواً

Here "رَابَطُوْا" (*raabitu*) means to make foolproof arrangements for one's security, or to remain united, or to continuously strive for a purpose.

"رَبَطَ اللهُ عَلَى قَلْبِهِ" (*rabatullahu ala qalbehi*): Allah gave him patience and strengthened his heart *{T}*.

Surah *Al-Anfaal* says:

8:11	So that he strengthens your hearts and makes you steadfast	وَلِيَرْبِطَ عَلَى قُلُوْبِكُمْ وَيُثَبِّتَ بِهِ الْاَقْدَامَ

"اِرْتِبَاطٌ" (*irtibaat*): to be tied with one another, to be in a relationship *{T}*.

R-B-Ain   ر ب ع

"اَرْبَعَةٌ" (*arba'ah*): the figure four (4). It is the masculine form (2:260).

"اَرْبَعَةٌ" (*arbaton*) is the feminine form (24:6).

"اَرْبَعُوْنَ" (*arba'on*), "اَرْبَعِيْنَ" (*arba'een*): forty (2:51).

"اَلرُّبْعُ" (*ar-rub'o*): one fourth (4:12).

"رُبَاعَ" (*ruba'a*): four each (3:2).

"رَابِعٌ" (*raabi-un*): fourth (18.22).

Ibn Faris says that besides meaning the figure four, the word means to be stolid, or to last and to elevate.

R-B-W ر ب و

"رَبَا" (*raba*), "يَرْبُو" (*yarbu*): to exceed, to be more, to be in excess, to increase, to swell {T, M}.

| 30:39 | So that the people's wealth grows | لِيَرْبُوَا فِى أَمْوَالِ النَّاسِ |

It also means for a vegetable to grow and swell {T, M}.

| 22:5 | He mixed water in with seeds and the seeds swelled | رَبَالسَّوِيْقَ |

"رَاب" (*raab*) with its feminine form "رَابِيَةٌ" (*raabiah*): that which climbs to the top.
"زَبَدَا رَّابِياً" (*zabadar raabia*): the scum that comes up on top (13:17).
"أَخْذَةً رَابِيَةً" (*akhzatan raabia*): strong grip, a grip which has grown very strong {T, M}. It means a grip which overshadows a man and overpowers him (69:10).
"أَرْبٰ" (*arba*): too much, very wealthy {T, M} 16:92.
"رَبْوَةٌ" (*rabwah*): high part of land, i.e. a plateau {T, M}.
"رَبَّيْتُهُ" (*rabbaituhu*): I fed him. (See heading (R-B-B)), as in 17:24.
"أَلرِّبَا" (*ar-riba*): interest which is received on a loan. To take more than the capital {M} (details further ahead).

Surah *Aal-e-Imran* says:

| 3:129 | Do not take interest. | لَا تَأْكُلُوا الرِّبٰو أَضْعَافاً مُضْعَفَةً |

You may think that it increases your wealth but in fact it decreases your national wealth. See under heading (Zd-Ain-F). The economic system proposed by the Quran has no place for interest. When in this system, the accumulation of wealth is forbidden, then the question of even loans hardly arises, leave alone interest,. In this system, nobody has any surplus money. It is distributed among the society. Whatever laws about loans are contained in the Quran belong to the era when a Quranic economic system had not taken shape.

Let alone interest, in this system no one can even make a gift hoping that he would get a bigger present in return.

| 30:39 | Whatever you give people more than what is due, hoping that it would be increased (in return) then in the system of God, it cannot be increased. | وَمَاآتَيْتُمْ مِنْ رِّباً لِيَرْبُوَا فِى أَمْوَالِ النَّاسِ |

Taj has said it means gift but we believe that this is said for everything that is more than due.

This has been explained at another place as follows:

| 74:6 | Do not do someone a favor in the hope of getting a better return | لَا تَمْنُنْ تَسْتَكْثِرْ |

This system is based on "اِيْتَا زَكوٰة" (**iyta zakat**). That is, to provide the means for others' development or nurture. That is why in 30:39 "زَكوٰةٌ" (**zakat**) has been used opposite to "رِباً" (**riba**) as interest.

The Quran has declared interest as forbidden by saying:

2:275	Allah has made trade as permissible and interest as forbidden.	وَاَحَلَّ اللّٰهُ الْبَيْعَ وَحَرَّمَ الرِّبٰو

The question is what **riba** or interest is? **Riba** according to the Quran is the opposite of business and trade. As to what business is, has been explained under heading (B-Y-Ain). Let us go over it briefly once more.

Whatever we get or take from others can be many different things as gift, remuneration, interest, profit in a business or a win on gambling. Let us see how they are different.

-   Gift: One has to do no labor or employ any capital for it. The giver gives it without any thought of getting anything in return. Thus, it cannot be brought under the category of give and take. Therefore, it is out of our present purview.
-   Remuneration: This is the payment for labor. No capital is needed to employ in it.
-   Interest: In this, capital is provided to somebody and something more than the capital given is received. There is no employment of labor in it.
-   Profit (in business and trade): In this, capital as well as labor is employed.
-   Gambling: Neither capital nor labor is employed in it.

The principle as related by the Quran is:

53:39	For a man there is nothing but the fruit of his labor	لَيْسَ لِلْاِنْسَانِ اِلَّا مَا سَعٰى

That is, only the compensation for labor is permissible while the compensation for the use of capital is not permissible. Since at that time this principle was not before the people at that time, they were unable to understand what the difference between profit and interest was.

A man purchases something for a hundred bucks, sells it for ten bucks more, and earns a profit of ten bucks. Another man lends a hundred bucks to someone and receives back a hundred and ten. He too receives ten bucks more. They argued that ten bucks were received by both over the principal amount. So where is the difference?

2:275	They used to consider both bai and riba as the same	ذَالِكَ بِاَنَّهُمْ قَالُوْ اِنَّمَا الْبَيْعُ مِثْلُ الرِّبٰو

But the Quran said that they are not the same. In **bai,** i.e. trade and business, both capital and labor are employed, the capital is returned and the profit in the form of compensation for the trader comes back. This is permissible. But in **riba** (interest) only capital is employed. There is no labor required from the investor. Therefore, whatever more is received back is the compensation for the capital which is forbidden. Therefore, according to the Quran, remuneration for labor is permisable but it is **haraam** to take back more than the capital.

If in trade too, one takes more than the compensation for his labor then that is interest (**riba**) which is forbidden. As to what is the correct remuneration for his labor, will be decided by the society. He can- not take above that. Therefore, any trade or business in which somebody only by employing capital gets back more than the capital is **riba** and according to the Quran it is forbidden, whether it is trade on land or being a sleeping partner in some business. This is called un-earned income. That is, the income which is received without any labor.

When neither capital nor labor is employed, then that is gambling. See heading (Y-S-R). Generally, it is though that business involves risk. That is, both profit and loss can be expected. And **riba** has no risk involved. This criterion is not right. If the criteria for an income be risk to make it permissible, then gambling should also be permitted because every hand involves a risk. The difference between **bai** and **riba** is that which has been explained above.

In trade or business, capital plus remuneration for labor is received back. And in **riba** capital plus the remuneration on the utilization of capital is received. The remuneration for capital is forbidden, whether it is called interest or profit. According to the Quranic economy, remuneration for capital can in no case be allowed. If an Islamic system is yet to be established in a society, when the responsibility for the needs of life is not on society, then the return of capital plus a day's labor of a shopkeeper can be compensated. Moreover, when the Islamic society fulfills the needs of a shopkeeper, then things will be supplied free of cost. God knows how much time man needs to establish an Islamic system. Nevertheless, whatever time it takes, man can get out of his self-made hell (**jahannum**) when he does establish such a system. The present system in which the remuneration for the utilization of capital is thought permitted and not impure, is a war against Allah's system (2:279).

R-T-Ain   ر ت ع

"رَتَعَ" (**rata**), "يَرْتَعُ" (**yarta-o**), "رَتْأَ" (**rataa**): to eat and drink in a green spot and to move around at will.

"رَتُّعٌ" (**rat-un**) is actually used for grazing of animals but later it began metaphorically to be used for humans too {T, M, R}.

"جَمَلٌ رَاتِعٌ" (**jamalun rati-un**), with plural "اِبِلٌ رِتَاعٌ" (**iblun rita un**): a camel which eats and drinks freely.

"أَلْمَرْتَعُ" (**al-marta-u**): grazing land.

"أَرْتَعَتِ الْأَرْضُ" (**arta atil ard**): the grass and fodder grew in the land in abundance {T, M, R}.

Surah **Yusuf** relates that **Yusuf's** (Joseph) brothers asked their father to allow them to take **Yusuf** out with them to the jungle:

12:12	So that he eats and drinks happily and plays around.	يَرْتَعْ وَيَلْعَبْ

"يَرْتَعْ وَ يَلْعَبْ" (**yartah wa yal'ab**): practically means what we call 'picnic' today.

R-T-Q   ر ت ق

"رَتْقٌ" (**ratq**): to fill a hole. It also means a joined thing.
"اِرْتَتَقَ الشَّيىْ" (**irtataqash shaiyi**): the thing was found and joined. There was no gap or hole left in it {T}.

Raghib says "اَلرَّتْقُ" (**ar-ratq**) means to join whether in creation or artificially.

The Quran has said about the earth and the skies:

21:30	in the beginning this universe was all joined together	كَانَتَا رَتْقاً فَفَتَقْنٰيهُمَا

Then different planets separated from this mass (79:30). The time is the 6th century AD, when nobody could even conceive this. Science has today confirmed this theory. However, at that time this truth could not be related by anyone except God!

R-T-L   ر ت ل

"اَلرَّتَلُ" (**ar-ratal**): teeth that are sparkling white, even and very beautiful. It basically means for something to be very properly balanced or arranged.
"اَلرُّتَيْلاءُ" (**ar-rutaila**): a kind of spider which spins a very proportionate and beautiful web {T, M}.

It is said about the Quran:

25:32	We have revealed the best of arrangements, proportion and arrangements.	وَ رَتَّلْنٰهُ تَرْتِيلاً

The Messenger (**pbuh**) has been addressed as:

73:4	You too implement it with that sort of administration and proportion.	وَ رَتِّلِ الْقُرْاٰنَ تَرْتِيلاً

R-J-J ر ج ج

"اَلرَّجُّ" (**ar-raju**): to shake, to shake violently, to cause a sort of quake, to shake something out of its place, to displace it.

"اِرْتَجَّ الْبَحْرُ" (**irtajjal bahr**): the sea became rough.

"اَلرَّجَاجَةُ" (**ar-rajajah**): the lion's den {T, M, R}.

The Quran says:

| 56:4 | when the earth will be shaky due to a violent movement | إِذَا رُجَّتِ الْأَرْضُ رَجَّاً |
| 99:1 | When the earth will be shaken | إِذَا زُلْزِلَتِ الْأَرْضُ زِلْزَالَهَا |

That is, it will be shaken with full force. Such utterances by the Quran could mean physical revolutions as well as social revolutions.

R-J-Z ر ج ز

"رِجْزٌ" (**rijz**) and "رُجْزٌ" (**rujz**) both mean continuous unease and permanent movement.

"اَلرَّجَزُ" (**ar-rajaz**): it's a kind of camel sickness in which its hind legs or back become so weak that when he tries to get up his legs begin to wobble and he can't stand up in first two or three attempts {T}.

"رِجْزٌ" (**rijz**) is the permanent unease that a nation suffers and it becomes so weak gradually that it is difficult to stand up again.

| 34:5 | The punishment which gives continuous unease | عَذَابٌ مِنْ رِجْزٍ اَلِيْمٌ |
| 29:34 | The destruction that comes from external events | رِجْزاً مِنَ السَّمَاءِ |

In surah **Al-Airaaf** such various types of destructions has been termed as "رِجْزٌ" (**rijz**), and that were faced by the nation of the Pharaoh (7:134).

Surah **Al-Anfaal** says that We (in the battlefield of Badr) removed the "رِجْزٌ" (**rijz**) from you that were created by the **shaitaan** (the resistance) and made you stable (8:11). This makes the meaning of "رِجْزٌ" (**rijz**) clear, which is to become unstable, or for such weakness to develop which creates weakness in the hearts and wavering the legs.

In surah **Al-Mudassar** when the Messenger (**pbuh**) was told that "you can now take up this revolutionary cause (invitation) to the people".

Along with it was said:

| 74:5 | shake off the weakness that produces wavering in the legs | وَ الرُّجْزَ فَاهْجُرْ |

Muster up the courage along with your friends to take up such heavy responsibility (of spreading Allah's message). This surah apparently addresses the Messenger (*pbuh*) but actually, the whole nation is being addressed. Such a revolutionary message (as of God's supremacy) can only be spread by a group or party that never wavers from its path.

R-J-S   ر ج س

"اَلرَّجْسُ" (*ar-rijs*): a harsh sound, a big and mixed sound, like an army on the move, or the onrushing of flood or thunder.

"رَجَسَتِ السَّمَاءُ" (*rajatis sama*): the thunder clapped loudly.

"اِرْتَجَسِ الْبِنَاءُ" (*artajasil bina'u*): the building moved audibly.

"اَلرَّجَّاسُ" (*ar-rajaas*): the sea, because it not only has the unease but also noise.

"رِجْس" (*rijs*) means the same as "اِلتباس" (*iltibaas*) i.e. doubt, sixes and seven, unease, not to be one-sided.

"هُمْ فِىْ مَرْجُوسَةٍ مِنْ أَمْرِهِمْ" (*hoom fi marjusatin min amrihim*): those people are in doubt over their matter {T}.

Ibn Faris says it basically means doubt and unease. Dirt is also called "رِجْسٌ" (*rijs*).

The Quran says:

| 10:100 | those who do not employ their intellect and thought, Allah puts filth over them | وَيَجْعَلُ الرِّجْسَ عَلَى الَّذِيْنَ لَا يَعْقِلُوْنَ |

Here "رِجْسٌ" (*rijs*) is the result of not using one's intellect. Therefore the meaning seems obvious i.e. doubt, unease. It also means such matters that are despicable to describe {T}, or unpleasant affairs.

The Quran says that:

| 5:90 | verily intoxication, gambling, sacrifice at alters and diving arrows are abomination from work of the shaitaan | إِنَّمَا الْخَمْرُ وَالْمَيْسِرُ وَالْأَنْصَابُ وَالْأَزْلَامُ رِجْسٌ مِّنْ عَمَلِ الشَّيْطَانِ |

It shows dislike, execration, unease too. Similarly forbidden edibles are called "فَإِنَّهُ رِجْسٌ" (*fa innahu rijsun*) in 6:146.

"رَجَسَهُ عَنِ الْأَمْرِ" (*rajasahu anil amr*): he stopped him from work {T}. Thus "رِجْسٌ" (*rijs*) are those deeds which create hurdles in the way of human development and which are a hindrance.

Taj-ul-urus says it means those deeds which take man towards destruction.

"مِرْجَاسٌ" (*mirjaas*) means a stone that is made to hang in a well to judge the depth {*T*}.

Surah *Al-Ahzaab* says about the family of the Messenger (*pbuh*):

33:33	Allah wants to remove rijs from you (Those hindrances that are an obstruction in your development)	يُرِيدُ اللَّهُ لِيُذْهِبَ عَنْكُمُ الرِّجْسَ اَهْلَ الْبَيْتِ

About those with faith, it is said that their chests open for Islam. Conversely, those who are on the wrong path, their chests are constricted. They pant for breath. After that, it is said:

2:129	Thus places Allah obstructions on those who do not believe	كَذَالِكَ يَجْعَلُ اللَّهُ الرِّجْسَ عَلَى الَّذِينَ لَا يُؤْمِنُوْنَ

This shows that "رِجْسٌ" (*rijs*) means narrowness of the heart, bias, narrow mindedness, dogmatism, not employing one's intellect and power of reasoning, doubts, unease. All these meanings are included in the connotation. This is why the hypocrites have been called "رِجْسٌ" (*rijsun*) in 9:95. That is, doubts, and being unsure, and obstruction in the right path, as against those with faith (9:124-125).

R-J-Ain ر ج ع

"رُجُوْعٌ" (*ruju*): to turn back and return, to come back {*T*}.
"رَجْعٌ" (*raj'a*): to turn back.

The meanings in which we [the Urdu-speakers of the sub-continent] use "رجعت" (*ruj'at*), is not the right one. We use this word to mean to fall back [retreat]. For somebody to move back from his position or for someone who is re-actionary. This has deterioration, lowliness and falling back in the connotation. However, in the Arabic language, it means to return to the former state, or in a better condition than before.

"اَلرَّجْعَةُ" (*ar-raja*) means to re-marry a woman after divorcing her. That is return to the prior state.
"لَيْسَ لِىْ مِنْ فُلَانٍ رَجْعٌ" (*laisa li fulanin raj'a*): I have had no benefit from that man. That is, nothing ever was returned by him.

The Arabs have a saying: "مَا هُوَ اِلَّا سَجْعٌ لَيْسَ تَحْتَهُ رَجْعٌ" (*ma huwa illa sajun laisa tahtahu raj'a*). This is only "رَجْعٌ" (*raj'a*) and there is no benefit in it.
"اَرْجَعَتِ الْإِبِلُ" (*arja'atil ibl*) means for a camel to fatten again after becoming weak.
"سَفْرَةٌ مُرْجِعَةٌ" (*safratun marji'ah*): is a journey in which there is some benefit.
"مَتَاعٌ مُرْجِعٌ" (*mata'un murje'un*): very beneficial thing.
"رَجِيْعٌ" (*raji*): a rope which has become unraveled but twined again {*T*}.

"رَجْعٌ" (*raj'a*) means to return, a thing which revolves comes back to the place it travelled from. In this manner, every revolving thing has "رَجْعٌ" (*raj'a*).

Surah *At-Tariq* says:

86:11	the heavenly bodies which are high in the atmosphere are revolving (and return to the place they have traveled from)	وَالسَّمَاءِ ذَاتِ الرَّجْعِ

Alternatively, it means the high atmosphere which turn backs (to their starting point) the heavenly bodies or things. And in their revolution, new aspects come forth. In meaning of turning back, this word has appeared in 67:36, where it has come opposite to "مُضِيّاً" (*muziyyah*), which means to go forward.

"رَجَعَ اِلَيْهِ" (*rajal ilaih*) means to turn for help towards, to have recourse to {Lane}.
"رَجْعٌ" (*raj'un*) also means reaction and for the results to be formulated.
As such, it is said "رَجَعَ الْعَلَفُ فِى الدَّابَّةِ" (*raja'al alfu fid dabbah*): the effect of the fodder was evident on the animal {T}. "رَجَعَ كَلَامِىْ فِيْهِ" (*raja'a kalami fieeh*): my talk affected him {T}. "اَلرَّجِيْعُ مِنَ الْكَلَامِ" (*ar-rajee-o minal kalami*): the talk which is returned to the speaker {T}.
"" (*rajj'a*) also means hail, because it gives back to the earth what it took from it (water). It also means rain {T}, as well as water which is on a surface {Kitaab-ul-Ashfaq}

The Quran says:

86:11	the height that returns vapors to the earth (in the form of rain)	وَالسَّمَاءِ ذَاتِ الرَّجْعِ

The Quran says "صُمٌّ بُكْمٌ عُمْىٌ فَهُمْ لَا يَرْجِعُوْنَ" (*summun bukmun umyun fahum la-yarjioon*) in 2:18. To understand the meaning of "يَرْجِعُوْنَ" (*yarjioon*) at such places, one thing must be understood as a prelude.

When Messenger *Mohammd (pbuh)* presented his message, there were two sorts of people in front of him. One party was of those with divine Books who at one time were on the right path but had later digressed. They were told to return to the right path. They denied doing so. Secondly, there were those for whom truth had been presented for the very first time. When they refused to come towards the truth, it was said that they do not turn towards the truth, but rather that they do not come to it at all. They do not pay attention towards it.

For this too, the Quran has used the word "لَايَرْجِعُوْنَ" (*la yarjeoon*). At the places where this word has appeared, the right translation would be 'to refer'.

Surah Taha says about *Moosa*:

20:40	We returned you towards your mother	فَرَجَعْنَاكَ إِلَى أُمِّكَ

Surah **An-Noor** says:

24:28	If the inmate of the house (or the man of the house) tells you to go back, then turn back.	وَإِنْ قِيْلَ لَكُمْ ارْجِعُوْا فَارْجِعُوْا

The returning of **Yusuf's** brothers to their father has been explained by words like " فَلَمَّارَجَعُوْا اِلَى أَبِيْهِمْ " (**falama raja-oo ila**) in 12:63.

Surah **An-Namal** says that when **Suleman** (Solomon) sent his envoy towards **Saba** (Sheba), he was told to return after giving her a letter, and not to wait for her reaction. "فَانْظُرْ مَاذَا يَرْجِعُوْنَ" (**fanzur maaza yarji-oon**) 27:28.

In surah **Qaf** the life after death has been called "رَجْعٌ" (**rajun**) in 50:3. That is, to return to life after death. Not return to this world but return to life after death in the hereafter.

Here it is necessary to dispel the wrong meaning that might have cropped up in people's minds due to the non-Quranic meaning of "رَجْعَت اِلَى اللهِ" (**raj'at ilal laah**). When we hear of someone's death, we say "اِنَّا للهِ وَ اِنَّا اِلَيْهِ رَاجِعُوْنَ" (**inna lillahi wa-inna ilaihi raajioon**), as it appears in 2:156. By this, we mean "**we belong to Allah and will return to Him**". This leads the mind to make two conclusions. One is that we were with God before being born (into this world) and after death will be gathered in a ground on the Day of the Judgment where God too will be present and thus we will return to Him. This concept is non-Quranic because it confines God to a certain place. This concept is false because God is not confined to a particular place.

He is everywhere - "هُوَ مَعَكُمْ اَيْنَمَا كُنْتُمْ" (**hua ma'akum ainama kuntum**) as stated in 57:5. What will be the condition of the life hereafter, how will good deeds be rewarded and bad deeds punished, these are things which cannot be understood in this world.

Whatever the Quran has said in this context shall not be discussed here, but one thing is clear that for the dead to go towards a place where God will be present is not a Quranic concept.

The Quran says:

89:22	Your Sustainer and the malaikah will come row upon row	وَجَاءَ رَبُّكَ وَالْمَلَكُ صَفًّا صَفًّا
89:33	That day jahannum will be brought.	وَجَائَئَ يَوْمَئِذٍ بِجَهَنَّمَ

The second situation that arises has been born due to Sufism. Vedant (Hindu Sufism) believes that the human soul is a part of the greater soul (God). This part, after being separating from the whole, has been bogged down and is impatient to join with the whole again. At last, the part will rejoin with the whole as birds return to their nests in the evening. This concept is shared by us in Muslim mysticism.

Virtuous people's souls will rejoin with their whole (God) and this is the success of life. Such people call death '*wisaal* (reuniting) because they think that a part will shall one day rejoin the whole.

This too is a non-Quranic concept because man and God are not part and whole. If a part departs, from a whole then the whole is incomplete and this signifies some fault in God. Therefore this concept cannot be accepted.

The concept of the human soul is wrong as well. For details, see under heading (R-W-H).

The meaning of direction or way is created by "رَاجِعُوْنَ" (*raajioon*) beside "اِلَيْهِ" (*ilaih*), or towards Him. Because we consider "اِلَيْهِ" (*ilaih*) or "اِلَيْنَا" (*ilaina*) to mean direction. Although everywhere in the Quran, it does not mean this.

For example, the Quran says:

| 25:45 | Have you not noted how your Sustainer elongates the shadows | اَلَمْ تَرَ اِلٰى رَبِّكَ كَيْفَ مَدَّ الظِّلَّ |
| 25:45 | If He wanted the shadows would neither be elongated or shorten. But he did not do so. He created the sun so that it was the cause of their lengthenin or shortening. | وَلَوْشَاءَ لَجَعَلَهُ سَاكَنًاثُمَّ جَعَلْنَا الشَّمْسَ عَلَيْهِ دَلِيْلاً |

After this it is said:

| 25:45 | then we pull (ilaina) it (the shadow) towards ourselves, | ثُمَّ قَبَضْنَاهُ إِلَيْنَا قَبْضاً يَسِيْراً |

Here the word "اِلَيْنَا" (*ilaina*) clearly shows that it does not mean any particular direction but it means that according to the laws of Allah, the shadows become shorter. Therefore, "اِلَيْهِ رَاجِعُوْنَ" (*ilaihi raajeeon*) may mean to move according to the law of Allah.

Surah *Aal-e-Imran* says:

| 3:82 | Whatever is in the heights or depths of the universe, bows to him, whether it likes it or not | وَلَهُ اَسْلَمَ مَنْ فِى السَّمٰوٰتِ وَالْاَرْضِ طَوْعًا وَّكَرْهاً وَاِلَيْهِ يُرْجَعُوْنَ |

And thus everything is revolving around that centre (of Allah's laws).

Surah *Yasin* says:

| 36.83 | God's personality is far beyond man's concepts of Him. Everything is run by Him | فَسُبْحٰنَ الَّذِيْ بِيَدِهِ مَلَكُوْتُ كُلِّ شَيْءٍ وَّاِلَيْهِ تُرْجَعُوْنَ |

Therefore, everything moves according to the laws created by Him. Everything operates according to His law, it cannot move away from it, and since man is included in 'everything', he too is not an exception to this rule. Every deed of his is tied to the natural chain of events. Thus, every step he takes is going towards Him.

We now go to the natural results of the human world (not the physical universe). In this connection the Quran has several dictums in which "وَاِلَیْہِ تُرْجَعُوْنَ" (*wa ilaihi turje-oon*) or similar phrases have been used.

As it is said:

When a man thinks he needs nobody (is independent of everybody) then he becomes rebellious.	كَلَّا اِنَّ الْاِنْسَانَ لَيَطْغٰى۔ اَنْ رَّاٰهُ اسْتَغْنٰى

Although the truth is that no matter how independent he thinks himself to be "اِنَّ اِلٰی رَبِّکَ الرَّجَعُ" (*inna ila rabbikar ruj'aa*) (35:4), he cannot go out of the circle of natural results. He has to come back to this law. This truth has been acknowledged as "وَتَقَطَّعُوْا اَمْرَہُمْ بَیْنَہُمْ" (*wataqatta'oo amrahum bainahum*) in 21:93, that is, here every human being is a member of the universal brotherhood. However, for the sake of their own interests they have divided it into many parts. "وَتَقَطَّعُوْا اَمْرَہُمْ بَیْنَہُمْ" (*wa taqatahu amrahum bainahum*) as in 21:93.

After that it is said "کُلٌّ اِلَیْنَا رَاجِعُوْنَ" (*kullun ilaina raaji-oon*), and after that:

21:94	Thus he who stays steadfast on the enabling program and he is also a momin (believer) then his efforts do not stay without result. We keep noting all of them (his efforts)	فَمَنْ يَّعْمَلْ مِنَ الصّٰلِحٰتِ وَہُوَ مُؤْمِنٌ فَلَاكُفْرَانَ لِسَعْيِہٖ وَ اِنَّا لَہٗ کَاتِبُوْنَ

This explains the meaning of "کُلٌّ اِلَیْنَا رَاجِعُوْنَ" (*kullun ilaina raajioon*). That is, all efforts of all men produce results according to the laws of Nature that nobody can escape. As the Quran appears to say, "By violating Our orders they think that they are going beyond our grasp, but they are in fact automatically being drawn to Us as per the laws of Nature." See also 2:281, 2:282 and 6:165, where the meaning of Law of Nature is made explicit.

About the results of deeds, it is generally believed that results will come before us in the life hereafter. This is a wrong notion. The results of deeds start to be compiled along with the commitment of the deeds, and then some results appear in this very life and some in the hereafter.

The Quran says:

29:9	You have to return to Me, then I will let you know about your deeds	اِلَيَّ مَرْجِعُكُمْ فَاُنَبِّئُكُم بِمَا كُنتُمْ تَعْمَلُونَ

It does not mean that when a man stands in front of God after dying, the results of his deeds will appear. It means that all your deeds circle around His laws of Nature, all results are formulated according to them. You cannot remain outside the purview of his laws. And, your results come before you according to it.

The Messenger (*pbuh*) himself was told:

| 40:78 | Some of the punishment which we are promising to the opponents may appear before your eyes too. And it may also possibly be after your death. But sooner or later, their deeds will result according to our law. They cannot go out of its purview. | فَإِمَّا نُرِيَنَّكَ بَعْضَ الَّذِى نَعِدُ هُمْ أَوْ نَتَوَ فَّيَنَّكَ فَاِلَيْنَا يُرْجَعُوْنَ |

But those results which do not appear in this world do appear in the hereafter. This is the place where it has been said that even after death you will "اِلَيْهِ تُرْجَعُوْنَ" (*ilaihi turjaoon*): will return towards Allah. i.e. do not think that now that you are dead, nobody has a grip on you or you are not accountable to anyone. You will be ruled by the law of Allah even after your death and you cannot escape it. This is the meaning of "اِلَيْهِ تُرْجَعُوْنَ" (*ilaihi turjeoon*) according to the Quran.

At certain places the word "رُجُوْعْ" (*ruju*) has appeared to mean what we mean turning towards someone. For example:

| 36:31 | These people do not ruju (refer or turn) to their messengers | أَنَّهُمْ اِلَيْهِمْ لَايَرْجِعُوْنَ |

In the light of these clarifications, the right meaning of "اِنَّا اِلَيْهِ رَاجِعُوْنَ" (*inna ilahi raajeoon*) will now be explained. In the Quran where it is said "اِنَّا اِلَيْهِ رَاجِعُوْنَ" (*inna ilahi raajeoon*), the verse before it mentions that in the establishment of Allah's system, there are a lot of difficulties. The difficulties are so extreme that one has to even lay down one's life in its path. After this the group of *momineen* has been told that you too will face various things. From the opponents or because of the opponents, you will face the fear of oppression, hunger, loss of life and property.

After that it is said:

| 2:156 | Give the news of good results to those, who face such events by saying that one should be ruffled by them. | الَّذِيْنَ اِذَا أَصَابَتْهُمْ مُصِيْبَةٌ قَالُوْا اِنَّا لِلّٰهِ وَاِنَّا اِلَيْهِ رَاجِعُوْنَ |

Our entire life is dedicated to establishing Allah's system and we turn to Allah's laws to be able to meet these challenges. In order to encounter these difficulties successfully, we turn to His laws, or since our entire lives are dedicated to establishing His system, these difficulties cannot make us waver from this path. Besides this, our every step moves towards Him.

Every move of ours revolves around this axis of "اِنَّا اِلَيهِ رَاجِعُوْن" (*inna ilaihi raa'jeoon*) and the results of our struggle will also be formulated as per His laws on which we have unwavering belief. Let as many difficulties come as they may. Let anyone put as many hurdles in our way as possible. We will not turn away from this path by being frightened or brow beaten. Our every step will in any case move towards this destination, which our God has determined for us and which is the aim and purpose of our lives.

After this, it is said:

| 2:155-157 | these are the people who are congratulated by Allah And these are the people who are on the right path | اُلِئِکَ عَلَيهِمْ صَلَوتٌ مَنْ رَبِّهِمْ وَرَحْمَةٌ وَأُولِئِکَ هُمُ الْمُهْتَدُوْنَ |

These verses make it clear that "الَيهِ رَاجِعُوْنَ" (*ilahi raa'jeoon*) does not mean that God is at any particular place and we have to return to that place to meet Him. Neither that our soul is a part of that whole (God) and will ultimately reunite with that whole. Instead it means that our entire life is dedicated to Allah's system "اِنَّا لله" (*inna lillah*), and despite all the difficulties and travails in the world, our steps move towards this very system. It gives us strength and the results of our deeds are formulated according to them. Every move of our lives moves around this axis. It is the centre of our lives. All our efforts are aimed towards this centre. Every deed of ours moves towards the natural cycle of events, and it cannot be detracted. It has to produce a result, whether the result becomes visible in this world or in the hereafter, because His laws are not confined only to this world.

R-J-F   ر ج ف

"اَلرَّجْفُ" (*ar-rajf*): for something to become mobile, or to shake up. Movement with unease or worry is included in this word's connotation.
"رَجْفُ الْقَلْبِ" (*rajful qalb*): severe palpitation of the heart due to unease {T, M}.

Raghib says it means severe unease *{R}*.

"اَلرَّاجِفُ" (*ar-raajif*): fever with shaking.
"أَرْجَفَتِ الرِّيْحُ الشَّجَرَ" (*ar-rajafatir reehush shajar*): the wind shook the trees.
"رَجَفَتِ الْأَرْضُ" (*rajafatil ard*): the earth moved, or shook.
"اَلرَّجْفَةُ" (*ar-rajfah*): earthquake.
"اَلْأَرَاجِيْفُ" (*ar-rajeef*): instigating news, news that makes one uneasy {T, M}.

The Quran says:

| 33:60 | people who spread news that causes unease or chaos without any reason | اَلْمُرْجِفُوْنَ فِى الْمَدِيْنَةِ |
| 7:78 | They (nation of Samood) were caught (trapped) by the earthquake. | فَأَخَذَتْهُمُ الرَّجْفَةُ |

| 79:6 | the day when that which shakes will shake | يَوْمَ تَرْجُفُ الرَّاجِفَةُ |
| 73:14 | the day when the common folk will be in an agitated state (the day on which the earth will shake up) | يَوْمَ تَرْجُفُ الْأَرْضُ |

R-J-L   ر ج ل

"رِجْلٌ" (**rajlu**): foot. Plural is "أَرْجُلٌ" (**arjul**): feet as used in 38:42.

"رِجَالٌ" (**rijaal**): pedestrian. It is the plural of "رَاجِلٌ" (**raajil**), as against "رُكْبَانًا" (**rukbana**) – 'mounted' as in 2:239. It is also used against "خَيْلٌ" (**khail**), which means cavalry (17:64).

"رَجُلٌ" (**rajul**): man. Plural is "رِجَالٌ" (**rijaal**): people, as used in 2:228 and 72:6.

Muheet says a man is called "رَجُلٌ" (**rajul**) because of his bravery and strength.

Raghib says that the meaning of "رَجُلٌ" (**rajul**) in 36:20, and 40:28 will be of a brave man {T, R, M}.

Ibn Faris says it basically has been derived from a word which means 'leg'. But "رَجُلٌ" (**rajul**) is different from this meaning.

R-J-M   ر ج م

Ibn Faris says "رَجْمٌ" (**rajm**) basically means to hit with stones, but later it began to mean kill as well. It is also used for accusing or abusing, or to scold and oust.

Taj says it means to leave someone or break relations with someone.

"اَلرَّجْمُ" (**ar-rajm**) also means to give someone a dressing down {T}.

"اَلرِّجَامُ" (**ar-rijaam**) means stones, and "مِرْجَامٌ" (**mirjaam**) means a sling which is used to throw stones {Lane}.

Surah **Yasin** says:

| 36:18 | if you do not cease, we will stone you (to death). | لَئِنْ لَمْ تَنْتَهُوا لَنَرْجُمَنَّكُمْ |

Surah **Ash-Shura'a** says:

| 26:116 | You will be among those who are stoned to death or killed | لَتَكُونَنَّ مِنَ الْمَرْجُومِينَ |

In surah **Al-Hijr** (15:34-35), the **Shaitaan** (the oppsition) has been called "رَجِيمٌ" (**rajeem**) which has been explained as "إِنَّ عَلَيْكَ اللَّعْنَةَ" (**inna ilaikal la'naa**). As such "رَجِيمٌ" (**rajeem**) and "مَلْعُونٌ" (**mal-oon**) are of the same meaning. For the meaning of "مَلْعُونٌ" (**mal-oon**) see heading (L-Ain-N). It means he who is deprived of God's benevolence, who is distanced from Him, with whom no connection whatsoever is maintained.

"رَجْمٌ" (*rajm*): guess work.

"حَدِيثٌ مُرَجَّمٌ" (*hadeethum- murajjam*) is a thought which cannot be verified *{T}*.

"رَجَّمَ الرَّجُلُ بِالْغَيْبِ" (*rajjamar rujul bilghaib*): that man has said something about the unknown.

"قَالَهُ رَجْماً" (*qaalahu rajma*): he simply made a guess {Lane}.

Surah *Al-Kahaf* says that people who state the number of people in the cave, is only "رَجْماً بِالْغَيْبِ" (*rajman bilghaib*) that is, mere guessing (18:32). Hence it means that they make guesses without knowing the truth.

In *Lataif-ul-Lugha* too, the meaning of "اَلرَّجْمَ" (*ar-rajm*) is 'to guess'.

In the old days, temples had astrologers used to tell people about the unknown. This is still the practice of the priests of temples and religious leaders in religious institutions. They used to claim that they got the news from the heavens. The Quran has said at several places that all this is mere guesswork.

Sometimes something comes true. For instance 2 out of 10 guesses may become true but they have no knowledge about the truth. (15:17-18, 37:69, 67:5, 72:8-9). After the advent of the Quran, the time for knowledge and awareness had arrived. Thus these superstitions had no place in human psyche. Now this nonsense "gets fiery whips by celestial forces".

As will be disclosed under the heading (L-Ain-N). According to the Quran, "لَعْنَت" (*laa'nat*) does not mean demeaning or curse word but a statement of reality. That is, due to the wrong way of life, deprivation from all those delights of life, those are a natural result of living according to the laws of Allah. Anybody who is deprived of these delights will be called "اَلرَّجْمَ" (*ar-rajm*). This is the meaning of "رَجِيْمٌ" (*rajeem*) as well. That is, he who is flung away or who is deprived of the delights, we are told to shun him. Any emotion that obstructs us from the right path or violates the principles of Allah (such people are the *shaitaan*, or the resistance, and must be stayed away from. This is "اَلرَّجْمَ" (*ar-rajm*) or "رَجِيْمٌ" (*rajeem*).

R-J-W ر ج و

"اَلرَّجَاءُ" (*ar-raja-u*) means hope, which is the opposite of "يَأْسٌ" (*yaas*). It is a hope that is not faint.

Raghib says this is a hope in which success is expected, but since hope and fear are inevitable together, later it started to be used for 'hope' that had fear in the expectation as well.

Muheet says that difference between "أَمَلٌ" (*amalun*) and "رَجَاءٌ" (*rija'un*) is that (*amal*) is used for pleasant hopes but "رَجَاءٌ" *rija* for both good and fretful hopes.

Azhari says when "رَجَاءٌ" (*raja*) is accompanied by a negative word it means fear *{T}*.

Ibn Qateeba too says that "لَايَرْجُوْنَ" (***la yarjoon***) means "لايَخَافُوْنَ" (***la yakhafoon***). {***Alqartain*** Vol.1}.

Ibn Faris also says that "لايَخَافُوْنَ" (***raja'a***) at times means fear.

"لايَخَافُوْنَ" (***al-irja'a***): to put off for later, to delay, to remove something, to postpone something.
"اَلرَّجَا" (***ar-raja'a***): edge, or edge of a well from top to bottom {***T***}. The plural is "اَرْجَاءٌ" (***arja***) as used in 69:17.
"مَرْجُوٌّ" (***marju***): with which hopes are linked (11:62).
"مُرْجَوْنَ" (***murja-un***): those who are kept waiting, those whose affair is postponed (9:106)

Surah ***Ash- Shu`ara*** says:

| 26:36 | They said postpone his affair | قَالُوْا اَرْجِه |

See 7:11 as well. Surah ***Al-Ahzaab*** says:

| 33:51 | You may defer whom you will of them, or you may take to yourself whom you will. | تُرْجِىْ مَنْ تَشَاءُ مِنْهُنَّ وَتُؤْوِىْ اِلَيْكَ مَنْ تَشَاءُ |

Here "تُرْجِىْ" (***turji***) means to keep something back, to remove away, and to put it off towards the edge. "تُؤْوِىْ" (***tuwi***) means to place close by, near oneself.

R-H-B   ر ح ب

"رَحُبَ الشَّيْءُ رَحْباً" (***rahabas shaiy-u rahba***): to be vast.
"اَرْحَبَه" (***arhabah***): he expanded it.

Ibn Faris too thinks that the root has the connotation of vastness or expanse.

"طَرِيْقٌ رَحْبٌ" (***tareequn rahb***): broad path.
"مَرْحَبأبِكَ" (***marhaba bika***): you came to a vast place, you will be treated here broad mindedly.
"رَحْبَةٌ" (***rahbah***): the open space in a house {***T***}.

The Quran says:

| 9:25 | The earth, despite its expansiveness, became narrow for you | وَضَاقِتْ عَلَيْكُمُ الْاَرْضُ بِمَا رَحُبَتْ |

Surah ***Saad*** says about the dwellers of ***jahannum***:

| 38:10 | There is no broad mindedness for you. Nobody welcomes you | لَامَرْحَباً بِكُمْ |

In a hellish life, nobody is pleased to see anybody, nobody welcomes a newcomer. Here there is no large heartedness, no lips smile at somebody's arrival. If it is, then it is only artificial, only for the sake of appearances. On the contrary, in their heart everyone is thinking "where did this trouble come from?"

R-H-Q   ر ح ق

"رَحِيْقٌ" (*raheeq*): very old, very pure, unadulterated and excellent wine. Every pure thing is also called "رَحِيْقٌ" (*raheeq*).

"حَسْبُ الرَّحِيْقِ" (*hasabur-raheeq*): thoroughbred.

"مِسْكٌ رَحِيْقٌ" (*miskun raheeq*): pure, unadulterated fine perfume {T, M}.

The Quran (83:25) has said about those in *janna* that they shall receive "رَحِيْقٍ مَخْتُوْمٍ" (*raheeqin makhtoom*) which means 'a pure drink', such that even later there is no chance of adulteration. Hence, this word means life's pure delights and happiness.

R-H-L   ر ح ل

"اَلرَّحْلُ" (*ar-rahl*): anything that is tied to the camel's back with the intent of sitting in it while traveling.

"رِحَالٌ" (*rihaal*) is plural of "رَحْلُ" (*rahl*).

"اَلرِّحْلَةُ" (*ar-rihlah*): journey, to the place where one travels to.

With time, this word has also been used for camel, camel seat, or where one alights, or for the house {T, M}. This word is also used for anything which is for loading goods on to the camel's back, or sacks (bags) {T, M}.

Surah *Yusuf* says:

| 12:62 | In their sacks (Bags). | فِيْ رِحَالِهِمْ |

Ibn Faris says that the basic meaning of this root is to keep on travelling or to continue with the journey.

The Quran says:

| 106:2 | The journeys of summer and winter | رِحْلَةَ الشِّتَاءِ وَالصَّيْفِ |

"اَلْمَرْحَلَةُ" (*al-marhalah*): the distance that a man travels habitually towards his destination {T}.

R-H-M   ر ح م

"رِحْمّ" (**rihm**), "رَحْمّ" (**rahm**), "رُحْمّ" (**ruhm**): the womb of a woman in which a child is nurtured and is protected from external effects {T, R}.

"رَحْمَةّ" (**rahmah**) is the gift that completes some shortcoming (and which is given according to the need) {T}. It means to gift a thing, which is given without any considerstion, as a benevolence. As such, "رَحْمَةّ" (**rahmah**) is the sustenance which man gets from God without any cost.

Surah **Ar-Rom** says:

| 30:36 | And when people experience Our benevolence, they start acting up, but when they land in trouble because of their own deeds, they become disappointed | وَإِذَا أَذَقْنَاالنَّاسَ رَحْمَةً فَرِحُوابِهَ وَ اِنْ تُصِبْهُمْ سَيِّئَةٌ بِمَا قَدَّمَتْ اَيْدِيهِمْ اِذَا هُمْ يَقْنَطُونَ |

Here "رَحْمَةّ" (**rahmah**) has been used against "سَيِّئَةّ" (**sayyia**). Therefore, it would mean all the delights of life. But the next verse mentions vastness or expanse, or large heartedness. It is obvious then that here "رَحْمَةّ" (**rahmah**) means the goods or accoutrements of life which we get from God without asking and at no cost.

In surah **Bani Israel**, the longing for parents by their progeny is mentioned:

| 17:24 | O God, look after them (nurture them) as they brought me up in childhood | وَقُلْ رَبِّ ارْحَمْهُمَا كَمَا رَبَّيْنِى صَغِيراً |

"رَحْمَةّ" (**rahmah**) also means rain which produces sustenance from earth (30:46, 42:28). Life's delights ("نَعْمَاءُ" - **na'maa**) which we get from God without any charge, are also "رَحْمَةّ" (**rahmah**), as in 11:9-10.

In the tale about **Moosa**, it is mentioned that the treasure belonging to two orphan kids was buried under a wall, which had been so buried as to be discovered by them when they became adults. This arrangement by God is called "رَحْمَةّ" (**rahmah**) in 18:82.

"رَحْمَةّ" (**rahmah**) also means to cover something or to provide with the means of protection {T}. That is why the noble Quran has used "رَحْمَةّ" (**rahmah**) against "ضَرَرّ" (**zarar**) which means 'harm' (30:33, 10:21), and against "سَيِّئَةّ" (**sayyia**) (30:31) and against "أَبْلَکَ" (**ahlaka**) (67:28).

Since God's sustenance is not only for a man's physical being, instead, it is also for human personality's development, which is the product of the life's order which Revelation gives us, therefore Revelation has also been called "رَحْمَةّ" (**rahmah**) in 43:23, 2:105. The truth which is the biggest source of man's development is the revelation which is totally given by God, which is why it is a special "رَحْمَةّ" (**rahmah**).

Since God is "رَبُّ الْعَالَمِيْنَ" (*rabbil aalameen*), or the one who provides development of the entire universe and develops the human personality as well, therefore He has taken upon Himself to provide Revelation through His Own sources.

6:54	Your Sustainer has taken upon Himself to provide the means of Sustenance without failure.	كَتَبَ رَبُّكُمْ عَلَى نَفْسِهِ الرَّحْمَةَ

Thus, He covers the entire universe in His blanket of benevolence (40:7). This is why in surah **Al-Fateha,** along with "رَبُّ الْعَالَمِيْنَ" (*rabbil aalameen*) also says "اَلرَّحْمٰنِ الرَّحِيْمِ" (*ar-rahman-ir-raheem*).

"رَحِيْمٌ" (*raheem*) means linguistically one who provides means of sustenance on continuous basis.
"اَرَحْمٰنُ" (*rahman*), on the other hand, is one who provides means of sustenance at a time of great need with overwhelmingness {**Al-Minar**}.

The first can be said to be an evolutionary means of provision of sustenance, while the second as an emergent provision.

Surah **Ar-Rahman** says:

55:29	Whatever there is in the heavens and on earth, is dependant on God for its sustenance	يَسْئَلُهٗ مَنْ فِى السَّمٰوٰتِ وَالْاَرْضِ كُلَّ يَوْمٍ هُوَ فِىْ شَانٍ

These things do not stay in one state and do not require the same sort of sustenance always. They keep changing with time. Thus, their demands for nourishment change as well with time. The needs of a foetus inside a mother's womb are quite different from the demands of bringing up a kid, and again for an adult, quite different. As long as something stays in a state, its sustenance is done by God's kindliness in a certain way. But as soon as it changes, its sustenance changes as well according to God's law. Thus in this way, everything reaches its completion from its beginning. This is the meaning of **Rabb, Rahman** and **Raheem.**

"رِحْمٌ" (*rihm*) also means kith and kin, relatives {**T, R, M**}.
"بَيْنَهُمَا رِحْمٌ" (*bainahuma rihm*): those two are closely related.
"اَرْحَامٌ" (*ar-haam*) is the plural of "رِحْمٌ" (*rihm*) (3:5) which also means relatives (60:3, 2:1).
"أُولُوا الْاَرْحَامِ" (*oolu al arhaam*): relatives (8:75).

Since "رِحْمٌ" (*rihm*) involves softness, therefore it also means that.

48:29	very hard against the opponents and very soft against each other	اَشِدَّاءُ عَلَى الْكُفَّارِ رُحَمَاءُ بَيْنَهُمْ

Surah **Al-Kahaf** says:

18:81	one who gives relations a big consideration	اَقْرَبَ رُحْماً

But **Ibn Faris** says that "اَلرُّحْمُ" (**ar-ruhm**) and "اَلرَّحْمَةُ" (**ar-rahmah**) are of the same meaning. This will make the meaning as one who is extra kind, extra sympathetic and faithful. **Ibn Faris** says it basically means softness and leaning.

Christians believe that every human child is born as a consequence of the sins of the parents and since this sin cannot be more than the deeds, therefore a man can be delivered only with God's mercy. This concept of mercy is against the Quranic teachings. According to the Quran, success is the natural result of deeds, and all this takes place according to the divine laws which are called the laws of nature.

The basic principle of these laws is that:

53:39	a man gets (in return) whatever he does	لَيْسَ لِاِنْسَانٍ اِلَّا مَاسَعَى

This means that good results for good deeds and bad results for bad deeds. Although for such deeds various capabilities are received by man as also guidance from God, free of cost, and these are included in "رَحْمٌ" (**rahm**). That is, all this for the development of man is received from God, free of cost. Now the man, who benefits from these things and develops his personality according to the laws of God, will be the beneficiary of life's blessings. He, who will not do so, will be deprived of them. This is the law of God (Nature). Therefore, man can reach his ultimate destiny, not due to the mere benevolence of God, but because of the result of his own deeds, in accordance with the laws of God. Based on this fundamental principal, Quran modifies such a nation that creates a heavenly society for itself with its utter most dedication.

"رَحْمٰنٌ" (**rahman**) rhymes with "فَعْلَانٌ" (**fa'lan**), as "تَطْشَانٌ" (**tatshan**) to "غَصْبَانٌ" (**ghasban**), while "رَحِيْمٌ" (**raheem**) rhymes with "فَعِيْلٌ" (**fa'eel**), as "عَلِيْمٌ" (**aleem**) with "حَكِيْمٌ" (**hakeem**) etc. "فَعْلَانٌ" (**fa'lan**) is used for qualities which are intense and of emergent, and "فَعِيْلٌ" (**fa'eel**) which are a must and continuous.

R-Kh-W ر خ و

"اَلرِّخْوُ" (*ar-rikhwu*): soft thing.

"رَخُوَ الشَّيْءُ" (*rakhush shaiyi*), "رِخِيَ" (*rikhi*), "رَخَأَ" (*rakha*): for something to become soft or loose.

"اِسْتَرْخَى" (*istarkha*) also means the same as above.

"أَرْخَاهُ" (*arkhah*), "رَاخَاهُ" (*rakhah*): he made him soft.

"أَرْخَى دَابَّتَهُ" (*arkha dabbatah*): he left the animal loose and let it have its way.

"اَلرُّخَاءُ" (*ar-rukha*): softened the speed {T, R, M}.

The Quran says:

| 38:36 | The (wind) used to blow softly and freely on His order | تَجْرِىْ بِأَمْرِهِ رُخَاءً |

"فَرَسٌ رِخْوَةٌ" (*faras-un rikhwah*): speedy and soft natured horse {T, R, M}.

R-D-A ر د أ

"اَلرِّدْءُ" (*ar-ridu*): heavy loads which are equal to each other in weight.

"رَدَأَالشَّيْءَ بِهِ" (*radish shaiyi bihi*): he boosted something with something, supported it, helped it.

Actually, "اَلرِّدْءُ" (*arid-u*) means helper {T}. When an animal is laden with weight on both sides in such a manner that both sides weigh the same, then each load is called "رِدْءٌ" (*rid-un*). When loads on each side are of the same weight, they support each other to maintain balance {T}.

The Quran says:

| 28:34 | send him as my helper | فَأَرْسِلْهُ مَعِىَ رِدْأً |

"رَدِىْءٌ" (*radi-un*): one who follows, but later it came to mean a condemned thing {R}, because generally that which comes behind is something with a fault.

Ibn Faris says it has two basic meanings, which are almost opposite. He says it means for something to deteriorate or become bad, and secondly to help.

R-D-D   ر د د

"رد" (**rud**), "يَرُدُّ" (**yarud**): to return (something) to somebody.

If it is followed by "على" (**ala**), then it has an element of insult and demeaning.
"رَدَّعَلَيْهِ الشَّىْءُ" (**radda a'laihi-shai'i**): he turned his back on that thing.

But if it is followed by "اِلَى" (**ila**), then it has the elements of respect, but it is not a principle

| 28:13 | We retuned Moosa honorably to his mother | فَرَدَدْنَاهُ اِلَى أُمِّه |

"اَلرَّدُّ" (**ar-rud**) means garbage.
"دِرْيَمٌ رَدٌّ" (**dirham rudd**): coin.
"لَامَرَدَّةَ فِيْهِ" (**la maraddata feeh**): it has no return (profit).
"اِرْتَدَّ الشَّىْءُ" (**irtadd ash shaiyi**): the thing returned, went back {T}.

Raghib says that "اَلْاِرْتِدَادُ" (**la-irtidaad**) means returning by the same path that one has come by.

"تَرَدَّدَ اِلَيْهِ" (**taraddada ilaih**): he came to him and returned repeatedly.
"تَرَدَّدَ فِى الْأَمْرِ" (**taraddad fil amr**): to be undecided on something {R}

Surah **Al-Baqrah** says:

| 2:228 | Their husbands have more right to take them back | وَبُعُوْلَتُهُنَّ أَحَقُّ بِرَدِّهِنَّ |

The Quran says:

42:47	the day which will not go away (which cannot be avoided or returned	يَوْمٌ لَا مَبَرَّدَلَهُ
19:76	beneficial in the end, as a result	خَيْرٌ مَرَدَّاً
42:44	Can there be some way in which it will turn back?	هَلْ اِلَى مَرَدٍّ مِنْ سَبِيْلٍ

"فَرَدُّوْا اَيْدِيَهُمْ فِىْ اَفْوَاهِهِمْ" (**faraddu aidiyahum fee afwaahihim**) as in 14:9. For the meaning of this verse, see heading (Y-D-Y).

This word has the connotation of 'at last'. Therefore, it is used generally for the result of deeds.

Surah **As-Sajdah** says:

| 41:47 | When the revolution shall take place, is known to none other than Allah | اِلَيْهِ يُرَدُّ عِلْمُ السَّاعَةِ |

We have to return to Him, and no one else. Only He knows how and where. Others can only make guesses. See heading (S-W-Ain).

"مَرْدُوْدٌ" (**mardood**): that which has been turned back, returned (79:10).

Surah **Hoodh** says:

11:77	Chastisement which cannot be turned back or returned	عَذَابٌ غَيْرُ مَرْدُودٍ

A verse in surah **An-Nahal** relates one of the basic principles of the system of sustenance of the Quran. God has said in it that different people have different capabilities for earning, due to which the different sectors in society run. This has been explained further in (43:23). See heading (S-K-R). But this does not mean that those who have capability to acquire more sustenance keep that which they acquire to themselves. That is, they should not believe that they have acquired it because of their capability and hence they should be the owners of it, regardless their need. This is a wrong concept.

16:71	Those who have received this excess capability do not let the sustenance reach those who are downtrodden. They fear that they will become holders of equal shares (despite their lesser capabilities)	فَمَا الَّذِيْنَ فُضِّلُوْا بِرَآدِّیْ رِزْقِهِمْ عَلَى مَامَلَكَتْ اَيْمَانُهُمْ فَهُمْ فِيْهِ سَوَاءٌ

"بِرَآدِّیْ" (**biraddi**) here is notable. The verse did not say that eyes should be given as alms. What is said is that the excess sustenance is for those who need it and are under them (the strong people). Therefore, the sustenance should be turned towards them. If you do not do this, it would mean that you think that the power or capacity for earning is not granted by God, or that you have received it from God, free of cost.

16:71	Do these people, who do not return their excess wealth to those who are needy, deny God's benevolence?	اَفَبِنِعْمَةِ اللهِ يَجْحَدُوْنَ

This is Quran's social order. (Details will be found in my book '**Nizaam-i-Raoobiyat**').

R-D-F   ر د ف

"اَلرَّدْفُ" (*ar-radf*), "اَلرَّدِيْفُ" (*ar-radeef*): one who rides double behind a rider. Similarly, anything that is behind another is called so as well.

"رَدِفَهُ" (*radifah*) and "رِدْفٌ" (*radafah*): to come behind something *{T}*.

The Quran says:

27:72	Perhaps it is approaching behind you	عَسَى اَنْ يَّكُوْنَ رَدِفَ لَكُمْ

This means, is very near you. It can also mean that it may have followed you.

"مُرْدِفٌ" (*murdif*): to make someone ride behind, and one who follows somebody *{T}*.

"مِنَ الْمَلَائِكَةِ مُرْدِفِيْنَ" (*minal malaiki murdifeen*): those who come one after the other, continuously (8:9).

"رَادِفٌ" (*raadif*): one who comes behind, or close up on you.

"تَتْبَعُهَا الرَّادِفَةُ" (*tatba-uhar raadifah*): the follower will follow him (79:7). That is the moment of reward and punishment, or God's law of natural results, the time for the results to appear, the result of deeds which follows inevitably.

Raghib says that "اَلْمُرْدِفُ" (*al-murdif*) means the rider in front who lets somebody ride behind him.

R-D-M   ر د م

"اَلرَّدْمُ" (*ar-ridm*): to close some gap or hole. "سَدَّ" (*sadda*) is its alternate, but "رَدَمَّ" (*radm*) is somewhat stronger than "سَدَّ" (*sadd*).

"رَدَمَ الْبَابَ" (*radamal baab*): to close the door, to shut one third of it *{T, R}*.

Ibn Faris says it basically means to close some gap with some sort of barrier.

Surah ***Al-Kahaf*** says:

18:94	They said "O Dhulqarnain, indeed Yajooj and Majooj are corrupters in this land. We would like to make a request to you that you create a barrier (sadda) between us and them.	قَالُوا يَا ذَا الْقَرْنَيْنِ إِنَّ يَأْجُوجَ وَمَأْجُوجَ مُفْسِدُونَ فِي الْأَرْضِ فَهَلْ نَجْعَلُ لَكَ خَرْجًا عَلَى أَنْ تَجْعَلَ بَيْنَنَا وَبَيْنَهُمْ سَدًّا
18:95	(He said) I will make a strong barrier (radma) between you and them.	أَجْعَلْ بَيْنَكُمْ وَبَيْنَهُمْ رَدْمًا

R-D-Y   ر د ی

"رَدَىٰ" (*radaa*) and "تَرَدَّىٰ" (*taradasa*): he fell into the well. "رَدِیْ" (*raddi*) is also used in this meaning. It may also mean that he fell from the mountain and died {T}.

92:11	When he will fall head over heels in the jahannum (state of destructions) his accumulated wealth will do him no good	مَا يُغْنِیْ عَنْهُ مَالُهُ اِذَا تَرَدَّىٰ

Raghib says that "تَرَدَّىٰ" (*taradda*) means to present you to destruction. That means, he who accumulates wealth and does not use it for the benefit of mankind calls in a way on forces of destruction to come his way.

"اَلْمُتَرَدِّیَةُ" (*al-mutaraddiyah*): an animal which falls to death. It has been declared by the Quran as forbidden for eating (5:3). Thereafter the word also means death in the ordinary sense.

"رَدِیَ فُلَانٌ" (*raddi falanun*): he was killed.

"فَهُوَرَدٍ" (*fahuwarid*): he is to be killed.

"اَرْدَاهُ غَیْرُهُ" (*ardahu ghairahu*): he was killed by someone {T}.

"اَلرَّدَىٰ" (*ar-radaa*): destruction, annihilation {R}.

"اَلرِّدَاءُ" (*ar-radaa'u*): sheet of cloth to cover oneself, especially the one used by Muslim women.

Surah **Taha** says "فَتَرْدَىٰ" (*fatardaa*): may you be annihilated or killed (20:16)

Surah **As-Sajdah** says: "اَرْدَاكُمْ" (*ardaakum*): to destroy and destruct (41:23).

"اَلْمَرْدِیُّ" (*al-mardiyyo*): a thrown stone {T}.

Ibn Faris says the root basically means to throw. He says that "اَلتَّرَدِّیْ" (*at-taraddi*) means to go to one's death playfully.

"رَادَىٰ عَنِ الْقَوْمِ" (*raada unil qaum*): he threw stones in defense of the nation {T}.

For the meaning of "رِدْءٌ" (*rid-un*), see heading (R-D-A).

R-Dh-L   ر ذ ل

"اَلرَّذْلُ" (*ar-razl*): a thing which is not liked or disliked for its uselessness {R}.

"اَلرَّذْلُ" (*ar-razl*), "اَلرُّذَالُ" (*ar-ruzal*), "اَلرَّذِیْلُ" (*ar-razeel*): a man who is of lower stature than others, i.e. a man of low stature {T}. It also means garbage, or something out of which the good things have been extracted, and the useless things are left behind {M}.

"اَلْأَرْذَلُ" (*al-arzal*): very lowly, cheap and useless. Plural is "اَرْذَلُوْنَ" (*arzaloon*).

The Quran says that the leaders of the nation of Nooh told him that the people who have joined his group were "هُمْ اَرَاذِلُنَا" (*hum arazilona*), meaning that they are people of lower class (11:27).

"اَرْذَلِ الْعُمُر" (*arzalil umur*): the fag end of life (16:70), or that part of old age.

"لَا يَعْلَمَ بَعْدَ عِلْمٍ" (*la ya'lama baada ilm*): the age when a man forgets even things which he once knew, i.e. when he becomes senile.

R-Z-Q   ر ز ق

"رِزْقٌ" (*rizq*): anything from which benefit can be derived, or the sustenance that living beings get from God. Rain is "رِزْقٌ" (*rizq*), and so is a fixed income. Therefore, "مُرْتَزِقَةٌ" (*murtaziqa*) are those people who have fixed salaries, ration or allowances. "رَزْقَةٌ" (*razqah*) is the ration which soldiers get *{T}*.

Ibn Faris says it means to give something at a fixed time. Thereafter the word began to be applied to every gift without regard to any time.

The Quran has termed all edibles as "رِزْقُ اللّٰه" (*rizqullah*), or Allah's *rizq* (2:60). In surah **Al-Hijr** "مَعَايِشَ" (*ma'ayish*) and "رِزْقٌ" (*rizq*) have been used in similar meaning (15:20), but for the Quran, life is not only man's physical life but this existence continues (in another form) even after death. That means that development is not only needed for the nurturing of the physical being but also for man's personality. Therefore the Quran has termed these means of sustenance even after death as "رِزْقٌ" (*rizq*) (22:58). This also shows that life in heaven is one of the evolutionary stages of life. There too, human life will continue to be developed. Details can be found in heading (J-N-N).

Thus, "رِزْقٌ" (*rizq*) is those means of sustenance which are required for the development of Man's physical being as well as his personality. The truth is that if the distribution of life's necessities takes place according to the law stated by Revelation, which is called the system of **Raboobiyah** or welfare, then a man's personality and his body can develop effortlessly.

Such a system is established by those about whom it is said:

2:3	whatever means of sustenance We give them, they keep available for humanity at large	وَمِمَّا رَزَقْنَاهُمْ يُنْفِقُونَ

This means that they do not collect it for themselves, nor do they block them (again for themselves). They keep them open. See heading (N-F-Q). Since this system is in obedience of Allah's laws, therefore it has been said:

17:31	it is Us who give this rizq	نَحْنُ نَرْزُقُكُمْ وَإِيَّاهُمْ
2:152	We give rizq to you as well as to your progeny	

In this way it is the responsibility of the establishment based upon Allah's laws to provide for every individual citizen (11:6), otherwise, if the division of *rizq* is according to man-made laws then (as we witness in the world today) millions of people die of starvation. There are further millions who are unable to feed themselves and their families properly. In the wrong sort of society there is hoarding, and the lower class is deprived of the means of sustenance. In a right kind of (Quranic) society, all sources of sustenance are available for everybody (41:10), because whatever is produced employs only man's labor. Everything else happens according to the law of Allah.

Therefore Man has right only to the remuneration for his labor. All the rest belongs to Allah, and therefore it should be distributed according to His laws (56:64-73). Details will be found in my book *Nizam-e-Rabboobiyat* where this division of sustenance has been dealt with from different angles.

The government which is established to enforce the laws of Allah is called an Islamic government. The basic principle of which is that the responsibility for providing every individual with the necessities of life rests with the state. In such a system, the fountainheads of sustenance are owned not by individuals but by the state and nobody has extra wealth. Therefore, every person works hard. He keeps what is needed for him and gives the rest for the sustenance of others. Thus, the state can fulfill the responsibility of providing for every individual. The purpose of an Islamic government is to distribute the sustenance given by God according to His laws among people who follow his laws.

Surah *Al-Waaqia* says "وَتَجْعَلُوْنَ رِزْقَكُمْ" (*wataja 'aloona rizqakum*) in 56:82. *Raghib* says that here it means luck or share, but the clear meaning is that you deny a book like the Quran, just so you may maintain your hegemony and keep your earning intact!

R-S-Kh   ر س خ

"رَسَخَ" (*rasakha*), "يَرْسُخُ" (*yarsukhu*), "رُسُوْخَاً" (*rusukha*): for something to be solid in its place. "رَسَخَ الْمَطَرُ" (*rasakhal mataru*): the rainwater was absorbed in the ground {T}. This is said when the water has gone so deep as to reach the ground's dampness.

The Quran has said:

3:6	the people who deeply imbibe knowledge (who become mature in knowledge)	اَلرَّاسِخُوْنَ فِى الْعِلْمِ

Raghib says "رَاسِخٌ فِى الْعِلْمِ" (*raasikhul fil ilm*) is one who has done so much research as to leave no doubt about the findings {T}.

The Quran presents its invitation or message on the basis of intellect and insight, and stresses on accepting it on the basis of deliberation and knowledge and research. Thus "رَاسِخٌ فِى الْعِلْمِ" (*raasikul fil ilm*) is one who reaches the truth of the results with research and thus his belief on God becomes solid.

For the meaning of verse, 3:6 see heading (H-K-M).

R-S-S   ر س س

"اَلرَّسُّ" (*ar-rus*): to dig, to bury. That is why to bury a dead man is also called "رَسّ" (*rus*). It also means an old well, whether paved or unpaved.

"اَلرَّسُّ" (*ar-rus*) also means the beginning of something.

"رَسَّ الْحُمَّى وَرَسِيْسُہُ" (*russul huma wa raseesah*): the initial indications of fever, such as yawning etc. {T}.

Raghib says it means the little effect that is present in something.

"اَبِلُ الرَّسِّ" (*ahlu- rus*): people who fabricate a lie first and then propagate it.
This has been derived from "" (*russa bainal qaum*): to create chaos and enmity {T}.

Ibn Faris says it means 'to solidify'.

The Quran says "اَصْحَابُ الرَّسِّ" (*as-habar-rus*) in 25:38. It has been used for some nation beside nations of **Aad** and **Thamood**. There are quite a few stipulations about it in the dictionary. One is that "اَلرَّسُّ" (*ar-rus*) is the name of a valley. Maybe this name was given to it due to some old well in this valley.
{R}.

But if figurative meaning is taken then it would mean that nation which used to fabricate wrong sort of talk and created chaos or unease among their people. Or, it was a nation with very little effect of their messengers left in them.

R-S-L   ر س ل

"رِسْلٌ" (*risl*) means for an obstruction to be removed and for a thing to proceed ahead smoothly with peace and ease {R}.
"نَاقَةٌ رَسْلَةٌ" (*naaqatun raslah*): slow camel.
"اِبِلٌ مَرَاسِيْلٌ" (*ibl maraseel*): slow camels.
"رَسُوْلٌ" (*rasool*): one who gets going, one who departs. Sometimes "رَسُوْلٌ" (*rasul*) is used to mean to get going. {R}.
"عَلَى رِسْلِكَ" (*ala rislik*): live peacefully as you want.
"اَلرَّسْلُ" (*ar-rasl*): slow in speed.
"اَلْاِسْتِرْسَالُ" (*al-istirsaal*): slowness in the animal's speed.

Ibn Faris says it basically means to get going. A group or herd is also called "اَلرَّسَلُ" (*ar-rasl*)

"جَاءَتِ الْخَيْلُ اَرْسَالاً" (*ja'atil khailu arsaala*): horses came in groups
"الارسال" (*al-irsaal*): to send (towards somebody)
"اَرْسَلَہُ عَلَيْہِ" (*arsalahu alaih*): he imposed himself on someone.

"اَلرَّسُوْلُ" (*ar-rasul*): the person who is sent towards men from God, as well as the message he conveys.

"رَسُوْلٌ" (*rasul*), "رِسَالَةٌ" (*risaalah*) and "مُرْسَلٌ" (*mursal*) appears for both messenger and the message itself *{T}*.

"اَلتَّرْسِيْلُ فِى الْقِرَاءَةِ" (*at-tarseelu fi alqira'ah*): to read slowly and beautifully *{T}*.

"اَلرَّسُوْلُ" (*ar-rasul*) would mean a person who gives the message from his sender continuously, gradually and with softness. His message too is called "اَلرَّسُوْلُ" (*ar-rasul*).

Men who got revelation from God and took it to the people are called Allah's "اَلرَّسُوْلُ" (*ar-rasul*). The Quran has called them "أَنْبِيَاءُ" (*ambia*), as well as "رُسُلٌ" (*rusul*). There is no difference between a *nabi* and a *rasul*.

Nabuwwa is to get the revelation from God and *risala* means to take it forward to the people. The details will be found under heading (N-B-A) where it has been clarified that the belief that a *nabi* is without *sharia* and *rasul* is with a *sharia*, is false. The Quran has made no such distinction. Every *nabi* had a holy book (2:213) and every "*rasul* did so as well (57:25).

As said above, a *rasul's* duty is to take Allah's message that he gets through Revelation, to the people.

Nooh told his nation that he was a *rasul* of Allah:

7:62	I bring you the messages from my Sustainer	اُ بَلِّغُكُمْ رِسٰلٰتِ رَبِّىْ

About *Muhammed* it is said:

5:67	Whatever that has been revealed to you by your Sustainer, take it to others	بَلِّغْ مَا اُ نْزِلَ اِلَيْكَ مِنْ رَّبِّكَ

As such, whatever *Muhammed (pbuh)* had received from God, he conveyed to people himself. He did not leave this task to others.

Rasul, who were selected to take Allah's message to the people, were human beings (18:110) and they were all men (16:43, 12:09, 21:7). *Rasul* was the first believer of the revelation that it was from God and was the truth (2:285). He was also the first member of this group (believers), that is, he would be the first member of the party that he would organize for establishing Allah's laws on this earth (40:66). He himself was a follower of the revelation and used to strive for establishing a system for practical life based on its teachings (4:64). He would never ask anyone to follow his own orders (and not that of Allah). Nor was this sort of things befitting for a messenger, such as to make people obey his own orders instead of Allah's (3:78-79). Thus obeying *rasul* was in a way obedience of Allah's orders (4:80), therefore this obedience was the obedience of the system which was established for implementing Allah's laws on this earth.

The revelation ended with **Muhammad (pbuh),** and thereafter followed the system which was established under the Quranic laws.

In this system, the successor (*khlifa*) of the **Rasul** performed the duties, which the messenger (pbuh) performed in his lifetime. That is, obeying Allah's laws and inducing others to follow them as well. But this system of following **Allah and Rasul** did not last very long. If that system is established once again, then that obedience can be established as well. This shall be equivalent to following Allah and **Rasul** in practical terms. These matters have been explained in my book "**Islami Nizaam**" (Islamic System), where it is said that **Allah and Rasul** have been mentioned together at many places in the Quran. But after that, the pronoun used is singular. It means that obedience to **Allah and Rasul** are not two different obediences, but the same. What is meant by them is the obedience to Allah's laws which is done by following the system established by the **Rasul** and which after his death is carried on by his followers.

Taj-ul-Uroos says that "أَلرَّسُوْلُ" (**ar-rasul**) also means a fellow archer although **Lissaanul Arab** says that the word "رَسِيْلٌ" (**raseel**) means this, but not "رَسُوْلٌ" (**rasul**). But Allah and His **rasul** are in fact fellow archers, because Allah's orders are implemented in this world by the strength of the **rasul** and his companions or followers.

That is why that at the time of the battle of **Badr**, God had said that:

8:17	it was not you who was shooting the arrows, but God himself	وَمَا رَمَيْتَ اِذْ رَمَيْتَ وَلٰكِنَّ اللّٰهَ رَمٰى

This is the closeness between God, His **rasul** and his companions and followers that brings into force the system of Allah. More details about this can be found in "قَابَ قَوْسَيْنِ" (**qaaba qauseen**) (53:9). See heading (Q-W-S).

As mentioned earlier, **nabi** and the **rasul** are two sides of the same coin. That is why the characteristics related by the Quran of a **nabi** do not differ from that of a **rasul**.

Note. There are letters about the obedience of **rasul** in "**Letters to Saleem** - vol. II"

For confirmation of this, view the many places where the characteristics of a **rasul** or **nabi** are defined in the Quran. For example, a **rasul** never orders anyone to follow his personal commandments, but only wants you to obey the laws of Allah (3:78). If he makes some mistake, then that is personal fault (not Allah's). He shows the right path in the light of Revelation (34:50). A **rasul** does not have the power even for his own good or bad (10:49). He never asks anyone to compensate him for the messenger-hood (10:72). **Rasuls** also had wives and children (13:38). All **rasul** came in their respective times and died as well (3:143), but after the advent of **Muhammad (pbuh)**, deliverance can only be obtained by following his dictum (7:158). **Rasul** always appeared in central places (28:59). Before getting into messenger-hood, the **rasul** were totally unaware that they would get such a task. (42:82, 28:89). Messenger **Muhammad** was illiterate before becoming a messenger, not afterwards (29:48). Messenger **Muhammad** was

Allah's last **rasul** (33:41), therefore no **nabi** or **rasul** can come now. **Rasul** only guided to the path of God, made others to follow it, but to make that happen was not in their power or their responsibility (28:56). To have trust in some messenger and to disbelieve others is **kufr** (denial) (4:150). These traits or characteristics and others have been ascribed to **rasuls** and **nabis** at different places in the Quran. This too has been said that (supposing) if the **rasuls** made any changes or amendments to the revelations, then they would face consequences as well as others. (17:74, 11:113, 10:5, 68:9).

Since the Quran is a complete code of life and since God has guaranteed its protection, the guidance of the human race does not end with the messenger-hood coming to an end. The question is of establishing the same system of God which the Messenger **Muhammad** (pbuh) had established. This system can be reestablished even today.

"اِرْسَالْ" (**irsaal**) means to leave or let go.
"اَرْسَلَ الْخَيْلَ فِى الْغَارَةِ" (**arsalal khail fil gharah**): reigns of the horses were let loose in the attack {T, M}.

The Quran has used this word to mean the opposite of "اِمْسَاكْ" (**imsaak**) which means to restrain.
"اَرْسَلَ عَلَى" (**arsala ala**): to impose on someone (19:83).

<h1 style="text-align:center">R-S-W   ر س و</h1>

"رَسَاالشَّيىْءُ يَرْسُوْ" (**rasash shaiyi yarsu**), "اَرْسَى" (**arsa**), "اِرْسَاءُ" (**irsaa**): for something to come to rest, to become immovable.
"رَسَتِ السَّفِيْنَةُ تَرْسُوْ" (**rasatis safaeenatau tarsu**): the boat anchored {T, M}.
"اَرْسَى السَّفِيْنَةَ" (**arsas safinah**): anchored the boat, made it stop.
"اَلْمِرْسَاةُ" (**al-mirsaah**): a boat's anchor {T, M}.
"مَجْرِبَا وَمُرْسٰهَا" (**majriha wa mursaaha**): for a boat to sail and anchor (11:41).

Surah **Al-Airaaf** says:

7:187	When shall it happen? When will it come before us?	اَيَّانَ مُرْسٰيَا

"مُرْسٰى" (**mursa**) can mean both the time to stop, as well as the stopping place.
"قُدُوْرٍ رَّاسِيَاتٍ" (**qudurir raasiyaat**): big cooking pots which are strongly fixed at one place (32:13).
"رَوَاسِىَ" (**rawasi**): fixed mountains (13:3). Singular is "رَاسِيَةٌ" (**raasia**).

R-Sh-D   ر ش د

"رَشَدَ" (*rashad*), "يَرْشُدُ" (*yarshud*), "رُشْدَا" (*rushda*), "رَشِدَ" (*rashid*), "يَرْشَدُ" (*yarshad*), (*rashadan*), "رَشَادَ" (*rashada*): the right solution of a matter, or to find the right path {T, M}.
"اَلرُّشْدُ" (*ar-rushd*): to be firmly on the right path {T, M}.

Ibn Faris says it means to firmly adopt a path.

"اَلرَّشَدُ" (*ar-rashadu*), "اَلرُّشْدُ" (*ar-rushdu*): the opposite of "غَيِّ" (*ghayyio*), and is used to mean the right guidance {R} (2:256).

Surah **An-Nisa** has used "رُشْدَا" (*roshda*) in 4:6, which means the ability to get to the bottom of things, or mature intellect.
"اِسْتَرْشَدَ فُلَانٌ لِأَمْرِهِ" (*istarshada fulanun li-amrih*): that man found the right solution to his problem.
"اَرْشَدْتُهُ" (*arshadtuhu*): I guided him to the right path.
"اَلرَّشِيْدُ" (*ar-rasheed*): one who shows the right way (11:87), and also a person who can judge things rightly or whose estimates can reach their climax without any help or failure {T}.

Surah **Al-Kahaf** says:

18:10	that the young men prayed to God, for them to be benevolent in the revolutionary struggle and to guide them on the right path	وَهَيِّئْ لَنَا مِنْ اَمْرِنَا رَشَدًا

After this it is said:

18:16	your benefactor will also give you the goods of His benevolence (And will also facilitate the successful completion of purpose)	وَيُهَيِّئْ لَكُم مِّنْ أَمْرِكُم مِّرْفَقًا

This shows that "رَشَدًا" (*rashada*) means not only to guide towards the right path but also to provide the tact and ease for reaching the destination successfully.

"اَلْمَرَاشِدُ" (*al-marashid*) are the ways which lead to the destination. In the Quran, "رَشَدًا" (*rashada*) has been used against "ضرّ" (*darru* – 'loss' (72:21). Thus "رُشْدُ" (*rooshd*) is a composite word which involves the tact and all measures to avoid loss on the way. That is why the messengers (i.e. those people who used to invite towards God) had been given "رُشْدُ" (*rooshd*) (21:51), and the group of **momineen** was called "رَاشِدُوْنَ" (*raashedoon*) (49:7). All this is received by obeying Allah's laws. That is why the Quran has made it clear that there is no "وَلِيٌّ" *wali* nor "مُرْشِدٌ" (*murshid*) except Allah (18:17), but we still consider some human beings as our religious leaders, or holy men, and hence are suffering because of that too!

R-Sd-D ر ص د

Ibn Faris says its root basically means to lie in ambush.

"رَصَدَه" (*rasadah*): he waited for him.
"اَلرَّاصِد" (*ar-rasid*): one who waits and watches the movements of someone.
"اَلرصِيْد" (*ar-raseed*): a wild animal that lies in wait to attack {T}.
"اِرْصَادٌ" (*irsaad*): to wait and while waiting, to prepare {T}.

The Quran says:

| 72:9 | he will find a ball of fire waiting for him | يَجِدْله شِهَابًا رَّصَدًا |
| 9:107 | for lying in wait for those who fight against Allah and His Rasul (i.e. against Allah's system) | إِرْصَادًا لِّمَنْ حَارَبَ اللّٰهَ وَرَسُوْلَهُ |

"اَلْمَرْصَدُ" (*al-marsad*), "اَلْمِرْصَادُ" (*al-mirsaad*): to ambush, or the place where the enemy is ambushed from. (89:14, 9:5){T}.

For God to be in "مِرْصَادٍ" (*mirsaad*) or to ambush, means that His law of Nature keeps full track of everybody and when the need arises, that is, when the time for result comes, then it clutches people in its grip (89:14). Nobody can escape this law. Every human deed travels the path fixed by the law of Nature created by God to reach its destination, and which is called its end or result. Therefore, no deed can be without a result, good or bad.

R-Sd-Sd ر ص ص

"رَصَّهُ" (*rassahu*), "يَرُصُّهُ" (*yarussuh*), "رَصَّا" (*rassa*): he integrated the elements of a thing strongly as if they were iron clad.
"اَلرَّصَاصُ" (*ar-rasaas*) means 'lead' (the metal).

The Quran says that *momins* fight in the way of their Sustainer:

| 61:4 | as if they were parts of a lead wall (i.e. an unshakeable wall) | كَأَنَّهُمْ بُنْيَانٌ مَّرْصُوْصٌ |

This can only happen when the hearts are integrated and when there is complete unity of thoughts and actions. The union of hearts comes from the code of life being homogenous. Consider the fate of the Muslim nations which are divided into different sects today, against this advice! But still we believe that we are the torch bearers of the system of Quran!

R-Zd-Ain   ر ض ع

"رَضَاعًا" (*razia*), "يَرْضَعُ" (*yarza*), "رَضَعَ" (*raza'a*), "يَرْضِعُ" (*yarzih*), "رَضُنْ" (*razun*), "رَضِعَ" (*raza-un*), "رَضَاعَةً" (*raza'a*): for an infant to suckle from its mother's breast {**T, R**}.

| 4:23 | your sisters who have suckled the breasts of the same woman (and which are forbidden for you to wed) | أَخَوَاتُكُمْ مِنَ الرَّضَاعَةِ |

"أَرْضَعَ" (*arza'a*): to suckle a child.
"الإِسْتِرْضَاعُ" (*al-istirza-u*): wanted to suckle {**T**}

| 4:23 | those mothers (those women) who have breast-fed you (they are also forbidden for you to wed) | وَأُمَّهَاتُكُمُ الَّتِى أَرْضَعْنَكُمْ |

"مَرَاضِعُ" (*maradih*): the place where you suckle, i.e. breasts {**Kishaf**}. Singular is "مَرْضَعٌ" (*marza'a*).

Surah **Al-Qasas** says:

| 28:12 | we stopped Moosa from suckling | وَحَرَّمْنَا عَلَيْهِ الْمَرَاضِعَ |

Here "مَرَاضِعُ" (*marazi'h*) could also be plural for "مَرْضَعٌ" (*marza'*), as well as of "مُرْضِعَةٌ" (*murziah*). In the first instance it would mean breasts. In the second those women who let a child suckle, that is, those who breast-fed the children.
"مُرْضِعَةٌ" (*murziah*): a woman who breast-feeds (22:2). The plural here too is "مَرَاضِعُ" (*marazih*).
"اِسْتَرْضَعَ" (*istarzah*): wanted the (woman servant) to breast-feed the child (2:233).

R-Zd-Y   ر ض ى

"رَضِيَ" (*razia*), "يَرْضَى" (*yarzi*), "رِضْوَاناً" (*rizwana*), "رِضاً" (*rizan*): to agree with someone, to approve someone. But there is heartfelt agreement and willingness in it and no compulsion whatsoever.
"تَرَاضِيَاهْ" (*taraziayah*): both have agreed on something, with mutual agreement, both are agreed upon it.

| 2:232 | when the two (husband and wife) mutually agreed | إِذَا تَرَاضَوْا بَيْنَهُمْ بِالْمَعْرُوفِ |

"رَضِيَهُ لِهَذَا الْأَمْرِ" (*raziahu lihaazil amr*): considered him capable of it. Considered him capable of serving him and selected him for the job.
"اِرْتَضَاهُ لِصُحْبَتِهِ وَخِدْمَتِهِ" (*irrazahu lisuhbatihi wakhidmatihi*): considered him to be worth of companionship and service and hence recruited him for this purpose.

"رَضِيْتُ الشَّىْءَ وَبِهِ" (*razeetush shaiya wa behi*): I liked that thing and adopted it {T, L}.

2:120	The Christians and the Jews will never agree with you. They will never be in agreement.	لَنْ تَرْضٰى عَنْكَ الْيَهُوْدُ وَلَا النَّصٰرٰى

The Quran says that *momineen* will be "رَضِيَ اللهُ عَنْهُمْ وَرَضُوْا عَنْهُ" (*razi Allahu unhum wa razu unhu*) in 9:100. It is generally translated as "Allah agreed with them, and they became content with Allah". Since to agree and disagree are human emotions, this diverts the mind as if Allah too is subject to these feelings. He too is happy about something and displeased with some. Allah is free of all such emotions. Therefore the meaning of this verse is different. One thing should be clarified first here. When the human mind was in its infancy, it had the concept of god, goddesses or Allah as the king or ruler before him and in which there was nobody stronger than the king. His mind too sat Allah on a throne like the king. Then he thought that like the king, Allah too had those close to him who have some say in his rule. Also he has guards etc. and His subjects who have no right against him.

If a human being wanted to present some request before Him, he would also have to accompany it with presents and all. Also the request would have to be presented before God through one of His close ones. So that he could intervene on his/her behalf. These requests (or the king's other orders) were not subject to any rule. They depended on the king's whims. If he was happy then he could well grant a person an entire village. If he was angered then the man would face his wrath. This state of the king's happiness or displeasure was not according to any rule. As such man should strive to maximum to keep God happy. Presents, gifts, sacrifice, all this was aimed at keeping the Deity happy and in agreement. So that He remained in agreement with his subjects.

The Quran (and before it the holy scriptures of the messengers through revelation) dispelled this superstitious concept of God and replaced it with the right concept. This was that God was not like a hedge monist ruler. He has fixed a rule for everything, and the entire affairs of the universe are conducted according to the laws formulated by Him. For human affairs too, He has formulated principles (which are now safe in the Quran and have come through the messengers). Every human deed results according to those laws. He, like the kings, does not reward anyone for nothing or on a whim, nor does he get angry on a frivolous thing and punish him.

Along with this, the Quran also said that God has a fixed purpose for the human life, and the laws He has given are ones according to which a human must live, and thus reach his ultimate destiny. This road for humans is favored by God. That is, if man takes this path then he lives according to God's wishes, and if he does not then he goes against God's wishes. "God's agreement" or his displeasure as mentioned in the Quran signifies these meanings.

As for example, surah *Al-Ma'idah* says:

5:3	I have chosen Islam (security) as your way of living	وَرَضِيْتُ لَكُمُ الْإِسْلَامَ دِيناً

If man lives according to this code of conduct, then he traverses a way that is favored by God. This has been said as "رَضِيَ اللهُ عَنْهُ" (***raziallahu unhu***). On the other side, a ***momin's*** state is such that he loves the path of God, and dislikes other ways against it.

49:8	But God has made trust beloved in your hearts and one to believe, and made denial, and hypocrisy, and sins as disliked. Such people are on the right path, this is a benevolence from Allah. And Allah is aleem and hakeem (He knows and is tactful)	وَلَكِنَّ اللهَ حَبَّبَ إِلَيْكُمُ الْإِيْمَانَ وَزَيَّنَهُ فِيْ قُلُوْبِكُمْ وَكَرَّهَ إِلَيْكُمُ الْكُفْرَ وَالْفُسُوْقَ وَالْعِصْيَانَ- أُولَئِكِ هُمُ الرَّاشِدُوْنَ- فَضْلاً مِنَ اللهِ وَنِعْمَةً - وَاللَّهُ عَلِيْمٌ حَكِيْمٌ

For trust to become so enamored in the hearts is "رَضُوْا عَنْهُ" (***razu unhu***).

This will make one understand the meaning of "رَضِيَ اللهُ عَنْهُمْ وَرَضُوْا عَنْهُ" (***razi Allahu unhum wa razu unhu***) as in 9:100, for Allah to be in agreement means to traverse the path set out by Allah. And to agree with humans means for Allah's recommended path to become the beloved path in their hearts.

The Quran explains this matter at another place as well. As in surah *At-Taubah* it is said about the hypocrites:

9:8	They agree with you by word of mouth but their hearts deny it	يُرْضُوْنَكُمْ بِأَفْوَاهِهِمْ وَتَأْبَى قُلُوبُهُمْ

Here "إِرْضَاءٌ" (***irzaa***) has come opposite "أَبَى" (***aabaa***) which means to refute strongly. As such "رَضِىَ" (***raziun***) would mean to agree from the heart. This meaning is also explicit in surah *Al-Baqarah*, when these hypocrites are told "اِتَّقِ اللهَ" (***ittaqillah***) in 2:206, or protect the laws of Allah, they do not do so. After that the ***momineen*** are mentioned. That they live a life of "ابْتِغَاءَ مَرْضَاتِ اللهِ" (***ibtigha'a marazatillah***) in 2:208, which means according to Allah's laws. Further ahead it is said:

2:208	Enter into (the domain of) God's obedience entirely	أُدْخُلُوْا فِى السِّلْمِ كَافَّةً
8:2-6	do not follow ungodly orders	لَاتَتَّبِعُوْا خُطُوَاتِ الشَّيْطِنِ

When all these pieces are kept in mind, it becomes clear what "مَرْضَاتِ اللهِ" (***marzaatillah***) means. That is, the obedience of Allah's laws with full willingness.
This is also the meaning of "رَضِيَ اللهُ عَنْهُمْ وَرَضُوْا عَنْهُ" (***raziullahu unhum warizwanuhu***). That is, due to following Allah's laws, these people live peacefully and in harmony. Their entire life is spent according to these laws, and the happy results of following Allah's laws accompany them.

The good results accompany them and due to this, their love for the love of Allah's laws increases.

This is called "اِتَّبَعَ رِضْوَانَ اللهِ" (**ittqba'a rizwanillah**) in 3:161 ز

Against which has been stated "بَاءَبِسَخَطٍ مِنَ اللهِ" (**ba'a bisakhatin minallah**). See heading (S-Kh-Th).

Surah **Mohammed** makes it clear that "رِضْوَانَهُ" (**rizwanahu**) means the same as "مَاأَنزَّلَ اللهُ" (**ma nazzalallahu**) (47:28). That is, the Quran.

Earlier it has been stated "كَرِهُوا مَاأَنزَّلَ اللهُ" (**karihu ma anzalallah**) in (47:26) and after it has been said "كَرِهُوا رِضْوَانَهُ" (**karihu rizwaanahu**) in 47:28. This means that "رِضْوَانَهُ" (**rizwaanahu**) is to follow the Quran and "سَخَطَ" (**sakhatun**) is following ungodly laws. Therefore **momineen** are wont to fully obey and follow the Quran "مَاأَنزَلَ اللهُ" (**ma anzalallah**). They tune their entire life to the Quranic laws. And the result as per the laws of Nature is the delights and pleasantness of life which accompany them. This sort of life is "عِيْشَةٍ رَّاضِيَةٍ" (**eeshatir raaziyah**) (101:7).

Surah **Maryam** says that **Zikaria** prayed to God for a son and said:

19:6	And make him pleasing of my Sustainer	وَاجْعَلْهُ رَبِّ رَضِيّاً

Here "رَضِيّاً" (**raziyyah**) means either beloved or favored or that he (the son) may be a person who lives his life according to Your laws.

Taj-u-Uroos says that "رَضِيٌّ" (**razzi**) means obedient.

Surah **At-Taubah** says that the **momineen** have been promised "جَنَّاتٍ" (**jannaat**) by Allah, and "مَسَاكِنَ طَيِّبَةً" (**massakinit tayyibah** – decent residences).

Later, it is said:

9:79	Allah's 'rizwaan' is greater than all this. And this is a great achievement.	وَرِضْوَانٌ مِّنَ اللهِ أَكْبَرُ ذَالِكَ هُوَ الْفَوْزُ الْعَظِيْمُ

This verse points to a great truth. The question is what happens due to trust and 'righteous deeds'? The human being is a compound of this physical life and his ego or personality. Life's success is that his physical being is good as well as the development of his ego. The development of a human being means that whatever latent capabilities he has, develops and is manifested. Allah's personality or persona is a complete persona, in which all His qualities are in full bloom. These very same qualities are present in humans too, but only to the extent a human being can have them. That is, on a much smaller scale. The development of human personality means that those traits grow. Now it is obvious that the more developed a human personality will be the more qualities of Allah he will reflect and to a greater degree.

With trust and good deeds the human personality is developed while he also gets the benefits of a good life. The Quran says that life's delights are very valuable too, and to get them is a big achievement. But the real success is that the human personality reflects the traits of God. " ذَٰلِكَ (*zalika huwal fauzil azeem*).

The result of good deeds is that on one's life becomes successful and delightful, and secondly his internal self also experiences a great change. This revolution (i.e. for human personality to be developed) is a very great success.

This has been said in another way:

| 50:35 | There will be everything in jannat which you may desire, and We have even more than that | لَهُمْ مَّا يَشَاؤُونَ فِيهَا وَلَدَيْنَا مَزِيدٌ |

This means that man's wishes can only be according to his mental level but in the life of *jannat*, this level will be raised and then they will wish for, and get that which is much beyond the level at present. That is, his personality will be developed in such a way that the present level of his comprehension is unable to grasp it.

But we should not overlook the fact that such development of a human personality can take place only in a Quranic society, not in secluded worship houses. Thus we see that "رضوان من الله" (*rizwaan minal lah*) or "مرضات الله" (*marazaatillah*) is the name of living according to the Quran and the good results that follow from it.

Surah *Al-Ambia* says:

| 21:28 | And they do not put in words for anyone, except for those who has His good pleasure | وَلَا يَشْفَعُونَ إِلَّا لِمَنِ ارْتَضَىٰ |

See heading (Sh-F-Ain).

R-Te-B   ر ط ب

"اَلرَّطْبُ" (*ar-ratb*), is the opposite of "يَابِسٌ" (*yaabis* - dry): i.e. moist, or fresh and dewy. Hence it means soft, fresh branch, green grass, green land etc.
"اَلرُّطَبُ" (*ar-rutab*): a kind of date *{T}*.

The Quran says:

| 19:25 | selected dates | رُطَبًا جَنِيًّا |
| 6:59 | Freshness of everything is found in the code of life for the universe. | وَلَا رَطْبٍ وَّلَا يَابِسٍ إِلَّا فِىْ كِتَابٍ مُّبِيْنٍ |

For "رَطْبٌ وَ يَابِسٌ" (*ratbi wa yabisun*), see heading (Y-B-S).

In verse 19:25, it is said that *Isa* (Jesus) was born in a season when trees were laden with ripe dates. This means that according to the Quran, *Isa* was not born in December, as generally believed. In that month there is a harsh winter in Palestine and it is not the season for fresh dates. Nowadays even the Christian historians are agreeing with the view that Jesus was not born on 25th December (Christmas). The Christians had borrowed this idea from the Iranians who thought that 25th December is Jesus' birthday. And 25th March as the Day of the resurrection. They also believed that *Mithra* (Zoroastrian deity) would return during the last days of the world. (See page 51 of by book *Meraaj Insaaniyat*).

R-Ain-B   ر ع ب

"رَعَبَ الحَوْضَ" (*ra'abal hauz*): filled the (small) pool.
"رَعَبَ السَّيْلُ الوَادِیَ" (*a'abas sailul wadi*): the flood filled the valley; to cut something.
"رَعَبَ السَّنَامَ" (*ra'abas sanaam*): he cut the hump (of the camel).
"اَلتِّرْ عِيْنَةُ" (*attareeba*): the hump that was cut {T}.

Raghib says that due to being filled with fear, "اَلرُّعْبُ" (*ar-roab*) means to become speechless {R}. This word is also used for just fear. Surah *Al-Kahaf* says:

| 18:18 | lest you become fearful due to it | وَلَمُلِئْتَ مِنْهُمْ رُعْباً |

The *momineen* should be so powerful that their opponents, upon seeing them in battle, shake with fear. But this is only possible when they bow before Allah's laws and of none else. This is what we know as "توحيد" (*tauheed*), while *shirk* (to follow other rules as well) definitely results in fear.

Surah *Aal-e-Imran* says:

| 3:150 | We will put fear into the hearts of these deniers, because they include others with Allah (in following laws) | سَنُلْقِیْ فِیْ قُلُوْبِ الَّذِیْنَ كَفَرُوا الرُّعْبَ بِمَآ أَشْرَكُوْا بِا اللهِ--- |

R-Ain-D   ر ع د

"رَعْدٌ" (*raad*): thunder. It also means to shake or tremble. It figuratively also means scolding or dressing down.
"اَلرَّعَّادُ" (*ar-ra·ad*): a man who talks tall, talks too much {T}.

Ibn Faris says it means basically movement and unease.

In the Quran this word has been used as meaning thunder (13:13, 2:19)

| 13:13 | Raad is busy in carrying out its ordained task | وَيُسَبِّحُ الرَّعْدُ بِحَمْده |

This means that it is an epitome of Allah's praise with its positive result See headings (S-B-H) and (H-M-D). Every force of the universe is engaged in its ordained task, and the collective result of their efforts is a constructive addition to the universe. When viewed separately, some of these forces evoke fear (like lightning and thunder) but collectively their result is constructive. And this is the manifestation of Allah's praise.

R-Ain-N   ر ع ن

"اَلرُّعُونَةٌ" (ar-rao'nah): means foolishness. It is also said that "رُعُونَةٌ" (rao'na) means sparseness of thought and "حُمْقٌ" (humaq) means refutation of intellect or thought {M}.

"اَلْأَرْعَنُ" (al-arun): a man who talks nonsense, fool, lazy and lackadaisical.
"رَعُنَ الرَّجُلُ" (ra-unir rajul): that fool talked nonsense and became loose.
"رُعِنَ" (ro'in): he fainted {T}.

Ibn Faris says its basic meanings are to be projected ahead and to be high or elevated. Second meaning is of nonsense, worries and unease.

"رَاعِنَا" (ra'ina): the Jews used to address the Messenger (**pbuh**) by this word (4:46). It was meant to tie him up with "رعونت" (ra-oonat) but they used to say it as "رَاعِنَا" (ra'ina) which means to condescend, to bear with us {R}, or as they say in English, "I beg your pardon".

For detailed meaning of "رَاعِنَا" (ra'ina), see heading (R-Ain-Y).

R-Ain-Y   ر ع ى

"اَلرِّعْىُ" (ar-riou): grass.
"اَلرَّعْىُ" (ar-raayou), "اَلْمَرْعَى" (al-mar'aa): to graze grass.
"اَلْمَرْعَاةُ" (al-mar'aa'a): grazing land, also the grass which is grazed.
"رَعَى" (ra-aya), "يَرْعَى" (yar'aa), "رَعْياً" (rayuia): the animals grazed, or left the animals to graze.
"اَلرَّاعِىُ" (ar-raee): shepherd, one of the plurals is "رِعَاءٌ" (riaa-un). See 28:32 {T}.

Raghib says "رِعْىٌّ" (ray'un) actually is to look after an animal and protect it in every way, whether it is to preserve its life by feeding it, or by protecting it from enemies etc. {R}. But later this word came into use for protecting and looking after everything.

"رَعَى أَمْرَهُ" (as-raee amrahu): looked after his affair and protected it.

"رَعَى النُّجُومَ وَرَاعَاهَا" (*raeen nujum wara'aha*): he kept track of the stars and their speed and looked after them *{T}*.

"مُرَاعَاةٌ" (*mura'atun*) means to look after something specifically, to protect someone.

"رَاعَىٰ أَمْرَهُ" (*raaya amruhu*): he looked after his affair very well and kept an eye on his wealth.

"اَلرَّعِيَّةُ" (*ar-raeeyah*): the animals which are looked after or which are left to graze. It also means those people who have some administrator for their affairs and who are watched over by someone *{T}*.

Ibn Faris says it basically means to protect and oversee.

Surah **Taha** says:

20:54	feed your cattle	وَارْعَوْا أَنْعَامَكُمْ

"اَلْمَرْعَىٰ" (*al-mar'aa*): grass or fodder (87:4).

Surah **Al-Hadees** says about Monasticism:

57:27	they could not protect it the way it should have been protected	فَمَا رَعَوْهَا حَقَّ رِعَايَتِهَا

Surah **Al-mominoon** says:

23:8	those who protect their goods and keep their promises sacred	وَالَّذِينَ هُمْ لِأَمَانَاتِهِمْ وَعَهْدِهِمْ رَاعُونَ

In surah **Al-Baqrah**, the group of **momineen** have been asked not to say "رَاعِنَا" (*raa ina*) like the Jews (2:102). The Jews used to twist the words while addressing the Messenger (*pbuh*) in order to change the meanings of the spoken words. The word "رَاعِنَا" (*ra'ina*) was among such twisted words. This was the peak of their lowliness that they had even given up normal courtesy and came down to street language.

They used to say the word in such a way, as to make it a derivative of "رُعُونَت" (*ra'onat*). See heading (R-Ain-Y). But **Al-Minar** says that "رَاعِنَا" (*raa ina*) is derived from "مُرَاعَاة" (*mura ah*). In this way "رَاعِنَا" (*ra'ina*) would mean that you concede to us and then we will concede to you. To use such words for the Messenger (*pbuh*) is open disrespect and unbecoming. *{Al-Minar* vol.1 page 410}. That is, the messenger should be obeyed unconditionally which actually is obedience of Allah and their life's duty. They should say "أُنْظُرْنَا" (*unzarna*) to the Messenger (*pbuh*) messenger. It means, look after us lest we become wayward, and they should not only listen to all his orders but obey them as well. "وَاسْمَعُوا" (*wasma'o*) (2:102).

But in my opinion, this verse tells even those who trust, to abstain from such acts and talk in which good and bad are mixed, or their difference is difficult to comprehend readily. If some saying or act has even a doubt that anything (word or deed) insulting the Messenger (*pbuh*), then that should be avoided and the purity of intent must not be cited for saying or doing them. Everything a Muslim says or does must be clear and unambiguous. There is no room for a poetic license sort of thing here.

R-Gh-B   ر غ ب

Ibn Faris says it means basically to demand or wish, and vastness.

"رَغْبَةٌ" (**raghbah**): actually it means for something to become vast or wide.

"رَغُبَ الشَّيِءُ" (**raghubash shaiyi**): the thing became vast.

"حَوْضٌ رَغِيبٌ" (**raghiba hauzun**): a vast pool.

"اَلرَّغْبَة" (**ar-raghbaha**), "اَلرَّغْبُ" (**ar-raghbu**): to wish very much, the vastness of intent {R}.

"وَادٍ رَغِيبٌ" (**raghib waadin**): a broad valley which can hold a lot of water.

"تَرَاغَبَ الْمَكَانُ" (**taraghabal makaan**): the place widened, became vast.

"أَرْغَبَ اللهُ قَدْرَکَ" (**arghabal lahu qadraka**): May God increase your respect or rank.

"اَلرِّغَابُ" (**ar-righaab**): animals which give a lot of milk and are very beneficial.

"رَغِيبٌ" (**ragheeb**): every vast and broad thing {T}

Raghib says "رَغِبَ فِيْهِ يا رَغِبَ اِلَيْهِ" (**raghiba fihi ya raghiba ilaih**): to wish for something and to long for it (with the broadness of intent). "اِنَّا اِلَى اللهِ رَاغِبُوْنَ" (**inna ilal lahi raaghiboon**) as in 9:59 also means the same. Also in 68:32 and "رَغِبَ عَنْهُ" (**raghiba unhu**) means to turn away one's liking from it {R}.

| 2:130 | Who can turn away from the leadership of Ibrahim? | وَمَنْ يَرْغَبُ عَنْ مِلَّةِ اِبْرَاهِيْمَ |

Also in 19:46 "رَاغِبٌ" (**raghib**) has been followed by "عَنْ" (**un**). At these places, this word means to take away liking from.

Surah **An-Nisa** says:

| 4:127 | you do not want to give widows and orphan girls what they should be given according to God's laws, and yet you want to wed them | لَا تُؤْتُوْنَهُنَّ مَاكُتِبَ لَهُنَّ وَتَرْغَبُوْنَ اَنْ تَنْكِحُوْهُنَّ |

Taj-ul-Uroos explains further that "رَغِبَ فِيْهِ" (**raghiba feeh**) means liked him, intended it.

R-Gh-D رغ د

"عِيْشَةٌ رَغَدٌ" (*eeshatun raghadun*) "رَغَدٌ" (*raghadah*): good, abundant and delightful earning.

"رَغِدَ عَيْشُهُمْ" (*raghida aishehum*): their lives became delightful and their earning (income) abundant or vast.

"أَرْغَدُوا مَوَاشِيَهُمْ" (*arghdiu mawashiahum*): they left their cattle to graze freely.

"أَرْغَدُوا" (*arghadu*): they reached a fertile land {T, M}.

"اَلرَّغَدُ" (*ar-raghadu*): abundant wealth, water, grass, earning etc. which causes no constriction and which is no cause for any worry {T}.

In surah *Al-Baqarah*, the characteristics of *janna* (heavenly society), have been detailed as that in which earnings will be "رَغَدًا حَيْثُ شِئْتُمَا" (*raghadan haisu shai'tuma*) (2:35). That is, life's necessities can be easily fulfilled from anywhere.

Surah *Taha* says in this context that in such a society the edibles, clothing and the basic necessities of life will be available without any effort (20:118), and man shall not be deprived of these.

Surah *An-Nahal* says:

16:112	The basic characteristic of such a heavenly society on earth is that every necessity of life is easily available to everybody, everywhere and in abundance	يَأْتِيهَا رِزْقُهَا رَغَدًا مِنْ كُلِّ مَكَانٍ

In such a society, people cannot inveigle the fountainheads of sustenance for themselves only. All means for development of the human being and his capabilities are freely available to all and it is the responsibility of that system that it ensures that nobody is deprived and everything is available to him in abundance.

"رَغَدًا حَيْثُ شِئْتُمَا" (*raghadan haiso shai'tuma*): available feely from wherever he wants.

R-Gh-M رغ م

"اَلرَّغْمُ" (*ar-raghm*), "اَلرُّغْمُ" (*ar-rughm*), "اَلرِّغْمُ" (*ar-righm*): dislike, abhorrence.

"اَلرَّغْمُ" (*ar-raghm*) or "اَلرَّغَامُ" (*ar-raghaam*) actually means 'dust'.

"أَرْغَمَ الذُّلَّ" (*arghanaz-zullu*): his face was rubbed in the dirt. This also means to make one obey forcibly.

"اَلْمَرْغَمُ" (*al-margham*) means 'nose' {T}.

"اَلْمُرَاغَمُ" (*al-muragham*): a place where one may go after running away, or after being angry with someone. Later it also came to mean fort, path, and spaciousness and abundance {T}.

Ibn Faris says it has two basic meanings. One is of dirt, while the other is of a path or a place to run away to.

The Quran says that anyone who migrates in order to establish Allah's system:

4:100	will find lots of sanctuaries in the world where he will find abundance	يَجِدْ فِى الْأَرْضِ مُرَاغَماً

And if the opponents have closed one door for him, then dozens of doors will open up.

R-F-T   ر ف ت

"رُفَاتٌ" (*rufaat*): chaff or that which falls off from a dry thing. Hence it means old pieces and bits.
"اِرْفَتَّ الْحَبْلُ" (*irfattal hubl*): the rope broke into pieces.
"رَفَتَهُ" (*rafatah*), "يَرْفُتُهُ" (*yarfutuh*): to break something, to pound or turn into small pieces. Like earth or old bones {T, R}.

Surah **Bani Israel** says:

17:49	will we be raised even after our bones turn to dust?	اَاِذَ اكُنَّا عِظَا ماً وَّ رُفَاتاً

Like today's materialists, they too thought that their life was confined only to their physical being. If the elements of life disintegrate, then life can't go on. Their thoughts have been dispelled by saying that God, who created them the first time, is capable of maintaining life without these physical elements as well (17:51). This is what life after death is.

R-F-Th   ر ف ث

"اَلرَّفَثُ" (*ar-rafas*) is a composite word and means everything to do with sexual intercourse, from the initial conversation to the climax {T}.

Muheet says it means a man who performs the intercourse {T, R}. It also means cases of sexual intercourse.

Raghib says it means sexual intercourse or talk about it, the mentioning of which is deemed improper.

Ibn Faris says it actually means sexual intercourse but is used for anything which a man feels shame to express.

"اَلرَّفَثُ" (*rafas*) means abuse or inappropriate talk as well.

In the context of *Hajj*, it is said "فَلَا رَفَثَ" (*fala rafas*) in 2:197. It means that during *Hajj* no dirty thought should enter the mind. No such act should be committed nor should any conversation which has a sexual overtone, be made.

About fasting, the Quran says:

2:187	you can go to your wives for sexual intercourse in the nights of the month of fasting	أُحِلَّ لَكُمْ لَيْلَةَ الصِّيَامِ الرَّفَثُ اِلٰى نِسَاءِكُمْ

Here the Quran by using "اِلٰى نِسَاءِكُمْ" (*ila nisaikum*) (your women), has made it clear that it means sexual intercourse.

R-F-D   ر ف د

"اَلرِّفْدُ" (*ar-rifd*): Gift, compensation. It also means something with which one gives support, help, share or luck.

"رَفَدَهُ" (*rafadah*), "يَرْفِدُهُ" (*yarfiduhu*), "رَفْدًا" (*rafda*): he helped him, or gave him aid.

"اَلْاِرْفَادُ" (*al-irfaad*): to help, to gift, to endow. It is actually the cloth or other soft material under the camel's seat so that it does not hurt the animal's back.

"رِفَادَةٌ" (*rifadah* .): piece of cloth to wipe the wound. It also means the contribution that was gathered in the days of ignorance by the *Quresh* tribe for the needy pilgrims forage.

"اَلْاِرْتِفَادُ" (*al-irtifaad*): to labor, to strive, to earn *{T, R}*.

Surah *Hood* says:

11:99	how bad a gift or compensation it is	بِئْسَ الرِّفْدُ الْمَرْفُودُ

That is, how bad is the help which has been given them or with which they have been supported.

R-F-Ain   ر ف ع

"رَفَعَ" (*raf'a*), "يَرْفَعُ" (*yarf'a*): to elevate.

Raghib has said sometimes "رَفْعٌ" (*rafa*) means to lift a material object, sometimes to build up a wall at the time of construction and take it to a height, sometimes to elevate fame or mention or sometimes to elevate the grade *{T, R}*.

Ibn Faris says it means basically means to elevate and pick. It also means to bring a thing closer, or to spread or make manifest.

"رَفَعَ" (*raf'a*) is used in various meanings. Its basic meaning contains the sense of intensity or exaggeration. That is to do whatever, quickly and intensely.

"رَفَعَ الْبَعِيرُ فِىْ سَيْرِهٖ" (*as-rafaal baeeru fi sairihi*): the camel increased his speed.

"رَفَعَ الْقَوْمُ" (**raf'al qaum**): the people went up to the heights.

"بَرْقٌ رَافِعٌ" (**barqun raaf'ih**): the lightning which shines high above.

"اَلرِّ فَاعَةُ" (**ar-rifa'ah**): the harshness of sound and intensity.

"رَفُعَ" (**raf'u**), "رِفْعَةٌ" (**rif'ah**): to be gentlemanly and of high stature {T}.

The Quran says:

| 2:63 | We raised the mount of Toor near your head | رَفَعْنَا فَوْقَكُمُ الطُّوْرَ |

That is, you were at the bottom and the mount was above you. In connotation of being the height of a building, it says in the context of the construction of the **Kaba**:

| 2:127 | when Ibrahim was raising the foundations of this house | إِذْ يَرْفَعُ إِبْرَاهِيْمُ الْقَوَاعِدَ |

"رَفَعَ صَوْتاً" (**rafa'a sautan**): raised voice.

"رَفَعَ صَوْتَهُ فَوْقَ صَوْتِهِ" (**rafa'a sautahu fauqa sautehi**): literally, it means to raise one's voice above another's, but figuratively it means to impose one's opinion over another's (49:2).

About the elevation of grade, it is said about **Idrees**:

| 19:57 | We granted him elevated grade | وَ رَفَعْنٰهُ مَكَاناً عَلِيّاً |

God has himself called himself "رَفِيْعُ الدَّرَجَاتِ" (**rafiud darajaat**) in 40:15, that is, he did not reach His elevated position gradually, but He is there from the beginning. That is, He is above the process of evolution and progress. It also means supremacy and authority.

"رَفِيْعُ الدَّرَجٰتِ" (**rafud darjaat**): of high grade, that is, of high ranks. It could also mean one who elevates stages or grades or ranks.

In surah **Al-Waaqiah** where "رَافِعَةٌ" (**raafiah**) has come opposite "خَافِضَةٌ" (**khafizah**), there too, it means this. That is, the one who gets elevated to great heights.

About **Isa** it is said "بَلْ رَفَعَهُ اللهُ اِلَيْهِ" (**bal rafahul lahu ilaih**) in 4:158, there too the meaning is that Allah elevated him and brought him close to Himself. If "رَفَعَ" (**rafa**) is taken to mean that he was lifted physically, then one would have to accept that God is at a certain place. Because whenever it is said that something has gone towards something, the thing towards which it has gone, has to be at a fixed place. It is against the Quran to believe that God is confined to any one place.

That is why "بَلْ رَفَعَهُ اللهُ اِلَيْهِ" (**bal rafahul laahu ilaih**) would mean that Allah elevated him and brought him closer to Him. Details will be found in my book **Sholayi Mastoor** in the tale about **Isa**.

About the Messenger **Mohammed** it is said:

94:4	we elevated your greatness	وَ رَفَعْنَالَكَ ذِكْرَكَ

For "رَفَعَ" (**rafa'a**) and "صَعِدَ" (**sa'ida**) as in 35:10, see heading (Sd-Ain-D).

R-F-F   ر ف ف

"رَفٌّ" (**ruff**) has a lot of meanings but the Quran only uses "رَفْرَفٌ" (**rafrafun**) in 55:76.
"رَفَّ الطَّائِرُ" (**raffat-tairu**) and "رَفْرَفَ" (**rafraf**): the bird opened up its wings in the air.
"اَلرَّفْرَفُ" (**ar-rufruf**): scattered leaves.
"اَلرَّفْرَفُ" (**ar-rafrufu**): mat, beddings, pillows, also green colored mattresses which are laid over floor covering to sleep. Some say it means the hem etc. of a tent's curtain, but generally it means floor covering or bedding *{T, R}*.

Ibn Faris says it means gardens, beddings, and green clothing.

R-F-Q   ر ف ق

"اَلْمِرْفَقُ" (**al-mirfaq**): elbow. Plural is "مَرَافِقْ" (**marafiq**). It also means softness and facility.
"رَفَقَ النَّاقَةَ" (**rafaqan naaqah**): the camel's elbow was fastened so that it does not run away.
"رِفَاقٌ" (**rifaaq**): the rope with which one's arm is tied (to its hind legs). This led to "اَلرُّفْقَةُ" (**al-rifqah**) meaning companion in the group (because while walking, their elbows touch each other). When the group disperses then the word "رِفْقَةٌ" (**rifqah**) is not used for them, but every companion can be called "رَفِيقٌ" (**rafiq**).
"اَلرُّفَاقَةُ" (**ar-rufaaqah**): group or party.
"اِرْتَفَقَ" (**irtafaq**): he leaned on the elbow.
"اَلْمُرْتَفَقُ" (**al-murtafaq**): anything which is leaned on, such as pillow or any other support {M}. Since this sort of leaning gives comfort, "اِرْتَفَقَ بِهِ" (**irtafaqa behi**) means benefited from it.
"رَفَقَ بِهِ" (**rafaqa behi**) or "رَفَقَ عَلَيْهِ" (**rafaqa ilaih**): dealt with him softly {T}.

Ibn Faris says that this root basically means to be close to one another and agree mutually without any violence or coercion.

The Quran says:

4:69	They are good companions	حَسُنَ أُولَئِكَ رَفِيقاً

Hence it means companions whose companionship during travel completes one's shortcomings so that the balance in his personality and the society is maintained. For 'elbow' this word has been used in 5:6.

Surah *Al-Kahaf* says:

| 18:16 | He will facilitate or provide ease in the purpose before you | يُهَيِّئْ لَكُمْ مِنْ اَمْرِكُمْ مَرْفَقاً |

The same surah calls *janna* (heavenly society) as حَسُنَتْ مُرْتَفَقاً" (*hasunat murtafaqa*) in 18:31 and *jahannum* (hellish society) as "سَاءَتْ مُرْتَفَقاً" (*sa'at murtafaqa*) in 18:29, that is, a place to lean on, or on whose support one can rise. Life in *jahannum* is such that man cannot traverse the evolutionary stages with its support. Life in *janna*, however, is such that it is the best support for rising high and going towards the heights. It is a support which never lets the balance be unbalanced, that is, "حَسُنَتْ مُرْتَفَقاً" (*hasunat murtafaqa*). Supports are present in a *jahannami* or hellish society too, but they are quite uneven. That is why they cannot support a man for standing on his own two feet. His personality's development can't be helped by them. Only *jannati* society's supports can help a man do so. And while keeping their balance, they progress ahead.

R-Q-B   رق ب

"اَلرَّقَبَة" (*ar-raqabah*): neck.
"رَقَبَهُ" (*raqabahu*): tied a rope around his neck, since when a man's necked is roped, he becomes obedient and thus this word generally began to mean a slave. Plural is "اَلرَّقَبُ" (*ar-raqab*).

"اَلرِّقَابُ" (*ar-riqaab*) means 'slave' as used in 2:177. Singular is "رَقَبَةٌ" (*raqabah*) as used in 4:92 {T}.

"رَقَبَ" (*raqab*), "يَرْقُبْ" (*yarqub*): to wait for, and to protect and look after.
"وَلَمْ تَرْقُبْ قَوْلِيْ" (*walam tarqub qauli*), as in 20:94. Here it can mean wait for, as well as to look after, and to consider. "يَتَرَقَّبُ" (*yataraqqab*) in 28:18 also has this meaning but with reference to the context, it may mean to wait anxiously, or more appropriate, be looking for something.

Taj-ul-Uroos says it means to expect something and to wait for it.

Raghib says it means to avoid something while waiting for something. That is, they used to raise their head to see whether someone was coming or not.

"اَلرَّقِيْبُ" (*ar-raqeeb*) means the protector, or one who looks after something, or one who waits for something, or one who looks after (1:4, 33:52)

Ibn Faris says it means basically to oversee something. The neck is also called "اَلرَّقَبَة" (*ar-raqabah*) because it remains erect and at attention when looking for something.

It may also mean to consider someone's feelings and to uphold someone's words. This word has been used in 9:8 and in 20:94.

"اِرْتَقَبَ الشَّیْءَ" (**artaqabash shaiyi**): to wait for something.

"اِرْتَقَبَ الْمَکَانَ" (**irtaqabal makaan**): to climb to some place, or to be raised.

"مَرْقَبَة" (**marqabah**): a place to climb.

"اِلرَّقْبَة" (**ariqbah**): protection and to fear, apprehend. It is used in both these meanings {T}.

Surah **Ad-Dukhaan** says "فَارْتَقِبَایَا" (**fartaqabaaya**) in 44:59, 44:10. Here it means to wait for.

Surah **Yunus** says:

10:102	Tell them to wait, and you as well wait with them.	قُلْ فَانْتَظِرُوْا اِنِّیْ مَعَکُمْ مِنَ الْمُنْتَظِرِیْنَ

R-Q-D   ر ق د

"اَلرَّقْدُ" (**ar-raqd**), "اَلرُّقَادُ" (**ar-ruqaad**), "اَلرُّقُوْدُ" (**ar-ruqud**): to sleep. In the Quran, this word has been used opposite "یَقَظْ" (**yaqaz**), or awakening.

18:18	you think they are awake whereas they are sleeping	وَتَحْسَبُهُمْ اَیْقَاظاً وَّهُمْ رُقُوْدٌ

"مَرْقَدٌ" (**marqad**): bedroom, sleeping place.

Surah **Yasin** says:

36:52	who awakened us from our sleeping places (bedrooms)	مَنْ بَعَثَنَا مِنْ مَرْقَدِنَا

Raghib says "اَلرُّقَادُ" (**aruqaad**) means a good nap {R}.

This clarifies the context of 18:18 in surah **Al-Kahaf** that they did not take a long sleep, they used to nap but that too with the caution that outsiders think that they were awake. This means that they were not oblivious of their safety at any time.

R-Q-Q   ر ق ق

Ibn Faris says it basically means fineness and softness.

"اَلرَّقُّ" (**ar-raq**), "اَلرَّقُّ" (**ar-riq**): thin membrane or skin used for writing.

"اَلرَّقُّ" (**ar-raq**): white page, white page with some writing on it {T, R}.

"اَلرَّقُّ" (**ar-raq**), "اَلرَّقِیْق" (**ar-raqeeq**): thin or fine thing.

"اَلرَّقَّة" (**ar-riqqah**): softness of the heart.

"اَلرَّقُّ" (**ar-riq**): slavery {T, R}.

The Quran says:

52:2-3	written book on fine, thin membrane	وَکِتَبٍ مَسْطُوْرٍ فِیْ رَقٍّ مَنْشُوْرٍ

R-Q-M ر ق م

"رَقَمَ" (*raqam*), "يَرْقُمُ" (*yarqam*), "رَقْماً" (*raqma*): to write.
"رَقَمَ الكِتَابَ" (*raqamal kitaab*): wrote the book with punctuation so that the book was clear.

The Quran says:

83:9	clearly written book	كِتَابٌ مَرْقُومٌ

"رَقَمَ الثَّوْبَ" (*raqamus saub*): to make lines on the cloth and make marks to determine the price.
"دَابَّةٌ مَرْقُومَةٌ" (*da-abbatun marqumah*): the animal which has branding marks on his legs or lines *{T}*.

Ibn Faris says it basically means writing and to make lines.

With reference to **Khalil**, he says "اَلرَّقْمُ" (*ar-raqm*) means to make clear the writing with the help of punctuation, and a book is called "كِتَابٌ مَرْقُومٌ" (*kitabum marqum*) when it is well punctuated. The Quran says "أَصْحَابُ الْكَهْفِ والرَّقِيْمِ" (*ashaabul kahfin warraqeem*) in 18.9. It is generally taken to mean that the affairs about the caved people was written on a metal plate and affixed outside the cave. Thus they were called "أَصْحَابُ الرَّقِيْمِ" (*ashabur raqeem*).

"مَرْقُومٌ" (*marqum*) means written, but recent research says that this is the same word which has been termed as "رَاقِيْمْ" (*raaqeem*) in the **Torah**. This was the name of a city which became famous as **Petra** and which the Arabs called **Batrah**. It was situated north of the **Sinai** and **Bay of Aqaba** on a plateau. When in the second century A.D, the Romans merged Syria and Palestine; this city became famous as a Roman colony. After the First World War, big caves were discovered there with ruins of buildings in and outside caves. It is believed that according to 18:9, the "أَصْحَابُ الْكَهْفِ والرَّقِيْمِ" (*ashaabul Kahafi war raqeem*) had taken shelter in one of these very caves where later a statue was built to commemorate them. Also see heading *ashaabul kahaf wir raqeem*.

R-Q-W ر ق و

"اَلرَّقْوُ" (*ar-raqwu*): small, sand dune.
"اَلرَّقْوَةُ" (*ar-ruqwah*): the upper part of the chest below the throat where one sees a man breathing, the collar bone. Plural is "تَرَاقٍ" (*taraq*) and "اَلتَّرَاقِیْ" (*at-taraaqi*) {T, M}.

75:26	When the breath comes above the chest (when you are about to die). When the end is near.	إذَ بَلَغَتِ التَّرَاقِی

The real meaning here is to climb.

"رَقَاالطَّائِرُ" (*raq at tair*) means the bird rose in its flight. See heading (R-Q-Y).

R-Q-Y   ر ق ى

"رَقِىَ" (*raqi*), "يَرْقَى" (*yarqa*), "رَقْيًا" (*raqya*), "رُقِيًّا" (*ruqiyya*): to climb, or to progress and prosper {T, M}.

The Quran says:

17:93	Or, climb up to the sky	أَوْتَرْقَى فِى السَّمَاءِ

"اَلتَّرْقُوَةُ" (*at-tarquwah*): collar bone where one can see the breath climbing. Plural is "تَرَاقٍ" (*taraqin*) and "اَلتَّرَاقِى" (*at- taraaqi*).

The Quran says:

75:26	When it reaches the collar bone	إِذَا بَلَغَتِ التَّرَاقِىَ

See also heading (R-Q-W).

"اَلرُّقْيَةُ" (*ar-ruqiyah*), "رَقَاهُ رَقْيًا" (*raqaho raqiya*) a sort of thing.
"وَرِقَةٌ" (*wariqah*), "وَرْقِيَةً" (*varqiyah*): He cast a spell over him or dispelled a spell.
"رَاقٍ" (*raaq*): one who cast spell.

The Quran says:

75:26	And is there anyone who can save himself by casting a spell?	وَقِيلَ مَنْ رَاقٍ

Note: Some scholars of the dictionary accept "ت" (t) in the word but I think that "ت" (t) is additional and the root of the word is (R-Q-W).

Ibn Faris has said that "رَقِّى" (*raqi*) means to climb, or spells etc.

"اَلْمَرْقَاةُ" (*al-marqatu*) and "اَلْمِرّ قَاةُ" (*al-mirqaat*): climbing ladder {T}.
"اَلرَّقَّاءُ" (*ar-raqa'u*): mountain climber {T}.

R-K-B   ر ك ب

"رَكِبَهُ" (*rakibahu*), "يَرْكُبُهُ" (*yarkubuh*), "رُكُوبًا" (*rukuba*): to climb something, to rise, to mount {T}, either on an animal or on boards a boat etc.

18:71	when the two got on board the boat	إِذَا رَكِبَا فِى السَّفِينَةِ

"رَاکِبٌ" (*raakib*): passenger. The plural is "اَلرَّکْبُ" (*ar-rakb*) as in 8:42. "رُکْبَانٌ" (*rukbaan*) as in 2:239, is the opposite of "رِجَالاً" (*rijaala*), which means on foot.

"اَلرِّکَابُ" (*ar-rikaab*): the camels which are ridden (59:6). The singular is "رَاحِلَةٌ" (*raahila*) which is from a different root.

"رَکُوبٌ" (*rakub*): an animal which is used for riding (36:72).

"رَکَّبَ" (*rakkaba*): to put one thing on top of another, or to fix {T}. To make something climb {M}, to arrange (82:8).

"مُتَرَاکِباً" (*mutraakiba*): one on top of another (6:100).

About man it is said in the Quran, that he has traversed various stages and will keep on traversing evolutionary stages and rise through them.

That is why surah **Inshiqaaq** says:

84:19	You climb from one condition to another and rise (up) in stages	اَلتَّرکَبُنَّ طَبَقاً عَن طَبَق

The present stage of the human life is not its ultimate. It has to go much further and be elevated. Therefore death does not end the system of life. Dust (earth's) particles have evolved biologically to evolve to the human form. But within this form the human personality is not the result of evolution.

Thereafter the next stage of evolution develops, i.e. instead of the evolution of the human form (body), the evolution of the human personality. This evolution begins in this life but continues in the life hereafter. That is, physical death does not stop it from going ahead. This verse may mean that humanity itself is rising by stages. History is a record of these stages.

R-K-D   ر ک د

"اَلرُّکُوْدُ" (*ar-rukud*): to be motionless.

"اَلرَّاکِدُ" (*ar-rakid*): immobile thing {T, R, M}.

"رَکَدَتِ السَّفِیْنَةُ" (*rakadatis safeenah*): the boat anchored {T, R, M}.

"اَلرَّوَاکِدُ" (*ar-rawakid*): the three stones (or bricks) used by the Arab gypsies as a make-shift stove, the stones are immobile {T}.

The Quran says about boats:

42:33	stay put on the sea	رَوَاکِدَ عَلَى ظَهْرِه

Become unable to move. That is, if God orders the winds to stop, then the sailing boats will stop moving.

R-K-Z   ر ك ز

"اَلرِّكْزُ" (*ar-rikz*): soft sound, tread, or sound which is low. Or human voice heard from afar like the bay of the hounds *{T}*.

Surah *Maryam* says:

19:98	Or do you even hear them making a whimper?	اَوْ تَسْمَعُ لَهُمْ رِكْزاً

"رَكَزْتُ كَذَا" (*rakaztu kaza*): I buried him secretly.
"اَلرِّكَازُ" (*ar-rikaaz*): buried treasure, as well as minerals which have been buried by God *{R}*.
"اِرْتَكَزَ" (*irtakaz*) means he stayed put and became stolid, because anything that is buried stays in its place *{T}*.
"رَكَزَ الرُّمْحَ" (*rakazar rumh*): he dug the spear into the earth.
"اَلْمَرْكَزُ" (*al-markaz*): the place where the spear has been dug in *{T}*.

Ibn Faris says it basically means to bury (dig) something into something so that it become immobile or static.

R-K-S   ر ك س

"اَلرَّكْسُ" (*ar-raks*): to bend something in such a way that the front end meets its rear end {M}.

"رِكَاسٌ" (*rikaas*): a rope, one end of which is tied to the camel's nose ring and the other end to its leg, and it is kept so tight that the camel's head remains bent and is in severe pain. All this is to train it.
"اِرْتَكَسَ" (*irtaks*): his head bent, he turned *{T}*.

The Quran says about the hypocrites:

4:88	Due to their (bad) deeds Allah made them lower their heads	وَاللّٰهُ اَرْكَسَهُمْ بِمَا كَسَبُوْا

It means that Allah's laws insulted and demeaned them, or put them into severe trouble, or turned them back to their state of denial. This meaning appears in 4:91 as well.

R-K-Zd   ر ك ض

"اَلرَّكْضُ" (*ar-rakz*): to spur a horse so that it runs fast. It also means for a bird to prepare its wings to fly.
It also means to run fast.

The Quran says:

21:12	They fled away from it	إِذَا هُم مِّنْهَا يَرْكُضُونَ
21:13	Do not flee.	لَا تَرْكُضُوا

"اَلْمَرْكَضُ" (*al-mirkaz*): the thing which is used to stoke the fire to make it burn brighter {T, R, M}.

In surah *Saad,* it has been said about *Ayub*:

38:42	move on	اُرْكُضْ بِرِجْلِكَ

To make your steps go fast. It can also mean put your leg into the water and move it.

Ibn Faris says "ركض" (*rikz*) basically means to move forward or to make mobile.

Surah *Al-Ambia* says "لَاتَرْكُضُوْا" (*la tarkuzu*) which points to a big truth. Its earlier verse says that the nations which have their social system follow other than God's laws, create chaos in society. It makes the distribution of wealth severely unbalanced and this leads to destruction. But they are drunk with power and wealth and do not realize that they are proceeding towards destruction. Until that destruction stares them in the eye, they try to run away from it. But at that time God's consequential law calls out to them and say "لَاتَرْكُضُوْا" (*la tarkuzu*) which means "do not try to run away, you cannot escape anywhere".

21:13	Go back to those places	لَاتَرْكُضُوْا

Go back to your palatial houses which you had adorned with the color of the blood of the poor. Go back so that you may be asked: where all this wealth came from and what right had you over these luxuries?

This is indeed a true picture of the result of capitalism which the Quran has drawn.

Verses before 21:13 say that those nations that build their economic systems on other bases than those given by Allah, contribute in spreading disorder which ultimately results in destruction. But they are so blinded by their wealth that they never realize their path towards destruction. Instead when destruction starts to knock at their doors, they try to run away from its wrath. That is the time when the consequential law of Allah calls them "don't try to run away, you can't escape your consequences".

21:13	Return to your palaces which you have created fron the earnings of the needy	وَارْجِعُوا إِلَى مَا أُتْرِفْتُمْ فِيهِ وَمَسَاكِنِكُمْ

Now go back to your previous states so you may be asked where your wealth came from and if you had any right to keep it as your own.

The Quran has made the whole system of capitalism with its many disadvantages crystal clear.

R-K-Ain   ر ك ع

"رَكَعَ" (*raka'a*): to bend face down or to fall down, whether the knees touch the ground or not, but the head should bow.

Raghib says "رُكُوْعٌ" (*rukuh*) means to bow. This word is spoken sometimes to bow physically and sometimes used for humility and submission whether that be in worship or not.

"رَكَعَ الشَّيْخُ" (*raka ash sheikh*): an old man, because in old age one bends a little due to weakness. If a man's condition becomes weak then too it is said "رَكَعَ فُلَانٌ" (*raka'a fulan*).

Ibn Faris too has said that it means to bow.

Taj-ul-Uroos says that in the era before the advent of Islam, the Arabs used to call a man "رَاكِعٌ" (*rakiun*) when he was not a worshipper of idols. Then they would say "رَاكِعٌ إِلَى اللهِ" (*rakiun ilal lah*) to him which means "the one who does not bend"

Zamkhishri has said that it means "he was content to turn towards Allah" *{T}*.

"رَاكِعٌ" (*raakiun*) has the plural as "رُكَّعٌ" (*rukka-un*).
"رُكُوْعٌ" (*ruku-un*) and "سُجُوْدٌ" (*sujod*) actually means to bow in submission to Allah's laws. In "سُجُوْدٌ" (*sujod*), there is more intensity (of submission) than "رُكُوْعٌ" (*ruku-un*), i.e. total submission and obedience. See heading (S-J-D).

In surah *Al-Baqrah* the Jews have been told:

2:43	the group which is genuflecting before Allah, you too join them and follow My laws like them	وَأَقِيمُوا الصَّلَوةَ وَآتُوا الزَّكَوةَ وَارْكَعُوا مَعَ الرَّاكِعِينَ

Since man's movements are an indication of his emotions (for instance, when we say 'no', our head automatically turns from side to side and when we say 'yes' then it automatically moves up and down), the display of bowing before Allah's laws is done by "رُكُوْعٌ" (*rukuh*) and "سَجْدَةٌ" (*sajdah*), i.e. by bending and genuflecting in prayer.

48:29	you see them in rukuh and sujud (bending and genuflecting)... the effects of their submission are evident from their faces	تَرَاهُمْ رُكَّعاً سُجَّدًا--- سِيمَاهُمْ فِيْ وُجُوْهِهِمْ مِنْ أَثَرِ السُّجُوْدِ

It is obvious that if a person bends and genuflects before Allah, but he actually follows other laws, then his *rukuh* and *sujud* will not be according to Allah's will, i.e. for a few minutes, he bends before Allah, but in his entire practical life he follows ungodly laws. Therefore his *rukuh* and *sujud* are not a true indication of his subservience to Allah. True *rukuh* and *sujud* are such that a man's heart submits to Allah's laws and along with his heart his head bends before Allah as well. This is what is desired by the congregations of prayer.

R-K-M   ر ك م

"اَلرَّكْمُ" (*ar-rakm*): to put things over each other and to build them into a layer by layer heap.
"فَيَرْكُمُهُ" (*fayarkumuhu*): he will turn them into a heap (8:37).
"رُكَامٌ" (*rukaam*): a heap of layer by layer {*T, M, R*}.

| 24:43 | then they are turned into layer upon layer of cloud | ثُمَّ يَجْعَلُهُ رُكَامًا |
| 52:44 | layer upon layer of cloud | سَحَابٌ مَرْكُومٌ |

"نَاقَةٌ مَرْكُومَةٌ" (*naaqatun markumatun*) is a camel which is very plump, which has layer upon layer of fat in its body {T, M, R}.

R-K-N   ر ك ن

"رَكِنَ" (*rakin*), "يَرْكَنُ" (*yarkan*): to lean towards someone and attain peace {T, M, R}.

Surah *Hoodh* says:

| 11:113 | Do not lean towards the rebellious people. (Do not be attracted to them) | وَلَا تَرْكَنُوا إِلَى الَّذِينَ ظَلَمُوا |

Surah *Bani Israel*:

| 17:47 | If We had not kept you firm then you might have leaned a little towards them | وَلَوْلَا أَنْ ثَبَّتْنَاكَ لَقَدْ كِدْتَّ تَرْكَنُ إِلَيْهِمْ شَيْئًا قَلِيلًا |

Messengers of Allah do not bend (from their stand), even though an ordinary man may (may it be for his mission's sake) bend a little. See 68:9 and 10:15.

"اَلرُّكْنُ" (*ar-rukn*): a thing which strengthens someone, support {T, R, M}.

Ibn Faris says that its basic meaning is strength.

"رُكْنٌ" (*rukn*) means the strongest element or part of a thing.

Surah ***Hoodh*** says:

| 11:80 | let me take the help of a strong support | اوِیْ اِلٰی رُکْنٍ شَدِیْدٍ |

Ibn Faris says "رُکْنٌ شَدِیْدٌ" (***ruknun shaded***) means respect and overpowering due to which nobody has the courage for opposition.

"اَرْکَانُ الشَّیْءِ" (***arkaanash shaiyi***): a thing's surroundings, the supports of that thing.

R-M-H   ر م ح

"اَلرَّمْح" (***ar-rumh***) means spear. Its plural is "رِمَاحٌ" (***rimah***) {T, R, M}.

The Quran says:

| 5:94 | that which your hands and your spears can reach | تَنَالُهُ اَیْدِیْکُمْ وَ رِمَاحُکُمْ |

Figuratively also this word "اَلرَّمْحُ" (***ar-rumh***) is used to mean poverty and starvation {M}.

Taj-ul-Uroos has mentioned it as "رَمَّاحٌ" (***rammah***) instead of "رُمْحٌ" (***rumh***).

R-M-D   ر م د

Ibn Faris says anything that is colored ash or dust is called "اَلْأَرْمَدُ" (***al-armadu***).

"اَلرَّمَادُ" (***ar-ramaad***) means ashes {T, R, M}.
"رَمَادَةٌ" (***ramadah***): annihilation, destruction.
"اَرْمَدَالْقَوْمُ" (***armadal qaum***): people faced drought and their animals were destroyed.

The Quran has likened the deeds of those who tread the wrong path as "رَمَادٌ" (***ramaad***) over which strong wind blows. Obviously if strong winds blow, ashes do not leave even a trace and are scattered. Wrong systems and deeds can't stand the strong currents of the times and like a heap of ashes which may seem to be very big, disperses easily.

R-M-Z   ر م ز

"اَلرَّمْزُ" (*ar-ramz*) means movement {M}.

Ibn Faris says it basically means movement or unease.

"اَلرَّمِيْزُ" (*ar-rameez*): means with a lot of movement {T}, this leads to its meaning signals, be it by lips, eyes, brows, mouth, hand or by the tongue, but there is no sound. Even if there is a sound it must be very low like that of whispering.

Surah *Aal-e-Imraan* says about *Zakariyah*:

3:40	you will not be able to talk to people for three days except in sign (language)	اَلَّا تُكَلِّمَ النَّاسَ ثَلٰثَةَ اَيَّامٍ اِلَّا رَمْزًا

In the traditions of the Jews, even talking was prohibited during fasting, or there was fasting in which the intent was to abstain from speaking. See 19:26.

R-M-Zd   ر م ض

"اَلرَّمَضُ" (*ar-ramz*): means for sand etc. to heat up in the sunlight.
"اَلرَّمَضُ" (*ar-ramzu*), "اَلرَّمْضَاءُ" (*ar-ramza'u*): intense heat {T}.
"شَهْرُ رَمَضَانَ" (*shahru ramazaan*): the month of *Ramadan*.

In ancient Arabic, this month was called "نَاتِقٌ" (*naatiq*), when the names of the months were changed (that too was before the advent of Islam) this month was called "رَمَضَانُ" (*Ramadan*) because it fell in the months of intense heat {T}.

The Quran began to be revealed during this month (2:185).

According to the lunar year, no month can fall in the same season every year. Hence this month of *Ramadan* can fall in winter as well as in summer, but it is called "رَمَضَانُ" (*Ramadan*) nevertheless. See heading (N-S-A).

R-M-M   ر م م

"رَمَّ الْعَظْمُ" (*rammal azm*): the bone became aged, and purified.

"رَمَّ الشَّىْءَ رَمَّاً وَارْتَمَّهُ" (*rammash shaiyi ramman wur tammah*): he ate the thing completely.

"اَلرِّمَّةُ" (*ar-rimmah*): old bones.

"اَلرُّمَّةُ" (*ar-rummah*): old rope, whatever is left of the past year's plants.

"اَلرَّمِيْمُ" (*ar-ramim*): any old and decrepit thing.

"اَلرِّمُّ" (*ar-rimmu*): broken or mashed dry grass, the garbage which floats on the surface of the water.

"اَلْاِرْمَامُ" (*al-irmaam*): to become quiet, silence.

"اَلرَّمُّ" (*ar-rammu*): to mend a decrepit thing {T, M, R}.

Ibn Faris has four basic meanings for it.
1) To mend or correct something
2) For a thing to become decrepit
3) To be quiet
4) To talk (this word means the opposites of the above).

The noble Quran says:

36:78	When the bones become decrepit, then who can make them live again?	مَنْ يُحْيِ الْعِظَامَ وَهِىَ رَمِيْمٌ

Surah *Zaariyaat* says about the destructive storm that had blown on the nation of *Aad*:

51:42	It did not spare anyone who came within its range and whoever did was reduced to smithereens (sawdust).	مَا تَذَرُ مِنْ شَىْءٍ اَتَتْ عَلَيْهِ اِلَّا جَعَلَتْهُ كَالرَّمِيْمِ

R-M-N   ر م ن

"اَلرُّمَّانُ" (*ar-rummaan*): pomegranate, whether tree or the fruit. Singular is "رُمَّانَةٌ" (*rummanah*), probably due to the effect which it has on the heart (it calms it down).

"رَمَنَ بِالْمَكَانِ" (*raman bilmakaan*): he resided there {T, M}.

The Quran has mentioned orchards of grapes, olives and pomegranates:

6:100	In jannat (heavenly society) there shall be grapes, olives and pomegranates	وَجَنّٰتٍ مِّنْ اَعْنَابٍ وَّالزَّيْتُوْنَ وَالرُّمَّانَ

R-M-Y رم ى

"رَمَى الشَّىْءَ" (*ramash shaiyi*), "رَمَى بِهِ" (*rami behi*): to throw something or lay it aside i.e. to discard.

"رَمَى السَّهْمَ عَنِ القَوْسِ" (*ramas sahma unil qaus*): shot the arrow from the bow.

"أَلْمِرْمَاةُ" (*al-mirmah*): small arrow.

"خَرَجَ يَرْتَمِى" (*kharaja yartami*): he went out to hunt with his bow.

"أَلْمَرْمَى" (*al-marma*): the target {T}.

Surah *Al-Murselaat* says:

77:33	it throws sparks	اِنَّهَا تَرْمِى بِشَرَرٍ

Surah *Al-Feel* says:

105:3	you stoned them	تَرْمِيْهِمْ بِحِجَارَةٍ

Surah *Al-Anfaal* says:

8:17	The shooting of arrows which was taking place from your side in the battle of Badar was actually being shot by Allah.	وَمَا رَمَيْتَ اِذْرَمَيْتَ وَلَكِنَّ اللَّه رَمَى

All these battles were fought for establishing the supremacy of Allah's system. When a commander fights a battle at the command of a government, he fights the battle on behalf of the government, or when the army attacks the enemy, the attack is deemed as an attack by the commander.

If "رَمَيْتَ" (*ramait*) is followed by different verbs, it has different meanings but here the talk is about battle and it has been made clear by saying "فَلَمْ تَقْتُلُوْبُمْ" (*falam taqtuluhum*) that here the killing of the enemies has been talked about. Therefore, "رَمَيْتَ" (*ramait*) would mean shooting arrows.

William Lane has written with different references, that when "رِامَيْتُهُ" (*ramaituhu*) or "مُرَامَةٌ" (*muramah*) appears alone, it means archery or stoning.

"رَمَاهُ بِقَبِيْحٍ" (*ramahu beqabeeh*): he linked her to evil {T}.

The Quran says:

24:33	Those who accuse puritan women, to accuse some puritan woman is worse than shooting arrows at her or stoning her	اِنَّ الَّذِيْنَ يَرْمُوْنَ الْمُحْصَنٰتِ

That is why the Quran has suggested very strong punishment for this crime (24:2).

R-W-H   روح

"رَاحْ" (*rah*), "رَوْحٌ" (*rauh*), "رُوْحٌ" (*rooh*), "رِیْحٌ" (*reeh*): these all derived from the same root, and from it are also "رَہاہ" (*rahah*), "رَوْحَةٌ" (*rauhah*), "اِسْتِرَاحَةٌ" (*istiraha*), "تَرْوِیْحَةٌ" (*tarviha*), "رَیْحَانٌ" (*raihaan*) etc.

"رَاحْ" (*rah*) basically means for the wind to blow, to feel the air *{T}*. Since air (wind) creates happiness for humans, has movement and strength, therefore all these connotations are included in words derived from its root.

Ibn Faris says it basically means vastness, expanse or large heartedness.

"اَلرَّوْحُ" (*ar-rauh*) means comfort, bliss, happiness, benevolence, vastness.
"مَکَانٌ رَوْحَانِیٌّ" (*makanun rauhaani*): a good and pure house *{T}*.
"اَلرِّیْحُ" (*ar-reeh*): wind.
"اَلرِّیْحَةُ" (*ar-reeha*): some part of the wind. "رِیَاحٌ" (*riyah*) is its plural.

Raghib says the Quran has used "رِیَاح" (*riyah*) to mean benevolence and happiness at various places, and "رِیْح" (*reeh*) for punishment.

Lataif-ul-Lugha says that when "اَلرِّیْحُ" (*ar-reeh*) or the wind is strong, it is called "اَلْعَاصِفُ" (*al-aasif*).
"مُبَشِّرَاتٌ" (*mubash shiraat*): that wind which brings clouds.
"اَلْمُعْصِرَاتُ" (*al-mu'seeraat*): those winds which bring rain.
"عَاصِفٌ" (*aasif*): winds in the valleys and deserts, or devastating winds.
"اَلْقَوَاصِفُ" (*al-qawasif*): those winds which raise a storm in the sea.
"اَلرِّیْحُ" (*reeh*): victory, power and overpowering, circulation, revolution, and turn *{T}*.

8:26	You will be out of wind (your strength will be lost)	وَتَذْهَبَ رِیْحُکُمْ

"تَرْوِیْحَةٌ" (*tarviha*): to sit and rest, to take a rest. Later it means the four sections prayer of *taraveeh* because after every four sections of it, there is a short rest period.
"اَلرَّوِیْحَةُ" (*ar-raviha*): to get some ease after constriction.
"رَاحَةٌ" (*raaha*): for the cattle to come back home in the evening for rest.
"اَلرَّوَاحُ" (*ar-rawah*) means evening or the period from when the sun starts setting till evening *{T}*.

In surah *Saba*, "رَوَاحٌ" (*rawah*) or evening journey appears opposite to "غُدُوٌّ" (*ghuduw*) or morning journey (34:12).

The *Muheet* says "اَلرَّوْحُ" (*ar-rauh*) means besides happiness and comfort and benevolence, also breeze and help.

It also means justice which gives the prosecution contentment and peace.

"اَلرُّوْحُ" (*ar-rooh*) means the human soul, as well as benevolence and revelation from God, and the noble Quran itself {M}. In verse 16:2, the meaning of "اَلرُّوْحُ" (*ar-rooh*) means Revelation. In Surah *Ash-Shura* verse 42:52, "رُوْحاً" (*roohan*) means the noble Quran itself.

Surah *Bani Israel* says:

17:85	they ask you about ar-rooh, tell them that ar-rooh is my Sustainers concern	وَيَسْئَلُوْنَكَ عَنِ الرُّوْحِ مِنْ اَمْرِ رَبِّىْ

Here "اَلرُّوْحُ" (*ar-rooh*) does not mean human soul, but Revelation, or Quran itself. The next verse explains this when it says "اَوْحَيْنَا اِلَيْکَ" (*auhaina ilaika*). The meaning is that these people want to know about what revelation is, tell them that it is a matter that belongs to the metaphysical world, it has no connection with the physical world so you cannot comprehend it even if you were to be explained. You will have to believe in it regardless, although you can understand its teachings.

They wanted to know about Revelation, and what the relationship between God and his Messenger is, etc. These things cannot be understood by someone who is not a messenger {*Al-Minar*}.

"رُوْحُ القُدُسِ" (*ruhul qudus*) as appeared in 2:87 means whose strength was available to *Isa* and which was the orders in *Torah* and *Bible* which he was endowed with through revelation. And which were the cause that a human being became exalted. Some think that "رُوْحُ القُدُسِ" (*ruhul qudus*) means *Jibrael* and have taken "رُوْحُ الْاَمِیْنُ" (*ruhul amin*) (26:193) to mean the same. {Al-Minar}.

Here the Quran has been said to be:

26:193	the trusted Spirit descended with it on your heart	نَزَل بِهِ الرُّوْحُ الْاَمِیْنُ عَلٰى قَلْبِکَ

This is supported by the verse of surah *Al-Baqrah* in which it is said about *Jibreel*:

2:97	Then indeed we brought it down on your heart by the announcement of Allah	فَاِنَّهٗ نَزَّلَهٗ عَلٰى قَلْبِکَ بِاِذْنِ اللّٰهِ

This clearly shows that "رُوْحُ الْاَمِیْنُ" (*ruhul amin*) is another title of "جبریل" (*Jibreel*).

Surah *An-Nahal* says "قُلْ نَزَّلَ رُوْحُ الْقُدُسِ" (*qul nazzalahu ruhul qudus*) in 16:102, thus "رُوْحُ الْقُدُسِ" (*ruhul qudus*) also means *Jibreel*. Since we cannot understand what Revelation is, we also cannot understand what *Jibreel* is. The word "اَلرُّوْحُ" (*ar-rooh*) points it to be a metaphysical being which reveals the Quran unto the Messenger's heart, and "مَلٰائِکَةٌ" (*malaika*) are those forces of nature in the universe which bear witness to God's being.

Therefore the Quran has used the terms *malaikah* and *rooh* separately as in 97:4, 78:38 and 70:4.

The initial links in the Quran about the creation of Man are the same as those which are known about common animals, but after that the humans have been elevated by saying:

32:9	God breathed His soul into it	وَنَفَخَ فِيْهِ مِنْ رُّوْحِهِ

And the result has been said to be:

32:9	The humans were endowed with eyesight and hearing	وَجَعَلَ لَكُمُ السَّمْعَ وَالْاَبْصَارَ وَالْاَفْئِدَةَ

This means that the means of gathering knowledge were induced in the mind and heart. It is obvious that here God's breath is that Godly strength which is known as personality or one's self, and which determines a man's characteristics. This self has been granted equally to each human being. It remains to be seen to what extent a man then develops it to. This is known as spiritualism and this development takes place only in an Islamic society.

Here it must be understood why God has called this 'force' as our soul. Is it a manifestation of God's personality? There are forces everywhere in the universe. They are more pronounced and visible in living things, this force is the result of materialist cause and effect, (or it comes into being as a consequence of physical laws). That is why it is called physical force. Human energy can also be classified under it, but humans have another sort of energy too which is manifested through his intent and authority. This force is stronger than the physical force and the physical force is subservient to it. This superior force has been attributed by God towards Himself. He has called it "روحنا" (*rohna*) or God's soul or force. What is meant to portray by this is that this force has no connection with the physical laws, but has been given to us directly by God. This is the character of human personality, and is attributed to divine force.

"الوہیاتی" (*aluhiati*) means a force which is not the product of matter but attributable directly to God. It must be noted here that the force which is not "الوہیاتی" (*aluhiati*) or divine is also created by no other than God. But it is created as per the laws which have been formulated by God in regard to matter. The human energy He has attributed to Himself in order to discriminate it from the physical forces.

This force is not a part of God's personality. The personality cannot be divided into parts; to think that it is a part which has separated from God, is a Hindu philosophy and a concept out of *Vedant*. Human personality is a gift of God which is not part of His overall personality, nor is its ultimate aim to reunite with the whole. This force is received in an undeveloped form and to develop it is the purpose of human life.

For this reason the Quranic society is formulated. Every human deed has an effect on his personality, and his personality does not end with the death of his corporeal self. The basic difference in the materialistic concept of life and the Quranic concept is this very thing. The materialistic concept believes that this corporeal self is all there is, that the machinery of this corporeal self is kept in motion by physical laws and when they cease to function then that individual is finished. According to the Quranic concept, human life consists of his corporeal self and his personality. His personality is not subject to physical laws, and therefore when the corporeal being ceases to function, even then nothing happens to his personality, it lives beyond.

Just as there are laws according to which a human body develops, so are there laws according to which a man's personality develops. These principals are called Permanent Values and are not a product of human intellect. They are received through Revelation and are now safe in the Quran. The difference between the developments of the two is that man's body develops when he himself eats or uses things, but the personality develops when a man helps others to develop. According to the Quran, the system of Quranic welfare is built on this very basis. As the human personality develops, it starts reflecting more and more the divine qualities (to a human extent, of course). More details can be found under heading (N-F-S).

The Quran has nowhere talked about the human "soul", but has always talked about the "soul of God". When this "God's soul" or the divine force is endowed to man, then in Quranic terms it is called "نفس" (*nafs*) as in 91:74-79. This is what is known as the human personality, Self or Ego.

When we say that the purpose of human life is the development of its personality, it does not mean that the human body and its development have no significance. According to the Quran the development of the human body is also very important because at the present level the human personality is developed through the development of the human body. As such, it is as important for the human body to be as healthy as for an egg to be healthy enough to become a strong chick. Although if it so happens that there is a tie between the interests of the body and the personality, then it is wiser to sacrifice the interest of the body over that of personality, as it becomes a test for belief and human dignity, just like the chick which breaks the shell when it gets too big for the eggshell. This is the essence of Quranic teachings, that is, to sacrifice physical demands for permanent values whenever there is a tie between them, this is what character building is.

The Quran has also used "اَلرَّيْحَانُ" (*ar-raihaan*) as in surah *Ar-Rahman*:

55:12	corn on the stalk, and aromatic crops	وَالْحَبُّ ذُو الْعَصْفِ وَالرَّيْحَانُ

"اَلرَّيْحَانُ" (*ar-raihan*) is a sort of fragrant grass, also initial vegetation if it is sweet smelling and flowering.

Faraa has said that the stalks are called "عَصْفٌ" (*asf*) and their leaves "رَيْحَانٌ" (*rehaan*).

"اَلرَّيْحَانُ" (*ar-raihaan*) also means progeny and sustenance.
"أَرَاحَ" (*arah*): he rested, left the cattle to rest in the pen in the evening.

R-W-D   ر و د

"رَوْدٌ" (*raud*): to come and go several times in quest of something, that is, to keep searching for something, to be continuously in movement.

"اَلرَّائِدُ" (*ar-ra'id*): means the handle of a grind wheel,

"رَائِدُ الْعَيْنِ" (*raa-idul ain*): the straw in the eye which keeps moving from one place to another {T, M}

"الْمَرَادُ" (*al-maraad*): the place or path where camels come and go, this path is called "رِيَادُ الْإِبِلِ" (*riyaadul ibl*).

"اَلرَّائِدُ" (*ar ra-id*): the man who is sent ahead of the caravan to look for water or fodder {T, M}.

Since "رَوْدٌ" (*raud*) has the connotation to strive or struggle for something, "اِرَادَةٌ" (*iraadah*) came to mean to desire something. But then "اِرَادَةٌ" (*iradah*) and demand were differentiated that desire is manifested by a man's talk or deed, but "اِرادَةٌ" (*iradah*) is sometimes undisclosed and sometimes disclosed {T}.

"اِرَادَةٌ" (*iradah*) actually means for the heart to be drawn towards something or hidden intent, or such leaning as a result of which some benefit is expected {M}

Raghib says "اِرادَةٌ" (*iradah*) means a force which includes desire, need, and wish, all, thereafter it also means for the heart to be drawn towards something or for decision only {R}. This led to "رَاوَدَهُ" (*ra-audawah*) meaning wanted him, or asked for him time and time again. If it is followed by "عَنْ" (*un*), then it means to demand a thing of someone against his willingness, as in 16:12 where it is related about **Yusuf's** brethren who said:

12:61	We will ask for him against his father's will (our father does not want us to take Yusuf with us but we will ask for him against his wishes)	سَنُرَاوِدُ عَنْهُ أَبَاهُ

"يُرِيْدُ" (*yureed*): he intends, it has meant this in 36:23 that is:

36:23	If the Raham intends to give me some pain	إِنْ يُرِدْنِ الرَّحْمٰنُ بِضُرٍّ

"رَاوَدَهُ عَنْ نَفْسِهِ وَعَلَيْهَا" (*rawaddahu un nafsehi wa alaiha*) means to deceive, to induce, to persuade {T, M}. It also means to have the desire to have sex with someone {T, M}. This makes the meaning of the verses such as 12:32 and 54:37 clear. The first verse points to the wrong intentions of **Aziz's** wife towards **Yusuf**, and the second towards the wrong ways of the nation of **Lot**.

"أَرْوَدَ فِىْ السَّيْرِ" (*arwada fis sair*): he traveled at a peaceful pace {T, M}.

From this it led to "رُوَيْدَ" (*ruwaid*) meaning to give time, breathing space. The Quran has used "رُوَيْدًا" (*ruwaida*) in this meaning,

86:17	so give the Deniers some time, a little time	فَمَهِّلِ الْكَافِرِيْنَ أَمْهِلْهُمْ رُوَيْدًا

God's intentions, which are mentioned at several places in the Quran, should not be taken as Man's intentions. Human intents are fulfilled and broken too. They are right and even wrong, are practical and sometimes while poetic at other times. But God's intentions are those truths according to which everything in the universe is working.

R-W-Ain   ر و ع

"اَلرَّوْغُ" (*ar-rau*): awe that is inspired by something's beauty or abundance.
"اَلرَّوْعَةُ" (*ar-rau'a*): awe, or the effect of something's beauty.
"اَلرَّوْغُ" (*ar-ru*): heart, fear and the place for palpitation *{T, R}*.

The Quran says:

11:74	When Ibrahim's heart overcame his surprise and palpitation	فَلَمَّا ذَهَبَ عَنْ إِبْرَاهِيمَ الرَّوْعُ

Rom   ر و م

"اَلرَّوْمُ" (*ar-room*): the Roman Empire.

Surah Rom or Rome says in 30:2 that the Romans were overpowered. This is the tale about the defeat which the Romans suffered at the hands of the Persian king **Khusru Pervaiz**, in which, province after province of the Romans fell to the Persians, and this continued till 615 A.D. At the very time when the Romans were in a weak condition, the Quran predicted that in a few years they will overpower the Persians, as such in 624AD. **Herkel** not only took his areas back from the Persians but also entered Persia and destroyed their place of fire worship. This happened in the year 2 H when the Muslims were victorious for the first time in the battle of **Badr**. The closest opponents of the Arabs were Persians. When the Persians were overpowering, even the Romans, the Arabs were distraught and worried, but within a short period of time, the Arabs, due to the Quranic system, became so strong that neither the Persians nor the Romans could stand up to them. This was all due to the strength that their Faith gave them.

R-He-B   ر ه ب

"رَهْب" (*rahb*), "رُهْب" (*rohb*), "رَهَب" (*rahab*), "رُهْبَة" (*ruhbah*), "رَهْبَة" (*rahbah*), "رُهْبَان" (*ruhbaan*).

This root means a fear which has caution in it, like one is afraid of burning and that is why we fear fire.

"اَلْمَرْهُوْب" (*al-marhoob*), "اَلرَّهِب" (*ar-rahib*): lion {*T*}. It also means to become weak.
"اَلرُّهْب" (*arrabu*) "اَلرُّهْبَى" (*ar-ruhba*) means a she-camel which is weak and tired after a journey.
"رَهِبَ الْجَمَلُ" (*rahibal jamal*): camel rose or stood up but again sat down due to weakness {*T*}.
"اَلرَّهْبَانِيَّة" (*ar-rahbaaniyyah*): includes all elements such as fear, caution, weakness, etc. in monastic, i.e. due to the fear of God, giving up all the pleasures of life ["اَلْأَرْهَاب" (*al-arhaab*): birds who do not prey {*T*}] and thus become weak, this sort of puritan is called "اَلرَّاهِب" (*ar-raahib*), its plural is "رُهْبَان" (*ruhbaan*) in 9:31. Some think that "رُهْبَان" (*ruhbaan*) is a Persian word, and it is a compound of the words "رُه" (*ruh*) and "بَان" (*baan*) which means a puritan {*T*}. This could be a Persian word because they too used to practise monasticism.

The Quran says:

| 7:116 | they tried to frighten the people | وَاسْتَرْهَبُوْهُمْ |

Surah *Al-Hashar* says:

| 59:13 | their fear of you is great | لَا أَنْتُمْ أَشَدُّ رَهْبَةً فِى صُدُوْرِهِمْ |

Here too "رَهْبَة" (*rahbah*) means fear.

Bani Israel were told:

| 2:41 | you must fear Me only | إِيَّايَ فَارْهَبُوْن |

To fear God means to fear the devastating results of violating God's laws and to uphold them and avoid rebelling against them.

"رَهَبَاً" (*rahaba*) basically means to fear and avoid.

Surah *Al-Ambia* says that the messengers were wont to:

| 21:90 | they used call on God (for help) to attain life's benefits | يَدْعُوْنَنَا رَغَبَاً وَرَهَبَاً |

This means that they used to call for help to attain life's benefits "رَغَبَاً" (*raghaban*) and to avoid its unpleasantness "رَهَبَاً" (*rahaban*). They used to refer towards Him in both cases. Obviously removing the ills and accruing the benefits are the emotions which motivate man or act as incentives for man.

Messengers used to obey the laws of God in both conditions, something which all *momins* should do as well. As far as "رَبْبَانِيَّتَ" (*rahbaniyaat*) or monasticism is concerned, that is, to give up on this world, the Quran says that it was created by the Christians themselves (it was not ordered by God) (57:27).

Along with it, the Quran has said:

| 57:27 | then they could not fulfill even this self-created condition | فَمَا رَعَوْهَا حَقَّ رِعَايَتِهَا |

This is what the Quran says about monasticism and which is the basis of Sufism and which (unfortunately) is considered to be our respectable Deen! When the Muslims let go of the Quran then all those ungodly elements to remove which the Quran had been sent, became part of Islam one by one. The total aneurism of the Romans, the racism of the Persians, the religious leadership and traditionalism of the Jews, and the monasticism of the Christians, all became part of Islam! Nowadays Islam is thought to be an amalgamation of all these! But this is no cause for hopelessness because God's **Deen** (way of life) is safe and intact with us within the Quran. As such, we can easily separate pure Deen from these adulterations, if we really intend to do so.

R-He-Th   ر ه ط

"اَلرَّهْطُ" (*ar-raht*): someone's nation, tribe. Some say that "رَهْطُ" (*raht*) is the party which has a membership of three to ten or seven to ten, but some say it is said even for less numbers or more but only men are included in it, not women.

Ibn Faris says it means a congregation of humans etc.

Surah **Hoodh** says:

| 11:92 | brotherhood or tribe | رَهْطُ |

Surah **An-Nahal** says about the nation of **Samood**:

| 27:48 | and there were nine men who used to raise chaos in the city | وَكَانَ فِى الْمَدِينَةِ تِسْعَةُ رَهْطٍ يُفْسِدُونَ فِى الْأَرْضِ |

It is a reference to the leaders of the nation who held the reins of power, every nation, government or country is ruled by some people in power and who are responsible for creating the imbalance in the country, and the rest of the country is destroyed by them.

R-He-Q   ر ه ق

"رَهِقَه" (*rahiqah*), "يَرْهَقُهُ" (*yarhaquhu*), "رَهَقَا" (*rahaqa*): to cover something or overshadow it. *Raghib* has added, with force. It means as well to join with something, to overtake it and besiege it {*T, R*}.

| 10:26 | Their faces do not turn bleak | وَلَا يَرْهَقُ وُجُوهَهُمْ قَتَرٌ |

"أَرْهَقَه" (*arhaqahu*): he forced him to do something beyond his power, put him into difficulty {M}.

Surah *Al-Kahaf* says:

| 18:80 | Make rebellion overpower them. (or involve them in rebellion) | يُرْهِقَهُمَا طُغْيَاناً |

"رَهَقٌ" (*rahaq*): foolishness, nonsense, impoliteness, harshness, commitment of evil deed {*T, R*}.

Ibn Faris says it means cheating, hastiness and oppression,

| 72:6 | so they increased their unawareness | فَزَادُوهُمْ رَهَقاً |

Azhari says it actually has been derived from "اِرْهَاق" (*irhaaq*) which means to coerce a man for doing that of which he is not capable {*T, R*}.

| 74:17 | I will involve him in great difficulty or stress | سَأُرْهِقُهُ صَعُوداً |

R-He-N   ر ه ن

"اَلرَّهْنُ" (*ar-rahn*): Something which is kept as a guarantee for something that you have taken temporarily.
"رِهَانٌ" (*rihaan*) is plural of "اَلرَّهْنُ" (*ar-rahn*). It also means a guarantee. In the dictionary "رَهْنٌ" (*rahn*) means proof and stability (to be stolid).

Raghib says "رَهْنٌ" (*rahn*) and "رِهَانٌ" (*rihaan*) are things which are kept as guarantee for a loan, but
"اَلرِّهَانُ" (*ar-rihaan*) is a thing which is kept as a guarantee in a bet. It is usually used in horseracing.

"اَلرَّاهِنُ" (*ar-raahin*): proven and ready, stolid and permanent.
"رَهَنَ الشَّىْءُ" (*rahanash shaiyi*): the thing remained stolid {*T*}.

Ibn Faris says it means to stick to one thing whether it is right or wrong.

"رِجْلَهُ رَهِيْنَةٌ" (*rijluhu rahina*): his foot is imprisoned or trapped *{T}*.
"أَنَارَهِيْنٌ بِكَذَا" (*anaraheen bikaza*): I am involved in that thing {M}.

The Quran says:

| 52:21 | everybody is hostage to his deeds (his life is dependent upon his deeds for results) | كُلُّ امْرِئٍ بِمَا كَسَبَ رَهِيْنٌ |

In surah *Al-Baqarah*, the advice that is given for lending says that if you are traveling and find no one to write down (the loan agreement) then:

| 2:283 | you must hold onto something as mortgage for the things that are lent | فَرِهٰنٌ مَقْبُوْضَةٌ |

To make this the basis for 'keeper's property' is an injustice (to God's laws), for example, a farmer takes a loan from somebody and mortgages some of his land for it. Thereafter the land will remain with the lender who will own the produce of the land till the loan is returned and will not even deduct the cost of the produce from the loan. If this is not a type of interest, then what is it? This means that it is indeed a type of interest, which is forbidden.

R-He-W   ر ه و

"اَلرَّهْوُ" (*ar-rahwu*): the space between the two legs, a place where water accumulates, also peace which is tranquil.
"اَلرَّهَاءُ" (*arraha-u*): level and expansive land.
"عَيْشٌ رَاهٍ" (*aishun rah*): a content and peaceful life.
"اَلرَّهْوَانُ" (*ar-rahwaan*): low land, a horse whose back while riding is soft *{T, R}*.

Kitab-ul-Ishteqaaq says that this word means the opposites, that is "هبوط" (*haboot*) or to come down, as well as "ارتفاع" (*irtafaa*), or to go up.

Ibn Faris says it has two basic meanings. One is of peace and contentment, and second is of a place which becomes high sometimes and at others becomes low. The Quran says when *Moosa* was taking along the nation of *Bani Israel* then he was told:

| 42:24 | to leave the sea in a calm state | وَاتْرُكِ الْبَحْرَ رَهْواً |

One meaning of this is verse is:
When *Moosa* reached it, the sea was peaceful, it was in ebb and it had receded and left some dry land behind.

Surah **Taha** says:

| 20:77 | for them take the dry path in the sea | فَاضْرِبْ لَهُمْ طَرِيقاً فِى الْبَحْرِ يَبَسًا |

Even if "رَبْوًا" (**rahwa**) is taken to mean broad or expansive, it will mean the path which has been broadened by the sea (by receding), take them by that way. The place where there was the sea at first would be low, when the sea recedes from there, then that land will be (as compared to the land which is still under water) be higher.

R-W-Zd   ر و ض

"رَوْضَةٌ" (**rauzah**): the land where there are beautiful flowers, trees and water, beautiful garden with a canal, any green place which has a canal adjacent to it. The plural forms are "رَوْضٌ" (**rauzun**), "رِيَاضٌ" (**riyazun**) and "رَوْضَاتٌ" (**rauzaat**). If there is no water, then it is not called "رَوْضَةٌ" (**rauzah**). It is a place where water collects.

"أَرَضَ الْقَوْمَ" (**aradal qaum**): he watered the whole nation, i.e, he benefited the entire nation.

"اَلرِّيَاضَةٌ" (**ar-riyazah**): to make somebody work hard to make him an expert at it, to train {T, R}.

Ibn Faris contends that its basic meanings contain vastness and expanse, as well as to soften something or to make some chore easier.

The Quran says:

| 30:15
42:22 | they will enjoy music in a green spot | فَهُمْ فِىْ رَوْضَةٍ يُحْبَرُوْنَ |

Its plural is "رَوْضَاتٌ" (**rauzaat**).

R-W-Gh   ر و غ

"رَاغَ الرَّجُلُ" (**raghal rajulu**), "رَوْغاً" (**ragha**): for some expedience, to turn to one side quietly, lean or to avoid {T, R}.

Ibn Faris says it basically means to lean and not to remain in one state.

"رَاغَ فُلَانٌ إِلَى فُلَانٍ" (**raagha fulanun ila fulaan**): that man secretly leaned towards him.

Faraa says that "رَاغَ إِلَى أَهْلِهِ" (**raagha ila ahlehi**) means that he returned to his family and kept the purpose of his coming back hidden from others.

"أَرَاغَ" (**aragha**), "إِرَاغَةٌ" (**iraagha**), "اِرْتَاغَ" (**wartaagh**): he intended and demanded.

"رِوَاغَةٌ" (**riwagha**), "رِبَاغَةٌ" (**ruyagha**): ring (as in boxing or wrestling) {T, R, M}.

In the tale of **Ibrahim**, the Quran relates "فَرَاغَ إِلَى أَلِهَتِهِمْ" (*faraagha ila aalihatihim*) in 37:91 and "فَرَاغَ عَلَيْهِمْ" (*faragha alaihim*) in 37:93. "رَاغَ إِلَى" (*ragha ila*) means to keep your intentions to yourself while attending to someone, and "رَاغَ عَلَى" (*raagha ala*) means to attack somebody overwhelmingly. As such, **Ibrahim's** tact was such that it contained the element of secrecy of intent and overpowering strength as well.

R-Y-B ر ی ب

"رَیْبٌ" (*raib*): actually it means psychological confusion, and uneasiness of "نفس" (*nafs*) {*Aqrabal Muwarid*}.

It also means doubt, and restlessness {*T*}, also guess or opinion and accusation {T, R, M}. Besides it, it also means the vicissitudes of life and need {*T*}.

Ibn Faris says it basically means doubt or doubt and fear.

"اَلرَّیْبُ" (*ar-raib*): anything which creates confusion. It also means need.
"رَابَنِی الْأَمْرُ رَیْباً" (*rabanial amru raiba*): that matter put me in doubt {*T*}.

In surah **At-Taubah,** in the context of **Masjid-e-Zarar**, it is said:

9:110	restlessness and confusion	رِیْبَةً فِی قُلُوبِهِمْ

In surah **Ibrahim** 14:9 and in surah **Saba** 34:54 and at other places, "مُرِیْبٌ" (*mureebun*) has come as an adjective of "شَکٌّ" (*shakk*), which means doubt.

"شَکٌّ مُرِیْب" (*shakkun mureebun*): doubt which creates uneasiness and confusion. In 40:34 "مُرْتَابٌ" (*murtaab*) has appeared, that is, one who doubts. In 29:48 is "اِرْتَابَ" (*irtaab*), that is, doubted.

Surah **At-Toor** says:

52:30	The vicissitudes of life which can be faced by realities but not by poetic or idealistic emotionalism.	رَیْبَ الْمَنُوْن

Therefore, "رَیْبٌ" (*raib*) would mean uneasiness of the mind due to doubt. The Quran has said about itself in the very beginning:

2:2	this is the code of life which leaves no doubt or create any confusion or unease in the minds (its teachings create complete peace and calm, it has no place for unease and confusion)	ذَالِکَ الْکِتَابُ لَارَیْبَ فِیْہِ

Aqrabal muwarid says that these meanings are cited for the word *ar-reebah*, because it is entirely based on logic and reasoning, and it is obvious that only reasoning can create complete peace, not by blind faith and superstitions.

R-Y-Sh   ر ی ش

"الرِّیْشُ" (*ar-reesh*), "الرَّاشُ" (*ar-raash*): the feathers of the birds with which their bodies are covered *{T}*.

"الرِّیْشُ" (*ar-rish*): human clothing and beautification. It also means wellbeing and economic freedom.

"رَاشُ فُلَاناً" (*raasha fulaana*): helped him earn and strengthened him, corrected his condition and benefited him.

"رَاشَ الرَّجُلُ" (*raashar rujul*): the man became rich and well to do *{T}*.

Ibn Faris says that the root basically means wellbeing, as well as the good things that one acquires in life.

The Quran says that your clothing covers your body and "رِیْشأ" (*reeshan*), also adorns you (7:26).

The Quran not only presents the utilitarian aspect of things but also gives equal importance to their aesthetic values. The beauty in the universe is a manifestation of this aspect of the creator. This means utilitarian and aesthetic values in everything. A *momin's* life too must be an embodiment of both these two aspects.

R-Y-Ain   ر ی ع

"رَیْعٌ" (*ree'a*): the projecting part of anything, also everything's best and first part.

"رَاعَ الطَّعَامُ" (*ra'at tu-aamu*): there was an increased production of crop, the crop production increased, was in abundance.

"رِیْعٌ" (*ri'a*), "رَیْعٌ" (*ra'a*): high land or high place. Every path or the path between two mountains, also mountain.

"کَمْ رِیْعُ أَرْضِکَ" (*kum ree-u ardika*): how high is your land?

"الرَّیْعُ" (*ar-ree'*): high dune, the high place of the valley along which water flows down, it is also used for church.

"رَیْعَانُ الشَّبَابِ" (*rai'aanus shabaab*): the early part of youth.

"نَاقَةٌ رَیْعَانَةٌ" (*naaqatun rai'aanatun*): a camel which gives a lot of milk *{T}*.

The Quran says:

26:128	Do you make a monument to yourself at every elevated place? (And that too unnecessarily?)	اَتَبْنُوْنَ بِكُلِّ رِیْعٍ آیَةً تَعْبُثُوْنَ

This means memorials are only for remembrance and have no utility as such. Only such things are good memorials which are beneficial to the coming generations.

<h1 style="text-align:center">R-Y-N   ر ى ن</h1>

"رَيْنٌ" (*rayn*): rust or dirt etc. *{T}*.

"رَانَ هَوَاهُ عَلَى قَلْبِهِ بِرَيْنٌ" (*raana hawahu ala qalbehi birayn*): his wishes controlled his heart.

"زِيْنَ بِالرَّجُلِ" (*reyna bir rujul*): the man was so involved in the confusion that it became difficult to extricate himself. It also means liquor, because it overwhelms the intellect {M}.

Ibn Faris says it basically means to cover.

Quran says:

83:15	their deeds overwhelmed their hearts as rust	رَانَ عَلَى قُلُوبِهِم مَّا كَانُوا يَكْسِبُونَ

Hearts are not sealed or close externally. A man's own deeds act as seals and rust for the heart. This is what has been described as "خَتَمَ اللهُ عَلَى قُلُوبِهِمْ" (*khatamallahu ala qulubihim*) in 2:7, because everything takes place according to the laws of God. The results of a man's deeds, which occur due to the law of nature, is that the man loses the ability to think rightly. He is so submerged by surface emotions that the road to thinking is closed to him.

Z-B-D   ز ب د

"اَلزَّبَدُ" (**az-zabad**): the foam that comes to the top of the water or other liquid *{T}*.

The Quran says:

13:17	The foam that mounts up to the surface...	زَبَدًا رَّابِيًا

"اَلزُّبْدُ" (**az-zubd**): cream which is later made into butter.
"تَزَبَّدَهُ" (**tazabbadah**): he took the gist *{T}*.

Ibn Faris says it means for a thing to be born out of another.
Raghib says that as a metaphor "زَبَدَة" (**zabadah**) is also for something which is in abundance.

Z-B-R   ز ب ر

"اَلزَّبْرُ" (**az-zubr**): to write.
"اَلتَّزْبِرَةُ" (**at-tazbirah**): writing.
"مِزْبَرٌ" (**mizbar**): pen.
"مَزْبُورٌ" (**maz-zaboor**): written material, book etc. *{T}*. The plural is "زُبُرٌ" (**zubur**).

Surah **An-Nahal** says that the messengers were sent with "اَلْبَيِّنَاتِ وَالزُّبُرِ" (**al-bayyinaati waz-zubur**) in 16:44, 26:196.
Here "زُبُرٌ" (**zubur**) means books. Similarly at other places i.e. "بِالْبَيِّنَاتِ وَالزُّبُرِ وَالْكِتَابِ الْمُنِيرِ" (**bilbayyinaati waz-zuburi wal kitaabil munir**) as in 35:25, 3:183, "زُبُرٌ" (**zubur**) is referred to the divine book providing guidance.

Surah **Al-Ambia** says:

21:105	Verily, We noted in **Zaboor** after the **zikr** (mention)	وَلَقَدْ كَتَبْنَا فِى الزَّبُوْرِ مِنْ بَعْدِ الذِّكْرِ

Some say that here "زَبُورٌ" (**zubur**) means "the Book of the Psalms" revealed on **Dawood**, and "ذِكْرٌ" (**zikr**) means **Torah**. But **Saeed Bin Jabeer** says that "زَبُوْرٌ" (**zaboor**) means every Divine Book (Revelation), i.e. Torah, Bible, Quran. Any of these books is "زَبُوْرٌ" (**zaboor**) *{T}*.

Surah **An-Nisa** says:

4:163	And we gave **Zaboor** to **Dawood**	وَآتَيْنَا دَاوُدَ زَبُوْراً

If "زَبُوْرٌ" (**zaboor**) means the book which was given to **Dawood**, then it would not have been said "زَبُوْرًا" (**zaboora**) which means one book. It should have been "اَلزَّبُوْرُ" (**az-zaboor**) which is a proper noun for "the book".

Ibn Faris says it basically means to read and write, and to strengthen or make something stolid.
Raghib says that any voluminous book is called "زَبُوْرٌ" (*zaboor*).

"اَلزُّبرَةُ" (*az-zubrah*): a big piece of iron *{T}*. Its plural is "زُبَرٌ" (*zubar*) and "زُبُرٌ" (*zubur*) as used in 18:96. This led it to mean sects or separate groups, as in 23:53

Since "زُبُرٌ" (*zubur*) is the plural of "زَبُوْرٌ" (*zabur*), as in 23:53, therefore it can also be interpreted as separate books.

Z-B-N   ز ب ن

"اَلزَّبْنُ" (*az-zabn*): to push, to shut out, to remove something from someone.
"اَلزُّبُنُ" (*az-zubun*): the one who pushes away someone with strong force.
"نَاقَةٌ زَبُوْنٌ" (*naaqatun zabun*): the she camel which kicks and pushes away who tries to milk her.
"حَرْبٌ زَبُوْنٌ" (*hurbun zaboon*): severe clash in an intense battle *{T}*. A battle is called "زَبُوْنٌ" (*zaboon*) because of its violance *{Kitab-ul-Ashfaq}*.

"اَلزِّبْنِيَةُ" (*az-zibniyah*): every brave or courageous person may be a soldier. The plural is "زَبَانِيَةٌ" (*zabaniyah*) as in 96:18. It is used for the fighters who go to war in defence of Righteousness.

Z-J-J   ز ج ج

Ibn Faris says it basically means for something to be thin, or fine.

"اَلزُّجُّ" (*az-zujj*) the iron piece at the back of a spear, the point of the elbow
"اَلزُّجَاجُ" (*az-zujaaj*): things made from glass, ceramics etc. Singular is "زُجَاجَةٌ" (*zujajah*) *{T, R}*.

The Quran refers to the lamp:

| 24:35 | ...within it a lamp.... | فِىْ زُجَاجَةٍ |

It also means a glass covering or a chandlier.
When the glass is full, it is called "كَأْسٌ" (*kaas*), and when empty, is called "زُجَاجَةٌ" (*zujajah*)
{Latif-ul-Lugha and *Fiqah-ul-Lugha}*.

Z-J-R   ز ج ر

"زَجَرَهُ" (*zajarah*), "يَزْجُرُهُ" (*azjuruh*), "زَجْرًا" (*zajran*), "اِزْدَجَرَهُ" (*izdajarah*): he stopped him (from something) and prevented and scolded him. Actually it means to shout at someone with a view to drive away or audibly scold someone or to give someone a dressing down.

"زَجَرَ الْبَعِيْرَ" (*zajaral ba-eer*): he scolded the camel and hushed it.

"اَلزَّجُوْرُ" (*az-zajor*): the she camel which cannot be milked unless shouted at, therefore this word has an element of scolding or talking harshly.

The Quran says:

37:2	Hence those who drive away with strength …	فَالزَّاجِرَاتِ زَجْرًا

This means the party of those fearless men who scold (or chastise) the oppressive forces to stop them from their excesses. A little later in the same surah:

37:19	that will only be one chiding	فَإِنَّمَاهِىَ زَجْرَةٌ وَّاحِدَةٌ

Surah *Al-qamar* says:

54:4	which contains such things as prevent from excesses	مَافِيْهِ مُزْدَجَرٌ

Still further ahead it is said:

54:9	they called him mad and ousted him chastising	مَجْنُوْنٌ وَازْدُجِرَ

Vested interests who have power and wealth always treat any messenger who calls them towards the Divine Guidance with contempt and arrogance.

Z-J-W   ز ج و

"زَجَاهُ" (*zajah*), "يَزْجُوْهُ" (*yazjuh*), "زَجْوًا" (*zajwa*), "وَاَزْجَى" (*wazja*), "اِزْجَاءُ" (*iz ja'a*): to drive something (egg on) softly *{T, R}*.

The Quran says:

24:43	Do you not reflect on the fact that God drives the clouds slowly and softly?	اَلَمْ تَرَ اَنَّ اللهَ يُزْجِىْ سَحَابًا

"زَجَا الْأَمْرُ" (*zajal amr*): the matter became easy and simple or straight forward.

"اَلْمُزْجَى" (*al-muzja*): Something in in small quantity *{T, R}*.

"بِضَاعَةٌ مُزْجَاةٌ" (*biza'atun muzjah*): a little capital or a small saving(12:88) *{T, R}*.

Ibn Faris says it basically means to throw away something without any hesitation or to drive, which can be easily culled and sent along.

"بِضَاعَةٌ مُزْجَاةٌ" (*biza'atun muzjah*): would mean a small sum which can easily be parted with and donated.

Z-H-Z-H   ز ح ز ح

"زَحْزَحَهُ عَنْهُ" (*zahzahahu unh*): removed it from him, put it to one side.

"هُوَ بِزَحْزَحٍ مَنْهُ" (*huwa bizahzahin minh*): he is at a distance from him.

"اَلزَّحْزَاحُ" (*az-zahzahu*): far, distant *{T}*.

Ibn Faris says these are its basic meanings.

The Quran says:

2:96	..but this will not save him from punishment...	وَمَاهُوَ بِمُزَحْزِحِهِ مِنَ الْعَذَابِ

Surah *Aal-e-Imraan* says:

3:185	...only he who is saved from the fire.	فَمَنْ زُحْزِحَ عَنِ النَّارِ

Z-H-F   ز ح ف

"زَحَفَ اِلَيْهِ زَحْفاً" (*zahafa ilaihi zahfa*): proceeded towards him, went forward towards him *{T}*.

Ibn Faris says it means to keep marching forward.

"زَحْفٌ" (*zahfin*) means when a a child moves forward by dragging on his bottom *{T}*. This word is also used to mean to move on the knees like children do *{M}*.

"زَحَفَ الْبَعِيْرُ" (*zahafal ba-eer*): due to tiredness, the camel started to drag its feet *{T}*.

"اَلزَّحَّافَةُ" (*azuh hafah*): reptiles, those creatures which crawl on ground, like a tortoise etc. *{M}*. Later it began to be used for the movement of armies because these, due to their size, move as if are dragging at a crawling pace.

"اَزْحَفَ لَنَا بَنُوْ فُلَانٍ" (*azhafu lana banu fulaan*): that tribe came from the above stated condition to fight us.

"تَزَاحَفُوْا فِى الْقِتَالِ" (*tazahafu fil qitaal*): they came face to face in battle.

"مَزَاحِفُ الْقَوْمِ" (*mazahiful qaum*): battle sites where a nation has fought battles *{T}*.

"اَلزَّحْفُ" (*az-zahf*): a brave army which is advancing towards an enemy.

Surah **Al-Anfal** says:

8:15	.... when you meet the enemy in battle .... (when they are advancing towards you)	اِذَالَقِيتُمُ الَّذِينَ كَفَرُوْا زَحْفاً

Z-Kh-R-F   ز خ ر ف

"اَلزُّخْرُفُ" (*az-zukhraf*): gold, which is used to make ornaments. This is its real meaning. Adornments were also called "زُخْرُفٌ" (*zukhraf*), and as a metaphor, for every exaggerated statements e.g. propaganda *{T, M}*.

"زُخْرُفٌ" (*zukhruf*) also used to explain the extreme beauty. In 43:35, this word means the things for adornment or adornment itself

The Quran says:

6:113	Decorative speech	زُخْرُفَ الْقَوْلِ
10:24	Until the earth takes its decoration	حَتّىٰ اِذَا اَخَذَتِ الْاَرْضُ زُخْرُفَهَا

"زُخْرُفاً" (*zukhurufa*): cosmetic make up, or other things one uses for own objectification and projection.

Muheet doubts that it either means gold or adornment *{M}*.
Raghib says it means artificial beauty *{R}*.
Ibn Faris says it basically means gold and also adornment. **Raghib** supports him on this.

Z-R-B   ز ر ب

"اَلزَّرْبُ" (*az-zarb*): entrance, a wooden enclosure for keeping goats in, etc.
"اَلزَّرَابِىُّ" (*az-zarabi*): the singular is "زُرْبِىٌّ" (*zurbi*) or "زَرْبِيَّةٌ" (*zarbiyah*) which means mattresses, bedding, any such thing which is used to lean upon or get support.
"اَلزَّرْبِيَّةُ" (*az-zurbiyyah*): good carpet or flooring *{M}*.

Fara says that "زَرَابِىُّ" (*zarabi*) means mattresses with frills. It is possible that this meaning may have developed with reference to "اَلزَّرَابِىُّ مِنَ النَّبْتِ" (*az-zarabiyyu minan nabt*) which means yellow and green plants which bear vegetables *{T}*.

Quran says:

88:16	floor covering of a high quality	زَرَابِىُّ مَبْثُوْنَةٌ

Ibn Faris says that "زَرْبٌ" (*zarb*) basically contains the connotation of some resting place.

Z-R-Ain   ز ر ع

"زَرَعَ" (*zara*), "يَزْرُعُ" (*yazra*), "وَزَرْعاً" (*zaruw*), "زِرَاعَة" (*zira'ah*): to put seed into the soil.

"اَلزَّرْعُ" (*az-zar'u*): to grow {T}.

"اَلزُّرَّاعُ" (*az-zurra*): those who till the soil, gardeners or farmers (48:29). The singular is "زَارِعٌ" (*zarih*).

"زَرْعٌ" (*zar'un*): crop, or what is produced by sowing {T} (6:141, 13:4).

Ibn Faris says with reference to **Khalil** that it basically means to develop or nurture something.

Therefore, as it will be explained later, it does not just mean to put seeds into the soil but also means to grow a crop. A man cultivates the land and sows the seeds and takes various precautions, but for the seeds to grow into a sapling and then into a plant is all according to Allah's laws and in this process no human effort is involved. That is why Allah has questioned:

56:64	Do you make the crops grow or it is Us?	ءَ اَنْتُمْ تَزْرَعُونَهُ اَمْ نَحْنُ الزَّارِعُونَ

The above verse explains that you only sow the seed while God's laws make it grow, thus how can you claim ownership of the entire produce ? Take what is due for your efforts and give Us Our share, i.e. give it to those who need it (56:73).

Z-R-Q   ز ر ق

"اَلزَّرَقْ" (*az-zaraq*): blue color.

"اَلزُّرْقَةْ" (*az-zurqah*): bluish, whiteness, greenish color in the blackness of the eye, for whiteness to cover eye's blackness.

"زَرِقَ" (*zariq*): his eyes' blackness was covered by whiteness. A person who has this is called "أَزْرَقْ" (*azraq*). Its plural is "زُرْقٌ" (*zurq*).

"اَلزَّرَقُ" (*az-zaraqu*) means blondness.

"زَرِقَتْ عَيْنُهُ تَزْرَقُ" (*zariqat anhu tazraq*): for the eyes to turn blue {T}.

The Quran says:

20:102	On the day of judgment, We will raise the criminals as blind, their blackness of the eyes will be covered with whiteness	نَحْشُرُ الْمَجْرِمِينَ يَوْمَئِذٍ زُرْقاً

"زُرْقٌ" (*zurq*) is plural and its singular is "أَزْرَقْ" (*azraq*).

Raghib says that "زُرْقاً" (*zurqa*) means blind whose eyes are bereft of sight{R}. Some linguists think that the Arabs had old enmity with the Romans and they were blue eyed. Thus every captive or enemy was called "أَزْرَقُ الْعَيْنِ" (*azraqul ain*) even though his eyes may not be blue {M, **Kashaf**}. But I think, the former meaning is more acceptable, because the Quran uses it in this context.

Later in the same surah, it is said:

| 20:124 | ..on the day of judgment we will raise them blind.. | نَحْشُرُهُ يَوْمَ الْقِيَامَةِ اَعْمَىٰ |

Z-R-Y   ز ر ی

"زَرَىٰ عَلَيْهِ عَمَلَهُ" (*zara ilaihi amalehi*): to chastise someone for his deed, to dress him down, to criticize him, to demean him and to accuse him {*T*}.

"اِزْدَرَاہُ" (*izdarah*): considered him to be low and insignificant.

"اِزْدَرَاہُ" (*al-muzdari*): one who thinks someone as inferior. {M, *Kashaf*}.

The Quran says:

| 11:31 | ...those who are lowly in your eyes .... | تَزْدَرِيّ اَعْيُنُكُمْ |

Z-Ain-M   ز ع م

"اَلزَّعْمُ" (*azza'am*), "اَلزُّعْمُ" (*az-zoam*), "اَلزِّعْمُ" (*az-zeem*): such a saying or utternace which could either be true or false, i.e. good or evil. But often it is used for things which are not true and not based on facts.

Lane has said when the Arabs say "ذَكَرَ فُلَانٌ" (*zakara fulanun*) then it means that the matter talked about is true, but when there is doubt about the veracity of the saying, then it is said "زَعَمَ فُلَانٌ" (*za'ama fulan*). Some say that "زَعْمٌ" (*za'am*) definitely means lie.

"اَلتَّزَعُّمُ" (*at-taza'am*): to fabricate lies; linguists say "زَعَمُوْا" (*za'amu*) means such things which have no authentication or proof, but are simply hear-say {*T*}. It includes the connotations of guesswork and expectation (may be true).

Muheet says "اَلزَّعْمُ" (*azza'am*) means doubtful talk or which is secretly believed to be false, some say talk without reasoning is "زَعْمٌ" (*za'am*). Some say it means to claim knowledge, some say that "زَعْمٌ" (*za'am*) means belief whether true or false {*R*}.

Raghib says that this word has always appeared in Quran when condemnation of the speaker is intended.

The Quran says:

| 64:7 | The unbelievers think that they can't be raised.... | زَعَمَ الَّذِيْنَ كَفَرُوْا اَنْ لَنْ يُبْعَثُوْا |

In Surah *Al-Anam* says:

| 6:137 | ...false belief.... | بِزَعْمِهِمْ |

"زَعَمَ بِهِ" (*za'ama bihi*): guaranteed it, accepted the responsibility for it.

"اَلزَّعِيْمُ" (*az-za'eem*): responsible for and patron (68:40, 12:72).

Ibn Faris has said that the root has two basic meanings. Firstly to say something which has not been verified, and secondly to accept the responsibility for something and become its patron.

Z-F-R   ز ف ر

"زَفَرَ" (*zafar*), "يَزْفِرُ" (*yazfir*), "زَفِيْرًا" (*zafeera*): to take the breath out *{T}*.

Raghib says it means to breathe heavily, as while sobbing the breath comes and goes. It is mostly used for the initial gasping sound of a donkey's braying. The last part of its voice is called "شَهِيْق" (*shaheeq*), while "زَفِيْرٌ" (*zafeer*) means to take the breath inside *{T}*.

The Quran has used both "زَفِيْرٌ" (*zafeer*) and "شَهِيْقٌ" (*shaheeq*) together in the same sentence 11:106. It means to sob, to cry out loud 21:100. It also means the sound of a fire flaring up (25:13), and it is also used for an unexpected misfortune.

"اَلزِّقْرُ" (*az-ziqr*): the load on one's back, a traveller's luggage, a skin container used by shepherds to store water, **Ibn Faris** says it can basicly mean both, load and noise.

Z-F-F   ز ف ف

"اَلزَّفِيْفُ" (*az-zafeef*) basically means for the wind to blow strongly, further the fast speed of an ostrich which is a combination of running fast along with flying *{R}*.
"زَفَّ الْبَعِيْرُ" (*zaffal ba-eer*): the camel moved faster.
"اَلزَّفْزَفُ" (*az-zafzaf*): a fast moving ostrich or a camel
"اَلزَّفِيْفَ" (*az-zafeef*) also means lightning.
"زَفَّ الْعَرُوْسَ اِلٰى زَوْجِهَا زَفًّا وَزِفَافاً" (*zaffal uroosa ila zaujihazaffa wa zifafa*): he presented the bride before the husband *{T}* (**Here the presenter's eagerness is involved**).

Ibn Faris says it basically means to be fast and slick in everything.

The Quran says:

37:94	they came towards him with alacrity	فَأَقْبَلُوْا اِلَيْهِ يَزِفُّوْنَ

(Here the emotive intensity is evident).

Z-Q-M زق م

"اَلزَّقْمُ" (*az-zaqm*): to take a mouthful, to swallow.

"أَزْقَمَهُ الشَّيْءَ" (*azqamahush shaiyi*): he gave him something as a mouthful and made him swallow {T}.

Raghib says "زَقَمَ" (zaqam) *and* "تَزَقَّمَ" (tazaqqam) *means to swallow something unpleasant {R}.*

"اَلزَّقُّوْمُ" (*az-zaqqoom*): means a wild plant which is bitter tasting and its small, round leaves are very ugly and it has big knots in its stalk.

The Quran says:

37:65	The shoots of its fruit-stalk are like the heads of devils.	طَلْعُهَا كَأَنَّهُ رُئُوْسُ الشَّيَاطِيْنِ

It is obvious why the Quran has used it as an allegory for a mental state of indivduals.

Soalub has said that "اَلزَّقُّوْمُ" (*az-zaqqoom*) means every edible thing that is poisonous and can kill {T}.

Muheet says that it is used when a person eats or does something that becomes a bane for him.

The Quran declares:

37:64	the tree that grows at the base of a hellish society	إِنَّهَا شَجَرَةٌ تَخْرُجُ فِيْ أَصْلِ الْجَحِيْمِ

It is obvious that this does not refer to an actual tree as no tree can grow in the fires of hell. It signifies such sustenance which may turns humanity into a very unhappy state of living in this world. It refers to powerful and rich people as long branches of the tree and their means of sustenance obtained through oppressive means. This has also been pronounced "شَجَرَةٌ مَلْعُوْنَة" (*shajaratun mal-oonah*) in 17:60 and "طَعَامُ الْأَثِيْمِ" (*tu'aamul aseem*) in 42:44. That is, such sustenance which makes a man weak and his potentials are stultified, and he is deprived of the true pleasures of life as defined by the Quran. This is sustenance of the people who have self-declared respect honour in a society due to the possession of wealth and power (44:49). This the group of *Mutrafeen* (56:45). The group which lives on the hard work of fellow human beings' labor (37:66). Such sustenance may temporarily satisfy their desires, but will be of no use for the development of humanity as whole.

In (17:60) which is referred above, it is also possible that it means .... as quoted in (14:26). This may mean wrong ideology of life; however, these all are allegorical and used to illustrate a state of individuals and society.

Zikriya   زكريا

The Quran has mentioned **Zikriyah** as one of the messengers belonging to **Bani Israel** (6:85). He is referred in surah **Aal-e-Imran** (3:37-40), surah **Maryam** (19:2-15), and surah **Al-Ambia** (21:89-90). These verses mention that he was old and his wife could not conceive, but the capability to give birth to a child was restored in her (21:90) and **Yahya** was born as **Zikriyah's** son. He was the patron of **Maryam** (3:37).

Loqa's Bible says that during the reign of king Herodis of Yahudia, this was the name of an astrologer, and his wife was from among the descendants of **Haroon** and was named **Al-yashba**. They had no child as **Al-yashba** was infertile.

The Torah (Old Testament) mentions a messenger named **Zakariah**, a very big official of the Jews was called **Nabi** (messenger) which was translated as astrologer. But the Quran's concept of a **Nabi** is entirely different from this, and the Quran has counted **Zikriyah** as one a **Nabi** (messenger receiving the revelaion).

Z-K-W   ز ک و

"زَكَاالْمَالُ وَالزَّرْعُ" (*zaka al-maal az-zar'o*), "يَزْكُوْ" (*yazku*), "زُكُوَّاً" (*zukuwwa*), "اَزْکیٰ" (*azka*): for crops or animals to grow, to develop, to increase, to prosper.

"اَزْکیٰ اللہُ الْمَالَ وَزَّکَاہُ" (*azka allahu-lmala wazzakkahu*): Allah gave prosperity and multiplied wealth.

"زَکَا الرَّجُلُ یَزْکُوْ" (*zakar rajuluh yazku*): someone prospered and his abilities developed. His life became happier, rich and blossomed in all respects.. {**Taj-ul-Uroos** and **Ibn Qateebah, Al-qartain.** Vol. I page 62}

Therefore, the basic meanings of "زَکَ" (*zaka*) are to develop, propsper, grow and blossom in all respects.

Raghib has stated this verse to prefer this meaning:

18:19	...find out which is the best food and bring some that satisfy your appetite ...	فَلْيَنْظُرْ اَيَّهَا اَزْکیٰ طَعَاماً

i.e. to select the food which has better overall nutritional value.

"اَلزَّکٰوۃُ" (*az-zakaat*) means to develop, to grow, to increase, to blossom {**T**}. It may also mean purity, probably in order to let the trees grow properly you have to pare the branches, etc, but this is not its basic meaning. In the Quran itself, in the same verse "اَزْکیٰ" (*azka*) and "اَطْهَرُ" (*at-har*) have been used separately in 2:232. Here "اَطْهَرُ" (*at-har*) is for purity and "اَزْکیٰ" (*azka*) for development. Purity is a negative virtue, i.e to stay away from impurities, but "زکٰوۃ" (*zakat*) is a positive virtue, that is to blossom, to grow, to increase, to progress, to realize potentials, etc.

Muheet writes with reference to *Baizaai* that the meaning of "اَلزَّكِىَّ" (*azikki*) is to grow with a view to enhance all around abilities, one who develops his potentials from one stage of life to later part of life. There is an implicit element of self-development and continuous evolvement in this term.

"أَرْض زَكِيَّةٌ" (*ardun zakiyyah*): lush green pasture which is very fertile and has abundant potential for growth.
"أَزْكىٰ" (*azka*) means very beneficial {M, F}.
"زَكَأً" (*zaka*) means the figure which is a pair {M, F}.

Surah *Al-Kahaf* Allah commits to bestow them a son who will have better abilities than their previous son:

| 18:81 | … better in character and conduct … | خَيْراً مِنْهُ زَكوةً |
| 18:74 | ..Individual with good character and conduct…. | نَفْساً زَكِيَّةً |

At another place it is said:

| 19:19 | … youth with good character and conduct.. | غُلٰماً زَكِيّاً |

In surah *Ash-Shams*, "زَكّٰهَا" (*zakkaha*) has been used against "دَسّٰهَا" (*dassaha*) (91:9-10).

"تَدْسِيَةٌ" (*tadsiyatun*) means to suppress someone, to bury someone alive (16:59), or to curb human development. As such "تَزْكِيَة" (*tazkiah*) would mean to remove all restrictions and obstructions which may be hampering someone's progress and to facilitate path to self-development.

The Quran refers to the following term repeatedly in many places e.g. (2:83, 2:177):

| 2:83 | Establish *Salah* and provide *Zakaah* | اَقِيْمُوْ الصَّلٰوةَ وَ اٰتُوْالزَّكوةَ |

Indeed these are the two basic pillars of the Quranic System which lay the foundations. For the detailed meaning of this term, see heading (Sd-L-W). You will find that its meaning is to establish a Quranic social order within the defined permanent values so that the individuals living within the society have the option to attain the aim of defined and explained self-development. The question is what then is the purpose of establishing such a social order? The aim is to "ايتائ زكٰوة" (*eetayi zakat*) i.e. to provide self-development. In other words, to provide the opportunity and environment to the mankind with requisite means for their individual and collective growth and development. This development and growth include both aspects: the nurturing of man's corporeal being and the development of his Self (personality).

In Sura **Al-Hajj:**

22:41	This is the group who when given power will establish the system of **salaah** and provide **zakaah**	الَّذِيْنَ اِنْ مَّكَّنّٰهُمْ فِى الْاَرْضِ اَقَامُوالصَّلٰوةَ وَ اٰتَوُ الزَّكٰوةَ

i.e. the basic responsibility of the Islamic State will be to provide *Zakaah* to others. The duty of an Islamic State would be to provide "الزَّكٰوةَ" (*zakaah*). It will provide sustainable means of growth (both aspects as mentioned above) to all in their society and the mankind at large.

At another place *momins* are defined as:

23:4	Those who strive for **zakaah** (development and growth for the mankind).	هُمْ لِلزَّكٰوةِ فَاعِلُوْنَ

Now the question that comes to our mind is, how will the Islamic State fulfill this huge obligation? It is obvious that to fulfill this responsibility all means of production must remain with the state so that it can distribute sustenance according to people's needs. Secondly, the individuals keep open (available) all that they earn above their needs, so that the state can take whatever and whenever it finds necessary for the provision of this collective responsibility. For this purpose, the Quran has not fixed any amount, all that is intended is to fulfill the need, so much so that it has been said that anything and all above one's needs can be handed over to the state (2:219). Seen from this angle, the entire income of such a state is geared towards this mentioned prosperity, or fulfilling the needs of society's individuals.

However, an Islamic \system can only be established gradually and in defined stages. Until the time that it shapes up completely, individuals will give, as in today's governments, voluntary donations and income taxes will also be imposed. The Quran has used the term "صدقات" (*sadaqaat*) for them. Commonly we believe "صدقات" (*sadaqaat*) and "زکٰوة" (*zakat*) to have same meaning, so much that the avenues of spending of "صدقات" (*sadaqaat*) by the Quran (9:60) are also taken to be avenues for spending "زکٰوة" (*zakat*), but the Quran has used these terms in different contexts.

It is obvious from the discussion so far that these are not simply individualistic issues according to the Quran but these are the departments of the Islamic State. Whatever one gives individually to help a fellow human beings will be charity. In an Islamic State, ultimately there is no need of individual charity because it becomes the duty of the state to provide for every ones needs which includes both aspects of self-development. Whatever the Islamic State takes is not a state tax and "زکٰوة" (*zakat*) is not Allah's tax as explained next.

This dualism of God and the sovereign is a product of Christianity, not of the Islam as revealed in the Quran. There is no place for this dualism whatsoever in Islam. In a state which is established for following Allah's Laws, everything that is given to the Islamic State is given to Allah. For details see headings (**R-B-B**), (**N-F-Q**) and (**Sd-D-Q**).

In Surah **An-Najam** the Quran declares:

53:32	do not decide on your own that your Self (*Nafs*) has been purified, He knows who is righteous (as per the Quran).	فَلَا تُزَكُّوا اَنْفُسَكُمْ هُوَاَعْلَمُ بِمَنِ اتَّقٰى

The criterion is explained in the Quran:

92:18	..he who gives his wealth for the development of others, has his Self-purified	الَّذِىْ يُؤْتِىْ مَا لَهٗ يَتَزَكّٰى
92:5	he who gives and thus attains righteousness (*taqwa*)	مَنْ اَعْطٰى وَاتَّقٰى
92:7	..for him the path (of life) becomes easy…	فَسَنُيَسِّرُهٗ لِلْيُسْرٰى

Z-L-F   ز ل ف

"اَلزَّلَفُ" (*az-zalaqu*), "الزُّلْفٰى" (*zulfa*), "الزُّلْفَةُ" (*zulfah*): nearness, rank or grade.
"اَلزُّلْفَةُ" (*az-zulfah*): the part (long or short) of the initial or later night. The plural is "زُلَفٌ" (*zulaf*).
"اَلْمَزَالِفُ" (*al-mazalif*): steps, which take a man closer to his objective. This term has both connotations of nearness and stages or grades in the achievement of an objective. "دَرَجَةٌ" (*darajah*) also means steps which take a man upwards.
"زَلَفَ اِلَيْهِ" (*zalafa ilaih*): he came closer to him.
"اَزْلَفَهٗ" (*azlafah*): brought him closer, gathered him.

Ibn Faris says it basically means to go forward in order to be closer.
Raghib says that "زُلَفٌ" (*zulaf*) means the stages of the night.
Kitabul Ashfaq says "اَلزُّلْفَةُ" (*az-zulfah*) means stages.

The Quran says:

67:27	At length, when they will see it close at hand..	فَلَمَّا رَاَوْهُ زُلْفَةً
34:37	..which brings you nearer to Us in stature…	تُقَرِّبُكُمْ عِنْدَنَا زُلْفٰى
26:64	and We brought the others closer over there	وَاَزْلَفْنَا ثَمَّ الْاٰخَرِيْنَ
11:114	both ends of the day and some parts of the night	اَقِمِ الصَّلٰوةَ طَرَفَىِ النَّهَارِ وَزُلَفًا مِنَ اللَّيْلِ

Also see heading (D-L-K) and (Th-R-F).

Z-L-Q   ز ل ق

"زَلِقَ" (*zaliq*), "يَزْلَقُ" (*yazlaq*), "يَزْلُقُ" (*yazluqu*) "زَلَقَ" (*zalaq*), "زَلَقاً" (*zalaqa*): to slip, to waver, to move from one's place.

"اَلزَّلَقُ" (*az-zalaq*): smooth ground on which one may slip. Ground which has no vegetation and plants.

"اَلزَّلْقَةُ" (*az-zalqah*): smooth rock. can also be mirror {T, R, M}.

Surah *Al-Kahaf* says:

18:40	It can become a smooth and plain field which has no vegetation whatsoever (like a mirror)	فَتُصْبِحَ صَعِيدًا زَلَقاً

"اَزْلَقَ فُلَاناً بِبَصَرِهِ" (*azlaqa fulanan bibasirih*): looked at him with sharp (angry) eyes, stared at him as if he will dislodge him from his place with his eyes {T, R, M}.

Surah *Al-Qalam* says about the non-believers:

68:51	they see you as if they will dislodge you from your place (deter you) with their very looks	لَيُزْلِقُونَكَ بِأَبْصَارِهِمْ

Z-L-L   ز ل ل

"زَلَّ" (*zal*), "زَلِيْلٌ" (*zalil*), "مَزِلَّةٌ" (*mazillah*): to slip, to waver.

"اَلْمَزِلَّةُ" (*al-mazillatu*), "اَلْمَزَلَّةُ" (*al-mazallatuh*): the place on which one slips.

"اَزَلَّهُ" (*azallahu*): misguided him (2:36).

"اَلزَّلَّةُ" (*azallah*): slip, to move from one's stance.

The Quran has used this word opposite "ثَبَتَ" (*sabat*) in 16:94, which means stability, firm position based on principles.

Ibn Faris says any word in which there is a "ل" (*laam*) after "ز" (ze) has a connotation to move (from one's place). In mutual conversation the term is used to waver, to change one's opinion, or to make a judgemental error.

Raghib says "زَلَّةٌ" (*zallah*) means a slip which is unintentional.

"اِسْتَزَلَّ" (*istazalla*): decide to persuade someone to move him away from his stance. (3:154).

"زَلِيْلٌ" (*zalil*) also means to transfer from one place to another.

"قَوْسٌ زَلَّاءُ" (*qausun zalla'u*): the bow, out of which the arrow shoots with high velocity.

"زَلْزَلَةٌ" (*zalzalah*): means to move or shake something very fast, or move it from its location {T}.

"زَلْزَلَ" (*zalzal*), "يُزَلْزِلُ" (*yuzalzil*), "زَلْزَلَةٌ" (*zalzalatu*), "زِلْزَالاً" (*zilzala*): shook it {T}.

99:1	When the earth is shaken to its convulsion	إِذَا زُلْزِلَتِ الْأَرْضُ زِلْزَالَهَا

Z-L-M ز ل م

"اَلزَّلَمُ" (*az-zalam*), "اَلزُّلُمُ" (*az-zulam*): the wooden part of the arrow which does not have feathers at its tail. Plural is "أَزْلَامٌ" (*azlaam*).

Ibn Faris says it basically means to be slim and smooth.

"أَزْلَامٌ" (*azlaam*) also means the arrows which the Arabs used in the period before Islam to carry out predictions or to foretell fate. Three arrows were used to be put into a bag. On one they used to write "اِفْعَلْ" (*if'al*) which means do, on the other "لَاتَفْعَلْ" (*la taf'al*), which means don't, and the third one did not have any writing. When a man intended to do something, he used to come to the priest and asked him to find out whether he should carry out what he intended to do. Thereupon the priest, as per his practice, used to take out one arrow and tell him according to what was written on the arrow. If the arrow without writing was picked then they would pick again. Some people used to carry such arrows and used them when the need arose *{T, M}*. These arrows were also used for making draws and to divide the meat of the animals, in gambling (5:3). For draw see heading (*Q-L-M*).

The Quran stopped all these practices, because in this way individuals instead of deciding according to their intellect and understanding leave themselves at the mercy of pure chance. Such practices bring them down from the level of the stature of humanity and consign them to the world of pure chances. The Quran helps man to develop his intellect, insight and understanding and teaches him freedom. Thus it prevented him from all of this which stultifies his intellect and his freedom of choice. The Quran gives him full freedom (while remaining within the bounds of Allah's laws) to exercise free will for deciding about his individual and collective affairs. However, without the guidance of the Quran the human condition has deteriorated to such extent that gambling has become common and is providing the basis of the capitalist system. Nations which are on the downfall not only give up their efforts but also leave the exercise of their intellect and reason and suffer the consequences as a result. A *momin* knows fully well that he is a living being, not a dead star. He does not depend on chances or coincidences, but acts within the permanent values and makes them subservient to his will.

Z-M-R ز م ر

"زَمْرٌ" (*zamr*): sound.

"اَلزَّمَّارَةُ" (*aza zammaratu*), "اَلْمِزْمَارُ" (*al-mizmaar*): flute.

"زَمَرَ" (*zamara*), "يَزْمُرُ" (*yazmuru*), "يَزْمِرُ" (*yazmiru*), "زَمْرَأَ" (*zamra*): to play the flute.

"اَلزُّمْرَةُ" (*az-zumrah*), the plural of which is "زُمَرٌ" (*zumar*), means scattered army or party, because all groups produce scattered sounds or noise *{T, M}*. This word is also used for gathering a group together by through blowing a bugle producing a high sound.

Raghib says it means a small party *{R}*.

The Quran says:

39:71	Those who reject the guidance will be led to hell in groups.	وَسِيقَ الَّذِينَ كَفَرُوْا اِلٰى جَهَنَّمَ زُمَرًا

The word "زُمَرٌ" (*zumar*) seems to connote small groups {*RIbn Faris* says it has two basic meanings. One is the paucity of something and the second is sound.

Z-M-L   ز م ل

"اَلزَّمِيْلُ" (*az-zameel*) is a man who sits atop a camel. It also means a companion who helps in arranging affairs before and during traveling.

"زَمَلَه" (*zamalahu*), "يَزْمِلُه" (*yazamiluhu*), "زَمْلًا" (*zamla*): he made him ride behind him or made him sit on the (camel's) howdah beside him.

"اَلزِّمْلُ" (*az-ziml*): load.

"اِزْدَمَلَ الحِمْلَ" (*izdamalil himl*): he lifted the entire load in one go.

"اَلْمُزَامَلَةُ" (*al-muzaamalah*): for riders of the same weight to ride a camel on both sides or to load the same type of loads for balancing on a camel.

There are usually two riders on a camel. On longer journeys, people who sit together on a camel, are usually of similar weight, and also compatible to each other with similar outlook to life. The reason for this is that if their weights are quite different then the camel will feel uncomfortable due to unbalance. If they do not have a psychological harmony the journey will be very uncomfortable for both of them. The leader of a caravan should be the one who is sensible and capable of selecting compatible companions in the journey from all respects.

When the Quranic system was revealed to the Messenger (*pbuh*), the most important duty before him was to adopt "زَمِيْلانَه" (*zammeelana*), that is, to select companions who were psychologically in tune with the message, because such a great system's success depended on selecting the right individuals. This was the duty towards which his attention was drawn by saying "يَا اَيُّهَا لْمُزَّمِّلُ" (*ya ayyohal muzammil*) in 73:1. Thereafter "تَزْمِيْل" (*tazmeel*), i.e. the selection of companions, carried out by the Messenger (*pbuh*) is unmatched in human history till now.

"اِزْدَمَلَ" (*izdamal*), "تَزَمَّلَ" (*tazammal*), "ازَّمَّلَ فِىْ ثِيَابِه" (*az-zammala fi siyaabehi*) also means that he got himself wrapped in his clothes. Hence "اَلْمُزَّمِّلُ" (*al-muzammil*) could also mean someone who is careless in his affairs and is slack in his work {*R*}. Obviously in "يَا اَيُّهَاالْمُزَّمِّلُ" (*ya ayyohal muzammil*), this meaning cannot be taken although it is a matter of surprise that a high caliber linguist like *Raghib* has said that it this term is used allegorically and means, who are careless in their affairs and slack in their work {*R*}.

Ibn Faris has written that this root basically means one who bears the load. He also mentioned that "اَلزُّمَيْلُ" (*az-zumayl*) could be a person who when faced with difficulties wraps himself tightly in his clothes and becomes like a 'bundle' of clothes.

"اَلْمُزَامَلَةُ" (*al-muzaamala*) means to load a camel with equal weights on both sides. This way, "اَلْمُزَمَّلُ" (*al-muzammil*) would mean one who is very careful and is keen in carrying out this task. "تَزْمِيْلُ" (*tazmeel*).

"اَلزَّمْلُ" (*az-zaml*) also means load and "اِزْدَمَلَ الْحِمْلَ" (*izdamalil himal*) means that he loaded the entire load at once *{T}*. From this aspect "مُزَمَّلُ" (*muzammil*) would be he who accepts and bears the responsibility which is incumbent in following the Message.

Kashaf says with reference to *Akramah*, that "يَا اَيُّهَا الْمُزَمَّلُ" (*ya ayyohal muzammil*) means "O you who bears a great burden of responsibility"

Tafseer Rooh Al-mu'aani says it means the bearer of the burden of the Message and its responsibilities. *Tafseer Khazin* also supports this. *Tastari* says in his book that "اَلْمُزَمَّلُ" (*al-muzammil*) is one who has adopted the attributes of Allah (this defines the highest scale in forming companionship with Allah to establish the Islamic System with a view to solve human problems).

Tafseer Fatahul Qadeer (*Shokaani*) says it means "مُزَمَّلُ بِالْقُرآن" (*muzammilu bil Quran*) i.e. one who takes on himself the responsibilities defined within the Quran. One who takes all guidance from the Quran.

Qurtabi has also supported these meanings and has attributed his interpretation to *Abbas (RAH)*. To conclude, when the Messenger (*pbuh*) was called "يَآيُّهَا الْمُزَمَّلُ" (*ya ayyohal muzammil*), it was a reference to his great responsibilities as a messenger, the purpose of which was to bring a great revolution for the good of mankind with the willing assistance of a group of *momineen*.

Some think that "مُزَمِّلُ" (*muzammil*) is a word which has originated from "مُتَزَمِّلُ" (*mutazammil*).

Z-M-He-R ز م ه ر

"اَلزَّمْهَرِيْرُ" (*az-zamharir*): intense cold. It also means the moon *{T, M}*.
"اِزْمَهَرَّ الْيَوْمُ" (*iz meharral yaum*): the day became very cold.
"اِزْمَهَرَّ الْوَجْهُ" (*iz maharral wajah*): the face was badly distorted and the teeth were visible.

The Quran says about *jannah*:

76:13	there will not be intense cold or intense heat	لَا يَرَوْنَ فِيْهَا شَمْساً وَّلَا زَمْهَرِيْراً

"اَلْمُزْمَهِرُّ" (*al-muz mahirru*) means a man with 'smiling' teeth *{T, M}*. This is probably taken from the chattering of teeth in intense cold.

Ibn Faris says it is possible that this word is based upon "زَبْرٌ" (**zahr**) with an additional "م" (**meem**).

"زَبْرٌ" (**zahr**) means to sparkle, shine.

"ازْمَهَرَّتِ الْكَوَاكِبُ" (**izmaharratil kawakib**): the stars sparkled. When it is winter or cold weather, stars appear to sparkle brighter.

Zanjabeel   زنجبيل

"اَلزَّنْجَبِيلُ" (**az-zanjabeel**): ginger. The Arabs used the term to define something which possess very fragrant smell {T}.

Muheet thinks that it was originally a Persian word "**shankabeel**" which got adopted in Arabic.

The Quran says:

76:17	it will be a mixture of ginger	كَانَ مِزَاجُهَا زَنْجَبِيلاً

For details, see heading (M-Z-J).

Z-N-M   ز ن م

Ibn Faris says "زَنَمَ" (**zanam**) basically means to hang a thing onto another, to latch onto another thing.

"اَلزَّنِيْمُ" (**az-zaneem**): a man who does not belong ancestrally to a tribe but is attached to the tribe {T}. "زَنَمَتَا الْعَنْزِ" (**zanata-lghuz**): a phrase which refered to two tit like things hanging from a goat's neck.

Ancestral lineage had great importance within the Arabs. This obviously had a consequence for a man who was not from a tribe i.e no descendant lineage or of unknown lineage but was living within a tribe, was consigned to a demeaning position.

From this "اَلزَّنِيْمُ" (**az-zaneem**) was referred to an individual who was known for being mean and wicked {T}.

"اَلزُّنْمَةُ" (**az-zunmah**): a tree which has no leaves {T}. The Quran has used the term "زَنِيْمٌ" (**zaneem**) in 68:13.

Z-N-Y   ز ن ی

"زَنٰی" (*zana*), "یَزْنِیْ" (*yazni*), "زِنیًٰ" (*ziniyan*), "زِنَاءً" (*zina*): fornication *{T, R}*. It means to have sexual intercourse without marriage.

17:32	do not go near *zina*	وَلَا تَقْرَبُوا الزِّنٰی

This means, not only stay from from *zina*, but do not even approach anything that has anything to do with *zina*.

Surah *Al-Furqaan* says:

25:18	do not commit *zina*	وَلَا يَزْنُوْنَ

"اَلزَّانِیْ" (*az-zaani*): a man who commits *zina*, "اَلزَّانِیَةُ" (*az-zaniyah*): a woman who commits *zina*. Each of them are to be lashed a hundred times as a punishment (24:2) within an Islamic State, as an exception if a married who was a slave in the past, (according to the customs prevalent in the pre-Islamic era) then the punishment is halved (4:25). This is because it is possible that a slave girl who has been brought up in an environment of low morality, may not show same level of character and conduct as a girl of good and strong upbringing. This serves as an indicator that how profoundly the Quran views moral conduct of human beings and takes into account the environmental factors which shape human personality and thus makes appropriate allowances. It must be noted that the Quran eliminated the institution of slavery once for all. Details can be found under the heading (*M-L-K*).

This should be noted that the punishment of stoning to death (or *rajm*) is not stated anywhere in the Quran.

This aspect has been done extensively researched in our times as to what effects sexual affairs have on the rise and fall of nations and to what extent the nations which do not respect the celibacy (before marriage) of its people descend low in character socially and morally. Anyone having an interest in this subject can refer to the book titled "*Letters to Saleem vol. III*".

Z-He-D   ز ه د

"زَبَدَ" (*zahad*), "یَزْبَدُ" (*yazhad*), "زُبْدًا" (*zuhda*): not to have a liking to something, turn away in dislike *{T}*, to avoid something, or to keep a distance *{T}*. The verb is "زَبَّدَ" (*zahid*).

In Surah *Yusuf* it is stated that the caravan people disposed off Yusuf at a small price because:

22:20	they did not have much interest in *Yusuf*	وَكَانُوا فِيهِ مِنَ الزَّاهِدِينَ

"اَلزَّبِیْدُ" (*az-zaheed*): little and insignificant *{T}*.
"اَلزَّاهِدُ" (*az-zaahidu*), "اَلزَّبِیْدُ" (*az-zaheed*): impolite man, somone with ill manners, or someone who eats little *{T}*.

Ibn Faris says it means the paucity of something, Something in short supply.
Muheet says that "زُبْدٌ" (*zuhd*) means to stop taking interest in in something. Cease liking something.

The term "زُبْدٌ" (*zuhd*) or "زابِدٌ" (*zahid*) commonly used in the Indian Sub continent in relation to e.g. mysticism or sufisim does not appear anywhere in the Quran. This is a term of ***tasawwuf (mysticism)*** in which giving up necessities and responsibilities of this world has great significence. This concept is against the Quranic teachings. ***Tasawwuf*** itself is an alien as far as the Quranic teachings are concerned. According to the Quran, a believer has a responsibility to bring natural forces under human control for the benefit of the mankind as a whole and enjoy the pleasures of this life within the values defined and explained in the Quranic. The Quran pronounces in no uncertain terms to challenge those who declare the bounties of this world which Allah has created for the benefit of mankind as forbidden (7:42). A ***momin*** only avoids those things which Allah has specifically forbidden otherwise he brings all other things of this world into use and benefits from them.

Z-He-R   ز ه ر

"اَلزَّبَرَةُ" (*az-zahrah*), "اَلزَّبَرَةُ" (*az-zaharah*): plant, or flower. Some say it is a flower in blossom.
"اَلزَّبَرَةُ مِنَ الدُّنْیَا" (*az-zahratuh minad duniya*): the scenic views e.g. greenery, water, hills, etc in the world. Beauty and splendour, the means of adornment (20:131).
"اَلزُّبَرَةُ" (*az-zuhrah*): whiteness *{T}*, beauty, brightness.
"اَلزَّبَرِیَّاتُ مِنَ الأَیَّامِ" (*az-zahriyyaat minal ayyam*): the spring season *{M}*.

Ibn Faris says that the basic meanings of this word are beauty, light, and cleanliness.

Z-He-Q   ز ه ق

Muheet says "زُهُوْقٌ" (*zuhuq*) means to come out/exit with difficulty.

"زَهَقَتِ النَّفْسُ" (*zahaqatin nafs*): he died with difficulty (that is he breathed his last with difficulty).

"اَلزَّاهِقْ" (*az-zahiq*): plump animal, also an animal which is very weak. The word can have opposing meanings.

"اَلزَّهُوْقُ" (*az-zahuq*): means deep well and also used for the path between two lofty mountains *{T}*. Whether with difficulty or ease, it means for something to exit *{T}*.

Ibn Faris says its basic meanings are to move forward, to pass away, or to surpass.

"زَهَقَتِ الرَّاحِلَةُ زُهُوْقاً" (*zahaqatir rahilatan zahuqa*): the she camel overtook the horses.

"زَهَقَ السَّهْمُ زُهُوْقاً" (*zahaqas sahmu zuhuqa*): the arrow went past the target.

"زَهَقَتْ نَفْسُه" (*zahaqat nafsuh*): he died *{T}*.

"تَزْهَقُ اَنْفُسَهُمْ" (*tazhaqu anfusahim*): they died (9:55).

"اَلزَّاهِقُ" (*az-zahiqu*): a defeated man *{T}*.

"اَلْمُرْهَقْ" (*al-murhaqu* the murdered one.

"زَهَقَ الشَّيْءُ" (*zahaqas shaiyi*): something was destroyed, or was ineffective *{T}*.

The Quran says about falsehood (batil):

21:18	every concept that is against the truth (*haqq*), creates destructive results and remains unsuccessful (gets defeated)	فَاِذَا هُوَ زَاهِقٌ
17:81	and say that truth (*haqq*) has arrived and falsehood (*batil*) is banished. In reality falsehood (by nature) is bound to parish.	وَقُلْ جَاءَ الْحَقُّ وَزَهَقَ الْبَاطِلُ ـ اِنَّ الْبَاطِلَ كَانَ زَهُوْقاً

In fact, *batil* is destined to be banished. Here "زَهُوْقٌ" (*zahuq*) means the same as "زَاهِقٌ" (*zahiq*) but with some exaggeration. *Batil* stays only till *haqq* (Allah's constructive program) does not arrive. Once it comes, *batil* gets defeated and wiped out. It does not have the ability to stay in when confronted by *haqq*. For more details see headings (H-Q-Q) and (B-Te-L).

"اَزْهَقْتُ الْاِنَاءَ" (*azhaqatul inaa*): I turned the pot over *{T}*.

Raghib says "زَهَقَتْ نَفْسُه" (*zahaqat nafsuhu*) means he died due to sorrow and grief *{R}*.

Z-W-J   ز و ج

"زَوْجٌ" (*zauj*): Two things which are compatible with each other e.g. a pair of shoes. "زَوْجَان" (*zaujaan*): Or two things which are opposing each other e.g. day and night.
In both cases, each one of them is called the other's "زَوْجٌ" (*zauj*).

"زَوْجٌ" (*zauj*) actually means someone who makes a combination or pairs with someone else, either in similarity or opposite.
"زَوَّجَ الشَّیْءُ بِالشَّیْءِ" (*zaujash shaiya bish shaiyi*): he paired a thing with something like similar to it.
"وَاِذَا النُّفُوْسُ زُوِّجَتْ" (*wa izan nafusu zuwwijat*): when every person will meet his companions and counterparts (81:7).

44:54	they will be made companions with *Hoor'een* (*Companions with high intellect*)	زَوَّجْنَاهُمْ بِحُوْرٍ عِیْنٍ

For the meaning of "حُوْرٌ" (*hoor*) see heading (H-W-R).

Lane says that everything of a homogenous variety is called "اَزْوَاجٌ" (*azwaaj*).

37:22	gather the oppressive parties and their ilk	اُحْشُرُوا الَّذِیْنَ ظَلَمُوْا وَ اَزْوَاجَهُمْ

With regards to the dwellers of *jannnat*, it is delared:

4:57	Therein shall be *azwaaj* with pristine intellect for you	لَهُمْ فِیْهَا اَزْوَاجٌ مُطَهَّرَةٌ

Here it does not only mean virtuous wives or husbands, but also companions with the same pure thoughts. In a heavenly society (*jannah*), there is existence of virtuous thoughts. Note that this heavenly society will be formed in this world. Here the relationship between husband and wife will include the responsibility of progeny as well. But such a concept of man and woman is not found in the Quran and the companionship in the hereafter will not be for progeny. This will be based on companionship; however, we cannot understand the nature of this at our present level of understanding and existence. The Quran has explained the hereafter concepts allegorically. Because of these meanings, the species of everything is called *zauj* {Lane}.
"اَزْوَاجاً مِنْهُمْ" (*azwaaja minhum*): people who are of different kind but of the same species, or things of many kind but of the same type (20:131).

26:7	We created different things of a good quality	كَمْ أَنْبَتْنَا فِيهَا مِنْ كُلِّ زَوْجٍ كَرِيمٍ
38:58	similar types of various punishments	وَآخَرُ مِنْ شَكْلِهِ أَزْوَاجٌ
51:49	We have created things which are zauj to one another, either similar or opposite	وَمِنْ كُلِّ شَيْءٍ خَلَقْنَا زَوْجَيْنِ

For example the sky is the *zauj* of the earth. They together make a pair or a combination. Winter is the *zauj* of summer, and a shoe is the *zauj* of the other shoe. *Zauj* also means whose companion is unique. This word can be used for either one of them; however, for the combination, we will use "زَوْجَانِ" (*zaujaan*) {*Lane*}.

"اِزْدَوَجَ" (*izdawaj*), "تَزَاوَجَ" (*tazawaj*): to make two parts go together; or words that rhyme; or for two problems to be related to each other.

"زَوْجٌ" (*zauj*) with plural "أَزْوَاجٌ" (*azwaaj*) means companion or friend {Lane}. It also means either husband or wife. The husband is the "زَوْجٌ" (*zauj*) of his wife and she is the "زَوْجٌ" (*zauj*) of her husband *{T, M}*. One complements the other. This is married (conjugal) life. The Quran has termed them each other's covering like a dress which covers the body. See heading (L-B-S). In verse 13:38, "أَزْوَاجًا" (*azwaaja*) means wives.

"تَزَوَّجْتُ اِمْرَأَةً" (*tazawajtu imra'ah*): I married a woman.

As per the Quran, it will be suffice to say that the term "تَزَوَّجَهُ النَّوْمُ" (*tazawwajahun naum*) is used allegorically when one is in a blissful sleep *{T, M}*. The relationship of a married couple is like a blissful sleep which is a source of pleasure to both partners. See heading (N-K-H). The wives and husbands in a heavenly society on earth will also be pure of heart and soul and good companions in the journey of life extending beyond death to the next life. The Quran has described their characteristics in different chapters. As far as the heaven in the next life is concerned, as mentioned earlier and in detail under the heading (J-N-N) that we cannot comprehend it at our present level of understanding. Hence, we are unable to say what the condition will be there. We cannot deny the fact that a companionship based on similar values and interests is blissful in this life as the Quran has stated in (2:221).

Z-W-D   ز و د

"اَلزَّادُ" (*az-zaad*): something more than the present needs and which is saved for later time. *{R}*. It means food (provision), whether for the present or future, especially the food which is prepared for a journey {F}.

"اَلْمِزْوَدُ" (*al-mizwaad*): tiffin carrier *{T}*.

"زَوَّدْتُهُ تَزْوِيدًا" (*zawwattuhu tazweeda*): I gave him food for the journey.

"تَزَوَّدَ" (*tazawwad*): he took food along for the journey *{T}*.

The Quran says in respect of *Hajj*:

2:197	Take a provision for the journey,, so you may not be dependent upon others???	وَتَزَوَّدُوا فَإِنَّ خَيْرَ الزَّادِ التَّقْوَىٰ

Ibn Faris says with reference to *Khalil*, that "تَزَوَّدَ" (*tazawwad*) means to take something good from one place to another.

Z-W-R   ز و ر

"اَلزَّوْرُ" (*az-zaur*): the upper part of the chest where the bones confluence. It is also used for a visitor.

"زُرْتُهُ" (*zartuhu*): I bared my chest before him (confronted him).

"اَلزَّوْرُ" (*az-zaur*) and "اَلزِّيَارَةُ" (*az-ziyarah*), "اَلْمَزَارُ" (*al-mazaar*): to meet, to visit.

"اَلزَّوْرُ" (*az-zaur*) also means the bent chest which leans on one side.

"اَلْأَزْوَرُ" (*al-azwar*): one who has a chest which is crooked or bent. One who leans his chest to one side more than the other while walking. One who looks from side of his eyes. The word means to lean to one side, as well as to move away from the right direction.

Ibn Faris says it means to lean to one side, as well as to move to onside.

It says in Surah *Al-Kahaf*:

18:17	the sun moves towards one side of their cave (i.e. does not shine directly into their cave)	تَزَاوَرُ عَنْ كَهْفِهِمْ

"زَوَّرَ عَنْهُ" (*zawwar unhu*): he shifted or moved away from it.

"اَلزُّورُ" (*az-zuur*) means to tell a lie.

"حَبْلٌ لَهُ زُورٌ" (*hablun lahu zuur*): a rope with twisted fibres or threads {*T, M, R*}.

Surah *Al-Hajj* says:

22:30	Avoid talk based on lies (traditional translation)	وَاجْتَنِبُوا قَوْلَ الزُّورِ

The above verse actually means to avoid any act or deed which is not in line with the defined righteous path. Every thought and action one takes away from the righteous path "صراط مستقيم"

(*sirat-e-mustaqeem*), would fall under "زُورٌ" (*zuur*). Islam is a M ovement, which has a definite aim. Therefore, there is no room for "زُورٌ" (*zuur*) in it. The next verse elaborates this:

22:31	turn away from all other paths and move towards the path defined by Allah (i.e the Quran)	حُنَفَاءَ اللهِ
22:31	do not mix it with an outside thought, emotion, and preference	غَيْرَ مُشْرِكِينَ بِهِ

This has also sated in Ssurah **Al-Furqan**:

| 25:4 | An injustice and a lie | ظُلْماً وَزُوْرًا |

"كَلَامٌ مُزَوَّرًا" (**kalamun muzawwar**): fabricated talk and a pack of lies.

"زَوَّرَ الشَّيْءَ" (**zawwarsh shaiyi**): to mix and garnish a matter with lies.

"تَزْوِيْرٌ" (**tazweer**) means to remove "زُوْرٌ" (**zuur**). Therefore it means to rehabilitate.

Ibnul Airabi says that "تَزْوِيْرٌ" (**tazweer**) would be used when something is improved, whether it is good or bad {T}.

It also means to meet or to be confronted. It is used in 102:2:

| 102:2 | until you reach your graves | حَتَّى زُرْتُمُ الْمَقَابِرَ |

Z-W-L ز و ل

"زَالَ" (**zaal**), "يَزُوْلُ" (**yazulu**), "يَزَالُ" (**yazaal**), "زَوَالاً" (**zawala**): for something to be lost, to change, to be depressed, to move to one side, to be removed, to go afar, to be parted, to desist.

The Quran has used this word opposite to "أَمْسَکَ" (**amsaka**) in 35:31, which means to prevent.

| 35:41 | Verily Allah's law is holding the sky and the earth so that they do not move from their places (do not leave their celestial places) | إِنَّ اللهَ يُمْسِکُ السَّمٰوٰتِ وَالْأَرْضَ اَنْ تَزُوْلَا |

"زَيَّلَ" (**zayyal**): to separate {T, M, R}

2:217	they will always be like this	لَا يَزَالُوْنَ
10:28	We will separate them	فَزَيَّلْنَا بَيْنَهُمْ
48:25	if they had separated	لَوْتَزَيَّلُوا

Raghib says "زَوَالٌ" (**zawaal**) refers to the movement of something which is initially stable and later becomes unstable.

Z-Y-T   ز ى ت

"زَيْتٌ" (*zait*): olive oil (24:35).

"زَيْتُوْنَةٌ" (*zaitoonah*): an olive tree, or its fruit (24:35, 80:29) *{R}*. It is considered to be a very useful and beneficial plant *{M}*.

The Quran says:

95:103	By *At-teen* and the *Az-zaitoon* and the *At-toor*	وَالتِّيْنِ وَالزَّيْتُوْنِ وَطُوْرِ

Here "اَلزَّيْتُوْنُ" (*az-zaitoon*) means a mount named "زيتا" (*zita*) in Palestine. *Lataif-ul-Lugha* has mentioned it as *Jabalash sham*. *Isa* or Jesus was born there, and "اَلتِّيْنُ" (*at-teen*) is the place where *Noah* received his Message. The Quran has said that messages towards *Noah's*, *Isa*, *Moosa* and *Muhammed* (pbuh) are from Allah. These are the divine invitations towards the establishment of Allah's social order and to educate mankind about the ultimate truth.

95:4-6	Indeed We created the Man...	لَقَدْ خَلَقْنَا الْإِنْسَانَ

Z-Y-D   ز ى د

"زَيْدٌ" (*zaid*) means to develop, be nurtured, to grow and blossom, to increase, to flourish..

"زَادَ اللهُ خَيْرأً" (*zadallahu khaira*), "زَيَّدَهُ" (*zayyadahu*) means to give more or to increase *{T}*.

"اِزْدَادَ" (*izdada*), "اِزْدِيَادأً" (*izdiyada*): to grow more, or to produce more *{M}*.

Surah *Ar-Raad* has used "اِزْدِيَادٌ" (*izdiyaad*) opposite to "غَيْضٌ" (*ghaiz*) in 13:8, which means to decrease, or go inside, or to be absorbed.

Surah *Yunus* has used the word "زِيَادَةٌ" (*ziyadatun*) in 10:26, while "مَزِيْدٌ" (*mazeed*) has been used in 50:35, which means the addition that is made after something has been completed.

Surah *Aal-e-Imran* says:

3:89	grow more (increase) in denial.	ثُمَّ ازْدَادُوْ اكُفْرأً

Surah *Al-Ahzaab* has mentioned *Zaid* in 33:37. This is the only companion of the Messenger (pbuh) who has been mentioned in the Quran. He was the son of *Harasa* and the Messenger's beloved servant and adopted son. He was married to the Messenger's cousin *Zainab*.

For the meaning of "اَلزَّادُ" (*az-zaad*), see heading (Z-W-D).

Z-Y-Gh   ز ی غ

"زَاغَ" (*zaagh*), "یَزِیْغُ" (*yazeegh*), "زَیْغاً" (*zaigha*): to lean to one side.
"زَاغَبِ الشَّمَسُ" (*zaaghatis shams*): the sun commenced setting *{T}*.

Raghib says that although "زَالَ" (*zaal*), "مَالَا" (*maala*), and "زَاغَ" (*zaagha*) express almost the same meaning, but "زَاغَ" (*zaagh*) means to move away from the right path towards the wrong direction *{T}*.

Muheet with reference to the procedure has explained that wherever the Quran has used the word "زَیْغُ" (*zaigh*), it means to lean to one side, except when it says "زَاغَتِ الْأَبْصَارُ" (*zaaghatil absaar*) which means the eyes to be opened wide, or to remain open (in amazement) *{M}*.

The Quran says:

61:56	When they diverted from Allah's guidance, the law of Requital made them lean towards that very path.	فَلَمَّا زَاغُوْا اَزَاغَ اللّٰهُ قُلُوْبَهُمْ

This verse reveals a great truth. Generally it is said that guidance or going astray is controlled by God (is in His hands). He can guide whoever He wishes and lead astray, whomever He wishes. He seals the hearts of those who are to be led astray etc. This concept is completely against the teachings of the Quran and the Law of Requital. The Quran declares that man is created with the freedom to act as he chooses, he decides for himself whether to go on the right path or otherwise. The type of decision makes him subject to the corresponding laws. If he takes the wrong path then all his abilities get utilized in traversing the wrong path and are wasted.

51:8	only he who wants to turn away from the right path gets turned away	يُؤْفَكُ عَنْهُ مَنْ أُفِكَ

It is not Allah's Will to coerce someone to adopt the right path if he wants to take the wrong path, or if a man wants to stay on the right path then he is not turned away from it. Only those who wish to follow the crooked ways have their hearts turned away from the truth. By virtue of possessing a free will the initiative is in man's own hands. Allah's laws help a person according to his own choice and decision to act – freedom to choose is at the heart of human functioning and with this comes the responsibility. For exmample, it is Allah's law that if we close your eyes, it will become dark for us, but if we open our eyes, we will be able to see in the light.

In Surah **An-Najam** with reference to the Messenger (**pbuh**):

53:17	your sight has neither moved away from the truth nor has it crossed the limit.	مَا زَاغَ الْبَصَرُ وَمَا طَغَى

Here "مَاطَغَى" (**ma tagha**) has made it clear that although a messenger's knowledge of the revelation is far greater than any other human being, it is still limited in comparison to Allah. It can't cross the limits set for it by Allah.

In Surah **Saba**:

34:12	..if any of them turned away from our command order..	وَمَنْ يَزِغْ مِنْهُمْ عَنْ أَمْرِنَا

"زَاغَتِ الْأَبْصَارُ" (**zaaghatil ansaar**) has been used at the times of chaos during a collective punishment (33:10). It either means that at times of fear, one's eyes do not stay at one point, or as **Muheet** says, it means that the eyes remain lifted (out of fear or bewilderment). In any case, the purpose is to describe a state of fear.

"زَيْغٌ" (**zaigh**) has been used to describe the change in one's opinion towards someone (38:63). Its meaning is given as being crooked, and lean towards falsehood (3:9). That is, instead of concentrating and be stolid on a point described by the Quran, move away hither or thither, to turn somewhere else, to follow one's wishes, desires and wishes. This is a very risky attitude; the right path is that which is defined by the Quran, irrespective of what what our hearts and minds wish.. What the Quran says is the truth, not what our leanings are. Anyone who goes to the Quran with preconceived ideas and with the intention of getting support for those ideas, can never find the right guidance.

To get the right guidance from the Quran, the mind must be free from all the preconceptions and preconceived beliefs. This is the reason that the Quran has described "زَيْغٌ" (**zaigh**) as the opposite of guidance (3:7). For more details see heading (H-K-M).

Z-Y-L   ز ى ل

See heading (Z-W-L).

Z-Y-N   ز ی ن

"اَلزِّيْنَةُ" (*az-zeenah*): the thing which is used to adorn something. Some say that something to be perceived by someone as beautiful is also called "زِيْنَةُ" (*zeenah*).

"زَيَّنَ" (*zayyan*): to adorn something, to make something appear more beautiful, this also covers flattery {T}.

Iblees declared:

| 15:39 | I'll make the earthly life appear so attractive (to men that they will decide to make it their destiny) (the concept of life will be materialistic) | لَأُ زَيِّنَنَّ لَهُمْ فِى الْأَرْضِ |

"اِزَّيَّنَ" (*iz-zayyan*): to be adorned or beautified (10:4).

| 20:60 | the day of adornment | يَوْمُ الزِّيْنَةِ |

Then about *Bani Israel* the Quran quotes:

| 20:87 | those things with which people of the community used to adorn themselves | أَوْزَارًا مِنْ زِيْنَةِ الْقَوْمِ |
| 7:148 | their jewelry | حُلِيِّهِمْ |

The Quran not only takes into account the utilitarian aspect of utilities but also considers the aesthetic aspects. That is why it not only allows us to add beauty to ourselves and to our environment but goes a step further by directing us to do so.

| 7:31 | Adopt beauty and adornment while following Our laws | خُذُوا زِيْنَتَكُمْ عِنْدَ كُلِّ مَسْجِدٍ |

The Quran declares: by saying:

| 7:32 | Say: who has forbidden the beautiful bounties of Allah which He has produced for His servants? | قُلْ مَنْ حَرَّمَ زِيْنَةَ اللّٰهِ الَّتِىْ أَخْرَجَ لِعِبَادِهِ |

This is for all to use:

| 18:7 | That which is on earth We have made it attractive and beautiful | إِنَّا جَعَلْنَا مَا عَلَى الْأَرْضِ زِيْنَةً لَّهَا |

Nothing is forbidden on this earth; however, it must be borne in mind that the pursuit of these things should not become the sole purpose of life (18:46). These should be used for helping in achieving the real purpose of life. In short, there is no harm in enjoying the adornments of life, but whenever there is clash with the laws mentioned in the Quran, those adornments and attractions should be sacrificed for upholding the Quranic values. This is the crux of the Quranic teachings and the main aim of Islamic System(*Deen)*.

For example The Quran has directed (in the context of veil) that when men and women go about outside they should lower their gaze and guard their modesty (24:30-31) and the women should:

24:31	Not display their beauty and ornaments except of which appears naturally	لَا يُبْدِينَ زِيْنَتَهُنَّ إِلَّا مَاظَهَرَ مِنْهَا

Here adornments mean things which women use for beautification, for instance jewelry etc.

This seems to be supported by the next part of the same verse where it is said:

24:31	they should not step hard on the ground so whatever they are hiding among their adornments is made obvious	وَلَا يَضْرِبْنَ بِأَرْ جُلِهِنَّ لِيُعْلَمَ مَايُخْفِيْنَ مِنْ زِيْنَتِهِنَّ

By stepping hard on the ground, the jewelry like anklets make a sound and draw attention, as far as the adornment of the upper part of the body is concerned, it is advised that they should cover their body with shawls (24:31) or put on "جلباب" (*jalbaab*) (33:59) which is the same sort of cloth as a longer and wider overall. This means that they should not exhibit the things of their adornment, although if it is done in front of men in their household then there is no harm (24:31).

Sexual attraction and urge are not like the pangs of hunger which arouses at its own as and when body needs it. This emotion is aroused on instigation and by thinking about it. The Quran directs us to stop those causes which lead to provoking such thoughts and consequently cause arousing this urges. One of the biggest instigations is by women to exhibit their adornment and provocative turn out in front of other men, and this what is forbidden by the Quran.

<u>Seen</u>   س

This letter appears in the beginning of "حرف مضارع" (*harf muzaarih*) which is such a verb that contains connotations of both future and present tense. But when it appears at the beginning of a word, the sentence is considered to only be about future. As for example "سَيَفْعَلُ" (*sayaf'al*) means that he will work.

It normally means near future tense, but near or distant future does not matter. Some say that it can also hold the meaning of infinity.

| 2:142 | These misguided will continue to say that… | سَيَقُوْلُ السُّفَهَاءُ |

Some even say that when it appears with some verb which refers to some promise or commitment, then it holds the meaning of stressing on an issue.

| 2:137 | Allah will surely be sufficient for you against them | فَسَيَكْفِيْكَهُمُ اللّٰهُ |

S-A-L   س أ ل

"سَأَلْتُهُ الشَّيْءَ" (*saaltuhush shaiya*): I asked him for a thing.
"سَأَلْتُهُ عَنِ الشَّيْءِ وبِهِ" (*sa altuhu unish shaiyi wabehi*): I enquired from him about something.
"أَسْأَلَهُ" (*asalah*), "سُؤْلَهُ" (*sulah*): met the need in question.
"ٱلسَّائِلُ" (*as-sa'il*): one who requests for something, needy {T}.
"ٱلْمَسْأَلَةُ" (*al-masa latah*): need, necessity {M}.

The Quran declares:

| 93:10 | Do not scold the needy (thinking him to be lowly) | اَمَّا السَّائِلَ فَلَا تَنْهَرْ |
| 55:29 | Everything in the universe is asking God to fulfil its needs. (everything is dependent on his system of sustenance for its development) | يَسْئَلُهُ مَنْ فِى السَّمٰوٰتِ وَالْأَرْضِ |

In Surah *As-sajdah* in reference to land and its produce:

| 41:10 | it should be kept open (or available) for all needy | سَوَاءً لِّلسَّائِلِيْنَ |

Since land is the main source of human sustenance, it should be freely available to all. This is the purpose of the creation of the earth. It is not the purpose that some should put barriers around the land and consider this to be their personal property. Allah has provided everything which is necessary for the sustenance of the human life.

14:34	And he provided for you everything you had asked for	وَآتَكُمْ مِنْ كُلِّ مَاسَأَلْتَمُوْهُ

This is part of His system of sustenance, and to consider it as means of nourishment for a particular class as a private property is a heinous crime.

It is also used as asking one another about some matter of mutual interest as used in surah **An-Naba**:

78:1	About what are they asking one another?	عَمَّ يَتَسَاءَلُوْنَ
37:24	who are questioned	مَسْئُوْلُوْنَ
20:36	Verily you are granted your request, **Moosa**	قَدْ أُوْتِيْتَ سُؤْلَكَ يُمُوْسٰى

Here "سُؤْلَ" (**suul**) means request, need, demand, or your demanded thing.

"سوال" (**sawaal**) or question basically means need or some necessity. When we question somebody, we are indeed demanding for some kind of an answer. The Quran has to be viewed carefully to determine the context in which it is used e.g. whether it means to demand or to question.

<h1 style="text-align:center">S-A-M   س أ م</h1>

"سَئِمَ" (**saim**), "يَسْأَمُ" (**yasaam**): to become tired of something.
"أَسْأَمَهُ" (**asaama**): he tired me out; he bored me {T}.
Some say that "سَأَمٌ" (**saam**) also means laziness {M}.

41:49	man does not get tired of desiring for wealth	لَا يَسْئَمُ الْإِنْسَانُ مِنْ دُعَاءِ الْخَيْرِ

This verse means that his demand is not just for fulfilling his needs but for becoming better than others, and thus his desires have no limits.

102:2	... till he meets his death	حَتّٰى زُرْتُمُ الْمَقَابِرَ
2:282	do not be tardy in writing down a loan agreement (do not be frustrated or tired of it).	وَلَا تَسْئَمُوْا اَنْ تَكْتُبُوْهُ

Saba سبأ

It was the name of the capitol city of a state which in the times of **Suleman** was ruled by a queen. The Quran has referred to this nation, its state and about its queen (34:15, 27:22). The fertility of the land has been specifically referred and then its subsequent destruction by floods. The people were creative and had built a very big dam for irrigating their lands and subsequently the flooding took place because the the dam was damaged due to lack of maintenance.

In 1955, an American archaeologist had discovered some ruins in southern Arabia, especially in the Yemen area. The name of his book is "Qataban and Sheba" and the author is Wendell Phillips. The ruins throw light on the tale told by the Quran, especially the dam and the destruction by floods because of damage to the dam (34:19).

"اَلسَّبَاءُ" (*as-saba*) means one who is in the liquor business, and "سَبَا الْخَمْرَ" (*saba al-khamr*) means that he bought liquor {*T, M*}. If the city was named with reference to this, then the mind goes towards the Taakistan which were abundant there. But "اَلسُّبْأَةُ" (*subah*) also means long journey {*T, M*}, and perhaps this capitol city was named with this reference.

The Quran says refers to the desire of the people as referred in this prayer:

| 34:19 | Our Sustainer, prolong our journey so that our trade increases | رَ بَّنَا بعِّدْ بَيْنَ اَسْفَارِنَا |

About queen of **Saba** and **Suleman**, see heading **Suleman**.

S-B-B س ب ب

"سَبَّهُ" (*sabbahu*), "سَبَا" (*sabba*): delinked it, sever it.
"اَلسَّبُّ" (*as-subbu*): to swear, because it affects and severs relations between people {*T*}.
"اَلسِّبُّ" (*as-sibbu*) and "اَلسَّبَبُ" (*as-sababu*): long strong rope with the help of which one climbs a tree etc. or which is used to reach to the bottom of the water well.

This gave it the meaning of something through which one reaches something {*T*}. A road too is called "سَبَبٌ" (*sabab*) {R, M}, because it joins one destination with another. Hence this word also means relationship, or relative.

The Quran says:

2:116	Their mutual relations will be cut off (The means the mutual interests and benefits which were connecting them will end)	وَتَقَطَّعَتْ بِهِمُ الْاَسْبَابُ
18:98	He then took another direction	ثُمَّ اَتْبَعَ سَبَبًا
22:15	Then let him extend a "ladder" to the Heavens	فَلْيَمْدُدْ بِسَبَبٍ اِلَى السَّمَاءِ
20:37	Means reaching towards the Heavens {*T*}	اَسْبَابَ السَّمٰوٰتِ

According to **Taj**, the word in 20:37 means steps or doors to the sky. **Abu zaid** says it means stages, *{T}*, and **Muheet** says it means steps, ways, surroundings or doors. The meanings of this word are wider and cover means and possibilities in carrying out some tasks.

Surah **Al-Kahaf** says:

18:84	And we provided him all thing as means	وَ اٰتَيْنٰهُ مِنْ كُلِّ شَيْءٍ سَبَبَاً

In the context of swearing , this root has been used in (6:108) where it is said that do not condemn or use bad language against the idols which the disbelievers worship, lest they react, and unconsciously further move away from Allah's guidance. Such like events of mutual condemnation can take place among religious debates at emotive level.

S-B-T   س ب ت

"اَلسُّبَاتُ" (*as-subaat*): sleep.

Ibn Faris says that the basic meanings of the word are of peace and tranquillity. Since peace and tranquillity meant that a man rested and stopped whatever he was doing, it got the meaning of ceasing to work or to cut it off *{T}*.

"سَبَتَ" (*sabat*), "يَسْبُتُ" (*yasbut*), "يَسْبِتُ" (*yasbitu*), "سَبْتًّا" (*sabta*): he rested *{T}*.

Raghib says that "سَبْتٌ" (*sabat*) means to close the business and to relax on a Saturday, to spend Saturday resting, to be around on a Saturday.

"سَبَتَ الشَّيْءَ" (*sabatas shaiya*) means to cut off something.
"اَلسَّبْتُ" (*as-sabt*) also means to shave something, like to shave the head.
"اَلْمَسْبُوتُ" (*al-masbuutu*): a corpse or an unconscious man. It also means a sick man who lies quietly with closed eyes *{T}*.

"يَوْمُ السَّبْتِ" (*yaumus-sabti*): the day of the week named Saturday. It is thought to be named so because on that day the Jews do not work *{T}*. Verse 2:65 has used this word in these meanings, and also to mean comfort and rest.

78:10	Created sleep to take to rest	وَجَعَلْنَا نَوْمَكُمْ سُبَاتاً

In surah **Al-Furqaan** this is referred to this meaning as well, and "نُشُوْرًا" (*nushura*) has been used opposite to it (25:47) which means to walk, to scatter, to get up.

It is mentioned in the Quran that a group of Jews broke the agreement not to do business on Saturdays (4:154, 2:65). Surah *Al-Airaaf* says that they used to catch fish on that day (7:163). In violation of this agreed arrangement (not to catch fish on Saturday) they suffered the consequences (4:27) and this state was as a consequence of not following one their commitment as a community which led to divisions and parting of ways (16:124). This makes it obvious that when a system is followed then even the very small restriction needs to adhere otherwise gradually the whole system gets affected. The restriction of not working on a Saturday is a small restriction; however, it tests the character of individuals. Those who cannot resist such a small temptation, and try to make inroads into this rule created for the benefit of the society, they cannot be expected to observe the stricter rules? Character develops through self-discipline and by resisting temptation. By relating this event, Quran means to highlight this very fact. The consequences of their conduct which **Bani Israel** faced for going against these agreed restrictions is detailed under the heading (Q-R-D).

Hastings has written in his Encyclopaedia of Religious Ethics, with reference to various testaments, that **Sabat** would start on Friday evening and lasted the whole of Saturday. During this time there were 38 other restrictions besides trading which were prohibited.

S-B-H   س ب ح

"سَبْحٌ" (*sabh*): to swim.

"سَبَحَ بِالنَّهْرِ" (*sabaha bin nahari*), "فِى النَّهْرِ سَبْحاً" (*fi nahari sabhan*), "سَبَاحَةً" (*sabaha*): he swam in a canal.

"أَسْبَحَهُ فِى الْمَاءِ" (*asbahu fil maa*): made him swim in water.

"اَلسَّابِحَاتُ" (*as-sabihaat*): boats.

"اَلسَّوَابِح" (*as-sawabih*): horses while running very fast move their limbs like a fast swimming action.

"اَلسَّبَّاحُ" (*as-sabbbah*): a good swimmer, on a same pattern also used for a fast horse or a fast camel *{T}*.

"سَبْحٌ" (*sabh*): to venture far and wide in the quest for earning a living *{T}*.

"اَلسَّبْحُ" (*as-sabh*) also means to experience travel through various lands *{Latif-ul-lugha}*.

Ibn Faris has said that it means a kind of pursuit , thus "سَبْحٌ" (*sabh*) means to strive very hard with utmost effort to achieve a goal, to strive with the maximum strength, to make sustained and continuous effort.

Taj-ul-Uroos has described a dream of **Ibn Shameel** in which he saw a person who was explaining the meaning of "سُبْحَانَ الله" (*subhan Allah*). He was explaining through the example of a horse which is going at a maximum speed like a fast swimmer. This means "سُبْحَانَ الله" (*subhan Allah*) to direct all efforts towards Allah as explained in the Quran and to remain steadfast in following the values *{T}*.

Raghib has also said that "سَبْحًا" (*sabha*) means to go very fast in water or through air. Later it was allegorically used for the stars in the sky.

"أَلسَّبِيْحْ" (*as-sabih*) means to make haste in Allah's obedience, but with passage of time the meaning expanded and was also used for spoken or practical worship {R}. Till this day "سُبْحَةٌ" (*subh*) means beads of a rosary. Although this is not common among the Arabs, since rosaries were used by Christians in their worship, something they probably borrowed from Buddhists.

The Quran mentions about the celestial bodies:

36:40	they are all floating in their orbits	كُلٌّ فِيْ فَلَكٍ يَسْبَحُوْنَ

About the Messenger (*pbuh*) the Quran quotes:

73:7	for you, the daily program is very extensive and you have to work hard to get through it	إِنَّ لَكَ فِى النَّهَارِ سَبْحاً طَوِيْلاً

About birds it is said:

24:41	Each one of them knows their flight directions , though their flight path is not signposted	كُلٌّ قَدْعَلِمَ صَلاَتَهُ وَتَسْبِيْحَهُ

It means that each bird knows how to go about its business, and each one is aware of its limits and the way it has to get means of subsistence.

57:1	Whatever there is in the universe is fully engaged in in carrying out the program designated for them through Allah's laws	سَبَّحَ لِلّهِ مَافِى السَّمٰوٰتِ وَالْأَرْضِ

The things in the universe are instinctively tuned towards carrying out their programs. This is what has been described in the tale about Adam as the "تَسْبِيْحْ" (*tasbeeh*) of the **Malaikas**: (2:31), or the "تَسْبِيْحْ" *tasbeeh*) of the thunder (13:13). But a man has to use his choice in order to complete the program. Hence believers are directed:

33:42	You should be engaged in carrying this program day and night (i.e. on continuous basis)	سَبِّحُوْهُ بُكْرَةً وَأَصِيْلاً

About the programme itself, the direction is:

56:66	to get busy in implementing Allah's laws of subsistence (**Rabubyah**), the programme on which the whole universe is functioning	فَسَبِّحْ بِاسْمِ رَبِّكَ الْعَظِيْمِ

In a human society, the struggle against the opposing forces which obstruct the programme of subsistence is also called "ذكر" (*zikr*) and "تَسْبِيْحْ" (*tasbeeh*). When **Musa (PBUH)** was directed to the Pharaoh, he too used these terms to define and explain his mission (20:34).

The system which Quran proposes for the believers places great importance on "صلوة" (*salaah*), which includes gathering for the prayer. These gatherings are physical manifestations of the group's acceptance of guidance from Allah. This is a manifestation in the form of "ركوع" (*ruku*) and "سجود" (*sajud*) which are translated to bowing and genuflecting. While doing this bowing and genuflecting, a believer agrees to follow and live according to Allah's laws and to spend his lifetime in implementing those laws in the society where he lives. The words in which this agreement is made are also termed as the "تَسْبِيْح" (*tasbeeh*) of Allah. Obviously if a person only says so but fails practically follow it , then these utterances are mere rituals. The movements in *salaah* are the manifestations of one's motive to follow the guidance as explained in the Quran. If these gatherings are not followed through any actions and these become an end it then nothing positive will emerge in the real life. It is evident that by simply enumerating the attributes of Allah and by counting the beads of a rosary are not the actions the Quran has directed us to do. These rituals can never produce any results and result in waste of precious human time.

"تَسْبِيْح" (*tasbeeh*), according to the Quran means to fully observe the laws of Allah by directing all efforts employing all resources to achieve desired results.

Lissan-ul-Arab says that "تَسْبِيْح" (*tasbeeh*) means transcendence. It is used for saying "سُبْحَانَ الله" (*subhan Allah*), or mention of Allah, praise of Allah etc. Since the aspect of intensity is implicit in it, therefore *tanzia* would mean to consider Allah free from all limitations and weaknesses.

This root has the element of intensity and strength. As such "كِسَاءٌ مُسَبَّحٌ" (*kisaaun musabbbah*) means very strong and tightly knit blanket. Hence "فَسَبِّحْ بِاسْمِ رَبِّكَ الْعَظِيْمِ" (*fasibbah bismi rabbikal azeem*) would mean to adopt the attributes of Allah as mentioned and explained in the Quran with total conviction and to propagate them widely for the benefit of others.

In Surah *As-Saffat* in context with *Yunus* it is noted:

37:143	He would have remained inside its belly until the Day of resurrection.	فَلَوْلَا اَنَّهُ كَانَ مِنَ الْمُسَبِّحِيْنَ لَلَبِثَ فِيْ بَطْنِهِ اِلٰى يَوْم يُبْعَثُوْنَ

If this word "مُسَبِّحِيْنَ" (*musabbihen*) had come from "سَبْح" (*sabh*), then it would have meant swimmer. But since the word is according to "سَبَّحَ" (*sabbaha*), it would mean one who struggles with full might. This has the automatic connotation of struggling hard in order to stay away from the fish's mouth and manage to swim ashore.

In the same surah it is said a little later:

37:162	We are verily to struggle very hard in this path	وَ إِنَّا لَنَحْنُ الْمُسَبِّحُوْنَ

These places too show that "تَسْبِيْح" (*tasbeeh*) means intensity, strength, and to engage in implementing Allah's laws with strength and persistence.

"سُبْحَانَ مِنْ كَذَا" (*subhaana min kaza*) is said at times of wonderment {T}.

It also means "distance":

| 37:159 | Allah is far from these wrong concepts in which they believe | سُبْحَانَ اللهِ عَمَّا يَصِفُونَ |

"سُبْحَانٌ" (**subhaan**) also means to be engaged in something {**T**}.

| 30:17 | You have to be engaged evening and morning in the duties assigned for you by Allah | فَسُبْحَنَ اللهِ حِينَ تُمْسُونَ وَحِينَ تُصْبِحُونَ |

S-B-Te   س ب ط

"اَلسَّبَطُ" (**sabt**) basically means abundance and plentiful in something {**M, T, Sulbi**}.

Ibn Faris says it means for something to be prolonged.

It also means a tree which has one root but the branches are quite spread out. It also means family and descendants.

"اَلسِّبْطُ" (**as-sabit**) means grandson, regardless of the maternal or paternal side. This word is also used for a Jewish tribe.
"أَسْبَاطُ" (**as-baat**) was a word used exclusive for the descendants of **Is-haq**, while "قَبَائِلُ" (**qabaa-il**) was used for the descendants of **Ismail**. The Arabs had kept this distinction to distinguish between the two branches of Ibrahim's descendants with a single word {**M, T, Sulbi**}. In the Quran too, the word "أَسْبَاطُ" (**asbaat**) has been used for the nation of **Moosa** (7:160). The Arabs used to call a non-arab as "اَلسَّبْطُ" (**sabt**), as they used to call the Arabs "جَعْدٌ" (**ja'd**). The Quran has also used "أَسْبَاطُ" (**asbaat**) for the descendants of **Yaqoob** (2:136)

S-B-Ain   س ب ع

"سَبْعٌ" (**sab-un**): means the figure seven, some think that in reality this word was "سَبْعَةٌ" (**sab-uh**) which means a lioness, because she attacks even faster than a lion. The Arabs thought the number seven to be a perfect number.

"اَلسُّبُعُ" (**as-subuh**), "اَلسَّبَعُ" (**as-sabah**) or "اَلسَّبْعُ" (**as-sab'u**): means a wild animal (5:3), some think that this is so because the Arabs considered seven animals to be in the category of beasts.

Raghib says that wild animals are called "سَبْعٌ" (**sabah**) because their strength is complete and the figure seven was also thought to be complete {**M, T, Sulbi**}.
Lane with reference to **Baizawi** has written that the Arabs not only meant seven by saying "سَبْعٌ" (**sabah**) but it is also used to mean "several" or "many".

"سَبْعُوْنَ" (*sab'on*) means seventy and "سَبْعِمِاءَةٍ" (*sabame'atah*) means seven hundred {*M, T, R*}. As we sometimes say twenties, fifties, hundreds and do not mean any fixed figure, or as we sometime say 'I have told you a hundred times' to put emphasis. It does not mean an exact hundred.

For example the Quran says:

9:80	Even if you ask forgiveness for them seventy times	اِنْ تَسْتَغْفِرْ لَهُمْ سَبْعِيْنَ مَرَّةً

It does not mean that if you ask for their pardon seventy times, we will not pardon them, but if you ask for their pardon more than seventy times then We will pardon them. It means that even if you ask pardon for them several times, they cannot be pardoned.

"سَبْعَ سَمٰوٰتٍ" (*sab'as samawaat*) is translated to numerous heavenly bodies (2:29). We also use the phrase 'across seven seas' by which we actually mean several seas.

2:261	Those who keep their wealth open i.e. spend for the benefit of other human beings, for them the wealth is like a seed which has seven saplings and there are a hundred grains in each sapling	اَلَّذِيْنَ يُنْفِقُوْنَ اَمْوَالَهُمْ فِيْ سَبِيْلِ اللّٰهِ كَمَثَلِ حَبَّةٍ اَنْبَتَتْ سَبْعَ سَنَابِلَ فِيْ كُلِّ سُنْبُلَةٍ مِائَةُ حَبَّةٍ

Obviously here "سَبْعَ سَنَابِلَ" (*sab-a sanabil*) means several.

The Quran says:

15:87	We have given you seven of the *misaani* and a great Quran.	وَلَقَدْ اٰتَيْنٰكَ سَبْعاً مِنَ الْمَثَانِيْ وَالْقُرْاٰنَ الْعَظِيْمَ

See the word "مثانى" (*misaani*) in heading (Th-N-Y).

S-B-Gh س ب غ

"اَلسَّبْغَةُ" (*as-sabhag*): vastness, expansiveness, generosity.
"سَبَغَ الشَّىْءُ" (*sabaghas shaiyi*), "سُبُوْغاً" (*subugha*): for something (clothes, armour etc) to be long and hanging.
"اَلسَّابِغَةُ" (*as-saabegha*): the armour which comes down to the level of knees or drags along the floor due to its length. Its plural is "سَابِغَاتٌ" (*saabeghaat*) (34:11).
"اَسْبَغَ شَعَرَهُ" (*asbagha sha'rah*): he let his hair grow very long.
"شَىْءٌ سَابِغٌ" (*shaiyun sabeghun*): a thing in full measure or abundance {*M, T, R*}.

Ibn Faris says that its basic meaning is of being in full measure or abundance.

"سَبَغَتِ النَّعْمَةُ" (*sabaghatin ne'mah*): for the benevolence to be expansive and in abundance {*M, T, R*}.

The Quran says:

| 31:20 | Allah endowed you with his benevolence in abundance | وَ أَسْبَغَ عَلَيْكُمْ نِعَمهُ |

S-B-Q   س ب ق

"سَبْقٌ" (*sabq*) basically means to get ahead in a race. Later "سَبَقَةُ" (*sabaqah*) began to be used to mean exceed in everything, get ahead.

| 31:20 | First the Messenger of Allah dies, and left the world, and after him **Abu Bakar** left the World as well | سَبَقَ رَسُوْلُ اللهِ وَصَلَّى أَبُوْبَكِرٍ |

"اَلسَّبَقُ" (*as-sabaqu*) is the prize which is given to the winner of any race e.g. horse race {*T*}. "اِسْتَبَقَا الْبَابَ" (*istabaqal baab*): both of them leaped towards the door with each trying to go out ahead of the other (12:25) {*T*}.

Muheet says that if this word is followed by "عَلَى" (*ala*), then the thing which goes ahead or comes first, is harmful and if it is followed by a "ل" (*laam*) then the thing is beneficial.

| 21:101 | ... welcomed them with pleasure and went forward to greet them | سَبَقَتْ لَهُمْ مِنَّا الْحُسْنَى |

Surah **An-Naqarah** says:

| 2:148 | Make effort to surpass one another in righteous deeds | فَاسْتَبِقُوا الْخَيْرَاتِ |

Psychologically, it is stated and believed that to compete and get ahead in life is a motivating force in people. It is the desire of competition and to get ahead that is something which keeps men busy. The Quran recognises this human emotion and asks us to develop it, and asks us to redirect our competitiveness into doing well for others. It says instead of getting ahead of others for personal gain try to excel one another in things which bring happiness to others. This will not only satisfy our desire (to get ahead) but will also prevent the chaos in society which would have occurred due to unbridled ambitions.

In surah **Al-Hijr**, this word of "تَسْبِقُ" (*tasbiqu*) has appeared to mean "يَسْتَأْخِرُ" (*yastakhir*) which means to fall behind (15:5). At another place "مُسْتَقْدِمِيْنَ" (*mutaqdemeen*) has appeared against "مُسْتَأْخِرِيْنَ" (*mustaakhireen*) in 15:24.

Therefore "سَبْقٌ اِسْتَخَارٌ" (*sabaqun istikhaaratun*) means the opposite of falling behind, and the same as "اِسْتَقْدَامٌ" (*istiqadaam*) i.e. to move forward.

Surah *Al-Waqiah* says "مَسْبُوْقِيْن" (*musbooqeen*) in 56:60 i.e. the one who is "مَغْلُوْبٌ" (*maghlub*), or surpassed.

Surah *Al-Ambia* says:

21:101	those for whom already our blessings have come (traditional translation)	إِنَّ الَّذِيْنَ سَبَقَتْ لَهُمْ مِنَّا الْحُسْنٰى

The above translation appears to imply as if God has already destined as to who will do good deeds and who will do evil deeds. This concept is against the Law of Requital explained in the Quran. The above mentioned verse means that those who take the right path will have the positive results (because the result of such deeds is such) and this thing has been predetermined and those who follow the wrong path will have the negative consequences. There is no exception to this principle.

Surah *Al-Hadeed* says:

57:21	try to outdo each other in going towards (seeking for) your Sustainer's Protection	سَابِقُوْا اِلٰى مَغْفِرَةٍ مِنْ رَّبِّكُمْ

S-B-L   س ب ل

Ibn Faris says that the basic meanings of this word are to hang, to leave and to elongate.

"أَسْبَلَ" (*asbal*): to hang, to leave.
"أَسْبَلَ الْإِزَارَ" (*asbalal izaar*): hanged *izaar*.
"أَسْبَلَ دَمْعَهُ" (*asbala dama'hu*): let his tears roll; let the tears roll so that they roll out of the eyes.
"أَسْبَلَتِ السَّمَاءُ" (*asbalatis sama'a*): it started to rain heavily from above.
"اَلسَّبَلُ" (*as-sabal*): rain, but this the rain which is suspended above as clouds but has not yet reached on the ground
"اَلسُّبْلَةُ" (*as-sublah*): rain on a wide scale.
"أَسْبَلَ الزَّرْعُ" (*asbalaz zar-u*): the ears began to hang in the crop {T}.
"اَلسَّبِيْلُ" (*as-sabeelu*) and "اَلسَّبِيْلَةُ" (*as-sabeelah*): path, an easy path where there is no harshness, or the distinct part of the path.
"سَبِيْلٌ" (*sabeel*) is both masculine and feminine but as feminine its usage is more common. The plural is "سُبُلٌ" (*subul*) {T}.

Ibn Faris says that because a path goes a long way (due to its length), it is called "سَبِيْلٌ" (*sabeel*).

"اَلسَّابِلَةُ مِنَ الطُّرُقِ" (*as-sabilah minat turuq*): the path that people traverse generally on, or on which they come and go for fulfilling their needs, that is, the traveller {T}.

The Quran has used the phrase "فِى سَبِيْلِ اللهِ" (*fi sabeel Allah*) several times (2:190). Against it has appeared "فِىْ سَبِيْلِ الطَّاغُوْتِ" (*fi sabeelit taghut*) as in 4:76. The **Momineen** go to war "فِى سَبِيْلِ اللهِ" (*fi sabeel Allah*) and the **kafirs** go to war "فِىْ سَبِيْلِ الطَّاغُوْتِ" (*fi sabeelit taghut*) as said in 4:76. "الطَّاغُوْتِ" (*at-taghut*) are those forces which are oppressive and force others to follow their dictates and establish the system of falsehood.

Therefore "فِى سَبِيْلِ اللهِ" (*fi sabeel Allah*) would mean for the observance of Allah's laws to establish Allah's system, and to traverse the path destined by Allah. They should do this act themselves as well as make others do the same. They should do this instead of following personal interests, and work for the interests of humanity at large. They should oppose the opposing forces. **Momineen** live and die for this very purpose. This also clarifies the meaning of "اتفاق فى سبيل الله" (*itifaaq fi sabeel Allah*) i.e. to keep one's wealth available or open for the benefit of mankind so that whatever is needed, can be taken from it.

"بْنُ السَّبِيْلِ" (*ibnus sabeel*): traveller who travels a lot. Some think it means a traveller whose food during a journey has finished {*T*}. The Quran has also included among the duties of an Islamic society to help travellers. This duty is of such importance that it is one of the purposes of spending **sadaqaat** (9:10). This includes facilities for any traveller in an Islamic society, and those who in their travels become needy for any reason to help them to reach their destination.

Muheet has also said that it means guests. In today's terminology "ابن السبيل" (*ibnus sabeel*) would be those who come to an Islamic state and are in transit (i.e. even non-citizens).

Surah **Aal-e-Imran** says about the people with the celestial book who used to say:

3:74	We can do whatever we want with these Arabs because they do not have a book, and nobody will hold us accountable	لَيْسَ عَلَيْنَا فِى الْأُمِّيِّنَ سَبِيلٌ

This sort of mentality is born of tribal bias. According to it a crime within the tribe is a crime but if committed outside the tribe is not a crime. But this is not restricted to tribal societies. Even the Romans believed that theft within their own nation was theft, but outside the nation was not. The fact is that whether it is religious grouping or political, they give rise to the mentality that all benefits should be confined to the party members and all others outside the party are despised. This is taking place even today as it was a practice for four thousand years ago. Nationalism prevalent today as a product of such thinking, and this very thing has turned the world into a sort of hell i.e. mutual conflicts. The Quran raised its voice against this sort of thinking and declared that a crime is a crime no matter it is against the people of your kind or others. There is no difference among nations or human beings in this respect. That is why any deed which is done "فِى سَبِيْلِ اللهِ" (*fi sabeel Allah*) is a good deed which is without any thought of remuneration or compensation, and is for the benefit of the whole mankind.

The Quran has said about the heavenly life:

| 76:18 | It has a spring which is named **salsabeel** | عَيناً فِيهَا تُسَمَّى سَلْسَبِيْلاً |

Muheet says that the root is "سَلْ سَبِيْلاً" (**sal-sabeela**) which means to find out about the way, i.e. to ask the way and move forward. It means the "river" that flows to satisfy the needs of all, and which does not differentiate.

At another place is said:

| 88:12 | flowing spring (the spring which flows all the time) | فِيْهَا عَيْنٌ جَارِيَةٌ |

The spring of life which keeps flowing forward; the eternal life which is the logical outcome of good deeds which goes forward continuously without interruption? It has no interruption whatsoever. It means that for human personality to keep traversing the path ahead. "سَبِيْلُ اللهِ" (**sabeel Allah**) is the path, the direction on which man sticks to "مَايَنْفَعُ النَّاسَ" (**ma yanfa unnaas**) for the good of mankind as mentioned in (13:17). This is the path towards which Allah's messenger invited mankind, because he knew the benefits of it through his insight which was developed through the evidence and the understanding of the Quran based on intellectual reasoning (12:108).

This is the right path as outlined by the Quran. By following this path the human abilities can develop to their utmost because "مَسَلَاالسَّكَاسَ إِلَى أَسْبَالِهَا" (**malal kaasa ila asbaalaha**): it is said to fill the cup to the brim {T}.

In surah **An-Nahal** the bee has been directed instinctively:

| 16:19 | Follow the path laid out by your Sustainer. | فَاسْلُكِيْ سُبُلَ رَبِّكِ ذُلُلاً |

This shows that the laws of nature are also the paths of God. For the mankind the right paths are the ones conveyed by the messengers as revealed to them through the revelation as noted in (14:12).

Surah **Al-Ankabuut** says:

| 29:69 | Those who struggle for Us are shown the way (the right path) by us. Allah is with those who do the righteous deeds. | وَالَّذِيْنَ جَاهَدُوْا فِيْنَا لَنَهْدِيَنَّهُمْ سُبُلَنَا - وَإِنَّ اللهَ لَمَعَ الْمُحْسِنِيْنَ |

There is only one path that leads towards Allah and that has been called by Him as "صِرَاطٌ مُسْتَقِيْمٌ" (**siraatul mustaqeem**) or the right path (1:5). But man is faced by new problems and challenges every now and then, as the life progresses. The Quran has broadly laid down the principles of life for the mankind, it is the duty of the believers to find the solution to these problems in the lightof these principles., Obviously this requires knowledge about the universe, about the social life of the nations of this world, an understanding of the needs of the times, and deep deliberation on the permanent values of the Quran. To struggle to find a solution to the problems facing us from the guidance which the Quran provides is called in the Quranic terms as "اجتهاد" (*ijtehaad*). It is Allah's promise that those who strive in this way, He will enhance their understanding and broaden their vision. This will help them to understand the issues of life and they will be able to resolve these as per the guidance of the Quran This direction is defined and explained by the Quran as the "سبل السلام" (*subul islam*) or the paths of tranquillity and protection.

At another place their purpose is described as:

| 5:16 | to bring them out of darkness into light | يُخْرِجُهُمْ مِنَ الظُّلُمٰتِ اِلَى النُّوْرِ بِاِذْنِهٖ |
| 5:16 | and thus they are guided to the right path | وَيَهْدِيْهِمْ اِلٰى صِرَاطٍ مُسْتَقِيْمٍ |

This also means that all these paths lead to the same "highway" called the guidance; whatever the group of *Momineen* decides while remaining within the confines of the Quranic values to meet the requirements of the time will always aim at the overall guidance which will serve as a criterion.

<h2 style="text-align:center">S-T-T   س ت ت</h2>

"اَلسِّتُّ" (*as-seet*), "اَلسِّتَّةُ" (*as-sittah*): the number of six. It was actually "سِدْسٌ" (*sids*) at first {*T*}.

The Quran says:

| 7:75 | created the earth and the heavens in six periods | خَلَقَ السَّمٰوٰتِ وَالْاَرْضِ فِىْ سِتَّةِ اَيَّامٍ |

There is a reference to the different stages through which the earth and other heavenly bodies have passed before these reached the present stage. For the correct meaning of "يَوْمٌ" (*yaum*), see (Y-W-M).
"سِتُّوْنَ" (*situun*) and "سِتِّيْنَ" (*sitteen*) means sixty (58:2).

S-T-R   س ت ر

"سِتْرٌ" (*sitr*): veil, some type of a cover which is used to hide something.

Surah *Al-kahaf* says:

18:90	they lived in the open ground so that there was no obstruction between them and the sun	لَمْ نَجْعَلْ لَهُمْ مِنْ دُونِهَا سِتْرًا

"أَلسِّتَارُ" (*as-sitar*): veil.
"سَتَرَ الشَّيْءَ" (*satarash shaiyi*): he hid that thing.
"إِسْتَتَرَ" (*istatar*): to hide {*T, R, M*}.

The Quran says:

41:22	You were not hidden	وَمَا كُنْتُمْ تَسْتَتِرُونَ

In Surah *Bani Israel* it is stated that when you recite the Quran, between you and the people who do not wish to believe in the life hereafter:

17:45	a veil descends	حِجَاباً مَسْتُوراً

Though this veil is not visible with eyes, but it can be understood as it prevents them from coming to the message. Their psychological state has been described as "حِجَابٌ مَسْتُورٌ" (*hijabun mastoor*), that is, a meta-physical cover. "مَسْتُورٌ" (*mistoor*) also means the same as "سَاعِرٌ" (*sa'ir*) which means one who hides. Likewise "مَسْحُورٌ" (*mashoor*) is the same as "سَاحِرٌ" (*saahir*) which means sorcerer. One of Gods attributes is "أَلسَّتَّارُ" (*as-sattar*) commonly referred, but this attribute has not been mentioned in the Quran.

S-J-D   س ج د

"أَلسُّجُودُ" (*as-sujud*): to bow the head.

Ibn Faris says it basically means to be low or to bend over.

"نَخْلَةٌ سَاجِدَةٌ" (*nakhlatun sajidah*): a date palm that is bent, especially one which bends under the weight of its fruit {*T*}.
"سَجَدَ الْبَعِيرُ" (*sajjadal baeer*): the camel bent its neck so that the man could mount on its back {*T*}.

Therefore, this root refers to (physically) someone bowing his head or some other thing to bend down(or bow). However, behind the human mannerism there is a philosophy and in modern terms it is called parallelism. It means that there is a profound connection between one's mind and body, and these two function in parallel. For example, if we are lying down and decide to do something, then we get up as the thought crosses our mind. When we wish to rest, we either sit down or lie down, or when we say 'yes' we nod our head (automatically and unconsciously). When we have respect for someone, our hand may rise to our forehead (for a salute) and if our respect transcends this, then we may even bow before that person to express out profound respect. These actions also affect our speech which is a translation of our bodily movements, or expresses the same emotions that the body movements signify. For example, when we say that he bowed his head at my order, you actually mean that he has accepted to carry out your order. When we say that he rebelled against the law of the state, then we mean that he has refused to accept the state's law and chose to go against it. Since the Quran speaks in a particular language (Arabic), it too uses the metaphors of this language to express itself clearly. In this context, it has used the words "سجده" (*sajdah*) to mean obedience and acceptance and is not referring to the act of physical bowing.

Surah *An-Nahal* says:

| 16:49 | And all living things which are in the highs and lows of the universe bow before Allah and do not rebel (following laws) | وَلِلَّهِ يَسْجُدُ مَا فِى السَّمٰوٰتِ وَمَا فِى الْأَرْضِ مِنْ دَابَّةٍ وَالْمَلٰئِكَةُ وَهُمْ لَا يَسْتَكْبِرُوْنَ |

Here "يَسْجُدُ" (*yashudu*) has been explained by "لَايَسْتَكْبِرُوْنَ" (*la yastakbiruun*), i.e. they do not disobey the orders of Allah but instead follow them.

The verse is further explained by:

| 16:50 | they carry out what they are directed to do | وَيَفْعَلُوْنَ مَا يُؤْمَرُوْنَ |

Therefore, the root of this word (S-J-D) must be kept in mind to determine whether it means a physical bowing or a figurative bowing which is to express obedience.

For the difference between religion and *Deen,* see headings (Dh-H-B) and (D-Y-N).

Another point should also be considered at this stage. When the human mind was in its infancy (like a child), it understood only the physical things and mostly used to express himself in physical terms. In today's terminology his knowledge was restricted to "sense perception". He had not yet reached the stage of having abstract concepts or to acquire knowledge through them. Therefore, his religion, like other things, was limited to this sense-perception. This means that he was still in the stage of formalism. To represent God, he had created idols. In worship etc. the stress was on the form of worship rather than the spirit. In fact, form had become the end in itself.

The Quranic teaching treats a man like an adult with developed intellect, reasoning, and perception. It can be said that the Quran wants human begins to come out of the nascent stage and into the adulthood. Therefore the Quran stresses on conceptual knowledge as well as on conceptual knowledge. In the matter of *Deen* the Quran stresses on the purpose while keeping the form without rejecting the later. This is because human beings wish some visible form to express their ideas. It stresses on the intention rather than the form, but it does not altogether do away with the form, but retains some part of it. We see that the great philosophers and thinkers use facial expressions and hands to explain ideas and concepts. This gesturing is part of human expression. In this way thinkers explain abstract truths with examples taken from physical world. This is the reason that the Quran, despite man having evolved much higher than the perceptual stage, has retained some form. The practice of bowing in prayers is a manifestation of this form. For example, in Surah *An-Nisa* (4:102) where observing prayer during a battle has been mentioned, it has also been said that one group may establish the prayer and when it is finished, then the other group observe their prayer.

Obviously here "سجده" (*sajdah*) means to physically bow one's head before God, like was the practice of our Messenger Muhammed (*pbuh*) and his followers. In the Quran, prayer and *Hajj* are two things in which some form has been retained. These two are collective prayers and it is necessary to have some uniformity in the collective form of worship. If in a collective gathering, every individual adopts his own form of worship, then one can well imagine the chaos this may create. More details about these matters can be found under the heading (Sd-L-W).

It is obvious that for a man to bow physically before God is the physical display of man's emotions and intentions towards God and that he accepts God's Laws willingly without any reservation. If his visible act of bowing is not a display of his inner feeling of acceptance and is purely a display of the worship procedure then this whole practice of worshipping is meaningless and this will never produce any positive result.

This is the truth for which the Quran has said:

| 2:177 | The righteousness is not to turn your face towards the east or the west, but it is whether you truly believe with conviction in Allah, the hereafter), universal forces, revelation through His books and the messengers who brought the revelation, and give wealth, despite the love of it, to relatives (who need it), orphans, needy, travellers, and the oppressed | لَيْسَ الْبِرَّاَنْ تُوَ لُّوْا وُجُوْهَكُمْ قِبَلَ الْمَشْرِقِ وَالْمَغْرِبِ وَلٰكِنَّ الْبِرَّ--- |

This means that "صلوٰة" (*salaah*) is actually a physical display of man's acceptance of the Quran as a book of guidance and a commitment to follow the values therein. If man takes the "صلوٰة" (*salaah*) only as an end in itself, then it holds no importance with God and man will never reap the benefits which one can only get by following the Quran as a whole.

Instead the Quran says:

107:5-7	There is loss to those who pray but ignore the essence of the prayer (as stated earlier) and perform the obvious trappings of the *salaat* to show people. Indeed the same people prevent the flow of the capital for the good of the wider public and hoard it for themselves.	فَوَيْلٌ لِّلْمُصَلِّيْنَ ٱلَّذِيْنَ هُمْ عَنْ صَلَاتِهِمْ سَاهُوْنَ ٱلَّذِيْنَ هُمْ يُرَاءُوْنَ وَيَمْنَعُوْنَ ٱلْمَاعُوْنَ

"ٱلْمَسْجَدُ" (*al-masjid*): forehead which touches the ground (during bowing), and "ٱلْمَسْجَدُ" (*al-masjid*) is the place where *sajdah* is performed *{T}*. This is a pronoun and can mean both the place where the *sajdah* is performed and the time when it is done.

Surah *Al-Kahaf* says that people built a *masjid* (or mosque) near the cave where these young men had escaped to (18:21). They were "مجاهدين" (*mujahideen*) i.e. those who struggled in life and lived a righteous life. But later (as usually happens) the truth disappeared and in their memory a monument was built which became a place for *sajdah* or worship.
In surah *Bani Israel* the *heckel* (a synagogue) of the Jews has been called *masjid* (17:7).

Surah *At-Taubah* also mentions the *masjid* or mosque during the times of the messenger (*pbuh*) which was based on "تقوىٰ" (*taqwah*) (9:109). It also mentions another mosque which was built with a view to create divisions among the Muslims, which the Quran has termed as *kufr* and the sanctuary for those fighting a war against Allah and His Messenger (*pbuh*) (9:107). The Quran has declared sectarianism as *shirk* (i.e. associating other gods with Allah His sharing sovereignty), and clearly stated that the *mushrikeen*, that is, those who follow other laws and associate these with Allah have no right to be in these *masjidsassociated with* Allah.

The Quran declared:

72:18	The *masjids* are only for Allah, so do not call on others along with Allah.	اَنَّ ٱلْمَسَاجِدَ لِلّٰهِ فَلَا تَدْعُوْا مَعَ ٱللّٰهِ اَحَداً

Sectarianism or causing divisions is forbidden and is declared a crime because it moves us away from the guidance and the values as revealed in the Quran and it prevents us from getting the benefits associated with the following of the Quran. If the believers follow the Quran then there cannot be any divisions as they will be moving away from their own desires which vary from individual to individual. The Quran has declared that there is no contradiction within the guidance (4:82) and those who follow it the way it is explained then they will be free from any contradiction as well.

Just as *sajdah* means not only to put your forehead on the ground but also to follow the Quranic Laws, so *masjid* is not just the place or building where people go for the prayer ritual. It means the centre which is the symbol for establishing Allah's laws on earth. The "كعبہ" (*kaaba*) Mecca has been declared "مَسْجِدِ الْحَرَام" (*masjidil haram*) in 28:27. This is not because people perform *sajda* there, but because it is the centre which represents the System which symbolises the Unity of Allah.. It is the centre for the Muslim nation because of being "مُسْلِمَةً لَّكَ" (*muslimata alak*) (2:128) i.e. a nation which symbolises the Quranic Laws.

Historically, after the Messenger's (*pbuh*) migration to Medina from Mecca, Medina was to become the centre of the Quranic system, therefore (regarding the night of migration) Medina has been called "مَسْجِد الأَقْصَا" (*masjid al-aqsa*) in the Quran, which means the mosque far away.

17:1	Glory to Allah Who did take His servant by a night journey from Mecca to the mosque far away, whose precincts We did bless- in order that We show him some of Our Signs.	سُبْحَنَ الَّذِیْ اَسْرٰی بِعَبْدِه لَیْلاً مِّنَ الْمَسْجِدِ الْحَرَامِ اِلَی الْمَسْجِدِ الْاَقْصَا الَّذِیْ بَرَكْنَا حَوْلَهُ لِنُرِیَهُ مِنْ اٰیٰتِنَا

After this, *Moosa(pbuh)* has been referred as noted in surah *Taha* where he has been ordered to go towards the Pharaoh. There too similar wording is used:

20:22	so that We show you Our big signs	لِنُرِیَکَ مِنْ اٰیٰتِنَا الْكُبْرٰی

This sign was *Moosa*'s success in the struggle against the Pharaoh. This was also the sign which after the Messenger's (*pbuh*) migration, from Mecca to Medina, was to be manifested as the later events indicate which ultimately led to the establishment of a model welfare state as directed in the Quran. It represents the victory of the believers over the forces which were defending the system based on human exploitation. This brings the fact before us that the building of a mosque is for a gathering of those who have one ideology and is to resolve the human issues within the values and boundaries laid down by the Quran . The human issues cannot be resolved through the existing concept of worship which is to satisfy some self - created emotional need to please a concept of god which is quite different from the concept of Allah explained in the Quran. The term used in the Quran has nothing to do with the concept of worship – it is about dealing with the human issues with a view to providing an environment for the development of the human self. This is to provide an option to those who think and reason to use their free will and deal with the human issues on a global basis. See heading (Ain-B-D) and any steps taken within the Quranic values are part and parcel of the concept of "عبادت" (*ibadat*). The existing gatherings for prayers do not achieve this purpose and have become ritualised and are in a gross need of revision in the light of the Quranic guidance.

Surah *Al-Airaaf* says:

7:31	O mankind take you adornment to every *masjid*	یٰبَنِیْ اٰدَمَ خُذُوْ زِیْنَتَكُمْ عِنْدَ کُلِّ مَسْجِدٍ

Here masjid has been used to mean to obey, to follow {*Lisan-ul-Arab*}.

In this verse, a great truth has been revealed. Christianity (and other religions) term monasticism as the height of obedience and worship, i.e. to give up the pleasures of this life and this world. This concept has been refuted by the Quran as it leads to lack of challenging environment which is required for the development of the human self, and the use of the adornment within the confines of the permanent values is a way forward and helps to enjoy this life and paving the way for the next one. As the Quran deals with the issues of the Self's development and wishes us to partake in this life as much as possible on a continuous basis through our physical self. More activity within the confines of these values widens the sphere of human choices at self's level. For example all those beliefs which hamper our decisions making disappear and very confident self emerges which has only one belief based on conviction and which uses Allah as an ultimate Self as a model. The self's sphere of choices increase which has no bounds and which extends beyond the geographical limits of this universe. One should of course benefit from world's good things while remaining within the limits defined within the Quran. The Quran invites us to use our body to develop our self which is the true entity and whose nourishment is the purpose of our life. The next part of this verse and the next verse has clarified this meaning by saying:

7:31	Eat and drink but do not transgress the limits. Allah does not like those who transgress the limits	وَكُلُوْا واشْرَبُوْا وَلَا تُسْرِفُوْا ۔ اِنَّ اللّٰهَ لَايُحِبُّ الْمُسْرِفِيْنَ
7:32	Say, who has forbidden the good things of this life which Allah has created (for the use of mankind)	قُلْ مَنْ حَرَّمَ زِيْنَةَ اللّٰهِ الَّتِيْ اَخْرَجَ لِعِبَادِهِ وَالطَّيِّبَاتِ مِنَ الرِّزْقِ۔

Two verses earlier say:

7:29	Say, Allah has directed you to be just and direct your faces towards his guidance and call upon him with total commitment and intensity	قُلْ اَمَرَ رَبِّيْ بِالْقِسْطِ وَاَقِيْمُوْا وُجُوْهَكُمْ عِنْدَكُلِّ مَسْجِدٍ وَّادْعُوْهُ مُخْلِصِيْنَ لَهُ الدِّيْنَ۔

Surah *Al-Fatah* says about the Messenger (*pbuh*) and those with him:

48:29	You will find them in *rukuh* and in *sajdah*	تَرَاهُمْ رُكَّعاً سُجَّداً

Here if literal meaning of *rukuh* and *sujud* are taken, then it would mean collective prayer and if figurative meanings are taken, then it would mean taking defined responsibilities and functioning within the confines of the limits defined by the Quran.

After this it is said:

48:29	they can be recognized by the signs on their faces	سِيْمَاهُمْ فِيْ وُجُوْهِهِمْ مِنْ اَثَرِ السُّجُوْدِ

This means that the peace and tranquillity which they get by following the permanent values as revealed in the Quran, become evident from their personality and body language. The internal stable state of the human Self displays its confidence and strength through its value driven decisions making and their results.

The Quran says:

| 55:41 | The criminals will be recognized from their personality and conduct | يُعْرَفُ الْمُجْرِمُونَ بِسِيْمٰهُمْ |

Here too an aspect of the human psyche is referred where the inner state at times gives clues through the body language and the face expressions. The calmness and the confidence which one gets through following the righteous path translate at times into our conduct and appearance.

S-J-R   س ج ر

"سَجَرَ التَّنُّوْرَ" (*sajarat tanur*), "يَسْجُرُ ةَ" (*yasjuruh*), "سَجْراً" (*sajra*): lighten a clay oven, putt maximum fuel to heat it up, to fill with fuel e.g. wood, coal.

"سَجَرَ النَّهْرَ" (*shajaran nahar*): he filled the canal.

"اَلسَّجُوْرُ" (*as-sajur*): the thing with which the oven is stoked.

"اَلْمِسْجَرُ" (*al-masjir*): wooden rod with which fuel in an oven is moved around so it may heat up quickly.

"اَلسَّاجِرُ" (*as-saajir*), "اَلْمَسْجُوْرُ" (*al-masjur*): immobile and filled thing. It also means to fill an empty thing, thus it means opposites {*Latif-ul-Lugha*}. It means the flood water which is more than the river can contain.

"سَجَرْتُ الْإِنَاءَ" (*sajartul ina'a*): I filled the pot.

"اَلسَّاجِرُ" (*as-saajir*): the plain from which the flood passes and fills it up the area.

"بِءْرٌ سَجِرٌ" (*beirun sajir*): a filled well {*T*}.

"سَجَّرَ الْمَاءَ" (*sajjarul ma'u*): for the water to make its own way {*T*}. This word means to flare up a fire as well as to fill something up and be full.

Ibn Faris says it means (1) to fill, (2) to meet up , and (3) to flare up or instigate.

The Quran says:

40:72	Then they will be pushed into the fire	ثُمَّ فِى النَّارِ يُسْجَرُوْنَ
52:6	Filled sea (or adjoining sea)	الْبَحْرِ الْمَسْجُوْرِ
81:6	The oceans will be busy with shipping all around	إِذَا الْبِحَارُ سُجِّرَتْ

If "بِحَارٌ" (*bihaars*) is taken to mean the settlings along the shores, then it would mean that ports and harbours will be inhabited and busy. However the meaning remains the same.

S-J-L   ل ج س

"اَلسَّجْلُ" (*as-sajl*): a big bucket (of the well) filled with water, philanthropist *{T}*.

"اَلسِّجِلُ" (*as-sijllu*): book, document, writer *{T}*.

"اَلسِّجِّیْلُ" (*as-sijjeel*): it is a Persian word that has been arabized from "سَنْگِ گُلْ" (*sang-e-gul*) i.e. clay which is hardened in fire. In the old days when people began to write, slates of clay were 'cooked' in the fire and hardened and were used to write on. This was called "اَلسَّجْلُ" (*as-sijl*). Later everything which was used to write was called "اَلسَّجْلُ" (*as-sijl*) *{R}*.

The Quran says that on the nation of *Loot*:

| 11:82 | were rained upon | حِجَارَةً مِنْ سِجِّیْلٍ |
| 51:33 | were rained upon | حِجَارَةً مِنْ طِیْنٍ |

At both places they were called "مُسَوَّمَةً عِنْدَ رَبِّكَ" (*musawwamatun inda rabbika*): (51:34, 11:83). That is, those who were marked by Allah for this purpose *{T}*. But "اَلسَّجْلُ" (*as-sijl*) has an element of writing and this too elaborates the meaning of "مُسَوَّمَةٌ" (*musawwamath*). Maybe they were "مَنْضُوْدٌ" (*manzood*) layer upon layer (11:82) or slates which were in a library atop the mountain and when the volcano erupted these fell on the inhabitations around it. This refers to the physical destruction caused in the historical context which affected the earlier nations from the past.

Surah *Al-Ambia* says:

| 21:104 | This will be the era when heights or people belonging to the upper echelons of society will be wrapped up like paper | یَوْمَ نَطْوِی السَّمَاءَ كَطَیِّ السِّجِلِّ لِلْكُتُبِ |

This verse is signifying that "their era has ended, now economic egalitarianism will take place" (39:67). If there is a reference to the celestial bodies in this verse then it would mean the wrapping up of the heavenly bodies.

Ibn Faris says the root basically means for something to be over filled and then spill over.

S-J-N   ن ج س

"سَجَنَ" (*sajan*), "يَسْجُنُ" (*yasjun*), "سَجْنًا" (*sajna*): to imprison someone {*T*}. (12:35, 12:25).
"اَلسِّجْنُ" (*as-sijn*): prison (12:33).

"سِجِّيْنٌ" (*sijjeen*): this word has appeared in surah *At-Tatfeef*:

| 83:3 | And what can make you know what this *sijjeen* is? | مَا أَدْرَاكَ مَا سِجِّيْنٌ |

Some have translated it as prisons. However, the Quran explained it by saying:
Some say that "سِجِّيْنٌ" (*sijjeen*) means prison, but the Quran has also said:

| 83:9 | It is a written scripture (a chronicle of deeds) | كِتَابٌ مَرْقُوْمٌ |

A chronicle of deeds a man does in his lifetime and record, like a written book with all details {*T, R*}.

S-J-W   و ج س

"سَجَا اللَّيْلُ يَسْجُوْ" (*sajjal lailu yasju*), "سَجْوًا" (*sajwa*): for the night to become silent, to stop, to become dark.

Ibn Faris includes tranquillity and to cover in its basic meanings.

"سَجَااللَّيْلُ" (*sajjal lail*) means for the night to be very dark and quiet.
"اَلْبَحْرُ السَّاجِىْ" (*al-bahru-saaji*): peaceful sea.
"الطَّرْفُ السَّاجِىْ" (*at-tarfus saaji*): quiet look.

Ibnul Airaabi says that "سَجَى اللَّيْلُ" (*sajjal lail*) means that the darkness of the night increased {T, R}.

The Quran says:

| 93:2 | The darkness of the night and the intensity of the darkness before dawn is a testimony | وَاللَّيْلِ إِذَا سَجَى |

This testimony is to the fact that this program of Allah's system will take some time to reach success and it will complete its stages before doing so. As such you find that despite your best efforts, the darkness of society is not being eliminated, then do not let this make you reach the conclusion that Allah's laws have left your side.

| 93:3 | Neither has your Sustainer left your side nor put you in trouble for nought | مَا وَدَّعَكَ رَبُّكَ وَمَا قَلَى |

With "وَالضُّحٰى" (*wadduha*) appearing with it, it can also mean that the changes of day and night are testimony to the fact that the opposition will always not remain so, and there will be a revolution, and that things will change for the better.

S-H-B   س ح ب

"سَحَبَ" (*sahib*): he pulled, dragged.

"ألمَرْأَةُ تَسْحَبُ ذَيْلَهَا" (*almar'atuh tashabu zailaha*): the woman drags the corner of her dress on the ground.

"اِنْسَحَبَ" (*insahab*): he dragged (along) on the ground.

"ألسَّحَابَةُ" (*as-sahabah*): which means dark clouds, a piece of cloud, because it pulls the water (from the sea), or the winds pull it, or it drags itself across the sky. The plural is "سَحَابٌ" (*sahaab*).

In the Quran, this word has been used both as singular and plural.

2:165	cloud which has been in control	ٱلسَّحَابِ ٱلْمُسَخَّرِ
13:12	very thick and dark clouds	ٱلسَّحَابَ ٱلثِّقَالَ
40:71	They will be pulled (or dragged) into the 'hameem' (hell fire)	يُسْحَبُونَ فِى ٱلْحَمِيمِ
54:28	The day they will be dragged to fire	يَوْمَ يُسْحَبُونَ فِى ٱلنَّارِ

S-H-Te   س ح ت

"ألسَّحْتُ" (*as-seht*): to uproot something, to pare something gradually.

"سَحَتَ الشَّحْمَ عَنِ اللَّحْمِ" (*sahatas sahma unil lahm*): pared off the fat from the surface of the meat {T},

The Quran says:

| 20:61 | He will punish them such that they will be eliminated | فَيُسْحِتَكُم بِعَذَابٍ |

"ألسُّحْتُ" (*as-suht*): everything which is forbidden to mention, a forbidden and dirty profession which is the cause of shame. Every forbidden and unacceptable sustenance which is deprived of the blessings of God {T}.

About the Jews it is said:

| 5:42 | their means of earning is execrable | أَكَّٰلُونَ لِلسُّحْتِ |

Commonly the Jews were prone to charging interest and their religious scholars did business under the cover of their religion i.e. gave religious edicts for profit. Not just the Jews, but capitalists and religious leadership is the same everywhere.

Muheet with reference to *Qeys* says that "سُحْتٌ" (*suht*) is that thing which is clearly forbidden and there is no doubt about it being so.

"حَرَامٌ سُحْتٌ" (*haraamun suht*) means forbidden and well known to everyone.
"أَرْضٌ سَحْتَاءُ" (*arzun sahta-u*) means a barren piece of land *{T}*.
"عَامٌ أَسْحَتُ" (*aamu ashat*): drought year during which there is no growth e.g. fodder *{T}*.

S-H-R   س ح ر

Muheet says "اَلسِّحْرُ" (*as-sehr*) basically means to turn, and figuratively it means to represent falsehood as truth.

Tahzeeb says it means to turn something away from the truth to untruth.
Taj-ul-Uroos says it means such things whose origin is such that it becomes difficult to separate fact from fiction. It is used for a deception of a sort that one cannot find out how the deception has been made. Later this word started meaning commony used techniques of cheating and deception {Ibn Qatebah}.

"سَحَرَه" (*saharah*) and "سَحَّره" (*sah-harah*): he was deceived.
"اِنَّمَا اَنْتَ مِنَ الْمُسَحَّرِيْنَ" (*nama unta minal musah hareen*): you all are among those who have been deceived, and are deceived time and again (26:153-158).
"عَنْزٌ مَسْحُوْرَةٌ" (*unzun mashurah*) means a goat which has big breasts but it produces little milk.
"اَلْمَسْحُوْرُ" (*almas-huur*) means someone whose mind has gone mad or someone who lost his mind *{T, M}*.

The opponents used to call the messenger (*pbuh*) as "رَجُلاً مَسْحُوْراً" (*rajulan mas huura*), that is, one who has been deceived, or one who is under a spell, or one whose intellect has been impaired (17:47). It also means the same as "سَاحِرٌ" (*saahir*), or one who deceives, as in 17:101.

Surah *Al-Mominoon* says:

| 23:89 | Ask them why have you been deceived? | قُلْ فَاَنّٰى تُسْحَرُوْنَ |

Aside from deception, this word also means lies. The Quran says:

| 11:7 | If you tell them that you will be raised after you are dead then the deniers will say that this is a lie. | وَلَئِنْ قُلْتَ اِنَّكُمْ مَبْعُوْثُوْنَ مِنْ بَعْدِ الْمَوْتِ لَيَقُوْلَنَّ الَّذِيْنَ كَفَرُوْ اِنْ هٰذَا اِلَّا سِحْرٌ مُبِيْنٌ |

"ﺍَﻟﺴَّﺤْﺮُ" (*as-sahar*) means the upper part of the chest, (lung, heart etc.). It means the corner of everything.

"ﺳَﺤَﺮٌ" (*sahar*) is the last part of the night, or just before dawn.

Raghib says that *sahar* means dawn, when the darkness of the night is changing into the light of day (54:34). The plural is "ﺃَﺳْﺤَﺎﺭٌ" (*ashaar*) as in 51:18 *{T}*.

Ibn Qateebah says that *sahar* means the beginning of a day, the time for commencing business.

History tells us that in the pas there has been a time which has been called the magical age. Western researchers have provided quite a bit of information about this era. **Sehr** or magic meant that people through various means tried to make various forces in the universe follow their orders or desires. This is what is known as sorcery as well. First came the era in which man pleaded to the forces in the universe, then came the era when he thought of forcing these forces to do what he wanted. Thus sorcerers had a very high stature in society, but if given careful thought, it will be seen that man's development from the era of worship to the era of magic was a first and childish attempt to develop rational thinking, 'Rational thought' means to find the cause of everything, to find out the cause and effect of everything. In the era of worship man thought, for instance, that a man suffers from fever because some deity was displeased with him. To get rid of this fever one needed to please that deity somehow. There was no cause and effect inquiry into the matter. From this man evolved to the era of magic, in others words, he thought if such mantra is read so many times, and in a certain way, then the aim will be achieved. That is, in his mind a faint linkage with deed and effect had begun to make a beginning. Allah's **deen** told him that everything in the universe is created by Allah. Every deed has a designated effect and this happens according to certain law. If man finds out about the laws then he can produce the effect any time he wants. This is the foundation on which our entire scientific structure rests, and the axis round which human life and his future revolves. Magic is false illusion only, because it does not have any concept of something happening due to a certain law, but because of reciting some mantras and to do some odd things.

The Quran invited mankind to rationally analyse everything in their world by using their intellect and reasoning. In the Quran, in the story about **Moosa**, there is mention of the sorcerers of the Pharaoh's nation and their sorcery. **Moosa** had dealt with them. If **sehr** means magic then at these places it will be taken to mean magicians, but if it means 'the worship of falsehood, then the figurative meanings of those verses will be taken accordingly.

If **sehr** is taken to mean magic, then one thing comes to fore. The Quran has said that these sorcerers deceived people's eyes (7:116), that is, the ropes they had thrown on the ground did not actually start to move. The sorcerers with sleight of hand or psychologically made the people think that they had moved. That is, this sort of magic only affects the power of thought and those things do not actually turn into something different. The magician affects the power of thinking of the people who are watching. Today's psychological advancement has proven that it can be done and is called illusion. That means that nothing more than our thoughts make this magic real. The point to note here is that the Quran exposed the existence of these types of tricks from the past which took place many centuries ago. Also see heading (Kh-Y-L).

The entire religion of the Jews seemed to have got infested and comprises of such sorcery and their places of worship were the centres of such sorcery. They used to attribute these things to **Suleman** (Solomon). **Ism azam** and **nuqooshi sulemaani** (the great name and the seal of Solomon) were their special gimmicks for creating such magic. The Quran refuted all this and said that the messengers of God have nothing to do with these deceptions and superstitions (2:102).

This is what the Quran said but the **Muslims** who are supposed to follow the Quran gradually got influenced by superstitions one after another, and by naming it spiritualism gave falsehood the appearance of the truth. They only deceived themselves.

The Messenger (**pbuh**)was accused to be:

17:47 25:8	he is under a spell	رَجُلًا مَّسْحُورًا

The Quran has denied this in 25:9. The personality of a messenger is so strong and developed through the useof intellect and reasoning within the values of the revelation that no sorcerer's psychological strength can influence it. The messenger could never have come under any spell, as it is impossible. In **Moosa's** story it has only been said that he thought that the ropes were moving, but this is a different thing, while to be under someone's spell and talk nonsense is quite different.. Messengers can never be under a spell. If in this tale about **Moosa**, sehr is taken to mean worship of false ideologies, then the meaning becomes clearer.

S-H-Q   س ح ق

"سَحَقَهُ" (**suhaqa**), "يَسْحَقُهُ" (**yashaquh**), "سَحْقًا" (**sahqa**): he hammered it or ground into fine (powder).
"اِنْسَحَقَ" (**insahaq**): he was ground (burdened).
"سَحَقَتِ الرِّيْحُ الْأَرْضَ" (**sahaqatir rihul ard**): the wind blew away the marks in the ground; it blew so hard as if it was grinding the earth.
"سَحَقَتِ الدَّابَّةُ" (**sahaqatil da-abbah**): the animal ran fast.
"اَلسُّحُقْ" (**as-suhuq**), "اَلسَّحُقْ" (**as-sahuq**) means to be distant.
"اَسْحَقَ فُلَانًا" (**as-haqi fulana**): he distanced him, killed him {**T, M**}.

Ibn Faris says it basically means enmity and distance, and to weaken something such that it becomes brittle.
"اَسْحَقَ الضَّرعُ" (**as-haqaz zar-u**): the nipples became dried of milk and withered.

Raghib says "سَحْقٌ" (*sahq*) means to turn something into smithereens.

The Quran says:

67:11	The dwellers of hell will be deprived from the good things of life	فَسُحْقاً لِأَصْحَبِ السَّعِيرِ
22:31	faraway place	مَكَانٌ سَحِيْقٌ

S-H-L   س ح ل

"سَحَلَهُ" (*sahalahu*), "يَسْحَلُهُ" (*yashalah*), "سَحْلاً" (*sahla*) he pared it, scraped it, filed it.

"الرِّيَاحُ نَسْحَلُ الْأَرْضَ" (*ar-riyaahu nashalul ard*): winds scrape the surface of the earth.

"اَلسَّاحِلُ" (*as-saahil*): river bank or sea shore which is worn away (gradually) or scraped by the water {T, R}.

The Quran says:

20:39	the river will put him on the shore	فَلْيُلْقِهِ الْيَمُّ بِا السَّاحِلِ

S-Kh-R   س خ ر

"سَخِرَ" (*saakhir*), "يَسْخَرُ" (*yaskharu*), "سَخَرًا" (*sakhrann*), "سَخْرًا" (*sakhran*), "سُخْرًا" (*sukhra*): means to joke with, and to play with somebody thinking him to be a character.

"رَجُلٌ سُخَرَةٌ" (*rajulun suharah*): a man who jests a lot and makes fun of people.

"سُخْرِيَّةٌ" (*sukhriyyah*), "اَلسُّخْرِىُّ" (*sukhriyaw*), "اَلسِّخْرِىُّ" (*as-sikhriyyu*): jest, joke.

"سَخَرَهُ" (*sakhara*), "يَسْخَرُهُ" (*yaskharu*), "سِخْرِيًّا" (*sikhriyyaw*), "سُخْرِيًّا" (*sukhriyya*), "سَخَّرَهُ" (*sakh-kharahu*), "أَسْخِيْرَأً" (*taskheera*): to take someone forcibly somewhere, to force someone to some work, to make someone work without pay, to subjugate somebody, to make someone follow orders {T}.

Ibn Faris says basically it means to consider lowly and to insult.

Surah **Az-Zakhraf** says:

43:32	So some of them are above others among them	لِيَتَّخِذَ بَعْضُهُمْ بَعْضاً سُخْرِيًّا

Here "سُخْرِيًّا" (*sukhriyya*) means to control or subjugate as related to getting work done {M}.

The above verse of surah **Az-Zakhraf** points to a very important reality. It says that individuals possess different abilities, capacities and affinities so that they may work for and with one another. If everyone had the same sort of qualities and abilities then nobody would work for nobody, or everyone would be doing the same thing. This is to facilitate division of labour to get work done in a society. But those with greater abilities are not permitted to rule over or subjugate others with lesser abilities. For the Quran, every human being is equal and the difference is only as far their abilities are concerned. For further details see the book titled "System of Sustenance" by G.A Perwaiz.

The Quran says:

45:13	And He has subjected to you all that is in the heavens and in the earth as per Law	سَخَّرَلَكُمْ مَا فِى السَّمٰوٰاتِ وَمَافِى الْاَرْضِ جَمِيْعاً مِنْهُ

This is done so that man should gain knowledge about those things and make use of them. As such, the nation which deliberates upon them and utilizes them will be the nation which makes the right use of th creation.

We should reflect in the revelation by the Quran which has revolutionized human thinking. Man used to be afraid of the forces of nature, he used to worship them, used to plead before them, or think that he was weak and powerless before them. The Quran said that this was a false concept. Every force in the universe is subservient to man. These forces do not have control him and are to be brought under his control and used for the benefit of the mankind. The *'malaikah'* or the forces of nature are subservient to man. This raised man's status above everything in the universe and the door to understanding and expl;oring the universe was thus opened. Any nation that acquires knowledge of the laws of nature will make these forces to come under their control and can take advantage of these resources. In this respect there is no differentiation between a *kafir* and a *momin*. Although a *kaafir* would use these forces of nature for own good, while a *momin* will use them for the overall good of mankind. This shows that man's status demands that he conquers the forces of nature and make use of them according to his will.

The status of a *momin* is that he conquers the forces of nature and utilizes them for the benefit of mankind as directed and explained in the Quran. He who does not conquer these forces in the first place, leaving the status of a *momin* aside, does not even deserve the status of a human being.

"سَخَّرَ" (*sakhira*) in the meaning of jest and satire has appeared at several places in the Quran as in 49:11, 37:12 and 21:41. Surah *Al-Momin* says "سِخْرِيّاً" (*sikhriyya*) in 23:110 which means the explained earlier.

S-Kh-Te ط خ س

"اَلسُّخْطُ" (*assukht*), "اَلسَّخَطُ" (*as-sakhat*): dislike, hatred, unwillingness, anger.
"سَخِطَ عَلَيْهِ" (*sakhita alaih*): he was angry at him.
"سَخِطَ" (*sakhit*): he disliked it, hated it.
"أَسْخَطَهُ" (*askhatah*): he annoyed him, made him angry.
"اَلْمَسْخُوطُ" (*al-maskhuut*): hateful, disliked {T}.

Raghib says "سَخَطَ" (*sakhat*) means extreme anger which demands punishment {R}.

But when this word is attributed to God, it will not have this meaning because God is high above such human emotions as anger. It becomes clear as noted in Surah **Muhammed**:

47:28	There is adversity for them because they do not follow Allah's guidance; they dislike things which are according to Allah's directions.	ذَلِكَ بِأَنَّهُمُ اتَّبَعُوا مَا أَسْخَطَ اللَّهَ وَكَرِهُوا رِضْوَانَهُ فَأَحْبَطَ أَعْمَالَهُم
47:26	They dislike the revelation: this results in their deeds going wasted i.e. without results	كَرِهُوا رِضْوَانَهُ يعنى كَرِهُوا مَانَزَّلَ اللَّهُ

That is, they do not produce the good results that they are expecting. As such "مَا أَسْخَطَ اللَّهُ" (*ma askhat allah*) means those things which are not according to Allah's laws and which result in their deeds being unproductive. There is no meaning of anger here. In 3:161, "سَخَطَ" (*sakhat*) has come opposite to "رِضْوَانٌ" (*rizwaan*).

Surah **Al-Ma'idah** says "أَنْ سَخِطَ اللَّهُ" (*un sakhitallahu*) which has been explained by "مَا قَدَّمَتْ لَهُمْ أَنْفُسُهُمْ" (*qaddamat lahum anfusahum*) in 5:80, which means the "natural outcome of ones actions".

For more details see heading (R-Zd-Y) and (Gh-Zd-B).

S-D-D د د س

"اَلسُّدُّ" (*as-sud*): obstruction, barrier, mountain. Some say "اَلسِّدُّ" (*as-sid*) is an obstruction that is manmade, and "اَلسُّدُّ" (*as-sodd*) means a natural obstruction like a mountain {T}, but others do not agree with this differentiation. In the Quran "اَلسُّدُّ" (*as-sudd*) has been used in meaning mountain (18:93) as well as for a man made obstruction (18:94). Surah **Yasin** uses this word to mean such causes and effects which obstruct human intellect and comprehension (36:9).

Ibn Faris thinks the basic meanings are to fill some gap and make it smooth.

"سَدَّدَ الرُّمْحَ" (*saddadar rumh*): straightened or corrected the (bent) spear.
"سَدَّدَ الثَّلْمَ" (*saddadas salam*): filled the gap {T}.
"رَجُلٌ سَدِيدٌ" (*rajulun sadeed*): a man who takes the right path.

"أَمْرٌ سَدِيْدٌ" (*amrun sadeed*): something that fills every gap there may be in the truth.

Raghib says it means balanced and moderate talk which includes no exaggeration whatsoever.

The Quran says:

4:9 33:70	very balanced, and straightforward and clear talk, which leaves no doubt	قَوْلاً سَدِيْداً

It is the Quranic teaching to be clear, straight, honest and truthful in dealing with others and talk without ambiguity, straight forwardly, and in a balanced manner. One should adopt a speech which is direct and to the point. It must not be meaningless and pointless.

"سُهُمٌّ سَدِيْدٌ" (*sahmun sadeeda*) is an arrow which finds the target straight away *{R}*.

Diplomacy is against the teachings of the Quran: See heading ***radam*** for the difference between "سَدٌّ" (*sudd*) and "رَدْمٌ" (*radam*).

S-D-R   س د ر

"أَلسِّدْرُ" (*as-sidr*): a lote tree. The singular is "سِدْرَةٌ" (*sidrah*). A lotetree has a good shade when it is in full blossom and when the Arabs are very tired from the heat of the desert, they rest under it. Therefore it symbolizes a heavenly place *{R}*. "فِىْ سِدْرٍ مَخْضُوْدٍ" (*fi sidrim makhzood*) is a tree which is laden with fruit and which has a good shade (56:28), or trees which have good shades but no needles to contend with. That is, comfort without any qualms.

In meaning of shade, this word appears at another place:

4:57	And We will admit them to thick shades	وَنُدْخِلُهُمْ ظِلاًّ ظَلِيْلاً

Here comfort and wellbeing both are implied. This tree is evergreen even in the desert climate, but according to ***Raghib***, though its fruit is not great in nutrients, but its shade is. The Quran says that when the ***saba*** area became barren after the floods, then some lote trees grew there in place of the very lush gardens.

34:16	And something of few plum trees	وَشَىْءٍ مَّنْ سِدْرٍ قَلِيْلٍ

"سَدِيْرُ النَّخْلِ" (*sadeerun nakhl*) means clump of date palms *{T}*.
"سَدَرَ" (*saadir*): he was surprised, he couldn't see due to intense heat.
"أَلسَّادِرُ" (*as-saadir*): a man who is mesmerised due to the intensity of the heat.
"سَدِرَ بَصَرُهُ سَدَراً" (*sadira basarahu sadara*): due to the intensity of the heat, his eyes opened wide with wonderment *{R}*.

Ibn Faris says it basically means surprise and bewilderment.

"اَلسَّادِرُ" (***as-saadior***): means one who is surprised.

Surah ***An-Najam*** describes the status of messenger-hood in a symbolic way. Note that the condition of revelation can only be related in a symbolic way because nobody except a messenger can ever understand the true state of it, although one can understand what is meant. It has been said that the place from where a messenger gets the revelation, the human intellect can only be surprised at it. Human intellect cannot understand what that state is.

The Quran says:

| 53:14 | The state where there is abundant surprise | عِنْدَ سِدْرَةِ الْمُنْتَهَى |
| 53:16 | when that which overshadows was overshadowing | إِذْ يَغْشَى السِّدْرَةَ مَا يَغْشَى |

Other than the messenger of Allah none can understand what the state was. For the eyes it was profound bewilderment like the expanse of the heated sand of the desert with mirages all around but despite that:

| 53:17 | the eye of the messenger did not take for a deception, it observed the truth as a clear reality and with no ambiguity. | مَا زَاغَ الْبَصَرُ وَمَا طَغَى |

But this only implies for those realities which are manifested before him, it cannot cross the limit set for him because the revelation does not come to him by personal effort, so it did not increase with his efforts. Truth is revealed to him i.e. only the part which is meant to be disclosed. As compared to ordinary human beings, a messenger's knowledge knows no bounds, but compared to God's knowledge, it has limits and it cannot go beyond those limits.

Raghib says that verse 53:16 points to the place or the same tree under which the messenger (***pbuh***) made the pact with God (48:18), but obviously here the word has more of a connotation of the state than meant to be some geographical location.

"اَلسَّدِيْرُ" (***as-sadder***): a fountainhead or reservoir of water, or river {*T*}.
"اَلسِّدْرُ" (***as-sidr***): sea. It can also mean the fountainhead of God.
"سِدْرَةُ الْمُنْتَهَى" (***sidratul muntaha***): the source of revelation where there is utter surprise for human intellect, but the messenger's eye sees it clearly.

S-D-S   س د س

"اَلسُّدْسُ" (*as-suds*), "اَلسُّدُسُ" (*as-sudus*): sixth part (4:11).

"اَلسِّتَّ" (*as-siit*): it was actually "سِدْسٌ" (*sids*) which later turned to "اَلسِّتَّ" (*as-siit*), i.e. six.

"سِتُّوْنَ" (*sittuun*), "سِتِّيْنَ" (*sittiin*): sixty {T} (58:2).

"سَادِسٌ" (*saadisun*): sixth (18:22).

Also see heading (S-T-T).

S-D-Y   س د ی

"اَلسَّدَىٰ" (*as-sada*): warp of the cloth.

"قَد أَسْدَىٰ الثَّوْبَ" (*qud asdayas saub*) and "سَدَّاهُ" (*saddah*): he straightened the warp of the cloth.

"اَلسُّدَىٰ" (*assudya*): camels which are left to roam on their own {T}.

"ذَهَبَ كَلَامُهُ سَدىًٰ" (*zaraba kal-uhu sudya*): his talk went waste {M}.

Ibn Faris says that "سدی" (*sudyah*) means to leave something roam free and at its own.

Khalil says "سَدْوٌ" (*sadwun*) is a child's game which is played with marbles and walnuts, in which they throw these things with their hands.

The Quran says:

| 75:36 | Does man think that he will be left unaccountable | اَیَحْسَبُ الْإِنْسَانُ اَنْ یُتْرَکَ سُدىً |

This meaning of this root needs careful attention. For weaving cloth, warp and weft both are required. Even if the warp is a hundred yards long, it is useless alone until it has weft, we cannot weave cloth without either one. Whatever social system man established was either like warp alone or weft alone. Sometimes he sought spiritualism and at other times he became completely materialistic. He has tried to keep the permanent values away from his political world. This is the reason his efforts to establish a system which can provide development of the self and prepare him for a higher purpose of life, have mostly evaded him. Humans either remained like warp or like weft but never became whole like cloth. The Quran declared that it is wrong for man to be either one entirely. He also needs the other part, but for this he will have to realize that his life has a great purpose before him. He is accountable for whatever he does in this life and his life in the hereafter will be based on his conduct here. Therefore the in this life he should use the right type of warp and weft to weave a cloth which fits into the design proposed by the Quran. This is called the righteous path. The human intellect alone cannot guide in this life as human beings do not have any internal guidance. The human intellect produces good results only when it works under the guidance provided by the divine revelation now preserved in the Quran.

Now consider the other meaning i.e. to let the camels go without someone to guide them. Allah has not left man rudderless in this way, but has provided guidance through the revelation. Therefore the correct option for man is to follow the guidance path defined and explained in the revelation i.e. the Quran. If he does not follow it, then all his efforts will go waste as noted and explained in the Quran (18:103-106). In the universe, except man, all other creations are bound to follow Allah's guidance which is inbuilt. They cannot do otherwise. This is what is called their nature (or instincts). God has formulated laws for human beings too but has given him the power to decide whether to follow them or not to follow them. However, he does not have the power to alter the effects of following the chosen path. He has the option to ignore Allah's laws but the results will definitely be compiled as per these laws. This is called the Law of Requital.

S-R-B   س ر ب

"اَلسَّرْبُ" (**as-sarb**): a camel, or grazing cattle.
"اَلسَّرِبُ" (**as-sarib**): flowing water.
"اَلسُّرْبَةُ" (**as-surbah**): path, road.
"اَلسَّارِبُ" (**as-saarib**): to roam in the land without any restriction and at will {*T, R*}.
"اَلسَّرَبُ" (**as-sarab**) and "السَّرِبُ" (**as-sarib**) means water that flows out of the leather containers.

Surah *Ar-Raad* says:

13:10	One who walks or moves by the day{T, R}.	سَارِبٌ بِالنَّهَارِ

Surah *Al-Kahaf* says:

18:62	This fish made its way in the river.	فَاتَّخَذَ سَبِيلَهُ فِى الْبَحْرِ سَرَاباً

This word connotes moving about without restriction and with complete freedom.
Azhari has said that "سَرَبَتِ الْإِبِلُ" (**sarbati ilibil**) is for camels to go freely where ever they may desire {*T, R*}.

Ibn Faris says that this root has the meaning of expanse and to move on the earth.
Raghib says it means water that leaks.

"سَرَابٌ" (**saraab**): mirage.

The Quran has likened the wrong path to a mirage (24:39). Living life without guidance is likened to looking for water by chasing a mirage which is deceptive and unreal. Our desires and deeds may look very attractive but bear on long lasting effects in life and like chasing a mirage the life ends wasted without any purpose. The Quran calls such a life as a path which leads to self-destruction.

Raghib says "السَّرَابُ" (**as-sarb**) means to go towards the low lying areas or slope, because the water flows towards the slope – freedom to flow is evident in this meaning. Low lying area.

S-R-B-L   س ر ب ل

"سِرْبَالٌ" (**sirbal**), with its plural "سَرَابِيْلٌ" (**sarabeel**) means shirts, or armour, or any dress that is worn on the upper part of the body like a shirt {T, M}. The Quran has used this word in both meanings.

16:81	He created your dress which protects you from the heat and created the armour which protects you in war	وَجَعَلَ لَكُمْ سَرَابِيْلَ تَقِيْكُمُ الْحَرَّ وَسَرَابِيْلَ تَقِيْكُمْ بَأْسَكُمْ

In surah **Ibrahim**, it is said about rebels of Islam that when their strength breaks:

14:50	their armour will turn to coal tar	سَرَابِيْلُهُمْ مِنْ قَطِرَانٍ

This means that their armour which protects them from the enemy, will stick to their bodies like coaltar instead of providing protection.

S-R-J   س ر ج

"أَلسِّرَاجُ" (**as-siraaj**) means a lamp or anything which gives out light {T, R}. Some think that it is the Arabized version of Persian word "چِراغ" (**chiraagh**) which means a lamp.

"أَلسِّرَاجُ" (**as-siraaj**) also means the sun {T, R}.

The Quran has said:

25:61	And made in it the sun	جَعَلَ فِيْهَا سِرَاجاً
71:16	The sun was made a lamp (to provide light)	وَجَعَلَ الشَّمْسَ سِرَاجاً

The Messenger (**pbuh**) has been called "سِرَاجاً مُنِيْراً" (**siraajaw muneera**) in 33:46.

"أَلسَّرْجُ" (**as-sarj**): saddle.
"أَلسَّرَّاجُ" (**as-saraaj**): saddle maker, one who tells a lot of lies {T, R}.

Ibn Faris says that this root basically means beauty, adornment, and good looks.
The lamp is called "أَلسِّرَاجُ" (**as-siraaj**) because of its light's beauty. A saddle is called "أَلسَّرْجُ" (**as-siraaj**) because it adorns an animal. "سَرَّجَ وَجْهَهُ" (**sarraja wajhahu**): he adorned his face, made it more beautiful.

S-R-H   س ر ح

"اَلسَّرْحُ" (**as-sarh**), "اَلتَّسِریْحُ" (**as-saareeh**): to let animals graze freely in a pasture in the morning {*T*}.

16:6	When you take them out for grazing	حِیْنَ تَسْرَحُوْنَ

"سَرَاحٌ" (**sarah**) and "تَسْرِیْحٌ" (**tasreeh**) mean to let free or to liberate from a contract like wedlock. Hence it may be used for divorce and to liberate {*T*}.

33:28	And to set you free (let you go) in a good manner	وَ أُ سَرِّحْكُنَّ سَرَاحاً جَمِیْلاً

This word has appeared against "اِمْسَاكٌ" (**imsaak**) which means to block in surah *Al-Baqrah*:

2:229-2:231	To keep obligated under contract	فَإِمْسَاكٌ بِمَعْرُوْفٍ أَوْتَسْرِیْحٌ بِاِحْسَانٍ

Ibn Faris says its basic meanings are to open up or to proceed to go.

S-R-D   س ر د

Ibn Faris says that "اَلسَّرْدُ" (**as-sard**) means to join one thing with another, like the links in armour.

It is also used to mean making armour and for sewing shoes or other leather goods.

"اَلسَّرْدُ" (**as-sard**): hole.
"اَلْمِسْرَدُ" (**al-misrud**): that with which a hole is made.
"اَلسَّرِیْدَ ةُ" (**as-sareedah**): leather string with which shoe etc. is sewn {*T*}.

The Quran says:

34:11	keep measure of the holes correctly so that the links of the armour may fit into them	وَقَدِّرْفِی السَّرْدِ

The second part of the verse refers to righteous deeds implying that these deeds tie together just like armour and provide protection in the long run.

S-R-D-Q   س ر د ق

"اَلسُّرَادِقُ" (*as-suraadiq*): that covering (of canvas or cloth) which is strung over the house patio, or any wall, or canvas wall which is strung or built around something. That is why it also means the cloud which spreads around a place and encircles it *{T}*.

Ibn Faris says "اَلسُّرَادِقُ" (*as-suraadiq*) means dust cloud.

Raghib says it is a Persian word that has been adopted in Arabic *{R}*.

The Quran says:

18:29	The fire of hell whose columns will surround them from all sides. (i.e. Hell will encompass them from all sides)	نَاراً اَحَاطَ بِهِمْ سُرَادِقُهَا

S-R-R   س ر ر

"اَلسِّرُّ" (*as-sirruh*): that matter which is kept secret *{T}*.

This root means to hide, but sometimes it also means the opposite i.e. to reveal {Latif-ul-Lugha} {F}.
"اَلسُّرُوْرُ" (*as-sururu*), "اَلْحُبُوْرُ" (*hubur*) and "اَلْفَرَحُ" (*al-farah*) are almost similar words but "اَلسُّرُوْرُ" (*as-surur*) is the happiness which remains in the heart and "اَلْحُبُوْرُ" (*hubur*) is the happiness which gets reflected through one's face. These are both good traits but "فَرَحٌ" (*farah*) is that happiness which produces false pride, and hence is bad *{M}*.

"سَرَّ ہ" (*sarrah*): made him happy.
"مَسْرُوْرٌ" (*masroor*): happy (84:9-13).
"اَلسِّرُّ" (*as-siir*): the beginning of anything, it's pure or basic part, the core. It is also used for prime land.
"سَرَارَة الْوَادِیْ" (*sararatul waadi*): the best part of the valley.
"اَلْمَسَرَّةُ" (*al-masarrah*): throne of flowers.
"اَلسَّرَّاءُ" (*as-sarra'a*): well being, abundance of prosperity, comfort and luxury *{T}*. This word is the opposite of "اَلضَّرَّاءُ" (*azzarra'a*) in 7:95.
"اَلسُّرِّيَّةُ" (*as-suriyyah*): a slave girl with whom sexual relations were established.
"اَلسَّرِيْرُ" (*as-sareer*): government, seat of government, seat, bed *{T}*, because only well established people have it.

Surah *An-Anaam* has used "سِرٌّ" (*sirrun*) opposite to "جَهْرٌ" (*jahr*) in 6:3. As such, "سِرٌّ" (*sirrun*) means secrets.

Surah *Al-Baqrah* has used words like "مَا يُسِرُّوْنَ" (*mayusirron*) and "مَا يُعْلِنُوْنَ" (*mayo'linun*) to mean secret talks in 2:77.

Surah **Ibrahim** says:

14:31	Whatever Allah has given them, whether unseen qualities or things of this world which one can see, are kept available for the benefit of mankind	وَيُنْفِقُوْ مِمَّا رَزَقْنٰهُمْ سِرًّا وَعَلَانِيَةً

It could also mean openly and secretly.

In Surah **Taha it** says:

20:7	He knows secrets and even more hidden things.	يَعْلَمُ السِّرَّ وَأَخْفٰى

Surah **Yunus** says:

10:54	They will try to hide their shame when they meet the punishment.	وَأَسَرُّوا النَّدَامَةَ

Some scholars say that this word means opposite of hiding, that is, to reveal, but hiding seems more appropriate here.

"سُرُرٌ" (*surur*) means wooden short seat (15:47). Singular is "سَرِيْرٌ" (*sareer*), and "سَرَائِرُ" (*saraa-ir*) means secret talks (86:9). Singular is "سَرِيْرٌ" (*sareer*).

"اِسْرَارٌ" (*israar*) means to talk about secret things, to hide from others and talk secretly (27:26).

S-R-Ain   س ر ع

"اَلسَّرَاعُ" (*as-sara'a*), "اَلسَّرِعُ" (*as-sari'h*), "اَلسُّرْعَةُ" (*as-sur'ah*): to become fast, to happen quickly, fastness, haste.
"سَرُعَ" (*saru'h*): fast wind, he hurried.
"اَلسَّرَعَانُ مِنَ الْخَيْلِ" (*as-sar'aanu minal kail*): horses which surge ahead *{T}*.

Ibn Faris says it basically means to make haste.

The Quran has said at various places:

2:202	Allah is quick in accountability	اللّٰهُ سَرِيْعُ الْحِسَابِ

According to the Law of Requital every cause has an effect. However, the results take time to materialise though the natural turn of events starts long before the result becomes evident. For example a plant starts its growth the moment a seed is planted in the ground and right environment is provided to the seed. However, the growth manifests itself after sometime when it erupts from the ground and one can see the branches and the stem of the plant. Likewise a our deeds start formulating results when the action is taken , but the consequence is manifested sometime later. This is how the turn of events is "سَرِيْعُ الْحِسَابِ" (*saree-ul hisaab*), or quick in holding accountability. The Quran has declared that every deed is accountable (45:21).

Surah *Al-Qaf* mentione "سِرَاعًا" (*sira'un*) which means something that happens quickly. "سَارَعَ" (*saara'a*), "مُسَارَعَةٌ" (*musara'ah*) and "سِرَاعًا" (*sira'an*) mean to make haste, to compete. "وَسَارِعُوْا اِلٰى مَغْفِرَةٍ" (*saari-u ila maghfirah*): make haste in going towards security (3:132).

<u>S-R-F</u>   س ر ف

"اَلسَّرَفُ" (*as-surf*): to cross the limit, to commit an excess *{T}*.

Ibn Faris says it means to do something foolish.

Surah ***Bani Israel*** says:

17:33	He should not exceed in killing	فَلَا يُسْرِفْ فِى الْقَتْلِ

This means that he should remain within limits, lest he kills the killer himself, by taking the law into his own hands in foolishness. In this case one should hand over the matter over to a court of law. This is explained further by "اِنَّهُ كَانَ مَنْصُوْرًا" (*innakana mansora*):

Surah ***Al-Furqaan*** uses this word against "قَتَّرَ" (*qatar*) in 25:67. "قَتَّرَ" (*qatar*) means miserliness and constriction. As such "اسراف" (*israaf*) would be "افراط" (*ifraat*) against "تفريط" (*tafreet*). That is, to spend more than necessary at a place i.e. to waste.

That is why it is said:

The mother fed too much milk to her child and spoiled his health	سَرَفَتِ الْأُمُّ وَلَدَهَا

This means for a thing to go waste because the intended benefit does not accrue.

"سَرَفُ الْمَاءِ" (*saraful ma'i*) means water to be wasted by giving no benefit when it flows across the floor *{T}*. That is why not keeping a thing where it is meant to be kept is called "اِسْرَافٌ" (*israaf*), and one who does so is called "مُسْرِفٌ" (*musrif*). The nation of ***Loot*** is called "قَوْمٌ مُسْرِفُوْنَ" (*qaumun musrifoon*) in 7:81, because they used to waste their reproductive ability by resorting to sexual perversion. The Quran warns us that these practices may not be taken serious when become prevalent; however, these have serious long term consequences in the life of nations and lead to their ultimate fall. Those who create chaos in the land are also called "مُسْرِفِيْنَ" (*musrifeen*) as in (26:151).

The above explanations show that "اِسْرَافٌ" (*israaf*) is not only being a wasteful spender (or one who spends needlessly), it also means to spend human energy, time, wealth or any other capability for a purpose which is not constructive, or to waste it for destructive results.

For the difference between "اِسْرَاف" (*israaf*) and "تَبْذِیْرٌ" (*tabzeer*) see heading (B-Dh-R).

S-R-Q   س ر ق

"سَرَقَةٌ" (*saariqah*): to take someone else's possession secretly. If it is taken openly, then this act will be called "اِخْتِلَاسٌ" (*ikhtilaas*), "اِسْتِلَابٌ اِنْتِہَابٌ" (*istilaab intihaab*) if the owner resists. But if it is still taken from him by force then it will be called "غَصْبٌ" (*ghasab*) *{T, M}*.

"سَرَقَ الشَّیْءُ" (*sariqas shaiyi*): the thing became hidden.
"ھُوَ یَسَارِقُ النَّظَرَ اِلَیْہِ" (*huwa yusaariqun nazara ilaih*): he is looking as glance at him.
"اِنْسَرَقَ عَنْہُمْ" (*insaraqa unhum*): to slip away quietly *{T, M}*.

Surah *Yusuf* says:

| 12:81 | Your son has stolen | اِنَّ ابْنَکَ سَرَقَ |

"اَلسَّارِقُ" (*as-saariq*): thief (5:38).
"اِسْتَرَقَ السَّمْعَ" (*istaraqas sam'a*): to eavesdrop *{T, M}* (15:18).

In 37:10 it has been said "خَطِفَ الْخَطْفَةَ" (*ikhifatil khatfitah*): to catch something in the air, or to get the whiff of something and to build mountain out of molehill.

For the punishment for a thief is "قَطْعِ یَدَ" (*qataa yud* as noted in (5:38) i.e. cutting hands. For details of this, see heading (Q-Te-Ain).

S-R-M-D   س ر م د

"اَلسَّرْمَدُ" (*as-sarmad*): permanent, a thing which always remains and which never ends.
"لَیْلٌ سَرْمَدٌ" (*lailun sarmad*): long night.

Raazi says "سَرْمَدٌ" (*sarmad*) has been culled from "سَرْدٌ" (*sard*) which means continuous and one after another. By adding "م" (*miim*) to it, the benefit of exaggeration has been obtained, thus it would mean continuous period *{T, R}*. *Ibn Faris* says this as well.

Muheet says that "اَلسَّرْمَدِیُّ" (*assarmadi*) is something which has no beginning or end *{M}*.

The Quran says:

| 28:71 | If Allah prolongs the night for you {T, R}. | اِنْ جَعَلَ اللہُ عَلَیْکُمُ اللَّیْلَ سَرْمَداً |

S-R-Y/W   س ر ی/و

"اَلسُّرىٰ" (*as-sura*): to walk the better part of the night.

"سَرىٰ" (*sara*), "یَسْرِیْ" (*yasri*), "سُرىٰ" (*surya*): to walk at night.

"أَسْرىٰ اِسْرَاءً" (*asrya isra'*): to walk during the night.

"اَلسَّرِیَّةُ" (*as-sarriyyah*): an army contingent, because it moves at night so that the enemy is not warned.

"اَلسَّرِیُّ" (*as-sariyyo*): small canal which goes towards an oasis {*M*}.

Surah **Maryam** says:

| 19:24 | there is a canal, down the slope | تَحْتَکِ سَرِیًّا |

"سَرَاةٌ" (*sarah*): the higher part of something, vast expanse of land.

Raghib and **Muheet** say that in 17:1, when it says "سُبْحٰنَ الَّذِیْ أَسْرىٰ بِعَبْدِہ" (*subhaanal lazi asra bi-abdehi*), the word "أَسْرىٰ" (*asra*) has not come from "سَرىٰ یَسْرِیْ" (*sarah yasri*) which means to walk at night, but rather from "سَرَاةٌ" (*sarah*), which means that God took his missionary to "سَرَاةٌ" (*sarah*), vast expanse of land.

"أَجْبَلَ" (*ajbala*) means that he went atop a mountain and "أَتْہَمَ" (*athama*) means that he went to the "تِہَامہ" (*tahamah*) {R, M}. Mecca had become a restricted land for the Messenger (*pbuh*) and his companions, so he migrated to Medina where the atmosphere for his mission was more favourable and there were more opportunities for his work.

But we consider that this "سَرىٰ" (*sarya*) is indeed from "یَسْرِیْ" (*yasri*) and *lilan* is an addition for stress. History tells us that the Messenger (*pbuh*) had commenced his migration journey at night.

Ibn Faris says it means physical courage and generosity and the word is spelled both as (S-R-Y) and (S-R-W).

Hence "اَلسَّرْوُ" (*assaro*) means to open something up

"سَرَ اَۃ ا لنَّہَارِ" (*saratun nahaar*): the peak of a day.

S-Te-H   س ط ح

"اَلسَّطْحُ" (*as-sath*): the roof of a house which is even/flat (smooth), or the upper part of anything.

"سَطَحَ" (*satash*), "یَسْطَحُ" (*yastah*): he spread out, smoothened it and laid out.

"اَلمَسْطَحُ" (*al-mastah*): smooth place where dates are dried {T, R}.

The Quran says:

| 88:20 | (don't you notice) at the earth, how it is spread out (for habitation) | وَاِلَى الْاَرْضِ کَیْفَ سُطِحَتْ |

S-Te-R   س ط ر

"سَطَرَ" (*satar*), "يَسْطُرُ" (*yastur*), "سَطْراً" (*satra*): to write (in straight lines).

Ibn Faris says its basic meaning is to make even rows, like the lines in a book or a row of trees. This has led it to mean writing.

68:1	By the ink pot and the pen, and what ever they write	ن وَالْقَلَمِ وَمَا يَسْطُرُونَ

This above verse is referring to the Quran and all the knowledge which man puts down in writing for safe keeping. All testify to this fact.

Surah *Bani Israel* says:

17:58	that which is written in the book	كَانَ ذَالِكَ فِى الْكِتْبِ مَسْطُوْرًا

"معنى مُسْتَطَرٌّ" (*mustatar*) has the same meaning as mentioned above (54:53).
"أَلْأَسَاطِيْرُ" (*al-asaateeer*) is the plural of "أُسْطُوْرَةٌّ" (*oosturah*), which means stories, tales. {T}.

Some have said that word means a story. The Quran says that when these people are told to deliberate on historical facts to find out what happened to the nations which indulged in what you too are practicing, they reply by saying:

6:25	These are tales from the past, which we have nothing to do with us	إِنْ هٰذَا إِلَّا أَسَاطِيْرُ الْأَوَّلِيْنَ

The Quran states that previous generations were warned that early nations got destroyed according to the Law of Requital and that the present generations will also experience the same outcome if their conduct remains the same.. The present day Mulims who read the Quran have the same attitude as those of the previous generations. When they are warned about the Law of Requital and what it did to the previous nations, they say that it was applicable to the Jews, or it was concerning the Christians, or this is about the pagans (*mushrikeen*) of Mecca, or this is about the hypocrites of Medina. In other words the entire Quran is only narrating the tales from the past which has no implications for the modern world. The present day Muslims claim that the only part that is relevant for us is, where there is a mention of the promises of paradise and heavenly life. The Quran states that this is their false claim and complacency and has nothing to do with the accountability process. Each individual is accountable for his deed (45:21). Since stories and tales are generally made up, "سَطَّرَ" (*sattara*), "تَسْطِيْرٌ" (*tasteera*) means to collect lies {T}, and since "سَطْرٌ" (*satrun*) means a straight line, therefore "أَلسَّطْرُ" (*as-satr*) also means to cut straight with the sword.

"أَلسَّاطُوْرُ" (*as-saatoor*) means knife {T}.
"سَيْطَرَ عَلَيْهِ" (*sversera alaih*): to stand straight as a row at someone's head.

This led it to mean "اَلْمُسَيْطِر" (*al-musatr*) which means overseer, guard, imposer *{R}*.

The Quran says:

88:22	You are not a guardian over them	لَسْتَ عَلَيْهِمْ بِمُصَيْطِر
52:37	Are they imposed ones?	اَمْ هُمُ الْمُصَيْطِرُوْنَ

In these verses the meanings are equivalent with "مَسَلَّطُوْنَ" (*masallatoon*) which means those who are imposed as guards on someone.

S-Te-W   س ط و

"سَطَا عَلَيْهِ وَبِهِ" (*sata alihi wabehi*), "سَطْوًا" (*satwun*), "سَطْوَةً" (*satwah*): to attack or to strongly overpower someone.

Raghib says to attack someone physically with bare hands is called "سَطْوَةٌ" (*satwah*). Actually it is derived from "سَطَا الْفَرَسُ" (*satal faras*) which means a horse to raise its forelegs and stand on its hind legs {T, R}.

The Quran says:

22:72	they might attack any moment (commit excesses on them)	يَكَادُوْنَ يَسْطُوْنَ

Ibn Faris says it basically means anger and overpowering, as well as height.

"سَطَا الْمَاءُ" (*satal ma-o*): water level has increased many folds.

S-Ain-D   س ع د

"سَعَدَهُ اللهُ" (*sa'adahul-lah*): Allah helped him
"يَسْعَدُهُ" (*yas-aduhu*), "سَعْدًا" (*sa'da*): he guided him.
"سَعِدَ" (*sa'id*), "يَسْعَدُ" (*yas'ud*), "سَعْدًا" (*sa'da*), "سَعَادَةً" (*sa'adah*): he was blessed.
"اَلْإِسْعَادُ" (*al-eesaad*), "اَلْمُسَاعَدَةُ" (*al-musa'adah*): to help.

Faraa says it means to follow Allah's guidance and His commandments.

"اَلسَّاعِدُ" (*as-sa'id*): the part of the hand from the elbow to the wrist wherein all the strength lies. This led to "اَلْمُسَاعَدَةُ" (*al-musa'idah*) meaning to help one another, that is because when people go on a mission to help one another, they walk hand in hand as close companions {T, R}.

The Quran quotes "سَعِدَ" (*saeedun*) which has appeared opposite to "شَقِى" (*shaqiun*) in (11:105) The later means going against Allah's guidance.

"شَقِيٌّ" (*shaqiyun*) too has come against "سَعِيْدٌ" (*sayedun*) in (11:106-108). That is, fortunate is is he who is close to Allah by opting to follow His guidance to go forward in life, and while "شَقِيٌّ" (*shaqiyun*) is he who ignores this guidance and thus remains deprived of its benefits. It is an unimaginable personal loss for those who reject the guidance of Allah as revealed and preserved in the Quran.

Raghib says "أَلسَّعْدُ" (*assa'du*) and "أَلسَّعَادَةُ" (*as-sa'adatah*) refers to the help which comes from Allah to those who opt to follow the guidance to help them reach virtue. We sometime hear people saying that such a thing is "سعد" (*sa'd*) lucky or such a thing is "نحس" (*nahas*) unlucky. Similarly this day is "سعد" (*sa'ad*) lucky or so and so day "نحس" (*nahas*) is unlucky. This is all non sense and the Quran warns us to stay from all such beliefs as these keep us away from the righteous path.

Nothing is lucky or unlucky. Any deed which has good result according to the criterion from the Quran is good and can be called "سعد" (*sa'ad*), and the day on which the result appears can be called "مسعود" (*masood*). Likewise, any deed whose result is bad using the Quranic criterion is called "نحس" (*nahas*) and the day on which this result appears can be called "منحوس" (*manhoos*). The days of the week have no significance at their own since these are simply measurements of time fixed by us to be aware of the passing time (and life). There is nothing "سعد" (*sa'ad*) or "نحس" (*nahas*) in the stars either. Stars follow their designed paths according to the known laws and the Quran makes it very clear. These have absolutely no connection to anyone's fate. Our fate is in our own hand and this is dependent on our deeds. More details can be found under the heading (N-H-Sd).

S-Ain-R   س ع ر

"أَلسُّعْرُ" (*as-so'ar*): the heat of the fire, hunger.

Ibn A'rfa says that "سُعْرٌ" (*so'ar*) means something that burns someone.

Faraa says it means to bother, hard work, severe pain, hardship.

"سَعَرْنَاهُمْ بِالنَّبْلِهِمْ" (*sa'rna hum bin nabl*): we shot arrows at them and pierced them {T}.
"مَسْعُوْرٌ" (*mas'or*) means a man who is very thirsty and hungry {T}. Also one who is greedy for more even though he has had his fill or one whose desire is never satisfied {M}.
"أَلسُّعَارُ" (*as-su'ar*): the heat of the fire, or intense hunger.
"أَلسُّعَارُ" (*as-sa'er*): fire, flaming fire {T}.

Surah **An-Nisa** says:

| 4:10 | Those who unjustly usurp the orphan's possessions, fill themselves with fire and they will be thrust into flaming fire | اِنَّ الَّذِیْنَ یَاْكُلُوْنَ اَمْوَالَ الْیَتٰمٰى ظُلْمًا اِنَّمَا یَاْكُلُوْنَ فِیْ بُطُوْنِهِمْ نَارًا ۔ وَسَیَصْلَوْنَ سَعِیْرًا |

What will happen to such people after death is to be seen over there (in the world hereafter). In this life such people are extremely greedy with unsatiable greed for riches, and they madly pursue easy money.. As such, "سُعْرٌ" (so'r) and "سُعُرٌ" (so'or) means madness as well {T}.

Ibn Faris says it basically means for something to flare up, to be raised, to be provoked.

"سَعَرَ" (sa'ar) and "سَعَّرَ النَّارَ وَالْحَرْبَ" (sa'aran naar wal hurb) would mean to intensify the battle and make it rage {T}.

| 81:12 | and when hell will be stoked | وَ اِذَا الْجَحِیْمُ سُعِّرَتْ |

This indicates the intensity of the punishment which will be intense according to severity of the committed crime.

S-Ain-Y   س ع ی

"سَعْیٌ" (sayun) means to intend, to walk fast or move fast, to arrange for something, or struggle for it.

Muheet says that when this word is used to mean go or run, it is followed by "اِلٰی" (ila), like in "فَاسْعَوْا اِلٰى ذِكْرِ اللّٰهِ" (fas-au ila zikril lah), and when it is used to mean struggle or strive for, then it is followed by "ل" (laam), like in "سَعٰى لَهَا السَّاعِیْ" (as-sa'aa laha)

"سعی" (as saee) one who tries, also one who collects charitable donations .

The Quran has used this word to mean run (2:260, 20:20), as well as to mean to strive (17:19). That is, running around, struggle, strive and take action, etc.

The Quran says:

| 53:39 | a man gets what he strives for | لَیْسَ لِلْاِنْسَانِ اِلَّا مَا سَعٰى |

This verse guides to a great principle. Economics also dictates that man should only receive the remuneration for his labour. To take something for nothing or to receive the returns on capital is not ligitimate as one has not worked for it. The benefits of a system which is built upon this principle can only be imagined by those who have insight. This principle highlights the fact that a man's place in society is determined by the labour he puts in, and not by virtue of his family or other references.

In the world of Deen this principle establishes the fact that deliverance and happiness accrue only through one's own efforts and not by someone's recommendation or favour.

The Quran has also refuted the concept that every child is born with the sins of his parents. Quran refutes that he is atoning for the sins committed during his last incarnation. A human being is born with a clean slate, and he becomes liable to get as many pleasantries of life as he struggles for doing good deeds. This principle also announces to the world of statesmanship and politics that every human child must get a level playing field. Nobody should be favoured in this respect nor obstructed. Is this not a revolutionary idea as a Quranic Principle to be put forward to the modern world?

S-Gh-B   ب غ س

"سَغَبَ" (*saghab*), "يَسْغَبُ" (*yasghab*), "وسَغِبُ" (*saghebu*), "يَسْغَبُ" (*yasghab*), "سَغْبأً" (*saghba*), "مَسْغَبَةً" (*musghaba*): to be tired and hungry.

Raghib says it also means to be thirsty.
Ibn Faris says the basic meaning of this root is hunger.

"المَسْغَبَةُ" (*al-masghabah*) means drought.

The Quran says:

90:14	Arrange for food of people when hunger and strife is all around		اِطْعَامٌ فِىْ يَوْمٍ ذِىْ مَسْغَبَةٍ

The Quran has compared it to climbing uphill (90:11-14). To earn with one's own efforts and to spend whatever more one earns which exceed his needs at a time when hunger is galore, is a great thing to do
This is what polishes human personality, and this is what Islam aims at. This is what is meant by establishing a system of 'raboobiyat' or welfare. In this connection, these verses of surah *Al-Balad* are a great manifestation of truth (90:11-16), and they should be studied in detail as a permanent value. Details can be found in the book titled Islamic System of Sustenance *by G.A.Parwez.*

S-F-H   س ف ح

"سَفَحَ الدَّمَ" (*safahad-dum*): he let blood flow, dropped blood, killed

"سَفَحَ الدَّمْعَ" (*safahad dum-a*): he shed tears

"سَفَحَ الدَّمْعُ" (*safahad dum-u*): tears rolled down

"اَلْمُسَافَحَةُ" (*al-musafaha*): to fornicate , because in it the human effort is wasted without any comittment. Thus in the pre-Islamic era of ignorance when Arabs invited a woman for marriage, they said "اِنْكِحِيْنِى" (*inkaheeni*) and when they invited only for illicit relationship they said "سَافِحِيْنِى" (*saafiheeni*).

"سَافِحِيْنِى" (*as-safeeh*) means the fourth arrow among the arrows of chance or gambling which had no marking and was plain, for which no one had to pay and which was without any result {*T*}.

The Quran has first listed the women with whom wedlock is forbidden, and then declared that besides them the marriage is permitted with the rest. This will be "مُحْصِنِيْنَ غَيْرَ مُسَافِحِيْنَ" (*muhsineena ghaira musaafeheen*) as in 2:24.

"مُحْصِنِيْنَ" (*musaafeheen*) means as related under heading (H-Sd-N).

"مُسَافِحِيْنَ" (*musaafeheen*) means to waste the human energy in the sexual act. This is meant to point to a great truth. Let us first see what is the difference between "نكاح" (*nikah*) marriage and "زنا" (*zina*) fornication. Both include the sexual act and its associated pleasure, but in the former, personal pleasure is not the only aim, whereas in the latter, only personal pleasure is intended. In fornication both man and woman try to avoid pregnancy. This is what is meant by wasting the human effort. As such, man should avoid any fornication which avoids the responsibilities of being married , and if the purpose is only to obtain sexual pleasure, then according to the Quran it is not permitted.

In the same surah, it is stated later:

4:25	Chaste, not immoral and not those who take secret relations	مُحْصَنٰتٍ غَيْرَ مُسٰفِحٰتٍ وَّلَا مُتَّخِذٰاتِ اَخْدَانٍ

For "اخذان" (*akhdaan*), see under heading (Kh-Dh-N), which means secret friendship, although this word has appeared in the context of a slave girl of that time as well.

These three terms would mean as under:

i.   "مُحْصِنِيْنَ" (*muhseneen*): the form of married relation in which all the limits, rights and duties, and purpose are kept in mind.

ii.   "اَلشَّفَاحُ" (*as-sifaah*): fornication which has no form of "*muhsinee*", no matter even if it becomes "acceptable" in a society.

iii.   "اِتَّخَاذِ اَخْدَانٍ" (*ittekhaazi akhdaan*): the fornication which is not permitted, even in permissive societies.

According to the Quran, only the form mentioned in (i) is permissible.

S-F-R ر ف س

"اَلسَّفْرُ" (*as-safr*) basically means to lift off a veil and make it evident.

Muheet says that "اَلسَّفْرُ" (*as-safr*) means to display or highlight the evident part of something and "اَلْفَسْرُ" (*al-fasr*), from which "تفسير" (*tafsser*) or explanation has been derived from, means to lay open the insides of something and to make it evident or clear. However, it means to unveil, distinct and make clear.

"سَفَرَتِ الْمَرْأَةُ" (*safaratil mar-ah*): the woman lifted the veil from her face {*R*}.

Ibn Faris says it means to open, to disperse and to be clear.

"اَلسَّفْرُ" (*as-safr*) also means to sweep clean.
"اَلْمِسْفَرَةُ" (*al-misfarah*) means broom.
"سَفَرَ" (*safar*) means to soil or make dirty.
"سَفَرَتِ الرِّيحُ الْغَيْمَ" (*as-safaratir reehul ghaim*) i.e. the wind dispersed the clouds.
"اَلسَّافِرُ" (*as-saafir*) means a traveller.
"اَلسُّفْرَةُ" (*as-sufrah*) food for the traveler which is prepared for the journey. After that it started meaning lunch box, and then "سُفْرَة" (*sufrah*) began to mean cloth, mat or plastic that is laid out on the ground as a table e.g. in some eastern cultures {*T*}.
"سَفِيْرٌ" (*safeer*) means one who arbitrates peace between nations, that is, an ambassador {*T*}, in a sense that he brings out what is in both the proponent's hearts and clears up the matter.
"اَلسَّفَارَةُ" (*as-safaaratu*), "اَلسِّفَارَةُ" (*as-sifaarah*): to try to make peace among nations {*T*}.
"اَلسِّفْرُ" (*as-sifr*) a great book or a book which highlights the truth, the plural is "أَسْفَارٌ" (*asfarah*) as in 62:5.
"سَفَرَ الْكِتَابَ سَفْرأً" (*safaral kitaaba safra*): wrote the book {*T*}.
"سَافِرٌ" (*saafir*) means writer, plural of which s "اَلسَّفَرَةُ" (*as-safarah*).
"أَسْفَرَ الصُّبْحُ" (*asfaras subh*): the day dawned (became bright).

The Quran says:

74:33	When the morning is well lighted (becomes bright)	وَالصُّبْحِ إِذَا أَسْفَرَ
80:38	some faces that day will be lighted (happy)	وُجُوْهٌ يَوْمَئِذٍ مُسْفِرَةٌ
80:15	in the hands of the writers	بِأَيْدِيْ سَفَرَةٍ
2:184	during travel	عَلَىٰ سَفَرٍ

S-F-Ain   س ف ع

"سَفْعٌ" (*saf'un*) means to pull after holding something, to singe, to mark. It also means to slap. "سَفَحَ بِنَاصِيَتِہ وِبِرِجْلِہِ" (*safaha bina siyatehi wabirijlihi*): caught him by the forelocks or the leg, and pulled him *{T}*.

The Quran says:

66:15	We will surely pull him by the forelocks (by catching hold of the forelocks), will pull them harshly	لَنَسْفَعاً بِالنَّاصِيَةِ

It means that at last these powerful and rich opposing the Truth will be demeaned and demoralized and will be overpowered and defeated.

"اَلسُّفْعَةُ" (*as-suf'ah*) means that heap of rubbish that lies in the ruins. Actually this word is used for blackish colour *{T}*.

Raghib says "سَفْعٌ" (*saf'un*) means to catch a horse by its black forelocks and pull.

Ibn Faris says it has two basic meanings. One is of blackish colour, and the second is to catch/hold something by hand.

S-F-K   س ف ك

"سَفْكٌ" (*safak*): to let flow, usually it means to shed blood *{T}*.
"اَلسَّفَّاكُ" (*as-saffaak*): one who sheds too much blood, or a man who is fluent in some language *{T}*.

The Quran says:

2:30	will shed blood	يَسْفِكُ الدِّمَاءَ

S-F-L   س ف ل

"اَلسِّفْلُ" (*siful*), "اَلسُّفْلُ" (*as-sufl*): lowliness. It is the opposite of "عِلْوٌ" (*ilwun*) and "عُلْوٌ" (*ulwun*) which mean height, stature etc.
"اَلْأَسْفَلُ" (*al-asfal*): very low, it is the opposite of "أَعْلَى" (*aala*) which means very high.
"سِفْلَةُ النَّاسِ" (*siflatun naas*): lowly, mean people *{T}*.

The Arabs also call a man "اَلسَّفِلَةُ" (*as-saafilah*), if he is a guest at a dinner and robs the host *{M}*.

The Quran says about the punishment of Loot's nation:

| 11:82 | turned the upper class into the lower class | جَعَلْنَا عَالِيَهَا سَافِلَهَا |

About the hypocrites, the Quran declares:

| 4:145 | they live in the lowest level of hell | فِى الدَّرْكِ الْأَسْفَلِ مِنَ النَّارِ |

This means that they live in a state of continuous inner turmoil. This refers to their state in this life, while in the hereafter they will face the worst consequences as a result of what they did in this life.

| 5:95 | the lowest, even worst | أَسْفَلَ سَافِلِينَ |

S-F-N   س ف ن

"سَفَنَ الشَّيْءَ" (*safanash shaiya*), "يَسْفِنُهُ سَفْنًا" (*yasfinuhu safna*): to pare something from the top or to rub it.

"سَفِينَةٌ" (*safeenah*) has been derived from it and means a boat, perhaps because boats were made by scraping out big trunks of trees in the old days. This was how a place to sit inside a boat was made. Or because when it sails, the boat seems to be parting the water.

"سَفَائِنُ الْبَرّ" (*safaa-inul bar*) means camels which are called boats of the desert *{T, M, R}*.

The Quran says:

| 18:71 | they both boarded the boat | رَكِبَا فِى السَّفِينَةِ |
| 18:76 | as far the matter related to the boat is concerned…. | أَمَّا السَّفِينَةُ |

S-F-H   س ف ه

"سَفَهَ" (*safah*) means stupidity, ignorance, nonsense, uneducated.

"سَفِهَهُ" (*safihahu*): to persuade someone to ignorance , or stupidity , to kill someone .

"سَفِهَ الشَّرَابَ سَفَهًا" (*safehash sharaaba safaha*): is said when a man drinks a lot but his thirst is not quenched.

"ثَوْبٌ سَفِيهٌ" (*saubun safyeh*): a poorly and roughly woven cloth, but its basic meanings are being nervous and in a hurry as well, which are an indication of being emotive and not rationally thinking.

"زِمَامٌ سَفِيهٌ" (*safyeeh*) is a person who is perturbed because of a camel which is not stable and its unpredictability causes concern to the rider - therefore can refer to immature intellect or poor logic *{M}*.

Those people whose hearts and minds are confused due to their inner psychological state which is in conflict and are called "سَفَاهَةٌ" (*sufaha-a*) by the Quran. Because of their such conduct they create imbalances in a society and behave like hypocrites (2:10-14). These people apparently consider themselves as very clever and smart but in reality they harm themselves while remaining unaware about the negative consequences of their wrong conduct (2:12).

At another place the word "سَفِيْهٌ" (*safeehun*) has been used for imbeciles in 2:282. In 6:141, by adding "سَفَهًا" (*safaha*) after "بِغَيْرِ عِلْمٍ" (*bighairi ilm*) i.e. without knowledge , it is declared that "سَفَاهَةٌ" (*safahah*) means not to use intellect and critical thinking . According to the Quran, not using human intellect and critical thinking is a very big mistake, as these people then cannot benefit from this ability to the maximum and as a consequence suffer in this life as well as in the next. *Momin* is the one who uses his intellect and critical thinking in the light of the Quranic values as revealed by Allah and takes full advantage of this life and then moves on to the next life with a developed Self. .

"سَفَاهَةٌ" (*safahah*) as used in 7:66 means foolishness, unawareness, ignorance.

Surah *Al-Baqrah* says:

2:130	who can be unmindful of the nation of *Ibrahim* except one who has not deliberated upon his very self, who has never even thought about how a personality develops and why it is important?	وَمَنْ يَّرْغَبُ و عَنْ مَّلَّةِ اِبْرَاهِيْمَ اِلَّا مَنْ سَفِهَ نَفْسَهُ

Muheet says that it means to demean and to devalue oneself – not giving oneself the significance which it deserves and not appreciating the possession of a free will which is only available to human beings.

The Quran highlights the significance of accepting the Quran as an external source of guidance with the permanent values. It also means that the belief in the existence of a Self and its ability to make choices is part of this conviction which requires guidance to develop itself. This possession of a free will which makes human beings superior to other creations in the world. Without accepting this fact the belief in God becomes meaningless as it does not bring any change in the Self. Further details can be found under the heading (N-F-S).

S-Q-R   س ق ر

"اَلسَّقْرُ" (*as-saqr*): heat of the sun.

"سَقَرَتْهُ الشَّمْسَ" (*saqaratus shams*): the sunlight melted it, burned him, and hurt him.

"اَلسَّاقُوْرُ" (*as-saqoor*): a branding iron.

"اَلسَّقَرُ" (*as-saqar*) also means to be distant and enmity *{T, M, R}*. The Quran has used this word to mean conditions existing in a state of hell

54:49	get a taste of the '*saqar*' which distances you (deprive you) from the pleasantries of life.	ذُوْقُوْا مَسَّ سَقَرَ

S-Q-Te   س ق ط

"سَقَطَ الشَّىْءُ" (*saqatash shaiyu*): for something to fall down, that is, to fall off the roof, or to fall down while standing {*T, M, R*}.

"سَاقَطَه" (*saaqata*): to make one do a thing continuously {*T, M, R*}.

The Quran says:

6:59	no leaf drops	وَمَا تَسْقُطُ مِنْ وَرَقَةٍ
19:25	that tree will drop fresh dates on you regularly	تُسَاقِطْ عَلَيْكِ رُطَباً جَنِيّاً
26:187	drop on us	فَأَسْقِطْ عَلَيْنَا
52:44	that which drops	سَاقِطاً

Surah *Al-Airaf* says about the **Bani Israel**:

7:149	they repented	وَلَمَّا سُقِطَ فِىْ أَيْدِيْهِمْ

Taj says it means to be ashamed and surprised. *Zajaj* says it means to repent on what one has done (regret).

Ibn Faris says it means to wring one's hand in repentance.

Muheet too says it means repentance. Similar meaning appears in the Quran for this word that is to repent at one's foolishness and mistakes.

S-Q-F   س ق ف

"اَلسَّقْفُ" (*as-saqf*): roof, plural is "سُقُفٌ" (*suquf*) (43:33).

Ibn Faris says its basic meanings are to be high and to be overshadowing.

"اَلسَّقِيْفَةُ" (*as-saqifah*): any place that has a roof over it. Usually it means a projected shed. The Arabs also term the sky as "سَقْفٌ" (*saqf*) because they think that it is the roof of the earth.

Surah *Al-Anbia* says:

21:32	we made the sky as a strong roof	وَجَعَلْنَا السَّمَاءَ سَقْفاً مَحْفُوْظاً

This means that the atmosphere is safe because whatever breakages take place in the heavenly bodies gets grounded or burned to dust in the atmosphere, and thus we are safe from it destruction, as if the sky is like a roof over the earth. In calling the sky as "سَقْف" (*saqf*), the Arabic metaphor is also at work, since Arabs used "سَقْف" (*saqf*) metaphorically to mean roof of the earth. The Quran too has used this word as a metaphor, it does not literally mean roof of a house.

"سماء" (*sama'a*) too does not mean the blue sky or 'roof' over our heads, but the atmosphere above us, or the heavenly bodies.

Details can be found in (S-M-W).

S-Q-M   س ق م

"اَلسَّقَامُ" (*as-saqaam*), "اَلسُّقْمُ" (*as-suqm*): illness, disease.
"هُوَ سَقِيمُ الصَّدْرِ عَلَيْهِ" (*huwa saqeemus sadri alaih*): he has prejudice against him.
"قَلْبٌ سَقِيمٌ" (*qalbun saqeem*): unhappy and frustrated heart {T}.

The nation of **Ibrahim** was idol-worshippers and star gazers. **Ibrahim** used to tell people to give up this practice of having multiple gods besides Allah, and invited them to unity. In this context the Quran says:

37:88	He deliberated on the star being god, judged it correctly and then said: I am very frustrated by your false gods	فَنَظَرَ نَظْرَةً فِي النُّجُومِ - فَقَالَ اِنِّي سَقِيمٌ
60:4	I am frustrated with you and those you follow other than Allah	اِنَّا بُرَءٰؤُ مِنْكُمْ وَمِمَّا تَعْبُدُونَ مِنْ دُونِ اللّٰهِ
6:77	I do not like such gods which change every second	لَا أُحِبُّ الْآفِلِينَ

S-Q-Y   س ق ى

"اَلسَّقْيُ" (*as-saqyu*): to give someone a drink.
"اَلسَّقْيَا" (*as-suqya*): made him drink, gave him to drink.
"اَلسَّقْيُ" (*as-saqyu*), "اَلْإِسْقَاءُ" (*al-isqaa*): These words have almost similar meanings. Some think that "سَقْيُ" (*saqyun*) means to make one drink by mouth and "اِسْقَاءُ" (*isqaa*) means to give water or point out water.

Raghib says "سَقَى" (*saqy*) means to give something to drink or make him drink, and "اِسْقَاءُ" (*isqa'*) means that you give someone a drink whether he drinks it or not. As such, "اِسْقَاءُ" (*isqaa*) is more composite than "سَقَى" (*saqy*).
"اَلسَّقَايَةُ" (*as-siqayaa*): the place where water is given to drink or the pot or utensil used for giving a drink (12:70), or the arrangement for drinking (9:19).
"اَلْإِسْتِسْقَاءُ" (*al-istisqaa*): to ask for a drink of water, or ask for rain.
"اَلسَّقِيُّ" (*as-saqiyyo*): the cloud which rains hard {M}.

Surah *Al-Baqrah* says "اسْتَسْقَى" (*istasqaa*) in 2:60, which means to ask for a drink or to ask for rain.

Surah *Ash-Shura* says:

26:79	it is God who gives me to eat and drink	وَالَّذِیْ یُوْ یُطْعِمُنِیْ وَیَسْقِیْنِ

Surah *An-Nahal* says:

16:66	We give you to drink what is in their body (honey in bees' stomach)	نُسْقِیْکُمْ مِمَّا فِیْ بُطُوْنِی

Surah *Ash-Shams* says about *Saleh's* camel:

91:13	look after God's camel and about its drink	نَاقَمَ اللَّهِ وَسُقْیَاہَا

In the story of *Yusuf* it is said "سِقَایَةٌ" (*siqayah*) in 12:70, this word has been used for a utensil which has also been called "صُوَاعٌ" (*swa'a*) in 12:72.

S-K-B   س ک ب

"سَکَبَ الْمَاءَ وَ الدَّمْعَ" (*sakabal ma'a wad dama'a*): he shed tears and let the water flow.
"سَکَبَ الْمَاءُ" (*sakabal maa-oo*): water flowed.
"مَاءٌ سَاکِبٌ" (*maa un saakibun*), "مَسْکُوْبٌ" (*maskub*): the water that flows on the earth's surface, which has not be dug out {T}. The scholars have also said it means to drop from above and flow. As such "مَاءٌ مَسَکُوبٌ" (*maaun masakub*) includes the meaning of a waterfall (which drops from a height). The Quran has used "مَاءٌ مَسْکُوْبٌ" (*maa-inn maskub*) in 56:31, which means that in a society based on the permanent values, the to get the necessities of life no one will not be exploited . This means that one will not have to dig a well to get water. But in a society not based on these values , one will have to strive extremely hard to get these basic necessities of life (20:117).

"رَجُلٌ سَکْبٌ" (*rajulun sakb*): a happy man {M}.
"فَرَسٌ سَکْبٌ" (*farasun sakb*): a fast horse.

S-K-T   س ک ت

"اَلسُّكُوْتُ" (*as-sakt*): to be quiet, not to speak.

The difference between "سُكُوْتٌ" (*sukut*) and "صَمْتٌ" (*samt*) is that the former one is said for things which are able to speak, but remain silent, and the later one is for things which cannot speak at all. In other words, "صَمْتٌ" (*samt*) can be said for anything whether it is able to speak or not.

"سَكَتَ الْغَضَبُ" (*sakat-al-ghazab*): his anger cooled down {*T*}.

The Quran says:

| 7:154 | when *Moosa's* anger cooled down | وَلَمَّا سَكَتَ عَنْ مُوْسَى الْغَضَبَ |

Raghib says "سُكُوْتٌ" (*sukut*) has a kind of peace, so here the word "سَكَتَ" (*sakat*) has been used to mean silence or peace.

S-K-R   س ک ر

"سُكْرٌ" (*sukr*): to be intoxicated.

Raghib says this is a condition which comes between a man and his intellect. Usually this word is used for intoxication but such condition can also be produced by anger and in passionate love {T, R}.

Ibn Faris says it basically means "surprise".

"سَكَرٌ" (*sakar*): alcohol, intoxication (16:67).
"سَكْرَةٌ" (*sakrah*): stupor, unconsciousness. This is a condition of stupor.

The Quran has said "سَكْرَةُ الْمَوْتِ" (*sakaratul maut*) in 50:18, which means unconsciousness of death.

Surah *An-Nisa* says:

| 4:43 | do not go near *salaah* when you are intoxicated | لَا تَقْرَبُوا الصَّلوةَ وَ اَنْتُمْ سُكَارَى |

Here the word "سُكَارَى" (*sukara*) is usually taken to mean stupor, but *Lissan-ul-Arab* says that it means overwhelming of sleep.

"سُكْرَى" (*sukaara*) has been used for people who are out of their senses due to fear and tribulation (22:2, 75:72).

"سَكْرَةٌ" (*sakrah*) has been used for the stupor that is produced by an overflow of emotions.

"اَلسَّكْرُ" (*as-sakr*): to close a canal.

"سَكِرَتِ الرِّيْحُ" (*sakiratir reeh*): the wind became still.

"اَلْمَاءُ السَّاكِرُ" (*al-ma'us saakir*): standing water.

"سَكَرَ الْبَابَ" (*sakarul baab*): closed the door {T, R}.

"سُكَّرَهُ" (*sak-karahu*): strangulated him.

Surah *Al-Hijr* says:

| 15:15 | our eyes have been blinded (we have been hoodwinked) | سُكِّرَتْ اَبْصَارُنَا |

In surah *An-Nisa*:

| 4:43 | when you are overwhelmed by sleep do not go near *salaat* | لَا تَقْرَبُوا الصَّلٰوةَ وَ اَنْتُمْ سُكَارٰى |

"سُكَارٰى" (*sukarya*) is the plural form of "سَكْرَانُ" (*sakran*) and "سَكْرَانَةٌ" (*sakranah*)

Later it is said:

| 4:43 | until you know what you are saying | حَتّٰى تَعْلَمُوْا مَا تَقُوْلُوْنَ |

This means in a condition (sleepy condition) when you do not even know what you are saying. There is no use of saying your prayers in such a condition. It is evident from this verse that if a person does not understand what *salaah* is about; there is no use in attending *salaah*. The first thing is that you should understand what you are saying in *salaah*. Only then *salaah* is of any benefit.

The Quran is to be studied with a view to benefit from the values in our life. To believe that to recite the words without comprehension can be of some use, is a sort of superstition that was prevalent in the magic age. . The Quran was revealed to end these false practices and invites us repeatedly to understand the guidance through the use of intellect and reasoning.

S-K-N   ن ک س

"سُكُوْنٌ" (*sukun*): not to move, to stop {T}.

"سَكَنَ" (*sakana*), "سَكَنًا" (*sakanan*), "سُكْنَى" (*sukna*): to adopt the style, or to reside {M}.

Raghib says that "سُكُوْنٌ" (*sukun*) means for a mobile thing to become immobile. That is why this word means to make some place in one's country or abode.

"اَلسُّکَّانُ" (*as-sukkaan*): a boat's oar.

"اَلسِّکِّیْنُ" (*as-sikkeen*): a knife (12:31), because according to **Raghib**, it turns the one who is slaughtered from mobility to immobility.

"مِسْکِیْنٌ" (*miskeen*): one whose movement has been reduced by hunger and deprivation. There is more of an element of being needy in it and refers to poverty.

"مِسْکِیْنٌ" (*miskeen*): he who is insulted and mean.

In surah **Al-Kahaf**, the boat people have been called "مَسَاکِیْن" (*masakeen*) in 18:79, because they were unable to do anything against the king's oppression *{T}*.

"اَلْمَسْکَنَۃُ" (*al-maskinah*): hardship and strife which makes a man helpless *{Al-fazul Mutaradif}*.

"سُکُوْنٌ" (*sukun*): poverty and lowliness and weakness *{T}*.

"سَکَّنْتُہُ تَسْکِیْناً" (*sakantuhu taskinah*): I removed his tribulations and gave him peace of heart, or made him immobile.

The Quran says:

| 6:97 | Allah made the night to give you peace | جَعَل اللَّیْل سَکَناً |
| 9:103 | your prayer is cause of peace for them | اِنَّ صَلَاتَکَ سَکَنٌ لَّہُمْ |

Ibn Faris says that "اَلسَّکَنُ" (*as-sakn*) means any favourite thing which provides peace and tranquillity.

"اَلسَّکِیْنَۃُ" (*as-sakinah*) means peace and contentment and honour.

Ar-rumani has said that this word means the same as "اَلتَّثَبُّتُ" (*at-ta'abbutu*), which means peace of mind *{Al-fazul Mutaradif}*.

"اِسْتَکَانَ" (*istakaan*) means to become demeaned and weak *{T}*. This is actually derived from (K-W-N) and not from *(S-K-N)*.

The Quran has used this root to mean to reside somewhere or settle somewhere (2: 35).

"وَہْنٌ" (*wahnuun*), "ضُعْفٌ" (*zo'fun*) and "اِسْتِکَانَۃٌ" (*istakanahu*) have been used in 3:145 to mean the same thing, but the order in which they have appeared shows that "اِسْتِکَانَۃٌ" (*istakanahu*) is used for extreme weakness. Since "اِسْتِکَانَت" (*istakanat*) is from *(K-W-N)*, we have also mentioned it under this heading.

"مَسْکَنَۃٌ" (*maskanah*) has been described as God's wrath (2:61), because it is that inertia due to which a nation becomes 'lifeless' and is devoid of progressing forward.

Surah **At-Taubah** has used the words "فُقَرَاءُ" (*fuqaraa*) and "مَسَاکِیْن" (*masakeen*) together in 9:60.

"مِسْكِيْنٌ" (*miskeen*) is one whose running business comes to a halt, or he is unable to take part in the struggle of life due to some mishap. In a Quranic system, no "مِسْكِيْنٌ" (*miskeen*) can be deprived of the necessities of life. He can acquire these things, not as a charity, but as his right.

Surah *Al-Balad* says:

| 90:15 | he who feels lonely in a crowd, and he who is isolated by a society | يَتِيْماً ذَا مَقْرَبَةٍ |
| 90:16 | he who falls down due to some weakness, is trampled upon, the Quranic society gets established to provide support to the weak and lonely | أَوْمِسْكِيْناً ذَامَتْرَبَةٍ |

S-L-B   س ل ب

"ٱلسَّلْبُ" (*as-salb*): to wrench something from someone. Some say it means to snatch something from someone when he is not attentive.

Ibn Faris says it means to take something swiftly, or snatch it.

"ٱلسَّلُوْبُ" (*as-saloob*): a female camel whose young one has been snatched from her {*M*}.
"شَجَرَةٌ سَلِيْبٌ" (*shajaratun saleeb*): a tree whose branches and leaves have fallen.
"ٱلسَّلِيْبُ" (*as-saleeb*): a woman whose child has died.
"ٱلسُّلْبَةُ" (*as-sulbah*): to be naked, to be without any clothes on the body {T, R}.

Surah *Al-Hajj* says:

| 22:73 | if a fly snatches away something from them | وَإِنْ يَسْلُبْهُمُ الذُّبَابُ شَيْئاً |

S-L-H   س ل ح

"ٱلسِّلَاحُ" (*as-silaah*), "ٱلسِّلْحُ" (*as-silah*): a weapon of war, anything used in a battle to fight or to attack, arms, metal part of a weapon, sword or its sharpness, a bow without tension, stick. Plural is "ٱسْلِحَةٌ" (*asleha*).

| 4.102 | should take their weapons along | | وَلْيَأْخُذُوا أَسْلِحَتَهُمْ |

"سَلَحَ" (*salah*), "يَسْلَحُ" (*yaslah*): for the birds to leave their droppings, but the Quran has not used this word in these meanings.

S-L-Kh   س ل خ

"سَلَخَ" (*salakha*), "يَسْلُخُ" (*yaslukhu*), "يَسْلَخ" (*yaslakh*): to skin an animal.

"سَلَخَتِ الْحَيَّةُ" (*salakhatil hayyah*): snake shed its skin.

"اَلسِّلْخُ" (*as-silkh*): snake skin.

"سَلَخَتِ الْمَرْأَةُ دِرْعَها" (*salaklhatil mar'atu dir'aha*): the woman took off her shirt {T}.

It also means to separate a thing from another in such a way that no residual mark is left behind.

The Quran says:

36:37	we draw the day away from the night	اَللَّيْلَ نَسْلَخُ مِنْهُ النَّهَارَ

This word as used in this verse points to the fact that day is drawn away from nigh in such a way that there is not even a trace of daylight left in night.

"سَلَخَ الشَّهْرُ وانْسَلَخَ" (*salakhash sharu wansalakh*): month passed {T} (9:5).

"انْسَلَخَ مِنْهُ" (*insalakha minhu*): leaving something, or donning it off. He has become naked or is devoid of it.

Surah *Al-Airaf* posts an example:

7:175	We gave him our laws and he put them on one side like a snake sheds its skin	أَتَيْنُهُ آيَتِنَا فَانْسَلَخَ مِنْهَا

This can be related to the state of the Muslims who claim to have the Quran as a book of guidance, but have abandone it as quoted in the verse earlier. But thanks to Allah, the Quran is preserved in its original text and and anyone looking for guidance can study it and can benefit from its permanent values.

S-L-S-L   س ل س ل

"اَلسَّلْسَلَةُ" (*as-salsalah*): to link a thing with another.

"اَلسِّلْسِلَةُ" (*as-silsilah*): a chain.

"تَسَلْسَلَ الْمَاءُ" (*tasalsalal ma'a*): the water went continuously down the throat {T, R}.

"سَلَّ" (*sall*): to pull something. See heading (S-L-L).

The Quran has used "سِلْسِلَةٍ" (*silsilah*) in 69:32 to mean chain, plural of which is "سَلَاسِلُ" (*salasil*) as in 76:4. One link gets linked to another and so on, and thus forms a chain.

S-L-Te   س ل ط

"اَلسَّلْطُ" (**as-sult**), "اَلسَّلِيْطُ" (**as-saleet**): hard and strong.

"اَلتَّسْلِيْطُ" (**at-tasleet**): to make dominating, to give domination and power.

"سَلَّطَهُ اللهُ عَلَيْهِ" (**sallatulaahu alaih**): Allah gave dominance and power over him (4:90).

Ibn Faris says it means domination and power.

"سَلْطَانُ النَّارِ" (**saltuwanun naar**): for the fire to flare up *{T}*.

"اَلسُّلْطَانُ" (**as-sultaan**): reason, proof, sign, evidence. *{T}*.

Mohammed bin yazeed has said that it has been derived from "سَلِيْطٌ" (**saleet**) which means olive oil which is used to provide light . As such, "سُلْطَانٌ" (**sultan**) will only be that argument which is based on reasoning and evidence with capacity to enlighten itself and show any matter like light *{T}*.

The Quran says:

| 37:156 | or do you have clear proof | اَمْ لَكُمْ سُلْطَانٌ مُبِينٌ |

But as per the meaning of "اَلسَّلْطُ" (**as-sult**), it also means domination and power. This word has been used several times by the Quran to mean this.

In surah *Ibrahim* it is said that God sent the messengers with "بَيِّنٰتٌ" (**bayyenaat**) clear reasoning (14:9), but the opponents refused to accept them saying that they would not obey until they are under their governance.

Iblees is told in surah *Al-Hijr*:

| 15:42 | you will have no power over those who decide to follow My guidance | إِنَّ عِبَادِئ لَيْسَ لَكَ عَلَيْهِمْ سُلْطَنٌ |

This word has also been used to mean capable or having the right to something in surah *Bani Israel* (17:33). Here domination is implied in the meaning.

Surah *An-Nisa* says:

| 4:153 | And We gave *Moosa* domination and power | وَأ تِيْنَا مُوْسَى سُلْطَانًا مُبِينًا |

Surah *Al-Haqq* also has used "سُلْطَانِيَه" (**sultaniah**) in this meaning (69:29).

In surah *Ar-Rahman* there is a verse which points to a great fact:

| 55:33 | If you have the power (the capability) to go beyond the planets or the stars, then do it , go beyond them | يٰمَعْشَرَ الْجِنِّ وَالْإِنْسِ إِنِ اسْتَطَعْتُمْ اَنْ تَنْفُذُوْا مِنْ اَقْطَارِ السَّمٰوٰتِ وَالْإِرْضِ فَانْفُذُوْا |

Here all mankind is addressed which includes both uncivilized and civilized people. Death is a mystery for human beings. The universe around us is also a mystery and modern man has tried hard to go beyond the earth's orbit to satisfy his inquisitiveness e.g. moon landing and sending probes to the mars. In this verse there is a pointer to an important sign saying you wish to go beyond the limits of this material visible universe. However, there is a limit of human physical self which cannot go beyond the physical world. The Quran has pointed to an ability which man can attain through the following of the permanent values which is called "سُلْطَانٌ" (*sultan*), i.e. the power to be attained through obeying Allah's laws.

The Quran has declared through the Messenger's (*pbuh*)*reference:*

| 17:80 | And bestow me with the helping power | وَاجْعَلْ لِيْ مِنْ لَّدُنْكَ سُلْطَاناً نَصِيْراً |

We know the fact that human physical self ultimately dies and has limitations. However, the Quran deals with the human Self which operates through choices and decision making in this life and has the ability to survive our death. The Quran points to this fact that if man chooses to live within the guidance then he can this power or "سُلْطَانٌ" (*sultan*). This helps self-development and strengthens it and gradually makes it develop ability to go beyond the physical boundaries of this visibsle universe. This is only possible by accepting the Quranic guidance. But this does not mean the so-called spiritual development propagated by monasticism. This "سُلْطَانٌ" (*sultan*) means such power and domination as annihilates all evil forces and establishes Allah's law effectively in a society. Physical forces can take man to the moon and stars, but they will keep him within this universe. Only human personality can go beyond, provided that it creates the "سُلْطَانٌ" (*sultan*) to which the Quran has pointed.

S-L-F   س ل ف

"سَلَفَ الْأَرْضَ" (*salafal arda*), "أَسْلَفَهَا" (*aslafaha*): to cultivate the land or to level it.
"سَلَفَ الشَّيْءُ" (*salafush shaiyi*): the thing passed, went ahead.
"سَلَفَ فُلاَنٌ" (*salafa fulan*): that man went ahead.
"أَسْلَفَ" (*aslafa*): sent ahead, presented.
"اَلسَّالِفُ" (*as-saalif*): the one who passes ahead
"اَلسَّا الِفَةُ" (*as-salifah*): predecessor who stays ahead in battle or travel {R}.

Ibn Faris says it means to be ahead and to supersede, to excel.

Surah *Al-Baqrah* says:

| 2:275 | that which has been taken earlier, belongs to him | فَلَهُ مَا سَلَفَ |

Surah *Az-Zakhraf* says about annihilated civilisations:

| 43:56 | we made them predecessors | وَجَعَلْنَاهُمْ سَلَفاً |

Above verse is referring to nations from the past whose history now remains as an example.

Surah **Al-Haqq** says:

69:24	whatever you did earlier	بِمَا أَسْلَفْتُمْ

S-L-Q   س ل ق

"اَلسَّلْقُ" (**as-salq**): this root basically means to rise or climb {*M*}.

"تَسَلَّقَ الْجِدَارَ" (**tasallaqil jidaar**): he climbed the wall.

"تَسَلَّقَ عَلَى فِرَاشِهِ" (**tasallaqa ala firashehi**): due to sadness and grief he couldn't sleep and kept changing sides in the bed.

"سَلَقَ فُلَاناً بِالسَّوْطِ" (**salaqa fulanan bis saut**): he skinned the man with his whip.

"اَلسَّلِيْقَةُ" (**as-saleeqah**): the footsteps and hoof marks on a treaded path , thin, fine bread, also temperament {*T*}.

Raghib writes that "اَلسَّلْقُ" (**as-salq**) means to lay down something forcibly, either with the hands or by word of motuh{*R*}, and "سَلَقَ فُلَاناً" (**salaqa fulana**) means he flattened him {*T*}.

The Quran says:

33:19	These people hurt you with their words (remarks)	سَلَقُوْكُمْ بِأَلْسِنَةٍ

Say accusations against you (the messenger), wish to control and overpower you with these satirical utterings.

Ibn Faris says it has so many different meanings that it is difficult to find a common thread though all.

However from its use in the Quran, the term predominantly has an element of causing hurt to someone else.

S-L-K   س ل ک

"سَلَکَ" (**salak**) actually means for one thing to enter another or make it to enter.

"سَلَکَ يَدَهُ فِى الْجَيْبِ" (**salaka yadahu fil jabeeb**): he put his hand into his shirt front {*T*}.

While explaining their difference, **Muheet** says that "خَيْطٌ" (**khait**) is any string that is either used for sewing or as a garland around the neck, but the string in which pearls etc. are put, is called "سِلْکٌ" (**silk**). The string which is already adorned with pearls etc. is called "سِمْطٌ" (**simt**) {*M*}.

"اَلسُّلُوْکُ" (**as-salook**) means to enter a path {*M*}.

"سَلَکَ" (**salak**) is to walk or make to walk, to enter or make to enter.

"اَسْلَکَ" (**aslak**): to make someone walk, to make someone or something to enter {*T*}.

The Quran says:

15:12	this way We enter it into the hearts of criminals	كَذَالِكَ نَسْلُكُهُ فِيْ قُلُوْبِ الْمُجْرِمِيْنَ
20:53	And made pathways for you (on the earth)	وَسَلَكَ لَكُمْ فِيْهَا سُبُلاً
71:20	so that you walk on them (travel on them)	لِتَسْلُكُوْا مِنْهَا

S-L-L   س ل ل

"اَلسَّلُّ" (*as-sal*): to extricate something quietly and with softness.

Ibn Faris has also added, extricating something secretly, in its basic meaning.

"سَيْفٌ" (*saifun saleel*): the sword that has been pulled out of the scabbard.
"اَلسُّلَالَةُ" (*as-sulalah*): the part that which is extricated {*T*}.
"اَلْمَسْلُوْلُ" (*al-maslool*): that which is extracted, the man or animal whose testicles have been removed (made impotent) {*M*}.

The Quran says that man was created from "سُلَالَةٍ مِنْ طِيْنٍ" (*sulaalatim min teen*) according to 23:14. Here it means a substance which has been culled from the matter both organic and inorganic. We know our body is composed of organic and inorganic matter such as found in the soil. .

"اِنْسَلَّ" (*insalla*) and "تَسَلَّلَ" (*tasallal*): he went away secretly, slipped away quietly.
"اَلسَّلَّةُ" (*as-sallah*): to steal secretly, theft.
"اَلسَّالُّ" (*as-saal*), "اَلسَّلَّالُ" (*as-sallaal*), "اَلْأَسَلُّ" (*al-asallu*): thief {*T*}.

Surah *An-Noor* says:

| 24:63 | those of you who slip away quietly | اَلَّذِيْنَ يَتَسَلَّلُوْنَ مِنْكُمْ |

S-L-M   س ل م

Since this is the root from which the word "اِسْلَامٌ" (*Islam*) is derived, its basic meanings must be comprehended properly, because these meanings will be used to explain various aspects of the word *Islam*.

"سَلِمَ" (*sa-lima*): he became clean (or free) from all sorts of faults, limitations, weaknesses. All his shortcomings were removed.
"سَلَمَ الدَّلْوَ" (*salamad dalau*): he prepared a strong bucket (e.g. for drawing water from a well).

In surah Al-Baqrah it is said about the cow of **Bani Israel**:

2:71	It is free from all bodily marks (faults) and is spotless	مُسَلَّمَةٌ لَا شِيَةَ فِيهَا

As such "سَلِمَ" (*sa-lima*): basically means to be pure and to be without any blemish. This is in realtion to the complete development of human abilities so that no failings and inadequacies remain in the Self.

The other meaning of this root is to be protected from dangers, accidents, or disasters.

Ibn Faris has said that it means more of health and wellbeing than anything else.

"سَلِمَ مِنَ الْأَفَةِ سَلَامَةً" (*salima minal aafateh salamah*): he remained safe from disasters.
"سَلَّمَهُ اللهُ تَسْلِيماً" (*sallamahullahu tasleemah*): Allah kept him safe from any disaster.

The Quran has mentioned one attribute of God as "اَلسَّلَامُ" (*as-salam*) in 59:23, which is generally taken to mean "free of all blemishes and weaknesses". However, Taj-ul-Uroos says that those who have used this meaning have committed a grave error. This is because "اَلسَّلَامُ" (*as-salam*) is something from which protection is sought, and "سَالِمٌ" (*salim*) is one who seeks protection, or someone who wants to be protected against evil or misfortune that is imminent. Thus Allah has been pronounced "اَلسَّلَامُ" (*as-salam*) because He has protected all creations from disasters and His system e.g. the Solar System is thus running well protected without interference from outside for a time appointed. Therefore, "" (*salaam*) would also mean to be safe from disasters and troubles. This is the second meaning of the root.

"اَلسُّلَّمُ" (*as-sullam*) means a ladder, i.e, a safe and dependable means for climbing. Thus the third meaning of this root is the means through which somebody can reach new heights safely and reliably.

"اَلسِّلْمُ" (*as-silm*) means to live peacefully and amicably. It means amity and thus the fourth meaning of this root would be to live peacefully and to establish peace and security for all in the world.

"تَسَالَمَتِ الْخَيْلُ" (*tasaalamatil khail*): horses moving together, synchronizing their feet and galloping in tandem, and for none of the horses doing something which may frighten other horses or cause stampede. This projects a concept of harmony and team work of an Islamic Society.

"اَلسِّلْمُ" (*as-silmu*), "اَلسَّلَامُ" (*as-salsaam*): obedience, to bow before. Therefore, the fifth basic meaning of the root would be to completely and willingly follow the laws of the Quran.

Nawab Siddiq Hasan Khan writes that S-L-M basically has the element of compassion and humility {*Al-ilm-ul-akhlaaq*}.

"اِسْتَسْلَمَ ثَكَمَ الطَّرِيقِ" (*istaslam akamat tareeq*): he walked in the middle of the road and kept straight path.

"قَالُوْا سَلَاماً" (*qaalu sal-ah*): they adopt the balanced path as defined in the Quran and do not do anything that is against the permanent values. Thus the sixth meaning of this root would be to adopt the balanced path of moderation and to avoid things which have negative influences and are obstructive.

"اِسْتَلَمَ الزَّرْعُ" (*istalamz zar-u*): the ears of corn came out. This is the seventh meaning of this root which refer to the multiplied reward of human righteous efforts. .

"اَلسَّلِمَةُ" (*as-salimah*): refers to a woman who is extremely pretty and attractive. Thus the eighth meaning of this root refer to beauty and pleasant looks.

To summarise all this Islam "اَلْإِسْلَامُ" (*al-islam*) is the name of a system in which all shortcomings of an individual are addressed and his potentials are fully developed. The system in which he/she is given protection from the negative forces and influences and he/she feels secure. The individual lives in peace and works to extend this peace to his fellow human beings across the world. He lives in complete harmony with others in his society and does nothing to cause annoyance to others and thus contribute to imbalance in the society. . This is only possible when he willingly follows the permanent values of the Quran He does not cross the defined limits knowingly and believes in the working of the law of requital. This way his efforts will be fruitful and do not go waste. Not only will his own personality be balanced and develop further, but he will contribute effectively for the well being of others.

This is the path that will result in success. If anyone adopts any other path, he will not be able to produce these results and he will ultimately be a loser (3:84). This is called Islam and is preserved within the folds of the Quran (20: 47). This means that Islam = The Quran.

The Quran has used the word "مُسْلِمٌ" (*muslim*) extensively that it is not possible to mention all references. Some selected ones are presented:

2:71	he is free from all faults and is impeccable	مُسَلَّمَةٌ لَا شِيَةَ فِيْهَا
2:33	when you have given (handed over)	إِذَا سَلَّمْتُمْ
8:43	(you had started to quarrel among yourselves) so Allah protected you from its destructive effects	وَلَكِنَّ اللهَ سَلَّمَ
52:38	reaching loftiness	سُلَّمٌ
8:61	amity	وَإِنْ جَنَحُوْا لِلسَّلْمِ
2:112	obedient	مَنْ أَسْلَمَ

Surah **Ar-Rom** has mentioned "اِسْلَامٌ" (**islam**) and "اِیْمَانٌ" (**iman**) separately (30:53). "اِیْمَانٌ" (**iman**) means to believe in something which is Ture and "اِسْلَامٌ" (**islam**) is to then follow it with complete unity of thought and conviction. As against those who have accepted the faith by word of mouth, but their hearts are devoid of the faith. They too are said to be "مُسْلِمٌ" (**muslim**), but not "مُوْمِنٌ" (**momin**) (49:14).

Surah **An-Namal** has used the word "مسلمین" (**muslemin**) to mean those who do not break the limits, or transgress them, but rather become obedient (27:3).

Surah **Maryam** has used the word "سَلَامٌ" (**salam**) opposite to "لَغْوٌ" (**laghu**) which means useless things – something which wastes time and energy.

A man with these characteristics has been called one with a "سلیم" (**saleem**) heart (26:89), and a nation with these characteristics is called "أُمَّةً مُسْلِمَةً لَّکَ" (**ummatan muslimal-laka**), or a nation which follows the laws of Allah (2:128). Every individual of this nation has a duty to say "سَلَامٌ عَلَیْکُمْ" (**salamun alaikum**) to everyone he meets (7:46). It means that I wish you peace and security and all the good things mentioned above. The other returns the same complements and thus the whole society rings with the sounds of "سَلَاماً سَلَاماً" (**salaman salaman**).

It is said in 3:66 about **Ibrahim** that he was neither a Jew nor a Christian, but rather "حَنِیْفًا مُسْلِماً" (**hanifan muslima**). This is the title used for followers of Allah's Deen, even before the advent of the Quran (22:78). To belong to some sect is against **Islam**, because sectarianism is against the Quranic teachings (30:32) - the Quran has declared mankind as one community (2:213).

"مسلم" (**muslim**) and "مشرک" (**mushrik**) are opposite of each other at thought and belief level, same is meant by "کفر" (**kufr**) and "اسلام" (**islam**) (9:74). It must be well understood that a **Muslim** can never be a criminal, if he commits a crime, then he is technically not a **Muslim** anymore. That is why the Quran says:

68:35	Would We make Muslims as criminals?	اَفَنَجْعَلُ الْمُسْلِمِیْنَ کَالْمُجْرِمِیْنَ

Therefore he who follows Allah's laws is a **Muslim**.

"اَلْإِسْلَامُ" (**al-islam**) is the code of conduct for life that Allah has designated for mankind available as an alternative and it is upto us to accept it or not to accept it. No other code of life is acceptable to Allah than Islam – because this is not based on human emotions and is based on the permanent values which do not change with time.

Surah *Aal-e-Imran* says:

3:82	Do these people prefer a **Deen** other than that designated by Allah?	اَفَغَيْرَ دِيْنِ اللّٰهِ يَبْغُوْنَ
3:82	(Even though) everything in the heavens and the earth is subjected to His laws accepting it willingly or unwillingly and at every step they have to follow his law	وَلَهُ اَسْلَمَ مَنْ فِى السَّمٰوٰتِ وَالْاَرْضِ طَوْعاً وَّكَرْهاً وَاِلَيْهِ يُرْجَعُوْنَ

After that it is said:

| 3:84 | And if man wants to experiment (another Deen) then he can try, but then he will find that ultimately he is the loser | وَمَنْ يَّبْتَغِ غَيْرَ الْاِسْلَامِ دِيْناً فَلَنْ يُّقْبَلَ مِنْهُ |

Anyone who adopts any other code of life except **Islam** will not be accepted i.e. will not get the benefit as one will get by following Islam. This is the same code of life that was given to all previous messengers and ultimately was completed with the advent of the Quran.

Allah has chosen this code of life for all humanity (5:3). As such, under the Sun, there is no other code of life other than that which Allah has termed "اَلْاِسْلَام" (al-islam), and is not to be found anywhere else except in the Quran. The followers of this **Deen** are called "مسلمین" (muslimeen), and a "مسلم" (muslim) is one who believes that the Quran is a complete code of life revealed by Allah . Since it is complete therefore there is no need for any other messenger.

S-L-W   س ل و

"سَلْوٰى" (*salwa*): anything which provides consolation, reassurance.
"اَلسَّلْوٰى" (*as-salwa*): honey, as well as meat *{T}*.
"سَلْوَةٌ مِنَ الْعَيْشِ" (*salwatun minal aish*): a comfortable life which is free from fear and tribulation *{M}*.
"سَلَاهُ عَنْهُ تَسْلِيَةً" (*salahu unhu tasleehi*): he made him forget his grief *{T}*.
"اَلسَّالِى" (*as-saali*): one who forgets sadness and grief *{M}*.
"سَلَاهُ" (*salaahu*): he gave up his memory and mitigated his sorrow *{T}*.
"اَلسَّلْوٰى" (*as-salwa*): a white coloured bird which the **Bani Israel** were given to eat in the valleys of **Sinai** (2:57) *{T}*.

Ibn Faris says it basically means a comfortable life with plenty of luxuries.

Raghib says that it means anything which gives solace.

Also see under heading (M-N-N)

Suleman سليمانَّ

Among the messengers of the **Bani Israel, Suleman** had a prominent position due to his fame and execution of power. He was the son of **Dawood** (38:30) and his heir (27:16). He was had great desire to acquire knowledge and had developed the ability make effective decisions (27:15). Although in those days the kingdom was acquired just for being the king's son, **Suleman** was designated king because of his special qualities. Civilized and uncivilized people (**djinn** and **inns**) were included in his armies and cavalry brigades (27:17). His naval fleet was also very famous at the time. The Quran has quoted saying that the winds were made subservient to him (21:28), meaning that he used his knowledge of the winds to employ his ships.. The rebellious mountainous tribes were brought under control by employing them on different tasks during his reign (21:82). They used to construct big buildings, design statues and draw pictures for him (34:12-13). During this period, the nation of **Saba** was ruling over the eastern part of Yemen, and they were Star worshipers. They were ruled by a queen. Suleman went to war with her nation which eventually became subservient to Allah (27:20-44). The Quran has noted some of this detail by stating that his army had passed through the valley of "نمل" (**namal**) (27:18-19). "هُد هُد" (**huud huud**) was an officer in this army (27:20-21).

Suleman was a grand and powerful king but his heir proved to be very weak (34:14). The Torah mentions him as Solomon in detail. As happens in human reporting of the history the Jews have fabricated a lot of stories of sorcery and superstition about him. The Torah carries some of these stories and narrations which are refuted by the Quran (2:102).

S-M-D س م د

Ibn Faris says that its basic meaning is to keep going without stopping.

"سَمَدَ" (**samada**), "سُمُوْدًا" (**samooda**): to raise the head high out of pride **{T}**.
"سَمَدَتِ الْإِبِلُ فِىْ سَيْرِبَا" (**samadatil ibilu fee saireha**): the camels went straight ahead with speed. From this the meaning is derived that they did so out of rebellion and pride, or that they did as they liked.
"سَمَدَ" (**samada**), "يَسْمَدُ" (**yasmadu**) means to be pushed high.
"سَامِدٌ" (**saamid**): one who is left standing in wonderment, perhaps because he too stands with his head high.

Ibn-ul Airabi says it means a man who is engaged in the pleasures of life and neglects his responsibility **{T}**.

Muheet says that "اَلسُّمُوْدُ" (**as-sumud**) means for the face to be distorted due to worries and grief **{M}**.

The Quran says about the opponents:

| 53:60-63 | You ridicule instead of worrying because you are unaware of the (bad) results that your deeds are going to produce | وَتَضْحَكُونَ وَلَا تَبْكُونَ وَ اَنْتُمْ سَامِدُونَ - فَاسْجُدُوْاِاللّٰهِ وَاعْبُدُوْ |

According to this sentence "سَامِدُوْنَ" (*samidoon*) would mean to be unaware.
But after that it is said "فَاسْجُدُوْ لِلَّه وَاعْبُدُوْا" (*fasjudul lahi wa'bedu*). Here "سَامِدُوْ" (*saamedoon*) would mean that you are very rebellious and proud, and do whatever suits you. It is better for you to leave this path and willingly follow Allah's guidance.

S-M-R   ر م س

"اَلسُّمْرَةُ" (*as-sumrah*): fair complexion (as colour of wheat).
"اَلسَّمْرَاءُ" (*as-samra'a*): wheat.
"اَلسَّمَرُ" (*as-samara*): night or conversation at night, nightly tales.
"اَلسَّامِرُ" (*as-saamir*): a congregation for story telling at night. It is also used for a story teller, singular as well as plural (23:67).
"اَلسَّمِيْرُ" (*as-sameer*) means story teller.
"اَلْمُسَامِرُ" (*al-musaamir*): a companion or fellow participant in a gathering at night for gossip and story telling.
"سِمَارَةُ اللَّيْلِ" (*simaratul lail*): to talk at night.
"سَمِيْرٌ" (*samiyar*) also means period, era {R}.
"اَلسَّامِرَةُ" (*as-saamirah*), "اَلسَّمَرَةُ" (*as-samarah*): a Jewish tribe. They differ in some things with the mainline Jews, for instance, they believe that no messenger will come after *Moosa*. They also believe in the caste system. They think that the city of *Nablus* (where they lived) is the holy city. There are two sects among them, *kushaan* and *dushaan.* These are the people whom the *samari* is said to have led to worship the golden calf built by him after *Moosa,* had gone up the mount to receive the commandments from God.

Muheet says "اَلسَّا مِرَةُ" (*as-saamirah*) is also a place in Palestine and a tribe as well which resides in *Nablus*. They are very few in number and believe that they become impure if touched by others {M} (20:97).

But modern day research shows that this chap was an individual of the *sameri* tribe, not *Bani Israel*. Three thousand years before Christ, there were two nations living in Iraq. One nation which had come from the south was Arab, and the other which probably came from the north was called Sameri.

Although Sameri tribe had Iraq as its motherland, it had spread out afar out. History has proven their relations with the Egyptians. It seems that this person who has been called *Sameri* by the Quran in 20:85 had become a disciple of *Moosa* and had left the place along with *Bani Israel*.

But it seems that *Moosa's* teachings had not affected him and he never accepted these from heart (20:96).

But if "اَلسَّامِرِيّ" (*as-saamiri*) has been derived from the root "سَمَرٌ" (*samara*), then it means story teller. The way the story tellers mislead the nation (simple folk) is known to everyone. Our own history is testimony to that fact that when we left the facts and truths of the Quran and diverted ourselves to myths and stories, we fell into ignominy. Gradually our Deen has turned into merely some mythical stories and the Quranic truths are ignored by the majority.

S-M-Ain   س م ع .

"اَلسَّمْعُ" (*as-sama*): hearing part of the ear. It also means listening, and sometimes even ear.
"سَمْعٌ" (*sama*): that which is listened to. It also means to listen and also one who makes one to listen, although some scholars have refuted the later meaning.
"اِسْتَمَعَ اِلَيْهِ" (*istama-a ilaih*) means to be attentive to someone, to lend an ear and to listen attentively.

The Quran has said "يَسْتَمِعُوْنَ اِلَيْکَ" (*yastami-oona ilaik*) for those who appear to be very attentive but actually are not listening (10:32). The Quran calls them deaf because they do not employ their intellect and thus do not benefit from listening (10:42).

4:46	listen to us, even if you are not heard	اِسْمَعْ غَيْرَ مُسْمَعٍ

Raghib says it is said satirically for someone to have turned deaf, and otherwise it is said as a prayer. Sometimes "سَمْعٌ" (*sama*) means understanding and method, i.e. "اَسْمَعَ" (*asma*) means to make someone understand too. This word is also used for obedience, i.e. "اِسْمَعُوْنِ" (*isma-oon*) means "أَطِيْعُوْنِ" (*atee-oon*) in 2:93.

"سَمِعَ لَهُ" (*sami-a lahu*): accepted it, agreed to it.

The Quran has mentioned eyesight and hearing and "قلب" (*qalb*) for acquiring knowledge. Eyesight and hearing are the senses through which a man knows about things. These are means for perceptual knowledge. The mind conceives an image after receiving data from these senses. Thus through eyesight, hearing and seeing it through intellect, one acquires knowledge.

The Quran lays a lot of stress on perceptual knowledge which helps us to develop concepts. These concepts are them used for furthering our knowledge through the use of critical thinking skills. It says that those who do not employ their hearing, eyesight and reasoning are dwellers of a society which is bound to be left behind and is equivalent of hell on earth (7:179).
Also see (Q-L-B) and (B-Sd-R). It also says that when a man's emotions overwhelm him, his means of acquiring knowledge do not let him reach the right conclusion (47:16-17). We notice how someone can become blinded in rage. One can sometime be overwhelmed by emotions.

In greed a man can do things which are otherwise laughable or silly. If biased, one can never accommodate the other's point of view. Just like when intoxicated, one's senses do not work properly, similarly these do not work properly when one is overwhelmed by emotions as well.

This is termed by the Quran as:

2:7	To be blinded, to be deaf , and hearts to be sealed	خَتَمَ اللّٰهُ عَلٰى قُلُوْبِهِمْ وَعَلٰى سَمْعِهِمْ وَعَلٰى اَبْصَارِهِمْ غِشَاوَةٌ

See heading (Kh-T-M). Knowledge can only produce good results under the guidance of the revelation, because it gives us those values of life which are free from human emotions. Human emotions bias our decision making and thus misguide us in the long run. Human intellect when alone will make any laws, these will never be free from the emotional bias and thus will have flaws.

(**istama**) to eavesdrop (72:1), to listen very attentively (42:38), not tinged with emotion. "سَمَّاعٌ" (**samma**) also means spy {*T*} (9:47)

Surah *Al-Kahaf* says:

18:20	how well he listens and how well he sees	اَبْصِرْبِهٖ وَاَسْمِعْ

Ibn Faris says "مُسْمِعٍ" (**mus-m'i**) and "مُسْتَمِعٌ" (**mustami'i**) also means praise of beauty and fame.

S-M-K س م ک

"اَلسَّمْکُ" (**as-samk**): height of a house or ceiling.
"قَدْ سَمَکَهُ" (**qad samakahu**): he made him lofty, raised him {*R*}.
"اَلسِّمَاکُ" (**as-simaak**): something used to make something lofty, or to raise something.
"اَلْمِسْمَاکُ" (**al-mismaak**): wooden pole with which a tent is raised.
"اَلسَّمَکُ" (**as-samak**) means fish, because it is high or raised (in the middle):

The Quran says:

79:28	God raised the height of sky (or its roof)	رَفَعَ سَمْکَهَا

It means that He raised the atmosphere to great heights. (The height of space is unlimited).

S-M-M   س م م

"اَلسَّمُّ" (*as-sum*): narrow hole like a needle's eye (7:40), or the openings of the ear and nose. May mean poison

"مَسَامٌّ" (*masaam*): pores on skin.

"اَلسَّمَامُ" (*as-samaam*): any light and fast moving thing.

"اَلسَّمُومُ" (*as-samoom*): fast, hot wind which generally blows in the summer months (in the hot regions) *{T}*.

The Quran says

| 56:42 | In scorching fire and scalding water | فِي سَمُومٍ وَحَمِيمٍ |
| 15:27 | Scorching fire | نَارِ السَّمُومِ |

Ibn Faris described the basic meaning of this root as the spot from where you enter something. He writes that poison is called "سَمَّ" (*samma*) because it enters into the body.

"سَمُومٌ" (*samom*) means hot air because it enters into the body due to its high velocity.

Raghib writes that "سَمَّهُ" (*sammah*) means that it entered something, while "سَمُومٌ" (*samom*) as that hot air that appears to affect like poison.

S-M-N   س م ن

"سَمِنَ" (*samin*), "سَمَانَةً" (*samanah*): he became plump, became fat.

"سَامِنٌ" (*saamin*), "سَمِينٌ" (*sameen*): the plural is "سِمَانٌ" (*simaan*) and means plump *{T}*.

The Quran says:

| 12:43 | fat cows | بَقَرَاتٍ سِمَانٍ |
| 51:27 | fat calf | بِعِجْلٍ سَمِينٍ |

"أَسْمَنَ الرَّجُلُ" (*asmanar rajul*): man became fat.

"أَسْمَنَهُ" (*asmanahu*): fattened him, put on weight *{T}*.

Surah **Al-Haashiya** says about the sustenance in a hellish society:

| 88:7 | It does not fatten (does not develop the body) | لَا يُسْمِنُ |

How can sustenance of ignominy can help to grow?

"اَلسَّمْنُ" (*as-samn*) means saturated butter, which is fattening.

S-M-W   و م س

"سَمَاءٌ" (*sama-a*), with plural form "سَمٰوٰتٌ" (*samawaat*) means sky because it is high and overshadows the earth. It actually means anything that is over you and overshadows you.

"سَمَاءٌ" (*sama-a*): every roof over your head. *Fuqah-ul-lugha* has also said that this word has this meaning:

Raghib says that everything is "سَمَاءٌ" (*sama-a*) in relation to a thing below it, and everything in relation to the thing above is called "أَرْضٌ" (*arz*).

Clouds and rain as well are called "سَمَاءٌ" (*sama-a*). Greenery and plants are called "سَمَاءٌ" (*sama-a*) as well because they are higher than the earth *{T}*, *{Ibn Qateebah}*.

"اِسْمٌ" (*ism*) means a sign with which one recognizes something.
Names are also called "اِسْمٌ" (*ism*). Plural is "أَسْمَاءٌ" (*asma-a*).
"سَمِيٌّ" (*sammi*) means of a similar name and equal.
"مُسَامَاةٌ" (*musaamah*) means mutual respect *{T}*.
"سَمَّى تَسْمِيَةً" (*samma tasmeeh*): to keep a name, to name something.
"اَلْمُسَمَّى" (*al-musamma*): name that is kept or given, said to be, nominated, designated, fixed and known *{T}*.

Mufardaat says:

until the "musamma" is known, names are of no use	مَعْرِفَةُ الْأَسْمَاءِ لَاتَحْصُلُ إِلَّا بِمَعْرِفَةِ الْمُسَمَّى

It means that *Adam* (human beings) has been given the ability to recognize things by their constituents and can characterise these by their properties and can identify them accordingly by giving them different names.

The Quran has used "أَرْضٌ وَسَمَاءٌ" (*arz o sama-a*) at many places. There is no doubt that this earth of ours is also called "أَرْضٌ" (*arz*) i.e. Earth, but everything in relation to (Sama) heavens seen as above is called "أَرْضٌ" (*arz*) as well. Therefore "أَرْضٌ وَسَمَاءٌ" (*arz o sama-a*) would mean the lows and highs of the universe as visible to us. When "أَرْضٌ" (*arz*) is to be used against "سَمَاءٌ" (*sama-a*) then "سَمَاءٌ" (*sama-a*) would also include the entire universe, and "أَرْضٌ" (*arz*) would refer to the society and civilization of humans. Therefore, "سَمَاءٌ" (*sama-a*) or "سَمٰوٰتٌ" (*samawat*) would not only mean sky and heavens, but also everything that is in the universe which includes galaxies so far discovered and those yet to be discovered and beyond. In other words, this word includes everything there is to be found.

Where ever the Quran has used the phrase of "أَرْضٌ وَسَمَاءٌ" (*arz o sama-a*), it needs to seen in the context in which it appears e.g. whether it implies loftiness and lowliness, whether it is in regard to physical things or in respect of ranks, or social life within a society. More details have appeared under the heading (A-R-Zd).

The Quran says:

| 2:31 | Adam has been taught the names of everything | وَعَلَّمَ آدَمَ الْأَسْمَاءَ كُلَّهَا |

Here **Adam** refers to all humanity or mankind. Also see under the heading (A-D-M). As mentioned earlier, knowing the names alone will do no good, until and unless you know what a thing is. As such, the meaning of the knowledge of names being given to **Adam** or man means that he has been given the potential and ability to discover and determine the characteristics of various elements and things in the universe. This is the reason the Quran declares that all the forces of the universe (the **Malaikah**) are within the reach and control of the man i.e. he has the potentials, attributes, and abilities to bring these to his use. The Quran does not differentiate this life from the next life when mentions these aspects of putting to the disposal of the human potentials. When man becomes aware of the law under which these forces of nature operate, all forces under that law become within his reach and are acchievable. The Quran refers to both parts of human life i.e. this physical existence and the life beuond death. It is upto us to explore both possibilities through the use of our intellect and reasoning. Therefore, a nation will become master of the universal forces according to the laws it becomes aware of. Further step is how to utilize those forces.

It has been said:

| 2:38 | Any nation which will utilize the guidance in the Quran they will have no fear and no grief. | فَمَنْ تَبِعَ هُدَايَ فَلَاخَوْفٌ عَلَيْهِمْ وَلَاهُمْ يَحْزَنُونَ |
| 2:39 | If a nation which masters the forces of the universe but utilizes these not for the benefit of the mankind then they will suffer the consequences of going agains the Quranic guidance. | أُولَئِكَ أَصْحَابُ النَّارِ هُمْ فِيهَا خَالِدُونَ |

What should be nation called then it neither masters the forces of the universe nor utilizes these forces as per the laws of God? A western doctor has written something very interesting as per his perception.

"Adam was made responsible for characterising things. This was a very husge responsibility, because the things whose characteristics and properties are not known remain undetermined and undefined. And if inaccurate characteriscis are given to things, the results can be very harmful". {Dr. M.L. Tyler in "**Homeo, drug pictures**" (preface)}.

This too signifies that acquiring knowledge about physical laws is a sign of being human.

The Quran says that those whom you think are your gods (other than the real God) are:

| 12:40 | Simply some names which you and your forefathers have fabricated | اَسۡمَاءٌ سَمَّيۡتُمُوۡهَا اَنۡتُمۡ وَآبَاؤُكُمۡ |
| 12:40 | Allah has not provided any support for this (not evidence and fact based) | مَا اَنۡزَلَ اللّٰهُ بِهَا مِنۡ سُلۡطَانٍ |

The big religious structures which have been erected from the past or those being erected now have no real significance other than the names given to them. These don't solve any human problems and issues except being used to project some mortals in high position to impress fellow mortals to influence them. The Quranic guidance explains the purpose of each human and thus takes away all the paraphernalia associated with the power, religious stature or wealth and helps us to look through to the reality. The right place of things is that which has been designated by Allah's law. His laws operate smoothly in the outer universe, and in the human world, the divine revelation is the right source and guide to these laws. Everything else may have a big name but gets exposed when analysed in the light of the guidance provided in the Quran.

S-N-B-L   س ن ب ل

"اَلسُّنۡبُلُ" (*as- sumbul*): An ear of grain, bunch of ears Singular is "اَلسُّنۡبُلَة" (*as-sumbulah*) as used in 2:261.

Plurals are "سَنَابِلُ" (*sanabil*) and "سُنۡبَلَاتٌ" (*sunbalat*)

"قَدۡ سَنۡبَلَ الزَّرۡعُ" (*qad sanbalaz zar-a*): corn grew ears {T}. This word is used to mean grain, not fruit.

S-N-D   س ن د

"اَلسَّنَدُ" (*as-sanad*): a thing which is used for support.

"سَنَدَ اِلَيۡهِ" (*sanada ilaihi*), "يَسۡنُدُ" (*yasnud*): he leaned (e.g. against a support) {T}.

"سَنَدَ الشَّيۡءَ" (*sanadash shaiyi*): he supported the thing and made it strong.

"اَلسَّنَدُ" (*as-sanad*): high mountain facing you .

"اَلسِّنۡدَانُ" (*as-sandaan*): an ironsmith's anvil over which heated iron is rested (to soften it) and then beaten (into a particular shape) {M}.

"اَلسَّنَدُ" (*as-sanad*): a sort of sheet that was made in Yemen.

"سَنَّدَ الرَّجُلُ" (*sanadar rajul*): man put a cloth sheet over him {T}.

The Quran says that the hypocrites are like "خُشُبٌ مُسَنَّدَةٌ" (*khushboon musannadah*) in 63:4, that is, they are like sticks which are leaning against the wall. It can also mean that they are like sticks which are wrapped up in human clothing. If we take the first meaning which will mean, a hypocrite is never self-confident and is always seeking support of others for his hypocrisy.

If we take the later meaning then it will mean a hypocrite is one thing inside and something else outside. Their exterior is always very appealing to people making use of various clothing, but deprived of all human qualities.

S-N-D-S   س ن د س

"سُنْدُسٌ" (*sundus*): silk of high quality (*Taj & Raghib*).

The Quran says:

| 18:31 | Clothes of green silk | ثِيَاباً خُضْرًا مِنْ سُنْدُسٍ |

S-N-M   س ن م

"اَلسَّنَامُ" (*as-sanaam*): camel's hump.
"اَلسَّنَمْ مِنَ النَّبْت" (*as-simu minan nabt*): a tall plant which has flowered or grown ears.
"سَنَّمَ الْإِنَاءَ تَسْنِيْماً" (*sannamal ina-a tasneema*): he filled the utensil or pot – filling to the extent that whatever is put into it (e.g. grain) rose above the edges.
"تَسَنَّمَ الْحَائِطَ" (*tasannamal ha-it*): he climbed the wall.
"أَسْنَمَتِ النَّارُ" (*asnamatin naar*): the flames of the fire rose high.
"سَنَامُ كُلِّ شَيْءٍ" (*sanaamu kulli shaiyin*): the best or highest part of something {*T, M*}.

Ibn Faris says it basically means loftiness and height.

The Quran has said about "تَسْنِيْمٌ" (*tasneem*) which has been explained further by saying:

| 83:28 | a spring out of which the righteous ones drink | عَيْناً يَشْرَبُ بِهَا الْمُقَرَّبُوْنَ |

This has the connotation of loftiness. That is, life's evolutionary stages, humanity's heights in righteousness, full development of human abilities and enhancement of potentials.

S-N-N   س ن ن

"اَلسِّنُّ" (*as-sinnu*): teeth {*T, M*} as in (5:45). Since the age of animals is determined by the number of teeth they have, it also means age.
"أَسَنَّ الرَّجُلُ" (*as-sannar rajul*): the man reached old age.
"اَلسُّنَّةُ" (*as-sunnah*): face, the open and distinct part of the face. It also means path, manner, custom, law. Its plural is "سُنَنٌ" (*sunan*).

"سَنَنَاتُ الطَّرِيْق" (*sananat tareeq*), "سُنَنُ الطَّرِيْق" (*sunanat tareeq*), "سِنَنُ الطَّرِيْقِ" (*sinanat tareeq*). These words are not plural forms of "سُنَّةٌ" (*sunnah*) which is a separate word. This means open and distinct part of a path. This led to its meaning of manner, sect, routine, and law:

The Quran says:

17:77	you will find no change in our way (system, law):	وَلَا تَجِدُ لِسُنَّتِنَا تَحْوِيلاً
35:43	now people appear to be waiting for whatever happened to the others to happen to them as well	فَهَلْ يَنْظُرُونَ إِلَّا سُنَّتَ الْأَوَّلِينَ
3:136	a lot of different systems and paths , and routines have passed before your time	قَدْ خَلَتْ مِنْ قَبْلِكُمْ سُنَنٌ

Ibn Faris says it means for something to continue, and for things to appear comfortably one after another.

"سَنَّ الشَّىْءَ" (***sannash shaiyi***) means to make something easy or to facilitate it {M}.
"سَنَّ التَّرَابَ عَلَى وَجْهِ الْأَرْضِ" (***sannat turaaba ala wajhil arda***): spread the soil smoothly on the ground till it turned into a dam {M}.

Regarding the creation of man, the Quran says:

| 15:26 | From putrefied mud | مِنْ حَمَإٍ مَسْنُونٍ |

Lane (with different references) has written that "سَنَنْتُ الْحَجَرَ عَلَى الْحَجَرِ" (***sananatul hajara alal hajar***) means that I put a stone on stone and rubbed it (grounded it). Occasionally putting water and rubbing stone on stone produces a kind of putrified matter which is called "سَنِينْ" (***saneen***). When it is allowed to remain for some time, it becomes hard {L}.

Some say that "مَسْنُونٌ" (***masnoon***) means wet and moist.
Abul heesham says that "سَنَّ الْمَاءُ" (***sannal maa-u***) means that water transformed {T}.

The Quran says that man was initially created from the soil. The soil which was mixed with water, i.e. life began with(inorganic & Organic) matter intermingling with water. When these two met and eons passed, there was a lot of metamorphosis in the matter and life began. This has been termed as "حَمَإٍ مَسْنُونٍ" (***hama inn masnoon***). Note that it explains how life began physically, but this does not mean that life is the product of this matter.

The Quran's has declared:

| 35:43 | There are no changes in the method of Allah | فَلَنْ تَجِدَ لِسُنَّتِ اللهِ تَبْدِيلاً |

This is an expression of a great fact, on which all scientific research rests, which is the basis of human living in the universe. Quran declared 1500 years ago that God's laws never change. Declaring such a fact is not the product of a human intellect. Humans have become aware of the concept of laws in the recent past . All scientific research is producing ever new results and we are becoming aware of the laws which never change. This understanding of these laws is giving us a new confidence in our functioning knowing fully well that these laws will never let us down and this has opened ever new spheres of scientific discoveries When man once understands the law made by God, he knows that these laws never change.

Just like Allah's immutable laws are operating in the physical world and the universe, so are His laws working in the human world. He has fixed some rules for the rise and fall of nations, and these rules never change. Any nation which follows these values will prosper and a nation which does not follow these values , will get destroyed.

This law based concept of God has brought a revolutionary change in the world. In the early human period man conceived God as a despot who did not follow any laws and values. For example He could go angry just like a human dictator or bestow rewards without any reason. Such a concept of God was became an object of fear lest He may become angry on a minor matter so man tried according to his own self-created belief and understanding to keep such a God happy with different offerings – the acts of worship.

The Quran made this revolutionary declaration that although God was all powerful and the highest authority, He had formulated laws for the physical universe, as well as for the human functioning sphere. And despite holding unlimited power, He has ordained that there will be no change in the laws He has formulated (no matter what happens).

So the decisions of human life too will be made, not whimsically, but according to His laws. That is, every human deed will produce results according to the laws framed by God and these are noted and explained in the Quran. For example the Quran declared: 'Allah created the heavens and the earth for just ends, so that every self finds the recompense of what it does in life; and none is treated unjustly' (45:22)

"وَ لَنْ تَجِدَ لِسُنَّتِ اللهِ تَبْدِيلاً" (*walan tajida lisunnatil lahi tabdeela*): and His laws will never change.

God only acts according to His law this is a law which never changes – we have verified it through our research in the scientific field. This change in human thinking has helped to change the face of the earth and the Quran has declared that: 'Soon will we show them Our signs in the furthest regions and in their own Self until it becomes manifest to them that this (The Quran) is the Truth....' (41:53). Those who understand the Quran and its thinking need to make others aware of the reality explained in the Book. This will help to bring change in the human thinking so that we can reduce the mutual conflicts and use this life to develop our self within the domain of the permanent values.

S-N-He   س ن ه

food and drink were spoiled or deteriorated	سَنِهَ الطَّعَامُ وَالشَّرَابُ سَنْهاً وَتَسَنَّهَ

"اَلتَّسَنُّهُ" (*as-sanahu*): to petrify, something to change due to passage of time. This word is used when bread becomes stale and drinks become stale and deteriorate.
"طَعَامٌ سَنِهٌ" (*tyaamu sanehun*): spoilt food.
"خُبْزٌ مُتَسَنِّهٌ" (*khubzun mutasannehun*): stale or spoiled bread.

The Quran says:

2:259	It was not spoiled	لَمْ يَتَسَنَّهْ

Even after passage of so much time, it did not metamorphose or change *{T, M}*.

Ibn Faris says that the meaning of "سَنَهَ" (*sanah*) is to depend on time.

"سَنَهَتِ النَّخْلَةُ" (*sanahatin nakhlah*): many years passed on the date palm.

Most scholars are of the opinion that "سَنَةٌ" (*sanah*) meaning of years has been derived from this root, but we have put "سَنَةٌ" (*sanah*) and its derivatives under heading (S-N-W).

S-N-W   س ن و

"اَلسَّنَةُ" (*as-sanah*) means years (its plurals are "سَنَوَاتٌ" (*sanawat*), "سِنُوْنَ" (*sinoon*) and "سِنِيْنَ"(*sineen*). There is some difference of opinion about its root. One school of thought says that its root is (S-N-H) because the Arabs say "سَانَهْتُ فُلَاناً" (*saanahtu fulana*) which means that I cut a deal with him on yearly rate.

Ibn Faris says the real meaning of "سَنَةٌ" (*sanah*) is dependent on a period of time.

"سَنَهَتِ النَّخْلَةُ" (*sanahatan nakhlah*): many years passed on the date palm. A second opinion says that its root is "سَنَوَّ" (*sano*) from which "يَسْنُوْ" (*yasnu*) has been derived, which means to go round and round a well.
"اَلسَّانِيَةُ" (*as-saaniyah*) means an animal which is made to go round and round a well in order to bring water out .
"اَلسَّنَةُ" (*as-sanah*) means one orbit of the sun. This is also called "دَارٌ" (*daar*), and since this orbit takes a full year, therefore "اَلسِّنَةُ" (*as-sinah*) means one year.
"اَلسَّنَةُ" (*as-sanah*) is a solar year while "اَلْعَامُ" (*al-a'am*) is a lunar year.
"اَلسَّنَةُ" (*as-sanah*) also means a year when there is drought and intensity, and "اَلْعَامُ" (*al-a'am*) is a year when there is prosperity and good harvest .

29:14	And he lived fifty less than one thousand years among his people	فَلَبِثَ فِيهِمْ اَلْفَ سَنَةٍ اِلَّا خَمْسِينَ عَامًا

Here "عَامًا" (*a'ama*) is the period without hardships and "سَنَةٌ" (*sanah*) is the period when there were hardships.

Lane says "سَنَةٌ" (*sanah*) also means crop of which there are four harvest in a year.

"اَلْفَ سَنَةٍ" (*alfa sanatin*) means two hundred fifty years, and "عَامٌ" (*a'am*) is one full year. So if "خَمْسِينَ عَامًا" (*khamseen aama*) are taken out from it, it leaves us with two hundred years, which could be a man's age. But these are all conjectures. When more historical facts come forth it will become clear what the Quran meant to say that *Nooh* lived fifty less than one thousand years among his people (29:14). Some say this is his period of messenger-hood, which commenced from the the era of an earlier messenger of Allah.

"سَنَّاهُ" (*sannah*) or "تَسْنِيَةً" (*tasniah*): opened it, facilitated it, made it easy *{T, M, R}*.

S-N-Y   س ن ى

"اَلسَّنَى" (*as-sana*) means light.
"اَلسَّنَاءُ" (*as-sana-u*) and "اَلسَّنَى" (*as-sana*) means loftiness and high stature.

The Quran says:

24:43	The dazzle of the lightning nearly blinded	يَكَادُ سَنَا بَرْقِهِ يَذْهَبُ بِالْاَبْصَارِ

Here "سَنَا" (*sana*) means dazzling light.
Ibn Faris says it basically means stature and loftiness.

S-He-R   ش ه ر

"سَهِرَ" (*sahir*), "يَسْهَرُ" (*yasher*), "سَهَرًا" (*sahara*): to be awake (at night).
"سَاهِرٌ" (*saahir*): one who wakes up at night, remaining awake at night *{T, M, R}*.
"اَلسَّاهِرَةُ" (*as-saahirah*): the upper part of the earth, the face of earth, or that part of the earth on which human beings live, or which is 'alive' because of them.

The Quran says:

79:14	There will be eternal life after the renaissance (life after death),	فَاِذَا هُم بِالسَّاهِرَةِ

It also means continuously in a state of awakening, or speed in development because "اَرْضٌ سَاهِرَةٌ" (*ardun saahirah*) is a land which grows plants very quickly *{T}*.

Since the state of life after death is incomprehensible to us, therefore the Quran relates those in terms of metaphors and examples only. Men having insight can have a faint glimpse at a inner reflection level of what it is meant by those examples and metaphors. Understanding more than this is not possible in this life –at least that is the level of understanding at the beginning of the 21st century. As further research is carried out on the Quranic message, more may be discovered by the later generations.

In Syrian language "اَلسَّاهُوْرٌ" (*as-saahoor*) means the same as "اَلْقَمَرٌ" (*al-qamar*) or the moon {F}, {*Kitab-ul-Ashfaq*}. In pure Arabic it means lunar eclipse {*Lane*}.

S-He-L   س ه ل

"اَلسَّهْلُ" (*as-sahal*), "اَلسَّهِلُ" (*as-sahil*): a soft thing.
"اَلسَّهْلُ مِنَ الْأَرْضِ" (*as-sahal minal arz*): soft ground. Plural is "سُهُوْلٌ" (*suhul*) {T}.

The Quran says:

| 7:74 | you build palaces on levelled and soft ground | تَتَّخِذُوْنَ مِنْ سُهُوْلِهَا قُصُوْراً |

S-He-M   س ه م

"سَهْمٌَاس" (*sahumas*): part. Its fundamental meaning is of an arrow which was used for balloting to apportion shares or to divide. It also means a corridor in a house.
"اَلسُّهَامُ" (*as-suhaam*): to become weak and change colour. It also means a camel disease in which they feel hot and thirsty.
"اَلسُّهُوْمُ" (*as-suhoom*): to be harsh due to some stress or worry.
"سَاهَمَ الْقَوْمَ" (*saahamal qaum*): he balloted with the nation {T, M, R}.
It also means to compete in archery, as well as to try overpowering each other.

The Quran says in reference to the story of *Yunus*:

| 37:141 | he balloted along with the others (traditional translation) | فَسَاهَمَ |

This verse is taken as part of a story of Yunus where he was in a boat and there was a ballot to ask one to leave the boat to lighten its load. However, this interpretation does not fit here and as explained later, more plausible meanings are taken for this term.

Allah has said that *Yunus* contested our laws (went against them or did not follow them) and it was his mistake.

| 37:141 | (as a consequence) he slipped | فَكَانَ مِنَ الْمُدْحَضِيْنَ |

Yunus got frustrated with the people of his nation and hastened in making a decision prior to receiving clear signs from Allah. . This hastening and leaving his people resulted in his getting in trouble in the water; however, he managed to come back to his people as explained in the Quran.

S-He-W   س ه و

"غَفْلَةٌ" "سَهَافِى الأَمْرِ" (*saha fil amr*): to forget something. Linguist scholars say that "سَهْوٌ" (*sahw*), "غَفْلَةٌ" (*ghaflah*) and "نِسْيَانٌ" (*nisyaan*) are all of the same meaning, but some say that "سَهْوٌ" (*sahw*) is slight neglect of something present in the human memory, and "نِسْيَانٌ" (*nisyaan*) is for something to go completely out of memory.

Ibn al-Asseer says that "سَهَافِى الشَّىْءِ" (*saha fish shaiyi*) means to give something up due to unawareness, and "سَهَاعَنْهُ" (*saha unhu*) means to give something up knowingly {T, R, M}.
"السَّهْوُ" (*as-sahw*): for something to be motionless and soft.
"السَّهْوَةُ" (*as-sahwah*): a bow which is easily stretched {T, R, M}.

Ibn Faris says most of the meanings of this word are connected with neglect and peace.

"جَاءَ سَهْواً رَهْواً" (*ja'an rahwan rahwa*): he came very peacefully.

The Quran says:

51:11	They are engaged in their doings and are unaware of the reality	هُمْ فِى غَمْرَةٍ سَاهُونَ
107:5	They are neglectful of their duties	الَّذِينَ هُمْ عَنْ صَلَاتِهِمْ سَاهُونَ
9:54	They are unaware of the reality of *salaah*	وَلَا يَأْتُونَ الصَّلَاةَ
107:6	and only believe in its physical form	الَّذِينَ هُمْ يُرَاؤُونَ

Because these can be very easily carried out and can gain respect in society through visible worship acts.

S-W-A   س و أ

"سَاءَهُ" (*sa-ahu*), "يَسُوءُهُ" (*yasu-uhu*): to say something to someone which is unpleasant.
"سَاءَ الشَّىْءُ" (*sa-ush shaiyi*): something bad happened.
"أَسَاءَ" (*asa-a*), "يُسِيءُ" (*yu-see*): to do something bad, to create imbalance and inequality, to create chaos and deterioration. It is the opposite of "أَحْسَنَ" (*ahsan*).
"السَّيِّئَةُ" (*as-sabeelah*): life's unpleasantness, problems in life {T}.

This is the opposite of "سَيِّئَةٌ" (*hasanah*) which means to give something complete balance and hence "سَيِّئَةٌ" (*sayyye-atah*) means imbalance. As such, "سَوْءٌ" (*sau-u*) means harm, chaos, and annihilation *{T}*, *{Latif-ul-Lugha}*. "حَسَنَةٌ" (*hasanah*) also means striking balance in actions and deeds "سَيِّئَةٌ" (*sayye-atah*) being opposite would mean exaggeration, disturbing the balance, going to extremes *{T}*.

"مَسَاوِيئُ" (*masaawi*): unpleasant things, faults *{T}* *{Latif-ul-Lugha}*.

Also see heading (H-S-N).

"اَلسَّوْءَةُ" (*as-sau-ah*): bad nature, bad thing or work, any talk or deed which if revealed will cause shame. It also means the male and female genitalia *{T}*. Plural is "سَوْءَاتٌ" (*saw'aat*) as in (7:20, 7:26).

The Quran says "سَيِّئَةٌ" (*sayyi-atah*) against "حَسَنَةٌ" (*hasanah*) at several places, as in (7:131), 3:119 etc. It also uses "اِقْتِصَادٌ" (*saa-a*) against "اِقْتِصَادٌ" (*iqtesaad*) which means striking balance (5:66).

To mean to be sad or have tribulations "سِيئَ بِهِمْ" (*siya behim*) has been used in (11:77). The effects of the righteous living is beauty and goodness in a society. In a society based on the permanent values, both human personality and society are balanced, and each member gets all the pleasantries of life. Acting against this way creates imbalance and as a consequence unpleasantness is created. This is why the Quran has said that people who live these opposing lifestyles can never be the same (40:58). The question that arises here is that if the balance of a society has gone awry, then what do we do to set it right?

The Quran says:

23:96	if you do righteous deeds , the imbalance within a society will (gradually) go away	اِدْفَعْ بِالَّتِي هِيَ أَحْسَنُ السَّيِّئَءَ
11:114	Indeed the good deeds remove the evil deeds	اِنَّ الْحَسَنٰتِ يُذْهِبْنَ السَّيِّئَاتِ

Surah *Al-Momineen* says that one of the characteristics of a true believer is:

13:22	They remove evil by virtue	يَدْرَءُ وْنَ بِالْحَسَنَ السَّيِّئَءَ

This does not mean that the Quran teaches us to present the other cheek if one is slapped or if someone takes off your coat (i.e. robs it forcibly), then you take off your shirt for him too. Such teachings only encourage the criminals . The Quran directs us to enforce justice which requires that steps to be taken to prevent crimes in a society and to punish criminals taking into account all circumstances. It also asks us to look at the causes of the crimes and to have a programme in place to rehabilitate those who are willing to reform themselves.

For example the Quran declares:

42:40 10:27	The punishment should always be commensurate to the crime,	جَزَاؤُ اسَيِّئَةٍ مِثْلُهَا

No crime should have more punishment than what it deserves – as noted earlier, all circumstances should be taken into account. . Also where reform can be expected, forgiveness is advocated. This verse makes it clear that evil should not be returned with evil. . Each member of the society should be made aware of the Law of requital i.e. what we sow so shall we reap.

41:27	verily we will punish them severely for the deeds they have committed	وَلَنَجْزِيَنَّهُمْ أَسْوَأَ الَّذِىْ كَانُوْا يَعْمَلُوْنَ

The foregoing explains how the Quran teaches to create balance in our personality and in a society at large.

Suw'a سُوَاعٌ

It was the name of an idol during the reign of **Nooh** (71:23). People of Arabia were well aware of this name. The tribe of **Banu Hazeel** used to worship an idol of this name.

S-W-D س و د

"اَلْأَسْوَدُ" (*al-aswad*) is the opposite of "أَبْيَضُ" (*abyaz*), which means black. Plural is "سُوْدٌ" (*suud*) as in (35:27).

"اِسْوَدَّ" (*iswad*), "يَسْوَدُّ" (*yaswud*): it became black:

"اَلسَّوَادُ" (*as-sawaad*): darkness, blackness, great wealth, the villages around a city, a large number, common folk, a big part of the nation.

"اَلسَّائِدُ" (*as-saa'id*): a leader of a smaller stature than "سَيِّدٌ" (*syed*) {T}.

"اَلسَّيِّدُ" (*as-syed*): leader, or one who has a big party , lord, or husband {T}.

"اَلسِّيَادَةُ" (*as-siyaadah*): leadership.

"اَلْأَسْوَدُ مِنَ الْقَوْمِ" (*al aswad minal qaum*): the most powerful and prominent man in a nation, a patron of a nation {T}.

"اَلْأَيَّامُ الْمُسَوَّدَةُ" (*al ayyamal muswada*): days of ill-being and pain {M}.

Raghib says "اِبْيِضَاضُ الْوُجُوْهِ" (*ibyidadul wujuh*) means happiness and pleasure and "اِسْوِدَادُ الْوُجُوْهِ" (*ibswidadul wujuh*) means sorrow and pain {R}. Also see heading (B-Y-Zd).

"سَيِّدًا" (*sayyeda*) meaning leader or head – this has been used by the Quran in (3:38). It means a man of respect, and meaning as a husband, has been used in (12:25); here it has been referred to a man in Egypt who was not only a husband , but was a leading figure as well. The Quran has not used it to mean an ordinary husband.

The Quran says:

| 16:58 | black, dark, or sorrowful | وَجْهُ مُسْوَدّاً |
| 3:105 | faces to blacken (be demeaned) | تَسْوَدُّ وُجُوهٌ |

It means when a face turns 'black', out of tribulation and trouble as an example. Against this the word used is (*tabyaz*) which means to be white meaning to be honoured.

S-W-R   س و ر

"سَارَ" (*saar*), "يَسُوْرُ" (*yasoor*), "سَوْرَةٌ" (*saurah*): to accost or attack someone.
"سُرْتُ الْحَاءِطَ و تَسَوَّرْتُه" (*surt ul-haa-ita wa tasawwaratuh*): I climbed the wall.
"اَلسُّوْرُ" (*as-soor*): a city in which one takes sanctuary. It also means loftiness, respect and honour.
"سَوْرَةُ السُّلْطَانْ" (*sauratus sultan*): a king's grandeur, respect etc.
"اَلسِّوَارُ" (*as-siwaar*): a bracelet which was at that time a sign of honour and stature. "أَسَاوِرُ" (*asaawir*) is its plural form.
"اَلْأُسْوَارُ" (*al-uswaar*) or "اَلْأَسْوَارُ" (*al-aswaar*): cavalry commander. It also means a very good archer and horseman *{T}*.

Ibn Faris has said that "اَلْإِسْوَارُ" (*al-iswaar*) is not an Arabic word.

"اَلسُّوْرَةُ" (*as-surah*) means rank and stature, respect, loftiness. It also means a building which rises majestically towards the sky *{M}*.

Many reasons are quoted about the Quranic chapters called "سُوْرَةٌ" (*surah*). Some think that these are called so because they contain higher level thoughts. Others think that the earlier chapters work as a stepping stone for the following chapters.. Still others say that since the chapters were revealed by stages and they all constitute the "building" of the Quran, therefore they are called "سُوْرَةٌ" (*surah*). Some say that they are called so because they are safe within the Quran, like a man seeking sanctuary is safe in a city which has provided protection *{T}*. A sign is also called a "سُوْرَةٌ" (*surah*) *{M}*.

"سُوْرٌ" (*soor*) also means strong, well-built camels of high breed *{T}*.

In the Quran itself, it has meant Quranic chapters (2:23) and as a sign of leadership. It has also come to mean hand bracelet in (35:33), (18:31) and (76:21).

Surah **Saad** says:

| 38:21 | when they climbed over the wall into the porch. | إِذْ تَسَوَّرُوا الْمِحْرَابَ |

The bracelets mentioned in heavenly society are referring towards power, grandeur and loftiness which believers will enjoy there (18:41). The Quran says that this is an allegory of the real thing. We cannot comprehend their reality with our present level of consciousness. See heading (J-N-N).

S-W-Te   س و ط

Ibn Faris says that "اَلسَّوْطُ" (*as-saut*) basically means to mix things with other things. It means to mix things so they get to confused and loose their true identites. *Ibn Faris* has noted these meanings.

"اَلسَّوْطُ" (*as-saut*) also means to whip because it mixes the skin with blood, or because it penetrates the skin or perhaps because the whip itself is woven by twisting different strands of leather. The plural is "أَسْوَاطُ" (*aswaat*).

Although it means to whip, the Arabs meant that any painful punishment was "سَوْطَ عَذَابٍ" (*as-sauta azaab*), or punishing whip.

Muheet and *Raghib* think that "سَوْطَ عَذَابٍ" (*sauta azaab*), as in (89:12) means different kinds of punishments, mixed together {T, R, M}.

Ibn Faris says "سَوْطَ عَذَابٍ" (*sauta azaa*) means a part of punishment.

S-W(Y)-Ain   س و (ى) ع

"سَاع" (*saa-a*), "يَسُوْعُ" (*yasoo*)

Muheet says that this root's real meaning is destruction, decline, and downfall *{T}*.

"سَاعَ الشَّىْءُ" (*sa-ash shaiyi*) means that a thing was wasted.
"هُوَ ضَاءِعٌ سَاءِعٌ" (*huwa zaa-i-un saa-ih*): he is to be wasted and annihilated.
"فَاقَةٌ مِسْيَاعٌ" (*faqatun misyaun*): a she camel which leaves her young one unprotected in the jungle where wild animals may kill it.
"أَسَاعَهُ" (*asa-a*): left it unprotected and let it go waste.
"رَجُلٌ مُسِيْعٌ" (*rajulun muse'un*) and "مِسْيَاعٌ لِلْمَالِ" (*mesa'u lilmaal*): a man who wastes his wealth.
"اَلسَّيِّعُ" (*as-sayyi'u*): water that flows on the ground.
"سَاعَ الْمَاءُ وَالشَّرَابُ" (*saa-al maa-u wa ash-sharaab*): water and wine fell to the ground and started flowing.
"تَسَيَّعَ الْبَقْلُ" (*tasayyi-al baql*): the vegetables began to dry *{T}*.
"أَسْوَعَ" (*aswa*): he transferred from one time frame to another, or went back one moment or stage *{T}*.

"سَوْعٌ مِنَ اللَّيْلِ" (*sau un minal lail*): a peaceful part of the night.

"اَلسَّاعَةُ" (*as-saa-ah*): portion of a time which passes continuously and the time which is lost.

Ibn Faris says it means to pass on a continuous basis.

It also means tough time , rivalry, and distance
"اَلسَّاعَةُ" (*as-saa'h*): those who are killed *{T}*.

The Quran has used the word "اَلسَّاعَةُ (*as-sa'h*)" extensively. The Quran repeatedly warns those who are on the wrong path that such a choice leads only to destruction and loss. It warns that if you do not change your ways then you will be destroyed as consequence of your actions. This is known as "اِنْذَارٌ" (*inzaar*) i.e. giving warning of the consequences of one's actions. These people do not heed this, and stick to their ways. Their wrong deeds keep piling up negative results until the time arrives when these results that are being compiled quietly but surely, become evident and the people are destroyed. This is called "اَلسَّاعَةُ" (*as-saa'h*), or the time of manifestation of the results. This change does not come at once, but is brewed for a long time. Despite this, it does make its appearance in a way that those who are unaware of its reality think that it has come upon them suddenly. Since this revolution mostly takes place through the hands of those who rise in the support of the truth - , this "اَلسَّاعَةُ" (*as-saa'h*) is in a way the last battle between good and evil, in which the forces of evil are defeated and destroyed. In short, the meaning of "اَلسَّاعَةُ" (*as-saa'h*) would be the manifestation of the result of deeds.
Surah ***Taha*** says that Allah informed ***Moosa*** in detail about how far the pharaoh's rebelliousness had gone, and then told him what he had to do. It is then said:

20:15	Know that the time for the last battle between good and evil has come.	إِنَّ السَّاعَةَ آتِيَةٌ

It means that it will come for sure. The pharaoh cannot be left to do as he pleases. The revolution is bound to come. Likewise the last Messenger (*pbuh*) was also told several times in the Quran:

15:85	the time for the last revolution is arriving	إِنَّ السَّاعَةَ لَأْ تِيَةٌ

Here it means that the revolution will definitely come and the opponents will be destroyed. The battle between truth and falsehood has been going on, on a small scale, and continues to do so. But it appears from the study of the Quran that as time moves ahead and the truths become revealed, there will be a big clash between the universal concept of meeting human basic needs and those who pursue selfish interests - , after which the earth will be illuminated by the universal concept of sustenance for all human beings as noted in (39:69). . This is the great "اَلسَّاعَةُ" (*as-saa'h*) pointing to a momentous change in the world and predicted by the Quran (89:22).

As per the Quran the human life does not end with death, nor do the results of deeds end with death. Thus in the life hereafter, results too have been called "اَلسَّاعَةُ" (*as-saa'h*). The context in which the term is used can be deduced from the study of the Quran i.e. whether referred to the present life to the life in the hereafter.

The cumulative effects of human actions take time to materialise, therefore the effects of the wrong path adopted by various nations take time to show their results. The Quran invites us to study the history from this aspect and see the consequences of following the wrong values.

In Surah *Al-Airaaf the Quran declares*:

| 7:187 | These people ask you as to when will that time of reckoning, with which you try to frighten us, will come? Tell them, only Allah knows. Nobody but Allah will reveal it at its time | يَسْئَلُوْنَكَ عَنِ السَّاعَةِ اَيَّانَ مُرْسٰهَا- قُلْ اِنَّمَا عِلْمُهَا عِنْدَ رَبِّى- لَا يُجَلِّيْهَا لِوَقْتِهَا اِلَّا هُوَ |

Also see 79:42-44.

At another place it is said:

| 33:63 | people ask you about the time of reckoning, tell them only God knows about it, and what do you know, that moment may be near | يَسْئَلُكَ النَّاسُ عَنِ السَّاعَةَ- قُلْ اِنَّمَا عِلْمُهَا عِنْدَ اللهِ- وَمَايُدْرِيْكَ لَعَلَّ السَّاعَةَ تَكُوْنُ قَرِيْباً |

At other places too it is said that only God knows when that moment will come (see 41:47, 43:85 and 31:34)

The Quran refers to the Bani Israel as an example to illustrate the rise and fall of nations from the history. The Bani Israel had messengers of Allah for about 1500 years and enjoyed the prosperity until they followed the revealed permanent values. However, when they went against these values, they suffered the consequences.

The last was *Isa* who told them clearly that if they do not reform their ways, then the power and prosperity will be taken away from them as per Allah's laws. But the reply they gave *Isa* is a historical fact and after that the time for revolution did come and the nation's grandeur and prosperity was taken away from them.

It is said about *Isa* in the Quran:

| 43:61 | His advent was to make the people aware of the great moment of truth. | وَ اِنَّهُ لَعِلْمٌ لِلسَّاعَةِ |

Also see 3:46-55, 43:63-66.

If the pronoun "اِنَّهُ" (*innahu*) is taken to refer to the Quran, then the verse would mean that this Quran tells about the great revolution which is imminent.

S-W-Gh   س و غ

"سَاغَ الشَّرَابُ" (*saghas sharaab*), "يَسُوْغُ" (*yasoogh*), "سَوْغاً" (*saugha*): for a drink to go down the throat easily.

"سَاغَ الطَّعَامُ" (*saaghat tu-aam*): the food went down the throat easily.

"أَلسِّوَاغُ" (*as-siwagh*): that which helps in getting something down the throat.

"شَرَابٌ سَائِغٌ" (*sharabun saa-igh*): pleasant drink which can easily be swallowed.

"طَعَامٌ سَيِّغٌ" (*tu-aamun sayyigh*): delightful food.

"سَاغَ النَّهَارُ" (*saaghun nahar*): the day passed easily or peacefully {T, R, M}.

The Quran says about the hell dweller:

| 14:17 | he will swallow it indeed but with difficulty | يَتَجَرَّعُهُ وَلَا يَكَادُ يُسِيغُهُ |

For details see heading (J-R-Ain).

Surah *An-Nahal* says about milk:

| 16:66 | it is very pleasant for whosoever drinks it (it is easily swallowed) | سَائِغاً لِلشَّارِبِينَ |

Sauf   سَوْفَ

"سَوْفَ" (*sauf*) is used like "سَ" (*seen*) for indication of some event taking place in the near future, soon.

Some say that "سَ" (*seen*) is used for the near future, while "سَوْفَ" (*sauf*) for distant future, but this is not a rule. Sometimes "لَ" (*laam*) comes ahead of "سَوْفَ" (*sauf*) to put stress on what is being said :

| 93:5 | And your Rabb will endow you with so much that you will become satisfied (it will be according to your wish). | وَلَسَوْفَ يُعْطِيكَ رَبُّكَ فَتَرْضَى |

S-W-Q   س و ق

"أَلسَّاقُ" (*as-saaq*): the calf (upper part) of a leg. The plural is "سُوْقٌ" (*suuq*) as in (38:33.)

"أَلسَّاقُ" (*as-saaq*) also means the trunk of a tree. Its plural is "سُوْقٌ" (*suuq*) as well, as in (48:29). But when Arabs relate something with stress or intensity, they link it with "سَاقٌ" (*saaq*) {T, R, M}. See heading (K-Sh-F) where it has been described in detail.

The Quran says:

68:42	The day that the shin will be laid bare	يَوْمَ يُكْشَفُ عَنْ سَاقٍ
75:29	And one leg will be joined with another	وَالْتَفَّتِ السَّاقُ بِالسَّاقِ
27:44	And she uncovered her legs	كَشَفَتْ عَنْ سَاقَيْهَا

In all the above, the connotation is of intensity.

"سَاقَ" (*saaqa*): to drive the animals from behind {T, R, M} as in 7:57.

"قَادَ" (*qaada*) means to pull animals from the front.

"سَائِقٌ" (*saa-iq*): one who drives (animals) {T, R, M} (50:21).

"مَسَاقٌ" (*masaaq*): place to drive animals

"ألسُّوقُ" (*as-sooq*): marketplace, or a place where people bring their animals for sale. Plural is "أسْوَاقٌ" (*aswaq*)

Nawab Siddiq Hasan Khan has written that (S-W-Q) connote intensity and gathering.

Ibn Faris says it basically means to drive.

"ألسَّاقُاس" (*as-saaq*) also means calf of leg because it supports the walker.

S-W-L   س و ل

"تَسْوِيْلٌ" (*tasweel*): to make something to be so attractive (usually something bad) that one is attracted to it {T}, {M}, {Al-ilm-ul-akhlaq}. It also means to turn some something bad to good {T, R}.

Surah Yusuf says:

| 12:18 | This is something your desires have made look good to you | بَلْ سَوَّلَتْ لَكُمْ أَنْفُسُكُمْ أَمْرًا |

Some say that it is from "سُوْلٌ" (*suul*) which means a desire which decks out something bad as good.

Surah *Muhammad* says:

| 27:25 | Their desires made it look good to them (and in this way misled them) | الشَّيْطَنُ سَوَّلَ لَهُمْ |

In surah *Taha* the *Saamri* says:

| 20:96 | in this way, my heart (mind) made it look good to me | وَكَذَالِكَ سَوَّلَتْ لِىْ نَفْسِىْ |

S-W-M   س و م

"سَوْمٌ" (*saum*) means to go out in search of something. The meaning is compound i.e. to go and search. Sometimes only the first meaning is taken, like "سَامَ الْإِبِلُ" (*sama al-ibl*) which means that camels went for grazing, or camels were let free to graze. At other times only the second meaning prevails, like "يَسُوْمُوْنَكُمْ سُوْءَ الْعَذَابِ" (*yasumoonakum su-ul azaab*) in (2:49) which means that they (bad) used to be looking for punishment to come to you (good). To treat others cruelly, to create difficulties deliberately.

"سَامَتِ الطَّيْرُ عَلَى الشَّيْءِ" (*saamatit tair alash shaiyi*): The bird kept hovering over it {T, M}.

"سَامَ فُلَاناً الْأَمْرَ" (*sama fulanal amr*): hurt him with something, made something must for him {T, M}.

"أَسَامَ الْإِبِلَ" (*asamal ibl*): left the camels to graze.

"اَلسُّوْمَةُ" (*as-suma*), "اَلسِّيمَةُ" (*as-seemah*), "اَلسِّيمَاءُ" (*as-seema-a*): sign, mark.

"سَوَّمَ الْفَرَسَ تَسْوِيْماً" (*saumul farsa tusma*): branded the horse.

"سَوَّمَ فُلَاناً" (*sawwama fulanan*): let him go free.

Surah *Aal-e-Imran* calls the *malaika* which are used to punish as "مُسَوِّمِيْنَ" (*musawwameen*) in (3:124).

The Quran says:

51:33	Those stones under Allah's law were earmarked to do the job	لِنُرْسِلَ عَلَيْهِمْ حِجَارَةً مِنْ طِيْنٍ مُسَوَّمَةً
3:14	And branded horses (horses which have been left to graze)	وَالْخَيْلِ الْمُسَوَّمَةِ
16:10	that in which you graze your cattle (the grazing fields)	وَمِنْهُ شَجَرٌ فِيْهِ تُسِيمُوْنَ
48:29	Signs (marks) on their faces	سِيمَاهُمْ فِيْ وُجُوْهِهِمْ

S-W-Y   س و ی

"اِسْتِوَاءٌ" (*istiwaa*) means for something to be perfectly balanced in itself, or for something to have its forces in the right places in the right proportion, and for it to have reached the peak of its development {T, M}.

Ibn Faris says it means solidarity and the balance between two things.

"اِسْتَوَى الرَّجُلُ" (*istawar rajul*): he reached his prime.

The Quran has described "اِسْتَوٰیٰ" (*istawa*) by saying "بَلَغَ أَشُدَّهُ" (*balagha ashud dah*) in (28:14).
Likewise in "اِسْتَوٰی عَلٰی سُوْقِهٖ" (*istawa ala suuqehi*) in (48:49) the meaning is clear i.e. for plants
to stand upright on their stems.

"اَلسَّوِیُّ" (*as-sawiyyu*) means which is safe from any exaggeration and in perfect proportion *{T, M}*.

"اَلصِّرَاطُ السَّوِیُّ" (*as-siraatus sawiyyu*) means balanced path (20:135).

"رَجُلٌ سَوِیٌّ" (*rajulun sawiyyu*): a man whose morals and manners are immaculate.

That is, he has good figure and has balanced personal;ity *{T}*.

Surah **Maryam** says:

| 19:17 | Then he assumed for her likeness a well-balanced man | فَتَمَثَّلَ لَهَا بَشَرًا سَوِیًّا |

"صِرَاطٍ مُّسْتَقِیْمٍ" (*siraatim mustaqeemin*) has come against "مُكِبًّا عَلٰی وَجْهِهٖ" (*mukibban ala wajhihi*)
in 67:22.

"سَوَّاهُ تَسْوِیَةً" (*sawwahu taswiyatah*) and "أَسْوَاهُ" (*aswah*) mean balanced him, made him balanced,
smoothed him *{T}*.

Raghib says it also means to make according to what sagacity demands e.g. meeting the
demands of human wisdom, the requirements to run human affairs as per the permanent values.

| 2:29 | made them with the right balance | فَسَوّٰىٰهُنَّ سَبْعَ سَمٰوٰتٍ |
| 82:7 | Allah is he who created and made you of the right proportion and balance as was needed | الَّذِیْ خَلَقَكَ فَسَوّٰاكَ فَعَدَلَكَ |

"اِسْتَوٰی اِلَی الشَّیْءِ" (*istaa alash shaiyi*): to arrive at some conclusion through individual thinking ,
or to intend to do something, or to be attentive to it *{T, M}*.

"اِسْتَوٰی عَلٰی" (*istawa ala*) has the connotation of overpowering and control*{R}*.

The Quran says:

| 43:13 | That you may sit firmly on their backs | لِتَسْتَوٗا اعلٰی ظُهُوْرِه |
| 23:28 | to sit tight (on an animal meant for riding, or on a boat) | اِسْتَوَیْتَ --- عَلَی الْفُلْكِ |

For Allah becoming "اِسْتَوٰیٰ" (*istawa*) on His throne, see the heading (Ain-R-Sh).

"سَوَاءٌ" (*sawa-un*) means for two things to be equal to each other.

"سَوَاءٌ زَیْدٌ وَ عَمْرُو" (*sawa-un zaidu wa um-run*): Zaid and Umru are of the same rank, are equals.

"اِسْتَوَیَا" (*istawaya*) and "تَسَاوَیَا" (*tasawiya*): for two things to be like each other, or similar.

"سَاوَیْتُ بَیْنَهُمَا مُسَاوَاةً" (*saawaitu bainahuma musaawah*): I made one equal to the other.

"سَوَاءٌ" (*sawa-un*) also means justice.

„سَوَّیْتُہُ بِہِ" (*sawwatahu behi*), or „سَوّیُ بَیْنَہُمَا" (*sawwaitu bainahuma*) means I did justice between those two.

„فَقُلْ اٰذَنْتُکُمْ عَلٰی سَوَاءٍ" (*fanbiz aihim ala sawa-inn*): I have told you about all things on equal account (21:109).

The Quran says:

| 41:10 | The earth should be available for use to all on equal basis | سَوَاءٌ لِّلسَّائِلِیْنَ |
| 20:58 | Both of us will have to follow these conditions (You and I will be in the same position) | مَکَانًا سُوًی |

Raghib says „مَکَانٌ سُوًی" (*makanun suwa*) means a point which is equidistant from both sides.

Ibn saidah writes that(*suwa*) means the place which has pointers so that people can find their way {T}.

„سُوًی" (*as-sawa-u*) means the middle or centre of a thing.

„سَوَاءَ السَّبِیْلِ" (*sawa as-sabeel*) means the middle of the road.

„سَوَاءِ الْجَحِیْمِ" (*sawa al-jaheem*): the centre of *jahanum* (hellish society) in (37:54).

„فَسَوَّاہَا" (*fasawwaha*): God levelled their cities to the ground (91:14) i.e. all their dwellings were destroyed {T}.

Surah **An-Nisa** says:

| 4:42 | If only they had been annihilated before hand | لَوْ تُسَوَّی بِہِمُ الْاَرْضُ |

Surah **Al-Kahaf** says „سَاوٰی" (*sawa*) to mean make it level (18:96)

„سِوْیٌ" (*siwyun*) and „اَلسِّوَاءُ" (*as-siwaa*) also mean 'other'.

„مَرَرْتُ بِرَجُلٍ سِوَاکَ وَسِوَائَکَ" (*marartu bi-rajulin siwaaka*): was spent time with someone other than yourself {T}.

Surah **An-Najam** (53:6) uses the term „فَاسْتَوٰی" (*fastawaya*) about the last messenger (*pbuh*) to refer to to describe his completely balanced personality which had all the characteristics of knowledge and vision which defined the upper most scales in the human self-development. The attributes of this personality are referred within the Quran as a model for us to follow through the study of the book. The selection for the revelation was based on a certain criterion by God and this is evident from the Quran. The messengers were then provided guidance as they lived their life through the revelation of the message. The final message has now been revealed to the mankind through the last messenger as the book has been completed.

S-Y-B ﺱ ﻯ ﺏ

"ﺳَﺎﺏَ" (*saab*), "ﻳَﺴِﻴْﺐُ" (*yaseeb*): he walked fast {T}.

"ﺳَﺎﺏَ ﺍﻟْﻤَﺎﺀُ" (*saabal maa-u*): the water flowed everywhere.

Ibn Faris says it means to move continuously.

"ﺳَﻴْﺐُ ﺍﻟْﻤَﺎﺀِ" (*saibul maa-i*): water started flowing.

"ﺳَﻴَّﺒْﺖُ" (*sayyabtu*): I freed that thing to go wherever it wants.

"ﺃَﻟﺴَّﺎﺋِﺒَﺔُ" (*as-sa'ibah*) is derived from this root as well.

During the period before the advent of Islam, the Arabs had a practice of letting an animal (camel, or cow etc.) go free in the name of some god. These animals could feed and drink from where ever they wanted and nobody would prevent them from doing this. The Quran says that Allah has not endorsed such superstitious practices and all these are self-made customs by your fore-fathers. The Quran directed to stop these (and others) superstitious practices (5:103).

S-Y-H ﺱ ﻯ ﺡ

"ﺳَﺎﺡَ ﺍﻟْﻤَﺎﺀُ" (*saahal maa-u*): for water to flow on the ground.

"ﺃَﻟﺴَّﻴْﺢُ" (*as-saih*): flowing water on the surface of the ground {T}.

Ibn Faris says it basically means to keep moving continuously.

"ﺃَﻟﺴِّﻴَﺎﺣَﺔُ" (*as-siyaha*): to move along the land, tourism (9:2). Some think that "ﺃَﻟْﻤَﺴِﻴْﺢُ" (*al-maseeh*) has been derived from this root. Still others say that it is not an Arabic word. See also heading (M-S-H).

"ﺃَﻟﺴَّﺎﺋِﺢُ" (*as-saa'ih*): one who travels for pleasure, tourist {T}.

The Quran has said that one of the characteristics of a Momin (believer) is that he is "ﺃَﻟﺴَّﺎﺋِﺤُﻮْﻥَ" (*as-sayihoon*) as noted in (9:112). For Momin women, it has used "ﺳَﺎﺋِﺤَﺖُ" (*sa-ihaat*) in (66:5). Although some say that it means those who fast, but *Raghib* has written that it means those who as per God's guidance go about in the land to gain knowledge, discover and learn new things and share it with others. This meaning seems more appropriate. This points to the fact that the Quran has included this character as a hallmark of the believing men and women and asked them not to remain confined in one part of the earth. This life is meant to be explored and discovered through learning and sharing for the good of mankind at large. Putting any restrictions on the free movement of men and women is directly against this value and Allah has disapproved it.

The Quran says:

| 22:46 | Have they not travelled through the earth? Do they not have understanding with which they can grasp, or ears with which to hear? It is not their eyes that are blind, but the hearts in their breasts are. | أَفَلَمْ يَسِيرُوا فِي الْأَرْضِ فَتَكُونَ لَهُمْ قُلُوبٌ يَعْقِلُونَ بِهَا أَوْ آذَانٌ يَسْمَعُونَ بِهَا فَإِنَّهَا لَا تَعْمَى الْأَبْصَارُ وَلَكِنْ تَعْمَى الْقُلُوبُ الَّتِي فِي الصُّدُورِ |

"اَلسَّاحَةُ" (*as-saahatuh*): open space, ground, open space between houses, the open space in front of a house.

"سَاحَةُ الدَّارِ" (*saahaqud daar*): terrace space (37:177)

S-Y-R   س ی ر

"اَلسَّيْرُ" (*as-sair*): to walk, to go, either in daytime or at night.

"سَرَىٰ" (*sara*) means only to walk at night (17:1, 15:65). See heading (S-R-Y).

"سَارَ الرَّجُلُ" (*saarur rajul*): the man walked.

"سَيَّرَهُ" (*sayyerah*): he made him walk, took him from one place to another.

"سِيرَةٌ" (*seerah*): way, speed, the way of walking, built, condition.

| 20:21 | we will return it to its former condition | سَنُعِيدُ هَاسِيرَتَهَا الْأُولَى |

"اَلسَّيَّارَةُ" (*as-sayyaarah*): the group which goes together, caravan (12:19).

The Quran repeatedly quotes historic facts as an evidence from the past:

| 6:11 | Move through the earth and see the fate of those who thought our laws were untrue | سِيرُوا فِي الْأَرْضِ ثُمَّ انْظُرُوا كَيْفَ كَانَ عَاقِبَةُ الْمُكَذِّبِينَ |

If those nations exist, then study their present condition and the level of development, but if these civilisations have ceased to exist, then through archaeology study their history and signs and learn lessons in the light of the permanent values revealed in the Quran.

S-Y-L   س ى ل

"سَالَ ٱلْمَاءُ" (*saalal maa-u*): the water flowed.

"أَسَالَهُ" (*a'saalah*): someone spilled it, or let it flow.

"مَاءٌ سَيْلٌ" (*maa-un seyl*): the water which flowed.

"ٱلسَّيْلُ" (*as-sayl*): abundantly flowing water, flood.

"ٱلسَّيْلَةُ" (*as-seelah*): the way or manner in which the water flows.

The Quran says:

13:17	valleys are flooded flood takes away the foam with it.	فَسَالَتْ اَوْدِيَةٌ - فَاحْتَمَل السَّيْلُ زَبَدًا
34:12	we made a copper spring flow for him	وَاَسَلْنَالَهُ عَيْنَ الْقِطْرِ
34:16	Big and fast flood	سَيْلَ الْعَرِمِ

Seen   سين

"ٱلسِّينْ" (*as-seen*) is a letter, but "يَسَ" (*yaseen*) (36:1) means O' man, or O' leader. The dictionary "طے" (tey) says that "يَسَ" (*yaseen*) means O' man.

Actually it is the abbreviation of the word "اِنْسَانْ" (*insaan*), and historically the Arabs at the time used to making abbreviations in their language.

"كَفَى بِالسَّيْفِ شَا" (*kafa bis saifi sha*) is an abbreviation for "كَفَابِالسَّيْفِ شَاهِدًا" (*kafa bis saif shahida*) which means that this is a verse by some poet.

"قُلْنَا لَهَا قِفِىْ لَنَا قَالَتْ قَافْ" (*qulna laha qifi lana qaalat qaf*). Here instead of saying "وَقَفْتُ" (*waqaftu*) it is only said "قَافْ" (*qaf*).

"ٱلسِّينْ" (*as-seen*) means pillar or support. If some link of the ceiling becomes weak then some "سِينْ" (*seen*) is put up to support it.

"سِيْنَاءُ" (*seena*) is a kind of stone.

"طُوْرِ سِينِيْنَ" (*toori seeneen*) as in (95:2), and "مِنْ طُوْرِ سَيْنَاءَ" (*min toori seena*) as in (23:20) is the mountain in Syria on which *Moosa* had gone to receive the revelation. See heading (Seen)

"ٱلسِّيْنِيْنَةُ" (*as-seeninah*) is a kind of tree.

Sh-A-M   ش أ م

"اَلْيَدُ الشُّوْمٰى" (al-yadush ashuma): left hand, as opposite of "اَلْيُمْنٰى" (al-yumna) which means right hand.

"اَلشُّوْمُ" (ash-shoom) is the opposite of "يُمْنٌ" (yumna) i.e. ill boding.

Taj-ul-Uroos says "شُوْمٌ" (shoom) means such deeds which are disliked and feared.

"قَدْشَأَمَهُمْ" (qad sha aamahum): he boded ill for them.
"رَجُلٌ مَشْءُوْمٌ" (rajulun mash-uoom): ill boded man {T}, {F}.

For the Quranic meaning of "نحوست" (nahusat), see heading (N-H-S).

The Quran (56:9) has used "اَصْحٰبُ الْمَشْءَمَةِ" (ashaab al-mash'amah), or people on the right hand, against

"اَصْحٰبُ الْمَيْمَنَةِ" (ashaab al-maymanah), or the ones on the left hand (the ill-fated ones)

Syria is called "شَأْمٌ" (sham) because it is to the left of the central (Mecca) {T}.

Sh-A-N   ش أ ن

"اَلشَّأْنُ" (ash-shaan): especially important matter, issue or condition {T}. Plural is "اَلشُّنُوْنُ" (ash-shu oon).

Raghib says it is said for matters or condition of great importance {T}.

"شَأَنَ" (shaana), "شَأَنَهُ" (shanahu): he intended it.
"شَأْنٌ" (shaan): important matters, because they are a thing of deliberate intent. It also means that he did something which he could do well.
"شَأْنُ الرَّأْسِ" (shaanur raas): the confluence of the small bones of the skull.
"الشَّأْنُ" (ash-shaan): a blood vessel which takes blood to the eye. It also means the path which brings tears to the eyes.
"شُنُوْنُ الْخَمْرِ" (shu-oonul khumr): that part of liquor which permeates the body {T}.

Ibn Faris says it basically mean to search, demand and intent.

Surah *Ar-Rahman* says:

	whatever there is in the highs and lows of the universe is dependent on the nurturer for its development	يَسْئَلُهُ مَنْ فِى السَّمٰوٰتِ وَالْاَرْضِ-
55:29		كُلَّ يَوْمٍ هُوَ فِى شَانٍ

This is the translation of the first part of the verse. In the second part "هُوَ" (*huwa*) is taken to mean Allah which is translated as Allah is in a different form of grandeur every moment. We think it is wrong, because Allah is a permanent entity which is constantly in a similar state of grandeur, though His powers may be displayed in different ways. As such, if in the second part of the verse above "هُوَ" (*huwa*) is taken to mean "مَنْ فِى السَّمٰوٰتِ وَالْأَرْضِ" (*mun fis samawati fil ard*), it be will be more appropriate. This way, the full verse would mean that everything in the universe is dependent on him for its development and the needs of things keep changing with time. In different situations their needs for development are different and Allah sustains them according to their changing needs (14:34). In this way, the development of things in the universe continues according to the law of evolution.

Sh-B-H   ش ب ه

"تَشَابَهَ" (*tashabah*) means for two things to be so similar that it becomes difficult to distinguish one from the other.

"شَبَّهَهُ اِيَّاهُ" (*shabbahu iyyahu*): he made that thing like the other thing, made them similar, look alike.

"اَلشِّبْهُ" (*ash-shibhu*), "اَلشَّبَهُ" (*ash-shabahu*), "اَلشَّبِيْهُ" (*as-shibyah*): alike, similar to.

"شُبِّهَ عَلَيْهِ الْاَمْرُ" (*shubbihah alaihil amr*): the matter became doubtful or unclear (ambiguous) for him {T}.

"تَشْبِيْهٌ" (*tashbih*): to describe a thing by referring to a similar thing.

"مُشَابَهَةٌ" (*mushabahah*): to resemble one another {T}, {M}.

The Quran says:

2:25	Similar	مُتَشَابِهاً
2:70	We can't understand what sort of cow should it be because all cows are similar to us and this throws us into doubt (or confusion)	إِنَّ الْبَقَرَ تَشَابَهَ عَلَيْنَا
2:119	their hearts are alike (are mutually agreed)	تَشَابَهَتْ قُلُوبُهُمْ
6:100	mutually alike and dissimilar	مُشْتَبِهاً وَغَيْرَ مُتَشَابِهٍ
6:144	mutually alike and dissimilar	مُتَشَابِهاً وَغَيْرَ مُتَشَابِهٍ

The noble Quran has two types of verses which are "مَحْكَمٰتٌ" (*muhkamaat*) and "مُتَشَابِهَاتٌ" (*mutashaabihaat*), as explained in 3:6. For detailed discussion on this, see heading (H-K-M) and (Th-N-Y).

Surah *An-Nisa* says in the tale about *Isa* that the Jews neither crucified Jesus nor murder him.

4:157	the truth became doubtful for them (what had actually happened)	وَلٰكِنْ شُبِّهَ لَهُمْ

For details see my book "*Shola-e-Mastoor*" in the part about Jesus.

Sh-T-T   ش ت ت

"شَتَّ" (*shattah*), "يَشُتُّهُ" (*yashuttuhu*), "شَتَّا" (*shatta*), "شَتَاتاً" (*shatata*): he separated or differentiated them, removed them.

"شَتَّ" (*shat*): he became different and unlike.

"أَمْرٌ شَتٌّ" (*amrun shat*): different matter {t, m}. The plural is "أَشْتَاتٌ" (*ashtaat*).

"جَاءُ وْا أَشْتَاتاً" (*ja'oo ashtata*): they came individually, and separately.

Surah **An-Noor** says "جَمِيْعاً أَوْ أَشْتَاتًا" (*jami'a au ashtata*) in 24:61 to mean together or separately.

Surah **Al-Lail** says:

92:4	your struggle is in different directions	إِنَّ سَعْيَكُمْ لَشَتَّى

This verse means that there is a purpose to every man's life and each has its own purpose.

There can be various aims in a man's life too, for the attainment of which he strives. The Quran says that although a man can have several purposes in life, but overall they can be classified into two categories. One is "أَعْطَى" (*aata*) as in 62:5, and the other is "بَخِلَ" (*bakhil*) as in 9:82. "أَعْطَى" (*aata*) means that a man gives from his earnings for the development of others, and "بَخِلَ" (*bakhil*) means that he keeps them only for himself. The previous case is the height of humanity and the other cause for demeaning of humanity.

Surah **Taha** says "نَبَاتٍ شَتَّى" (*nabaatin shatta*) in 20:53 to means various types of herbs and plants.

"شَتَّى" (*shatta*) is the plural of "شَتِيْتٌ" (*shateet*) which means that which has been separated, differentiated, individualised.

Sh-T-W   ش ت و

"اَلشِّتَاءُ" (*ash-shita*): winter. The Arabs divided the year into two parts. One was "شِتاء" (*shita'a*) and the other "صيف" (*saif*). Furthermore, "شِتاء" (*shita'a*) was divided in two parts of. The last three months of this period were "رَبِيْعْ" (*rabih*), and last period was "صَيْفْ" (*saif*) which had the last three months of "قَيْظْ" (*qaiz*). Since in winter the Arabs hardly went out of their homes to go and make a living, in these months there was dearth of fodder and grain. Therefore "اَلشِّتَاءُ" (*ash-shita'a*) also meant drought, and "صَاحِبُ الشَّتْوَةِ" (*saahibush shatu*) as a person whom got frustrated of winter and drought, and sought for help {T, M}.

The Quran says about the caravans of the **Quresh** tribe:

106:2	their travels in winter and summer (all year around)	رِحْلَةَ الشِّتَاءِ وَالصَّيْفِ

Sh-J-R   ش ج ر

"شَجَرٌ" (*shajar*) means anything that disperses after gathering together *{T}*.

"شَجَرَ بَيْنَهُمْ" (*shajara bainahum*) means to quarrel among themselves because of differences.

The Quran says:

2:65	mutual disagreement	فِيمَا شَجَرَ بَيْنَهُمْ

"شَاجَرَ فُلَانٌ فُلَاناً" (*shajarun fulanun fulana*): so and so differed with so and so.

"اَلشَّجَرُ" (*ash-shajar*): tree. This is the plural while singular is "شَجَرَةٌ" (*shajarah*), probably because it has one trunk but many different branches. This is the basic meaning of "شَجَرٌ" (*shajar*).

Taj-ul-Uroos says that "تَشَاجَرَ" (*tashajar*) means for the armies to engage in hand to hand combat. Since the branches of a tree are also seemingly engaged with each other, this is why a tree is called "شَجَرٌ" (*shajar*), but the former meaning is more plausible i.e. for a tree having one trunk but many branches.

Ibn Faris says it means for something to be lofty or high and its elements to be engaged with others.

In the Quran, in the tale about ***Adam***, it is said:

2:35	do not go near that tree	فَلَا تَقْرَبَا هٰذِهِ الشَّجَرَةَ

As related in the tale about ***Adam***, the tale is actually a detailed account of human story. Man prior to his civilized life used to exist on a few needs and the food supply was abundant, hence there were no differences between them. Later when humans began civilized life, they got led to clash of interest between individuals and tribes, and this led to differences among them:

10:19	mankind was one group earlier but later they began to differ among themselves	وَمَا كَانَ النَّاسُ إِلَّا أُمَّةً وَاحِدَةً فَاخْتَلَفُوا

Humanity has to reunite once again, but this unity is not possible without the guidance of revelation (2:213). This is the connotation of 2:35. That is, they were all told that their reality (beginning) was the same, therefore, they should not develop mutual differences. Later on, self-interests which teaches every individual to protect his own interests, and is a devilish intellect, led them to selfish interests and thus they became each other's enemy (2:36). As such, at this point "شَجَرٌ" (*shajar*) would mean those mutual differences among human beings which arouse because of pursuing selfish interest.

And which can be resolved only by living according to the system of the revelation (2:38), which teaches us to equally share the available sustenance.

Sh-H-H   ش ح ح

"اَلشُّحُّ" (**ash-shuh**): to comprehend he right meaning of this word we have to visualize very harsh summer time when there is very little water and lot of thirsty people. In this situation people would certainly try to get ahead of each other in order to get a drink. This situation is called "تَشَاحَحَا الْمَاءَ" (**tashaha ha ma'a**), or "تَشَاحَّاهُ" (**tashah ha hu**) {T}.

The Quranic system is that everyone should prefer the need of others over those of themselves. So "شُحِّ نَفْس" (**shuhhin nafsi**) would be opposite to this system.

Surah *Al-Hashar's* verse makes this clear when it says the following for a Momin:

59:9	A *Momin's* trait is that he may be in dire straits himself, but he prefers the needs of others to before his own	يُؤْثِرُونَ عَلَى اَنْفُسِهِمْ وَلَوْكَانَ بِهِمْ خَصَاصَةٌ
59:9	remember, those he who protect themselves from *shuh hi nafs* (selfish interests), are the ones whose crops grow well	وَمَنْ يُوقَ شُحَّ نَفْسِهِ فَأُولَئِكَ هُمُ الْمُفْلِحُونَ

In other words, a Momin is he who prefers watering the fields for someone else.

"تَشَاحَّ الْقَوْمُ" (**tashah halqum**): people tried to get ahead of each other, lest the thing remains out of their reach.
"تَشَاحَّا عَلَى الْأَمْرِ" (**tashah ha aslal amr**): they both quarrelled in the matter, and none was ready to let the matter go {T}.

Ibn Faris says it basically means to withhold something.

With this meaning "تَشَاحَّ الْقَوْمُ" (**tashah hul quum**) would not only mean that nations tried to get ahead of one another, but also that in order to get ahead, they tried to stop others from doing so. This makes the meaning of "شُحُّ" (**shuh**) clear. It is the psychological attitude to get ahead and grab something for you, and to stop others from getting to it.

According to this connotation, "اَلشُّحُّ" (**ash-shuh**) would mean the worst type of selfishness which has both greed and miserliness in it. Some say that miserliness is confined only to wealth but "شُحُّ" (**shuh**) is used for miserliness or confining all sorts of things for self-including wealth {T}. Not only for reserving for self but also for stopping them from reaching anyone else.

Raghib says it is "شُحُّ" (**shuh**) when this habit is found habitually in a person.

"اِبِلٌ شَحَائِحُ" (**iblun shaha-ih**): a camel which gives very little milk.
"زَنْدٌ شَحَاحٌ" (**zandun shuhah**): fire stones which do not spark fire.
"مَاءٌ شَحَاحٌ" (**ma-un sha-ha**): very little water {M}.

Surah *Al-Azaab* says "أَشِحَّةً" (*ashihah*) in 13:19. Singular is "شَحِيْحٌ" (*shahih*) which means to be miser and greedy.

Sh-H-M   ش ح م

"اَلشَّحْمُ" (*ash-shahm*): fat. Plural is "شُحُوْمٌ" (*shuhoom*).
"اَلشَّحْمَةُ" (*ash-shahmah*): piece of fat.
"اَلشَّحْمُ" (*ash-shahm*): a camel's hump {*T, M, R*}.

The Quran says:

6:147	fat (of cows and goats) was made forbidden for them	حَرَّمْنَا عَلَيْهِمْ شُحُوْمَهُمَا

Sh-Kh-Sd   ش خ ص

"شَخْصٌ" (*shakhs*): everything seen from afar. With reference to height it is said "شَخَصَ الْجُرْحُ" (*shaksal jurh*): the wound became high i.e. worsened, or swelled.
"شَخَص شُخُوْصًا" (*shakhas shakhusa*): he rose.
"شَخَصَ السَّهْمُ" (*shakhasas sahm*): the arrow went above the target {*T, M, R*}.

Ibn Faris says there is a sense of height in its basic meaning.

"شَخَصَ بَصَرَهُ" (*shakhasa basarah*): he kept his eyes open without blinking, or when someone's eyes remain wide open due to terror {*T, M, R*}.

The Quran says:

14:42	the eyes will be opened wide at the time of that great revolution	تَشْخَصُ فِيْهِ الْأَبْصَارُ
21:97	the deniers of this system will have their eyes wide opened	فَإِذَا هِيَ شَاخِصَةٌ أَبْصَارُ الَّذِيْنَ كَفَرُوْا

Sh-H-N   ش ح ن

"شَحَنَ السَّفِيْنَةَ" (*shahamnas safeenata*) or "يَشْحَنُهَا" (*yash-hanuha*): loaded the boat with whatever goods were to be loaded {T, R}.

The Quran says:

26:119	Laden boat	اَلْفُلْكِ الْمَشْحُوْنِ

"اَلشِّحْنَةُ" (*ash-shihnah*): the goods that are loaded on a boat.

"اَلشِّحْنَةُ" (*ash-shihna*): the fodder for animals which is collected and is enough for the animals for a day and a night.

"شَحَنَ" (*shahan*), "شَحْنًا" (*shahna*): to reply to someone harshly, to scold, and also to distance.

"اَلشِّحْنَةُ" (*ash-shihnah*): the administrator for some area appointed by the king.

"اَمْشَاحِنٌ" (*al-mushaahin*): one who is secretly opposed {T, R}.

Ibn Faris says it basically means both, to fill and to distance, but there seems to be no link between them.

Sh-D-D   ش د د

"اَلشِّدَّةُ" (*al-shiddah*): hardness.

"شَدَّ" (*shud*): he strengthened and solidified it.

"شَيْءٌ شَدِيْدٌ مُشْتَدٌّ" (*shai-un shadeedun mushtad*): very strong thing.

"اَلشَّدُّ" (*ash-shud*): to tie someone up strongly.

"اَلشِّدَّةُ" (*ash-shiddah*): bravery and solidarity of heart.

"اِنَّهُ لِحُبِّ الْخَيْرِ لَشَدِيْدٌ" (*inna lihbi alheer ash-shadeed*): brave, strong, miser (100:7)

"اَلْاَشُدُّ" (*al-ashuddu*): maturity.

"وَاشْدُدْ عَلَىٰ قُلُوْبِهِمْ" (*wushdud ala qulubhim*): seal their hearts (10:88) {T, M}.

It means maturity and guidance as in 40:67, 6:153 and 17:44.

Surah *An-Nisa* says:

4:6	oversee the wealth of orphans till they reach "age of *nikah*"	وَابْتَلُوا الْيَتَامَىٰ حَتَّىٰ إِذَا بَلَغُوا النِّكَاحَ

At other places, such as in 17:34 and 6:135 it has been said to watch over their assets till they reach maturity. This clearly shows that the age for wedding is when one grows up, not old age. This is what has been said about the orphans whose wall was about to fall down and which *Moosa's* companion had repaired without any charge.

In 22:5 it has been used for the youth of ordinary folk. In 28:14, the same has been said about *Moosa*.

In surah *Yusuf* the word "شِدَادٌ" (*shidaadun*) has been used to mean harsh years (12:48). It is the plural of "شَدِيْدٌ" (*shaded*). Its plural is also "أَشِدَّاءُ" (*ashidda'a*).

Surah *Al-Fatah* describes a Momin as:

48:29	They are very hard against the opponents	أَشِدَّاءُ عَلَى الْكُفَّارِ

"أَشَدُّ" (*ashaddu*): very hard and strong (2:74).
"اشْتَدَّ" (*ishtaddu*): to attack fiercely or to walk fast (14:18).

Sh-R-B   ش ر ب

"شَرِبَ" (*shariba*), "يَشْرَبُ" (*yashrab*): to drink, to be satiated.
"اَلشَّرَابُ" (*ash-sharaab*): anything which is swallowed and not chewed (2:259).
"اَلْمَشْرَبُ" (*al-mashrab*): water, to drink water, place to drink water, time or place of drinking, the manner in which the water is drunk {*T, M*}.
"طَعَامٌ ذُوْمَشْرَبِةٍ" (*tu-aam un zu mashrabah*): food which after eating one gets very thirsty {*Aqrab-ul-muwarid*}.

The Quran says "مَشْرَبَهُمْ" (*mashrabahum*) in 2:60 to mean a place to drink or water itself.
"شِرْبٌ" (*shirb*) as in 26:155 means the portion to drink water or turn to drink, or the time to drink.
"شُرْبٌ" (*shuurb*) as in 56:55 means to drink.
"شَارِبٌ" (*shaarib*) as in 47:15 means one who drinks water. The plural is "شَارِبُوْب" (*shaariboon*) or "شَارِ بِيْنَ" (*shaaribeen*).

Surah *Al-Baqrah* says "يَطْعَمْهُ" (*yat-umhu*) after "شَرِبَ" (*sharib*) in 2:249. Here "شَرِبَ" (*shariba*) means to drink to the fill and "طَعِمَ" (*ta-im*) means to taste the water:

The tale of *Bani Israel* relates:

2:93	the calf lay in their hearts	وَأُشْرِبُوْا فِيْ قُلُوْبِهِمُ الْعِجْلَ

But it means figuratively that the calf's sanctity had permeated their hearts, or that its love found its way to their hearts.

Sh-R-H   ش ر ح

"شَرْحٌ" (**sharh**): to open, or make clear {*T, M*}.

Raghib says it means to spread the flesh. It also means to widen and expand, as well as comprehension.

"شَرَحَ الْبَابَ" (**sharahal baab**): opened the door.
"شَرَحَ الْكَلَامَ" (**sharahal kal**): comprehended a matter {*M*}.

The Quran says that anybody whom the Quran wants to guide:

6:126	Widens his chest for Islam (makes it more accommodating)	يَشْرَحْ صَدْرَهُ لِلْإِسْلَام

This word includes the connotations of comprehension, the ability to accept the right thing, and the courage to adopt the right path. It also means conversely. About those on the wrong path is said:

6:126	It constricts his chest, narrows it	يَجْعَلْ صَدْرَهُ ضَيِّقاً حَرَجاً

The truth is that "شَرَحَ صَدْراً" (**sharah sadr**) is a very big specialty for whoever gets it, or to comprehend something without being biased on merits, to appreciate the truth wherever it is found, and to accept it. In other words, accept the truth despite all opposition and to propagate it in as much detail and clarity. To be courteous to everyone, be expansive towards enemies, and not be narrow minded anywhere. All these are included in "شَرَحَ صَدْراً" (**sharah sadr**). That is why the messengers have always prayed to God to give them this "شَرَحَ صَدْراً" (**sharah sadr**) as in 20:25, and the Messenger (*pbuh*) has been told as much that it is because of "شَرَحَ صَدْراً" (**sharah sadr**) that his difficult mission became so easy and the burden which was breaking his back was made light (94:1-2). Otherwise the opponents were acting in a way as to make one unable to breathe (15:97).

Therefore, as per the Quran, for matters to become easy "شَرَحَ صَدْراً" (**sharah sadr**) is necessary (94:1, 20:25-29). It must be every Muslim's trait (6:126). Anyone who is narrow minded or lacks in courage, has not his chest widened to accept real Islam. In 39:22, this has been likened to "شَرَحَ بِهِ صَدْراً" (**sharaha behi sadra**) which means to accept something gracefully, or to open one's heart for it (16:106).

Sh-R-D   ش ر د

"شَرَدَ الْبَعِيْرُ" (*sharadal ba-ir*): the camel ran way after stampeding.
"اَلتَّشْرِيْدُ" (*at-tashreed*): to scold, to oust, to disperse, to make someone balk and run away.

Raghib says that "شَرَدْتُ بِہ" (*sharadat behi*) means that I acted in such a way that nobody will ever follow it. They will stay away from such acts and balk at doing so.

The Quran says:

8:57	give them such a taste (teach them such a lesson) that those who are following with the same designs run away at seeing their condition (become frustrated).	فَشَرِّدْ بِہِم مَّنْ خَلْفَہُمْ

Ibn Faris says its basic meanings are to balk and to be distanced.

Sh-R-Dh-M   ش ر ذ م

"شِرْذِمَةٌ" (*shir zimah*): a small group, a group that is breakaway.
"ثِيَابٌ شَرَاذِمُ" (*si-aabun sharazim*): rags {T, R}.

The Quran says:

26:54	an insignificant group	شِرْذِمَةٌ قَلِيْلُوْنَ

Ibn Faris says that the "ذ" (*dhal*) is additional in this word, which is actually derived from "شَرَمْتُ الشَّيْءَ" (*sharamtush shaiyi*), which means to tear something to bits. A small group is called "شِرْذِمَةٌ" (*shirzimah*) because it breaks away from a bigger party.

Sh-R-R   ش ر ر

"شَرٌّ" (*sharr*) is the opposite of "خَيْرٌ" (*khair*) i.e. Goodness (99:8).

Lissan-ul-Arab says that "شَرٌّ" (*sharr*) means evil or badness i.e. "سُوْءٌ" (*suu*).
The author of ***Misbaah*** says that it means oppression and chaos.

"اَلشَّرَارُ" (*ash-sharaar*), "اَلشَّرَرُ" (*ash sharer*): the sparks that fly from a fire. Singular is "شَرَارَةٌ" (*sharaarah*) and "شَرَرَةٌ" (*shararah*) as in 77:32.
"شَرَّ الْمَاءُ مِنَ الْقِرْبَةِ" (*sharrul ma-un minal qaryah*): water continued to drip from the water bag (of leather).

"اَلشَّرُّ" (**ash-sharru**) means intensity, happiness, anger, rage, greed and morally decrepit. It also means everything that is not according to one's personality, or that which obstructs the attainment of his needs *{M}*.

Ibn Faris says its basic meanings are to scatter, to fly away hither and thither and to disburse.

Raghib says that "خَيْرٌ" (*khair*) and "شَرٌّ" (*sharr*) are ambivalent words. While a thing may be *khair* or good for someone, it could be *sharr* or bad for someone else *{R}*.

Since the word is the opposite of *khair*, the heading (Kh-Y-R) should also be consulted.

Ibn Faris says this word means for the spending of human capability and strength to be so spent, wasted, scattered away or disperse so as not to produce any positive result.

Conversely *khair* would mean for human forces to produce good or constructive results. When water flows within the boundaries of a river's banks, its result is only good, but when it overflows the banks as flood, it produces negative results. When breeze blows slowly, it is cause for pleasure, but when it turns into a storm, it can only wreak havoc. When forces gets scattered or frittered away and become unbridled, they cause *sharr*. This very thing applies to human personality. If ones strengths are diffused, ones capabilities cannot develop. If they are concentrated, then they solidify.

Surah *Al-Falaq* says:

| 113:2 | be safe from whatever that has been created | مِنْ شَرِّ مَاخَلَقَ |

This makes it clear that *sharr* is not something which has been created as such i.e, bad, as it was believed in the old days. Nothing in the universe is good or bad by itself. Everything has an evil aspect and a good aspect. One should try to avoid its evil element and adopt the good element. If water stays under the boat then it is good, but if it comes into the boat then it is not good. To utilize everything under the guidance of God's revelation is *khair*, and to use it for human destruction is *sharr*. As far as our social evils are concerned, they are the product of our wrong social system. If a society is established under the guidance of the Quran then all the social ills will disappear. This is the same situation with individualistic pain. As human knowledge progresses, the pains are lessened.

Then there are the emotional problems which trouble us. If man is brought up in the right way, he can overcome those problems as well. When a man's point of view is changed his whole perspective is changed. That is why "*Iblees*" has been told:

| 15:22 | truly, you will have no power over my missionaries | إِنَّ عِبَادِئ لَيْسَ لَكَ عَلَيْهِمْ سُلْطَنٌ |

Khair and *sharr* have appeared quite many times in Quran which reveal the truths mentioned above. Not that the Quran has not argued about good and evil in a philosophical manner, because its subject matter is not philosophy. Its purpose is to provide guidance so that **sharr** may not remain i.e. strengths do not disperse and do not produce destructive results, but consolidate in an organized way and produce constructive results. As mentioned earlier, it is the way we use things which makes them good or bad. As far as the permanent values which have been given to man through the revelation are concerned, they are inherently **khair** or good, such as justice, benevolence etc. They are opposite to bad or **sharr**: Likewise the things which have been classified by the Quran as forbidden, produce **sharr** or evil.

Sh-R-Te   ش ر ط

"ٱلشَّرَطُ" (*ash-shart*): mark or sign that is fixed by the people. Plural is "أَشْرَاطٌ" (*ash-raat*). "ٱلشُّرْطَةُ" (*ash-shurtah*): the first part of anything, or the front rank of the army which is ever ready to lay down lives. It also means the governor's brigade and body guards, because they wear signs which distinguish them {*T, R, M*}. The singular is "شُرْطِىٌّ" (*shurti*).

The Quran says about the "ٱلسَّاعَةُ" (*sa-a*) or the imminent revolution, after that the decisive time, when the opponents were so defeated that they could not recover, will come.

Sh-R-Ain   ش ر ع

"ٱلشَّرِيعَةُ" (*ash-shareeya*): the spot where people and animals come to drink, but the water must be coming from a continuous spring which never ceases and is open on the surface. Ergo no effort is needed to get to the water. If it is accumulated rain water, then it is not "شَرِيعَةٌ" (*shari'ah*) but "كَرَعٌ" (*kara'a*).
"ٱلشَّارِعُ" (*ash-shaareh*): thorough fare:
"ٱلشَّرْعُ" (*ash-shara'a*): straight path which is distinct and open.

Ibn-ul-Airaabi says that "شَرَعَ" (*shara*) means "ظَهَرَ" (*zahar*), i.e. was made evident, and disclosed.
"شُرِعَتِ الرِّمَاحُ" (*shuri-atir rimaah*): spears were straightened.
"أَشْرَعَ الشَّىْءَ" (*ashra-ash shaiyi*): he granted it loftiness.
"ٱلشِّرَاعُ" (*ash-shira'a*): a boat's sail.
"ٱلشَّرِيعَةُ" (*ash-shari'ah*): thresh hold.
"ٱلشَّرِيعَةُ" (*ash-shari'ah*), "ٱلشِّرْعَةُ" (*ash-shir'ah*): straight and distinct path {*T, M*}.

Ibn Faris says it means to open something lengthwise i.e. to open it in such a way that the whole thing can be viewed.

Surah **Ash-Shura** says:

| 34:13 | Allah has highlighted this way of life (**Deen**) for you | شَرَعَ لَكُمْ مِنَ الدِّينِ |

Surah **Al-Jaasiah** says:

| 45:18 | then we put you on an open and distinct path in the matter of **Deen** | ثُمَّ جَعَلْنَاكَ عَلَى شَرِيْعَةٍ مِنَ الْأَمْرِ |

These verses talk about **Deen** or the path fixed by God.

Surah **Al-Ma'idah** says that we have revealed this book to you with truth, which is going to prove true the truths that were revealed in prior celestial books. It is the safe keeper of those truths, so in matters that they differ decide according to Allah's laws. When the truth has come to you then do not just follow whims and fancies.

After that it is said:

| 5:48 | and for each one of you we had designated a path and manner | لِكُلٍّ جَعَلْنَا مِنْكُمْ شِرْعَةً وَّ مِنْهَاجاً |

Here **Deen** does not mean those unchanging rules which have been the same from **Nooh** to our Messenger Muhammed (**pbuh**) (42:13). Here **Deen** means those sub laws or rules which were given to earlier messengers temporarily according to their time, and which have been kept changing with the times.

The Quran says that the Jews and the Christians object saying that why does some of Quran's orders are opposed to their **Shariat**, they should realize that there are some principles of **Deen** and some sub-rules. The principles do not change but the sub rules do so according to the needs of the times. Therefore, if some of these are different from that of previous nations then it cannot be concluded that the Quran is not come from God.

This meaning is confirmed by that verse of surah **Al-Hajj** which says:

| 22:67 | We had imposed for every nation (the practical ways of implementing the deen) which they followed | لِكُلِّ أُمَّةٍ جَعَلْنَا مَنْسَكاً هُمْ نَاسِكُوْهُ فَلَايُنَازِعُنَّكَ فِى الْأَمْرِ |

There can be difference in these, but not the **Deen** itself. Therefore let them not raise an issue with you as far as the real **Deen** is concerned.

22:67 could also mean that we do not coerce anybody to follow this **Deen**, or way of life. Everyone has the right to follow the way he wants. Our job is to introduce them to this way, but it is on the humans themselves to whether follow this way or some other. This meaning is confirmed by the next verse which says:

| 5:48 | If Allah wanted, He could have made you all follow the same way of life. | وَلَوْشَاءَ اللهُ لَجَعَلَكُمْ أُمَّةً وَّاحِدَةً |

But this would have usurped your free will, and this would be against God's wishes.

We treat **Deen** and **shariat** separately or to mean different things. **Shariat** is taken to mean those sub laws which are to be followed by the followers of Islam. The Islamic system is based on principles outlined of none other than Allah. These principles and some orders given in the Quran will never be changed, but staying within their parameters, and make sub laws in their accordance, is a requirement every nation can meet. The Quranic principles will remain unchanged but these sub laws will keep changing with time. If these sub laws can be called **shariat**, then **shariat** will keep changing as per the times, but the Quranic principles will remain constant.

The characteristics of the **shariah**, i.e. the sub rules prepared by mutual consultation by the nation within the parameters of the broader and unchanging Quranic principles, should be clear, distinct and notable. It must also be a path that is the same for everybody, such as water from which everyone can drink. Which is reachable by everyone, which is continuous and should not be like accumulated rain water which depletes after a time. As such, **shariat** must not be stagnant but should be changing continuously, along with the changing requirements of time. If it is stagnant, then like standing water, it too will develop a bad smell, and will no longer be life giving.

Surah **Al-Airaaf** has used "حِيتَانُهُمْ شُرَّعًا" (*heetanuhum shurra'a*) in 7:162

"شُرَّعاً" (*sharra'a*) is the plural of "شَارِعٌ" (*shaari'*) and means a fish that raise its head high and come to the surface of the water {M}.

Ibn Faris says that it means a fish which keep its heads low. He writes that "تَشْرَبُ" (*tashrab*) means to drink water, but this could be a printing error and the right word is could be "تَسْرَبُ" (*tasrab*). But the point at which this has been used in the Quran, shows that the earlier meaning is more appropriate.

Bani Israel used Saturday as a holiday and did not work on that day. Therefore their fishermen did not catch fish on that day. When fish or other animals from continuous experience find no danger at a certain time, they openly come within human presence without fear. But the greedy among **Bani Israel** used to take advantage of this trait of the fish and used to catch it, even on the day of **Sabbath**. See details under heading (S-B-T).

Sh-R-Q   ش ر ق

"اَلشَّرْقُ" (*as-sharq*): an opening.
"شَرَقَ الشَّاةَ" (*sharaqash shah*): split the ear of the goat.
"اَلتَّشْرِيْقُ" (*at-tashreeq*): to cut the flesh or tear it apart.
"اَيَّامُ التَّشْرِيقِ" (*ayyaamush shareeq*): three days of **Eid-ul-Azha** (when animals are slaughtered as a sacrifice to Allah) *{T}*.

Ibn Faris says that this word basically means to enlighten and to open.

"شَرَقَتِ الشَّمْسُ" (*sharaqatis shams*): the sun rose.
"اَشْرَقَتِ الشَّمْسَ" (*ashraqatis shams*): the sun illuminated.
"اَيَّامُ التَّشْرِيقِ" (*ayaamuttashreeq*): days when meat is sundried.
"اَلشَّرْقُ" (*ash-sharq*) also means the sun, when it has risen or has been illuminated.
"طَلَعَتِ الشَّرْقُ" (*tala'tish asharq*) means the sun came out, "غَرَبَتِ الشَّرْقُ" (*gharabitish sharq*) is never used.
"اَلشَّرْقُ" (*ash-sharq*): for the sun to come up, the place from where the sun rises, that is, the east.
"اَلشَّارِقُ" (*ash-shaariq*): the sun, at the time when it is rising *{T, M}*.
"شَرَقَ النَّخْلُ" (*sharaqan nakhlu*) and "اَشْرَقَ" (*ashraq*): date palms became tall or white flowers bloomed on them.
"شَرِقَ الدَّمُ فِيْ عَيْنِهِ" (*shariqad damu fi ainihi*): his eye became red *{T, M}*.
"اَلْمَشْرِقَانِ" (*al-mashriqaan*): two points at which the sun rises in summer and the winter *{T, M}*.

The Quran has used "مَشْرِقٌ" (*maghrib*) as against "مَغْرِبٌ" (*mashriq*) in 2:115. Surah **Saad** has used "بِالْعَشِيِّ" (*bil ashiyyi*) against "اَلْإِشْرَاقِ" (*al-ishraaq*) in 38:18.

Surah **Ar-Rahman** says:

55:17	Sustainer of the extreme points of summer and winter from which the sun rises and sets	رَبُّ الْمَشْرِقَيْنِ وَرَبُّ الْمَغْرِبَيْنِ

The whole world is meant by it. Likewise "مَشْرِقٌ" (*mashariq*) and "مَغْرِبٌ" (*magharib*) has also been used for the east and west in 70:40 and only "مَشَارِقُ" (*mashaariq*) has also been used in 37:5.

Surah **Al-Airaaf** says that **Bani Israel** was made the owners of the lush lands in the "مَشْرِقٌ" (*mashariq*) as well as in "مَغْرِبٌ" (*magharib*) in 7:137. This means all parts of the blessed land which were situated in the east and west, or the entire area, because the Quran has further said:

2:115	the entire universe	وَلِلّٰهِ الْمَشْرِقُ وَالْمَغْرِبُ

Surah **An-Noor** says:

24:35	He is above the relationships of the *mashriq* or *maghrib* (the whole universe).	لَا شَرْقِيَّةٍ وَ لَا غَرْبِيَّةٍ

His light illuminates the entire universe. Just as God is the God of all humanity, so are His laws light (enlightenment) for all humans, and his system of sustenance is for all humans.

39:69	This is the light which at long last will illuminate the whole world	وَأَشْرَقَتِ الْأَرْضُ بِنُورِ رَبِّهَا

"اِشْرَاقٌ" (*ishraaq*) has been used by the Quran for the day to proceed in 38:18, while 15:72 has used "مَشْرِقِيْنَ" (*mushriqeen*). This means that they faced punishment when there was sunlight, or at the time of sunrise.

Sh-R-K   ش ر ک

"اَلشِّرْکُ" (*as-shirk*) basically means to stick to, to hang on to, become inter mingled.
"شَارَکْتُ فُلَانًا" (*shaaraktu fulanan*): became companion or friend.
"اِشْتَرَکَ الْأَمْرُ" (*ishtarkal amr*): the matter got confused or intermingled.
"مُشَارَکَةٌ" (*musharakah*): to be partners in something.
"فُلَانٌ شَرِيْکُ فُلَانٍ" (*fulanun sharikun fulanun*): he is his partner or companion. It also means to marry a girl and be part of her family. The plural is "شُرَکَاءُ" (*shuraka'a*).
"اَشْرَکُ" (*ash-sharaku*): the net of a hunter, the small pathways that emerge from a bigger path "أُمُّ الطَّرِيْقِ" (*ummut tareeq*), and end after going some way. Singular is "شَرَکَةٌ" (*sharakah*).

"شِرْکٌ" (*shirk*) is a particular term of the Quran. It means to consider non godly things as Allah's contemporary, or to consider that others also have the same powers as Allah. It can be understood as considering man-made laws to be equal to that of Allah's laws, or to accept the right of others where Allah's right should be acknowledged. The Quran teaches that everything in this universe has been subjugated to man and all men are equal. No one has the right to make anyone obey him. As such, there is no power higher than man on this earth, i.e. humans are all equal and everything else in the universe is subservient to them. Only one being, that is, Allah is above humans. Hence accepting anyone other than Allah to be superior to him is an insult to mankind.

This is what "شِرْکٌ" (*shirk*) is. It makes no difference to Allah's divinity. Man himself falls from the high pedestal of humanness by indulging in "شِرْکٌ" (*shirk*). This is why Quran says that "شِرْکٌ" (*shirk*) is the greatest crime or sin.

"مُشْرِکِیْنَ" (*mushrikeen*) are those who fall from man's stature, and consider others then Allah to be superior to them. "توحید" (*tauheed*) or oneness means the obedience of one Allah's laws (which He has given through the revelation and which are preserved in the Quran) and the conquering of the entire universe. Even a little digression in this is considered "شِرْکٌ" (*shirk*).

"أَشْرَکَ" (*ashrak*): he was guilty of *shirk*, or of sharing Allah's place with others.
"مُشْرِکٌ" (*mushrik*): one who commits *shirk*. The plurals are "مُشْرِکُوْنَ" (*mushrikoon*) and
"مُشْرِکِیْنَ" (*mushrikeen*).

At the time Quran was being revealed, there was one group of people which was claiming to be obedient to God's revelation. These people were called the ones with the book. They are the Jews and Christians. The other group was not obedient to any celestial law. They were followers of self-made customs and traditions. According to their own concept, they were obedient to Allah but were as well obedient to other Gods. These people were called *mushrikeen*, or those who think Allah's divinity was also shared by other forces. Since both of these groups were deniers of the Quran, they were called *kafireen*, or the deniers. These terms do differentiate between them but the fact is that even those with the book were not really obeying Allah's laws, but were actually following man made laws. They followed the religion given to them by their religious scholars. The laws of Allah in their real shape were no longer with them at all, and whatever they had was also a formality. Their deeds or acts were dependent on the writ of the scholars. As such, in deed they too were *mushrikeen*, as the Quran calls them in 2:135:

Deen of oneness is the right path, and the different sects are those small pathways which mislead man to other directions and meet a dead end after going some way. That is why the Quran has called sectarianism as *shirk* in 30:31-32, because in sects the last authorities are human beings and not Allah. In *Deen*, any argument or the last word belongs to Allah's laws only.

As such *shirk* not only means to worship idols and statues, it is also means to give man-made laws the status of Allah's law (and this is big *shirk*). In this way they divide God's *Deen* into different sects.
The Quran says that those who do this call themselves *Momin*, but in fact are *mushrik*.

12:106	most of them believe in Allah but in such a way as to be *mushriks*	وَمَا يُؤْمِنُ اَكْثَرُهُمْ بِاللّٰهِ اِلَّا وَهُمْ مُشْرِكُوْنَ

Just as Quran discusses one-ness or unity of Allah all through the book, it also discusses *shirk* and its elements. The Quran's basic teaching is to obliterate *shirk* and establish oneness.
"لَا اِلٰهَ اِلَّا اللّٰہ" (*la ilaha illal lah*) is aimed towards this meaning. That is, denial or refusal to obey any law except Allah's law and to accept Allah's law whole-heartedly and practically. Muslims and *mushrik*s are opposites of one another (3:63), and the believers on non-godly forces and the acceptors of devilish authority are "مُشْرِکِیْنَ" (*mushrikeen*) (16:99-100).

A point should be clarified here. There will be several places in the Quran where waging war against the *mushrikeen* is advocated. This does not mean that *Muslims* go to war against the world's **mushrikeen** in any case. At these places the **mushrikeen** at the time of revelation of the Quran are meant, that had created conditions that led to battles. Thus war will be waged only against those who create that sort of conditions. In other words, there will be no war against **mushrikeen** only because they are **mushrikkeen**. War will be fought only with those who create war-like conditions. For this there are detailed orders in the Quran.

But the position of the **mushrikeen** and the relationship with them which the Quran has determined will remain the same always.

Whatever has come above means that:

- To think that anyone shares the forces and authority reserved for Allah alone, is **shirk**.
- To think that one is subservient or obedient to any force or human being except Allah, or is bowed before is **shirk**.
- To accept the supremacy of anyone or anything except the Quran is **shirk,** and to follow any law excepting this law is **shirk**.
- **Deen** formulates unity within the nation of believers of Allah. To be divided into sects is **shirk**.
- One God, one code of life given by Him, its followers is one nation, one system for this nation. This is what oneness is. Anything besides it is **shirk**.

Sh-R-Y ش ر ى

"شَرَىٰ" (*shara*) means to buy as well as to sell. The word "بَيْعٌ" (*bai*) also has similar meanings. When barter system was the mode of trading, goods were exchanged in return for goods and not currency, because currency had not yet been invented. Thus buying and selling used to take place simultaneously since object were echanged instead of being paid for with money. As such, this word meant both, buying and selling {T, R, M}.

"شَرَىٰ" (*shara*) actually means to give up possession of a thing and take another thing in one's possession instead.

"اِشْتِرَاءٌ" (*ishtira'a*): giving up one way and adopting another {T}.

Raghib says "شَرَىٰ" (*shara*) is for selling and "اِشْتَرَىٰ" (*ishtaras*) is mostly used for buying.

The Quran says "يَشْرِىٰ نَفْسَهُ" (*yashri nafsehi*) in 2:208 to mean sell oneself. It says in 12:20 "وَشَرَوْهُ بِثَمَنٍ بَخْسٍ" (*washrauhu besamanin bakhs*). Here as well it means to sell away, but "اِنَّ اللهُ اشْتَرَىٰ" (*innallahash tara*) in 9:11 means to buy.

Quran says in 2:16 "أُوْلَٰئِكَ الَّذِيْنَ اشْتَرَوُا الضَّلَٰلَةَ بِالْهُدَىٰ" (*oolaikal lazeenaash tara wuz zaalatah bil hudaa*). Here it means to give up the right guidance and to be misled.

"شَرْيَانٌ" (*sharyaan*), "شَرَايِيْنُ" (*shiryaan*) is a kind of tree whose wood is used to make bows. It also means that vein of the human body which keeps throbbing. The plural is "شَرَايِيْنُ" (*sharayeen*).

"شَرَىٰ" (*shara*) also means to spread *{T, M, R}*.

Ibn Faris writes that the connotations to be agitated and to rise are also found in this word. "شَرِىَ الْبَعِيْرُ فِى سَيْرِهٖ" (*sharial ba-ir fi saa irehi*) is used for a fast walking camel *{F}*.

The Quran says:

9:111	Verily, Allah has bought (traded) their lives and wealth in return for the *jannat* (heaven)	إِنَّ اللّٰهَ اشْتَرَىٰ مِنَ الْمُؤْمِنِيْنَ اَنْفُسَهُمْ وَاَمْوَا لَهُمْ بِاَنَّ لَهُمُ الْجَنَّةَ

This is not just a concept but the very basis of an Islamic republic and state. In it, the system of the state which is formulated for establishing the laws of Allah makes a pact with the individuals. This pact trades the lives and wealth of the citizens in exchange for a heavenly society on earth. It is obvious that if a nation's life on this earth becomes heavenly, it also gets heaven after death. Details can be found in my book *Nizaam-e-Raboobiyat*.

Sh-Te-A   ش ط أ

"اَلشَّطْءُ" (*ash-shat'u*): date or the crops needles (vermiculites), new saplings.
"اَلشَّطْءُ مِنَ الشَّجَرِ" (*ash-shat uminal shajar*): branches that sprout near the root of the tree.
"شَطْأُالْوَادِىْ وَ النَّهْرِ" (*shat ul-waadi wan nahar*): the edge of the valley or bank of a river, or beach *{T, M, R}*.

The Quran says:

48:29	like the crop which sprouts needles or plant hairs	كَزَرْعٍ اَخْرَجَ شَطْأَهٗ
28:30	from the edge of this blessed valley	مِنْ شَاطِىءِ الْوَادِ الْاَيْمَنِ

Sh-Te-R   ش ط ر

"اَلشَّطْرُ" (*ash-shatr*): a part which is separated from the whole. Later it began to be used to mean one side of anything, no matter if it is not separated from it.

It also means ends, towards, environs, direction etc. It also means to be distanced.
"اَلشَّطِيْرُ" (*as-shateer*) means foreigner, stranger, also far, distant,
"مَنْزِلٌ شَطِيْرٌ" (*manzilun shateer*): a distant destination.
"اَلشَّاطِرُ" (*ash-shaatir*): a fast horse used for taking mail *{T}*.

"شَطَرَ" (*shatara*): direction

"شَطَرَهُ" (*shatrahu*): he intened to go towards him.

"اَلشَّطْرُ" (*ash-shatr*): the half of something *{M}*.

The Quran has used this word to mean direction and manner:

2:114	towards *masjid-ul-haraam*	شَطْرَ الْمَسْجِدِ الْحَرَامِ

Ibn Faris says "شَطْرٌ" (*shatr*) is said when the connotation of distance is also included.

Sh-Te-Te   ش ط ط

"شَطَّ" (*shat*), "يَشُطُّ" (*yashut*), "شَطَّ" (*shatta*): to be distanced, to surpass the limit, to be unjust.

"اَشَطَّ" (*ashatt*) is also used for the latter meaning *{T, M, R}*.

The Quran says:

38:22	decide justly between us and do not be unjust	فَاحْكُمْ بَيْنَنَا بِالْحَقِّ وَلَا تُشْطِطْ

That is, do not take us away from the truth, or be distanced from it.

Surah *Al-Kahaf* says:

18:14	we will say something that is far away and distanced from the truth.	لَقَدْ قُلْنَا إِذًا شَطَطًا

"تُشْطِطْ" (*wala tushtit*) in 38:22 means do not lean to any (one) side.

Sh-Te-N   ش ط ن

"شَطَنٌ" (*shatan*) means strong, long rope.

"بِئْرٌ شَطُونٌ" (*beirun shatun*): a deep well.

"شَطِينٌ" (*shateen*) or "شَاطِنٌ" (*shaatin*): anything that is very far.

Ar-Rumani says "شَطَّ" (*shatt*), "شَطَنَ" (*shatan*) and "بَعُدَ" (*ba'ad*) means to be distanced, and are of the same meaning *{Al-fazul Mutaradifa}*.

Ibn Faris too says it means to be distanced.

"شَطَنَ" (*shatan*) means that he went too far.

"شَطَنَ صَاحِبَهُ" (*shatana sahibahu*): he opposed his companion, and intended to oppose him, to be rebellious *{T}*.

The word "شَيْطَانٌ" (*shaitaan*) has been derived from it, which will mean:

- to be far away or distance from Allah's blessings, removed or deprived of life's happiness.
- one who gives up the right path and adopts the wrong way by being rebellious.
- an ugly snake.

"رُءُوْسُ الشَّيَاطِيْنِ" (*ru-oosush-shverseeen*): a head snake (cobra) {T}.

Ibn Faris too says these are its basic meanings.

Some think that *shaitaan* has been derived from "شَاطَ" (*shaat*) or "يَشِيْطُ" (*yasheet*).

"شَيَطَ" (*shait*) means to be incinerated, to be killed.
"شَاطَ الشَّيْءُ" (*shata- shaiyi*): the thing burned up.
"شَاطَ السَّمْنُ وَ الزَّيْتُ" (*shaatas samanu waz zait*): the oil heated up so much that it almost caught fire.
"شَيْطَانٌ" (*shaitaan*) would hence mean fiery, rebellious, and producing negative results.

In the Hebrew language, *shaitaan* means one who obstructs.

The Quran says:

| 19:44 | *shaitaan* is rebellious against Allah's orders | إِنَّ الشَّيْطَنَ كَانَ لِلرَّحْمَنِ عَصِيًّا |

Surah *Al-Qasas* says that when *moosa* hit the *qubti* a punch in anger which killed him, he said:

| 28:15 | This is a *shitaani* deed | هَذَا مِنْ عَمَلِ الشَّيْطَنِ |

Thus it is obvious that anything done when overwhelmed by emotions (in this case anger) is attributed to *shaitanat* (devilishness), as in 12:5. The leaders of the people rebellious to Allah's orders were also termed as "شَيَاطِيْنْ" (*shayateen*):

| 2:14 | when they go to their party leaders | وَإِذَا خَلَوْا إِلَى شَيٰطِيْنِهِمْ |

The wild and rebellious tribes which *Suleman* had subjugated and made to work for him are also called *shayateen* (38:37, 21:82). To mean snake, this word has been used in the tale about *Ayyub* (38:41). In the *Gharib-ul-Quran* by *Mirza Abul Fazal*, it has been mentioned with reference to *Qamoos*, that "شَيْطَانٌ" (*shaitaan*) also means the intensity of thirst.

In the tale about *Ayyub* it is said:

| 38:41 | the snake to have touched (or the overwhelming of thirst) | إِنِّى مَسَّنِى الشَّيْطَانُ |

Also 8:11 says "رِجْزَ الشَّيْطَانِ" (*rijzas shaitaan*) where the meaning could be the weakness and trouble born out of thirst.

The Quran says:

37:65	whatever sprouts from it is like a snake's head which is broad like a cobra's	طَلْعُهَا كَأَنَّهُ رُئُوسُ الشَّيَاطِينِ

Astrologers have also been called "شَيَاطِيْنُ" (*shiyateen*) in 67:5, 37:7.

Any force, according to the Quran that rebels against Allah's laws, is "شِيَاطِيْنُ" (*shaitaan*), whether it is man's own rebellious emotions or the leaders of nations which are opposed to Allah's system. Rebelliousness and mutiny is their basic characteristic, and their job is to obstruct the establishment of the right systems.

"شَيْطَانٌ" (*shaitaan*) and "طاغوت" (*taghoot*) are one and the same thing because "طاغوت" (*taghoot*) is anything that is non-godly (2:256, 4:76).

For more information about *shaitaan*, see heading (B-L-S) and (Ain-B-D).

Sh-Ain-B   ش ع ب

"اَلشَّعْبُ" (*as-shobe*): to gather together and to differentiate, to split and create a gap (it has opposite meanings):

Raghib says "اَلشَّعْبُ" (*as-shobe*) means to gather and scatter because "اَلشَّعْبُ مِنَ الْوَادِى" (*ash-shobe minal waadi*) is a place where one end meets the valley, but the other end departs from it. When viewed it seems that a thing is being parted, and when you see the other ends it seems as if the two ends are meeting together. So the word means both to gather together and to separate {R}.

Ibn Faris says that it connotes collectiveness together with parting:

"اَلشَّعْبُ" (*ash-shobe*): big tribe, the line of descendants to which all the tribes belong. The plural is "شُعُوْبٌ" (*shu-ub*) as in 49:13. Tribe is smaller than "شَعْبٌ" (*sha'ab*),
"شُعْبَةٌ" (*shoa-bah*) means branch, or a part that has broken away, the space between two horns of branches. Plural is "شُعَبٌ" (*shu-ab*) as in 77:30.
"اَلشُّعْبَةُ مِنَ الشَّجَرِ" (*ash-shobatus minal shajr*): spread out branches of tree:
"اَلشِّعْبُ" (*asheeb*): the path between two mountains.
"شَعْبَانُ" (*shaabaan*): the month before the month of fasting (*ramadaan*). In this month the Arab gypsies use to spread out in search of water and loot {T}. Hence it also means to scatter.
"شُعَيْبٌ" (*Shoaib*): is the name of a messenger who was sent towards the nation of *Madyan*. Some say that he was *Moosa's* father-in-law {M}. For more details see heading *Shoaib*.

The Quran teaches that all mankind is one nation, one universal brother hood (2:213), but in order to be recognized, they were divided into many different races and tribes. The difference is only for recognizing them just as we give different names to our sons in order to distinguish between them. It is not to signify any superiority or bias. Therefore, no nation or tribe or caste is superior to others. All humans are respectable (17:70). The standard or rank is deed and he who is better in deeds is the more respectable.

This verse has this meaning.

| 29:13 | Just as by dividing a city it is easier to recognize the parts so was the human race divided for recognition | وَجَعَلْنَاكُمْ شُعُوْباً وَّ قَبَائِلَ لِتَعَارَفُوْا - اِنَّ اَكْرَمَكُمْ عِنْدَ اللهِ اَتْقَكُمْ |

If this purpose could be served some other way then this difference would no longer be necessary. As far as ranking is concerned, it is determined by the humanism in individuals.

Sh-Ain-R   ر ع ش

"شَعْرٌ" (*sha'run*) and "شَعَرٌ" (*sha-arun*): the hair that grows on a human body. A camel's hair is called "وَبَرٌ" (*wabarun*) and a sheep's hair is called "صُوْفٌ" (*suuf*). All these three words have been used in 16:80, although *Zamkhishri* says that "شَعَرٌ" (*sha-arun*) can be used for human as well as animal hair *{T}*.

"اَلشَّعْرُ" (*ash-sheru*) and "اَلشَّعْرُ" (*ash-sha'ru*) is to comprehend something, to know, to judge, to understand the finer points, to comprehend something by using the senses. The verbs that are derived from it are "شَعَرَ" (*sha'ar*), "يُشْعُرُ" (*yush-ur*), "شَعُرَ" (*sha-ur*), "يَشْعُرُ" (*yash-ur*). Prominent from the nouns derived from it are "اَلشِّعْرُ" (*ash-sher*), "اَلشَّعْرُ" (*ash-sha'r*), "اَلشُّعُوْرُ" (*ash-shu'ur*), "اَلشِّعْرَى" (*ash-shera*).

"اَشْعَرَهُ" (*ash-ara*): told him, made him aware. Some say it means to judge or comprehend something by the senses *{T}*.

Mental philosophy and abstract concepts were not "شعور" (*shu-ur*) to the Arabs. It is an *ajami* (non arab) practice which was of a Greek concept. "شَاعِرٌ" (*shaa-ir*) or poet is called so because he comprehends meanings by using his intelligence which eludes the common man. Sometimes "شِعْرٌ" (*she'r*) means a lie and "شَاعِرٌ" (*shaa-ir*) means a liar. Since exaggeration is mostly present in poetry, it became a saying that the best poetry is the most exaggerated. Opponents used to call the Messenger (*pbuh*) as poet and the Quranic verses as poetry in these very meanings *{T}*.

"شِعَارٌ" (*shi-aar*): code words (as are used in the war).

"شِعَارُ الحَجّ" (*sha'ir-ul-hajja*): all those deeds performed in pilgrimage, which are done to express obedience to God. The place where these deeds are done is called "شَعِيْرَةٌ" (*mash'ar*). The plural is "شَعَائِرُ" (*sha-ir*).

"شِعْرَىٰ" (*shi'ra*) is the name of a star which is seen in very hot weather and is very bright.

The Quran mentions "رَبُّ الشِّعْرَىٰ" (*rabbush shera*) in 53:49.

In the period before the advent of Islam, some Arab tribes worshipped this star {*Lisan-ul-arab*}. But if "شَعْرَىٰ" (*sheyra*) is taken to have come from "شَعَرَ" (*sha'ar*) then it would mean intellect and comprehension.

The Quran has mentioned intellect, comprehension, awareness, deliberation etc. at several places. By deliberating on them with reference to context, we can glean their fine differences. But all have one thing in common, that is, those who do not utilize their intellect and consciousness, are thought to be worse than animals and the fuel for *jahannam* (hellish society).

The Quran has opposed poetry but that does not mean that prose is preferable to it and poetry not. The Quran does not bother with the style of relating. By poetry it means that emotionalism which is not concerned with facts.

In surah *Yasin*, the Quran says:

| 36:69 | We have not taught poetry to this Messenger (*pbuh*) | وَمَا عَلَّمْنٰهُ الشِّعْرَ وَمَا يَنْبَغِيْ لَهُ |

Neither is poetry befitting the revolution that a messenger brings. Then it says:

| 26:69 | Whatever We have given the messenger (*pbuh*) is historical facts and life's basic principles and rules | إِنْ هُوَ إِلَّا ذِكْرٌ وَقُرْآنٌ مُبِيْنٌ |

And their purpose is:

| 36:70 | Those who have the ability to be alive, to warn them (through the Quran about the destructive results of the wrong ways of life) | لِيُنْذِرَ مَنْ كَانَ حَيّاً |

This means that the Quran is concerned with historical facts and the solid facts of life. As against it, poetry plays with man's emotions. Therefore it has likened it to a camel which is driven hither and thither by false thirst. See heading (H-Y-M). The poets traverse the land of emotions and their entire life they say what they do not practice (26:225-226). This way of life is not befitting the stature of a messenger (and his followers). According to Biographical literary by *Coleridge*, the opposite of poetry is not anti-thesis (prose), but science. The Quran argues scientifically, and therefore poetry (which is removed from facts) can not be accepted by Allah.

Here it must be noted that like other nations (the Greeks etc.) the Arabs too believed that like astrologers and fortune tellers, poets also receive divine messages. Even today poets in the west are thought to be 'inspired' people. The Quran clearly distinguishes between human capabilities and the Revelation, so that it becomes clear that direct inspiration from God can only be had through the revelation and only messengers had this. Since messenger hood has come to an end, it can not be available to anyone anymore. It gives no credence to '*kashf*' and '*ilhaam*' (both mean inspiration) and does not think them to be direct knowledge from God. It says that this 'inspiration' is actually the product of human emotionalism or the product of psychological power which have no relevance to knowledge and fact. This is why the Quran says that a messenger is not a poet, just as he is not a fortune teller, sorcerer, or astrologer. Revelation towards a messenger is from God, and it does not have any mixture of his own wishes and thoughts (53:3-4). The Arabs did not have the term '*tasawwuf*' in their language but the specialty that *tasawwuf* was thought to be present in poets, astrologers, sorcerers etc. By rejecting these elements, the Quran has actually rejected "*tasawwuf*"too. If the Arabs were familiar with the term of '*tasawwuf*', they would also say that '*tasawwuf*' is not befitting a messenger. Instead the Quran has said that a messenger is not an astrologer or sorcerer. He gets knowledge directly from God which creates revolutionary changes in man's world, but "*tasawwuf*"cannot do all this.

The Quran says about the hypocrites:

| 2:9 | These people try to deceive God and the group of believers, but actually they are deceiving themselves, but they do not realize this | يُخٰدِعُوْنَ اللّٰهَ وَالَّذِيْنَ اٰمَنُوْا ۔ وَمَا يَخْدَعُوْنَ اِلَّا اَنْفُسَهُمْ وَمَا يَشْعُرُوْنَ |

This means that consciously they try to deceive others but sub-consciously they are deceiving themselves. Note how well this difference between conscious and subconscious conditions has been related.

Surah *Al-Ma'idah* says:

| 5:2 | Do not desecrate the symbols of God | لَا تُحِلُّوْا شَعَآئِرَ اللّٰهِ |

Islam is a way of living which takes shape in the form of a state. A state has some symbols. Respecting them means that that you respect its way of life, or state like the flag of a state. The flag is actually a piece of fabrics but it is also the symbol of a state and is therefore respected. Respecting the flag means that one respects that state. These symbols are called "شَعَائِرُ" (*sha-a'ir*), therefore "شَعَائِرُ اللّٰهِ" (*sha-a-irillah*) would mean the symbols of a state which is established to implement the Quranic laws.

The respect of those symbols would mean respecting the laws themselves. These symbols will not be worshipped, only respected, and that too while keeping in mind that in themselves these symbols hold no value. Their respect is the respect of God's laws, and that is that.

Sh-Ain-L   ش ع ل

"اَلشُّعْلَةُ" (*as-sholah*): the flames of the fire. The wood or fuel which helps to flares up a fire.

"اَلشَّعِيْلَةُ" (*as-sha'eelah*): a dwelling on fire.

"اَلْمَشْعَلُ" (*al-mash'al*): lamp.

"شَعَلَ النَّارِ فِى الْخَطَبِ" (*sha-alan naara fil yaseeb*): he lighted a fire among the wood.

"اِشْتَعَلَتِ النَّارُ" (*ishta-alatin naar*): the fire was alighted and flared up {T, R}.

Ibn Faris says it means for the edges of something to fray, or when a fire flares up.

"اِشْتَعَلَ الرَّأْسُ شَيْباً" (*ishta-alar raasu shaiba*): for white hairs to proliferate in the head and in this way the head to flare up with whiteness {M}, or for white hair to appear in the head.

In surah *Maryam*, these words have been used for *Zikria* in 19:4.

Shoaib   شعيب

One of *Ibrahim's* sons (from his third wife, *Qatura*) was named *Madyan*.

He settled in an area adjacent to north *Hijaaz* and his descendants came to be known as the nation of *Madyan*. Their period is taken to be around 2000 B.C. This nation flourished here for about four hundred years. Later *Shoaib* was sent to them. When *Moosa* had escaped from Egypt (after the murder incident) he had come to *Madyan*. The Quran says that here he lived with and old man (and his daughters) and became a shepherd. This old man married off one of his daughters to him (28:22-28, 20:40). This old man has not been described further, but some believe that it could have been *Shoaib*.

The Torah has named him *Raaweel*, and also *Yasru* as well as *Hubaab*. Historians think that *Hubaab* is indeed the name of *Shoaib*   {Torah 10:29}, while these other names are of his pseudonyms and that *Hubaab* is called *Shoaib* in the Quran. This way the time of *Shoaib* and *Moosa* is the same i.e. approximately 1700 to 2000 B.C.

The Torah says *Madyan's* brother was named *Yaqshaan*. His son *Duwaan* settled near his uncle. This was a very green area and swamped by thick forests. The Quran says that *Shoaib* was sent towards the nation of *Madyan* (29:36), and *Ashabul aika* (26:176-177). Researchers think that *Ashaabul aika* were the descendants of *Duwaan*. The Quran has talked about the nation f *Madyan* and *Ashaabul aika* as if they were people of the same tribe.

From what **Shoaib** advised them, one can glean what things they were indulging into:

7:58	My nation, be obedient to Allah, be subservient no one else is your Allah except him	يَقَوْمِ اعْبُدُوا اللهَ - مَالَكُم مِنْ إِلهٍ غَيْرُهُ
7:58	You should measure fully (not less). Do not give people less (than they bargain for). After the country has reformed, do not bring chaos in it	فَأَوْفُوا الْكَيْلَ وَالْمِيزَانَ وَلَاتَبْخَسُوا النَّاسَ أَشْيَاءَ هُمْ وَلَاتُفْسِدُوا فِي الْأَرْضِ بَعْدَ إِصْلَاحِهَا ذَلِكُم خَيْرٌ لَّكُم إِن كُنتُم مُّؤْمِنِينَ

This shows that there were serious inequities in that society for removing, which **Shoaib** had been sent to them (as a messenger).

He brought his message to them and as usual, the capitalist section or the wealthy section of society opposed him strongly and warned that if he and his people did not accept their religion, they will be banished (7:88).

Surah **Hoodh** talks about one objection they made which points to a great fact about the way of Islam as well.

They had said:

11:87	Shoaib, does your salah teach you to tell us to leave worshipping the gods that our forefathers worshipped, or that we can not spend our wealth as we wish?	قَالُوا يَا شُعَيْبُ أَصَلَاتُكَ تَأْمُرُكَ أَن نَّتْرُكَ مَا يَعْبُدُ آبَاؤُنَا أَوْ أَن نَّفْعَلَ فِي أَمْوَالِنَا مَا نَشَاءُ إِنَّكَ لَأَنتَ الْحَلِيمُ الرَّشِيدُ

This shows how deep the connection between **salah** and economics in Islam is. **Salah** means to follow the laws of Allah, and the laws of Allah also encompass economics. As such, **salah** and economics go hand in hand.

That nation did not reform and kept on its erring ways until it was totally destroyed.

Surah **Al-Airaaf** says:

7:91	earth shaking doom overtook them	فَأَخَذَتْهُمُ الرَّجْفَةُ

Surah **Hoodh** mentions "اَلصَّيْحَةُ" (**as-saihah**). It means a harsh voice or sound.

Surah **Ash-Shora** says "يَوْمِ الظُّلَّةِ" (**yaumi zullah**) in 28:189, that is, the day of the shadow. It seems that an earthquake occurred with a deadly sound and volcanoes emitted clouds of smoke. In this way that nation was destroyed.

To understand what the relationship between physical or natural calamities and Allah's punishment is, see the heading **Nooh** in my book "**Jooy-e-noor**".

Sh-Gh-F   ش ع ف

"اَلشَّغَافُ" (*as-shaghaaf*): the veil over the heart, or the membrane over the heart.
"شَغَفَهُ" (*shaghafah*): reached his heart's veil.
"شَغَفَهُ الْحُبُّ" (*shaghafahul hoob*): love reached the veil of his heart, or love penetrated the membrane of his heart and entered in it {T}. Therefore, the height of love is also called "اَلشَّغَفُ" (*as-shaghaaf*) {M}.

Surah *Yusuf* says:

| 12:30 | Yusuf's love penetrated her heart(into the depths of her heart) | قَدْ شَغَفَهَا حُبًّا |

Sh-Gh-L   ش غ ل

"اَلشُّغْلُ" (*as-shugl*), "اَلشُّغُلُ" (*as-shughul*), "اَلشَّغْلُ" (*as-shaghl*), "اَلشَّغَلُ" (*as-shaghal*): engagement, hobby, an activity which engages one's entire attention.
"اِشْتَغَلَ فِيْهِ السَّمُّ" (*ishtaghala fihis samm*): the poison penetrated into him.
"مَالٌ مَشْغُولٌ" (*misalun mashghool*): capital invested in trade or business.

Ibn Faris says this word is opposite of "فَرَاغٌ" (*faraaghun*) which means to be empty, vacant or free.

The Quran says:

| 48:11 | We are so much occupied in our wealth that we have no time to spare for other things. | شَغَلَتْنَا أَمْوَالُنَا |

Surah *Yasin* says about the dwellers of *jannah*:

| 36:55 | They will be engaged in something happily all the time (which will be very pleasing to them) | فِيْ شُغُلٍ فَكِهُوْنَ |

Sh-F-Ain   ش ف ع

"شَفْعٌ" (*shaf'un*) basically means to join one thing with another, or to join two things together, or to make them become a pair {M}.
"وَتْرٌ" (*watrun*) means to be single and "شَفْعٌ" (*shafun*) means to be part of a pair, or the former is odd and the latter even {T}.

Raghib says it means to join one thing with another similar thing or to integrate them, and "شَفَعَّ" (*shaf'ah*) means to join one while helping or commiserating with him.

"شَفَاعَةٌ" (*shuf'ah*) means to strive and mix something with one's own things and thus make them additional {T}. In *Faqahi* terms, it means to pay the price of something which is asked for, and thus make it one's own, i.e. to buy at a price {M}.

"عَيْنٌ شَافِعَةٌ" (*ainun shaafi'ah*): the eye which due to lack of focus sees double.

"نَاقَةٌ شَافِعٌ" (*naaqatun shafi'ah*): a she-camel who has one child following her, and a second in the womb.

"نَاقَةٌ شَفُوعٌ" (*naaqatun shafoo*): a she-camel which gives twice as much milk as usual {T}.

"اَلشَّفَاءِعُ" (*as-shaafi'o*): different types of grass which grows together {T}.

Ibn Faris says "اَلشَّاةُ الشَّافِعُ" (*ash-shatush shaafi'o*) is a goat with its kid with her.

The above meanings show that "شَفْعٌ" (*shaf'un*) means for one thing to be added to another and thus make two. Later "شَفَاعَةٌ" (*shaf'ah*) began to mean recommendation because in this a man stands with someone else for the recommendation or for helping him with his support {T}. It also means to pray {T}.

Ibn Faris says "شَفَعَ فَلَانٌ لِفُلَانٍ" (*shafa-a falanun lifulaan*) means a man who comes with someone and recommends whatever he wants (supports him in whatever he wants).

The Quran preaches collective life because the development of a man's capabilities takes place only in a collective life. Thus everyone of the group of ***Momineen*** is the "شَفِيعٌ" (*shafi*) of every other individual. That is, always there if he needs help and the centre of this system is the "شَفِيعٌ" (*shafi*) of everyone. He does not let anyone feel that he is alone. This companionship is his basic characteristic.

This "شَفَاعَةٌ" (*shaf'ah*) goes beyond the members of the group of ***Momineen***, because it is their duty for sustenance towards the whole of mankind. They have been told to "بِرّ" (*birr*) and "تَقْوَىٰ" (*taqwa*). That is, to co-operate with others big heartedly, according to the laws of Allah. They are told conversely to "اِثْم" (*ismun*) and "عُدْوَ" (*udwaan*), or not to co-operate in malpractices (5:2).

It has been said as:

4:85	He who helps others in good deeds also gets his share of the benefits, and so does one get equal share of punishment if he helps someone in bad deeds	مَنْ يَشْفَعْ شَفَاعَةً حَسَنَةً يَكُنْ لَهُ نَصِيبٌ مِنْهَا وَمَنْ يَشْفَعْ شَفَاعَةً سَيِّئَةً يَكُنْ لَهُ كِفْلٌ مِنْهَا

Note that in co-operation, one does help another but in *shafa-at* one is by the other's side.

We believe that on the Day of Judgment the criminal will be judged and designated to hell. Then those who are close to God i.e. the messengers, especially Messenger Muhammed (*pbuh*)) will intervene on their behalf and God will pardon them and grant them ***Jannat***. This is called ***shafa-***

at. It is evident that this belief demolishes the entire structure of **Deen** which is based on the consequential law, i.e. as you do so you reap.

| 99:7-8 | every deed produces a result and is manifested | مَنْ يَعْمَلْ مِثْقَالَ ذَرَّةٍ خَيْرًا يَرَهُ وَمَنْ يَعْمَلْ مِثْقَالَ ذَرَّةٍ شَرًّا يَرَهُ |

It seems that the concept is a product of the era of hegemony. When the friends of the oppressive rulers recommended amnesty for the criminals and criminals were pardoned, and even rewarded. This concept seems to be like the Christian belief and lends support to it that **Isa** (Jesus) will at last atone for the wrongs of people and thus they will be pardoned. But your Messenger (*pbuh*), it was said by them, can do nothing in this regard. Thus, in response to this, the concept of *shafa-at* came into existence, which says that after the criminals are so adjudged on the day of the judgment, our Messenger (*pbuh*) will go into bowing before God and will himself not go into *jannat* until God pardons all.

This did answer the Christians but demolished the entire structure of the **Deen** and the Muslim nation which believed this, went into ignominy. There is no such certification from the Quran, nor can there be any leeway for this. It has been said clearly:

| 2:48 | nobody can do anything for anybody, nor will anybody *sahafa-at* be accepted nor will any body let off after paying any compensation, and nobody will be able to help the criminal | وَاتَّقُواْ يَوْمًا لاَّتَجْزِى نَفْسٌ عَن نَّفْسٍ شَيْئاً وَلاَيُقْبَلُ مِنْهَا شَفَاعَةٌ وَلاَيُؤْخَذُ مِنْهَا عَدْلٌ وَلاَهُمْ يُنصَرُون |

To support the concept of *shafa-at*, such verses are presented as:

| 2:225 | who can recommend or plead without his permission | مَن ذَاالَّذِى يَشْفَعُ عِنْدَهُ إِلَّا بِإِذْنَهِ |

It is concluded from this that with God's permission, recommendations can be made and the Messenger Muhammed (*pbuh*) will recommend his followers with God's permission indeed.

But to draw these conclusions from this verse is wrong because it goes against the natural law, which runs throughout the Quran. So if the concept of recommendation or *shafa-at* is also in the same Quran then it will mean (God forbid) that the Quran has contradictions.

The verse before the one above says:

| 2:224 | O believers, whatever Allah has given you, keep it open (available) for the sustenance of the needy, before such a time comes when neither can one pay for one's crimes and enter the *jannat*, nor will the friendship of any elder be of any advantage, and neither will anybody's *shafa-at*. | لَا بَيْعٌ فِيهِ وَلَا خُلَّةٌ وَلَا شَفَاعَةٌ |

In the next verse, if the meaning is taken to mean that Allah will accept (any) recommendation, then there will be an open contradiction, which there is none of in the Quran.

That raises the question of what this verse really mean? According to the law of nature, every deed's results begin to be formulated right from when the deed starts. In order to make one understand the truth about reward and punishment, the Quran has drawn a picture before us as if people are presented in court for judgment. There is a judge, the accused, the prosecutor, witnesses, and policemen etc. The Quran has used these as allegories. At one place in the Quran it is said that the one who is being questioned will stand alone in the witness stand.

6:95	you will be presented alone before us…..there will be nobody with you (to help you or recommend you or plead for you)	وَلَقَدْ جِئْتُمُونَا فُرَادَى-- وَمَا نَرَى مَعَكُم شُفَعَاءَ كُم

And "the policeman" (the *malaikah*) will push you from behind and bring you before Us:

50:21	everyone will have one to drive him forward: there will also be witnesses	وَجَاءَتْ كُلُّ نَفْسٍ مَعَهَا سَائِقٌ-- وَشَهِيْدٌ

These witnesses will not stand with the criminal on their own. Whoever, those who will be called, will come forward and will be allowed to present evidence. These are the "شَفِيْعٌ" (*shafi-un*) which have been mentioned in the Quran.

2:255	Who can stand with anyone (support anyone) without Allah's permission	مَنْ ذَا الَّذِى يَشْفَعُ عِنْدَهُ إِلَّا بِإِذْنِهِ

These witnesses will also be messengers who are said to be:

5:109	The day when Allah will gather the messengers together and ask them as to the response they had received from the people?	يَوْمَ يَجْمَعُ اللهُ الرُّسُلَ فَيَقُوْلُ مَاذَا أُجِبْتُمْ

And the *Mala-ikah* too will be called to appear:

78:38	The day when the *arruh* and the *malaikah* will be standing in rows and only he will speak who has been granted permission to do so	يَوْمَ يَقُوْمُ الرُّوْحُ وَلْمَلَٰءِكَةُ صَفًّا لَّا يَتَكَلَّمُوْنَ إِلَّا مَنْ اَذِنَ لَهُ الرَّحْمَٰنُ وَقَالَ صَوَابًا

Therefore in these verses the meaning of *shafa-at* seems to be to give evidence. To present the right evidence for somebody is a very great help too. The Quran has explained this itself:

43:86	Those other than Allah whom they call upon have no power for *shafa-at*. Only who gives true evidence has the power to give *shafa-at*.	وَلَا يَمْلِكُ الَّذِيْنَ يَدْعُوْنَ مِنْ دُوْنِهِ الشَّفَاعَةَ إِلَّا مَنْ شَهِدَ بِالْحَقِّ

That is, *shafa-at* means evidence. This is why the messenger (*pbuh*) has been called *shaheed*, or witness (16:89), but never *shafi*. About the concept of *shafa-at* which others have, the Quran has said:

74:47	The *shafa-at* or recommendations or pleadings of their recommenders will do no good	فَمَا تَنفَعُهُمْ شَفَاعَةُ الشَّافِعِينَ

This because Allah's law says that:

6:165	No man can lift another's burden	لَا تَزِرُ وَازِرَةٌ وِزْرَ أُخْرَىٰ

Jannat is begotten only in exchange for good deeds:

7:43	to acquire the *jannat* (heaven) through recommendation is born in nations which have lost the will or power to do good deeds	تِلْكُمُ الْجَنَّةُ أُورِ ثْتُمُوهَا بِمَا كُنتُمْ تَعْمَلُونَ

This sort of concept prevailed among the Jews when they were at the lowest ebb. They used to say that they will not stay in *jahannam* or hell. They shall perhaps stay there for a few days (after which they will be rescued by their holy people). At this the Quran says to ask them if there is some pact about this between Allah and them. Then it says to tell them that such beliefs are false. Allah's law dictates that anyone who commits bad acts will be destroyed, and he who has faith and does good deeds will be among the heirs to the *jannat,* or heaven (2:81-82).

It is obvious from these explanations that in this world *shafa-at* would mean to be with someone to help him. If the work assisted is good, then he too will be equally rewarded, if not then he will also be punished. In the life hereafter the concept of *shafa-at* is as if a witness chooses to give true evidence. It is an allegorical statement.

For the criminals to go scot free on somebody's recommendation or *sifarish* or for someone to get what one does not deserve as such, is against the basic teachings of the Quran. Therefore, this is not the right meaning of *shafa-at*. Wherever it appears in the Quran, reference must be made to the context to determine its true meaning.

Surah *Al-Fajar* says "وَالشَّفْعِ وَالْوَتْرِ" (*wush shaf-ee wal watr*) in 89:3. It either means the stars which move together or which exist together or which move separately or exist separately. That is, the stars which seem to be together and the stars which seem separate.

Sh-F-Q ش ف ق

"الشَّفَق" (*ash-shafaq*): the redness that remains in the sky from sunset till darkness falls. "شَفَقٌ" (*shafaq*) also means edge *{T}*.

Raghib says that "شَفَق" (*shafaq*) means daylight at time of sunset intermingling with the darkness of the night.

The Quran says:

84:17	But no, I sweat by the dwelling glow	فَلَا أُقْسِمُ بِالشَّفَقِ

Ibn Faris says its basic meaning is weakness in something.

"الشَّفَقُ" (*ash-shafaq*) or "الشَّفَقَةُ" (*ash-shafaqahk*): to have apprehensions about the welfare of someone.

"اَشْفَقَ مِنْهُ" (*ash-faqa minhu*): feared it, was bothered.

"اَشْفَقَ عَلَيْهِ" (*ash-faqa alaih*): looked after him out of love (or sympathy) and feared lest anything bad befalls him *{T}*. Such a well-wisher is called "مُشْفِقٌ" (*mushfiq*) or "شَفِيقٌ" (*shafiq*).

"الشَّفَقَةُ" (*al-shafaqah*) also means weakness, since fear is also weakness.

"ثَوْبٌ شَفَقٌ" (*saubun shafaq*): fragile cloth *{M}*.

Since this word signifies a weakness, it is not used for God.

Raghib says that when this word is followed by "مِنْ" (*min*), the element of fear is dominant, and when it is followed by "فِی" (*fi*), the element of love, sympathy and well-wishing is more prominent. *But Taj-ul-Uros* has used "عَلَی" (*ala*) instead of "فِی" (*fi*), and this seems more appropriate.

Surah *Al-Azaab* says:

33:72	they feared it (they were afraid of misappropriating what was trusted to them)	اَشْفَقْنَ مِنْهَا

Surah *Al-Ambia* says:

21:28	They are afraid (of the destructive results of going against the laws) and fear the results	وَهُمْ مِنْ خَشْيَتِهِ مُشْفِقُونَ

In other words, they think it would be in their own interests to abide by these laws.

Sh-F-H   ش ف ه

"شَفَهَ" (*shafahu*), "عَنْهُ شَفْهاً" (*unhu shafha*): he put him to work that made him oblivious of other things.

"شَفَهَ" (*shafahu*): struck his lips.

"شَافَهَهُ" (*shafahu*): talked to him in person.

"شَفَةٌ" (*shafatun*) means a single lip. The pair of lips is called "شَفَتَانِ" (*shaftaani*) as well as "شَفَتَيْنِ" (*shaftaini*). The plural is "شِفَاهٌ" (*shifah*) and "شَفَوَاتٌ" (*shafawaat*) {T}.

Some scholars think that "شَفَتَيْنِ" (*shafah*) is actually from "شَفْوٌ" (*shafwun*). That is why we have listed it under (Sh-F-W), which may as well be referred to there.

Sh-F-W   ش ف و

"اَلشَّفَا" (*ash-shafa*): edge, the limit of everything.

Ibn Faris says that this word may have been culled from "شَفَا" (*shafa*), which is from the root (Sh-F-W), and it is also possible that "ف" (*fa*) has been exchanged with "ب" (*ba*), that is, "شبا" (*shiba*) has changed into "شفا" (*shifa*).

When the sun is setting, they say "مَابَقِيَ مِنْهُ إِلاَّ شَفَى" (*ma baqiya minhu illa shafa*). That is, very small part of it remains {M}. This has the connotation of being near death.

"شَفَتِ الشَّمْسُ" (*shafatish shams*): the sun is about to set {T}.

The Quran says:

| 9:189 | at the edge of the beach | عَلَى شَفَا جُرُفٍ |
| 3:102 | at the edge of the hole | شَفَا حُفْرَةٍ |

"اَلشَّفَةُ" (*as-shafah*) means lip. The plural is "شَفَوَاتٌ" (*shafawat*) and "شِفَاهٌ" (*shifah*). From this it became "مُشَافَهَةٌ" (*mushafah*) i.e. to talk person to person {T}.

The Quran says:

| 90:9 | two lips | شَفَتَيْنِ |

Sh-F-Y   ش ف ى

"شَفَهَ" (*shafah*), "يَشْفِيهِ" (*bi-shafihi*), "شِفَاءً" (*shifa-a*): gave him health (freedom from sickness). "اَلشَّفَاءُ" (*ash-shifa-o*) means to recover from an illness. Later it began to be used for medication and treatment too *{M}*.

The noble Quran has used this word as against sickness:

| 26:80 | when i fall sick, it is he who gives me health | وَإِذَا مَرِضْتُ فَهُوَ يَشْفِينِ |

It also to mean medicine, as in:

| 16:69 | it has recovering power for people (cure) | فِيهِ شِفَاءٌ لِلنَّاسِ |

Ibn Faris says that this root basically means to come to the edge and peep over it. He thinks that the cure overpowers the disease and that is why "شَفَاء" (*shiffaa*) is called so.

Sh-Q-Q   ش ق ق

"شَقَّهُ" (*shaqqah*), "يَشُقُّهُ" (*yash-uqquhu*), "شِقَّا" (*shaqqa*): to tear something up, to make a hole in it.
"اِنْشَقَّ" (*inshaqq*): was torn.
"الشَّقُّ" (*ash-shaqq*): the morning *{T}*.
"اِنْشَقَّتِ الْعَصَا" (*inshaqqatil asa*): the elements shattered, or mutual differences cropped up.
"شَقَّ عَصَا الْمُسْلِمِينَ" (*shaqqa asal muslimeen*): it created fissiparous tendencies among the group of ***momineen***.
"اَلْمُشَاقَّةُ" (*al-mushaqqah*), "اَلشَّقَاقُ" (*ash shiqaaq*): opposition, enmity, mutual differences *{T}*.
"شِقٌّ" (*shiqq*): hard labor, problem, to become tired after exerting to the full, tiredness.
"شَقَّ عَلَيْهِ الْأَمْرُ" (*shaqqa ilaihil amr*): the matter weighed heavy on him.
"شَقَّ عَلَيْهِ" (*shaqqa alaih*): put him in trouble *{T}*.
"شَقَّ عَلَيْهِ" (*ash-shuqqah*): the opposition of distance, distant journey *{T}* as in (9:42), or the destination which is reached with difficulty.

The Quran says "شَقٌّ" (*shiqq*) to mean splitting of stones and for springs to spring forth, as break of dawn (2:74). Surah ***Saad*** has used "شِقَاقٍ" (*shiqaaaq*) to mean opposition, and it has been used in 59:4 for opposition and differences.

Surah ***Al-Abas*** says:

| 80:26 | Then we split the earth in a physical way | ثُمَّ شَقَقْنَا الْأَرْضَ شَقًّا |

Surah **Al-Qasas** says:

| 28:27 | I do not want to be harsh with you or to give you a difficult responsibility | وَمَاأُرِيْدُ اَنْ اَشُقَّ عَلَيْكَ |

Surah **An-Nahal** uses "شِقٌّ" (*shiqq*) to mean hard work (16:7).

"شَاقَّ" (*shaqq*) means to oppose intensity and constriction, deprivation and hopelessness. It means to adopt a different way, create a difference, to part with each other (4:35).

Surah **Al-Qamar** says:

| 54:1 | the time of revolution neared and **al-qamar** is about to split | إِقْتَرَبَتِ الساعَةُ وَانْشَقَّ الْقَمَرُ |

For its meaning, see heading (Q-M-R).

Sh-Q-W(Y)   ش ق و (ى)

"اَلشَّقَاءُ" (*ash-shaqa'a*): intensity and constriction, deprivation.
"شَقِيَ" (*shaqiya*), "يَشْقَى" (*yash-qa*), "شَقَاوَةً" (*shaqawah*), "شِقُوَةً" (*shiqwah*): to be ill fated, have bad luck.
"شَقَاوَةٌ" (*shiqawah*) is the opposite of "سعادة" (*saa-dat*) or faithfulness, and since "شَقَاوَةٌ" (*siqawat*) has tiredness and trouble in it, that is why it also means tiredness and trouble or bother.

Ibn Faris says its basic meanings are intensity and to bear hard labor. It is also the opposite of facility, softness, faithfulness and good luck.

"اَلْمُشَاقَاةُ" (*al-mushaqah*): to bear trouble, to bear harshness.
"اَلشَّاقِى مِنَ الْجِبَالِ" (*ash-shaaqi minal jibal*): a mountain which juts out and overhangs, and which is very difficult to climb.

The Quran has said "شَقِيٌّ وَسَعِيْدٌ" (*shiqiyyun wa saeed*) in 11:105. Here "شَقِيٌّ" (*shiqiyyun*) is the opposite of "سعادة" (*saa-dat*).
Zikriyah says in surah **Maryam**:

| 19:4 | And I have not been deprived and hopeless in your supplication, my Sustainer. | وَلَمْ اَكُنْ بِدُ عَاءِكَ رَبِّ شَقِيًّا |

Surah **Taha** says:

| 20:2 | We have not revealed the Quran to you for depriving you of life's blessings and to throw you in trouble | مَا اَنْزَلْنَا عَلَيْكَ الْقُرْاَنَ لِتَشْقَى |

This "تَشْقَى" (*tash-qa*) has been explained a little further on where **Adam** has been told that life's necessities are plenty in this heaven (20:118), but if you listen to **Iblees**, he will cause your exit from *jannat* (20:117). The result will be that you will be deprived of all the blessings and be involved in great difficulties.

Surah **Al-Lail** says he who is "اَشْقَى" (*ash-qa*), goes to *jahannam* of great ill fate (92:15). In other words, he will be deprived of happiness, but against this has come "اَتْقَى" (*atqa*) in 92:17. Therefore "اَشْقَى" (*ash-qa*) may also mean rebellious.

Surah **Maryam** says:

| 19:32 | Insolent unblessed | جَبَّاراً شَقِيَّاً |

Surah **Al-Mominoon** says about those in *jahannum* who will say:

| 26:106 | bad luck befell us | غَلَبَتْ عَلَيْنَا شِقْوَتُنَا |

Remember that this ill fate is the result of man's own bad deeds. Good luck or bad luck is not man's destiny.

Sh-K-R   ش ک ر

"اَلشُّكْرُ" (*ash-shukr*): to fill up and to express *{M}*.

Ibn Faris says it has different meanings, one of which is to be filled and abundant.

"شَكِرَتِ النَّاقَةُ" (*shakaratin naaqah*): the camel's teats became full of milk.
"اَلْمِشْكَارُ" (*al-mishkaar*): an animal which may have little fodder but still its teats are full of milk.
"ضَرَّةٌ شَكْرَى" (*zarratun shakra*): teat full of milk.
"اَلشَّكِرَةُ" (*as-shikrah*): a female camel whose teats are full of milk *{T}*.
"شَكِرَتِ الشَّجَرَةُ" (*shaakiraatish shajarah*): branches sprouted on the tree trunk.
"اِشْتَكَرَتِ السَّمَاءُ" (*ishtakaratis sama-u*): it rained very hard.
"اِشْتَكَرَ الْحَرُّوَالْبَرْدُ" (*ishtakaral harru wal bard*): the winter and summer were fulsome.
"شَكَرَ فُلَانٌ" (*shakara fulan*): that man was greatly benevolent and gave a lot to people.

Taj-ul-Uroos says that "شُكْرٌ" (*shukr*) means obedience and the performance of must to do duties, as also the expression of thankfulness, God's full response to this "شُكْرٌ" (*shukr*), or to give much in return for little.

For example if a person helps someone else a little, even at his own cost, then this little sacrifice on his part will be considered greater than giving something to someone that is more than one's necessities. This is what it means by giving ample return for little benevolence.

If we keep the basic meaning of "شُکْر" (*shukr*) in mind, then we can easily comprehend the meaning of "سعی مشکور" (*sa-ee mushkoor*) or that effort which fetches good results. That is, more than the effort warranted, so complete like the teats of a goat which are full of milk.

"شَاکِر" (*shaakir*) is one who makes one's effort fetch full results, and also the one whose efforts fetch such complete results. The word "شُکْر" (*shukr*) has been used for the efforts going waste, against "خُسْر" (*khusr*) in 39:65-66. A man's efforts which produce good results is also called "شَکُوْر" (*shakoor*) in 14:5.

"شَکُوْر" (*shakoor*) has more exaggeration than "شَاکِر" (*shaakir*).

Since "شُکْر" (*shukr*) means to highlight or make evident. That is why "کُفْر" (*kufr*) or denial has been used against it in 14:7. It is meant for covering up or bury.

Surah *Al-Baqrah* says:

2:154	Always keep God given blessings uncovered or available so that the human race can benefit from it (do not hide them or cover them)	وَاشْکُرُوْ اِلیْ وَلَا تَکْفُرُوْنِ

Among the first of God given gifts are the capabilities which a human being possesses. The development of capabilities and them to be evident is also "شُکْر" (*shukr*), and this thing is produced by doing good deeds. Therefore, good deeds become the cause of "شُکْر" (*shukr*) of God's benevolence.

Surah *Al-Ahqaaf* relates this very fact when it is said that you should ask for:

46:15	O my nurturer, give me the capability of thanking you (for committing *shukr*) for your benevolence. (I may do such deeds as to develop them)	رَبِّ اَوْزِعْنِیْ اَنْ اَشْکُرَ نِعْمَتَکَ--- وَاَنْ اَعْمَلَ صَالِحاً

At another place, it is said:

31:12	He who covers up or hides Allah's benevolence (hides or does not disclose), does Allah no harm, but he who uncovers them develops his own capabilities (he harms himself). Allah in his personality needs no thanks (He is not dependent on you)	مَنْ یَّشْکُرْ فَاِنَّمَا یَشْکُرُ لِنَفْسِہِ وَمَنْ کَفَرَ فَاِنَّ اللّٰہَ غَنِیٌّ حَمِیْدٌ

To uncover God's gifts or to disclose them means to utilize them as God has ordered. That is, they should be kept available for humanity at large. This fact has been highlighted with the help of an example. A dwelling was plentiful, but they started covering God's benefits (16:112), and the result was that they started facing punishment of hunger and fear. Allah's messenger was sent to them but they rejected him too. Then the **momineen** have been warned not to do likewise.

| 16:112 | Keep Allah's gifts uncovered | فَكَفَرَتْ بِأَنْعُمِ اللهِ |
| 16:114 | If you follow his laws only, then obviously you will keep open whatever Allah has given you | وَاشْكُرُوْا نِعْمَتَ اللهِ |

Denial of those gifts means to hide them (according to yours self made laws):

| 16:114 | For what they used to do on their own | إِنْ كُنْتُمْ إِيَّاهُ تَعْبُدُوْنَ |

This has been made further clear in surah **Al-Airaaf** that "شَاكِرِيْنَ" (*shaakireen*) are those who do not follow the way of the **Iblees** and do not fall into his trap (7:17).

Surah **Al-Baqrah** says about **Bani Israel**:

| 2:56 | We gave your life after death so that you could be "thankful" | ثُمَّ بَعَثْنٰكُمْ مِنْ بَعْدِ مَوْتِكُمْ لَعَلَّكُمْ تَشْكُرُوْنَ |

This makes it clear that nations regain life or are resurrected after death so that they can develop their capabilities. Those nations which do not do so are not 'alive', nor can they exist.

For efforts to be thankful or "مشكور" (*mash-koor*) means for them to produce full results, that is, they produce the fullest results and become fully fruitful.

To be thankful means to uncover the blessings or gifts that God has given:
- A) That he makes his latent capabilities fully evident or develops them.
- B) Keep the means of development spread in the universe open for the benefit of mankind and not hide them for himself.

This is only possible when Allah's laws are fully followed. This will be 'thankfulness' of man. "شُكْرٌ" (*shukr*) from Allah's side means that He makes man's efforts produce full results, and it is a particularity of Allah's law that if followed, they produce the fullest possible results.

Surah **Adh-dhahar** says:

| 76:3 | We have shown the right path through revelation. Now it is upot him (man) to adopt it, or some other way | إِنَّا هَدَيْنٰهُ السَّبِيْلَ إِمَّا شَاكِراً وَإِمَّا كَفُوْراً |

Here "شُكْرٌ" (*shukr*) means to treat the path as a great gift and adopt it.

Surah **An-Nisa** says:

| 4:147 | If you value this guidance then believe (have faith or **eeman**) | اِنْ شَکَرْتُمْ وَاٰمَنْتُمْ |

34:13 has used "شَکُوْرٌ" (**shakur**) or "شَاکِرٌ" (**shaakir**) which means to benefit from the gift you have been given.

Surah **Saba** says:

| 34:13 | O descendants of **Dawud**. Act (according to our laws) by benefiting from the gifts given | اِعْمَلُوْا اٰلَ داؤد شُکْرًا |

That is, utilize the multiple benefits and avail of the benefits in the universe and thus be thankful for them.

Ibn Faris says it also basically means to be content with little means.

"فَرَسٌ شَکُوْرًا" (**farasin shakoor**) means a horse which is fat, so even a little fodder is enough for it. When one's capabilities are developed, then even few external supports are sufficient to produce profuse results.

Sh-K-S   ش ک س

"شَکَاسَةُ الْاَخْلَاق" (**shakaasatul akhlaaq**): to be impolite or discourteous.
"شَاکَسَہ" (**shakasahu**): he treated him shabbily, harshly.
"اَللَّیْلُ وَالنَّھَارُ یَتَشَاکَسَان" (**al-lailu wan nahaaru yatash-a kasan**): day and night are opposed to each other.
"تَشَاکَسُوْا" (**tash-akasu**): they opposed each other, or they acted narrowly in their dealings.

The Quran says:

| 39:29 | Partners in business who keep quarrelling as they are bad tempered and narrow minded in their dealings | شُرَکَاءُ مُتَشَاکِسُوْنَ |

Sh-K-K   ش ک ک ک

"اَلشَّکُّ" (*as-shak*): it is the opposite of belief.

Raghib says that when two quite different things begin to look similar to a person, then this condition is called "شَکٌّ" (*shak*).

Muheet says with reference to ***Keys*** that just as knowledge begins with belief, "شَکٌّ" (*shak*) begins with doubt. See heading (R-Y-B). This is why it is said "شَکٌّ مُرِیْبٌ" (*shakkun mureebun*) but not "رَیْبٌ مُشَکِّکٌ" (*raibun mushakkik*)

Ibn Faris says it basically means for one thing to diffuse in another.

As such, "شَکَکْتُہ بِالرُّمْح" (*shakatuhu bir rumh*) means that I pierced the spear into his body. "شَکٌّ" (*shakk*) is like that one thing which seems to have entered another, and nothing is certain (doubt).

Raghib says that "شَکَکْتُ الشَّیْءَ" (*shakaktu shaiyi*) means that a thing which has a hole through it. A thing like that cannot be depended upon to be reliable. There is a thought that it is from a proverb which says for the arm to stick to the side. This word would therefore mean for two opposing things to enter into one another so that the distinction is no longer clear {R}.

"شَکُّوا بُیُوْتَہُمْ" (*shakku buyutahum*) means that they built all their homes to be similar {T, R}.

These examples make the meaning of "شَکٌّ" (*shak*) clear. That is, for two opposite things to look similar and not be clearly distinguishable from one another. Hence it also means to be hard for a person to reach the right conclusion about something.

About the matter of crucifixion of Christ, it has been said that:

4:157	Indeed, those who differ in it, are surely in doubt about it	إِنَّ الَّذِیْنَ اخْتَلَفُوْا فِیْہِ لَفِیْ شَکٍّ مِنْہُ

This makes the meaning of "شَکٌّ" (*shak*) clear, i.e. there was so much resemblance between ***Isa*** (Jesus) and the man they had arrested, that it was difficult to differentiate one from the other. Therefore, they are still in doubt as to what had actually happened. Details can be found in my book "***Shola-e-mastoor***" in the subject of ***Isa***.

Sh-K-L ش ك ل

"اَلشِّكْل" (*ash-shikl*), "اَلشَّكَل" (*ash-shakal*), "اَلشُّكَل" (*ash-shukal*): similar, alike.
"فِىْ فُلَانٍ شَكْلٌ مِنْ اَبِيْهِ" (*fi fulanun shaklin min abih*): that man resembles his father very much {T}.

Surah **Saad** says:

| 38:58 | Various punishments of the same kind | وَاٰخَرُ مِنْ شَكْلِهٖ اَزْوَاجٌ |

The plural is "اَشْكَالٌ" (*ash-kaal*) which means different matters and needs.
"شَكَلَ الْاَمْرُ" (*shakalal amr*): the matter became complex and dubious {T}.
"اَلشِّكَالُ" (*ash-shikaal*): the rope with which an animal's fore and hind legs are secured so that it can only take measured steps as the rope's leeway allows.
"شَكَلَ الدَّابَّةَ" (*shakalad dabbah*): he bound the legs of the animal with "شِكَالٌ" (*shikaal*)

Ibn Faris says that most meanings of this word are derived from similarity and likeness. He says "شَكَلْتُ الدَّابَّةَ" (*shakalad dabbah*) is so said because one leg of the animal is secured to a similar leg.

"اَلشِّكَالُ فِى الرَّحْلِ" (*ash-shikaalun fir rahl*): the rope with which the camel's seat ends are tied {T}.
"شَاكِلٌ" (*shaakilun*) has come from it, the feminine of which is "شَاكِلَةٌ" (*shaakilah*) as in 17:84, that is which binds.

Surah **Bani Israel** says:

| 17:84 | Say that each works on its manner | قُلْ كُلٌّ يَعْمَلُ عَلٰى شَاكِلَتِهٖ |

To comprehend the meaning of this verse, we first have to understand that everything has potential. A mango seed has the capability to grow into a mango tree and bear sweet fruit. But although the cactus seed also turns into a tree, it bears only needles. The inner destiny of a mango seed is the fruit of the mango, while that of the cactus tree are the thorns.

Like the animal which cannot go beyond or above its "شَاكِلَةٌ" (*shaakilah*), so can nothing go beyond its inherent limits. Nothing can go beyond the limit nature has proscribed for it. As far as man is concerned, he too has limited "شَاكِلَةٌ" (*shaakila*), but death is not his limit. He can go beyond it (55:33). Heredity, initial environment, upbringing, education, emotional leanings etc. are the shackles which arrest his feet, but the right kind of society can produce vastness in his scope.

The Quran formulates a system which gives every man the chance to develop his latent capabilities and talents. The prohibitions in such a society are there only in order to create this expansiveness (2:286).

In a Quranic society, everyone will be held accountable according to his "شَاكِلَةٌ" (*shaakilah*), although his limits will also be tried to be extended. The climax of an animal's progeny is that it becomes like its father, but the human child can go much farther than his fore fathers. Modern day science is testimony to the fact that today man is much ahead of his forefathers. The next generation will be much advanced than the present generation. Just like the capabilities of men differ in any era, so do the possibilities of different generations of man differ, and their possibilities increase as their knowledge and awareness increases. Note that these possibilities are present in everybody's personality, which are equal.

Lataif-ul-lugha says that "أَلشَّواكِلُ" (*ash-shawakil*), which is the plural of "شَاكِلَةٌ" (*shaakilah*) means the roads which lead from the main highway *{T}*. This is referring to the different ways of life men adopt according to their capabilities.

Humans have the power to do as they like, but their powers are limited. For instance, a man can raise one foot and keep standing but he cannot raise both feet and still keep standing. In so far as they have the power to exercise their right, they are totally independent and there is no interference in it what so ever. See details in the heading (Q-D-R).

Sh-K-W(Y)   ش ک و)ی)

"شَكْوَةٌ" (*shakwah*) means a leather bag with an opening at one end, used for holding water or milk.
"شَكْوٌ" (*shakwun*) means to open the opening so that whatever it holds comes out or becomes evident. This leads to "شِكَايَةٌ" (*shikayah*) i.e. to come out with whatever one may have in his heart *{T}*.

Raghib says it means to make one's unpleasing thoughts known.

Surah *Yusuf* says:

| 12:86 | I relate or express my troubles to my Allah. | إِنَّمَا أَشْكُوبَثِّيْ وَحُزْنِيْ إِلَى اللهِ |

At another place it is said:

| 58:1 | She was relating her condition to Allah | وَتَشْتَكِيْ إِلَى اللهِ |

"أَلْمِشْكٰوةٌ" (*al-mishkaat*): a hole in the wall which is not through that wall. Some have said it means a place where lamps are kept (24:35).
"أَلشَّكْوَىٰ" (*ash-shakwa*): complaint *{T}*.

Sh-M-T   ش م ت

"شَمِتَ الْعَدُوُّ شَمَاتَةً" (*shamital aduwwu shumatah*): for someone's enemy to be happy at one's plight:

"اَشْمَتَهُ بِعَدُوِّهِ" (*ash-matahu bi-aduwwih*): made him happy by hurting or troubling his enemy: {*T*}.

When in anger **Moosa** dragged his brother by his heard. His brother **Haroon** had said:

| 7:150 | do not give the opponents a chance to be happy at my expense or to laugh at me | فَلَا تُشْمِتْ بِىَ الْأَعْدَاءَ |

"اَلتَّشْمِيْتُ" (*at-tash-mit*) means to pray for somebody who sneeze. Like saying "bless you", or to remove this "شماتت" (*shumatat*) by one's prayer, like "تَمْرِيْضٌ" (*tamreez*) means to remove sickness from someone:

Sh-M-Kh   ش م خ

"شَمَخَ الْجَبَلُ" (*shamakhal jabal*): for a mountain to be very high and long.
"اَلْجِبَالُ الشَّوَامِخُ" (*al-jibalu-shawamikh*): very high and long mountains.
"شَمَخَ الرَّجُلُ بِأَنْفِهِ" (*shamakhar rajulu bi-anfehi*): The man raised his nose (high in the air): showed pride: {*T, M, R*}.

Ibn Faris says the root means to be big and high.

The Quran says:

| 22:77 | big mountains that are firmly in their place | رَوَاسِىَ شٰمِخٰتٍ |

Sh-M-Z   ش م ز

"اَلشَّمْزُ" (*ash-shamz*): for the human palate to be displeased or revolted with unpleasant things.

"تَشَمَّرَ وَجهُهُ" (*tash-ammaz wajhu*): his face distorted, changed colour.

"اِشْمَأَزَّ" (*ash-maazz*): to fear and be uneasy, for hair to stand on its end in fear, to stand, to be stifled, to feel constricted.

"اِشْمَأَزَّ الشَّيْءَ" (*ishmaazash-shaiyi*): he dislikes that thing.

"اَلْمُشْمَئِزُّ" (*almushma-izz*): to dislike: one who dislikes: one who is frightened. {*T, M, R*}.

Surah *Az-Zumr* says:

| 39:45 | When only Allah is mentioned before those who do not believe, their hearts become constricted | إِذَا ذُكِرَ اللهُ وَحْدَهُ اشْمَأَزَّتْ قُلُوبُ الَّذِيْنَ لَا يُؤْمِنُوْنَ بِالْآخِرَةِ |
| 39:35 | when others (except Allah) are mentioned, they get very happy | وَإِذَا ذُكِرَ الَّذِيْنَ مِنْ دُوْنِهِ إِذَاهُمْ يَسْتَبْشِرُوْنَ |

Happy with personality cults and pure obedience to Allah is only displeasing to him, because men can easily be won over by emotions but law makes concessions for no one. The system or law that the Quran has chosen for mankind seeks only to obey Allah and no one else. Personality cults have no place in this system, but personality cults have so distorted Allah's **Deen** that a human being is the last word nowadays on anything. The law of Allah as the final authority has no place in this system! This has extended to that stage that if anyone is invited to only follow Allah, he becomes displeased! This is the great truth which the Quran points to in the above verse.

Sh-M-S   ش م س

"اَلشَّمْسُ" (*ash-shams*): the sun: 2:285 the sunlight.

Ibn Faris says it basically means to be of different colours, to be fickle, and transient.

"اَلشَّمُوْسُ مِنَ الدَّوَابِّ" (*ash-shamusu mid dawaab*): the four legged animal which is uneasy.

"اَلشَّمْسُ" (*ash-shams*) is used for the sun because it keeps on moving along with its heat which is not constant.

| 76:13 | They will neither feel the sun, or freezing cold | لَايَرَوْنَ فِيْهَا شَمْساً وَلَا زَمْهَرِيْرًا |

"مَطْلِعَ الشَّمْسِ" (*matli-ash-shams*): is the place from where the sun seems to be rising, or the east (18:90).

"مَغْرِبِ الشَّمْسِ" (*maghrib ash-shams*): the spot at which the sun seems to be setting, or the west (18:86).

Gharib-ul-Quran says that the sun was the national symbol of the Persians just as the moon was the national symbol of the Arabs before Islam {*Mirza Abul Fazal*}. For these meanings of the sun and the moon, see heading (Q-M-R).

Ibn Kalbi says that "اَلشَّمْسُ" (*ash-shams*) is the name of an ancient idol {F}. Probably that is why the Arabs of old, named their boys *Shams*. Some think that it was the name of a famous water spring {F}.

Sh-M-L   ش م ل

"اَلشِّمَالُ" (*ash-shimaal*): the left side. It is the opposite of "يَمِيْنٌ" (*yameen*), or right side (18:17).
"يُمْنٌ" (*yumnu*): a symbol of happy tidings.
"اَلشِّمَالُ" (*ash-shimaal*): the sign of ill fate.
"زَجَرْتُ لَہُ طَيْرَ الشِّمَالِ" (*zajaratun lahu twairush shimaal*): I scolded the bird of his ill-fate {T}.

The Quran says "اَصْحَابُ الشِّمَالِ" (*ash-abush shimaal*) in 56:41, meaning the fellowship of the ill-fated ones. It has appeared to mean those who live in *jahannam* (hellish environment). These are the people who will be given the list of their deeds in their left hand (69:25).

"اَلشَّمَالُ" (*ash-shamaal*): the north wind which is usually very cold. This wind is cold and dry and if it blows for more than a week, the undertakers get ready for brisk business because the Egyptians could not tolerate the wind for long {T}.

"اَلشِّمَالُ" (*ash-shimaal*) also means the cover that is put on the teats of the goat (to protect them from other's eyes).
"اَلشَّمْلَۃُ" (*ash-shamlah*): is the blanket in which a man wraps himself {T}.

Raghib has said that "شِمَالٌ" (*shimal*) is used for that cloth in which something gets wrapped from left.
"اَلِاشْتِمَالُ بِالثَّوْبِ" (*ishtimaalu bis saub*): is to be wrapped up in cloth in a way that its end is to the left {R}.
"اِشْتَمَلَ عَلَی الشَّیْءِ" (*ishtamala alash- shaiyi*) means to overshadow something and include it in itself {M}.

According to *Ibn Faris*, this above mentioned is included in its basic meaning.

"اَلرَّحِمُ تَشْتَمِلُ عَلَی الْوَلَدِ" (*ar-rahimu tash-tamilu alal wald*): the womb encompasses the child or has taken the child within it.

| 6:145 | that which is in the wombs of the mothers | اَمَّا اشْتَمَلَتْ عَلَیْہِ اَرْحَامُ الْاُنْثَیَیْنِ |

Habit and temperament is also called "اَلشَّمَالُ" (**ash-shimaal**). Plural is "شَمَائِل" (**shamaa-il**). We have already said that "يَمِيْنٌ" (**yameen**) means symbol of happiness and "شِمَالٌ" (**shimal**) the symbol of ill fate. The Quran has termed those in hellish environment as "أَصْحَابُ الشَّمَالِ" (**as-haabish shimaal**) and those in heaven as "أَصْحَابُ الَيَمِيْنِ" (**as-haabul yameen**). This does not mean that the Quran also believed or accepted these symbols as the Arabs in those days did. Since the Quran has been revealed in the Arabic language, it uses the metaphors of that language to express its meaning clearly. This point should always be kept in mind that the Quran did not believe in things like the Arabs did, but only used the terms of their language so that it would be easier for them to understand.

Sh-N-A   ش ن أ

"شَنَأَهُ" (**shana-ah**): to be dead against somebody {T, R, M}.

Muheet says it involves enmity with rudeness.

The Quran says:

| 5:2 | Some nation's strong enmity | شَنَانُ قَوْم |
| 108:3 | your enemies (those who had enmity with you) | إِنَّ شَانِئَكَ هُوَ الْأَبْتَرُ |

Ibn Faris says the root of the word contains the connotations of having enmity and of avoiding.

Sh-He-B   ش ه ب

"اَلشَّهَبُ" (**ash-shahab**): white colour with a blackish tinge, just like the flame of the fire which in intense heat seems white with a blackish centre, or a mountain covered with snow.
"سَنَةٌ شَهْبَاءُ" (**sanatun shah-baa**): a drought year with no greenery to be seen and the land seems white and barren.
"شِهَابٌ" (**shihaab**): the flame of fire which rises, or the flame which is seen till afar in the sky. It is called a broken star {**T, R**}.

In the old ages (dark ages) it was thought that man's luck or destiny was connected with the stars, and therefore astrologers traced the movement of the stars to find out about man's destiny. This is practiced even now and astrologers are given much importance. The Quran says that when the world was less knowledgeable, such things (astrology) could be accepted, but when the light of knowledge has come, then such guess work is not tolerable. If somebody makes such claims these days (as astrology does) then they should be dispelled by the whip of knowledge, which discloses the myth of such predictions (72:9, 37:9, 15:18).

Sh-He-D   ش ه د

"شَهِدَ" (*shaheda*), "يَشْهُد" (*yush-hud*) means to be present, to present one.

"شَهَادَةٌ" (*shahadah*): to present truthfully whatever is known to one through actual viewing or through insight {T, R}. One who does this is called "شَاهِد" (*shahid*) or "شَهِيدٌ" (*shaheed*).

"مُشَاهِدَةٌ" (*mushahidah*) means to observe, according to scholars, but if the meaning is stretched then it would mean for anything to come within the grasp of the senses.

The word "غَيْبٌ" (*ghaib*) has come against "شَهَادَةٌ" (*shahadah*) in 59:22.

"غَيْبٌ" (*ghaib*) means that which is oblivious to the eyes, invisible. See heading (Gh-Y-B).

As such, "شَهَادَةٌ" (*shahadah*) would mean things which can be seen and felt and "غَيْبٌ" (*ghaib*) would mean those things or forces which are latent. So "شَهَادَةٌ" (*shadah*) or "مَشْهُودٌ" (*mash-hoodh*) are those things and forces which appear as palpable realities. "غَاِبُ الْفَرَ" (*ghaibul fars*) is that force of the horse which it preserves while running and "شَاهِدُ الْفَرَسِ" (*shahidul fars*) is the strength which he uses up in running.

"شَهِدَ" (*shahida*) also means to be at home and "غَابَ" (*ghaab*) means to go away on a journey. {*Lane*}.

| 2:185 | Those of you who are traveling (in the midst of travel) should fast in this month | فَمَنْ شَهِدَ مِنْكُمُ الشَّهْرَ فَلْيَصُمْهُ |

Travellers have a different set of orders.

"اِمْرَ أَةٌ مُشْهِدٌ" (*imra atun mush-hid*): a woman whose husband is not at home {T, R}.

"مَشْهَدٌ" (*mush-hud*): the place one presents oneself, or the place where all hidden results appear palpably (19:37).

"يَوْمٌ مَشْهُودٌ" (*yaumun mash-hoodh*): means such time (11:103).

Surah *Bani Israel* says:

| 17:87 | Indeed the forthcoming of the Quran teachings have appeared in palpable form | إِنَّ قُرْآنَ الْفَجْرِ كَانَ مَشْهُودًا |

Here "مَشْهُودٌ" (*mash-hoodh*) means that the results appear in palpable form. About the meaning of "فَجْر" (*fajr*), see heading of that name.

"شُهَدَاءَ كُمْ" (*shuhada akum*): your helpers (2:23).

God has been called "شَهِيدٌ" (*shaheed*) because everything is before him to witness (22:17) and a messenger is a "شَاهِدٌ" (*shahid*) as well (28:2), because the facts that he sees as a messenger, he unveils exactly before others. This is a main function of messenger-hood.

"اَلشَّهْدُ" (*ash-shahd*), "اَلشُّهْدُ" (*ash-shohd*): honey which is not yet taken out of the hive.

"شَهِدَ" (*shahida*) means to give evidence, be a witness and to swear:

"شَهِدَ عَلَيْهِمْ" (*shahida alaihim*): 41:21 will give evidence against them:

"شَهِدَ عَلَى كَذَا" (*shahida ala kaaza*): also means to give full report or news about someone {M, *Arab-ul-Muwarid*}{T, R}.

Gharib-ul-Quran (with reference to *Ibn Abbas*) says that "شَهِدَ" (*shahida*) also means to decide as in 12:21, or one who decides, as in 6:19. It also means watchman (2:143).

Whatever the form this word takes the meanings include the sense of being present, to present, to keep within sight, in all of them.

The Quran has not used the term "شَهِيْدٌ" (*shaheed*) for those who give their lives in the way of god. Such a man has not been described by the Quran as "شَهِيْدٌ" (*shaheed*). Even a man alive, as well as a dead man can be "شَهِيْدٌ" (*shaheed*). Anybody who by practical example, gives evidence of "مَا أَمَنَ بِهِ" (*ma amana behi*), what he believes, is a "شَهِيْدٌ" (*shaheed*), whether it is through life, or wealth, or with any other thing, and stays steadfast with it for his entire life. To give one's life in the way of God is the biggest evidence of one's belief.

According to the Quran (2:143), the entire nation of Muslims is "شُهَدَاءَ عَلَى النَّاسِ" (*shuhada'a alan naas*), i.e. the nation that kept watch over all the nations of the world, and their centre (Rusool), acts as safe keeper of their deeds (2:143). Recall the duty of the nation of Muslims of yours, and the high stature it enjoyed for this responsibility and then compare that to the nation of Muslims of today. Today we are dependent on others for the barest needs. The reason of this is obvious. That nation of before considered the Quran as its code of life and acted upon it, but we seem to have been lost in superstitions and myths.

Sh-He-R   ش ه ر

Taj-ul-Uros says that "اَلشُّهْرَةُ" (*ash-shohrah*) means for a bad thing to be famous or well known.

Johri says it means for something to become known completely. In the urdu language, "شہرت" (*shohrat*) is used for good things to become famous, and "تَشْهِيْر" (*tash-heet*) for bad things to be famous.

"اَلشَّهِيْرُ" (*ash-shaheer*): famous, respected *{T}*.

"اَلشَّهْرُ" (*ash-shahru*) means the moon because it heralds the advent of a month. A month is also called "شَهْرٌ" (*shahr*).

Ibn Faris says that it basically means to be evident and clear. This is probably why the moon is also called "اَلشَّهْرُ" (*ash-shahar*).

"شَاهَرَهُ مُشَاهَرَةً" (*shaharahu mushaharah*): employed him at a monthly salary *{T}*.

The Quran says ''شَهْرُ رَمَضَانَ'' (*shahru ramazan*) in 2:185, where this word has appeared for the month of **Ramadan**.

The plural is ''أَشْهُرٌ'' (*ash-har*) and ''شُهُوْرٌ'' (*shuhur*), as in 9:36.

Sh-He-Q   ش ه ق

''شَهَقَ الرَّجُلُ'' (*shahaqar rajul*), ''يَشْهَقُ'' (*yash-haq*), ''شَهِيْقاً'' (*shaheeqa*): the sound of the voice of his crying came out of his chest haltingly.
''شَهِيْقُ الحِمَارِ وَتَشْهَاقُه'' (*shaheequl aari wa tash-ahaquh*): the sound of a donkey braying.
''اَلشُّهُوْقُ'' (*ash-shuhuq*): to rise.
''اَلشَّهْقَةُ'' (*ash-shahqah*): a scream {T, R}.

The Quran says:

11:106	to shout and make a din	زَفِيْرٌ وَشَهِيْقٌ

Zajaaj says this word means the voices of people in plight, and ''شَهِيْقٌ'' (*shaheeq*) means a loud sound of crying in pain. This word is from ''جَبَلٌ شَاهِقٌ'' (*jabalun shahiq*) which means a very high mountain, climbing which is very difficult {T, R}.

Ibn Faris says it basically means to be high.

''فُلَانٌ ذُوْشَاهِقٍ'' (*fulana zu shahiq*) means that he is very hot tempered.

The Quran has also used the word ''شَهِيْقٌ'' (*shaheeq*) to mean **jahannam** (hellish environment) in 67:7. In such a hellish society, there is chaos, cries and shouts everywhere, whether it is hell in this world or the hereafter.

Sh-He-W   ش ه و

"شَهَاءٌ" (*shahu*), "اَشْتَهَاءٌ" (*ashtahah*): to wish for something, to lean towards it, desire it.

Raghib says that "شَهْوَةٌ" (*shah-watun*) means temptation towards the things one wants or likes.

Sometimes a thing which is wanted is called "شَهْوَةٌ" (*shahwah*) as well and sometimes this emotion is called "شَهْوَةٌ" (*shahwah*) {T}.

"شَيْءٌ شَهِيٌّ" (*shaiyi shaiyyun*): tasty thing.
"طَعَامٌ شَهِيٌّ" (*tayamun shahi-yun*): the food that one likes {M}.

In the verse (3:13) "شَهَوَاتٌ" (*sahahawatun*) is the plural of "شَهْوَةٌ" (*shahwah*) which according to *Raghib* means goods that are liked (3:13).

Muheet says that "الشَّهَوَات" (*shahawaat*) is an exaggeration meaning.

"مُشْتَهِيَاتٌ" (*mushtahiyat*) means favourite things or leanings (27:56). Along with other words, it has appeared for sexual leanings.

The Quran has described life of *jannat* as:

41:31	Every good thing will be available there (whatever your heart desires).	وَلَكُمْ فِيهَا مَا تَشْتَهِيْ اَنْفُسُكُمْ

Surah *Maryam* says:

19:59	After that such people came who shunned *salawaat* and pursued sexual interests.	فَخَلَفَ مِنْ بَعْدِهِمْ خَلْفٌ اَضَاعُوا الصَّلوةَ وَاتَّبَعُوا الشَّهَوَاتِ

This means that instead of following Allah's laws, they started pursuing their temptations and wishes. If human desires are met under the laws of the revelation then the pleasantries of a heavenly life are begotten. Instead, if the laws of revelation are broken, and such desires are met, then the result is destruction Also see heading (H-W-Y).

Sh-W-B   ش و ب

"اَلشَّوْبُ" (*ash-shaub*): to mix together.

"شَابَ الشَّيءَ شَوْباً" (*shaabash shaiyi shauba*): he mixed that thing, he adulterated that thing. From this "اَلشَّوْبَةُ" (*ash-shauba*) came to mean deception.

"اَلشَّوَائِبُ" (*ash-shawa-ibu*): is the plural of "شَائِبَةٌ" (*shaa-ibah*) which means the adulterations, the faults, and dangers.

"شَوْبٌ" (*shaub*) also means honey because it also is mixed with wax, and it is also mixed with herbs for medication {*T, M, R*}.

The Quran says about those in *jahannam*:

37:67	On top of it, they will be given hot mixture (to drink)	إِنَّ لَهُمْ عَلَيْهَا لَشَوْباً مِنْ حَمِيمٍ

This means that they will have unpleasant environment, troublesome existence, life full of difficulties, deceitful existence.

Sh-W-R   ش و ر

"شَارَ الْعَسَلَ" (*shaaral asal*): took the honey out of the hive and collected it.

"اَلْمَشَارُ" (*al-mash'aar*): the hive out of which the honey is taken.

"اَلشَّوْرُ" (*as-shaur*): the honey which is taken out of the hive.

"اَلْمِشْوَارُ" (*al-mishwaar*): the stick which is used to take the honey out (of the hive).

"الْمِشْوَارَةُ" (*al-mishwaarah*): the honeycomb.

Ibn Faris says it basically means to make evident or present, and to take something away.

"شَاوَرَ" (*shawar*), "مُشَاوَرَةً" (*mushawarah*), "تَشَاوَرَ" (*tash-awar*): to consult mutually, to get the gist of others' opinions and arrive at a conclusion {*R*}. Hence it means deposition of the thoughts, opinions etc. so that the opinions may lead to some conclusion.

If it is taken to mean honey itself, then it would mean to collect all the honey from the hive.

The string of a bidder's bow is also called "اَلْمِشْوَارُ" (*al-mishwaar*) {*T*}.

As such the principal for "مشوره" (*mashwarah*), or consultation would be the thrashing of opinions and then reaching a conclusion through them.

"أَشَارَ اِلَيْهِ" (*ash-aaral ilaih*): pointed to him {*T*}. (19:29).

"اَلشَّوْرَةُ" (*ash-shaurah*), "الشَّارَةُ" (*ash-harah*): beauty, style, dress, clothing, plumpness, look, adornment.

"شَارَ" (*shaara*), "يَشُورُ" (*yash-oor*): trained the horse or made it run in order to display it to a customer. {*T*}.

The Quran has given laws for the humanity, which are never changing. A Quranic system is one in which people formulate sub laws by consultation according to needs of their times under the broader framework of these laws.

That is why it is said about the **Momineen**:

42:38	their matters will be decided by mutual consultation	وَ أَمْرُهُمْ شُوْرَىٰ بَيْنَهُمْ

Since the first ever Quranic system was established by the Messenger (*pbuh*) himself, he was told:

3:158	Consult these Momineen in such matters	شَاوِرْهُمْ فِى الْأَمْرِ

Since the consultation is for all **Momineen,** their system can never be rigid or static. They can, with mutual consultation, not only amend old laws but also make new sub laws in keeping with the needs of their times. Thus while the never changing laws of Quran will always be constant, the sub laws will keep changing from time to time. This is what Quran means by consultation. The Messenger (*pbuh*) himself did this, and the Quran is testimony to it. Therefore all **Momineen** of all times are supposed to do this (4:115). In the western style of governance, nothing is changeable. The nation is free to decide what it wants. They do not have to follow any parameters.

It is called the secular form of governance. In the other hand, the fundamentalists think that nothing is changeable and the decisions that have been made some time back should always hold. Contrary to both, the Quranic system says that the basic unchangeable laws are that of the Revelation, and staying within their parameters sub laws can be changed with consultation as per the need of the times. This is a very good mix of permanence and change, and human life will be able to progress smoothly in this manner.

Sh-W-Ze   ش و ظ

"اَلشَّوَاظُ" (*ash-shawaaz*), "اَلشِّوَاظُ" (*ash-shiwaaz*): flame which has no smoke *{T, M, R}*. These words also mean the heat of the fire and smoke, the heat of the sun, to shout and cry, and the intensity of thirst.

The Quran says:

55:35	a fiery flame will be sent towards your two groups	يُرْسَلُ عَلَيْكُمَا شُوَاظٌ مِنْ نَارٍ

Sh-W-K   ش و ک

"اَلشَّوْکَةُ" (*ash-shaukah*): the cutting of a tree, or a weapon as in 8:7.

"أَرْضٌ شَاکَةٌ" (*ardun shaakah*): land of thorns.

"اَلشَّوْکَةُ مِنَ الْقِتَالِ" (*ash-shaukatu minal qitaal*): the intensity of battle.

"شَوْکَةُ السِّلَاح" (*shaukatus silaah*): the sharpness of a weapon. {*T, M, R*}.

Ibn Faris says it means for something to be rough as well as to be sharp and pointed.

Sh-W-Y   ش و ی

"شَوَی اللَّحْمَ" (*shawil lahwa*), "یَشْوِیہِ شِیًّا" (*ashwihi shaiya*): to fry meat.

"اَلشِّوَاءُ" (*ash-shiwa'u*): fried meat or barbequed meat.

"شَوَی الْمَاءَ یَشْوِیہِ" (*shawil ma-a yash-wih*): he heated the water, or boiled it.

"اَشْوَی الْقَمْحُ" (*ash-wal qamh*): the wheat grains became so hard that they could be brought out by rubbing between the bare hands and to fry them {*T, M*}.

Surah *Al-Kahaf* says:

| 18:29 | which will burn their faces or singe their faces | یَشْوِی الْوُجُوہَ |

"اَلشَّوَی" (*ash-shawa*): means the skin of the hands and legs and the skull. Singular is "شَوَاةٌ" (*shawah*). Some think that all the parts of the body which if hit, do not cause death are "شَوَی" (*shawa*). Thus a non-crucial or valueless thing is also called "شَوَی" (*shawah*).

Surah *Al-Ma'arij* says about the fire of *jahannam*:

| 70:16 | It pulls out the hands and legs perforce | نَزَّاعَةً لِلشَّوَی |

This means that it makes people completely helpless, or that it pulls the skin of the head. It means both ignominy and plight, or that which robs of strength and cripples.

Ibn Faris says it means an ordinary thing or valueless thing.

Sh-Y-A ش ى أ

"شَاءَ" (*sha'a*), "يَشَاءُ" (*yasha'u*), "شَيْئاً" (*shaiya*), "مَشِيئَةً" (*mashiyah*): to intend.

Most scholars have not differentiated between will and intent, but there is a difference.

"مشيت" (*mashiyat*) or will, means to invent or create and intend means to want *{T, M}*.

Raghib says that "اَلشَّيىِ" (*ash-shaiyi*) can be used for anything which is present, whether it is present physically or otherwise. "شَيىِ" (*shaiyi*) can also be used for anything which can be known about or about which some news can be given *{R}*.

Scholars have argued a lot as to what are things that "شَيىِ" (*shaiyi*) can be used for. Some even say that things which are hidden or latent can also be said to be "شَيْىِ" (*shaiyi*). But we will not go into the academic discussion here because the Quran is not about academic disagreements.

The Quran has said at various places:

| 2:20 | Indeed, Allah is ordinator on every thing | إِنَّ اللهَ عَلَى كُلِّ شَيىِْ قَدِيرٌ |

Here "شَيىِْ" (*shaiyi*) means thing, or matter, or issue or affair.

Surah **Al-Baqrah** says:

| 2:48 | (the day) when nobody can be of help to anybody | لَا تَجْزِى نَفْسٌ عَنْ نَفْسٍ شَيْئاً |

It must be understood as to what is meant by Allah's will. We think that for Allah to have power over all things is that He acts without any law or rule like a despot, that He may grant estates if He is happy, and annihilate a whole village if He is angry at something (God forbid) *{T}*, *{M}*, *{R}*.

For details about God being all powerful, see heading (Q-D-R). For now, let it suffice to say that for God being all powerful the above meaning is quite wrong. For God's will does not mean that it is exercised without any law or rule (or justification).

It is scientific observation that everything is bound by the system of cause and effect, but if we go backwards from this, a point will surely come when we will have to acknowledge that there is some effect which has no discernible cause. This is the point where everything in the universe and the universe itself began according to purely God's will. If somebody inquires as to why and how this universe was created by God, he can only be answered that all this was made as per God's will. At this point, as we believe, His will is not restricted or bound by any law or rule (the law and rule is as He willed).

The Quran says:

| 36:82 | At this point God says be, and the thing comes into being | اِنَّمَا اَمْرُهُ اِذَا اَرَادَ شَيْئًا اَنْ يَقُوْلَ لَهُ كُنْ فَيَكُوْنَ |

"Say" does not mean that God utters the words from his mouth, i.e. He simply intends and that thing starts being created. When we observe, we find that everything in the universe follows a certain law or rule. At this point God has subjected everything to certain laws:

| 33:39 | here everything starts following the law that god has made for these things in the first phase of creation | وَكَانَ اَمْرُ اللّٰهِ قَدَرًا مَقْدُوْرًا |
| 65:3 | Allah has fixed a law or rule or standard for everything | قَدْ جَعَلَ اللّٰهُ لِكُلِّ شَيْءٍ قَدْرًا |

All these laws of nature have been made by Allah, but He has decided not to interfere in them:

| 33:61 | you will never find change in Allah's rules | لَنْ تَجِدَ لِسُنَّةِ اللّٰهِ تَبْدِيْلاً |

Here Allah's "مشيت" (*mashiyat*) or will would mean the laws that are being followed in the entire universe, and nothing in the universe has the power to go against these laws. The first phase (of creation) in which all laws were created by Allah as per His will alone, is out of our comprehension and we can't and do not know anything about it. Whatever we can learn about Allah is through studying these laws which are at work in the universe. In other words, this phase of Allah's will can be understood by us through knowledge and experience.

God has given man the power to obey or disobey the laws that have been created for this life:

| 18:29 | Whosoever wishes can adopt the path of acceptance and whoever wants can choose denial | فَمَنْ شَاءَ فَلْيُؤْمِنْ وَ مَنْ شَاءَ فَلْيَكْفُرْ |

That is, contrary to other creations in the universe, man can exercise the right to obey or disobey the laws that have been made for him, but at the same time he has been told that while he can indeed choose whichever way he wants, he has no power over the results. The result of every deed will be as has been created by Allah, i.e. good result for good deeds and bad result for bad deeds. For instance, man can choose between eating poison and sugar but he cannot create the result eating sugar while eating poison. The laws as to which deed will produce what sort of results have been given to man through the revelation, which today are safe in the Quran. So when man wants to understand something about Allah, he will have to understand the laws of nature along with the laws created for him. When man deliberates on both these laws, then he can get to the truth that both these laws are actually branches of the same tree.

Wherever in the Quran has been said "مشيت" (*mashiyat*) i.e. "as Allah wills", it will have to be seen with reference to the context as to which phase of His will is being talked about. To take the same meaning everywhere would create confusion due to which one may wrongly believe that it is the Quran which is contradictory! It does not have any contradiction. Our own lack of understanding creates the confusion and contradiction.

The Quran also says in 2:142 "يَهْدِئ مَنْ يَّشَاءُ" (*yahdi mun yash-a*). It clearly means that Allah gives guidance to whosoever so wishes. "مَنْ يَّشَاءُ" (*mun yash-a*) means whichever person wants, but if it is taken to mean whoever Allah wishes, as it is generally understood, then it would mean that guidance from Allah is received by whoever He wants.

Surah *Al-Ma'idah* says:

5:16	Allah grants guidance through this Quran to anybody who wants to follows its laws	يَهْدِئ بِهِ اللّٰهُ مَنِ اتَّبَعَ رِضْوَانَهُ

The thing is very clear that the guidance will come from Allah, no doubt, but the initiative will have to be man's i.e, he must want it. If man follows Allah's laws, he will get guidance to the right path, but if he rejects them or goes against them then he will definitely meet destruction.

61:5	When they adopted the crooked ways (wrong ways), their hearts were also turned.	فَلَمَّا زَاغُوْا اَزَاغَ اللّٰهُ قُلُوْبَهُمْ

This fact has been displayed or clarified in another way. The **Bani Israel** demanded a commander. Allah appointed *Taloot* as their commander. **Bani Israel** objected to his appointment as they thought there was no outstanding-ness as to wealth. The messenger told them that *Taloot* was selected because of sagacity and bodily strength, i.e. they were told in other words that Allah's selection is not random, but well thought out and as per a certain law.

Whatever is received by anyone is because he deserves it:

2:247	Power and statehood is received from Allah according to his law (his will or certain scheme), not blindly.	زَادَهُ بَسْطَةً فِى الْعِلْمِ وَالْجِسْمِ وَاللّٰهُ يُؤْتِى مُلْكَهُ مَنْ يَّشَاءُ

This also clarifies the meaning of surah *Aal-e-Imran's* verse which says:

3:25	Receiving power and statehood and losing them depends on Allah's scheme, or will	تُؤْتِى الْمُلْكَ مَنْ تَشَاءُ وَتَنْزِعُ الْمُلْكَ مِمَّنْ تَشَاءُ۔

That is, all this happens according to a law which is based on the principle that he, who deserves power and authority to rule, gets it (21:105). He who loses this capability loses them.

The above explanations show that there are three phases of Allah's will or scheme. The first phase in which laws for all things are created and everything is created according to His plan, or as He sees fit. We cannot comprehend anything about this phase. The second phase is that of the external universe where everything is bound to follow the laws made for it. These do not change ever. Man can find out (he has been given the capability) about these laws by deliberation. The third phase is that of the human world. In one part of his life, (the physical part) the same laws apply as to other things in the universe, but on the human level, the laws that he needs, are given through divine revelation. These laws too are not changeable but man, contrary to other things in the universe, has been given the right (power) either to follow them or go against them, but the results of his deeds, whatever they may be, will definitely be according to his deeds i.e. good results for good deeds and bad results for bad deeds (as per god's plan).

This is what is known as the turn of events, law of nature, which too is not changeable.

This is what is meant by god's "مشیت" (*mashiyat*), or will. Do note that the space, in which man has been given freedom to choose, is never interfered in by Allah. And he has been told:

41:40	In this phase, do as you wish. We will not interfere.	اِعْمَلُوْا مَا شِئْتُمْ

Although the results of whatever you do will be according to the laws of nature. There is one verse which causes confusion because of its right meaning not being explained.

Surah *Ad-Dahar* says:

76:29	This noble Quran is a reminder, and anyone who wants may obey Allah	اِنَّ هٰذِهِ تَذْكِرَةٌ فَمَنْ شَاءَ اتَّخَذَ اِلٰی رَبِّهِ سَبِیْلاً

Up to this point the meaning is very clear, i.e. the revelation has been given by Allah, now whosoever wants, can adopt the way suggested by it, and whoever wants can adopt some other way. Ahead it is said:

76:30	and you cannot want that which god does not want (general translation)	وَمَا تَشَاءُوْنَ اِلَّا اَنْ يَشَاءَ اللّٰهُ

This meaning is not only contradictory to what has been said before but it also demolishes the entire structure of human freedom. This would mean that whatever you wish is not your own decision but Allah makes you do what He wants, and that man is helpless in this regard.

Aside from surah *Ad-Dahar* , more or less the same verse has also appeared in surah *Al-Mudassar* (74:54-56) and surah *At-Takweer* (81:28-29). "مَا تَشَاءُوْنَ" (*ma tash-aoon*) means 'you do not want', but according to the Arabic grammar, it also means "no, do not do it".

Mukhtasiral maani says in page 232 that the speaker wants that it may so happen, or the speaker wants to avoid a direct order (and wants the other to do what he wishes), or says this in order to instigate the other (to do it), because the one spoken to does not want to belie the speaker.

Zamkhishri has explained this point in his book *Kishaaf*.

Surah *Al-baqrah* (2:83) says that you cannot want that which God does not want (general translation)
Here "لَاتَعْبُدُونَ" (*la ta'badoon*) does not mean a negative. The translation of the verse is:

"When we made *Bani Israel* agree that they will not follow anyone except Allah, and be in good behaviour with parents, and orphans and needy". After that it is said "be nice (kind) to people".

Here these words are taken in a negative term, like "تَذْهَبُ إِلَى فُلَانٍ" (*tazhabu ila fulanan*) or " تَقُوْلُ " "لَهُ كَذَا" (*taqulu lahu kaza*). Here "تَذْهَبُ" (*tazhab*) and "تَقُوْلُ" (*tazaru*) are pronouns but they mean 'do it'. It is further written that this style is more effective than giving a direct order to do or not to do.

There are other examples too of this style in the Quran, for instance, the same surah says:

| 2:227 | do not spend, except in the way of Allah | وَمَا تُنفِقُونَ اِلاَابْتِغَاءَ وَجْهِ اللّٰهِ |

In the light of these explanations, the meaning of "وَمَاتَشَاءُ وْنَ اِلَّا اَنْ يَّشَاءَ اللّٰهُ" (*wama tash-aaoona illa un yash-a allah*) becomes clear i.e. "you should homogenize your intent with Ours". In other words "You should live according to Our principles, and We want you to live according to Our principles".

Surah *Az-Zumr* says:

| 39:7 | If you go against his laws (what harm can you bring to him i.e., nothing. He is not dependant on you at all) | اِنْ تَكْفُرُوْا فَاِنَّ اللّٰهَ غَنِيٌّ عَنكُمْ |
| 39:7 | But He does not like denial from His followers. He wants you to be thankful. | وَلَايَرْضَى لِعَبَادِهِ الْكُفْرَ- وَاِنْ تَشْكُرُوْا يَرْضَهُلَكُمْ |

As such, a man must willingly accept and homogenise with Allah's will or "مشیت" (*mashiyat*).

Sh-Y-B   ش ى ب

"اَلشَّيْبُ" (*ash-sheeb*): old age, white hair or the whiteness of the hair {*T, M*}.

Surah *Maryam* says:

| 19:4 | The head due to whiteness of the hair (seems aflame) | وَاشْتَعَلَ الرَّأْسُ شَيْباً |

Or it means white hair has appeared in abundance in the head.

Surah *Ar-Room* uses "شَيْبَةً" (*shaibah*) for old age (30:54).

Surah *Al-Muzammil* says:

| 73:17 | The day whose difficulty will turn the young ones old | يَجْعَلُ الْوِلْدَانَ شِيْباً |

Ibn Faris says it basically means for one thing to be mixed with another.

"شَيْبٌ" (*shaib*) is called so because in it the whiteness of the hair mixes with the blackness of the hair.

Sh-Y-Kh   ش ى خ

"اَلشَّيْخُ" (*ash-sheikh*): an old man, an old camel, a teacher, a scholar, a leader, head of a tribe, expert.
"اَلشَّيْخَةُ" (*ash-shaikha*): old woman etc.
"شَيْخُوْخَةٌ" (*shaiku khah*): old age {*T, M*}.

The Quran has used the word "شَيْخٌ" (*sheikh*) in 11:72 and 12:78 to mean old man, but has not used "اَلشَّيْخَةُ" (*ash-shaikha*) anywhere. "اَلشَّيْخُ" (*ash-shaikhu*) and "اَلشَّيْخَةُ" (*ash-shaikhah*) is nowhere to be found in the Arabic dictionaries to means married man or married woman.

Sh-Y-D   ش ی د

"شَادَ الْبِنَاءَ" (*shaadal bana-a*), "يَشِيْدُهُ" (*yash-eeduhu*), "شَيَّدَهُ" (*shaiyaduhu*): to plaster a building and raise it higher.

"اَلشَّيْدُ" (*ash-sheed*): the material (limestone etc.) with is used to plaster the building.

"اَلْمَشِيْدُ" (*al-masheed*): the building which is made of limestone etc. and raised high, solid, and strong {*T, M*}.

The Quran says:

| 22:45 | to raise the voice | قَصْرٍ مَشِيْدٍ |
| 4:78 | high and mighty forts | اَلْإِشَادَةُ |

Ibn Faris says the root means to raise something higher.

Sh-Y-Ain   ش ی ع

"شَاعَ الْخَبَرُ فِی النَّاسِ" (*sha-al khabaru fin naas*): the news spread among the people {*T, M*}.

The Quran says:

| 22:19 | the people who want dirty things to spread. | إِنَّ الَّذِيْنَ يُحِبُّوْنَ اَنْ تَشِيْعَ الْفَاحِشَةُ |

"هٰذَا شِيْعُ هٰذَا" (*haaza shaiyu haza*): it is like, similar to {*T, M*}.

Surah *Saba* says:

| 34:54 | like it was done with people like them | كَمَا فُعِلَ بِأَشْيَاعِهِمْ مِنْ قَبْلُ |

Surah *Al-Qamar* says:

| 54:51 | we have annihilated people like you | وَلَقَدْ اَهْلَكْنَا اَشْيَاعَكُمْ |

"اَلشِّيَاعُ" (*ash-shiya'u*): the flute or voice of the shepherd with which he calls together the spread out animals of the flock. Those who give a call, invites {*T, M*}. It also means to follow behind the caller.

"شَيَّعَهُ عَلٰی رَأْیِهِ" (*shayyi-ahu ala raabihi*): he followed his opinion, supported him.

"هٰذَا شِيْعُ هٰذَا" (*haaza shiyu haaza*): this is the child who was born after that child. This is said for two children who were born one after the other and no child was born in between them.

"اَلْمُشَايِعُ" (*al-mushaa-iyu*): one who is always found with someone or attached to someone.

"شِيْعُ نِسَاءٍ" (*shaiyun nisaa-un*) means one who is always found among women.

"اَلشَّاعَةُ" (*ash-sha'atuh*) means wife, because she is always with her husband {*T, M*}.

Ibn Faris says it basically means to help one another.

These meanings explain what "شِیْعَة" (*shiyah*) means. That is, the people who become one party by following the same person, and thus be one another's strength and support. If it is obedience of Allah's law (which they all are following) in which there is co-operation in good deeds, then it is a party of the *Momineen*, to be with whom is a matter of pride and honour.

As such, after talking about the *Momineen* of the nation of *Nooh*, it is said:

37:83	Verily, *Ibrahim* was one of them (their successor)	إِنَّ مِنْ شِیْعَتِهِ لَا إِبْرَاهِیْمَ

But if such grouping is made in obedience of some human idol, then the Quran calls it *shirk*.

Therefore, it has told the Muslim nation very clearly:

3:103	All of you attach yourself to this book and do not be divided into sects	وَاعْتَصِمُوْا بِحَبْلِ اللهِ جَمِیْعاً وَلَا تَفَرَّقُوْا
30:32	Do not be like those people who have divided themselves into sects and formed groups. (do not turn into *mushrik* once you have accepted Islam).	وَلَا تَكُوْنُوْا مِنَ الْمُشْرِكِیْنَ - مِنَ الَّذِیْنَ فَرَّقُوْا دِیْنَهُمْ وَكَانُوْ شِیَعاً - كُلُّ حِزْبٍ بِمَا لَدَیْهِمْ فَرِحُوْنَ

The result is that every sect claims and believes to be on the right path while all other sects (in its opinion) are not. Since Quran prohibits sectarianism itself, there is no question as to which sect is right and which wrong. Sectarianism, according to the Quran is *shirk*. That is why the Messenger (*pbuh*) has been told:

6:159	Those who forms groups in *Deen*, you have no connection with them	إِنَّ الَّذِیْنَ فَرَّقُوْا دِیْنَهُمْ وَكَانُوْا شِیَعًا لَسْتَ مِنْهُمْ فِیْ شَیْءٍ

Since there are so many groups today among the Muslims, how can they all be united? The method to eliminate the differences among these sects is suggested by Quran itself. It says to consider the book of Allah as the centre and to establish a system according to it. This is the only way. By doing so, the sects will dissipate by themselves. If personalities are removed from within, and only one system (according to the Quran is followed) then the sects will be forced to perish. To follow the Quran is very important. To follow Allah according to what one individually believes creates sectarianism. If only Allah's system is followed then it maintains unity. This may be kept in mind that sectarianism is not only division in religion but also in politics, not only among the *Momineen*, but in every nation. Sectarianism and grouping in politics too has been prohibited by Allah, and termed as punishment (6:65). The Quran has said that the Pharaoh (*Firouni*) authority or the oppressive forces always divides and rules (28:4). For more details, see heading (F-R-Q).

The Quran has termed "شِیَعٌ" (*shiya-un*) to mean nations or tribes (15:10).

End of volume I

الْحَمْدُ لِلّهِ رَبِّ الْعَالَمِينَ

Made in the USA
Las Vegas, NV
16 October 2022